"Value-packed, accurate, and comprehensive..."
—*Los Angeles Times*

"Unbeatable..."—*The Washington Post*

LET'S GO:
ITALY

is the best book for anyone traveling on a budget. Here's why:

No other guidebook has as many budget listings.

In Rome, we found 38 hotels or hostels for under $27 a night. In the countryside we found hundreds more. We tell you how to get there the cheapest way, whether by bus, plane, or train, and where to get an inexpensive and satisfying meal once you've arrived. There are hundreds of money-saving tips for everyone plus lots of information on student discounts.

LET'S GO researchers have to make it on their own.

Our Harvard-Radcliffe researchers travel on budgets as tight as your own—no expense accounts, no free hotel rooms.

LET'S GO is completely revised every year.

We don't just update the prices, we go back to the places. If a charming café has become an overpriced tourist trap, we'll replace the listing with a new and better one.

No other budget guidebook includes all this:

Coverage of both the cities and the countryside; directions, addresses, phone numbers, and hours to get you there and back; in-depth information on culture, history, and the people; listings on transportation between and within regions and cities; tips on work, study, sights, nightlife, and special splurges, city and regional maps; and much, much more.

LET'S GO is for anyone who wants to see Italy on a budget.

Books by Let's Go, Inc.

Let's Go: Europe
Let's Go: Britain & Ireland
Let's Go: France
Let's Go: Germany, Austria & Switzerland
Let's Go: Greece & Turkey
Let's Go: Israel & Egypt
Let's Go: Italy
Let's Go: London
Let's Go: Paris
Let's Go: Rome
Let's Go: Spain & Portugal

Let's Go: USA
Let's Go: California & Hawaii
Let's Go: Mexico
Let's Go: New York City
Let's Go: The Pacific Northwest, Western Canada & Alaska
Let's Go: Washington, D.C.

LET'S GO:

The Budget Guide to

ITALY

1993

Lorraine S. Chao
Editor

Steven V. Mazie
Assistant Editor

**Written by
Let's Go, Inc.**
a wholly owned subsidiary of
Harvard Student Agencies, Inc.

**ST. MARTIN'S PRESS
NEW YORK**

[handwritten: Feb 1993 St V'Day — May May this aid you in your future journey in 1994 — Michele]

Helping Let's Go

If you have suggestions or corrections, or just want to share your discoveries, drop us a line. We read every piece of correspondence, whether a 10-page letter, a tacky Elvis postcard, or, as in one case, a collage. All suggestions are passed along to our researcher/writers. Please note that mail received after May 5, 1993 will probably be too late for the 1994 book, but will be retained for the following edition. Address mail to:

Let's Go: Italy
Let's Go, Inc.
1 Story Street
Cambridge, MA 02138

In addition to the invaluable travel advice our readers share with us, many are kind enough to offer their services as researchers or editors. Unfortunately, the charter of Let's Go, Inc. and Harvard Student Agencies, Inc. enables us to employ only currently enrolled Harvard students.

Maps by David Lindroth, copyright © 1993, 1992, 1991, 1990, 1989, 1986 by St. Martin's Press, Inc.

Distributed outside the U.S. and Canada by Pan Books Ltd.

ISBN: 0-312-08241-X

First edition
10 9 8 7 6 5 4 3 2 1

Let's Go: Italy is written by the Publishing Division of
Let's Go, Inc., 1 Story Street, Cambridge, Mass. 02138.

Let's Go® is a registered trademark of Let's Go, Inc.
Printed in the U.S.A. on recycled paper with biodegradable soy ink.

Editor	Lorraine S. Chao
Assistant Editor	Steven V. Mazie
Managing Editor	Tim Whitmire
Publishing Director	Paul C. Deemer
Production Manager	Mark N. Templeton
Office Coordinator	Bart St. Clair
Office Manager	Anne E. Chisholm

Researcher-Writers

Rome	Alexis Averbuck
Calabria, Basilicata, Tuscany, Liguria	
Naples	Sam Brown
Emilia-Romagna, The Marches, Abruzzo	
Molise, Apulia	John Dorfman
Rome	Kristin Kimball
Rome, Lazio (except Rieti, Viterbo,	
Civitavécchia, and the Pontine Islands)	Margaret Meserve
Veneto, Friuli-Venezia Giulia, Trentino	
-Südtirol/Alto Adige, The Lake Country,	
Lombardy, Valley D'Aosta	Stephanie Rosborough
Sicily, Tunisia	Anthony Schinella
Umbria, Sardinia, Campania (except Naples)	
Rieti, Viterbo, Civitavécchia, Pontine	
Islands	Peter Sroka

Sales Group Manager	Tiffany A. Breau
Sales Group Representatives	Frances Marguerite Maximé
	Breean T. Stickgold
	Harry J. Wilson
Sales Group Coordinator	Aida Bekele
President	Brian A. Goler
C.E.O.	Michele Ponti

Acknowledgments

If anything can be called vicarious pleasure, it is editing a travel guide about Italy. Cooped up in our little cockroach-infested office soaring three floors over Harvard Square, we sifted through and pored over hundreds of pages of glorious beaches, delectable pastas, quaint towns, canals, museums, and castles. All of it prepared and delivered courtesy of a worthy basketball team of researcher/writers. Power forward Anthony "Mad Dog" Schinella's sardonic writing and insight into Saharan tourism were without equal. Point guard Stephanie Rosborough breezed through Northern Italy, sending back invariably thorough research. Center Sam Brown tackled and completed a herculean itinerary and managed to provide us with lucid prose throughout. We commend shooting guard Peter "San Pietro" Sroka for his candid copy and for adjusting to the Thailand-Italy switch on such short notice. Rounding out the crew, forward John Dorfman scoured Central Italy and relayed his research with clarity.

Lorraine's summer, brought to you by the letter T, was made wonderful by the rest of Team Thai: Steven Victor Mazie, Chuckra Chai, and Tim Whitmire. Steve made my job much easier with his competent editing and my summer very special with his friendship. Chuckra Potewiratananond, he of the shredded groin, kept me laughing throughout the summer with revolting culinary fantasies. Tim, my dear bubber, was always giving and provided patient support every step of the way. Lorraine would also like to remember the original Putnam Place: Blythe Grossberg, Bart St. Clair, Emily Drugge, polished metaphor among trite similes Josh Grossberg, Kemp's Frozen Yogurt, and raw cookie dough. Blarth, won't you be M.I.N.E.? I love you guys. Thanks also to Mark Templeton (to whom admiration and gratitude are also owed), Liz Stein, Copake, Jen Medearis, René Celaya, Muneer Ahmad, Chris Caps, Mike Balagur, and Tennis, all of whom lessened the burden of being in the office. Thank you Román for the inspiration and crossword frenzy, David Henry for the new angst-free you, and Beth Ann for enduring friendship. My gratitude and love for Mom, Dad, Michael, and Mark are immeasurable.

Steve heaps thanks on Lorraine Chao, his skilled editrix and confidant, who brightened an already bright Cambridge summer and made *Let's Go* fun; Galway-bound Tim Whitmire, for providing support, friendship, t-shirts, and frequent comestibles; production dude Mark Templeton, who maintained his affability and sanity through countless typesetting hours; and perma-grinned Chuckra Chai for amusing company and investment savvy. Sher. Thanks also to office buds Jen Medearis, Liz Stein (and—*sigh*—her glorious Copake retreat), René Celaya, tennis pro Chris Caps, wrasslin' partner Blythe Grossberg, Bart "Ivanisevic" St. Clair, Muneer Ahmad, G.O.P. posterboy Harry Wilson, fellow-Feelies (R.I.P.)-fan Andrew Kaplan, and bandanna-meister Mike Balagur, who was generous enough to include me in his acknowledgements. Thanks to Dave Geist in Alaska, Ken Katz in Israel, Robert Gordon in Little Rock, Robert Tobin in Ireland, Phil Rubin in Manhattan, John Simpkins in Boston, and wacky Iowa men Jon Taylor, Josh Gibson, Matt Shors, and Adam Svenson. And to Barna, Julie, Gary, July, Tim and Dave—players in a real-life soap opera we call Liptubs '92—it was a wonderful summer. This book is dedicated to the memory of Nana Marcella , to Nana Mickey and Grandpa Fred, and to Mazies everywhere: Jeff and Carol and Rachel and Josh in L.A., Barb in Ann Arbor, and Mom and Dad in Des Moines, whose love and inspiration are beyond thanks.

Lorraine and Steve thank Managing Editor Tim Whitmire; Production Manager Mark Templeton; Publishing Director Pete Deemer; Office Manager Ann Chisolm; Office Coordinators Bart St. Clair and Aida Bekele; eagle-eye proofers Mike Balagur, Jane Yeh, Patrick LaRivière, Nicole Nazzaro, and Chuckra Chai; GI-padded Rome squad Kayla Alpert, David Thorpe, Alexis Averbuck, Margaret Meserve, and Kristin Kimball; *Let's Go:Italy* 1992 editor Jessica Goldberg; erstwhile Thailand researchers Paul Boni, James Chattra, Danna Harman, Brett Janis, Marlies Morsink, and Patrick Walker

—LSC
—SVM

Managing Editors don't usually write acknowledgments, but given that this is my last guide of a three year *Let's Go* career, Lorraine and Steve have seen fit to let me say a few words. At the end of the day, it's hard to put it all together, but I'll try to be brief (never a strong point of mine...).

First thanks are due to Team THAI / ITA: Lorraine, Steve, and Chuck. They spent the spring preparing the most ambitious Let's Go project ever—*Let's Go: Thailand 1993.* Circumstances avoidable and unavoidable took Lorraine and Steve to *Italy,* where they did a magnificent job in tough circumstances, while Chuck laid the groundwork for a first-rate 1994 guide to Thailand. All three are numbered among my favorite people; though my travels will soon take me far from them, it would take much more than the vagaries of the travel guide business or even life in the Real World to take them far from my heart.

Zan, Jamie, and Chris gave me my start at *Let's Go* and will always represent to me the very best of the "old guard." Pete, the oldest of the old guard, brought me back for a final *Let's Go*-round and I only wish that I had always merited the respect he showed me. July, Blythe, Caps, and Mark joined the long winter's journey into autumn, from snowed-in Cape Cod hotels to the final desperate September hours of MEing and type-setting—the totality of the experience renders acknowledgments pointless.

My ME group was amazing, essentially making my job that of a proofreader with a nice chair. Gary, Rick, Jonathan, Carolyn, and Peter all shared a devotion to their work that awed me; anyone who buys *LG: Britain and Ireland, London,* or *Israel and Egypt 1993* is purchasing a true labor of love. I especially thank Jonathan for his steady support in a summer when I probably more often seemed in need of therapy than a reliable boss. To Carolyn, who joined me in discovering more about friendship than any pair of 21-year-olds wants to believe they still have to learn: thank you for your honesty. In return I can offer nothing more or less than eternal devotion to our friendship.

As always, all my love to my family, in all its extended permutations. Ivan and Sherief, I can't tell you guys how much I miss you—life after Harvard will be good, but it won't be the same. And finally, my most profound thanks to Alison for all that has been and yet will be. Because of you I believe; because of you I will return.

—TRW

About Let's Go

A generation ago, Harvard Student Agencies, a three-year-old non-profit corporation dedicated to providing employment to students, was doing a booming business booking charter flights to Europe. One of the extras offered to passengers on these flights was a 20-page mimeographed pamphlet entitled *1960 European Guide,* a collection of tips on continental travel compiled by the HSA staff. The following year, students traveling to Europe researched the first full-fledged edition of *Let's Go: Europe,* a pocket-sized book with tips on budget accommodations, irreverent write-ups of sights, and a decidedly youthful slant.

Throughout the 60s, the series reflected the times: a section of the 1968 *Let's Go: Europe* was entitled "Street Singing in Europe on No Dollars a Day." During the 70s *Let's Go* evolved into a large-scale operation, adding regional European guides and expanding coverage into North Africa and Asia. In the 80s, we launched coverage of the United States, developed our research to include concerns of travelers of all ages, and finetuned the editorial process that continues to this day. The early 90s saw the introduction of *Let's Go* city guides.

1992 has been a big year for us. We are now Let's Go, Incorporated, a wholly owned subsidiary of Harvard Student Agencies. To celebrate this change, we moved from our dungeonesque Harvard Yard basement to an equally dungeonesque third-floor office in Harvard Square, and we purchased a high-tech computer system that allows us to typeset all of the guides in-house. Now in our 33rd year, *Let's Go* publishes 17 titles, covering more than 40 countries. This year *Let's Go* proudly introduces two new entries in the series: *Let's Go: Paris* and *Let's Go: Rome.*

But these changes haven't altered our tried and true approach to researching and writing travel guides. Each spring 90 Harvard University students are hired as researcher-writers and trained intensively during April and May for their summer tour of duty. Each researcher-writer then hits the road for seven weeks of travel on a shoestring budget, researching six days per week and overcoming countless obstacles in the quest for better bargains.

Back in Cambridge, Massachusetts, an editorial staff of 32, a management team of six, and countless typists and proofreaders—all students—spend more than six months pushing nearly 8000 pages of copy through a rigorous editing process. By the time classes start in September, the typeset guides are off to the printers, and they hit bookstores world-wide in late November. Then, by February, next year's guides are well underway.

A NOTE TO OUR READERS

The information for this book is gathered by Let's Go's researchers during the late spring and summer months. Each listing is derived from the assigned researcher's opinion based upon his or her visit at a particular time. The opinions are expressed in a candid and forthright manner. Other travelers might disagree. Those traveling at a different time may have different experiences since prices, dates, hours, and conditions are always subject to change. You are urged to check beforehand to avoid inconvenience and surprises. Travel always involves a certain degree of risk, especially in low-cost areas. When traveling, especially on a budget, you should always take particular care to ensure your safety.

CONTENTS

List of Maps

EUROPE BY YOURSELF

WITH THE YOUTH & STUDENT TRAVEL SPECIALISTS

FROM ROME TO

	return	return
Athens	$ 310	200
Cairo	$ 540	-
London	$ 215	340
Tunis	$ 260	-
Istanbul	$ 370	220
Los Angeles	$ 780	200
New York	$ 620	200

FROM LONDON TO

	return	return
Amsterdam	£. 75	57
Athens	£. 133	265
Berlin	£. 126	96
Madrid	£. 124	167
Paris	£. 64	70
Rome	£. 120	170
Venice	£. 150	157
Los Angeles	£. 285	-
New York	£. 220	-

FROM PARIS TO

	return	return
Amsterdam	ff. 910	488
Berlin	ff. 1480	1121
Rome	ff. 1100	1008
Madrid	ff. 1580	1042
New York	ff. 2450	-
Sydney	ff. 8425	-

Prices are valid for summer '92
Domestic and international tickets.
Discounted and regular international
train tickets. Hotel reservations. Tours
and pocket holidays worldwide.

**YOUTH & STUDENT
TRAVEL CENTRE**

ROME	via Genova, 16 - Tel. (06) 46791
ROME	corso Vittorio Emanuele II, 297 - Tel. (06) 6872672 - 6872673
ROME	Air Terminal Ostiense - Tel. (06) 5747950
FLORENCE	via dei Ginori, 25/R - Tel. (055) 289721/289570
MILAN	via S. Antonio, 2 - Tel. (02) 58304121
NAPELS	via Mezzocannone, 25 - Tel. (081) 5527975/5527960
VENICE	Dorso Duro Ca' Foscari, 3252 - Tel. (041) 5205660/5205655
LONDON	44 Goodge Street, W1P 2AD - Tel. (004471) 5804554/6375601 Metro Goodge Street
LONDON	220 Kensington High Street, W8 7RA - Tel. (004471) 9373265 Metro High Street Kensington
PARIS V°	20, rue des Carmes - Tel. (00331) 43250076 Metro Maubert Mutualitè

LET'S GO: ITALY

General Introduction

US$1 = 1082 lire(L)
CDN$1 = L905
UK£1 = L2147
AUS$1 = L775
NZ$1 = L586

L1000 = US$0.92
L1000 = CDN$1.10
L1000 = UK£0.46
L1000 = AUS$1.29
L1000 = NZ$1.71

> *You may have the universe if I may have Italy.*
> —*Giuseppe Verdi*

Let's Go is a helpful companion that introduces the budget traveler to the many faces of Italy. Our researchers travel on a shoestring budget, so their concerns are the same as yours: how to travel, eat, drink in the sights, enjoy evenings, sleep, and luxuriate in the most economical way possible. We list the best of the least expensive accommodations and restaurants in each town. And we suggest lots of ways to save money.

Let's Go also guides you through everything you need to do before you go. This General Introduction supplies details about applying for passports, visas, and student IDs; suggestions on what to pack and how to book an inexpensive flight; and procedures for sending mail and money overseas. We help you decide what kind of trip to take and whether it makes sense to invest in a railpass or a hostel card. Finally, we provide capsule accounts of political and cultural history, Italian customs, and culinary glories. The practical information in the introduction is supplemented at the back of the book by an Italian phrase list, a glossary, and an Italian menu reader.

Let's Go: Italy divides the country into 20 regions, corresponding to the historically and administratively autonomous entities to which most Italians claim allegiance. Small neighboring regions are occasionally grouped together. We arrange Italy roughly north to south, beginning in Venice and traveling west across the Po Valley to the Alps before descending into the peninsula proper. The mainland is divided into three large sections: northern, central, and southern. This breakdown reflects the areas' widely different offerings and the country's transportation network but ignores the more traditional North-South split at Rome. *Let's Go: Italy* completes its coverage of Italy with Sicily and Sardinia, the country's two major islands, then continues down to African Tunisia. Each regional division begins by introducing you to the flavor of the cities and the texture of the countryside—the traditional villages of inland Sardinia; little known medieval and Renaissance towns in Tuscany and Umbria; and the caves, castles, and conical houses of the Apulian plain.

Practical Information sections for each town supply you with essentials. We include the town's accessibility from other points in the country; directions into the city center from the train and bus stations; the addresses and phone numbers of the local tourist offices; currency exchange; the telephone and post offices (with their telephone and postal codes); the train and bus stations; taxi services; car, bicycle, and motorcycle rental agencies; pharmacies; the police and hospitals; and the emergency telephone number. For larger cities, *Let's Go* also provides you with street maps and basic information about airports, student travel offices, American Express offices, metropolitan transportation, swimming pools, bookstores, public baths, libraries, and laundromats. We also list schedules and fares of the various forms of transportation.

Ranked lists of accommodations and restaurants—compiled with both your wallet and your comfort in mind—follow each town's practical information section. Each sec-

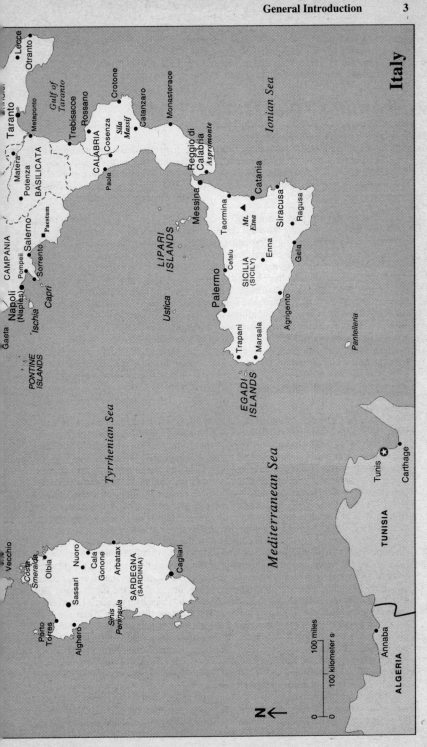

Italy

tion concludes with a detailed write-up of the town's sights, festivals, and nightlife, and a description of possible daytrips to nearby countryside.

Use *Let's Go* as a starting point for your explorations. As you begin to scour Italy, you'll find that some of the best travel secrets are the ones you discover for yourself.

Planning Your Trip

> ### A Note on Prices and Currency
>
> As we go to press, the value of the lira is being depreciated to fit the parameters of the European Economic Community. Prices (in lira) may be up to 30% more than those listed in this guide. This book was researched in the summer of 1992, and the exchange rates above compiled in August 1992. Since rates fluctuate considerably, be sure to confirm them before you go by checking a newspaper.

For a successful trip, plan ahead. Read up on the places you'd like to go, ways to get there, and things to do along the way. Travel is one of Italy's largest industries; you'll have no trouble loading up on information. Take the time to write to some of the organizations listed in *Let's Go's* general and regional introductions, and ask specific questions about local cuisine, hiking, entertainment, festivals, or whatever else interests you. Talk with friends who have been there and check your local library. Remember that small towns are just as Italian as the large cities, and usually considerably less congested. "Doing" Florence, Venice, and Rome may be a time-honored tradition, but it is also one of the most expensive of all possible Italian vacations. Visiting one of these cities, and then exploring the region around it, will give you a much better sense of Italy. It will also ensure that you don't spend all of your time amid other tourists.

Allow for leisure time in your itinerary—zipping through all of Italy in two weeks will sap both your sight-seeing energy and your social time. If you make an effort to be polite and friendly, so will most of the people you meet. And any attempt to speak Italian, however bungled, will be enthusiastically received.

Geography

Italy presents a lumpy Christmas stocking of gifts to the traveler. Where there aren't hills, there are mountains: half-a-dozen Alpine ranges and the Dolomites cover the north; the Apennines drift down the body of the mainland; the Gargano and Sila Massifs, respectively, enliven the spur and toe of the boot; individual peaks such as Mt. Etna and Mt. Vesuvius preside over ancient cities; and just to round things off, baby volcanos bubble near Naples—you can swim in the craters of their extinct cousins north of Rome. The verticality of the landscape is broken by three substantial areas of plain: the vast valley of the Po stretches from the rice paddies of Piedmont through a collection of low-lying Lombard cities and across the farmlands of Emilia-Romagna; a coastal plain runs along the Tyrrhenian Sea from southern Tuscany through Lazio; and the *tavoliere* (chessboard) of the heel makes Apulia another rich farming region. The situation is not much different on the islands. Most of the smaller islands are mountains rising from the ocean, with the exception of the flat Égadi archipelago off the west coast of Sicily and Ventotene off the coast of Lazio. Sicily and Sardinia have mountainous interiors, though many of the major cities are tucked along the flatter coast. This geography ensures that hill towns dominate the landscape everywhere. The average Italian grandmother carrying home the groceries can beat the average American teenager up a hill, and the country has bred a unique form of human being, capable of simultaneously negotiating 3-inch heels, 13th-century stone cobblestone paving and a 60° incline. Though the largest Italian cities (*e.g.* Rome, Milan, Turin, Naples) now feature urban sprawl, the vast majority of the landscape remains a symbiotic mixture of well-tended countryside and well-enclosed cities. In some cities, notably Siena, farms and olive groves grow inside the old city walls.

Girding a peninsula roughly 1000km long and 150-250km across, the Italian coastline seems endless. In summer, though, the beaches are hard-pressed to accommodate what appears to be Italy's entire population, sun-crazed and sand-happy. (Most Italians don't swim at their beaches—presumably to avoid the filth of Mediterranean water.) Much of the coast will surprise only with its dullness, but the long wastelands serve to set off the preposterously beautiful Amalfi coast (south of Naples), the crescent of Liguria (the Italian Riviera), and the Gargano Massif (the spur jutting into the Adriatic). Other attractive mainland seashores include Calabria's Tyrrhenian coast, the wee southern coast of Lazio (near Gaeta), and the Monte Cónero cliffs (just south of Ancona); the rest of the Adriatic, Tyrrhenian, and Ionian provide only lessons in resort life, the Ionian in its least populous incarnation. Much of Sardinia's coastline is pretty, if pretty similar. Sicily's coast boasts Greek ruins in romantic settings, as well as lots more sand. If you *must* swim, venture to any of the smaller Italian islands, though you may be elbowed off the beach as the summer crowds expand past carrying capacity (particularly at Cápri and Elba).

Other significant geographic features include the Lake Country (six glamorous bodies of water at the foot of the Alps), a series of lagoons along the Adriatic coast between Venice and Ravenna, and cave systems in the north and south—the karst of Friuli-Venezia Giulia and Apulia, where limestone has eroded in remarkable ways. The wilds of Italy have been whittled away over the millennia, but are selectively preserved in the great national parks. Abruzzo National Park shelters chamois, lynxes, bears, woodpeckers, and a variety of songbirds in a beech, yew, and maple-covered corner of the Apennines; set in the Alps between Valle D'Aosta and Piedmont, Gran Paradiso National park may afford a glimpse of the ibex. The Sila Massif in Calabria contains virgin forests, artificial lakes, and the occasional wolf.

When to Go

The densest swarms of tourists choke Italy in July and August; almost as many arrive in June. If you come with them, you'll have to brave booked-beyond-belief hotels, hour-long lines to see Michelangelo's David, German colonists in Elba, and a view of the ocean obstructed by seven levels of lounge chairs. Hotels charge more in high season; some may demand full pension. But summer also finds Italy open for tourist business. Though many of the best restaurants are closed for holiday in August, every youth hostel and hotel is open (some youth hostels and many campgrounds open *just* for the summer), and museums and tourist offices maintain expanded hours. If you do travel in summer, try to make reservations by calling a few days in advance. If you want to sleep on Cápri, Elba, the Amalfi coast or other summer hot spots, make reservations at least six months in advance (specific recommendations for the advance notice required to find a bed in high season are found in the regional introductions and the Accommodations sections of individual towns). Be aware that some areas have a *second* high season. The Dolomites and Alps are popular skiing destinations for Europe's wealthy; high season includes the two weeks after Christmas, mid-February to mid-March, and Easter. Easter week in Rome gets a little tight, as does Christmas in Venice. In general, though, visiting Italy between September and May means enjoying the benefits of the off-season. Hotels, museums, and streets will be less crowded, prices more reasonable, and local residents more relaxed. You'll be able to attend the fall wine harvests, the first olive pressings of early winter, or Holy Week processions in April. Traveling outside the summer months should give you a more accurate picture of Italian life. Whenever you go, try to plan a rough itinerary based on the season: weather, festivals, and likely tourist congestion should all be considerations. A winter camping plan would face endless rain; a February visit that doesn't include a Carnevale celebration seems a loss.

Italy and August. A final word of warning: if you choose to travel in August, reservations are a matter of necessity; most Italians take their own vacations in August, and close up their businesses and restaurants. Some of the industrial cities of the north become complete ghost towns (scarcely one in a hundred Milan establishments remains open); many other cities remain alive only as tourist-infested infernos.

Useful Organizations and Publications

Tourist Offices

Centro Turistico Studentes coe Giovanile (CTS), via Genova, 16, 00184 Roma (tel. (06) 467 91, fax (06) 467 92 05). With 90 offices throughout Italy, CTS provides travel, accommodation, and sight-seeing discounts, as well as information for students and young people. Sells the International Student Identity Card (ISIC) and International Youth Cards (FIYTO card). Branch offices in London, Paris, and Athens.

Italian Cultural Institute, 686 Park Ave., New York, NY 10021 (tel. (212) 879-4242); 496 Huron St., Toronto, Ontario, M5R 2R3 (tel. (416) 921-3802). The Italian Government's cultural agency abroad. Information on Italian art, music, literature, and current events, including the occasional concert, exhibition and lecture series. Consider calling them even if you don't bother writing anywhere else—they're friendly and helpful (though very busy in summer). Other offices in Los Angeles (tel. (213) 207-4737), Montréal (tel. (514) 849-3473), Chicago (tel. (312) 822-9545), San Francisco (tel. (415) 788-7412), Washington, DC (tel. (202) 328-5590), Ottawa (tel. (613) 236-0279), and Vancouver (tel. (604) 688-0809).

Italian Government Travel Office (ENIT), 630 Fifth Ave., #1565, Rockefeller Center, New York, NY 10111 (tel. (212) 245-4822); 500 N. Michigan Ave., Chicago, IL 60611 (tel. (312) 644-0990); 360 Post St., San Francisco, CA 94108 (tel. (415) 392-6206); 1, pl. Ville Marie, 1914, Montréal, Qué. H3B 3M9 (tel. (514) 866-7667); 1 Princes St., London, England WIR 8AY (tel. (01) 408 12 54). Write for their detailed (and indispensable) guide *Italia: General Information for Travelers to Italy* and for regional information.

Italian Embassies and Consulates

U.S., Italian Consulate General, 12400 Wilshire Blvd., #300, West Los Angeles, CA 90025 (tel. (310) 820-0622); other consulates or embassies of Italy at 2590 Webster St., San Francisco, CA 94115 (tel. (415) 931-4924); 500 N. Michigan Ave., #1850, Chicago, IL 60611 (tel. (312) 467-1550); 630 Camp St., New Orleans, LA 70130 (tel. (504) 524-2271); 100 Boylston St., #900, Boston, MA 02116 (tel. (617) 542-0483); 535 Griswold St., #1840, Detroit, MI 48226 (tel. (313) 963-8560); 690 Park Ave., New York, NY 10021 (tel. (212) 737-9100); student office, 686 Park Ave., New York, NY 10021 (tel. (212) 879-4242); 421 Chestnut St., Philadelphia, PA 19106 (tel. (215) 592-7329); 1300 Post Oak Blvd., #660, Houston, TX 77056 (tel. (713) 850-7520).

Canada, Embassy of Italy, 275 Slater St., Ottawa, Ont., K1P 5H9 (tel. (613) 232-2402); Consulate of Italy, 3489 Drummond St., Montréal, Qué. H3G 1X6 (tel. (514) 849-8351).

U.K., Embassy of Italy, 14 Three Kings Yard, London, W1 (tel. (071) 629 82 00); Consulate General of Italy, 38 Eaton Place, London, SW1X 8AN (tel. (071) 235 93 71); Consulate General for Scotland and Northern Ireland, 32 Melville St., Edinburgh, EH3 7HA (tel. (031) 220 36 95, (031) 226 36 31 for passport/visa inquiries); Italian Consulate in Manchester, 111 Piccadilly, Manchester, M1 2HY (tel. (061) 236 90 24).

Australia, Embassy of Italy, 12 Grey St., Deakin, A.C.T. 2000, Canberra, G.P.O.B. 360 (tel. 73 33 33).

New Zealand, Embassy of Italy, P.O. Box 463, 38 Grant Rd., Wellington (tel. 473 53 39, fax. 472 72 55).

Budget Travel Services

Compagnia Italiana Turismo (CIT), 544 Broadway #307, New York, NY 10012 (tel. (800) 248-8687); 1450 City Councillors St., Montréal, H3A 2E6 Qué. (tel. (514) 845-9101). New York office sells rail tickets wholesale; Montréal office specializes in individual and group tour packages. Other branch offices in Chicago, Los Angeles, and Toronto.

Council on International Educational Exchange (CIEE/Council Travel), 205 E. 42nd St., New York, NY 10017 (tel. (212) 661-1414). Information on academic, work, volunteer, and work opportunities worldwide. Sells the ISIC, FIYTO and ITIC cards. Write for their free biannual *Student Travels* (postage $1). Also available are *Work, Study, Travel Abroad: The Whole World Handbook* ($12.95, postage $1.50), *Going Places: The High School Student's Guide to Study, Travel, and Adventures Abroad* ($13.95, postage $1.50), and *Volunteer! The Comprehensive Guide to Voluntary Service in the U.S. and Abroad* ($8.95, postage $1.50). **Council Travel** and **Council Charter** are CIEE's two budget subsidiaries. Council Travel has offices throughout the U.S. and in Europe and Asia (tel. (212) 661-1450; same address as CIEE), and sells Eurail and individual country railpasses, guidebooks, travel gear, discounted flights, ISIC, FIYTO, and ITIC cards and IYHF memberships. Council Charter offers charters and scheduled flights to most major European cities, which can be purchased through the New York office or any Council Travel office in the U.S. Address mail inquiries to the New York office.

Educational Travel Centre (ETC), 438 N. Frances St., Madison, WI 53703 (tel. (608) 256-5551). Flight information, HI cards, and Eurailpasses. Write for their free tour and flight information pamphlet *Taking Off.*

Federation of International Youth Travel Organizations (FIYTO), Islands Brygge 81, DK-2300 Copenhagen S., Denmark (tel. (31) 54 60 80). Issues the International Youth Card (IYC). Free annual catalog lists over 10,000 discounts available to cardholders. Organizations that sell the IYC in Italy include:

CTA, via G. Marcora, 18, Roma (tel. (06) 584 04 46).

EAS (Experience America Society), via Pantano 4, 20112 Milano (tel. (02) 8901 0893 or 863 273, fax (392) 889 3301) and Piazza Velasca, 4, 20122 Milano (tel. (02) 805 39 03). Also at via Argiro, 25, 70122 Bari (tel. (080) 521 26 91 and Piazza di Espagna, 12, 00187 Roma (tel. (06) 678 4565).

EUROPA YSTC, via Mezzocannone, 119, 80134 Nápoli (Naples) (tel. (081) 552 06 92). Also at via G. Guglielmi, 10, Salerno (tel. (089) 23 15 82).

ATG, via dei Barbieri, 3A, 00186 Roma (tel. (06) 687 55 38 or 687 70 41). Also at via de Amicis, 4, 20123 Milano (tel. (02) 894 050 75) and via San Bragio, 14, 35100 Padova (tel. (049) 895 07 94).

CTS, via Genova, 16, 00184 Roma (tel. (06) 467 92 71).

ETLI, Youth Section, via Leopold Serra, 19, 00153 Roma (tel. (06) 554 38 33).

Turismo Universitario, via Aquileia, 50/3, P.O. Box 18, 33100 Udine.

International Student Travel Confederation (ISTC), ISIC Association, Gothersgade 30, 1123 Copenhagen K, Denmark, (tel. (31) 93 73 77, fax (31) 93 93 03). **US,** CIEE/Council Travel Services (see separate listing above). **Canada,** Travel CUTS (seeseparate listing below). **U.K.,** London Student Travel, 52 Grosvenor Gardens, London WC1 (tel. (071) 730 34 02). **Ireland,** USIT Ltd., 7 Anglessa St., Dublin 2 (tel. (01) 77 81 17). **Australia,** SSA/STA, 220 Faraday St., Carlton, Melbourne, Victoria 3053 (tel. (03) 347 69 11). **New Zealand,** Student Travel, Courtenay Cham-

bers, 15 Courtenay, 2nd floor, Wellington (tel. (04) 85 05 61). The ISTC is the issuer of the ISIC card.

Let's Go Travel Services, Harvard Student Agencies, Inc., Thayer Hall-B, Harvard University, Cambridge, MA 02138 (tel. (617) 495-9649). Managed by the same people who produce these swell books. Sells Eurailpasses, American Youth Hostel memberships (valid at all HI youth hostels), International Student and Teacher ID cards, International Youth cards for nonstudents, maps and travel guides (including the *Let's Go* series), discount airfares and a complete line of budget travel gear. All items are available by mail.

STA Travel, 17 E 45th St., New York, NY 10017 (tel. (800) 777-0112); 48 E. 11th St., New York, NY 10003 (tel. (212) 986-9470); 7202 Melrose Ave., Los Angeles, CA 90046 (tel. (213) 934-8722); 74 Old Brompton Rd., London SW7 3LQ, England (tel. (071) 937 99 21 for European travel, (071) 937 99 71 for North American travel, (071) 937 99 62 for the rest of the world); 222 Faraday St., Melbourne, Victoria 3053 (tel. (03) 347 69 11); 10 High St., Auckland, New Zealand (tel. (09) 309 9995); other offices worldwide. A worldwide youth travel organization that provides ISIC cards, American Youth Hostel memberships, railpasses, insurance, bargain flights, and travel services.

Travel CUTS (Canadian Universities Travel Service), 187 College St., Toronto, Ont. M5T IP7 (tel. (416) 979-2406), with offices in Victoria, Vancouver, Halifax, Edmonton, Saskatoon, Winnepeg, Ottawa, Montréal, and London. Offers student rates on both domestic and international travel. Sells ISIC, HI, and International Youth cards as well as Eurailpass and Eurail Youthpass. Arranges adventure tours and work abroad. Their newspaper, *The Student Traveler,* is free at all offices and on campuses across Canada.

Books

Forsyth Travel Library, 9154 W. 57th St., P.O. Box 2975, Shawnee Mission, KS 66201 (tel. (800) 367-7984 or (913) 384-3440). A mail-order service that stocks a wide range of European city, area, and country maps, as well as guides for European train and boat travel. The sole North American distributor of the Thomas Cook *European Timetables,* a compilation of European train schedules ($24.95, $4 shipping). Write or phone for a free newsletter and catalog.

John Muir Publications, P.O. Box 613, Sante Fe, NM 87504 (tel. (505) 982-4078, fax (505) 988-1680). Publishes over 75 books on travel and environmental explorations, including the *Kidding Around* series of itinerary planners for the junior traveler, several books by veteran traveler Rick Steves, including his *Europe through the Back Door* ($17.95), which shows you how to avoid tourist traps, and an Italian phrasebook ($4.95).

Travelling Books, P.O. Box 77114, Seattle, WA 98117 (tel. (206) 367-5848). Provides a mail-order service from their extensive catalog of books, maps, language aids and sundry accessories. The catalog, which includes travel tips and information, is free.

Superintendent of Documents, U.S. Government Printing Office, Washington, DC 20402 (tel. (202) 783-3238, fax (202) 275-2529). Open Mon.-Fri. 8am-4pm. Publishes *Your Trip Abroad* ($1), *Safe Trip Abroad* ($1), *Health Information for International Travel* ($5), and "Background Notes" on all countries.

Wide World Books and Maps, 1911 North 45th St., Seattle, WA 98103 (tel. (206) 634-3453). Publishes a free catalog listing the most recent guidebooks.

Documents and Formalities

Passports

You will need a valid passport both to enter Italy and to reenter your home country. As a precaution, carry a photocopy of it showing the number, and date and place of issue. **Keep this separate from your passport.** Consulates also recommend that you carry an expired passport or an official copy of your birth certificate in a separate part of your baggage (you can request a duplicate birth certificate from the Bureau of Vital Statistics in your state or province of birth). It's also wise to carry a few extra passport-type photos. If you lose your passport, notify the local police and the nearest consulate immediately. Remember that your passport is a public document that belongs to your nation's government, and may not be withheld or used as collateral without your consent.

U.S. citizens can obtain a 10-year passport ($65) or, if under age 18, a five-year passport ($40). Apply at any U.S. Passport Agency office or at one of the several thou-

Always travel with a friend.

Get the International
Student Identity Card,
recognized worldwide.

For information call toll-free **1-800-GET-AN-ID**.
or contact any Council Travel office. (See inside front cover.)

 Council on International Educational Exchange
205 East 42nd Street, New York, NY 10017

sand federal and state courts and post offices that accept passport applications. All travelers to Italy, including infants, must have a passport in their name. If this is your first U.S. passport, if you are under 18, if your current passport is more than 12 years old, or if it was issued before your 18th birthday, you must apply in person (although parents may apply on behalf of children under 13). With your application, you must submit proof of U.S. citizenship (a certified birth certificate), proof of identity (an unexpired document with photo and signature, such as a driver's license), and two identical 2in. x 2in. photographs (you can get these taken at most camera stores).

To renew your passport by mail ($55), you must submit a previous U.S. passport issued not more than 12 years ago and have been at least 16 years of age the first time you applied for a passport. Submission of the old passport fulfills the requirements of proof of citizenship and identity; you need only to enclose two recent, identical 2in. x 2in. photographs along with it. The passport office normally requires three to four weeks to process an application, but it is wise to apply *several months in advance*, especially during the busy period from February to July. You should also be aware that some countries forbid entrance if your passport is due to expire in less than six months, and that returning to the U.S. with an expired passport subjects you to a $100 fine.

Rush service is available for travelers who are willing to pay a fee for express mail service and can prove (with an airplane ticket) that they are departing the country within five working days. If your passport is lost or stolen, report the loss to the nearest U.S. embassy or consulate and the local police immediately. For more information, call the U.S. Passport Information's 24-hour recording (tel. (202) 647-0518) or contact the Washington Passport Agency, 1425 K St., Washington, DC 20524-0002 (tel. (202) 647-0518, recorded information (202) 647-0518).

Canadian citizens may apply for a five-year passport in person at one of 26 regional offices or at the Passport Office, Promenade du Portage, Place du Centre, Hull, Ottawa; by mail at the Passport Office, Department of External Affairs, Ottawa, Ont. K1A 0G3; or, outside Canada, at the nearest Canadian embassy or consulate. Applicants should submit evidence of Canadian citizenship verified by a "guarantor" (a professional who has known you for at least two years), two identical passport photos co-signed by you and the same guarantor, a completed application (available at passport and post offices, and travel agencies), and CDN$35. The Passport Office recommends that you apply in winter if possible. Expect a five-day wait if applying in person, three weeks if applying by mail. No rush service is available. For more information, refer to the pamphlet *Bon Voyage, but...* , free from the passport office.

British citizens should apply in person at a local passport office. You must present original copies of your birth certificate; two identical, recent passport photographs, signed and countersigned by a qualified person; a completed application co-signed by that same person; and a copy of your marriage certificate (if applicable). The fee is £15 and your passport is valid for 10 years, five years if you are under 16. The process takes four to six weeks. Family passports may be issued, but children age 16 and up require separate passports. Rush service is available upon proof of need for immediate departure. Applicants should count on a month of processing time, more during the busy season between February and August.

Irish citizens should pick up an application at a local guard station or request one from one of the two passport offices. If you have never had a passport, you must send your birth certificate, the long application, and two identical pictures to Passport Office, Setanta Centre, Molesworth St., Dublin 2 (tel. (01) 711 633) or Passport Office, 1A South Mall, Cork, County Cork (tel. (021) 272 525). To renew, send your old passport, the short form, and the photos. Passports cost £45 and are valid for 10 years. Apply for a passport as soon as you know you will need it, though rush service is available.

Australian citizens must apply for a passport in person at a local post office, where an appointment may be necessary, through a passport office, or through an Australian diplomatic mission overseas. A parent may file for an applicant who is under 18 and unmarried. With your application you must turn in proof of citizenship, proof of your present name, two photographs and other forms of identification. Proof of citizenship can be an Australian passport valid for more than two years and issued after November

22, 1984, a birth certificate, or a citizen certificate from the Department of Immigration. The photographs (45mm x 35mm) must be identical, not more than six months old, and signed as instructed in the application. Other acceptable ID includes driver's license, credit card, rate notices, etc. Application fees are adjusted every three months; call the toll free information service for current details (tel. 13-12-32 or (008) 02-60-22). There is also a departure tax when a citizen over 11 years old leaves the country.

Applicants for a **New Zealand passport** must contact their local Link Centre, travel agent, or New Zealand Representative for an application form. Completed applications must include evidence of New Zealand citizenship (such as a previous New Zealand passport or an original birth or citizenship certificate) and two properly certified identical photographs. They should be mailed, along with the application fee, to the New Zealand Passport Office, Documents of National Identity Division, Department of Internal Affairs, Box 10-526, Wellington (tel. (04) 474 8100). For an application lodged in New Zealand, the fee is NZ$56.25 for adults and NZ$25.30 for children under 16; applications lodged overseas cost NZ$110 and NZ$49.50. All children are now required to have separate passports; their names can no longer be endorsed in the passport of their parents or guardians. A child's passport is valid for five years. Children whose names are already endorsed in their parents' or guardians' passports will be able to travel using such documentation until either their 16th birthday or the passport's expiration date, whichever occurs first, but only when accompanied by the passport holder. The standard processing time is three weeks, but urgent applications will be given priority. A New Zealand citizen who is overseas may send or take a passport application to the nearest New Zealand Embassy, High Commission, or Consulate which is authorized to issue passports. Unless the passport is urgently required, the application will be processed in New Zealand. For more information, contact the **New Zealand Passport Office**, Documents of National Identity Division, Department of Internal Affairs, Box 10-526, Wellington.

Visas

A visa is a stamp placed on your passport by a foreign government that permits you to visit that country for a specified purpose and period of time. Tourists from the United States, Canada, Great Britain, Australia, and New Zealand do not need a visa to visit Italy for three months or less. If you wish to remain longer and can prove that you are a bona fide tourist with adequate means of support, you may obtain a one-time three-month extension from any local police station (*questura*). The Bureau of Consular Affairs warns, however, that visa extensions are granted infrequently. If you intend to travel for more than three months, consider obtaining a long-term visa before departure. Travelers from countries other than those listed above should be sure to check with the Italian Government Travel Office or the nearest Italian Embassy or consulate; Italy does require visas from citizens of many countries in Asia, Africa, and the Middle East.

Entrance to Italy as a tourist does not include permission to study or work there. To apply for a student visa, you need a letter of acceptance from the institution you will be attending and either a statement of financial support from your parents or a letter from your bank or accountant confirming that you have sufficient financial resources to fund your schooling. To obtain a work visa, you must submit a written promise of a job that no available Italian can fill.

Italy requires foreigners to register at a local police station within three days of arrival in the country. Hotels are responsible for registering their guests, but if you aren't staying in a hotel, the responsibility is yours. The U.S. Department of State provides two 50-cent pamphlets, *Americans Abroad* and *Foreign Entry Requirements,* and the helpful *Your Trip Abroad* for $1. Send a check to the **Consumer Information Center,** R. Woods, Consumer Information Center—2B, P.O. Box 100, Pueblo, CO 81009 (tel. (719) 948-3334). You can get a visa (and more information) from the nearest Italian embassy or consulate; Americans can also get information on visa requirements from the **Bureau of Consular Affairs,** 1425 K St. NW, Washington DC 20524 (tel. (202) 647-0518). In case you find yourself really in an enormous rush for your visa, you can also try **Visa Center, Inc.,** 507 Fifth Ave., New York, NY 10017 (tel. (212) 986-0924). Service costs vary with passport requirements but average $10-15.

Student and Youth Identification

The **International Student Identity Card (ISIC)** is the most widely accepted form of student ID and is often required for student flights, trains, and clubs. Cardholders qualify for over 8000 discounts, including reductions on museum admission, theater tickets, movies, and transportation. Make a habit of presenting it and asking about student discounts wherever you go. (Ask: *c'è uno sconto studentesco?*— CHAY oo-noh SCON-toh stoo-dehn-TEHS-coh.) The annual *International Student Travel Guide* lists some of the discounts available with the ISIC card. Pick it up when you apply or write to CIEE for a copy. When issued in the U.S., the card provides repatriation insurance of $3000, medical/accident insurance of $3000, plus $100 coverage of per-day, in-hospital care for up to two months, $1000 all-risk accidental death and dismemberment coverage, and $10,000 emergency medical evacuation insurance. To apply for the card ($15), you must supply current, dated proof of your student status (a letter on school stationery, signed and sealed by the registrar, or a photocopied grade report from fall 1992, spring 1993, or summer 1993 sessions); a 11/2 in. x 2 in. photo with your name printed on the back; and the name, address, and phone number of a beneficiary (in the event of the insured's death, payment will be made to the beneficiary). The card is valid for 16 months, from September 1 through the end of the following calendar year. However, you cannot purchase a new card in January unless you were a student during the fall semester; if you are about to graduate, get the card now.

Some of the student travel offices who issue the ISIC are **Council Travel,** 205 E. 42nd St., New York, NY 10017 (tel. (212) 661-1450); **Let's Go Travel Services,** Harvard Student Agencies, Thayer Hall-B, Harvard University, Cambridge, MA 02138 (tel. (617) 495-9649); and **Travel CUTS,** 187 College St., Toronto, Ontario M5T 1P (tel. (416) 979-2406).

With the increase in the use of phony ISIC cards, many airlines and other establishments may request double proof of student status; student travelers may want to bring a along a school picture ID or signed statement from their school registrar as well as the ISIC card.

Anyone under 26 can take advantage of the **International Youth Card (IYC)**—$10 without insurance, $15 with—issued by the Federation of International Youth Travel Organizations (FIYTO). Also known as the FIYTO card, the IYC gets you discounts on transportation, accommodations, museums, restaurants, lessons, and activities. When applying, you must include your passport number, proof of birthdate (photocopy of a valid driver's licence, birth certificate, or the personal data page of your passport), and a passport-sized photograph with your name printed on the back. Further information can be obtained by contacting CIEE, or any Council Travel office.

International Driver's License

All foreign drivers in Italy must be in possession of both an **International Driver's Permit** and an **International Insurance Certificate,** (also known as the green card), which certifies that you have liability insurance. If you've held a U.S. driver's license for at least a year, driver's permits are available for $10 from the **American Automobile Association (AAA).** Contact your local AAA office or call their main office at 1000 AAA Dr. (Box 75), Heathrow, FL 32746-5063 (tel. (407) 444-7000). Specific inquiries about the IDP should be addressed to **AAA Travel Agency Services** (mail stop 100), Heathrow, FL 32746-5063 (tel. (407) 444-7883). For CDN$10, Canadian drivers can get a permit from the **Canadian Automobile Association (CAA),** 2 Carlton St., Toronto, Ont. M5B 1K4 (tel. (416) 964-3170). Applicants must hold a valid license and submit two passport-sized photos, and proof of age (drivers must be 18 years of age or older). You may obtain a green card through your own insurance company (if your policy applies abroad), or through rental and travel agencies.

Customs

Before you leave home, record the serial numbers of all valuables you take on your trip and, if possible, carry receipts to prove that you did not buy them abroad. Be especially careful to document items manufactured abroad. A customs agent at your point of departure may be able to stamp or certify your list of serial numbers. If you are bringing prescription medicine across any border, be sure the bottles are clearly marked and have the prescription ready to show the customs officer.

Non-residents may import Italian or foreign banknotes and bearer securities up to 20 million lire before declaring the amount to customs. You can export up to 20 million as well; check with the tourist offices or the embassy for further details. Portable radios may require a small license fee upon entering Italy. Except for the currency limit, few export restrictions apply, except on antiques and precious art objects, which require the authorization of the *Sovrintendenza delle Antichita e Belle Arti, Ministero dei Beni Culturali e Ambientali.*

Upon returning to your home country, you must declare all goods acquired abroad and pay a duty on any articles exceeding an established value or quantity. Holding onto receipts for purchases made abroad will help establish values when you return. Keep in mind that items you buy at duty-free shops abroad are *not* exempt from duty when you return. "Duty-free" means only that you don't have to pay taxes in the country of purchase. **U.S. citizens** may bring back $400 worth of goods duty-free; the next $1000 is subject to a 10% tax. All items included in your duty-free allowance must be carried with you—none may be shipped separately. Goods must be for personal or household use and may include up to 100 cigars, 200 cigarettes (1 carton), and 1 of wine or liquor. You must be 21 or older to bring liquor into the U.S. If you stay abroad for less than 48 hours, or if you have claimed any part of your $400 exemption within the previous 30 days, you are eligible for an exemption of only $25, including 50 cigarettes, 10 cigars, 150ml (4 oz.) of alcohol, and 150ml of perfume. All items included in your allowance must accompany you. The exemptions of persons traveling together may be combined.

You may mail unsolicited gifts back to the U.S. duty-free if they're worth less than $50 and do not contain liquor, tobacco, or perfume. Write "Unsolicited Gift," with a description of the price and nature of the gift, on the outside of the package before mailing. If the parcel is worth more than $50, the Postal Service will collect the duty and a handling charge from the recipient. If you mail home personal goods of U.S. origin, mark the package "American goods returned." For more information, request the brochure *Know Before You Go,* available from the U.S. Customs Service, 1301 Constitution Ave., Washington, DC 20229 (tel. (202) 566-8195). You can also receive this brochure for 50¢ by writing R. Woods, Consumer Information Center, Pueblo, CO 81009; request item 477Y.

Canadian citizens may bring back CDN$20 worth of goods after a 24-hr. absence, any number of times per year. After 48 hours, you may bring back goods valued up to CDN$100. Written declaration may be required. After seven or more days, once per calendar year, you may bring back goods valued up to CDN$300. Only the 48-hr. and seven-day exemptions may include alcohol (40 oz. of wine or liquor, *or* 24 12-oz. bottles or cans of beer) and tobacco (200 cigarettes, 50 cigars, and two 200gm containers of loose tobacco). The age at which you may import liquor varies by province. Values above the exempted limits are taxed at about 20%. You may also send gifts up to a value of CDN$60 duty-free, but you cannot mail alcohol or tobacco. Before leaving, list the serial numbers of all your valuables on a Y-38 form at a Customs Office or your point of departure. Write to the Canadian Customs and Excise Department, Mackenzie Ave., Ottawa, Ont. K1A 0L5 (tel. (613) 957-0275) for the booklet *I Declare/Je Déclare.* Another helpful booklet, *Bon Voyage, But...,* is available from the Department of External Affairs (tel. (613) 996-2825).

British citizens may claim an exemption of £32. If you are over 16, you may include tobacco (200 cigarettes or 100 cigarillos or 50 cigars or 250g of tobacco) and alcohol (2 of still table wine, plus 1 of alcohol over 22% by volume or 2 of alcohol not over 22% by volume). If you have obtained these goods in the EC (of which Italy is a member), the amount which you can import increases. Direct questions to Her Majesty's

Customs and Excise Office, Custom House, Nettleton Rd., Heathrow Airport, Hounslow, Middlesex TW6 2LA (tel. (01) 382 54 68).

Irish citizens may import a maximum of IR£34 per adult traveler duty-free (IR£17 per traveler under the age of 15). Travelers over 17 may bring in 200 cigarettes, 100 cigarillos, 50 cigars, or 250g of tobacco, and 1 of alcohol over 44 proof or 2 of alcohol under 44 proof. You may import as much currency into Ireland as you wish. For more information, write Division 1, Office of the Revenue Commissioners, Dublin Castle, Dublin 1 (tel. 679 27 27).

Australian citizens are allowed an exemption ("concession") of AUS$400, including 1 of wine, beer, or liquor, and 250g of tobacco or 250 cigarettes. Australians under 18 receive a concession of AUS$200 and may not import alcohol or tobacco. Before leaving, register new or expensive items on the appropriate form available from any local Customs office, and have the list stamped at Customs before departure. Exports of more than AUS$5000 without the permission of the Reserve Bank of Australia is prohibited. For more information, request the brochure *Customs Information for All Travelers* from a local office of the Collector of Customs or from an Australian consulate abroad. **Citizens of New Zealand** may bring in NZ$700 worth of duty-free goods as long as the goods are intended for personal use or as unsolicited gifts. Travelers 17 or older are allowed 200 cigarettes (1 carton) or 50 cigars or 250g of tobacco or a mixture of all three not to exceed 250g. You may also bring in 4.5 of beer or wine and 1.125 of liquor. The *New Zealand Customs Guide for Travelers* and *If You're Not Sure About It, DECLARE IT* are both available from any customs office. For more information, contact New Zealand Customs, P.O. Box 29, Auckland (tel. (9) 773 520). The U.S. Customs Service has proclaimed that "a vital part of customs's role is screening out items injurious to the well-being of our nation." The U.S., Canada, U.K., Australia, and New Zealand all prohibit or restrict the import of firearms, explosives, ammunition, fireworks, plants, animals, lottery tickets, obscene literature and film, and controlled drugs.

Money

A word of warning. For many tourists, especially students, budget travel quickly turns into a destructive—and even dangerous—budget obsession. This disorder is the consuming desire to spend as little money as possible: to stay in the cheapest lodgings no matter how miserable, to eat grim, tasteless food, to spend fewer lire than the day before just for the sake of saving money. Perhaps the worst sin of the entire *Let's Go* series is that it perpetuates this mind-set among travelers, many of whom spend years living on a regimented budget to save enough money to go abroad only to skimp on their travel once overseas.

When you hit the budget travel doldrums, devote a little cash to cushioning the shocks. Force yourself to have a really nice meal. Spend the night in a quiet *pensione* overlooking a garden. You can go to the most luxurious *caffè* in town and drink a cappuccino with five people tending to your every need; such a mini-luxury break might cost you L6000 at most, and you'll feel rich and pampered rather than destitute and ignored. And remember that length of stay isn't everything: Grinding out four weeks in the smelly cheap housing near the docks in Genoa will only depress you; for the same money, you can spend three weeks enjoying yourself—the Italians and other tourists will appreciate your company more, and you'll return home happier.

Currency and Exchange

The Italian monetary system is based on the lira (plural: lire). The smallest denomination of Italian currency is the L10 coin (although these are now becoming as rare as they are worthless; the L50 coin is now the more common lowest denomination), and the smallest note is the L1000 bill. Before leaving home, most people buy about $50 worth of lire to save time and hassle upon arrival, but the rates you encounter at the airport or train station will often be better than those at home (albeit the worst in Italy).

When exchanging money, look for *"cambio"* signs and shop around. Avoid exchanging money at luxury hotels and restaurants as well as train stations and airports;

Don't forget to write.

Now that you've said, "Let's go," it's time to say, "Let's get
American Express® Travelers Cheques." Because when you want
your travel money to go a long way, it's a good idea to protect it.
So before you leave, be sure and write.

the best deals are usually found at banks such as the Banco d'Italia or the Banco Nazionale del Lavoro, where the rates are far more favorable, although you should still expect to pay a commission of 1-2%. Changing currency is best done in the morning; banking hours are usually Monday through Friday, 8:35am until 1:35pm with an extra hour in the afternoon (usually 3-4pm, but this varies). Remember that unless a percentage rate is charged, you will lose a fixed chunk of money each time you convert. To minimize your losses, exchange large sums at once, but never more than you can safely carry around. It also helps to plan ahead: If you are caught sans lire at night or on a Sunday, when banks and exchange bureaus are closed, you may be forced into a particularly disadvantageous deal.

Traveler's Checks

No facet of your trip is likely to cause you more headaches than money—even when you have it. Carrying large amounts of cash, even in a money belt, is unwise. Traveler's checks, which can be replaced if lost or stolen, are far safer. Although not all Italian establishments, including banks, accept traveler's checks, your peace of mind will far outweigh the occasional inconvenience. American Express is probably the best-known traveler's check today. Buying AmEx traveler's checks will also grant you to access to some of the services at their offices (*i.e.* mail—see Keeping in Touch below) for free, even if you aren't a cardholder.

None of the major companies listed below supplies traveler's checks in lire, so buy checks in your home currency—changing money from one foreign currency to another will cost you dearly. Buy mostly in large denominations but also get a few smaller checks. While large notes spare you long waits at the bank, small notes minimize your losses if you just need a little cash to tide you through the wait in Bríndisi. Given the tendency for Italian exchanges to charge flat commissions, changing small checks generally serves to make bad rates much worse. If you're forced to change in a small town, grit your teeth and change a reasonable amount of money—you probably won't lose more than a few thousand lire. If you change five $20 checks in five different places during your trip because you can't bear a rotten exchange, you will end up spending L20,000 in extra commissions.

In the event of theft or loss, a fair amount of red tape and delay will complicate even the best circumstances. If you need replacement checks, showing receipts will speed up the process dramatically. (Keep them in a safe place separate from your checks.) To protect yourself from clever thieves who take just one or two checks from the middle of the pile to escape detection, record the number of each check as you cash it. That will make it easier to identify exactly which checks are missing if some do disappear. Also leave a list of check numbers with someone at home.

Most banks and many agencies sell traveler's checks, usually for face value plus a 1-2% commission. Consult your bank or phone book for the nearest vendor. All of the following agencies operate affiliated offices in Italy from which you can obtain replacement checks or emergency funds.

American Express, tel. in the U.S. and Canada (800) 221-7282; in the U.K (0800) 52 13 13; in Australia (02) 886 0689. Call (801) 964-6665 for referral to offices in individual countries. Available in 7 currencies. A new option allows 2 people traveling together to share 1 set of checks. Offices cash their own traveler's checks free. A free list of all offices is available at any Travel Office. For more information, write: American Express Company, Traveler's Check Division, Salt Lake City, UT 84184-3406.

Bank of America (WorldMoney), tel. in the U.S. (800) 227-3460, collect from elsewhere (415) 574-7111. Available in U.S. dollars only. A commission rate of 1% per $100 is charged for non-bank members. For more information, write: Bank of America, P.O, Box 37010, San Francisco, CA 94137.

Barclay's, tel. in the U.S. and Canada (800) 221-2426; in the U.K. (202) 67 12 12; collect from elsewhere (212) 858-8500. Affiliated with Visa. Available in U.S. dollars, British pounds and German marks; Canadian dollars available in Canada. Charges a commission rate of 1%. To report lost checks call (800) 227-6811 in the U.S.; collect from elsewhere (415) 574-7111.

Citicorp, tel. in the U.S and Canada (800) 645-6556, collect from elsewhere (813) 623-1709. Available in U.S. dollars, British pounds, German marks, and Japanese yen. Charges 1-11/2%

You can't eat pasta without bread.

When in Rome, it's not a problem if your cash supply runs dry. Because with Western Union you can receive money from the States within minutes, in case the situation arises. Plus it's already converted into lire.

Just call our number in Rome, 39 02 95 457 305, or in the United States, 1-800-325-6000, and then hop on a gondola to the nearest Western Union location.

Oh, and enjoy your dinner.

WESTERN UNION | MONEY TRANSFER®

commission. Checkholders are automatically enrolled in Citicorp's Travel Assist Hotline (tel. in the U.S. (800) 523-1199, collect from elsewhere (215) 244-1740) for 45 days after purchase and may avail themselves of the World Courier Service which guarantees hand-delivery of traveler's checks anywhere in the world.

MasterCard, tel. in the U.S. and Canada (800) 223-9920, collect from elsewhere (609) 987-7300. Available in 11 currencies.

Thomas Cook, tel. in the U.S. (800) 223-7373, collect from elsewhere (609) 987-7300. Affiliated with MasterCard. Available in 11 currencies.

Visa, tel. in the U.S. and Canada (800) 227-6811; in London (071) 937 8091; collect from elsewhere (212) 858-8500. Available in 13 currencies. Commission depends on individual bank.

Credit Cards

Credit cards are of limited use to the budget traveler because low-cost establishments, particularly in southern Italy, rarely honor them (though acceptance is on the rise). A card can, however, prove invaluable in emergencies. Moreover, if you need to make a major purchase of any sort in Italy (hiking gear, for instance), you might save a substantial amount of money by charging: in calculating the bill, credit card companies use gracious exchange rates you can only dream about encountering abroad. Major credit cards such as **Visa** and **American Express,** and, to a lesser extent, **MasterCard,** offer you instant cash advances at many banks throughout Europe. This infusion of cash might be your most convenient source of money for several days (section below on sending money abroad outlines the difficulties in getting money from home). In addition, holders of most major credit cards can now get instant cash around the clock at automated teller machines (ATMs) throughout Europe. In order to use this service, however, one must have a PIN number, which American credit cards usually do not have. You must obtain this from a bank; check with your issuing bank about conversion charges, interest rates, and ATM locations as well. Also be forewarned that the shaky transatlantic electronic connection still often impedes successful transactions.

American Express (tel. (800) 528-4800) provides an assortment of useful services to cardholders. Full-service offices will honor a personal check of up to $1000 every seven days (up to $200 in cash, the rest in traveler's checks). They will also wire to replace lost or stolen cards. American Express's free "Purchase Protection Plan" insures against loss or theft of any item bought with the American Express Card, within 90 days of purchase. Cardholders can use the American Express offices sprinkled around Italy as mailing addresses for free; others must pay (or show American Express traveler's checks) to pick up mail. Perhaps the greatest bonus for holders of U.S.-issued cards is Global Assist, a 24-hr. help line that provides information and monetary aid in cases of personal medical emergency or document loss. You can also send urgent messages home through this service. *The Traveler's Companion,* a list of full-service offices throughout the world, is available at American Express Travel Offices. While many of these services are also available to holders of other cards, primarily **Visa,** it varies according to the bank which issues the card (Citibank, Chase, Signet etc.); check with your individual bank before going abroad.

Unless otherwise stated, every American Express office mentioned in this book offers the following services: mail holding and messages; exchange (usually at mediocre rates but without commission on AmEx traveler's checks, making these rates the best around); cashing cardholder's checks; money wiring; selling traveler's checks; and a travel agency (if you're there already, bringing your train schedule or price questions to them might save you a wait at the station). Some American Express offices also have ATM machines; the availability of ATM machines, and other special services, is listed by individual office for each city.

If your income is low, you may have difficulty acquiring an internationally recognized credit card. However, if a family member already has a card, it's easy to get an extra one. American Express will issue a second green card for $30 per year ($35 for a gold card); bills go to your loved ones. Check with your bank for details on obtaining an extra Visa or MasterCard.

Convenient as they may be, credit cards require extra vigilance. Lost or stolen cards should be reported *immediately,* or you may be held responsible for forged charges. Write down the card-cancellation telephone numbers for your bank and keep them in a safe place separate from your cards. Always be sure that the carbon has been torn into pieces, and ask to watch as your card is being imprinted; an imprint onto a blank slip can be used later to charge merchandise in your name, eventually resulting in a pitched battle with your credit card company.

Sending Money

The easiest way to get money from home is to bring an **American Express Card.** American Express allows cardholders to draw cash (up to $200 in local currency) from their checking accounts (checkbook welcomed but not required) at any of its full-fledged offices and many of its representatives' offices, up to $1000 every 21 days (no service charge, no interest). With someone feeding money into your account back home, you'll be set. The next best approach is to wire money through the instant international money transfer services operated by **Western Union** (tel. (800) 225-5227) or **American Express** (tel. (800) 543-4080). The sender visits one of their offices or calls and charges it to a credit card; the receiver can pick up the cash at any overseas office abroad within minutes (American Express charges about $25-35 to send $250, $70 for $1000; Western Union charges $50 for $1000). To pick up the money, you'll either need to show ID or answer a test question. The simplest and stodgiest route is to **cable money** from bank to bank. Find a local bank big enough to have an international department; bring the address of the receiving bank and the destination account number. Usually both sender and receiver must have accounts at the respective institutions. Transfer can take up to a few days; the fee is usually a flat $20-30. Outside American Express offices, avoid trying to cash checks in foreign currencies as they usually require weeks and a $30 fee to clear.

Finally, if you are an American in a life-or-death situation, you can have money sent to you via the State Department's **Citizens Emergency Center,** Bureau of Consular Affairs, CA/PA, Rm. 5807, U.S. Department of State, Washington, DC 20520 (tel. (202) 647-5225 or, in an emergency after business hours, (202) 634-3600). For a fee of about $25, the State Department will forward money within hours to the nearest consular office, which will then disburse it according to instructions. The agency prefers not to send sums greater than $500, and will enclose a message upon request. The quickest way to get money to the State Department is through Western Union.

Value-Added Tax

The Value-Added Tax (VAT) is a form of sales tax levied in the European Economic Community. VAT is generally part of the price paid on goods and services. In Italy, the amount varies from item to item but averages 19%. At certain large stores, visitors from outside the EEC can request exemption from the VAT on merchandise costing L625,000 or more. Ask for an invoice when you make your purchase and present both the certificate and goods to a customs officer upon leaving the country. Once you leave the country, you can claim a refund from the store by mail as long as it is still within 90 days of the date of purchase. Payment by credit card may speed up the processing of the refund check.

Bargaining

Bargaining is common in Italy, but use discretion: it is appropriate and warranted in dealings at markets, with street vendors, and over unmetered taxi fares (always settle your price *before* getting into the cab). But haggling over prices is out of place most everywhere else, especially in large stores. Hotel haggling is most often done in uncrowded, smaller *pensioni* or for *affitta camere* (*Let's Go* mentions when such activity is common). If you speak no Italian, memorize the numbers. Let the merchant make the first offer and counter with one-half to two-thirds of her bid. Never offer anything you are unwilling to pay—you are expected to buy if the merchant accepts your price.

Packing

Pack light. Separating extras from essentials is crucial for maximum comfort and sanity. The convenience of traveling light far outweighs the disadvantages of a limited wardrobe—no one's likely to notice that you've worn the same two outfits for the last six weeks when you're moving from town to town. A tried-and-true method suggests setting out everything you think you'll need and then packing only half of it. Leave expensive jewelry and watches at home; save room for gifts and souvenirs. The more you have to lug around, the less you'll enjoy zipping about. Invest first in a money belt or, even better, a neck pouch that will tuck securely *under* your clothing. Guard your money, passport and other valuables here and keep it with you *at all times*.

Luggage

Determining which type of luggage best suits your needs is critical. Consider a light suitcase if you're going to stay in one city or town for a long time. Those who wish to travel unobtrusively might choose a large shoulder bag that closes securely.

If you're planning to cover a lot of ground by foot, bus, or thumb, a sturdy backpack with several compartments is unbeatable. Packs come in two varieties—external frame and internal frame. Each type has its own advantages. Internal packs are sturdier and more compact. Because they mold well to the back and maintain a lower center of gravity, internals are easier to carry over rough terrain. And the straps usually zip away out of sight, helping to reduce damage in airline baggage compartments. The main advantage of external frame packs is that they lift weight off the back, allowing greater ventilation (of prime importance if you plan to hike in summer) and distribute weight better (which may provide greater comfort over long distances). For normal loads, when the pack functions primarily as a suitcase, an interior-frame model will be less cumbersome and easier to transport. A front-loading pack, in contrast to a top-loading model, will free you from groping for hidden items in the bottom of your pack. Whatever you choose, don't buy a cheap pack. Bargain backpacks have bad zippers, shabby construction, and—worst of all—wimpy straps that will maul your shoulders after a week of hard traveling. A good internal frame pack should run $90-300. Try out several models at a good camping store—packs, like clothes, fit different people differently. When you find one, fill it with weights in the store and take it for a spin. When packing, put all your gear into the pack, then simulate Italian conditions by walking to the nearest cathedral and then up and down a flight of steps a dozen times to make sure you can manage the weight. To minimize tottering, place heavy items up against the inside wall near your center of gravity, and lighter items toward the bottom and top.

No matter what kind of luggage you choose, a small daypack is indispensable for plane flights and sightseeing. You can tote lunch, your camera and other valuables, and a stock of toilet paper to counter its sporadic presence in Italian restrooms. Label every piece of baggage with your name and address and purchase a few small combination locks for your bags (these tiny padlocks pass through two zippers, holding a bag shut). Knife-wielding overnight train robbers won't be dissuaded, but lazier kleptomaniacs may bypass your belongings for more permeable packs.

Sleeping bags are useful for both the serious camper and the budget traveler in winter, when many hostels and *pensioni* save fuel at the slight expense of their patrons' circulation and happiness. When shopping for a sleeping bag, primary consideration should be given to the climate of your intended destination (check the brief temperature table at the end of the General Introduction, or request the climate chart from IAMAT—see Health below). Down-filled bags are fluffy and warm, but expensive ($150-400) and impractical (they're useless when wet). Cheaper bags filled with synthetic insulation (like Quallofil) dry faster, retain their insulation even when soaked, and are lighter and more durable ($100-175). Unless you are traveling in the Italian Alps in the winter, a synthetic bag will suffice for Italy (see Camping section below for further details on sleeping bags).

Don't let bad water ruin your trip.

One out of two world travelers will get sick. Drinking contaminated water is the number one cause. PŪR water purifiers make the water safe to drink.

You're planning a great trip—investing lots of time and money. You don't want to miss a thing. But you worry. You've heard stories. Will you get sick? Is any water really safe? Will you be out enjoying the day as planned? Or will you be spending your days with cramps and diarrhea, hoping the medications will work?

Don't let bad drinking water turn your trip-of-a-lifetime into a nightmare. Wherever you travel, before you drink the local water, purify it with PŪR™ water purifiers—The only ones that instantly remove Giardia and eliminate all other microorganisms including bacteria and viruses.

PŪR water purifiers are affordable, lightweight, and easy to use.

Don't let bad water ruin your trip. Make sure it's safe. Make sure it's PŪR.

For more information or to order,

Call 1-800-845-PURE

Water Purifiers

"My fellow travelers experienced stomach upset and worse while I was completely fine."
—Ellen R. Benjamin, Ph.D.

Clothes and Shoes

Climate should determine your travel wardrobe. Dark-colored items will not show the wear and tear they're bound to suffer, but light colors will be cooler and more comfortable in hot weather. Natural fibers usually beat synthetics. Especially during Italy's summers, cotton or cotton blends keep you cooler and happier, and are easy to wash in a sink.

No nation outdresses Italy. This is not only the country that gave the world Armani and Gucci, it's the country that buys most of that absurdly expensive fashion. Any attempt to compete or blend in will likely prove futile (and financially irreparable), but do bring appropriate clothing for visits to Italy's art-encrusted cathedrals and churches, where shorts, skirts above the knee, and sleeveless and cut-off shirts are usually forbidden—some of the more famous churches even employ clothing guards to keep the immodest away. If you maintain a neat, conservative appearance, you'll fare better when dealing with hotel owners or attempting to hitchhike. Women travelers may avert some harassment by eschewing miniskirts and tank tops (see the Women Travelers section below for further details). In any case, if you want to attend a Papal audience in Rome, women will need to wear a dress and keep their arms and head covered, and men will need a tie and jacket (for both genders, garments should be dark or subdued in color).

Footwear is not the place to cut corners. Lace-up walking shoes provide better support and Italian social acceptability than running or tennis shoes. Again, check the climate—for the rainy fall or spring, you may want to buy a pair of good waterproof shoes with a strong grip. If your plans include Alpine forays, good hiking boots are essential. You may want to try light-weight boots instead of the traditional leather ones. The former are easier to break in, more comfortable and less expensive. They are also ususally better ventilated. But be forewarned: many lightweights that feel nice and cushy in the store will be falling apart after only a few weeks on the trail—look for durability when shopping, and opt for the sturdier leather boots if you plan to hike extensively. Toss some light shoes into your luggage for evening strolls, beachcombing and club-hopping—or buy a pair of Italian leather sandals once you get there. *Break in your shoes before you go.* Sprinkling talcum powder on your feet and inside your shoes and wearing two pairs of socks helps prevent chafing and blisters, while moleskin will protect any blisters that do develop. Bring lots of good socks: grungy or threadbare socks promote blisters and youth hostel ostracism.

Sundries

One pocket of your backpack should be devoted to sundries—a flashlight, Swiss Army knife, first aid kit, Star Wars action figures, travel alarm, water bottle, safety pins, some cord, and a needle and thread. Toiletries should be available, so you won't need extra tubes of toothpaste. Laundry services in Italy are absurdly expensive and inconvenient. Washing clothes in your hotel sink is a better option. A mild liquid soap (available in camping stores) can serve the range from dish detergent to shampoo. Don't forget a plug for the sink; often a rubber squash ball is just the right size to stop the drain, or you can buy a stopper at a hardware store. A mess kit will also be extremely useful, since feasts are easily and readily purchased at the market. Carrying a metal plate (one with high sides that can double as a salad bowl) may look silly when you're packing, but picking salad ingredients out of your lap will look even sillier.

Camera equipment is expensive, fragile, and heavy. The less you bring, the fewer your worries and back ailments. Film availability is limited and prices inflated in smaller towns and tourist centers, so bring supplies along or pick them up in larger cities. Despite disclaimers to the contrary, airport X-ray equipment often fogs film—the higher the speed, the greater the likelihood of damage. Resist the pleas of personnel to send your camera and film through and have it hand-checked. For extra heavy protection, purchase a lead-lined pouch and stash your rolls in it.

Your favorite electrical appliances will require an electric converter. Voltage is generally 220v AC throughout Italy, although some hotels offer 110v. Check before plugging in or you could fry your appliance into oblivion. Since Italy's prongs are not flat but round, U.S. and Australian gadgets need an adapter, available in Italy or from most travel stores. The **Franzus Company,** Murtha Industrial Park, P.O. Box 142, Railroad

Ave., Beacon Falls, CT 06403 (tel. (203) 723-6664, fax (203) 723-6666) publishes the free pamphlet *Foreign Electricity Is No Deep Dark Secret* (which contains, among other things, a voltage list for countries including Italy) and sells a variety of adaptors and converters (Italian adaptor $3.50, kit of 1600-watt converter and 4 adaptor plugs $27.50).

Safety and Security

Large cities demand extra caution. Carry all your valuables (including your passport, railpass, traveler's checks and airline ticket) in a **money belt** or a **necklace pouch** stashed securely *inside* your clothing (both available at any well-stocked travel store). If you carry a purse, buy a sturdy leather one with a secure clasp, and carry it crosswise on the side away from the street with the clasp against you. Even these precautions do not always suffice: moped riders who snatch purses and backpacks sometimes tote knives to cut the straps. As far as packs are concerned, buy some small combination padlocks which slip through two zippers, securing a pack shut; they weigh next to nothing, and their presence will intimidate potential thieves and pickpockets. Never put valuables in your back pocket or the outside pocket of your daypack (what could be an easier target?). Be particularly watchful of your belongings on buses, don't check baggage on trains, especially if you're switching lines, and don't trust anyone to "watch your bag for a second," whether they're from your country or not. Ask the manager of your hotel or hostel for advice on areas to avoid, and if you feel unsafe, look for places with either a curfew or a night attendant. Keep your valuables on you in low-budget hotels where someone else may have a passkey, and always in dormitory-style surroundings—otherwise a trip to the shower could cost you a passport or wallet.

While traveling, steer clear of empty train compartments, particularly at night. A larger padlock to secure the straps of your pack through the luggage holder is a good idea (see the Once There—Transportation section below). If you plan to sleep outside (an option we do NOT recommend), or simply don't want to carry everything with you, store your gear in a train or bus station locker, but be aware that these are occasionally

broken into. Women should consult the section on Women Travelers in Additional Concerns below. For more notes on the habits and hangouts of Italian criminals, consult the Practical Information sections of individual cities (especially Rome and Naples).

If you are ever in a potentially dangerous situation anywhere in Italy, call the **EMERGENCY ASSISTANCE NUMBER—113 or 112.** 113 is the Public Emergency Assistance number for the State Police, and usually has an English interpreter on hand; 112, the Immediate Action Service of the Carabinieri, should be your second choice. 115 is the nationwide telephone number for the fire department, and 116 will bring the ACI (Italian Automobile Club) if you need urgent assistance on the road.

Insurance

The firms listed below offer insurance against theft or loss of luggage, trip cancellation/interruption, and medical emergency. Bear in mind that most policies do not insure items against theft, only against loss or damage by an identifiable third party. Beware of unnecessary coverage. Check to see whether your homeowner's insurance (or your family's coverage) provides against theft during travel. Homeowner's policies will generally cover theft of travel documents (passports, plane tickets, rail passes, etc.) up to $500.

University term-time medical plans often cover summer travel. Buying an ISIC card in the U.S. provides $3000 worth of accident and illness insurance and $100 per day for up to 60 days of hospitalization while the card is valid. Also included is $1000 all-risk accidental death and dismemberment coverage; $10,000 emergency medical evacuation coverage; and $3000 repatriation of remains insurance. CIEE offers an inexpensive Trip-Safe plan with options covering medical treatment and hospitalization, accidents, baggage loss, and even charter flights missed due to illness; STA offers a more expensive, more comprehensive plan. (For CIEE and STA addresses, see Useful Organizations—Budget Travel Services above.)

Remember that insurance companies usually require a copy of the police report for thefts, or evidence of having paid medical expenses (doctor's statements, receipts) before they will honor a claim. Have these written in English, if possible, and make sure that you return home within the specified time limit to file for reimbursement. Always carry policy numbers and proof of insurance.

Travel Assistance International, 1133 15th St. NW, #400, Washington, DC 20005 (tel. (800) 821-2828). Medical and travel insurance up to $30,000. Frequent Traveler plan offers $15,000 coverage for up to 90 days of travel during a single calendar year. Short-term plans available.

Access America, Inc., 6600 W. Broad St., P.O. Box 90310, Richmond, VA 23230 (tel. (800) 234-8300). A subsidiary of Blue Cross/Blue Shield that offers travel insurance and assistance. Covers everything from trip cancellation/interruption, to bail money, to emergency medical evacuation. 24-hr. hotline.

The Travelers Insurance Co., 1 Tower Sq., Hartford, CT 06183 (tel. (800) 243-3174 or (203) 277-2138). Baggage, trip cancellation/interruption, disruption/default, accident, and emergency medical evacuation and assistance coverage.

Travel Guard International, 1145 Clark St., Stevens Point, WI 54481 (tel. (800) 782-5151). Offers a comprehensive "Travel Guard Gold" package, including free medical evacuations and repatriation of remains. The ScholarCare program is tailored to students and faculty spending time abroad.

Edmund A. Cocco Agency/Globalcare Travel Insurance, 220 Broadway, #201, P.O. Box 780, Lynnfield, MA 01940 (tel. (800) 821-2488). Coverage for travel, accident, sickness, and baggage, as well as on-the-spot payment of medical expenses. Services include legal assistance, emergency cash transfers, and medical transportation. Protection against bankruptcy or default of airline and cruise tickets also offered.

Wallach and Company, Inc., 107 West Federal St., P.O. Box 480, Middleburg, VA 22117-0480 (tel. (800) 237-6615, fax (703) 687 3172). Optional trip cancellation, accidental death, and baggage protection plans. 24-hr. worldwide emergency assistance.

Drugs

Travelers should avoid drugs altogether. Italy enacted a "zero-tolerance" law in 1991; possession of any amount of narcotics or even "soft drugs" (i.e. marijuana) is now illegal. Sentences for violations are stiff: up to 15 years in jail and fines of up to L.200,000,000. Travelers have been jailed for possessing as little as 3g of marijuana. Your home government is completely powerless to interfere with the judicial system of a foreign country and all foreigners are subject to Italian law. Consular officers can only visit the prisoner, provide a list of attorneys, and inform family and friends; they cannot repatriate you to a prison in your home country and they cannot reduce your sentence.

Even if you don't use drugs, beware of the person who asks you to carry a package or drive a car across the border. For more information, write for the pamphlet *Travel Warning on Drugs Abroad* from the **Bureau of Consular Affairs,** #5807, Department of State, Washington, DC 20520 (tel. (202) 647-1488).

Health

Don't cut corners on health—few things are as disappointing as a trip ruined by illness or accident. The basic advice: Eat well and avoid exhaustion. Follow a reasonable itinerary to prevent physical and psychological strain. Don't be too anxious to embrace all the local customs—-watch the caffeine intake; one man's 10 cups of espresso a day is another's poison. Protein is an excellent source of sustained energy, and fluids are essential. Italian water is safe to drink unless marked "*acqua non potabile*." Relying on bottled mineral water for the first few weeks minimizes chances of a bad reaction to the few unfamiliar microbes in Italian water.

Italy, especially the south, scorches in the summer. Be wary of over-exertion and heatstroke. Drink plenty of non-alcoholic fluids, don a brimmed hat that shades your head completely and stay indoors during peak sun hours (10am-2pm). Heatstroke can occur even without exposure to the sun; symptoms include headache, flushed skin, excessive sweating, and fever. You'll feel better by getting out of the sun immediately,

covering yourself with cold, wet towels, and drinking fruit juice or salty water (to ward off dehydration). People with asthma or allergies should be aware that Rome often has visibly high levels of air pollution, particularly during the summer. If you're planning on spending time beneath the open sky, be sure to use sunblock. Remember that the sun's rays are more powerful at higher altitudes, and that UV rays penetrate clouds. Biking or driving through the countryside may summon allergies that you didn't even know you had. If you're worried about any of the above, see your physician before leaving; in any case, you should check with her or him and make sure your inoculations are up to date. Perhaps consider joining **International SOS Assistance** (tel. (800) 523-8390). Members receive emergency medical care, including transportation to hospitals or appropriate care units. Weekly ($40), monthly ($80) and annual memberships ($275) are available.

Even if you are in good health at home, you can't be sure how your body will react to the stress of traveling in a foreign country. It's a good idea to include a small **first-aid kit** among your traveling accessories. You can make one at home, or purchase a ready-made one from a hardware store, and stock it according to your needs. Items you might want to include are: bandages, antiseptic soap or an antibiotic cream, a thermometer in a sturdy case, a Swiss army knife (with tweezers), moleskin, sunscreen, insect repellent, aspirin, a decongestant, something for motion sickness, an antihistamine, and a remedy for diarrhea.

If you wear glasses or contact lenses, take an extra pair or a prescription with you, and make arrangements with someone at home to send you a replacement pair in an emergency. If you wear contacts, you should take along a pair of glasses to rest tired eyes. Bring extra solutions, enzyme tablets, and eyedrops—the price for lens solution in Italy can be exorbitant, and under-cleaning your lenses risks serious eye injury.

Travelers with a chronic medical condition requiring medication should consult their physician before departing. Always carry up-to-date prescriptions and/or a statement from your doctor, especially if you will be bringing insulin, syringes, or any narcotics into the country. Carry an ample supply of all medications, since matching your prescription with a foreign equivalent may be problematic. And when flying, tote all medication in your carry-on bag. If you have diabetes, contact your local **American Diabetes Association** office, where they can assist you in obtaining an ID card. Request a copy of their information sheet which includes ways to state that you are diabetic and request help in several languages.

Travelers with medical conditions that cannot be easily recognized (e.g. diabetes, allergies to antibiotics, epilepsy, heart conditions) should consider obtaining a **Medic Alert Identification** tag ($35 for a steel tag, $40 for silver, $50 for gold). This internationally recognized emblem identifies the medical problem and provides the number of Medic Alert's 24-hr. hotline. Medical personnel can call this number to obtain information about the member's medical history. Write to Medic Alert Foundation International, 2323 North Colorado St., Turlock, CA 95381-1009 (tel. (800) 432-5378).

Abortion is legal in Italy, although not as a means of birth control. Local health units called *consultori* advise women on rights and procedures. In Milan, the office is **Consultorio Familiare ANCED,** corso Buenos Aires, 75 (tel. (02) 670 15 79). There are also hospitals in most large cities that administer "morning after" contraceptives—as always, be sure they fully explain the side effects to you.

Before leaving home, you may wish to join the **International Association for Medical Assistance to Travelers (IAMAT),** 417 Center St., Lewiston, NY 14092 (tel. (716) 754-4883); in Canada, 40 Regal Rd., Guelph, Ont. N1K 1B5 (tel. (519) 836-0102); in Australia, 575 Bourke St., 12th Floor, Melbourne 3000; in New Zealand, P.O. Box 5049, Christchurch 5. Along with a variety of useful brochures (*How to Adjust to the Heat, How to Adapt to Altitude, How to Avoid Traveler's Diarrhea*), members receive an ID card, a chart detailing advisable immunizations for 200 countries and territories, and a worldwide directory of English-speaking physicians who have had medical training in Europe or North America. Membership is free (a donation is requested) and doctors are on call 24 hrs. a day for IAMAT members. Contributors of $25.00 or more to IAMAT will also receive a packet of 24 World Climate Charts detailing climates, seasonal clothing, and sanitary conditions of water, milk, and food in 140 cities around the world. Throughout Italy, American Express and Thomas Cook offices can help you find English-speaking doctors. Remember that First Aid Service (*Pronto Soccorso*) is available in airports, ports, and train stations. At every drugstore (*farmacia*) in Italy, there is a list of pharmacies open all night and on Sundays.

Useful health information is available from a variety of sources. Write the **Superintendent of Documents,** U.S. Government Printing Office, Washington, DC 20402 (tel. (202) 783-3238) for *Health Information for International Travel* ($5). **The Pocket Medical Encyclopedia and First-Aid Guide** ($4.95) might also be helpful. Write Simon and Schuster, 200 Old Tappan Rd., Old Tappan, NJ 07675, Attn: Direct Order Dept. (tel. (800) 223-2348).

Alternatives to Tourism

Work

The employment situation in Italy is grim for natives (especially in the South) and even worse for foreigners. Work visas are extremely difficult to obtain since you must find a job that cannot be filled by an Italian. Openings are coveted by herds of would-be expatriates, so competition is fierce. Unfortunately, the innocent dream of a glamorous job in Rome is illegal without a real-life visa, and stiff punishment can be a very real consequence of bending the laws. Foreigners are most successful at securing harvest work, restaurant or bar work, housework, or work in the tourism industry, where English-speakers are needed. Teaching English can be particularly lucrative. Local language schools, usually called "The Cambridge School" or "The Oxford School" are listed in the phone book. Some schools simply post signs in stores, hair salons, or *caffès*. No more than minimal Italian is necessary to teach conversation.

On the other hand, there is the cash-based, untaxable, underground economy—*economia sommersa* or *economia nera*--which makes up as much as one-third of Italy's economy. Your best bet is to work connections. Friends abroad may be able to expedite work permits or arrange informal work-for-accommodations swaps at their uncle's

trattoria or their cousin's farm. Many permitless agricultural workers go untroubled by local authorities, who recognize the need for seasonal labor. European Community citizens can work in any other EC country without working papers, and if your parents or grandparents were born in an EC country, you may be able to claim dual citizenship or at least the right to a work permit. Students can check with their university's foreign language departments, which may have official or unofficial access to job openings abroad. If you're convinced that you can get a legitimate job, *The Directory of Overseas Summer Jobs* ($14.95) may help. This listing of 50,000 volunteer and paid openings worldwide is available from Peterson's Guides, 202 Carnegie Center, P.O. Box 2123, Princeton, NJ 08543 (tel. (800) EDU-DATA (338-3282); in New Jersey (609) 243-9111). Peterson's also distributes *Work Your Way Around the World* ($16.95), a collection of practical advice and creative job-hunting ideas. For publications and organizations with information on work in Italy, check *Work, Study, Travel Abroad: The Whole World Handbook,* compiled by CIEE ($12.95, $1.50 postage). The *Directory of Summer Jobs Abroad* lists 30,000 vacancies in a variety of fields (£7.95). Write to Vacation Work Publications, 9 Park End St., Oxford OX1 1HJ, England (tel. (0865) 24 19 78). In Italy, check the help-wanted columns in the English-language papers *Daily American* and the *International Daily News. Wanted in Rome* is available in English-language bookstores or from their office at via dei Delfini, 17, 00185 Roma (tel. (06) 679 01 90). In Milan, you can place a free advertisement in the weekly *Secondamano* (also good for finding rides); in Rome, contact *Porta Portese,* via di Porta Maggiore, 95 (tel. 73 37 48). The magazine *AAM Terra Nuova* (L6000 per issue), good for agricultural jobs, can be obtained by writing to Casella Postale 2, 50038 Scarperia (tel. (055) 840 15 84). Radios will usually broadcast free advertisements, and prospective *au pairs* should consider placing advertisements in women's magazines.

Summer positions as a tour group leader are available with **Hostelling International (HI)** and **American Youth Hostels (AYH)**, P.O. Box 37613, Washington, DC 20013-7613 (tel. (202) 783-6161). You must be at least 21, take a week-long leadership course ($295, room and board included) and lead a group in the U.S. before leading a trip to Europe. The **Experiment in International Living (EIL)** requires language fluency,

leadership ability and extensive overseas experience for similar positions. You must be at least 24. EIL also runs an exchange program for high school students (P.O. Box 676, Kipling Rd., Brattleboro, VT 05302, tel. (800) 345-2929).

Teaching is another work option in Italy. The **Institute of International Education (IIE)** publishes *Academic Year Abroad,* a directory of teaching opportunities in over 100 countries worldwide. To purchase a copy ($31.95 plus $3.80 shipping), send a check made out to the IIE to Communications Division, Box TF, Institute of International Education, 809 United Nations Plaza, New York, NY 10017 (tel. (212) 883-8279). You may be able to secure a teaching position with an American school in Italy through one of these organizations: **U.S. Department of State,** Office of Overseas Schools, Room 245 SA-29, Department of State, Washington, DC 20522-2902 (tel. (703) 875-7800), which can send you a list of English-language K-12 schools abroad which you can then contact directly; the **U.S. Department of Defense,** 2461 Eisenhower Ave., Alexandria, VA 22331 (tel. (202) 325-0885); and **International Schools Services,** P.O. Box 5910, Roszel Rd., Princeton, NJ 08540 (tel. (609) 452-0990). The ISS, which operates and assists English-speaking schools abroad, publishes a free pamphlet entitled *Your Passport to Teaching and Administrative Services Abroad.* The *ISS Directory* ($29.95, $5.75 postage) can be obtained through Peterson's Inc. ISS also publishes a free pamphlet, available upon request.

Long-term employment is difficult to secure unless you have skills in high-demand areas, such as medicine (including nursing) or computer programming. If you're determined to have a glamorous, international career, Eric Kocher has compiled job-hunting strategies in *International Jobs: Where They Are, How To Get Them* ($14.66, postage included), published by Addison-Wesley, 1 Jacob Way, Reading, MA 01867 (tel. (800) 447-2226). For jobs in private industry, contact the Italian consulate for a listing of firms, or consult the *Directory of American Firms Operating in Foreign Countries,* published by World Trade Academy Press, 50 East 42nd St., #509, New York, NY 10017 (tel. (212) 697-4999). Although the three-volume set costs $195, World Trade also offers excerpts containing lists of American firms in specific countries (averaging $10-15 per country).

The **Association for International Practical Training (AIPT)** is the U.S. affiliate of the International Association for the Exchange of Students for Technical Experience (IAESTE). AIPT offers on-the-job training and internships in more than 80 countries for full-time students with at least two years of university study in engineering, computer science, math, the natural sciences, applied arts, or agriculture. Apply ($75) to IAESTE Trainee Program, c/o AIPT, 10400 Little Patuxent Parkway, Suite #250, Columbia, MD 21044 (tel. (410) 997-2200).

Volunteering

Volunteering is also a good way to immerse yourself in a foreign culture. Besides the personal satisfaction, you may even receive room and board for your work. *Volunteer! The Comprehensive Guide to Voluntary Service in the U.S. and Abroad,* ($8.95, postage $1.50) offering advice and listings, is available from CIEE (See Budget Travel Services—Useful Organizations).

Volunteers for Peace, 43 Tiffany Rd., Belmont, VT 05730 (tel. (802) 259-2759) publishes *The International Work Camp Directory* ($10 postpaid) and a free newsletter. The organization arranges placement in 34 different countries ($125 placement fee). Though few openings are available, you can volunteer as a camp counselor for the **YMCA** in Italy by contacting their International Camp Counselor Abroad Program (ICCA), 356 W. 34th St., New York, NY 10001 (tel. (212) 563-3441). Applicants must be over 17 and U.S. citizens.

Archeological Digs

For information on archeological digs, write to the **Centro Camuno di Studi Preistorici,** 25044 Capo di Ponte, Valcomonica (Brescia) (tel. (0364) 420 91). This research center offers volunteer work, grants, tutoring, research assistant positions, and training and apprenticeship in scientific art and editing. The **Archeological Institute of America,** 675 Commonwealth Ave., Boston, MA 02215 (tel. (617) 353-9361) puts out the *Archeological Fieldwork Opportunities Bulletin* ($10.50 non-members) which lists

over 200 field sites throughout the world, available from Kendall/Hunt Publishing Co. (tel. (800) 338-5578).

Study

There are several comprehensive guides available on international study programs. A good place to start is *Work, Study, and Travel Abroad: The Whole World Handbook* ($12.95, $1.50 postage), which describes over 1000 study programs and lists eligibility requirements and application timetables for each. For more information, contact the Campus Information and Student Services Department, CIEE, 205 E. 42nd St., New York, NY 10017 (tel. (212) 661-1414). Senior travelers should consider a course with **Elderhostel** (see Senior Travelers—Additional Concerns). The **Institute of International Education (IIE)** publishes several annual reference books. *Vacation Study Abroad* ($26.95, postage $3) and *Academic Year Abroad* ($31.95, postage $3) describe a myriad of study-abroad programs. *Vacation Study Abroad* details over 1000 summer and short-term programs. Order from 809 United Nations Plaza, New York, NY 10017 (tel. (212) 883-8200). IIE also recently compiled *Financial Resources for International Study* ($36.95, $5.75 postage), which lists 630 foundations that offer grants to the cosmopolitan scholar (available from **Peterson's Guides,** see above). The tourist office of the **Centro Turistico Studentesco e Giovanile (CTS),** via Genova, 16, 00184 Roma (tel. (06) 467 91; fax (06) 467 92 05) is connected with the Italian Ministry of Foreign Affairs and the Italian Ministry of Education. They provide information on foreign study in Italy. The **American Institute for Foreign Study,** 102 Greenwich Ave., Greenwich, CT 06830 (tel. (800) 727-2437 or (203) 869-9090) offers summer, semester, and year-long courses in Italian language, art history, and studio art in Florence in cooperation with Italian universities. (Intensive orientation in Siena. Semesters $6700, full year $12,250.) The **American Field Service (AFS)** offers both summer- and year-long opportunities in Italy for high school students, ages 15-18. Write to AFS International/Intercultural Programs, 313 E. 43rd St., New York, NY 10017 (tel. (800) 237-4636 or (212) 949-4242).

If your Italian is fluent, consider enrolling directly in an Italian university. Universities are overcrowded, but you will probably have a blast and develop a real feel for the culture. For an application, write to the nearest Italian consulate. In Rome, contact the Segretaria Stranieri, Città Universitaria, piazzale delle Scienze, 2, Roma. Remember that visas are required of foreign students in Italy. Contact these organizations for more advice:

Amicizia, Casella Postale 42-PG I, 06100 Perugia (office address: via Fabretti, 59; tel. (075) 202 12). International student organization for work and study in Italy.

Ufficio Centrale Studenti Esteri in Italia (UCSEI), via Monti Parioli, 59, 00197 Roma (tel. (06) 320 44 91 or 321 89 01). National organization for foreign students in Italy.

Another option is studying at an institute designed for foreigners but run by an Italian university. Write to the Italian Cultural Institute for a complete list of programs (see Useful Organizations). The following schools and organizations offer a variety of classes.

ABC Centro di Lingua e Cultura Italiana, via G. Carducci, 3, 50121 Firenze (tel. (055) 247 92 20). Italian Language School in Florence offering language, studio art, art history, and cooking courses for 1-24 weeks.

Centro Linguistico Italiano Dante Alighieri, via B. Marliano, 4, 00162 Roma (tel. (06) 832 01 84, fax (06) 860 42 03); via dei Bardi, 12, 50125 Firenze (tel. (55) 234 29 84, fax (55) 234 28 77). Language classes, cultural daytrips, extracurricular activities. Write 1- 2 months in advance.

Instituto per l'Arte e il Restauro, Palazzo Spinelli, borgo Santa Croce, 10, 50122 Firenze (tel. (055) 24 48 08 or 24 48 09). Summer and year-long courses on Italian language, art, and art restoration.

Italiaidea, p. della Cancelleria, 85, 00186 Roma (tel. (06) 683 07620, fax (06) 689 29 97). Organizes language, arts, and culture courses throughout the year, including vacation courses at the seaside or in the mountains during summer months.

Koinè, Centro Koinè, via de' Pandolfini, 27, 50122 Firenze (tel. (055) 21 38 81, fax (055) 21 69 49). Offers group and 1-on-1 courses on Italian language and culture. Instruction centers in Florence and Lucca all year round, also Cortona and Orbetello during spring and summer.

Università Italiana per Stranieri, Palazzo Gallenga, p. Fortebraccio, 4, 06100 Perugia (tel. (075) 643 44). Language classes, cultural instruction, daytrips, and extracurricular activities.

Keeping in Touch

Mail

The postal system in Italy has justly drawn snickers from the rest of Western Europe, and now ranges from barely decent to deplorable. Aerograms and airmail letters from Italy take anywhere from one to three weeks to arrive in the U.S., while surface mail—much less expensive—takes a month or longer. Since postcards are low-priority mail, send important messages by airmail letter. Letters and small parcels rarely get lost if sent *raccomandata* (registered), *espresso* (express), or *via aerea* (air mail). Stamps *(francobolli)* are available at face value in *tabacchi* (tobacco shops), but you should mail your letters from a post office to be sure they are stamped correctly. Overseas letters are L1150; overseas postcards are L1050. Letters and postcards within Europe are L750 and L650 respectively.

Make sure anyone sending you mail from North America allows it at least two weeks to reach you. Mail from home can be sent to a hotel where you have reservations, or you can collect mail from most American Express offices if you have an American Express card or carry their traveler's checks. Have the sender write "Client Mail" on the envelope with the office's complete address.

Letters addressed to the post office with your name and the phrase "Fermo Posta" (General Delivery) will be held at the post office of any city or town. You must claim your mail in person with your passport as identification, and you may have to pay L250 per piece of mail. In major cities like Rome, the post office handling *Fermo Posta* usually is efficient and has long hours (though they close at noon on Saturdays and the last day of the month, and are also closed on Sunday). Since a city may have more than one post office, write the address of the receiving office if possible. It's also a good idea to have the sender capitalize and underline your last name to ensure proper sorting. Before writing a letter off as lost, check under your first name, too.

If you need to get something to or from Italy with celerity, both **Federal Express** and **DHL** operate in Italy, as do several Italian competitors. Shipments from North America to anywhere in Italy are guaranteed to arrive within 48 hours; shipments (up to 500g) from Italy are guaranteed anywhere in the world within two days. The cost from the U.S. to Italy for under 220g of documents is about $25; shipping anything but documents usually involves filling out a commercial invoice. Contact the companies directly for more information.

Telephones

Italian phone numbers range from two to eight digits in length. *Let's Go* makes every effort to get up-to-date phone numbers, but everyone is at the mercy of the Italian phone system, which this year is undergoing yet another change in a seemingly endless series of major overhauls. Everywhere, phone numbers change with bothersome frequency; in Rome they change as quickly as traffic lights. If you call an old number, you may hear a recording of the new number in Italian, possibly even in English. For directory assistance, dial 12. Insert L200 if you are calling from a pay phone—the coins will be returned when you complete your call. Phone books often list two numbers: the first is the number at the time of printing, the second (marked by the word *prendera*) is what the number will be at some future, unspecified time. For an English-speaking operator, dial 170.

There are three types of telephones in Italy. Hold-outs from the dark ages of telecommunications take only tokens (*gettoni*) which are available (though increasingly rarely) for L200 from machines in train and bus stations, coffee shops, and telephone booths. *Gettoni* are also accepted as L200 coins, so there's no need to worry about buying too many. Instructions are posted on all phones; one *gettone* buys five minutes. You should usually deposit three or four, even if your call is local. If you underestimate, you may be cut off in the middle of your conversation. At the end of your call, press the return button for unused *gettoni*. To place long-distance calls, deposit six *gettoni* initially, and continue to feed the machine at every beep. For intercity calls, deposit eight or more. Thankfully, *gettoni* machines are being phased out. When using them, be sure to dial slowly as they sometimes misdial and disconnect if you treat them roughly. Expect a couple of tries to get through successfully.

Scatti calls are made from a phone run by an operator (who may simply be the proprietor in a bar). Every town has at least one bar with a *telefono a scatti*, which can be used for international calls. A meter records the cost of your call, and you pay when you finish. Check with the operator before you lift the receiver, and remember that he or she may tack on a substantial service fee.

The third type of phone is most common, and accepts either coins (L100, 200 or 500) or **phone cards**. Cards are an appealing, modern method. Cards can be bought for L5000 or L10,000 from machines, usually found near the phone. When you insert the card, a meter subtracts lire from it as you speak and displays the remaining value. Partially used cards can be removed and re-used. If you happen to run out in the middle of a call, you must insert another card, so buy more than one if you're planning a long conversation.

For the most part, it is not difficult to make **long-distance calls within Europe.** A person-to-person call is *con preavviso,* and a collect call is *contassa a carico del destinatario* or *chiamata collect.*

Intercontinental calls can be made from phone card pay phones. In some small towns, however, international calls must be made from telephone company offices (SIP or ASST), generally found near the main post office and sometimes in major train stations, or from a *telefono a scatti.* To place a call at a telephone office, fill out a form at the counter. You will be assigned a specific booth. Some offices ask for a L10,000 deposit. When direct-dialing is possible, dial two zeros and then the country code (U.S. and Canada 1, Ireland 353, Great Britain 44, Australia 61, New Zealand 64), followed by the area code and number. Calls to the U.S. cost L10,000 for three minutes and L3000 for each minute thereafter. Rates are highest on weekdays 8:30am-1pm, decrease after 6:30pm on weekdays and Saturdays from 1 to 10pm, and are at their lowest 11pm-8am, on holidays, and between 2:30pm on Saturday and 8am on Monday. Perhaps the simplest way to call long-distance is to use the **AT&T Direct Service;** dialing a single number will connect you to an overseas, English-speaking operator who will then dial your collect call for you (you can also use a calling card). When calling the U.S. from most major cities in Italy, you can reach an AT&T operator by dialing 172 10 11 or an MCI operator with 172 10 22. For MCI customer service call 1678 790 73. You may want to consider getting a calling card from either company if you plan to make a lot of international calls; the cost is significantly lower. In order to receive a card with the AT&T Direct numbers for most European countries, call AT&T at 1-800-874-4000. Remember that getting through often takes several tries.

Calls to Italy must be preceded by the country code (39) and the city code. When direct-dialing, the zero should be dropped from the beginning of each city code. Italians usually yell into the phone when calling long-distance, and you'll know the reason if you attempt an international call. The best connections are often abysmal; don't bother hanging up and trying again—it'll probably get worse. Work those lungs, lose your inhibitions and bellow if you want to communicate with your loved ones.

Telegraphs and Fax Machines

The surest way to get an important message across the ocean is by wire service. **Telegrams** are sent from the post office and cost L815 per word, including the address. Night letters are wired and then delivered (L370 per word up to 22 words). In Rome, telegrams can be sent from the post office at p. San Silvestro during business hours at booths #73-76. **Faxes** may be sent and received at #77. At night, use the Telegraph Office (p. San Silvestro, 18, next door to the post office; tel. (06) 675 55 30) for sending telegrams or receiving faxes. The night office is open whenever the post office is closed. The staff claims faxing to or from the U.S. is impossible, but insist. Fees are

about L10,000 a page. If you have difficulty with a public fax service, try asking the concierge of an upscale hotel. Explain your situation and offer to pay all charges.

Additional Concerns

Senior Travelers

Senior travelers are entitled to a number of travel-related discounts—always ask about these. A perfect example: **Hostelling International** welcomes seniors; memberships are available to those over 55 at a discounted $15. For more information, contact AYH, P.O. Box 37613, Washington DC, 20013-7613 (tel. (202) 783-6161) or any AYH-affiliated hostel federation. The following organizations and publications provide information on discounts, tours, and health and travel tips for traveling seniors.

American Association of Retired Persons, Special Services Dept. 601 E St., NW, Washington, DC 20049 (tel. (202) 434-2277 or (800) 227-7737). U.S residents over 50 and their spouses are eligible for group and individual discounts on lodging, car and RV rental, air arrangements and sightseeing. For AARP-arranged tours and cruises call (800) 927-0111. Annual membership $8.

Bureau of Consular Affairs, Superintendent of Documents, U.S. Government Printing Office, Washington, DC 20402 (tel. (202) 783-3238). Their *Travel Tips for Older Americans* ($1) provides information on passports, visas, health, and currency.

Elderhostel, 75 Federal St., 3rd floor, Boston, MA 02110 (tel. (617) 426-7788). Several Italian universities participate in this miniaturized-study abroad program ($2200-$2800, including airfare from New York). Available to people over 60 and their over-50 spouses, courses are offered in a variety of academic fields and last 2-4 weeks.

E.P. Dutton Publishing Co., Inc., Penguin USA, 120 Woodbine St., Bergenfield, NJ 07621 (tel. (800) 331-4624). Publishes *The Discount Guide for Travelers Over 55* by Caroline and Walter Weintz ($7.95, postage $1.50).

National Council of Senior Citizens, 1331 F St. NW, Washington, DC 20004 (tel. (202) 347-8800). For an annual membership fee of $12 or a lifetime fee of $150, members receive information on discounts and travel abroad, hotel and auto discounts, and supplemental Medicare insurance.

Pilot Industries, Inc., 103 Cooper St., Babylon, NY 11702 (tel. (516) 422-2225). Publishes the newly-revised *Senior Citizens' Guide to Budget Travel In Europe* ($5.95) and *The International Health Guide for Senior Citizen Travelers.* ($4.95). Postage for either book is $1.

Travelers with Disabilities

Italians are making an increased effort to meet the needs of people with disabilities. The **Italian Government Travel Office (ENIT)** provides listings of accessible hotels and associations for people with disabilities in various Italian cities and regions. When making arrangements with airlines or hotels, specify exactly what you need and allow time for preparation and confirmation of arrangements. In most **train stations**, a porter will assist you for L500 to L1000 per bag. Major train stations will provide aid as long as you make reservations by telephone 24 hrs. in advance. Italy's rail system is modernized, so most trains are wheelchair accessible. For more information, call Italy's state rail office in New York (tel. (212) 697-2100).

If you plan to bring a seeing-eye dog to Italy, contact your veterinarian and the nearest Italian consulate. You will need an import license, a current certificate of your dog's inoculations, and a letter from your veterinarian certifying your dog's health (See the section below on *Pets*).

These organizations may prove helpful:

American Federation for the Blind, 15 W. 16th St., New York, NY 10011 (tel. (212) 620-2159 or (800) 232-5463). Offers information, recommends travel books, and issues ID cards ($10, useful for discounts) to the legally blind. Write for an application, or call the Products Center at (800) 829-0500.

Directions Unlimited, 720 North Bedford Rd., Bedford Hills, NY 10507 (tel. (800) 533-5343). Specializes in individual and group vacations, tours, and cruises for people with disabilities.

Disability Press, Ltd., Applemarket House, 17 Union St., Kingston-upon-Thames, Surrey KT1 1RP, England (tel. (081) 549 6399). Publishes the *Disabled Traveler's International Phrasebook* (£1.75), a compilation of useful phrases in 8 languages, including Italian. Supplements also available in Norwegian, Hungarian, and Serbo-Croation (60p each).

Mobility International, USA (MIUSA), P.O. Box 3551, Eugene, OR 97403 (tel. (503) 343-1284, voice and TDD). Provides information on travel and exchange programs, accommodations, organized tours, and more. Contacts in over 30 countries. Publishes *A World of Options: A Guide to International Educational Exchange, Community Service and Travel for Persons with Disabilities* ($14 to members, $16 otherwise, postage included).

The Society for the Advancement of Travel for the Handicapped (SATH), 345 Fifth Ave. #610, New York, NY 10016 (tel. (212) 447-SATH (7284), fax (212) 725-8253). Advice and assistance on trip-planning. Publishes a quarterly travel newsletter and information booklets (free for members, $2 for nonmembers). Annual membership $45, students and senior citizens $25.

Travel Information Service, Moss Rehabilitation Hospital, 1200 W. Tabor Rd., Philadelphia, PA 19141 (tel. (215) 456-9600). Brochures on tourist sights, accommodations, transportation and travel accessibility services mailed for a $5 fee.

Evergreen Travel Service, 4114 198th St. SW, Suite #13, Lynnwood, WA 98036 (tel. (800) 435-2288 or (206) 776-1184). Provides travel information and arranges tours worldwide for people with disabilities. In the U.S., their "Wings on Wheels" tours feature charter buses with wheelchair accessible facilities; they also offer tours for the blind and "lazy bones" tours for travelers who like a slower pace.

Whole Person Tours, P.O. Box 1084, Bayonne, NJ 07002-1084 (tel. (201) 858-3400). Organizes international tours and publishes *The Itinerary,* a magazine for travelers with physical disabilities. 1-year subscription (6 issues) $10, 2-year subscription (14 issues) $20.

Gay and Lesbian Travelers

Gay and lesbian travelers may find Italians unwelcoming, particularly in the South. Holding hands or walking arm-in-arm with someone of the same sex, however, is common in Italy, especially for women, and sexual acts between members of the same sex are legal for those above the age of consent (16). People in large cities—Bologna, Milan, and Turin—tend to be more tolerant: just last year, Italians elected their first openly gay candidate to Parliament. Gay bars dot the nightclub scene in most cities (they also provide a refuge for women of all persuasions who want nightlife without incessant ogling), and a few gay beaches (*spiagge gay*) dot the shores. The Italian national gay organization, **ACRI-gay,** is linked to the Communist Party in Bologna, p. di Porta Saragozza, 2, P.O. Box 691, 40100 Bologna (tel. (051) 43 67 00). *Babilonia,* a national gay magazine, is published monthly. Women's organizations and lesbian groups are often one and the same in Italy. The best source is once again connected to the Communist Party: the **ACRI-Co-ordinamento Donne** (at via F. Carrara, 24 in Rome; tel. (06) 35 791) publishes the bimonthly newsletter *Bolettino associazione Lesbiche Italiane.* The following sources should prove helpful in planning your trip; before ordering any publications, try the gay and lesbian sections of your local bookstores.

Spartacus International Gay Guide ($27.95) provides over 1000 pages of information for gay men, covering almost every country in the world. Order from 100 E. Biddle St., Baltimore, MD 21202 (tel. (301) 727 5677), or Bruno Gmünder Verlag, publisher, Worldwide Sales and Distribution, Luetzowstrasse 10, P.O. Box 30 13 45, D-1000, Berlin 30, Germany (tel. (030) 254 98 200).

Giovanni's Room, 345 S. 12th St., Philadelphia, PA 19107 (tel. (215) 923-2960). An international feminist, gay, and lesbian bookstore and mail-order house. They stock most of the publications listed here, as well as many others of interest to gay and lesbian travelers.

Ferrari Publications, P.O. Box 37887, Phoenix, AZ 85069 (tel. (602) 863-2408), publishes *Places of Interest* ($12.95), *Places for Men* ($12.95), and *Places of Interest to Women* ($10). Ferrari also publishes *Inn Places: USA and Worldwide Gay Accommodations* ($14.95).

The Women's Traveler, ($12), a travel guide for the lesbian community, provides listings of bars, restaurants, accommodations, bookstores, and services in over 50 cities worldwide. Available only in the U.S. or Canada from the Bob Damran Co., P.O. Box 11270, San Francisco, CA 94101 (tel. (415) 255-0404).

Random House publishes a similar touring book for gay and lesbian travelers called *Are You Two Together?* by L. van Gelder for $18.

Women Travelers

Women traveling in Italy must take extra precautions, especially if they're going solo. The native men are often quite friendly. Spotted on neon vespas, brandishing mirrored Ray-bans and sporting quite a bit of hair gel, these Romeos show a remarkable interest in your origin, your destination and your general well-being. While the constant barrage of queries and catcalls can become annoying, sometimes plain offensive, take it in stride. Italian males consider flirtation both an art form and a game; most comments should not be taken seriously. Women, whether alone or in groups, can avoid most harassment by adopting the attitude of Roman women: Walk like you know where you are going, avoid eye contact (sunglasses are indispensable), meet all advances with silence and dignity, and, if still troubled, walk or stand near older women or couples until you feel safe. If you can, tell a police officer that you are being followed. A walkman with headphones tells potential harassers that you're not listening (but be careful—purse-snatchers and pickpockets will take note of your musical oblivion as well). Wearing tight or suggestive clothing can attract unwanted attention, but so can attire that is perfectly modest but obviously American (sweatshirts, college t-shirts, sneakers, hiking shorts, even jean jackets). If you are physically harassed on the bus or in some other crowded space, don't talk to the person directly (this only encourages him); rather, use body language, like a well-aimed knee or elbow, to make your point. Stepping hard on toes works admirably. Again, if you sense real trouble ask the people around you for help. With luck, you may get the satisfaction of seeing your tormentor get an indignant, rapid-fire Italian tongue-lashing. When traveling on Italian trains, avoid empty compartments, especially at night. Look for compartments with large nuns for maximum safety. For more detailed advice, the *Handbook for Women Travelers* is available for £4.95 from Judy Piatkus Publishers, 5 Windmill St., London W1, 1P HF England (tel. (01) 631 07 10). Memorize the emergency number (113 or 112) and keep enough money handy for telephone calls and bus or taxi rides.

Budget accommodations occasionally mean more risk than savings. Avoid small dives and city outskirts; go for university dormitories or youth hostels instead. Centrally located accommodations are usually safest and easiest to return to after dark. *Let's Go* notes individual accommodations that are particularly safe or unsafe for women and includes, wherever possible, locations and numbers of women's centers, special accommodations for women, and rape crisis centers. Some religious organizations also offer rooms for women only. For a list of these institutions, contact the city's archdiocese or write to the provincial tourist office. Also helpful is the **Associazione Cattolica Internazionale al Servizio della Giovane,** which runs hostels for women throughout Italy. Their main offices are at via Urbana, 158, 00184 Roma (tel. (06) 482 79 89), and corso Garibaldi, 121a-123, 20121 Milano (tel. (02) 659 52 06 or 659 96 60).

Traveling with Children

Despite now having the lowest birthrate in Europe, Italians are well known for their love of children, and you will probably encounter more cooing than complications. Most hotels will put a cot in your room for a 30% price increase. Most large cities have permanent amusement parks (Rome in particular), a welcome respite from museums and churches. Even picky children tend to enjoy the simplest (and cheapest) of Italian foods: pizza, spaghetti (*al sugo* or *al ragù* will bring a red meat sauce), and *gelato*. Even so, planning ahead and drawing up a detailed itinerary are especially useful for those traveling with small children. Remember that you may have to slow your pace considerably, and keep in mind that all the new sights and experiences are especially exhausting for kids—you may want to leave room for a mid-afternoon nap for everyone. Allow plenty of flexibility in your plans, book your rooms ahead of time and plan sight-seeing stops that both you and your children will enjoy (besides amusement parks, water slides, circuses, and beach or lake breaks are some of the most common diversions). In addition, train systems in Italy sometimes offer discounts for groups or families. There are discount Eurailpasses for groups and children (children under 12 travel at half-price, children under four usually travel free), and an Italian kilometric ticket can be used by up to five at once. For some families, it may be more convenient to travel by rental car, but train travel will often be cheaper, reduce the fidgets, and pro-

vide a novel, absorbing experience for North American children. See the Transportation section below for more details. **Wilderness Press,** 2440 Bancroft Way, Berkeley,
CA 94704 (tel. (415) 443-7227) distributes *Backpacking with Babies and Small Children* ($8.95) and *Sharing Nature with Children* ($6.95), which present useful tips for
the outward-bound family. **Lonely Planet Publications,** 155 Filbert St., Oakland, CA
94607 (tel. (510) 893-8555 or (800) 229-0122) publishes *Travel With Children* ($10.95,
$1.50 postage), a book chock-full of user-friendly tips and anecdotes; they also publish
a free quarterly newsletter full of general travel advice and anecdotes. To order from
overseas, write: P.O. Box 617, Hawthorn, Victoria, 3122, Australia.

Pets

If you are bringing your cat or dog into Italy, you must have a veterinarian's certificate stating the breed, age, sex and color of the pet, the owner's name and address, and
certification that the beastie is in good health and has been vaccinated against rabies
between 20 days and 11 months before entry into Italy. Both the Italian Government
Travel Office and your local Italian Embassy have these forms, which are valid for 30
days. Parrots, parakeets, rabbits and hares also need these certificates, and Customs
will examine them upon entry into Italy (cats and dogs may be examined too, although
not in all cases). Bring a leash or muzzle if you have a dog; one or the other is required
in public.

Specific Diets

Jewish travelers who keep kosher should consult local tourist boards for a list of kosher restaurants. Also useful is *The Jewish Travel Guide* ($10.95, $1.50 postage) from
Jewish Chronicle Publications, 25 Furnival St., London EC4A 1JT, England; the U.S.
and Canadian distributor is Sepher-Hermon Press, Inc., 1265 46th St., Brooklyn, NY
11219 (tel. (718) 972-9010). The guide lists synagogues, kosher restaurants, and Jewish institutions in over 80 countries.

Vegetarians should write the **Società Vegetariana Italiana,** via dei Piatti, 3, 20123
Milano, for information on vegetarian restaurants, foods, and stores. A vegetarian
should have few problems in Italian restaurants, since the majority of first courses (*primi,* the pasta course) are meatless, and most restaurants will also supply you a mixed
plate of their vegetable side dishes upon request (ask for *cortoni cotti senza carne*—
cooked side dishes without meat or *vedure miste* (mixed vegetables). If you carry along
your own dish, you'll also be set to buy fruits, vegetables, breads, and cheeses from
corner shops or open-air markets. *Let's Go* includes some vegetarian restaurants and
you can always ask for a dish *senza carne* (without meat), though you may face incre-
dulity. For more information, contact the **Vegetarian Society of the U.K.,** Parkdale,
Dunham Rd., Altrincham, Chesire WA14 4QG (tel. (061) 928 07 93). They publish the
international *Vegetarian Travel Guide* (£3.99), listing vegetarian and health-conscious
restaurants, guesthouses, societies, and health food stores throughout the world (be
warned: half the book is devoted to the U.K.). The guide is also available for $16, $2
postage) from the **North American Vegetarian Society,** P.O. Box 72, Dolgeville, NY
13329 (tel. (518) 568-7970).

Consult the Food and Wine section below for general comments on eating in Italy.

Getting There

From North America

Constantly fluctuating prices and market conditions make estimating airfares impossible, but a few general rules do apply. Off-season travelers enjoy lower fares and face
much less competition for inexpensive seats, but you needn't travel in the dead of winter to save. Peak-season rates usually apply from late May to mid-September. If you
manipulate your travel dates carefully, you can travel in summer and still save with
low-season fares. You may also be able to take advantage of cheap flights at home to
reach an advantageous point of departure. If you plan on traveling elsewhere in Europe,

consider beginning your trip outside of Italy; a flight to Brussels or Frankfurt could cost considerably less than one to Milan or Rome.

Have a knowledgeable travel agent guide you through the options outlined below. Nothing facilitates successful travel arrangements like an amicable relationship with a competent travel agent, so ask around and try to find someone whom you both like and trust. If you don't have time to do this footwork, keep in mind that commissions are smaller on cheaper flights and some travel agents will be less than eager to help you dig up the best deal; it may be helpful to check with more than one agent. Check the travel section of the Sunday *New York Times* or another major newspaper for bargain fares. Also consult CIEE, Travel CUTS, Let's Go Travel, and other student travel organizations.

Since inexpensive flights from Canada cost substantially more than the lowest fares from the U.S., Canadians may want to consider leaving from the States. Be sure to check with Travel CUTS for information on special charters.

Charter Flights

In general, charter flights are the cheapest. You can book charters up to the last minute, but most flights in early summer fill up well before the departure date. Later in the season, companies may have trouble filling their planes and will either cancel flights or offer special prices. With charters, you may stay abroad for as long as you like and may often fly into one city and out of another. Charters do not, however, allow for change. You must book specific departure and return dates and you lose most, if not all, of your money if you cancel your ticket.

In addition, charter flights can be unreliable. Companies reserve the right to change the dates of your flight, add fuel surcharges after you have made final payment, or even cancel the flight. The most common problem is delay. Charter companies usually fly a single plane to and from Europe, so delays accumulate and one mechanical failure can delay an entire lineup of flights.

Council Charter, 205 E. 42nd St., New York, NY 10017 (tel. (800) 800-8222; (212) 661-0311), CIEE's subsidiary, is America's oldest charter company. It offers a combination of charters and regularly scheduled flights to most major European cities including Rome and Milan. A \$30 cancellation waiver allows passengers to cancel for any reason up to three hours prior to departure from the U.S. and receive a full refund. Tickets can also be purchased at any Council Travel office in the U.S. Flights are very popular, so reserve early.

Airline Ticket Consolidators

These agencies advertise prices lower than most charters and sell unused tickets on scheduled flights. There are several discount travel agencies worth contacting. **Bargain Air,** 655 Deep Valley Dr., Rolling Hills, CA 90274 (tel. (800) 347-2345 in CA only or (310) 377-2919, fax (310) 377-1824) offers discounted flight to most European cities, including Milan. Check also with **Discount Travel International,** Ives Bldg., #203, Forrest Ave., Narberth, PA 19072 (tel. (215) 668-7184 for reservations); **Last Minute Travel Connection,** 601 Skokie Blvd., #224, Northbrook, IL 60062 (tel. (900) 446-8292 or (708) 498-3883); or **UniTravel,** P.O. Box 12485, St. Louis, MO 63132 (tel. (800) 325-2222 or (314) 569-0900). For \$25, **Travel Avenue** will search for the lowest international airfare available and then discount it 8-25%. They are located at 641 W. Lake St., Chicago, IL 60606-3691 (tel. (800) 333-3335).

Air Hitch, 2901 Broadway, #100, New York, NY 10025 (tel. (212) 864-2000) offers a commercial-jet hitchhiking assistance program, for those with wanderlust but no specified destination. Travelers indicate a region, rather than a city, pay in advance, and receive a "flight indication" listing of three possible flights, one of which they will be booked on. (East Coast to Western Europe \$160, West Coast to Western Europe \$269, and \$229 to Europe from anywhere else in the continental U.S.)

Commercial Carriers

If you decide to make your transatlantic crossing with a commercial airline, you'll be purchasing greater reliability, security, and flexibility—usually at a higher price. The

Calabria

the heart of the Mediterranean

come, Calabria is waiting for you

National Parks, mountains
running from the Sila plateau
to the Serre region, and down to
Aspromonte. Lakes + rivers in an
unblemished landscape
surrounded by 780 km.
of colourful coasts: the red sands
of Crotone, the coast of jasmine,
the purple coast, the white sands
of Tropea.

This project has been carried out by the CTS Travel UK Ltd on behalf
of the group "Dimension Calabria", CTS Catanzaro - Italy.

major airlines offer two options for the budget traveler. The first is to fly **standby.** Tickets may be purchased in advance on a private basis or through a ticket consolidator, but you are not guaranteed a seat on any particular flight. Seat availability is known only minutes before departure, and standby seating varies from airline to airline. Since you are not tied to a particular departure, standby travel affords greater flexibility, but it makes traveling on a fixed itinerary problematic. In addition, standby tickets are harder to come by and may be more expensive than economy round-trip fares on certain routes.

Your second option on a commercial airline is the **Advanced Purchase Excursion Fare (APEX).** This plan provides confirmed reservations and flexible ports of arrival and departure, but you must tailor your trip to meet strict minimum/maximum length requirements, usually seven to 60 or 90 days. Tickets (often non-refundable) must be purchased three or four weeks in advance. Book APEX fares early—by June you may have difficulty getting your desired summer departure date. **Alitalia,** Italy's national airline, is geared primarily to executives and well-heeled travelers, but they do offer APEX and off-season youth fares. Since reservation systems are often messy, you should have your ticket in hand as early as possible and arrive at the airport at least two hours before departure. In some cases, you may get a discount for early reservations.

Courier Flights

Anyone who can handle traveling light should consider flying as a courier. The company hiring you will usually use your checked luggage space for freight (some will give you carry-on documents instead); you're left with the carry-on allowance. Restrictions to watch for: most flights are round-trip with fixed-length stays (usually under two weeks); the deals often involve only single tickets so you'll be going solo; and most flights from North America originate in New York (including a pleasant visit to the courier office in the scenic suburbs near JFK airport); most to Italy arrive in Milan. Round-trip fares from the U.S. range from $175 to $400. **Now Voyager,** 74 Varick St., #307, New York, NY 10013 (tel. (213) 432-1616) acts as an agent for many courier flights worldwide from New York, although some flights are available from Houston, and they are planning to expand their service. You'll have better luck (and more disengaged phone lines) working directly through the courier companies; pick up a copy of *The Air Courier's Handbook* ($12.95) at your bookstore for a list. **Travel Unlimited,** P.O. Box 1058, Allston, MA 02134-1058, distributes comprehensive monthly newsletters detailing all possible options for travel on air couriers—often at 50% off commercial fares. Couriers do not advertise, so this is an invaluable source of cheap fares (1-year subscription $25—$35 outside U.S.).

From Europe

Travel agents in your home country can often give you specific information on travel within Europe, but it's simpler, and usually cheaper, to make arrangements once you arrive there. Check newspapers, travel agencies, and student travel organizations. Look into **STA Travel,** 74 and 86 Old Brompton Rd., London SW7 (for international travel, tel. (071) 937 99 62; North American, (071) 937 99 71; European, (071) 937 99 21). Also check with **Kilroy Travels International A/S** (formerly Scandinavian Student Travel Service), Skindergade 28, DK-1159, Copenhagen K, Denmark (tel. (33) 91 03 00), for student and youth charter flights.

By Plane

Budget fares are available on high-volume flights between northern Europe and Italy, but usually only in the spring and summer. Carriers within Europe often offer student discounts. There are many good charter flights from London.

Air Travel Group Ltd., 227 Shepherds Bush Rd., London W6 7AS (tel. (081) 748 1333), acts as an umbrella organization for three services. **Italy Sky Shuttle** programs flight assignments from seven UK hubs to 21 Italian cities, **Magic of Italy** offers resort holidays in choice villas and **Italian Escapades** handles travel itineraries, booking flights, renting autos, and making motel reservations. They also operate branch offices in Manchester, Bologna, Milan, Naples, Rome, and Palermo. **London Student Travel,** 52 Grosvenor Gardens, London SW1W 0AG (tel. (01) 730 34 02), offers competitive fares all over the continent, and there's no age limit for many of their flights. Also check with **Magic Bus,** 20 Filellinon, Syntagma, Athens, Greece (tel. (01) 32 37 471-4), which operates inexpensive flights within Europe, despite its name.

By Train

The great majority of budget travelers in Europe use the economical and efficient train system. **Eurailpasses** may be used to get to Italy from a number of European countries and are also valid for travel within Italy. If you're under 26, you may purchase BIJ tickets, which cut regular second-class train fares on international runs by about 50%. BIJ tickets are sold by **Transalpino** and **Eurotrain.** Neither organization has a representative in the U.S., so Americans will have to purchase these in Europe. If you cannot find a Transalpino or Eurotrain office, try a large student or budget travel organization such as Council Travel, ISTC, or STA Travel. When you buy a BIJ ticket, you must specify both your destination and route, and you have the option of stopping off anywhere along that particular route for up to two months. The fare between London and Venice is about $75, round-trip $140; between London and Rome, about $75, round-trip $150. Fares from Paris, Zurich, Frankfurt, or Brussels will be less expensive. The regular, second-class one way train fare between Zurich and Milan is $26, between Paris and Milan $62. On an overnight ride, you might want also to purchase a **cuccetta,** the economy version of a full sleeping berth (about $15).

By Bus

Few people think of buses when planning travel to Italy, but they are available and cheap. **Magic Bus** runs direct service between many major cities in Europe. Their main office is located at 20 Filellinon, Syntagma, Athens, Greece (tel. (01) 32 37 471-4), but information is available from cooperating offices in many other cities. **London Student Travel** at 52 Grosvenor Gardens, London SW1W 0AG (tel. (01) 730 34 02) operates express buses from London to destinations in Italy.

Once There

Tourist Offices

Most Italian towns maintain an information office for the town and surrounding area. These offices are especially useful in summer when local festivals and special events abound. The staff is usually helpful and friendly and includes an English-speaker. Be sure to collect the readily available, outrageously glossy brochures.

The **Ente Nazionale Italiano di Turismo (ENIT)** is a national tourist office with bureaus in Rome (via Marghera, 2) and abroad. In provincial capitals, look for a branch of the **Ente Provinciale per il Turismo (EPT),** which provides information on the entire province. Many towns also have an **Azienda Autonoma di Soggiorno e Turismo** (city tourist board). The Azienda tends to be the most useful and approachable; the bureaucratic EPT is less accustomed to dealing with tourists, and generally has no better information. The smallest towns sometimes sport a privately run **Pro Loco** office. Recently, a new brand of tourist office, the **Azienda di Promozione Turismo** has popped up. Watch out for these, because they are allowed to present you with a list of only those hotels that have paid to be listed; some of the hotels we recommend may not be on the list. Keep an eye out for the student-oriented **Centro Turistico Studentesco e Giovanile (CTS)** and the **Compagnia Italiana Turismo (CIT),** the government-subsidized travel agency that specializes in outdoor activities such as camping and boating. Offices are listed in the Practical Information section of each town.

Embassies and Consulates

Your home country's embassy or consulate in Italy can provide you with legal advice and a list of doctors and will contact relatives in an emergency. All embassies provide consular and passport services, plus a 24-hr. referral service for emergencies; however, consulates are generally better equipped than embassies to handle travelers' problems. All nations have embassies in Rome, and most maintain consulates in major cities. Below is a partial list of foreign embassies in Rome.

U.S., via Veneto, 119/a, 00187 Roma (tel. (06) 467 41).

Canada, via G. B. de Rossi, 27, 00161 Roma (tel. (06) 85 53 41).

U.K., via XX Settembre, 80a, 00187 Roma (tel. (06) 475 54 41).

Australia, via Alessandria, 215, 00198 Roma (tel. (06) 83 27 21).

New Zealand, via Zara, 28, 00198 Roma (tel. (06) 85 12 25).

Emergencies

Few legal systems are as convoluted and ambiguous as Italy's. Interpretations of the law are as varied as the dialects of the land. Your consulate will provide an attorney and advice, but after that you are on your own; you will be subject to Italian law.

If you can't avoid the police system, at least know with whom you are dealing. The **Polizia Urbana,** or **Pubblica Sicurezza** (emergency tel. 113), are the non-military police who deal with local crime. Try to contact them first if you are robbed or attacked. The **Carabinieri** (emergency tel. 112) are actually a part of the Italian Army. They usually deal with the most serious crimes, such as terrorism (hence their intimidating, well-armed presence at airports). The **Vigili Urbani** manage less violent, less serious offenses, such as traffic violations. They also give directions to lost tourists. This book provides listings of police offices and medical emergency numbers in the Practical Information section of individual cities. Consult the Safety and Security section above for further notes on avoiding touristic misfortune.

Transportation

Plane

Italy's train system is so efficient and airline prices so high that it makes little sense to fly Italy's three domestic airlines, **ATI, Alitalia,** or **Alisarda,** unless you need to go a long distance in speed-of-light time. Ask about discounts on domestic travel at one of their many offices.

Train

Ferrovie dello Stato (FS), the Italian State Railway, is one of the last European train systems to provide inexpensive service. The fare between Rome and Venice, one of the longer trips in Italy, is only $32 one way second-class. Moreover, passengers between the ages of 12 and 25 are eligible for reduced rates (see below). Italian trains retain the romance and convenience that American railways have lost. Unfortunately, they are not always safe. While passengers sleep deeply, they may be molested, robbed or even attacked. Padlocking your pack to an immobile object (like the luggage rack) is a good idea; sleep wearing your money belt or neck pouch and, if you are traveling with a companion, try to sleep in shifts. Overnight travelers should know that compartments are sometimes gassed—be sure you open a window to thoroughly ventilate your compartment, and try to travel during the day whenever possible. (Women travelers should be cautious of empty compartments even during the day.)

Although the traveler touring only Italy will lose money on a **Eurailpass,** consider buying one if you will be traveling outside Italy as well. The Eurailpass is valid for unlimited travel in 17 European countries and also entitles you to free passage or reduced fares on some ferries and buses. If you're under 26, you can purchase the **Eurail Youthpass,** valid for one ($425) or two months ($560) of second-class travel. If you're over 25, you must purchase a first-class Eurailpass, ranging from 15 days of unlimited travel ($390) to three months ($1042). Eurailpasses may be bought only outside of Europe and are available only to those who do not reside in Europe. The **Eurail Flexipass** allows time to tour as well as traverse Italy. Passes available include those for five days of first-class travel within 15 days of validity ($230), nine days of travel within 21 days of validity ($398), and 14 days of travel within one month of validity ($498), with half-price for children under 12. Travelers under 26 are eligible for a longer term second-class **Youth Flexipass,** which allows a three-month window for 15 days ($340) or 30 days ($540) of travel. Eurail also offers the **Saverpass,** a 15-day, discounted first-class pass for unlimited travel for two or more people traveling together ($298 per person). During tourist season (April 1 to September 30), three or more people must travel together. For more information or to purchase a pass, contact Council Travel, Travel CUTS, Let's Go Travel Services, or a travel agent.

The Italian State Railway offers its own passes, valid on all train routes within Italy. The **BTLC "Go Anywhere"** train pass is available in first- or second-class. Second-class passes cost $136 for eight days, $172 for 15 days, $198 for 21 days, and $240 for 30 days. Travelers must have the dates of validity stamped on the BTLC ticket at the first station of use. Unless you travel at a furious pace, however, there's no way to make this pass worth its price—train fares in Italy are simply too cheap.

The **Italian Kilometric Ticket** is good for 20 trips or 3000km (1875 mi.) of travel, whichever comes first, and can be used for two months by up to five people. Three thousand kilometers is a long way in Italy, so it's virtually impossible for one person to break even on the Kilometric Ticket. For a couple or a family traveling reasonably widely, however, it can pay off. Ticket holders may travel on Intercity, Eurocity, Rapido and ETR450 (Italy's newest and fastest train providing express service to major cities), but must pay a supplemental fare. When used by more than one person, mileage per trip is calculated by multiplying the distance by the number of users. Children under 12 are charged half of the distance traveled, and those under four travel free. A first-class kilometric ticket is $238, second-class, $140, plus a $10-per-person fee. When buying the ticket, be sure the sales agent stamps the date on it, or you may find yourself with a useless pass. Either pass may be bought from the **Italian State Railway representative,** 666 Fifth Ave., New York, NY 10113 (tel. (212) 697-2100), or in Italy

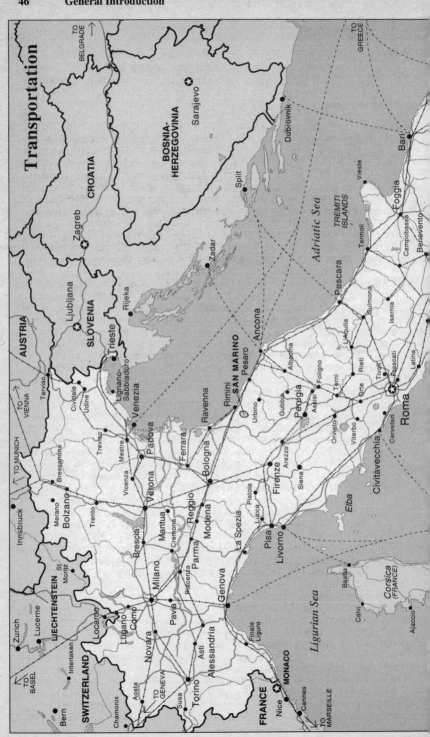

Transportation

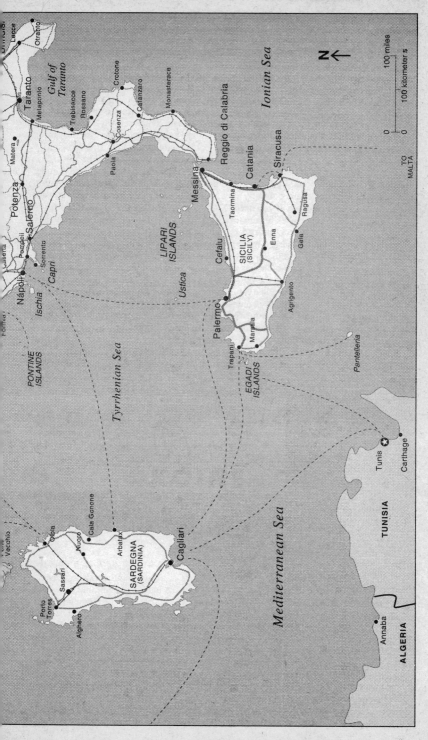

(where purchase price is slightly lower) at major train stations and offices of the **Compagnia Italiana Turismo (CIT).** Be aware that while using this pass, you must go to the ticket booth and have your mileage stamped, otherwise you will pay hefty fines assessed for buying a ticket on the train.

The Italian railway recently introduced the **cartaverde,** available to anyone under 26. The card costs L40,000, is valid for three years, and entitles you to a discount of 20% on any state train fare. They can be purchased only in Italy and if you're under 26, it should be your *first* purchase upon arrival. Families of four or more, or a group of up to five adults traveling together, qualify for discounts on Italian railways. Anyone over 60 with proof of age can get a 30% discount if they buy a *cartargento* ("silver card"), good for a year for L10,000. The discount is not available from June 26 to August 14 and December 18 to 28. These discounts apply only to tickets purchased in Italy.

The Italian train system involves four kinds of regular trains. The *accelerato,* more commonly (and appropriately) referred to as a *locale,* usually stops at every station along a particular line and is painfully slow, sometimes taking twice as long as a faster train. Travel on a *locale* only if you need to get off at an obscure stop or want to soak in the scenery. The *diretto* makes fewer stops than the *locale,* and the *espresso* stops only in major stations. The air-conditioned *rapido,* or *intercity (IC)* trains stop only in the largest cities. You will be charged more for a *rapido* ticket (waived for Eurail or BTLC holders), but it's often worth the money on long hauls (but check your train schedule; sometimes an *espresso* train is just as fast). Some *rapido* trains do not have second-class compartments, rocketing the cost of a ticket out of the budget traveler's range, and a few require reservations. On overnight trips, consider paying extra for a *cuccetta,* a fold-down bunk which typically comes six to a compartment; the cost will vary depending on the length of the journey (usually around $15). If you're not willing to spend the money on a *cuccetta,* consider taking an *espresso* train for overnight travel—they usually have compartments with fold-out seats.

Finally, *freccie* trains run directly between cities that are normally connected only through other cities. There are 14 *freccie* that cover Italy, each running once per day.

Bus

Regularly scheduled bus routes are seldom used in Europe for long-distance travel. They are slower than *diretto* trains and no cheaper. Still, buses in Italy are more punctual than trains, comfortable and frequent, and they serve many points in the countryside that are inaccessible by train. Buses are also often crowded, so buy tickets in advance. Italy's bumpy terrain requires a strong stomach; even those with vast experience elsewhere may find themselves prone. Be sure to bring a motion sickness remedy (dramamine is okay, but prescription ear patches are better—talk to your doctor), and remember that while an empty stomach ensures nothing comes up, it bounces more. As a reward, the scenery from many Italian buses often outshines the beauty of any final destination. Bus rides in the Southern Tuscan hills and the route from Bolzano to Cortina D'Ampezzo in the Dolomites are among the most incredible (and most nauseating).

You must purchase a bus ticket before boarding in many Italian cities and may be fined if you don't. Purchase tickets at train stations and CIT offices.

Car

If you're pressed for time, or touring with friends or a large family, traveling by car may prove the most enjoyable and practical way to see Italy. Keep in mind, however, that much of Italy's infrastructure was constructed before the age of the automobile. Some towns will prove virtually unnavigable; consider parking on the outskirts and walking to town centers. On the other hand, the Italian *Autostrada* are the worthy successors to the Roman roads, fantasies in engineering that barrel through mountains and soar over valleys on piers. They charge equally stunning tolls: the ride from Rome to Bologna will run you on the order of L40,000 in booth stops alone. A word to the wise: plan your route ahead of time. Reckless drivers are not uncommon in Italy, and the convoluted street system often inflames tempers. Moreover, gas costs around L1500 a liter. The Italian government does offer a "Tourist Incentive Package," where for a single price you receive gasoline coupons which will save you up to 15% on gas costs, a toll card, the right to breakdown services and other services. The package may be purchased at the Fiumicino Airport, Auto Club of Italy (ACI) border offices and ENIT offices in Europe, only with foreign currency. The ACI is located at v. Marsala, 8 00185 Roma (tel. (06) 499 81); you may want to inquire about a temporary membership while planning your trip. You may also wish to write for David Shore and Patty Campbell's book *Europe Free! The Car, Van, & RV Travel Guide,* 1842 Santa Margarita Dr., Fallbrook, CA 92028 (tel. (619) 723-6184).

Unfortunately, a car can cut severely into your budget. Gas *(benzina)* computes to about $5 a gallon and renting a four-seater for one week will run around $290. If you need a car for three weeks or more, leasing will be less expensive than renting. Most firms lease to drivers over 17 and rent to those over 20. The minimum rental age in Europe is rarely, if ever, under 21. Many companies also require a major credit card, and some offer discounts to foreigners.

Several U.S. firms offer rental and leasing plans in Italy. If you are a student or faculty member, inquire about special discounts or contact Council Travel or CTS. Reserving in the U.S. is usually much cheaper than renting once you've arrived. Many agencies require advance reservation made in the U.S. The major firms renting in Italy are **Auto-Europe,** #10 Sharp's Wharf, P.O. Box 1097, Camden, ME 04843 (tel. (800) 223-5555); **Avis Rent-A-Car,** 900 Old Country Rd., Garden City, NY 11530 (tel. (800) 331-1084); **Budget Rent-a-Car,** 200 N. Michigan Ave., Chicago, IL 60601 (tel. (312) 580-5000), **Europe by Car,** Rockefeller Plaza, New York, NY 10020 (tel. (800) 223-1516 or (212) 581-3040); **Foremost Euro-car, Inc.,** 5430 Van Nuys Blvd., #306, Van Nuys, CA 91402 (tel. (800) 272-3299); **Hertz Rent-A-Car** (tel. (800) 654-3001); **Kemwel Group, Inc.,** 106 Calvert St., Harrison, NY 10528 (tel. (800) 678-0678); and **Maiellano Tours,** 441 Lexington Ave., New York, NY 10015 (tel. (212) 687-7725 or (800) 223-1616).

Do not leave valuables visible in your car. If you wish to leave an important or expensive article behind, try to find a parking garage (plentiful in major cities) where you can leave your car for around L4000 per day.

Foreign drivers in Italy need both an international driver's permit (or, if you are driving your own car, your license accompanied by a translation) and an international insurance certificate (or "green card") good for no more than 45 days. Remember that all *Autostrada* direction signs are marked in green, all secondary roads in blue. Maps are essential, or you may find yourself confounded by Italy's labyrinth of small roads. It's good to have more than one map, as each emphasizes different roads. For any serious driving emergency, call the 24-hr. nationwide auto service at 116 (charges apply).

Mopeds and Scooters

Mopeds and scooters, an enduring feature of Italian life, provide an enjoyable way to tour the country, especially in coastal areas where the view demands frequent attention. Mopeds cruise at an easy 40kph and don't use much gas. They are, however, dangerous in the rain and extremely unpredictable on rough roads or gravel. Always wear a helmet and never ride wearing a backpack. If you've never been on a moped before, Italy is not the place to start. The Vespa-style motorbikes with small wheels and a center platform for your feet are particularly hazardous. Rentals are difficult to arrange in many places, but ask at bicycle and motorcycle shops. Rates are between L25,000 and L50,000 a day.

Bicycle

A bicycle's pace lets you feel truly a part of Italy. Anywhere outside the flat Po Valley, Italy's hills require a purpose-built touring or mountain bike with very low gears for any sustained expedition, along with an excellent set of lungs and legs. Since roads are generally in good condition, a touring bike with its more comfortable dropped bars and narrower, faster tires is probably preferable. Draw your pedaling inspiration from Karen and Gary Hawkins' book *Bicycle Touring in Europe* ($11.95) available from Random House, Inc., 400 Hahn Rd., Westminster, MD 21157 (tel. (800) 733-3000); for practical advice refer to Raymond Bridge's exhaustive *Bike Touring: The Sierra Club Guide to Outings on Wheels,* published by Sierra Club Books in San Francisco.

You can take your bicycle on the plane with minor disassembly (usually only the seat, handlebars, wheels, and pedals need to come off) and a suitable box, both available at bike stores. Check with individual airlines for restrictions and costs. You may also be able to purchase an appropriate bike once you reach the home of Campagnolo and Bianchi.

If you want to transport your bicycle by train within Italy, label it and bring it to the *ufficio bagagli* at the railroad station; it should arrive within three days. If the train has a *bagagliaio* (baggage compartment), you and your bike can ride the rails together. The Touring Club Italiano publishes a helpful book (in Italian) called *Manuale Pratico di Cicloturismo.*

Long- and short-term rentals are readily available. The **French National Railroad (SNCF),** 610 5th Ave., New York, NY 10020 (tel. (800) 848-7245 or (212) 582-2110) rents bikes and has representatives in 11 countries, including Italy. With a ticket or railpass and identification, you can rent a bike for about $3 a day with a $20 deposit. They also stock schedules and maps of train routes throughout Europe.

Getting all the necessary equipment together may be your biggest hassle. It is definitely worthwhile to buy proper equipment for touring; riding a bike with a frame pack strapped on it or your back is about as safe as pedaling blindfolded over ice. Bicycle accessories—panniers and other touring bags, lighting equipment, racks—are cheaper and of better quality in the U.S. Local bike shops can provide helpful information, but their prices tend to be high. Fortunately, mail and telephone ordering has been perfected to a fine art in the U.S. Don't spend a penny before you scan the pages of *Bicycling* magazine and the **Performance** bicycling catalog for the lowest sale prices. **Bike Nashbar,** P.O. Box 3449, Youngstown, OH 44513-0449 (tel. (800) 627-4227) almost always offers the lowest prices, but when they don't, they cheerfully subtract 5¢ from the best price you can find. If you call their toll-free number, the parts will usually be on their way the same day. They regularly ship anywhere in the U.S. and Canada, and to overseas military addresses. Their own line of products, including complete bicycles, is the best value. The first thing you should buy is a **bike helmet.** At about $50, it's a lot cheaper and more pleasant than neurosurgery.

Fixing a modern derailleur-equipped bike is something that just about anyone can do with a few simple but specialized tools and some good advice. *Bicycling Magazine's Basic Maintenance and Repair* ($6.95) is an easy-to-carry, easy-to-use guide published by Rodale Press, Inc., 33 E. Minor St., Emmaus, PA 18049 (tel. (800) 441-7761). *The Bike Bag Book* ($3.95, postage $1.25), a common-sense approach to common problems, is published by **10-Speed Press,** Box 7123, Berkeley, CA 94797 (tel. (800) 841-2665).

To increase the odds of finding your bike where you left it, buy a U-shaped lock made by **Citadel** or **Kryptonite.** They may seem expensive ($20-40) until you compare them to the price of buying a new bike in Italy. Each company insures its locks against theft for one or two years, up to a certain amount of money. Be sure to secure your wheels and seat within the lock if they have quick-release mechanisms.

Thumb

> Be sure to consider the risks involved before you hitch. *Let's Go* does not recommend hitching as a means of travel.

Italy has an excellent network of tollroads (*Autostrade*) linking major cities. They run east-west, between Venice, Milan, and Turin, and north-south, connecting Milan, Rome, and Naples. Hitching on the *autostrada* itself is illegal (as well as dangerous). Travelers more intent on seeing the countryside and meeting Italians than on making time often hitch the primary road system, which carries a large volume of short-range traffic.

Women who decide to hitchhike should be forewarned: some men will consider you fair game for sexual harassment or worse. Those who choose to hitch usually do so with a companion; bulletin boards at hostels are often cited as a good place to start looking. Likewise, newspapers and university message boards sometimes carry ads-seeking passengers to share driving and costs.

Hitchhiking adepts usually refuse rides in the back seat of a two-door car, and they keep the door unlocked and their belongings close at hand—in case a quick escape becomes necessary, luggage locked in the trunk will probably stay that way. They also take care never to fall asleep in cars—some drivers may consider it tantamount to a wholesale sexual invitation. If a situation becomes uncomfortable for any reason, hitchers firmly ask to be let out, regardless of how unfavorable the spot seems for finding another ride. Hitching for women reportedly becomes more dangerous the further south or off the mainland one goes, and anywhere near a large city poses a particular risk.

The lighter hitchers travel, the easier rides are to find. They usually stack baggage carefully in a tight pile—many drivers whip by if the belongings seem excessive. A sign with the destination written in large letters is also reportedly useful. If long-distance traffic is scarce, some hitchers aim for the next large town on the road and scrawl out a new sign.

Accommodations

Hostels

Hostels are great places to meet travelers from all over the world; if you are alone, there is no better place to find a temporary traveling companion. Italian youth hostels, *Ostelli Italiani,* are inexpensive and open to travelers of all ages; many are situated in historic buildings and areas of great natural beauty. They offer inexpensive meals and often provide services unavailable at hotels, including kitchen privileges, laundry facilities, and bike rental. On the other hand, you must adapt to curfews, daytime lockouts, and separate quarters for men and women (some hostels do have doubles). You should also be warned that many hostels close in late fall and winter. Hostels are not as abundant in Italy as in northern Europe, and their locations are often inconvenient. Security is also less certain than in a hotel room, so keep your valuables with you, or check them at the office.

Hostel accommodations usually consist of bunk beds, each with a mattress and blanket, in dormitory rooms. You may be required to use a **sleep sack,** a special sheet; you can purchase them from a number of travel and camping store, but most hostels which require them also provide them. Hostels usually receive guests from 6-11:30pm during the summer, and 6-10:30pm from October to April, and you must settle your account by 9am or pay for another night. The curfew is usually midnight in summer and 11pm in winter; some hostels turn off lights and hot water after this time. Rates vary by hostel, ranging from L10,000 to L17,000 per person including breakfast; dinners cost between L5000 and L13,000 (less for just a pasta course).

To stay in youth hostels affiliated with the **Hostelling International (HI),** formerly International Youth Hostel Federation (IYHF), often you must be an HI member. In most countries, membership cards are available while you wait from certain budget travel agencies. The cost varies by country (in the U.S., $25, under 18 $10, over 54 $15), and membership is good through the calendar year. The HI affiliate in Italy is **Associazione Italiana Alberghi per la Gioventù (AIG),** via Cavour, 44, 00184 Roma (tel. (06) 487 11 52 or 474 67 55, fax (06) 474 12 56). Membership cards are available in Italy from major hostels, AIG offices throughout Italy, and student travel services. AIG hostels vary in the strictness with which they observe membership requirements; a number of hostels not affiliated with the AIG exist as well, and do not require HI membership. Specific requirement information is included in individual listings of hostels throughout the book. Buying a card before you leave home avoids problems (as not all hostels requiring cards sell them); they can be purchased through any of the HI affiliates listed below.

U.S.: American Youth Hostels (AYH), 425 Divisadero St. #310, San Francisco, CA 94117 (tel. (415) 863-9939).

Canada: Canadian Hostelling Association (CHA), 1600 James Naismith Dr., Gloucester, Ontario, K1B 5N4 (tel. (613) 748-5638).

U.K.: Youth Hostels Association (England and Wales), Trevelyan House, 8 St. Stephen's Hill, St. Albans, Herts, AL1 2DY (tel. (07 27) 552 15).

Australia: Australian Youth Hostel Association, Level 3, 10 Mallett St., Camperdown, NSW 2050 (tel. (02) 565-1699).

New Zealand: Youth Hostels Association of New Zealand, P.O. Box 436, Corner of Manchester and Gloucester St., Christchurch 1 (tel. (03) 79 99 70, fax (03) 65 44 76).

Hotels

A provincial board inspects, classifies, and registers all hotels. No hotel can legally charge more than the maximum permitted by inspection, but some proprietors double their prices at the sound of a foreign voice—remember that an official rate card must adorn the inside of the door of each room, and that you should ask to look at the room (and the card) before committing to anything. Keep in mind that showers and breakfast often cost extra, and prices rise from year to year. The prices listed in the book shouldn't be off by more than 10%, but occasionally hotels upgrade their services to a new class level and rates jump accordingly.

Given this system, you are unlikely to get ripped off by checking into the first place you find, or to find an unusual bargain by shopping around for hours. Differences between hotels of the same class are largely a matter of location and character, rather than price or facilities. In general, the most charming places are near the historic town center, while cheaper, nastier joints reside near the train and bus stations.

Hotels in Italy have recently been classified on a five-star system. Under this system, all accommodations should be called *hotels;* be aware, however, that a number of establishments retain their old classifications as *pensioni* (small one-to-three star hotels) or *locande* (the cheapest, usually one star, if any). *Albergo* is synonymous with hotel.

Prices fluctuate regionally; expect higher prices in the north and in Rome and Florence. The cheapest non-institutional singles generally start at about L18.000 and dou-

bles at L26,000. Rates tend to be lower per person in a shared room. A room with a double bed is called a *matrimoniale* (though marriage is no longer a prerequisite). A double with separate beds is called a *camera doppia,* and a single is a *camera singola.* Showers, which are rarely in the room, usually cost L1000-2500 extra. Many rooms have a bidet, good for chilling wine, washing socks, or soaking tired feet. Some places offer only full pension, meaning room and board (3 meals per day), or half-pension, meaning room, breakfast, and one other meal. Rooms with a private bath cost 30-50% more.

Italian law establishes a high and low season for areas popular with tourists. Remember that off-season months are different for alpine regions and seaside resort areas. When there is a difference in high and low season dates, *Let's Go* mentions it. Except in summer tourist spots such as Florence, Venice, the Riviera and Cápri, you usually needn't write for reservations. If you do write for reservations, be aware that Italian law considers a booking legal once a deposit has been paid, and you probably won't be able to get your deposit back if you have to cancel. Without reservations, start looking for a room in the morning during high season, or call a day in advance. Pick up a list of hotels and their prices from the local tourist office (you can also call the tourist office and have them quote rates over the phone). If you plan to arrive late, call and ask a hotel to hold a room for you. However, few hotels accept phone reservations more than a day in advance. Many small places don't have an English speaker, but this shouldn't dissuade a non-Italian speaker from calling. Instructions on making a room reservation in minimal Italian are included at the back of the book, and most *pensione* proprietors are used to receiving this type of call.

In many smaller towns (and some larger ones), householders rent rooms in their homes to passing travelers, sometimes with the blessing of the tourist authorities, sometimes without. Look for *affitta camere* signs posted around town or notes in store windows. Rates vary wildly; be prepared to bargain, but don't expect to pay much less than than what a reasonable one-star *pensione* in town would cost.

Alberghi diurni (day hotels), found in town centers and near railroad stations, are good places to go when you need to clean up but don't have a room. Most are open 6am to midnight, and offer showers, barbershops, and luggage storage.

Student Accommodations

Student residences in Italy are inexpensive and are theoretically open to foreign students during vacations and whenever there is room. In reality, these accommodations are often nearly impossible to arrange. All university towns operate a *Casa dello Studente* to which you can apply. A useful source of information on student housing is the *Guide for Foreign Students,* from the **Italian Ministry of Education,** viale Trastevere, Roma. The following university towns have a *Casa dello Studente,* which will usually send you an application upon request (get complete addresses from the Ministry of Education): Bari, Bologna, Catania, Ferrara, Florence, Genoa, Messina, Macerata, Modena, Milan, Naples, Parma, Pavia, Perugia, Pisa, Rome, Salerno, Sássari, Siena, and Urbino. Other possibilities are *Casa Fusinato,* via Marzolo, Padova; *Casa del Goliardo,* Palermo; and *Foresteria dell'Istituto di Ca' Foscari,* Venice. The tourist office in university towns can also provide specific information.

The **Relazioni Universitarie** of the *Associazione Italiana per il Turismo e gli Scambi Universitari* operates a low-price-accommodations service for foreign students throughout the year in many of the major university towns. Discount student travel services also available. The main office is at via Palestro, 11, 00185 Roma (tel. (06) 475 52 65).

The **Centro Turistico Studentesco e Giovanile (CTS)** is the Italian student and youth travel organization. Their offices, located throughout Italy, help you find and book accommodations in *pensioni* or dormitories. The London, Paris, and Athens offices can reserve a room for you in Italy for the first few nights. The central office is at via Genova, 16 Roma (tel. (06) 467 91).

Camping

Lakes, rivers, the ocean and the Alps are common backdrops for Italian camp-grounds. Though there's often little space between sites, peaceful seclusion is usually only steps away. In August, arrive early—well before 11am—or you may find yourself without a spot. Rates average L6000 per person and another L6000 for the car. Many of the campgrounds are downright luxurious, boasting everything from swimming pools to campground bars, while others may be more primitive—you may want to shop around. The **Touring Club Italiano** (Corso Italiano, 10, 20122 Milano) publishes an annual directory of all camping sites in Italy, *Campeggi in Italia,* available in book-stores throughout Italy. A free map and list of sites is available from the Italian Government Travel Office or directly from **Federcampeggio,** via V. Emanuele, 11, Casella Postale 23, 50041 Calenzano (Firenze).

Camping requires preparation. Spend some time perusing catalogs and questioning knowledgeable salespeople before buying any equipment. There are many reputable mail-order firms—use them to gauge prices and order from them if you can't do as well locally. **Campmor,** 810 Rte. 17N, P.O. Box 997-LG91, Paramus, NJ 07653-0997 (tel. (800) 526-4784), offers name-brand equipment at attractive prices. Open 24 hours and absolutely every day, **L.L. Bean,** 1 Casco St., Freeport, ME 04033 (tel. (800) 221-4221), has plenty of its own equipment and some national brands. Even better, though less accessible, is the northwest U.S.'s long-time favorite, **Recreational Equipment, Inc. (REI),** P.O. Box C-88125, Seattle, WA 98188 (tel. (800) 426-4840). They carry excellent equipment and clothing for nearly every outdoor activity. They also distribute the guide *Europa Camping and Caravanning* ($13) and, like L. L. Bean, have a mail-order catalog.

Good **sleeping bags** are rated for specific minimum temperatures. The lower the mercury, the higher the price; expect to pay between $100 and $300. Anticipate the most severe conditions you may encounter, subtract a few degrees, and then buy a bag. Remember, the warmest bag will keep you *warm,* so don't overpurchase if you need a bag just for the summer. Back-saving **ensolite pads** to go under your bag cost about $10 for simple foam pads and $50 for the best foam/air hybrids. (The cheapest foam varieties are plenty comfortable; buy one that's at least three-quarters-body length.) Some bags now include internal pad holders so you won't find yourself sleeping next to your pad when you awake.

Modern **tents,** remarkably clever contraptions in primary colors, are self-supporting (equipped with their own frames and suspension systems) and can be set up quickly. Up-to-date versions of simpler designs are made of modern materials and have effective insect netting and integral floors. Make sure you have and use the tent's protective rain fly (dew can be quite soggy). Backpackers and cyclists will require especially small, light models; single-person tents are available from under 1kg (2.2 lbs), two-person from under 1.4kg (3 lbs). Two reputable U.S. manufacturers of lightweight tents are Sierra Designs and Eureka. Expect to pay at least $95 for a simple two-person tent, $125 for a serviceable four-person model; the lightest and most durable tents will set you back $100 to $250. For the best deals, look around for last year's merchandise, par-ticularly in the fall; tents don't change much, but prices may be reduced by as much as 50%.

Other camping basics include a battery-operated **lantern** (*never* gas) for use inside the tent, and a plastic **groundcloth** or **tarp** to put under the tent. If you want to do a lot of cooking, **campstoves** come in all sizes, weights, and fuel types, starting at about $50. Bring some **waterproof matches** (and some cooking equipment) or the stove might prove useless. Sufficient equipment to cook may prove more of an albatross than a convenience—consider your eating requirements and preferences carefully. A **canteen, Swiss army knife,** and **insect repellent** are small, essential items to throw in with your gear.

Before leaving home, you may want to write to the **Automobile Association,** Fanum House, Basingstoke, Hampshire RG21 2EA, England, for their publication *Camping and Caravanning in Europe. Camp Europe by Train* ($16.95) is available from **Ariel Publications,** 14417 SE 19th Pl., Bellevue, WA 98007 (tel. (206) 641-0518). The **Na-**

tional Campers and Hikers Association, Inc., 4804 Transit Rd., Bldg. #2, Depew, NY 14043 (tel. (716) 668-6242) distributes travel guides for campers and sells the International Camping Carnet ($23), required for entry to some European campgrounds.

Camping on beaches, roads, or any flat, inconspicuous plot is illegal, but not uncommon, in Italy. Campers who don't make fires or litter lessen their chances of being disturbed. Respect for property rights is extremely important—always ask permission when camping within sight of a farmhouse.

Alternative Accommodations

Italian history comes alive when you stay in the guest house of a Roman Catholic **monastery.** Guests need not attend services but are expected to make their own beds and, often, to clean up after meals. Found in rural settings, monasteries are usually peaceful, and you shouldn't stay in one unless you want a quiet and contemplative experience. Carrying an introduction on letterhead from your own priest, pastor, or rabbi may facilitate matters, although many monasteries will accept only Catholic guests. For more information about specific regions and a list of convents, monasteries and other religious institutions offering accommodations, write to the archdiocese (*arcivescovado*) of the nearest large town. Many regional tourist boards also maintain a list of monasteries with guest houses.

For a quiet, non-religious atmosphere, stay in a **rural cottage** or **farmhouse.** Usually, you will be given a small room and asked to clean up after yourself, but you will have freedom to come and go as you please. For more information, write to the main office of **Agriturismo,** corso V. Emanuele, 101, 00186 Roma (tel. (06) 651 23 42) or contact any of their offices in the region that you will be visiting.

If you plan to hike in the Alps or the Dolomites, you should contact the **Club Alpino Italiano,** via Ugo Foscolo, 3, 20122 Milano, which owns about 600 huts (*rifugi alpini*) in the mountain districts and publishes a book with a map and information (including rating by difficulty). The **Touring Club Italiano,** corso Italia, 10, Milano, (tel. (02) 852 61) publishes a number of books giving detailed hiking itineraries which include stopovers in the mountain refuges.

The **Associazione Cattolica Internazionale al Servizio della Giovane—Protezione della Giovane (PDG),** is a religious organization that helps women find inexpensive accommodations in its own hostels, convents, and *pensioni* throughout Italy. If you don't mind the occasional 10:30pm curfew, this service is extremely convenient. The PDG staffs offices in train stations of major cities and maintains centrally located bureaus in many towns.

You should also consider contacting international host organizations. **Servas,** for example, is dedicated to promoting understanding among cultures. Members stay free of charge in host members' homes in over 90 countries. Stays are limited to two nights, unless you are invited to stay longer. Prospective members are interviewed and asked to contribute $45 plus a refundable $15 deposit for the list of hosts. To apply, write U.S. Servas Committee, Inc., 11 John St., #407, New York, NY 10038 (tel. (212) 267-0252).

Volunteers for Peace is a work camp organization with similar goals. VFP publishes a newsletter and an annual directory to workcamps in 30 countries, primarily in Eastern and Western Europe ($10). Write to VFP, Tiffany Rd., Belmont, VT 05730 (tel. (802) 259-2759).

Sleeping in European train stations is a time-honored tradition, but while free and often tolerated by local authorities, it is neither fun, nor comfortable, nor safe (particularly dangerous for women and solo travelers).

Life and Times

History and Politics

If Italian history seems a confusing mish-mash of events, personalities, and political parties, take heart: it is. No overview here could keep pace with events in all the separate duchies, kingdoms, republics, and Empires that have washed over the Italian peninsula, a region united only under the Roman Empire and, after a lapse of 1400 years, by 19th-century nationalism.

With the 1979 discovery of a million-year-old village in Isernia, Molise, archeologists date the earliest human settlement in Italy to the beginning of the Paleolithic era (1,000,000-70,000 BC). Italic *tribes* are thought to have inhabited various areas of the peninsula starting about 2000 BC, and a vestige of their passing persists in the names of Italian towns and regions: the Umbrii and Picentes around Umbria and the Marches (Áscoli Piceno), the Samnites around Campania, the Massapians in Apulia, the Sabines and Latins in Lazio, the Sikels in Sicily, and the more advanced Sards of Sardinia.

Invaders: the Etruscans and the Greeks

A number of these peoples were subjugated following the arrival of the belligerent yet cultured Etruscans in central Italy around 1200 BC. Scholars still debate the possibility that the Etruscans were locals, but it doesn't seem likely: tradition, their non-Indo-European tongue, and archeologists' studies show them as emigrating from somewhere in Asia Minor. They founded a number of cities in Tuscany and Lazio— Volsinii (Orvieto), Volaterrae (Volterra), Cortona, Arretium (Arezzo), Clusium (Chiusi), and Perusia (Perugia) are still in existence; at Tarquínia, Veio, and Cervéteri, you can see the remains of their largest metropolises. By the 8th century BC, their 12-state confederation (the Dodecapolis) was the strongest power in Italy, and their cultural remains show trading links to Greece and Carthage.

Beginning in the 8th century BC, the Greeks, who had already been trading and exploring around the boot for more than a millennium, began to settle in southern Italy, first along the Apulian coast, later founding such metropolises as Sybaris, Croton, Naxos, and Syracuse in Calabria and Sicily, Cuma and Neapolis in Campania. This arc of settlement for a period outshone its homeland in cultural and martial achievement, earning the title of *Magna Graecia* (Greater Greece). These cities introduced a pastime which was to prove irresistible to future generations of Italians: interminable intercity warfare. Many Greek cities killed each other off in this fashion between the 6th and 5th century BC, and those that were left spiraled into an irreversible decline. The Etruscan federation, which by the same period ruled most of Northern Italy, eventually found itself losing ground in the North to the barbarian Gauls, and then in the South to the emerging Roman war machine.

Rome

Myth has it that the twins **Romulus and Remus** founded Rome in 753 BC. Wary of sharing power, Romulus slew Remus, initiating a grand tradition of ruthless, bloody politics. The new kingdom flourished during two centuries of Etruscan rule, until the son of **Tarquinius Superbus** raped the virtuous Roman maiden Lucretia. Lucretia committed public suicide, and the enraged Roman populace expelled the Tarquins in 509 BC.

The monarchy thus gave way to the Roman republic, and the liberated city quickly set about conquering its neighbors. Over the next hundred years the Etruscans were conquered along with the Latin tribes and the Umbrii. The defeat of the Etruscans spurred on territorial expansion; winning a pair of Samnite wars in the 3rd century BC gave Rome control of the entire peninsula except for the Greek cities. The Greeks invited Pyrrhus of Epirus in to defend them, but while winning a series of battles against the republic, Pyrrhus failed to press his advantage, ensuring eventual defeat (hence the term Pyrrhic victory). After losing to Rome at Beneventum in 275 BC, Pyrrhus abandoned the effort, leaving the entire mainland to Rome.

Having conquered the Italian peninsula, the republic waged its most important battles, the three **Punic Wars** (260-146 BC), against Carthage for control of the Mediterranean. During the second of these wars, the Carthiginian general **Hannibal** unexpectedly transported his army—elephants and all—across the Alps, surprising and slaughtering the unsuspecting Roman military and sacking the capital. Rome, led by the evasive Fabius and the vindictive Scipio, and egged on by Cato the Censor, retaliated in the Third Punic War by razing Carthage in 146 BC, sowing its fields with salt to prevent the city from ever thriving again. It was during the Punic Wars that Rome first began to envision itself a pre-eminent world power, conquering and subjugating Spain, Sicily, Sardinia, Corsica, and North Africa, consolidating its control over Mediterranean trade and shipping and extending its military potency to the economic sphere.

While traditional Roman society had been austere and religious, Rome's many successful conquests left her bathed in riches, an environment ripe for corruption. Yeoman farmers who formed the venerated foundation of Roman agricultural society were pushed off their land by avaricious politicians and driven into slavery or starvation. Social upheaval quickly followed; by 131 BC, slave, farmer, and plebeian demands for land redistribution led to popular riots against the corrupt patrician class, culminating in the **Social War** (91-87 BC), in which tribes throughout the peninsula successfully fought for extension of Roman citizenship and the corresponding social and economic benefits. Sulla, the general who had led Rome's troops during the conflict, then led the Roman army into Rome (an unprecedented and taboo move), taking control of the city in a bloody military coup, during which over 1600 knights and senators were executed.

In the wake of this latest upheaval, **Spartacus,** an escaped gladitorial slave, led a 70,000-man army of slaves and farmers in a two-year rampage down the peninsula. When the dust cleared, **Pompey the Great,** a close associate of Sulla, had taken effective control of the city, but soon found himself in conflict with his sometime co-ruler **Julius Caesar.** Caesar, the charismatic conqueror of Gaul, finally emerged victorious, but a small faction, fearful of Caesar's growing power, assassinated him on the Ides (15th) of March in 44 BC. His power eluded several would-be heirs before falling to his nephew, Octavian, who consolidated and concentrated power, assumed the title of **Augustus Caesar,** and inaugurated an imperial government in 27 BC.

His reign (27 BC-14 AD) is generally considered the golden age of Rome, ushering in the *Pax Romana* (200 years of peace). The population swelled to 80 million citizens, Rome gained a virtual monopoly on all Mediterranean trade, and the Latin language developed fixed rules to ensure that it was both "perfect" and universally spoken.

Like its sacred symbol the Capitoline wolf, Rome continued to hunt for territorial prey as long as its power remained. Although many of Octavian's successors were less august than himself, Rome reached its maximum expansion under **Trajan** (98-117 AD) and clung to its status as *caput mundi* (capital of the world) until the death of **Marcus Aurelius** in 180 AD.

The Moribund Empire and the Dark Ages

Weak leadership and the southward invasions of Germanic tribes combined to create a state of anarchy in the 3rd century AD. **Diocletian** secured control of the fragmented empire in 284 AD. He then established order, divided the empire into eastern and western halves, and escalated the persecution of Christians—a period that became known as the "age of martyrs." The persecution began in 64 when the Emperor Nero, a poetaster and dedicated sadist, needed a scapegoat for the immense destructive fire he was widely believed to have started. The Roman people were diverted and entertained by the sight of Christians dressed in the hides of animals and torn to shreds by savage canines, or set on fire as lamps so law-abiding citzens could do a little reading before bed. The Christians who died came to be known as martyrs, from the Greek for "witnesses"— an apt term for those who experienced firsthand the full extent of Roman cruelty.

While subsequent, more tolerant, emperors turned their attention to enemies their own size, popular prejudice—and the torture and murder of Christians—persisted. Many Romans were hostile toward Christians, regarding them as a threat to the Roman lifestyle. Christians looked forward to a time when Christ would return to earth and Rome would be consumed by flames. Converts, the Democrats of early Rome, challenged traditional Roman family values by opting out of rituals, particularly those dedicated to pleasure. And Christian pacifism, exemplified by their refusal to serve in the Roman army, was interpreted (rightly) as subversive. At the same time, zealots eager to prove their fidelity to Christ were often willing participants in their own martyrdom. At the Colosseum, crowds cheered on hungry lions who tore hapless Christians limb from limb. Christians were also used as disposable targets for archery and as scrap for wood-chopping exercises. Despite this remarkably hazardous environment, by the end of Diocletian's violent reign approximately 30,000 Christians remained in Rome.

The fortunes of local Christians took a turn for the better when **Constantine,** Diocletian's successor, saw a huge cross in the wartime sky along with the letters, *"In hoc signo vincit"* (By this sign you shall conquer). Sure enough, victory followed the vision, and Constantine, combining military strategy with spiritual conversion, conquered his co-emperor Maxentius in 312 and declared Christianity the state religion in 315 AD. But Constantine hastened the end of Rome's supremacy by moving the capital of the empire east, to the newborn city of Constantinople. As city officials lost touch with their far-off imperial government, Christian bishops began to assume some traditional civic duties, such as caring for the poor and the hungry. Meanwhile huge armies of barbarian mercenaries broke through neglected fortifications along the empire's northern borders and descended on the city. In 410 **Alaric,** king of the Visigoths, deposed the last of Rome's western emperors and sacked the city. The ensuing scramble for power wasn't fully resolved until 476, when **Odoacer,** an Ostrogoth chieftain, was crowned King of Italy. Sacker-extraordinaire **Attila the Hun** arrived on tour in 452; despite the absence of an opposing army to greet him in Rome, fast-talker Pope Leo I convinced him to pillage elsewhere.

The bisection of the empire increased its instability; over the next two centuries, at least one of the two empires was at war. The eastern Roman (Byzantine) emperor **Justinian** declared war on the western division in 526, subjugated it, and imposed the *corpus juris,* the codified law of the empire, which eventually served as the legal model for European nations for half a millennium. Much of the quarrel between the two divisions of the empire revolved around the ownership of Rome itself, a struggle which led to its temporary concession to the protection of the papacy.

The papacy thus grew in power, but threatened by German Lombards, the Pope was forced to call for Frankish assistance. On Christmas Day, 800, Pope Leo III crowned **Charlemagne** "Emperor of the Romans," and a period of relative stability ensued.

Medieval Anarchy

Unfortunately, peace was short-lived. Charlemagne's death in 814 AD led to 150 years of near-anarchy, as Italian city-states dissipated their political energy and military strength in constant bickering, leaving themselves vulnerable to Hungarian attacks from the north and Saracen assaults on Sicily, Sardinia, and the western coast. The ascension of **Otto I** of Germany and his subsequent founding of the **Holy Roman Empire** in 962 re-established order, which was maintained until the death of his grandson, **Otto III,** in 1002 AD. Italy's relapse into near-chaos paved the way for increased papal authority. Although he was unable to repel the devastating Norman invasion of 1084, led by **Robert Guiscard, Pope Gregory VII** (1073-1085) did much to free Italy from outside rule, and from the 11th to 13th century, Rome grew as the administrative hub of the Roman Catholic Church.

The 14th century brought new martial tribulations to Rome; in 1309, **Pope Clement V** was forced to flee Rome for the city of Avignon while warring noblemen ravaged the city. The papal seat returned to Rome in 1378, but the half-century of separation had significantly eroded papal influence.

The Renaissance

Although the papacy eventually reasserted itself, the leaders who clasped the fallen scepter in the 14th through 16th centuries were secular politicos ruling the individual city-states. Left to their own devices, the leaders of these *communi* concentrated on extending their own economic and territorial power. Toward this end, they initiated a political fragmentation that would typify Italian history for centuries. Ironically, such instability planted the seeds of the greatest intellectual and artistic flowering of history—the **Renaissance**. Great ruling families like the Gonzaga in Mantua, the d'Este in Ferrara, and the Medici in Florence instituted important reforms in commerce and law, fertilizing the already rapid cultural and artistic flourishing of their respective cities. Princes, bankers, and merchants channeled their increasing wealth into patronage for the artists and scholars whose work defined the era. Unfortunately, power-hungry princes also cultivated the dark side of the Renaissance—constant warfare, usually among mercenaries. The weakened cities yielded easily to the Spanish invasions of the 16th century; by 1556, both Naples and Milan had fallen to King Ferdinand of Aragon.

Disease and Disaster

Along with the humanist ideals of Petrarch, the brilliant creations of Michelangelo and Raphael, and the licentious exploits of *Carnivale*, Renaissance Italy encountered a humiliating arrest to its achievements: **syphilis**. The disease was probably imported to the continent in 1494 from either Africa or the West Indies, or from (egads!) America by Christopher Columbus's crew. French soldiers contracted the disease from prostitutes in Naples and nicknamed it the "Neapolitan disease"; in turn, the Italians called it *morbo gallico* (disease of the Gauls). In Rome, the disease spread wildly, infecting seventeen members of the Pope's family and court, including Cesare Borgia (illegitimate son of the pope, Rodrigo; murderer; and protagonist of Machiavelli's *The Prince*).

To add to the city's horrors, the Tiber produced a violent **flood** in 1495. Water gushed into the streets and surged through churches and homes until it was suppressed by the fortified walls of the city's palaces. Many people drowned, including the inmates of the fearsome Tor di Nona, a stark prison overlooking the (now-called) Ponte Umberto. The Nona boasts two famous alums: astronomer-*cum*-heretic Giordano Bruno and sculptor-*cum*-jewel thief Benevento Cellini.

The ascetic Florentine Dominican friar **Girolamo Savonarola** soon proclaimed these calamities the wages of sin to be paid by the decadent Church and inaugurated an war on the papal and municipal excesses of Rome. He condemned the Church for its whoring and its profligacy. He warned the city of famine, pestilence, and general catastrophe if it failed to clean up its act—he even envisioned a black cross rising from the hills of Rome emblazoned with the words, "The Cross of God's Anger." The pope (**Pius III**) tried to shut up the pesky friar, first by a papal decree forbidding him to speak, then by offering him a cardinal post. The friar refused the official hat, claiming that one "red with blood" would be more appropriate for the corrupt position. The pope finally just excommunicated him. Savonarola persevered with a vengeance until the Florentines themselves got sick of his continual haranguing and tortured, burned, and hanged him.

Jews in Renaissance Italy

Pope Sixtus IV (1464-71) was a strong and vocal defender of the Jews; at the same time he commissioned the Sistine Chapel as a great monument to Catholicism. Nevertheless, to the consternation of the Roman Jewry, he paid no attention to the first stirrings of the Spanish Inquisition. Later, with the help of some prodding by his talented Jewish physician, Sixtus IV warned King Ferdinand and Isabella (the sponsors of Christopher Columbus, who may have been a Jew himself) to loosen their anti-Semitic strictures. Sixtus IV even took pains (via papal edicts and arm-twisting) to silence the rampant anti-Jewish sentiment among certain monks and intellectuals, some of them recent converts from Judaism.

The Inquisition and expulsion of the Jews from Spain in 1492 sent many of them packing to Italy (a kinder, gentler nation) and to Rome to join the well-established Jewish community, where they set up shops and businesses. Many towns and cities, such as Livorno, did welcome their services as merchants and moneylenders; Jews were exempt from the ancient Church injunction against usury (loan interest), and even when their money-lending practice was threatened by law, it went underground. Shakespeare's *The Merchant of Venice* illustrates the prevailing antipathy toward (and simultaneous financial dependency on) Jews in 16th-century Italy in its cruel depiction of Shylock, the Jewish money-lender.

Pope Leo X (1513-22), known more for his intense patronage of the arts than his religious devotion, involved a select number of Jews in his court. He even made a small, subversive gesture in favor of the Jews during his formal entry into the Vatican. During all popes' first procession, the Jews gathered at the Ponte Sant'Angelo with their rabbi to present their book of law to prove that they were worthy citizens; by tradition, the pope would reject the Jewish faith, voice some pre-scripted foolishness about the Jews' general unworthiness, sinfulness, and inferiority, and then begrudgingly confirm their privileges. At the inauguration of each pope, the Jews also decorated the popes' parade routes with elaborate tapestries and banners; this was generally the most contact with the pope that the Jews had. When the rabbi met with Leo X, the new pope uttered the prescribed indignities and disrespect with a certain expression of reluctance and shame. Leo's own Jewish court companions included the handsome musician Jacopo di Sansecondo (who also served as a model for Raphael), as well as an advisor, a physician, and one Giovanni Maria, a flautist who pleased the Pope so much that he was made a count and received a healthy allowance.

Continuing this trend of relative papal tolerance of Jewish culture, Leo's successor, Julius II, in a burst of respect for the Old Testament, commissioned Michelangelo's Moses statue.

However, the Counter-Reformation ushered in a new period of intolerance toward the Jews. **Pope Paul IV** (1555), a Neapolitan who vowed that he "would burn his father at the stake if he were a heretic," revived the hatred and intolerance of the Spanish Inquisition once more, searching out heretics for the Church bonfire. Torture was widely practiced and some people were burned at the stake. While the Catholics' attack was aimed more directly at the Christian heretics, Jews were also regarded as enemies. In 1556 all Roman Jews were herded into the Ghetto, a small, low-lying malarial district near the Tiber. Under the scrutiny of the Mattei family, the gates were locked at night, and during the day Jews were forced to wear yellow caps (for men) or yellow veils (for women) if they ventured beyond the dreary zone. Jews were only allowed to work in outdoor markets or rag shops, though many pursued mystical practices, such as astrology and fortune-telling to make a living; it was not unheard of for patrician ladies of Rome to regularly have their palms read in the Ghetto. The walls of the Ghetto remained for two centuries.

The Borgia Family

One of Italy's leading Italian families, the Borgias have long been immortalized on stage, in song, and in print. Victor Hugo airbrushed the events of Lucrezia Borgia's life in a play he wrote about her; Gabriel Donizetti made her the protagonist of one of his operas. Her reputedly equally captivating brother Cesare inspired the title character of Machiavelli's *The Prince*. A close look at the history of the Borgia family makes it seem peculiar that they should be cast as heroes and heroines rather than as villains. All of 15th-century Europe trembled at the mere mention of this unscrupulous but charismatic family. While the very first Borgia Pope, Calixtus III, was harmless enough, his nephew and successor **Rodrigo Borgia,** (1430-1503) who bore the papal name of Alexander VI, was intent on founding a kingdom which would be ruled by his multitudinous progeny. The pitter-patter of little feet was heard all over the Vatican in the 1470s: Rodrigo and his mistress—with whom he lived openly—had four children together; he fathered six others by other mistresses. Rodrigo wasn't all business, though; he outraged republican Rome by throwing bash after decadent bash. Although Rodrigo was said to be bewitchingly attractive and had no trouble getting dates, he still found the need to hire 50 prostitutes to dance a ballet entirely naked. You can still see Rodrigo's insatiable appetites in his face, captured in the unflattering frescoes done by Pinturic-chio in the Vatican Museums.

While Rodrigo ruled in Rome, his son **Cesare Borgia** (1476-1507) went about the bloody business of carving out a new kingdom in Europe. Cesare, who had inherited his father's comely appearance, became the original "Valentino" after subduing the Duchy of Valentois. Cesare swiped title after title from conquered nobles, ruthlessly pillaging cities as large as Urbino; Venetians and Florentinians were certain they would be next. It could be as dangerous being Cesare's friend as it was to be his enemy. Noto-rious for his nonchalance while witnessing murders, he once invited four high-ranking officers to a banquet and continued munching on a drumstick while they were strangled in front of him. Historians suspect Cesare of murdering his elder brother, as well as his brother-in-law, both of whom he saw as threats to his power.

Rodrigo and Cesare acquired immense holdings but never managed to establish their own kingdom. Rodrigo's younger sister **Lucrezia Borgia** (1480-1519) certainly did her part to help out, marrying five times by the time she was 22, each time for a strate-gic purpose. Lucrezia's first (at age 11) and second betrothals were mutually dissolved. Her third marriage (at age 13) was to a member of the Sforza clan, Milan's most pow-erful family. When the Sforzas were no longer useful to the Borgias, Lucrezia had no problem getting an annullment from the Church—her father, after all, was the pope. Her fourth husband was murdered—and given her history, her fifth husband, the duke of Ferrara, was an understandably reluctant groom. Their "shotgun" wedding (Rodrigo held an army to the duke's head) was one of the most extravagant European royalty had ever seen.

In contrast to history's long-term view of her family, Lucrezia's personal story had a happy ending. Her marital bliss was crowned by a brood of children. Rodrigo and Ce-sare, on the hand, got their just deserts; the former may have been poisoned and the lat-ter was struck down in battle. In their heyday, the Borgias were reviled and feared by Italians; it's no surprise that shortly after their deaths outrageous and often supernatural tales were spun, many of which survive today. Perhaps the most well-known is the sup-posed incestuous relationships of Rodrigo and Cesare with Lucrezia, for which there is no hard evidence.

After the Renaissance: Italian Irrelevance

Sixteenth century Spaniards brought a wonderful gift to Italy, in addition to their in-vading armies: the **Inquisition** became the primary method of suppressing Protestant-ism and the Jesuits, and rolling back the Counter-Reformation. Its victims included such noted intellectuals as Galileo Galilei and Giordano Bruno. The end of the 16th century brought the attenuation of Spanish control over the Italian states and a corre-sponding rise in the temporal power of the papacy. The War of Spanish Succession against Austria a century later (1701-16) ended Spanish rule in Milan and Naples; Aus-trian rulers replaced them. At the same time, the Duke of Savoy, Victor Amadeus II, extended his territorial control in Piedmont, leaving Italy a patchwork of political re-gimes.

The rise of **Napoleon** ushered in the new century. He united Italy for the first time since antiquity by bringing the southern provinces together with the Kingdom of Na-ples and the Roman Republic in 1798. Napoleon further stimulated Italian patriotism by arousing national resentment against the Austrian presence. After Napoleon's fall in 1815, the **Congress of Vienna** carved up Italy anew, shuffling kingdoms and granting considerable control to Austria.

The Italian Nation

In subsequent decades, strong sentiment against foreign rule prompted a movement of nationalist resurgence called the **Risorgimento,** ultimately culminating in national unification in 1870. Success of the Risorgimento rests primarily with three Italian he-roes: **Giuseppe Mazzini,** the movement's intellectual leader; **Giuseppe Garibaldi,** the military leader and commander of the "red-shirts"; and **Camillo di Cavour,** the political and diplomatic mastermind.

Although the much-revered Garibaldi and his army of 1000 defeated the Bourbons in the south, the credit for Italy's birth as a nation belongs to Cavour. In 1858, he and **Napoleon III** of France strengthened an alliance against the Austrians that freed Lombardy from foreign control. The new Kingdom of Italy, under **Vittorio Emanuele,** (whose statesmanship is commemorated by a *via* or *piazza* in seemingly every town) went on to annex Romagna, Parma, Mòdena, and Tuscany. In 1866, the Prussians forced the Austrian Habsburg Empire to surrender Veneto to Italy, and France ultimately relinquished Rome on September 20, 1870, the pivotal date in modern Italian history. Once the elation of unification wore off, however, age-old provincial differences reasserted themselves. Northern regions wanted to shield their relative prosperity from the economic stagnation of the agrarian south, central city-states were wary of surrendering too much power to a central administration, and the Pope, whose Roman empire had been seized by the new kingdom, threatened Italian Catholics (98% of the population is Catholic, mind you) with excommunication for participating in politics. Cavour's death in 1861, coupled with the sudden economic decline of farmers relative to those employed in the modern sector and the strife of *trasformismo,* alienated people from politics. Disillusionment increased as Italy became involved in World War I and fought to gain territory and vanquish Austria. Italy's war aims were met, but at a high price: half a million dead, rising inflation, economic dislocation, and a huge war debt.

The chaotic aftermath of World War I paved the way for the rise of **fascism,** with its promise of order and stability. The Bolsheviks had recently gained control in Russia, and **Benito Mussolini** politically milked an Italian "red scare" to destroy his strongest domestic opponents. Seeking to regain for Italy the glory of imperial Rome, "Il Duce" conquered Ethiopia in 1936.

In 1940, Italy entered World War II and joined the Axis alliance. Success came quickly, but was short-lived: When the Allies landed in Sicily three years later, Mussolini fell from his pinnacle of power. By the end of 1943, the government had changed direction, and declared war on Germany, which promptly invaded and occupied its former ally. Some of the most savage fighting took place as the Allies struggled up the peninsula; skirmishes between supporters of the deposed Fascist government and its democratic replacement further ravaged Italy.

The Postwar Republic

Modernity has not brought simplicity to Italy. The end of World War II ushered in sweeping changes in the Italian polity, but no clear leader emerged to marshal the republic in its turbulent early years. The Constitution adopted in 1948 established a new Italian Republic with a president, a bicameral Parliament with a 315-member Senate and 630-member Chamber of Deputies, and an independent judiciary. The president, elected for a seven-year term by an electoral college, is the head of state and appoints the prime minister. Chief executive authority rests with the prime minister and his Council of Ministers, subject to legislative approval.

Within this framework, the **Christian Democratic Party** (DC), bolstered by American money and military aid, bested the Socialists and surfaced as the consistent ruling party in the newly fashioned republic. But domination by a single party has not given the country stability; the republic has been mired in political turmoil, with more than 50 different governments since World War II. With the exception of one brief Socialist stint in the 80s, though, the Christian Democrats have led the government all the while and the strong left has remained in the opposition. The Italian party system traditionally follows a pattern of "polarized centrism"—a multiparty system with most voters belonging either to the right-leaning Christian Democrats, or to one of the left-leaning parties: the **Socialist Unity Party** (PSU, though usually referred to by its old name, the PSI) or the **Democratic Party of the Left** (PDS, a much less radical version of the old Communist Party, the PCI). A small minority of Italian voters belong to one of the several centrist parties that bridge the ideological gap. Since no single party can claim a majority of the voters, Italian governments are formed with volatile and tenuous coalitions forged between parties. Before the 1989 fall of the Eastern European regimes, the Communists exerted a great deal of influence, especially in the south, and received about 30% of the vote in most national elections. Recently, however, the picture has grown fuzzy; the revamped PDS continues to slide. In the elections of April 1992, PDS support declined to under 17% from its strong 27% showing in 1987.

The instability of the postwar era, in which the Italian economy sped through industrialization at an unprecedented rate, gave way to violence and near-anarchy in the 1970s. The *autunno caldo* (hot autumn) of 1969, a season of strikes, demonstrations, and riots, came on the heels of the international mayhem of 1968 and foreshadowed the violence of the 70s; twenty percent inflation (and the corresponding devaluation of personal savings), spiraling unemployment rates, and the proliferation of terrorist groups left the Italian government at a loss to respond. Perhaps most shocking was the 1978 kidnapping and murder of ex-Prime Minister **Aldo Moro** by the Brigate Rosse (Red Brigades), a leftist terrorist group formed in Turin in 1970. This assassination, which capped years of public violence against judges, senators and deputies, spurred the government to launch major anti-terrorist campaigns that achieved mild success in restoring order.

Current Politics

Although leftist terrorism has declined, Italian politics remain just as dangerous—and are even more scandalous. In 1989, the Radical Party's candidate **Ilona Staller,** the ex-porn star "La Cicciolina," was elected to the house of deputies in Viareggio. The buxom pol celebrated her win by baring her breasts in a victory parade. (In 1991, she married a well-known artist whose works include an enormous sculpture of the couple forming the beast with two backs atop a snake-surrounded bed in the Garden of Eden.) In another tabloid news item, the Christian Democrats' support took a dive after the **P2** Masonic lodge scandal broke and revealed bribes, kickbacks, and corrupt dealings among the DC hierarchy, right-wing fringe groups, and the heads of large banks.

Although the extent of **mafia** power has waned somewhat in recent years, the loosely affiliated leaders of the nebulous organization still command great control over Italy's society, politics, and economy, especially in the *Mezzogiorno* (Mediterranean region) and Sicily. As the leaders of the black market, the mafia has become the pillar, however crooked, of the Italian economy. Some of the *mafiosi's* success stems from the cultural acceptance of their activities (at one time, most members were regarded not as thugs, but as men of honor and strength who simply followed their own peculiar code of morality). But today's mafia—with its heightened passion for drug-running and violence—inspires near-universal fear and resentment among Italians. The Italian Parliament passed an unprecedented anti-mafia law in 1982, followed by the Palermo *maxi processi* (maxi-trials), the largest mafia trial in history. Sicily-based *La Rete* (the Network), a new political party with a strong anti-mafia platform, has become the most influential in Palermo—it won 15 Parliament seats in the April 1992 elections.

Divisions in Italy are not just between frightened citizens and organized criminals. Because the nation of Italy is still very young, city and regional bonds often prove stronger than nationalist sentiment. The most pronounced split exists between the north's highly industrialized European areas and the south's agrarian Mediterranean territories. Despite the many obstacles to modernization in the south, Italy has expanded with astonishing rapidity since World War II, and has surpassed even Britain in economic rankings. Yet over the last 15 years, regional parochialism has been on the rise and northern patience with the wayward south is wearing thin. In response, regional government has been granted more autonomy, but some northerners want more: the right-wing **Lombard League** seeks to unite the fattest part of the north and rejects Rome and the South. The Lombards scored a major victory in the April 1992 elections—a 9% share of the electorate up from less than 1% in 1987—with a platform advocating a new federal system which would cut off subsidies to the dependent south. Present-day Italy's most important task—and it is by no means an easy one—is to harness meaningful political participation on a national level and attempt to heal its destructive divisions. But the Lombard League's remarkable surge shows that northerners aren't ready for true Italian unity. And recent Italian politics, characterized by instability, querulousness, and scandal, isn't well-suited to attack these problems. To make matters worse, political participation is among the lowest in Europe.

The chaos of Italian politics disillusions even its leaders. After three long years, Socialist Bettino Craxi, lamenting his inability to work with the Christian Democratic majority, resigned from the prime minister's chair in March 1987. After Craxi's fall, three Christian Democrats took office in quick succession. Then, following a rare period of relative stability, the musical chairs of Italian politics returned in April 1992: Christian Democrat Giulio Andreotti, who had been Prime Minister since July 1989, resigned, and President Francesco Cossiga also announced his retirement, citing Italy's "disastrous financial situation, the prominence of bad in our society, public disservice, and institutional paralysis." In the 1992 elections, the Christian Democrats gathered less than 30% of the vote for the first time since 1946, but managed to hold on to the presidency. On May 27, 1992, after disputes over voting procedures, a fist-fight between the neo-fascists and Christian Democrats (honest!), and 10 days and 15 rounds of voting that produced no majority, Oscar Luigi Scalfaro was finally elected Italy's new president.

In his victory, Scalfaro garnered the support of two parties that were once anathema to the ruling coalition—the PDS (the new Communists) and the Greens, a party committed to protecting the environment. Scalfaro, Italy's ninth president since 1948, has pledged his support for significant institutional reform of government, including a streamlining of the cabinet. And Giuliano Amato, the new prime minister appointed by Scalfaro, is a Socialist—only the third non-Christian Democrat to occupy the seat since the Republic's founding. With a Socialist prime minister and a new left-of-center coalition in power in Italy, there is hope that the government may emerge from its destructive past and make progress in addressing some of the country's most damaging problems: budget deficits twice as bad as the United States', a public debt that exceeds the country's GNP, 6% inflation, uncontrollable crime, and, of course, omnipresent political fragmentation.

Art and Architecture

> *Lump the whole thing! Say that the Creator made Italy from designs by Michael Angelo.*
>
> *—Mark Twain*

Any study of Italian art begins with the Roman Empire. The glory of Roman architecture is based on the **arch**, a deceptively simple innovation which yielded the famous Roman aqueducts, bridges, vaulted roofs, and triumphal arches. Although the Greeks provided a model for many aspects of Roman society, the arch had little place in Hellenistic building; the Romans made it the base of their art and their infrastructure, and proceeded to conquer the world with its simple geometry. Rome's **Colosseum** (80 AD) typifies this marriage of Greek aesthetics and Roman technology; its **Pantheon** (117-125 AD), however, is proof that the arch was far more than a piece of architectural technology—it was a stroke of aesthetic genius.

The collapse of the Roman Empire and the rise of Christianity marked the beginning of a search for new aesthetic forms. The most pressing concern was the modification of the Roman temple to accommodate the Christian mass; for this purpose, the structure of Roman market-halls called "basilicas" were adopted, creating space for religious paintings, mosaics and architectural innovation. New trends in painting were slower to emerge; the color, composition, and treatment of subjects in catacombs (5th-7th centuries) recall classical Roman wall painting, with Bacchic figures representing Christ and the Apostles. As early as the 5th century, however, Pope Gregory the Great was calling for art which would edify the illiterate masses and exalt the world beyond—not glorify the individual or the transient temporal world. The Christian art which emerged in the

Middle Ages was thus crafted by men with an eye fixed firmly on heaven. Viewers will be struck by the lack of proportion, the disregard for the body and the landscape cluttered with obscure symbols. These paintings combined a disregard for the physical world with a diminution of the individual in a larger, protective hierarchy of symbols and belief.

Although inspired by a different philosophy, Byzantine art (emerging from Constantinople, capital of the Eastern Roman Empire as of 330 AD) was also religious and highly stylized. Byzantine architecture was notable both in the blueprint form of the Christian basilica and the domes and vaults atop these churches. Italian examples of Byzantine construction include the Church of San Vitale in Ravenna (547) and the Church of San Marco in Venice (1063-1073); the brilliant mosaics of the latter are also characteristically Byzantine.

Following these early years of the millenium, two great styles emerged to dominate art and architecture: Romanesque and Gothic, perhaps best understood in relation to one another. From 500-1200 AD **Romanesque** dominated Europe, with churches easily identified by small, rounded arches resting on massive stone piers. When you spot a Romanesque church, check inside for characteristic Romanesque art—either as distorted, stylized, Byzantine-type artwork or as classical relief sculpture in the stone of the buildings themselves—and note how little light invades the interior. Great Italian Romanesque churches include the Cathedral of Pisa, San Ambrogio in Milan, the cathedral of Massa Marittima, and San Miniato in Florence.

The **Gothic** style of the 12th to 14th centuries resulted from the combination of the pointed arch and the flying buttress—together, they supported the heavy roof and allowed the majestic Romanesque wall to be replaced by the glorious Gothic window. The Gothic church can be spotted by its telltale pointed windows, but you won't find any in Italy: For some unknown reason, Italian Gothic never adopted the flying buttress and thus the incredible light-filled churches of France and Germany are absent in Italy. Still, the pointed arches and ribbed vaults mark a dramatic departure from Romanesque building, especially when compared side-by-side (do this as you wander through a city). San Petronio in Bologna and the Cathedrals of Milan and Siena are lovely examples of this style. Gothic art is marked by a nascent emphasis on the natural over the symbolic—a principle that would become fully enunciated in the approaching Renaissance. Great Gothic artists include **Simone Martini** and **Pietro Lorenzetti** (especially his Crucifixion in San Francesco, Siena).

As the 14th century neared, the economic and political conditions which nurtured the Renaissance were taking shape; the art was beginning to change as well, most notably with the work of **Giotto di Bondone** (1267-1337). Giotto presented the viewer with fully-rounded figures who move naturally in three-dimensional space; in contrast to Byzantine and medieval art, Giotto used realistic proportions and backgrounds. His approach constituted a dramatic break with medieval concerns in art while at the same time his contemporary Dante was accomplishing a similar feat in the field of literature. For a good example of Giotto's work, see his *Death of St. Francis* (Bardi Chapel of Santa Croce, Florence). His successor, **Masaccio** (1401-1428), is also worth noting for his work with light, shadow and color. The work of these men foreshadowed the developments of the Renaissance, a period characterized not only by the art and literature which it produced, but also by the new humanism which would prosper in the attitudes of artists and politicians.

The **Renaissance** (14th-16th centuries), a period of renewed interest in humanity and its products, welcomed a flood of innovation and a rejection of dogmatic authority. No longer was man viewed merely in his relation to the heavens—the Renaissance brought a new emphasis on man as an individual. The rediscovery of the human body as an object of beauty and of human beings as creatures of worth influenced all parts of Renaissance culture. The nude was rediscovered in Renaissance art, for example, but its realistic portrayal was informed by the science of anatomy, a study which enjoyed a similar reawakening during this period. Though a religious perspective no longer dominated the artist, religious art did not disappear altogether; it merely changed form. In *The Creation of Adam* in the Sistine Chapel, for example, the perfect anatomy of Adam—and the detail in his hand and in God's—contrasts sharply with medieval paintings. Renaissance art portrays human beings as individuals, often captured in action, and inserts them into specific, realistic backgrounds.

These new techniques revolutionized painting, sculpture, and architecture in Italy. One of the most prominent **early Renaissance** sculptors was **Lorenzo Ghiberti** (1378-1455), although his magnificent Gates of Paradise—the bronze doors of the Florence baptistery—draw heavily upon Gothic influence. The creation of the doors took decades, however, and required the creation of a Florentine workshop for students which produced, along with the doors, the most influential artist of the 15th century, **Donatello** (1386-1466). Donatello revered the Roman style while producing some of the most original work of his time. He was the first sculptor to give movement to niche-statues, and his bronze *David* (in the Florentine Bargello) was the first free-standing nude since antiquity. His close study of anatomy not only informed his sculpting, but made his statues the inspiration for anatomical accuracy and realism among later Renaissance painters. (Legend has it that he used to cry, "Speak, speak!" to his statues as he worked on them.)

The two most important architects of the early Renaissance are **Filippo Brunelleschi** (1377-1446) and **Leon Alberti** (1404-1472). Brunelleschi was an extraordinary engineer, often credited with the "discovery" of linear perspective in painting. His greatest accomplishment was raising the first great dome of the Renaissance over Santa Maria del Fiore in Florence. Alberti, whose style was less grandiose but more practical than Brunelleschi's, was the first to confront architecture in the context of town-planning; he also constructed San Sebastiano and Sant'Andrea in Mantua and Rucellai Palace in Florence. In the high Renaissance, their mantle would be taken up by **Donato Bramante** (1444-1514), who would redefine 16th-century architecture with his tribune of Santa Maria della Grazie in Milan and his plans for St. Peter's in Rome (significantly altered by Michelangelo after Bramante's death).

There is no doubt, however, that the peak of the Renaissance (1450-1520) was dominated by three men known as the Triumvirate of the High Renaissance: **Leonardo da Vinci** (1452-1519), **Michelangelo Buonarroti** (1475-1564), and **Raphael** (1483-1520).

The first of these three, da Vinci, was the original Renaissance Man—artist, scientist, architect, engineer, musician, weapons designer—and although he seldom finished what he started, his achievements were extraordinary. His monumental painting *The Last Supper* (Santa Maria delle Grazie in Milan) is a veritable handbook on Renaissance individualism in a religious theme. He also perfected the use of aerial perspective, defined standards of human proportional perfection, and stylized the use of *sfumato,* a technique that enables the artist to move smoothly from color to color and which revolutionized painting technique throughout Europe. That another genius of da Vinci's caliber existed at the same time—and in the same place—is stupefying. But Michelangelo painted and sculpted with as much skill as his contemporary—and perhaps with even greater results. The beautiful ceiling of the Sistine Chapel remains his great achievement in painting (after completing the project, he didn't paint again for 25 years). His architectural achievements are equally noteworthy—the master's designs for St. Peter's elevated Italian architecture to new heights. But sculpture is where Michelangelo's true genius lay. Classic examples are the formal, tranquil *Pietà* in St. Peter's, its half-finished, anguished counterpart in the Castello Sforzesco in Milan, the majestic, virile *David* in Florence's Academy, and the powerful *Moses* in Rome's San Pietra in Vincoli. Raphael is notable for his prolificacy and his technical perfection; he laid the foundation for modern history paintings with unyielding accuracy and attention to detail. Raphael invented the seated three-quarter-length portrait and the group portrait, and his frescoes in the Papal apartments in the Vatican are a must for lovers of Renaissance art.

When Rome was pillaged in 1527 by German and Spanish mercenaries, economic instability and theological conflict brought an end to the golden age of the Renaissance. The widespread disillusionment that followed was reflected in the emerging style of **mannerism,** so-called because the school pursued the manner but not the spirit of their predecessors. Borrowing from the previous styles, but exaggerating them in an attempt at originality, mannerists flouted Renaissance rules even as they revered them. This odd school was a short-lived link between the Renaissance and Baroque periods. A precursor to the Baroque period was the great architect **Andrea Palladio** (1508-1580), the originator of Palladian architecture (known for its classical, centralized proportions). Palladio's most important works were the Villa Capra at Vicenza and Il Redentore in Venice. The most lasting contribution to his art, however, may have been his *Four Books of Architecture,* which influenced many American and English architects (including Inigo Jones and Christopher Wren).

The Baroque period that followed lasted into the 18th century. It signaled a concern for balance and wholeness, a new **realism.** At the beginning of this era, **Michelangelo de Caravaggio** (1573-1610) urged a return to naturalism—a commitment to portraying nature as is, whether ugly or beautiful. He was scornful of some realists who obsessed over clean lines, feared the sometimes distasteful realities of nature, and portrayed apostles as common laborers; look for the harsh, glaring light in his pictures. **Gian Lorenzo Bernini** (1598-1680), the most prolific artist of the high Baroque, designed the ornate colonnades of St. Peter's (and so many other works that the city of Rome has been called a "Bernini museum"). **Tiepolo** (1696-1770) was the last of the great Italian decorative painters, and his sunny palate and strong frescoes marked the end of the tradition begun with Giotto.

Through French influence, the decorative **rococo** style and the sterner formalities of **neoclassicism** succeeded the Italian Baroque, to be succeeded themselves by the major trends of the 20th century. Two of Italy's greatest artists of this period were expatriates. **Amadeo Modigliani** (1884-1920) drew inspiration from the varied sources of mannerism, Renaissance art, and African primitivism in his masterful composition of portraits and nudes, and did all his major work in France. **Giorgio de Chirico** (1888-1978), a sporadic expatriate, originated **metaphysical painting,** a precursor of surrealism, characterized by mysterious, threatening shapes moving in ambiguous space.

Other modern Italian artists include **Sandro Chio** and **Enzo Cucci,** both neo-expressionists. **Francesco Clemente,** one of Italy's most talented new artists, paints to evoke dissatisfaction or disgust. Marcello Piacentini's monstrous fascist architecture looms at EUR in Rome. To trace the current path of Italian art, you can visit modern art galleries in most major cities as well as at the Canova Museum at Passagno.

For further reading, you might want to try the bestseller (as of 1550) *Lives of the Artists,* a gossipy, informative glimpse into the artists of the Renaissance by Vasari, court artist for the later Medici. Ferdinand Shevill's *The Medicis* is an accessible look at the most influential family of the High Renaissance, while general books like H.W. Janson's *The History of Art* or E.H. Gombrich's *The Story of Art* contain everything you would ever need to know about art—Italian or otherwise.

Literature

Greek and Roman Mythology

Ovid's work—particularly his *Metamophoses*—is a principal source for our knowledge of Greco-Roman mythology, a set of stories second only to the Bible in its influence on the Western imagination. When the Romans plundered Greece, they even stole its divine pantheon; take your favorite Greek myths, latinize the gods' names, and *presto,* instant Roman mythology. Myths were passed from generation to generation and region to region, where they were embellished and interpreted to reflect local concerns. The anthropomorphic gods and goddesses lived as immortal beings with divine power, yet often descended to earth to intervene romantically, mischievously, or combatively in human affairs, sometimes disguised as animals or humans. Traditionally, 14 major deities preside: **Jupiter** (Zeus, in Greek), king of gods; his wife **Juno** (Hera), who watches over child-bearing and marriage; **Neptune** (Poseidon), god of the sea; **Vulcan** (Hephaestus), god of smiths and fire; **Venus** (Aphrodite), goddess of love and beauty; **Mars** (Ares), god of war; **Minerva** (Athena), goddess of wisdom; **Phoebus** (Apollo), god of light and music; **Diana** (Artemis), goddess of the hunt; **Mercury** (Hermes), the messenger god and patron of thieves and tricksters; **Pluto** (Hades), lord of death; **Ceres**

(Demeter), goddess of the harvest; **Bacchus** (Dionysus), god of wine; and **Vesta** (Hestia), goddess of the hearth.

Jupiter was a sexual gymnast, and Juno was equally inventive in plotting revenge on his lovers. **Danae,** imprisoned in a tower by her father, was impregnated by Jupiter in the form of a golden shower, and **Ganymede,** a handsome Trojan shepherd, was snatched up from earth to be the cup-bearer of the gods. **Europa** was ravished by Jupiter disguised as a bull. Worse still for mortals, Juno, powerless to injure her philandering husband directly, directed her vengeance at the objects of his affection: **Io** was turned into a cow and chased pitilessly by an enormous gadfly; **Leto**, pregnant with Diana and Phoebus, was forbidden to rest on solid ground until the itinerant island of Delos lent its tiny shore for her to give birth upon, and **Callisto**, who got off relatively easy for her dalliance with Jupiter, was changed into a bear. **Semele**, one of the few willing consorts of Jupiter, dissolved into ash when he appeared to her in his full Olympian brilliance. Both **Edith Hamilton's** and **Bullfinch's** *Mythology* are eminently readable retellings of these and other myths.

Literature of the Empire

The same historical circumstances which nurtured art and architecture in Italy inspired an outpouring of literature that embraces Roman wars and modern feminism with equal fervor. As the Etruscan language remains completely opaque to modern scholars, the accessible Italian literary tradition begins with the Romans.

Early republican literature is not particularly inspiring; **Plautus's** farces, for instance, can best be seen as antique sitcoms. The poetry of Verona's **Catullus,** on the other hand, set a high standard for passion. **Livy** set down the authorized history of Rome during the first years of empire. **Julius Caesar** gave a first-hand account of the final shredding of the Republic; his *Commentaries* recount his experiences on the front lines of the Gallic wars.

With Caesar's close contemporary **Cicero** (bumped off by Mark Antony within a year of Caesar's fatal Ides of March), Latin prose is said to have reached its zenith: the dialogue *De Republica* explores a fundamental question of political philosophy—is it better to be a statesman or a philosopher?—and resolves it magically with Scipio's dream, the inspiring tale which closes the work. Cicero's *Brutus,* meanwhile, offers a history of Roman oratory.

The Rome of Augustus, despite a government prone to sudden banishment of the impolitic, produced the greatest Latin authors of antiquity. **Virgil** (Publius Vergilius Maro), revered as the only Roman poet worthy of comparison with Homer, wrote for the newly imperial city a creation myth worthy of its glory. The *Aeneid* links the founding of Rome with the fall of Troy through the wanderings of the Trojan Aeneas, who is told by the oracle of Apollo to "seek your ancient mother; there the race of Aeneas shall dwell and reduce all other nations to their sway." After protracted journeys around the Mediterranean and into the underworld, Aeneas settles in the Tiber valley (surprise!) where his descendents, Romulus and Remus, would found the all-conquering Rome. Robert Fitzgerald's blank verse translation is probably the best approach to this epic; it would take a brave and well-trained soul to stuff the original into a backpack for train-ride reading. More entertaining forays into the golden age of poetry include **Ovid's** racy *Amores* and his virtuoso collection of transformation myths, the *Metamophoses*. Official Rome preferred **Horace,** whose martial lyrics (*Dulce et decorum est, pro patria mori*—"Sweet and fitting it is to die for one's country") were more compatible with the sentiments of Augustus.

From the post-Augustan empire, **Petronius's** *Satyricon* is a bizarre, blunt look at the decadence of the age of Nero, while **Tacitus's** *Histories* summarize Roman war, diplomacy, scandal and rumor in the years following the death of Nero with unblinking even-handedness. His *Annals* look down from the upright Rome of Trajan's reign onto the scandalous activities of the Julio-Claudian emperors (Tiberius is a favorite target). Finally, **Marcus Aurelius's** *Meditations* bring us the musings of a philosopher-king on the edge of a precipice—it was all downhill after Marcus.

Italy had no *Beowulf* to brighten the Dark Ages, but the silence of a millennium was broken in brilliant fashion by a quite characteristic Italian cultural formation: a triumvirate. Any good Italian bookstore seems to devote a least a ceiling-to-floor case to annotated and critical editions of the works of **Dante Alighieri** (1265-1321), one of the first European poets to eschew Latin. He is consequently considered as much the father of the modern Italian language as of its literature. After suffering the death of his young love Beatrice in 1290, and exile from Florence in 1302, Dante began writing his masterpiece, *La Divina Commedia,* partially as a form of solace. Dante peopled his allegorical journey through the afterlife with famous figures from his own lifetime; among the *Commedia's* chief virtues are Dante's acid opinions of Italian cities and their inhabitants. Most English translators complain of the struggle to transform the euphonic *terza rima* of Dante's verse into even vaguely melodious English; Italian students whine about their struggle to comprehend *Il Poetà's* obsolete vocabulary and grammar. A good annotated version will get an interested reader through the difficulties of the Italian; otherwise, Ciardi and Mandelbaum have produced the best English versions.

If Dante is aptly described as a man with one foot in the Middle Ages and one in the Renaissance (quite a straddle), **Petrarch** (Francesco Petrarca, 1304-74) chose his side so emphatically as to be considered "the first modern man." Reading his *Il canzoniere,* one begins to notice that the poet seems less concerned with the unattainable Laura (who died in the Black Death of 1348) than with precisely summarizing his feeling for her; his subtle self-examination marks an individual, personal style unprecedented in medieval literature.

The third member of the medieval literary triumvirate was a close friend of Petrarch's, but the style of **Giovanni Boccaccio** owes little to his melancholy chum. Boccaccio took Dante to task in his lectures for descending to write in the vernacular, but claimed the same pleasure for himself in his most celebrated work, the *Decameron.* This collection of 100 stories told by ten young Florentines fleeing their plague-ridden city ranges in tone from bawdy and mocking to prim and earnest, featuring pious maidens, licentious priests, carefree nobles, more licentious priests, pathetic paupers, scads of licentious widows, and the occasional licentious nun. Considered the first Italian novelist, Boccaccio was the first author since antiquity to claim the privilege of writing not to edify or to preach, but merely to entertain the bored ladies of the leisure class. Boccaccio makes the best Italian companion for long journeys: the hundred tales are set along the length of the peninsula, with properly snide Florentine asides on the appearance and habits of Italians from the Friuli to Sicily. The innovations of these three men had an immeasurable impact on the coming Renaissance. However, the Renaissance veneration for the Romans meant that much of the writing of the next century shuns the Italian vernacular in favor of Latin.

Renaissance Literature

Fifteenth- and 16th-century Italian authors were forced to create new genres to accommodate their expansive accomplishments. **Leon Battista Alberti** and **Palladio** (Andrea di Pietro) wrote treatises on architecture and art theory at either end of the Renaissance; **Baldassre Castiglione's** *The Courtier* instructed the inquiring Renaissance man on deportment, etiquette, and other fine points of behavior; **Vasari** took time off from ruinous redecorations of Florence's churches to produce a primer on art history and criticism *(The Lives of the Artists).* The most lasting work of the Renaissance, **Niccolò Machiavelli's** *Il Principe (The Prince)* was the first purely secular treatise ever written on politics. This sophisticated assessment of what it takes to gain and hold political power is candid, brutal, direct, Mansfieldian. *The Prince* is probably best-seen as a handbook for reunifying Italy; some, however, look at Machiavelli's circumstances (in exile and desperately trying to win the favor of Lorenzo de' Medici, to whom he dedicated the book) and consider it self-serving. Choosing Cesare Borgia as a role model probably didn't help Machiavelli's reputation; few remember today that he was also the Renaissance's finest playwright.

Both of the great Renaissance epic poets lived off the patronage of the same fabulously wealthy family—the Este clan of Ferrara. **Lodovico Ariosto's** *Orlando Furioso* is a study in irony; its gentle mocking of the literature of chivalry was the springboard off which *Don Quixote* leapt. **Torquato Tasso,** considered the most important poet of the period, killed himself after his life's work, *La Gerumsalemma liberata,* suffered a poor reception by the emerging academies.

This being the Renaissance, people with perfectly good jobs in other areas felt compelled to add strings to their bows. Among Renaissance artists, **Benvenuto Cellini** wrote about that most interesting of all subjects, himself, in *The Autobiography;* **Michelangelo** wrote enough sonnets to fill a rather thick volume, while **Leonardo da Vinci** wrote about everything and anything *(The Notebook).* **Lorenzo de' Medici** had enough time on his hands while ruling Florence to pen hundreds of poems and songs. The scathing and brilliant **Pietro Aretino,** professional parasite and publicist, created new possibilities for literature when he began accepting payment from notable targets for *not* writing about them.

As Italy slid into international inconsequence, literary production again foundered. The Venetians frittered their time to the best effect; **Casanova's** *Life* makes good bedtime reading. Meanwhile, the prolific dramatist **Carlo Goldoni** transformed the traditional theater of the *commedia dell'arte* by replacing its stock figures with original, unpredictable characters in such works as *Il ventaglio.* He wrote in Venetian dialect, so unless you're an insatiable linguist, an English translation is recommended.

The publication of **Alessandro Manzoni's** sprawling, romantic epic *I promessi sposi* (*The Betrothed*) marks the birth of the modern novel in Italy. A devout Catholic, Manzoni probed the suffering of humanity through the seemingly random course of history in this work and in his two tragedies, *Il conte di Carmagnola* and *Adelch.*

20th-Century Literature

The 20th century has seen an explosion in literary innovation throughout Europe, and Italy has not been left behind.

Theatre

Early in the 20th century, the playwright **Luigi Pirandello** (1867-1936) became the father of modern experimental theater with his dramatic explorations of the relativity of truth, exemplified by *Sei personaggi in cerca d'autore* (*Six Characters in Search of an Author*). At the same time, the Triestino **Italo Svevo** produced unconventional masterpieces which were ignored in Italy for decades before Svevo caught international fancy. His three great works on the bourgeois mind are *Una vita* (*A Life*), *La coscienza di Zeno* (*The Confessions of Zeno*), and *Senilità* (*Senility*).

Poetry

Italy was also a center of Modernist innovation in poetry. The most flamboyant and controversial of the early poets is **Gabriele d'Annunzio,** whose cavalier heroics and sexual escapades earned him as much fame as his eccentric, over-the-top verse. **D'Annunzio** was a true child of pleasure, or *Il Piacere*, the title of his novel set in Rome. In the mid- and late-20th century, **Salvatore Quasimodo, Eugenio Montale** and **Giuseppe Ungaretti** dominated the scene. Montale and Quasimodo founded the "hermetic movement" (also known as "obscure poems dropped from an airless ivory tower"), but both became more accessible and politically committed after the Second World War. Both snagged Nobel Prizes along the way. Ungaretti brought to Italy many of the innovations of the French Symbolists; his collection *L'allegria* set a trend toward increased purity of language and clarity of meaning in Italian poetry. Ungaretti was drawn to Rome to study Keats and Shelley, and during his stay he disseminated his ideas to hundreds of admiring college students.

Among the welter of great modern writers, another unique Italian contribution was the Roman dialect poets. Three of the greatest were **G.G. Belli** (1791-1863), **Trilussi** (1871-1950), and **Cesare Pascarella** (1858-1940). In his fictional history *ABBA ABBA*, **Anthony Burgess** imagines a conversation in which Belli explains the advantages of local dialects over national language: "A language waves a flag and is blown up by politicians. A dialect keeps to things, things, things, street smells and street noises, life." Writing nearly 3000 sonnets, Belli was known for his vulgar caricatures of important Risorgimento figures. *ABBA ABBA* includes English translations of Belli's poems.

Prose

The 1930s heralded in the heyday of a generation of Italian writers who were much influenced by the experimental narratives and themes of social alienation in the works of U.S. writers like Ernest Hemingway, John Dos Passos, and John Steinbeck. This school included **Cesare Pavese, Ignazio Silone, Vasco Pratolini,** and **Elio Vittorini**. One of the most representative works of 1930s Italian literature is Vittorini's *Pane e Vino* (Bread and Wine), written while the left-wing intellectual and political activist author was in exile. The most prolific of these writers, **Alberto Moravia**, wrote the ground-breaking *Gli Indifferente* (The Time of Indifference) which launched an attack on the Fascist regime and was promptly censored. To evade the stiff government censors, Moravia employed experimental, surreal forms in his subsequent works. His later works, up to the 1970s, use sex to symbolize the violence and spiritual impotence of modern Italy.

The downfall of fascism resulted in a postwar explosion of long-repressed power and innovation in the neo-realist literary movement. Many of these writers fictionalized their own experiences during the war; the greatest of these books is **Carlo Levi's** *Cristo si è fermato a Eboli* (*Christ Stopped at Eboli*), in which the hero finds himself exiled to an isolated, impoverished village untouched either by civilization or by Christ.

As Italian literature approaches the end of the century, it is more difficult to determine what is a lasting masterpiece and to identify what schools are being developed. A traveler wishing to find something modern and relevant may take advantage of the tradition of regional writing, which need be neither provincial nor banal. The Sicilian novelist **Leonardo Sciscia**, for example, ostensibly writes a murder mystery in his *Il giorno della civetta* (*Mafia Vendetta*), about a policeman from the North investigating a Mafia murder, but the novel also provides an intimate and deep portrait of Sicily and its people. **Giorgio Bassani**'s *Il giardino dei Finzi-Contini* (*The Garden of the Finzi-Continis*) is a profoundly moving account of the persecution of the Jews in Ferrara before the war; **Natalia Ginzberg**'s *Lessico famigliare* (*Family Sayings*) lovingly depicts the ties of a northern Italian family during the war; **Gina Lagario**'s bestselling *Tosca dei gatti* (*Tosca of the cats*) tells the tale of a dying caretaker in the Piedmont and the journalist who befriends her.

The works of the greatest of modern Italian authors, **Italo Calvino**, are unsurprisingly most widely available in English. Calvino's writing—full of intellectual play and magical-realism—is exemplified in *Invisible Cities,* a collection of cities described by Marco Polo to Kubla Kahn. The more traditionally narrative *If on a winter's night a traveler...* is a boisterous romp about authors, readers, and the insatiable urge to read, but perhaps most enjoyable for the traveler is *Italian Folktales,* Calvino's collection of traditional regional fairytales.

Most recently, **Umberto Eco's** wildly popular *The Name of the Rose,* a richly-textured mystery set in a 14th-century monastery, somehow managed to keep readers on edge while making the history of the revolutionary crisis in medieval Catholicism vaguely intelligible. *Foucault's Pendulum,* his latest, becomes rather precious in its complications, but wraps the story of the Knights Templar and half-a-millennium of conspiracy theories into a neat pocket-size package for transport.

Music

The Italians are musical tyrants, as anyone who's studied the piano, belonged to a school band, or belabored a violin can attest. The *piano, crescendo,* and *allegro* are there for a reason, since Italians invented the systems for writing musical notation that persist today: **Guido D'Arezzo** came up with the musical scale, and a 16th-century Venetian printed the first musical scores with movable type. Cremona brought forth violins by Stradivarius and Guarneri; the piano (actually the *pianoforte,* which just means soft-loud, the way it plays) is an Italian invention. Even so, for Italians, vocal music has always occupied a position of undisputed preeminence. The seeds of this musical legacy took their time in flowering, although there was a brief upsurge of indigenous music in the 14th century with the sensuous *Fenice Fu* of **Jacopo da Bologna** in the north and the exotic *Ecco La Primavera* of the Florentine **Francesco Landini.** After this interlude, indigenous music languished until the 16th century, when Italians re-asserted themselves and native pupils succeeded their northern teachers as choirmasters of the great cathedrals. In Venice, the Church of San Marco served not merely as a place of worship but also as a public showplace for the glory of the Venetian Republic. To befit a sanctuary of such splendor, church officials disregarded the more austere taste of Rome, calling for religious music with thunderous volume and dramatic instrumental accompaniment. **Gabrieli's** works for two or three choirs, multiple organs, and a variety of instruments scattered throughout the basilica filled the bill nicely. **Palestrina** and his Roman colleagues, worried that the Council of Trent might banish the use of polyphony in the liturgy, pre-empted such repression by eschewing Venetian flamboyance in favor of crystalline harmonies. At the same time, **madrigals,** free-flowing secular songs for three to six voices, grew in popularity.

The 16th century brought the greatest musical innovation in Italian history: opera. Born in Florence, nurtured in Venice, and revered in Milan, **opera** is Italy's most cherished art form. Invented by the **Camerata,** an artsy clique of Florentine poets, noblemen, authors, and musicians, opera began as an attempt to recreate the dramas of ancient Greece (which they decided had been sung) by setting their lengthy poems to music. After several years of effort with only dubious success, one member, Jacobo Peri, composed *Dafne* in 1597, the world's first complete opera. Although *Dafne* has since been lost (not a great loss, according to all contemporary accounts), a school of operatic composers soon emerged, eager to master the Camerata's new genre of music. As opera spread from Florence to Venice, Milan, and Rome, the styles and forms of the genre also grew more distinct. Much of early opera featured *stile recitativo,* a style which attempted to recapture the simple, evocative singing and recitation of classical drama. The first successful opera composer, **Monteverdi,** drew freely from history, blithely juxtaposing high drama, concocted love scenes, and bawdy humor. By charming his patroness the Duchess of Mantua, Monteverdi's jewel *Orfeo* (1607)—still performed today—assured the survival of the genre.

Contemporaneous with the birth of opera was the emergence of the **oratorio,** which sets biblical text to dramatic choral and instrumental accompaniment. Introduced by the Roman priest, **Saint Filippo Neri,** who liked to preach against a background of dramatic music, the oratorio was soon incorporated into masses throughout Italy.

Instrumental music began to establish itself as a legitimate genre in 17th century Rome. **Corelli** developed the concerto form with its contrasting moods and tempos, adding drama and emotion to technical expertise. **Vivaldi** wrote over 400 concertos while teaching at a home for orphaned girls in Venice. Under Vivaldi the concerto assumed its present form in which the virtuoso playing of the soloist is opposed to and accompanied by the concerted strength of the orchestra.

Eighteenth-century Italy exported its music; Italian composers coined the established musical jargon, their virtuosos dazzled audiences throughout Europe. At mid-century, operatic overtures began to be performed separately, resulting in the creation of a new genre of music; the **sinfonia** was modeled after the melody of operatic overtures and simply detached from their setting. Thus began the symphonic art form, which later received its highest expression in the hands of Italy's northern neighbors. At the same time, the composer **Domenico Scarlatti** wrote over 500 sonatas for the harpsichord and **Sammartini's** creative experimentation furthered symphonic development. In opera, baroque ostentation yielded to classical standards of moderation, simplicity, and elegance. Italian opera stars, on the other hand, had no use for moderation; many a soloist would demand showy, superfluous arias to showcase his or her skill.

To today's opera buffs, Italian opera means Verdi, Puccini, Bellini, Donizetti, and Rossini—all composers of the late 19th and early 20th centuries. With plots relying on wild coincidence and music fit for the angels, 19th-century Italian opera continues to dominate modern stages. **Verdi** became a national icon by mid-life, so much so that *Viva Verdi* was a battle cry of the Risorgimento. Acting as altar boy at the age of seven, Verdi became so distracted by the music of the mass that a harried priest kicked him off the altar; when he returned home bleeding and his parents asked him what had happened, he replied only, "Let me learn music." The music which he wrote as a man includes both the tragic, triumphal *Aïda* and *Il Traviata,* whose "foul and hideous horrors" shocked the London Times. Be aware as you listen that much of Verdi's work promoted Italian unity; his operas include frequent allusions to political assassinations, exhortations against tyranny, and jibes at French and Austrian monarchs. Another great composer of the era, **Rossini,** boasted that he could produce music faster than copyists could reproduce it, but he proved such an infamous procrastinator that his agents resorted to locking him in a room with a single plate of spaghetti until he completed his compositions. His *Barber of Seville* remains a favorite with modern audiences. Finally, there is **Puccini,** composer of *Madama Butterfly,* noted for the beauty of his music and for the strength, assurance and compassion of his female characters. Relying on devilish pyrotechnical virtuosity and a personal style marked by mystery and incessant rumors, violinist **Niccolò Paganini** brought musical Europe to its knees and filled its ears with, in the words of Brahms, "angelic singing."

Italian music continues to grow in the 20th century. **Ottorino Respighi,** composer of the popular *Pines of Rome* and *Fountains of Rome,* experimented with shimmering, rapidly shifting orchestral textures. **Gian Carlo Menotti,** now a U.S. resident, has written short, opera-like works such as *Amahl and the Night Visitors,* but is probably best known as the creator of the Two Worlds Art Festival in Spoleto (see the Spoleto—Umbria—listings below). **Luigi Dallapiccola** worked with serialism, achieving success with choral works such as *Canti di prigionia* (*Songs of Prison*) and *Canti di liberazione* (*Songs of Liberation*); both protest fascist rule in Italy.

Rock came to Italy in the 1960s, a reflection of musical trends set in America and Britain, but endowed with a unique and indigenous character that blended Italian folk songs and Mediterranean rhythms with pop beats. **Luigi Tenco** adapted the sound of be-bop to spirited folk melodies while **Lucio Dalla** produced socially conscious rock. Both rock and politics continued to grow more radical over the next decade as epitomized by the band **Area,** whose lyrics both reflected and strengthened the political unrest of the 1970s.

No single trend has emerged to characterize Italian music over the last dozen years; a look at Italy's most popular performers reveals a surprising diversity of musical genres. **Luciano Pavarotti** remains universally adored; his cathedral-filling voice draws packed audiences. Although Italian discos rely primarily on English and American bands, when not dancing the night away, young Italians prefer the native singers and Italian lyrics of *musica leggera,* (light Italian rock), as performed by **Claudio Bagliori, Bennato Edoardo,** and **Gianni Morandi.**

Opera season runs December to June. The productions at the Teatro alla Scala in Milan, the Teatro San Carlo in Naples, the Teatro dell'Opera in Rome, and La Fernice in Venice are especially spectacular, but Bari, Bergamo, Genoa, Mòdena, Trieste and Turin are also quite prestigious. Tickets are surprisingly cheap; a decent seat can be obtained for under $15. Don't despair if you miss the season; throughout summer, you can enjoy open-air opera at the Baths of Caracalla in Rome, the Roman Arena in Verona, and at many major music festivals including the *Maggio Musicale Fiorentino* in Florence from May to June. The **European Association of Music Festivals,** 122, rue de Lausanne, 1202 Geneva, Switzerland (tel. (22) 732 28 03, fax (22) 738 40 12) publishes the booklet *Festivals 1993,* which lists the dates and programs of major European music and theater festivals. Don't be discouraged by high prices; student rates and standing room are often available.

Film

The Birth of Film

For Rome's contributions to the arts in this century, don't go to the museum—go to the movies. Years before there was Hollywood, there were the **Cines** studios in Rome. Constructed in 1905-6, Cines created the so-called Italian "super-spectacle," extravagant, larger-than-life re-creations of momentous historical events. The first "blockbuster" picture in film history was the 9-reel *Quo Vadis*, directed by Enrico Guzzani for Cines studio in 1912. The film featured real chariot races, real Christian-eating lions in the Colosseum, 5000 extras, mountainous three-dimensional sets, and a burning-of-Rome sequence that blazed the way for the scorching of Atlanta in *Gone With The Wind*.

Soon after the international success of *Quo Vadis*, the advent of World War I and the subsequent rise of fascist government brought an end to the Italian super-spectacle. Recognizing the popular power of cinema and its possibilities for propaganda, Mussolini did, however, create the *Centro Sperimentale della Cinematografia*, a national film school (the first outside the Soviet Union), and the gargantuan **Cinecittà studios**, both of which are located in Rome. The presence of famous director and covert Marxist, **Luigi Chiarini**, attracted many students who would themselves rise to directorial fame in the celebrated postwar boom in Italian cinema. Among these were **Roberto Rossellini** and **Michelangelo Antonioni.** When the group surrounding Chiarini started publishing a film journal, a rival publication was founded by none other than Vittorio Mussolini, the dictator's son. Mussolini himself avoided the aesthetic questions of film, except to enforce the occasional "imperial edict," one of which forbade Italian audiences to laugh at the Marx Brother's *Duck Soup*. Hail Fredonia!

With the fall of fascism, a generation of young filmmakers was suddenly free to express itself, unconstrained by the regulations of the discredited regime. Mussolini's nationalized film industry (which lasted until 1943) produced no great films, yet sparked the subsequent explosion of **neo-realist cinema** (1943-50). The new style was characterized by the rejection of sets and professional actors in favor of location shooting and authentic drama. Such low production values, soon to shape a revolution in film, were determined in part by postwar economic circumstance, in part by the vigorous new aesthetic (itself not unrelated to economics) that was emerging. Neo-realists first gained attention in Italy with **Luchino Visconti's** 1942 *Ossessione,* a film based on James Cain's pulp-novel *The Postman Always Rings Twice.* (Hollywood would later turn the story into a film-noir classic by the same name.) **Roberto Rossellini's** 1946 tale of a Resistance leader trying to escape a Gestapo manhunt, *Roma, città aperta* (Open City), was filmed largely on the streets of Rome, just two months after the city's liberation. The neo-realist documentary style and the authentic setting led some audiences to believe the movie was actually newsreel footage. The film won world-wide acclaim for the neo-realists and holds a place in film history on par with *The Birth of A Nation, The Cabinet of Dr. Caligari,* and *Citizen Kane.* Perhaps the most famous and commercially successful neo-realist film, **Vittorio de Sica's** *The Bicycle Thief* (1948), is also set in Rome.

When neo-realism turned its wobbly camera from the Resistance to social critique, it lost its popular interest and, after 1950, gave way to individual expressions of Italian genius. Post-neo-realist directors **Federico Fellini** and **Michelangelo Antonioni** rejected logical narrative construction, turning away from the mechanics of plots and characters to a world of moments and witnesses (Oh, the humanity!). Fellini employed a closed system of recurring signs and symbols to create the personalized universe that pervades many his films. In the autobiographical *Roma*, a gorgeous stand-in for the director encounters an otherwise grotesque cast of characters. *La Dolce Vita* (1960), regarded by many outside Italy as the representative Italian film, scrutinizes the stylish Rome of the 1950s. In this film Fellini takes up Italy's ongoing fascination with it's decadent aristocracy (a theme Antonioni would pursue a year later in *L'Avventura*) and questions the country's postwar love affair with American culture. The film features Swedish starlet Anita Ekberg wading in the Trevi Fountain with a kitten on her shoulder. (When the Pope viewed *La Dolce Vita*, he promptly placed it on the index of banned films.) Antonioni's Italian films include *L'Eclisse* (1962), *Deserto Rosso* (1964), and the more accessible *Blow-Up,* his 1966 English-language hit about mime, murder, and mod London. Antonioni's *L'Avventura*, the story of a group of bored, young aristocrats, has been hailed as the second greatest film of all time—so maybe the idea was still original back then.

Pier Paolo Pasolini, perhaps the most controversial of Italian directors, was also one of the greatest. Pasolini—who spent as much time on trial for his politics and atheism as he did making films—began his artistic career as a poet and screenplay writer. Already regarded as Italy's premier poet when he took over the director's chair, Pasolini brought an intensely lyrical poetic vision to the screen. Always suspicious of his own tendency to aestheticism, the ardent Marxist set his first films in Italian shanty neighborhoods and in the underworld of Roman poverty and prostitution. With *Hawks and Sparrows*, regarded by many, including Pasolini himself, as the director's masterpiece, Pasolini abandoned his preoccupation with the subproletariat and embarked upon an investigation of the philosophical and poetic possibilities of film. Beyond these contributions to Italian cinema, Pasolini is generally credited with having helped introduce the problems of structuralist linguistics to the theory of film, radically influencing the way critics, feminist film theorists, and progressive filmmakers have thought about film over the last thirty years.

By the late 60s it was clear to international critics that there were few young directors capable of carrying on the legacy of the previous two decades. Most of the "old Leopards" were considered to have passed their creative peaks and, by the early 70s, were dying off in rapid succession. Factional disputes regarding politcs led to the disbanding of the National Association of Italian Filmmakers and the collapse of the Venice Film Festival in 1968. The free-flowing American bucks that had backed so many productions in the 50s and 60s were sucked back home as hard economic times hit the U.S. and inflation rose in Italy. Despite this, the great tradition of Italian film has refused to choke and die. One of the most important and controversial Italian filmmakers of the seventies was **Lina Wertmuller;** her film *Swept Away* (1974), in which a rich Milanese woman is stranded on a desert island with a provincial sailor, was an ironic approach to feminism which left many feminists furious. Those familiar with **Bernardo Bertolucci's** *Last Tango in Paris* and *Last Emperor* should see his 1970 *Il Conformista* (The Conformist), the story of a man hired to assassinate his former teacher. Other major modern Italian films include de Sica's *Il giardino dei Finzi-Contini* (Garden of the Finzi-Continis) and **Francesco Rosi's** *Cristo si è fermato a Eboli* (Christ Stopped at Eboli), both based on the books of the same titles. In the 1980s, the **Taviani** brothers were catapulted to fame with *Kaos,* a film based on five stories by Pirandello, and *La notte di San Lorenzo* (Night of the Shooting Stars), recounting the ludicrous and tragic final days of World War II in an Italian village. The Oscar-winning *Cinema Paradiso,* directed by Giuseppe Tornatore, is the most recent invasion of America by Italian cinema.

Food and Wine: La Dolce Vita

A food glossary at the back of this book describes items commonly found on menus throughout Italy. Regional introductions and food sections of individual city listings describe local specialties.

Don't plan to lose weight in Italy. Any ground gained in health through monounsaturated olive oil and complex carbohydrate-rich pasta will certainly be buried under waves of *gelato,* cheesy pizza, indispensable coffee pit-stops, inescapable fried calamari, and the cholesterol heaven of the Italian dessert tray.

Italian cuisine, like virtually every other aspect of Italian life, differs by region. The north lays culinary claim to creamy sauces, exotic mushroom dishes, stuffed pasta, and flat, handmade egg noodles. Piedmont is best known for its delectable (but pricey) truffles, as is its southern neighbor Umbria; Lombardy specializes in cheeses and *biscotti* (sweet, shortcake-like biscuits); the coastal region of Liguria is noted for its seafood, pesto, and olive oil, while Germanic and Austrian influence on the Trentino-Südtirol/ Alto Adige and Veneto regions have popularized dumplings, referred to as *gnocchi,* typically made of potatoes and flour, but occasionally of more exotic additions (from prunes to cornmeal to cheese). Central Italy serves richer, spicier dishes. The Emilia-Romagna region is the world's pasta palace, serving the richest cuisine in Italy. Food here is loaded with meat, cream, cheese, and butter sauce. Tuscany draws justifiable acclaim for its pricey olive oil and bean dishes, while the Abruzzo is known for spicy, pepper-strewn food and a wealth of game meats. The food of the south is a bit coarser, but far less expensive than in the rest of Italy. Tomato sauces and tubular pasta originated in Campania, the birthplace of the most renowned "Italian" food; pizza as we know it hails from Naples. Greek influence can be detected in Calabrian cuisine, with its use of figs, honey, strong spices, and eggplant. Sicily produces luscious deserts, such as *cannoli,* sweet pastry stuffed with sweet cheeses and chocolate, and *cassata,* a rich ice cream. If you like fish, Italy will not disappoint. The lakes and endless coastline provide an astounding array of delicacies.

In the heyday of the Roman republic, citizens ate only two meals a day, *prandium* (a light mid-day meal) and dinner. The custom of eating a morning meal of cereal and fruit evolved during later centuries. Dinners were typically lavish, festive affairs, with entertainment and music considered as vital as food. The gusto of the Italian appetite is still clearly evident, as is the seriousness Italians ascribe to their meals; you will be hard-pressed to find the equivalent of TV dinners and instant breakfasts here. Most Italians begin the morning in a *bar* (a café) with a *cappuccino* and a brioche. **Lunch** is the main meal of the day in Italy. Almost everything closes down between 1 and 4pm, so you might as well take advantage of tradition. Though many Italians now take an American-style business lunch hour, most still find time to linger at midday over a few courses in a *trattoria.* Restaurants generally close from about 2pm until suppertime. If you don't want a big meal, grab lunch at an inexpensive *tavola calda* (literally, "hot table") or *rosticceria* (grill), or pick up a snack from one of the ubiquitous *pizzerie.* Buy picnic materials at a *salumeria* or *alimentari,* both grocery stores. Fresh fruits and vegetables are best purchased at the open markets. A fitting cap to lunch is a leisurely stroll with world-famous Italian ice cream: **gelato.**

Italian **dinners** begin considerably later and last much longer than their American counterparts. The farther south you travel, the later dinner is served. Milan eats at about 7:30pm, Florence at 8pm, and Rome at 9pm. Small towns usually dine around 8pm. A full supper at an *osteria, trattoria,* or *ristorante* (in order of increasing expense) begins with an *antipasto* (appetizer), which can be as simple as *bruschetta,* a type of garlic bread, or as fancy as *prosciutto e melone,* thin strips of ham with melon. Next comes the *primo piatto* (the first course, usually pasta or soup), followed by the *secondo,* which consists of meat or fish. After dinner, help yourself to a piece of cheese or fruit and sip a *digestivo* (liqueur). Ordering a *caffè* will get you strong Italian espresso; ask for *caffè macchiato* (literally "spotted coffee") if you would like some milk in it. The most important thing to remember about eating in an Italian restaurant is not to let the menu intimidate you. You don't have to eat all the courses, nor must you eat them in any prescribed order.

The *menù turistico* (referred to by *Let's Go* as *menù*) isn't always such a bargain. Since the government ensures fair dealing by controlling what is served, you will encounter no surprises. This may reassure non-Italians, but it also means the food is rather run-of-the-mill. The fixed price has been rising steadily, but you can still find a few bargains. When selecting a restaurant in Italy, keep in mind that family-run establishments charge less (by a couple thousand lire) than those with hired help.

The billing at Italian restaurants can be a bit confusing. Most restaurants add a *pane e coperto* (cover charge) of about L1500 to the price of your meal, as well as a *servizio* (service charge) of 10-15%. In city restaurants, you may want to tip if the bill does not include service, but in family-run establishments without hired servers, tipping may be considered offensive. In a *bar,* look for a sign stating either *servizio compreso* (service included) or *servizio non compreso* (not included). In the case of the latter, drop some cash into the kitty on the bar (purr). Café prices are lower—often half-price—if you don't sit down. The *Ricevuta Fiscale* (receipt) is an irritating device intended to hamper tax evasion. A restaurant must legally make up an R.F. and hand a copy to the client, who then must keep it until 60m from the restaurant (seriously!). If you are stopped (this happens rarely) and caught without it, both you and the restaurant may be fined.

Italy's rocky soil, warm climate, and hilly landscape have proven themselves ideal for growing grapes, and Italy produces more **wine** than any other country. Wine is the staple beverage (even served, slightly diluted, to children as young as 6). Italy's three greatest wine growing regions are Piedmont, Tuscany, and Veneto, but most every region has something to offer. Wines from the north tend to be heavy and full-bodied; most touted (and expensive) are Piedmont's *barolo* and *barbera,* but the equally famous and more affordable *Asti spumante* deserves a swig. Tuscany is regarded as Italy's wine-making capital; its rich *chianti,* similar to claret, is a universal favorite. For a Tuscan spending spree, buy a *brunello di Montalcino,* a ruby wine that ages beautifully for up to 30 years. Other good heavy red wines include *salerno* from Naples and *valpolicella* from the Venetian district. White wine connoisseurs should sample *soave* from Verona, *frascati* from Rome, *orvieto* from Umbria, *lacrima Christi* (Christ's Tear) from Naples, and *tocai* and *pinot grigio* from Friuli. Sparkling wines are also common in the north, and sipping them just before dinner at dusk imparts a sense of the *dolce farniente* (sweet apathy). The hotter climate of southern Italy and her islands produces stronger, fruitier wines than the north. Try the Sicilian *marsala,* which resembles a light sherry, or *cannonau,* from Sardinia.

You can usually order by the glass, carafe, or half-carafe, although bars rarely serve wine by the glass. *Vecchio* means "old," and *stravecchio* means "very old." *Secco* means "dry" and *abboccato* means "sweet." When in doubt, request the local wine—it will be cheaper (typically around L3500 a liter) and best suited to the cuisine of the region. Before going, you might want to go to your local library and check out *The Wine Atlas of Italy* by Burton Anderson (Simon and Schuster, $40), winner of numerous awards including the competition for Wine Book of the Year, and packed with regional information including culinary specialties and travel tips.

Sports and Recreation

Spectator Sports in Ancient Rome

When Juvenal wrote that "bread and circuses" were all that were necessary to keep the Roman populace happy, he was referring in part to the free snacks and wild, violent goings-on staged in the 50,000-person-capacity Colosseum. In order to keep the city's large numbers of unemployed occupied, emperors depended on the distracting powers of ceremonial pageantry and calculated violence of gladiatorial combats: gladiators would first ride around the arena in chariots, then walk around it, attended by slaves toting their awe-inspiring battle gear—plumes in the helmets added a dash of color. Shirtless, nipples hard from the excitement, the gladiators would make the traditional salute to the emperor (right arms swept out from across their chests) and bark out the haunting refrain "Hail Emperor! We men who are about to die salute thee!"

After the intensity of this opening ceremony, much-needed comic relief was supplied by performers: vertically-efficient men, particularly *zaftig* women, and people with disabilities. Finally a piercing horn section announced the main attraction. The gladiators wore whatever suited their individual fighting styles: those who favored speed over strength wore almost no protective gear and carried only a net and spear to trap and then stab an opponent. Buffer gladiators wore all the armor they could and carried heavy swords and lances. Professional gladiators had a chance to test out what would work best at gladiatorial schools. While attendance was mandatory for some criminals and prisoners of war, occasionally free men would go to gladiatorial school just to get a date: the grueling practices, revolting accommodations, and occupational hazards were well worth the attention that foxy ladies bestowed on a gladiatorial victor.

Long before Brecht and 20th-century drama, gladiatorial combats broke down the fourth wall between performer and audience. The crowds exhorted the combatants to beat the crap out of each other, whipping themselves into an ear-shattering frenzy. Fallen, injured gladiators could make a sign begging for mercy. While the Emperor was mulling over his decision, the blood-thirsty crowd howled and screamed for a thumbs down. Usually they were appeased. Most Romans, even the cultural elite, saw nothing wrong with these savage spectacles. The writings of Seneca, the famous tutor of Nero (go figure), proved a rare exception: "It is pure murder...the spectators call for the slayer to be thrown to those who in turn will slay him, and they demand that the victor be kept for another butchering."

The second most popular event at the Colosseum was the killing of wild, often exotic, animals. Lions, tigers, bears, crocodiles, giraffes, and camels were all released from an underground network of tunnels into a simulated forest. Professionals (*venatores*) would work the frightened animal into a fevered pitch and draw out its death as long as possible.

There was some good clean fun in imperial Rome. Over at the Circus Maximus, Romans placed wagers on old-fashioned horse and chariot races. As many as 10 horses at a time would pull chariots decorated in colors representing a particular stable. The horses themselves sparkled with jewels, pearls in their manes and flashy doo-dads attached to their armor. Crashes were common, and chariot, horse, and rider disappeared into towering clouds of dust, which of course was what the Romans liked best.

Modern Sports

In Italy, **il calcio** (American soccer, or European football) far surpasses all other sports in popularity. Many Italian youth grow up playing the game, and some claim that Italy's victory in the 1982 World Cup did more for national unity than any political movement could have ever hoped to achieve. The Argentinian Diego Maradona, despite a recent cocaine-laced fall from grace, plays professionally in Italy and is a national god. The Italian love of soccer divides as well as unites the Italian people, however; by kindling the deepest feelings of city loyalty, inter-urban rivalries—especially that between Naples and Rome—too often find expression in heated brawls.

Bicycling is also popular in Italy. Besides manufacturing some of the best bikes in the world, Italians host the **Giro d'Italia,** a 25-day cross-country race in May. The Giro is similar to the Tour de France—it attracts premier bikers from all over the world.

As the only country to encompass the entire 1400km arc of the Alps (along with the equally long stretch of the Apennines), Italy attracts thousands of **skiers** from December to April. **Summer skiing** is available on glaciers surrounding the resorts of Bardonecchia, Aosta, Courmayeur, Cervinia, Stelvio Pass, and others, as is hiking and mountain climbing throughout the north, in Abruzzo's national park, and in the Sila Massif in Calabria. **Swimming** has become rarer and riskier as Mediterranean pollution worsens. Try the beaches in the less-populated deep south (Calabria, Apulia, and the Basilicata), any of the Italian islands, or a lake (in the Lake region of the north, or at the four large volcanic lakes of central Italy). **Spear fishing** and **scuba diving** are legal in most places as long as you don't combine them (use a snorkel if you must hunt fish). **Horseback riding** information is available from the Federazione Italiana Sport Equestri, v. Tiziano, 70 Roma.

Other major sporting events include the annual Italian Grand Prix Car Race held in Monza, and the Equestrian Show Jumping Championship and International Italian Tennis Championship, both held in Rome.

Festivals and Holidays

Despite a dearth of national holidays, Italy suffers no shortage of town festivals. Although such revelry comes and goes according to the whims of the local administration and budget, you will probably happen upon a few without even trying. Most commemorate local historical or religious events and often include elaborate ceremonies and re-enactments.

The most common excuse for a local festival is the celebration of a religious event. Virtually every town has a patron saint and has hosted a miracle or two, all of which are enthusiastically celebrated. An unmentionable number of festivals occur Easter weekend, with especially lavish celebrations in Assisi, where the coming of spring is greeted by rites dating back to the Dark Ages, and Florence, where you can see fireworks exploded by a mechanical dove. The *Fiera di Sant'Orso* occurs in Aosta at the end of January, as it has for a millennium, and from May 1-4 Cagliari hosts a parade for St. Efisio involving thousands of pilgrims in period dress. More bizarre is the May celebration of *Festi di San Domenico Abate* in Coculla, where people march through the city carrying a likeness of the saint draped with live snakes.

Less reptilian, though perhaps equally stomach-wrenching, is Italy's glut of jousting festivals, which tend to be held in late summer—notably in Arezzo on the first Sunday in September and Foligno the Sunday after that. Another medieval legacy, the Sienese *Palio,* features a bareback horse race in the town square; once in July and once in August, the audience stands in the middle and the horses careen off mattress-padded storefronts. On the third Sunday in July, Venetians commemorate the end of the epidemic of 1575 with a gondola procession. Venice celebrates *Carnevale* in February with masks and some discreet street revelry, but the Carnevale action is much better in Ivrea, where anyone not wearing a red hat is likely to get dyed orange in the *Battle of Oranges.* Every June Florence stages a soccer match with its players in 16th-century costume to commemorate a match between the Florentines and the soldiers of Charles V, who were then laying siege to the city.

Italy also hosts plenty of food and art festivals. A food *festa* is rarely well publicized; but if you happen upon one, thank your patron saint—local cuisine is celebrated by gorging to the accompaniment of music, dancing, and general frolic. Arts festivals flourish in the summer, with Venice, Verona, Taormina, Sorrento, and Messina all hosting major film festivals, and local musical festivals sponsored by Naples, Lucca, and Viterbo. Where food festivals and religious celebrations often end at nightfall, art festivals may span weeks or months. The month-long *Festival dei Due Mondi* (Festival of Two Worlds) in Spoleto, a delightful hodge-podge of classical art and cultural exhibits, follows this trend. Celebrations are one of the best reflections of the Italian national character; try to include a few of these in your itinerary. For a list of festivals, write to the **Italian Government Travel Office,** 630 Fifth Ave., #1565, Rockefeller Center, New York, NY 10111 (tel. (212) 245-4822).

In addition, various festivals of music, drama, ballet, and film also take place throughout the year. Plays are often performed at sites that were famous during the classical era, such as Syracuse, Paestum, and Pompeii.

Take holidays, both legal and religious, into account when planning your itinerary. Banks, shops, and almost everything else shuts down, but merriment abounds. Italy officially closes on the following dates: January 1 (New Year's Day); January 6 (Epiphany); Easter Monday; April 25 (Liberation Day); May 1 (Labor Day); August 15 (Assumption of the Virgin); November 1 (All Saints' Day); December 8 (Day of the Immaculate Conception—that's the conception of Mary, not of Jesus, of course); December 25 (Christmas Day); and December 26 (Santo Stefano). Offices and shops in the following cities also shut down for feast days in honor of their respective patron saints: Venice (April 25, St. Mark); Florence, Genoa, Turin (June 24, St. John the Baptist); Rome (June 29, SS. Peter and Paul); Palermo (July 15, Santa Rosalia); Naples (Sept. 19, St. Gennaro); Bologna (Oct. 4, St. Petronio); Cagliari (Oct. 30, St. Saturnino); Trieste (Nov. 3, San Giusto); Bari (Dec. 6, St. Nicola); and Milan (Dec. 7, St. Ambrose). Be prepared for other surprises as you travel. A calendar of some of the best festivals (of all varieties) should help you wade through the possibilities as you plan.

Climate

Due to the cooling waters of the ocean and the protective Alps encircling the north, Italy's climate is for the most part temperate. The north grows fairly warm (and, in some places, very rainy) in the summer, while the south bakes in arid dry heat. Beware of Venice in August: the air is still, the canals stagnate, and the visitor swelters. In treeless Florence, it's a rare breath of air that musters up enough energy to provide relief. A breeze off the sea, however, cools the coast. Winter in the Alps is very cold, while Milan, Turin, and Venice turn chilly, damp and foggy. Tuscany fares better, with temperatures in the 40s, although rain is a sure bet. Southern temperatures usually remain in the 40s and 50s during the winter.

The following information is drawn from the International Association for Medical Assistance to Travelers' *World Climate Charts* (see IAMAT above in Health section). In each monthly listing, the first two numbers represent the average daily maximum temperature in degrees Celsius and Farenheit, with the minimum temperature following.

	January		April		July		October	
Bologna	5/4	11/30	18/64	10/50	30/86	20/68	20/68	12/54
Cápri	11/52	8/46	16/61	12/54	27/81	21/70	20/68	16/61
Florence	9/ 48	2/36	19/66	8/46	30/86	18/64	20/68	11/52
Genoa	11/52	5/41	17/63	11/52	27/81	21/70	20/68	15/59
Milan	5/41	0/32	18/64	10/50	29/84	20/68	17/63	11/52
Naples	12/54	4/39	18/64	9/48	29/84	18/64	22/72	12/54
Rome	11/52	5/41	19/66	10/50	30/86	20/68	22/72	13/55
Palermo	16 /61	8/46	20/68	11/52	30/86	21/70	25/ 77	25/61
Venice	6/43	1/34	17/63	10/50	27/81	19/66	19/66	11/52

Weights and Measures

°C = (°F-32) X 5/9

1 centimeter (cm) = 0.39 inch
1 meter (m) = 1.09 yards
1 kilometer (km) = 0.62 mile
1 gram (g) = 0.036 ounce
1 kilogram (kg) = 2.2 pounds
1 liter = 1.06 quarts

°F = 5/9 X °C 32

1 inch = 2.54cm
1 yard = 0.92m
1 mile = 1.61km
1 ounce = 28g
1 pound = 0.45kg
1 quart = 0.94 liter

NORTHERN ITALY

Veneto

The Veneto stretches from the Carnic Alps near the Austrian border down across the foothills of the Dolomites and the Venetian Alps to the fertile plain of the Po and its desolate delta. The territory encompasses not only an extremely wide range of terrains, but a multitude of culturally independent towns and cities nominally lumped together on account of having once succumbed to the predatory forces of La Serenissima. The Venetian Empire didn't direct its interests inland until the 14th century, by which late date the character of the region had already been molded by Germanic and Milanese influence. Consequently, the dissolution of the expanded empire, brought about by the Napoleonic invasions of the 18th century, did little more than ruffle the surface.

The greatest indication of unity in the region is found in the transcendent medium of cuisine. Rice and *polenta* vie for preeminence as the starch of preference, the latter—a cornmeal concoction best described as "mush"--the filling base of most local seafood dishes. Wine is strictly regional, featuring the dry white *soave,* the dry \T sparkling *prosecco,* the light red *bardolino,* and the full-bodied *valpolicella.* The cities of the Veneto are united by another shared claim: each falls in the most touristed region in Italy, as good an indication as any of the enormous appeal and scope of its attractions.

Venice (Venezia)

She is the Shakespeare of cities—unchallenged, incomparable, and beyond envy.
—John Addington Symonds

Born of a most fortuitous marriage of sea and sky, Venice is a shimmering phantasm unaccountably made flesh. First driven by Attila's hordes, then by conquering Lombards, Roman refugees joined fishermen on the low barrier islands of the swampy lagoon. An unsuccessful attack by Charlemagne in 810 led to the settlement of the inner islands that underlie the modern city. The early community's commerce blossomed from a booming market for salt, and the theft of St. Mark's remains from Alexandria by two Venetian merchants in 828 further established the city's eminence under a new patron saint. By the 11th century, ties to Constantinople and the fees collected for ferrying Crusaders to the Middle East had established Venice as the dominant entrepôt for trade with the Middle East. In 1204, Venice sent the penniless armies of the Fourth Crusade to raid Constantinople; over the course of three days the Venetians, thus aided, depleted what had been the wealthiest metropolis in the world of its greatest works of art. The spoils filled Venetian squares and treasuries, and new territories throughout the eastern Mediterranean bolstered their prosperity. The republic rallied to the 14th-century threat posed by Genoa by consolidating its oligarchic government; after defeating its rival in 1380, Venice expanded onto the Italian mainland. Over the next three centuries, jealous European powers to the west and the unstoppable Ottoman Turks to the east whittled away *La Serenissima's* empire, while the discovery of ocean routes to the Far East robbed it of its monopoly on Asian trade. By the time Napoleon conquered it in 1797, idle Venice was little more than a decadent playground. French and Austrian rule capped off the city's glory days for good as the development of industry at Mestre drew away the archipelago's working population. Venice maintains her magnetic charm even today—every year drawing millions of visitors to her car-free streets and *piazze.* Most Venetians you'll encounter will probably have some connection with the tourist indus-

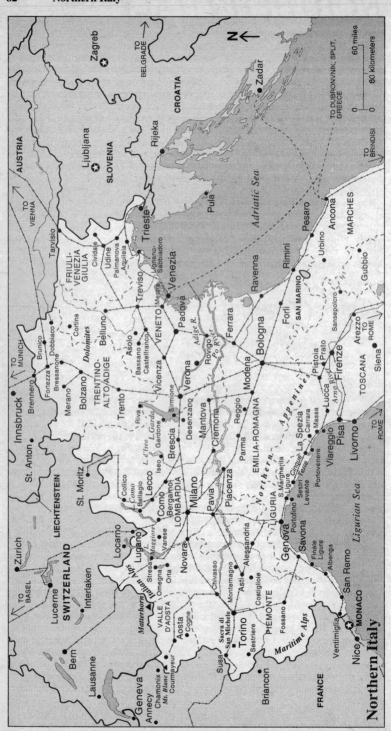

Northern Italy

try; look for natives in bars and residential areas far from Venice's tourist thorough-fares. Shops in La Serenissima are chic and expensive, catering largely to tourists with *lire* to burn. Avoid Venice in August when it's absolutely infested with photo-snapping foreigners; escape the late-summer "invasion" by coming in late spring or early sum-mer.

Orientation

Venice is composed of 117 bodies of land distributed throughout the Venetian la-goon, and is protected from the full force of the Adriatic by the Lido, which lies 2km further out to sea and runs parallel to the coast. A 4km causeway links the canal-riddled land mass of this urban center to the mainland. The **Santa Lucia Train Station** (or simply *ferrovia*) lies on the northwestern edge of the city, while the garages, car rentals, and bus terminals are across the Grand Canal in nearby **piazzale Roma**—the last stop for all land-bound transportation. If you're in a rush to get to San Marco (and the cen-tral tourist office) from the station or piazzale Roma, take *vaporetto* #2. For a splendid introduction to the *palazzi* along the stately Grand Canal, take #1 or 34. You can also make the 40-minute walk to San Marco by heading left as you exit the station onto lista di Spagna and following the signs.

Ubiquitous yellow signs mounted on the sides of buildings mark streets and point the way to major sights, but a good map renders Venice far more navigable. The tourist of-fice distributes a free plan of the city; the ACTV information office in p. Roma also hands out helpful freebies with less detailed street information, but including a tremen-dously useful schema of Venice's many *vaporetti* lines. The best free map, if you can locate it, is put out by "Venice Shops." The best map for sale is the one with a red cover published by Edizioni Foligraf Mestre-Venezia (L3500), but you will almost certainly get lost within the Venetian labyrinth anyway, so your money would be better spent on *gelato* or pastry to maintain your energy while you wander.

Orientation begins with a fundamental comprehension of the *sestieri*, the sections of the city. Within each section, there are no individual street numbers, but merely one long and haphazard sequence of numbers (roughly 6000 per *sestiere*). Every building, however, is also located on some type of a "street"—*fondamenta, salizzada, calle, via, campo*, or *piazza*. To add to the confusion, it is often unclear which *sestiere* you are in at any given moment as the boundaries are not clearly indicated. *Let's Go* supplies the *sestiere*, the number, then the street name when possible, and supplements this by men-tioning the nearest landmark; beyond that, try asking the locals.

The **Grand Canal,** the central artery of Venice, can be crossed on foot only at the **ponti** (bridges) **Scalzi, Rialto,** and **Accademia.** *Traghetti* (gondola-like ferry boats) may seem too picturesque for practical use, but in fact they are used quite frequently for canal crossings where there is no bridge. North of the Canal, from the station to about the Rio dei Santi Apostoli lies the *sestiere* **Cannaregio.** Continuing clockwise around the Canal, **Castello** is just south of the Rio di S. Giovanni Crisotomo, and **San Marco** extends from the Mercerie and p. San Marco to the Ponte Accademia. The east-ernmost extension of Venice is the **Santa Elena** *sestiere*. Cross the Rialto bridge from p. San Bartolomeo, and you will find yourself in the **San Polo** district. West of San Polo and encompassing piazzale Roma is the *sestiere* of **Santa Croce.** Now trace an imaginary line from Cà Rezzonico on the Grand Canal to the church of Santa Maria Maggiore on the *rio* of the same name: the land south of this and hooking around to the Punta della Dogano is **Dorsoduro.** All of this looks very nice and tidy on paper, but since you will most likely be winding through Venice's twisted alleys without a com-pass at your disposal, bear in mind that much is lost in the translation from page to re-ality. Getting lost in Venice is actually one of the greatest pleasures the city has to offer; the carless quiet of the less touristed paths provides relief from encounters with the camera-happy throngs who fill San Marco. One caveat: if lost and in a hurry, do not run with your eyes on your map. Picturesque alleyways often end abruptly at canal's edge, and a plunge into the sadly polluted green waters would be a most unwelcome free bath. And don't make the mistake of trying to rinse off your sticky *gelato*-laden hands

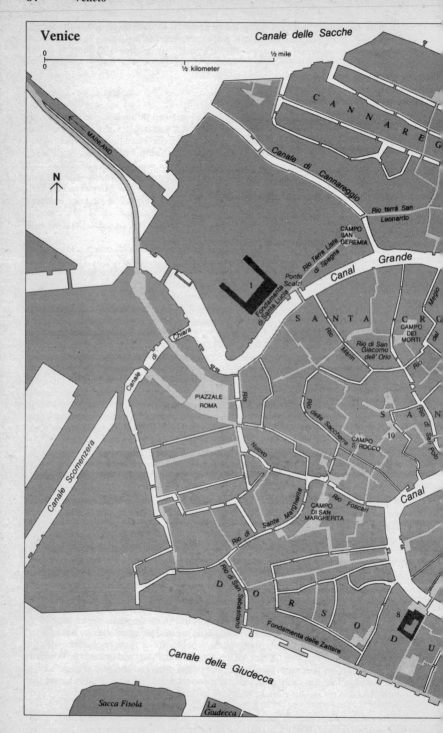

Venice

Canale delle Sacche

0 _____ ½ mile
0 _____ ½ kilometer

N
↑

MAINLAND

CANNAREG

Canale di Cannareggio

Rio terrà San Leonardo

CAMPO SAN GEREMIA

Rio Terrà Lista di Spagna

Ponte Scalzi

Canal Grande

Fondamenta di Santa Lucia

1

SANTA   CRO

Rio Mann

Rio di San Giacomo dell' Orio

CAMPO DEI MORTI

Meglio

di

Chiara

Rio

Canale di

PIAZZALE ROMA

Rio

Rio della Sacchere

CAMPO S. ROCCO

S   A   N

Rio di San Polo

10

Nuovo

Santa Margherita

Rio Foscari

Canal

CAMPO DI SAN MARGHERITA

Rio di

Rio di San Sebastiano

D   O   R   S   O

8

D   U

Fondamenta delle Zattere

Canale della Giudecca

Sacca Fisola

La Giudecca

Canale Scomenzera

1   Train Station
2   Post Office
3   Amex
4   IYHF
5   Piazza San Marco
6   Palazzo Ducale (Doge's Palace)
7   Campo San Salvatore
8   Gallerie dell'Accademia
9   Church of S. Maria Della Salute
10   Campo dei Frari
11   Church of San Zaccaria
12   Campo S. Giorgio
13   Campo SS. Giovanni e Paolo
14   Church of S. Maria Formosa
15   Teatro Goldoni

in the Canal—those stone stairs leading into the water have been gathering moss since Michelangelo was a boy.

If you do get lost, make use of the city's invaluable yellow signs to head in the direction of the district of your choice; look for signs to Rialto (the bridge connecting San Marco and San Polo), the Accademia (Dorsoduro), San Marco (at the border of San Marco and Castello), piazzale Roma (Santa Croce), and the *ferrovia* (Cannaregio).

High tides (usually Nov.-April) cause *acque alte,* the periodic floodings that swamp parts of the city, notably San Marco, under as much as three feet of water. If you don't like wet feet, check ahead with the tourist office and consult the signs posted at all ACTV landing stages. *Acque alte* usually last two to three hours, and planks or platforms are laid out across most major thoroughfares.

If you plan to drive to Venice, parking on the Tronchetto "car park island" could cost you as much as L30,000 per day, while parking in the garages at the p. le Roma runs L9000-22,000. Motorists should consider leaving their cars in the parking lot at the Mestre train station on the mainland (about L7000 per day) and taking a train into Venice (L1000 each way; all trains into and out of Venice stop at Mestre).

Vaporetti

The alternative to walking is taking the **vaporetti** (motorboat buses), which ply the Venetian waterways. Most principal boats run 24 hrs. but frequencies are reduced after 11pm. A 24-hr. *biglietto turistico,* available at any ticket office, allows you unlimited travel on all boats except #2 (L12,000). You can also purchase a three-day ticket for L17,000. Neither is really worthwhile unless you're on a kamikaze tour. If you plan to stay more than four days on Giudecca, or plan to visit some of the outlying islands, a **Cartavenezia** might be useful. With this, the *diretto* is only L800 and the *accelerato* L700. It's valid for one month. (Bring L10,000 and a passport photo to the information office at fondamenta Nuova.) The ACTV office offers a special three-day ticket for holders of the Cartagiovane Youth Pass (see tourist offices under Practical Information) for L13,000.

Not all stations sell tickets all the time; buy extras, but make sure to get the type that can be machine-validated (upon boarding) at any station. Tickets may be bought both at the booths in front of the *vaporetti* stops and at various self-serve dispensers (located at the ACTV office at p. Roma and at the Rialto stop). Tickets may also be bought from the conductor after boarding (L500 surcharge). Be sure to count your change carefully when buying tickets at the station booths. Tourists dashing for a departing *vaporetto* sometimes find themselves short a few *lire* once the boat is on its way. The fine for riding the *vaporetti* without a ticket is L15,000, but enforcement can be lax. The major lines include:

#1: Roma-Ferrovia-Rialto-San Marco-Lido and back with 15 obscure intermediary stops along the Grand Canal. Every 10min. 7am-11pm. L2200.

#2: Rialto-Ferrovia-p. Roma-Accademia-San Marco-S. Elena-Lido. A *diretto* with no intermediary stops. Every 10min. 7am-11pm. L3300.

#5: Circolare Destra—Zaccaria-Guidecca-p. Roma-Ferrovia-fondamenta Nuove-Murano; **Circolare Sinistra**—Murano-fondamenta Nuove-Ferrovia-p. Roma-Giudecca-San Zaccaria. Every 15min. 7am-11pm. L1800.

#8: San Zaccaria-Giudecca-Tronchetto. An alternative to #5 for getting to the youth hostel from San Marco. Every 15min. 7am-8pm. L2200.

#12: fondamenta Nuove-Murano-Burano-Torcello-Treporti. Every hr. 5am-11pm. L3300.

#16: Fusina-Zattere. To the camping-hostel from the Zattere bank in Dorsoduro, which faces the island of Giudecca. Every 30min. L3300.

Traghetti: These run across major canals. Riva Santa Maria del Giglio to Riva di San Gregorio daily 8am-6pm; Riva di San Samuele to Riva di San Baranabà (Palazzo Grassi to Cà Rezzonico) Mon.-Sat. 7:30am-2pm; Riva di San Tomà (near the Frari) to Riva di Cà Garzoni Mon.-Sat. 7am-9pm, Sun. 8am-8pm; Riva del Vin to Riva del Carbon Mon.-Sat. 7:45am-2pm; Riva di San Sofia to Riva Peschiera (the Rialto fish market) daily 7am-9pm; Riva di San Marcuola to Riva del Fontego dei Tedeschi Mon.-Sat. 7:30am-2pm; from in front of the train station to fondamenta San

Simeon Piccolo Mon.-Sat. 7:30am-2pm. At roughly L500, these are a fun ride for some spare change.

Practical Information

Tourist Offices: APT (tel. 71 90 78), at the train station. Helpful and organized, but usually mobbed. One of the 2 lines (the longer one) is just for accommodations. If you are 15-26 years old, they will issue you a free Cartagiovane (Youth Pass), which is valid for all sorts of discounts detailed in their extensive brochure. Bring a passport-sized photo (can be taken at the machine in the station, L2000) and a valid ID. Be sure to ask for a map and a copy of *Un Ospite di Venezia* (A Guest in Venice), a bilingual biweekly (monthly in the winter) booklet with tons of information and entertainment listings. Office in train station is open Mon.-Fri. 9am-noon and 3-6pm, Sat. 8am-2pm. The main office is at **San Marco**, Ascensione, 71/F (tel. 522 63 56), under the arcade at the far end of the *piazza*. Exhaustive information on sights. English spoken. Shorter lines. Open Mon.-Sat. 8:30am-7pm. A 3rd office is on the **Lido** at Gran Viale 6/A (tel. 526 57 21). Open Mon.-Sat. 9am-2pm. **Hotel Information (AVA),** p. Roma, 540/D (tel. 522 86 40) makes reservations in 1- and 2-star hotels with a deposit. Open daily, officially 9am-10pm; Oct.-April 9am-9pm, but in practice at the management's whim. Also an office inside the train station (tel. 71 50 16), in the same cubbyhole as the tourist office.

Budget Travel: Centro Turistico Studentesco (CTS), Dorsoduro, 3252 (tel. 520 56 55) on fondamenta Tagliapietra. Off the Dorsoduro-to-San Marco route not far from campo S. Margherita. Take calle Piove to calle Larga Foscari and turn right after crossing the bridge, on the bank of Rio Foscari. Open Mon.-Fri. 9am-12:30pm and 3:30-7pm. **Transalpino** (tel. 71 66 00) has an office to the right as you exit the train station. Open daily 8:30am-8:30pm.

Consulates: U.K., Dorsoduro, 1051 (tel. 522 72 07). Open Mon.-Fri. 9am-noon and 2-4pm. The closest **U.S., Canadian,** and **Australian** consulates are in Milan; **New Zealand** citizens should contact their embassy in Rome.

Currency Exchange: for the best rates, think about changing money in Padua. Otherwise, try **Banca Ambrosiano Veneto** on calle Larga XXII Marzo, San Marco 2378, between San Marco and the Accademia. Open Mon.-Fri. 8:20am-1:20pm and 2:35-4:05pm. Fixed L4500 commission. (Many banks cluster around the same *calle*. You can shop here for the best rates, but watch out for sky-high commissions.) If you insist upon changing money at the station, spare yourself the lines and get slightly better rates by walking 400m to the bank by the bridge spanning the canal.

American Express: San Marco, 1471 (tel. 520 08 44), off p. San Marco. Take calle Seconda dell'Ascensione from the end of the *piazza* opposite the basilica and follow it for a couple of blocks (look for the AmEx directional mosaic underfoot). L1500 inquiry charge on mail for those without card or traveler's checks. Mediocre **exchange** rates but no commission. Office open Mon.-Fri. 9am-5:30pm, Sat. 9am-12:30pm. Exchange service open Mon.-Sat. 8am-8pm.

Post Office: San Marco, 5554 (tel. 528 93 17), on salizzada Fontego dei Tedeschi near the eastern end of the Rialto bridge off campo San Bartolomeo. Fermo Posta at desk #4; stamps at #11 and 12. Open Mon.-Sat. 8:15am-7pm. Branch office through the arcades at the end of p. San Marco. Open Mon.-Fri. 8:15am-1:30pm, Sat. 8:15am-12:10pm. Stamps are sold in the *tabacchi* at the station. Inquire at the main office about the locations of smaller branches in the other *sestieri*. (All have the same hours.) **Postal Code:** 30124.

Telephones: ASST, train station. Open Mon.-Fri. 8am-7:45pm, Sat. 8am-1:45pm. Also at San Marco, 5551, next to the main post office. Open daily 8am-7:45pm. **SIP,** in p. Roma and along viale Santa Maria Elisabetta on the Lido. Open daily 8am-9:30pm. **Telephone Code:** 041.

Flights: Aeroporto Marco Polo (tel. 541 54 91). ACTV local bus #5 runs to the airport every 30min. (30min., L1000), or take the ATVO coach with luggage space for L5000.

Trains: Stazione di Santa Lucia (tel. 71 55 55; **lost and found** 71 61 22). Information office in station across from tourist office; city maps available. To: Padua (every 15min., 30min., L3200); Bologna (14 per day, 1hr. 30min.., L12,100); Milan (18 per day, 2hr. 30min.-3hr., L18,700); Florence (6 per day, 2hr. 30min.-3hr., L18,700); Rome (4 per day, 5hr. 15min., L52,000). **Luggage Storage:** L1500. Open 24 hrs.

Buses: ACTV and **ATVO** buses depart from p. Roma (tel. 528 78 86). Roughly every 30min. to: the villas on the Riviera del Brenta (Malcontenta L1000, Mira L2300, Strà L3100), Padua (L3800), Mestre (L1000), Treviso (L2600). Ticket office open daily 7:30am-11pm. Information office open Mon.-Sat. 8am-6:30pm. The fine for riding without a ticket is L30,000.

Car Rental: Europcar, p. le Roma, 496/H (tel. 523 86 16). The best rates in Venice, which ain't saying much. Open Mon.-Fri. 8am-1pm and 2-7pm, Sat.-Sun. 8:30am-noon. **Avis,** p. le Roma, 496/G (tel. 522 58 25). Open Mon.-Sat. 8am-8pm, Sun. 8am-1pm; Nov.-March Mon.-Sat. 8am-noon and 3-7pm.

English Bookstore: Il Libraio a San Baranabà, Dorsoduro, 2835/A (tel. 522 87 37), fondamenta Gherardini, off campo San Baranabà. Classics, all American fiction set in Venice, and—joy of joys—the *Let's Go* budget travel series. Claims to be open Mon.-Tues. and Thurs.-Fri. 10:15am-1pm and 3:15-8pm, Wed. and Sat. 10:15am-1pm.

Laundromat: Lavaget, Cannaregio, 1269 (tel. 71 59 76), on fondamenta Pescaria off rio Terà San Leonardo beside the Ponte Guglie. Self-service. Do your wash for L11,000, soap included. Open Mon.-Fri. 8:15am-12:30pm and 3-7pm.

Public Baths: Albergo Diurno (Day Hotel), San Marco, 1266 (tel. 528 55 67), in the *ramo secondo* (2°), off the west end of p. San Marco. Showers L4000. Toilets L500. Luggage storage L2000-3000. Showers open daily 8am-4pm. Also in the station—next to *binario* 1. Showers L4000. Soap and towel each L500. Open daily 7am-8pm. Toilets are scattered throughout town. *Gabinetti* (also *toilette*) can be found on either side of the Rialto, on the waterfront near p. San Marco, and under the Dorsoduro side of the Accademia bridge (L200), to name but a few locations.

Late-Night Pharmacy: check the *Ospite di Venezia* or call 192.

Hotel Crises: Questura, on fondamenta San Lorenzo in the Castello (tel. 520 32 22). These are the people to contact if you suspect your hotel keeper is pulling a fast one on you.

Emergencies: tel. 113. **Police: Carabinieri,** p. Roma (tel. 523 53 33 or 112 in an emergency). **Medical Assistance:** tel. 529 45. **Hospital: Ospedali Civili Riuniti di Venezia,** campo SS. Giovanni e Paolo (tel. 529 45 17). **Boat ambulances,** tel. 523 00 00. **Ufficio Stranieri** (Foreigners' Office): tel. 520 07 54.

Accommodations

Plan on spending slightly more on rooms here than elsewhere in Italy, but bask in the disarming hospitality Venetians have perfected during this once-great republic's 200-year touristic afterlife. In summer, reservations, preferably made as much as a month in advance, will preserve your sanity. To avoid the crowds and expense of summertime stays in Venice, visit the city while based in one of the towns nearby (Padua and Treviso, each 30 minutes away, are good places to secure a room). Many *locande* will hold a room until 10 or 11am. The **APT** at the train station and the **AVA** hotel service near the bus station will book rooms, but a disadvantage to using such a service is that hotels must stick to their quoted, maximum price; if you go there directly they are often willing to bargain. Singles listed below vanish in summer. If the situation becomes desperate, you can always resort to one of the campgrounds at Mestre or Padua's youth hostel (closes at 11pm). The police frown on impromptu crashing in parks or on beaches.

Dormitory-type accommodations are always available in Venice without reservations, even during August and September. Such accommodations often have irregular operating seasons, so check with the tourist offices to see which are open. In *pensioni,* look out for L10,000 breakfasts and other forms of bill-padding, and always agree on what you'll pay before you hit the sack or surrender your passport.

Institutional Accommodations

Ostello Venezia (HI), fondamenta di Zitelle, 86 (tel. 523 82 11), on Giudecca. Take *vaporetto* #5 (*sinistra*) from the station (25min., L2200), #5 (*destra*) or #8 from San Zaccaria near San Marco (5min., L2200). Get off at Zitelle and walk right. In a renovated *palazzo* on the canal, but with a few too many stairs and far too many dormers. English spoken. In summer it's necessary to arrive in the morning to secure a place—the tourist office at the train station will let you know if they're already full. Open 7:30-9am and 6-11pm. Curfew 11pm, lights out 11:30pm. L18,000 per person, membership required. HI cards L30,000. Breakfast included. Full meals L12,000. Phone reservations not accepted.

Suore Cannosiano, fondamenta del Ponte Piccolo, 428 (tel. 522 21 57), also on Giudecca. Take boat #5 to Sant'Eufemia, and walk to your left and over the Ponte Piccolo bridge as you descend. Women only. Run by solicitous nuns. You can arrive at any time of day to leave your bags. Check-out 6-8:30am. Lockout 8:30am-4pm. Curfew 10:30pm. Five-bed or dorm-style rooms L14,000 per person.

Domus Civica, ACISJF, San Polo, 3082 (tel. 522 71 39), across the street from a bar in both directions, on the corner of calle Chiovere, calle Campazzo, and S. Rocco, between the Frari Church and p. le Roma. Along the road, follow the yellow arrows between p. le Roma and the Rialto. Women only, otherwise everything else the heart could desire: cheery nuns, ping-pong tables, a TV room, and a piano. Check-out 7:30-10am. Curfew 11:30pm. Singles L25,000. Doubles L44,000. Showers included. Open mid-June to mid-Oct.

Instituto Ciliota, San Marco, 2976 (tel. 520 48 88), in calle delle Muneghe off calle delle Botteghe and campo Morosin. *Vaporetto:* #34 to San Samuele. Near San Marco and the Accademia, yet off the major thoroughfares. Friendly staff extends their welcome to single men and unmarried couples. English spoken. Curfew 11pm. Singles L42,000, with shower L50,000. Doubles L72,000, with shower L83,000. Approximately L12,000 discount with a *cartagiovane.* Breakfast included. Open mid-June to mid-Sept.

Foresteria Valdese, Castello, 5170 (tel. 528 67 97). Take the *vaporetto* to San Zaccharia, then walk to campo Santa Maria Formosa (5min.). From the campo, take calle lunga S. M. Formosa; the building's over the 1st bridge. The 18th-century guesthouse of Venice's biggest Protestant church. Engaging frescoes and ebullient management. Check-in 9am-1pm and 6-8pm. Lockout 1-6pm. Dorms with bunk beds for 8, 12, or 16 people L25,000 per person for 1 night, L20,000 each additional night. Breakfast included. Reserve 1 month ahead for their 2 beautiful doubles (L54,000). Two apartments with bath and kitchen, L80,000 for 2; L15,000 for each additional bed up to maximum 5 in the apartment.

Suore Mantellate, Santa Elena, calle Buccari, 10 (tel. 522 08 29). A breathtaking 40-min. walk east from San Marco. Take *vaporetto* #1 or 2 to San Elena, and walk across the park. Friendly nuns and large rooms. Curfew 10:30pm. Doubles L32,000 per person. Showers and breakfast included. Open Sept.-July. Reserve ahead.

Archie's House, Cannaregio, 1814/B, San Leonardo (tel. 72 08 84), where San Leonardo meets campiello Anconetta, on the side of the street closest to the Grand Canal. Privacy, location, and price compare favorably to the youth hostel. Archie (who speaks 12 languages) and his wife loathe rowdy guests. Rooms have 3-5 beds. One person L20,000. Two or more people L18,000 per head. Less in off-season. Cold showers included. Hot showers L1000.

Instituto San Giuseppe, Castello, 5402 (tel. 522 53 52). From p. dei Leoncini to the left of San Marco, take calle dei Specchieri to campo San Zulian, then go right on campo de la Guerra over the bridge, and turn left immediately. For families only. 5- or 6-bed rooms in the center of town, with a garden. Curfew 11pm. L25,000 per person. Closed Easter and Christmas. Reserve 1 month ahead with deposit.

Hotels Cannaregio (From the Station to the Rialto)

Pensione Smeraldo, Cannaregio, 1333 (tel. 71 73 55). Over the Ponte Guglie bridge on Rio Terà San Leonardo. Located in an old palace, it has gone from regal to rickety, but the high-ceilinged rooms stay cool in summer. Singles L35,000. Doubles L50,000. Quad L20,000 per person. Owner always willing to make a deal. AmEx, DC, Visa. Also try **Rooms Biasin,** Cannaregio, 1252 (tel. 71 72 31) to your left on calle del Spizier just after the Ponte Guglie bridge and run by the same management. Two small singles, L25,000. Doubles L50,000, with bath L75,000. AmEx, MC, Visa.

Orsaria Rooms, Cannaregio, 103 (tel. 71 52 54), on calle Priuli, about 50m from the train station. Take a left immediately after the relatively diminutive Chiesa Scalzi, and collapse into clean, well-maintained, and incredibly convenient accommodations. Singles L35,000. Doubles L60,000. Triples L85,000. Quads L100,000.

Alloggi La Gondola, Cannaregio, 180 (tel. 71 52 06 or 524 16 79), on calle del Forno, a tiny alley to the right off lista di Spagna immediately after the Hotel Continental. Convenience, not luxury. Only 5 rooms, so call ahead. Single L27,000. Doubles L50,000. Triples L69,000. AmEx, MC, Visa.

Hotel Minerva and Nettuno, Cannaregio, 230 (tel. 71 59 68), on your left on Lista di Spagna from the station. Spacious, remodeled rooms and convenient locale make this a prime choice. Singles L38,000, with bath L52,000. Doubles L50,000, with bath L80,000. Breakfast L9000. MC, Visa.

Locanda Rossi, Cannaregio, 262 (tel. 71 51 64). From the train station, follow lista di Spagna about 100m, taking a left on calle della Procuratie before campo San Geremia. An oasis of calm. Sterile, post-modern rooms. Curfew 1am. Singles L43,500, with bath L57,500. Doubles L61,000, with bathroom L91,000. Showers L3000. Breakfast included. Open Feb.-Dec. AmEx, MC, Visa.

Villa Rosa, Cannaregio, 389 (tel. 71 65 69), on the corner of calle della Misericordia and calle Pesaro. Turn left onto calle della Misericordia from Lista di Spagna. Comfortable rooms in a residential part of town. Singles L40,000, with bath L55,000. Doubles L60,000, with bath L90,000. Breakfast included. MC, Visa.

Locanda Antica Casa Carettoni, Cannaregio, 130 (tel. 71 62 31), along rio Terà Lista di Spagna, to the left of the station. Rooms steeped in antiquity described by the proud proprietor as "truly Venetian." Singles L26,000. Doubles L46,000. Triples L66,000. Open March-July and Sept.-Jan.

Alloggi Calderon, Cannaregio, 283 (tel. 71 55 62), in p. San Geremia at the end of lista di Spagna. Functional rooms with hall bathrooms, but only a short walk from the station. Singles L35,000. Doubles L50,000. Triples L75,000. Quads L80,000. Breakfast L3500. Reserve ahead Aug.-Oct.

Albergo Adua, Cannaregio, 233/A (tel. 71 61 84), on lista di Spagna. Courtly rooms with flowery wallpaper, most with wall-to-wall carpeting. Small, family-run, and quiet for the neighborhood. Singles L38,000. Doubles L55,000, with bath L80,000. Discounts for larger rooming groups. Breakfast L9000. MC, Visa.

Dorsoduro and Santa Croce

Cà Foscari, Dorsoduro, 3887/B (tel. 522 58 17), on calle della Frescata, at the foot of calle Crosera where it hits calle Marconi. Take *vaporetto* #1 or 34 to San Tomà. Look for the camouflaged sign. Family-run, with pride. Tastefully decorated rooms. Singles L35,000. Doubles L57,000, with bath L70,000. Breakfast included. Call in advance—rooms held until noon. Open Feb.-Nov.

Locanda Montin, Dorsoduro, 1147 (tel. 522 71 51). From campo San Barnabà, go south through the passageway Casin dei Nobili, across the bridge, right on the fondamenta Lombardo, and around the corner onto fondamenta di Borgo. Modern paintings and restored antiques abound. Singles L40,000. Doubles L65,000. Showers and breakfast included. Reserve with 1 night's deposit. Closed 20 days in Jan. and 10 days in Aug. AmEx, DC, MC, Visa.

Alloggi Al Gallo, S. Croce, 197/G (tel. 523 67 61), on calle Amai very close to p. Roma. Shortly after the 2nd bridge, if heading from p. Roma to Rialto or coming from the station, cross the Grand Canal, turn right, then left on fond. del Tolentini and look for calle Amai on your left. A few modern rooms over a family-run pizzeria. No breakfast, but there's an espresso machine for caffeine addicts. Doubles L65,000, with bath L74,000. Closed 2 weeks in Nov.

Casa Messner, Dorsoduro, 217 (tel. 522 74 43), near the Chiesa della Salute, and closest to the #1 stop of that name. Discounts can be arranged for large groups. Singles L55,000. Doubles L74,600. Breakfast included. Accepts AmEx, DC, MC, Visa.

San Marco (From the Basilica west to the Grand Canal)

Locanda San Salvador, San Marco, 5264 (tel. 528 91 47), on calle del Galliazzo, off campo San Bartolomeo. Good views and a spacious terrace. Right in the middle of the action. Singles L42,000. Doubles L60,000, with bath L75,000. Breakfast included.

Locande San Samuele, San Marco, 3358 (tel. 522 80 45). Follow calle deghe Botteghe from campo San Stefano and take a left on salizzata San Samuele. Rooms and bathrooms are small and somber. Giovanni, the manager, is fun, though. Singles L37,000. Doubles L47,000, with bath L78,000. Breakfast L7000.

Alloggi Alla Scala, San Marco, 4306 (tel. 521 06 29). From campo Manin find corte Contarini del Bovolo. Colorful rooms *alla carnevale.* Doubles L65,000, with bath L75,000. Showers included. Breakfast L6500. Reserve with 1 night's deposit. Closed 15 days in Aug.

Alloggi Massetto, San Marco, 1520/A (tel. 523 05 05), on ramo Primo Corte Contarina at the Boca de Piazza west of San Marco. Good prices and prime locale. Singles with bath L25,000. Doubles with bath L40,000. Triples with bath L50,000.

Locanda Casa Petrarca, San Marco, 4386 (tel. 520 04 30). From campo San Luca, go south on calle dei Fuseri, take the 2nd left and then turn right onto calle Schiavone. English spoken. Singles L29,000, with bath L39,000. Doubles L54,000. Triples L74,000. Breakfast L6000.

Castello (From San Marco to the Island of Sant'Elena)

Pensione Casa Verardo, Castello, 4765 (tel. 528 61 27). Take rimpetto la Sacrestia out of campo SS. Filippo e Giacomo (just east of San Marco) across the bridge. Without a doubt *the* find in this part of town—run by a hospitable, outgoing family. English spoken. Singles L35,000. Doubles L55,000, with bath 65,000. Showers included. Reserve with 1 night's deposit. They have another establishment, **Hotel da Bepi,** Santa Croce, 160 (tel. 522 67 35), on the fondamento Minotto, near p. Roma. Singles L45,000. Doubles L70,000, with bath L90,000. Breakfast included. Accepts MC, Visa.

Casa Bettina, Castello, 4388 (tel. 523 90 84), 1min. from S. Zaccaria stop and across campo S. Giovanni Novo from the Museo Giodi. A small establishment whose owner will talk as long as you'll listen. Doubles L40,000, with bath L46,000. Breakfast L5000.

Hotel Caneva, Castello, 5515 (tel. 522 81 18 or 520 86 73), a 2-min. walk from the Rialto. Take calle Stagneri from p. S. Bartolomeo, cross the bridge, and turn right after campo della Fava. Off a quiet, alternative route to S. Marco. 17 of the 23 rooms overlook a canal and about half are carpeted. Singles L30,000, with bath and breakfast L55,000. Doubles L50,000, with bath and breakfast L75,000. Triples L60,000. Quads L70,000. Breakfast L5000. From Nov.-March, prices drop by L10,000.

Locanda Corona, Castello, 4464 (tel. 522 91 74; *vaporetto:* San Zacchria). Head north on Sacrestia, from campo SS. Filippo e Giacomo, take the 1st right, and then the 1st left onto calle Corona. Gregarious proprietors. Fine rooms, limited hot water supply. Drop by the Fucina degli Angeli (Angel's Forge) next door for a look at glass-blowing. Singles L34,000. Doubles L48,000. Showers L3000. Breakfast L8500.

Locanda Silva, Castello, 4423 (tel. 522 76 43). Take calle dell'Anzolo (it starts next to San Marco), then make the 2nd right, continue across the bridge, and go left when you hit fondamenta del Rimedio. On a charming canal. Large and fastidiously kept. Singles L45,000. Doubles L65,000, with bath L80,000. Triples L90,000. Includes breakfast. Open Feb.-Nov.

Locanda Sant'Anna, Castello, 269 (tel. 528 64 66). Take via Garibaldi, which becomes fondamenta Santa Anna, turn left on ponte Santa Anna, then right at corte del Bianco (*vaporetto:* #1 or 4 to Giardini). Worth the hike. Friendly family proprietors and a refreshing absence of tourists on the far eastern frontier of Venice. Starched sheets and sparkling rooms. TV downstairs. Curfew midnight. Singles L47,000. Doubles L68,000, with bath L76,000. Triple L94,000, with bath L99,000. Showers and breakfast included. Reserve ahead with 1 night's deposit.

The Outskirts of La Serenissima

Ugly, industrial Mestre on the mainland and Litorale del Cavallino, on the Lido, have the lowest prices and most frequent vacancies around Venice. To reach Mestre, cross the lagoon (all trains out of Venice stop there), and walk up via Cappuccina to the right of the station. Turn right on via Grozzi and right again onto via Parini, until you reach **Hotel Vidale** at #2 (tel. 531 45 86). Rents spacious, spotless rooms. Singles L32,000. Doubles L45,000, with bath L66,000. Triples L60,000. Visa.

Ridiculously cheap accommodations cluster in the less accessible region of **Litorale del Cavallino** on the Lido. Take *vaporetto* #14 from San Marco to Punta Sabbioni (40min., L3300). Then take bus #5 (L2200) from the *vaporetto* stop to via Faro 10km away. Of the 14 one-star hotels, the champion price slasher is **Da Giovanni,** via del Faro, 35 (tel. 96 80 63). (Singles L15,000. Doubles L30,000. Breakfast L5000.) **Al Buon Pesce Da Aldo** (tel. 96 80 64) is at #31. (Singles L18,000. Doubles L31,600. Breakfast L5000.)

Camping

The **Litorale del Cavallino,** on the Adriatic side of the Lido, east of Venice, is one endless row of campgrounds on the beach. From San Marco, *vaporetto* #14 winds its way to Punta Sabbioni (40min., L3300). **Camping Miramare** (tel. 96 61 50), about 700m along the beach to your right as you descend from the Punta Sabbioni *vaporetto* stop, charges L4100-5500 per person and L6600-9500 per tent depending on the time of year. Bungalows L32,000-65,000. Open April-Sept. **Cà Pasquall,** via Poerio, 33 (tel. 96 61 10), charges a mere L4500 per person and L12,000 per tent space. (Open May 10-Sept. 17.)

Another option is **Campeggio Fusina,** via Moranzani, in the locality of Malcontenta (tel. 547 00 55), which costs L7000, tent included. (English spoken. Call ahead.) From

p. Roma, take bus #4 (L1000) to Mestre and change to bus #13 (across the street from Supermarket Pam). Ride to the last stop (1hr., last bus at 9pm). The boat trip is more picturesque and convenient but also more expensive. Take *vaporetto* #5 (L2200) left to Zattere and then take #16 (L3300) for 20min. to Fusina.

Food

The secret to eating well and cheaply in Venice is **bar snacks.** Venetians have long cultivated the august tradition of the between-meal repast, known as the *cicchetto,* always washed down by *un'ombra,* a glass of local wine. Visit any *bar* or *osteria* in town and make a meal from the vast display of meat- and cheese-filled , tidbits of seafood, rice, and meat, and *tramezzini,* triangular slices of soft white bread with every imaginable filling. Stray from the tourist thoroughfares to avoid microwaved pizza slices, anticipate L1000-4000 per snack.

It is becoming difficult to actually sit down to a good meal in Venice at terrestrial prices. Stop at an *osteria* for appetizers and a *bar* for dessert to avoid an outrageous restaurant bill, and always shop around first before deciding on a place to eat. Good deals on tourist *menùs* converge along the broad **via Garibaldi,** a lovely 15-min. walk along the waterfront from p. San Marco.

If you're going to spend big bucks on dinner, try one of the local seafood dishes. *Seppie in nero* is a tasty, soft squid coated with its own ink and usually served with *polenta,* a bland cornmeal mush. A plate of *pesce fritta mista* (mixed fried seafood, at least L9000) usually includes *calamari* (squid), *polpo* (small octopus), shrimp, and the catch of the day. *Fegato alla veneziana* is a simple but celebrated dish of liver and onions. For dessert, try a slice of *tiramisù* (literally "pick-me-up"), a gloriously gloppy layered cake soaked in liquor-laced espresso, filled with a creamy sweet cheese custard and topped off with powdered chocolate.

Kosher food is served in Europe's oldest Jewish quarter, in Cannaregio at the end of a series of Hebrew and Jewish signs. Call ahead to reserve a space at the **Casa Israelitica di Reposo,** 2874 (tel. 71 80 02), located across the campo del Ghetto Nuovo from the Museo Ebraico. (Open Sun.-Fri. 8:30am-12:30pm.)

Gastronomie, rosticcerie (take-out restaurants), and *pasticcerie* (pastry shops) are halfway between dining out and eating supermarket foods. The pizza at **Cip Ciap,** Castello, 5799/A (tel. 523 66 21), at Ponte del Mondo Novo, off fondamenta Santa Maria Formosa, southwest of the campo, deserves highest praise (L5000-10,000, slices L1200); the *disco volante* (literally "flying saucer," stuffed with mushrooms, eggplant, ham, and salami, L9000) is out of this world. (Open Dec.-Oct. Wed.-Mon. 9am-9pm.) For take-out deli food, the best and most central is **Aliani Gastronomia,** San Polo, 655 (tel. 522 49 13), on ruga Vecchia San Giovanni, after a left off ruga Orefici, the street that leads to the Rialto bridge on the San Polo side. Cheeses and cold cuts, lavish lasagna (L1550 per *etto*), roasted half chicken (L9800), and veggies are yours for the munching. (Open mid-Aug. to July Mon.-Sat. 8am-1pm and 5-8pm.)

Incorrigible sweet-tooths may decide to skip the main course altogether and subsist solely on confections. *La dolce vita* thrives at **Pasticceria Pitteri,** Cannaregio, 3844, on Strada Nova, the central street (open Mon.-Sat. 7:30am-8:30pm.) Buy the dense and nutty *pane dei dogi* (L2500 per *etto*) and repent at your leisure. Or stop by **A. Rosa Salva,** San Marco, 5020 (tel. 522 79 34), on Marzaria San Salvador near the Rialto bridge. Locals claim that this is Venice's premier bakery; the renowned *budino di semolino* (a rich pudding cake), (L1000 each), affirms their assertion. (Open Mon.-Sat. 8am-8pm.)

The best place to buy fish and produce is at the large **market** every morning at the Rialto bridge (in San Polo), or just past the Ponte Guglie in Cannaregio. Locals shop on the side streets near **campo Beccarie** in San Polo near the Rialto. Less entertaining but more convenient are the **alimentari.** In Dorsoduro, go to **Mega 1** at campo Santa Margherita, 3019/B, an unmarked entrance between a phone booth and a *caffè.* (Open Thurs.-Tues. 9am-1pm and 4:30-7:30pm, Sat. until 7:45pm, and Wed. 9am-1pm.) In Castello near San Marco, there's **Su. Ve.,** 5816, on calle del Mondo Novo off campo Santa Maria Formosa. (Open Thurs.-Sat. 8:45am-7:30pm, Wed. 8:45am-1pm.)

Near the Train and Bus Stations

Mensa DLF (tel. 71 62 42), to the left as you leave the tracks. Portions are large, food decent, and clientele congenial. Full meal L11,700. Wine L2000 per half-<liter>. Open Mon., Wed., Fri.-Sun. 12:30-1:30pm and 6-9pm, Tues. and Thurs. 6-9pm.

Trattoria alle Burchielle, Santa Croce, 393 (tel. 523 13 42), on the fondamenta Burchielle, right off the corner of p. Roma over the bridge at campazzo Tre Ponti, the 3-bridge intersection. Regional delights served along the banks of the small canal. Pasta L6000. Wine L8000 per . Cover L1500. Service 10%. Open Tues.-Sun. 9am-10pm.

Shanghai, Cannaregio, 101 (tel. 71 62 32), on calle Priuli, to the left and left again from the train station—altogether a 45-second walk. Good, hot, non-Italian food and adorable children. Appetizers begin at L2000, main courses at L5000. *Menù* L15,000.

Cannaregio

Vini da Gigio, Cannaregio, 3628/A (tel. 528 51 40), back on the right hand side of Chiesa S. Felice, off strada Nova near Ponte Nova. Dine among sedate locals at one of the few restaurants that doesn't feature an English translation of their menu. Fresh seafood dishes range from L8000-21,000. Open Tues.-Sat. noon-3pm and 7-10pm, Sun. noon-3pm.

Ristorante al Ponte, Cannaregio, 2352 (tel. 72 07 44), quite literally *on* Ponte del'Anconeta, the 2nd bridge after you turn left from the station, just past p. San Geremia. The reasonable *menù* (L12,500) includes everything but beverage and spotlights regional specialties such as *seppie nere alla Veneziana* (black cuttlefish in a sauce of oil, white wine, and tomatoes). Cover L3000. Service 12%. Open Wed.-Mon. 11:30-2:30pm and 6:30-9:30pm.

Ai Promessi Sposi, Cannaregio, 4367 (tel. 522 86 09). From the strada Nova, take a left on calle del Duca just before campo S. Apostoli, then a right on calle dell'Oca. Mellow music and magnificent meals. Try their specialty, *spaghetti bigoli in salsa* (thick spaghetti with anchovies and onions, L7000). *Menù* L14,000. Cover L1500. Open Thurs.-Tues. noon-2:30pm and 7-10pm.

Trattoria Casa Mia, Cannaregio, 4430, on same alley as Promessi Sposi. One look at the family-filled interior and you may choose to make it *la casa tua* for the evening. *Bigoli in salsa* is L5500 per person for a minimum of 2, and fish entrees begin at L10,000. Cover L1500. Service 12%. Open Wed.-Mon. noon-3pm and 7-10pm.

San Polo and Santa Croce

Mensa Universitaria di Cà Foscari, S. Polo, 2480 (tel. 71 80 69), on calle del Magazen. Full meals including drink and dessert L4000 with *cartagiovane* or other student ID. Open Mon.-Sat. 11:45am-2:30pm and 6:30-8:30pm, Sun. noon-2pm.

Trattoria da Ignazio, S. Polo, 2749 (tel. 523 48 52), on calle Saoneri, an extension of salizzada S. Polo. Take the latter from campo S. Polo. A bit pricey, but get your money's worth by lolling indefinitely in their pleasant garden. Partake of the *agnolotti alla panna e prosciutto* (meat-stuffed pasta with cream and prosciutto, L5000) and *tartufo* (*gelato* truffle, L4000) for dessert. Cover L2500. Service 12%. Open Sun.-Fri. noon-2:30pm and 6:30-9:30pm.

Da Bepi, S. Croce, 158 (tel. 522 67 35), on fondamenta Minotta. Follow fond. Tolentini around the bend to the left when heading away from the station. A half-carafe of *tocai* or *prosecco* (a dry, bubbly Veneto wine) is L3500. Try the *tagliolini salmone* (flat pasta with salmon, L8500). Open Tues.-Sun. noon-2:30pm and 7:30-10:30pm.

Cantina Do Spade, San Polo, 860 (tel. 521 05 74), in sottoportego delle Do Spade near the Rialto. Tucked away under an archway before the Do Spade bridge south of the fish market. Really a winery, but serves sumptuous little sandwiches (L1200-1800). Try the house wine (L600 per glass) or any of the hundreds of Friuli and Veneto whites and reds. Especially good is *inferno* from the Val Telina (L2000 per glass). Open Sept.-July Mon.-Sat. 9am-1pm and 5-8pm.

Cantina Do Mori, San Polo, 429 (tel. 522 54 01), down the street from the above. Venetians have frequented this cavernous snack-and-wine bar since 1571. Wine L1200-7000 per glass. *Tramezzini* L1400. Open Aug. 20-July Mon.-Tues. and Thurs.-Sat. 8:30am-1:30pm and 5-8:30pm, Wed. 8:30am-1:30pm.

Alla Rivetta, S. Polo, 1479 (tel. 522 42 46), on canal's edge in campiello dei Melon on the way to Rialto. Expect better prices than service. Fried fish an unbeatable L8000. Wine L6000 per . Cover L1500. Service 10%. Open Tues.-Sun. 7am-9:30pm.

Dorsoduro

El Chef, Dorsoduro, 2765 (tel. 522 28 15), on calle Lombardo, under the archway from campo S. Barnabà. If a dish of fish is not your wish, go elsewhere. Local wines to wash it all down are L8500 per . Open mid-March to Dec. Tues.-Sun. noon-3pm and 6:30-10pm.

Da Silvio, Dorsoduro, 3748 (tel. 520 58 33), on calle S. Pantalon near the *campo* of the same name. Delicious fare served up in the *trattoria's* garden. *Calamari fritti* (deep-fried squid) only L7500. A daunting array of scallop options. Pasta from L3500. 15% discount with *cartagiovane*. Open Mon.-Sat. 9am-3:30pm and 5:45-11pm.

Crepizza, Dorsoduro, 3757 (tel. 522 91 89), on calle San Pantalon off calle Crosera across from da Silvio. Look for the hanging sign. Crêpes (about L7500, sweet crêpes from L5000) and pizza (L4500-9500) served with zeal. Cover L1000. Service 10%. Open Wed.-Mon. noon-2:30pm and 7-10:30pm.

San Marco

Rosticceria San Bartolomeo, San Marco, 5424/A (tel. 522 35 69), in calle de la Bissa off campo San Bartolomeo near the Rialto Bridge, under a sign for Rosticceria Gislon. Top-notch self-service food. Venetian specialties like *seppie con polenta* (cuttlefish with cornmeal pudding, L14,000). 15% discount with *cartagiovane*. Open Feb.-Dec. Tues.-Sun. 10am-2:25pm and 4:50-9pm.

Leon Bianco, San Marco, 4153 (tel. 522 11 80), on salizzata San Luca which runs between campo San Luca and campo Manin, northwest of p. San Marco. Snarf tasty food while standing at marble counters, shoulder to business-suited shoulder. Main courses L5500. *Risotto* L4000. *Tramezzini* L1300. Tasty fried snacks L1000-1300. Open Mon.-Sat. 8am-8pm.

Vino, Vino, San Marco, 2007/A (tel. 523 70 27), on calle del Sartor da Veste, off calle Larga XXII Marzo, which runs from the Ponte Moisè due west of p. San Marco. Praised in the *New York Times,* and, like the paper, its black and white, and red all over. A river of wines (L1000-8000 per glass) and a sea of tourists. Cover L1000. Open for drinks Wed.-Mon. 10am-11:30pm; for eats, noon-4pm and 6-11pm.

Castello

Osteria Al Mascaron, Castello, 5225 (tel. 259 95), on calle longa Santa Maria Formosa, which runs off campo Santa Maria Formosa, northeast of p. San Marco. The ultimate in informal *osteria* eating. Filled with chattering Venetians taking a wine break or enjoying delicious specialties like *spaghetti alle vongolenere* (with black clams, L12,000). Cover L2000. Open mid-Jan. to mid-Dec. Mon.-Sat. 10:30am-3pm and 7-10:30pm.

Trattoria Alla Rivetta, Castello, 9625 (tel. 528 73 02). Off campo SS. Filippo e Giacomo which lies just east of p. San Marco—the restaurant's squeezed in to the right before the Ponte San Provolo. One of the only genuine and reasonable places in the area. Try the *pesce fritta mista* (large portion L13,000). Cover L1500. Service 12%. Open Aug. 15-July 15 Tues.-Sun. 11am-11pm.

Antiche Botteselle, via Garibaldi, 1621 (tel. 523 72 92), on a broad street that penetrates Castello near the Arsenale stop, about a 15-min. walk from S. Marco. Economical *menù* L13,000 if you mention *Let's Go,* otherwise L12,000 plus cover and service. Thirty-six types of pizza (L4800-8000). *Primi* L5000-14,000. *Secondi* L6000-19,000. Wine L8000 per . Open Thurs.-Tues. 9:30am-1:30am.

Al Vecio Portal, Castello, 3990 (tel. 528 77 69), in campiello Pescheria. Set back from the Riva degli Schiavo behind the Hotel Gabrielli. Choose individual dishes over the unimaginative *menù*. Scallops cooked to suit are L9000. *Primi* L5000-7500. *Secondi* L7000-13,000. Cover L2000. Service 12%. Open Wed.-Mon. 11:30am-3pm and 6:30-10:30pm.

Trattoria Chinellato, Castello, 4227 (tel. 523 60 25), on calle Albanesi a few doors down from campo SS. Filippo e Giacomo. Gregarious proprietor will make you feel right at home. Get your salivary glands going by peeking through the window first. *Seppie nere* L14,000, or try the *gnocchi della casa* L9000. Cover L1500. Service 12%. Open Wed.-Mon. 9am-9pm.

Gelaterie

Each of the *gelaterie* listed below is a favorite hangout with locals and the sort of meeting place that is the Venetian substitute for a *passeggiata*.

Gelateria Santo Stefano, San Marco, 2962 (tel. 522 55 76), in the northwest corner of campo Morosini San Stefano, is professed to have the best *nocciola* (hazelnut) and *panna* (whipped cream) in the world. Cones L1000-4000. Open Tues.-Sun. 7:30am-midnight; Oct.-Nov. and Feb.-Mar. 7:30am-9pm. Closed Dec. and Jan.

Gelati Nico, fondamenta Zattere, 922 (tel. 522 52 93), in Dorsoduro near the *vaporetto* stop of the same name, is the pride of Venice. The prices are similar to San Stefano's, but the portions are huge. *Gianduiotto,* a slice of dense chocolate hazelnut ice cream dunked in whipped cream, is their specialty (L2700). Open in summer Fri-Wed. 7am-11pm; mid-Jan. to mid-Dec. 7am-9pm.

Il Doge, campo Santa Margherita, Dorsoduro, 3058/A (tel. 523 46 07) is seldom without a line of salivating customers. Tasty *granite* (flavored ices, L2000), and *frappé* (fruit shakes, L3000), along with *gelato* comprise the holy frozen trinity. Open for worship Feb.-Oct. Tues.-Sun. 10:30am-midnight.

Causin, across the campo, is a *caffè-gelateria* that has pleased customers since 1928 and has certificates to show for it. The best and cheapest place in Venice. Two-scoop cone L1500. Five-scoop bowl L3000. Open daily 8am-8pm.

Sights

If you'd like to see the splay of the land before you start, take *vaporetto* #1 (L2200) down the Grand Canal for an introduction to both Venetian architecture and the sinuous curve of its main waterway. Tourists jam **San Marco,** while the commercial district of town lies in **Rialto.** Compared to these wealthy districts, the buildings in **Cannaregio** seem ungainly, plain, and densely packed. **Castello,** originally separated from the rest of Venice by marshes, still maintains the feeling of a quiet, isolated village. **Dorsoduro, Santa Croce,** and **San Polo** all preserve some quaint Venetian corners. Outside of San Marco, churches tend to approximate the timetable of 9am-12:30pm and 3-6pm.

If the plethora of Venetian museums strikes your fancy, consider buying the city's **Biglietto Cumulativo** (Special Museum Ticket, L16,000). This ticket gets you into the Palazzo Ducale, the Museo Correr, the Museo del Risorgimento, the Cà Rezzonico Museo del Settecento, the Galleria d'Arte Moderna di Cà Pesaro, the Museo Vetrario di Murano, the Palazzo Mocenigo, the Museo Guidi, and the Casa di Goldoni. It is available at any of the above museums and is valid through the end of the calendar year. Also keep your eyes peeled for special art exhibits tucked away in churches and schools.

Toby Cole's *Venice, A Portable Reader,* narrates city history as encountered by personalities from Casanova to Mark Twain (Frontier Press, L22,000). Mary McCarthy's *Venice Observed* (Penguin, L15,000) is a trenchant, absorbing collection of essays. James Morris's *Venice* (Faber and Faber, L20,000), is an entertaining and insightful description of the art, history, and character of the city.

The Grand Canal

The Grand Canal has always been the living heart of Venice. The facades of the opulent *palazzi* that crowd its banks testify to a history of immense wealth. Sit back on *vaporetto* #1 or 34 and cruise the channel. The palaces share the same structure despite the external decorative features, which reflect the styles of various historical periods. From early on, cramped island life didn't permit the luxury of a central courtyard. Instead, Venetian *palazzi* were constructed with central halls running front to back, providing the necessary air circulation and light. The ground floor (*androne*) served as an entrance hall, while the living quarters occupied the *piano nobile* (second floor). The overall effect, unlike that of the "closed" fortress-palaces of the Florentine Renaissance, is one of inviting openness.

The oldest surviving palaces, some from the 13th century, were influenced by Byzantine and early Christian tastes. Look for rounded arches in low relief, like those on the **Cà da Mosto,** the *palazzo* on the S. Marco side of Grand Canal shortly past the Rialto bridge towards the train station. The **Fondaco dei Tedeschi,** on the Rialto side of the Cà da Mosto, functioned as a German trading center in the 13th century, but was rebuilt in 1505. Further on toward the station on the same side of the canal is the **Cà d'Oro** whose name derives from the gold leaf that once adorned the tracery of its renowned facade. Built in 1440, the Cà d'Oro represents the pinnacle of the Venetian Gothic (see Cannaregio below).

On the other side of the canal, one can see what is now the **Gallery of Modern Art.** The majestic Baroque edifice is known as the **Palazzo Pesaro**—for the grotesques grimacing out from its facade. Closer to the station stands the **Fondaco dei Turchi,** a Veneto-Byzantine palace that was a Turkish warehouse until 1838. Today, the **Natural History Museum** stands in lieu of the Ottoman merchants.

Many of Venice's Renaissance edifices are the works of three major Venetian architects: Mauro Coducci, Jacopo Sansovino, and Michele Sanmicheli. Coducci's early **Palazzo Corner-Spinelli** (1510) and **Cà Vendramin Calergi,** both on the east bank, were the first *palazzi* to depart from the traditional Venetian style, infusing classical and Byzantine elements. Coducci's leadership inspired Sansovino's stately **Cà Corner** (1550) and Sanmicheli's **Palazzo Grimani,** also on the east bank.

San Marco and Castello Piazza San Marco and Environs

Bustling **piazza San Marco** is the city's nucleus. Water and land traffic merge at the molo and riva degli Schiavoni, whence Venice radiates in unsurpassed magnificence. The numerous domes and spires of the church of San Marco, along with the pink, rococo decorations of the Doge's Palace contrast with the classical façade of Sansovino's. The classical theme is further reinforced by the disciplined porticoes of the two Procuratie that flank the large *piazza.*

Above the piazza soars the solid brick **campanile** (tel. 528 99 00; open daily 10am-6pm. Admission L3000). A fine photo spot, though cheaper admission, shorter lines, and better views are available at the **Campanile di San Giorgio** across from p. San Marco on the small island of San Giorgio (see *Outlying Sights* below).

Construction of the **Basilica of San Marco** (tel. 522 52 05) began in the 9th century, when two Venetian merchants stole St. Mark's remains from Alexandria, packing them in pork to hoodwink Arab officials. The caper is commemorated in a mosaic to the left of the three entrance arches. The basilica's cruciform plan and five bulbed domes, a direct architectural reference to the Church of the Holy Apostles in Constantinople, suggest a prestige which was intended to rival both Byzantium and St. Peter's. Rebuilt after a fire in the 10th century, it was enlarged and embellished without cease over the next half-millennium. The result is a unique synthesis of Byzantine, Western European, and Islamic influences from across the centuries. (Open daily 9:45am-5pm. Admission L2000.)

The four Hellenistic bronze horses over the door are replicas. Brought from Chios to Constantinople by Constantine the Great, abducted in 1204 by the Venetian Fourth Crusade, and temporarily removed (to Paris) at the close of the 18th century by Napoleon II, the original members of this well-traveled quartet have moved to a permanent home inside the basilica. The church sparkles with mosaics of all ages—perhaps the best are those on the atrium's ceiling (shadow a tour group for an exhaustive rundown). Underfoot, 12th-century confections of marble, glass and porphyry confuse the eyes with endless geometric intricacies. The basilica's main treasure is the unbearably gaudy **Pala d'Oro** (tel. 522 56 97), a Veneto-Byzantine gold bas-relief encrusted with precious gems. In the area behind the screen are Sansovino's bronze reliefs and his sacristy door. The ticket to this area will also get you into the small **treasury,** a hoard of gold and relics left over from the spoils of the Fourth Crusade. (Open Mon.-Sat. 9:45am-5pm, Sun. 1:30-5pm. Admission L2000.) Through a door in the atrium is the **Galleria della Basilica** (tel. 522 52 05)—worth it for a better view of the mosaics on the walls and floors. The recently restored *Horses of St. Mark* (the originals) are on display here. (Open daily 10am-5pm. Admission L2000.) *Remember, here as in all Venetian churches no shorts or sleeveless shirts are allowed.* Guided tours of the basilica are given April-June and Sept.-Oct. Mon.-Sat. at 11am. Call the **Curia Patriarcale** for further information (tel. 520 03 33). English spoken.

As you come out of San Marco you'll find Coducci's ornate **Torre dell'Orologio** (1499), a florid arrangement of sculpture and sundials on your right. Two oxidizing bronze Moors strike the hours. (Closed for restoration in 1992.) The arch below marks the beginning of the **Mercerie,** Venice's main commercial street leading to the Rialto.

Between San Marco and the lagoon stands the **Palazzo Ducale** (Doge's Palace; tel. 522 49 51). The *palazzo,* built in the 14th century after the original was destroyed by a fire, is a magnificent example of Venetian Gothic. The sculpted Virtues of Temperance, Fortitude, Prudence, and Charity that adorn the **Porta della Carta** are attributed to the 15th century duo of Giovanni and Bartolomeo Bon. At the side of San Marco stand the *Quattro Mori,* statues of four Roman emperors that crusaders "borrowed" from Constantinople in 1204. Rizzo's **Scala dei Giganti,** sweeping up to the second floor in the left end of the courtyard, is crowned with Sansovino's *Mars and Neptune.* Up his famous **Golden Staircase** preside the Senate Chamber and the Room of the Council of Ten (the much-feared secret police of the Republic), both shrouded in paintings. Come while daylight illuminates the dark Tintorettos and Veroneses. The route then returns to the second floor, where after passing some enormous globes, you can wander through the echoing **Grand Council Chamber.** The room contains the huge, resplendent *Paradiso* by Tintoretto as well as Veronese's *Apotheosis of Venus.* Portraits of all the doges of Venice except Marin Falier also adorn the walls of this room. An empty frame commemorates this over-ambitious doge, who was executed for treason after his unsuccessful coup attempt in 1355. Throughout the building are slits in the walls where secret denunciations were inserted to be investigated by the Ten. (Open daily 9am-7pm. Admission L8000.)

From the Council Chamber, a series of secret passages leads across the **Ponte dei Sospiri** (Bridge of Sighs) from the back of the palace to the prisons. Casanova was among those condemned by the Ten to walk across into the hands of sadistic inquisitors. The name alludes to the bitter groans of prisoners pondering the slim prospects of ever regaining their freedom.

Facing the Palazzo Ducale across p. San Marco are Sansovino's greatest hits, the elegant **Libreria** (1536) and the **Zecca** (mint, 1547). The main reading room of the **Biblioteca Marciana** (tel. 520 87 88), on the second floor, is adorned with frescoes by Veronese and Tintoretto, among others. (Entrance at #12. Open Mon.-Fri. 9am-1pm. Prior permission required.) Venetian artists received their quota of classical cultivation from the sculptures in the **Museo Archeologico** (tel. 522 59 78), next door. (Open Mon.-Sat. 9am-2pm, Sun. 9am-1pm. Admission L4000.) Close by is the 99m **Campanile di San Marco.** First completed in 912, the bell tower abruptly crumbled into a pile of rubble only ten years before its millennium. An identical replacement was erected in time for the big birthday. (Open daily 10am-6pm; shorter hours during the winter. Admission L3000.)

Under the portico at the opposite end of the *piazza* from the church is the entrance to the **Museo Civico Correr** (tel. 522 56 25). It houses a couple of Bellinis and Carpaccio's *Courtesans,* not to mention such sundry curiosities of daily Venetian life as the foot-high platform shoes once worn by sequestered noblewomen. (Open Wed.-Mon. 9am-7pm. Admission L5000, students L2500.)

Two famous *caffè* face off in the *piazza.* Eighteenth-century supporters of the Austrians ruling the city patronized **Caffè Quadri,** p. San Marco, 120-123, on the side of the *piazza* farther from the water. (Tel. 523 92 99. Open daily 10am-midnight; Oct.-April Tues.-Sun. 10am-midnight. Less filling.) Patriotic Venetians frequented **Caffè Florian,** across the *piazza* at San Marco, 56/59. (Tel. 528 53 38; open daily 9am-midnight; Oct.-April Thurs.-Tues. 9am-midnight. Tastes great.) There is no more seductive way to spend a Venetian evening than to sit in the *piazza,* listening to the competing orchestras while sipping a cappuccino. Both *caffè* have a L3500 cover charge during "concerts," so if you sit down with a caffé (L4500), you might as well take off your coat and make yourself at home. A lowbrow way to absorb the atmosphere without letting the atmosphere absorb your wallet is to get a coffee-to-go at the nearby Wendy's (L1000) and plunk yourself down on the steps that run along the base of the surrounding *loggia* (doesn't taste so great, but more filling than an authentic Italian espresso). **Harry's Bar,** favored hangout of "Ernesto" Hemingway and real men ever since, lies on calle Vallaresso, in front of the San Marco *vaporetto* stop. (Drinks L7500. Service 20%. Open Tues.-Sun. 10:30am-11pm.)

The Mercerie

Starting under the arch of the Torre dell'Orologio in San Marco, the shop-filled and tourist-clogged Mercerie leads up to the **Church of San Giuliano,** commissioned by the Venetian doctor Tommaso Ragone as a monument to himself. His portrait by Sansovino glowers over the door, framed by inscriptions and allegories.

The Mercerie then passes by **campo San Salvatore.** The local church resolves the architectural discrepancy between the square Greek cross and the long Latin cross in off-beat form: it consists of three square crosses stuck together. Don't miss Giovanni Bellini's *Supper in Emmaus* and Titian's *Annunciation* (1566). The latter failed to suit Venetian tastes, hence Titian's own scrawl at the bottom reads *Titianus. Fecit. Fecit.* insisting twice to the skeptical public that the work is indeed complete, and by him.

A few steps east of the *campo* along calle dell'Ovo lies the **Casa Goldoni** (tel. 523 63 53). The museum displays the original manuscripts of Carlo Goldoni's plays. (Open Mon.-Sat. 8:30am-1:30pm. Free.)

Around San Marco

North of p. San Marco stands the **Church of Santa Maria Formosa.** At the bottom of the campanile leers a carved head, which, to Ruskin, "embodied the type of evil spirit to which Venice was abandoned, the pestilence that came and breathed upon her beauty." Revive your overtaxed sensitivity to all things beautiful with a glance at this hideous mug. Coducci's Greek-cross plan, a rebuilding of an ancient church, houses Palma il Vecchio's painting of St. Barbara, here the exemplar of female beauty in Renaissance Venice. Across the bridge, a twisted alleyway leads to the haunting **Palazzo Querini-Stampalia** (tel. 522 52 35), whose intriguing aristocratic rooms house paintings dating from the 14th through 18th centuries. (Open Tues.-Sun. 10am-12:30pm. Admission L5000.)

North of campo Santa Maria Formosa, calle Lunga and calle Cicogna lead to campo **SS. Giovanni e Paolo** and to the church of the same name (*San Zanipolo* in the Venetian dialect). This grandiose Gothic structure, built by the Dominican order over the course of two centuries (mid-13th to mid-15th), resembles a brick barn, and the monuments to various doges along the sides are no improvement. However, there is a wonderful polyptych by Giovanni Bellini hanging over the second altar of the right-hand nave. From the left transept you enter the **Cappella del Rosario** (Rosary Chapel) which, although damaged by a fire in 1867, still preserves four marvelous paintings by Veronese. In the *campo* stands an equestrian statue of Bartolomeo Colleoni by Andrea del Verrocchio, a famous Venetian *condottiere* (mercenary captain). Upon his death, Colleoni left the Senate all his loot on the condition that it erect a statue to him in p. San Marco; the Senators claimed, however, that the exact wording of the will allowed them to raise the statue not in the *piazza,* but in front of the **Scuola di San Marco.** If you cross the Ponte Rosso and go straight, you'll come to the Lombardos' masterpiece, the **Church of Santa Maria dei Miracoli.** Inside, the pilasters stand in carved underbrush; coy *putti* peer out from leafy crevices.

To the east of San Marco, off the riva degli Schiavoni, stands the beautiful 15th-century **Church of San Zaccaria.** Coducci designed this striking facade, an enlarged version of his San Michele. Inside, the second altar on the left houses Bellini's masterpiece *The Madonna and Saints.* Around the corner, on the waterfront, is Massari's **Church of the Pietà,** containing celebrated Tiepolo frescoes. Vivaldi was concertmaster here at the beginning of the 18th century, and concerts featuring his music are held in the church throughout the summer.

For a real treat, make your way through the *calli* to the **Scuola di San Giorgio degli Schiavoni** (tel. 522 88 28). Here, between 1502 and 1511, Carpaccio decorated the ground floor with some of his finest paintings, depicting episodes from the lives of St. George, St. Jerome, and St. Trifone. (Open Tues.-Sat. 9:30am-12:30pm and 3:30-6:30pm, Sun. 9:30am-11am. Mon. 9:30am-12:30pm. Admission L4000.) The nearby **Museo dei Dipinti Sacri Bizantini** (tel. 522 65 81), at Ponte dei Greci, displays religious paintings from the Byzantine and post-Byzantine periods. (Open Mon.-Sat. 9am-1pm and 2-5pm. Admission L4000.) For the tale of *La Serenissima's* maritime supremacy, visit the **Museo Storico Navale** (tel. 520 02 76) on the waterfront of the Castello district where via Giuseppe Garibaldi hits riva dei Sette Mártiri. (Open Mon.-Sat. 9am-1pm. Admission L2000.)

A bit farther down the waterfront lie the mysterious and overgrown grounds of the biennial International Exhibition of Modern Art, known as the **Biennale.** Since 1895 countries have graced the Biennale with modern art ranging from the gripping to the mind-boggling; over 40 nations have permanent pavilions. Beyond the exhibition grounds, across the bridge, the open space of the **Parco delle Rimembranze** welcomes all comers. While in this remote corner of the world, pay a visit to the **Arsenale,** the shipyard which was once the keystone of Venice's economic success. A Renaissance arch, the **Great Gateway,** was erected in 1460 as a monument to the Republic's military and mercantile prowess.

Cannaregio From the Rialto to the Ghetto

Heading north from the Rialto bridge on salizzada San Giovanni, you reach the last of Coducci's churches, **San Giovanni Crisostomo,** a refined Greek cross. The interior contains works by Giovanni Bellini and an altarpiece by Sebastiano del Piombo. Marco Polo supposedly lived under the arch in corte Seconda del Milione.

From the Crisostomo church, head left toward the *rio* of the same name. Cross two bridges and two small squares to find the **Church of SS. Apostoli,** with an unassuming Tiepolo painting of Santa Lucia's first communion. The church is at the foot of the broad Strada Nova, which was rammed through crowded slums so that Napoleon's horsemen might pass. Nearby is the **Cà d'Oro** (whose inaccessible front door taunts you from the Grand Canal), where the **Galleria Giorgio Franchetti** (tel. 523 87 90) opened in 1984. This formerly private collection displays works of minor Flemish painters and a few major pieces, among them Titian's *Venus,* Mantegna's *St. Sebastian* and Durer's *Deposition.* (Open Mon.-Sat. 9am-1:30pm, Sun. 9am-12:30pm. Admission L4000.) North of here the **Church of the Gesuiti** boasts a florid green-and-white marble interior and Titian's *Martyrdom of St. Lawrence.* In the northern corner of Cannaregio the **Church of Madonna dell'Orto** patiently awaits the venturesome. Take scenic *vaporetto* #5 (*destra*) to the Madonna dell'Orto stop (L2200). Arguably the only attractive Gothic church in Venice, this far-flung building has made off with a pirate's hoard of Tintorettos, notably his *Sacrifice of the Golden Calf, Last Judgement* and *Presentation of the Virgin.*

Between the church and the train station lies the **Jewish Ghetto,** the first in Europe. The term *ghetto* itself originated in Venice, as the quarter was named after the knife-grinders who previously worked here. Established by ducal decree in 1516, the Ghetto Nuovo remained the enforced enclave of the Jews in Venice until Napoleon's victory over the Venetian Republic in 1797. The area contains five synagogues, of which three are open to the public. The **Sinagoga Grande Tedesca** is less opulent but more intriguing than the **Sinagoghe Spagnole** and **Levantina.** Tedesca is also the oldest, dating back to 1528. Drop by the **Museo Ebraica** (tel. 71 53 59) in the campo del Nuovo Ghetto for a diminutive but fascinating exhibit documenting five centuries of Jewish presence in Venice. Inquire here about guided tours of the Old Ghetto. (Museum open June-Sept. Sun.-Fri. 10am-7pm; Oct.-May Sun.-Fri. 10am-4pm. Admission L4000, students L2000. Guided tour an additional L4000, students L3000.)

San Polo and Santa Croce

The **Ponte Rialto,** spanning the Grand Canal, is the entrance to this commercial district. In the center of the **Erberia,** the grocery section of the open market, is the **Church of San Giacomo di Rialto,** the oldest in Venice. A stubby column with a staircase to the top stands in front of it, supported by a bent stone figure. The column served as a podium from which state proclamations were issued; the statue, called *il Gobbo* (the hunchback), has served as a bulletin board for public responses since Roman times.

From the **Rialto** bridge, drift with the crowd down the ruga degli Orefici, then turn left and follow ruga Vecchia San Giovanni to the **Church of San Polo** (*San Apponal* in the local dialect); the young Giandomenico Tiepolo completed the dramatic 14 stations of the Cross in the chancel. Nearby, in the great Gothic Franciscan **Basilica dei Frari**

(1340-1443; tel. 522 26 37), Donatello's wooden *St. John the Baptist* keeps company with a later Florentine statue of the saint by Sansovino and three purely Venetian paintings: Giovanni Bellini's triptych of the *Madonna and Saints* over the sacristy, Titian's famous *Assumption of the Virgin,* and his *Madonna of Case Pesaro.* (Open Mon.-Sat. 9am-noon and 2:30-6pm, Sun. 3-5:30pm. Admission L1000, Sun. and holidays free.)

The *scuole* of Venice were a combination of guilds and religious fraternities. Members paid annual dues for the support of their needy fellow members and for the decoration of the *scuola's* premises. Among the richest and most illustrious was the **Scuola Grande di San Rocco** (tel. 523 48 64), across the *campo* at the end of the Frari. Note the detail of the exterior, such as the grotesques at the bottom of the columns. Tintoretto, who set out to combine, in his words, "the color of Titian with the drawing of Michelangelo," covered the inside with 56 paintings; the result of 22 years of labor nearly lives up to his ambition. To see the paintings in chronological order, start on the second floor in the Sala dell'Albergo and follow the cycle downstairs. (Open daily 9am-5:30pm. Admission L6000, with *cartagiovane* L5000.)

You can also visit the less embellished **Scuola dei Carmini** (tel. 528 94 20), nearby in campo Carmini off campo Santa Margherita, whose ceiling Giambattista Tiepolo apparently had a swell time painting. (Open Mon.-Sat. 9am-noon and 3-6pm. Admission L5000.) Across the Rio Nuovo from the campo Sta. Margherita (the far end from c. Carmini), the church of **San Pantalon** sports Venice's most absurdly delightful *trompe l'oeil* ceiling, the life's work of Giovanni Fumiani.

Dorsoduro

The Ponte dell'Accademia crosses the Grand Canal at the **Gallerie dell'Accademia** (tel. 522 22 47). This temple of Venetian-school art should top your list of things to see. Among the galleries, Room II stands out for Giovanni Bellini's *Pala di San Giobbe,* a sublime marriage of perspectival sense and Venetian sensibility. Room IV encloses more Bellinis (Giovanni and father Jacopo both) as well as an early Piero della Francesca, but Room V surpasses this, with a pair of certifiable Giorgione canvases, *La Tempesta* and *La Vecchia.* Rooms VI-IX build up High Renaissance anticipation, which receives its payoff in Room X. Displayed here, Veronese's huge rendition of the Last Supper enraged the leaders of the Inquisition with its indulgent improvisation—a Protestant German and a monkey figure among the guests—and Veronese was forced to change the name to *Supper in the House of Levi* to avoid having to make changes at his own expense. This room also contains several brilliant Tintorettos and Titian's last work, a brooding *Pietà.* Rounding off the collection are a number of works by Tiepolo, Canaletto, and Longhi, whose refined cityscapes are considered the height of early urban art. The wonderful cycle of *The Legend of St. Ursula* by Carpaccio (1490-95) in Room XXI boasts a great scene of Ursula, 11,000 virgins in tow, trooping off to Cologne to meet martyrdom at the hands of the marauding Huns. (Open Tues.-Fri. 9am-7:30pm, Mon. and Sat. 9am-2pm., Sun. 9am-1pm. Admission L8000.)

The **Cà Rezzonico** (*vaporetto* stop of the same name) is on the fondamenta Rezzonico, across a bridge from campo San Baranabà. Designed by Longhena, it's one of the great 18th-century Venetian palaces. Inside, recall notorious intrigues and love affairs in the **Museo del Settecento Veneziano** (Museum of the 18th Century; tel. 522 45 43). Step out on the balcony and look out over the Grand Canal at the newly restored Palazzo Grassi across the way. The small bedrooms and boudoirs on the second floor house delightful works by Tiepolo, Guardi, and Longhi. (Open Sat.-Thurs. 9am-7pm. Admission L5000; seniors, students, children under 12 L3000.)

The **Collezione Peggy Guggenheim,** Dorsoduro, 701 (tel. 520 62 88), housed in the late Ms. Guggenheim's Palazzo Venier dei Leoni, near the tip of Dorsoduro, is an small and eclectic collection of modern art. It has rapidly become one of Venice's most popular museums, and deservedly so. Aesthetic and tasteful presentation complements the diversity of the collection itself. The collection includes works by Brancusi, Marino Marini, Kandinsky, Rothko, Max Ernst, and Jackson Pollock. The grounds also feature a sculpture garden. (Open Wed.-Fri. and Sun.-Mon. 11am-6pm, Sat. 11am-9pm. Admission L7000; students with ISIC card, children, and seniors L5000. Free Sat. 6-9pm.)

The **Church of Santa Maria della Salute,** standing at the tip of Dorsoduro, is the most theatrical piece of architecture in Venice. It was designed by Longhena as the site of the dramatic *Festa della Salute* (Nov. 21), which celebrates the deal struck by the church and the festival with God, a deal that purportedly saved Venice from the plague of 1630. In the sacristy are several Titians and a Tintoretto. (Open daily 8am-noon and 3-6pm. Admission to sacristy L500.)

A bit north of fondamenta Zattere, toward the western end of town, lies the 16th-century **Church of San Sebastiano.** It was here that Paolo Veronese took refuge in 1555 when he fled Verona, apparently after killing a man. By 1565 he had filled the church with some of his finest paintings and frescoes. On the ceiling, you'll marvel at his breathtaking *Stories of Queen Esther.* To get a closer look at the panels, climb to the nuns' choir. Here you'll also see the artist's moving fresco *St. Sebastian in Front of Diocletian.* Ask the custodian to turn on the lights (tip L500). Approach the church by sea from the San Basilio stop on *vaporetto* #5 or 8 (L2200).

Outlying Sights

Many of Venice's most beautiful churches are a short boat ride away from San Marco. Two of Palladio's most famous churches are visible from the *piazza.* The **Church of San Giorgio Maggiore,** across the lagoon (take boat #5 or 8; L2200), graces the island of the same name. The church houses Tintoretto's famous *Last Supper.* Ascend the **campanile** (tel. 528 99 00) for a superb view of the main islands. (Open daily 9am-1pm and 2-6pm. Admission L2000.)

A bit farther out on the next island, Giudecca, is Palladio's famous **Church of II Redentore** (the Redeemer). During the pestilence of 1576, the Venetian Senate swore that they would build a devotional church and make a yearly pilgrimage there if the plague would leave the city. Palladio accommodated the pilgrims by enlarging the church's tribune and still managed to preserve the coherence of the building's layout. Take *vaporetto* #5 or 8 (L2200).

The tiny **Church of San Michele in Isola,** on its own island on the far side of the lagoon, is a Venetian masterpiece. Begun by Coducci in 1469, the pristine marble facade with its delicate scallops was Venice's first Renaissance structure. Venice's attachment to its idiosyncratic, essentially medieval architecture meant that the ideas of Alberti and Brunelleschi took a long time to drop anchor in the lagoon. When they did, they mixed with Byzantine influences, as this facade attests. The small hexagonal chapel to the left is a later addition. Take *vaporetto* #5 to the *cimitero* (cemetery) stop (L2200).

The Islands of the Lagoon

Accessible by *vaporetto* #1 and 2, the **Lido** was the setting for Thomas Mann's *Death in Venice* and Visconti's haunting film version, both of which give an unforgettable impression of the sensuality and mystery for which Venice is famous. Lovers of the *belle époque* will enjoy a visit to the fabled Grand Hôtel des Bains. From the *vaporetto* stop, follow the crowd that troops daily down Gran Viale Santa Maria Elisabetta or take bus A (L700).

Boat #12 departs from fondamenta Nuove, near campo dei Gesuiti, for the islands of Murano, Burano, and Torcello. (Murano is also serviced by the #5.) **Murano** has been famous for its glass since 1292, when Venice's artisans decided to transfer their operations there. Today, serious glass-making and tourist-oriented enterprises coexist, affording numerous opportunities to witness the glass-blowing process. For a look at the most successful efforts of past masters, visit the **Museo Vetrario** (tel. 73 95 86) on fondamenta Giustinian, along the main canal, with a splendid collection dating from Roman times onward. (Open daily 9am-7pm. In off-season Thurs.-Tues. 10am-3pm. Admission L5000, students, seniors and children L3000.) Also located on Murano is the exceptionally pretty **Basilica SS. Maria e Donato,** originally built in the 7th century but owing its exterior a 12th century renovation.

Burano, a half-hour out of Venice by boat #12 (L3300), caters to tourists. It is famous for its lace, which is hawked all over Venice; the small **Scuola di Merletti di**

Burano (tel. 73 00 34) documents the craft. (Open Tues.-Sat. 9am-6pm, Sun. 10am-4pm. Admission L5000.)

Today **Torcello,** the remaining island, is the most rural of the group. Of the first-time visitor to Venice, Englishman John Ruskin wrote "Let him not...look upon the pageantry of her palaces...but let him ascend the highest tier of the stern ledges that sweep round the altar of Torcello." The **Cathedral of Torcello** (tel. 73 00 84), founded in the 7th century and rebuilt in the 11th, leaves much to be desired from the outside, but the Byzantine mosaics inside are so incredible that a 19th-century restorer took a few back to Wales with him. (Cathedral open daily 10am-12:30pm and 2-5pm. Admission L1500. Adjacent **museum** open Tues.-Sun. 10am-12:30pm and 2-5:30pm. Admission L3000.)

Never too far from water, prosperous Venetians built their farming villas along the Brenta River which connects Venice and Padua. To call on the villas, take the ACTV buses from p. Roma. **Villa Malcontenta** (also called "Villa Foscari"), built by Palladio on a temple-like plan, is one of the most revered in the western world. (Tel. (041) 547 00 12. Open May-Oct. Tues., Sat., and the first Sun. of the month 9am-noon. Admission L10,000.) **Mira** (also "Palazzo Foscari"), one of the most attractive villas on the Brenta, is now open for tours. (Tel. 42 35 52. Open Tues.-Sun. 9am-noon and 2-6pm. Admission including guided tour L7000, seniors L5000.) **Strà** (also "Villa Pisani"; tel. (049) 50 20 74) is renowned for its grand design by Figimelica and Preti and its interior decoration by Urbani and Giambattista Tiepolo. (Open Tues.-Sun. 9am-6pm. Admission L6000.) To get to Villa Malcontenta, take bus #16 from p. Roma (L700). To reach the other two villas, hop on the bus (not the direct line) that leaves about every half-hour for Padua (L1700-2400).

Entertainment

The weekly booklet *Un Ospite di Venezia* (free at tourist offices) lists current festivals, concerts, and gallery shows. Also ask for *Venice, 1993 Events.* There are concerts once or twice a week in the larger churches such as San Marco and the Frari. The **Teatro La Fenice** (tel. 521 01 61) has an excellent summer program, featuring mostly music, with many guest artists (admission L10,000-30,000, with *cartagiovane* half-price). The **Festival Vivaldi** takes place in early September. In summer, Vivaldi's music is also featured in a concert series in the church of **Santa Maria della Pietà**, where he was choirmaster.

For a historical introduction to the city, check out Steven Wolf's three-talk series *Venice in English: The Art and History of Venice,* an entertaining way to gain perspective on what's around. (Mon.-Sat. 7pm at the Hotel San Cassiano at S. Croce, 2232. Tel. 524 17 68.) From the Rialto Bridge, follow the signs to the Contemporary Art Museum Cà Pesaro until you find directions for the Hotel San Cassiano. Free aperitifs are served during the break. (Admission L10,000, students L7000. The third talk is free, but one should be sufficiently enlightening.)

Mark Twain called the **gondola** "an inky, rusty canoe," but only the gentry can really afford to ride one. The authorized rate starts at L70,000 for 50 minutes, which inflates to L90,000 after sundown, but mercenary gondoliers will frequently quote prices in the six-digit range. Rides are most romantic if procured about 50 minutes before sunset, and barely affordable if shared with as many people as possible. There is, however, a sneaky way to get a cheap ride just for the experience. There are several points along the Grand Canal where many Venetians need to cross, though there is no bridge. To solve the problem, *gondole* operate a short, cross-canal service. Each trip lasts only a minute or so, but this stand-up style of transportation averages a mere L500. (See *Traghetti* in Orientation for a complete listing of departure points.)

Venice's selection of nightclubs is paltry; most people seem to prefer mingling and dancing in the city's streets. Try **El Souk** (tel. 520 03 71), a swanky place in calle Contarini Corfù, 1056/A, near the Accademia. It's a kasbah run like a private club. (Open 10:30pm-4am. Cover L15,000 includes first drink.) Beyond this, the Lido is your best choice; there you can hit **Nuova Acropoli** (tel. 526 04 66), at lungomare Guglielmo Marconi (go right after you hit the beach).

The famed **Venice Biennale,** centered east on Canal San Marco, takes place every even-numbered year, with a gala exhibit of international modern art. (Admission to all exhibits L10,000, less to see individual bits and pieces.) The **Mostra Internazionale del Cinema** (Venice International Film Festival; tel. 520 03 11) is held annually from late August to early September. Tickets (about L10,000-30,000) are sold at the Cinema Palace on the Lido (where the main films are screened) and at other locations—some late-night outdoor showings are free. Contact the tourist office with questions about cinema. The city has a toll-free number—198.

After an absence of several centuries, Venice's famous **Carnevale** was successfully (in a monetary if not entirely festive sense) revived as an annual celebration in 1979. During the ten days preceding Ash Wednesday, masked Venetians and camera-happy tourists jam the streets. Write to the tourist office in December for dates and details, and be sure to make lodging arrangements months in advance. (Feb. 14-23 in 1993.) Venice's next most colorful festival is the **Festa del Redentore** (third Sun. in July). The Church of Il Redentore is connected with Zattere by a boat-bridge for the day, and a magnificent round of fireworks shoots off between 11pm and midnight on the Saturday night before. (July 18 in 1993.) On the first Sunday in September (Sept. 5 in 1993), Venice stages its classic **regata storica,** a gondola race down the Grand Canal, preceded by a procession of decorated gondolas. The religious festival **Festa della Salute** takes place on November 21 at Santa Maria della Salute, with another pontoon bridge constructed, this time over the Grand Canal.

Every year since 1954, Venice, Pisa, Genoa, and Amalfi have celebrated their collective heritage as former Mediterranean maritime republics with a historical pageant and regatta. Although the pageant caters somewhat to tourists, the **Regata delle Quattro Repubbliche Marinare** (Old Republics' Maritime Regatta) is taken quite seriously by the locals. The competition alternates between cities every four years. (Venice was host in 1992.)

The **Vogalonga** is a recently invented and very popular boating course of 30km, threading through the islands of the lagoon. For L5000, anyone in any kind of boat can row in this all-inclusive event, which takes place the Sunday before or after the Day of Ascension. Official race headquarters functions out of a pastry shop (tel. 521 05 44).

If **shopping** is your bag, a few caveats are in order. Do not make purchases in p. San Marco or around the Rialto bridge. Not only do shops outside these areas boast products of better quality and selection, they charge about half the price. Venetian glass is best bought toward the Accademia bridge from San Marco, and between the Rialto and the station in Cannaregio, though for fun you may want to look in the showroom at the glass-blowers' factory behind the Basilica of San Marco. The brochure accompanying the *cartagiovane* lists many shops offering reductions to pass-holders. For the most concentrated and varied selections of Venetian glass and lace, trips to the nearby islands of Murano and Burano, respectively, are in order. If you've got your heart set on a piece of Burano lace, a bit of crafty bartering with the shopkeeper could save you a third of the originally quoted price. *Vaporetto* #5 (L2200) serves Murano while #12 (L3300) serves both Murano and Burano. Both boats leave from the fondamenta Nuove stop.

Padua (Pádova)

In 602, Padua fell victim to marauding Lombards, and the once-prosperous Roman municipal center was reduced to a pile of rubble. Five and a half centuries later, the city had recuperated sufficiently to declare its independence from Byzantine and Lombard rule. The new republic quickly made up for lost time as, despite a series of tyrannical rulers and military defeats, Padua became one of the intellectual hubs of Europe. The "Bo" was founded in 1222, and is second in seniority only to Bologna among Italy's universities. Luminaries such as Dante, Petrarch, Galileo, and Copernicus all contributed to the collective genius, while the visual arts flourished, abetted by the visits of Florentines Giotto and Donatello and by the local brush of Mantegna. Reconstruction following World War II has given rise to a number of eyesores that threaten to engulf the once picturesque town, but the flourishing university and wealth of mid-millennium masterpieces safeguard Padua's reputation as a city of culture.

Orientation and Practical Information

Intercity buses and its location on the Venice-Milan and Venice-Bologna train lines make Padua a convenient destination any way you slice it. The train station is at the northern edge of town, just outside the 16th-century walls. A 10-min. walk down the corso del Popolo—which becomes corso Garibaldi—will take you into the modern, commercially minded heart of town. Another 15min. will bring you to **Il Santo**, the cathedral of Padua's patron saint, Anthony. **ACAP** city buses #3, 8, and 18 (L1000) will take you directly downtown. For L3000, you can purchase a 24-hr. tourist ticket valid for all urban lines.

Tourist Office: in the train station (tel. 875 20 77). Accommodations information and bus schedules for villas outside Padua. No accommodations service. Pick up a map and a copy of the sometimes-available entertainment brochure, *Padova Today. Domeniche in Bicicletto* gives superb bike itineraries. Open Mon.-Sat. 9am-6pm, Sun. 9am-noon. A 2nd office in the Museo Civico (tel. 875 11 53) is open daily 9:30am-12:30pm and 1:30-4:30pm.

Budget Travel: CTS, via Santa Sofia, 94/96 (tel. 875 17 19), at via Gabelli. Student IDs and travel information. BIJ and other train tickets. English spoken. Open Mon.-Fri. 9:30am-12:30pm and 3:30-7pm.

American Express: Tiare Viaggi, via Risorgimento, 20 (tel. 66 61 33), near p. Insurrezione. No exchange service. Open Mon.-Fri. 9am-1pm and 3-7pm, Sat. 3-7pm.

Post Office: corso Garibaldi, 25 (tel. 820 85 17). Open Mon.-Fri. 8:15am-7:30pm, Sat. 8:15am-12:20pm. **Postal Code:** 35100.

Telephones: ASST, corso Garibaldi, 3 (tel. 65 17 60). Open 24 hrs. **SIP** (tel. 66 60 88), in the passageway by Caffè Pedrocchi. Open daily 8am-9:30pm. **Telephone Code:** 049.

Trains: p. Stazione (tel. 875 18 00), in the northern part of town at the head of corso del Popolo, the continuation of corso Garibaldi. To: Venice (every 15min., 30min., L3200, round-trip L4800); Verona (every hr., 1hr. 30min., L6500); Milan (every hr., 2hr. 30min., L17,100); Bologna (18 per day, 1hr. 30min., L8800). Open daily 7:20am-7pm. **Luggage Storage:** L1500. Closes for lunch 2-3:30pm.

Buses: ATP, via Trieste, 42 (tel. 820 68 11), near p. Boschetti, 5min. from the train station. To: Bassano del Grappa (every 30min.., 1hr. 15min., L5000); Vicenza (every 30min., 30min., L4200); Venice (every 30min., 45min., L4200); Strà (every hr., L1700). Buses operate roughly between the hours of 6am-9pm.

Bike Rental: in p. del Municipio at the Comune di Padova. To the right as you exit the train station. L1000 per hour, but you must have a car to leave as collateral.

English Bookstore: Draghi Libreria Internazionale, via Cavour, 17-19 (tel. 876 03 05). An alcove full of classics (including the *Let's Go* series). Open Tues.-Sat. 9am-12:30pm and 3:30-7:30pm, Mon. 3:30-7:30pm.

Laundromat: Fast Clean, via Ogni Santi, 6 (tel. 77 57 59), near the *portello* and the *segretaria* of the university. Take bus #7, 9, or 15. Self-service. 1-4kg L6500; 4-7kg L8500. Soap L500. Dryer L1000. Open Mon.-Fri. 9:30am-12:30pm and 4:30-8pm, Sat. 9:30am-12:30pm.

Swimming Pool: Stabilimento Comunale di Nuoto "A. S. Padova Nuoto," via Decorati del Valor Civile (tel. 68 13 00), south of Prato della Valle off via Cavalletto. Catch bus #5 or 22 at Prato della Valle and tell the driver you want to get off at the *piscina.* Open daily 9:30am-7pm; Sept.-May 9:30am-1pm. Admission L6000, Sun. L7000.

Emergencies: tel. 113. **Police:** via Santa Chiara (tel. 876 03 33). **Ufficio Stranieri** (Foreigners' Office), riviera Ruzzante, 13 (tel. 66 16 00). English interpreters available Mon.-Fri. 10am-12:30pm. **Hospital: Ospedale Civile,** via Giustiniani, 2 (tel. 821 11 11), off via San Francesco.

Accommodations

Cheap lodgings abound in Padua, but tend to fill quickly. If you can't get into the places listed below, try any of the hotels near **piazza del Santo,** or call 828 31 11 to check the availability of summer housing at Padua's university. In summer, start your search as early as at 7am.

Ostello Città di Padova (HI), via Aleardi, 30 (tel. 875 22 19), off via Camposampiero. Take bus #3, 8, or 12 from the station. Get off near the Basilica or Prato della Valle, a 10-min. walk to the hostel. Quiet location with large, immaculate, crowded rooms. Accommodating staff. English spoken. There's a cheap and friendly hostel bar in back—the best place to meet local travelers. Flexible 5-day max. stay. Open daily 8-9:30am and 6-11pm. Register and drop off your stuff any-time Mon.-Fri. Relaxed about daytime lockout and lights out. Curfew 11pm. L15,000 per person, hot showers and breakfast included. Dinner available in the bar (open same hours). *Primi* L3800, *secondi* L5000-7000. If out-of-the-way castles suit your imagination, consider staying at the hostel in Montagnana (see description under Near Padua).

Casa della Famiglia (ACISJF), via Nino Bixio, 4 (tel. 875 15 54), off p. Stazione. Go right as you leave the station—it's a small street to the left. Women under 29 only. Their reception office in the station is open daily until 5pm (tel. 364 57). The good sisters reserve the right to turn away "undesirables." Curfew 10:30pm. Modern and tidy doubles, triples, and quads about L17,000 per person.

Pensione Bellevue, via L. Belludi, 11 (tel. 875 55 47), off Prato della Valle. Gorgeous rooms over-looking ivy-covered courtyard. Singles L30,000, with bath L45,000. Doubles with bath L58,000.

Casa del Pellegrino, via Cesarotti, 21 (tel. 875 21 00), along the northern side of Sant'Antonio. Another quasi-institutional set-up. This 129-room place targets pilgrims to the adjoining basilica. Ascetic rooms. English spoken. Flexible midnight curfew. Singles L30,000, with bath L46,000. Doubles L47,000, with bath L67,000.

Hotel Verdi, via Dondi dell'Orologio, 7 (tel. 66 34 50), in the center of town. From the station take bus #6 and get off at Teatro Verdi stop. Kind proprietors tend clean, sunny rooms. Singles L30,000. Doubles L38,000. Showers included. Closes at midnight.

Albergo Pavia, via del Papafava, 11 (tel. 66 15 58), right down the street from the Pace. Rooms in front of the garden boast wooden floors; rooms in back have been recently renovated. Rooftop clotheslines where the management will let you have a corner for your laundry. Singles L30,000. Doubles L38,000.

Camping: Montegrotto Terme, strada Romana Apponanse, 104 (tel. 79 34 00). A 15km bus ride from Padua. L12,000 per person, L8000 per tent. Open Mar.-Oct.

Food

Markets are held on both sides of the Palazzo della Ragione. During the academic year, student *mense* pop up all over town, so ask around. You can sample a glass from the nearby Colli Euganei winery district, or try the sparkling *lambruschi* of Emilia Romagna. Two of the most distinctive whites are produced by **Nane della Giulia,** via Santa Sofia, 1, off via San Francesco, and **Spaccio Vini Carpanese,** via del Santo, 44 (tel. 305 81; open Mon.-Sat. 9-11:30am and 4-6pm). Delicious wines run L1000-2500 per glass.

Mensa Universitarià, via San Francesco, 122 (tel. 66 09 03). The most pleasant and convenient *mensa*. Come for the bulletin boards, helpful if you're looking for a used car or motorcycle or a summer sublet. Padovese students receive L3000 discounts on the full-meal price of L7000.

Al Pero, via Santa Lucia, 72 (tel. 365 61), near via Dante. Bustling neighborhood eatery with fantastic food. To visit Veneto without tasting *polenta* is a sin. Fulfill your vows by ordering the *salamini arrosti con polenta* (with small roasted sausages, L4000). *Primi* L3500, *secondi* L4500-5000. Wine L4000 per. Cover L1500. Open Sept.-July Mon.-Sat. noon-2:45pm and 7:15-10pm.

Ristorante Vecchia Padova, via Zabarella, 41 (tel. 875 96 80). Avoid the pricey dinnertime table service. At lunch, the same gourmet food can be relished cafeteria-style in the cheerful, air-conditioned dining room. Generous salad bar. Full meals with wine L13,000-16,000. Open Sept.-late July Tues.-Sun. noon-2:30pm and 7pm-midnight.

Alexander Bar, via San Francesco, 38 (tel. 65 28 84), off via del Santo, which runs roughly parallel to via Roma 2 blocks east. One hundred beers and about 60 types of *panini* (L2200-4000). Open late, so you can take your time deciding. Open Mon.-Sat. 8:30am-2am.

Sights

Despite four centuries of Venetian dominance, Padua proudly preserves its distinct civic identity, taking pride in the legend of its founding by the Trojan Antenor, in paying tribute to its local saint, the Franciscan Sant'Antonio (the patron saint of lost and found and target of an unbelievable number of hopeful pilgrims), and in its illustrious university. The frugal may buy a ticket good at most of the museums of Padua (**Cappella degli Scrovegni, Museo Civico, Orto Botanico, Palazzo della Ragione, Battistero del Duomo,** and the **Oratorio di San Giorgio).** It costs L10,000 (L7000 for students and groups), is available at any of the above sights, and is valid for one year.

The **Cappella degli Scrovegni** alone merits a pilgrimage to Padua. The chapel contains the master fresco cycle of the celebrated Florentine Giotto. Executed over the course of three years between 1303 and 1305, these thirty-six perfectly preserved panels illustrating the Redemption story are one of the most influential works of art from this period. Giotto's ability to realistically portray the third dimension was unprecedented in medieval art, and his achievements affected Italian painting for centuries to follow. (Open April-Sept. daily 9am-7pm; Oct.-March Tues.-Sun. 9am-6pm. Admission L8000. School groups L3000 per person. Tickets must be bought at the Museo Civico and are good for both the chapel and museum.) The adjoining **Museo Civico** houses an art gallery with Giorgione's *Leda and the Swan* and a Giotto crucifix.

Next door, the **Church of the Eremitani** boasts an imposing exterior and a beautifully carved wooden ceiling that was successfully reconstructed after a devastating bombing in 1944. Unfortunately, the cycle of frescoes by Andrea Mantegna that once rivaled the Giotto next door in innovative beauty were almost entirely lost. (Open Mon.-Sat. 8:15am-noon and Sun. 9am-noon and 3:30-6:30pm; Oct.-March Mon.-Sat. 8:15am-noon and Sun. 9am-noon and 3:30-5:30pm.)

A complex of buildings on p. del Santo pays homage to Il Santo, as Padua's patron is familiarly called. The **Basilica di Sant'Antonio** (tel. 66 39 44), where the saint is entombed, is a medieval architectural splurge, a blissfully absurd conglomeration of eight domes, a pair of octagonal campaniles, and some supporting minarets. The mecca of progressing pilgrims looking for everything from lost love to lost limbs, the church is perpetually packed. The rather garish brilliance of the frescoed arches of the interior provide an odd backdrop to Donatello's bronze sculptures on the high altar. These seven statues, watched over by the artist's *Crucifixion,* must be grouped together in the mind (their present arrangement dates to the mid-19th century) in order for one to appreciate the subtle interplay of their expressive postures. The **Cappella di San Felice** on the right displays the 14th-century works of Altichiero da Zevior, one of Giotto's preeminent students. Saint Anthony's tongue and jaw are contained in an appropriately head-shaped reliquary in the apse of the church. (Basilica open daily 6:30am-7:45pm; off-season 6:30am-7pm.)

The adjoining **Oratorio di San Giorgio** houses fine examples of Giotto-school frescoes, and the **Scuola del Santo** on the corner contains more excellent frescoes, including three by the young Titian. (Both open daily 8:30am-12:30pm and 2:30-6:30pm; Oct.-Nov. and Feb.-March 9am-12:30pm and 2:30-4:30pm; Dec.-Jan. 9am-12:30pm. Admission L1000 for each.)

In the center of p. del Santo sits Donatello's pioneering bronze equestrian statue of **Gattamelata,** a mercenary general remembered for his agility and ferocity in all fields (his name means "calico cat"). In true Renaissance spirit, Donatello modeled the statue after the Roman equestrian statue of Marcus Aurelius at the Campidoglio in Rome.

A verdant refuge lies a block away in the **Orto Botanico** (tel. 65 66 14), the oldest in Europe (est. 1545), where Goethe and other prurient vegophiliacs studied the sex lives of plants. (Open Mon.-Sat. 9am-1pm and 3-6pm, Sun. 9am-1pm; in winter Mon.-Sat. 9am-1pm. Admission L3000, students L1500.)

The **university** campus is scattered throughout the city but its headquarters is found in Palazzo Bò (tel. 828 31 11). (In Venetian dialect *bò* means steer or castrated bull and derives from the sign of the inn that formerly occupied the *palazzo's* site.) The **teatro anatomico** (1594), the first of its kind in Europe, hosted the likes of Vesalius and the Englishman William Harvey, who discovered the circulation of blood. Almost all Venetian noblemen received their mandatory instruction in law and public policy in the Great Hall, and the "chair of Galileo" is preserved in the **Sala dei Quaranta,** where the physicist used to lecture.

Caffè Pedrocchi (tel. 755 20 20), across the street, was the headquarters for 19th-century liberals who supported Mazzini. When it was first built, the *caffè's* famous neo-classical facade had no doors and was open around the clock; every university student was entitled to a free newspaper and a glass of water. The battle between students and Austrian police here in February 1848 was a turning point in the Risorgimento. Capture the spirit for the price of a cappuccino (L2200; open Tues.-Sun. 7:30am-1am).

Entertainment

Padua's nightlife is elusive; the best way to get the inside scoop on the goings on of the collegiate crowd is to keep your eyes peeled for posters around the university and to scan the *mensa* bulletin. The evening *passeggiata* fires up in p. Garibaldi and up via Cavour. The walkway is lined with *caffè*, Pedrocchi among them. The *caffè* in nearby p. delle Frutta also come to life at night, and prices here are a bit easier to stomach. Check the posters around Palazzo Bò or pick up a copy of the newspaper *Il Mattino* for concert and film listings. In July the city organizes the **Cinema Città Estate,** a film series presented in the Arena Romana (tickets about L6000). Call the tourist office (tel. 875 20 77) or the Assessorato di Turismo (tel. 820 15 30) for further information. On February 8, Padua celebrates the **Festa della Matricola,** in which students and professors take the day off from classes, don ancient academic garb, and play practical jokes on each other.

Near Padua

The **Colli Euganei** (Eugan Hills), southwest of Padua, offer a feast for the senses. Padua's tourist office has pamphlets suggesting various itineraries. The volcanic hills revel not only in rich soil, the consequent richness of their wines, and hot mineral springs, but in an abundance of extraordinary accommodation options as well. For an inexpensive tryst with nature, contact the **Agritourist** office at via Mártiri della Libertà, 9 (tel. 66 16 55), in Padua for information on staying in a true-as-dirt hillside farm. Most of the participating farms offer a bed in a double or triple for about L25,000, including breakfast and showers. If you've always dreamed of life in a castle, realize your regal aspirations with a night at the **Youth Hostel (HI)** in **Montagnana.** The town is just outside of the *colli,* an hour by bus from either Vicenza or Padua (round-trip L10,000). The hostel (tel. (0429) 81 07 62) is a 70-bed affair within the Rocca degli Alberi, one of the town's two turreted edifices. For L12,000, enjoy a soft bed and hot showers under the auspices of a warm-hearted management. The Montagnana **tourist office** is in p. Maggiore (tel. (0429) 813 20). Take the bus to Pojana and walk the two or three kilometers.

Treviso

Treviso means "three faces" and, while the name may be without historical significance, it seems particularly well-suited to this provincial capital. The tourism industry promotes the first two faces, *città d'acque* (city of water) and *città dipinta* (painted city). On the water side, rivulets from the Sile loop through town, disappearing only to resurface where least expected, and as for the paint, the frescoed facades of the buildings that line the city streets still display hints of their former glory. The third face of Treviso needs no glossy brochures to catch the visitor's eye: Treviso is rolling in dough. Benetton was born here, and though there are only four official outlets in town, Benetton's lucre-laden wings hover over the whole province. For those of you who wish to buy your B's from the source, a warning: buy big. For Treviso is also the birthplace of that most dastardly of desserts: *Tiramisù.*

Orientation and Practical Information

Treviso lies a half-hour inland from Venice. The historic center is contained within the old city walls which are bordered alternately on the inside and outside—sometimes both—by flowing water. Via Roma is the inevitable entrance to town, and a curving street that changes names at each bend eventually leads to p. dei Signori, the geographic and social center of Treviso. A stroll down pedestrian-dominated via Calmaggiore will take you to the *duomo*.

Tourist Office: via Toniolo, 41 (tel. 54 06 00 or 54 76 32). Via Roma becomes corso del Popolo as you cross the Fiume Sile; take this to p. della Borsa, easily identified by the face-off of rival banks. Via Toniolo is to the right. An abundance of glossy literature—choose from a dozen equally beautiful brochures, but don't miss *Treviso Città Dipinta* which includes a walking itinerary of the best-preserved exterior fresco-work. There's also info galore on the Ville Venete (see Central Veneto below). Open Mon.-Fri. 8:30am-12:30pm and 3-6pm, Sat. 8:30am-noon.

Post Office: p. Vittoria, 1 (59 72 07). Stamps and Fermo Posta at #1. Open Mon-Sat. 8:15am-7:30pm. **Postal Code:** 31050.

Telephones: SIP, via XX Settembre, 1. Between p. della Borsa and p. dei Signori. Open Mon.-Sat. 9am-12:30pm and 3-7:30pm. **Telephone Code:** 0422.

Trains: p. Duca d'Aosta (tel. 54 13 52), at the southern end of town. Treviso lies on the Venice-Udine line. To: Venice (every 30min., 30min., L2400); Udine (every 30min., 1hr. 30min., L8800); Milan (every hr., 3hr. 30min., L18,700). **Luggage Storage:** L1500, open daily 6am-8:30pm.

Buses: lungo Sile Mattei, 21 (tel. 54 58 47 or 54 62 68), to the left just before corso del Popolo crosses the river. Comprehensive service throughout the Veneto and to the villas. To: Padua (every 30min., L6700); Vicenza (every 30min., L5800); Bassano (9 per day, L5100); Ásolo (15 per day, L4400).

Emergencies: tel. 113. **Hospital: Unit Sanitaria Locale,** tel. 40 50 50. Take bus #1.

Accommodations and Food

Your top choice for housing should be **Le Beccherie,** p. Ancilloto, 1 (tel. 566 01 or 54 08 71), behind the Palazzo dei Trecento, a genteel place with rustic woodwork and a tasty restaurant downstairs. Singles L30,000. Doubles L50,000, with bath L85,000. Otherwise, try **Al Cuor,** p. Duca d'Aosta, 1 (tel. 41 09 29), an impersonal hotel with a greater number of rooms (mostly doubles) and the convenience of sharing a *piazza* with the train station. Just turn right. Singles L28,000, with bath L49,000. Doubles L48,000, with bath L76,000.

Treviso is famous for its cherries, *radicchio* (red chicory), and *tiramisù,* a heavenly local creation of espresso-and-liquor-soaked cake topped with sweet cream cheese. Cherries peak in June, *radicchio* in December. If *primi* and *secondi* seem to be merely an inconvenient delay, begin with dessert at **Nascimben,** via XX Settembre, 3 (tel. 15 12 91), a posh *pasticceria* that will satisfy every gastronomic dream (open Tues.-Sun. 7am-2am). The unnamed liquor store (look for the *Birra Vini* sign) at via Mura di S. Teonista at the end of borgo Cavour is living proof of *radicchio's* celebrated status in the community; admire the artistically labeled bottles of *grappa al radicchio rosso* (L15,000). More conventional table wines begin at L3000 a bottle. For your basics, shop at **Pam Supermarket,** p. Borso, 18 (tel. 539 13) in the corner of the piazza behind Banca Nazionale del Lolvoro. (Open Thurs.-Tues. 8:30am-1pm and 3-7:30pm, Wed. 8:30am-1pm.) If your food needs are still unfulfilled, sit down at **Casa Mia,** p. S. Maria dei Battuti, 13, near p. S. Leonardo. Don't be fooled by the sign saying "la boutique della gastronomia," a joking reference to the clothing boutiques on either side. This tiny store serves up regional specialties at prices that will always be in style. Choose from their well-dressed vegetable and seafood salads-to-go (L1500-6000 per *etto)*. The Casa is open Tues.-Sat. 9am-1:30pm and 5-7:30pm, and Sun. 10am-1pm. **All'Oca Bianca,** vicolo della Torre, 7 (tel. 54 18 50), on a side street off central via Calmaggiore, is a casual, family-style *trattoria* in the thick of things. Delight in inexpensive drinks and pastries. Main courses average L10,000. (Open Thurs.-Tues. 8am-4pm and 6pm-midnight.)

Sights

The **Palazzo dei Trecento** (54 17 16), which abuts p. dei Signori loudly asserts Treviso's successful reemergence from a 1944 air raid (on Good Friday), which demolished half the town. Ascend the stairs on the outer wall and look for the clearly marked signs underfoot which mark the pre-bomb extension of the walls. Post-war reconstruction and new building blend harmoniously with the original townscape, and spiraling prosperity allows the city to devote its resources to endless restoration. (Open Mon-Sat. 8:30am-12:30pm. Free.)

Treviso is known not only for its exterior frescoes, but for interior ones as well, most notably those of Tomaso da Modena, Giotto's star pupil, who did little work outside Treviso. A sample of his work can be seen in the Romanesque **Chiesa di Santa Lucia,** also in p. Monte. The adjacent church of San Vioto houses damaged Veneto-Byzantine frescoes from the 12th century.

Back in p. dei Signori, one can join in via Calmaggiore's endless *passeggiata* and stroll beneath the arcades to the seven-domed, patchwork-style **duomo.** The original structure was erected in the 12th century and bore an understandable resemblance to the contemporaneous church of San Giovanni Battista (the Baptistry) next door before undergoing six centuries' worth of modifications. The most famous addition is the **Cappella Malchiostro** which was inserted in 1519 and contains frescoes by Pordenone and Titian's *Annunciation.* The combination is as strange as it is beautiful, for the two artists were sworn enemies. (Open daily 8:15am-12:30pm and 3-8pm.)

From p. del Duomo, via Risorgimento leads to the large Dominican church of **San Nicolò.** The mammoth, 14th-century brick structure sports a triple apse, along with some frescoed saints by Tomaso da Modena. The grandiose rendering of St. Christopher is believed to be the work of Antonio da Treviso. Don't miss da Modena's engaging take of forty high-profile Dominicans in the *Seminario Vescovile* (tel. 54 17 16) next door; each portrayal is remarkably individual and expressive. (Open in summer Mon.-Fri. 8am-noon and 3:30-7pm; in winter Mon.-Fri. 9am-noon and 3-5:30pm. Free.)

The **Museo Civico** at borgo Cavour, 22 (tel. 513 37) houses Titian's *Sperone Speroni* and Lorenzo Lotto's *Portrait of a Dominican,* conveniently hung in the same room. The ground floor protects Treviso's archeological finds, most impressive among which are the 5th-century BC bronze discs from Montebelluna. (Museum open Tues.-Sat. 9am-noon and 2-5pm, Sun. 9am-noon. Admission L1000.)

From the museum, head up via Caccianiga to the nearly intact northern wall. The pathway on top of the wall affords a pleasant walk to the other side of town. Via Manzoni meets with via San Francesco leading to the Romanesque-Gothic church of that name. The church's main attractions are two more frescoes by Tomaso da Modena.

The Tomaso da Modena tour finishes up with his greatest work in the church of Santa Caterina. Via Manzoni becomes via Carlo Alberto and leads to within eyeshot of the deconsecrated church. The magnificent fresco cycle located here was closed for restoration in 1992; check with the tourist office.

Bassano del Grappa

At the foot of imposing Monte Grappa, secluded Bassano del Grappa is a hideaway for refined Italian and Austrian tourists. Lofty tile-roofed, flower-trimmed buildings cluster around the Brenta, a rushing Alpine torrent in winter and a refreshing green river in summer. Mushrooms, wrought iron, pottery, *grappa* brandy, and the emblematic covered bridge have all earned the city fame, but Bassano is known, above all, as the birthplace of the 16th-century painter Jacopo da Ponte (Bassano).

Practical Information

Tourist Office: largo Corona d'Italia, 35 (tel. 243 51). From the station, walk down via Chilesotti, across the larger viale delle Fosse, and through the gap in the stone wall to the new office complex. The tourist office is the older, detached building to the right. Well-informed staff will inundate you with Bassano reading. The monthly, trilingual *Bassano Mese* is invaluable. Bicyclists and motorists looking to tackle the region will benefit from *Bici e Vai,* an itinerary-packed brochure of the nearby towns. Open Mon.-Fri. 9am-12:30pm and 3-6:45pm.

Post Office: (tel. 221 11), on via XI Febbraio, at the southern end of the city near the *duomo.* Open Mon.-Fri. 8:15am-7:45pm, Sat. 8:15am-6:40pm. **Postal Code:** 36061.

Telephones: Caffè Danieli, p. Garibaldi (tel. 293 22). Open daily 7am-9pm. **Telephone Code:** 0424.

Trains: at the end of via Chilesotti (tel. 250 34), a couple blocks from the historic center. To: Padua (11 per day, 1hr., L3900); Venice (15 per day, 1hr., L5000); Trent (8 per day, 2hr., L7200); Vicenza via Cittadella (8 per day, 2hr., L3200).

Buses: in p. Trento (tel. 250 25). As you come up via Chilesotti, turn left on viale delle Fosse. More direct and much more frequent than trains. To: Padua (every 30min., L5000); Vicenza (every 30min.., L3600); Masèr (6 per day, L2900); Asiago (5 per day, L4400); Maróstica (every hr., L1500); Thiene (every hr., L2900).

Bike Rentals: Signora Ernesto at the **Cooperativo Feracina,** via delle Fosse (tel. 202 44), near a big park.

Emergencies: tel. 113. **Police:** via Cá Rezzonico (tel. 21 22 22). **Hospital: Ospedale Civile,** viale delle Fosse, 43 (tel. 21 71 11).

Accommodations and Food

Low-budget hotels seem to be in danger of extinction in Bassano. Reserve ahead or consider accommodations elsewhere—the town makes a perfect daytrip.

Albergo Nuovo Mondo, via Vittorelli, 45 (tel. 52 20 10), near p. Garibaldi. The central location and regal, if faded, decor justify the added expense. Singles L28,000, with bath L40,000. Doubles L45,000, with bath L60,000.

Locanda Hotel Bassanello, via Fontana, 2 (tel. 353 47), on the other side of the tracks. Family-run; inexpensive rooms. Singles L25,000. Doubles L38,000, with bath L55,000. Breakfast L5000. Closed Sat.

Ostello Asiago (HI), via Costalunga, 9/10 (tel. (0424) 46 27 77) in the town of Asiago, a 25km bus ride from Bassano. L16,000 covers bed, breakfast, and hot showers in this former ski lodge. Unfortunately open only half the year and the management doesn't necessarily adhere to the printed schedule. Open Jan.-March and June 20-Sept. 10.

The town's most spirited claim to fame is *grappa,* a potent liquor distilled from the seeds and skins of grapes. For authenticity, buy a bottle from the **Nardini** distillery by the Ponte degli Alpini. The distillery was founded in 1779 and is the oldest of its kind. Bassano is also famous for its white asparagus. Depending on the season, this and other produce can be purchased at the **open-air market** on Thurs. and Sat. 8am-1pm in p. Garibaldi. For sumptuous cooked food on the run, try the gourmet, deli-style fare at **Venzo** on via da Ponte or **Guido Merlo** around the corner at via Roma, 15.

Al Saraceno, via Museo, 60 (tel. 52 25 13). A local hangout with seafood specialties and an impressive pizza repertoire. *Primi* L5000-7000, *secondi* L5000-12,000. Pizza L4500-7000. Cover L2000. Open Tues.-Sun. 10am-2:30pm and 5:30pm-1am.

Mensa Ferroviaria, via de Blasi, 9 (tel. 291 50), to the right as you exit the train station. A windowless cafeteria with pink tablecloths and plenty of spirit. Full meals only L7500. Open daily 11am-3pm and 6-10pm.

Ottone Birraria, via Matteotti, 50 (tel. 222 06). Runs the gamut from Hungarian goulash (L12,000) to hot club sandwiches (L5000-7000) to a more elegant *menù.* Pasta L8000. Open Wed.-Sun. 9:30am-3:30pm and 6:30pm-1:30am, Mon. 9:30am-3:30pm.

Sights and Entertainment

Bassano's charm is epitomized in the small **Ponte degli Alpini,** a covered wooden bridge dating from 1209 and redesigned by Palladio (1568-70) to resemble a fleet of ships anchored in midstream. The bridge acquired its name, a tribute to the Alpine soldiers who gave their lives in the defense against Austrian and German attacks on Mt.

Grappa, after World War I. Save one or two hours to stop by the **Museo Civico** in p. Garibaldi (tel. 222 35). The museum's collection bespeaks the genius of the local da Ponte (better known under their adopted name Bassano), one of the later Renaissance's great painting families. The most illustrious member of the family, Jacopo da Bassano (1517-1592), won accolades for his luminous *Flight into Egypt* and the gentle *St. Valentine Baptizing St. Lucilla.* The museum also contains sculptures and chiaroscuro sketches by Antonio Canova (1757-1822), the master of neoclassicism and toast of Europe for most of his career. (Open Tues.-Sat. 10am-12:30pm and 2:30-6:30pm, Sun. 10am-12:30pm. Admission L2000, students L1000.)

Next door looms the Romanesque-Gothic church of **San Francesco,** completed in the early 14th century. The spacious interior unfortunately has few traces left of the original frescoes, but the *Madonna and Child* by Lorenzo Martinelli beneath the arches of the entrance has recently been restored. On the altar rests a wooden sculpture of Christ by Guariento of Padua (1400).

For information on local events, consult the calendar in *Bassano Mese,* and inquire at the tourist office about the summer concert series in the villas of the Veneto.

Near Bassano

Before World War I, Bassano was known simply as Bassano Veneto. The city assumed a new name after the war to honor the Italian soldiers who died defending the strategic mountain nearby. The mountain figured significantly again in the subsequent World War, this time as the venue of a bloody battle against fascist forces. On the summit of Mt. Grappa stands an eerie war memorial honoring the soldiers that died during WWI. Less conspicuous, but more impressive, are the tunnels that were carved into the mountain by the Italian Engineer Corps in 1918. The subterranean passageways slice through over 5km of the mountain's interior.

Ten kilometers from Bassano are the **Oliero Grotte,** four caves open for public exploration (March-Oct. Tues.-Sun.). Pick up a brochure at the Bassano tourist office or call the *grotte* directly (tel. 993 63 or, during office hours, 999 91). Groups may book visits during other periods of the year, but if it's raining you'll need a Plan B; the caves lack a modern drainage system and scuba diving is not allowed.

Vicenza

This quiet provincial city boasts one of the highest average incomes in Italy, thanks to a recent boom in high-tech manufacturing and services that now augments the traditional industries of textiles and gold-working. Vicenza is most renowned, though, as the city of architect Palladio (Andrea di Pietro, 1508-1580), whose extremely influential designs--Renaissance interpretations of the classical Roman canon--mingle with Venetian Gothic on the city's streets.

Orientation and Practical Information

Vicenza lies in the heart of the Veneto. The train station is in the southern part of town. **AIM** city buses #1 and 7 run to the center of town and p. Matteotti (L1000). Next to the train station is the intercity **FTV** bus station. To walk into town, orient yourself with a glance at the helpful map outside the station and set out on viale Roma. Take a right on corso Palladio (the central street), and turn right; p. Matteotti is at the other end, 10 minutes away.

Tourist Office: p. Matteotti, 12 (tel. 32 08 54), next to the Teatro Olimpico. Provides a map of the Venetian villas and information on how and when to visit them. For the disabled, there's a city map of wheelchair-accessible facilities. Open Mon.-Fri. 9am-12:30pm and 2:30-6pm, Sun. 8:30am-12:30pm; mid-Oct. through mid-March Mon.-Fri. 2-5:30pm.

Budget Travel and Car Rental: AVIT, viale Roma, 17 (tel. 54 56 77), before you reach the supermarket PAM. BIJ/Transalpino tickets. Avis and Hertz rental cars. Open Mon.-Fri. 8:30am-12:30pm and 3-7pm, Sat. 9:30am-12:30pm.

Post Office: contrà Garibaldi (tel. 32 24 88), near the *duomo*. Stamps at window #11; Fermo Posta at #6. Open Mon.-Fri. 8am-7:30pm, Sat. 8am-1pm. **Postal Code:** 36100.

Telephones: SIP, p. Giuseppe Giustu, 8 (tel. 99 01 11), off corso SS. Felice e Fortunato. Open daily 9am-1pm and 3-7pm. After 7pm, go to **Ristorante La Taverna,** p. dei Signori, 47 (tel. 54 73 26). Open until 1am. **Telephone Code:** 0444.

Trains: p. Stazione (tel. 32 50 45), at the end of viale Roma. To: Venice (every 30min., 1hr., L5000); Padua (every 30min., 30min., L3200); Milan (every 30min., 2-3hr., L13,800); Verona (every 30min., 30min., L4300). **Luggage Storage:** L1500, open daily 6am-10pm.

Buses: FTV, viale Milano, 7 (tel. 32 31 30), to the left as you exit the train station. To Bassano (every hr., L4100); Asiago (every hr., L5100); Padua (every 30min., L4200); Thiene (every 30min., L3300); Schio (every 30min., L3300); Montagnana (3 per day, L4900). All buses run approximately 6am-9:30pm.

Swimming Pool: Piscina Comunale, via Giurato, 103 (tel. 51 37 83), northwest of town, near the U.S. army base. Open Mon.-Fri. 10am-7pm, Sat.-Sun. 9am-7pm. Admission L4800. Also at via Ferrarin (tel. 92 47 31). Open Mon.-Fri. 10am-6:30pm, Sat.-Sun. 9am-6:30pm. Admission L5000, under 18 L4000.

Emergencies: tel. 113. **Police:** via Muggia, 2 (tel. 50 77 00). **Medical Emergency:** tel. 99 31 11. **Hospital: Ospedale Civile,** viale Rodolfi, 8 (tel. 99 31 11).

Accommodations

Vicenza's bourgeois inclinations render it an unpromising home for inexpensive *pensioni*. To compound the problem, many establishments close for vacation in early August, and most are packed in September during the annual architecture course. Consider the youth hostels in Verona or Asiago (see Bassano del Grappa).

Hotel Vicenza, stradella dei Nodari, 5/7 (tel. 32 15 12), off p. Signori in the alley across from Ristorante Garibaldi. Meticulously scrubbed and centrally located. Management makes room for you to store your luggage after check-out. The babble of voices in the square, however, continues to the wee hours of the morning and is hardly a lullaby. Singles L30,000, with bath L45,000. Doubles L46,000, with bath L70,000.

Albergo Alpino, borgo Casale, 33 (tel. 50 51 37), near the stadium. Bland but acceptable. Singles with bath L25,000. Doubles L40,000, with bath L50,000. Includes breakfast. Closed 2 weeks in Aug.

Albergo Due Mori, contrà Do Rode, 26 (tel. 32 18 86), around the corner from Hotel Vicenza. Bright, sparkling, newly furnished rooms. Singles with bath L50,000. Doubles L65,000.

La Conchiglia D'Oro, viale Trissino, 62 (tel. 50 42 02), most easily reached by bus #3 or 15 which stop right in front. Spotless, modern rooms in a family-run organization that gets everyone involved. Phone in advance to check on vacancy if you're planning to arrive on a Monday. However, they don't take reservations. Doubles with bath L54,000. Triples with bath L68,000.

Camping: Campeggio Vicenza, strada Pelosa, 241 (tel. 58 23 11), out past the main U.S. army base. Take bus #1 from the train station (20min.). L6800 per person. L8000 per tent, with car L16,000.

Food

Produce is marketed outdoors every day in p. dell'Erbe behind the basilica, and on Tuesday and Thursday mornings you can hunt for edibles among the bizarre clothes that are sold in the central *piazza*. Thursday's market is the biggie, winding throughout the town. Cheese, chicken, and fish tend to proliferate in p. del Duomo. For more staid shopping, turn to **Supermercato PAM,** viale Roma, 1 (open Mon.-Tues. and Thurs.-Sat. 8:30am-1pm and 2:30-7:30pm, Wed. 8:30am-1pm).

Righetti, p. del Duomo, 3 (tel. 54 31 35), with a better marked entrance at contrà Fontana, 6. Self-service with reasonable prices and great ambience. *Primi* L3000, *secondi* L5000, and a L500 cover that includes unlimited bread. Open. Sept.-late July Mon.-Fri. noon-2:30pm and 7-10pm.

Al Bersagliere, contrà Pescheria, 11 (tel. 32 35 07), off p. Erbe. A hole-in-the-wall with great prices and a relaxed, if inelegant, atmosphere. *Primi* L3500-5000. *Secondi* L5000-10,000. Cover L1500. Open Mon.-Sat. 8am-2am.

Al Grottino, p. Erbe, 2 (tel. 32 34 94), tucked away under the basilica. Sample local wines for L1600-3000 per glass in this cave-like *enoteca* while whetting your appetite with petite sandwiches (*panini*) for L1000-2000. Open Mon.-Sat. 8am-2pm and 4pm-2am.

Sights

Piazza dei Signori is the town center; it was the town's forum when Vicenza was Roman and the town's showpiece when it was Venetian. Palladio began and ended his architectural career in this square; his treatment of the **basilica** first made the young architect famous. In 1546, Palladio's patron, the wealthy Giovan Giorgio Trissino, agreed to fund his proposal to shore up the collapsing Palazzo della Ragione, a project that had frustrated some of the foremost architects of the day. Ingenious variation of pilaster widths in the twin *loggie* masks with Renaissance harmony the irregular Gothic structure beneath. Palladio continued to work on the basilica until his death. Look at the **Torre di Piazza** next door to get an idea of the basilica's former appearance. (Basilica open Tues.-Sat. 9:30am-noon and 2:30-5pm, Sun. 9:30am-noon.)

Across the *piazza*, the **Loggia del Capitano** illustrates a later Palladian style. Palladio left the facade unfinished at his death, having completed only the three bays and the four sets of gigantic columns. The two symbolic columns of Venice complete the *piazza*.

Behind the Loggia del Capitano, the **Palazzo del Comune** faces **corso Palladio,** Vicenza's main street. Vicenzo Scamozzi's precise design for the *palazzo* demonstrates a much sharper interpretation of classical architecture than that embodied in the buildings of Palladio, his mentor. Corso Palladio, lined with Renaissance *palazzi,* runs the length of Vicenza, from Porta Castello in the east to the Teatro Olimpico on the banks of the Bacchiglione River. In p. Castello, a medieval gate is all that remains from the castle that once guarded the town's entrance. In front of the gate, on the left, the two bays of the **Palazzo Porto-Breganze** are an imposing fragment of the structure begun by Scamozzi according to Palladio's designs. Scamozzi did manage to finish the **Palazzo Bonin,** also designed by Palladio (at #13 on the right-hand corner of corso Palladio).

Contrà Vescovado leads out of the *piazza* next to Palazzo Porto-Breganze to the **duomo,** a large Gothic structure in brick with a graceful apse and a Palladian cupola. The **Casa Pigafetta** on nearby via Pigafetta hints that Palladio wasn't the only architect to influence Vicenza; this unique early Renaissance house successfully fuses Gothic, Spanish, and classical styles.

Farther south, on the banks of the Retrone near Ponte San Michele, stands the **Palazzo Civena,** an early Palladian home.

The area north of corso Palladio is crammed with Renaissance *palazzi,* each striving to outdo its neighbors in conspicuous expenditure. For more Palladio, try the **Palazzo Valmarana-Braga,** corso Fogazzaro, 16, the sculpted figures on the corners distinguish it from its neighbors. Vasari considered Palladio's unfinished **Palazzo da Porto-Festa** on contrà Porti the most magnificent of all, but others prefer the other two on the street, either the grandiose **Palazzo Porto-Barbaran** or the **Palazzo Thiene,** a felicitous blending of Palladio's and Lorenzo da Bologna's architectural genius. The **Palazzo Schio** is a refreshingly non-Palladian masterpiece.

At the far end of corso Palladio, on what was once a lawn sloping to the river, Palladio built the villa-like **Palazzo Chiericati** which now houses the well-stocked **Museo Civico** (tel. 32 13 48). The collection in the *pinacoteca* on the first floor includes some of Bassano's best endeavors, works by Bartolomeo Montagna (notably *Madonna Enthroned),* a Memling *Crucifixion,* Tintoretto's *Miracle of St. Augustine,* and a rare and refined *Madonna* by Cima da Conegliano. (Open Tues.-Sat. 9:30am-noon and 2:30-5pm, Sun. 10am-noon. Admission L4000, Sun. L3000. Admission good for the Teatro Olimpico.)

The nearby **Teatro Olimpico** (tel. 32 37 81) embodies the same classicism cultivated by the 16th-century *palazzo*-building patrons. The *Accademia Olimpica,* as the noble literati called themselves, met in the pseudo-Roman theater for performances of their own plays. The city still hosts productions here every year June through September, with both local and imported talent. (Open Mon.-Sat. 9:30am-12:20pm and 3-5:30pm,

Sun 9:30am-12:20pm; Oct. 16-March 15 Mon.-Sat. 9:30am-12:20pm and 2-4:30pm, Sun. 9:30-12:20pm. Admission L4000, Sun. L3000.)

Entertainment

Manifestazioni 1992, available at the tourist office, will guide those in search of high culture. Besides the performances in the **Teatro Olimpico** (tel. 32 37 81; admission L15,000-40,000, students L12,000-20,000), there is the summer concert series **Concerti in Villa.** Check with the tourist office for the foreign film series. Vicenza hosts **jewelry fairs** in January, June, and September. For a wider range of options, ask for a copy of *Informacittà.*

Dance clubs promote big nights by leaving cards in McDonald's-caliber fast food joints; movie and club listings are posted where corso Palladio passes under the arch at p. Castello.

Near Vicenza

Though most of the Palladian villas scattered through the Veneto are a bit of a strain to get to (see Ville Venete below), there are a few great villas close to town. Goethe considered the **Villa La Rotonda** (also called Villa Capra; tel. 32 17 93; walk from town or take bus #8 or 13 from near the station) one of the most magnificent architectural achievements ever. Everyone seems to have agreed—this villa was a model for Palladian buildings in France, England, and the U.S., most notably Jefferson's Monticello. (Interior open March 15-Oct. 15 Wed. only. Exterior open Tues.-Thurs. 10am-noon and 3-6pm. Admission L5000, to the exterior L2000.) Palladio's unfinished **Villa Thiene** (tel. 55 68 99 or 55 90 09) is stately and a bit forlorn, remaining aloof despite the encroaching suburbs of Quinto Vicentino. (Open Mon.-Sat. 8:30am-12:30pm. Free.)

Central Veneto

The arc of land stretching from Treviso through Bassano del Grappa to Vicenza makes up the heartland of the Veneto. This region happily bore the brunt of the celebratory Venetian decoration of the *terra firma,* leaving a choice collection of indefensible castles, strikingly charming towns, and Renaissance villas. Two small train lines run through the region, one linking Treviso to Vicenza by way of Castelfranco Veneto and Cittadella, and the other traveling north from Padua through Castelfranco to Bassano del Grappa. Most of the other sights in the region can be reached easily by bus, but the unwieldy schedules (see Treviso, Bassano, and Vicenza Practical Information) might prompt you to hop on a bike or moped, or gather a group to rent a car.

The Towns

The small hill town of **Ásolo** lies 16km east of Bassano, but buses are easiest to find in Treviso. Queen Caterina Cornaro, the 15th-century ruler of Cyprus, got the short end of the stick when big, bad Venice took her kingdom and grudgingly ceded her this one town as compensation. The diminutive realm, however, flourished under her court and attracted swarms of artists with its darling mountain base setting and refined atmosphere. Later Venetians would take over the town and populate it as a refuge from the summer heat of their city. The **Rocca,** a medieval fortress constructed on top of a Roman predecessor, commands a panoramic view of the lovely town below, including the queen's **castello** and garden.

The walled city of **Castelfranco Veneto** was founded by the citizens of Treviso at the end of the 12th century to keep out their rivals from the neighboring province of Padua. Within the walls, the cathedral and **Casa del Giorgione** displays works by the native-born teacher of Titian. In the *duomo* lies Giorgione's brilliant *Madonna and Child* (unfortunately in a locked chapel—track down the sacristan to see it). **Cittadella,** less than half an hour away, was Padua's rebuttal to Castelfranco. The *duomo* shows off the *Supper at Emmaus* by Jacopo Bassano, but the city's greatest claim to fame rests in its virtually intact 13th-century walls and ramparts. The **tourist office** is at Galleria Garibaldi (tel. (049) 597 09 86). Both Cittadella and Castelfranco lie along the Vicenza-Treviso local train line (16 per day, 25min. to Cittadella from Vicenza, 40min. to Castelfranco from Vicenza, L2100 and L2800 respectively).

Closer to Bassano is the fortress town of **Maròstica,** another altogether perfect medieval town complete with upper and lower castle and 13th-century walls. If you are in this corner of the world on the second weekend in September of an even-numbered year, don't miss the **Human Chess Game,** played between Vicenza and Bassano. In this reenactment of a match between two nobles played on an equally grand scale in 1454 for the heart of a fair maiden, human chess pieces in 15th-century costumes do battle on the giant checkerboard *piazza.* For information and reservations, contact the **Pro Loco** at 36063 p. Castello Inferiore (tel. (0444) 721 27).

Ville Venete

Venetian expansion to the mainland which began in the early 15th century provided infinite opportunity for Palladio's talents. As Venice's wealth accumulated and its maritime supremacy faded, its nobles began to turn their attention to the acquisition of real estate on the mainland. The Venetian Senate stipulated that they build villas rather than castles to preclude any possibility of becoming independent warlords. The architectural consequences were stunning: Veneto is now home to hundreds of the most splendid villas in Europe.

There are 3000 villas in the Veneto, but they are difficult to reach, have unpredictable schedules, and often allow tours of their exteriors only. Phone ahead or contact the **Amministrazione Provinciale Assessorato al Turismo** in Vicenza on via Gazzolle (tel. 39 91 55). The affable staff has mountains of well-written booklets on the villas. The tourist offices in Vicenza and Treviso provide good literature on Palladio's works, but they have written information only on the villas in their immediate provinces. The only complete map, *Ville Venete,* put out by the Istituto Geografico de Agostini and available at most newsstands and bookstores, is helpful but difficult to read. Check for *How to Visit the Villas of the Veneto,* at tourist offices (almost invariably out of stock).

The bus from Vicenza to Bassano stops at Thiene. Here, make the change to head for the tiny village of **Lugo** to see two famous Palladian villas at close range (5 per day, 2 on Sun., L3200). The simple **Villa Godi-Valmarana** (a.k.a. "Malinveri," tel. (0445) 86 05 61) was the architect's first. (Interior open March-Nov. Tues., Sat.-Sun., and holidays 2-6pm. Admission L5000). A few yards up the street is the more elegant and expansive **Villa Piovene** (tel. 86 14 81). The villa may be viewed only from the outside; for a close look, pay L3000 to enter the wonderful park around it. (Open daily 2:30-7pm.)

Seven kilometers to the east of Ásolo lies the most famous of the villas, the **Villa Barbaro-Volpi,** at **Masèr.** Built in 1560 by Palladio, the building rests on a gentle hillside covered with pines. The elegant central pavilion is flanked by arcaded wings that hide unglamorous necessities such as stables, while adding grandeur to the facade. The interior is throroughly adorned with Paolo Veronese's splendid frescoes. At one end of the series of doorways running through the house, Veronese left a portrait of himself, and ever since there has been speculation that the distant woman who gazes at him was his mistress. Wander to the base of the hill to see the exquisite circular temple that Palladio built for the owners. (Interior open Tues., Sat.-Sun., and civic holidays 3-6pm; Oct.-May Tue., Sat.-Sun., and civic holidays 2-5pm. Admission L6000. Call (0423) 56 50 02 for more information.) Masèr is an easy bus trip from Bassano (6 per day, L2900).

Consummate your immersion in Palladian architecture with a train ride from Castelfranco to Fanzolo (on the Padua-Belluno line) to see **Villa Emo** (tel. (0423) 48 70 40). Considered along with Masèr to be one of the most characteristic Palladian villas, the interior frescoes balance fluently with the architecture and are the masterworkings G.B. Zelotti. (Open Feb.1 to mid-Dec. Sat. 3-6pm, Sun. and holidays 3-7pm. Admission L5000, groups L4000.)

Every summer an **entertainment series** of operas, ballets, plays, and musical concerts sparks life in Ville Venete. For information about plays, refer to the tourist offices of Recoaro Terme (tel. (0445) 751 58), Asiago (tel. (0424) 46 22 21), or Villaverla (tel. (0445) 85 60 73). For information about the opera, call the **Ufficio Opere Estate Festival di Roassano Veneto** (tel. (0424) 845 02).

Verona

> There is no world with Verona walls but purgatory,
> torture, hell itself. Hence banished is banish'd from
> the world, and world's exile is death ...
> > Romeo and Juliet

Maybe Shakespeare went a little overboard, but the city of rose-colored marble still casts a romantic spell with every full moon. There is a distinctly Venetian air in Verona, and in fact, Venice's Lion of San Marco ruled here for three centuries. But the city's artistic strength derives from its two-thousand-year stint as a major metropolis. Even during its formative years as a Roman colony, Verona was an important crossroads, and the remarkably well-preserved remains are tangible evidence of the colony's preeminence in the classical world. In the 13th and 14th centuries, Verona experienced another cultural heyday under the rule of the della Scala clan. A synthesis of statuesque remains and opulent *palazzi* defines today's Verona, whose gracious interweaving of past and present manifests itself best in the celebrated summer opera season held within the Arena, an amphitheater of epic proportions erected in 100 AD.

Orientation and Practical Information

Between piazza Brà and the aforementioned Arena beats the heart of the city, and corso Porta Nuova is the artery that leads south to the bus and train transportation. Most of the scenic portions of town are contained within the lazy loop of the ambivalent Adige River; several bridges enable you to cross to the other side. Piazza Brà is a 20-min. walk up corso Porto Nuova from the train station, or a ride aboard **AMT** bus #2. Bus tickets (L1000) are available at the booth across from the station, as are day passes (L2500).

Tourist Office: via Dietro Anfiteatro, 6 (tel. 59 28 28), which translates to "behind the amphitheater." Obliging, multilingual staff will locate anything for you on the free map, and distributes a trio of glossy, useful brochures. Accommodations consultations, but no reservations made. Open Mon.-Sat. 8am-8pm, Sun. 8:30am-1:30pm. An equally helpful branch awaits tourists in p. Erbe, 38 (tel. 803 00 86), on the end intersected by corso Borsari. Open Mon.-Sat. 8am-8pm.

Budget Travel: CIT, p. Brà, 2 (tel. 59 17 88). Student discounts on plane, train, and bus tickets, including Transalpino. Open Mon.-Fri. 9am-1pm and 3-7pm, Sat. 9am-1pm. **Centro Turistico Giovanile,** via Seminario, 10 (tel. 800 42 92), across the river off via Carducci, on the 3rd floor. Mellow staff sells student and hostel cards, BIJ tickets, and Transalpino tickets. Open Mon.-Fri. 3-7pm. **CTS,** largo Pescheria Vecchia, 9/A (tel. 803 09 51), near the Scaligeri tombs. The usual: IDs, Transalpino, BIJ, etc. Open Mon.-Fri. 9:30am-12:30pm and 4-7pm.

Currency Exchange: Cassa di Risparmio, p. Brà, centrally located on the corner of via Roma. Open Mon.-Fri. 8:20am-1:20pm and 2:35-4:05pm.

American Express: Fabretto Viaggi, corso Porta Nuova, 11 (tel. 800 90 40), a couple of blocks down on the left from p. Brà. Won't sell traveler's checks, but changes them at reasonable rates for no commission after 4pm. Open Mon.-Fri. 8:30am-12:30pm and 3-7pm.

Post Office: p. Poste (tel. 59 09 55), also known as p. Francesco Viviani, adjacent to p. Indipendenza near Ponte Nuovo. Stamps and Fermo Posta at #13, 14, and 16. Open Mon.-Sat. 8:15am-7:30pm. **Postal Code:** 37100.

Telephones: SIP, via Leoncino, 53, as you leave p. Brà. Open Mon.-Sat. 9am-12:30pm and 3-7:30pm. 24-hr. phone bank and *schiede* dispenser 3 doors down. **Telephone Code:** 045.

Trains: p. XXV Aprile (tel. 59 06 88), linked with p. Brà by corso Porta Nuova. To: Venice (every hr., 2hr., L8800); Milan (every hr., 1hr. 30min., L10,500); Bologna (every hr., 2hr., L8800); Trent (every hr., 1hr., L7200); and Rome (6 per day, 6hr., L36,900). **Currency exchange** open 7am-9pm, but with the commission they charge, you might as well just flush your traveler's checks down the toilet. **Luggage Storage:** L1500. Open 24hrs.

Buses: APT, p. XXV Aprile (tel. 800 41 29), across from the train station. To: Riva del Garda (every hr. 7:45am-6:45pm, L7400); Sirmione (every hr., L3500); Brescia (every hr., L3900); Montagnana (3 per day, L7800). Ticket window open daily 6am-8:30pm.

Taxis: tel. 53 26 66.

Car Rental: Hertz (tel. 800 08 32), at the train station. Be sure to ask for their "Affordable Europe Rates." L661,000 per week, tax included. Open Mon.-Fri. 8am-noon and 2:30-7pm, Sat. 8am-noon.

Bike Rental: Paolo Bellomi, via degli Alpini (tel. 800 70 40), opposite the arena off p. Brà. L4000 per hr., L15,000 per day. Open daily 9:30am-10pm; off-season 10am-7pm.

Swimming Pool: Centro Nuoto Piscina Coperta, via Col. Galliano (tel. for outdoor pool 56 78 25; indoor pool 56 76 22). Take bus #7 from p. Erbe or Castelvecchio to the beginning of corso Milano and ask for directions. Both pools are Olympic-sized. Olympic-caliber people-watching to boot, despite unflattering mandatory headwear. Open in summer daily 10am-8pm. Admission L5500, half-day L4000, over 60 or under 14 L3500.

English Bookstore: The Bookshop, via Interatto dell'Acqua Morta, 3 (tel. 800 76 14), across Ponte Navi and to the left. Many guides (including *Let's Go*) and phrase books, comforting classics, and even books for babies. Also a community bulletin board with occasional bargains of an unpredictable nature. Open Tues.-Fri. 9:15am-12:30pm and 3:30-7:30pm, Mon. 3:30-7:30pm, Sat. 9:15am-12:30pm.

Emergencies: tel. 113. **Police: Questura,** tel. 59 67 77. **Ufficio Stranieri,** lungoadige Porta Vittoria. Interpreter available Mon.-Fri. 8:30am-12:30pm. **Hospital: Ospedale Civile Maggiore,** borgo Trento, p. Stefani (tel. 93 11 11).

Accommodations

Make reservations during the opera months of July and August. Student-style accommodations are plentiful, cost the least, expand to take in extra people if necessary (especially the magnificent youth hostel), and neither impose an age limit nor require a hostel card.

Ostello Verona (HI), salita Fontana del Ferro, 15 (tel. 59 03 60), on the southern slope below Castel San Pietro. From the train station or downtown, take bus #2 (or #32, Mon-Sat. during the day or #59 after 8pm) across the river (on Ponte Nuovo), and get off in p. Isolo. Walk ahead to via Ponte Pignolo at the end of the *piazza*, turn right (you'll see the hostel sign), go to the end (3 blocks), then turn left, take the first right, and finally the first left. One of the most beautiful and well-run hostels in Europe, and the only one adorned with 15th-century frescoes. The restoration of the building, the Villa Algarotti-Francescati, has been a labor of love for Prof. Fiorenzo Scarsini. Read the posted explanations of the work-in-progress as you munch unlimited bread at breakfast. Rudi, the multilingual master chef, will even cater to herbivores if notified in advance, and fabulous Fabio (Fab Fab) has become legendary. You can also **camp** in the villa's garden. Rooms open at 6pm, but arrive earlier to register and drop off your stuff. Curfew 11pm, with special provisions for opera-goers. Hostel L13,000 per person, including hot showers, breakfast, and sheets that give starch new meaning. Camping L7000 per person, all-inclusive (L5000 without tent). Restaurant-caliber dinners L10,000.

Casa della Giovane (ACISJF), via Pigna, 7 (tel. 59 68 80), off via Garibaldi, accessible via the ubiquitous bus #2. From buses #3, 4, or 5, it is a 5-min. walk from p. della Vittoria. Women only. Spotless rooms (mostly doubles and triples) in an optimal location. Flexible lockout 9am-6pm. Curfew 10:30pm, unless you have opera tickets. L15,000 per person in 8-bed rooms. Singles L20,000. Bed in a double L19,000, in a triple L17,000. Women can also head to **Casa della Studentessa,** via Trezza, 16 (tel. 800 52 78), across the river and 5-10min. from the youth hostel. Take bus #1, 2, or 8 across Ponte Nuovo and walk down via Carducci, turn right on via San Vitale, and left on via Trezza. Cozy and respectable. Curfew 11pm, but they often stay open later, especially for operas and important concerts. Bed in a double L22,000, in a triple L20,000. Showers included. Reserve ahead.

Locanda Catullo, vic. Catullo, 1 (tel. 800 27 86), set off from via Catullo between 1/D and 3/A, off via Mazzini. Gorgeous rooms; some of their newly redone doubles have French doors and mini-terraces (L3000 more in summer). Singles L26,000. Doubles L35,000, with bath L55,000.

Locanda Volta Cittadella, via Volta Cittadella, 8 (tel. 800 00 77), near p. Cittadella. Spartan but clean rooms. Singles L27,000. Doubles L36,000.

Camping

Campeggio Castel S. Pietro, via Castel S. Pietro, 2 (tel. 59 20 37), over the hill from the hostel, just down and around the bend from the castle. Take bus #3 to via Marsala. Hot showers, a bar, and other conveniences. L5500 per person, L4000-7000 per tent depending on size, L3000 per car. Caravans not allowed. Open mid-June to mid-Sept.

Campeggio Romeo e Giulietta, via Bresciana, 54 (tel. 851 02 43), inconveniently located on the road to Peschiera de Garda. Take APT bus to Peschiera from train station (L1000); alert bus driver that you wish to get off at the campground. The last bus from Verona leaves at 8pm. Hot showers, plenty of space, grocery store, and swimming pool, but alas, no romantic balconies. L5200 per person, L6800 per tent. Open year-round.

Food

Verona is famous for its wines: *soave* (dry white), *valpolicella,* and *bardolino* (both red). This fecund area also supplies Italy with luscious peaches and other produce. The vendors in p. Isolo offer better prices than those in p. delle Erbe. Or visit **Supermarket PAM,** via Dei Mutilati, 3, near p. Brà off corso Porta Nuova. (Open Mon.-Tues. and Thurs.-Sat. 8:30am-7:30pm, Wed. 8:30am-noon.)

In the Center

Trattoria Fontanina, piazzetta Chiavica, 5 (tel. 803 11 33), down the street from the tombs of the Scaligeri. Streetside terrace. *Primi* L7000, *secondi* L8000-12,000. Cover L1500. Service 12%. Open Wed.-Sun. noon-2pm and 7-9:30pm, Mon. noon-2pm.

La Bottego di Nonno Francesco, via Leoni, 4 (tel. 59 67 37), near Ponte Navi. Gastronomic goodies to go. Open Mon.-Tues. and Thurs.-Sat. 8:15am-1:45pm and 4:30-7:45pm, Wed. 8:15am-1:45pm. Closer to the Arena, try **Élite Gastronomica,** corso Porta Nuova, 2 (tel. 803 00 74). Make a picnic of their tempting seafood salads in the shade of piazza Brà's park. Open Mon.-Tues. and Thurs.-Sat. 9am-1pm and 4-7:30pm, Wed. 9am-1pm.

Oreste dal Zovo, via S. Marco in Foro, 7/5 (tel. 803 43 69), off corso Porta Borsari. Congenial owner has shelves of every wine imaginable. Serve yourself *grappa* from a mini-barrel (L2500) and crunch on microscopic snacks (L100) or more substantial but still small *panini* (L1000).

Across the River

Unless the gravitational tug of the Arena proves overwhelming, cross the water to this university quarter when in search of satiation.

Nuovo Grottina, via Interrato dell'Acqua Morta, 38 (tel. 803 01 52), off via Carducci by Ponte Nuovo. A favorite with students during the school year, and priced to stay that way. Pizza L4500-8500. *Menù* L13,000. Wine L3000 per half-liter. Cover L1000. Open Fri.-Wed. 9:30am-2:30pm and 6pm-1am.

Trattoria Al Cacciatore, via Seminario, 4 (tel. 59 42 91), the 4th left off via Carducci, which begins at Ponte Nuovo. A genuine neighborhood joint with delicious food. *Primi* L3500, *secondi* L7500. Cover L1500. Open Mon.-Fri. 8:30am-2:30pm and 6:30-10pm, Sat. noon-2:30pm.

Trattoria dal Ropeton, via San Giovanni in Valle, 46 (tel. 300 40), below the youth hostel. Very authentic, very popular, and very hard to get the best courtyard tables. Consider reservations. *Primi* L6000, *secondi* L11,000. Cover indoors L1500, courtyard L2500. Open Wed.-Mon. 12:30-3pm and 7:30-11pm.

Il Grillo Parlante, vicolo Seghe San Tomaso, 10 (tel. 59 11 56), tucked in a tiny corner alley behind the old bus station in p. Isolo. Bright red doors and a tropical motif mark Verona's vegetarian hotspot. *Primi* L6000, *secondi* L6500-7000. Cover L2500. Open Fri.-Sun. and Tues.-Wed. noon-2pm and 7:30-10pm, Thurs. noon-2pm.

Sights

The majestic pink **Arena** (tel. 800 32 04) in p. Brà dates back to 100 AD, and among Roman amphitheaters it is surpassed in size only by the one at Capua and the Colosseum. The Arena's superb condition testifies to Verona's municipal pride. In the 16th century, a special committee was set up to restore the amphitheater, and the theater has been kept in healthy working order ever since. (Open Tues.-Sun. 8am-6:30pm; in opera season 8am-1:30pm. Admission L6000, students L1000.)

From p. Brà, via Mazzini takes you into **piazza delle Erbe,** the former Roman Forum. The center of the *piazza* holds the Madonna Verona fountain, installed by Cansignorio della Scala in 1368. At the far end rises the 1523 column of St. Mark, the symbol of four centuries of Venetian domination. Various *palazzi* and towers, dating from the 11th through 17th centuries, enclose the *piazza.* The **Gardello Tower,** built in 1370, stands between the imposing Baroque **Palazzo Maffei** and two buildings with frescoed facades and spacious terraces that Verona's first families, the Scaligeri (della Scala) and the Mazzanti, once called home. The medieval **Casa dei Mercanti** on the corner of via Palladio, with its crenellation and two-arched windows, merits a closer look. In the center of the *piazza,* almost hidden by fruit vendors' awnings, stands the Berlina—during medieval times, convicts were tied to the marble structure to be pelted with rotten fruit.

The **Arco della Costa,** called the "Arch of the Rib" for the whale rib hung from it, separates p. delle Erbe from **piazza dei Signori.** The delicate **Loggia del Consiglio** (1493), built in the Venetian Renaissance style, stands adjacent to the *prefettura.* The gray **Palazzo della Ragione** (Palace of Reason, a court of law built in 1193) stands on the corner. This densely knit brick and marble ensemble was the seat of the della Scala family dynasty for centuries. The Scala were a violent and dogged lot, as their names suggest: Cangrande (Big Dog) was the clan's head, succeeded by Mastino II (The Mastiff), and then Cansignorio (Head Dog). Yet, like many of their brutish peers, the della Scala were also sensitive patrons of the arts. Dante passed many months here as the guest of Cangrande, and eventually dedicated his *Paradiso* to the powerful warlord. A sculpture of the poet stands in the center of the *piazza.*

Through the arch at the far end of p. dei Signori lie the peculiar outdoor **Tombs of the Scaligeri,** further testimony to the Scala family temperament. A copy of the statue of Cangrande preens under a Gothic canopy. Big Dog, naked sword in hand, slouches arrogantly on his hollow-eyed steed. (The original resides in the Castelvecchio museum.) Over the door of the neighboring **Church of Santa Maria Antica** looms the tomb of Cangrande I. Indulge your literary curiosity by visiting the houses where Romeo and Juliet supposedly grew up. **Casa di Romeo,** long the home of the Montecchi family (model for the Montagues), may disappoint; the dilapidated building is now a coffee bar (around the corner from p. dei Signori at via Arche Scaligori, 2). At Casa Capuletti, via Cappello, 23, more commonly known as **Casa Giulietta** (tel. 803 43 03), you will find a tall, ivy-covered wall next to a balcony where you can wait your turn in line to brood where Juliet once did. Good luck spotting your Romeo among the tourists and trinket stands. The house, though more appropriately romantic than the Casa di Romeo, has less historic merit; the feuding dal Capellos (Capulets) never lived here. (Open Tues.-Sun. 8am-6:30pm. Admission L5000, students L1000.)

At the other end of via Arche Scaligeri, corso Sant'Anastasia will bring you to the Gothic **Basilica of Sant'Anastasia** whose interior bulges with art treasures. Don't miss Pisanello's *St. George Freeing the Princess* (in the Giusti Chapel at the end of the left transept), considered one of his best paintings, and the frescoes by Altichiero and Turone. Terra cottas by Michele da Firenze adorn most of the apse. Walk down via Duomo from the basilica to the **duomo,** decorated with medieval sculpture by local stone carvers. The first chapel to the left features Titian's ethereal *Assumption of the Virgin.* The **Biblioteca Capitolare** (tel. 59 65 16), the oldest library in Europe, maintains a priceless medieval manuscript collection, which shameless sinners can see by donning a specious scholarly visage to trick the priest. (Cathedral open daily 7am-noon and 3-7pm. Library open Mon., Wed., and Sat. 9:30am-12:30pm, Tues. and Fri. 9:30am-12:30pm and 4-6pm. Free.)

Over the Roman Ponte Pietra (across the Adige) bows the recently uncovered **Teatro Romano** (tel. 800 03 60), now a venue for Shakespearean plays. The theater was built during the Augustan and Flavian years at the foot of what is today called St. Peter's Hill. The Romans built a fortress on the hilltop; the current castle dates from the 19th-century efforts of the French and Austrians. There's a wonderful view of Verona from up here, especially in the evening. (Complex open Tues.-Sun. 8am-6:30pm, off-season and performance days Tues.-Sun. 8am-1:30pm. Admission L5000.)

At the bottom of the hill, the Interatto dell'Acqua Morta leads to the 15th-century **Church of Santa Maria in Organo.** Although Sammicheli made a significant contribution to the facade, the most delicate inlay work was completed by Giovanni da Verona. Behind the church the **Giardino Giusti** (tel. 803 40 29), a delightful 18th-century garden, beckons. (Open daily 9am-8pm. Admission L5000.)

The della Scala fortress, the **Castelvecchio** (tel. 59 47 34), was carefully reconstructed after devastation during World War II. The many-leveled interior is decked out with walkways, parapets, an extensive collection of sculptures and paintings including Pisanello's *Madonna and Child,* Luca di Leyda's *Crucifixion,* which balances passion and compositional rhythm, and works by Andrea Mantegna, Francesco Morone, Tintoretto, and Tiepolo. (Open Tues.-Sun. 8am-6:30pm. Admission L5000.) The **Scaligeri Bridge,** spanning the Adige from the *castello* to p. Sacco e Vanzetti, is the most impressive of the 15 bridges spanning the river.

Upstream from the Castelvecchio looms the church of **San Zeno Maggiore,** one of the finest examples of Italian Romanesque architecture. Built and expanded upon from the 10th to 12th centuries, the massive brick church of Verona's patron saint surpasses its more central counterparts in artistic wealth. The 48 panels of the 11th-century bronze doors depict scenes from the Old and New Testaments in bold relief. These doors, the first undertaken since antiquity, sparked a craze for bronze portals throughout Italy. The interior structure is notable for its wooden "ship's keel" ceiling and the spacious crypt area, where 42 columns create the impression of a forest. The altarpiece is an oft-stolen Renaissance work by Andrea Mantegna. Pay to light it up—its position makes it hard to see its splendid coloring on any but the brightest days. The two-story apse intersperses 12th-century carvings with capitals from Roman temples. (Open daily 8am-noon and 3-7pm.)

Entertainment

Verona has parlayed the romance of its pervasive rosy marble and vast Roman arena into the city's premier cultural event, as the not-so-ruined ruins come alive in July and August for an opera and ballet extravaganza. Ticket prices start at L22,000 for unreserved gallery seats. For more information, call 59 01 09 or 59 07 26, or go directly to arch #8 or 9 to make a reservation or a purchase (tel. 59 09 66 or 59 01 09). If you opt for general admission seating, be prepared to encounter crowds of operaholics who camp out up to two hours before the gates open to ensure for themselves marginally better views.

The **Teatro Romano** stages Shakespeare productions every summer—a tad odd in Italian (L17,000 for the cheapest seats). (Reserve ahead at arch #18. Open in season Mon.-Sat. 10:30am-1pm and 4-7pm. For information call 807 71 11, for reservations 59 00 89.) *Verona for You* (available at the tourist office) lists current exhibits and events.

Friuli-Venezia Giulia

Overshadowed by the heavily touristed cities of Veneto and the loftier mountains of Trentino-Alto Adige, Friuli-Venezia Giulia has traditionally received less than its fair share of recognition. Trieste has been the one long-standing exception to this rule, and today increasing numbers of beach-goers flock to the developing coastal resorts of Grado and Lignano, the least expensive on the Adriatic.

Friuli-Venezia Giulia was once a number of distinct provinces, as its mouthful of a name suggests. Successive invasions by Romans, Goths, and Lombards each left their mark upon the region until finally the local clergy unified around the Patriarchate of Aquileia and maintained autonomy from the church and other states from the 6th to 15th centuries. The entire region was then appropriated by the Venetian Republic, only to be reabsorbed, Venetians and all, into Austria-Hungary. The present region is the product of a union between Udihe, Pordenone, Gorizia, and Trieste which took place after World War II. The historical differences between these provinces, and the area's vulnerability to Eastern forces given its marginal geographic location in the north of Italy, combine to give Friuli-Venezia Giulia a hybrid character and culture. The mix of political intrigue and coffee-culture elegance brought by the Austro-Hungarian Empire attracted intellectuals of varied provenance to turn-of-the-century Friuli: James Joyce lived in Trieste for 12 years, during which he wrote the bulk of *Ulysses;* Ernest Hemingway's *A Farewell to Arms* draws part of its plot from the region's role in World War I; Sigmund Freud and Rainer Maria Rilke both worked and wrote here. The bubbling mixture of Slovenian, Friulian, and Italian peoples has produced an indigenous literary tradition of its own, which includes the novelist Italo Svevo and the poet Umberto Saba.

In defiance of a long history of military invasions, the interior of the region promotes a quiet tourist-free lifestyle. The Tagliamento and Natisone River Valleys shelter fertile farmlands, and local dialect and hearty culinary traditions are the legacy of the society's peasant origins. The Carnian Alps to the north and the Julian Alps to the east present copious opportunities for hiking, rock-climbing, and skiing, and provide an alternative climate to the beaches of the southern coast.

Trieste

The unofficial capital of Friuli-Venezia Giulia lies at the end of a narrow strip of land sandwiched between Slovenia and the Adriatic. Given its strategically placed harbor and proximity to Austrian and former Yugoslavian borders, Trieste has been a bone of contention over the centuries. Even as an independent city from the 9th to 15th centuries, and Venice's main rival in the Adriatic until La Serenissima gobbled it up, Trieste was always coveted by the Austrians. Austria finally got its crack at a real Adriatic port in the post-Napoleonic real estate market, and proceeded to rip the medieval heart from Trieste, replacing it with neo-classical bombast. The equally heavy-handed style of government the Habsburgs brought succeeded in turning the mostly Italian population into fervent *irredentisti* clamoring for the return of the vaguely Italian province to Italy. They emerged victorious in 1918 when Italian troops occupied the Friuli, but unification only brought more trouble: Mussolini's thicket of fascist statuary provided appropriate counterpoint to the Austro-Hungarian architecture, while his policies of cultural chauvinism offended anyone not already alienated by the Habsburg rulers. The achievement of its citizens' dream also succeeded in wiping out Trieste's reason for existing: Italy already had a choice collection of Adriatic ports.

Today, evidence of Trieste's multinational history lingers in the numerous buildings and monuments of Habsburg origin and the Slavic nuances in the local cuisine. The city's Italian identity, on the other hand, is vehemently asserted by the persistence of fascist and anti-Slav parties, and more tangibly in the formidable **p. Unità d'Italia.** The cumulative product of these conflicting forces is a cosmopolitan transportation hub—a logical departure point for travelers to Eastern Europe whether they opt to travel by land, air or sea.

Orientation and Practical Information

Trieste is a direct train ride from Venice or Udine, and several trains and buses cross over daily to neighboring Slovenia and Croatia. Less frequent ferry service runs the length of the Istrian Peninsula. The gray, industrialized quays catering to ferries and fishermen taper off into Trieste's equivalent of a beach—a stretch of tiered concrete, strewn with well-bronzed bodies, which runs 7km from the edge of town out to the castle at Miramare. Moving inland one encounters **piazza Oberdan,** which opens onto the ever-busy **via Carducci.** Consumers conduct kamikaze shopping sprees on the fashion-oriented streets that intersect with this central artery near p. Goldoni. The artistically inclined can head to the gargantuan **p. Unità d'Italia,** the square that looks out to the harbor and is Trieste's pride and glory. Public transportation runs throughout the city, and most buses stop in the immediate vicinity of the train station. Everything in Trieste except public services is closed on Monday.

Tourist Office: in the train station (tel. 42 01 82), around the corner to the left after exiting from the main entrance. Copious information on Trieste including a list of *manifestazioni* (cultural events) occasionally encompassing international programs as well. English spoken. Open Mon.-Fri. 9am-1pm and 4-7pm, Sat. 9am-1pm. Another branch is located in the **Castello di San Giusto** (tel. 30 92 98).

Budget Travel: Aurora Viaggia, via Milano, 20 (tel. 602 61), 1 block from via Carducci. Information on transportation and lodging in the former Yugoslavian territory. Open Mon.-Fri. 9am-12:30pm and 4-7pm, Sat. 9am-noon.

Consulates: the **U.S.** no longer has a consulate here, but it does have an honorary representative at via dei Pellegrini, 42 (tel. 91 17 80; available Mon., Wed., and Fri. 10am-noon); otherwise try the consulate in Milan. **U.K.,** vicolo delle Ville, 16 (tel. 30 28 84), available Tues. and Fri. 9am-12:30pm. The closest **Canadian** and **Australian** consulates are in Milan; **New Zealand** citizens should contact their embassy in Rome. To check on the current state of visa requirements for travel east, contact the **Consulate General of Yugoslavia,** strada del Friuli, 54 (tel. 41 01 25). Open Mon.-Fri. 9am-noon.

Currency Exchange: Banca d'America e d'Italia, via Roma, 7 (tel. 63 19 25). Cash advances on Visa cards. Open Mon.-Fri. 8:20am-1:20pm and 2:35-3:35pm.

Post Office: p. Vittorio Veneto, 1 (tel. 36 67 42), along via Roma, the 2nd right off via Ghega coming from the train station. Fermo Posta at counter #21, stamps at #30. Open Mon.-Sat. 8:05am-7:30pm. **Postal Code:** 34100.

Telephones: SIP, viale XX Settembre. Open Mon.-Sat. 8:30am-12:30pm and 3:30-7:30pm, Sun. 8:30am-3:30pm. Another office at p. Oberdan. Open Mon.-Fri. 8:30am-noon and 1:50-3:50pm. **ASST,** via Pascoli, 9, off p. Garibaldi. Open 24 hrs. **Telephone Code:** 040.

Trains: p. della Libertà (tel. 41 82 07), down via Cavour from the quays. To: Udine (14 per day, 1hr. 30min., L6500, round-trip L9700); Venice (16 per day, 2hr., L12,100); Milan (5 per day, 5hr. 30min.-7hr. 30min., L30,300); Ljubljana (6 per day, 3hr. 30min., L13,000). **Storage** L1500, open 24hrs.

Buses: corso Cavour (tel. 37 01 60), in the fringe of p. della Libertà near the train station. To: Udine (7 per day, L5400); Rijeka/Fiume (5 per day, L12,000). **Luggage storage** L1500. Open daily 6:20am-9:20pm.

Ferries: Agemar Viaggi, p. Duca degli Abruzzi, 1/A (tel. 36 37 37), by the waterfront next to the canal. Will arrange trips with **Adriatica di Navigazione.** To: Grado (15min., L5900); Izola (45min., L5300); Piran (1hr. 30min., L5900); Umag (2hr. 30min., L9100); Novigrad (3hr. 15min., L11,700); Porec (4hr., L14,400); Rovinj (4hr. 15min., L15,400); Pula (4hr. 30min., L19,100). Those intent on seeing the entire Yugoslavian coast from a deck chair can take the 31hr. cruise to Durrës, Albania (Aug. 19-July 15 L110,000, July 16-Aug. 18 L145,000). Prices do not include harbor tax.

Taxis: tel. 545 33 or 30 77 30.

Swimming Pool: Piscina Communale "Bruno Bianchi," riva Gulli, 3 (tel. 30 60 24), along the waterfront. Indoor. Open Mon.-Sat. noon-3pm, Sun. 9am-1pm. L3000. Lockers L1000.

Laundromat: via Ginnastica, 36 (tel. 36 74 14). Coin-operated. Open Mon.-Fri. 8am-1pm and 4-7pm.

Public Baths: p. della Libertà, slightly to the right in front of the train station. Showers L5000. Open Mon.-Tues. and Thurs.-Sat. 8am-6pm, Sun. 8am-noon.

Late Night Pharmacies: tel. 192.

Emergencies: tel. 113. **Police:** via del Teatro Romano (tel. 603 11), off corso Italia. **Hospital: Ospedale Maggiore,** p. dell'Ospedale (tel. 77 61), up via Tarabocchia from via Carducci. **Ambulance:** tel. 310 310.

Accommodations

Watch out for weekdays, when companies often fill up the smaller *pensioni* with workers. Consult the tourist office, which leaves a helpful list of Trieste's hotels and *pensioni* taped to the door for those who arrive after hours.

Ostello Tegeste (HI), viale Miramare, 331 (tel. 22 41 02). From station take bus #6 (L8000) from *across* the street from the tourist office. Get off at the last stop and take bus #36 to the hostel. New furniture and a waterfront view make this an enjoyable hostel. Average of 4 bunks per room. Hot showers included, but hot water only available 5hr. per day. HI members only. Registration noon-11:30pm. Checkout 9:30am. Lockout 9:30am-noon. Curfew 11:30pm. L17,000 includes showers and breakfast. Also serves lunch and dinner (*menù* L12,000). Call or write ahead to reserve a bed during suntanning season.

Locanda San Nicolò, via San Nicolò, 2 (tel. 36 65 32), off riva III Novembre. Friendly proprietor gives you keys so you can stay out as long as Trieste keeps hopping. Dimly lit but spacious rooms. Singles L22,000. Doubles L32,000-35,000. Showers L2000.

Pensione Venezia, via Genova, 23 (tel. 684 80), off riva III Novembre. Rooms clean as a new penny managed by a pleasant family. Doubles L30,000. Showers L1000.

Albergo Canciani, via Carducci, 8 (tel. 73 20 68). Walk up 1 flight and turn left down the unmarked, unlit hallway. This nook consists of only 4 rooms so call ahead. Single L29,000. Doubles L46,000. Triples L60,000.

Camping

Marepineta (tel. 29 92 64), along the coast, provides beachside luxury. L7000 per person, L13,500 per tent and car (or any sort of camper). Hot water, electricity, and a bar included. Open May-Sept. Alongside the campground is a charming 2km trail billed as the **Rilke Sentiere** after the poet Rilke, who lived in **Duino**, the village at the other end of the trail. Duino presides over the haunting ruins of the **Duino castle.** (Open by reservation only; tel. 20 81 20.) Camping Marepineta is located in Sistiana; buses leave from the terminal every hr. (L2300).

Camping Obelisco, strada Nuova Opicina (tel. 21 16 55), is 7km from Trieste in Opicina, a suburb on the rocky *carso*—a sparsely beautiful place to camp for those not umbilically attached to the beach. Fewer facilities than Marepineta, and correspondingly lower prices. L4000 per person, L3500 per tent, light L1500. Trains leave frequently from the station (L2500), or take the tram from p. Oberdan (L1600).

Food

Many dishes in Trieste's restaurants have Eastern European overtones (usually Hungarian) and are often loaded with paprika. The city is renowned for its fish; try *sardoni in savor* (large sardines marinated in oil and garlic). Monday is a non-day in Trieste: many shops and restaurants close. To fend for yourself, visit one of the several **alimentari** on via Carducci or try the **Bosco Supermarket** in p. Goldoni (open Tues. and Thurs.-Sat. 8am-1pm and 4:30-7:30pm, Mon. and Wed. 8am-1pm). While in town, sample a bottle of **Terrano del Carso,** a dry red wine with a low alcohol content that has been valued for its therapeutic properties since the days of ancient Rome. To purchase grapes in their unadulterated form, stroll through the open-air **market** in p. Ponterosso, by the canal. (Open Tues.-Sat. 8am-5:30pm.)

Antica Taverna: Arco di Riccardo, via del Trionfo, 3/A, very much off the beaten track. Walk up the right-hand side of the stairs to S. Maria Maggiore, and turn right in the little alley in p. S. Silvestro. Riccardo's Roman arch still abuts the building whence flows the chatter of an exuberant and well-fed Italian clientele. *Primi* begin at L5500 with *secondi* about L12,000. Cover L1500. Open Tues.-Sun. 1-3pm and 8pm-12:30am.

Paninoteca Da Livio, via della Ginnastica, 3/B (tel. 75 58 14), inland off via Carducci. Small, smoky shop boasts monster *panini* (L2000-6000), dozens of brands of beer, and hordes of customers. Open Mon.-Sat. 8:30am-3pm and 5-10pm. Closed 2 weeks in June and July.

Pizzeria Barattolo, p. Sant'Antonio, 2 (tel. 64 14 80), along the canal. Amazing pizza (L6000-12,000). Also bar and *tavola calda* offerings. Open Tues.-Sun. 8am-1am.

La Massaia Gastronomica, on via Carducci at via Ginnastica (tel. 66 33 45). A gourmet take-out deli. Sublime, and reasonably priced. Most dishes L1500-3000 per *etto*. Open Tues.-Sat. 8:30am-1pm and 5-7:15pm, Sun. 8:30am-1pm. Closed 2 weeks in June and July.

Sights

In honor of the Habsburg empress, 19th-century Viennese urban planners carved out a large chunk of Trieste to create borgo Teresiano, a district of straight avenues bordering the waterfront and the canal. Facing the canal from the south is the district's one beautiful church, the Serbian Orthodox **San Spirideone.** Unfortunately, the church is surrounded by a steel barricade, so you'll have to admire it from afar. The **Municipio** at the head of **piazza dell'Unità d'Italia,** a monument to the limits of ambition, sags under the weight of its heavy ornamentation and oversized tower. In the corner of the *piazza* stands an allegorical fountain with statues representing four continents. The surreal effect is completed by the stone warehouses rotting slowly along the waterfront.

The 15th-century Venetian **Fortress of San Giusto** presides over **Capitoline Hill,** the city's historic center. You can take bus #24 (L800) from the station to the last stop at the fortress, and ascend the hill via the daunting Scala dei Giganti (265 steps) rising from p. Goldoni. Face the sea from the west tower; downtown Trieste is on your right. Within the walls is a huge outdoor theater where film festivals are held in July and August (pick up a copy of *Trieste '93, Eventi Luglio-Agosto* at the tourist office). Directly below are the remains of the old Roman city center, and across the street is the restored **Cathedral of San Giusto.** Its irregular plan is due to its origin as two churches built simultaneously from the 5th through 11th centuries, one dedicated to San Giusto, the other to Santa Maria Assunta. Inside are two splendid mosaics in the chapels directly to the left and right of the altar. Walk around the ramparts of the castle (open daily 8am-7pm), or peek into the museum, which has temporary exhibits in addition to its permanent collection of weaponry (tel. 76 69 56; open Tues.-Sat. 9am-12:45pm; admission L3000).

Down the other side of the hill, past the *duomo,* lies the eclectic **Museo di Storia ed Arte** and **Orto Lapidario** (Museum of History and Art and Rock Garden; tel. 37 05 00 or 30 86 86) at v. Cattedrale, 15, in p. Cattedrale. The museum provides archeological documentation of the history of Trieste during and preceding its Roman years, and boasts a growing collection of Egyptian art and artifacts from southern Italy. (Open Tues.-Sun. 9am-1pm. Admission L3000, students with ID L1500.) Descending the hill towards the ruins of the *teatro romano* you end up only a few short blocks from p. Unità d'Italia.

A delightful collection of drawings and a delightless selection of paintings by Tiepolo, Veneziano, and others has been moved from the Capitoline Hill to an elegant 18th-century villa at largo Papa Giovanni XXIII, 1, which is now the **Museo Sartorio** (tel. 30 14 79). The museum is easily reached by walking along the quays, a short distance from the center. (Open Tues.-Sun. 9am-1pm. Admission L3000.)

Back in the thick of things, stop at the **Museo del Risorgimento** in a *palazzo* by Umberto Nordio off p. Oberdan. The museum contains the cell of Guglielmo Oberdan, the 19th-century Irredentist who met his death at the hands of the Austrians in 1882 and posthumously gave his name to the *piazza.*

Entertainment

The regular opera season of the **Teatro Verdi** runs November to May, but a six-week operetta season is held in June and July. Purchase tickets or phone for reservations at p. Verdi, 1 (tel. 36 78 16; open Tues.-Sun. 9am-noon and 4-7pm; seats from L10,000). Inquire at the tourist office about other performances in the **castle** or **Teatro Romano.**

Caffè Tommaseo, in p. Tommaseo along the canal, and **Caffè San Marco,** on via Battisti, preserve the city's turn-of-the-century coffee culture (the latter frequently offers live musical performances). The liveliest *passeggiata* takes place along viale XX Settembre; if you don't feel like participating, you can sit with a cappuccino in p. Oberdan and watch aimless adolescents watch each other.

Near Trieste

West of Trieste you can sunbathe along the rocky coast and visit the **Castello Miramare** (tel. 22 41 43), the Disneyesque castle of Archduke Maximilian of Austria, who ordered its construction in the middle of the 19th century. Maximilian didn't live to see the completion of the grounds; he went to serve as Napoleon III's "Emperor of Mexico" and ended up being shot. Miramare acquired a bad reputation after Maximilian's widow Carlotta went mad; it was rumored that anyone spending the night here would come to a bad end, a belief helped along by the decision of Archduke Ferdinand to spend the night here on the way to his assassination at Sarajevo. Poised on a high promontory over the gulf, Miramare with its white turrets is easily visible from the Capitoline Hill in Trieste or from the train on the journey through the *carso*. Miramare's extensive parks are open to the public at no cost and range from marble fountains to secluded, bark-strewn paths. To reach Miramare, take bus #6 to the end and transfer to #36 (30min., L800). (Castle museum open Tues.-Sat. 9am-1:30pm and 2:30-6pm, Mon. 9am-12:30pm. Admission L6000, L7500 with guided tour.) In July and August, a series of sound and light shows transforms Miramare into a high-tech playground. Paging Tinkerbell...

Near the castle, a **marine park** (tel. 22 41 47) sponsored by the World Wildlife Fund conducts several programs throughout the year, including guided introductions to the coast's marine life.

About 15km from Trieste in Opicina, you'll find the **Grotta Gigante** (tel. 32 73 12), the world's largest accessible cave. Staircases wind in and around the 90m-high interior, which the brochure claims could hold the whole of St. Peter's. (Open Tues.-Sat. 9am-noon and 2-7pm; Nov.-Feb. 10am-noon and 2:30-4:30pm. L8000 for round-trip transportation from p. Oberdan and admission.)

Aquileia, Grado, and Palmanova

Aquileia was founded in 181 BC on the banks of the now-defunct Natisone-Torre River. Between 200 and 452 AD it flourished as the Roman capital of the region, serving as the gateway to the Eastern Empire and as the principal trading port of the Adriatic. The Patriarchate of Aquileia was established here in 313, but as the Huns and Lombards descended to sack the city in the 5th and 6th centuries, the Patriarch hightailed it to Grado and then moved on to Cividale del Friuli. Aquileia finally regained control in 1019, celebrating by rebuilding its great basilica, and from here the Patriarchate successfully defied the popes until it faded into obscurity. Meanwhile, the port silted up and malaria set in. The disgruntled Patriarch moved on to Udine and dwindled into an archbishop, leaving behind a perfect open-air museum of Roman and early Christian art, the most important archeological remains in northern Italy.

Aquileia can be reached by bus from Udine (16 per day, 1hr., L3600), and local buses travel to Cervignano, a train station on the Trieste-Venice line (every 30min., L1200). The **tourist office** (tel. (0431) 91 94 91; open April-Oct. Fri.-Wed. 9am-1pm and 4-6pm) is a block from the bus stop in p. Capitolo.

Across the *piazza* from the tourist office stands Aquileia's **basilica.** The basilica is a tribute to the town's artistic heritage, offering a sampling of artwork from across the centuries. The floor, a remnant of the original church, is a 4th-century mosaic of unequalled magnitude, animating over 700 square meters with geometric designs and realistic bestial depictions. The 9th-century crypt beneath the altar contains several 12th-century frescoes illustrating the trials of Aquileia's early Christians and scenes from the life of Christ. In the *Cripta degli Scavi,* directly to the left upon entering, excavation has uncovered three distinct layers of flooring, providing vivid evidence of the building's varied history. (Basilica open daily 7:30am-7:30pm; in winter 8am-12:30pm and 3-6pm. Crypt open Mon.-Sat. 9am-3pm., Sun. 9am-1pm.)

Omnipresent yellow signs and clearly delineated tourist maps make it easy to find the various ruins, but the cypress-lined alley behind the basilica runs parallel to the once-glorious **Roman harbor** and is a pleasant alternative to via Augusta as a path to the **forum.** Continue from there to the **Museo Paleocristiano** (tel. 91 11 30), where displays explain the transition from classical paganism to Christianity, and moss covers the ubiquitous mosaics. (Open Tues.-Sat. 9am-6:30pm, Sun. 9am-1pm and 2-6:30pm, Mon. 9am-2pm; in winter Mon.-Sat. 9am-2pm, Sun. 9am-1pm. Free.)

Camping Aquileia, via Gemina, 10 (tel. (0431) 910 42; in winter 910 37), up the street from the forum, is a shady spot with a swimming pool. (L4500 for adults, L5500 July-Aug.; under 12 L2800-3500. Tent sites L7200-L8500, wooden bungalows or caravans for two L26,000-50,000. Open May 15-Sept. 15.) The **Albergo Aquila Nera** (tel. (0431) 910 45), down via Roma in the p. Garibaldi, offers more central accommodations. (Singles with bath L35,000. Doubles with bath L60,000. Additional bed L10,000. Breakfast L7000. Complete dinner for about L18,000—be sure to ask the proprietress for a glass of local white wine. Open April-Dec.) The **Desparo Supermarket** on the Udine end of via Augusta is a penny-pincher's salvation (open Tues.-Sat. 8am-1pm and 4pm-midnight, Sun. 8am-1pm), and the **Trattoria Augusta** upstairs serves a decent *menù* for L15,500 (open Tues.-Sun. 9am-3pm and 5pm-midnight).

Buses from Udine continue past Aquileia to **Grado** (16 per day, 1hr., L3600), a seaside resort rapidly growing in popularity. Once Aquileia's port city, Grado has become a haven for sun-seekers, attracting tourists with its well-maintained beaches and thermal baths. Although most of Grado's written history was destroyed by a fire in the 9th century, much of its early architecture has survived. Two nature reserves alongside the natural lagoon round out the list of Grado's attractions. For more information contact the **tourist office** (tel. (0431) 89 92 10).

Palmanova, a town girded by a nine-sided Venetian fortress, lies between Udine and Aquileia on the bus route to Grado (16 per day, 20min., L2100). With a hexagonal central *piazza* and six main streets radiating out to the ramparts, Palmanova is an exceptionally well-preserved example of Renaissance military planning. The **tourist office,** borso Udine, 4/C (tel. (0432) 92 91 06) is on the ground floor of the **Museo Civico,** which displays manuscripts and artifacts documenting Palmanova's military history. (Both open Tues.-Sun. 10am-noon.)

Udine

If you venture here you should congratulate yourself on your unorthodox itinerary: Udine is an unexpectedly captivating town. In addition to Italian, natives speak some German, some Serbo-Croatian, and the old Friulian dialect, an obscure relative of equally obscure Swiss Romansch. The linguistic intermingling of Central European, Balkan and Italian influences typifies the exotic composite of Udinese life. Given its turbulent history—conquered by Venice in 1420, appropriated by Austria in the late 18th century, and heavily bombed during WWII—Udine is fortunate to have escaped with its landmarks intact. The present town is notable primarily for its graceful Gothic and Renaissance architecture,and for works of the rococo pioneer Giambattista Tiepolo.

Orientation and Practical Information

Udine's train and bus stations are both on viale Europa Unita in the southern part of town. All bus lines pass by the train station, but only buses #1, 3, and 8 run from viale Europa Unita to the center of town, by the p. della Libertà and Castle Hill. You can also make the 15-minute walk: from the station, go right to piazzale D'Annunzio, then take a left turn under the arches to via Aquileia. Continue up via Veneto to p. Libertà.

Tourist Office: p. 1° Maggio, 7 (tel. 29 59 72). From p. della Libertà, turn right on via Manin and left on p. 1° Maggio, then look for the pink-arched facade, or take bus #2, 7, or 10 to p. 1° Maggio. Wonderful maps, copious information. Be sure to pick up the booklet *Udine: Eight Itineraries* for an exhaustive overview. Open Mon.-Fri. 9am-1pm and 3-6pm.

Currency Exchange: Credito Italiano, via Manin, 2 (tel. 50 32 33), near p. della Libertà. Open Mon.-Fri. 8:20am-1:20pm and 2:35-4:05pm, Sat. 8:20am-11:50pm.

Post Office: via Veneto, 42 (tel. 50 19 93). Fermo Posta and stamps through the left door at desk #9. Open Mon.-Sat. 8:15am-7:40pm. Also a smaller branch at via Roma, 25, straight ahead from the train station. Open Mon.-Fri. 8:10am-4:15pm, Sat. 8:05am-1pm. **Postal Code:** 33100.

Telephones: SIP, via Savorgnana, 13 (tel. 27 81), off p. Duomo. Open Mon.-Sat. 9am-12:30pm and 3:30-8pm, Sun. 8:30am-3:30pm. **Telephone Code:** 0432.

Trains: on viale Europa Unita (tel. 50 36 56). **Information** office open 7am-9pm. Trains to: Venice (26 per day, 2hr., L10,500); Trieste (18 per day, 1hr. 30min., L6500); Milan (4 per day, 5hr., L27,000); Vienna (5 per day, 7hr., L55,000). **Luggage storage,** L1500. Open daily 8am-10:15pm.

Buses: on viale Europa Unita (tel. 20 39 41), 1 block to the right of the train station as you exit. Comprehensive and efficient service throughout the region. To: Trieste (9 per day, 1hr., L5700); Lignano (11 per day, 1hr., L5700); Venice (2 per day, 2hr., L10,500); Grado (16 per day, 1hr., L4800); Palmanova (16 per day, 20min., L2200); Aquileia (16 per day, 40min., L3800); Cividale (20 per day, 30min., L2200).

Mountain Information: the bulletin board of the Associazione Guida Alpina Italiana is under the arcades of the city hall on via B. Odorico. Information on upcoming trips and skiing. For information on hikes within the Friuli-Venezia Giulia, contact **Gruppo Attività ed Informazione Ambientali,** via Monterotondo, 22 (tel. 60 18 92).

Swimming Pool: Piscina Comunale, via Ampezzo, 4 (tel. 269 67 or 269 29), near p. Diacono. Indoor pool open Sept.-May; outdoor June-Aug. Open Mon.-Sat. 2-7pm, Sun. 10am-1pm. L5000; under 10 L3000.

Emergencies: tel. 113. **Police:** via Prefettura, 16 (tel. 50 28 41). **Medical Emergency:** tel. 118. **Hospital: Ospedale Civile** (tel. 55 21), in p. Santa Maria della Misericordia. Take bus #1 north to the last stop.

Accommodations

First the good news: the large map outside the train station is clearly marked with the locations of Udine's hotels, and some are steals. Now the bad news: local workers probably snagged the best spots long ago.

Suite Inn, via di Toppo, 25 (tel. 50 16 83). Take bus #1 from the station, get off at via Gemona or piazzale Osoppo, and walk up via di Toppo. Sweet proprietor is eager to please. Cozy sitting room with TV and piano. Tidy rooms, spotless bathrooms, and phones. Singles L29,000. Doubles L46,000. Breakfast L5000.

Locanda Da Arturo, via Pracchiuso, 75 (tel. 299 70). Take bus #4 from the station, get off at p. Oberdan, and walk down via Pracchiuso on the far side of the *piazza.* Restaurant downstairs has a *menù* for L16,000. Quiet, with only a few rooms. Call ahead for reservations. Singles L18,000. Doubles L36,000. Closed either July or Aug.

Locanda Piccolo Friuli, via Magrini, 9 (tel. 50 78 17). From p. Garibaldi take via Brenari to via Poscolle and continue on vicolo Gorgo. A bit more expensive, but worth it. Creaky wood floor, big sitting room, and frescoes create the quaint atmosphere. Singles with bath L40,000. Doubles with bath L60,000. Triples with bath L80,000. Breakfast L8000.

Food

A pastiche of earthy Italian, Austrian, and Slovene, Udinese cuisine tends more toward the hearty than the *haute.* A typical regional specialty is *brovada e museto,* a stew made of marinated turnips and boiled sausage. Shop for produce weekday mornings in the **open-air market** at p. Matteotti near p. della Libertà, or head for via Redipuglia or p. 1° Maggio on Saturdays between 8am and 1pm. Buy staples at the **Desparo Supermarket,** at viale Volontari della Libertà, 6, off p. Osoppo. (Open Tues.-Sun. 8:30am-12:50pm and 3:50-7:30pm.)

Zenit, via Prefettura, 15. A cross between a 50s diner and a pre-school cafeteria in decor, but reasonable as a self-service joint. Popular with local businessfolk. *Primi* L3500-5000. *Secondi* L6000-8000. Cover L500. Open Mon.-Sat. 11:45am-2:30pm and 6:30-9:30pm.

Ristorante/Pizzeria Ai Portici, via Veneto (tel. 50 89 75), under the arcade before p. della Libertà. Pizza for L6500 is a reasonable price, given the chic ambience. *Primi* L5000-6000. *Secondi* L7000-15,000. Cover L1500. Open Wed.-Mon. 9am-midnight or 1am.

Spaghetti House, via Cividale, 27. Next to Albergo Clocchiati. Over 20 different types of spaghetti (L5000-8000) generously doled out in an amusement park-like setting. Also a fun place for that late-night ice cream binge. Pizza L4500-12,000. Full meal L15,000. Open Tues.-Sun. 11am-3:30pm and 5:30pm-2am.

Sights and Entertainment

The heart of Udine is **piazza della Libertà,** an elegantly elevated square. Along its higher side runs the Renaissance **Arcade of San Giovanni.** The two symbolic columns of Venice in the *piazza* commemorate the conquest of Udine by the Venetian Republic; while across the *piazza* stands the delicate, candy-striped **Loggia del Lionello,** an architectural reminder of the conquerors' presence in Udine. Originally built in 1448, the beloved *loggia* was severely damaged by a fire in 1876, but reconstructed shortly thereafter by popular demand.

The rugged **Arco Bollani** (1556, designed by Palladio), in the corner near the clock tower, allows you through the walls enclosing the **Chiesa di Santa Maria** and the **castello** of the Venetian governors. The *castello* is home to the **Museo Civico,** which exhibits a myriad of notable frescoes including a frieze and several *putti* by Giambattista Tiepolo. (Open Tues.-Sat. 9:30am-12:30pm and 3-6pm, Sun.-Mon. 9:30am-12:30pm. Admission L3200, students L1600.)

Back in p. del Duomo, 50m from the more hectic p. della Libertà, stands the fine Roman-Gothic **duomo,** with several Tiepolos on display in the Baroque interior (the first, second, and fourth altars on the right side). There is a small **museum** (tel. 50 68 30) in the squat brick *campanile,* which is comprised of two chapels with 14th-century frescoes by Vitale da Bologna. (Museum closed for renovation in 1992.) Udine has been called the city of Tiepolo, and some of this Baroque painter's finest works adorn the **Oratorio della Purità** (tel. 50 68 30), across from the *duomo.* The *Assumption* frescoed on the ceiling (1759) and the *Immaculate Conception* of the altarpiece represent Tiepolo's world of light, air, and awe. (Ask the cathedral sacristan to let you in. Tip expected.)

A sizeable sampling of earlier Tiepolo frescoes is housed in the **Palazzo Arcivescovile** (tel. 50 43 14), p. Patriarcato, 1, at the head of via Ungheria. Here, from 1726 through 1730, Tiepolo executed an extensive series of Old Testament scenes. (Open Mon.-Fri. 9am-noon. Free. Closed for restoration in 1992.) Several blocks south from p. della Libertà along via Stringher, off p. XX Settembre, stands the **Chiesa di San Francesco.** This architectural gem of the early Renaissance is considered Udine's most beautiful church. Unfortunately, it opens only for exhibitions.

There are also a number of interesting museums, including an excellent **Gallery of Modern Art** at p. P. Diacono, 21 (tel. 29 58 91), on the ring road that circles the old city. The museum transports you to the idiosyncratic world of De Kooning, Lichtenstein, Chagall, Picasso, and every major 20th-century Italian artist. (Open Tues.-Sat. 9:30am-12:30pm and 3-6pm, Sun. 9:30am-12:30pm. Admission L3000, students L1500.) The **Friulian Museum of Popular Arts and Traditions,** via Viola, 3 (tel. 50 78 61), northeast of the p. XXVI Luglio, exhibits a collection of regional costumes and folk art. (Open Tues.-Sat. 9:30am-12:30pm and 3-6pm, Sun. 9:30am-12:30pm. Admission L3000, students L1500. Closed for restoration in 1992.)

Cividale del Friuli

At the far edge of Italy and unknown to most travelers, sleepy Cividale saw its glory days come and go during the darkest of the Dark Ages. In the 6th century AD, land-hungry Lombards seized what was then *Forum Iulii* and made the vanquished Roman trading center the capital of the first Lombard duchy. By the 8th century, things were so hopping that the Patriarch of Aquileia moved in to grab a piece of the action, setting off a building frenzy. Since then things have been generally quiet, despite devastating earthquakes that have twice crumbled the city's monuments. Thus Cividale remains the only place in Italy to see magnificent art from the least known century of Italian history.

Orientation and Practical Information

Cividale is easily reached by train from Udine, which lies at the end of a *locale* line that connects the two cities (every hr., 20min., L1900). The train and Rosina bus stations open onto viale Libertà and are a brief walk from the **center** and **tourist office** at largo Boiano, 4 (tel. 73 13 98). From the train station head directly onto via Marconi, turning left through the **Porta Arsenale Veneto** when the street ends. Bear right in the p. Dante, then left onto largo Boiano. The staff is extremely helpful (open Mon.-Fri. 9am-1pm and 3-6pm, Sat. 9am-1pm). The **post office,** at largo Boiano, 37 (tel. 73 11 57), is just down the street from the tourist office (open Mon.-Fri. 8:30am-5:30pm and Sat. 8:30am-1pm). The **postal code** is 33043. In case of **emergency,** call 113, or seek out the **police** on p. A. Diaz (tel. 73 14 29). The **hospital (Ospedale Civile)** is in p. dell'Ospedale (tel. 70 81).

Accommodations and Food

Accommodations are certainly not Cividale's forte. **Al Pomo d'Oro,** p. S. Giovanni (tel. 73 14 89), has singles with bath for L48,000, doubles with bath for L75,000, and breakfast for L5000. The specialties of the area are *gubana* (a fig- and prune-filled pastry laced with *grappa,* the local brandy) and *Picolit,* a pricey dessert wine rarely sold outside of the Natisone Valleys. Most bars stock pre-packaged *gubana,* but for fresh mouth-watering rings, look for the "Gubana Cividalese" sign on your right as you near the **Ponte del Diavolo,** located at corso D'Aquileia, 16. Piazza Diacono hosts Cividale's **open-air market** every Saturday from 8am to 1pm. The management of **Trattoria da Renza,** stretta Stellini, 18 (tel. 73 37 63), is tremendously proud of its wide assortment of home-made pasta and almost as proud of its collection of signatures of Italian celebs. Ask to sit outside in the vine-roofed area with a view of the **Chiesa S. Francesco's** tower next door. Complete dinners run from L20,000 to L23,000, but two rounds of *primi* (L5000) will satisfy for less. (Cover L2000; open Sun.-Fri. 8:30am-3pm and 6-10:30pm.)

Sights and Entertainment

Built and expanded upon over a period of centuries, Cividale's *duomo* (directly on your left as you leave the tourist office) is an odd melange of architectural styles, but most of the credit is given to Pietro Lombardo, who completed the bulk of the construction in 1528. Walk to the far end of the *duomo* to view the 12th-century silver **altarpiece of Pellegrino II,** with its 25 saints and pair of archangels. Move on to the Renaissance **sarcophagus of Patriarch Nicolò Donato,** located to the left of the entrance. Annexed to the *duomo* is the **Museo Christiano.** This free display includes the **Baptistery of Callisto,** a wonderfully sculpted piece of architecture commissioned by the first Aquileian patriarch to move to Cividale. More significantly, the museum houses the **Altar of Ratchis,** a delicately carved work from 749, one of the few surviving masterpieces of the Middle Ages. Both the museum and the cathedral are free. (Open Mon.-Sat. 9:30am-noon and 3-7pm, Sun. 3-6:45pm. Museum also open Sun. 9am-noon.)

The greatest Italian work of the 8th century can be found downhill and upstream at the **Tempietto Longobardo** (follow the signs). Although the "little temple" suffered greatly from the earthquakes of 1222 and 1976, exhaustive efforts have restored a famous sextet of 8th-century stucco figures to their original form. The beautiful 14th-century wooden stalls partially compensate for the loss of the original frescoes. Another bonus is the spectacular view of river and mountains, obtained from the entrance. (Open Mon.-Sat. 9am-2pm, Sun. 9am-1pm. Admission L2000, students L1000.) For a similarly stunning vista, try the **Ponte del Diavolo,** an impressive stone bridge of indeterminate age. For a better look at the bridge itself, descend the stair to the water on the far side.

On the sixth of January, the **Sword Mass** follows a procession to the *duomo.* This event commemorates the investiture of the Patriarch Marquando of Randek, and the sword used today is the gift presented to him by the townspeople in 1336.

Lignano-Sabbiadoro

Just a generation ago, Lignano-Sabbiadoro's spectacular beach served only as the launching point for the town's fishing fleet. Nowadays, the tourist board uses the golden sand to lure that even-more-lucrative catch: *lire*-laden tourists with skins to burn. Go to Lignano to sunbathe and swim, but not to pick up local culture—there ain't none.

Orientation and Practical Information

The resort is actually a peninsula, with Lignano-Sabbiadoro at the eastern end and Lignano-Pineta and Lignano-Riviera farther west. The frequent trains on the Venice-Trieste line will deposit you at the town of **Latisana.** When you exit the station, proceed straight for two blocks to Bar Rossitto (on your left), where you can buy an SGEA ticket to Lignano-Sabbiadoro, the last stop (every hr., 30min., L2700).

Tourist Office: in Sabbiadoro, via Latisana, 42 (tel. 718 21). In **Pineta**, via dei Pini, 53 (tel. 42 21 69). Zealous and efficient. An essential stop for accommodations in high season. *Lignano For You's* index lists every imaginable service. Open Wed. and Fri.-Sun. 8am-8pm, Tues. and Thurs. 9am-12:30pm and 3:30-8pm; July-Aug. daily 8am-8pm.

Post Office: in Sabbiadoro, viale Gorizia, 37 (tel. 716 85). Open Mon.-Fri. 9:30am-5:30pm, Sat. 8:30am-1pm. In Pineta, p. Rosa dei Venti (tel. 42 23 82). Open Mon.-Fri. 8:10am-1:15pm, Sat. 8am-1pm. **Postal Code:** 33054.

Telephones: SIP, in Sabbiadoro, via Codroipo, 9. In Pineta, raggio dell'Ostro, 8. Both open daily 8am-midnight. Public telephones in bars and hotels are marked on the tourist office's map, which is posted around town. **Telephone Code:** 0431.

Buses: Ferrari SGEA (tel. 713 73) and city buses leave from viale Gorizia, 28. From Lignano, there is frequent bus service to Udine (15 per day, 1hr. 30min., L5400).

Bike Rental: Graziella, via Friuli, 16. Other rental shops throughout town. Bicycles L5000 per hr.; mopeds L14,000 per hr.; dirt-bikes L7000 per hr.; "tridems"—pedal-operated carts that will seat three—L9000 per hr.

Emergencies: tel. 113. **Police:** via dei Platani, 74 (tel. 714 32). **Hospital: Ospedale Civile di Latisana,** via Sabbionera (tel. 508 11 or 51 03 81). **Medical Assistance:** parco San Giovanni Bosco, 20/A, on the beach in Sabbiadoro (Open May-Sept.). **First Aid:** tel. 710 01.

Accommodations

Forget arriving unannounced in Lignano between August 1 and 20. If you do, head to the tourist office before 10am to pounce on cancellations. From April to June and September through October, the weather is beautiful and mild, and Lignano is one of the cheapest beach resorts in Europe. Most places offer much better deals if you take full or half-pension and stay at least three days. The city essentially closes down in winter.

Pensione Amalfi, via Udine, 80 (tel. 715 33), 1 block from town center. Large, impersonal, and close to the beach. Singles L16,000-20,000. Doubles L32,000, with bath L40,000. Open mid-March-mid-Sept.

Mueblè Splendid, via Carnia, 27 (tel. 714 87), near via Tolmezzo. The name fits both the rooms and the cheery owners. Make reservations. Singles L30,000. Doubles L45,000. Triples L60,000. Extra bed L15,000. Open mid-March-mid-Sept.

Pensione Ornella, via Adriatica, 11 (tel. 712 62), off viale Venezia, about 5 blocks to the right from the tourist office. Airy and spotless. Singles L30,000. Doubles L50,000. Breakfast L6000.

Camping Sabbiadoro, via Sabbiadoro, 8 (tel. 714 55), about halfway to Lignano-Pineta. The most expensive, but centrally located. L7800 per person, L12,800 per site. 4-person bungalows L42,000-105,000. Light L1000. Showers included. Open May-Sept. For information on campgrounds in Lignano-Riviera, call **Camping Pino Mare** (tel. 42 85 12).

Food and Entertainment

Food prices here are insane. The inexpensive alternatives to pizza and sandwiches are the numerous *tavole calde* and *gastronomie* catering to beachgoers. Also try the fruit stands throughout the town and the **Tutto Sconto Supermarket** at via Carnia, 17. (Open Mon.-Sat. 8am-1pm.)

Discos and travel agencies threaten to take over every last building in Lignano. The former levy hefty cover charges (L10,000-15,000, less on weeknights). Try dancing on the beach at the **Terrazza a Mare,** in a funky building.

Inquire at the tourist office about free trips to **Marano Lagoon,** a bird-watching and nature preserve. For manufactured excitement, visit the **Luna Park** amusement park on via Centrale next to the big garage. The **Aqua Splash** on viale Europa—"the biggest park of water games in Europe"—has an impressive number of slides swooping into a 1500-square-meter pool, next to the "bumper boats." (Open in summer daily 10am-7pm. Admission L20,000, children L15,000.) The **Parco Zoo Punta Verde** houses about 2000 animals. (Admission L10,000, children L7000; consult the tourist office for hours.)

Trentino-Südtirol/ Alto Adige

"Grüss Gott!" Travelers to Italy's northern reaches often hear this and fear they have stumbled into Austria. And they have in all but name; the influence of Austrian culture exceeds that of Italian in much of the region. Trentino in the south is predominantly Italian-speaking, while Südtirol (South Tirol) in the north is largely German-speaking and encompasses most of the mountain region known as the Dolomites. Long an integral part of the Holy Roman Empire, the provinces were conquered by Napoleon only to pass into the hands of the Austro-Hungarian Empire. At the end of World War I, however, Trentino and the Südtirol fell under Italian rule. Germany curtailed Mussolini's brutal efforts to Italianize the Südtirol during the 1920s, but not before he had supplied every German name in the region with an Italian equivalent.

Tensions still simmer: Germanic secessionist terrorist bombings rocked the region during the 1960s and again in the 1980s, and an anti-Germanic party has recently been gaining support among ethnic Italians. At the same time, the advent of "complete provincial autonomy" a decade ago has meant, among other things, that all official publications must be in both languages. North of Bolzano, you may get better service by trying to speak German; in Trent, Italian is the ticket. The intermingling of Austrian and Italian traditions permeates everything from art to cuisine. Squat, earth-colored castles, an extreme departure from the less defense-oriented architecture further south, cluster in deep green valleys where swift rivers course beneath towering, snow-covered peaks. The sight of white-whiskered men in blue aprons might make you want to yodel. Indulge yourself: in moments of joy, the Südtirolese natives go at it full force.

The entire region, especially the north, is highly susceptible to seasonal vagaries. From Christmas to Easter and between July 15 and September 10, hotels and resort facilities run at full capacity and prices run about 20% higher. In the low seasons, services open and close unpredictably.

Dolomites (Dolomiti, Dolomiten)

Stunning limestone spires shoot skyward from billowing fields and pine forests. These amazing peaks—fantastic for hiking, skiing, and rock-climbing—start west of Trent and extend north and east to the Austrian frontier.

Finding accommodations in the Dolomites is as easy as sliding down a bunny slope. Least expensive are the hundreds of alpine huts and the rooms in private homes advertised by the *zimmer/camere* signs. Pick up the complete *Südtirol Hotel Guide,* free at the provincial office in Bolzano and in local tourist offices. These offices also provide complete listings of about 40 legal campgrounds in the region, but travelers camp almost anywhere—with discretion. Keep in mind that hiking at high altitudes without proper equipment borders on the suicidal.

The **SAD** (Società Automobilistica Dolomiti) deploys an armada of **buses** that covers virtually every paved road in the area with surprising frequency. If you plan to move around, pick up a free *SAD Orario* (bus schedule with map) at the Bolzano/ Bozen bus station. **Car rentals** run L70,000-90,000 per day, weekend specials L150,000, gas not included. A major credit card helps, and you must be over 21. Keep in mind that map distances in this region may appear short, but progress along tortuous mountain roads is slow.

Hiking

Even the least intrepid can become avid Dolomitists. The terrain varies from wide, gentle trails to vertical cliffs. You can purchase hiking boots (*scarponi da montagna*) and rock-climbing equipment in Alto Adige, but better buys are more likely in Trent or Verona. **Alpine huts** (*rifugi*) abound, making forays into the mountains easier and safer. All huts are clearly marked on the *Kompass Wanderkarte,* the best map of the region, available at most newsstands and bookstores. Huts generally operate from late June through early October, but at higher altitudes the hut season is likely to be shorter. The provincial tourist offices in Trent and Bolzano supply information in English on their respective provinces. The Alpine desk of the office in Bolzano is run by Dr. Hannsjörg Hager, a noted Alpinist who speaks English and can help you pick a suitable route, making sure the huts are open before you get into the mountains.

Hut prices increase with altitude, but average about L12,000 per dormitory cot and L18,000 per bed. All offer a *menù* for roughly L10,000; bring your own food if possible. Pick up information about winter walking paths from the tourist office. For further information about Trentino huts, contact the SAT at via Manci, 57 (tel. 98 18 71 or 98 64 62), in Trent.

Skiing

The Dolomites offer amazingly popular downhill skiing enhanced by generally sunny skies and perfectly powdery snow. The **tourist office** in Bolzano is a good source of information; ask for *Ski Panorama: South Tyrol* or their pamphlet for cross-country skiers. The **tourist office** in Trent will supply you with *Snowy Planet.* When you write, explain your price range and the kind of skiing that interests you, and request a specific recommendation for a ski area. Major ski centers near Trent include **Folgaria, Brentonico, Madonna di Campiglio,** and **Monte Bondone** (especially close to the city); near Bolzano, **Alta Venosta** (around Lake Resia) and **Colle Isarco;** near Bressanone, **Val d'Isarco,** the **Zona dello Sciliar,** and **Val Gardena;** and near Corvara, **Alta Badia.** The **Skiarena Ortler,** Reutweg 4 (tel. (0473) 763 48), 39026 Prad am Stilfserjoch, around and to the east of Merano, sells a six-day pass good on 63 lifts in 11 areas (about L120,000; mid-Jan.-mid-Feb. L200,000). One of the cheapest and most convenient ways to enjoy a skiing holiday in the Dolomites is to get a **settimana bianca** (white week) package deal from any CTS or CIT office. Prices start around L500,000 and include a week's room and board and ski passes. If you want to travel the region by bus or car, or if you're planning to stay in the region of interlocking trails around the Gruppo Sella, consider purchasing the **Superski Dolomiti** pass, good on all 430 cable-cars and lifts in the Dolomite area (around L40,000 per day, L200,000 per week). Ski rental costs about the same everywhere: cross-country L25,000, downhill L35,000. Christmas and early February to mid-March are considered high season, when prices are significantly higher than those quoted above. Regional passes cost considerably less.

Trent (Trento, Trient)

Trent has a history of cultural confrontation. Sandwiched between the Latin and German realms, the city seemed the perfect site for a summit on the challenge posed to Rome from beyond the Alps, and in the 16th century the Council of Trent pondered the problems of Lutheran contagion for 18 ineffective and inefficient years. Cultural and physical ownership of the city itself was contested in the 19th century, but the question of national identity was settled once and for all at the conclusion of World War I when Trent was chalked up as a Habsburg loss. Over the past few decades, the once-disputed land has led a life of undisturbed tranquility, and the calm of the city's frescoed *piazze* and numerous parks makes Trent a relaxing stop on any tour of northern Italy.

Orientation and Practical Information

Behind Trent's train station flows the Adige River; in front are the public gardens. A right turn on via Pozzo will take you past a helpful signboard map at the corner of the garden to via Orfane which becomes via Cavour and leads to p. del Duomo. An earlier left on via Roma leads in the direction of the Castello del Buonconsiglio. Virtually everything of importance is concentrated within the small historic center.

Tourist Office: Azienda Autonoma, via Alfieri, 4 (tel. 98 38 80), diagonally across p. Dante and the public gardens to the right from the train station. Ask for the glossy English text *Trento,* which is pretty enough to be kept as a souvenir after its use. Open Mon.-Sat. 9am-noon and 3-6pm, Sun. 10am-noon. **Azienda per la Promozione Turistica del Trentino,** corso III Novembre, 134 (tel. 98 00 00), a 15-min. walk away on the continuation of via Santa Croce. A library's worth of literature on the Trentino province is yours for the asking. *Splash of Colours* provides photos and data on the various areas within the province. If you're driving, ask for the Trentino road map with photos and itinerary suggestions.

Budget Travel: CTS, via Cavour, 21 (tel. 98 15 33), near p. del Duomo. Student IDs, Transalpino tickets, and occasional organized outings. Open Mon.-Fri. 9am-noon and 3:30-6:30pm, Sat. 9am-noon.

Post Office: via Calepina, 16 (tel. 98 72 70), at p. Vittoria. Open Mon.-Fri. 8:10am-7:40pm, Sat. 8:10am-1pm. Another office to the left from the train station on via Dogana. Same hours. **Postal Code:** 38100.

Telephones: SIP, p. della Portella, the 1st right from via Pozzo. Open Mon.-Sat. 8:30am-12:15pm and 3:30-7pm, Sun. 8am-1pm. **Telephone Code:** 0461.

Trains: tel. 82 36 71. To: Verona (every hr., 1hr., L7200); Bolzano (every hr., 45min., L4300); Bologna (11 per day, 3hr., L15,400); Venice (7 per day, 3hr., L12,100). **Luggage Storage:** L1500. Open 24 hrs.

Buses: next to train station (tel. 98 36 27). To Riva del Garda (every hr., 1hr., L4600). Extensive local service. Ask at the information booth in the station for schedules.

Bike "Rental": p. Mostra, in front of the Castello del Buonconsiglio. ID and a L10,000 deposit get you a free bike for 3hr. Look for the parking-lot-keeper of the castle in a blue shirt and cap. Other depots at via Torre Vanga, the youth hostel, and p. Garzetti. Open Mon.-Fri. 8am-8pm, Sat. 8am-1pm.

Hiking Equipment: Rigoni Sport, p. Battisti, 30/31 (tel. 98 12 39). Open Tues.-Sun. 9:10am-noon and 3-7pm, Mon. 3-7pm. **Mountain Shop,** via Buonarotti, 4 (tel. 82 42 58), near the campground. Inexpensive.

English Bookstore: Libreria Disertori, via M. Diaz, 11 (tel. 98 14 55), near p. Battisti. One case full of English-language volumes in the front left corner as you enter. Open Tues.-Sat. 8:30am-noon and 3:30-7pm, Mon. 3:30-7pm.

Swimming Pool: Nuova Lido Piscina Coperta, via Fogazzaro, 4 (tel. 91 10 06), off viale Verona, a continuation of corso III Novembre. Outdoor and indoor. Open daily 9am-8pm. Admission L4500, children L2000.

Emergencies: tel. 113. **Police: Questura,** p. Mostra (tel. 98 61 13). **Hospital: Ospedale Santa Chiara,** largo Medaglie d'Oro (tel. 92 51 25), past the swimming pool and up via Orsi. **Alpine Emergency: CAI-SAT hotline,** tel. 23 31 66. The **fire station,** tel. 115, can also reach alpine help.

Accommodations

Trent teems with rooms for rent except in August, when private rooms are impossible to find without reservations. The hostel is by far the best option. Check with the tourist office about Agriturismo.

Ostello Giovane Europa (HI), via Manzoni, 17 (tel. 23 45 67), a continuation of via Torre Verde. Hotel turned hostel. Director S. Ferrari opened the hostel in 1989 as a favor to the city. 1- to 6-person rooms. Bar and TV. Check-in from 7:15am. Lockout 9am-5:30pm. Curfew midnight. L15,000 per person; breakfast included. Lunch and dinner for groups only (L12,000).

Casa della Giovane, via Prepositura, 58 (tel. 23 43 15). Take a right off via Pozzo from the station at the 1st real intersection, and turn left at p. da Vinci. Set back from the street behind a housing complex that doubles conveniently as soundproofing. Spotless rooms with the latest in modern plumbing. Filled with students Sept.-early June. Check-out by 9:30am. Curfew 11pm. Singles L18,000, with bath L20,000. Doubles with bath L18,000 per person. Women only.

Hotel Venezia, p. Duomo, 45 (tel. 23 41 14), a *dipendenza* of the hotel of the same name around the corner. Both have clean, standard rooms, some with a view of the *duomo.* Quality and prices are the same. Singles L30,000, with bath L45,000. Doubles L52,000, with bath L70,000. Breakfast L6000.

Al Cavallino Bianco, via Cavour, 29 (tel. 23 15 42), down the street from the *duomo.* Spacious rooms, but the main draw is the uninhibited paint job in the living room—enjoy the great outdoors from the comfort of your hotel! No breakfast option, but an espresso machine brews a cup for a measly L500. Singles L30,000, with bath L45,000. Doubles L50,000, with bath L70,000. Triples with bath L93,000. Closed in Dec. and 1 week in June.

Camping: Camping Trento (tel. 82 35 62), on lungadige Braille, a 20-min. walk upstream along the river. Take bus #2. After the Centrale Elettrica, walk 500m up to the pharmacy. Reception closes at 11pm. L5500 per person,L7500 per site. Open March-Oct. 15. Closed for repairs in 1992; will reopen in 1993.

Food

The **market** in p. Lodron behind the *duomo* does its thing every morning from 8am to noon and occasional afternoons. **Open-air markets** spring up on Thursday in vie Maffei, Prati, Esterle, Torrione, and Borsieri, as well as p. d'Arogno. Budget buys await at **Supermarket Orvea,** via Belenzani, 49 (tel. 96 03 33; open Mon.-Fri 8:30am-12:30pm and 3:30-7:30pm, Sat. 8:30am-12:30pm).

Birreria Pedavena, via S. Croce, 15 (tel. 98 62 55). Leave p. del Duomo on via S. Vigilio and go with the flow. A good introduction to the north-south hybrid cuisine. *Pasta e fagiole* L4500, *wurstel* dishes L5500-7000. Warm up to the atmosphere with a *bier* at the bar. Cover L1500. Open Aug.-June Wed.-Mon. 8:30am-midnight.

Ristorante/Pizzeria Chistè, via delle Orne, 4 (tel. 98 18 46). Serves huge portions that are popular with the locals. *Primi* about L5500. Pasta about L11,000. Cover L1000.

Pizzeria Duomo, p. Duomo, 22 (tel. 98 42 86). Pizza any way you want it. Loosen your belt and tackle the *luna,* a double-calzone specialty (L10,000). Open Sun.-Fri. noon-2pm and 6-10:30pm. Closed for remodelling in 1992; scheduled to reopen in 1993.

La Cantinota, via S. Marco, 24 (tel. 98 03 61), at the other end of via Manci from via Roma. Enjoy the irreproachable cuisine, and humor the management by dropping by the piano bar after dessert. *Risotto* for at least 2 people L9000; *wurstel alla griglia* L12,000. Cover L2000. Open Aug.-June Fri.-Wed. 11:30am-2:30pm and 7pm-2am. Piano bar open 10pm-2:30am.

Sights and Entertainment

The pointed dome of Trent's Gothic-Romanesque **duomo,** also known as the **Cathedral of Saint Vigilio,** rises in modest emulation of the looming Alps. Inside, two unusual twin-arcaded staircases climb the walls of the nave, while the remains of 13th- and 14th-century frescoes decorate the transept. The famed Council's decrees were delivered in front of the huge cross in the Chapel of the Holy Crucifix. A group of fascinating "knotted" columns, miracles of medieval stonemasonry, support the eastern end of the building outside. (Open daily 6:30am-noon and 2:30-8pm.) The remains of a 6th-century paleochristian basilica were recently uncovered beneath the *duomo.* Admission to this underground church is included in the admission to the **Museo Diocesano** (tel. 23 44 19), housed in the 12th-century Palazzo Pretorio. The museum contains famous Flemish tapestries as well as Council memorabilia. (Open mid-Feb. to mid-Nov. Mon.-Sat. 9:30am-12:30pm and 2:30-6pm. Admission L2000, students L1000.) The fountain of Neptune in the center of the *piazza* was erected in the 18th century. (Open Mon.-Sat. 9am-noon.)

Walk out of p. del Duomo and along **via Belenzani,** a Renaissance-era street with intricate frescoes from the 19th century. Take a right at the end of the street onto via Roma to continue to the **Castello del Buonconsiglio,** Trent's other main sight. Once the home of the bishop-prince who governed Trent, the castle was incorporated into the city walls. The disparate elements were finally merged in the 17th century by the patron-bishop Bernardo Clesio, who joined the corpulent round tower, part of the **Castello Vecchio,** to the Renaissance **Magno Palazzo,** built in 1536. The castle houses the **Museo Provinciale d'Arte** with frescoes by Dosso Dossi in the Sala Grande and the remarkable "frescoes of the 12 months" by an anonymous 15th-century artist in the **Torre dell'Aquila.** (Castle and museum tel. 23 37 70. Open Tues.-Sun. 9am-noon and 2-5:30pm; Oct.-March Tues.-Sun. 9am-noon and 2-5pm. Admission L4000 for ages 18-60; free on the first and third Sundays of the month.)

The diminutive church of **Santa Maria Maggiore** also merits a visit. Built in 1520, this Renaissance house of worship hosted the last meeting of the Council of Trent. When exiting, don't miss the bizarre heads protruding from the more recent building to the left on the edge of via Prepositura. The facade resembles a group of aristocrats peeking out to see who rang the doorbell. Consult the tourist office for a schedule of guided tours of Trent's monuments.

While you're at it, pick up the brochure for **If in Trentino in Summer a Castle,** a series of concerts, dance, and other media presentations held in castles around Trentino from June to September. (Admission free-L20,000.)

Mountains Near Trent

Monte Bondone rises majestically over Trent and begs for pleasant daytrips and overnight excursions. Check with the tourist office (tel. 94 71 28) in **Vaneze,** halfway up the mountain, about accommodations, ski lifts and maps. **Ski School Monte Bondone** (tel. 472 11) gives lessons and rents equipment. Pick up a map at the tourist office in Trent, and then catch the cable car from ponte di San Lorenzo, between the train tracks and the river, to **Sardagna,** a great picnic spot (cable car runs daily 7am-6:30pm, L2500). From there, a 10-12km hike takes you to the **Mezavia Campground.** (tel. 94 81 78; L5000 per person, L7000 per tent; open June to mid-Sept.)

Removed from the other Dolomites, the **Dolomiti di Brenta** (Brenta Group) are among the most spectacular. The brochure *I Rifugi della S.A.T.,* available at the tourist office in Trent, contains all hut information for the Brenta Group. Prices run L12,000-15,000 per night, and they are usually open June 20 to September 20. The best base for exploring this area is **Molveno,** a small lakeside town that can be reached by Atesina bus from Trent. From here, a classic hike is the climb to **Rifugio T. Pedrotti** (2491m), a large Alpine hut beneath the Bocca di Brenta (tel. (0461) 58 60 42). From Molveno, take the chairlift to **Rifugio Pradel** and pick up trail #340. Continue on this trail until you reach **Rifugio Selvata** (1630m), where you can transfer to trail #319. This path will take you to the summit (4hr.). Once you reach the top take trail #318 right away unless you have rock climbing equipment and want to tackle the world-famous **via della Bocchette.** Follow #318 under the via della Bocchette toward Madonna di Campiglio (4hr. to Pedrotti-Madonna). From Madonna di Campiglio, you can take the bus to Trent. Some opt to hitch.

Bolzano (Bozen)

Bolzano attempts to ease linguistic feuds with mandatory instruction in both Italian and German for its youth. The disproportionately large number of fair, rosy-cheeked bilinguists, however, reveals the city's true Austrian bent. Happily, underlying tensions have not interfered with Bolzano's growing prosperity. The historic center is an attractive combination of spacious *plätze/piazze* and arcaded alleys, presenting a congenial face to the mountain-bound traveler.

Orientation and Practical Information

Bolzano's historic center rests in the hollow of the converging Isarco and Talvera rivers, and is linked by bridge to the more modern, industrial sectors to the west. Bolzano's street signs somewhat comically manifest its bilingualism, redundantly repeating themselves bilingually in both languages repetitiously (the insufferable linguistic chauvinists at *Let's Go* generally include only the Italian name). A brief walk up via Stazione from the train station, or via Alto Adige if you've arrived by bus, leads to the epicenter of the old town, p. Walther.

Tourist Office: p. Walther, 8 (tel. 97 56 56 or 97 06 60). Lists of every accommodations option, including Agriturismo. *Walks and Hikes* suggests nearby hikes of varying lengths and difficulty. *Manifestazioni* includes several pages of tourist-oriented phone numbers. If you plan on spending 3 or more nights, ask about the **Visitor's Pass (Carta di Ospite)** which entitles you to several desirable freebies and discounts. Open Mon.-Fri. 8:30am-12:30pm and 2-6pm, Sat. 9am-12:30pm. **Provincial Tourist Office for South Tyrol,** p. Parrocchia, 11 (tel. 99 38 08), just down from p. Walther, across from the *duomo*. A must for those setting out for the mountains. Plan ahead and pick up the detailed hotel listings for the region. Dr. Hannsjörg Hager (tel. 99 38 09) is the resident hiking guru. Open Mon.-Fri. 8:30am-12:30pm and 2-5:30pm. Dr. Hager arrives at 9am.

Budget Travel: CTS, via Rovigo, 38 (tel. 93 41 46), across the river, off via Milano just past p. Matteotti. Open Mon.-Fri. 9am-12:30pm and 3:30-7pm, Sat. 9am-noon. **CIT,** p. Walther, 11 (tel. 97 85 16). Transalpino tickets and skiing packages. Open Mon.-Fri. 8:30am-12:30pm and 3-6:30pm.

Currency Exchange: Banca Nazionale del Lavoro, at the end of via Stazione at p. Walther. The best rates, and full Visa services. Open Mon.-Fri. 8:20am-1:20pm and 3-4:30pm.

Post Office: via della Posta, 1 (tel. 97 84 32), by the *duomo*. Open Mon.-Fri. 8:15am-5:15pm, Sat. 8:15am-12:45pm. **Postal Code:** 39100.

Telephones: SIP, p. Parrocchia, 17 (tel. 99 11 11), to the left of the post office. Open Mon.-Sat. 8:30am-12:15pm and 3:30-7:45pm, Sun. 8am-1pm. **ASST,** via Roma, 36/M, across the river near p. Adriano. Open Mon.-Sat. 8am-8pm. **Telephone Code:** 0471.

Trains: p. Stazione (tel. 97 42 92). To: Trent (19 per day, 45min., L4300); Verona (14 per day, 1hr. 15min., L10,500); Merano (every 45min., 45min., L3200); Milan (2 per day, 4hr., L20,400). **Information** open daily 8-11:55am and 2:20-5:25pm. **Luggage Storage:** L1500. Open 24 hrs.

Buses: via Perathoner, 4 (tel. 97 51 17), between the train station and p. Walther. To: Alpe di Siusi (7 per day, 1hr. 30min., L5200); Collalbo (5 per day, 50min., L2600); Cortina d'Ampezzo (4 per day, 3hr. 30min., L13,700); Merano (3 per day, 1hr., L3800); Brunico (8 per day, 1hr. 45min., L8100).

Car Rental: Avis, p. Verdi, 18 (tel. 97 14 67). **Hertz,** via Alto Adige, 30 (tel. 97 71 55).

Bike "Rental": via Stazione, near p. Walther. Borrow a bike for 4hr. by leaving a L10,000 deposit and ID information.

Hiking Information: Club Alpino Italiano (CAI), p. Erbe/Obstplatz, 46 (tel. 97 81 72), and **Alpenverein Südtirol (AVS),** via dei Bottai/Bindergasse, 25 (tel. 97 87 29). These are, respectively, the Italian and Austrian Südtirol Alpinist clubs. Weekend daytrips about L15,000 (CAI trips Sun. only). *Kompass Wanderkarte* for the area, billboard with offers of used ski equipment. CAI open Mon.-Fri. 11am-12:30pm and 5-7pm. AVS open Mon.-Fri. 3:30-7:30pm.

Camping Equipment: Sportler, via dei Portici/Laubengasse, 37/A (tel. 97 40 33). Expensive, extensive selection. Open Mon.-Fri. 9am-12:15pm and 2:30-7pm, Sat. 9am-12:15pm.

Swimming Pool: Piscina Coperta, viale Trieste (tel. 91 10 00), across the river. Indoor pool. Open Oct.-June Tues.-Fri. 12:30-2:30pm and 7-9pm, Sat. 4-6pm and 6:30-8:30pm, Sun. 3-6pm and 6:30-8:30pm.

Laundromat: Lavanderia Automatica Westinghouse, p. Matteotti, 3 (tel. 91 44 46), across the river off via Torino. The luxury of washing your own clothes can be yours for the price of a good dinner (L15,000). Open Mon.-Fri. 8am-noon and 2:30-7pm.

Emergency: tel. 113. Police: tel. 94 76 11. Medical Emergency: tel. 90 83 30. Hospital: Ospedale Regionale San Maurizio, via Lorenz Böhler (tel. 90 81 11). Medical Assistance: White Cross, tel. 27 44 44.

Accommodations and Camping

Bolzano has budget deals up the wazoo in the spring and fall; in summer and winter, however, you'll have to keep your eyes peeled to find anything affordable. Given the magnificent surroundings, it is almost a pity to stay in the city. Try the mountain options or ask about the Agriturismo program at the tourist office.

Magdalena Weinstube, Sta. Maddalena di Sotto, 22 (tel. 97 43 80). Worth the hike toward St. Magdalena. Beautiful farmhouse with a stupendous view of the city. All rooms with bath. L20,000 per person, but you must stay more than 1 night. Breakfast included.

Pensione Reiseggerhof, Sta. Maddalena di Sotto, 24 (tel. 97 86 94), uphill from Weinstube. More great views, along with heart-warming floral trim on the furniture in the sunny doubles. All rooms with bath. Doubles L25,000 per person. Breakfast included.

Albergo Klaus, via della Mostra/Kohlernstraße, 14 (tel. 97 12 94), 1km above town. Walk to the right from the station down via Renon, then go under the tracks and over the river. Question your sanity as you climb into the "Kohlerbahn" cable car, and pat yourself on the back when you discover the Edenic retreat at the other end. A real farmhouse with friendly people and a noticeable drop in temperature from the valley below. All rooms with bath. L22,000 per person. Breakfast included. Funicular L5000 round-trip, L6000 with luggage (last at 8pm).

Hotel Regina Angelorum, via Renon, 1 (tel. 97 21 95), across from the train station. A dependable last resort if you can't find accommodations elsewhere. All rooms with bathrooms attached, and breakfast is an all-you-can-snarf, self-service affair. Singles L46,000, low season (Oct.-June) L44,000. Doubles L78,000, low season L72,000. Triples L99,000, low season L92,000. Quads L130,000, low season L122,000. Closed in Nov.

Camping: Moosbauer, via San Maurizio, 83 (tel. 91 84 92). Take bus #8 from the station (last at 8:30pm). L6500 per person, L11,000 per site.

Food

Rindsgulasch is a delicious beef stew, *Speck* is tasty smoked bacon, and *Knödel* (dumplings) come in dozens of rib-sticking varieties. Fall spotlights the local vineyards with the week-long Südtiroler Törgelen tasting spree. Festive p. dell Erbe (Obstplatz) has an all-day produce **market** every day but Sunday, and two **Despar supermarkets** thrive at via della Rena, 40, and via dei Bottai, 29 (both open Mon.-Fri. 8:30am-12:30pm and 3:45-7:15pm, Sat. 8am-12:30pm). For baked goods, revel among the delectable selections at **Panificio/Backerei Lemayr,** via Goethe, 17 (open Mon.-Fri. 7am-12:30pm and 3:30-7:15pm, Sat. 7:30am-12:30pm).

Restaurant Weisses Rössl, via dei Bottai/Bindergasse, 6 (tel. 97 32 67), the continuation of via Laurin and via dei Grappoli, at the end of via dei Portici. A cheap place with great Austrian atmosphere. Nearly 100 regional and Italian dishes listed plus a daily *menù* (L7500-12,000). Open Aug.-June Mon.-Fri. 7am-1am, Sat. 7am-3pm.

Spaghetti Express, via Goethe, 20 (tel. 97 53 35). A noisy, fun place with a young crowd. Try any of the umpteen kinds of pasta (L7000-9500)—the dish with crabmeat, cream, and brandy is great. Cover L1500. Open Mon.-Sat. noon-2pm and 7-10pm.

Sights and Entertainment

Piazza Walther is altogether clean and attractive—even the McDonald's on the corner is tasteful. The 14th-century Gothic **duomo,** which presides over the *piazza/platz,* reaches skyward with a tower of lace-like delicacy designed by Johann Lutz. The interior presents an interesting juxtaposition of medieval fresco fragments and postmodern pink marble altars. (Open Mon.-Fri. 9:30am-6pm, Sat. 9:30am-noon.) The 14th-century **Church of the Francescani** rests in a peaceful garden off the *piazza.* (Open daily 6am-noon and 2:30-6pm.) The firetowers of the 13th-century **Castel Mareccio** (tel. 97 66 15), on passeggiata lungo Talvera, are later additions. (Open Mon.-Sat. 10am-noon and 3-6pm.)

Across the Talvera River, the quarter around p. Gries boasts two imposing churches. Martin Knoller frescoes grace the 1770 **Church of the Benedictine Abbey of Muri** (tel. 28 11 16) on the *piazza,* a mighty Baroque construction. (Open 9-11:30am and 3-6pm. Ring side bell.) Michael Pacher carved the delicate whorls of the retable altarpiece (1471-80) inside the **Gries Parish Church** (tel. 28 54 87), off the *piazza.* (Open Feb.-Nov. Mon.-Fri. 10:30am-noon and 2:30-4pm. Call ahead.) Free guided tours of the town sights depart from the tourist office Wednesday and Saturday mornings at 9:30am.

The bike-borrowing option is the best way to visit the castles that cluster in the nearby valleys. **Castello Mareccio,** closest to the center, has a core structure which dates back to the 13th century. A 15-minute ride up via Weggerstein to via S. Antonio will take you past **Castello Roncolo** (tel. 98 02 00), the most impressive of the lot. Guided tours of the frescoed rooms are available for groups, preferably by reservation. (Open April-Nov. Tues.-Sat. 10am-5pm. Admission L1000.)

Abundant annual cultural events include **provincial wine exhibitions** (March-April) and the **F. Busoni International Piano Competition** (late Aug.-early Sept.). The monthly information booklet contains a day-by-day listing of events, including English-language movie showings.

The Dolomites around Bolzano

The mountains around Bolzano beg to be explored on foot. Pick up a *Kompass Wanderkarte* from any newsstand or tobacco shop and consult Dr. Hager at the Alpine Desk of the provincial tourist office.

To get a feel for the mountains without expending much energy, take a daytrip to **Soprabolzano** (Oberbozen/auf dem Ritten) and **Collalbo** (Klobenstein). The **Funivia del Renon** (Renon cable car, or Rittnerbahn) climbs to scenic Soprabolzano from Bolzano's via Renon, to the right of the train station (round-trip L7200). From there, a train will take you the 7km to Collalbo (every hr., round-trip L3800). Both the villages and their environs invite leisurely hikes.

Fortunately, the **Alpe di Suisi/Seiseralm** and the **Catinaccio/Rosengarten** Group are close to Bolzano. These spectacular sights have the highest concentration of *rifugi* in the region. Four or five buses per day leave Bolzano for almost every town in the area, many of which are only 40 minutes away.

Enter the Sciliar/Schlern Group from the west at **Fiè allo Sciliar/Völs** or **Tiers.** Four hours on easy footpaths puts you at **Rifugio Bolzano di Monte Pez/Schlernhaus** (tel. (0471) 61 20 24; open late June-Oct. 5). Yet another hike (3-4hr.) brings you from Tiers to **Rifugio Bergamo/Grasleitenhütte** (tel. (0471) 64 21 03; open late June-Sept. daily 8am-8pm). Both are breathtaking refuges built in the 1880s by the Alpine clubs.

To get into the Catinaccio Group from the south, catch a bus to Passo di Constalunga/Karer Pass, and get off at the Alpenrose Hotel, where a chairlift runs to **Rifugio Paolina.** (Tel. (04710) 61 20 08; open June-Oct. 20 and Dec. 24-Easter daily 9am-noon and 3-6pm.) To continue toward the Sciliar/Schlern Group, you can follow one of two possible routes. If you feel energetic, follow trail #550, which climbs steeply up to Passo delle Coronelle (2630m) and then descends (meeting trail #541) to Rifugio Vaiolet. The huts mentioned are only a few out of the 20 or so packed into a relatively small area. Consult local Alpinists and your map to discover others.

Merano

Merano recently celebrated its 150th anniversary as Italy's most popular spa. A protective shield of tall mountains to the north, coupled with a lack of the same to the south, have given the town a sunnier, less variable climate than many of its neighbors. The enthusiastic patronage of Austrian royalty during the late 1800s added a veneer of *fin de siècle* elegance to the medieval architecture at the town's core.

Thirty kilometers northwest of Bolzano, Merano is a quick train or bus ride away (5 trains per day, 40min., L2800; 3 **SAD** buses per day, L3800). Both buses and trains stop in p. Stazione/Bahnhofplatz. From here, via Europa departs to the right, intersecting corso Libertà/Freiheitsstrasse at p. Mazzini. Follow this to the center of town and the **tourist office** at corso Libertà/Freiheitsstrasse, 45 (tel. 352 23), where the staff provides in-depth accommodations information and a free map supplying useful numbers and addresses. The post office is at via Roma, 2, across the Postbrücke from the center (open Mon.-Fri. 8am-12:30pm and 3-6:30pm, Sat. 9am-noon and 3-5pm). The region's four-hour free **bike "rental"** deal operates from the parking lot next to the station— bring ID and a L10,000 deposit (open daily 9am-6pm). Whether you plan to tackle the slopes by foot or wheel, consult the **Alpine Association,** via Galilei, 45 (tel. 371 34; open Mon.-Fri. 9:30am-noon), or the **CAI** office, corso Libertà, 188 (tel. 489 44), for up-to-date information. CAI has unpredictable hours, so call ahead. To relax afterwards, try the **Health Spa Center,** across the river from the Kurpromenade. It has every facility imaginable, but luxury has its price. Call for a full run-down of options (tel. 377 24). In cases of **emergency,** dial 113, or try the **police** (via Manzoni, tel. 493 33). The local **hospital, Ospedale Locale,** is at Goethestrasse, 50 (tel. 461 11).

The downtown area is bursting at the seams with luxury hotels. The soil must be different on the surrounding hillsides, however, for here homey guesthouses have sprung up boldly in the midst of the more grandiose upstarts. The **Villa Pax,** via Leichter, 3/A (tel. 362 90), is a nun-run establishment that houses local female students during the off-season and opens its doors to travelers of both sexes from March to November. Walk up via Cavour or take bus #1A (which stops at the station and the tourist office, L1000) to Brunnerplatz. Turn right on via Dante, and left shortly thereafter. Comfortable rooms and a friendly atmosphere more than compensate for the mildly institutional exterior. The benevolent proprietresses have even installed a tiny kitchenette to shield their guests from Merano's soaring restaurant prices. All rooms come with bath. (L23,000 per person; breakfast included.) Reserve ahead for August and September. The nearby **Casa Pallotti/Pallottiheim,** via delle Piante, 7/9 (tel. 301 32), is a bright white building boasting a pool, garden, and good green countryside all in addition to its sunny rooms (all with bath). Only men are welcome. Following the directions to Brunnerplatz, take a left on via Virgilio, and look for via delle Piante on your right after 10-15min. (L22,000 per person, breakfast included.)

Restaurants and hotels are analogously priced, but with a little hunting the budget traveler can fend off starvation. The **A&O supermarket** at via dei Portici, 213, has cheap picnic material; shady parks and benches throughout Merano offer ample space for a makeshift meal. (Open Mon.-Sat. 8:30am-12:15pm and 4-6pm.) A weekly **market** floods the area around the railway station with edibles and inedibles alike on Friday mornings from 8am to 12:30pm. To reach **Ristorante Merano/Meraner Weinstube,** p. Duomo, 4 (tel. 361 83), walk down a couple of stairs, down a hallway, into a not-so-bright dining room—and enjoy a hearty meal for a harmless price. A culturally confused *menù* is L13,500, with more modest combination plates available for L7000. The unambiguously named house specialty, *Meraner Weinstubenplatte,* is L36,000 for two people, all garnishings included. (Open Fri.-Wed. 11am-2pm and 6-9pm.)

Merano's primary attraction lies in its capacity for enhancing personal well-being; the theme here is *relaxation.* Pick up *Merano, Programma Manifestazioni e Concerti,* a biweekly brochure which covers everything from celluloid festivals to cellulite control. For visual entertainment, the **Kurhaus** dominates the Kurpromenade with its recently restored art nouveau splendor, and the rival edifices throughout town provide an eyeful from any angle. The **Castello Principesco** is situated in the historic center behind the town hall. Its 15th-century atmosphere has been dutifully preserved and the rooms are almost overbearingly quaint. (Open Mon.-Sat. 9am-noon and 2-6pm. Admission L4000.) The nearby town of **Tirolo** derives its fame from the **Castle Tirolo,** which gave its name to the entire region. The castle can be reached by bus and a short walk; consult the tourist office for additional information.

Near Merano lies the Giogáia di Tessa/Texelgruppe mountain range, an appendage to the eastern Alps. The **nature park** here accommodates humans with two high paths girdling the mountains, the **Meraner Hohenweg.** The southern road is dotted with farms and refuges, making a short visit manageable at whim, while the northern road offers more isolated hiking but a scarcity of huts. Consult the tourist office in Merano for more information.

Brunico (Bruneck)

Northeast of Bolzano and just a snowball's throw from Austria sits little Brunico. The quaint streets of the city center look like the fruits of a toddler's enthusiastic labors with pastel Crayolas, while the surrounding farmlands and mountains suggest that the young artist misplaced everything but the lushest shade of green.

Orientation and Practical Information

The Brunico train station sits at the head of via Europa, which arcs its way past the bus station and tourist office almost all the way to the center of town. Via Centrale and via Oberragen together compose the central walkway. The two streets curve to accommodate the Schlossberg, on which rests the Castello di Brunico, the fortress whose construction paved the way for the settlement of the village.

Tourist Office: AAST, via Europa, 22 (tel. 857 22), upstairs from the bus station at the midway point of the street's 90° turn. Pick up the little book *Kronplatz,* and the pamphlet *Brunico; Focus for a Wide Variety of Holidays.* Extensive information on accommodations, although the helpful staff draws the line at actually reserving a room for you. Open Mon.-Fri. 8am-12:30pm and 2-6pm, Sat. 8am-noon.

Post Office: via Europa (tel. 853 08), just before the bus station. Open Mon.-Sat. 8:15-6:45pm. **Postal Code:** 39031.

Telephones: SIP, at the bus station. Open until about 11pm. **Telephone Code:** 0474.

Trains: beginning of via Europa (tel. 858 26). To: Fortezza (12 per day, 30min., L2800) and Bolzano via Fortezza (4 per day, 1hr. 30min., L5700). Ticket window open 6am-8:10pm. Open 6am-9pm.

Buses: SAD, via Europa, 22, downstairs from the tourist office. Some breathtaking, stomach-wrenching rides through the Dolomites. To: Bolzano (10 per day, 1hr. 30min., L8100); Merano (3 per day, 2hr. 30min., L10,900); Cortina D'Ampezzo (4 per day, 1hr. 30min., L6700); Innsbruck (1 per day, 2hr. 30min., L12,600). The ticket office is closed on Sunday, so buy your tickets in advance.

Bike Rental: Velo, via S. Lorenzo (tel. 208 44), a continuation of via Michael Pacher. L4000 per hr., L15,000 per day.

Emergencies: tel. 113. **Police:** via S. Lorenzo, 17 (tel. 851 18). **Hospital:** via Ospedale (tel. 853 33 or 203 33). **Alpine Emergency:** tel. 305 50. **Mountain Rescue Service:** tel. 844 44.

Accommodations and Camping

The tourist office distributes a list of rooms in private homes, which may be your best bet if you have your heart set on staying downtown.

Pension Notburgaheim, via Bruder Willram, 4. Directly alongside the river with a view of the castle, the bulbous steeple of the Rain Church, and their very own vegetable garden. All the bathrooms are down the hall, but the central location offers some solace. L19,000 per person. Breakfast included.

Ragen Haus, via Bruder Willram, 29 (tel. 848 18). Down the street from Notburgaheim and across the river from the Parish Church. A very square building with a garden. All rooms with bath, most with a terrace. L28,000 per person, low season L25,000. Breakfast included.

Camping: Campeggio Bersaglio (tel. 413 26), by the Schiesstand. 8000 square meters of forest with a restaurant. L2100 per person, L5000 per site. Open May-Sept.

Food

The **weekly market** on Wednesday mornings on via Europa provides an opportunity to browse and nosh, but on other days Stadtgasse/via Centrale do almost as well. The

G. Meinl Supermarket at Stadtgasse, 11, has shelves of cheap staples, while their kitchen whips up a different regional menu every day (open Mon.-Fri. 8:30am-12:15pm and 3-7pm, Sat. 8:30am-noon). The **H. Frisch bakery** two doors down (look for the brass pretzel) has mounds of bread and oodles of multi-flavored strudel (L1000 per piece). (Open Mon.-Sat. 7am-12:15pm and 4-7pm.)

Hotel Krone, via Oberraggen, 8 (tel. 852 67). *Primi* L2800-5000, and *schnitzel*-laden *secondi* L6500-8000. Open Sun.-Fri. noon-2pm and 7-9pm.

Mensa KVW (tel. 850 56), in back of the big white and yellow building on via Tobl. Packed with laborers, it's the best buy in Alto Adige. *Menù* L6500. Open daily 11:30am-3pm.

Sights and Entertainment

Brunico is better known for its natural wonders than for its art, but there is enough of interest to fill the restful hours after an outdoor excursion. In 1250, the Bishop of Bressanone gave orders to have a castle built atop the modest elevation of the Schlossberg, and the single street of houses below rapidly expanded into a thriving village. The **Castello di Brunico,** also known as the **Bishop's Castle,** underwent several renovations throughout the Gothic era, but the overall effect is still that of a stolid fortress. Inquire at the tourist office about visits to the royal rooms and chapel.

The **Rain Church** sends forth its onion-shaped steeple from halfway up the Schlossberg. The church was rebuilt in the Baroque style in 1675, but is not as exciting an attraction as its elegant spire would have you believe when seen from the streets below. More gripping is the **Parish Church,** by the town cemetery. Brunico was the hometown of the Gothic woodworker Michael Pacher, and this monochrome manila place of worship shelters a crucifix by the native whittling whiz, as well as the Südtirol's largest Mathis organ.

Near Brunico

Brunico lives for the mountains and you'll find the attitude contagious. Skiing is splendid in winter, hiking unbeatable in summer. The tourist office in Brunico burgeons with appropriate info, although much of it comes only in German and Italian. Try to squeeze an English translation out of the staff. In winter, the **Skirama Kronplatz-Plan de Corones** ski pass, which is sold for about L180,000, gets you a week of unlimited mileage on the neighboring peaks of San Vigilio and Valdaora in addition to the supreme Kronplatz. For hiking, purchase a map of foot paths and trails near Brunico at the tourist office. A list of alpine guides is also available. The experts will help with your itinerary for hiking or skiing.

Several trails lead out from the towns around Brunico. **Riscone,** the toe to Mt. Kronplatz's foot, lies only 10 minutes away by bus. Swanky **Cortina d'Ampezzo** lolls in ostentation one hour to the south. Overpriced and crowded, this jet-set reserve makes an interesting daytrip—you too can glimpse Beautiful People as they forage through boutiques. Stand back and watch carefully: when they spot appealing merchandise they'll charge it in an instinctive display of conspicuous-consumption aggression. Other than this fascinating fauna, however, there is little of affordable or enduring interest in Cortina.

The Lake Country

The Italian Lakes have the rare ability to turn even a great writer into a puddle of romantic goo. Although some of Stendhal's most florid prose was engendered by his attempt to describe the region, we at *Let's Go* hope to avoid that fate. After you've visited (and you really must visit), you too can bore your friends with the sort of breathless, enchanted effusions 19th-century Romantics produced by the dozen.

To properly discriminate among the ooh-aah candidates, you should bear in mind the differing personalities of the lakes. Garda draws a younger crowd with sailboard-speckled waters by day and an assortment of nightclubs after sunset. Como hosts the sophisticates from nearby Milan, while Lago Maggiore doggedly retains a supine elegance with its elderly luxury hotels lining the shore. The cleaner waters of Garda and Orta are preferable for swimmers, but any lake will do if you prefer to contemplate placid ripples from *terra firma.*

Restaurant prices have soared to rival the mountains; plan on a picnic or two (small *alimentari* abound). Local cheeses include *robiola* (a cream cheese), *caprino* (goat cheese), the soft, tangy *taleggio,* and the piquant *fontale.* All cost about L1200 per *etto,* enough for several sandwiches. A specialty of the Como region is *agone,* sun-cured fish from the lake. *Brianza* is the trademark name of most local wines.

Lake Garda (Lago di Garda)

Garda is the grandest of the Italian lakes and also the most popular, thanks to its breezy summer and mild winter. Overlooked in favor of its western neighbors in the last century, it now boasts a more contemporary air. Of the lake's major towns, only three warrant a visit: Riva for its seclusion, reasonable prices, and splendid swimming; Gardone Riviera for the morbidly fascinating villa of Gabriele D'Annunzio; and Sirmione for its extensive Roman ruins and beautifully situated medieval castle. If you're coming from Verona, consider a daytrip to the tiny but stunning bay at **Punta San Vigilio** (just past Garda) for swimming, sunning, and picnicking.

Desenzano lies on the Milan-Venice train line, two hours from Venice, 25 minutes from Verona and Brescia, and one hour from Milan. Once there, it's easy to get to the lake towns by bus or the more expensive hydrofoils and ferries. Check the schedules carefully and plan ahead, as buses and ferries stop running early in the evening. For shorter trips take the ferry—it's cheaper and you can sit on deck. However, the hydrofoil makes the Riva-Desenzano trip in only two hours (L20,800), while the regular ferries leave infrequently and take four hours (L10,400). **Campgrounds** surround the lake but are concentrated between Desenzano and Salò; unofficial camping is discouraged. Many private residences rent rooms (mostly doubles) in Lake Garda's larger towns. Get a list of these from the tourist office, and then head out, ready to bargain.

Sirmione

Alas, shrewd developers realized the potential of what Catullus once lauded as the "jewel of peninsulae and islands," and Sirmione's natural beauty is consequently in danger of extinction. The Space Boat Disco has landed just off-shore, and the expansive Garda Village is forthcoming. In the off-season, however, the crowds thin out, and the surviving cypress and olive groves that cluster at the peninsula's farthest point provide an attractive haven from the man-made wonders in the center of town.

Buses run to Sirmione every half-hour from Brescia and Verona (1hr., L3500 and L3900 respectively), and from Desenzano, the closest train station (L1500). The ride down the peninsula's central artery concludes in Sirmione on viale Marconi, next to the **tourist office** in the disk-shaped building at #2 (tel. 91 61 14), where you can arm yourself with maps and accommodations information. (Open Mon.-Fri. 9am-12:30pm and 3-7pm, Sat. 9am-12:30pm.) **Bikes** can be rented at **Green Walk,** via Verona, 47 (tel. 990 40 34) or on via XXV Aprile (L3000 per hr., L17,000 per day). The **postal code** for Sirmione is 25019; the **telephone code** for both Sirmione and Desenzano is 030. In **emergencies,** dial 113; for **medical emergencies,** call toll-free 1678 21049.

Sirmione is best visited on a daytrip; if you arrive in July or August without a reservation, plan on sleeping in the lake. Ask the tourist office for a list of private rooms as a possible last resort. **Albergo Flora,** at San Salvator, 7 (tel. 91 60 27) has large rooms for reasonable prices (singles L33,000; doubles L50,000, with bath L64,000). Campers have three options: **Sirmioncino** (tel. 91 90 45), in Colombare behind the Hotel Benaco, usually has space (L6400 per person, L1400 for tent and site). Lugana boasts two campsites in **Il Tiglio** (tel. 990 40 09) and **Lugana Marina** (tel 91 91 73).

Food prices drop marginally outside the castle's immediate vicinity. If the inescapable waterfront views have you craving seafood, the **Osteria del Pescatore** does the trick at via Piana, 20. Try the *trota dorato alla saliva,* a tasty trout dish fried in butter and sage, whose merits overshadow any juvenile misinterpretations of its name (L9000). Sirmione's **market** at piazzale Montebaldo shakes, rattles, and rolls on Friday mornings from 7:30am to 1pm.

Sights

Dominating the central *piazza* is the conspicuous **Rocca Scaligora,** built in the 13th century by Mastino I della Scala. You can roam around the interior and climb the lofty towers for the equally lofty sum of L6000 (open Tues.-Sun. 9am-6:30pm, in winter 9am-1pm). At the far end of the peninsula, the **Grotto di Catullo** offers views of native vegetation and the ruins of a Roman villa and bath complex (open Tues.-Sun. 9am-6pm; admission L6000). Between the ramparts and the ruins lie a clean and quiet public beach and the refreshingly modest **Church of San Pietro in Mavino.** The hilltop house of worship was originally constructed in the 9th century, and the interior retains some admirable 13th-century frescoes.

Gardone Riviera

Home to Lake Garda's most famous sight, D'Annunzio's villa **Il Vittoriale,** Gardone Riviera entices crowds of German hedonists with the frisson of fascism and the promise of a tan. Still, the hills behind Gardone are threaded with walking paths, and aging lemon groves scent the air.

Orientation and Practical Information

Tourist Office: corso Repubblica, 35 (tel. 203 47), in the center of Gardone Sotto. When you get off the boat, turn left onto the *corso*. Pamphlets are few, but the affable staff fills in the gaps. Ask for the map of nearby walks. Information on rooms, but no reservations. Open Mon.-Sat. 9am-12:30pm and 3:30-6:30pm, Sun. 9am-12:30pm; in winter Mon.-Sat. 9am-12:30pm and 3-6pm.

Post Office: via Roma, 8 (tel. 208 62). Open Mon.-Fri. 8:10am-1:30pm, Sat. 8:30-11:40am. **Postal Code:** 25083.

Telephone Code: 0365.

Buses: To and from Brescia (every 30min., L3400), Desenzano (6 per day, 2hr. 30min., L2500), Milan (3 per day, 3hr., L11,400), and Riva (6 per day, 1hr. 15min., L3700).

Emergencies: tel. 113. **Medical Assistance:** tel. 413 nights and holidays.

Accommodations and Food

Do the daytrip thing to Gardone. Rooms are expensive and breakfast is often required. If you must stay, the views from **Pensione Hohl,** via del Colli, 4 (tel. 201 60), might ameliorate the financial pain (singles L30,000; doubles L44,000). **Pizzeria/Ristorante Sans Souci,** vicolo al Lago off corso Repubblica on the lake side, serves food in the cool calm of a cellar and veranda. *Primi* run L5000-10,000 and pizza goes for L4500-9000. (Open Tues.-Sun. noon-3pm and 6pm-3am.)

Sights and Entertainment

Above Gardone sprawls the sunset playground of Gabriele D'Annunzio (1863-1938), the poet, novelist, and latter-day Casanova with a fondness for a well-roasted baby. Parked in the garden is the prow of the battleship *Puglia,* the emblem of D'Annunzio's popularity. After World War I, he raised an army of poetry lovers and steamed across the Adriatic to snatch Fiume from infant Yugoslavia, to the embarrassment of diplomats and the cheers of nationalists.

In 1925 Mussolini presented a lovely rural villa to the poet in an attempt to shut him up; even Il Duce found D'Annunzio's ultra-nationalist squawking embarrassing. D'Annunzio promptly christened the villa *Il Vittoriale,* after Italy's recent victory over the Austrians, and proceeded to kitschify it into a castle of self-commemorative gloom only he and Vincent Price could call home.

D'Annunzio regularly went into debt to stuff his house with the most expensive, useless, and unattractive bric-a-brac available; the fascist jumble-sale effect is most pronounced in his bathroom, which is strewn with 2000 weird and wacky objects. The *Sala del Mappamondo* contains a huge globe (*mappamondo*) on which to dream dreams of global conquest, while the *Sala del Lebbroso* guards the cradle/coffin in which D'Annunzio would lie to contemplate death and the surrounding leopard skins.

The Vittoriale is up the hill from Gardone, best reached along via Roma and via dei Colli. Visit the house early—before the crowds arrive. Taped tours of the house play in German, English, French and Italian; if you're lucky they will play your tongue. (Open Tues.-Sun. 9am-12:30pm and 2-6:30pm, until 5:30pm in winter. Admission L5000 to grounds, L15,000 for both grounds and house.) Visit the **botanical gardens** laid around a stately villa halfway up the hill to Il Vittoriale to recover from the perversity. (Open March-Oct. daily 8:30am-7pm. Admission L4000.)

The **Fondazione "al Vittoriale"** puts on a summer program of plays, concerts, and dance in the outdoor **Teatro del Vittoriale** (mid-July to early Aug., cheapest seats L15,000).

Riva del Garda

Presiding over Lake Garda's northernmost point, Riva's dramatic juncture of mountain and water announces the lake's extension into the Trentino region. This is the riveting landscape that once lured Thomas Mann and Friedrich Nietzsche to come and ponder. A trench-encircled off-limits·expanse during World War I, Riva wavers between its Austrian heritage, a legacy of Habsburg rule up to 1918, and its more recent affiliation with Italy. The question is partly settled by the Teutonic firmness with which weekending families take over the town. Join the flotilla of windsurfers at play in Riva's steady breezes, or explore the drier options afforded by a network of nearby hiking trails.

Orientation and Practical Information

Riva is easily reached by bus from Trent (8 per day, 1hr., L4300), and buses run frequently to and from the closest train station at Roverto (20min., L2100). The Roverto Sud exit of the Brennero Autobahn is only 15km away.

The **tourist office,** Giardini di Porta Orientale (tel. 55 44 44), to the left of the castle as you face the water, is helpful and informative even when closed for lunch. The electric board out front will help you locate hotel vacancies, and the maps posted in back will summon forth the latent hiker in you. Ask for a schedule of events to get the dope on Riva and other nearby lake towns. (Open Mon.-Sat. 9am-noon and 2:30-6:30pm.) **Bike rental** is available at via Fiume, 19, off p. Gazzoletti. Regular bikes cost L10,000 per day; mountain bikes run L15,000. The **hospital** is inland from the center on largo Inviolata (tel. 55 40 04). Riva's **telephone code** is 0464; its **postal code** is 38066.

Accommodations and Camping

Riva is one of Lake Garda's few affordable destinations. Still, come in off-season or make reservations for July and August many months ahead of time.

Ostello Benacus (HI), p. Cavour, 9 (tel. 55 49 11), next to the church in the center of town. Renovated in 1988, with new doubles and triples for women. Hot showers. Reception open 8-10am and 6pm-midnight, but the happy proprietor never stays away for long and the daytime lock-out is not enforced. Members only. L12,000 per person, breakfast at the adjacent *mensa* L3000. In summer advance reservations (with 30% deposit) are recommended. Open March-Oct.

Garni Carla, via Negrelli, 2 (tel. 55 21 40). From the Church of the Inviolata walk up viale dei Tigli, turn left on via Rosmini, then right onto via Negrelli. Sparkling rooms, cool balconies, and a small garden with some peculiar tropical shrubbery. Singles with bath L30,000. Doubles with bath L60,000. Additional L2000 charge if you are staying for only 1 night.

Locanda La Montanara, via Montanara, 20 (tel. 55 48 57). Central. Singles L22,000. Doubles with bath L44,000. Breakfast L5000. Half- and full pension provided in cozy downstairs *trattoria*. Reserve at least a month ahead for summer. Open April-Oct.

Villa Minerva, viale Roma, 40/A (tel. 55 30 31), near the Inviolata. A step up in decor and price. Singles L31,000, with bath and breakfast L38,000. Doubles L52,000, with bath and breakfast L60,000.

Camping: Bavaria, viale Rovereto, 100 (tel. 55 25 24), on the road toward Torbole. *Pizzeria*-equipped and right on the water. L13,500 per person, tent included. Open April-Oct.

Food

A large **open-air market** comes to Riva every other Wednesday on vias Dante, Prati, and Pilati, while the **supermarket** inland from the tourist office provides less sporadic service.

Alimar SRL, p. Cavour, 6 (tel. 55 49 11), next to the hostel. The usual *mensa* combo of cheerless appearances and heavenly prices. *Primi* L4500, *secondi* L6000. All-inclusive meals L10,000. Open Mon.-Fri. 11am-3pm and 6:30-8pm, Sat. 11am-3pm.

Birrera Spaten, via Maffel, 7 (tel. 51 36 70). The tablecloths in this centrally located eatery burst with all the color that the *mensa* threw away. Good food, garish plaids; beware the onset of fashion nausea. Pizza begins at L5500, *primi* at L5000. *Secondi* run L4000-9000. Open daily 10:30am-3pm and 5:30pm-midnight; off-season Tues.-Sun.

Sights

Riva's most prominent structure is the 12th-century **Rocca** (castle), surrounded by water and graced by a small shady park. The Austrian-influenced **Church of the Inviolata** (1611), up viale Roma, is an unusual example of Baroque architecture. Its octagonal exterior has three sets of finely carved wooden doors. **Cascata Varone** (3km from Riva) makes for an enjoyable excursion. The natural gorge that surrounds this 100m waterfall is breathtaking. Buses to Varone from Riva are few and oddly timed, but you can hike or rent a bike. Hitching is not uncommon. **Musica Riva** in July is an internationally known festival of performances by well-known young musicians with concerts held in churches, auditoriums, and the courtyard of the Rocca. (Admission free-L15,000.)

Lake Como (Lago di Como)

An air of poetic sublimity lingers over Lake Como's northern reaches. The shores combine the atmospheres of the Mediterranean and of the mountains—lavish villas tucked into a craggy backdrop, warmed by the heat of the Riviera sun and cooled by lakeside breezes. The "lake" itself is actually a forked amalgam of three long lakes joined in the Centro Lago area of Bellaggio, Tremezzo, Menaggio, and Varenna. The dense green slopes are peppered with villages—take the boat for Colico and get off at the first stop that strikes your fancy. Varenna is one of the best-preserved fishing hamlets on the lake. Regular boat service connects towns in all three areas of the lake, as do convenient buses.

Como

Situated on the southwestern tip at the receiving end of the Milan rail line, Como is the lake's token industrial center. The city is famous for silk manufacturing, and the preponderance of hyper-efficient lunch-time pit-stops removes the city from the languorous atmosphere permeating most lake towns.

Orientation and Practical Information

Como is a half-hour from Milan by train (every hr., L2700). As you leave the station (tel. 26 14 94), the town is straight ahead and the lake is to your left. There is another train station on the other side of town, **Ferrovia Nord Milano** (tel. 26 63 13), on via

Manzoni off lungo Lario Trieste, which serves only Milan (every 30min. morning and evening, every hr. 2-5pm, L4600).

Tourist Office: p. Cavour, 16 (tel. 27 40 64), in the largest lakeside *piazza* near the ferry dock. From the train station, walk down to via Gallio which becomes via Baribaldi and leads to the inland side of p. Cavour by way of p. Volta. Extensive information on the city, and an excellent guide to campsites on the lake. Open Mon.-Sat. 9am-12:30pm and 2:30-6pm.

Currency Exchange: Banca Nazionale del Lavoro, p. Cavour, 34, across from the tourist office. Dependable rates and cash advances on Visa. Open Mon.-Tues. and Thurs.-Fri. 8:20am-1:20pm and 2:30-4pm, Wed. 8:20am-5:50pm. Sat. and 4-6pm, try the tourist office.

Post Office: via T. Gallio, 4 (tel. 26 93 36). Stamps at #11. Open Mon.-Fri. 8:15am-7:30pm, Sat. 8:15am-noon. There is another office in the center of town at via V. Emanuele, 99 open Mon.-Fri. 8:15am-1:30pm, Sat. 8:15am-11:40am. **Postal Code:** 22100.

Telephones: SIP, via Bianchi-Giovini, 41, off p. Cavour in a magnificent 15th-century palace. Open Mon.-Sat. 9:30am-12:30pm and 2:30-7:30pm, Sun. 9am-1pm. **Telephone Code:** 031.

Buses: SPT, Matteotti (tel. 30 47 44), at the bend in lungo Lario Trieste. To: Menaggio (L3800); Bellaggio (L3500); Gravedona (L5600); Bergamo (L6700). **Information** open Mon.-Fri. 8am-noon and 3-6pm, Sat. 8am-noon.

Ferries: tel. 27 33 24 or 26 02 34. Daily to all lake towns. Fares L1300-11,200. Departures from the piers along lungo Lario Trieste, in front of p. Cavour. Pick up the booklet *Orari e Tariffe* for a comprehensive listing of prices and departures.

Swimming Pool: Lido Villa Olma. Sad to say, Como's dirtied waters no longer permit ablutions. The grassy plot here is more lawn than beach, but the pool does the job—it's wet. L7000, L5000 if you buy tickets at the youth hostel. Open daily 10am-6pm.

Bike Rental: the youth hostel rents them for a mere L6000 per day.

Emergencies: tel. 113. **Police:** viale Roosevelt, 7 (tel. 27 23 66). **Hospital: Ospedale Valduce,** via Dante, 11 (tel. 32 41).

Accommodations

Less expensive campsites and hostels line the shores of the lake, but if you must stay in town...

Ostello Villa Olmo (HI), via Bellinzona, 6 (tel. 57 38 00), on the inland side of Villa Olmo. From the station it's a 20-min. walk down via Borgovico (which becomes Bellinzona) to your left or take bus #1, 6, 11, or 14 (L800). Multilingual staff, bar facilities, and discounts on assorted tickets (e.g. pool and *funivia*). Slightly crowded rooms with lockers. Play it safe and call ahead in summer. Curfew 11pm. L13,000 per person with breakfast. Full meals L12,000. Bag lunches L10,000. Open March-Nov. daily 7-9:30am and 5-11pm; off-season, groups by reservation only.

Protezione della Giovane, via Borgovico, 182 (tel. 57 43 90), on the way to the youth hostel. Take bus #1, 2, or 6. Women only. Clean but shabby singles and doubles, some more modern than others. A spacious building with a central courtyard and garden. Kitchen available. L15,000 per person. Washing machines available at reduced rates. Lunch or dinner L15,000.

Albergo S. Antonio, via Coloniola, 10 (tel. 30 42 77), behind the bus station. Neat rooms with showers, and a good restaurant downstairs (*menù* L18,000). Singles L38,000. Doubles L55,000.

Food

Many of Como's residents eat lunch *alla Milanese,* downing a quick, satisfying meal in an inexpensive self-service joint. The food is wholesome, the atmosphere energetic, and cover charges rare. Unfortunately, similar options are not available in the evening, and finding an affordable dinner can be a challenge. Picnickers will appreciate the long hours of the **G.S. supermarket** on the corner of via Recchi and viale Fratelli Rosselli, across from the park. (Open Mon. 2-8pm, Tues.-Sat. 8:30am-8pm.) Lakeside benches are great for free *al fresco* dining, although solowomen may attract unwanted attention from Romeos who want to share a breadstick. *Panettone* fans should sample Como's variation on Milan's "big bread"; mountainous loaves of *matalok* can be purchased at the **Franzi bakery** at the corner of via Vitani and via Francensco Muratto.

Ristorante Carducci, via Carducci, 4 (tel. 27 63 88), in the old part of town near the Basilica di San Fedele. An inexpensive ACLI-run *mensa* in a functional room. Full meals L8500. Open Mon.-Fri. 11:30am-2:15pm, Sat. 11:30am-1:30pm. Closed 2 weeks in Aug.

Geral's, via Bianchi Giovani, 8 (tel. 30 48 72), off p. Cavour. Inhale decent food elbow-to-elbow with complete strangers. This green-tiled feeding machine will suck you in and spit you out in less than 30min., but you'll eat well if you don't get lost in the sea of consumers. *Primi* L4000, *secondi* L5500. Bar open Mon.-Sat. 7am-8pm, meals lunchtime only.

Taverna Messicana, p. Mazzini, 5/6 (tel. 26 24 63). Inexpensive *primi* and *secondi* (from L6000 and L6500 respectively) and a million variations on the pizza theme ranging from L5000 to 12,000 (for a salmon and vodka adventure). Cover L2000. Open Tues.-Sun. 11am-2pm and 6:30pm-midnight.

Sights and Entertainment

Como's **duomo** harmoniously combines Gothic and Renaissance elements. The vigorous sculptures that animate the exterior of the church are the work of the Rodari brothers; note especially Como residents Pliny the Elder and Pliny the Younger on either side of the door. Against the *duomo* is the sturdy **Broletto,** the former communal palace, with thick pillars, colonnaded windows, and colorful marble balconies. The **Church of San Fedele,** two blocks from the *duomo,* bears an unsurprising resemblance to Ravenna's Byzantine churches, since the oldest parts of the church (notably the altar and the blind arcade) were built by the Lombards during the same period.

After visiting Como's monuments, take the *funicolare* up to **Brunate** for excellent hiking and eye-exploding views. The cars leave from the far end of lungo Lario Trieste every half-hour (L3300; round-trip L5800, L4000 if purchased through the youth hostel; children L2000, round-trip L3500). Be aware that the last car comes down from Brunate at 10:30pm. The other option is spending the night in one of the three rough-and-ready *baite* (guesthouses) along the trail, which provide room and board in either private or dormitory-style rooms. Most serve three meals daily, but only breakfast is included in the overnight cost (about L25,000 per person). Check with the tourist office in the off-season to make sure they're open.

On the last weekend of June, Como celebrates the **Sagra di San Giovanni,** two days of folk arts and fireworks. Check with the tourist office for the location of this year's festival.

Centro Lago

The endless villas and towns of the Centro Lago can be explored at your leisure while staying at one of the two excellent youth hostels in **Menaggio** (on the west shore) and **Domaso** (on the north side). In Menaggio, **Ostello la Prinula (HI),** via IV Novembre, 38 (tel. (0344) 323 56), is one of the jollier and better-kept hostels around; family-run, it offers great cuisine (dinner L10,000), family suites, a washing machine, and even cooking equipment. (Lockout 10am-5pm. Curfew 11pm. L11,500 per person. Open mid-March to mid-Nov.) The **hostel (HI)** in Domaso is at via Case Sparse, 4 (tel. (0344) 960 94); it lies 16km from Como by bus, but the boat is more convenient. (L12,000 per person. Open March-Oct.) You can also crash at one of the secluded **campsites** that dot the northwest shore of the lake, between the lucid waters and towering mountains. Walk from where the Como buses let you off, or take the bus from Menaggio to Porlezza on Lake Lugano, and then take the scenic loop through S. Bartolomeo, S. Nazzaro, and Cavargna. Here, as in the upper region of Lake Como, tents and sleeping bags are a must. The Como tourist office has complete camping information.

Once your baggage is properly ensconced, hop on a ferry and hop off whenever a villa, castle, or village charms you. Among the innumerable possibilities, we humbly suggest whistle stops at **Varenna,** on the western shore, for its perfect cluster of houses below the castle Vezio, and **Isola Comacina,** also on the western shore, for its breathtaking "Oratory of San Giovanni". Also take the time to ogle the magnificent Villa Balbianello (on the extreme tip of the headland that cradles Comacina) during the boat ride for, unfortunately, it's closed to the public.

Lake Maggiore (Lago Maggiore)

Lacking only the hustle of its easterly cousins, Lake Maggiore cradles the same temperate mountain waters and picture-perfect shores. A glaze of opulence coats the waters here, and a stroll past any of the grandiose shore-side hotels reveals that Maggiore is a preferred watering hole of the elderly elite. Modest *pensioni* tucked away in the shadows of their multi-storied superiors, however, enable travelers to partake of the lake's sedate pleasures for a surprisingly reasonable sum.

Stresa

Stresa retains much of the charm that brought visitors here in droves during the 19th and early 20th centuries. Splendid views of the lake and the mountains around it lie at each turn of the cobbled streets. Only an hour from Milan on the Milan-Domodossola train line (L5300), the town is a convenient base for further expeditions in the region. The **tourist office** (tel. 301 50 or 304 16) is at via Principe Tomaso, 72; from the station, turn right on via Carducci and follow the signs. (Open Mon.-Sat. 8:30am-12:30pm and 3-6:15pm, Sun. 9am-noon; Oct.-April Mon.-Fri. 8:30am-12:30pm and 3-6:15pm, Sat. 8:30am-12:30pm.) The **post office** is at via Roma, 5, near p. Congressa. (Open Mon.-Fri. 8:15am-6:30pm, Sat. 8:15-11:40am.) Stresa's **telephone code** is 0323. For **emergency medical assistance** (*Guardia Medica*), phone 318 44. The funky sign at via De Martini, 20, reading **"Hopital,"** is, in fact, the place to go with a medical complaint (tel. 304 28).

Accommodations and Food

Albergo Luina, via Garibaldi, 27 (tel. 302 85), offers quiet comfort in the thick of the cobbled center. The kind, English-speaking proprietors reserve the right to request a minimum three-day stay during high season, but almost invariably take pity on those who look young, poor, and innocent (just do your best). (Singles L40,000. Doubles with bath L75,000.) **Orsola Meublé,** via Duchessa di Genova, 45 (tel. 310 87), offers a resting place just downhill from the station. Some rooms have terraces. (Singles L35,000. Doubles L40,000.) Go uphill and pass under the tracks to find the beautiful breezy rooms of **Hotel Mon Toc,** via Duchessa di Genova, 67-69 (tel. 302 82). (Singles L35,000. Doubles L52,800. Occasionally mandatory full pension L65,000 per person.)

Taverna del Pappagallo, via Principessa Margherita, 40 (tel. 304 11), serves up appetizing and affordable fare in this area bereft of a supermarket. *Primi* begin at L5000, *secondi* at L10,000. Pizza hovers around L8000. (Cover L2000. Open Thurs.-Mon. 11:30am-2:30pm and 6:30-10:30pm.) Follow the diagonal continuation of via de Amicis past via P. Tomaso, and you'll stumble upon a number of appetizing dining opportunities. The sweet-tooth hotline calls attention to the local cookies, *margheritine,* available in any of Stresa's *pasticcerie,* and reports that the fresh fruit *granite* at the *gelateria* next door to Taverna del Pappagallo, deserve the highest praise (L2000-2500). Try the mango, if they've got it.

Entertainment

From the last week in August to the third week in September, some of the finest orchestras and soloists in the world gather in Stresa for the internationally acclaimed **Settimane Musicali di Stresa.** (Student prices of L15,000 available for certain concerts.) Write or call the ticket office for information (Palazzo dei Congressi, via R. Bonghi, 4, 28049 Stresa; tel. 310 95). You can also ask about the **Estate Chitarristica sul Lago Maggiore,** an international extravaganza of classical guitar held in August in nearby Verbania; many of the concerts are free.

Near Stresa

The beauty of the **Borromean Isles, Isola Madre, Isola Bella,** and **Isola dei Pescatori,** has been amply touted with endless superlatives over the past 300 years. Daily excursion tickets allow you to hop back and forth among the islands at liberty. L9200 will buy a ticket to Pallanza and the intermediate islands. The L11,200 variety allows you to extend your itinerary even further to **Villa Tàranto** with its impressive botanical gardens (open daily April-Oct. 8:30am-7:30pm; admission L8000, ages 6-14 L5000). Enclosed gardens are a recurring theme in any tour of this end of the lake, and if you save your money by eschewing the flora, you will often find yourself with only a small plot of land to pace upon while waiting for the next ferry to rescue you. **Isola dei Pescatori** is the only garden-free island, and vendors have capitalized on the unrestricted space by erecting souvenir stands on all sides. You have the run of the island, but midday tourist congestion makes it difficult even to walk.

Isola Madre (tel. 312 61 for information) is the longest and quietest of the three islands. Lancelotto Borromeo was the first of the noble family to begin work on the palaces and gardens, renting the island in 1502. Count Renato bought it in 1609 and continued the project. The result is an elegant 16th-century villa and its magnificent classical Italian garden. The palace contains a great number of portraits of the family and, no expense having been spared for the Borromeo *bambini,* a famous collection of dolls and marionette stages and props. The botanical garden has a stupendous array of exotic trees, plants, and flowers. Pick up the free guide from the ticket office. (Open March 27-Oct. 24 daily 9am-noon and 1:30-5:30pm. Admission L9000, ages 6-15 L4000.)

The sprawling opulence of the Palazzo e Giardini Borromeo has made **Isola Bella** (tel. (0323) 305 56) the most famous of the islands. The palace, built in 1670 by Count Borromeo for his wife Isabella, is a monument to the Baroque obsession with ornamentation. The ten terraces of the gardens, liberally punctuated with statues, rise up in true wedding-cake fashion to the Borromeo family emblem, the unicorn. The effect is theatrical and the garden was, in fact, used as a theater, by boat-borne performers. Music was also composed specifically for choirs to perform in the garden. By the way, the Borromeo family motto is "Humilitas." (Same hours and prices as Madre.)

Pallanza, on the far side of Isola Madre, offers little of artistic interest, but lakeside dining is cheaper here and you might consider having a meal before cruising "home." Stresa's navigation offices are located in p. Marconi, and tickets are sold from 8am-8pm. For additional information, contact the central office at Arona, viale Barracco, 1 (tel. (0322) 466 51).

Lake d'Orta (Lago d'Orta)

Lake d'Orta remains the Lake Country's unspoiled refuge, surrounded by hills and forests and graced by several small towns. Known as "Cusius" in ancient times, Orta has wrapped itself in legends and history which complement its enchanted setting. Nietzsche retreated here in 1883-1885 to script his final work, *Thus Spoke Zarathustra.* Lake d'Orta lies on the Novara-Domodossola **train** line (10 per day from Novara, 1hr. 30min., L6900). Get off at Orta Miasino, 3km above Orta, and then either walk down or catch one of the four buses that travel to Orta. Like any true retreat, the lake is cursed—and thus blessed—by a dearth of public transportation. Connections from nearby Lago Maggiore are difficult and indirect, but on weekdays in summer **buses** leave twice a day from Baveno and Stresa (contact the tourist offices). Beware the train station's peculiar hours if you're counting on an evening departure (open 6:20-11:30am and 1:30-3:30pm).

Orta's **tourist office** is at via Olina, 9/11 (tel. 903 54; open Tues.-Sat. 9am-noon and 3-5:30pm, Sun. 10am-noon and 3-5pm). If you arrive on a Monday or are bound for a different town, check the office at via Panoramica across the street and down from the Eastern-influenced Villa Crespi (tel. 90 56 14; open Mon. and Wed.-Fri. 10am-1pm and 4-7pm, Sat.-Sun. 10am-1pm and 4-8pm). The **post office** is at p. Ragazzoni. (Open Mon.-Fri. 8:30am-noon and 2-6pm, Sat. 8:30-11am.) The **postal code** is 28016; the **telephone code** is 0322.

Restaurant prices (and the solicitous treatment accorded tourists) are a relief after those of the more commercialized lakes, but affordable accommodations await only a happy few. **Ristorante Olina** (tel. 90 56 56), across from the tourist office, boasts beautiful doubles with private baths (L65,000; use of kitchen L5000). Family suites with kitchens are also available, some with glimpses of the lake. The **Taverna Antico Angello,** via Olina, 18 (tel. 902 59), offers central one-star economy hung with wisteria. (Singles L28,000; doubles L38,000.) **Conca d'Oro** (tel. 902 52), to the left on the descent into town, offers a greater number of lesser rooms. (Singles L35,000; doubles L54,000.) A good-sized **open-air market** sells out on Wednesday mornings in p. Motta. For warmer comestibles, consider hopping on a boat to **Ristorante San Giulio,** with an 18th-century dining room and lakeside terrace, on the tiny island of the same name. The setting is peaceful and romantic, and the *menù* is rich with local fare. *Primi* run L4000-6000 and *secondi* are L10,000; the cover is L2000.

Set high in the cool, verdant hills above town is the **Sacro Monte,** a monastic complex devoted to St. Francis of Assisi. The sanctuary was founded in 1591, and its 20 chapels boast some 376 life-sized statues and 900 frescoes whose combined forces tell the life story of Italy's patron saint. **Isola di San Giulio,** across from Orta, has an interesting Romanesque **basilica** from the 12th century, built on 4th-century foundations. (Open Mon.-Sat. 9:30am-11pm and 2-7pm, Sun. 9:30-10:45am and 2-7pm.) A circular route around the island snakes through the narrow streets past ivy-covered walls and tiled roofs. Bring L3000 to buy a bag of *pane di San Giulio* from the nuns in the adjacent convent. A light ring on the doorbell will produce a covered head at the window in a fraction of a second, and the dense little loaves are guaranteed to stick to your ribs and the roof of your mouth for hours to come. Small motor boats weave back and forth constantly during the summer (round-trip L2000; tickets sold on board). Winter service is restricted to just a couple of runs per day.

Lombardy (Lombardia)

Over the centuries Roman generals, German emperors, and French kings have vied for control of Lombardy's bounty. The agricultural riches of the region have since been augmented by industrial and financial resources, making it the cornerstone of the Italian economy. Italy's wealthiest region may seem to have more in common with its northern neighbors than with the rest of the peninsula—this perception has led to an anti-southern prejudice. Lombardians make periodic calls for secession and an end to the subsidization of the Roman bureaucracy and the historically backward South. Yet since World War II Lombardy's "new Italy" has attracted legions of ambitious southerners, and the province has recently become a magnet for immigrants from North Africa and the Middle East. Tension between long-time denizens and immigrants persists, but thanks in part to this diversity residents of Lombardy are today among the least provincial Italians.

Although cosmopolitan, Milan, with its international reputation for high style and finance, may loom largest in foreigners' perceptions of the region, Lombardy is in fact far more than a metropolis and its countryside. Cities such as Pavia and Cremona are themselves the focus of smaller provinces; Bergamo, Brescia, and Mantua, with their hints of Venetian influence, are culturally foreign to their western neighbor. The beginnings of the Alps in the lake country are not far from the southern plain, yet have an elusive atmosphere that combines an Italian climate with strains of Swiss and Austrian culture.

Milan (Milano)

In a country often inclined to rest on its cultural laurels, Milan is a fresh exception—a frenetically industrious city where the achievements of modernity seem most to outstrip historical legacy. Even the *duomo,* the city's sophisticated emblem, anticipates its 20th-century skyscraping counterparts.

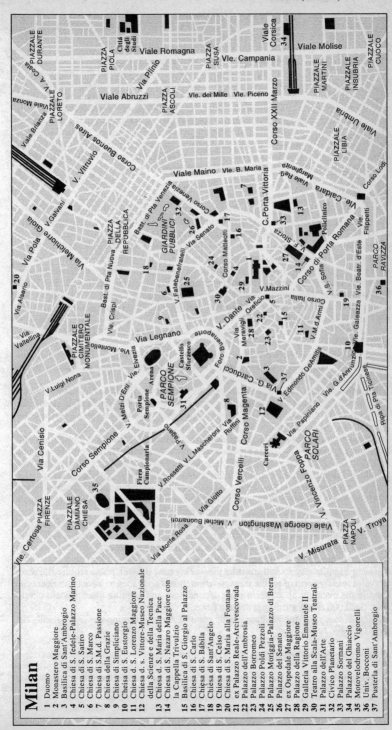

Milan

1 Duomo
2 Monastero Maggiore
3 Basilica di Sant'Ambrogio
4 Basilica di S. fedele-Palazzo Marino
5 Chiesa di S. Satiro
6 Chiesa di S. Marco
7 Chiesa di S.M.d. Passione
8 Chiesa della Grazie
9 Chiesa di Simpliciano
10 Chiesa di S. Eustorgio
11 Chiesa di S. Lorenzo Maggiore
12 Chiesa d. s. Vittore-Museo Nazionale della Scienze e della Tecnica
13 Chiesa d. S. Maria della Pace
14 Chiesa di S. Nazaro Maggiore con la Cappella Trivulzio
15 Basilica di S. Giorgio al Palazzo
16 Chiesa di S. Carlo
17 Chiesa di S. Bábila
18 Chiesa di Sant'Angelo
19 Chiesa di S. Celso
20 Chiesa di S. Maria alla Fontana
21 ex Palazzo Reale-Arcivescovada
22 Palazzo dell'Ambrosia
23 Palazzo Borromeo
24 Palazzo Poldi Pezzoli
25 Palazzo Moriggia-Palazzo di Brera
26 Palazzo del Senato
27 ex Ospedale Maggiore
28 Palazzo della Ragione
29 Galleria Vittorio Emanuele II
30 Teatro alla Scala-Museo Teatrale
31 Palazzo dell'Arte
32 Civico Planetario
33 Palazzo Sormani
34 Palazzo del Ghiaccio
35 Motovelodromo Vigorelli
36 Univ. Bocconi
37 Pusteria di Sant'Ambrogio

The Romans founded Mediolanum in the 3rd century BC after conquering an existing settlement at that site. The new colony rapidly overcame its humble origins to become the capital of the western half of the Roman empire between 286 and 402 AD; an evolving Milan enjoyed the prestige of being the region's principal metropolis throughout the Middle Ages. The Visconti and Sforza dynasties ushered in the Renaissance to Milan; in the 15th century Lodovico Sforza's patronage attracted Leonardo da Vinci and Donato Bramante to his court, earning Milan the title of "the new Athens." The modern era arrived when the French troops—with their revolutionary ideals—entered the city in 1797. The city later became headquarters of the Italian unification movement in the mid-19th century. After suffering heavy bombing during World War II, Milan was speedily rebuilt, and much of the center was surgically replaced with steel and glass. Milan is relentless in its pursuit not of erstwhile glory but of the modern—a preoccupation that makes it an international center of *haute couture*.

Orientation

Milan is linked by train to all major cities in Italy and Western Europe. The layout of the city resembles a giant target, encircled by a series of concentric ancient city walls. In the outer rings lie suburbs built during the 1950s and 60s to house southern immigrants. The **duomo** and **Galleria Vittorio Emanuele II** comprise the bull's-eye, roughly at the center of the downtown circle. Within this inner circle are four central squares: **largo Cairoli,** near Castello Sforzesco; **piazza Cordusio,** connected to largo Cairoli by via Dante; **piazza Duomo,** at the end of via Mercanti; and **piazza San Babila,** the business and fashion district along corso Vittorio Emanuele. Northeast and northwest lie two large parks, the **Giardini Pubblici** and the **Parco Sempione.** Farther northeast is the **Stazione Centrale,** Mussolini's colossal train station built in 1931; the area around the train station is a mishmash of skyscrapers dominated by the sleek **Pirelli Tower** (1959), one of the tallest buildings in Europe. From the station a scenic ride on bus #60 takes you to the downtown hub, as does the more efficient commute on subway line #3. The station is also connected to the downtown area by **corso Buenos Aires,** where prices for clothing are actually palatable.

The **subway** (Metropolitana Milanese, abbreviated "MM") is the most useful branch of Milan's extensive public transportation network. **Line #1** (red line) connects the *pensioni* district east of Stazione Centrale to the center of town and extends as far as the youth hostel (Molino Dorino fork). **Line #2** (green line) links Milan's three train stations and crosses MM1 at Cadorno and Loreto. The new **Line #3** (yellow line) runs from just north of the Stazione Centrale to previously uncharted lands in the southern sprawl of the city and provides a bridge between its two forerunners, intersecting with line #2 at Stazione Centrale and #1 at the *duomo*. The subway operates from approximately 6am to midnight. Among the many useful train and bus routes, **trams #29** and **30** travel the city's outer ring road, while **buses** #96 and 97 service the inner road. **Tram #1,** which runs during the wee hours, also departs from Centrale and runs to p. Scala, near the *duomo*. Tickets for buses, trams, and subways must be purchased in advance at newsstands or from ticket machines; bring small change. A ticket (L1000) is good for one subway ride or 75 minutes of surface transportation. All-day passes (L3500) are available from the **ATM** office at the Duomo and Centrale stops. Those planning a longer stay should consider the weekly pass (L8400, photo required). Passes are valid for any form of public transportation. It is a good idea to have extra tickets on hand in the evening, as *tabacchi* close around 8pm and vending machines are unreliable. (L20,000 fine for riding without a ticket.)

Milan closes shop for vacation during most of August, leaving the city virtually deserted.

Practical Information

Tourist Office: APT, via Marconi, 1 (tel. 80 96 62), in the "Palazzo di Turismo" in p. del Duomo, to the right as you face the *duomo*. Everyone here speaks some English and is helpful. Comprehensive local and regional information, and an especially useful map and museum guide. Will not reserve rooms but will phone to check for vacancies. Open Mon.-Sat. 8am-8pm, Sun. 9am-

12:30pm and 1:30-5pm. Branch offices at **Stazione Centrale** (tel. 669 05 32 or 669 04 32; open Mon.-Sat. 8am-6pm) and **Linate Airport** (tel. 74 40 65; open Mon.-Fri. 9am-4:30pm). For hotel information and reservations, call the hotel owners' association, **Hotel Reservation Milano** (tel. 76 00 60 95), which may request a deposit during busy periods. The **Associazionne Turistrea Giovanile,** via del Amicis, 4 (tel. 89 40 50 75), near the Porta Ticinese, has some discounts and helpful information for young travelers. Open Mon.-Fri. 9:30am-1pm and 2-6:30pm, Sat. 9:30am-1pm.

Budget Travel: CIT, Galleria Vittorio Emanuele (tel. 86 66 61). The most central travel agency. Also **changes money.** Open Mon.-Fri. 9am-5:50pm. Another office at the **Stazione Centrale** (same hours). **Centro Turistico Studentesco,** via S. Antonio, 2 (tel. 583 041 21). Open Mon.-Fri. 9:30am-6pm, Sat. 9:30am-noon; Sept.-May Mon.-Fri. 9:30am-1pm and 2:30-6pm, Sat. 9:30am-noon. **Transalpino Tickets:** Next to the train information office in the upper atrium of Stazione Centrale (tel. 670 51 21). Open Mon.-Sat. 8am-8pm, Sun. 8:30am-12:30pm and 2:30-6:30pm. When closed, go to **Italturismo,** to the right from the station, tucked under the grand drive-thru. Open daily 6:45am-8pm; Sept.-July Mon.-Sat. 6:45am-8pm.

Consulates: U.S., largo Donegani, 1 (tel. 290 018 41). Open Mon.-Fri. 9-11am and 2-4pm. **Canada,** via Vittor Pisani, 19 (tel. 669 74 51). Open Mon.-Fri. 9am-5pm. **U.K.,** via S. Paolo, 7 (tel. 869 34 42). Open Mon.-Fri. 9:15am-12:15pm and 2:30-6:30pm. **Australia,** via Borgogna, 2 (tel. 760 133 30). Open Mon.-Thurs. 9am-noon and 2-4:30pm, Fri. 9am-noon. **New Zealand** citizens should contact their embassy in Rome.

Currency Exchange: All **Banca d'America e d'Italia** and **Banca Nazionale del Lavora** branches give cash advances on Visa cards. (The former are usually open Mon.-Fri. 8:30am-1:30pm and 2:45-4:15pm, the latter Mon.-Fri. 8:20am-1:20pm and 2:30-4pm.) The **Banca Nazionale delle Comunicazioni** at Stazione Centrale has pretty standard rates if you need to change money right away. (Open Mon.-Sat. 8am-6:30pm, Sun. 9am-1pm.)

American Express: via Brera, 3 (tel. 855 71), on the corner of via dell'Orso. Walk through the Galleria, across p. Scala, and up via Verdi. Holds mail free for American Express members, otherwise L800 per inquiry. Will accept wired money for a fee of US$30 per US$1000. Open Mon.-Fri. 9am-5:30pm.

Post Office: via Cordusio, 4 (tel. 869 20 69), near p. del Duomo in the direction of the castle. Stamps at #1 and 2. Fermo Posta c/o the CAI-POST office to the left upon entering. Open Mon.-Sat. 8:15am-7:40pm. **Postal Code:** 20100.

Telephones: SIP, in Galleria Vittorio Emanuele. Open 7am-midnight. **ASST,** in Stazione Centrale, past the tourist office. Open 7am-midnight. **Linate Airport: ASST,** open 7am-11:45pm. **Malpensa Airport,** open 7am-8pm. **Telephone Code:** 02.

Flights: Malpensa Airport, 50km from town. Intercontinental flights. Buses leave every half hour in the mornings, hourly in the afternoon from p. Luigi di Savoia, on the east side of Stazione Centrale (L8500). **Linate Airport,** 7km from town. Domestic/European flights and intercontinental flights with European transfers. Much easier logistically. The bus to Linate leaves Stazione Centrale every 20min. 5:50am-9pm (L2900). It's cheaper (L1000) to take bus #73 from p. San Babila (MM1). **General Flight Information** for both airports, tel. 74 85 22 00.

Trains: Stazione Centrale, p. Duca d'Aosta (tel. 675 00), on MM2. The primary station. To: Genoa and Turin (both every hr., 1hr. 30min. and 2hr., L10,800); Venice (20 direct per day, 3hr., L16,700); Florence (every hr., 3hr., L27,000 with supplement); Rome (every hr., 5hr., L53,800 with supplement). Information office (at far left of station when facing tracks) open daily 7am-11pm. Eurail passes and *Cartaverde* available just outside the building, on the far left as you face the entrance. **Luggage Storage:** L1500. Near information. Open 4am-2am. **Lost and Found:** (tel. 67 71 26 77) next to *binario* 21. Open daily 7:20am-8:45pm. **Stazione Nord** (tel. 851 16 08) connects Milan with Como, Erba, and Varese; **Porta Genova** (tel. 835 03 82) has local lines to the west (Alessandria-Asti); **Porta Garibaldi** (tel. 655 20 78) links Milan to Lecco and Valtellina to the northwest.

Buses: ATM (tel. 87 54 95), in the p. del Duomo MM station. Municipal buses require pre-purchased tickets (L1000). Day passes for non-residents L3500. Open Mon.-Sat. 8am-8pm. Also at **Stazione Centrale** (same hours). **Intercity** buses are less convenient and more expensive than the trains, but **SAL, SIA, Autostradale,** and many others depart from p. Castello and the surrounding area (MM: Cairoli) for Turin, the lake country, Bergamo, Certosa di Pavia, and points as far away as Rimini and Trieste.

Taxis: In p. Scala, p. del Duomo, p. S. Babila, and largo Cairoli. Or contact them by radio (tel. 67 67 or 83 88). The official Milan taxis are yellow and uniformly expensive, starting at L4000, with a nighttime surcharge of L4000. Yipes.

Car Rental: Hertz (tel. 204 83, Galleria delle Carrozze office 670 30 62). Outside the station, to the left as you exit. Tourist rates are about two-thirds those for Italians, but you must make arrangements ahead of time in your country of departure. If done here, the **Guida Italia** package offers a Fiat for 7 days for under L500,000, with reservations a week ahead. Daily rental around L125,000, with taxes and insurance. Open Sept.-July Mon.-Fri. 7:40am-8pm, Sat. 7:40am-2:10pm. Also check with **Europacar** (tel. 1678-68088) and **Avis** (tel. 669 02 80) at the same place: same rates, similar hours.

English Bookstore: The American Bookshop, via Camperio, 16 (tel. 87 09 44), at largo Cairoli. The best selection in Milan. Open Tues.-Fri. 10am-7pm, Sat. 10am-1pm and 3-7pm, Mon. 3-7pm. Closed 2 wks. in Aug. **Hoepli Libreria Internazionale,** via Hoepli, 5 (tel. 86 54 46), near p. Scala. Respectably sized mixed collection on the second floor. Open Mon.-Sat. 9am-7pm. Try any store with a sign reading *Libreria Internazionale.*

Library: United States Information Service, via Bigli, 11A (tel. 79 50 51), near p. S. Babila. Library with U.S. publications for perusal. Open Mon.-Tues. and Thurs. 9:30am-1pm and 2:30-6pm, Wed. 9:30am-1pm. **British Council Library,** via Manzoni, 38 (tel. 78 20 16), near USIS. Open Tues.-Wed. 10am-7:30pm, Thurs.-Fri. 10am-6pm, Sat. 10am-12:30pm.

Day Hotel: Albergo Diurno (tel. 669 12 32), beneath p. Duca d'Aosta, reached by stairs underground as you leave the center of the Stazione Centrale. Toilets L500, with soap and towel L2000, with shower L5000, with bath L8000. Open Thurs.-Tues. 7am-8pm. Also **luggage storage** (same hrs.), L1500 per 24 hrs.

Laundromat: Lavanderia Automatica, corso Porta Vittoria, 51 (tel. 55 19 23 15), beyond largo Augusto behind the *duomo.* The most central, but consult the yellow pages for the *lavanderia* nearest you.

Swimming Pool: Cozzi, viale Tunisia, 35 (tel. 659 97 03), off corso Buenos Aires. Out of a dozen, the closest to Stazione Centrale. Open Tues.-Sat. 12:30-6:30pm; admission L4500. In summer, move outdoors to **Giulia Romano,** viale Ponzia, 35 (tel. 29 22 24). **Lido di Milano,** p. Lotto, 15 (tel. 36 61 00), near the youth hostel. Open daily 11am-7pm. Admission L4500. Indoor pool open Sept. 10-June 10am-5:30pm.

Late-Night Pharmacy: Though nocturnal duty rotates among Milan's pharmacies (call 192 to find out who is on the night shift), the one in Stazione Centrale never closes (tel. 669 07 35 or 669 09 35). During the day, try the **Italo-English Chemist's Shop** on corso Europa, 18 (tel. 76 00 18 28 or 78 16 02).

Hospital: Ospedale Maggiore Policlinico, via Francesco Sforza, 35 (tel. 551 16 55), 5min. from the *duomo* on the inner ring road.

Emergencies: tel. 113. **Police:** tel. 772 71. **"SOS for Tourists":** tel. 545 65 51 for legal complaints. **Medical Emergency:** tel. 38 83. **Ambulance:** tel. 77 33.

Accommodations

There are over 50 apparent on-paper bargains in Milan, but if you want a clean room in a safe and reasonably convenient location, only a few choices are worth your while. Every season is high season in Milan (except August), and a single room in an upright establishment for under L35,000 is a real find. Even resort areas like the Riviera and the Alps offer better bargains than Milan. For the best deals, it is advisable to make the trip from the station to the city's center or its southern periphery. In all cases, make reservations well ahead of time.

Hostel

Ostello Pietro Rotta (HI), viale Salmoiraghi, 2 (tel. 39 26 70 95). From any train station, take MM2 to Cadorna and change to MM1 going out to Molino Dorino. Get off at QT8—a district in the leafy outskirts. Modern hostel with 6 bedrooms, a sunny garden, and helpful staff, but run on a mechanized regimen. English spoken. HI card strictly required, but foreigners can purchase it at the hostel (L30,000). Open 7-9am and 5-11:30pm (you should arrive in the evening). Beware of unbending enforcement of daytime lockout. Depending on the management's bio-rhythms, lights suddenly die between 11:20pm and midnight. Curfew 12:30am. L20,000 per person. Breakfast and lockers included. Use of washing machine or dryer L6000 each. Individuals may not make reservations, but in the summer groups should (deposit 50%). Open Jan. 13-Dec. 20.

Near Stazione Centrale

Due Giardini, via Settala, 46 (tel. 29 52 10 93 or 29 51 23 09; MM2: Caiazzo). Go left from the station on via Scarlatti; via Settala is the 4th road on the right. Neat rooms, but the main attraction is the expansive garden outside. Open all night. Singles L40,000. Doubles L60,000. No reservations taken; come early in the morning.

Hotel San Marco, via Piccinni, 25 (tel. 204 95 36 or 29 51 63 16; MM1-2: Loreto). From station head left to p. Caiazzo and turn onto via Pergolesi which becomes Piccinni. Comfortable rooms with TV and telephone and a reassuring atmosphere of calm. Friendly management. Singles L37,000, with bath and breakfast L58,000. Doubles L72,000, with bath and breakfast L80,000.

Near piazza Loreto

Albergo "Villa Mira," via Sacchini, 19 (tel. 29 52 56 18; MM1-2: Loreto), off via Porpora 2 blocks from p. Loreto. A family-run establishment with rooms out of a Mr. Clean commercial, plus a bar downstairs. Singles L37,500. Double with bath L54,000.

Hotel Winston, via Catalani, 21 (tel. 266 47 80; MM1-2: Loreto), off via Porpora. A quiet retreat of modern rooms, some overlooking a garden of tranquility. Singles L32,000. Doubles L45,000.

Hotel Ca' Grande, via Porpora, 87 (tel. 26 14 52 95 or 26 14 40 01; MM1-2: Loreto), about 7 blocks in from p. Loreto in a free-standing building protected by a spiked fence. Clean, serviceable rooms, but the street side can be noisy. Good English spoken here. Singles L38,000. Doubles L60,000, with bath L78,000.

Hotel Catalani, via Catalani, 71 (tel. 284 63 61; MM1-2:Loreto), north off via Porpora. Large, mess-free rooms, some with balconies. Singles L35,000. Doubles L60,000, with bath L65,000. Make reservations.

Around corso Buenos Aires

All of these hotels are near the Porta Venezia stop on MM1.

Viale Tunisia, 6. This building houses two budget hotels, each equidistant from the station and the city center. Some English is spoken at the **Hotel Kennedy** (tel. 29 40 09 34), 6th floor. Very tidy rooms, with dreamscape decor imported from the 60s. If you can't stand baby blue, however, look elsewhere. Singles L45,000. Doubles L60,000, with bath L80,000. Triples with shower L105,000. Reservations are recommended, and you may lose them if you arrive after 4pm and haven't paid in advance. Closes at midnight, checkout by 10am. The **Hotel S. Tomaso** (tel. 29 51 47 47) is on the 3rd floor. Orderly rooms with hardwood floors, some overlooking a courtyard. Communication in English is not a problem. Singles L40,000, with bath L45,000. Doubles L70,000. Prices may be a bit higher in Sept. and Oct., a bit lower in Dec. and Jan.

Hotel Aurora, corso Buenos Aires, 18 (tel. 204 92 85 or 204 79 60). Street noise is muted by the interior courtyard, and behind a grungy facade lies a spotless labyrinth of modern rooms, again swathed in baby-blue. English spoken. Singles L50,000, with bath L65,000. Doubles with bath L80,000. TV for L5000 more. Open Sept.-July.

West and South of the City Center

Hotel Jolanda, corso Magenta, 78 (tel. 46 33 17; MM1: Conciliazione), in a quiet neighborhood popular with university students. Tasteful, wood-floored rooms that are essentially unattainable without a reservation 2 wks. in advance. Those who arrive after 1pm may lose their reservations if not paid for in advance. Singles L35,000. Doubles L65,000, with bath L90,000. Open Sept.-July.

Hotel Cesare Correnti, via C. Correnti, 14 (tel. 87 07 25), the continuation of via Torino, on the right after intersection with Carrobbio, a 10-min. walk southwest of the *duomo*. Snow-white, recently redone rooms are a pleasure—even Grumpy would approve. Some rooms overlook a serene courtyard. Singles L35,000. Doubles L55,000. Call 2-3 days ahead or reserve by mail.

Pensione Cantore, corso Genova, 25 (tel. 835 75 65; MM2: Genova), a 15-min. walk southwest of the *duomo*, farther down via C. Correnti. A bit out of the way, but grand and immaculate rooms. Friendly atmosphere. Closes at 1am. Doubles L55,000. Reserve ahead.

Camping

Il Bareggino (tel. 901 44 17; MM1: Molino-Dorino line), on via Corbettina in Bareggino. Hard to reach without a car, though you can take an *extraurbane* bus from p. Lotto. L5000 per adult, L2600 per child, L4900 per tent.

Autodromo (tel. (039) 38 77 71), in the park of the Villa Reale in Monza. Take a train or bus from Stazione Centrale to Monza, then a city bus to the campground. A step down. L3200 per person and per tent, L2000 per child under 6. Open April-Sept.

Food

Like its fine *couture*, Milanese cuisine is classic, understated, and overpriced. Specialties include *risotto giallo* (rice with saffron), *cotoletta alla milanese* (a breaded veal cutlet with lemon), and *cazzouela* (a mixture of pork and cabbage). *Pasticcerie* and *gelaterie* crowd every block. Try the Milanese sweet bread *panettone*, made with raisins and citrons.

Avoid eating in the area neighboring the train station; instead, walk south on viale Tunisia. The entire city—including most restaurants—closes for vacation in August, so you may have to explore and improvise to stay sated at the end of the summer. The newspaper *Il Giornale Nuovo* lists all the restaurants and shops open in the city. The largest **markets** are around via Fauché or viale Papiniano on Saturday and sometimes Tuesday, and along via Santa Croce on Thursday. On Saturday, the **Fiera di Sinigallia** occurs on via Calatafimi—a 400-year-old extravaganza of the commercial and the bizarre.

Splurge on the local pastry at **Sant'Ambroeus** (tel. 76 00 05 40), a Milanese culinary shrine, under the arcades at corso Matteotti, 7. (Open Tues.-Sat. 8am-8pm, Mon. 3:30-8pm.) For supermarkets, try **Pam,** off corso Buenos Aires at via Piccinni, 2 (tel. 20 27 15), or the air-conditioned store at via Piane, 38B. (Both open Tues.-Sat. 8:30am-7:30pm, Mon. 2-7:30pm.) There is also a useful **S & B Market** further down at via Casati, 3 (open Tues.-Sat. 8:30am-1pm and 3:30-7:30pm, Mon. 8:30am-1pm). For a balanced meal at reasonable rates, sit down with the Milanese office workers at one of the countless self-service restaurants that now cater to professionals under time constraints. **Brek** and **Ciao** are both chains of such restaurants with branches scattered throughout the city. The Brek restaurant on via Lepetit by Stazione Centrale and the strategically positioned Ciao in p. del Duomo are particularly convenient. (At both, *primi* average L4500, *secondi* L7500.)

South of Stazione Centrale and near corso Buenos Aires

Pizzeria del Nonno, via Andrea Costa, 1 (tel. 26 14 52 62; MM1-2: Loreto), off p. Loreto. Surprisingly genteel decor for a hungry, rowdy crowd. Enormous pizzas (L5000-8000) keep their mouths full. Special of the day runs L6000-8000. Cover L1000. Open Tues.-Sat. noon-2:30pm and 7pm-12:30am, Sun. 6pm-12:30am.

Moby Dick, via Porpora, 161 (tel. 70 63 05 91; MM1-2: Loreto). Work up an appetite during the 9-block haul, or take the bus down via Porpora. Pizza with pizzazz. Upscale clientele. Try the *Simpatía* with tomatoes, ricotta, olives, oregano, and prosciutto (L7000). The Moby Dick is loaded with salmon (L12,000). Pasta dishes L7000-10,000. Cover L2500. Open Thurs.-Tues. noon-2pm and 6:30-11:30pm.

Tarantella, v. le Abruzzi, 35 (tel. 29 40 02 18), just north of via Plinio. Lively and leafy neighborhood place with sidewalk dining. Great *antipasti*. Immense specialty salads L10,000. Pizza L7500-8500 (try the *gorgonzola*). *Primi* begin at L8000, *secondi* range from L14,000 to seafood fantasies in the L20,000 range. Open Sept.-July Sun.-Fri. noon-3pm and 7-11:30pm.

La Piccola Napoli, viale Monza, 13 (tel 285 33 97; MM1-2: Loreto). A haunt for night owls. Pizza L7000-10,000. Open mid-Aug. to mid-July Tues.-Sun. 6pm-3am.

Trattoria da Paolo, viale Monza, 6 (tel. 261 32 14; MM1-2: Loreto). The fare is cheap and filling, served in a home-kitchen atmosphere. Convenient to the piazza. Pasta and meat dishes L4000-9000. Cover L1500. Open Sun.-Fri. noon-2:30pm and 7pm-12:30am.

Near piazza del Duomo

Flash, via Bergamini, 1 (tel. 58 30 44 89; MM1: Duomo), at p. San Stefano. Mobbed—and with good reason. The chef spins delectable Neapolitan pizza (L7000-11,000). Wine L5000 per . Many types of delicious *panini* (including vegetarian) at the bar (L3500-4000). Open Tues.-Sun. noon-3pm and 7pm-1am.

Peck, via G. Cantù, off via Dante near the *duomo*. Milan's premier *rosticceria*. Pizza and pastries by the kilo—L3000 will buy a large slice of either. You simply mousst try the chocolate mousse (about L3000). Open Tues.-Sat. 8am-1pm and 3:30-7pm.

Between Largo Cairoli and piazza Cordusio

Le Briciole, via Camperio, 17 (tel. 87 71 85 or 80 41 14), 1 street over from via Dante. Popular with lively young folk. Pizza L6500-9000. Spectacular *antipasto* buffet L9500, *secondi* L7500-14,000. Cover L2500. Open Tues.-Fri. and Sun. 12:15-2:30pm and 7:15pm-midnight.

Near via Torino and corso di Porta Ticinese

This once-affordable neighborhood is muddling through the early stages of gentrification. Leap into the chic v. cheap battle before chic wins out (and you can't afford to leap anywhere near here).

Be Bop Caffè/Ristorante, viale Col di Lana, 4 (tel. 837 69 72; MM2: Sant'Agostino or Genova), off the far side of p. XXIV Maggio. Understated decor with a jazz soundtrack, except after hours when the young staff pumps up the volume. Salads are generously proportioned here, in every sense (L13,000-16,000). All-inclusive lunch *menù* L14,000. Open Sept. to mid-Aug. Mon.-Sat. noon-2:30pm and 7:30pm-1am.

La Crêperie, via C. Correnti, 24 (tel. 837 71 24), the continuation of via Torino. Fruit crêpes L3000, desserty liqueur crêpes L4000, and the "real food" variety L5000. L8000 lunch special combo. Sip a lemon-and-celery juice to the non-stop music. Open Mon. and Wed.-Fri. noon-midnight, Sat. noon- 1:30am, Sun. 5pm-midnight.

Mergellina, via Molino delle Armi, 48 (tel. 89 40 13 33), in a banana-colored building by the actual Porta Ticinese. 10-min. walk from the *duomo*. Terrific pizzas L6000-10,000. Cover L2000. Open Sept.-July Thurs.-Mon. 11am-3pm and 7pm-1:30am, Wed. 7pm-1am.

Portnoy, via de Amicis, 1 (tel. 837 86 56), at corso di Porta Ticinese. Ultra-hip: where black will always be "in." Young, socially conscious management displays new paintings and poetry. Writers give readings of their work followed by discussion. *Panini* about L3500. Open Mon.-Sat. 7am-2am. Poetry readings 7:30-8:30pm; no showings in Aug. Some classical music nights also (no extra charge).

Between via Pontaccio and piazza XXV Aprile

Pizzeria Grand'Italia, via Palermo, 5 (tel. 87 77 59). Go for pizza at L3500-6000, or sample a multitude of other dishes. Open Wed.-Sun. 12:15-3pm and 7:15pm-1:30am.

Spaghetteria Enoteca, via Solferino, 3 (tel. 87 27 35; MM2: Moscova) in the basement. A monument to the tangled and inextricably wonderful world of spaghetti. Everything is prepared *all'instante* (on the spot). *Assagini* (small portions) of 5 types of spaghetti L8500. Cover L2000. Open Sept.-July Tues.-Sun. from 7:30pm. Lively *birreria* next door.

Gelaterie

After World War II, a man named Viel began selling tutti-frutti *gelato* from a little cart outside the *duomo*. Soon a brother was opening a store of his own on one street corner, a cousin on another, and a son on a third. Today the name Viel is synonymous with exotic, fresh fruit *gelati* (L1700-4000) and *frullati* (whipped fruit drinks, L2500) in Milan. For the freshest and fanciest, take your taste buds to the jolly **Viel Frutti Esotici Gelati** on the left as you face the Castello from Largo Cairoli (MM1: Cairoli). Esotici specializes in fruit *frappés* (*frulatti di frutta*), fruit flavors, and fruit toppings. Outdoor seating is available. If you need a fix while sightseeing, try **Odeon Duomo,** on p. del Duomo facing the cathedral. At **Viel Celso,** via Marconi, 3E, next to the tourist office, you can buy a cone packed with four scoops and take it to the outside tables, one of the cheapest places to sit near the *duomo* (L2200-4500 for a large cup).

Jack Frost Gelateria, via Felice Casati, 25 (tel. 669 11 34; MM1: Porta Venezia), off corso Buenos Aires at via Lazzaretto. Creamy *gelato* and fairy-tale decor. Try their *bacio* (a chocolate and hazelnut "kiss"). Open Thurs.-Tues. 10:30am-1am.

Gelateria Milanodoc, p. Cantore, 4 (tel. 89 40 98 30), near the Navigli. A household word in Milan. Under a thatched roof enclosed by hedges. Open Tues.-Sun. 8am-1am.

Sights

Around the Duomo

The **piazza del Duomo** marks both the geographical and conceptual focus of Milan. The **duomo,** a terrifying, radically vertical Gothic creation with vaguely classical proportions, presides over the *piazza*. Gian Galeazzo Visconti founded the cathedral in 1386, hoping to flatter the Virgin into granting him a male heir. Construction proceeded sporadically over the next four centuries; it was finally completed at Napoleon's command in 1809. In the meantime, 2245 statues, 135 spires, 96 gargoyles, and kilometers of tracery accumulated. The unusual triangular facade, perpetually under restoration, juxtaposes Italian Gothic and Baroque elements under a filigree crown. Inside, the 52 columns rise to canopied niches that shelter statues reaching almost the full height of the ceiling—48 meters. The church, a five-aisled cruciform, seats 40,000 worshipers. Narrow side aisles extend to the grand stained-glass windows, said to be the largest in the world. The imposing 16th-century marble tomb of Giacomo de Medici in the right transept was inspired by Michelangelo. From outside the north transept, you can climb to the top of the cathedral, where you will find yourself surrounded by florid outbursts of turrets and spires (admission L3000, with elevator L5000). This roof-top magical kingdom terminates at the central tower (1765-69), which is crowned by a gold-plated Madonna. For a terrestrial adventure, go around to see the magnificent apse windows decorated with great swirls of tracery. (Open daily 7am-7pm; Oct.-May 9am-4:30pm. No shorts, miniskirts, or sleeveless shirts or dresses.)

The **Museo del Duomo,** p. del Duomo, 14 (tel. 86 03 58), is across the *piazza* in the Palazzo Reale. The newly renovated museum hosts a collection of treasures from the cathedral. (Open Tues.-Sun. 9:30am-12:30pm and 3-6pm. Admission L4000.) It also houses the **Museo d'Arte Contemporanea.** The ground floor accommodates temporary exhibitions. Upstairs is a fine permanent collection of Italian Futurist art, though Picasso figures in among the assembled Boccionis, De Chiricos, and Marinettis. (Open Tues.-Sun. 9:30am-12:15pm and 2:30-5:15pm. Free. Access for people with disabilities.)

On the north side of the *piazza* is the monumental entrance to the **Galleria Vittorio Emanuele II.** The four-story arcade of *caffè,* shops, and offices is covered by a glass barrel vault and a beautiful glass cupola (48m). The designer died in a fall from the top a few days before its grand opening in 1878. A meander through the gallery from the *duomo* leads to the **Teatro alla Scala** (also known as **La Scala**), the world's premier opera house, a simple neoclassical building completed in 1778. La Scala rests on the site of the Church of Santa Maria alla Scala, from which it took its name. To see the many-tiered, lavish hall, enter through the **Museo Teatrale alla Scala** (tel. 805 34 18). Here a succession of petite rooms are lined floor to ceiling with opera memorabilia, including plaster casts of the hands of famous conductors, Verdi's mythologized top hat, pencil depictions of his last hours on earth, and photographs of divine diva Maria Callas. (Open Mon.-Sat. 9am-noon and 2-6pm, Sun. 9:30am-12:30pm and 2:30-6pm; Oct.-April Mon.-Sat. 9am-noon and 2-6pm. Admission L4000.)

Passing the 16th-century Palazzi Marino, which is opposite La Scala and is now the mayor's office, and the side of the church of San Fedele (1569), you arrive at the curious **Casa degli Omenoni** (1565). The exterior of this compact Renaissance palace is embellished with eight giant figures of the worldly Atlas. The street ends at **piazza Belgioioso,** a pleasant square of old Milan dominated by the 18th-century Belgioioso *palazzo* and the picturesque house of 19th-century novelist Alessandro Manzoni, who wrote **I Promessi Sposi** (The Betrothed). The **Museo Manzoniano,** at via Morone, 1 (tel. 87 10 19), is devoted to his life and works. Among the portraits of his friends is an autographed likeness of Goethe. The museum also contains a small library. (Open Tues.-Fri. 9am-noon and 2-4pm. Free. Closed in 1992 for restoration.) Further traipsing down via Morone brings you to **via Manzoni.** A fitting beginning for this street, medieval **Porta Nuova** is a Roman tomb sculpture and a Gothic niche cradling statues of saints. The real gem on the *via* is the **Museo Poldi-Pezzoli** (at #12; tel. 79 48 89), an outstanding private collection of art bequeathed to the city in 1879, housed in the former home of the founder. The museum's masterpieces are hung in the Golden Room, which overlooks a luscious garden (visible through a Palladian window). The paintings include a Byzantine *Virgin and Child* by Andrea Mantegna; Bellini's *Ecce Homo; St. Nicholas* by Piero della Francesca; the magical *Gray Lagoon* by Guardi; and the museum's signature piece, Antonio Pollaiolo's *Portrait of a Young Woman.* (Open Tues.-Sun. 9:30am-12:30pm and 2:30-5pm; April-Sept. closed Sun. afternoon. Admission L5000.)

Near Castello Sforzesco

After the cathedral, the enormous 15th-century **Castello Sforzesco** (tel. 62 36 39 47, MM1: Cairoli), restored after heavy bomb damage in 1943, is Milan's best-known monument. Its majestic tower provides a delicate touch to an otherwise overwhelming exterior. The sheer vastness of the first interior court makes it difficult to appreciate any architectural detail, while the more enclosed, lesser courtyards are noted for their Renaissance arcades. On the ground floor around the Ducal Court is the excellent sculpture collection renowned for Michelangelo's unfinished *Pietà Rondanini,* his last work. The picture gallery features paintings by Mantegna, Bellini, Lotto, and other Renaissance masters, as well as an outstanding *Madonna with Angels* by Filippo Lippi. There is an Egyptian collection and an overwhelming display of Roman, Greek, and Etruscan artifacts in the basement. Five centuries of musical instruments are on display on the first floor. (Open Tues.-Sun. 9:30am-5:30pm. Free.)

Via Verdi, alongside La Scala, leads to **via Brera,** another charming street lined with small, brightly colored palaces and art galleries just a few steps from the *duomo* (MM1: Cordusio; for doorstep service, catch bus #61 from MM1: Moscova). The **Pinacoteca di Brera** (Brera Art Gallery), via Brera, 28 (tel. 80 83 87), glories in a 17th-century *palazzo* and presents a truly impressive collection of paintings. The courtyard encloses a two-storied *loggia* and a magisterial statue of Napoleon as a victorious Roman Emperor. Paintings include Bellini's intense *Pietà* (1460); Andrea Mantegna's brilliantly foreshortened *Dead Christ* (1480); Raphael's *Marriage of the Virgin* (1504); Caravaggio's delectable *Supper at Emmaus* (1606); and Piero della Francesca's 15th-century *Madonna and Child with Saints and Duke Federico di Montefeltro.* The vibrant, animated frescoes by Bramante from the *Casa dei Panigarola* (Rm. 24) provide comic relief from the dramatic intensity of these works. A limited but choice collection of works by modern masters including Modigliani and Carlo Carrà serves as an even more striking contrast. (Open Tues.-Thurs. 9am-6pm, Fri.-Sat. 9am-2pm, Sun. 9am-1pm. Admission L8000.)

The **Church of Santa Maria delle Grazie,** on p. di Sta. Maria delle Grazie and corso Magenta off via Carducci (MM1: Cairoli, or take bus #21 and 24), is renowned for the splendid tribune Bramante added in 1492. Note the eccentric pilasters in the shape of a candelabra rising from a base carved with medallions representing saints. Inside, the Gothic nave with its tunnel-like vaults is juxtaposed with the airiness of the Bramante addition. To the left, a door leads to an elegant square cloister, the artist's other contribution to the church. (Open Mon.-Sat. 7:30am-noon and 3-7:30pm, Sun. 3-7:30pm.)

Next to the church entrance in what was the monastery's refectory is the **Cenacolo Vinciano** (tel. 498 75 88), containing Leonardo's *Last Supper.* In late afternoon, the natural light that streams through the windows elegantly complements the lighting in the fresco. From the far end of the room, you can see how Leonardo used converging lines to simulate a third dimension. The fresco captures the apostles reaction to Jesus' prophecy that "One of you will betray me." Take the time to examine the expression of Doubting Thomas with his raised forefinger; the sad profile of lonely Philip, who leans forward with arms folded in fear that he unknowingly is the betrayer; and Peter, partially blocked by an ungainly Judas who springs forward, clutching his 30 pieces of silver. Scaffolding for an eternal restoration project covers only the bottom of the fresco, leaving the rest in full view. (Open Tues.-Sun. 9am-1:15pm. Admission L6,000. Access for people with disabilities.)

If you are still in pursuit of the spirit of Leonardo, explore the **Museo Nazionale della Scienza e della Tecnica "Leonardo da Vinci,"** via San Vittore, 21 (tel. 46 27 09,

MM1: San Ambrogio or bus #50 or 54), off via Carducci. A large section is devoted to applied physics and a huge room is filled with wooden models of Leonardo's most ingenious and visionary inventions. Open Tues.-Sun. 9am-5pm. Admission L6000.)

The **Church of Sant'Ambrogio** (MM1: San Ambrogio), which served as a prototype for Lombard-Romanesque churches throughout Italy, is the most influential medieval building in Milan. An atrium guarding fragments of ancient tombstones and frescoes fronts the low-pitched facade. The high altar, encased in glass, retains the original 9th-century reliefs in brilliant silver and gold, inlaid with enamel and gems. The crypt contains the gruesome skeletal remains of Sant'Ambrogio and two early Christian martyrs. The tiny 4th-century **Chapel of San Vittore,** with exquisite 5th-century mosaics adorning its cupola, is through the seventh chapel on the right. As you leave the church on the left, you will pass under the peculiar **Portico della Canonica** (1492) by Bramante, the end columns of which have notches resembling those of tree trunks. Also by Bramante are the two exquisite courtyards in the adjacent **Università Cattolica,** originally the monastery of Sant'Ambrogio.

Continue your spiritual pilgrimage to the land of the dead. The vast grounds of the **Cimitero Monumentale,** several blocks east of Stazione Porta Garibaldi, are a labyrinthine network of three-story mausoleums in architectural styles ranging from Egyptian pyramids to art deco jukeboxes. If you've made it this far, you might feel like becoming one of their number.

From corso di Porta Romana to the Navigli

This part of town may lack the grandeur of downtown Milan, but several interesting monuments warrant a visit. The distances between sights are greater here; consider using public transportation.

At the **Church of San Nazaro Maggiore,** on corso di Porta Romana (accessible from the *duomo* by tram #13), a medieval Lombard-Romanesque structure conceals the remnants of a 4th-century basilica. The Renaissance funerary chapel of the Trivulzio in front is the work of Bramante's pupil Bramantino (1512-1547). The tomb bears the famous epigraph: "Qui numquam quivit quiescit: Tasc"—"he who never knew quiet now reposes: Silence." (Open daily 8:30am-noon and 3-6:30pm.)

The **Church of San Lorenzo Maggiore,** on corso Ticinese (MM2: Porta Genova, then bus #59), the oldest church in Milan, testifies to the greatness of the city during the paleochristian era. The building began as an early Christian church in the mid-4th century, and although it was rebuilt later (12th-century campanile and 16th-century dome), it retains its original octagonal plan. On the four cardinal sides are large, semicircular screened spaces behind which runs an ambulatory, in the manner of San Vitale at Ravenna. To the right of the church meditates the 14th-century chapel of Sant'Aquilino. Inside is a beautiful 4th-century mosaic of a young, beardless Christ among his apostles. A staircase behind the altar leads to the remains of an early Roman amphitheater. (Church open Mon.-Sat. 8am-noon and 3-6pm, Sun. 10:30-11:15am and 3-5:30pm.) Near the front of the church is the 12th-century **Porta Ticinese.**

Farther down corso Ticinese (bus #15) stands the **Church of Sant'Eustorgio,** founded in the 4th century to house the reputed bones of the Magi, spirited off to Cologne in 1164. The present building (erected in 1278) has a typical Lombard-Gothic interior of low vaults and brick ribs supported by heavy columns. The real gem of this church, and one of the great masterpieces of early Renaissance art, is the **Portinari Chapel** (1468), attributed to the Florentine Michelozzo (L500 to open the gates in the back of the apse). Similar to Brunelleschi's Pazzi Chapel in Florence, the plan of the chapel involves a square crowned by a dome with a smaller niche on one side also surmounted by a dome. A *Dance of Angels* is carved around the base of the multicolored dome, and frescoes depict the life and death of Peter the Martyr. In the center of the chapel is the magnificent Gothic tomb of St. Eustorgius (1339), sculpted by Giovanni di Balduccio of Pisa. (Church open daily 8am-noon and 3-7pm.)

Through the neoclassical Arco di Porta Ticinese (1801-1814) or outside the Porta Genova station (MM2), you will find the Amsterdam of Italia: canals, small footbridges, open-air markets, picturesque alleys, and trolleys. This is the **navigli district,** part of the medieval canal system (whose original locks were designed by da Vinci) that linked northern cities and lakes.

South and East of the Duomo

One of the largest constructions of the early Renaissance is the 1456 **Ospedale Maggiore** on via Festa del Perdono near p. Santo Stefano. The "General Hospital"—now the University of Milan—boasts nine courtyards. The inside arches are covered by multicolored circles and diamonds and the Gothic frames by medallions. Inside is a magnificent 17th-century court and a gracious smaller one credited to Bramante. In 1479, Bramante designed the mystical **Church of San Satiro** on via Torino, a few blocks (or a few minutes ride on bus #15) from the *duomo*. Despite its modest proportions, the interior creates the illusion of wide spaces. Compare the imaginary and the real by standing at the back of the church and then behind the high altar. The octagonal baptistery, also by Bramante, contains a beautiful frieze of *putti.*

Following via Spadari off via Torino and then making a right onto via Cantù will deposit you at the lilliputian but lovely **Pinacoteca Ambrosiana,** p. Pio XI, 2 (tel. 80 01 46). The 14 rooms of the Ambrosiana house exquisite works from the 15th through 17th centuries, including Botticelli's *Madonna of the Canopy;* Leonardo's *Portrait of a Musician;* Raphael's cartoon for the *School of Athens;* Caravaggio's *Basket of Fruit,* the first example of still-life painting in Italy; and the two plush paintings of *Earth* and *Air* by Breughel. (Open Sun.-Fri. 9:30am-5pm.)

East of the *duomo,* **corso Vittorio Emanuele,** between p. del Duomo and p. San Babila, is the major shopping street of the city. Except for the **Church of San Carlo al Corso** (another neoclassical building modeled after the Pantheon), the street was entirely rebuilt after the war. Off p. San Babila, **Via Monte Napoleon,** the most elegant street in Milan, is lined with early 19th-century *palazzi* and late 20th-century Armanis and Cardins, now used by the most exclusive of city businesses and the most exquisite of its *ateliers* (designer show rooms). The part of **corso Venezia** bordering the Giardini Pubblici is a broad boulevard lined with sumptuous palaces. Don't miss a stroll through the English-style **Giardini Pubblici** on a sunny afternoon. (Open roughly 7am-10pm.) A small zoo lies within the grounds (open 9:30am-5pm).

The **Galleria d'Arte Moderna,** via Palestro, 16 (tel. 70 23 78), is next to the Giardini Pubblici in the neoclassical Villa Comunale (MM2: Porta Venezia). Napoleon lived here with Josephine when Milan was capital of the Napoleonic Kingdom of Italy (1805-1814). Important modern Lombard art is displayed here, as well as works by Picasso, Matisse, Renoir, Gauguin, and Cézanne. (Open Wed.-Mon. 9:30am-12:15pm and 2:30-5:30pm. Free.) Another worthwhile museum is the **Museo di Milano** (tel. 70 62 45) on via Sant'Andrea, 6, which shows Italian art and shares an 18th-century mansion with the petite **Museo di Storia Contemporanea** (Museum of Contemporary History; tel. 76 00 62 45; MM2: San Babila). (Both open daily 9:30am-3:30pm. Free.) Also check out the **Museo Civico di Storia Naturale** (Museum of Natural History) on corso Venezia, 55, in the Giardino Pubblico (tel. 62 08 54 05). This quarters extensive and worthwhile geology and paleontology collections, including a room of complete dinosaur skeletons. (Open daily 9:30am-5:30 pm. Free.)

Entertainment

Music and Theater

Emblematic of the pastiche of populism and posh that characterizes the arts scene in Milan is the **Musica in Metro** program, a series of summer concerts performed by local music students dressed in their black-tie best in subway stations. These kids probably hope to perform someday at **La Scala,** which traditionally opens its season on December 7. Opera performances continue through early June. La Scala is closed mid-July through August, gone to the beach with the rest of Milan. The summer season, primarily during June and September, features recitals, operas, and concerts, as well as some ballet. Though good tickets are usually sold out long in advance, gallery seats (notorious for inducing altitude sickness) go for as little as L18,000. (Box office (tel. 72 00 37 44) open Tues.-Sun. 10am-1pm and 3:30-5:30pm. On performance days tickets go on sale 5:30-9:30pm; unsold gallery seats and standing room are available 1hr. before curtain.) The **Conservatorio,** via del Conservatorio, 12 (tel. 76 00 17 55 or 76 00 18 54), near p. Tricolore, offers more classical music, while the **Teatro Lirico,** via Rastrelli, 6 (tel. 80 00 46), south of the *duomo,* is Milan's leading stage, offering everything from ballet to avant-garde plays. (Ticket office open Mon.-Sat. 10:30am-6:30pm; admission from L20,000). Summer brings special programs of music and culture: **Milano d'Estate** (Milan in Summer) in July, and **Vacanze a Milano** (Vacation in Milan) in August.

The **Piccolo Teatro,** via Rovello, 2 (tel. 87 76 63), near via Dante, began in the postwar years as a socialist theater and is now owned by the city. (Performances Tues.-Sun. nights.) **Ciak,** via Sangallo, 33 (tel. 71 34 01), near p. Argonne east of the *duomo,* is a favorite haunt of young *milanesi* for theater, films, and occasionally cabaret. Take train #5 from Stazione Centrale to viale Argonne.

The **Teatro di Porta Romana,** corso di Porta Romana, 124 (tel. 518 11 26 or 518 11 44; bus #13 from via Marconi off p. del Duomo), is building a reputation for experimental productions and first-run, mainstream plays (admission about L17,000). In what has become an annual project, the **Teatro dell' Elfo,** via Ciro Menotti, 11 (tel. 71 67 91), sponsors the **Festival dei Festival,** showcasing the best of the many local theater festivals staged throughout Italy. (Performances throughout July. Admission about L25,000.) For a different brand of street theater, the **Carnivale** in Milan is increasingly popular. As the crowds in Venice sport fewer costumes and more cameras each year, many come here instead for the friendlier atmosphere. Tickets for all performances are sold at the corresponding venue but can also be purchased through **La Biglietterra,** corso Garibaldi, 81 (tel. 659 01 88 or 659 89 56).

Movies and Nightlife

Milan's cinematic scene thrives. Theaters such as the **Angelicum,** p. Sant'Angelo, 2 (tel. 659 27 48, admission L9000) off via Moscova, and the **Anteo,** via Milazzo, 9 (tel. 659 77 32, admission L9000), specialize in showing films in their original languages. Check any Milanese paper (especially the Thursday edition) for showings and general information. The **Mexico,** via Savona, 57, southwest of the *duomo,* has a good variety (L8000). Between late June and late August, the **Cinema nel Parco** festival offers outdoor showings of recent films (L3000). Old movies can be seen at the **Cineteca Italiana/Museo del Cinema,** via Manin, 2/B (tel. 79 92 24; open Mon.-Fri. 3-6:30pm; admission L3000).

The **Navigli** and **Porta Ticinese** areas, once the lairs of prostitutes and black-marketeers, are now alive with clubs, *birrerie* (beer halls), and *paninoteche* (sandwich bars). Another safe, attractive, and chic district lies by **via Brera;** here you'll find art galleries, small clubs, and restaurants.

Rock and all that's Hot: After Bologna, Milan supports the best rock scene in Italy. **Prego,** via Besenzanica, 3, is one of the best clubs. Cover L15,000. Open Tues.-Sun. until 2am. **Rolling Stone,** corso XXII Marzo, 32, east of the *duomo.* Easy on hip and heavy on chic. Cover L10,000. Open Thurs.-Sun. until 2:30am. **Plastic** (officially **Il Killer Plastico**), is not far away at viale Umbria, 120. Verging on disco, it swings between a punk/new wave and a fashionable New York crowd. Cover L15,000, Sat. L18,000. Open Tues.-Sun. until 2:30am. **Bella Epoque,** p. XXIV Maggio, 8 (MM2: Porta Genova, then bus #59). Looks back to the golden era of rock'n'-roll. Come here for a quick Beatles fix. Open Fri.-Sun. until 3am.

Jazz and Folk: Capolinea, via Ludovico il Moro, 119. Walk out corso Italia toward the Navigli and Porta Ticinese, south of the *duomo.* A student crowd. Open Tues.-Sun. until 1:30am. **Le Scimmie,** via Ascanio Sforza, 49, beyond the Capolinea. Milan's premier jazz spot. Open daily 8pm-2am. **Biblo's,** via Madonnina, 17, in the Brera area, welcomes folk performers. Open daily. Admission L10,000-15,000.

Discos: USA, via B. Cellini, 2, near corso Porta Vittoria. One of Milan's top discos, but expensive. Cover L15,000-20,000. Open Wed.-Sun. 11:30pm-3am. **American Disaster,** via Boscovich, 48, near Stazione Centrale. Tacky (don your glow-in-the-dark shirts) but less expensive. Open Thurs.-Sat. **No Ties,** foro Buonaparte, 68. A chic, both gay and straight place with a long line at the door. Cover L10,000-12,000, Wed. 2-for-1 admission. Open Wed.-Sun. 10pm-3am. **Nuova Idea,** via de Castillia, 30 (MM2: Gioia). A huge and notably gay hangout, famous throughout Italy. Cover

L8000-10,000. Open Tues. and Thurs.-Sun. 9:30pm-1 or 2am. **Contatto,** corso Sempione, 76 (MM1: Cairoli, then bus #57), behind the Castello Sforzesco. Another gay club.

Neither Fish nor Fowl: Zimba ("lion" in Swahili), via Gratosoglio, 108. Has shocked xenophobes by becoming one of the city's biggest hangouts. Conga, rhythm and blues, and Carribean music. Open Tues.-Sun. **Magia Music Meeting,** via Salutati, 2 (MM2: San Agostino). New bands looking for a break start out here. Go for dinner while you listen (about L8000). Open daily until 3am.

Shopping

Milan's most elegant boutiques are found between the *duomo* and p. S. Babila, especially on the excessively chic **via Monte Napoleone.** If you can tolerate the stigma of being an entire *season* behind the trends, famous designer brands may be purchased from **blochisti** (wholesale clothing outlets). Try **Monitor** on viale Monte Nero (MM2: Porta Genova, then bus #9), or **Il Salvagente,** on via Bronzetti off corso XXII Marzo (bus #60). **Fiorucci's** original shop is at Galleria Passarella, 1 (tel. 70 00 80 33; MM1: San Babila), at corso Vittorio Emanuele. (Open Tues.-Sat. 10am-7pm, Mon. 3-7pm.) More affordable, yet still well-designed, is the clothing sold along **corso Buenos Aires,** and both **via Torino,** near the *duomo,* and **via Sarpi,** near porta Garibaldi, are decked out in inexpensive department stores and boutiques catering to a younger crowd. Shop around the area of corso di Porta Ticinese for *chic ma non snob* (hip) attire (MM2: Porta Genova, then bus #59). **Eliogabalo,** p. Sant' Eustorgio, 2 (tel. 837 82 93), named after a Roman Emperor renowned for his preoccupation with matters sartorial, offers the latest in *haute couture.* Lacking both the cachet and expense of boutiques, the department store **Rinascente,** downtown across from the *duomo,* carries reasonably priced essentials. Reasonable prices for everything from clothes to groceries can be found at the **STANDA** department store at via Torino, 37 (tel. 86 67 06), five blocks from the *duomo.* Photo booth (L500), photocopy machine (L100), and shoe repair on the third floor. (Open Tues.-Sun. 9am-7:30pm and Mon 2-7:30 pm.) True Milanese bargain hunters attack the giant street markets on Saturday and Tuesday to buy their threads. These are on **via Fauché** (MM2: Garibaldi) and **viale Papinian** (MM2: Sant'Agostino); or try the 400-year-old **Fiera di Sinigallia** on nearby via Calatafimi (Sat. only). For used clothing try the Navigli district or corso Garibaldi. Shop at the end of July for the pre-Ferragosto sale wars (20-50% off). (Clothing stores are generally open Mon. 10am-noon, Tues.-Sat. 10am-noon and 2-7:30pm.)

Pavia

Once an important Roman outpost, Pavia weathered Attila the Hun in 452 and Odoacre the Goth in 476 before earning time in the limelight as the Lombard capital during the 7th and 8th centuries. The city retained both power and privilege through the subsequent dominion of Charlemagne, but in 1024 the last of the political bigwigs took off for Milan. But this minor fall from grace was nothing compared to the humiliation of foreign occupation. Spanish, Austrian, and French forces governed Pavia in rapid succession from the 16th century until 1859, when Italy's movement for national independence—a particular concern for Pavia—liberated the city.

The Pavia of today has returned to a state of prosperity with the help of agricultural and industrial development. Romanesque churches dating from Pavia's tranquil years as a Milanese satellite are scattered throughout the historic sector, and the 14th-century university continues to flourish. The once-prominent city's status as an offbeat tourist locale is evinced by the confidence with which non-Italians persevere in mispronouncing its name (hint: emphasize the second syllable).

Orientation and Practical Information

Pavia is a mere 35km south of Milan, on the train line to Genoa (30min.). The city sits on the banks of the Ticino river not far from its intersection with the Po. The train station overlooks piazzale Stazionale in the modern, west end of the town, which is linked to the historic center by corso Cavour.

Tourist Office: via F. Filzi, 2 (tel. 221 56), in a characterless section of town. Take a left on via Trieste from station and then right on Filzi. Good map of the city. Ask for the booklet *Pavia and its Province: Discovering the Pavia Area. Appartamenti* provides seasonal listings of events. Open Mon.-Sat. 9am-12:30pm and 2:30-6pm.

Post Office: p. della Posta, 2 (tel. 269 19), off via Mentana, 1 block over from corso Mazzini. Stamps and Fermo Posta at #5. Open Mon.-Sat. 8am-7pm. **Postal Code:** 27100.

Telephones: SIP, via Galliano, 8 (tel. 30 45 11), around the corner from the post office. Open Mon.-Sat. 9am-12:30pm and 2:30-7:30pm, Sun. 9am-2pm.

Trains: at the head of viale V. Emanuele II at the western end of town (tel. 230 00) . To: Genoa (every 1/2-hr., L7000); Milan (every hr., L2400); Cremona (4 per day, L4700); Mantua (1 per day, L8200). **Luggage Storage:** L1500. Open 6am-9:30pm.

Buses: SGEA, departing from the new space-age station on via Trieste (left from the train station). To Milan (every hr. 6am-10pm, 50min., L3500) via the *certosa* (charterhouse; 10min., L1500).

Emergencies: tel. 113. **Police:** p. Italia, 5 (tel. 112). **Hospital: Ospedale S. Matteo,** p. Golgi, 2 (tel. 38 81). **Medical Assistance:** tel. 39 01, nights and holidays tel. 52 76 00.

Accommodations

A dearth of reasonably priced places to stay makes Pavia most appealing as a day-trip. Inquire at the tourist office about the current condition of the youth hostel at Vaghera.

Hotel Splendid, via XX Settembre, 11 (tel. 247 03), off corso Cavour near p. del Duomo. Indeed ironic, but the Splendid is the last of Pavia's one-stars that has not been converted to student housing. Friendly management, but less than sparkling rooms, and the smell may haunt you for days. Look out for beds that go bump in the night. Singles L30,000. Doubles L54,000.

Camping: Ticino, via Mascherpa, 10 (tel. 52 53 62). Walk down viale Vittorio Emanuele II from the station. At the statue of Athena, the wise thing to do is turn right and cross the bridge. Swimming pool. L6200 per person, L4000 per tent.

Food

Coniglio (rabbit) and *rana* (frog) are the local specialties, but if you don't eat things that bounce, stick to the local pastries on display in shop windows along corsos Cavour and Mazzini. **Esselunga** is an intimidatingly oversized supermarket at the far end of the mall complex between via Trieste and viale Batisti (open Tues.-Sat. 8am-8pm, Mon. 1-8pm).

Trattoria da Andrea, via Teodolina, 23 (tel. 242 10), off p. del Duomo. A homey room saturated with tantalizing smells. The brothers in charge perfected their art long ago. *Menù* L16,000. Pasta around L6000. Wine L8000-14,000 per bottle. Open Sat.-Thurs. noon-3pm and 6:30-11pm.

Ristorante Pizzeria Marechiaro, p. Vittoria, 9 (tel. 237 39). Delicious pizza with exquisite crust, prepared before your eyes, for L5000-9000. Crowded, cozy atmosphere; delighted diners overflow onto the pretty *piazza.* Cover L2000. Open Tues.-Sun. 11am-3pm and 7pm-3am.

Gelateria de Cesare, via Garibaldi, 15c (tel. 250 74), parallel to corso Mazzini on the river side. The pride and glory of Pavia's *gelato* connoisseurs, this modest cubbyhole has none of the glitz of its competitors, but scoops out mighty fine *gelato.* Open Sept.-July Tues.-Sun. 9am-midnight.

Sights and Entertainment

For centuries the **Church of San Michele** (tel. 260 63) was the favored venue for coronations of Northern Italian kings, including Charlemagne in 774 and Frederick Barbarossa in 1155. The original 7th-century church was entirely rebuilt in the Romanesque style at the end of the 11th century following a serious earthshaker. The massive yellow sandstone facade is divided into three parts and topped with a Lombard-Romanesque *loggia.* Vigorously sculpted griffins, snake-tailed fish, monsters, and struggling human figures symbolizing the battle of good and evil adorn the three doorways and the columns of the raised crypt inside. Decorating the chancel are a 1491 fresco of the *Coronation of the Virgin* and bas-reliefs from the 14th century. The 8th-century silver crucifix of Theodote graces the chapel to the right of the presbytery. To get to San Michele, go down corso Garibaldi and turn right after via della Rochetta. (Open Tues.-Sat. 9-11:30am and 2:30-6:30pm, Sun. 9am-noon.)

From San Michele it's a short walk to what's left of Pavia's layered brick **duomo.** The **Torre Civica,** adjoining the *duomo,* collapsed in the spring of 1989, killing several people and taking with it a good portion of the *duomo's* left-hand chapel, as well as some nearby houses and shops. Disputes over what ought to be done with the rubble have led to a lackadaisical restoration--the *piazza* is ever-garnished with barricades and scaffolding. The shaky brick exterior of the *duomo,* recently reinforced by concrete columns, conceals an impressive interior. Begun in 1488 and influenced by the designs of Bramante, Macaluso, and Leonardo, the *duomo* was one of the most ambitious undertakings of the Renaissance in Lombardy—naturally, much of it was not actually completed until 1895-1933. The huge interior space in the form of a Greek cross is typical of a Renaissance central-plan church.

The prestigious **University of Pavia,** founded in 1361 (tel. 382 38 71), sprawls along strada Nuova. It claims such famous alumni as Petrarch, Columbus, and the Venetian playwright Goldoni. The university's most electrifying exponent, however, was the physicist Alessandro Volta (his experiments are on display at the university). And the patron of the university, Galeazzo II of Visconti, earned notoriety for his research into human torture. The three towers rising from the university's property on p. Leonardo da Vinci are vestiges of the more than 100 medieval towers that once pierced the city's skyline and as of summer 1992 were fenced off and swaddled in scaffolding on account of the city's understandable concern with structural failure.

Strada Nuova ends at the **Castello Visconteo** (1360), a colossal medieval castle set in a park that once extended to the Certosa di Pavia, the Visconti's private hunting ground 8km away. The castle's vast courtyard is bordered on three sides by richly colored windows and elegant terracotta decoration. The fourth wall was destroyed in 1527 during the Franco-Spanish Wars. Pavia's **Civic Museum** (tel. 338 53), located here, houses a picture gallery and an extensive Lombard-Romanesque sculpture collection. (Open June-Nov. Tues.-Sat. 9am-1:30pm, Sun. 9am-1pm; off-season Tues.-Sat. 9am-1:30pm. Admission L5000.)

From the front grounds of the castle, you can see the low rounded forms of the **Church of San Pietro in Ciel d'Oro** (tel. 30 30 36). Another exquisite example of the Lombard-Romanesque style, it was consecrated in 1132. Inside on the high altar is a marble reliquary containing the remains of St. Augustine in an ornate Gothic ark. (Open daily 7am-noon and 3-7:30pm.)

Each September, folklore and concerts jazz up the city for 15 days in the **Settembre Pavese** festival. The **Festa del Ticino** (first week in Sept.) is a city-wide extravaganza that prompts shops to stay open late and castlekeepers to lower the drawbridges, welcoming rock stars and ballet impresarios alike. (For a schedule of performances contact the tourist office.) If you prefer modern rites, join the rowdy masses who throng in May or June to watch the **Coppa Città di Pavia,** a national soccer tournament held in the **Campo Sportivo Frigirolo.**

Near Pavia

Eight kilometers north of Pavia stands the **Certosa di Pavia** (Charterhouse of Pavia; tel. 92 56 13; ask to speak with polyglot Padre Tebreab). Both buses and trains can deposit you nearby. **Buses** leave Pavia from p. Piave opposite the station (L1500) and Milan from p. Castello (L2600). From the bus stop, the *certosa* awaits you at the end of a long road lined by trees; from the **train** station, go to the left around the outside wall of the monastic complex and turn inside to the right at the first opening. This Carthusian monastery and mausoleum was built for the Visconti who ruled the area from the 12th to 15th centuries, and summarizes four centuries of Italian art, from early Gothic to Baroque. The exuberant facade (late 1400s-1560) revels in sculpture and inlaid marble, representing the apex of the Lombard Renaissance. The interior of the church basks in a wealth of masterworks including those of Bergognone and Amadeo. Solari's monument to Lodovico il Moro Visconti and his child bride Beatrice d'Este is especially remarkable. The Old Sacristy houses a Florentine triptych carved in ivory, with 99 sculptures and 66 bas-reliefs depicting the lives of Mary and Jesus.

The monks lead delightful tours of the complex whenever a large enough group has gathered (usually every 45min.), leaving from inside the church. (Open Tues.-Sun. 9-11:30am and 2:30-6pm; March-April. and Sept.-Oct. Tues.-Sun. 9-11:30am and 2:30-5pm; Nov.-Feb. Tues.-Sun. 9-11:30am and 2:30-4:30pm. Free.)

Cremona

Agriculturally prosperous Cremona is home to some of the most remarkable architecture in Lombardy. For the past 500 years, however, it has been Cremona's musical contributions that have made the world take note. In 1530, Andrea Amati created the violin and established the Cremonese violin-making dynasty. Having learned the fundamentals as apprentices in the Amati workshop, Antonio Stradivari (1644-1737) and Giuseppe Guarneri (1687-1745) lifted the art of violin-making to unprecedented heights. The world's greatest violinist, Nicolò Paganini, received ovations throughout Europe with a Guarneri violin in hand. Antonio Stradivari created nearly 1200 stringed instruments (mandolins, lutes, cellos, and violas) with a tone and timbre so remarkable that, upon hearing them, people spoke of angelic voices. Students from all over the world still come to learn the legendary craft at the International School for Violin-Making, ever hopeful of stumbling upon the formula of Stradivari's secret varnish. Today, Cremona's magnificent earth-toned buildings create an atmosphere of staid sobriety, but continuing interest in all things musical and an ever-active concert season at the Ponchielli Theater lend the city a more than compensatory dose of color and life.

Orientation and Practical Information

Via Palestro undergoes a double metamorphosis, becoming first **via Campi** and then **via Verdi** en route from the train station to the cluster of *piazze* at the core of the historical center. A left at p. Cavour or p. Pace leads to the architecturally rich p. del Comune, home to a number of impressive edifices and the indispensable tourist office. If the 15-min. walk doesn't appeal, jump on bus #1 (L900). Most Cremonese desert the city in July and August.

Tourist Office: p. del Duomo, 5 (tel. 232 33), in front of the *duomo*. The staff is bubbly and obliging, but you may have difficulty communicating in English. *Cremona, Art City* has a map and some historical background. Open Mon.-Sat. 9:30am-12:30pm and 3-6pm.

Post Office: via Verdi, 1 (tel. 226 19). Open Mon.-Fri. 8am-7pm, Sat. 8am-1pm. **Postal Code:** 26100.

Telephones: SIP, p. Cavour, 1 (tel. 239 11). Open Mon.-Sat. 9am-12:30pm and 2:30-7:30pm, Sun. 9am-1pm. **Telephone Code:** 0372.

Trains: via Dante, 68 (tel. 222 37). Ask for p. Stazione. To: Milan (9 per day, 1hr. 30min., L6500); Pavia (4 per day, 1hr. 15min., L5700); Mantua (15 per day, 1hr., L5000); and Brescia (12 per day, 45min., L4300).

Buses: Autostazione di via Dante (tel. 292 12), to left of the train station. To Milan (7 per day, 2hr., L5500); Bergamo (5 per day, L7300); and Brescia (almost every hr., L5000). Tickets at **La Pasticceria Mezzadri,** via Dante, 105 (tel. 257 08), or at the station, open 7:20am-1pm and 2:15-6:30pm.

Emergencies: tel. 113. **Police: Sicurezza Pubblica,** via Tribunali, 6 (tel. 233 33). **Medical Assistance:** tel. 37 74. **Hospital: Ospedale** (tel. 40 51), past p. IV Novembre to the east.

Accommodations and Camping

While lodging runs cheap in Cremona, it can be difficult to find a room, especially during the week. If you want to stay, reserve far ahead in summer.

Albergo Touring, via Palestro, 3 (tel. 213 90). From the station, walk across via Dante and straight down via Palestro. Singles L25,000. Doubles L37,000, with bath L45,000. Closed for renovation in 1992.

Albergo Brescia, via Brescia, 7 (tel. 43 46 15). An unpleasant 20-min. walk to the left down via Dante and a left at p. Libertà, or take bus #1, 3, 4, or 6 from the station. Nice management and functional rooms that are booked solid during the week. Singles L35,000. Doubles L45,000. Open Aug. 10-July 10.

Albergo Bologna, p. Risorgimento, 8 (tel. 242 58). Very small singles only. L25,000. Open Aug.-first week of July.

Camping: Parco al Po (tel. 271 37), on via lungo Po Europa southwest of town. From p. Cavour, walk 20min. down corso Vittorio Emanuele. L4900 per person, L4200 per tent. Electricity L1500. Open May-Sept.

Food

First whipped up in the 16th century, Cremona's best-known dish, the bizarre *mostarda di Cremona,* consists of a hodgepodge of fruits—cherries, figs, apricots, melons—preserved in a sweet mustard-flavored syrup and served on boiled meats. Bars of *torrone* (nougat with an egg, honey, and nut base that comes in a variety of flavors) are less adventurous but equally steeped in Cremonese confectionary lore. *Mostarda di Cremona* can be found in most local *trattorie,* while *torrone* can be purchased in the elegant sweet shops on via Solferino. **Spelari,** at via Solferino, 25, has been keeping dentists in business since 1836, and sells homemade *torrone* pies for L9800. (Open Tues.-Sat. 8:30am-12:30pm and 3:30-7:30pm, Mon. 8:30am-12:30pm.) The booming local dairy industry is known for its provolone and *grana padana* cheeses. On Wednesday and Saturday from 8am-1pm, food vendors hold an **open-air market** in p. Marconi, past p. Cavour on corso Verdi. Two **supermarkets** compete on p. Risorgimento (open 8am-12:45pm and 4-7:45pm).

Italmense Agnello Ristorante, via Vianello Torriani, 7 (tel. 221 19), off via Boccaccio north of the *duomo.* Popular with students and office workers. Pasta L3000. *Secondi* L5500. Full meals L8900. Open Mon.-Fri. noon-2pm. Closed 2 weeks in Aug.

Pizzeria allo Stagnino, corso Garibaldi, 85 (tel. 391 53), at via Oberdan. Bronzed and boisterous soccer players come here after games. In their absence, relative calm prevails. Family-run, and families run about. Pizzas L5500-9000, wine begins at L6500 per . Cover L2000. Open Sept.-July Wed.-Mon. 10am-2:30pm and 6pm-2am.

La Bersagliera, p. Risorgimento (tel. 213 97). Cremonese cognoscenti lavish praise on this family-owned establishment. Pizzas L9000. Wine L7000 per . Cover L2000. Open Fri.-Wed. noon-12:30pm and 6:30-10pm.

Sights and Entertainment

Violins and their production are the primary attraction in Cremona. Closest to the train station, the small **Museo Stradivariano,** at via Palestro, 17 (tel. 293 49), provides a fascinating introduction to Stradivari's art. Also exhibited are finished examples by such modern masters as Giuseppe Lecchi and Gaetano Sgarabotto. (Open Tues.-Sat. 9:30am-12:15pm and 3-5:45pm, Sun. 9:30am-12:15pm. Admission L5000, includes the Museo Civico around the corner and the Violin Room.) When school is in session, the **International School of Violin-Making** workshop in the Raimondi Palace on corso Garibaldi entertains with artisans in action. If you stand and stare long enough, someone will explain what's going on. On the second floor of the **Palazzo del Comune** in p. del Comune, a plush town hall decorated with 16th-century Renaissance terra-cottas, the **Saletta dei Violini (Violin Room)** showcases five masterpieces attributed to Andrea Amati (1566), his grandson Nicolò Amati (1658), Stradivari (1715), and Guarneri (1734). (Open June to mid-Aug. Mon.-Sat. 9am-noon and 3-6:45pm, Sun.

9am-noon; mid-Sept. to May Mon.-Fri. 9am-noon and 3-6:45pm, Sat.-Sun. 9am-noon. Hours sometimes change according to the whims of the guard. Admission L5000—includes Museo Stradivariano and the Museo Civico.)

Directly facing the *palazzo* is the pink marble **duomo,** a fine example of the 12th-century Lombard-Romanesque style. Its central, two-story Gothic porch shelters a statue of the Madonna and two saints (1310) above a charming frieze that depicts the Labors of the Months. Though the interior is dark, you'll have no trouble beholding the luminous cycle of 16th-century frescoes by Boccaccio Boccaccino, Gianfrancesco Bembo, and others. (Open Mon.-Sat. 7am-noon and 3-7pm, Sun. 7am-1pm and 4-7pm.) To the left of the cathedral stands the late 13th-century **Torrazzo,** at 108m the tallest campanile in Italy (beating out Siena's Torre di Mangia by 6m). A massive brick structure lightened by an octagonal marble crown, it bears Cremona's coat-of-arms and a 16th-century clock. (Scale the heights mid-March to Oct. Mon.-Sat. 10am-noon and 3-6:30pm. Sun. 10am-12:30pm and 3-7pm. Admission L5000.) The dome of the solid 1167 **baptistry** rises in a perfect, unadorned octagonal pattern to a small oculus. (Open daily 9am-12:30pm and 3-7pm. Closed for restoration in 1992.) The **Loggia dei Militi,** across from the baptistry, completes the square. Erected in 1292 in Gothic style, it functioned as a meeting place for the captains of the citizens' militia. The Gothic **Church of Sant'Agostino** (1345), near via Plasio, contains Bonifacio Bembo frescoes and a *Madonna with Saints* by Perugino (1494).

Cremona is also endowed with fine Renaissance buildings. For a prototypical piece look for the **Palazzo Fodri** (1499) at corso Matteotti, 17. Its elegant terra cotta shelters a courtyard embellished with panels depicting famous battles. The columns in the courtyard bear French royal insignias in homage to Louis XII of France, who occupied the duchy of Milan in 1499. The **Palazzo Affaitati** (1561), via Ugolani Dati, 4, flaunts an impressive grand staircase of marble that leads to the **Museo Civico** (tel. 293 49). The museum's collection of paintings from the Cremona school (15th-18th centuries) includes the illustrious families of Bembo, Campi, and Boccaccino. Caravaggio's San Francesco contemplates a *memento mori* (skull), and the 15th-century codices harken to Renaissance politicking. (Hours and prices same as at Museo Stradivariano. Entrance included with admission to Museum.)

Take via Ghisleri from p. della Libertà (20min.) or bus #2 from p. Cavour to the remarkable 15th-century **Church of San Sigismondo** on via Marmolada. When the duchess Bianca Maria Visconti wed Francesco Sforza, scion of a rival clan, her family, the rulers of Milan, presented this church to Cremona as her dowry.

Cremona is alive with the sound of music all year long. **Cremona Jazz** in March and April eases the way into the summer season with a series of concerts throughout the city (tickets begin at L10,000). **Cremone Rock** gets serious at the stadium at the end of June, and they'll be dancing in the streets with **Salotto in Piazza,** evenings in June and July when p. del Comune becomes an outdoor piano bar. On a more sedate note, **Luglio in Musica** is a series of free concerts of sacred works in the Church of San Sigismondo. The September **Festival di Cremona** kicks off the Teatro Ponchielli fall season with a classical series heavy on the strings (tickets L12,000-30,000), and it all reaches a crescendo with the opera season, also in the Teatro Ponchielli, from mid-October through early December (tickets begin at L18,000). For ticket information on the Festival or the *Tradizionale Stagione Lirica,* contact the Teatro Ponchielli ticket booth at corso Vittorio Emanuele, 52 (tel. 40 72 73).

Mantua (Mantova)

Despite a bit of fame as the home town of Virgil, Mantua's early years as a Roman colony passed by in relative obscurity. These days were followed by an equally luster-less adolescence during which the city helplessly changed hands between each new invader. After enduring periods of Byzantine, Longobard, and Frankish dominion, Mantua achieved sudden glory in 1328 with the unexpected ascension of the Gonzaga family. The new powers-that-were sprouted from peasant roots to become one of the most formidable Renaissance dynasties, rivaling the Visconti and Medici. In the years that followed, Mantua went to finishing school, or, more accurately, finishing school came to Mantua. The Gonzagas zealously sought to obliterate any taint of provincialism by importing known artists and cultivating whatever promising talent existed locally. Leon Battista Alberti designed their churches of San Sebastiano and Sant'Andrea, Claudio Monteverdi spun madrigals for their pleasure, and Andrea Mantegna painstakingly applied his paints to their palace walls. Today's industrial eyesores sprawl along the outskirts of the modern city, but the artistically rich historic center preserves much of the unhurried rustic flavor its rulers sought so fiercely to repudiate.

Orientation and Practical Information

A few kilometers north of the Po, Mantua is girded on three sides by the torpid waters of the Minro lagoons, producing a stubby, peninsular projection in which the better part of the historic center is concentrated. The unrestricted land at the far end has given way to modern expansion. The train station lies a 10-min. walk along via Solferino e S. Martino and via Fratelli Bandiera if you embark from Mantua's three central *piazze:* p. Mantegna, p. Concordia, and p. Marconi.

Tourist Office: p. Mantegna, 6 (tel. 35 06 81), adjacent to the church of Sant'Andrea. From the train station take via Solferino through p. S. Francesco to via Fratelli Bandieri and turn right on via Verdi. Efficient and amiable staff. Ask for *Mantova e la Festa Padana,* a yearly calendar of events throughout the province, and inquire about the *agriturismo* program. Open Mon.-Sat. 9am-noon and 3-6pm.

Currency Exchange: Banks are a dime a dozen. **Banca Nazionale del Lavoro,** p. Cavallotti, 3, where corso Vittorio Emanuele II becomes corso Umberto, has dependable rates and cash advances on Visa. Open Mon.-Wed. and Fri. 8:20am-1:20pm and 3-4:30pm, Thurs. 8:20am-5:50pm.

Post Office: p. Martiri Belfiore, 15 (tel. 32 64 03), up via Roma from the tourist office. Open Mon.-Fri. 8am-7pm, Sat. 8:20am-1:20pm. **Postal Code:** 46100.

Telephones: SIP, via Corridoni, 17 (tel. 32 77 11), leaving from p. Martiri Belfiore. Open Mon.-Fri. 8:30am-noon and 2-4:30pm. **Telephone Code:** 0376.

Trains: p. Don Leoni (tel. 32 16 46), at the end of via Solferino e S. Martino, southwest of town. To: Cremona (every hr., 45min.., L5000); Verona (every hr., 40min., L3200); and Milan (6 per day, 2hr. 30min., L12,100). **Luggage Storage** L1500, open 6:10am-9:15pm.

Buses: APAM p. Mondadori (tel. 32 72 37), across and to the right as you leave the train station. Cross corso Vittorio Emanuele II to via Caduti. Buses to Brescia (15 per day, 4hr., L5700). Tickets sold Mon.-Sat. 7am-1:15pm and 3-7:15pm.

Bike Rental: Ferrari Umberto, via Conciliazone, 6 (tel. 92 30 92), off corso Vittorio Emanuele II near the bus station. L2500 per hr., L12,000 per day. Open Tues.-Sat. 8:30-11:15am and 3-7pm, Mon. 3-7pm.

Emergencies: tel. 113. **Police:** p. Sordello, 46 (tel. 32 63 41). **Hospital: Ospedale Civile,** viale Alberoni, 1-3 (tel. 33 71).

Accommodations and Food

Apart from the beautiful youth hostel, bargains are few.

Ostello Sparafucile (HI) (tel. 37 24 65), in the nearby hamlet of Lunetta di San Giorgio. From the train station, exit to your right and walk left down corso Vittorio Emanuele to p. Cavallotti (5min.), then take bus #2 or 9 from in front of the UPIM, or walk through p. Sordello along via S. Giorgio and bridge-like via Legnano to the stone tower at the far end (1km). This lovingly restored 16th-century tollbooth is, as its name implies, the supposed hangout of the thug in Verdi's *Rigoletto.* Lockout 9am-6pm. Curfew 11pm. HI card required. L14,000 per person. Open April-Oct.15.

Locanda La Rinascita, via Concezione, 4 (tel. 32 06 07), near p. Virgiliana. From the train station, walk left on viale Pitentino (15min.), then right on via Zappetto, which intersects with via Concezione. Breezy, reasonably clean rooms and cordial proprietor. Gossip can be passed easily from balcony to balcony. Singles L22,000. Doubles L33,000. Reserve 4 or 5 days in advance.

Albergo Roma Vecchia, via Corridoni, 20 (tel. 32 21 00), down from p. Belfiore. Another entrance around the corner at via Buozzi, 1. Large, clean rooms with good mattresses. Management will give you a key should you desire to prowl the streets nocturnally. Doubles L42,000, with bath L50,000. Triples L51,000, with bath 65,000. Towels L2000. Open Aug. 23-Dec. 19 and Jan. 4-July 31.

Camping: Sparafucile tel. 37 24 65, next to the youth hostel. In a comfortable setting. L4000 per person, L3500 per tent. Cold showers included. Hot showers L1000. Light L2500. Breakfast served in the adjoining hostel at 7:30am.

Self-Service Virgiliana, p. Virgiliana, 57 (tel. 32 23 77). From p. Sordello, take via Fratelli Cairoli to p. Virgiliana and seek out the left corner of the *piazza*. A clean *mensa* with excellent values. Tasty full meals under L11,000. Open Mon.-Fri. noon-2pm.

Ai Ranari, via Trieste, 11 (tel. 32 84 31), the continuation of via Pomponazzo, near Porto Catena. A slightly more chic place specializing in regional dishes. *Primi* L7000-8000, *secondi* L9000-14,000. Don't leave without trying the Mantuan delight of *tortelli di zucca* (L7500). Wine L8000 per . Cover L1500. Open Thurs.-Tues. noon-3:30pm and 7-11pm.

Sights and Entertainment

Cobblestoned **piazza Sordello** forms the center of a vast complex built by the Gonzaga. The **Palazzo Ducale** (tel. 32 02 83) dominates the *piazza*. One of the most sumptuous palaces in Europe, it stands as a monument to Gonzagan "modesty." The 500 rooms and 15 courtyards, constructed over a period of 300 years (14th-17th centuries), now house an impressive collection of antique and Renaissance art. The **Magna Domus** and the **Captain's Palace,** two 14th-century Gothic structures, constitute the main part of the palace. Near the entrance is the Hall of Dukes where you'll find Antonio Pisanelli's frescoes (1439-44), discovered in 1969 under thick layers of plaster. Pass through the early 17th-century apartment of Guastalla and the New Gallery to the Tapestry Rooms. Here hang duplicates of 16th-century tapestries made from the Raphael cartoons in the Vatican. The Gonzaga's Summer Room looks out onto a hanging garden (1579) bordered on three sides by a splendid portico. The Hall of Mirrors displays paintings of mythological and allegorical scenes. Some have unusual optical effects—the arms of the figure in the fifth lunette from the left appear to follow you from one side of the room to the other. From the Paradise Chambers you enter the Dwarves' Apartments, tiny low rooms built as much to amuse the court as to house its substantial dwarf contingent.

Just as the tapestries and 16th-century murals begin to cloy, the tour enters the **Castello di San Giorgio** (1390-1406), the most formidable structure in the palace complex. Formerly a fortress, the imposing *castello* was converted into a wing of the palace when the Gonzaga no longer required its military capacity. Andrea Mantegna's famed frescoes of the Gonzaga family (1474) in the **Camera degli Sposi** (Marriage Chamber) spin about the walls. (Open Tues.-Sat. 9am-1pm and 2:30-4pm, Sun.-Mon. 9am-1pm. Admission L10,000.)

Despite its 18th-century facade, the **duomo** was conceived centuries earlier: witness the Romanesque campanile and the Gothic elements on its side. Its interior by Giulio Romano (1545) hails from the late Renaissance, but the baptistry in the lower chamber of the campanile was frescoed in the 13th century. (Open daily 8:30am-12:30pm and 3:30-7:30pm.)

Piazza delle Erbe, just south of p. Sordello, opens onto the **Rotonda di San Lorenzo.** The circular, 11th-century Romanesque rotunda (rebuilt early this century) is also known as the Matildica for the powerful noblewoman who, expiring heirless, left the rotunda to the pope. Observe another specimen of warped Italian fountain humor in the gushing grotesque that adorns the lower right end of the *palazzo's* facade.

Opposite the rotunda rises Mantua's most important Renaissance creation, Leon Battista Alberti's **Church of Sant'Andrea** (1471-1594). The unique facade, combining the classical triumphal arch motif—barrel-vaulted portal and flanking pilasters—with that of an antique pedimented temple front, evidences the beginning stages of early Renaissance three-dimensionality. The gargantuan interior was the first monumental space constructed in classical style since imperial Rome. It was also one of the first Renaissance churches with matching interior and facade. The plan—a vaulted church with a single aisle, flanking side chapels, and a domed crossing—served as a prototype for ecclesiastical architecture for the next 200 years. The first chapel to the left houses the tomb of painter Andrea Mantegna.

The **Palazzo d'Arco** (tel. 32 22 42), off viale Ritentino, elevates astrology to high culture. The star of the *palazzo* is the zodiac chamber, an extravaganza of ambers and ochres by Fontanello. From p. Mantegna, follow via Verdi to the *palazzo*. (Open Tues.-Wed. and Fri. 9am-noon, Thurs. and Sat.-Sun. 9am-noon and 3-5pm; Nov.-Feb. Sat.-Sun. 9am-noon and 2:30-4pm, Thurs. 9am-noon. Admission L4000.)

Mantua's greatest musical moment occured in 1770, when the beautiful **Teatro Accademico Biliena** (tel. 32 76 53) debuted with a cameo performance by 14-year-old Mozart. (Open 9am-12:30pm and 3-5:30pm. Admission L1000.)

Contrast to the luxurious palaces and academies can be found at the spartan, boxlike house of the artist **Mantegna** on via Acerbi, 47 (tel. 36 05 06). Built in 1476, it stands open for visits and frequently hosts traveling exhibits. (Open 9am-12:30pm and 3-6pm. Free.) Opposite the house stands Alberti's **Church of San Sebastiano** (1460), whose Greek cross layout initiated the Renaissance fad of centrally planned churches. (Closed for restoration in 1992.)

A trek through p. Veneto and down largo Parri leads to the opulent **Palazzo Te** (tel. 32 32 66 or 36 58 86), one of Italy's most famous 16th-century villas. It was built by Giulio Romano as a suburban retreat for Francesco II Gonzaga. The rooms inside demonstrate the Renaissance fascination with all things Roman, as well as the desire to play with the original forms. Idyllic murals of Psyche, remarkable for their vividness and eroticism, fresco Francesco's banquet hall. Another wing of the palace features regular shows of modern Italian artists alongside a collection of Egyptian art. Reservations are a must if you are traveling with a group and want to see the Egyptian collection. (Open Tues.-Sun. 10am-6pm. Admission L8000, under 18 L4000. Prices double when touring exhibits come to Te.)

The **Teatro Sociale di Mantova,** p. Cavallotti (tel. 32 38 60), off corso Vittorio Emanuele, stages operas in October and plays November through May. (Cheap seats around L20,000.) Some of the best productions in the country stop here, albeit only for a couple of nights. The **Spazio Aperto** series brings dance, music, and cinema events to various *piazze* and *palazzi* around town. Check for the **Festa Internazionale di Chitarra Classica** in August. Mantua also hosts a chamber music series in April and May which attracts local and foreign artists. Most fun is the **Concorso di Madonnari** on August 15; the *madonnari,* street artists whose chalky madonnas wash away with the first rains, hold a competition in nearby Grazie di Curtatone.

Near Mantua

Make the trip to **Sabbioneta,** 33km southwest of Mantua, founded by Vespasiano Gonzaga (1532-91) as the home for his feudal court. Its importance as an artistic center in the late Renaissance earned it the title "Little Athens of the Gonzagas." Inside the well-preserved 16th-century city walls lie the **Ducal Palace,** the **Olympic Theater,** and the **Palazzo del Giardino,** all fascinating Renaissance structures. The best way to see the town is to take the guided walk, which enables you to visit the otherwise inaccessible interiors of buildings. There is also an elegant 16th-century church, Santa Maria Assunta. The 45-min. tour in Italian (L6000) leaves roughly every 20min. from the **tourist office,** via Gonzaga, 31 (tel. (0375) 520 39; open Tues.-Sat. 9:30am-12:30pm and 2:30-6pm, Sun. 2:30-6pm). Seven buses per day go to Viadanna via Sabbioneta. In summer Sabbioneta stages a **Festival di Musica e Danza,** and from mid-March to mid-April antique aficionados come for the exhaustive **mercato del Antiquariato.**

A unique way to discover the rich cultural heritage and natural beauty of the Mantuan province is to participate in the tourist office's well-established **Agriturismo** program. Starting at about L15,000 per night, you can stay at one of 10 gorgeous old villas in the countryside, in proximity to the region's less renowned artistic treasures, and participate in the daily workings of a farm. For information and reservations, contact the tourist office in Mantua.

Bergamo

Bergamo, like the *Commedia dell'Arte* it invented, is endowed with a multitude of personalities. A bustling commercial and industrial center, an artistic hot-spot, and a focal point of both history and legend, the city is divided physically and spiritually into two parts. The hilltop *città alta* recalls its medieval origins with narrow, cobbled streets shaded by solemn ecclesiastic facades, while the rapid-paced *città bassa* below is a temporal world apart. Whether the totality strikes you as a harmonious synthesis of complementary traits or a municipal Jeckyll-and-Hyde, the juxtaposition of Venetian fortress and trade metropolis cannot fail to intrigue.

Orientation and Practical Information

Poised at the juncture of the Brembana and Seriana valleys, Bergamo is an easy train ride from Milan, Brescia, and Cremona. The train station, bus station, and budget hotels are all in the *città bassa.* To get to the more interesting *città alta,* take bus #1 or 3 (L900) to the funicular, which ascends from viale Vittorio Emanuele II to the Mercato delle Scarpe (every 15min., L900), or walk up the old footpath to the city, starting from behind the funicular station on viale Vittorio Emanuele II (10-20 min).

Tourist Office: APT (*città bassa*), viale Papa Giovanni XXIII, 106 (tel. 24 22 26), straight ahead through p. Marconi from the train station, on the left hand side. Open Mon.-Fri. 9am-12:30pm and 3-6pm. On weekends head to *città alta:* **APT,** vicolo Aquila Nera, 2 (tel. 23 27 30), off p. Vecchia. Open daily 9am-12:30pm and 3-6:30pm. Both offices stock the same materials. Ask for maps of both cities and the polylingual *Bergamo Itinerari di Città e Provincia.*

Currency Exchange: Banca Nazionale del Lavoro, via Petrarca, 12 (tel. 39 81 11), off viale Vittorio Emanuele II near p. della Libertà. Good rates and Visa deals. Open Mon.-Tues. and Thurs.-Fri. 8:20am-1:20pm and 3-4:30pm, Wed. 8:20am-5:50pm. After-hrs. money exchange at **Hotel Excelsior San Marco,** p. della Repubblica, 6 (tel. 23 21 32), off viale Vittorio Emanuele II. Cash only.

Post Office: via Masone, 2A (tel. 21 22 70), at via Locatelli. Take via Lelasco from viale Vittorio Emanuele II. Stamps and Fermo Posta at #7. Open Mon.-Fri. 8:15am-8pm, Sat. 8:30am-1pm. **Postal Code:** 24122.

Telephones: SIP, largo Porta Nuova, 1 (tel. 21 92 95), where viale Papa Giovanni XXIII becomes viale Vittorio Emanuele II. Open Mon.-Sat. 9am-12:30pm and 2:30-7pm., Sun. 9am-1pm. After hours, go to **Hotel Cappelle d'Oro,** v. Papa Giovanni XXIII, 12 (tel. 21 83 65). In *città alta,* try **Caffè Tasso,** p. Vecchia, 3 (tel. 23 79 66).

Trains: p. Marconi (tel. 24 76 24). To: Milan (every hr., 1hr., L4500); Brescia (15 per day, 1hr., L4500); Cremona (6 per day, 1hr. 30min., L6500). Information open daily 7am-8:30pm. **Luggage Storage:** L1500. Open 6am-10pm.

Buses: across from the train station (tel. 24 81 50). To: Milan (every 30min. 5:40am-10:30pm, L6000); Cremona (every 30min. 5:05am-7:30pm, L7300); Como (9 per day 6:55am-6:20pm, L6700); Brescia (8 per day 6:50am-6:45pm, L5600).

Emergencies: tel. 113. **Police:** via Monte Bianco, 1 (tel. 27 61 11). **Medical Emergency:** tel. 25 02 46. **Hospital: Ospedale Riuniti,** largo Barozzi, 1 (tel. 26 91 11).

Accommodations

The higher the altitude, the higher the price; alas, *città alta's* fortress walls conceal no budget gold mines. Ask the tourist office about Agritourism and other rural alternatives.

Ostello Città di Bergamo (HI), via G. Ferraris, 1 (tel. 34 23 49). Take bus #14 from Porta Nuova to località Monterosso. The uphill hike is rewarded with an unparalleled view of an unattractive apartment complex, and the ambience and suburban isolation may send your spirits on a downspin. On the positive side, a well-stocked supermarket serves the community at the base of the hill. Open 7-9am and 6pm-midnight, but you can lounge around downstairs during the day. L12,000 per person, breakfast included. Meals L11,000. (Closed for renovation in 1992.)

Albergo S. Antonino, via Paleocapa, 1 (tel. 21 02 84), a left off viale Papa Giovanni XXIII past the tourist office. The dishearteningly grungy exterior disguises a store of clean, dependable rooms. ACLI *mensa* downstairs (see below). Curfew midnight. Singles L20,500, with bath L25,000. Doubles L32,000, with bath L37,000.

Locanda Caironi, via Torretta, 6 (tel. 24 30 83), off via Borgo Palazzo. About a 20-min. walk, or take bus #5, 7, or 8 out on via Angelo Maj. A family-run affair in a quiet, residential neighborhood. The *trattoria* downstairs is considered one of Bergamo's best-kept culinary secrets. Singles L18,000. Doubles L30,000.

Food

Casonsei, a meat-filled ravioli dish, is a Bergamasco culinary delight, as are the *branzi* and *taleggio* cheeses. *Valcalepio* red and white wines have distinguished local viniculture. Streets in *città alta* are lined with *pasticcerias* selling yellow *polentina* confections topped with chocolate blobs intended to resemble dead birds. Be forewarned about this sweet (and pricey) take-off on Bergamo's most ancient culinary tradition: many natives have never tasted these for-tourists-only treats. The real *polenta,* served with bird meat (especially during the fall hunting season), originated when the area's first inhabitants used the birds they caught to make their corn-based *polenta* meals more substantial. For necessities, shop at **Roll Market,** on the right-hand side of viale Vittorio Emanuele II just before the hill to *città alta* (open Tues.-Sat. 8:30am-1pm and 3:30-8pm, Mon. 8:30am-1pm).

Città Bassa

Mensa ACLI, via Paleocapa, 1, in the basement of the Albergo S. Antonino. 2 dishes, *contorno,* and bread for L10,500. Wine L800. Open Mon.-Fri. 11am-2:15pm and 7-8:15pm.

Trattoria Casa Mia, via S. Bernardino, 20 (tel. 22 06 76), off via Zambonate. Follow via Tiraboschi from Porta Nuova. An inviting, unpretentious place serving complete meals (including wine, water, coffee, bread, and service) for under L14,000. Open Sept.-July Mon.-Sat. 8am-3pm and 5:30-10:30pm.

Ristorante Self-Service Dany, via Taramelli, 23/B (tel. 22 07 55). From the station walk down viale Papa Giovanni XXIII, turn right on via San Francesco d'Assisi, then left. *Primi* from L2000, *secondi* from L3500. Open Mon.-Fri.

Città Alta

Though you may withstand the temptations of the first bakery you pass on via Colleoni or via Gombito, be prepared to undergo the same trial at 20m intervals. The makings of a moderately balanced meal, however, lurk among the sweets. Ham-filled pastries and gourmet pizza by the slice provide flavorful alternatives to the standard *panino.*

Forno Tresoldi, via Colleoni, 13 (tel. 24 39 60). Costs a little more than three coins, but the spinach pizza is otherworldly (about L2500 per slice). Open Tues.-Sun. 9am-1pm and 3-7:30pm.

Trattoria Barnabò, via Colleoni, 31 (tel. 23 76 92), past p. Vecchia. One of the finest restaurants in Bergamo, with *menù* under L15,000. They sculpt a vast menagerie of *polenta* breads—enhanced with cheese, mushrooms, and sausage—in various zoological forms. Open Sept.-June Fri.-Wed. noon-2:30pm and 7pm-midnight.

Trattoria 3 Torri, p. Mercato del Fieno, 7/A (tel. 24 43 66), a left off via Gombito when heading away from p. Vecchia. This enticing little corner establishment entertains with elegance, and is always full. Try the *real* polenta (L12,000). *Menù* around L30,000, but *primi* begin at L8000. Cover L2000. Open Thurs.-Tues. noon-2:30pm and 7-10pm. Reservations strongly recommended.

Sights

Città Bassa

Begin a tour of the city at **p. Matteoti,** the heart of Bergamo Bassa and a favorite meeting place for the evening *passeggiata.* In the **Church of San Bartolomeo,** at the far right of the *piazza,* rests a superb altarpiece of the *Madonna and Child* by Lorenzo Lotto. Via Tasso on the right of San Bartolomeo leads to the **Church of Santo Spirito;** note the strange infernal-looking sculpture on the facade. Its fine Renaissance interior (1521) houses paintings by Lotto, Previtali, and Bergognone. **Via Pignolo** connects the lower city with the upper and winds past a succession of handsome palaces (16th to 18th centuries). Along the way is the tiny **Church of San Bernardino,** whose polychromatic interior is the humble backdrop to a splendid altarpiece by Lotto. A right on via San Tommaso brings you to the astounding **Galleria dell'Accademia Carrara,** one of the most important art galleries in Italy. Housed in a glorious neoclassical palace, the 15 rooms of the second floor boast an impressive array of paintings with particular emphasis on the Lombard and Venetian schools. Virtually all the Italian notables are represented, and their works are joined by the canvasses of such international luminaries as Brueghel, Van Dyck, and El Greco. (Open Wed.-Mon. 9:30am-12:30pm and 2:30-5:30pm. Admission L3000, students free.)

Città Alta

From the Carrara gallery, a terraced walkway (via Nora) ascends from the lower city to **Porta Sant'Agostino,** a 16th-century gate built by the Venetians as part of their fortifications for the city. Via Porta Dipinta leads to the heart of Bergamo Alta, first passing the Romanesque **Church of San Michele** (12th-13th centuries), decorated inside with colorful frescoes, and then the neoclassical **Church of Sant'Andrea,** which contains a fine altarpiece by Moretto. The street continues as narrow and steep via Gombito, lacing by a massive 12th-century tower of the same name. The *città alta* can also be reached along the white marble **Porta San Giacomo,** which overlooks the *città bassa's* main thoroughfare. This route leads to via Gambito by way of via S. Giacomo, whose left-hand wall is adorned with several monstrous but easily overlooked leering grotesques.

Via Gambito ends in **piazza Vecchia,** a majestic ensemble of medieval and Renaissance buildings flanked by restaurants and *caffè.* On the right is the white marble **Biblioteca Civica** (1594), the repository of Bergamo's rich collection of manuscripts, modeled after Venice's Sansovino Library. Across the *piazza* is the **Palazzo della Ragione** (the Palace of Reason, 1199), massive and angular with a robust arcade. Note the stately Gothic window and the recently added lion of St. Mark that testify to the Venetian domination of the city. To the right, and connected to the *palazzo* by a 16th-century covered stairway, stands the 12th-century **Torre Civica** (Civic Tower). Its 15th-century clock sounds the curfew at 10pm.

A passage between the two buildings leads to **piazza del Duomo.** Ahead is the multicolor marble facade of the masterful **Colleoni Chapel** (1476). It was designed by G. A. Amadeo (also responsible for the Charterhouse of Pavia) as a tomb and chapel for Bartolomeo Colleoni, a celebrated Venetian mercenary. (Open daily 9am-12:30pm and 2-6pm.)

To the right of the chapel is the octagonal **baptistry** graced by a red marble gallery. It is actually a reconstruction of a 14th-century baptistry that at one time stood in the **Basilica of Santa Maria Maggiore.** This basilica, which adjoins the Colleoni Chapel to the left, was constructed in the second half of the 12th century. The understated Romanesque exterior contrasts sharply with the flourishing Baroque interior. Donations and additions by various artisans and trade guilds adorn the basilica—note the measuring instruments lodged in the wall outside. Grocery-laden townspeople often take a shortcut through its cool interior. Other points of interest include Flemish and Tuscan tapestries, the magnificently preserved 1347 fresco on the left wall, and the Victorian tomb of the composer Gaetano Donizetti (1797-1848). (Open Mon.-Sat. 8:30am-noon and 3-7pm. Sun 9am-12:45pm and 3-7pm.) For a romantic conclusion to the tour, return to p. Mercato delle Scarpe and proceed left on via alla Rocca. Sitting on a site occupied by fortifications since Roman times, the present Rocca is home to the **Risorgimento Museum,** and the surrounding grounds have been dubbed the **Park of Remembrance** in honor of those soldiers who died for the Italian cause. If you can escape Bergamo's self-absorbed, twentysomething couples, the hilltop greenery is a pleasant place to recuperate before the final descent.

If you find yourself in Bergamo during concert season, you might be drawn into more sedentary pursuits. The **drama season,** featuring Italy's most prestigious companies, occupies center stage at the Donizetti Theater from November to April at which point the spotlight shifts to the two-month-long, universally acclaimed **International**

Piano Festival, co-hosted by Brescia. In September, Bergamo unabashedly celebrates its premier native-born composer with a festival of Donizetti's lesser-known works. This operatic interlude serves as a mellifluous transition into the traditional opera season in October and November. For further information, contact the tourist office or the theater itself at p. Cavour, 14 (tel. 24 96 31).

Brescia

Situated between Milan and Verona, Como and Garda, Brescia has long been overlooked by tourists bound for bigger things. The comparatively slow pace of tourism may be a by-product of the city's multifaceted character, which defies succinct promotional slogans. Roman ruins and fascist *piazze* co-exist within the thoroughly urbanized center, and, lest a single style of cathedral be thought undiplomatic, Brescia has not one *duomo* but two. Relative prosperity has been the one constant over the years. Brescia thrived under Lombard dominion in the 11th and 12th centuries, and again prospered under the covetous supervision of the Venetian Republic (1426-1797). Today the city owes its place in the prosperous Lombardian economy to weapons production, ensuring that Brescia has the frenetic pace of a modern industrial center.

Orientation and Practical Information

Brescia is approximately midway between Milan (1hr.) and Verona (45min.) on the direct train line to Venice, and is the main point of departure for buses to the western shores of Lake Garda. Most of the city's architectural gems are concentrated in the *piazza*-packed *centro storico,* linked to p. della Repubblica by corso Martiri della Libertà and via Porcellaga. Continuing through the center and out the other end, you will come to two aptly named streets, via del Castello and via del Musei. The first leads uphill to the castle; the latter slopes down to museum row and the Roman archaeological site.

Tourist Office: corso Zanardelli, 34 (tel. 434 18), the arcaded continuation of corso Palestro which branches to the right off corso della Libertà/via Porcellaga en route to the center. Set off slightly from the street. Helpful map. Open Mon.-Fri. 9am-noon and 3-6:30pm, Sat. 9am-12:30pm.

Post Office: p. Vittoria, 1. Stamps and Fermo Posta at #6. Open Mon.-Fri. 8:15am-5:30pm, Sat. 8:15am-1pm. **Postal Code:** 25100.

Telephones: SIP, via Moretto, 46 (tel. 512 74). Open Mon.-Sat. 9am-12:30pm and 2:30-7:30pm, Sun. 9am-1pm. **Telephone Code:** 030.

Trains: at the opposite end of viale Stazione from p. della Repubblica. To: Milan (every 45min., 1hr., L6500); Verona (every hr., 45min., L5000); Venice (every hr., 2hr. 15min., L13,800); Bergamo (15 per day, 1hr., L3900); Padova (every hr., 1hr. 45min., L10,500); Vicenza (every hr., 1hr. 15min., L8800); Cremona (8 per day, 50min., L4300). Information open 8am-noon and 1-8pm. **Luggage Storage:** L1500. Open 24 hrs.

Buses: by the train station (tel. 582 37 or 440 61). East-bound buses are to your right and under the bridge from the train station. To: Verona (6:45am-7:50pm, 2hr., L5500); Mantua (6am-7:15pm, 1hr., L5700); Cremona (6:30am-7:50pm, 1hr., L5000). West-bound buses leave from the SIA station, just to the left of the train station. Ticket office open Mon.-Sat. 6am-8pm, Sun. 7-11am and 3-6pm. Daily to Milan (5:50am-9:20pm, 1hr. 45min., L9500).

Emergencies: tel. 113. **Police:** (tel. 425 61), on via Boticelli. **Medical Assistance:** tel. 399 55 45. **Hospital: Ospedale Civile,** tel. 399 51.

Accommodations

Accommodations are reasonably priced in Brescia, but often fill with businesspeople during the week; weekends are better. Call a week in advance for reservations. You'll be fortunate to find any sort of bargain in the historic center—the dorms and hotels on the periphery are your best bet.

Servizio della Giovane (ACISJF), via Fratelli Bronzetti, 17 (tel. 553 87). From the station, take viale Stazione to p. della Repubblica, and pick up via dei Mille on the far side. Via Filli Bronzetti is on the right after a couple of blocks. Women only. Run by friendly nuns. Spotless bathrooms off triples that are so newly furnished they look like promotional photos. Kitchen facilities another perk. Curfew 10pm. L10,000 per person.

Albergo Rigamonti, via Mansione, 8 (tel. 403 32). Modern, tidy, and respectable. TV room, bar, and car park. Singles L30,000, with bath L43,000. Doubles L45,000, with bath L55,000.

Albergo San Marco, via Spalto S. Marco, 15 (tel. 455 41). From the station take via Foppa, turn right on via XX Settembre, make the next left, and turn right onto via Emanuele, which becomes via Spalto S. Marco. Rooms are clean, the clientele young and fun. Often occupied by workers during the week—call ahead. Singles L23,000. Doubles L40,000. Closed in Aug.

Albergo Vellia, via Calzavellia, 5 (tel. 29 04 25), 1 street over from via Pace between via Dante and corso Mameli. Spacious rooms. Downstairs bathroom has a tub. Singles L30,000. Doubles L42,000, with bath L50,000.

Food

Open-air vendors do their thing in p. Mercato and p. Rovetta (Tues.-Fri. 8am-noon and roughly 3-6pm). The **Oviesse** clothing store off p. Rovetta at corso Mameli, 23, conceals a grocery store in its basement (open Tues.-Sat. 9am-12:25pm and 3-7:20pm, Mon. 3-7:20pm). Whatever and wherever you choose to eat, or even if you're not eating at all, be sure to submerge yourself in one of the local wines. *Tocai di San Martino della Battaglia,* a dry white wine, *groppello,* a medium red, and *botticino,* a dry red of medium age, are all favorites in Brescia and beyond.

Ristorante Rosticceria Mameli, corso Mameli, 53 (tel. 595 02), near p. Loggia. An enticing array of prepared foods sold downstairs for take-out, and upstairs in the restaurant. Salads L1500-5000 per *etto. Primi* around L7000, *secondi* L11,000. Open Tues.-Sun. 8am-midnight.

Trattoria Al Frate, via Musei, 25 (tel. 514 69), by the base of the ascent to the castle. Plentiful food; the ever-present imbibers who rise only for a refill are living testimonials to the fine wines. *Primi* L8500, *secondi* L11,000-17,500. Cover L3500. Wine begins at L9600 per liter. Open Tues.-Sun. 10:30am-3pm and 5pm-2am.

Sights and Entertainment

Down from **piazza della Vittoria,** the first sight encountered in the center of town, is the **piazza della Loggia,** built when Venice ruled the city. On one side of this square stands the **Torre dell'Orologio,** modeled after the clock tower in Venice's p. San Marco, with an astronomic clock and two stone fellers that strike the hours. Across from the tower, the Renaissance **loggia,** the work of a gaggle of architects including Sansovino and Palladio, boasts intriguing carvings. An elaborate door underneath the portico leads to a monumental staircase and a room adorned with paintings from the 16th century.

The **piazza del Duomo,** across via X Giornate, is dominated by its heavily manneristic **duomo nuovo** (1604-1825). The green cupola is the third highest in Italy. Next door is the old *duomo,* or **Rotonda,** a refreshingly simple Romanesque building with endearing patchwork and uneven windows scattered over its two-story circular plan. Within is a *stauroteca,* a reliquary allegedly containing fragments of the True Cross. (Open Wed.-Mon. 9am-noon and 3-7pm. Contribution desired, but not required.) Behind the cathedrals, at via Mazzini, 1, is the **Queriniana Library,** with 300,000 volumes and medieval manuscripts. The **Broletto Palace,** next to the *duomo nuovo,* is a typical Lombard medieval town hall crowned by an 11th-century tower.

Down via dei Musei from the center is Emperor Vespasian's vast **Tempio Capitolino,** part of the yield of ongoing archaeological efforts to unearth monuments from Brescia's classical incarnation as the Roman colony of Brixia. Upstairs is a small museum with assorted mosaics, a medieval road map, and excellent bronzes, the best of which is a life-sized **Winged Victory,** a copy of the Praxiteles original. (Museum and temple open Tues.-Sun. 10am-12:45pm and 2-6pm. Admission L2000.)

A few paces farther down via dei Musei you'll find the 16th-century **Church of Santa Guilia,** now the home of a **museum of Christian art.** Its greatest treasure is the 8th-century cross of Desiderius, encased in silver and encrusted with hundreds of jewels and cameos; note especially the inset 3rd-century portraits. Also look for the biblical carvings on a 4th-century ivory chest. (Open daily 10am-8:30pm. Admission L5000. Closed for restoration in 1992.)

From the Tempio Capitolino walk through p. Foro to via Gallo, which becomes via Crispi and leads to Brescia's principal attraction, the **Pinacoteca Tosio-Martinengo.** The solemn 22-room *palazzo* displays a good collection of works by Brescian masters (notably Moretto), but better still is the serene, effeminate *Cristo benedicente* by Raphael. There are also first-rate works by Veneziano, Tintoretto, Clouet, Vicenzo Foppa, and Lorenzo Lotto. (Open Tues.-Sun. 9am-12:30pm and 2-5pm. Admission L4000.)

Fender-benders should check out the **Museo della Chitarra** (Guitar Museum), via Trieste, 34. (Open Mon.-Tues. and Thurs.-Fri. 2:30-7:30pm. Free.) If you have more time, visit the **castello** hovering on the high ground behind via dei Musei. This array of architectural styles houses a sad little zoo, an observatory, the Risorgimento Museum (with mementos from 17th- and 18th-century Brescia), and the Luigi Marzoli Museum of Arms (Italy's most extensive collection with hundreds of armaments from every era). On the grounds, whose praises Catullus once sang, is the **San Pietro in Oliveto Church** (reconstructed in 1510), surrounded by gnarled olive trees. Down via Piamarta is an intact Roman gate.

The bulk of Brescia's high-brow cultural events take place amidst the golden, Baroque splendor of the Teatro Grande. December to April marks the annual **Stagione di Prosa,** a long-running series of dramatic performances. From April to June, the focus shifts to keyboards with the onset of the **Festive Pianistico Internazionale,** now in its 29th year, and co-hosted by nearby Bergamo. October ushers in a two-month opera season, occasionally rounded out with ballet. (Contact the tourist office for specific ticket information.) **Estate Aperta** includes an impressive series of concerts, theatrical performances, and films, held June through September in churches, courtyards, and *piazze*. Pick up a schedule at the tourist office, or call the coordinating forces at the Centro Teatrale Bresciano (tel. 377 11 11). Tickets for theater and dance average L10,000, cinema L7000, and concerts a surprisingly affordable L5000.

Piedmont (Piemonte)

The source of the mighty Po River, fertile Piedmont basks in the bounty that has put it on the gastronomic map as a capital of fine food and wine. From the 11th century the region's robust resources served the French House of Savoy, whose fortunes became increasingly intertwined with those of Italy. In the early 19th century, after Napoleonic occupation, Piedmont became the crucible for the unification movement. It was the Savoy king Vittorio Emanuele II and his minister Camillo Cavour who ushered in the *Risorgimento,* enlisting France's help to drive the Austrians out of Italy in 1859. From 1861-1865 Turin was the capital of the newly formed Kingdom of Italy. But first Florence and then Rome usurped this title. The suddenly idle Piedmontese aristocracy quickly turned its hand to industry; today, only Lombardy exceeds the region in wealth and productivity. Piedmont also continues to bubble with political ferment: Both the Red Brigades and latter-day monarchists have based their operations here.

The area falls into three zones. The Alpine, with the two stellar peaks of Monviso and Gran Paradiso, contains a string of ski resorts and a huge national park that spills across the regional border into Valle D'Aosta. The Pianura, the beginning of the fecund Po valley, encompasses industrial Turin, the wine-soaked Asti region, and Italy's only rice paddies. And the hills north and south of the Po shelter many of the region's isolated castles.

Turin (Torino)

Behind Turin's peaceful facade lies the work of crafty, hard-working urban planners. Just beyond the train station, cars circle neatly around the putting-green grass of p. Carlo Felice, where only the occasional jogger disturbs well-rooted cosmopolitans perusing their morning *La Stampa*. P. Castello, the city center, pulses with university students and Armani-clad businessmen. The Turin you're likely to encounter is cultured and courteous, but it can't be mere coincidence that the train station sends you out facing north. Employees of the Fiat auto company, an institution synonymous with Turin, live and work in the south end in the giant modern slum of Mirafiori, the birthplace of the Red Brigades. These radical crimson troopers of the 1970s drew on the same legacy of revolutionary ideology that established Turin as the fountainhead of Italian political unification in the 18th and 19th centuries. The presence of this turbulent Turin, the side that makes the city a capital of Italian extremism, is something you may not suspect, as you admire the Baroque downtown.

Orientation and Practical Information

Turin lies on a broad plain on the north bank of the Po River, flanked by the Alps on three sides. **Stazione Porta Nuova,** in the heart of the city, is the best place to disembark. The city itself is an Italian rarity in that its streets meet at right angles; it's a cinch to get around either by bus or on foot. The three main streets are **corso Vittorio Emanuele II,** running past the station to the river; the elegant **via Roma,** housing the principal sights and running north through p. San Carlo and p. Castello; and **via Garibaldi,** stretching from **piazza Castello** to **piazza Statuto** and the **Stazione Porta Susa.**

Tourist Office: APT, via Roma, 226 (tel. 53 59 01), under the left arcade on p. CLN, the small divided *piazza* just before p. San Carlo. Extensive literature on Turin and its province. Open Mon.-Sat. 9am-7:30pm. Smaller office at the **Porta Nuova** train station (tel. 53 13 27; open Mon.-Sat. 9am-7pm.) Both offices will help you find a room. **Informa Giovani** ("Youth Information"), via Assarotti, 2 (tel. 57 65 49 76), off via Garibaldi between p. Castello and Porta Susa. From feminist groups to flea markets to fortune tellers, they'll give you the word. Youth hostel membership (L25,000 plus photo), as well as information on renting bikes, getting a job, or finding an apartment in Turin. Open Mon. and Wed.-Sat. 10:30am-6:30pm.

Budget Travel: Centro Turistico Studentesco, via Camerana, 3 (tel. 53 43 88), 2 streets over to the left of the station as you exit, and 1 block off corso Vittorio Emanuele II. Travel information, discount train (BIJ) and air tickets for students under 26. ISIC cards. English spoken. Open 9:30am-12:30pm and 3-6:30pm, Sat. 9:30am-12:30pm.

Currency Exchange: The banks along via Roma and via Alfieri offer good rates, as does an automatic exchange machine by the tourist office at p. CLN, 226.

Post Office: via Alfieri, 10 (tel. 53 58 91 or 562 81 00), off p. San Carlo. Telex, fax and telegram service. Open Mon.-Fri. 8:15am-2:20pm, Sat. 8:15am-1pm. Fermo Posta open 9am-noon and 3-7pm. **Postal Code:** 10100.

Telephones: ASST, via Arsenale, 13, off via S. Teresa, around the corner from the post office. Open Mon.-Sat. 8am-7:45pm. Coin- and card-operated phones available 24 hrs. at the **SIP,** via Roma, 18, where you can purchase phone cards from a machine. **ASST** office in Porta Nuova, open daily 8am-7:45pm. **Telephone Code:** 011.

Flights: Caselle Airport, tel. 577 84 31 or 577 84 32. European destinations. Take a bus from the ATIV agency on corso Siccardi, 6, at via Cernaia (every 45min. 5:15am-11:15pm, L5000; ticket office open Mon.-Fri. 9am-1pm and 2-7pm, Sat. 9am-1pm, but you can also purchase tickets on the bus). From Caselle to Turin, buses leave approximately every 30min. 6:30am-11:30pm, 35min., L5000. Stops at p. XVIII Dicembre (near Porta Susa) and the station at corso Inghilterra, 3. From there, take city bus #9 or 15 (L1000) to Porta Nuova.

Trains: Porta Nuova, tel. 561 33 33. To: Milan (every 30min., 1hr. 45min., L12,100); Venice (11 per day with change at Milan, 4 per day direct, 4hr. 30min., L30,300); Genoa (every hr., 2hr., L12,100); Rome (9 per day, 9-11hr., L63,600); Paris (3 per day, change at Lyon, 7hr. 30min.-10 hrs., L80,000). **Luggage Storage:** in Porta Nuova, L1500. Open 24 hrs.

Buses: Autostazione Terminal Bus, corso Inghilterra, 3 (tel. 44 25 25). Timetable available from tourist office. Take bus #9 or 15 from Porta Nuova to the station. Buses serve ski resorts, the Riviera, and the western valleys of Susa and Pinerolo. To: Courmayeur (21 per day, 3hr., L13,200); Aosta (every hr., 2hr., L10,300); Milan (15 per day, 2hr., L17,500); Chamonix (3 per day, 3hr. 30min., L28,500).

Metropolitan Transit: City buses cost L1000. Tickets must be bought at *tabacchi* before boarding. The system is easy to navigate and a helpful map is available at most terminal offices.

Taxis: tel. 57 37, 57 30, 57 44, or 57 48. L4000 plus L1000 per km. L3000 surcharge at night and L1500 Sun. and holidays.

Bike Rental: on viale Matteoti in Parco Valentino, a 15-min. walk down corso Vittorio Emanuele as you exit Porta Nuova to the right. Open Tues.-Sun. 9:30am-12:30pm and 3-7pm. L2000 per hour, L7000 per day. You must leave an ID and a L5000 deposit.

Lost Property: Ufficio Oggetti Smarriti, via Chatillon, 19 (tel. 85 54 37), open 8:30am-12:30pm. Also at Porta Nuova (tel. 55 69 33 15), open 8am-noon and 3-7pm.

English Bookstore: The British Bookstore, Libreria Internazionale Luxembourg, via Accademia delle Scienze, 3 (tel. 561 38 96), across from Palazzo Carignano. A wide and worldly selection. Open Tues.-Sat. 9am-7:30pm.

Laundromat: Lavanderia Graziella, via S. Secondo, 30 (tel. 54 58 82). Wash and dry: 4 kg, L12,000, 6 kg, L15,000. Open Mon.-Fri. 8am-12:30pm and 3-7:30pm, Sat. 8:30am-12:30pm.

Public Baths: Albergo Diurno (tel. 54 49 72), just outside Porta Nuova, on the left side as you leave the tracks. Clean and elegant. Showers L7500. Towels included. Toilets L1500. Open Mon.-Sat. 7am-7pm, Sun. 7am-noon.

Swimming Pool: Piscina Comunale Stadio Civile, corso G. Ferraris, 294 (tel. 319 93 09). Take bus #41 from corso Vittorio Emanuele near the station. Open June-Sept. Tues.-Sun. noon-7pm, L5000, Sun. L7000. Changing room L3000.

Late-Night Pharmacy, corso Vittorio Emanuele II, 66 (tel. 53 82 71), open 24 hrs. Ring to summon the pharmacist after dark.

Emergencies: tel. 113. **Police:** corso Vinzaglia, 110 (tel. 558 81). **Medical Assistance:** tel. 57 47. **Hospital: Mauriziano Umberto,** largo Turati, 62 (tel. 508 01). **Red Cross:** tel. 51 77 51.

Accommodations and Camping

Hotels abound but prices can be steep, even for the most bare-bones of rooms. Accommodations are actually easier to find in summer than during the rest of the year, and more easily uncovered on weekends than during the week.

Ostello Torino (HI), via Alby, 1 (tel. 660 29 39), a small street off via Gatti. Take bus #52 from Stazione Porta Nuova. Get off at the third stop after crossing the Po River, and follow the road uphill immediately to your right through piazzale Luserna. Via Alba branches off viale Thovez at the top of the *piazzale;* the hostel is at the corner of via Gatti. Located in a hilly residential neighborhood speckled with art nouveau mansions. Contemporary, clean, and comfortable. Desk open 7-9am and 6-11:30pm, Oct.-March 7-9am and 6-10:30pm. Curfew 11:30pm, in winter 10:30pm. L16,000 per person. Breakfast and sheets included. HI card required, or pay L5000 extra, or purchase one (L30,000).

Pensione San Carlo, p. San Carlo, 197 (tel. 55 35 22), on the fourth floor. In the midst of the action, yet set back from the noisy *piazza.* Clean rooms and cheerful management. Singles L40,000, with bath L50,000. Doubles L50,000, with bath L70,000. Triples L70,000.

Locanda Studium, via Carlo Alberto, 47 (tel. 839 56 81), 3 blocks east of via Roma, *scala* (stairway) C, third floor. Pleasant management helps dispel funereal atmosphere of rooms. Doubles L36,000. One triple L45,000.

Pensione Alfieri, via Pomba, 7 (tel. 839 59 11), under the right archway where the *piazza* deadends. Caring owners, but a dearth of rooms. Often occupied by long-term residents. Singles L20,000. Doubles L35,000. Reserve ahead.

Hotel Bellavista, via Galliari, 15 (tel. 669 91 21), on a street slightly behind and to the right of Porta Nuova as you exit. Large, airy rooms and a sunny hallway. Singles L40,000. Doubles L60,000, with bath L80,000.

Hotel Magenta, corso Emanuele, 67 (tel. 54 26 49), left of the train station. Very chic. If it's not full you can probably talk the manager's price down. All rooms have TV. Singles L54,000, with bath L87,000. Doubles L64,000, with bath L104,000.

Camping: Campeggio Villa Rey, strada superiore Val S. Martino, 27 (tel. 819 01 17). L4000 per person, L3500 per tent. Open mid-June to early Oct.

Food

Piedmontese cuisine is a sophisticated blend of northern Italian peasant staples and elegant French garnishes. Butter replaces olive oil in cooking; cheese, mushrooms, and white truffles edge out tomatoes, peppers, and spices. *Agnolotti* (ravioli stuffed with lamb and cabbage) are the local pasta specialty, but *polenta,* a cornmeal mush often topped with fontina cheese, is the more common starch. Many *secondi* involve flesh or fowl simmered in wine sauces, a testament to a region that produces some of Italy's noblest wines. Plan to spend extra in Turin's supermarkets or restaurants on the three outstanding red wines: Barolo, Barbaresco, and Barbera.

Turin serves delectable local pastries, including the remarkably rich *bocca di leone,* a doughnut filled with whipped cream, fruit, or chocolate (about L2500). You can sample it at **Cossolo il Pasticciere,** via Gramsci, 1, and via Garibaldi, 9. Their *sospiri* (chocolate rum pastries, L1100) are as light as air and almost as cheap. (Open Mon.-Sat. 7:30am-8:30pm).

Several trendy *gelaterie* ice the near side of p. Castello coming from the station. Try the spiffy **Bar Blù** (tel. 53 14 24, open Tues.-Sun. 7am-2am) or **Ra Palino** (tel. 89 82 82, open Tues.-Sun. 11:30am-1am), where you can sample the exotic flower flavors *rosa* and *viola.* The **open-air market** at p. della Repubblica runs Mon.-Fri. 8am-1pm. On Saturday (8am-6pm), an assortment of non-edibles are also sold here—everything from baskets to underwear. Get gastronomy-to-go at **Market Rossini,** via Rossini, 1 (tel. 839 77 13), at the corner of via Lagrange. Open Mon.-Tues. and Thurs.-Sat. 8:30am-1pm and 4-7:30pm, Sun. and Wed. 8:30am-1pm. To mingle with the fashion nobility, try **Caffè Torino,** via Roma, 204, on p. San Carlo (tel. 54 51 18), a Turin institution. If you're in an extravagant mood, sit down and savor the solicitous service provided by tuxedo-clad waiters. (Cappuccino L5500 if you sit, L1500 if you stand. Open Wed.-Mon. 7:30am-1am.)

Torino 1, via Lagrange, 43/B (tel. 54 21 26), parallel to via Roma. Excellent cafeteria fare—even businessmen deign to eat here. *Primi* L1800, *secondi* L3500. Open Mon.-Sat. 11:45am-2:30pm and 6:45-9pm.

Ristorante Taverna Fiorentina, via Palazzo di Città, 6 (tel. 54 24 12), off p. Castello. A small, family-run restaurant. Try the *capretto Sardo al forno* (baked lamb, Sardinian-style, L7000). Plate of the day L6000-9000. Cover L2500. Open Aug.-June Sun.-Fri. noon-3pm and 7-10pm.

Trattoria Amelia, via dei Mercanti, 6 (tel. 562 84 78), off via Garibaldi. A homey *trattoria* in the center of town. Family-style cooking. *Primi* L5000. *Secondi* L7000-8000. Tourist menu L15,000. Open Sun.-Fri. noon-2:30pm and 6:30-9:30pm.

Trattoria Messico, via Bernadino Galliari, 8 (tel. 650 87 98), 2 streets south of via Vittorio Emanuele, near Porta Nuova. No sombreros here, just tourists afraid to stray too far from the station and a smattering locals. Terrific pasta and *fettuccini al messico* (L6000). Wine L6000 per liter. Cover L2000. Open Mon.-Sat. noon-2pm and 7-10pm.

Trattoria Toscana, via Vanchiglia, 2 (tel. 812 29 14), off p. V. Veneto near the university. This hit with locals rewards those who undertake the walk. Don't miss the *bistecca di cinghiale* (boar steak, L6500), which clashes with the rose-covered tables. Open Sept.-July Sun.-Fri. noon-4:30pm and 7-9:30pm.

University Mensa, via Principe Amadeo, 48 (tel. 812 71 60), past via Rosine. Cafeteria-quality food. Student ID required on pain of death. Full meal L7000. Open Sept.-July Mon.-Sat. noon-2pm and 7-8:30pm.

Seven-Up, via Andrea Doria, 4 (tel. 54 25 82). Eat crêpes or silky *risotto* (both L6000) in a crisp-and-clean, no caffeine atmosphere. Pizza too (L4500-8500). Open Tues.-Sun. noon-2:30pm and 6:30-11pm.

Sights

It's hard to say which the Turinese revere more: the sooty secularism of the successful auto industry or the (now tarnished) cultural clout of the Holy Shroud. Whatever the preference of locals, the city has much to offer those who are neither religious pilgrims nor auto buffs. Among Turin's attractions are a multitude of museums, architectural sights, and serene gardens.

Down via Roma from the Porta Nuova station, **piazza San Carlo** displays all the formality and grandeur the 17th-century Baroque was capable of bestowing. Resting in the center of this perfect rectangle, the statue of Duke Filiberto Emanuele assesses the crowds—and cars—from his horse. This *piazza's* elegant embellishment comes in the shape of Baroque buildings and the form of the twin churches of **Santa Cristina** and **San Carlo,** both the work of Filippo Juvarra, architect to King Vittorio Amadeo II.

Beyond p. San Carlo, via Roma ends in **piazza Castello,** the historic center of the city, dominated by the imposing **Madama Palace** (tel. 57 65 38 19), so-called because the widow of Vittorio Amadeo I, "Madama Reale," Marie Christine of France, lived here. (Natives often refer to it as the Palazzo Reale, however, which is a bit confusing as there is another royal palace in Turin.) The colossal two-story pilasters and columns are set against Juvarra's richly decorated facade, which hides a jumble of fragments—including a Roman gate and a 13th-century castle— all incorporated in the building. The **Museo Civico di Arte Antica** (tel. 57 65 38 19) inside contains a fine collection of medieval and Renaissance objects. (Both palace and museum were closed for restoration in 1992.) The **Armeria Reale** (Royal Armory) of the House of Savoy (tel. 54 38 89) is located just across the piazza Castello at #191, and contains the best collection of medieval and Renaissance tools of war in the world. Before visions of swords and spears overwhelm you, duck upstairs to the library and hunt out Leonardo da Vinci's self-portrait (*autoritratto*) in red ink. (Open Tues. and Thurs. 2:30-7:30pm and Wed. and Fri.-Sat. 9am-2pm. Admission L6000.)

Though the city owes its glory to political rather than ecclesiastical leadership, unadulterated splendor blesses the the interior of the **Church of San Lorenzo** in p. Castello. Constructed between 1668 and 1680, it is Guarini's most original creation—follow the moldings as they weave in and out of side chapels, or count the myriad columns, of every color, shape, size, and texture imaginable. The dome is the highlight, a multi-layered kaleidoscope of wishbones and starfish with ribs whirling about like the tails on whizzing comets. (Open 7:30am-noon and 4-7:30pm.) Cross the courtyard to see the **Palazzo Reale** (tel. 436 14 55), a plain apricot building that the Princes of Savoy called home from 1645 to 1865. Its red-and-gold interior is a frigid Las Vegas—all glitter with no gusto—but it does protect an outstanding collection of Chinese porcelain vases. The small but sumptuous garden was designed by Louis le Nôtre (1697), who is more famous for his work on the *jardins* of Versailles. (Palace open Tues.-Sun. 9am-1:15pm. Admission L6000. Gardens open daily 9am-6pm. Free.)

The **Cathedral of San Giovanni,** behind the Palazzo Reale where via XX Settembre crosses p. San Giovanni, is also a must-see, although it houses a has-been. Guarini's remarkable creation, the **Cappella della Santa Sindone** (Chapel of the Holy Shroud, 1668-1694), rests here. His unrestrained, whirling black marble dome (under renovation in 1992, but still open to tourists) caps the somber rotunda that houses a silver vessel containing one of the strangest relics of Christianity, the **Holy Shroud of Turin.** This is the piece of linen in which it was thought that Christ was wrapped for burial after his crucifixion. Although scientists have finally refuted the claim that this was Christ's shroud, they haven't been able to account for it. The piece apparently dates from the 12th century, but no one has been able to explain the unique front and back impressions of a crucified body. Before leaving the cathedral, don't miss Luigi Gagna's oil reproduction of Leonardo's *Last Supper* above the front door, considered the world's best copy of the Renaissance masterpiece. (Tel. 436 15 40. Chapel open Tues.-Sat. 9am-noon and 3-6pm, Sun. 9am-noon. *Duomo* open daily 7am-noon and 3-7pm.)

The **Palazzo dell'Accademia delle Scienze,** at #6 of the via of the same name, houses two of Turin's best museums. Crammed into two floors of this Guarini masterpiece, the **Egyptian Museum** (tel. 54 40 91) hoards the finest collection of Egyptian artifacts in the world outside Cairo. Here you will find several copies of the Egyptian *Book of the Dead* and an intact sarcophagus of Vizier Ghemenef-Har-Bak, which stands out among the large sculptures and architectural fragments on the ground floor. Upstairs is the fascinating and well-furnished tomb of 14th-century BC architect Kha and his wife, one of the few tombs spared by thieves. (Museum open Tues.-Sun. 9am-2pm. Admission L10,000.) The third and fourth floors house the **Galleria Sabauda** (tel. 54 74 40). This gallery, with masterpieces from the House of Savoy, is renowned for its paintings by Flemish and Dutch artists: van Eyck's *St. Francis Receiving the Stigmata,* Memling's *Passion,* van Dyck's *Children of Charles I of England,* and Rembrandt's *Old Man Sleeping.* The Sabauda also swells with mannerist and Baroque paintings, including a noteworthy Poussin, several Strozzis, and Volture's *Decapitation of John the Baptist.* Major works from Palazzo Madama reside here while it undergoes restoration. (Open Tues.-Sun. 9am-2pm. Admission L6000.)

The **Museo di Antichità,** north of p. San Giovanni at corso Regina Margherita, 105 (tel. 521 22 51), houses several beautiful Greek and Roman busts, a collection of Greek and Cypriot ceramics, and pieces from the treasury of Marengo. There are also several pre- and proto-historic artifacts from the Piedmont and Valle d'Aosta regions. (Open Tues.-Sat 9am-1pm and 3-7pm, the first and third Sundays of the month 9am-1pm. Admission L6000.) The **Galleria d'Arte Moderna,** via Magenta, 31 (tel. 48 83 43), off largo Emanuele, contains representative works of late 19th- and 20th-century masters, including Chagall, Picasso, Courbet, and Renoir. (Closed for restoration in 1992.)

The **National Cinematographic Museum,** p. San Giovanni, 2 (tel. 436 11 48), occupies the Palazzo Chiablese, although it may have moved by 1993—check with the APT. The film museum was also closed for restoration in 1992. The museum contains an excellent collection of pre-cinematic and cinema stills, and maintains a library (tel. 521 47 84). Turin was the birthplace of Italian cinema; the seminal silent film *Cabiria* was filmed along the banks of the Po. (Library open Tues.-Sat. 10am-noon and 3-6pm. Check with the APT for current museum location, hours and admission costs.)

The Palazzo Carignano contains the **Museo Nazionale del Risorgimento Italiano** at via Accademia delle Scienze, 5 (tel. 562 11 47), but enter from p. Carlo Alberto on the other side. One of the great Baroque palaces of Europe, its facade is a masterpiece of white marble relief and elegant statues. In the 19th century, this palace housed the first Italian parliament and the cradle of Prince Vittorio Emanuele II. The museum today contains historic documents and other paraphernalia of national interest. On Sundays from 10:30am to noon there is a free guided tour of the exhibits. (Open Tues.-Sat. 9am-6:30pm, Sun. 9am-12:30pm. Admission L5000.)

For the culture-weary, a siesta in the shady **park** at p. Cavour is ideal, as is an amble along the banks of the Po through gorgeous gardens to the **Valentino Castle** (tel. 669 93 72). A "medieval" castle built in 1884 for a world exposition, it looks like something from *Alice in Wonderland.* The guide takes you through room after room of enchanting objects—a sink in the shape of a castle, a throne that converts to a potty. Unfortunately, both the dungeons and towers are inaccessible. (Open Tues.-Sat. 9am-6pm, Sun. 10:30am-6pm. Admission L6000, Fridays free.)

Every Italian city needs its vertical expression of civic virility; in modern Turin, you can skip prowess-testing stairs and take a glass elevator to the top. The **Mole Antonelliana,** via Montebello, 20 (tel. 839 83 14), a few blocks east of p. Castello, began, in a flurry of political intrigue, as a synagogue, but ended up as a Victorian eccentricity—a two-story Greek temple perched atop a giant glass pyramid and crowned by a lighthouse. The view inside the dome as you ascend to the top is dizzying. (Open Tues.-Sun. 9am-7pm. Admission L3000.)

Entertainment

The newspaper **La Stampa** publishes an excellent section on current events, all types of music, cinema, and theater, as well as annual festivals. Turin comes alive with the sound of music, theater, and dancing shoes from the beginning of June through July 6 when the city invites international companies to the **Sere d'Estate** festival. For information and programs, contact the **Assessorato per la Cultura,** p. San Carlo, 161. (Tel. 57 65 37 40. Open Mon. 3-7pm, Tues.-Sat. 9am-1pm and 3-7pm. In winter, open Mon. 2-6:30pm, Tues.-Sat. 9am-6:30pm. Admission to events will run you between L15,000 and L30,000.) **Settembre Musica** is a month-long extravaganza of classical concerts performed all over the city. Contact the Assessorato for a program.

Cinemas are prevalent in Turin, offering the latest in both big-budget blockbusters and less popular art films. During the academic year, a number of foreign films are shown in their original languages. For a list of the titles, times and locations, contact the Informa Giovani.

During his time as a student in Turin, Erasmus said that magic pervaded the city, and Turin has since extended its reputation as a center of the occult. Get your palm read at the porta Pila, or flirt with the world of black garb and magenta walls at **Inferno,** via Carlo Alberto, 55 (tel. 83 25 02) and via Po, 14 (tel. 839 74 42). Local punks come to chat more than to shop. (Both open Mon. 3:30-7:30pm, Tues.-Sat. 9:30am-12:30pm and 3:30-7:30pm.) If you seek more traditional attire, but can't afford the chic shops lining via Roma, try the **department store** at via Lagrange and via Teofilo Rossi.

Near Turin

When Turin was besieged by the French on September 6, 1706, King Vittorio Amadeo II made a pact with the Virgin Mary to build a magnificent cathedral in her honor if the city could resist. Turin was unconquered, and the result was the magnificent **Basilica of Superga** (tel. 89 00 83), erected on the summit of a 672m hill. The Basilica's neoclassical deep-porched form and high drum support a magnificent dome. From the spacious terrace, you can survey the city, the Po Valley, and the Alps. Half the fun is getting there. Take tram #15 from via XX Settembre to Stazione Sassi and then board a small cable railway for a 20-minute ride through fragrant countryside. (Open daily 8am-noon and 2:30-6:30pm. Free.) The funicular departs on the hour from June to Sept. (L1600). The tourist office also has information about boat trips on the Po, which normally run mid-June to mid-Sept. (L3000-8000).

Turin is about two hours from many excellent **hiking areas** and **ski slopes** in the Alps. An hour up the nearest mountain, alpine refuges begin beckoning. **Sestriere** (2035m), an hour and a quarter from Turin, boasts the most comprehensive resort with four cableways, 20 ski lifts, excellent runs, and a skating rink. Bus service connects the area with Oulx (on the Turin-Paris train line) and Turin. The **Venini,** a *rifugio alpino* (alpine hut) on the town's outskirts, supplements the town's conventional lodgings. For more information contact Sestriere's **tourist office,** piazzale Agnelli, 11 (tel. (0122) 75 54 44). **Alagna Valsesia** (1200m), 156km from Turin and 138km from Milan, boasts the second-largest lift in the area. Farther north looms **Macugna** (1327m), 183km from Turin and 141km from Milan, with its own enormous ski lift (1540m). The ski season runs November through May; ask in Turin about snow conditions before boarding a bus. All areas are linked with Turin by bus and train. For more information and a list of accommodations, write to the tourist office in Turin and request a booklet on *settimane bianche* ("white weeks," cheaper weekly skiing deals), as well as an *Annuario Alberghi* and their booklet *Orizzonte Piemonte: Dove la Neve è "Più Neve."*

Susa

Though far from Rome, Susa never lets the visitor forget its Roman origins. Surrounded by mountains and divided by a river, this tiny hamlet was once the seat of the Gaul Cottius, a prefect of the Empire. Stuffed with Roman artifacts and graced with a beautiful cathedral, Susa is the perfect escape from Turin's occasionally oppressive elegance and a pleasant ruin-infested stopover on the way to the culturally vacuous ski resorts further up the Susa Valley.

A typically Italian historical jumble, Susa's cultural wealth centers on its collection of antique Roman remnants and operational medieval constructions. Medieval Susa centers on the **Cathedral of San Giusto,** a 1029 structure that houses the 14th-century *Triptych of Rocciamelone,* a Flemish portrayal of the Virgin and saints in brass, and a fine 10th-century baptismal font, carved in serpentine. Beside the cathedral, the **Porta Romana** (5th century) hints with many-windowed splendor at the Roman remains around the town. From the front of the cathedral, in p. Savoia, follow the yellow signs uphill to the **Arco d'Agosto** (draped in scaffolding in 1992), the **Castle of Maria Ade-**

laide, and the Roman **aqueduct.** If the two-minute uphill walk tuckers you out, drink the delicious spring water pouring from the "mouth" of a "man" by the arch. Cottius, then a mere chieftain, built the arch as a brown-nosing tribute to the Emperor Augustus in 9 BC; Augustus returned the favor by elevating Crottius to a prefecture in the Roman Empire. If archeological treasures aren't enough, you can savor the spectacular mountain vistas from the grounds of the castle. Around the town, the complete Roman tour takes in the **Amphitheater** and the **Baths** (follow the ubiquitous yellow signs), while the medievalist can continue on to the Romanesque church of **Santa Maria Maggiore,** graced by a comely campanile. Finish up with medieval churches by heading to the Gothic 13th-century **Convento di San Francesco** which boasts a lovely little cloister and a Savoy founder. When the Savoys came to town, they holed up in the collection of 12th- and 13th-century houses along **borgo dei Nobili,** reached by heading down via S. Francesco from the convent.

To get to Susa from Turin, take the train to Bussoleno (10 per day) and change there for Susa (Turin-Susa 53 km, 1hr., L3500). From the station, walk up corso Stati Uniti 50m to your right. The white stand at the corner of the small park is Susa's friendly **Pro Loco,** a friendly tourist office with maps and brochures. (Open daily 8:30am-7:30pm, in winter Tues.-Sat. 8:30am-noon.) The SAPAV **bus** line (tel. 62 20 15) serves Susa, with departures to Turin, Oulx (L10,000), and Sestriere, the most fashionable of the Piedmont ski resorts. Buses leave from outside the train station, corso Stati Uniti, 33. **First aid** (*pronto soccorso,* tel. 316 31) is across the street from the train station, up toward the tourist office. If you plan to stay, Marco and Loris will be your hosts-with-the-most at **Hotel Stazione,** c. Stati Uniti, 2 (tel. 62 22 26), just across from the station. They'll fill you in on Susa's history, and give you spotless rooms as well. (Singles L27,000, with bath L33,000. Doubles with bath L52,000.) Tuesday mornings a **market** offering everything from clothes to fresh cheese slithers the length of via Palazzo di Città and via Martiri della Libertà. Tasty, fresh *focaccia* (large round cakes served in slices—L1200) is happily available at via Mazzini, 2 (right by the bridge, open Mon.-Sat. 9am-1pm and 4-7:30pm). Susa's **postal code** is 10059; its **telephone code** is 0122.

Sacra di San Michele

Perched on a bluff 1000m above the town of Avigliana, the massive stone **Sacra di San Michele** (tel. 93 91 30) looms in evocative splendor over the approaching traveler. *The Name of the Rose* was not filmed here, but that was only the filmmaker's error; Eco did base the monastery of the book on the edifice here, and even in summer it's not hard to imagine monks falling to snowy deaths from the windows, or turning up in a vat of pig's blood stowed in some creepy corner. Although it's easier going by car, the 12km hike from nearby Avigliana (easily reached by train—15 per day, L2400—from Turin) will make you feel like a proper pilgrim. From p. del Popolo in Avigliana follow the main road, corso Laghi, around Lago Grande. Every time the road splits, take the right fork until you hit via Sacra di San Michele on its steep and winding tour up the mountainside (allow two to three hours for the entire walk). Passing motorists are few once you hit via Sacra di San Michele, but workers on the Sacra's four-year-old restoration project occasionally pass by on their way to the summit. **Buses** to the top leave only on Sundays in July and August at 8am from p. Carlo Felice in Turin. (Martoglio bus line, tel. 937 60 28, round-trip L10,000.) The Sacra, a monastery founded in 1000 AD, perches atop Mt. Pirchiriano, making the place notable both for its interior and for the views its location affords. Upon entering the structure, the impressive "Stairway of the Dead," an immense set of steps helping to buttress the building leads outside to the beautifully carved wooden doors depicting the arms of St. Michael with the Serpent of Eden. As you enter the vast Romanesque-Gothic interior, the fresco to your left depicts the *Burial of Jesus, the Death of the Virgin,* and the *Assumption,* by Secondo del Bosco (1505). Peek into the shrine of St. Michael, down the small steps in the middle of the nave. As your eyes get accustomed to the dark, you'll see three tiny chapels. The largest one, to your left, with a back wall of solid rock, was built in 966 AD by St. John Vincent and supposedly consecrated by angels—and is the most sacred spot in the Sacra. In the crypt you'll find the tombs of medieval scions of the Savoy family. (Sacra open Mon.-Sat. 9am-12:30pm and 3-6pm, Sun. 9am-noon and 3-6pm. Oct.-March Mon.-Sat. 9am-12:30pm and 3-5pm, Sun. 9am-noon and 2:30-5pm.) There are **public toilets** outside the entrance, but bring your own paper. For more information, contact Avigliana's **Informazione Turistica** (tel. (011) 93 86 50), where cordial workers will supply you with maps. (Open Mon.-Sat. 9am-12:30pm and 3-6pm.)

Asti and the Monferrato Area

Vineyards provide Asti with both economic revenue and winespread renown. The sparkling Asti Cinzano and Asti Spumante begin their effervescing here. Many wineries remain under family control, and a warm reception awaits the curious tippler who takes time to explore less-trafficked areas. In addition to wine, paleontology storms ahead at **Cinaglio, Valleadona,** and **Villafranca d'Asti,** where remains of mastodons, rhinoceri, and other gargantuan fauna have been unearthed. So important are the discoveries that a paleological epoch has been named after the area, the Astian period.

The City of Asti

Modern Asti takes its name from the ancient Lugurian village "Ast" ("high hill"). In 89 BC, the settlement became one of the most important Roman outposts in ancient Liguria, "Hasta Pompeia," and by the 13th century, Asti had emerged as one of the richest and most powerful provinces in Italy. For the next 500 years, control of the region bounced between native princes and the House of Savoy. Although the resulting wars destroyed the city several times, 120 13th-century towers survive.

Orientation and Practical Information

Asti is easily accessible by train from Turin (every 30min., 40min., L4300) and Alessandria (every 30min., 20min., L3200). A direct train leaves daily for Milan (2hr., L10,500). The train station in p. Stazione (tel. 503 11) is a few short blocks south of the heart of the town, **piazza Vittorio Alfieri.**

Tourist Office: p. V. Alfieri, 34 (tel. 50 357). Assists in finding accommodations (but no reservations made) and information on daytrips to wineries and castles. Pick up the *Guide to Asti and its Province* and the indispensable map of town. English spoken. Open Mon.-Fri. 9am-12:30pm and 3-6:30pm, Sat. 9am-12:30pm.

Currency Exchange: Instituto Bancario di San Paolo di Torino, p. Alfieri and c. Dante. Change located on the second floor. Open Mon.-Fri. 8:25am-1:25pm and 2:40-4:10pm.

Post Office: corso Dante, 55 (tel. 59 28 51), off p. V. Alfieri. Open daily 8:15am-7pm. **Postal Code:** 14100.

Telephones: SIP, p. Alfieri, 10 (tel. 550 11). Open Mon.-Fri. 8:30am-12:30pm and 3-7pm, Sun. 9am-4pm. Automatic phones next door, open daily 7am-10pm. **Telephone Code:** 0141.

Buses: p. Marconi (tel. 536 72), across the *piazza* from the train station. To: Costigliole (7 per day, 30min., L2500) and Isola d'Asti (every hour, 10min., L1600), as well as Acqui (2 per day, 1hr., L 4400), and Canelli (9 per day, 45min., L3100). Buy tickets on the bus.

Emergencies: tel. 113. **Police:** corso XXV Aprile, 5 (tel. 41 81 11). **Hospital: Ospedale Civile,** via Botallo, 4 (tel. 39 21). **Red Cross:** tel. 21 78 83.

Accommodations and Food

Across from the train station, **Hotel Cavour,** p. Marconi, 18 (tel. 502 22), offers modern, clean singles for L35,000, with bath L45,000. Doubles are L50,000, with bath L60,000. (Open Sept.-July.) Though you'll be a good hike from the action, you might want to take bus #2 to the corner of corso Torino and corso XXV Aprile (L800) to **Antico Paradiso,** Corso Torino, 329 (tel. 21 43 85) with singles for L31,000 and doubles for L46,000. In the center of it all, **Hotel Reale,** p. V. Alfieri, 6 (tel. 502 40), holds true to its "royal" title, renting singles for L70,000 and doubles for L120,000. You can camp at **Campeggio Umberto Cagni** (tel. 27 12 38). From p. Alfieri, turn onto via Aro, which becomes corso Volta. Make a left onto via Valmanera, 152. (L4000 per person, L4000 per tent. Open Apr.-Sept.)

At the **Campo del Palio,** across the street from the station, vendors hawk everything from leather to lettuce to lampshades (open Mon.-Sat. 8:30am-1pm). Mornings also rouse a market into action at p. Catera, off via Carducci in the heart of town. The **Super Gulliver Market,** via Cavour, 81, could feed an army of Lilliputians *and* a horde of Houyhnhnms. (Open Mon.-Sat. 8:30am-7:30pm.) **Pizzeria da Gianni,** corso Alfieri, 83, toward the hospital, throws pizza for L4000-7500, *primi* for L3000-4000, and *secondi* for L6000-7000. The house specialty is *lumache alla parigiana* (Parisian snails, L7000). Cover is L2000. (Open Wed.-Mon. 6pm-1am.)

Sights

From **piazza Vittorio Alfieri,** the heart of the town, a short walk west on via Garibaldi will take you to quiet p. Santo Secondo and the 18th-century **Palazzo di Città** (City Hall), as well as the medieval **Collegiata di San Secondo,** patron saint of Asti. The Romanesque-Gothic church was built on the very spot where San Secondo, Asti's patron saint, was decapitated. (Open daily 7am-noon and 3:30-7pm.) On corso Alfieri stands the **Torre Rossa** (Red Tower), also known as the **Tower of San Secondo** because of the saint's imprisonment there. Asti's oldest tower, this 16-sided, cylindrical-looking work of art has foundations dating back to the time of Augustus. The tower adjoins the elliptical 18th-century **Church of Santa Caterina.** If you walk to the left of the *piazza* as you exit the church, you'll be able to see the dome of the **Santuario della Madonna del Portone** (Sanctuary of the Madonna of the Gate). This splendid Byzantine church can be reached by going south on p. S. Caterina to via S. Anna.

North of corso Alfieri, several medieval streets lead to p. Cattedrale, dominated by the eclectic **Cathedral of Asti,** whose size and grandeur make it one of the most noteworthy Gothic cathedrals in Piedmont. The cathedral was begun in 1309; in the 16th and 17th centuries local artists, including native son Gandolfino d'Asti, covered every inch of the walls with frescoes. Decaying 11th-century mosaics blanket the floor of the altar. If you wander about for a few minutes, the caretaker might come out and give you an exhaustive private tour (open daily 7:30am-noon and 3-7pm). Up via delle Valle from corso Alfieri (not far west of p. Alfieri) is the **Torre Troyana.** Built in the 13th century, at 38m it is the highest tower in Piedmont. Asti also has its own wine cellar, near p. Alfieri, which can be visited on Wednesdays (ask at the tourist office). The **Giardini Pubblici,** between p. Alfieri and campo del Palio, provide refreshing flora for picnicking fauna (of the human variety). On the far end of the *corso* is the 15th-century **Church of S. Pietro** with a 12th-century octagonal baptistry. (Open Tues.-Sat. 9am-noon and 3-6pm, Sun. 10am-noon.) Often, exhibits of local artists are shown in the baptistry and the complex stays open later. The church served in WWII as an army hospital; Romans, friars, and war dead all share the space beneath the courtyard.

Seasonal Events

The series **Asti Teatro,** held during the first three weeks of July, offers theatrical productions from the medieval to the modern. The venue varies, so call for information; reservations are suggested. (Teatro Alfieri, via L. Grandi, 16; tel. 35 57 23 or 576 67. Open daily 2:30-7:30pm. Admission around L18,000, discounts for children and students.) The theatrical takes to the streets with the **Palio di Asti,** held annually on the third Sunday of September. The Palio recalls the town's liberation in 1200 with man and mare alike draped in medieval garb. A procession commences at 2pm from the cathedral, passes through the town, and ends at the piazza Alfieri, where the horses are relieved of their costumes for the festival's racing finale. Astian vintners have made a tradition of courting prospective buyers with annual Bacchanalias, each dedicated to a different fruit of the vine. In spring you can celebrate the exposition **Vino Nuovo del lunedì Marzo,** during the last week of March in the Salone delle Manifestazione, p. Alfieri. In September, agricultural Asti revels in the **Douja d'Or,** a week-long festival celebrating the splendor of the grape.

The Monferrato and Le Langhe

Many vineyards and castles near Asti merit a trip. **Costigliole,** a brief bus ride away, is home to a medieval castle complete with drawbridge. Costigliole's **tourist office** can be reached at (0141) 96 60 31. Also a short distance from Asti and accessible by bus are **Isola d'Asti,** with its two medieval churches (the bus passes Isola d'Asti on its way to Costigliole), and **Canelli,** surrounded by the muscat vineyards which produce the fruity *Asti spumante.* (Ask at Asti's tourist office for the *Carta dei Vini a D.O.C. Della Provincia di Asti,* a map of vineyards in the region offering wine tastings). If medieval castles fortify you, press on to enchanting **Alessandria,** from Asti, about 30 minutes by rail .

Valle d'Aosta

With the collapse of Cogne's mining industry and the decline of agriculture, Valle d'Aosta's economy has taken a turn to Tourism with a capital T. Vacationing French and Swiss breeze through the bilingual valleys and even the most remote villages cater to the needs of finicky travelers. The enduring attraction of the region is the *towns*— remote villages separated from their neighbors by miles of vast countryside. The gorgeous Valdostan expanse inspires torrents of superlatives. Skiers and hikers visiting the area often swear they've found paradise—that is, until they inspect Aosta's sky-high price-tags.

Train service in the region runs only as far as Pre-St-Didier, but fearless buses bank 180-degree turns with gut-wrenching efficiency to make most of the valley accessible. The most spectacular entrance to the area is indisputably the international cable car connection from Chamonix (about L65,000). Be aware that in Courmayeur, the connection on the Italian end, prestige doesn't come cheap. This Mont Blanc resort has combined forces with Cervinia to try to bring the Olympic games to Valle d'Aosta, and if unchecked inflation were the only criterion, the ambitious twosome would stand a good chance. Unless you've got lots of money to burn, head to the lesser-known valleys and enjoy the high peaks at lower prices.

Hiking

The Valle d'Aosta is a paradise for hikers. Each valley's tourist office provides information on routes (usually very well-marked) and the comprehensive network of huts and refuges, which allows the intrepid to stay high for days at a time. Trails often bring you above 10,000 feet, so dress and pack carefully. You'll need a sweater, a windbreaker, a pair of gloves, heavy wool socks with polypropylene liners, a compass, and a first-aid kit. Don't forget that the strength of the sun intensifies with altitude—wear plenty of sunscreen even on cloudy or chilly days. And because even the easiest trails have tricky stretches, you'll need a pair of good hiking boots. The best time of the year to hike is in July, August, and the first week of September, when all the snow has melted. Avoid hiking in April and May, when thawing snow often causes avalanches. Obtain a reliable map—*Kompass* maps are the most accurate. Also beware of poisonous snakes, which have flourished as the birds that normally gobble them fall victim to illegal hunting. Be especially careful on rocky tracts at low altitudes.

The tourist offices in Aosta and in each smaller valley give out a list of campgrounds, bag-lunch (*al sacco*) vendors, and mountain huts and bivouacs (ask for the *elenco rifugi bivacchi*). Most regional offices also carry the booklet *Alte Vie* (High Roads) with maps, photographs, and helpful advice pertaining to the two serpentine mountain trails that link many of the region's most dramatic peaks. Both routes are subdivided into shorter hikes and assessed with regard to difficulty and availability of food and accommodations. Long stretches require virtually no expertise and offer panoramic views and a taste of Alpine adventure.

Similarly, **rifugi alpini** (mountain huts) are not the exclusive abodes of veteran mountaineers. Some are only a cable car or a half-hour walk from main roads, and many offer half-pension (L28,000-33,000). Public refuges, or *bivacchi,* though generally empty shells, are free, while those run by caretakers cost L13,000-18,000 per night. For more detailed information on all things mountainous, contact **Interguide,** at via Monte Emilius, 13 (tel. 409 39), in Aosta, or the **Club Alpino Italiano,** open Mon., Wed.-Thurs. 5-7pm, Tues. and Fri. 8-10pm, above Aosta's tourist office. They offer insurance and membership deals with discounts on refuges.

Skiing

Skiing in Valle D'Aosta is sublime, but it's not the bargain it used to be. **Settimane bianche,** "white-week" packages for skiers, are a welcome source of discount rates and may keep you from devoting the bulk of your *après-ski* hours to the contemplation of financial woes. In off-season, one-star full pension runs about L320,000, half-pension L280,000, and bed and breakfast L200,000, while weekly lift passes average L150,000. In high season, prices jump by as much as 20%. Winter reservations should be made in writing directly through the hotels. For more specific information, write to the **Ufficio Informazioni Turistiche,** p. Chamonix, 8, 11100 Aosta, and request their pamphlet **White Weeks: Winter Season, Aosta Valley.**

Courmayeur and **Cervinia** are the best known resorts in the 11 ski-worthy valleys, basking in the reflected glory of Mont Blanc and the Matterhorn. **Val d'Ayas** and **Val di Gressoney** offer equally challenging terrain for lower rates. If cross-country is more to your taste, head to **Cogne,** or to the community of **Brusson** half-way down Val d'Ayas.

In Cervinia and Courmayeur, tank tops replace parkas for **summer skiing** (play it safe and bring both), and in June and late September it's possible to find a room without reservations. Arrange summer package deals, similar to those available in winter, through the tourist office in either Cervinia or Courmayeur (they're still quite expensive).

Other Sports

Kayaking, rafting, and swimming in the rivers of Valle d'Aosta provide cheaper adrenaline fixes than skiing. The most navigable rivers are: the **Dora Baltea,** which runs through the valley; the **Dora di Veny,** which branches south from Courmayeur; the **Dora di Ferre,** which wanders north from Courmayeur; the **Dora di Rhêmes,** which flows through the Val di Rhêmes; and the **Grand Eyvia,** which courses through the Val di Cogne. Seven kayaking lessons and a week of camping on the Dora Baltea cost about L260,000 through the **Scuola di Canoa di Courmayeur,** c/o Emanuele Pernasconi, Casella Postale, 11013 Courmayeur. A day-long rafting expedition will set you back L75,000. (Courses offered June 29-Sept. 6.) **Rafting Adventure,** in Villeneuve, also offers group trips (tel. (0165) 950 44). The latest hit with the adventurous is **mountain biking;** the Aosta tourist office distributes a list of rentals throughout the valleys. Bungy jumping can't be far behind.

Aosta

Aosta is the metropolitan hub—if a city of 40,000 qualifies as a metropolis—of a region whose economy is increasingly dependent upon tourism. And while Aosta itself sits in the flatlands, its prices have more in common with the nearby peaks of Monte Emilius (3559m) and Becca di Nona (3142m). On the plus side, Aosta has benfitted aesthetically from its 2000-year history as a substantial city in a region of diminutive hamlets. Remains of bridges, triumphal arches, and theaters recall Aosta's importance as a Roman center, and a hodgepodge of towers and churches provide architectural diversity from the Middle Ages. Day trips to the *real* alpine valleys from Aosta are tricky to schedule if you want to return before night falls, so plan ahead. The tourist office distributes an invaluable train/bus/cable car schedule, as well as dozens of other encyclopedic freebies.

Orientation and Practical Information

Aosta sits roughly in the center of the region bearing its name, and is most easily reached by train from Turin (11 per day, *diretto* 2 hr., *locale* 4 hr., L9300). Alp-bound visitors arriving from the east should change trains at Chirasso. Trains stop at p. Manzetti, which lies at the opposite end of the Avenue du Conseil des Commis from p. Chanoux, Aosta's central *piazza*. Buses stop just around the corner from p. Chanoux in p. Narbonne.

Tourist Office: p. Chanoux, 8 (tel. 356 55), straight ahead and down Avenue du Conseil des Commis from the train station. Ask for the booklets *Aosta: Architecture, Art, Archeology* and *Aosta Valley,* and pick up copies of the regional listings of hotels, campgrounds, and mountain huts *(rifugi).* The compact yearly *Orari* contains comprehensive schedules of Val d'Aosta's transportation services, including cable cars. Open daily 9am-1pm and 3-8pm, Sun. 9am-1pm.

Currency Exchange: Banco Valdostano A. Berard and C., p. Chanoux, 49. Efficient, friendly, and visa-adept. Open Mon.-Fri. 8:20am-1:20pm and 2:40-4pm.

Post Office: p. Narbonne (tel. 36 22 87). Open Mon.-Fri. 8:15am-7:30pm, Sat. 8:15am-1pm. **Postal Code:** 11100.

Telephones: SIP, viale Pace, 9 (tel. 439 97), off via Chanoux. Open Mon.-Fri. 8:15am-12:15pm and 2:30-6:30pm, Sat. 8:45-12:15pm and 3-6:30pm, Sun. 8am-3pm. **Telephone Code:** 0165.

Trains: p. Manzetti (tel. 36 20 57). Frequent service to Chivasso and the intermediate stations at Chatillon, Verrès, and Pont-St-Martin which offer access, respectively, to the valleys of Valtournenche, Ayas, and Gressoney. To: Chivasso (15 per day, 1hr. 30min., L6300) with stops at Chatillon (L2100), Verrès (L2800); Pont-St-Martin (L3800). Also to Turin (11 per day, 2-4 hr., L9300) and to Milan (9 per day with a transfer at Chivasso, 3hr.-4hr. 30min., L13,700). **Luggage Storage:** L1500; open 9am-12:30pm and 2:30-6:30pm. **Photocopy machine:** L100 per copy.

Buses: p. Narbonne (tel. 36 20 27), off p. Chanoux on via Ribitel Arcidiacono. To: Cogne (9 per day, 50 min., L2100); Courmayeur (12 per day, 1hr., L3000), Great St. Bernard Pass (2 per day, 45 min., L6000); Fenis (5 per day, 30min., L1600); Valtournenche (7 per day, 2 hr. 15min., L4800); Ask at the information desk in front of the station for the timetable.

Alpine Information: Club Alpino Italiano, p. Chanoux, 8 (tel. 401 94), upstairs from the tourist office. Open Mon., Wed., and Thurs. 5-7pm; Tues. and Fri. 8-10pm. During the rest of the week, try contacting the **Società Guide,** via Monte Emilius, 13 (tel. 444 48).

Snow Conditions: tel. 324 44.

Emergencies: tel. 113. **Police:** corso Battaglione Aosta (tel. 36 15 45). **Hospital: Ospedale Regionale,** viale Ginevra, 3 (tel. 30 41). **Ambulance:** tel. 30 42 11. **Alpine Emergency: Società Guide,** tel. 444 48.

Accommodations

"High season" in Aosta Valley varies among hotels, but is generally considered to be from late December to mid-January, all of February and March, and the second and third weeks of April. In high season, most hotels will not accept reservations for fewer than three nights. What's more, ancient Valdostan tradition decrees that all advance reservations be done by mail with a 30% deposit.

La Belle Epoque, via d'Avise, 18 (tel. 36 22 76), centrally located off via Aubert. Good-sized clean rooms; palatial hall bathroom. Singles L26,000. Doubles L46,000. The best deal in the Aosta Valley.

Mancuso, via Voison, 32 (tel. 345 26). From the station, hang a left on via Carducci as you exit, and another left under the tracks. Peaceful, family atmosphere, and a chummy restaurant downstairs to boot (*menù* about L15,000). All rooms with bath, some with terraces facing Pila. Singles L35,000, doubles L58,000; off-season L34,000 and L50,000 respectively.

Monte Emilius, via Carrel, 9 (tel. 356 92), a skip and a jump to the right from the train station. Friendly management, and dulcet serenading nightly by passing traffic. Singles L22,000. Doubles L36,000.

Camping: Camping Ville d'Aoste (tel. 328 78 or 25 07 79), in Les Fourches, 1km from Aosta. The cheapest. L4300 per person, L4500 per tent. Open June-Sept. **Camping Milleluci** (tel. 442 74), in Roppoz, also 1km from Aosta. L5800 per person, L5400 per tent. Open year-round.

Food

The strategy of any frugal gourmet in Aosta should be to supplement a hearty one-dish meal with a sampling of local cheeses. Prospective picnickers feast their eyes and imaginations on the food shops lining via de Tillier and via Pretoriane; the siren song of pastries will entice you to hurl yourself upon the local bakeries. The most divine divas are *tegole,* wafer-thin cookies containing an assortment of ground nuts, though the generous *krapfen* at **La Corbeille à Pain,** via P. Pretoriane, 22, are worth a try (L1000), as are the L900 *brioches d'Aosta* at the *panettoria* at via de Tillier, 24. The **STANDA supermarket** on via Torino sells more generic merchandise (open Mon.-Sat. 8:30am-12:30pm and 3:30-7:30pm). Cross under the tracks for the shopping experience of a lifetime at **Gros Cidac,** via Paravera, 4, which specializes in low prices and bulk sales. You might feel out-of-place if you're shopping for less than an army, but entertain yourself by watching local bargain-hunters maneuver overflowing flatbed carts down the aisles (open 8:30am-noon and 2:30-6pm; closed Sat. afternoon and Mon. morning).

Trattoria Praetoria, via S. Anselmo, 9 (tel. 443 56), just past the Port Pretoriane. An intimate dining room where Valdostan chatter flows as freely as the wine. *Primi* L6000-8000, *secondi* L9000-12,000. Cover L3000. Open Fri.-Wed. noon-2:30pm and 7-10pm.

Grotta Azzurra, via Croce di Città, 97 (tel. 36 24 74), uphill from where via de Tillier becomes via Aubery. Fake wood paneling and delicious fare. Try the *gnocchi alla gorgonzola* (L7000). Cover L2000. Service 15%. Open Aug.-June Thurs.-Tues. noon-2:30pm and 7-10pm.

Sights

Ruins dating from the time of Augustus (the town's original name was "Augusta Praetoria") have given Aosta its nickname "Rome of the Alps." The town was founded in 23 BC when the region served as an important passageway into Gaul. The virtually intact **Arco d'Augusta,** constructed to honor the Empire's top banana, hails the entrance to the ancient town. The **Porte Pretoriane,** toward p. Chanoux down via Sant'Anselmo, stands at the eastern limits of the old city walls. Within the Roman bounds, active excavation continues to unearth a growing number of historical monuments. The sprawling remains of the **Roman Theater** are the most spectacular, although in 1992 a veneer of scaffolding detracted somewhat from the stony magnificence. (Open daily 9:30am-noon and 2:30-6:30pm; off-season 9:30am-noon and 2-4:30pm.) More discreet examples of Roman masonry can be seen around and virtually underneath the *duomo.* Admire the cathedral-side excavations from the railings, and enjoy the forum's present incarnation as a tiny, sub-ground-level park, the **Criptoportico Forense.** (Open daily 10am-noon and 2:30-6pm; off-season 10am-noon and 2:30-4:30pm.) Jump ahead 400 years to the 5th century AD and round off the archeological tour with a visit to the digging sites at the **Church of San Lorenzo.**

Begin your medieval itinerary at the **Church of St. Ursus,** better known as **Sant'Orso,** whose Romanesque campanile towers over Aosta's pygmy horizon at a height of 46m. The Sant'Orso complex combines an 11th-century structure with a Gothic facade; a 12th-century cloister is annexed to its right flank. The result is an intriguing, earth-colored architectural melange that has become one of the town's primary attractions. St. Ursus, who pioneered the orthodox canonic community after fleeing the heretical practices of delinquent Bishop Placcano, lies interred in the barren crypt, and the story of his life is narrated in the 40 sculpted capitals of the columns that gird the adjacent cloister. Don't fail to pay your respects to Aosta's leafy landmark—the 1000-year-old lime tree gracing the Sant'Orso property recently received official recognition as an historic monument. Dating from the same period, the **Tour Fromage** stands squat and mute by the remains of the amphitheater. No cheese to be seen, but the renovated tower frequently hosts traveling art exhibits, often of jarringly contemporary work.

Entertainment

Those with a penchant for royalty should come to Aosta to witness an annual coronation ritual with a decidedly Valdostan twist. Every October brings the **Bataille de Reines** (Battle of the Queens), a bovine head-butting bash in which approximately 200 well-trained Bessies engage in elimination rounds of brain-battering. The winner is proclaimed Queen and awarded a collar of victory and a bell; whether or not Her Majesty's pommeled skull allows the victor to appreciate their significance is left to speculation. On a more sedate note, the **Foire de St-Ours,** held during the last days of January, is the region's oldest and most prestigious crafts fair. 1993 marks the 992nd staging of the event, which includes exhibitions and a candle-lit procession made all the jollier by an abundance of mulled wine.

Near Aosta

Pick a castle, any castle. Turreted fortresses jut up all over the valley; flip through the photo-strewn pages of *Castelli della Valle d'Aosta* at a local bookstore or the free booklets at the tourist office, and then embark on your chosen quest. **Fénis** and **Issogne** represent the crème de la crème of the crop. Fénis (tel. (0165) 76 42 63) is a monument to the glories of indecisive architecture, flaunting turrets of all shapes and sizes. The interior of the castle is equally noteworthy for its 14th-century Gothic paintings. (Open Wed.-Mon. 9:30am-noon and 2-5:30pm; Dec.-Feb. 9:30-11:30am and 2-4pm.) The castle is easily reached by bus from Aosta (5 per day, 1/2-hr., round-trip L2900). Farther down the valley, 1km from Verrès (15 trains per day, 35 min., L3200), rests the artistic treasure trove of the Issogne fortress (tel. 92 93 73). The collection of 15th-century Gothic and Renaissance art pays tribute to the aesthetic tastes of Prior George di Challant, patron of the arts and a member of the valley's premier nobility. (Open Tues.-Sun. 9:30am-noon and 2-5:30pm; Dec.-Feb. 9:30-11:30am and 2-4pm.)

Valle del Gran San Bernardo

This sparsely populated valley links Aosta to Switzerland via the Great St. Bernard Pass. Napoleon trekked through here with 40,000 soldiers in 1800, but the pass is better known for the **Hospice of St. Bernard,** founded in 1505, the home base for the charitable ministrations of the patron saint of alpinists and skiers and dogs' best friend. Today, the famous dogs are still around, although frequently in cat-sized souvenir form; legendary life-saver Barry was stuffed for posterity and may still be seen if you drive through the pass—sadly, he's a bit worse for the wear. The hospice (just across the Swiss border—bring a passport) continues to offer counseling, although its present slant is toward tourism. A brisk walk uphill past the dog museum (bow WOW!) to the summit of a crag offers amazing views of international peaks. **Mont Velan** (tel. 782 07) down in Saint-Oyen charges L18,000 per person, and **Des Alpes** (tel. 78 09 16) in Saint-Rhêmy steps up a notch in price and altitude with singles for L20,000 and doubles for L39,500. **Camping Pineta** (tel. 781 13) in Saint-Oyen offers riverside plots for L5500 per person and per tent (open year-round). The smaller branch of the valley leading to Ollomont and Oyace is even more serene and offers longer hikes. **Mont Gelé** (tel. 732 20) in Ollomont charges L24,000 per single, L40,000 per double (L2000 less for each in off-season). For more information, contact the tourist office in Aosta or call the St-Oyen/St-Rhêmy **ski-lift office** (tel. 78 09 13 or 78 09 28). The valley is in the Aosta telephone area and uses the **telephone code** 0165.

The first of the spectacular bus rides departs from Aosta at 8am; the last return bus at 4:15pm (4 per day, 1 hr. 15min., L6000, round-trip L9200). L14,100 will take you from Aosta to Martigny in Switzerland (4 per day, 3-4 hr. with a stopover at the pass).

Valtournenche

The **Matterhorn** ("Cervino" in Italian) is a wonder to behold. **Cervinia-Breuil** is not. Slapdash, opportunistic architecture characterizes this popular resort, and the nondescript buildings differ only in purpose: some serve expensive food, others offer expensive accommodations, and those remaining rent expensive sports equipment. Many fresh air fiends, however, consider these man-made deterrents a small price to pay for the opportunity to climb up or glide down one of the world's most famous glaciers. (True mountaineers, however, might consider approaching from the more spartan Swiss side, which features trails, huts, more trails, and a blessed dearth of tourists. It is, however, accessible only by expensive private railroad; see *Let's Go: Germany, Austria and Switzerland.*) A cable car provides year-round service to **Plateau Rosa** (round-trip L30,000) where summer skiers frequently tackle the slopes in swimming gear. Don't forget to tuck your passport into your Speedo since a number of the trails spill over into Switzerland. Hikers can forgo the lift tickets and attempt the three-hour ascent to **Colle Superiore delle Cime Bianche** (2982m), with tremendous views of Val d'Ayas to the east. Ninety minutes on the same trail leads to the emerald waters of **Lake Goillet.**

The **tourist office** (tel. 94 91 36) on the main street inundates visitors with information on white weeks and *settimane estive,* their summer equivalent (open 8:45am-noon and 2:45-6:30pm). **Du Soleil** (tel. 94 95 20), across from the tourist office, lacks many of the luxuries of its glitzier, ritzier competitors, but has the best rates going (half-pension L230,000). Six-day lift passes are L205,000 for the unrestricted, international variety. If you plan to stick it out for a week during the summer months, look into the *Carta Estate,* a guest pass providing discounts on multitudes of post-ski activities.

Hotel Lac Bleu (tel. 94 91 03), 2km downhill from Cervinia, offers low-season singles at L25,000 and doubles at L45,000 (high season L30,000 and L50,000). Also quite reasonable is **Leonardo Carrel** (tel. 94 90 77; singles L29,000, doubles L49,000 year-round) in the locality of Avouil. **Guide del Cervino** (tel. 94 83 69) can be reached by three hours thirty minutes of trekking or by the cable car to Plateau Rosà. **Theodule** (tel. 94 94 00), a half-hour walk or 10 minute schüss from Plateau Rosà, has the odd distinction of tendering summer yoga classes. Both *rifugi* cost in the ballpark of L12,000 nightly, half-pension available at L38,000. For outdoor escapades complete with a fearless leader, contact the **Società Guide** (tel. 94 81 69), which organizes group outings.

Restaurant prices are as steep as the Matterhorn itself, so consider raiding the **Despar supermarket** by the bus stop. You can also save some dough by buying bread at the bakery across the street and then heading for the nearest *Fontina* sign to purchase sandwich fillings. If the nippy air forces you indoors, try **Pizzeria Copa Pan** (tel. 94 91 40), a few doors past the tourist office, which is one of the only restaurants to serve dishes in the four-digit price range (open Fri.-Wed.). Downhill in Valtournenche, an **outdoor market** is held on Friday mornings in summer. Fuel up at the inexplicably-named **Big Ben,** with a surprisingly affordable L12,000 *menù.*

Six buses per day run to Cervinia-Breuil from Châtillon on the Aosta-Turin train line. Two direct buses also arrive daily from p. Castello in Milan. The **telephone code** is 0166.

Val d'Ayas

The scattered villages of the Val d'Ayas remain unscathed by the chaotic flashiness of the region's more high-profile resorts, and sports enthusiasts who value economy over name-dropping should consider stopping here and bypassing the more ostentatious pleasure grounds to the west.

In Brusson, **Beau Site** (tel. 30 01 44) has the best deal on white weeks: L250,000 for full board except at Easter and Christmas when prices leap up to L280,000. **Cai Casale** (tel. 30 76 68), a hostel/hut in St. Jacques, 3km north of Champoluc, has nightly rates of L15,000 per person, L38,000 with full pension. **Aquila** (tel. 30 01 26) in Brusson is a stone's throw from 45km of cross-country trails, and asks L20,000 per person. In Crest, 4km from from Champoluc and accessible by cable car, **Cre Fornè** (tel. 30 71 97) lets singles for L19,000 (high season L21,000) and doubles for an unbeatable L25,000 (high season L28,000). Bring James, Martin and a sleeping bag to **Camping Deans** (tel. 30 02 97), also in Brusson (L5000 per person, L4000 per tent; open year-round).

Mountain bikes and skis can be rented at **Sport 4** (tel. 30 65 30) on the way into Champoluc, or at myriad other spots as well. Contact the **Società Guide** (tel. 30 71 94) for hiking advice, or read through the list of proposed itineraries on the mountaineering map in Champoluc's central *piazza.* The valley's *telecabina* will take you up to the mountain community of Crest, a convenient base for further excursions (lift operates daily 8am-12:50pm and 2-5:50pm, round-trip L8000). Before setting off, fuel up with a *crostata salata Valdostana* (L2000 per *etto*) or one of the meatier varieties of pastries at the *gastronomia/salumeria* between the Champoluc bus stop and the cable car.

Eight buses run daily to Champoluc from the train station at Verrès (1 hr., L3200, round-trip L5500). Thirteen trains run to Verrès from Aosta (40 min., L3200, round-trip L5400), while a comparable number cover the 90 minutes of track from Turin, making connections fairly painless. If you can spare some time from outdoor pursuits, visit the **parish church** in Antagnod which shelters several artistic works of interest including a sculpted saint (possibly from the workshop of Michael Pacher) and the most ornate Baroque high altar in all of Val d'Aosta.

The central **tourist office** in Brusson (tel. 30 02 40) and smaller branches in Champoluc (tel. 30 71 13) and Antagnod (tel. 30 63 35) provide trail maps and hotel information. The **telephone code** for the Ayas Valley is 0125.

Val di Gressoney

Val di Gressoney is situated at the eastern edge of Val d'Aosta, where a medieval influx of Germanic Swiss tribes induced a lasting change in atmosphere (especially in comparison to its Frenchified neighbors). The skiing complex at Gressoney-Saint-Jean and La Trinité is linked to Champoluc in the adjacent valley, and lifts run year-round to the foothills of the formidable Mt. Rosa.

Full board packages to accompany your lift tickets can run a bit high, but **Weissmatten** (tel. 35 54 32) in Saint-Jean and **Casa dei Larici** (tel. 36 62 84), in La Trinité offer affordable week-long bed-and-breakfast deals (both L175,000). **Grizzetti** (tel. 36 61 38) in La Trinité wins the daily rates contest with singles for L25,000 and doubles for L45,000. **Argentina** (tel. 35 59 44), in Saint-Jean, charges L25,000 for singles and L40,000 for doubles (in high season L30,000 and L50,000). Campers can knock a digit off their bill and head to **La Pineta** (tel. 35 53 70) in Saint-Jean (L4500 per person, L4800 per tent).

If the fresh mountain air fails to exhilarate you, head to Gressoney-Saint-Jean on June 24, when traditional **S&M paraphernalia** is paraded down the streets in honor of the town's warped patron saint. In mid-August, the instruments come out again—this time in honor of the tourists. Most of the valley's less suggestive artistic treasures are contained within the **parish church** at Issime.

The best way to get to the valley is to hop a train to Pont-Saint-Martin (15 per day from Aosta, 50 min., L4300, round-trip L7400), and then bus to La Trinité (at least 7 per day, 1hr. 15min.). Summer service also links p. Castello in Milan to Pont-St.-Martin's p. IV Novembre, adjacent to the striking Roman bridge that gives the town its name.

Regional **tourist offices** are conveniently located in Gressoney-Saint-Jean (tel. 35 51 85) and Gressoney-La-Trinité (tel. 36 61 43), while offices in the smaller towns distribute local information. For additional information, consult **Aldebaran International Club** (tel. 36 63 15) in Gressoney-La Trinité. This northernmost township has the monopoly on alpine associations. Contact the **Club Alpino Italiano** (tel. 36 62 59) there. In Saint-Jean, try the efficient, handsome **Nando Laurent** (tel. 35 51 48). A seven-day ski pass good for all resorts in both the Gressoney and Ayas Valleys ranges from L157,000 to L178,000. The **telephone code** is 0125.

Val di Cogne

Cogne's iron mines were once the keystone of Valdostan industry. When the mines ran dry in the 1970s though, the townspeople resorted to more genteel pursuits—delicately prying cross-country skiers apart from their money. The quiet village has consequently become a harmonious blend of authentic and slightly self-conscious rusticity: Women in traditional garb make lace and craftsmen sculpt wood in the open air for the entertainment of the daily visitor. In winter, Cogne functions as the head of a 50km entanglement of cross-country trails. A cable car transports Alpine addicts to the top of the modest downhill facilities (round-trip L10,500, L112,000 for a 7-day pass). In summer, however, the pastoral community is better known as the gateway to the **Gran Paradiso National Park.**

Given the resemblance of the whole of Val d'Aosta to a mammoth nature reserve, one might wonder what sets this park apart from its surrounding areas. The answer: ice and fauna. In addition to offering a seemingly endless network of hiking trails and a population of 5000 ibex (an endangered species that has become symbolic not only of the park but of Alpine fauna in general), the park hosts the highest glacier (4061m) to exist entirely within Italian borders..

In Cogne, stay at quaint **Hotel Stambecco** (tel. 740 68; L28,000 for a single, L41,000 for a double). **Du Soleil** (tel. 740 33), on the main strip into town, has singles for L28,000 and doubles for L43,000. The latter also advertises the most economical *settimana bianca*—L200,000 for a week of bed and breakfast. Campers can choose between **Camping Gran Paradiso** (tel. 741 05; open June-Sept.), which charges L4500 per person and L4400 per tent, or the more popular **Lo Stambecco** (tel. 741 52; open June-Sept. 20) in the *località* of Valnontey (L5000 per person, L4800 per tent).

Valnontey is a wee hamlet in the midst of the national park, notable for its convenient *alimentari,* its cluster of two-star hotels, and the **Giardino Alpino Paradisia.** The inspiration for constructing a botanical garden amidst a barren scrubland at an altitude of 1700m struck during the Cogne Mountain Festival in 1955, no doubt aided by the downing of several bottles of wine. Practical complications notwithstanding, the thriving gardens boast a wide array of rare alpine vegetation, including—for all you insatiable thallophytophiles out there—a comprehensive display of lichen. (Open June 15-Sept. 15 9am-12:30pm and 2:30-6pm. Admission L3000.)

Cogne's **tourist office** (tel. 740 40) distributes maps of the park, a list of nearby *rifugi,* a brochure with bus schedules, and their ultra-helpful *Guide to Walks and Excursions,* which outlines hikes for all levels. Cogne is an easy bus ride from Aosta (8 per day, 50 min., L2100). The **telephone code** is 0165.

Courmayeur

Italy's oldest Alpine resort has become the jet set's newest playground. **Monte Bianco** (Mont Blanc) is the main attraction: its jagged ridges and unmelting snowfields lure tourists with unsurpassed opportunities for hiking and skiing. Prices are astronomical and rooms are booked solid summer and winter (reserve 6 months ahead), but in June the city shuts down while the shopkeepers take their own vacations.

The **AGIP** station at strada Regionale, 76 (tel. 84 24 27), 1km north on via Roma, charges the lowest rates in the city, singles going for L20,000, and doubles for L35,000 (L5000 more for each during high season). **Venezia** (tel. 84 24 61), up the hill to the left from p. Monte Bianco, has spiffy, genteel singles for L30,000 and doubles for L46,000.

Picnicking is the best option in this town of Michelin-starred eateries. At **Pastificio Gabriella,** passaggio del Angelo, 94, toward the *strada regionale* end of via Roma, you'll find excellent cold cuts and pâté garnished with Alpine violets. (Closed for 2 weeks in July.) **Il Fornaio,** at via Monte Bianco, 17, serves up scrumptious breads and pastries. Try the *Veneziane* (L1000). Wednesday is **market day** (8:30am-2pm) at nearby Dolonne (1km from Courmayeur).

Even white-week specials are exorbitant; bed-and-breakfast deals under L230,000 are a dream. Ski passes average L190,000, falling to L160,000 during the summer months. As always, nordic skiing, hiking, and boarding remain the cheapest alternatives. Pick up the seasonal brochure *Courmayeur; Mont Blanc* for a complete list of athletics facilities and rental shops. For even pricier thrills, take the *Funivia del Monte Bianco* to the border summit (L23,000, round-trip L32,000); from here, a descent into French Chamonix costs 153F (about L39,000). The swaying journey suspended among needle spires and a wasteland of snow and ice is a safe window into a savage land.

For hiking excursions in Italy, snag the bus that departs hourly from viale M. Bianco to **Combal Lake.** A beautiful six-hour hike awaits you on the road up the valley past *Rifugio Elisabetta* to where the path (marked by a "2" in a triangle) branches off to the left and clambers up to the Chavannes Pass (2603m). The trail then runs along Mont Perce, beneath the crest, until it reaches Mont Fortin (2758m), where it descends once again to Lake Combal. The view from Mont Fortin is breathtaking. The bus finally deposits you back at Courmayeur. A map is crucial on these jaunts; arm yourself with tips at the **Ufficio delle Guide** (tel. 84 20 64) in p. Abbe-Heurl, facing the stone-steepled church (open 9am-12:30pm and 3:30-7pm).

The English gentlemen who launched the first climbing expeditions of Monte Bianco in the 19th century brushed off the **Giro del Monte Bianco** as a two- or three-day tour for "less adventurous travelers who want to avoid the difficulties and dangers of the High Alps." Today, more level-headed local guides suggest that travelers take a week or more to complete the trip. The trail leads around Monte Bianco, past Chamonix and Courmayeur, and even into Switzerland. Refuges and hotel dormitories are spaced five or six hours apart all along the route. You need not invest a fortnight: one leg of the larger trail makes an ideal daytrip, and two sections can amply fill a weekend. This is serious mountaineering for which you should be properly and thoroughly equipped before you head out.

Buses access Courmayeur from all directions: Aosta (11 per day, 1 hr., L3100); Turin (6 per day, L11,000); and Chamonix (8 per day, L9000). Pick up a schedule at the **tourist office** (tel. 84 20 60), on p. Monte Bianco at the base of the town by the main road. The same omnipotent office complex houses the **bus station** (tel. 84 93 17), **currency exchange** (open 7:30am-8pm), and **post office** (tel. 84 20 42, **postal code:** 11013; open Mon.-Fri. 8:15am-6:30pm and Sat. 8:15am-1:40pm).

Liguria (Italian Riviera)

The crescent-shaped coastal strip of Liguria stretches 350km along the Mediterranean between France and Tuscany. Genoa, in the center, divides the coast into the Riviera di Levante (rising sun) below and to the east, and the Riviera di Ponente (setting sun) above and to the west. Ligurians are known for their cultural isolation; claiming Nordic, not Latin, ancestry, they have their own vocabulary and an accent incomprehensible to other Italians, let alone foreigners. Its distinctive character, however, has not prevented Liguria from playing a leading role in the unification of the Italian peninsula. Giuseppe Mazzini, known as the father of the *risorgimento*, and Giuseppe Garibaldi, the most popular hero of the *risorgimento*, were both Ligurians (although Garibaldi was actually born in Nice). Also, the famous red-shirted army that liberated southern Italy from the Bourbon monarchy was led by Ligurian sharpshooters.

Today, the region is one of Italy's most prosperous, led by Genoa, Italy's principal port. The maritime Alps tumble down to the ocean and protect Liguria from ugly northern weather, allowing the region to draw flowers, lemons, and olive oil from its soil, and visitors to its shores year-round. In summer the landscape comes ablaze with deep reds and purples, while lemon and almond blossoms scent the air; in winter, the olive trees that shade the robust flower beds produce what may be Italy's best oil (a slippery title contested by Tuscany).

The character of the Italian Riviera differs from that of its French neighbor. Here you'll find neither the arrogance nor the cultural sterility of Cannes or St. Tropez. The palm-lined boulevards and clear turquoise water are the same, but above these rise *città vecchie* or *alte* (old or upper cities), distinctly Italian mazes of narrow cobblestone streets. Unless you're gliding in languidly from France, you might do best by starting at the eastern edge of Liguria and working your way only as far as Genoa. Slightly more expensive, the eastern (Levante) coast is also more inviting. This region is less congested than Ponente, and the dramatic juxtaposition of Alps and ocean here creates a landscape where pine forests hover thousands of feet above the water, and where wee pebble beaches are often shaded by sharply chiselled escarpments. If you plan to stay closer to the French border in Ponente, consider Finale Ligure, a resort town with medieval ambience and infinite stretches of sandy beach. The area of the Ponente from mperia to the French border, known as the Riviera dei Fiori (Riviera of Flowers), nestles against gaudy Sanremo and other hyped-up vacation spots; it's the least alluring portion of the coast.

Getting around Liguria is no problem as all the coastal towns are linked by frequent trains on either the Genoa-La Spézia or Genoa-Ventimiglia line, and even more frequently by intercity buses that pass through all major towns. Boats connect the resort towns, and local buses run to the hill towns inland.

Riviera di Ponente

Ventimiglia

A former Roman municipality, Ventimiglia has long lost all vestiges of the splendor of its ancient and medieval past. The relics of a Roman theater remain to the east of town, and the 11th-century old city's winding streets across the river to the west manage to enchant some, nonetheless, modern Ventimiglia serves primarily as a point of departure for the French Côte d'Azur, within reach of all the famous Riviera oases. Unlike these retreats, however, Ventimiglia is also within reach of even the thinnest of money belts.

Orientation and Practical Information

Right on the French-Italian border, Ventimiglia is an important gateway in and out of the country. Frequent buses link it to the rest of the Riviera dei Fiori and parts of France while trains run to the Italian and French Riviera. (Nice: 10-25 per day, 40min., L6900; Genoa: 15 per day, 2hr. 30min., L12,100; Cannes: 25 per day, L18,800; Marseille: 9 per day, L35,100.) From the train station, cross the street and walk down via della Stazione. The second cross road is **via Cavour,** and the third is **via Roma.** Much of what you will need lurks on these two streets.

Tourist Office: via Cavour, 61 (tel. 35 11 83). Angela and Anna are the sweetest and most helpful officials on the Riviera. Pick up a town map and lots of brochures. Open Mon.-Sat. 9am-1pm and 3-7pm, Sun. 9am-noon and 3-6pm.

Currency Exchange: via Stazione 3/A (tel. 35 12 15), outside the station. No commission. Open Mon.-Sat. 8am-12:30pm and 2:30-7pm. Also in the train station. Open 24 hrs.

Post Office: via della Repubblica, 8 (tel. 35 13 12), toward the water. Open Mon.-Fri. 8:10am-5:30pm, Sat. 8:10am-noon. Closes at noon on the last working day of each month. **Postal Code:** 18039.

Telephones: At the restaurant in the train station (tel. 35 19 35). Open 24 hrs. **Telephone Code:** 0184.

Buses: Riviera Trasporti, via Cavour, 61 (tel. 35 12 51), next to the tourist office. Open Mon.-Sat. 7:30am-noon and 4-7pm, Oct.-March Mon.-Sat. 8:30am-noon and 4-7pm. On Sundays, get tickets at **Pasticceria Viale,** via Cavour, 626 (open daily 8am-noon and 3-8pm). To: San Remo (L2200), Bordighera (L1500), Imperia-Porto Maurizio (L5000, change in San Remo), as well as other local towns.

Bike Rental: Eurocicli, via Cavour, 85/A (tel. 35 18 79). L3000 per hour, L10,000 per day. Open Mon.-Sat. 8:30am-7:30pm, Sun. 9am-7:30pm; mid-Oct.-May Mon.-Sat. 8:30am-7:30pm.

Emergencies: tel. 113. **Police:** p. della Libertà, 1 (tel. 35 75 75 or 35 75 76). **Hospital: Ospedale Santo Spirito,** on via Basso (tel. 35 67 35).

Accommodations and Food

Ventimiglia is one of the Riviera's most inexpensive places to flop, but reserve rooms in July and August. Consider crossing the border and staying in the **youth hostel** (tel. (033) 93 35 93 14) in the nearby French town of Menton (15min. by train, L1600).

Cavour, via Cavour, 3 (tel. 35 13 66). Make a right on via Cavour as you come from the station. Respectable rooms and polite management. Doubles L36,500, with bath L45,000. Showers included.

XX Settembre, via Roma, 16 (tel. 35 12 22). Friendly and clean. Singles L16,000. Doubles L28,000. Full pension L50,000, half pension L36,000. Its restaurant serves a well-prepared L17,000 meal. Restaurant open Fri.-Wed. noon-3pm and 7:30-9:30pm. May be closed for vacation in June—call ahead.

Hotel Vittoria, via Hanbury, 5 (tel. 35 12 31). Make a left on the 1st cross street after exiting the station. Sparkling rooms and sweet owners. Curfew 12:30am. Singles L30,000. Doubles L60,000. Breakfast included. MC, Visa.

Camping Roma, via Peglia, 5 (tel. 335 80 or 35 76 13), 400m from the waterfront. Across the river from the station side of town, or at the "right" side of the old town as you approach it. L12,000 per person, L12,000 per tent; Sept.-July L7000 per person, L7000 per tent.

You will pay dearly for quality, sit-down meals. The two restaurants in the *pensioni* above serve good meals. Another excellent option is **Self-Service Hotel Suisse,** p. Battisti, 34 (tel. 35 11 28), outside the train station. Daily pasta specials start at L5000, entrees with side veggies at L7000; cover runs L1000. (Open daily noon-2:30pm and 7pm-midnight.) The covered **open-air market** which sprawls every morning along via della Repubblica, via Libertà, via Sant'Ambrosio, and via Roma is the best place to grab fresh produce. **Supermercato STANDA,** at the corner of via Roma and via Ruffini, is well-stocked with staples. (Open Mon.-Sat. 8:30am-7:30pm.) Many of the *pizzerie* lining the beach prepare personal-size take-out pizzas for about L2000.

Sights and Entertainment

Most of Ventimiglia's "entertainment" is centered on its **beach,** but a few treasures await the adventurous traveler willing to risk a decline in tan maintenance. To reach the **Cathedral** with its intricate Gothic portal and adjoining 11th-century baptistry, follow via Banchieri after the bridge into the old town and from there take via Falerina. **San Michele,** a Romanesque church of the same vintage is on the other side of town. Follow the signs off via Garibaldi to piazza Colleta (open Sun. 10:30am-noon). The well-preserved **Roman theater** anchors the **archeological zone** (tel. 381 31) off corso Genova to the east of the town. Turn left on via Cavour, and continue about 1km to find it between gas stations and railroad tracks. (The zone is now "closed," but you can view it perfectly well from corso Genova.)

A trip to the **Balzi Rossi** (Red Cliffs, tel. 381 13), 9km from Ventimiglia toward France, offers you a glimpse of an even earlier civilization. Take the blue Riveria Trasporti bus from the corner of via Cavour and via Ruffini in Ventimiglia (9-12 per day, 20min., L1500) to view the remains of Cro-Magnon troglodytes and the caves they time-shared. The most spectacular artifacts are housed in Balzi Rossi's **Prehistoric Museum** near the seaside. (Open Tues.-Sun. 9am-1pm and 2:30-6:30pm. Admission L4000, under 18 free.) Take the blue Riveria Trasporti bus (L1500) from via Cavour and via Martiri della Libertà to La Mortola to laze a day in the **Hanbury Gardens** (tel. 229 507). These world-famous botanical gardens stretch from the summit of Cape Mortola down to the sea and contain some of the world's most exquisite and exotic flora, culled from three continents. (Open daily 9am-6pm; off-season Thurs.-Tues. 10am-4pm. Admission L8500.)

Near Ventimiglia

Of the many valleys fanning inland from Ventimiglia, **Val di Nervia** is the most accessible. On foot, continue past the Roman theater to the Val di Nervia road on your left. You can also take the blue Riveria Trasporti bus from the train station in Ventimiglia (Campo Rosso is the nearest; 15min., L1500).

Riviera Trasporti also runs buses to the surrounding castle-topped hills. **Dolceacqua,** 9km from Ventimiglia, is crowned by a medieval castle and an old city whose narrow, twisting stone streets still bustle (L1800 by bus from the Ventimiglia train station). Turn right at the bottom of the new city and walk across the arched Roman bridge to the orange, pink, and green rococo **cathedral** at the bottom of the old city, then continue up the narrow streets to the wonderful **Castello dei Doria.** (Open Sept.-June daily 9am-noon and 3-7pm, July-Aug. Wed.-Mon. 10am-noon and 3-5:30pm. Admission L2000.) Pilgrims troop from Ventimiglia and the surrounding countryside to Dolceacqua for the biggest and tastiest pizza in the region at **Pizzeria La Rampa,** via Barberis, 11 (tel. 20 61 98), on the left side of the main *piazza* in the new town (overlooking the bridge and old city). (Open daily 7pm-midnight.) On August 15, the village celebrates **Ferragosto** with swirling regional dances, traditional costumes, and mouth-watering local pastries.

Bordighera

Bordighera is known as the "City of Palms." Legend has it that Sant'Ampelio brought the seeds from Egypt and planted them in the town's fertile soil. Today, the city proudly supplies the Vatican with the palm leaves for Holy Week. One of the most popular resorts on the Riviera di Ponente, balmy, palmy Bordighera has hosted an upscale crowd in its dramatically situated gardens and fortified old town ever since the British claimed this chunk of the Riviera.

Orientation and Practical Information

The bus from Ventimiglia (15min., L1300) drops you off along the main street, **via Vittorio Emanuele II,** which runs west from the city's train station. Most of the offices and shops line via Vittorio Emanuele, while the residential area sits uphill and farther inland.

Tourist Office: via Roberto, 1 (tel. 26 23 22), just past the small park. From the train station, go left on via Vittorio Emanuele, then take the 1st right on via Roberto. Doles out maps, hotel listings and information in English. Does not book rooms, but makes good suggestions. Open Mon.-Sat. 9am-12:30pm and 3:30-6pm, Sun. 9am-noon; Oct.-May Mon.-Sat. 9am-12:30pm and 2:30-5:30pm.

Post Office: (tel. 26 16 74), in p. Eroi della Libertà, also known as p. Stazione, next to the station. Open Mon.-Fri. 8:10am-6:30pm, Sat. 8:10am-noon. **Postal Code:** 18012.

Telephones: SIP, via Roberto, 18, across from the tourist office. Pay phones only. Open daily 8am-8pm. **Telephone Code:** 0184.

Emergency: tel. 113.

Accommodations and Food

In summer, most hotels want clients to stay several days and require that they accept full or half-pension.

Villa Loreto, via Giulio Cesare, 37 (tel. 29 43 32). Take via Vittorio Emanuele left from station for 200m then go right on orange-tree-lined via Rossi and left on via Aldo Moro, which leads into via Cesare. Women and married couples only. A hike, but the nuns provide the lowest prices and best company around in their palatial, tranquil residence graced by palm and lemon trees. Curfew 10:30pm; Sept.-June 9pm. They only give rooms with full pension (L48,000-53,000 per person, depending on the size of the room and whether it's with bath).

Villa Miki, via Lagazzi, 14 (tel. 26 18 44), off via Vittorio Emanuele about 100m down from the station. Small rooms, but a serene setting, firm beds, and balconies overlooking the town and valleys. L28,000 per person. Showers and breakfast included. Full or half-pension required during summer and Easter, L45,000-55,000 per person.

Albergo Nagos, p. Eroi della Libertà, 7 (tel. 26 04 57). A warm reception and private showers await you at this friendly pension. Singles L25,000. Doubles L35,000. Full pension (L48,000) required July-Aug., half-pension (L43,000) required May-June and Sept.

The *trattorie* in the old city serve the cheapest sit-down meals. For picnics, try the **mercato coperto,** p. Garibaldi (open Tues.-Sat. 7am-1pm) or the **Supermercato STANDA,** via Libertà, 32 (open Mon.-Sat. 8:30am-12:30pm and 3:30-7:30pm). **Trattoria degli Amici,** via Lunga, 2 (tel. 26 15 79), in the *città alta,* serves *lasagne con funghi porcini* (with fresh mushrooms) for L8500. Cover runs a hefty L4000. (Open Jan.-Oct. Tues.-Sun. noon-2pm and 7-11pm.)

Sights and Entertainment

If you're game for a lovely but lengthy walk, head east along via Romana. Fork off onto via Rossi, where cannons still stand sentinel above an awesome expanse of deep blue sea. Take the steps down to the **Church of Sant'Ampeglio,** built around the grotto where Ampeglio the hermit holed up. (Open Sun. at 10am or knock on the door. Also open May 14, for the festival of Sant'Ampeglio.) Bordighera's omnipresent **beach** is presided over by lungomare Argentina, so dubbed because Evita Peron herself inaugurated it.

In late July and August, Bordighera holds the **Salone Internazionale Umorismo** (tel. 26 17 27), an international humor festival with performances and exhibits in the Palazzo del Parco (the same building as the tourist office).

Sanremo

The first and still the largest resort on the Italian Riviera, Sanremo was once the glamorous retreat of high-rolling heirs and heir-seeking flappers (not to mention high-rolling heiresses and heiress-seeking gigolos). The high prices persist, though tawdry casinos, shabby cabanas, and hyperactive tourism are all that remain of its one-time eminence. Like Sestri Levante on the Riviera di Levante, Sanremo is an expensive, avoidable annoyance—don't stop unless you're looking for a gambling opportunity. The terminally hopeful can relive Sanremo's glory days at the Edwardian **Casino,** corso Inglesi, 18 (tel. 53 40 01). The entrance fee is only L15,000, though you must be 18 to enter and men must wear coat and tie. Blackjack begins at 8:30pm, but early gamblers can play roulette starting at 2:30pm. The "American Room" of one-armed bandits has neither dress code nor entrance fee, and lures early risers with its 11am opening. All the "fun" stops at 2:30am.

Dolcedo

An unforgettable excursion into the Ligurian hinterland can be launched from Imperia (an unpleasant modern town along the Riviera). A 7km trip through sunny groves that produce Liguria's best olive oil leads to the medieval village of **Dolcedo.** Stroll across the bridge on which the Knights of Malta carved "mcclxxxxii die 3 juli hoc opus perfectum fuit" ("on 3 July 1292 this work was finished") to the old market square. Make a right on via de Amicis to the **Church of San Tommaso.** Inspired by the pink and green exterior, the decorators went wild inside, leaving one half pink and green and the other blue and gold. Stop for lunch at the moderately priced **Ristorante Da Tunu** (tel. 28 00 13), where a full meal costs less than L15,000, wine L5000 per three-quarters of a liter. *Cinghiale* (wild boar) is an autumn specialty. (Cover L1500. Open Tues.-Sun. noon-2:30pm and 7-9:30pm.) Riviera Trasporti buses (towards Prela) leave p. Dante in Imperia for Dolcedo 11-15 times per day. Buy tickets at any *tabaccheria* in town (L1800).

Cervo, a medieval hillside village by the sea, enchants with white houses, red roofs, and stone archways. Take the *locale* along the Ventimiglia-Genoa line. Cervo hosts an international chamber music festival in July and August, held in front of the Baroque **Church of San Giovanni Battista.**

Finale Ligure

Eschewing the glamor and arrogance of other Riviera towns, Finale Ligure welcomes weary backpackers with soft sand, luxurious flora, and inviting oceanside tea-rooms.

Orientation and Practical Information

The city divides into three sections, **Finalmarina** in the center, **Finalpia** to the east, and **Finalborgo,** the old city, to the west. The **train station** is in Finalmarina, as are most places listed below.

Tourist Office: IAT, via San Pietro, 14, (tel. 69 25 81 or 69 25 82), on the "real street" overlooking the sea (as opposed to the *lungomare*, which isn't a proper "street"). Loquacious Luisa has been here for over 30 years and knows her stuff. Motherly help for all of your problems, as well as a great map. Open Mon.-Sat. 8am-1pm and 4-7pm; off-season Mon.-Sat. 8am-1pm and 3-6pm, Sun. 8:30am-12:30pm. The **Associazione Alberghi** (tel. 69 42 52), across from the station in a camper-like office, helps you find rooms in the summer. Open June-Sept. 15 Mon.-Fri. 9am-8pm, Sun. 9am-8:30pm.

Currency Exchange: Try the Casa di Risparmio, via Garibaldi, 3. Open Mon.-Fri. 8am-1:45pm and 2:45-4:30pm, Sat. 8am-1pm. The San Paolo bank takes liberties with a L5000 commission.

Post Office: via Concezione, 29 (tel. 69 28 38). Open Mon.-Fri. 8:10am-6pm, Sat. 8:10-noon. **Postal code:** 17024.

Telephones: SIP, via Roma, 33. Pay phones, directories, and vending machines selling tokens and phone cards. Open June 1-Sept. 30 8am-11pm; Oct. 1-May 31 8am-8pm. If it's late, try the phones at **Bar Casanova,** via Brunenghi, 75 (tel. 69 56 15), behind the train station. Open Mon.-Sat. 6:30am-1:30am. Also a phone in the station. **Telephone Code:** 019.

Trains: p. Vittorio Veneto (tel. 69 27 77). Constant service to: Genoa (L5000), Ventimiglia (L6500), and Santa Margherita Ligure (L7200).

Buses: SAR, via Aurelia, 28 (outside and to the left of the train station). Ticket office open Mon.-Sat. 7am-1pm. On Sunday, buy tickets at Bar Sport, across the *piazza,* or at one of the other listed agents. To: Borgo Verezzi (L1100), Savona (L2800), Albenga (L2200), and other towns. All buses leave from in front of the station. Orange **city buses** to Finalborgo, L1000.

Bike Rental: Oddone, via Colombo, 20 (tel. 69 42 15), on the street behind the tourist office. Bikes: 9am-12:30pm, L8000; 3-8pm, L10,000; 9am-8pm L15,000. Tandems: 9am-12:30pm, L20,000; 3-8pm, L22,000; 9am-8pm, L25,000. Mountain bikes: L10,000 for 1hr., L30,000 half-day, L50,000 full day. You must leave your passport and a deposit. Open daily 8am-12:30pm and 3-8pm. MC, Visa.

Pharmacy: via Ghiglieri, 2, off via Pertica. Open Mon.-Fri. 8:30am-12:30pm and 4-8pm. A posted sign shows which pharmacies are open when this one isn't.

Emergencies: tel. 113. **Police:** via Brunanghi, 68 (tel. 69 26 66). **Guardia Medica:** 8pm-8am and Sat. 2pm-Mon. 8am, tel. 64 77 77. If you need to get to the **hospital** (tel. 69 07 95), call one of the following *AUTO LETTIGA* service numbers—cheaper and more reliable than a taxi: (tel. 69 23 33 in Marina, 69 13 25 in Borgo, 69 83 32 in Varigotti, 64 66 66 for the hospital's own service).

Accommodations

Go to the Associazone Alberghi first—it could save you a trek. The hostel is your best bet in July and August. Rooms in private homes can be arranged through the tourist office.

Youth Hostel: Castello Uvillermin (HI) (tel. 69 05 15), on via Generale Caviglia in a turreted castle overlooking the sea. From the station, take a left onto v. Torino. At the tiny p. Milano, turn left and go up the stairs. Cross the street and continue uphill (via staircase); when you get to the top, turn right onto v. Caviglia. A small sign and, yes, another set of steps marks the way up to the castle, on your left. The view makes the climb worthwhile. Crowded in summer, with the (somewhat rustic) facilities strained to their breaking point, but still cheap and convivial. Cristina fixes great meals (L12,000). No phone reservations, and no groups in July-Aug. Reception open 7-9:30am and 5-10:30pm. Curfew 11pm; July-Aug. 11:30pm. Check-in 5pm, but you can leave your bags 7-9:30am. Doors locked until 7am. L14,000 per person, sheets and breakfast included. HI card required, and can be bought for L30,000, or pay L5000 extra. Open March 15-Oct. 15.

Albergo San Marco, via della Concezione, 22 (tel. 69 25 33), the street facing the beach, down from the station. Spotless rooms, all with bath. You could eat off the floor (yum!). Doubles L60,000. Triples L70,000. Breakfast included. June-Sept. full pension required: L55,000 per person in June, L62,000 in July, L70,000 Aug. 1-15, L65,000 Aug. 16-31, L57,000 Sept. 1-15, L52,000 Sept. 16-30. Closed Oct.

Albergo Cirio, via Pertica, 15 (tel. 69 23 10), in the center of town. Super-friendly family atmosphere. Singles L25,000, with bath L30,000. Doubles L50,000, with bath L60,000. Triples L60,000, with bath L70,000. Breakfast included. In July-Aug. half-pension is required at L45,000 per person. AmEx, MC, Visa.

Camping: Il Mulino (tel. 60 16 69), on via Piemonte. To get here from the station, take the bus for Calvisio from the stop outside at via Torino and get off at the Boncardo Hotel. From here, take via Porro, go left under an arch onto via Castelli; follow it uphill and look for the signs for the campsite. Believe it or not, this is the closest campground to the beach. Bar and restaurant on the premises, but no proper laundry. L7000 per person, L6000 per tent; off-season L6000 and L4500. Open April-Sept.

Food

Trattorie and *pizzerie* line the streets closest to the beach. Pay less for comparable fare farther inland along via Rossi and via Roma.

Spaghetteria Il Posto, via Porro, 19. An elegant and creative pasta house with an unusual menu. Try the *penne zar* (pasta with salmon and caviar, L8500) or the *penne pirata* (with shrimp and salmon, L8500). Cover L1500. Open Tues.-Sun. 7:30-10:30pm. Closed for approx. 1 month after Easter.

Salumeria Della Chiesa, via Pertica, 13 (tel. 69 25 16), near the train station, is the perfect place to pack a picnic lunch for the beach. *Insalata di mare* (seafood salad) L3500 per *etto.* Lasagna L1500 per *etto.* Open daily 7:30am-1pm and 4-8pm; Oct.-May Mon.-Wed. and Fri.-Sat. 7:30am-1pm and 4-7pm, Thurs. 7:30am-1pm. The same management runs a restaurant around the corner on via Gandolino, with *primi* from L6000. Open Mon.-Sat. noon-2pm.

Paninoteca Pilade, via Garibaldi, 67 (tel. 69 22 20), off p. Vittorio Emanuele. Some of the best *panini* on the Riviera (L3000-5000). Pizza by the slice (L1800). MTV, old Coke posters, and cheap food. What more do you want? Beer L2500-4000, wine L1300. Open daily 10am-1am; off-season 10am-2:30pm and 4-8pm.

Bei Gisela, via Colombo, 2. *Jawohl!* If you're hankering for kitsch, a bit of Deutschland, or just good beer on tap, here's the place. Löwenbräu memorabilia everywhere. *Primi* from L6000, beer on tap L2200. Open daily 10:30am-2:30pm and 6:30-10:30pm for dinner, 3:30pm-midnight for boozing and schmoozing. Sept.-June closed Wed.

Sights and Entertainment

Enclosed within its still-intact ancient walls, **Finalborgo,** a 1km walk up via Brunenghi from the station, is a Renaissance city in miniature. The Baroque **Basilica di San Biago,** inside the city walls through the *Porta Reale* entrance off via Brunenghi, boasts an elegant 13th-century octagonal clock tower. The looming 12th-century **Castel San Giovanni** is closed to the public. The **Chiostro di S. Caterina,** a five-minute walk across town from the *Porta Reale,* is a 14th-century edifice housing the **museo civico.** (Open Tues.-Sat. 10am-noon and 3-6pm, Sun. 9am-noon; Oct.-May Tues.-Sat. 9am-noon and 2:30-4:30pm. Admission L3000.)

Closer to the beach at the waterfront in **Finalmarina,** you can climb the steps at the intersection of via Colombo and via Torino to the lofty 14th-century **Castelfranco.** World War II ravaged much of this structure, but it has recently been restored, and the view is tremendous. (May be closed in 1993; ask at the tourist office for hours and admission charge, if any.)

The towns surrounding Finale Ligure invite discovery. Take an SAR bus to tiny **Borgo Verezzi.** Get off at the first stop in the town of Borgio. From here, five buses leave daily for Verezzi. From mid-July through August, performances animate **Teatro di Verrezzi,** the town's outdoor theater in the main *piazza.* The performing company is one of Italy's most renowned, featuring many noted Italian thespians. (Admission about L25,000. Call the Borgo Verezzi tourist office at (019) 61 51 54 or 61 51 16 for details.)

Nighttime fun in Finale throbs and splashes at the **Sporting Club** (tel. 69 13 22), a combination swimming pool/disco. The club runs a free shuttle, which leaves every hour 10am-midnight from the Hotel Boncardo, corso Europa, 4, to the club in nearby San Bernardino. (Open June-Sept. 15 for swimming only, daily 11am-7pm, L8000 per person; for swimming and dancing, daily 9:30pm-3am, Sun.-Fri. L15,000 per person, Sat. L25,000 per person. One non-chlorinated drink included.) Or try the pricey, meat-markety **Scotch Club,** on via S. Pietro (tel. 69 24 81).

Genoa (Génova)

An entanglement of dispiriting, shop-filled streets, Genoa exists today as a rank, wild trading port. A strategic location has brought it security and trade; by the late 13th century, having defeated Pisa, the reach of the Genoan empire extended as far as North Africa, Syria, and the Crimea. Crusades and colonial profits allowed its leading families to endow the city with parks, palaces, and a generous store of art. Venice overwhelmed Genoa in 1380, and the city languished under foreign domination until it was swept up in the fires of the Risorgimento. Renowned *Genovesi* include Christopher Columbus, the Risorgimento ideologue Giuseppe Mazzini, and virtuoso violinist Niccolò Paganini. Thinly spread between craggy hills and the sparkling waters of the Mediterranean, Genova occupies three dimensions, north-south, east-west, and, most importantly, up-down. The most useful form of public transportation in this city of rapidly ascending streets are the prolific public elevators and cog-rail trollies. Heavily rebuilt after World War II bombing, the city's commercial center does not merit a visit. Instead, stick to the *creuze,* the narrow footpaths that wind their way upwards among houses, overhanging gardens, and numerous cats; these trails offer spectacular views and a peaceful respite from the chaos of the modern city.

Orientation and Practical Information

Unlike most Italian cities, Genoa's center does not lie at the *duomo,* or even in the oldest quarter of the *centro storico,* but around the decidedly more modern 19th-century p. de Ferrari. Most visitors arrive at one of Genoa's two train stations, **Genova Principe** or **Genova Brignole.** Buses #33 and 37 connect the two stations (25min., L1000). From Brignole take bus #40 and from Principe take #41 to the center of town at p. de Ferrari. The city stretches along the coast; the main streets leading west to Stazione Principe from p. de Ferrari are **via XXV Aprile, via Garibaldi** and then **via Balbi. Via XX Settembre** runs east in the direction of Stazione Brignole. The tourist offices give out free maps, but their street indexes are woefully inadequate, and most of the smaller streets' names aren't marked. This map will probably serve only to get you completely lost, especially if you attempt to venture into the *centro storico.* Procure a decent map; Genoa's tangled streets can stump even a native.

Genoa's double sequence of street numbers (red for commercial establishments, black for residential or office buildings) is incredibly confusing, especially since dirty red numerals often appear black. Don't be fooled if you come to the supposed address of a place and it is not there; chances are that you have simply come to the number of the wrong color.

The *centro storico* preserves many of Genoa's most important monuments; unfortunately, it is also the city's most dangerous quarter, riddled with drugs and prostitution. The problem is complicated by the labyrinthine streets; you'll need a sixth sense of navigation, even with a map, and it's an extremely bad place to get lost. Don't wander the area after dark or on shop-closed Sundays; and be cautious in deserted Genoan August. But do visit: the sights are well worth seeing.

Tourist Office: EPT, via Roma, 11 (tel. 54 15 41, fax 58 14 08), up 2 flights off p. Corvetto. From Stazione Brignole, go right on via de Amicis to p. Brignole, then continue up via Serra to p. Corvetto. Friendly but seems disorganized. Archaic information on hotels and museums. Pick up a copy of *Succede a Genova,* a glossy handout jam-packed with listings of upcoming cultural events and tons of useful information. English spoken. Open Mon.-Fri. 8am-1:30pm and 2-5pm, Sat. 8am-1:30pm. There are train station **branches** at both Principe (tel. 26 26 33) and Brignole (tel. 56 20 56). Open daily 8am-8pm.

Budget Travel: CTS, via San Vincenzo, 117r (tel. 56 43 66), off p. Verdi near Stazione Brignole. Student fares to all destinations. **Associazione Albergatori per la Gioventù,** via Cairoli, 2 (tel. 29 82 84), near p. Nunziata. HI cards. Both open Mon.-Fri. 9am-12:15pm and 3-7:30pm.

Consulates: U.S., p. Portello, 6 (tel. 28 27 41). Business matters and emergencies only. For passports and visas contact the consulate in Milan (tel. (02) 290 018 41). Open Mon.-Fri. 9am-noon. **U.K.,** via XII Ottobre, 2 (tel. 56 48 33). Open Mon.-Fri. 9am-noon and 4-7pm.

Currency Exchange: Banks abound: Sat.-Sun. head to the train station, which gives slightly lower rates, but only takes L500 commission. Open daily 7am-10pm.

American Express: Viatur, piazza Fontane Marose, 3 (tel. 56 12 41), inside a travel agency. L3000 for mail inquiry without AmEx card or AmEx traveler's checks. Does not actually handle money, but will authorize **check cashing** for cardmembers (they give you an authorization, which you take to a bank to get your *lire*). Open Mon.-Fri. 9am-12:30pm and 3-6:45pm.

Post Office: Central office, via Dante, off p. de Ferrari, may very well still be under renovation in 1993. If so, go to the office at v. D'Annunzio, 34 (tel. 160 for central information at either office) for **Fermo Posta** or express mail service. From piazza de Ferrari, follow via Dante 2 blocks to p. Dante; take via D'Annunzio, on your right. The post office will be on the left-hand side, on the pedestrian level above the roadway. Both the central office and the temporary main office at via D'Annunzio keep the same hours. Open Mon.-Sat. 8:15am-7:40pm. Tel. 160 for **central information** at either office. Convenient offices (without Fermo Posta) in the Stazione Principe and across the street from the Stazione Brignole. All open Mon.-Fri. 8:15am-8pm, Sat. 8:15am-1pm. **Postal Code:** 16100.

Telephones: ASST, in the post office, has the shortest lines. Open daily 8am-8pm. Other ASST phones at via XX Settembre, 139 (open Mon.-Sat. 8am-11:50pm, Sun. 8am-9pm) and Stazione Brignole (open 8:15am-9:15pm). **Telephone Code:** 010.

Flights: C. Colombo Internazionale (tel. 24 11), in sestiere Ponente. European destinations. Buses depart for the airport from the last platform in the *piazza* 1hr. before scheduled flights (L4000).

Trains: Stazione Principe (tel. 241 21), in p. Acquaverde. **Stazione Brignole** (tel. 58 63 50), in p. Verdi. For train information, call 28 40 81, 7am-11pm. Trains run from both stations to points along the Ligurian Riviera and to major Italian cities. To Turin (10 per day, 2hr., L12,100) and Rome (15 per day, 5-6hr., L33,600).

Buses: AMT, via D'Annunzio, 8r (tel. 599 71). 1-way fares L1000. All-day tourist passes L3000 (foreign passport necessary).

Ferries: Stazione Marittima, tel. 26 14 66. Major destinations are Porto Torres (Sardinia), and Palermo, but each could be reached more cheaply and conveniently from elsewhere. Listed fares are 1-way deck class. **Grandi Traghetti** (tel. 58 93 31 or 26 71 28). To Sicily (22hr., July 23-Aug. 10, L100,000). **Tirrenia** (tel. 25 80 41). To Sardinia (L41,800-53,500). **Corsica Ferries:** (tel. 59 33 01). To Corsica (6hr., L44,000).

Boat Excursions: Cooperativa Battellieri del Porto di Genoa, tel. 26 57 12. Guided boat tours of Genoa's port from the Stazione Marittima (daily at 10am and 2pm, 40min., L4000). Trips to the Cinque Terre (L17,000, round-trip L27,000) and Portofino (L10,000, round-trip L17,000).

Hitchhiking: Hitchers take bus #17, 18, 19, or 20 from Stazione Brignole to the Genoa West entrance, where highways lead to points north and south.

English Bookstore: Bozzi, via Cairoli, 2r (tel. 29 87 42). Open Mon.-Fri. 8:30am-7pm, Sat. 8:30am-8:30pm. Closed 1 wk. in Aug.

Public Baths: Diurno, sottopassaggio de Ferrari, 67r (tel. 56 49 80), in the underpass in front of the bombed-out theater in p. de Ferrari. Showers L3500, bath L5000. Towels L1000. Shampoo L500. Open Mon.-Sat. 7:45am-7:30pm, Sun. 7:45am-noon.

Swimming Pool: Piscina Communale, via G. B. d'Albertis. Admission L2500. Open Mon., Wed., and Fri.-Sat. 8:30am-noon and 4-7:30pm.

Pharmacies: tel. 192 for the name of an all-night pharmacy. **Pescetto,** via Balbi, 185r (tel. 26 26 97), is usually open all night.

Laundry: Lavanderia Contini, p. Paolo da Novi, 37 (tel. 56 24 83). Near Stazione Brignole. L9000 per load for washing, L11,000 for drying. (Figure out a way to air-dry your clothes!) Open Mon.-Fri. 8:30am-12:30pm and 3:30-7:30pm.

Emergencies: tel. 113. **Police:** via Diaz (tel. 536 61). Ask for the *ufficio stranieri* (office for foreigners). **Hospital: Ospedale San Martino,** viale Benedetto XV, 10 (tel. 353 51). **Ambulance:** tel. 570 59 51.

Accommodations and Camping

Genoa must have more one-star hotels per capita than any other city in Italy, so finding cheap shelter isn't a problem. Finding someplace you'd also want to stay is. Almost without exception, budget lodgings in the *centro storico* (historical center) and near the port prefer to rent rooms by the hour, and no one should stay here at night. Go for the hostel, or stick to the area around Stazione Brignole; the establishments are substantially nicer and more secure. Rooms get scarce only in October, when Genoa hosts nautical conventions.

Ostello Per La Gioventù (HI), via Costanzi, 120 (tel. 24 22 457). From Stazione Principe, take bus #35 for 5 stops, then transfer to bus #40 (which you can take direct from Brignole). Ride #40 to the end of the line, just uphill from the hostel. Brand-spanking new, with panoramic views of the city and incredible facilities: free luggage lockers outside each room, reading lights by each bed, elevators, bar and self-serve restaurant (L12,000 per meal). TV and reading rooms, laundry (L12,000 for 8kg) and maps and brochures. Excellent wheelchair access. Parking and payphones available, too. Checkout 9am; office closed 9am-6pm. Curfew 11:30pm. Max. 3-day stay. HI card required. L18,000 per night, sheets and breakfast included. Open year-round.

Casa della Giovane, p. Santa Sabina, 4 (tel. 20 66 32 or 28 18 02), near p. Annunziata. Women only. An excellent deal, it's clean and feels safe. Rooms most plentiful on weekends and in the summer. Strict curfew 10:45pm. Singles L20,000. Doubles L36,000. Triples L45,000. Quads L52,000. Breakfast included. Meals in restaurant only L10,000.

Pensione Mirella, via Gropallo, 4 (tel. 83 93 772). From Stazione Brignole, go right on via de Amicis to p. Brignole and go right again. In a beautifully maintained and secure building. Large, clean, and elegantly furnished rooms and pleasant proprietor. Singles L30,000. Doubles L45,000. Make reservations. **Albergo Carola** (tel. 89 13 40), 2 flights up. An excellent alternative. Singles L27,000. Doubles L46,000.

Pensione Barone, via XX Settembre, 2 (tel. 58 75 78), off via Fiume. Small establishment on the 3rd floor. Handsome rooms with baroque designs on the ceilings. Curfew 1am. Singles with shower L30,000, with shower and private toilet L35,000. Doubles with shower L46,000, with shower and private toilet L55,000. MC, Visa. If they are full, ask about their other hotel, **The Garden,** which should be restored by '93.

Camping: The area around Genoa teems with campgrounds, but many are booked solid during July and Aug. Options in the city are scarce and often unsavory; try for something on the beach. **Villa Doria,** via Vespucci, 25 (tel. 68 06 13), in Pegli. Take the train or bus #1, 2, or 3 from p. Caricamento to Pegli, then walk or transfer to bus #93 up via Vespucci. The closest campground west of the city. English spoken. L5000 per person, L12,000 per tent.

Food

Partaking of the culinary offerings of Genoa may inflict grave damage on your waistline, but your purse and palate will be most pleased. The *trattoria* is still very much alive in this city, and local specialties abound. *Pesto,* the Genovese pride and joy, is an incomparable pasta sauce made from ground basil, pine nuts, garlic, and *parmigiano,* and served with olive oil. Although *pesto* has spread joy throughout the world, you can only taste the real product in Genoa, for the basil has a special smooth quality to it, without the slight taste of mint; eat it in the traditional manner, over *trenette* cooked with potatoes. Other Genovese specialties include *pansotti,* ravioli stuffed with spinach and ricotta, served with a creamy walnut sauce; also try the *parinata,* a fried bread made from chick-pea flour, and the *polpettone,* a baked composite of mashed potatoes and beans sprinkled with bread crumbs. Accompany any meal with loads of oil-soaked *foccacia,* a delicious flat bread topped with herbs, olives, onions, or cheese, and a specialty of nearby Recco. The *centro storico* hosts the best *trattorie* at the best prices, so eat a big lunch and skip dinner, because you don't want to navigate this area at night. Near Brignole, borgo Incrociati teems with small family-run restaurants; wander around to check out the daily specials—your best bet for dinner.

Osteria da Colombo e Bruno, borgo Incrociati, 44r. A traditional *trattoria* frequented at lunch by local workers. The *menù* (L11,000), including *primo, secondo,* vegetable, fruit, bread, water, and wine, can't be beat. Open Mon.-Sat. 12:30-2:30pm and 7:30-10pm. Closed in Aug.

Sa Pesta, via Giustiniani, 16r, near p. Matteotti. Sa Pesta knows *pesto;* everyone from doctors to dockworkers converge here for lunch to wolf down incomparably prepared "Zenovese" specialties like *farinata* and *minestrone alla genovese* (with *pesto*). Primi L5000-7000; *secondi* L6000-8000. Fixed-price menu offered. Open Mon.-Sat. noon-2:30pm. Closed in Aug.

Bakari, vicolo della Fieno, 16r, off p. Soriglia in the *centro storico.* A chlorophyll-colored restaurant that packs 'em in at lunch. Choose from 6 different fixed-price *menùs,* including 3 different vegetarian dinners. Prices range from L10,000 for a beggar's banquet to L20,000 for a regal feast. All meals include at least *primo, secondo,* vegetable, dessert, water, wine, and bread. Open Mon.-Thurs. noon-2:30pm and 7-9:15pm, Fri. noon-2:30pm. (Dinners cost 10% more than lunch.)

Kilt 2 Self Service, vicolo Doria, in the shade of p. San Matteo in the *centro storico.* A cafeteria set-up that dishes out otherworldly gourmet meals for a fixed price of L12,500. Menus change daily, but keep an eye out for the *mussels marinara*—they would send even Julia Child into ecstasy. Open Mon.-Sat. noon-2:30pm.

Brera Express, on via Brera, (tel. 54 32 80). Just off via XX Settembre, near Stazione Brignole. *Pizzeria* and full-service, but the best deal is the cafeteria-style *prezzo fisso* menu—L14,500 for a full meal including beverage. Open Mon.-Fri. 11:30am-3pm and 7pm-midnight. (Self-service closes at 10pm.)

Focacceria Daniel, via San Vicenzo, 185r (tel. 56 67 70), off v. XX Settembre. Bakes up a wide variety of tasty *focaccie* (L1600 per *etto*). Open daily 7am-7:30pm.

Sights

From Principe to the Centro Storico

Genoa's commercial connections have procured fine collections of Oriental, Flemish, and Italian art. Witness the city's penchant for exquisite architecture in the open and airy Stazione Principe, graced by a small square with a statue of Christopher Columbus, and also in the distant view of the port. Nearby, just before the *palazzo*-lined **via Balbi** on via S. Giovanni, lies one of Genoa's oldest monuments, the Romanesque church **San Giovanni di Pre'.** The stone vaulted roof and the feeble light that filters into the church heighten its Romanesque weight and cavernous solidity. Next door, **La Commenda,** built in the late 12th century, quartered the Knight Commanders of St. John.

Via Balbi, the heart of Genoa's university quarter, preserves some of the most lavish *palazzi* in Genoa. At #17, the fine courtyard of the 18th-century **Palazzo Reale** (Royal Palace) once opened onto a beautiful seaside garden; now it looks out on a major road and construction cranes. Upstairs, the **Galleria d'Arte** (tel. 20 68 51) provides a glimpse into the lifestyles of 18th-century Genovese nobility, with paintings by Tintoretto, van Dyck, and Bassano. (Open daily 9am-1:30pm. Admission L4000. Under 18 free.) The street runs into p. Nunziate, formerly called "Gaustato" (broken) for the large number of ruins in the square. Today it typifies the Genovese square: small, irregular, and distinguished by formal *palazzi.* The severe neoclassical façade (1843) of the **Church of SS. Annunziata** (1591-1620) conceals incongruously rococo innards which resemble King Midas's personal residence. The gold-washed interior was almost entirely reconstructed after suffering heavy damage during World War II bombing raids. Although the chapels that line the aisles do not preserve any great masterpieces, they form an impressive gallery of 17th-century art. (Open daily 6:30am-1:30pm and 3:30-6:30pm.)

Wander down the bookstore-strangled via Cairoli to **via Garibaldi,** the most impressive street in Genoa, bedecked with elegant *palazzi.* Wander into their courtyards; each *palazzo* conceals impressive frescoes, fountains, or leafy gardens complete with goldfish pools.

The **Palazzo Bianco** (1548, rebuilt 1712) at via Garibaldi, 11 (tel. 29 18 03), now houses one of the city's most important collections of Ligurian art as well as its grandest gathering of Dutch and Flemish paintings. (Open Tues.-Sat. 9am-7pm, Sun. 9am-noon. Admission L4000. Under 18 free.) Next door at via Garibaldi, 9, **Palazzo Doria Tursi,** now the city hall, showcases Niccolò Paganini's violin, the *Guarneri del Gesù.* The sounds of this instrument broke the hearts of many, drove others to suicide, and persuaded the rest that they were hearing angels singing. The violin is still used on rare occasions to perform Paganini's works, but with less extreme consequences. (Open Mon.-Sat. 9am-noon and 2-5pm. Free.) **Palazzo Rosso,** via Garibaldi, 18, built in the 17th century, houses magnificent furnishings and a lavishly frescoed interior. Today it plays host to the **Galleria di Palazzo Rosso** (tel. 28 26 41). Several full-length van

Dyck portraits grace the second floor, as does Bernardo Strozzi's masterpiece, *La Cuoca.* (Open Tues.-Sat. 9am-7pm, Sun. 9am-noon. Admission L4000. Under 18 free.)

The *galleria* faces the vigorous Renaissance façade of the **Palazzo Municipale** (1564-70) and its beautiful roof gardens. The courtyard of the **Palazzo Podestà** (1565), via Garibaldi, 7, contains an unusual grotto fountain and an intriguing stucco decoration of a merman. **Palazzo Parodi** (1578), via Garibaldi, 3, boasts an elegant doorway with noseless telemons, a tribute to the owner's ancestor, Megollo Lecari, who took revenge on his enemies by chopping off their noses and ears. Via Garibaldi spills into p. Fontane Marose, from which p. del Portello is the base for a public elevator (L400) that whisks you up to **p. Castelletto.** The *piazza* maintains an extraordinary vista over the entire city and port. From p. Portello a *funicolare* (L1000) also departs for the **Chiesa di Sant'Anna.** A harmonious Renaissance work, Sant'Anna is also notable for its location, poking out precariously from the steep hillside among leafy gardens. One of Genoa's most beautiful and peaceful *creuze* (footpaths) descends from the church among trees, *palazzi,* and omnipresent felines.

From p. Fontane Marose, salita di Santa Caterina takes you to piazza Corvetto. The **Villetta Di Negro** spreads out along the hill to your left, inviting you to relax amid waterfalls, grottos, and terraced gardens. At its summit stands a fantastic museum of Oriental art, the **Museo d'Arte Orientale E. Chiossone** (tel. 54 22 85). The first floor houses impressive sculptures; check out the dimunitive dog-dragon. (Open Tues.-Sat. 9am-7pm, Sun. 9am-12:30pm. Admission L4000. Under 18 free.) From p. Corvetto, via Roma leads to **piazza de Ferrari,** the city's bustling and pompous center, home to a monstrous fountain resembling a raised hubcap.

Off p. de Ferrari lie p. Matteotti and the **Palazzo Ducale,** once the home of the city's rulers. Inside, visit the two beautiful courtyards, one punctuated by an elegant 17th-century fountain. Standing kitty-corner to this imposing palace is the ornate **Church of the Gesù** (also known as SS. Ambrogio e Andrea; 1549-1606). This Baroque edifice features *trompe l'oeil* effects, double cupolas, and two important Rubens canvases, *The Circumcision* and *St. Ignatius Healing a Woman Possessed of the Devil.*

The Centro Storico

The unkempt and often dangerous historical center is a mass of duplicitous streets bordered by the port, via Garibaldi, and p. de Ferrari. Due to its crime, prostitution and drugs, the historic center is an advisable spot for tourists only during weekdays when stores are open; at night the quarter's underground elements crawl out and not even the police venture in. But the *centro storico* is also home to Genoa's most memorable monuments: the *duomo* S. Lorenzo, the church of San Luca, and the medieval Torre Embraici. Keep an eye out for the numerous sculpted and painted tabernacles, or "Madonette," that adorn the corners of buildings (about 3m up the walls).

Off p. Matteotti resides the **Duomo San Lorenzo.** Already in existence in the 9th century, the church was enlarged and reconstructed in the 12th through 16th centuries, resulting in the characteristically striped Gothic façade and uncharacteristically lopsided appearance—only one of the two planned bell towers was completed. The carved central portal decorated with lions, sirens, and vines opens to a severe and simple interior. The chapel of St. John the Baptist along the left wall is decorated with statues of Adam and Eve by Matteo Civitali. A vintage American bomb adorns the right wall of the church, miraculously unexploded after having crashed through the roof during World War II. (Open Mon., Wed., and Fri.-Sat. 10am-noon and 2-5pm, Sun. 10am-noon.) Behind the *duomo* via Arrivescovato leads to Genoa's most characteristic and charming square, **piazza San Matteo.** It contains the houses and family chapel of the Doria family, members of the medieval oligarchy that ruled Genoa. The animal reliefs above the first floor are the trademarks of the masons who built the houses. Chiseled into the **Church of San Matteo** (1125) are descriptions of the Dorias' great deeds. To the left, a small door protects a lovely 14th-century cloister, with slim, twin columns topped by human and animal figures. Nearby, down violo delle Vigne, resides one of Genoa's oldest churches, **Chiesa Santa Maria delle Vigne.** Dating from the 10th century, it still maintains its Romanesque arc-spired bell tower (open 8am-noon and 3:30-7pm).

555

From here head down via Greci to **via San Luca,** the main artery of the old quarter, where you'll find many of Genoa's most important monuments. The **Church of San Siro** was Genoa's first cathedral (rebuilt 1588-1613). A dome crowns the little **Church of San Luca,** a 12th-century treasure in the shape of a Greek cross. (Both open Mon.-Sat. 7am-noon and 3-7pm. Free.) **Palazzo Spinola,** in p. di Pellicceria, 1 (follow the yellow signs), exemplifies Genoa's mercantile wealth from the 16th through 18th centuries. In the *palazzo's* rooms, which retain most of their original decoration and furnishings, works of art donated by the Spinola family mingle with later additions, constituting the **Galleria Nazionale di Palazzo Spinola** (tel. 29 46 61). Don't miss the portraits of the four evangelists by van Dyck in the Sala da Pranzo. (Open Tues.-Sat. 10am-7pm, Sun. 9am-1pm. Admission L4000. Under 18 free.)

Medieval arcades (Portici di Sottoripa) border one side of piazza Caricamento, by the port on the other side of p. Banchi. Across the *piazza,* the **Palazzo San Giorgio,** a part-Gothic, part-Renaissance structure, once housed the famous Genovese bank of St. George. Intense World War II bombing left much of the area in need of reconstruction, but some interesting churches remain scattered among the old tenements and medieval ruins. The **Church of Santa Maria di Castello,** a labyrinth of chapels, courtyards, cloisters, and gardens, once served as a crusaders' church and hostel. In the chapel to the left of the high altar check out the *Crocifisso Miracoloso*—Jesus' beard supposedly grows longer every time crisis hits the city. Nearby, the medieval **Torre Embraici** looms over Santa Maria di Castello, with Guelph battlements jutting out from the rough stone surface. Head down vico della Pace to piazza San Cosimo to visit the **Chiesa di Santi Cosma e Damiano,** built in the 1100s and typical of Genovese Romanesque architecture. The church features a austere façade and a beautifully preserved octagonal campanile.

Finally, the newest addition to the old city, the **Museo dell'Architettura e Scultura Ligure** occupies the former monastery of Sant'Agostino at p. di Sarzano (tel. 20 16 61). This museum attempts to explicate Genoa's history through its surviving art. Giovanni Pisano carved the museum's most outstanding piece, the funerary monument of Margherita of Brabant, in 1312. Fragments of this monument have been scattered to various corners of the continent; the museum optimistically awaits reassembly. (Open Tues.-Sat. 9am-7pm, Sun. 9am-noon. Admission L4000.) From piazza Sarzano head back up via Ravecca to the medieval **Porta Soprana,** which flaunts its enormous twin towers and noble arched entryway, the emblem of this district. Walk past the reputed boyhood home of Christopher Columbus (his father was the gatekeeper of Soprana) and the ruins of the 12th-century cloister of the **Church of Sant'Andrea.**

To pay tribute to Italy's greatest patriot and political thinker (save, of course, Nicolò Machiavelli), take bus #34 from Stazione Principe to the **Cimitero di Staglieno.** Here, in one of Europe's only modern necropolises, lies the **Tomb of Giuseppe Mazzini** (1805-1872), which honors the Genovese native known as the father of the Risorgimento. Other national figures such as Lorenzo Pareto (1800-1865), the famous Italian scientist and scholar, have also chosen to spend eternity here. (Cemetery open daily 8am-5pm.)

Entertainment

In July **Genoa Jazz** presents jazz concerts at Villa Imperiale, drawing musicians from Europe and the United States. Seats start at about L15,000, but you can buy a ticket for the entire series for about L60,000. For information check with the tourist office, or call Kamarillo, via San Vincanzo, 109r (tel. 58 74 55). For listings of other music, theater, and dance performances, pick up a copy of *Succedere a Genova* at any tourist office.

Nightlife booms at **Charlie Christian,** via S. Donato, 20r, a smoky bar with live jazz and blues, hiply named after the father of jazz guitar (open Mon.-Sat. 8pm-1am). Hoofers head to **Cristina's,** in piazza Tommasei (tel. 36 86 52), where they can vogue to the latest vibes. (Open Tues.-Sat. 10pm-2am.) In summer the action moves to **Nervi,** only minutes away by train or bus, where people bar-hop or stroll along the *lungomare* lapping *gelato.*

Riviera di Levante

Camogli

Camogli takes its name from the wives who ran the town while their husbands manned its once-huge fishing fleet ("Camogli" is a contraction of "Casa Mogli"—"Wives' House"). Lest this generate any unenlightened visions of long-gone tranquility, bear in mind Dickens's evaluation of Camogli: "the saltiest, roughest, most piratical little place." The husbands are back now, for better or for worse, and this "piratical little place" has mellowed into a small, peaceful resort.

The town climbs uphill from the sea into pine and olive groves; below, a promontory separates the pebble beach from the fishing harbor. Like many Riviera towns, Camogli came into money long after its six-story, blank-walled houses had been built. The *nouveau riches* Camogliesi hired painters to decorate their homes with *trompe l'œil* balconies, pilasters, moldings, and rustication, and other fripperies. After a long absence, the style has re-emerged and the solid, green-shuttered homes once again sport fanciful façades.

Camogli is famous nationally and internationally for its enormous fish-fry, the Sagra del Pesce. On the second Sunday in May, tourists descend on Camogli to partake of the free fish, fried up in a giant, four-meter-across pan, which holds 2000 sardines at once, and adorns a wall at the entrance to the town when not in use. Though Camogli is best-known for its pebble beach and holiday atmosphere, don't pass up a peek into the **church** off p. Colombo in the old town. From the church, stone steps lead left to the **Acquario Tirrenico** (aquarium; open daily 10am-noon and 3-7pm; admission L4000).

Camogli can be reached by *locale* train on the Genoa-La Spézia line (from Genoa 20 trains per day, 40min., L1600; from La Spézia 10 trains per day, 1hr. 30min., L5000; from Sestri Levante 35 per day, 30min., L2400) or from Santa Margherita by bus (35min., L1700) or train (10min., L1500). **Tigullio** buses depart across from the station to nearby towns. Buy tickets at Bar Aldo, next to the station. (To: Santa Margherita, 18 per day, L1700; Portofino Vetta—*not* Portofino Mare, the port—3 per day, L1400.) Buses also stop at p. Schiaffino, across from the tourist office (on via XX Settembre). You can buy tickets close by at the *tabaccheria* at via Repubblica, 25. Ferries are more expensive, but offer incredible views of the peninsula's cliffs. From Camogli, **Golfo Paradiso,** via Scala, 2 (tel. 77 20 91) ferries take you around the rugged headland to **San Fruttuoso** (May-Sept. 15 7-12 per day, L6000, round-trip L10,800). They also run a nighttime trip to Portofino (leaving at 9:30pm and returning at about 11:45pm; round-trip L16,000). Buy tickets on the boat. Or you may just want to forget all about the boats and make the three-hour hike to San Fruttuoso; pick up the Camogli tourist office's useful trail map if you do, or just follow the double blue dots of the well-marked path.

The **tourist office** at via XX Settembre, 33 (tel. 77 10 66), to your right as you leave the station, helps you find a room and cheerfully answers even the zaniest questions, all in broken English. They also have **telephones.** (Open Mon.-Sat. 9am-12:30pm and 4-7pm, Sun. 9am-12:30pm; Sept.-June Mon.-Sat. 9am-12:30pm and 3:30-6:30pm.) Camogli's **telephone code** is 0185. The **post office** accepts doomed-to-be-late mail at via Cuneo, 1 (tel. 77 01 14), to the left of the station. (Open Mon.-Fri. 8:10am-6pm, Sat. 8:10-4pm.) The **postal code** is 16032. You'll find a **pharmacy** at via Repubblica, 6 (open Mon.-Sat. 8:30am-12:30pm and 3:30-7:30pm).

Albergo La Camogliese, via Garibaldi, 55 (tel. 77 14 02), is a steal. Walk down the looong stairway near the train station to #55, near the seafront. The clean, commodious rooms are a joy, and the proprietors have indisputably found their calling. They refer to *Let's Go* readers as "Let's Go amici" and offer them special discounts. (Singles with bath L40,000. Doubles L55,000, with bath L60,000-80,000, depending on size and view. Breakfast L4000. Show them your book and make reservations.) The pleasant **Pensione Augusta,** via Schiaffino, 100 (tel. 770 592), at the other end of town, has clean and simple rooms enlivened by the ceaseless rumbling of nearby trains. (Singles

L50,000; doubles L67,000-75,000. All rooms with bath.) If these are full, walk left from the station past the post office to **Albergo Selene,** via Cuneo, 16 (tel. 77 01 49). (Singles L45,000. Doubles L74,000.) If you still can't find anything, talk to the owner of La Camogliese and he will probably be able to find you a reasonable room in town. By 1993, a **trattoria** associated with La Camogliese (and much less expensive than the **Ristorante La Camogliese,** where *primi* go for a shocking L12,000) should be open. Ask at the *albergo* for details. For a do-it-yourself meal, the scores of foodstuff shops on via Repubblica should suffice. **Revello,** via Garibaldi, 183 (tel. 77 07 77), at the end of via Garibaldi, offers a stupendous smattering of snack sensations. Locals make a morning stop there for the Riviera's best *focaccia,* but their secret treat is the *camogliese al rhum,* a chocolate-covered cream puff with a rum-spiked filling (both are L2600 per *etto*). These sinfully delicious treats were born here in January, 1970, and have been pleasing visitors ever since. (Open daily 7:30am-1pm and 3:30-7:30pm.)

San Fruttuoso

The tiny fishing hamlet of San Fruttuoso, set in a natural amphitheater of pines, olive trees, and green oaks by the sea, is much too expensive for a prolonged stay or even a meal, but it's still a fabulous daytrip. The town is accessible by foot (11/2hr. from Portofino Mare or Portofino Vetta) or by boat. Both **Golfo Paradiso** (tel. (0185) 77 20 91; 12 boats per day from Camogli, L6000, round-trip L10,000) and **Servizio Marittimo del Tigullio** (tel. (0185) 28 46 70; 15 boats per day from Portofino, L6000, round-trip L10,000) provide service.

For a great view, walk to the left of the bay to the medieval **lookout tower,** constructed by the Doria family. Fifteen meters offshore and 18m underwater stands a bronze statue with upraised arms, the *Christ of the Depths,* erected in memory of casualties at sea. The statue now serves as protector of scuba divers, and, in late August, the townlet sponsors a **festival** commemorating those lost at sea. Be sure to visit the Benedictine **Abbazia di San Fruttuoso di Capo di Monte** (tel. (0185) 77 27 03), for which the town was named. Here the non-amphibious can see an exact replica of the *Christ of the Depths* and activate a musical nativity scene. (Open May-Oct. Tues.-Sun. 10am-1pm and 2-6pm; Nov.-Jan. Sat.-Sun. 10am-1pm and 2-4pm; Mar.-Apr. Tues.-Sun. 10am-1pm and 2-4pm. Admission L5000.)

Portofino

Gorgeous Portofino was discovered long ago by the well-to-do. Today the yachts of the wealthy fill the harbor and boutiques line the streets, but the curve of the shore and the tiny bay may be enjoyed by paupers and princes alike. A nature reserve surrounds Portofino; trek through it to San Fruttuoso (90min.) or Santa Margherita (21/2hr.). If you choose to hang around town, you can escape to the cool interior of the simple yellow **Chiesa di San Giorgio** by following the signs uphill from the *piazza* at the bay. A few more minutes up the road to the **castle** will set you in an enchanting garden with a fairy-tale view of the clear bay. Look for the footpath marked "Al faro" to reach the lighthouse (20min.—don't step on the salamanders!) and a breathtaking coastline vista. The *gelateria* here is open April-Sept. daily 9:30am-8pm.

There's no train to Portofino, but Tigullio **buses** run along the coastline to and from Santa Margherita. (Every 30min., L1400; make sure you take the bus to Portofino Mare, not Portofino Vetta, and buy tickets on board.) Maps and English brochures are available at the **tourist office,** via Roma, 35 (tel. 26 90 24), on the way to the waterfront from the bus stop. Some English spoken. A large signboard of the arrivals and departures from Sta. Margherita is posted outside. (Open Mon.-Tues. and Thurs.-Sat. 8:30am-7pm, Wed. 9am-12:30pm, and Sun. 9:30am-noon; off-season, Mon.-Sat. 9am-6pm, Sun. 9am-1pm.) Portofino's **telephone code** is 0185; use the **telephones** at the tourist office. To sustain yourself on the hike to San Fruttuoso, head to **Alimentari Repetto,** under the arches to the left of the bay, for warm *focaccia* and cool drinks (open daily 7am-10:30pm).

Santa Margherita Ligure

Santa Margherita Ligure lies close to secluded villages and exquisite beaches but away from teeming tourist throngs. Like Camogli's, Santa Margherita's buildings have been decked out in colorful *trompe l'œil* façades. Blessed with the character and affordability of a small town, it has the accessibility of a large one, with so many *pensioni* that impecunious travelers can dump their backpacks here and spend their days exploring the more exclusive Riviera nooks.

Orientation and Practical Information

Tourist Office: via XXV Aprile, 2b (tel. 28 74 85). Turn right from the train station onto via Roma, then right on via XXV Aprile. Information, town map, and accommodations service. English spoken. Open daily 8:45am-12:30pm and 3:30-7pm.

Post Office: via Roma, 36 (tel. 28 88 40), to the right of the station. Open Mon.-Fri. 8:10am-6:30pm, Sat. 8:10am-noon. **Postal Code:** 16038. **Telephone Code:** 0185.

Trains: (tel. 28 66 30), in p. Federico Raoul Nobili at the summit of via Roma. To: Genoa (3 per hr. 4:30am-midnight, L2400); La Spézia (2 per hr. 6am-2am, L5000). **Luggage Storage:** L1500 per piece. Ticket window and luggage storage open Mon.-Sat. 5:45am-7:50pm, Sun. 6:15am-8:35pm.

Buses: Tigullio buses depart from p. Martiri della Libertà at the small green kiosk on the waterfront. *Biglietteria* open daily 7am-8pm. Service to Camogli (15km, L1700) and Portofino (5km, L1400). Tickets can easily be bought on board for Portofino.

Ferries: Tigullio, via Palestro, 8/1/B (tel. 28 46 70). Boats leave from the docks at p. Martiri della Libertà. To: Portofino (L4000, round-trip L7000); San Fruttuoso (L9000, round-trip L15,000); and Cinque Terre, Monterosso, or Riomaggiore (July-Sept. 15 only, L18,000, round-trip L25,000).

Bike Rental: Motonoleggio, via Pagana, 5b (tel. 28 34 08). From the waterfront, follow via Gramsci up the hill past the Hotel Helios. Bikes L10,000 for 3 hours, L20,000 per day. Tandems and motorbikes for slightly higher prices. Open June-Sept. daily 9am-12:30pm and 2:30-7:30pm. Oct.-May open sporadically, but you can call ahead and try to reserve.

Emergency: tel. 113. **Police:** (tel. 28 71 21), on via Vignolo. **Hospital: Ospedale Civile di Rapallo,** p. Molfino, 10 (tel. 502 31), in Rapallo near the train station. For late-night and weekend medical attention, **Guardia Medica:** tel. 60 333 or 27 33 82.

Accommodations

Stay away from the water. Your room won't have a view and you'll have to trek a bit, but the reward will be peace, quiet, and an extra L10,000 in your pocket.

Hotel Fasce, via Luigi Bozzo, 3 (tel. 28 64 35, fax 28 35 80), off corso Matteotti. Signor Arry and his British wife Jane offer one of the best deals in this book. Their sparkling, contemporary rooms are each equipped with private telephone (L5000 per collect call), a safe for valuables, and a color TV with English language channels. But wait, there's more! If you act now, you'll receive free parking, laundry service (L20,000 per load), and a sun deck with bar service. By 1993, they should have 12 bicycles, which they will loan out to *Let's Go* guests for free. It is a first-class hotel by every standard but price, an incredible L40,000 per person, with bath L47,500. Breakfast included. A 3-course dinner in their restaurant runs L25,000. 10% discount Oct.-May 15. AmEx, MC, Visa. Be sure to show them your *Let's Go.*

Corallo, via XXV Aprile, 20 (tel. 28 67 74), about 3 blocks from the tourist office, through the garden. The kindly gent who runs the place has been in the business for years. His tidy, simple rooms have been recently repainted, and he's now turning his attention to the garden in front. Curfew 2:30am (get keys in the Bar Vanni out front to get in after midnight). Singles L24,000. Doubles L40,000. Call ahead, and show up before noon.

Albergo Annabella, via Costasecca, 10 (tel. 28 65 31), off p. Mazzini, not far from the beach. Capacious, clean, and contemporary rooms. Singles L35,000. Doubles L50,000. Triples L66,000. Showers L2000. Breakfast L6000. In high season, they like their guests to take half-pension, at L55,000 per person.

Albergo La Piazzetta, via Gramsci, 1 (tel, 28 69 19, fax 28 80 26). Clean rooms, with pretty ceilings, tiled floors and modern furnishings. Singles L40,000, with bath L49,000. Doubles L60,000, with bath L70,000. Breakfast included. MC, Visa.

Food

Supermarkets, bakeries, fruit vendors, and butcher shops line corso Matteotti. On Fridays from 8am to 1pm, the shops oust the cars and spill onto the *corso.*

Trattoria Baicin, via Algeria, 9 (tel. 28 67 63), off p. Martiri della Libertà near the water. Papà Tomaso is the master chef, Mamma Beatrice rolls the pasta and boils the sauces, and brothers Piero and Rossano work the tables, making for a friendly and traditional Ligurian meal courtesy of the Famiglia Giovanuzzi. Try Mamma's homemade *Trofie alla Genovese gnocchi* mixed with potato, string beans, and pesto (L6000). A full meal sets you back L18,000 (cover included, 10% service not). Cover L1800. Open Tues.-Sun. noon-3pm and 6:45-midnight. Reserve ahead for Sat. night and all of Sun. All credit cards accepted.

Trattoria Da Pezzi, via Cavour, 21 (tel. 28 53 03), offers the most interesting daily specials in town, including *ravioli di verdura e ricotta in salsa noci* (vegetable ravioli in sweet walnut-cream sauce) on Thurs. and Sun. (L4500). Cover L1000. Open Sun.-Fri. 11:30am-2:15pm and 6-9:30pm. Also a snack bar and take-out service at the entrance—open Sun.-Fri. 10am-2:15pm and 5-9:20pm.

Pestarino, via Palestro, 5; back entrance at via Cavour, 4. Just plain delicious. Rice salad L2000 per *etto, torta di verdura* L1800 per *etto,* curried turkey L3500 per *etto.* They'll warm up anything for you. Open daily 8am-1pm and 4-8pm; in winter closed Tues.

Rosticceria Revelant, via Gramsci, 15 (tel. 28 65 00), east of p. Martiri della Libertà. Scrumptious take-out meals. Try the lasagna (L1350 per *etto*). Open Thurs.-Tues. 8am-1pm and 4:30-8:30pm, Sun. 7:30am-1pm.

Trattoria San Siro, corso Matteotti, 137. Something out of the past: a plain black-and-white sign on the outside, a small barrel-vaulted dining room and real Italians on the inside. Full meals L18,000 (cover included). Try the *pansoti* (rounds of pasta stuffed with mixed greens in a walnut sauce, L6000). Pasta with pesto only L4000. Cover L2000. Open Jan.-Nov. Sun.-Mon. 11am-4pm and 6-11pm.

Maitò Nel Blu, via XXV Aprile, 21 (tel. 28 84 11). A chic, air-conditioned place. Try the *penne a maison* (pasta with tomatoes, cream, and cheese, L6000) or their savory *antipasto del mare* (L12,000). English spoken. Open Tues.-Sun. noon-2:30pm and 7:30-11pm. AmEx, MC, Visa.

Sights and Entertainment

As big as Santa Margherita is, its main attraction remains its tranquility and proximity to Camogli and Portofino. From 8am to 12:30pm, you can ogle the day's catch at the local **fish market** on lungomare Marconi, or come between 4 and 6pm to watch the fleet bring in its haul. (Market closed Wed. afternoon.) More exalted sights include the rococo **basilica** on p. Caprera, dripping with gold and crystal, which houses some good Flemish and Italian works. To reach the **Church of the Cappuccini,** a favorite feline hangout, walk along the waterfront past p. Martiri della Libertà and mount the stone ramp behind the stone castle. For human companionship, chalk up a pool cue at the **Old-Inn Bar,** p. Mazzini, 40 (open daily 7am-1am).

Sestri Levante

Lauded in the lofty verse of Dante and Petrarch, the serene beauty of Sestri Levante is today as dead as the poets. Nature blessed this paradise with a lovely peninsula dividing the Bay of Silence from the Bay of Fables, and humanity has responded by blighting the outcrop with an endless block of development. Trains arrive here en route from La Spézia to Santa Margherita, and cruel gods will strand you in Sestri if you attempt to catch the last train from the Cinque Terre in hopes of reaching Santa Margherita. If you're stuck here, walk down to the **Baia del Silenzo** (Bay of Silence), east of p. Matteotti. The people at **Albergo Leda,** via XX Settembre, 15 (tel. 414 01), speak a little English, and the rooms are airy and clean. (Singles L30,000. Doubles L45,000. Triples L60,000. Quads L75,000.)

Cinque Terre

The Cinque Terre (Five Lands) are comprised of five isolated fishing villages clinging precariously to a small stretch of cliff above the sea. Unfortunately, the only sea creatures bobbing in the now-sterile Mediterranean are swimming tourists. Attractions of the Cinque Terre include enrapturing vistas and a sweet white wine called *sciacchetrà*.

The five towns, in order of increasing distance from Genoa, are: Monterosso, Vernazza, Corniglia, Manarola, and Riomaggiore, among which Monterosso is the biggest, easiest to reach, and least charming.

Orientation and Practical Information

The listings here are for Monterosso, which is easily accessible by local train from all the villages.

Tourist Office: via Fegina, 38 (tel. 81 75 06), below the train station. The only tourist office in the Cinque Terre, well-stocked with the straight dope on boats, hikes, and hotels. Accommodations service for Monterosso and **currency exchange** (good rates). Open April-Oct. Mon.-Sat. 9am-noon and 5:30-8pm, Sun. 9am-noon.

Post Office: via Loreto (tel. 81 75 27). Open Mon.-Fri. 8:30am-6pm, Sat. 8:30am-noon. **Postal Code:** 19016.

Telephones: Cartolecia, p. Garibaldi, 16, near the port on the south side of town. Open 8am-12:30pm and 2:30-7:30pm. **Telephone Code:** 0187.

Trains: via Fegina, on the north end of town, to the right as you face the water. To: Vernazza, Corniglia, Manarola, and Riomaggiore (every hr., 5-20min., L1500). Also to Genoa (15 per day, 1hr. 30min., L5600).

Boats: Navagazione Golfo dei Poeti (tel. 96 76 76), at the port to the right of the beach in the south end of town. Trips to Manarola and Riomaggiore (5 per day, L7000, round-trip L11,000).

Boat Rental: on the public beach, through the tunnel from the station. Pedal boats L10,000 per hr., L50,000 per day. 3-person motorboats L29,000 per hr., L145,000 per day. 5-person motorboats L35,000 per hr., L175,000 per day.

Beaches: There are only 2 public beaches in the Cinque Terre, one on the south side of Monterosso (to the left as you face the water), and the other a long strip of pebbles between Corniglia and Manarola. You can also swim off of the rocky outcrops between Manarola and Riomaggiore.

Emergencies: tel. 113. **Police: Carabinieri,** tel. 81 75 24. **Medical Emergency: Guardia Medica,** tel. 80 04 09.

Accommodations

Accommodations are plentiful in the Cinque Terre; finding a room should be no problem except during late July and August. Get help from the tourist office if you're having trouble finding a place to stay, but remember that they won't be able to find you *affitta camere*—cheap and picturesque rooms in private houses in Corniglia and Vernazza.

Hostel: Mamma Rosa, p. Unità, 2 (tel. 92 00 50), in Riomaggiore, across from the bar at the Riomaggiore train station. Short on rules and regulations, long on hospitality. No separate-sex rooms. No curfew. L18,000 per person. Showers included. Cooking facilities available.

Albergo Barbara, p. Marconi, 21-23 (tel. 81 22 01), in Vernazza. Ask about the hotel in the Trattoria Capitano at #21. Clean and comfy rooms with a fantastic view of Vernazza's colorful port. Singles L40,000. Doubles L55,000.

Affitacamare E. Guelfi, via Fieschi, 222 (tel. 81 21 78), in Corneglia. Only 1 of the more than 20 *affitta camere* that hide in this excruciatingly cute fishing village. Rooms with views of the water. Singles L25,000. Doubles L50,000.

Camping: Acqua Dolce, Levanto (tel. 80 84 65), near the water. Just a few minutes by train from the Cinque Terre. Near the water and easy to reach by foot. L6000 per person, L6000 per tent. Open April-Oct. 15.

Food

Each town's main street is lined with fruit and vegetable stores and a port teeming with respectable *trattorie*. First known for its white wine, the Cinque Terre still maintain a worthy tradition of viniculture which produces an intensely flavored white wine called **Sciacchetrà;** it runs an expensive L10,000 to L15,000 per bottle due to the lack of suitably arable terrain in the area.

Ristorante Cecio, in Corniglia. On the small road that leads from Corniglia to Vernazza; follow the signs at the top of the stairs that lead to town from the train station. A small restaurant overlooking the hills and water, with absolutely fantastic food. *Primi* L6000-8000; get the *gnocchi al pesto* for an out-of-body gastronomic thrill. *Scallopine al limone* (veal with lemon) L7000. If you eat too much to make it home again you can crash here too. (Doubles with bath L50,000.)

Focacceria Il Frontoio, via Goberti, 1, in Monterosso. The wood-burning oven fires up every kind of mouth-watering *focaccia* imaginable: with olives, onions, herbs, or stuffed with different fillings. Slices only L1500-2500. A great place to stock up before heading out on a hike. Open March-Oct. daily 9am-1:15pm and 4:30-8pm.

Sights

Nature is responsible for the Cinque Terre's best sights—the savage cliffs and lush tropical vegetation surrounding these stone sea villages. The best views are afforded from the narrow goat paths that link the towns, winding through vineyards, streams, and dense foliage clotted with cacti and lemon trees. Come with a good pair of walking shoes, and you can cover the distance between Monterosso and Riomaggiore in one day; or take strolls between frolics in the water. The best hikes lie between Monterosso and Vernazza (1hr. 30min.), Vernazza and Corniglia (1hr. 30min.), and Corniglia and Manarola (1hr.). The "via dell amore" that links Manarola and Riomaggiore is more notable for the easy access it affords to the water than for its view.

In Monterosso visit the **Convento dei Cappuccini,** which perches on a hill between the two halves of town. The convent preserves an impressive *Crucifixion* by Flemish master Van Dyck, who sojourned in this area during some of his most productive years. (Open daily 9am-noon and 4-7pm.)

Portovénere

A mosaic of multicolored dwellings and home to many, many cats, Portovénere sits on and among rocks, seemingly removed from the rest of the world. This venerable port is dominated by its **Castello Doria,** built by Genoa in the 16th century to defend the Republic from the threat of Pisan attacks. The castle rises on pre-existing fortifications dating back to the Roman period, and is surrounded by ruined mills, a cemetery, and an orchard. The view from the top of the surrounding gulf is breathtaking. (Open daily 10am-noon and 2-6pm.) Take the steps of via Cappellini, 80, up to the **Church of San Lorenzo,** built in 1116 and consecrated by Pope Innocent II in 1130. The church holds the city's most revered relic, the **Madonna Bianca,** which supposedly floated to town inside a log sometime in the 13th century. A jaunt through town leads to the **Church of San Pietro.** As you approach the church, a bronze statue of *Mater Naturae* looks out over the gulf. This figure was a gift to the city by the sculptor Scorzelli. A bit further on, to your right, is the **Grotta Byron,** dizzyingly near the crashing waves. A sign marks this spot as having inspired Byron, "who, as a daring swimmer, defied the waves of the sea from Portovénere to Lerici." (We wouldn't advise following in his wake.) The optically intriguing church itself, whose black-and-white-striped façade appears from a distance to be an extension of its steps, is built over part of a 6th-century paleochristian church. The present edifice served as a bivouac of Austro-Russian troops during the Napoleonic wars; the French, though they tried, weren't able to destroy it. The view from its 9th-century *loggia* is unmatched.

Portovénere has no train station but is easily accessible from La Spézia (see below) by bus P (L1800). The tiny **tourist office,** p. Bastreri, 7 (tel. (0187) 90 06 91), sells bus tickets. (Open Wed.-Mon. 10am-noon and 5-7pm.) The only reasonable lodging option in Portovénere is **Il Genio,** p. Bastreri, 8 (tel. (0187) 90 06 11). Unfortunately, they only take reservations for minimum stays of a week in the summer. (Singles with bath L56,000. Doubles with bath L75,000. Triples L100,000. Open Feb.-Dec.) Savor a rustic local meal at the century-old **Antica Osteria del Carrugio,** via Cappellini, 66 (tel. (0187) 90 06 17; open Dec.-Oct. Fri.-Wed. 12:15-2:30pm and 7:15-8:30pm). For cheaper eats, try the **Rosticceria/Salumeria** next door (tel. (0187) 90 10 54; open June-Aug. daily 7am-8pm, Feb.-May and Sept.-Oct. Wed.-Mon. 7am-2pm and 3:30-9pm).

The islands **Tino, Tinetto,** and **Palmaria,** the last famed for its **Grotta Azzurra,** await offshore. In summer, take one of the eight ferries leaving Portovénere daily for the *giro delle isole* (tour of the islands, L8000). Six ferries leave daily for the islands from La Spézia, as well. Buy tickets ahead of time at the docks.

La Spézia

La Spézia, a major commercial and naval port, serves as a departure point to Corsica and as an excellent anchor from which to visit the surrounding coast. Enjoy the merits of the city by following the locals in their evening *passeggiata* down car-free via del Prione.

If the city fathers see fit, there should be a **Tourist Information Booth** within the train station in 1993. If not, well, it's no great loss; there's not much to see here, and the hotels and restaurants we list are all pretty easy to locate.

La Spézia is the most convenient Italian port for Bastia, Corsica. Two lines operate out of La Spézia. **Corsica Ferries,** molo Italia (tel. 212 82), in the round ticket booth, runs daily at 8:15am, May to late September. Additional evening departures are available June through July, Friday and Saturday at 7:30pm, and in August, on Fridays, most Saturdays, and some Sundays, also at 7:30pm (5hr., L32,000, L38,000 on and around weekends in June-Aug.). **Navarma Lines,** molo Italia, in the round ticket booth next to Corsica Ferries' booth, or in the office at via Tolone, 14 (tel. 218 44), provides service late June to mid-September daily at 8:15am; additional evening sailings Friday and Saturday at 8:15pm from late June through August (5hr., L31,000-38,000).

Basically, the only real reason to stay in La Spézia is if you can't find a room in the nearby Cinque Terre or Portovénere—it's only a few minutes to either by train or bus. If you're stuck for a Rivieran room, try **Albergo Terminus,** via Paleocapa, 21 (tel. 372 04), on the left as you exit the train station. The impressive lobby was once part of a church, and foreshadows the lofty rooms found within. (Singles L30,000. Doubles L40,000, with bath L50,000. Showers included. Breakfast L5000.) **Albergo Spézia** lies on via Cavallotti, 31 (tel. 351 64)—make a right off via del Prione, one street before via Carpenino coming from the station. The spacious, carpeted rooms boast squishy mattresses. (Singles L24,000. Doubles L34,000, with bath L45,000. Showers included. Call ahead in summer.) If these are full, stop by **Albergo Giglio Rosso,** via Carpenino, 31 (tel. 31 374), off via Prione. Its dark singles run L30,000; doubles are L40,000. While in La Spézia, try *mesciua,* a thick soup that combines beans, cornmeal, olive oil, and pepper. At **Osteria con Cucina "del Prione,"** via Prione, 270 (tel. 391 34), the friendly waiters cater to your every whim. *Primi,* including a mean *penne boscaiola,* (with cream, ham, mushrooms, and tomatoes) start at L6000, *secondi* at L7500, pizzas at L4500. (Cover L1500. Open Mon.-Sat. 6-10:30pm.) Or dive into the high life at **Ristorante Da Sandro,** via del Prione, 268 (tel. 372 03), one of the best in La Spézia. The cook recommends *trittico della casa,* a combo plate of seafood pastas (L8000), or *gnocchi gorgonzola* (L7000). (Wine L4500 per . Cover L2000. Full meals L14,000-21,000. Open Sat.-Thurs. noon-2pm and 7:30-10pm. AmEx, MC, Visa.)

CENTRAL ITALY

Emilia Romagna

Go to Florence, Venice, and Rome to sightsee. Come to Emilia Romagna to eat. Italy's wealthiest wheat and dairy producing region covers the fertile plains of the Po river valley and boasts the finest culinary traditions on the Italian Peninsula. Plan to go over budget while in Emilia Romagna, as you gorge on Parmesan cheese and prosciutto, Bolognese fresh pasta and *mortadella,* Ferrarese *salama* and *grana* cheese. Complement these with the respectable selection of regional wines, including reds like the sparkling *lambrusco* from Parma and Sangiovese from Romagna.

The Romans settled the region originally, but the terrain is dominated by medieval remnants. Developed as autonomous *comuni* during this chaotic time, the towns of the region later fell under the rule of great Renaissance families: the Malatesta in Rímini, the Bentivoglio in Bologna, the Farnese in Parma and Piacenza, and the Este in Ferrara and Mòdena. At the beginning of the 16th century, Pope Julius II conquered Emilia and Romagna, inaugurating the three centuries of rule from Rome during which these provinces were considered the property of the Papal States. In the 19th century the Italian Socialist movement was born here. The area remains a stronghold of the left; Bologna is the buckle of Italy's "Red Belt," which extends from Emilia-Romagna through Tuscany and Umbria and has been governed by the Communists since World War II.

Emilia Romagna's look is unusual for Italy. Muted yellows and browns predominate, and the farm buildings are low, square, and flat-roofed. The uninterrupted plains give the sense of infinite space. The illusion of distance is magnified by the cold gray fog of winter—replaced in summer by a silver haze and stifling heat that make distant towns shimmer. Anonymous sculpture from the period of the communes gives even the smallest towns artistic fame. A naturalistic spirit imbues the local architecture—cathedrals' arches seem to have grown into their places, and cloisters' carved columns resemble ivy-clad trees. And if Tuscany artistically outshone its northern neighbors during the Renaissance, Emilia Romagna has vindicated itself, giving the world such modern luminaries as conductor Arturo Toscanini, tenor Luciano Pavarotti, and filmmakers Antonioni and Federico Fellini.

Bologna

With one forkful of Bologna's *tortellini,* it becomes clear that this city appreciates the better things in life. Indulgence of the mind began 900 years ago when the city founded the first university in Europe. The **Università di Bologna** has since graduated the likes of Dante, Petrarch, Copernicus, and Tasso, and has made Bologna the urban epitome of culture and prestige. The wisdom and eloquence of its scholarly halls spills over into the streets, where endless porticoed walks, *nobili signori* and *signore,* and a general opulence belie wealthy Bologna's contradictory position as the outpost of the Italian Communist Party.

Bologna continues to live up to its nicknames "La Dotta" (The Learned) with its huge student population, and "La Grossa" (The Fat) with its complacent prosperity and tremendous appetite for rich foods.

Orientation and Practical Information

At the heart of northern Italy, Bologna is the hub for rail lines to all major Italian cities, as well as to both the Tyrrenian and Adriatic coasts. Buses #25 and 30 shuttle between the train station and the town's historical center at p. Maggiore (tickets L1200 at most *tabacchi* and newspaper stands). On the northern edge of p. Maggiore is piazza

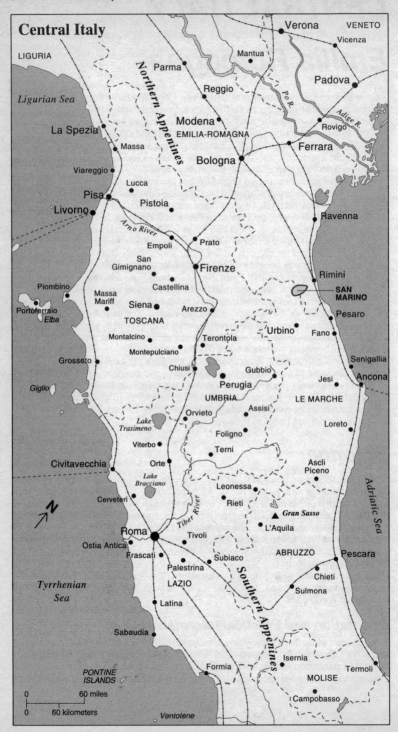

Central Italy

LIGURIA

Ligurian Sea

VENETO

Verona

Vicenza

Mantua

Northern Appenines

Parma

Reggio

Po R.

Padova

Adige R.

Modena

EMILIA-ROMAGNA

Rovigo

La Spezia

Massa

Ferrara

Viareggio

Bologna

Lucca

Ravenna

Pisa

Pistoia

Livorno

Arno River

Prato

Empoli

San Gimignano

Firenze

Rimini

SAN MARINO

Piombino

Castellina

Massa Mariff

Siena

Arezzo

Pesaro

Portoferraio

Elba

TOSCANA

Urbino

Fano

Montalcino

Terontola

Senigallia

Montepulciano

Chiusi

Gubbio

Jesi

Ancona

Grosseto

Perugia

Giglio

UMBRIA

LE MARCHE

Orvieto

Assisi

Lake Trasimeno

Foligno

Loreto

Viterbo

Terni

Ascli Piceno

Civitavecchia

Orte

Lake Bracciano

Leonessa

Cerveteri

Tiber River

Rieti

▲ *Gran Sasso*

N

Roma

Tivoli

L'Aquila

Ostia Antica

Subiaco

ABRUZZO

Pescara

Frascati

Palestrina

Chieti

LAZIO

Sulmona

Tyrrhenian Sea

Latina

Sabaudia

Southern Appenines

Isernia

Termoli

PONTINE ISLANDS

Formia

MOLISE

0   60 miles

0   60 kilometers

Campobasso

Ventolene

del Nettuno. From here, **via Ugo Bassi** runs to points west, **via dell'Indipendenza** runs north, back toward the train station, and **via Rizzoli** runs west to **piazza Porta Ravegnana,** site of the two towers.

Tourist Office: Main office in Palazzo Comunale, p. Maggiore, 6 (tel. 23 96 60), in the building on the right side of the *piazza* as you face the basilica. Modern, genial, and efficient. Computer terminal "Tutto Bologna" at the entrance provides reams of information in English on everything from museums to banks (keep an eye out for branch terminals sprinkled throughout the city, though this is the only one in the *centro storico*). Open Mon.-Sat. 9am-7pm, Sun. 9am-1pm. In the **train station** (tel. 24 65 41), near the main exit to the street. Stop here to book a room free; they have up-to-the-minute information on hotel vacancies, sparing you hours of trudgery. Check to see if they have a spare copy of *A Guest In Bologna,* for the latest information on sights and entertainment. Also pick up the respectable free map, with listings of monuments and museums. Open Mon.-Sat. 9:30am-12:30pm and 2:30pm-6:30pm. Another well-stocked **branch office** at the airport, near the international arrivals (tel. 38 17 22). Open Mon.-Sat. 9am-1pm.

Budget Travel: Centro Turistico Studentesco (CTS), via delle Belle Arti, 20 (tel. 26 48 62). Reliable and popular, and one of the few agencies open in late summer. ISIC cards. Open Mon.-Fri. 9:30am-12:30pm and 3:30-6:30pm, Sat. 9:30am-noon. **University Viaggi,** via Zamboni, 16/E (tel. 22 85 84 or 23 62 55). Open Mon.-Fri. 9am-12:30pm and 3-6pm; closed 2 weeks in Aug. Both issue BIJ tickets and HI cards. Big discounts on sea and air travel. Arrive in the early morning to avoid lines.

Currency Exchange: banking hours Mon.-Fri. 8:20am-1:20pm and 2:30-3:30pm or 2:45-3:45pm, or change at the *cambio* at the train station (L800 commission, decent rates). Open 7am-12:30pm and 3-7:30pm. After 7:30pm, go to ticket booth #1.

Post Office: p. Minghetti (tel. 22 35 98), southeast of p. Maggiore, off via Farini. Fermo Posta at #20 in the Casellario Abbonati wing. Open Mon.-Fri. 8:15am-6:40pm, Sat. 8:15am-12:20pm. **Postal Code:** 40100.

Telephones: ASST, p. VIII Agosto, 24, off via dell'Indipendenza. Open 24 hrs. **SIP,** via Fossalta, 4/E, off p. Nettuno. Open daily 8am-9:30pm. Also at the train station. **Telephone Code:** 051.

Flights: Aeroporto G. Marconi (tel. 31 15 78 or 31 22 59), at borgo Panigale northwest of town center. Take blue (suburban) bus #91 from the station. European flights. Many charters available.

Trains: Information, tel. 24 64 90. Open 8am-8pm. The harried staff rarely answers the phone. Instead try the tourist office in p. Maggiore, where they will make free copies of any national train schedule. Trains to: Florence (every 30min., 1hr.-1hr. 30min., L6300); Venice (every hr., 2hr.-2hr. 30min., L10,800); Milan (every hr., 2hr. 30min.-3hr., L13,700); Rome (every hr., 3hr.-3hr. 30min., L27,100). After dark women should take the bus instead of walking to the town center, or stick to via dell'Indipendenza.

Buses: ATC buses for nearby cities depart from the terminal on the far side of p. XX Settembre (tel. 24 83 74). Walk left from the train station. Bologna's efficient urban buses, also run by ATC (tel. 35 01 11), get crowded in early afternoon and evening. Inner-city tickets cost L1200 and are valid for 1 hr. after they are punched. Fine for evaders L50,000.

Taxis: tel. 37 27 27, 37 37 50, or 37 47 18. Fare L7000 for the first 2 km, L1400 for each additional km.

English Bookstore: Feltrinelli, via dei Giudei, 6/C (tel. 26 54 76), off p. Porta Ravegnana. Browse with the university students at this huge store. Small selection of English books. Open Mon.-Fri. 9am-7:30pm, Sat. 9am-1pm and 3-7:30pm.

Laundromat: Self-Service Acqua Lavasecco, v. Todaro, 4 (tel. 24 07 40). Open daily 8am-11pm.

Public Baths: Diurno, in town center at via Montegrappa, 2 (tel. 22 84 09), off via dell'Indipendenza. Showers (*semplice*) L9000. Shampoo and 2 towels included. Bathrooms L500. Open Mon.-Fri. 8:30am-12:30pm and 3:30-7pm, Sat. 8:30am-12:30pm. Another day hotel at p. Re Enzo, 1/B, bordering p. Maggiore to the north. Showers with shampoo and towels L10,000. Bathrooms L1000. Same hours.

Late-Night Pharmacy: at the train station (tel. 24 66 03) and at p. Maggiore, 6 (tel. 23 85 09) in the town center. (Open Mon.-Sat. 7:30am-11pm, Sun. 8am-10pm.)

Emergencies: tel. 113. **Police:** p. Galileo, 7 (tel. 33 71 11). **Ufficio Stranieri** (Foreigners' Office): tel. 33 74 73 or 33 74 75. **Medical Emergency:** tel. 33 33 33. **Hospital: Ospedale Policlinico Sant'Orsola-Malpighi,** tel. 636 21 11 or 636 31 11.

Accommodations

Prices are high and rooms scarce due to the glut of students and business travelers. The situation improves very slightly in January, July, and August. But don't despair: Bologna has an affordable youth hostel.

Ostello Di San Sisto (HI), via Viadagota, 14 (tel. 51 92 02), in the Località di San Sisto 6km northeast of the center of town, off via San Donato. Ask at the tourist office for the map giving specific directions. Take bus #93 running away from p. dei Martiri from via Irnerio/dei Mille, which peels off via dell'Indipendenza 3 blocks from the train station. (Mon.-Sat. every 30min., last bus at 8:15pm). Get off at the 2nd stop after the rotary and follow the signs. On Sun. and Aug. 1-24 you must take bus #20 or 301, both of which head from town center toward the station on via dell'Indipendenza and turn onto via Irnerio. Get off at the 1st stop after the bus leaves via San Donato, and walk the 1.5km to the hostel. A villa set among green pastures. Open 7-9am and 5-11:30pm. L11,000 per person, nonmembers L15,000. Breakfast included. Dinner 5-8pm L10,000.

Protezione della Giovane, via Santo Stefano, 45 (tel. 22 55 73), off p. Porta Ravegnana. Women only. Clean, but often filled with students in the winter. Curfew 10:30pm. L17,000 per person. Breakfast (7:30-9am) and shower included. Lunch and dinner L10,000 each. Reservations recommended.

Albergo Panorama, via Livraghi, 1 (tel. 22 18 02). Off via Ugo Bassi, near the intersection with via N. Sauro. True to its name this cozy hotel has large rooms with panoramic views of the hills behind Bologna. Very clean, super-friendly management. Singles L35,000. Doubles L60,000.

Albergo Apollo, via Drapperie, 5 (tel. 22 39 55). Near p. Maggiore, off via Rizzoli. Clean white rooms with plenty of space; couldn't be closer to the center of town. Singles L36,000. Doubles L60,000, with bath L76,000.

Pensione Marconi, via Marconi, 22 (tel. 26 28 32). Bear right from the station onto via Amendola, which becomes via Marconi. Spotless. Desk is monitored all night. Singles L35,000. Doubles L58,000, with bath L70,000.

Albergo Minerva, via de' Monari, 3 (tel. 23 96 52), off via dell'Indipendenza about a 10-min. walk from the station. Optimal location, pleasant management, and decent rooms (but without baths). Singles L30,000. Doubles L45,000.

Albergo Il Guercino, via L. Serra, 7 (tel. 36 98 93). Turn left out of the station and go left over the tracks on via Matteotti. Turn left on via Tiarini and then immediately right on via Serra. The best of the high-priced "budget" hotels in Bologna, but an inconvenient location. The young, friendly English-speaking owner lets quiet and comfortable rooms with phones. Midnight curfew. Singles L38,000, with bath L65,000. Doubles L60,000, with bath L85,000.

Albergo Arcoveggio, via Spada, 27 (tel. 35 54 36). Behind the train station, take via Matteoti. New hotel with clean rooms and friendly management. Singles L35,000. Doubles L60,000, with bath L72,000.

Food

Bologna's cuisine centers around fresh hand-made egg pasta in all shapes and sizes, from long strands of *tagliatelle,* to wide flat sheets stuffed with any imaginable filling. The best of the stuffed pastas are *tortellini,* bursting with ground meat, and *tortelloni,* made with ricotta cheese and spinach. Don't miss Bologna's namesake dish, *spaghetti alla Bolognese,* pasta with a hefty meat and tomato sauce. Bologna is also renowned for salamis and hams of all kinds, including (surprise!) "bologna," known locally as *mortadella.*

Restaurants cluster on side streets only minutes away from the town center; the areas around via Augusto Righi and via Piella, as well as the neighborhood of via Saragozza, are especially good for cheap, traditional *trattorie.* **Mercato Ugo Bassi,** via Ugo Bassi, 27, a vast indoor market, sells a wide variety of produce, cheeses, and meats. (Open Mon.-Wed. 7:15am-1pm and 5-7pm, Fri. 7am-1pm and 4:30-7:30pm, Thurs. and Sat. 7:15am-1pm.) Or you can go to Bologna's crowded **outdoor market** in via Pescherie Vecchie, off p. Maggiore (same hours). You'll find the large, American-style **Supermarket Coop** off via dei Mille at p. Martiri. (Open Tues.-Sat. 8:30am-7:30pm and Mon. 2:30-7:30pm.)

Mensa Universitaria, p. Puntoni, 1, where via Zamboni meets via delle Belle Arti. Show the guard a student ID to buy a meal ticket (L1000-7800) which entitles you to pasta, *secondo, contorno, vino,* and *frutta.* Rambunctious students are generally eager to meet foreigners; strike up a conversation while waiting in the long lines. Inside is a bulletin board listing jobs and apartments. Open Sept.-July Mon.-Sat. 11:45am-2:30pm and 6:45-9pm.

Trattoria Da Maro, via Broccaindosso, 71/D (tel. 22 73 04), off strada Maggiore. Students and locals gather here to lunch on satisfying plates of *tagliatelle* or *tortellini* (L5000) and any of the standard *secondi* (L7000). Cover L2000. Open Sept.-July Mon.-Fri. noon-3pm.

Trattoria Della Santa, via Urbana, 7/F. Pasta that would make your Italian fairy godmother cry her heart out, but portions are petite. *Tortelloni* made with ricotta, spinach and herbs, L7000. Tasty grilled meat *secondi* (starting at L8000). Open Sept.-July Mon.-Sat. 12:30-2:30pm and 7:45-10:30pm.

Oggi Si Vola, via Urbana, 7/E (tel. 58 53 08). A rare sight in Italy: an entirely macrobiotic restaurant. Cheerful and homey interior with an open kitchen. Miso soup and such macrofaves as grilled vegetables, L8000. Open Mon.-Sat. noon-2:30pm and 8-10:30pm.

Antica Trattoria Roberto Spiga, via Broccaindosso, 21/A (tel. 26 00 67). A modest, miraculous Bolognese relic: one room, a couple of servers, and a surfeit of good food. Complete meals L18,500 with wine or water. Sublime *gnocchi* L5000. Wine L1000 per glass. Open Mon.-Sat. noon-2pm and 7-10pm.

Trattoria Da Danio, via S. Felice, 50 (tel. 55 52 02). A 10-min. hike up via San Felice off via Ugo Bassi rewards you with a large and appetizing menu at this humble, authentic *trattoria*. Try the *lasagne verdi* or the *tagliatelle verdi pancetta e pomodoro* (L7000 each). Daily pasta specials L7000. Cover L2500. Open Sept.-July Mon.-Sat. noon-2:30pm and 7:30-10pm. Closed for 2 weeks in August.

Lazzarini, via Clavature, 1 (tel. 23 63 29), off p. Maggiore. Touristy but affordable snack bar with an exquisite self-service restaurant upstairs. The menu changes daily, but look for the *tortellini alla panna* L5800. Other pasta dishes L6000. Entrees L7000-9000. Restaurant open Mon.-Fri. 11:30am-3pm. Snack bar open Mon.-Sat. 7am-8pm.

Ristorante Clorofilla, strada Maggiore, 64 (tel. 23 53 43), near p. Porta Ravegnana. Although the name sounds like a throat medicine, the food here is innovative, healthy, and almost exclusively vegetarian. Bulletin board is the communication center for local environmental and social action groups. Try one of their imaginative salads (L5500-8000), or tea (L3000). Desserts L3500-5000. Open Mon.-Sat. 11am-3pm and 7pm-midnight, in the winter tea served 4-7pm. A small **health-food market** a few doors down sells whole-wheat bread, organically grown fruit, and delicious cookies. Open Mon.-Fri. 8am-1pm and 4-7pm, Sat. 8am-1pm.

Pizzeria La Mamma "Self Service," via Zamboni, 16. A popular hangout frequented by boisterous university and military students (any student ID will get you a 10% discount). Table service also available. Delicious pizza (L5500-10,000). Open daily noon-2:30pm, 7-10pm.

Caffè Rinascimento, via Oberdan, 2 (tel. 22 19 04), off p. Porta Ravegnana. An elegant caffè and piano bar. Expensive coffee, pastries, and hours of intimate conversation among Bologna's beautiful people. Avoid the "petit restaurant;" the prices are *grossi*. Open daily 8am-11:30pm.

La Torinese, p. Re Enzo 1/A (tel. 23 67 43), off p. Maggiore. Bologna's favorite *gelato*. Open Mon.-Sat. 7am-9pm; Sept.-July Fri.-Wed. 7am-9pm.

Sights

Bologna's most remarkable sight is the endless series of porticoes lining buildings throughout the city. Begun during the 14th century, porticoes offered a solution to the housing crisis of a growing city; buildings expanded into the street while leaving room for mounted riders to pass underneath. The building frenzy lasted several centuries, resulting in a diverse mix of architectural styles, from Gothic to Renaissance to Baroque. You will be hard-pressed to find two porticoes with the same design and decoration, though all serve the same function and are roughly the same size.

The yawning tranquility of **piazza Maggiore,** the heart and center of the city, reflects both Bologna's historical wealth, exhibited in its collection of tidy monuments, and its modern-day prosperity, evidenced by the city's commitment to maintaining the *piazza* in well-swept repair. The **Basilica di San Petronio,** designed by Antonio da Vincenzo (1390), was built to overawe. The Bolognese originally planned (like many cocky Italian towns) to make their basilica larger than St. Peter's in Rome, but the jealous Church ordered that the funds be used instead to build the nearby Palazzo Archiginnasio. The marble facade of the *duomo,* displaying the town's heraldic red and white, extends to the magnificent central portal. Jacopo della Quercia (1367-1438) carved the eroded marble *Virgin and Child* and the expressive Old and New Testament reliefs. The cavernous Gothic interior has played host to such historic events as meetings of the Council of Trent (when not meeting in Trent) and the 1530 ceremony in which Pope Clement VII gave Italy to the German king Charles V. According to legend, the pomp and pageantry of the papal exercises here drove a disgusted Martin Luther to reform Germany. The chapels to the left contain a few additional curiosities. Check in the north aisle for the extravagant *St. Roch* by Parmigianino. The zodiacal sundial on a nearby wall is the largest in Italy—it measures hours, days, and months when the sun shines through the ceiling opening onto the floor. The seventh chapel has a 15th-century Lorenzo Costa *Madonna and Saints.* Finally, don't miss the eighth chapel, with Jacopo di Paolo frescoes of *Heaven and Hell.* (Open daily 7:30am-7pm.)

Behind San Petronio, through one of Bologna's busiest porticoes, visit the **Palazzo Archiginnasio,** formerly a university building, covered with memorials to and crests of notable scholars. It now houses the town library; there's an old anatomical theater upstairs, but you have to ask the *portiere* to open it. Shattered during the bombing of 1944, the theater was subsequently reconstructed from thousands of rubbly bits. (Open Mon.-Sat. 9am-12:30pm. Free.)

Piazza del Nettuno adjoins p. Maggiore. The famous 16th-century bronze *Neptune and Attendants* statue and fountain, the work of Giambologna, grace the square. Affectionately called "The Giant" by town citizens, Neptune reigns over the seas and a collection of extremely erotic sirens and water-babies. To the right, a clock tower, a beautiful terra-cotta *Madonna* by Nicolò dell'Arca, a Menganti bronze statue of Pope Gregory XIV, and some Gothic windows by Bologna's favorite Renaissance architect, Fioravante Fioravanti, punctuate the large brick block of the **Palazzo Comunale.** (Open Tues.-Sat. 9am-2pm, Sun. 9am-12:30pm. Free.) The Romanesque **Palazzo del Podestà,** across the *piazza* (facing San Petronio) was remodeled by Fioravanti's son Aristotle, who later designed Moscow's Kremlin.

Via Rizzoli leads from p. Nettuno to **piazza Porta Ravegnana,** where seven streets converge in Bologna's medieval quarter. The two towers here are the emblem of the city. Of the 200 towers built in the 12th and 13th centuries by aristocratic Bolognese families only a dozen or so remain. Legend has it that the two principal families of Bologna, the Asinelli and the Garisendi, competed to build the tallest and best-looking tower. The Garisendi plunged into the construction of their tower without suitably reinforcing the foundation. It sank on one side and the upper portion fell off; all that remains is the leaning section. The Asinelli were more cautious and built their tower to a sleek 97m (number four on the big list of tallest Italian towers—after Cremona, Siena, and Venice, in case you're keeping score). Reality tells a simpler, if less dramatic, story: land movement botched an attempt to build an observation tower for the civic defense system (the lower, tilting tower), so the city started again and found greater success nearby. Climb the **Torre degli Asinelli** for an amazing view of the city; the arches of Lorraine ogli Estara are particularly breathtaking. (Open daily 9am-6pm. In winter, 9am-5pm. Admission L3000.)

Going down via Zamboni to p. Verdi, one enters the **Zona Universitaria,** Europe's oldest university campus. Keep your eyes peeled, though, or you might miss it. The buildings are non-descript, disjunct, and don't appear to be affiliated to a university. Only the signs over the doors let you know that these are the ancient halls of the learned. The political posters plastered everywhere reflect the idealistic bent of Bologna's college crowd. If you're in town in June, look for the traditionally vulgar posters lampooning the lives of graduating students.

Back at the two towers, the Strada Maggiore leads east past the **Basilica of San Bartolomeo.** Stop here and see the exquisite *Madonna* by Guido Reni in the left transept before proceeding to the **Church of Santa Maria dei Servi,** a remarkably intact Gothic church. Inside columns alternate with octagonal pillars to support a unique combination of ogival arches and ribbed vaulting. In a left-hand chapel behind the altar hangs

Cimabue's great *Maestà*. Giovanni Antonio Montorsoli, a pupil of Michelangelo, executed the exquisite Renaissance altar.

Via Santo Stefano leads from the two towers past the pointed arches of the portico of the **Palazzo di Mercanzia,** opening onto the triangular **piazza Santo Stefano.** The **basilica's** four interlocking Romanesque churches are all that remain of the original seven. The most spectacular church, the round **Chiesa del San Sepolcro,** is the center of the group. San Petronio, patron saint of Bologna, lies here, buried under the pulpit. In the courtyard in the rear is the **Basin of Pilate**--the governor supposedly absolved himself of responsibility for Christ's death in this bath-size tub. Flanking San Sepolcro is the oldest church in the group, the **Church of SS. Vitale e Agricola.** Its arched interior incorporates bits of Roman temples, capitals, and columns. A labyrinth of little chapels opens off the side of "Pilate's courtyard," and in the back you'll come upon the dark **Church of the Trinity.** You can skip the small religious museum on the top story with a good conscience. (Open daily 9am-noon and 3-6pm. Admission L2000.)

From p. Maggiore, follow via dell'Archiginnasio to via Farini and then via Garibaldi to the **Church of San Domenico.** San Domenico, founder of the Dominican order, is buried here. Nicolò dell'Arca earned his nickname for the work he did on the saint's tomb, or "ark." His statues rival the Michelangelos in the tomb and the softly modeled 13th-century reliefs by Nicola Pisano. To tell whose work is whose, consult the informative schema hanging near the entrance to the chapel. Look for Filippino Lippi's *Visit of St. Catherine* at the end of the right aisle.

The **Church of San Giacomo Maggiore,** in p. Rossini is a successful mélange of the Romanesque and Gothic styles. The edifice was designed in the late 13th century, when the Dominican and Franciscan brotherhoods, who favored the Gothic design, began to influence the aristocratic clergy, adherents of the Romanesque style. The chapels enclose paintings by Caracci, Veneziano, Tibaldi, and Barocci, and a tomb sculpture by Jacopo della Quercia hangs high on the wall of the ambulatory. The adjoining Romanesque **Oratorio di Santa Cecilia** (ask the sacristan to let you in through the back of the church) presents a calm cycle of Renaissance frescoes by Amico Aspertini, contrasting sharply with those of Tibaldi. Behind, in the ambulatory, is the **Bentivoglio Chapel,** commissioned by these 15th century tyrants of Bologna. Lorenzo Costa painted the frescoes on the wall; one depicts the Bentivoglio clan. On the altar is a magnificent Francesco Francia altarpiece.

The **Museo Civico Archeologico,** via Archiginnasio, 2 (tel. 23 38 49), exhibits an excellent collection of prehistoric and Etruscan artifacts. Innumerable Roman inscriptions and Bronze and Stone Age tools are on display along with various artistic antiquities. (Open daily 9am-1pm, 3:30-7pm. Admission L5000, students L2500.)

The **Pinacoteca Nazionale,** via delle Belle Arti, 56 (tel. 22 32 32), ranks among Italy's best galleries. Follow the progress of Bolognese artists from primitivism to mannerism and beyond. Bolognese artists may have missed the boat on the Renaissance but the Pinacoteca doesn't. The first section contains a Giotto altarpiece, and the Renaissance wing contains Raphael's *Ecstasy of Santa Cecilia,* Perugino's *Madonna in Glory,* Guido Reni's *Madonna,* and Parmigianino's *Madonna di Santa Margherita.* One room holds great works by the three Carracci, Bolognese natives who helped spark the Baroque revolution. (Open Tues.-Sat. 9am-2pm, Sun. 9am-1pm. Admission L6000.)

The **Museo Civico Medioevale e del Rinascimento** (tel. 22 89 12), in the 15th-century Palazzo Ghisilardi Fava at via Manzoni, 4, contains, in addition to a number of exquisite curios, a superb collection of the sculpted tombs of medieval Bolognese professors, which typically show the professor reading to students. The diligent students are shown dozing, daydreaming, and gossiping. Other important pieces include the huge gilt bronze statue of Pope Boniface VIII and the "Stone of Peace," which depicts the Virgin and Child flanked by kneeling students who came to terms with the *comune* in 1321 after protesting the execution of a fellow student. (Open Mon. and Wed.-Sat. 9am-2pm. Sun. 9am-1pm. Admission L5000, students L2500.)

The **Santuario della Madonna di San Luca** is a distinctive landmark outside the city on Monte della Guardia—you'll probably notice it from the train when arriving in Bologna. Built in the early 1700s by Carlo Dotti, the sanctuary houses the painting *Madonna and Child,* undoubtedly the work of a 12th-century Byzantine artist, though attributed to St. Luke. The sanctuary's eye-catching 4km portico stretches from Bologna's southwest city gate, the Porta Saragozza, up the hill to the church. Constructed between 1674 and 1793, the walkway encloses 665 arches. To get to the Santuario, take city bus #20 from behind p. Nettuno to Villa Spada, outside of town. From here, take the private **Casepuri** bus to the sanctuary (round-trip L2000).

The *piazzola*, a large and diverse **open-air market**, takes place on p. VIII Agosto (Sept.-July Fri.-Sat. 8am-2pm). Literature buffs may want to drop by the **museum and house of Giosuè Carducci**, p. Carducci, 5, to see the poet's works and sundry possessions. (Open Mon.-Sat. 9am-noon and 3-5pm, Sun. 9am-1pm).

Entertainment

Bologna Spettacolo News available at the tourist office (free) or any newsstand (L800) has all the information you need about upcoming concerts and music festivals, whether it be 17th-century chamber music or a 20th-century love-in. The city sponsors daily **open-air discos,** in July and August in Parco Cavaioni, on the outskirts of the city. (Action begins about 10pm. Free. The main disco is called "Frigo".) To get to the park, take bus #52 from p. Minghetti into the hills 5km out. Once there, make friends fast, as bus service may end by 10pm. Bologna's newest nighttime summer entertainment is the city-sponsored **Bologna Sogna** (Bologna Dreams) series, which features concerts at *palazzi* and museums around town through July and August. Ask the tourist office for a schedule of events.

During the academic year, current **English-language movies** are screened every Monday at **L'Adriano,** via S. Felice, 52 (tel. 55 51 27; admission L6000).

Bologna's tremendous university population makes for lively nighttime diversion during the academic year. Try *osterie* and bars in the university district, particularly along via delle Belle Arti and on p. Verdi. Also check out **Cantina Bentivoglio** at v. Mascarella, 4/B for jazz, and the **Old West Pub** at v. Saragossa, 55 for folk music.

Mòdena

It is fitting that Mòdena is the hometown of Luciano Pavarotti, avid eater and operatic tenor virtuoso as well as Ferrari and Maserati factories—like all of the above, Mòdena purrs with prosperity. Conquered by the Romans in the 3rd century BC, the city owed its early prominence to its location: the region's principal road, the via Emilia, ran through the heart of this town. In 1598, the Este family lost Ferrara to the pope and reestablished their duchy in Mòdena. The city is best visited as an excursion from Bologna or Parma or as a stopover between the two.

Orientation and Practical Information

Mòdena lies roughly midway between Parma and Bologna. From the train station, take bus #7 or 11 (L1000) to **piazza Grande** and the center of town. The alternative is a walk that takes you left on via Crispi, right down corso Emanuele, right around the Palazzo Ducale, and finally to **via Emilia** (Mòdena's main street) and the **piazza** by way of via Battisti

Tourist Office: via Scudari, 30 (tel. 22 24 82). From p. Grande, walk right on via Emilia. Friendly and helpful. Happy to unload free maps and brochures. Open Mon.-Fri. 9am-12:30pm and 3:30-4:30pm, Sat. 9am-12:30pm. **Informa Giovani,** via Scuderi, 12 (tel. 20 65 83). Just a few doors down from the tourist office. An information office geared specifically to young people, they dole out a fantastically useful publication called *La Città in Tasca,* with listings of everything from bike shops to banks. The office also keeps bulletin boards with job & housing notices. Drop by to check out their material, or just chat with the staff. Open Mon.-Tues. and Thurs.-Sat. 10:30am-12:30pm and 4-7pm.

Budget Travel: Hersa Viaggi (CTS), via Emilia Est, 429 (tel. 37 28 63). Information and numerous student discounts. Open Mon.-Fri. 8am-12:30pm and 3-7pm, Sat. 8am-12:30pm; closed Aug. 9-24. Also try **Agenzia Viaggiatori Iter,** via S. Carlo, 5 (tel. 22 23 70), off via Emilia 1 block from

p. Grande. Similar discount services. Open Mon.-Fri. 8:30am-12:30pm and 3-7pm. Closed 1 week in Aug.

Post Office: via Emilia, 86 (tel. 24 20 30). Open Mon.-Sat. 8:15am-7:40pm. **Postal Code:** 41100.

Telephones: SIP, via Università, 23, off corso Canal Grande. Open daily 8am-8pm. **Telephone Code:** 059.

Trains: p. Dante Alghieri (tel. 21 82 26). To: Bologna (every 30min., 20min., L2800); Parma (every 30min., 30min., L3800); and Milan (16 per day, 1hr. 45min., L12,200).

Buses: ATCM, via Fabriani (tel. 30 88 00), off viale Monte Kosica, which leads from the train station. Bus #7 to Ferrara (every hr., L5400), bus #7 to Maranello (several daily, L3500). Also a bus to Bologna (L4000).

Emergencies: tel. 113. **Police:** viale Rimembranze, 14 (tel. 22 51 72). **Hospital: Nuovo Policlinico,** tel. 36 10 24. Take bus #7 east and get off at via del Pozzo.

Accommodations and Camping

Here, as throughout Emilia Romagna, reserve ahead if you plan on sticking around for a night or two.

Locanda Sole, via Malatesta, 45 (tel. 21 42 45), off via Emilia at p. Muratori, west of p. Grande. Only 100m from town center. Cool, basic rooms catering to students. Singles L27,000. Doubles L45,000. Showers included.

Albergo del Pozzo, via del Pozzo, 72/A (tel. 36 03 50), slightly east of town center. Take bus #7 east and get off at via del Pozzo. Adequate accommodations but often full; call 2-3 days before arrival. Singles L27,000. Doubles L36,000, with bath L55,000.

Albergo Astoria, via Sant'Eufemia, 43 (tel. 22 55 87), parallel to and south of via Emilia, off p. Grande. Fifty slightly dilapidated budget rooms—kept clean by incredibly friendly management. Singles L25,000. Doubles L40,000. Showers L3000.

Camping: International Camping Mòdena, via Cave Ramo, 111 (tel. 33 22 52), in Località Bruciata. Take bus #7 to the bus station and then #12 (without a bar through it) to within half a kilometer of the site. L6200 per person, L4500 per tent. Open March 15-Oct.

Food

Luxuriating in the low plains area around the Po river basin, the city and its environs till one of the most fertile soils in the Italian peninsula. Mòdena, like nearby gastronomic centers Bologna and Parma, produces unsurpassed *prosciutto crudo,* and the bright, sparkling *lambrusco* red wine (best chilled). Mòdena's own claim to gastronomic fame derives from the curiously tame but fragrant and full-bodied *balsamic* vinegar, which Modenese sprinkle liberally over salads, vegetables, and even fruit. Balsamic vinegar can be aged for decades, and the finest vinegars can do damage upwards of L50,000 for a lilliputian bottle. Top off a meal with the local *Vignola* cherries, considered to be among the tastiest in Italy (travelers continuing on to the Veneto can compare them to Ásolo's famed crop and sip in red-lipped bliss).

Stock your picnic basket at the **STANDA supermarket,** via Emilia, 119, across from the post office (open Mon.-Wed. and Fri.-Sat. 8:30am-12:30pm and 3:30-7:30pm, Thurs. 8:30am-12:30pm). To watch local Modenese society in action, drop into **Bar Molinari,** via Emilia next to STANDA, immediately before lunch and dinner or in the evening. Small pastries L1100, large ones (all you'll need for lunch) L3000. Try the delicate *torta Elizia.* (Open daily 7am-12:30am.)

Trattoria Da Omer, via Torre, 33 (tel. 21 80 50), off via Emilia across from p. Torre. Look for the hand-painted sign among the jewelry and fur stores. Chef Omer is the saving grace of Mòdena with his reasonably priced, meticulously prepared delicacies. *Tortellini fiocco di neve,* filled with fresh cheeses and seasoned with butter and sage, is pasta at its prime for L8000. Zesty vegetable buffet L4000. *Secondi* L9000. *San Giovese* wine L9000 per : Cover L2000. Open Mon.-Fri. 12:30-2:30pm and 7:30-10:30pm.

Ghirlandina Mensa, via Leodoino Vescovo, 9 (tel. 23 72 55). From the *duomo* take largo Sant'Eufemia and turn left onto via Leodoino Vescovo; the mensa hides on your left. One of Mòdena's best cafeterias: tasty food and consistent quality. Menu changes daily. *Primi* L2500-3000. *Pasta al salmone* L3000. Secondi L4000-5000. Open Sept.-July Sun.-Fri. noon-6pm and 7-9pm.

Cioè, viale Monte Kosica, 140 (tel. 21 03 96), behind the bus station in a rougher part of town. Traditional Italian fare. Pasta L5000. *Secondi* L7000-10,000. Open Aug.20-Aug.10 Mon.-Fri. noon-2:30pm. Closed for two weeks in Aug.

Italy, Italy, via dell'Università, off corso Canal Grande. A modern, informal Italian fast-food restaurant actually patronized by Italians. Extremely congenial staff. Marble and glass interior complements decent pasta offerings (L4000). All-you-can-eat salad bar L5000 (small plate L2800). Open Tues.-Fri. 10am-11pm, Sat.-Sun. noon-10pm.

Sights

One of the best-preserved Romanesque cathedrals in Italy, Mòdena's **duomo,** in p. Grande, dates from the early 12th century. The lions on the south portal show Lombard influence, but the rest of the cathedral deviates substantially from orthodox Lombard-Romanesque style. Its patron, the Marchioness Matilda of Canossa, held a fief that included Tuscany, Parma, Ferrara, and Mantua. Although Matilda professed Guelph sympathies, much of her territory backed the Holy Roman Emperor, especially the merchant *comune* of Mòdena. Thus the stylistic innovations on the religious buildings sponsored by the Marchioness often bore political significance. Since her Ghibelline opposition was based in Lombardy, Mòdena's *duomo* displays a trussed (rather than a Lombard vaulted) roof.

The master sculptor Wiligelmo and his school decorated most of the *duomo* with stylized carvings that draw on local, Roman, Biblical, and even Celtic themes. Carvings enrich the cathedral's several entrances. On the front doorway off the *piazza,* look for floral carvings that represent heaven and Christ's genealogy. Scenes from the Old Testament surmount the left and central portals. A heart-wrenching depiction of Adam and Eve being evicted from the Garden of Eden graces the left side of the central portal. Over the right entrance, carvings show San Gimignano, Mòdena's patron saint, traveling to Asia. The entrance facing via Emilia displays locally inspired Labors of the Months. (*Duomo* open daily 7am-noon and 3:30-7pm.) The **Museo Lapidario del Duomo** (tel. 21 60 78), across the street on the via Lanfranco side, is closed indefinitely for restorations.

Looming high over the *duomo* is the 95m **Ghirlandina Tower,** Mòdena's symbol. Built in the late 13th century, it incorporates Gothic as well as Romanesque elements. A memorial to those who died fighting the Nazis and Fascists during World War II has been added to the base. The tower opens only a few days a year—the porter at the *municipio* (town hall) in p. Grande can tell you the next date of opening. Tourist officials advise caution for visits to the tower.

The **Palazzo dei Musei,** in largo Sant'Agostino at the western side of via Emilia, contains both the **Biblioteca Estense** (Este Library, tel. 22 22 48) and a picture gallery. The library's permanent display of masterpieces includes elaborate 15th- and 16th-century bindings, a 1501 Portuguese map of the world, a 1481 copy of Dante's *Divine Comedy,* and a series of exquisitely illuminated manuscripts. Don't miss the **Bible of Borso d'Este,** a 1200-page tome partially illustrated by Taddeo Crivelli, a 15th-century Emilian painter. (Open Mon.-Sat. 9am-1pm. Free.)

The **Galleria Estense** (tel. 22 21 45 or 23 50 04), on the floor above the library, is a well-stocked and meticulously organized collection. Bernini's bust of Francesco d'Este I, who assembled much of the collection, presides from an alcove as you enter. Turn right into a long gallery that begins with earthy Emilian primitives and peaks in Cosmè Tura's expressionistic *St. Anthony of Padua.* Beyond, a remarkably strong Flemish section features Joos van Cleve's *Virgin and Child with St. Anne.* A room of Anthonio Begarelli's elegant terra-cotta sculptures is trailed by another room loaded with Dosso Dossi's eccentric creations. Mannerist and Baroque galleries follow, with some Venetian works by Tintoretto and El Greco, as well as Velàzquez's famous portrait of Francesco I d'Este. Included are Emilian paintings ranging from Correggio's delicate *Madonna and Child* (1489-1534) to Guercino's explosive *Martyrdom of St. Peter* and

Parmigianino's peculiar elongated portraits. (Open Tues.-Wed. and Fri. 9am-2pm, Thurs. and Sat. 9am-7pm, Sun. 9am-1pm. Admission L4000.) On the second floor of the *palazzo dei Musei* discover the newly restored **Archeological Museum,** which cradles a vast and eclectic collection of archeological, anthropological and artistic objects. The various thematic galleries focus on topics such as the art of Florentine paper-making, early electromagnetic experiments, and paleolithic stone tools. The museum also contains an especially colorful exhibit of relics from South American native peoples, collected in the early 1800s. (Open Tues.-Sat. 9am-1pm. Tues. and Thurs. 3-6pm. Sun. 9am-1pm. Admission L3000.)

Mòdena's real claim to international fame is the **Ferrari** automobile. The factory is located southwest of Mòdena in **Maranello.** (Bus #7 from the bus terminal, every hr., 30min., L3500.) Though you're not allowed to sniff around the inner-workings of this top-secret complex, you can, however, view a truly astounding display of antique and modern Ferrari cars and Formula One racers, as well as trophies at the nearby **Galleria Ferrari,** the company museum, via Dino Ferrari, 43 (tel. (0536) 94 32 04). To reach the museum from the Ferrari factory stop, zoom down the road in the same direction as the bus for about 200 yards, and then screech a right at the sign that says Galleria Ferrari; the museum is nestled in an oversized glass-and-steel amalgamation on the left, about 100 yards down the street. The upstairs of this bi-level building houses the trophies collected over the years by unsurpassable Ferrari racing cars. Quake in front of the monstrous beasts that make the wheels churn in the next aisle, then head downstairs to worship the cars themselves. Over twenty Ferraris are on display; drool and fantasize over the stately antiques of yesteryear or the flashy turbos of the 90s. (Open Tues.-Sun. 9:30am-12:30pm and 3-6pm. Admission L7000.) On your way back to the bus, check out the memorabiliafest in the souvenir shop. (Open Mon.-Wed. and Fri.-Sat. 9am-12:30pm and 3:30-7pm.)

Entertainment

The city sponsors a summer music, ballet, and theater series called **Sipario In Piazza** with performances in p. Grande during July and August. If the stars are properly aligned, you might happen on a performance by virtuoso native son, Luciano Pavarotti. Contact the Ufficio Sipario in *piano terra* Palazzo Comunale, piazza Grande (tel. 20 64 60), for information and tickets (L10-20,000). Winter brings **opera** to Mòdena's **Teatro Comunale,** corso Canal Grande, 85 (tel. 22 51 83), next to the Ghirlandina Tower. On the fourth weekend of every month, the city puts on the **Fiera d'Antiquariato** at the Ex Ippodromo park, northwest of the town center (take bus #7), a boisterous celebration of food, wine, and local customs. To experience Modenese life in the fast lane, check out the list of **discos** at the **tourist office** or at the office of **Informa Giovani,** where they can also give you tips and up-to-the-minute information on what is to be done.

Parma

Parma's place in the international limelight derives not from its splendid history or culture but from the dedication with which "i Parmigiani" (people from Parma) craft their incomparable delicacies. Parmesan specialties include a sweet and buttery-smooth *prosciutto cruolo,* the sharp and crumbly *Parmigiano* (Parmesan) cheese, and a bright sparkling red wine called *Lambrusco.*

But there is more to Parma than just food. The city's market-town prosperity has long financed its robust cultural activity: here 16th-century mannerist painting came to full bloom under Il Parmigianino, while Giuseppe Verdi became so enamored of the local countryside that he remained in Parma to compose his greatest music. Stendhal, then an unknown French functionary, made the city the setting of his 1839 novel *The Charterhouse of Parma,* loosely based upon events in the life of Alessandro Farnese (Pope Paul III), who created the Duchy of Parma and gave the city to his natural son. Twentieth-century Parma has given the world maestro Arturo Toscanini.

Today Parma cultivates an air of mannered elegance and prosperity recalling the refinement of 19th-century rule. The town is blanketed in tranquility, overtrafficked by neither cars nor tourists.

Orientation and Practical Information

Parma lies about 200km northwest of Bologna, conveniently served by the Bologna-Milan train line. The historical center lies on the eastern side of the Torrente Parma, a dry river bed during the heat of the summer, which bisects the city. Walk left from the station to via Garibaldi, then right 1km to the town center. Turn left on via della Repubblica to reach **piazza Garibaldi.** The main streets branch off this *piazza,* with via Mazzini running west, strada Cavour heading north toward the *duomo,* via della Repubblica extending east, and strada Farini branching south in the direction of the **Cittadella,** Parma's park and the site of its youth hostel.

Tourist Office: p. del Duomo, 5 (tel. 23 47 35). From the station, walk left and turn right down via Garibaldi, then make a left onto strada Pisacane. Wonderfully helpful, multilingual staff offers a detailed city map and information on all nearby towns. Does not make hotel reservations, but has a price list of Parmesan accommodations. Open Mon.-Fri. 9am-12:30pm and 3:30-6:30pm, Sat. 9am-12:30pm; Oct.-April Mon.-Fri. 9am-12:30pm and 3-6pm, Sat. 9am-12:30pm.

Currency Exchange: Credito Romagnolo, via Mazzini, 6. Open Mon.-Fri. 8:20am-1:20pm and 3-4pm, Sat. 8:20-11:20am. Try the **train station** as a last resort. Open 5:25am-11pm, but avail yourself of this option only on weekends, when the banks are closed.

Post Office: on the street that runs between strada Garibaldi and strada Cavour, near the *duomo.* Open Mon.-Fri. 8:15am-6:40pm, Sat. 8:15am-12:20pm. Also a **branch** across the street from the station, at via Verdi, 250. Open 8:30am-6:40pm; in Aug. 8:30am-2pm. **Postal Code:** 43100.

Telephones: SIP, (tel. 23 84 81), in p. Garibaldi in the front of the city hall. Beware: loud and chaotic at night. Open daily 8am-10pm. **Telephone Code:** 0521.

Trains: tel. 77 11 18, rarely answered. To: Milan (20 per day, 1 hr. 20 min., L10,500); Bologna (34 per day, 1 hr., L6500); Florence (7 per day, L13,800).

Buses: (tel. 23 38 13), on viale P. Toschi before the ponte Verdi. More convenient than trains to provincial towns. To: Colorno (6 per day, L2200); Fontanellato (nearly every hr., L3200); Torrechiara (nearly every hr., L3200); Busseto (6 per day, L5250); Bardi (5 per day, L6200); Montechiarugolo (several daily, L2200).

Emergencies: tel. 113. **Police: Questura,** borgo della Posta (tel. 23 88 88). **Hospital: Ospedale Maggiore,** via Gramsci, 14 (tel. 967 20), across the river beyond the Ducal Palace.

Accommodations and Camping

Parma's budget hotels fill up quickly. Call in advance to reserve a place at the hostel.

Ostello Cittadella (HI), via Pasao Buole (tel. 58 15 46). Take bus #9 (make sure you ask the driver if he's going towards the *ostello*) from in front of the station (last bus 8pm; L700). Get off after about 15 min. when you see a small white sign that says *ostello.* Walk down via Pasao Buole until you reach a large white portico surrounded by ancient walls; walk inside to the hostel on your left. From p. Garibaldi, take bus #2 or 6. The hostel occupies a 17th-century Farnese fortress. Spacious, 6-bed rooms, fresh bathrooms (ask downstairs for toilet paper), and luxurious showers with hot water. Three-day max. stay. Reception open all day. Lockout 9:30am-5pm. Curfew 11pm. HI members only, but sometimes accepts student ID. L12,000 per person.

Casa della Giovane, via del Conservatorio, 11 (tel. 28 32 29). Women only. Beautiful rooms, sturdy furniture, and polished wood floors. Clean and very friendly. When rooms are tight (usually Sept.-June) younger women receive preference. Curfew 9:30pm; women over 18 can stay out until 11:30pm on Thurs. Doubles and triples: L25,000 for women under 25, full board, L17,000 for room only. Women over 25 (exceptional cases only) L32,000 for full board, L20,000 for room only.

Albergo Croce di Malta, borgo Palmia, 8 (tel. 23 56 43). Peaceful rooms kept sparkling. Singles L30,000. Double L45,000.

Locandà Lazzaro, via XX Marzo, 14 (tel 20 89 44). No sign, but upstairs from the restaurant of the same name. A few homey rooms. Singles L28,000, with bath L35,000. Doubles with bath L52,000.

Albergo Leon d'Oro, viale Fratti, 4 (tel. 77 31 82), off via Trento. From the station, go 2 blocks left. Functional rooms (no baths), and convenient to the center. Singles L25,000. Doubles L35,000.

Camping: at the Ostello Cittadella (above). The only campground near Parma. Has electrical outlets and a public park nearby. Three-day max. stay. L5000 per person, L6000 per tent. Open April-Oct.

Food

The cuisine of Parma is unequalled, yet surprisingly affordable. Native Parmesan cheese, famous prosciutto, and an abundance of local sausage varieties are all proudly displayed in the windows of via Garibaldi's numerous *salumerie.* (Most open Mon.-Wed. and Fri.-Sat. 8am-1pm and 4-7pm, Thurs. 8am-1pm.) *Lambrusco* is the wine of choice. When exported, this sparkling red loses its natural fizz so carbon dioxide is added—this is your chance for the real thing. An **open-air market** can be found at p. Ghiaia, off viale Mariotti, past Palazzo Pilotta (8am-1pm and 3-8pm). Shop for basics at **Supermarket 22,** via XXII Luglio, 27/C. (Open Mon.-Wed. and Fri.-Sat. 8:30am-1pm and 4-8pm, Thurs. 8:30am-1pm.)

Trattoria Corrieri, via Conservatorio, 1 (tel. 23 44 26). A gorgeous, classy *trattoria,* with white-washed arches, brick columns, and hanging salami and cheeses. Devour traditional *tortelli di zucca* (ravioli stuffed with sweet squash in a cheese sauce, L6000) or try the *tris,* a mix of *tortelli* with *zucca, asparagi* (asparagus) and *erbette* (greens) for L8000. *Piatti del giorno* L7000. *Lambrusco* L6000 per . Cover L2000. Open Mon.-Sat. noon-2pm and 7:30-10pm.

Le Sorelle Pachini, strada Farini, 27. Near p. Garibaldi. Open lunch only, so skip dinner! A delightful traditional *salumeria* which hides one of the best *trattorie* in town in the back. Seems to be a well-kept local secret; you won't find many tourists here. Menu changes daily to suit the sisters' fancies; *primi* L8000, *secondi* L10,000-12,000. Cover L3000. Open Mon.-Sat. noon-2:30pm

Ristorante Nuovo Giardinetto, borgo Santa Chiara, 10/A (tel. 23 55 51), off borgo Tommasini, which is off via della Repubblica. Pasta, a main course, and a *contorno* for L6700—an inspired bargain. Wine L1200 per half-. Open Sept.-July Mon.-Fri. noon-2pm and 7-9pm.

Pizzeria La Duchessa, p. Garibaldi (tel. 23 35 28). An excellent *trattoria* with a grand variety of *pizze* as well. Large outdoor dining area is a great people-watching forum in the evening. Be prepared to wait for a seat. Pastas average L8000, pizza L5500-10,000, and *secondi* L12,000. Open Tues.-Sun. noon-3pm and 7-10pm.

Antica Gelateria Fiore, strada Petrarca, 1/A. Huge variety of flavors, all delicious. Cones start at L1500.

Sights

Parma's *duomo* and baptistry repose in p. Duomo amidst the characteristic calm magnificence that permeates the entire city (though restoration of both buildings currently dispels both calm and majesty). Masterpieces jam the 11th-century Romanesque **duomo.** The interior houses the *Descent from the Cross* bas-relief by the master Benedett-o Antelami in the south transept, and the *Episcopal Throne* supported by piers in the apse. In the cupola Correggio's *Virgin* rises to a gold heaven in a spiraling gyre of white robes, pink *putti,* and blue sky. The impression of depth is stunning; you'll practically have to stand beneath one corner and look straight up to convince yourself the scene isn't sculpted. (Some of the art is hidden by restoration work, now nearing completion. Open 7:30am-noon and 3-7pm.)

The **baptistry** (tel. 23 58 86), in the final stages of exterior renovation, is an architectural miracle born of the transformation of Romanesque into Gothic. Begun in 1196, the basic structure was completed in 1216, while ornamentation continued until the 1260s. In the absence of the scaffolding, you'd notice the baptistry's asymmetry—in the Middle Ages, symmetry connoted death. Through the beautifully sculpted portals by Antelami, the interior showcases a beautiful dome, the work of Byzantine masters, and 13th-century frescoes of an anonymous local artist. (Open daily 9am-noon and 3:30-8pm. Admission L3000.)

Behind the *duomo* in p. San Giovanni lurks the **Church of San Giovanni Evangelista** (tel. 390 67). Again, restoration efforts currently obscure the Correggio frescoed cupola. Along the left nave over the first, second, and fourth chapels are frescoes by Correggio's mannerist contemporary, Parmigianino. (Open daily 6:30am-noon and 3:30-8pm. Admission L3000.)

Walk back toward the river on strada al Duomo, turn right on strada Cavour, then pull a quick left-right to reach Correggio's **Camera S. Paolo** (tel. 23 33 09) in the small courtyard behind the gate that opens off via M. Melloni (actually out the back door of the post office). If Correggio's lively, lusty scenes of gods and *putti* are any indication, her position as abbess did not prevent Giovanna Piacenze, who commissioned the decoration in 1519, from indulging in life's pleasures. In fact, Giovanna's face appears over the fireplace as the goddess Diana. (Open daily 9am-2pm. Free.)

From the Camera, cross via Garibaldi and p. Marconi to find the gigantic complex of the **Palazzo della Pilotta** hunkering by the river. Constructed in 1602, the palace expresses the authoritarian ambitions of the Farnese dukes. Parma developed from antiquity as a series of distinct clusters of buildings, controlled by religious and civic powers. The Farnese built two new clusters, the Pilotta Palace and the **Cittadella** (now a park), in an attempt to unify the city. The never-completed palace was partially destroyed during World War II. Today it houses several museums, the most important being the **Galleria Nazionale** (tel. 23 33 09). Enter the gallery through the **Farnese Theater,** itself built in 1615 in imitation of Palladio's Teatro Olimpico in Vicenza. In the spectacular Farnese style, this much larger version boasts a moveable stage set. A labyrinth path winds into the gallery proper. This extraordinary collection includes works of the Ferrarese and Parmesan schools, most prominently those of Correggio and Parmigianino, as well as miscellaneous Italian and European masterpieces. Be sure not to miss *Testa di una Fanciulla* (Head of a Young Girl) by Leonardo da Vinci, all of Dosso Dossi's work, and the *Pietà* by Cima da Conegliano. (Theater and gallery open Tues.-Sat. 9am-2pm. Admission to theater L4000.)

Also in the Palazzo della Pilotta, the sizeable **Museo Archeologico Nazionale** (tel. 23 37 18) lodges coins, bronzes, and sculptures of Greek, Etruscan, Roman, and Egyptian origin. Visits to the museum can be made only with advance notice; contact the tourist office. (Open Tues.-Sun. 9am-2pm. Admission L4000.)

Outside the *duomo* district a French flavor lingers, the aftertaste of the rule of Napoleon's wife Marie-Louise over the city and from the more general Gallic influences of the 16th and 18th centuries. The **Museo Glauco Lombardi,** in the Palazzo di Riserva at via Garibaldi, 15 (tel. 23 37 27), has a collection of period pieces devoted to Parma during the reign of Marie-Louise. (Open Tues.-Sat. 9:30am-12:30pm and 4-6pm, Sun. 9:30am-1pm; Oct.-April 9:30am-12:30pm and 3-5pm, Sun. 9:30am-1pm. Free.) Unfortunately, many of the French *palazzi* were blasted to flinders during the war, but enough of the older buildings survive to convey the sophistication depicted by Stendhal.

To remedy cultural overload, retreat to the green flourish of Baroque **Ducal Park,** located west of the Pilotta Palace over the ponte Verdi bridge. (Open 6am-midnight; Oct.-April dawn-dusk.) South of the park on borgo Rodolfo Tanzi, the birthplace of **Arturo Toscanini** (1867-1957), conductor *extraordinaire,* now houses a small museum with memorabilia from the maestro's life. (Tel. 28 54 99. Open Tues.-Sun. 10am-1pm. Free.)

Witness the complex production processes of either *Parmigiano* cheese or *prosciutto di Parma* by contacting the **Consortio di Parmigiano** (tel. 29 27 00) at via Gramsci, 26/A, or the **Consortio di Prosciutto** (tel. 20 81 87) at via M. Dell'Arpa, 8/B. They'll tote you around on a guided tour of the facilities, and throw in a tasty free sample at the end.

Entertainment

The city of Parma sponsors a fine summer music festival, **Concerti Nei Chiostri,** featuring classical music in the area's churches and cloisters. (Tickets L20,000, available at the door.) Contact the tourist office for information, and ask them for their brochure *Andare per Coucche, pieri e castelli,* which lists the local summer concerts and festivals, including starlit concerts in neighboring castles.

Near Parma

Enthusiasts of Italian opera and architecture aficionados will be pleased by the offerings of the cities and towns around Parma. No composer better embodies the Italian soul than opera giant Giuseppe Verdi, whose native hamlet of **Roncole Verdi** rests on the Parma plain 3.5km outside the city of **Busseto** (15 buses daily to Roncole and Busseto, 30min., L4200 and L5200 respectively). To see where this son of a poor innkeeper received his earliest inspiration, visit the house and museum at **Verdi's birth site** (tel. (0524) 922 41) in Roncole. In Busseto proper, within the walls of the ancient **Rocca,** you'll find the famous **Teatro Verdi,** opened in 1868. The best of Verdi's pupils came here to perform during the winter opera season. (Birth site and theater open Tues.-Sun. 9am-noon and 3-7pm; closed Dec.-Mar. except to special groups or by appointment. Admission to both L4000.) Three kilometers away from Busseto (on the same bus) lies the **Villa Sant'Agata** (tel. (0524) 922 10), Verdi's residence during sabbaticals from his work in Milan. Parts of this mansion are open to the public and remain unaltered from the time of his death in 1901. (Open April-Oct. Tues.-Sun. 9-11:40am and 3-6:40pm. Admission L5000.)

Piacenza

Tucked into the distant northwest corner of Emilia Romagna, almost bordering on Piemonte, Piacenza eschews a tourist economy to embrace home-grown prosperity. True to its name, this town is pleasantness incarnate. Piacenza is home to several noteworthy monuments of the Renaissance and Middle Ages, making it a worthwhile stopover on your way through to Parma or Bologna. Piacenza lies on the main rail line between Milan (L5100) and Bologna (L9300), as well as on a secondary line that connects Piacenza to Turin (L12,200) through Alessandria. From the station walk straight across the park on the other side of v. Sant'Ambroglio, take a right on via Alberoni, another right onto via Roma, and then a left off corso Cavour, which leads directly to the **piazza dei Cavalli.** This central square is named for the two massive equestrian statues by Francesco Mochi, cast between 1612 and 1625. Even though the statues were intended as tributes to their riders, Duke Rannucio I (1592-1622) and his father Duke Alessandro Farnese (1545-1592), the horses seem to dominate their masters. Both dukes ruled Piacenza when, together with Parma, it comprised the Farnese kingdom. The true masterpiece of the *piazza,* however, is the gothic **Palazzo del Comune,** now called **Il Gotico.** Built in 1280, the building recalls Piacenza's glory days as a leading member of the Lombard League (a powerful trading group of city-states in northern Italy). Note Il Gotico's excellent preservation, the soaring crenellated battlements, and the sense of depth achieved through the use of a recessed nave surrounded by a massive outer portico of pointed Gothic arches. Constructed between 1122 and 1233, the **duomo** at the opposite end of via XX Settembre broods with a somber interior laid out in three round-pillared aisles. The crypt, with its maze of thin columns, is one of the most beautiful as well as the spookiest in Italy; grab a friend's hand and go check it out. (*Duomo* open Mon.-Sat. 7am-noon and 3:30-7:30pm, Sun. 10-11am and 4-7:30pm.)

The Renaissance **Church of the Madonna di Campagna,** in piazzale Campagna (take via Garibaldi from the center), is in the shape of a Greek cross, lacking the typical long nave with aisles. Designed and built by A. Tramello, the church was completed in 1528. Numerous frescoes by Pardenone adorn the cupola. (Open 8am-noon and 4-7pm.)

The **Palazzo Farnese,** in p. Cittadella, was begun in 1588 but, like its counterpart in Parma, was never completed; walk into the courtyard and note the missing fortifications on its back wall. The *palazzo* houses the **Museo Civico** which boasts the famed Etruscan sheep's liver believed to have been used for divining, as well as a sublime Botticelli fresco depicting the birth of Jesus. (Open Tues.-Wed. and Fri. 9am-12:30pm,

Thurs. and Sat.-Sun. 9am-12:30pm and 3-6pm. Admission L5000.) For art-viewing of a more modern variety, head over to **Galleria Ricci Oddi**, via Sirio, 13 (tel. 207 42), south of p. Sant'Antonino. The museum boasts a good collection of contemporary and modern art, including works by Klimt and A. Bocchi.

The **tourist office** in p. Mercatini, 10 (tel. 293 24), tucked in the back of the Municipio near p. dei Cavalli, distributes a map full of useful information on hostels and sights. (Open Mon.-Wed. and Fri.-Sat. 9am-12:30pm and 4:30-6:30pm.)

As in any Italian town, specialty shops selling meats, cheeses, bread, and fruit are omnipresent. An especially good place to try is via Calzolni, near the center. Local specialties include *tortelli* pasta filled with spinach and ricotta, and *pisarei e fasö,* a hearty bean-and-pea soup. You can sample either at **Trattoria Due Stelle** via Alberoni, 85, a busy little family-run restaurant whose pasta dishes run L4000. *Secondi* are all L6000. (Cover L2000. Open Mon.-Sat. noon-2:30pm and 6:30-9pm.) Or head away from the station to **Osteria Del Trentino,** via del Castello, 71, off p. Borgo, a charming restaurant where you can eat indoors or out back in the leafy garden. *Primi* average L7000 and *secondi* L10,000. (Cover L2000. Open Mon.-Sat. noon-2pm and 8-11pm.) Also try **Ristorante da Renato Angello,** via Calzolai, 2. *Primi* average L7000, *secondi* L10,000. (Open Tues.-Sun. noon-2:30pm, 7-9:30pm. Cover L2000.) The most convenient lodging option is the **Hotel Moderno,** via Tibini, 31 (tel. 38 50 41/2; fax 38 44 38). Just walk along the left side of the park in front of you, directly onto via Tibini. True to its name, it offers modern rooms with new and sturdy furniture and well-scrubbed bathrooms. (Singles L28,000, with bath L36,000. Doubles L40,000, with bath L48,000.) Piacenza's **postal code** is 29100; its **telephone code,** 0523.

Ferrara

Ferrara earned its laurels as the home turf of the Este dynasty from 1208 to 1598. In between murdering sundry relatives or merely plotting to do so, these sensitive aesthetes proved themselves some of the most enlightened (and also bloodthirsty) patrons of their age. Their court and university attracted Petrarch, Ariosto, Tasso, Mantegna, Pisanello, and Titian, among others. Ercole I's early 16th-century city plan broke new ground with its spacious, harmonious design, and here the modern theatre, with curtains, stage, and seated audience, was invented. But the balding dukes eventually went heirless, and Ferrara succumbed to two and half centuries of papal control and cruel neglect. Today, an air of retrospective melancholia permeates the deserted *palazzi* and hangs heavy above the medieval town center.

Orientation and Practical Information

Ferrara lies on the train line between Bologna and Venice. When you walk out of the train station, turn left and then right on viale Cavour, which leads to the Castello Estense at the center of town (1km). Buses #1, 2, and 9 also travel this route (L800).

Tourist Office: p. Municipio, 19 (tel. 20 93 70). Well-stocked. Exceptionally knowledgeable folk eager to discuss everything from local politics to your dining preferences. Open Mon.-Sat. 9am-1pm and 2:30-7pm, Sun. 9am-1pm.

Post Office: viale Cavour, 27 (tel. 345 04), 1 block toward the train station from the *castello.* Open Mon.-Fri. 8am-7:30pm, Sat. 8am-1pm. **Postal Code:** 44100.

Telephones: SIP, largo Castello, 30 (tel. 497 91), off viale Cavour at the castle. Open 8am-8pm. From midnight to 8am, try **Hotel Ripagrande,** via Ripagrande, 21 (tel.76 52 50). **Telephone Code:** 0532.

Trains: Information, tel. 77 03 40; open Mon.-Sat. 8:30am-noon and 3-7pm. To Bologna (33 per day, 40min., L3000, round-trip L5000); Venice (24 per day, 1hr. 30min., L7000, round-trip L12,000); Ravenna (14 per day, 1hr., L4700, round-trip L8000).

Buses: ACFT and **GGFP,** tel. 20 52 35. Main terminal on via Rampari San Paolo. Most buses can also be taken from the train station (buy tickets at **Bar Fiorella,** across from the train station), or from p. Municipio (buy tickets from the information booth at p. Municipio, 10). To Ferrara's beaches (12 per day, 1hr., L4800). Buses to Mòdena depart from the train station (11 per day, 1hr. 30min.-2hr., L4800).

Swimming Pool: via Porta Catena, 103 (tel. 75 03 67). Take bus #3 and get off at the corner of viale XXV Aprile. Go up via Azzo Novello and turn right on via Porta Catena. Open June 11-Aug. Admission L10,000, children L5000.

Emergencies: tel. 113. **Police:** corso Ercole I d'Este, 26 (tel. 20 75 55), off largo Castello. For assistance in English, dial 269 44 and ask for the *Ufficio Stranieri* (office for foreigners). **Hospital: Ospedale Sant'Anna,** corso Giovecca, 203 (tel. 29 51 11).

Accommodations and Camping

Ferrara's decent budget accommodations are likely to be full. Reserve at least a day or two in advance if possible.

Albergo San Paolo, via Pescherie Vecchie, 12 (tel. 76 20 40). Walk down corso Porta Reno from the *duomo*, turn left on via Carlo Mayr, take the 1st right, and then the 1st left. Entrance on via Baluardi, 9. Ferrara's best option. Brand new rooms in a quiet, central location. Singles L30,000, with bath L50,000. Doubles L50,000, with bath L65,000. Reservations advised.

Albergo Nazionale, corso Porta Reno, 32 (tel. 20 96 04), on a busy, loud street that runs between the castle and the *duomo*. The clean rooms fill quickly. Friendly manager knows more about America than any newspaper. Matrimonial suite with 2 beds. Singles L35,000, with bath L40,000. Doubles with bath L70,000.

Albergo Tre Stelle, via Vegri, 15 (tel.10 97 48). Basic, bathless, clean rooms. Impossible to squeeze in—call ahead for reservations. On a romantic, cobblestoned street. Singles L18,000. Doubles L28,000.

Albergo Alfonsa, via Padiglioni, 5 (tel. 20 57 26). Great location but simple rooms verge on the grim and unkempt. Singles L26,000, with bath L35,000. Doubles L40,000, with bath L50,000. If full, the English-speaking owner has another place 1.5km away (take bus #7), **Albergo Daniela,** via Arginone, 198/A (tel. 77 13 98). Singles L18,000, with bath L23,000. Doubles L28,000, with bath L30,000.

Camping: Estense, via Gramicia, 5 (tel. 75 23 96). Take bus #11. L5000 per person, L4000 per child. Open Easter-Oct.

Food

Ferrara produces an enticing array of local specialties. Don't miss the chance to gorge on *capelletti,* delicious triangular meat *ravioli* served in a broth, or *capellacci,* stuffed with squash and parmesan cheese and served in a light sauce of butter and sage. The gastronomic symbol of the city is its robust *salama da sugo,* an aged, ball-shaped sausage of meats soaked with wine, served hot in its own juices. The traditional Ferrarese dessert consists of a chunk of luscious *pampepato,* a chocolate-covered almond and fruit cake. **Negozio Moccia,** via degli Spadari, 19 (tel. 353 75), sells the renowned *pampepato Estense* brand in half-kg (L7950) and 1-kg (L13,500) sizes—the lowest prices in town. (Open Mon.-Sat. 9am-1pm and 4:30-9pm.) For picnic goodies, stop by the **Mercato Comunale,** via Mercato, off via Garibaldi next to the *duomo,* or **Supermarket Conad,** corso Garibaldi, 51/53 (open Mon.-Wed. and Fri.-Sat. 8:30am-7:30pm, Thurs. 8:30am-1pm). All shops in Ferrara close on Thursday afternoon.

Trattoria da Giacomino, via Garibaldi, 135 (tel. 215 96). The best place in town. The *tortelloni di ricotta* are the tastiest pumpkin-filled pasta around (L5500). Or try the *scallopine al Marsala,* meat cutlets with wine, lemon, and mushrooms (L7500). Cover L2000. Open Sept.-July Sun.-Fri. noon-2pm and 7:15-9:30pm.

Trattoria Da Noemi, via Ragno, 31/A (tel. 76 17 15), off corso Porta Reno. The smells of Ferrarese cooking have wafted out of this *trattoria* for over 30 years. The *salamina* (L8000) is as succulent as ever, and a plate of their home-made *gnocchi* (L6000) makes a divine dinner. A veranda stretches out back. Cover L2500. Open Sept.-July Mon.-Sat. noon-2:30pm and 6:30-10pm.

Osteria Al Brindisi, via G. degli Adelandi, 11 (tel. 370 15). The oldest *osteria* in Italy, originally named "Hostaria del Chiuchiolino,"—the restaurant of the drunkard—in 1435. Recently blessed by a full-fledged cardinal, so you can dig in without fear of divine reprisal. Copernicus and Cellini did. No joke. Try delicious sandwiches (L4500) paired with one of their 600 varieties of wine. Open Mon.-Sat. 10am-11pm.

Al Postiglione, vicolo Chiuso del Teatro, 4 (tel. 259 18). Pasta dishes L2500-3500. Delicious sandwiches like the *paradiso,* with prosciutto, artichokes, mushrooms, tomato, and cheese (L4500). Wine L1000 per glass. House specialty is *lasagne* (L5000). Open Mon.-Sat. 8am-3pm and 5-10pm.

Ristorante Asia, viale Cavour, 23A (tel. 486 81). For the rare person who wearies of Italian cuisine. Creative Chinese fare. Try *vitello con funghi e bambu,* an incredible, cheap veal dish (L7000), or the *omelette con carne di granchio,* an unusual scramble of eggs and crabmeat (L4000). Open Sun.-Tues. and Thurs.-Sat. 11am-3pm and 5pm-midnight.

Sights

Towered, turreted, and moated, the awesome *castello* stands precisely in the center of town; the Estes originally constructed it as a refuge from attack by their subjects. Corso della Giovecca lies along the former route of the moat's feeder canal, partitioning the medieval section of town from that which was planned by the d'Este's architect, Biagio Rossetti. The ducal apartments begin at the hanging garden facing p. del Duomo and stretch inside the *palazzo;* they are reached via the grand staircase in the rear courtyard of the building. The Salone dei Giochi and the surrounding rooms retain rich frescoes on their ceilings, the best of which are in the Loggetta degli Aranci. The Lombardesque **Cappella di Renata di Francia** (Chapel of Renée of France) seems a bit out of place here—as Renée herself, a Protestant married to a Catholic, must have felt. Parisina, the wife of Duke Niccolo d'Este III, was killed with her lover, the Duke's natural son, Ugolino in the damp prison underneath. This domestic spat beneath the castle's surface of unruffled elegance inspired Browning to pen "My Last Duchess." (Open Tues.-Sun. 9am-1pm and 2:30-6:30pm. Admission L4000. Entrance inside the courtyard.)

Walk down corso Mártiri della Libertà to p. Cattedrale and the *duomo.* Alongside the church under the double arcade, little shops and vendors operate much as they did in the Middle Ages; today, however, they sport Fendi and Fiorucci logos. Reshaped by every noble with designs on Ferrara, the cathedral and the castle remain the effective center of town. The tall slender arches and terra-cotta that ornament the apse were designed by Rossetti, the town planner; Leon Battista Alberti (1404-1484), the Florentine theorist whose precepts Rossetti had in mind as he worked, executed the pink campanile covered with Estense seals and crests. Notice the *faux* rose windows in the left and right portions of the facade. (Church open Mon.-Sat. 6:30am-noon and 4-7:30pm, Sun. 7:15am-1pm and 4-7:45pm.) The best pieces now reside in the **Museo della Cattedrale** upstairs: Cosmè Tura's 15th-century *San Giorgio* and *Annunciation* from the Ferrarese school, and Jacopo della Quercia's *Madonna della Melagrana.* (Museum open Mon.-Sat. 10am-noon and 3:30-5:30pm. Free.)

The **Palazzo del Municipio** faces the cathedral across the *piazza.* Atop the protruding arch, Nicolò III sits on horseback, clutching the reins of power. Enter the *palazzo* and ask the custodian at the desk to see the *stanzino delle Duchesse,* a small, ornately painted 16th-century powder room used by the Ferrarese duchesses. (*Palazzo* open Mon.-Sat. 9am-2pm. Free.) Exit into **piazza del Municipio** to admire the elegant staircase and its domed landing, designed by Benvenuti. Back in p. Cattedrale, the **Torre dei Ribelli,** in the southwest corner of the *piazza,* incorporates remnants of some rebellious nobles' houses, displaying the fate of those who tried to get the better of the d'Este. The streets of the medieval town south of the cathedral bristle with fortified houses. Medieval quintessence finds expression in arch-filled **via delle Volte,** a back alley for the *palazzi* along the now-receded Po River.

On the fringes of the city center stand the d'Este *palazzi.* Only the carved door of the **Palazzo Schifanoia,** via Scandiana, 23 (tel. 641 78), hints at the wealth of frescoes inside. The magnificent frescoes in the Saloni dei Mesi offer one of the most accurate and vivid depictions of 15th-century courtly life. (Open daily 9am-7pm. Admission L2500, the second Sun. and Mon. of the month free.) The **Palazzo Ludovico Il Moro,** via XX Settembre, 124, features a courtyard designed by Rossetti. Inside, the **Museo Archeo-**

logico Nazionale houses extensive finds from the Greco-Roman city of Spina and an outstanding collection of Athenian vases.

The **Casa Romei,** via Savonarola, 30 (tel. 403 41), was the 15th-century dwelling of the Ferrarese merchant Giovanni Romei. Tour this abode to ogle some of the most beautifully decorated and frescoed rooms of the period. The museum in the basement displays statues and frescoes salvaged from destroyed churches in Ferrara. (Open Tues.-Sun. 8:30am-2pm. Admission L4000.)

The **Palazzo dei Diamanti,** at corso Ercole I d'Este and corso Rossetti (the continuation of corso Porta Po), on the other side of town, outshines all other ducal residences. Inside, the **Pinacoteca Nazionale** (tel. 20 58 44) contains the best work of the Ferrarese school. Most impressive are the *Passing of the Virgin* (1508) by Carpaccio and the incredibly overworked *Massacre of the Innocents* by Garofalo. (*Sale* 300-400-600 and Sala Bastianino open Tues.-Sat. 9am-2pm, Sun. 9am-1pm. The rest of the museum is open Tues.-Sat. 9-11:30am, Sun. 9-11am. Admission L6000.) On the ground floor, the **Galleria Civica d'Arte Moderna** often mounts special exhibits by well-known contemporary Italian and European artists. (Open daily 9am-1pm and 3-5:30pm. Admission varies from exhibit to exhibit.) Down corso Porta Mare at #9 you'll find the **Palazzo Massari** museum complex. The most interesting museum is the original **Museo Documentario della Metafisica** (tel. 20 69 14), which documents the inception of metaphysical art in a collection of works by Giorgio de Chirico, Carlo Carrà, Tino Puenté, and Giorgio Morandi, Italy's greatest 20th-century painters. Other museums in Palazzo Massari include the **Museo Boldini,** filled with paintings by the 19th-century Italian painter Giovanni Boldini; the **Museo Ferrarese dell'Ottocento,** which houses a hodge-podge of 19th-century Italian paintings; and the tiny **Galleria della Fotografia** and **Galleria Civica,** both of which display local work. (All museums in the complex open daily 9am-1pm and 3-5:30pm. Admission L5000, students and on first Sun. and Mon. of the month free.) Fans of Italian literature will want to make a pilgrimage to the **tomb of Ariosto** and the **Biblioteca Ariostea** in the **Palazzo Paradiso,** via Scienze, 17 (tel. 20 73 92). (Open Mon.-Fri. 9am-7:30pm, Sat. 9am-1pm; the tomb was closed for restoration in 1992.)

At #170 on the Giovecca visit the recently restored **Palazzina di Marfisa d'Este,** a splendid palace in miniature. (Open Mon.-Sat. 9am-12:30pm and 3-6pm, Sun. 9am-12:30pm. Admission L2000.) Walk by the **Palazzo dei Bentivoglio,** at via Garibaldi, 90, a fantastic showpiece of the mannerist liberties that evolved into the Baroque style. The pervasive sense of history in Ferrara is nowhere stronger than in the **Cimitero Israelitico** (Jewish cemetery) at the end of via delle Vigne off corso Porta Mare. Here the Finzi and Contini are buried as well as most of Ferrara's 19th and 20th-century Jewish community. Ring the bell and the custodian will let you in. Look for the monument to Ferrarese Jews murdered at Auschwitz.

Entertainment

In July and August, Ferrara hosts **Ferrara Estate,** a music and theater festival that brings diverse performances to the city's *piazze* (contact the tourist office for specific information). During the rest of the year, avant-garde theater shakes up the **Sala Polivalente,** corso Porta Mare, 7, behind Palazzo Massari. For more information, contact the Museo della Metafisica (tel. 20 69 14). At the end of June, the city sponsors the **Aterforum,** a series of classical music concerts in Ferrara's churches and palaces. Check with tourist office for more information. Buy tickets (L8000-10,000) at the **Teatro Comunale,** corso Giovecca, 10/12 (tel. 20 26 75), or at the performance site. Each year on the last Sunday of May, Ferrara re-creates the ancient **Palio di San Giorgio.** This event, dating from the 13th century, is a lively procession of delegates from the city's eight *contrade* (districts) followed by a series of four races in p. Ariostea: the boy race, the girl race, the donkey race, and finally, the great horse race. The flag-waving ceremony of the eight *contrade* takes place two weeks earlier in p. del Municipio. During the summer, local bands play next to the *duomo* for free (tel. 76 20 02). The **Apollo,** piazza Carbonne, 37 (tel. 76 20 02), shows four films, usually contemporary American movies dubbed in Italian. The theater is closed in summer and on Mondays. Try

Casanova, via Frizzi, 14 (tel. 20 91 90), a stylish but not terribly cheap *enoteca* and bar where many students and young folks hang. (Closed Mon.)

Near Ferrara

The **Abbazia di Pomposa,** one of the oldest and most beautiful Benedictine abbeys in Italy, lies one hour from Ferrara in the town of Pomposa. The oldest parts of the church date from the 8th century, but most of the structure now bears a Romanesque stamp.

Inside the church, intricate 12th-century mosaics and stonework decorate the pavement, and 14th-century frescoes adorn the walls. The reliefs of fantastic, orientalized beasts now found in the museum once decorated the church. (Free.)

The abbey is equipped with an amiable **tourist office,** in front of the church inside the 11th-century **Palazzo della Ragione** (the abbots' grandiose quarters). (Tel. (0533) 71 01 00. Open May-Oct. 9am-1pm and 3-7pm.) The romantic abbey serves as the site for the **Musica Pomposa** concert series, with high-quality classical performances every Saturday and many Wednesday evenings in July and August. Write to the Pomposa Abbey tourist office at via Pomposa, 4, or to the Ferrara tourist office for the 1993 brochure.

Unfortunately, you'll have a hard time getting to the abbey from Ferrara without a car. The bus between Ferrara and Pomposa only runs from June 15 through August, and makes one trip to Pomposa at 8am, returning to Ferrara at 6pm (L7200).

Twenty minutes south from Pomposa the village of **Comacchio** boasts an illustrious history. A great producer of salt in the 15th century, Comacchio was once the equal of powerful Venice. The salt industry has now dried up, but the town remains a beautifully melancholy place. The **tourist office,** via Buonafede, 12 (tel. (0533) 31 28 44), dispenses information on tours of Comacchio's lagoons, which contain ingenious fishing devices developed over the centuries. (Open daily 10am-noon and 4-7pm.) Comacchio also sponsors a number of jazz concerts and an **International Ballet Festival.** Should you want to stay, **Albergo La Pace,** via Fogli, 21 (tel. (0533) 812 85), overlooking a canal, lets singles at L18,000 and doubles at L34,000, but consider taking full room and board for L45,000 since the food here is fabulous. Five buses per day leave from the Ferrara bus station for Comacchio (L7200).

Five kilometers from Comacchio stretches a vast expanse of beach. The most uncluttered spot is **Lido di Spina,** the beach farthest south. A scenic campsite here, **Spina Camping** (tel. (0533) 33 01 79), charges L6000 per adult, L4200 per child; off-season prices drop to L5250 and L3150. Twelve buses run daily from Ferrara's bus station, the first out at 7:30am and the last back from Lido Nazione at 9:15pm. Comacchio is also convenient to and from Ravenna, with six ACFT buses making the one-hour run daily (4 on Sun., L7200; catch the bus at via Tre Ponti near the large COOP store).

Ravenna

> *Of all the cities in Romanian lands The chief and*
> *most renowned Ravenna stands.*
> > *——Dryden*

Ravenna's moment of geopolitical superstardom came—and went—14 centuries ago, when Justinian and Theodora, rulers of the Byzantine Empire, made Ravenna the headquarters for their attempt to restore order to the anarchic west. In this they were unsuccessful, but Ravenna remained the seat of the Exarchs of Byzantine Italy for two centuries, and the artistic legacy of the period includes the most important examples of Byzantine art outside stanbul. Ravenna is currently a small city, home to some of the world's most inspiring mosaics, a few stunning churches, Dante's bones, and providing access to crowded beaches.

Orientation and Practical Information

Visit Ravenna as a daytrip from Bologna (5 trains per day, L6500) or Ferrara (9 per day, L5300). There are also frequent trains to Ferrara, where you can change for Venice (L11,300). Take a train to Bologna via Castelbolognese and Florence (1hr. 30min., L9300, round-trip L15,800) via Faenza. To go south along the Adriatic coast, take the Rímini line. The train station sits at the east end of town in p. Farini. Viale Farini leads from the station straight into via Diaz, which runs to p. del Popolo, the center of town.

Tourist Office, via Salara, 8 (tel. 354 04). From p. del Popolo, take via Muratori to p. XX Settembre, go right on via Matteotti, follow it to its end, go left on via Cavour, then take your 1st right. Useful maps and accommodations information. Open daily 8am-2pm and 3-6pm; Oct.-May Mon.-Fri. 8am-2pm and 3-6pm, Sat. 8am-2pm.

Budget Travel: CTS, via Mazzini, 11 (tel. 399 33). Friendly office. English spoken. ISIC cards sold, but no HI cards. Discount airfares. Open Mon.-Fri. 9:30am-12:30pm and 4-7:30pm, Sat. 9am-1pm.

Currency Exchange: Via Diaz is lined with banks that give good rates. Most are open Mon.-Fri. 8:20am-1:20pm and 2:45-3:45pm, Sat. 8:20-11:20am.

Post Office: p. Garibaldi, 1, off via Diaz before p. del Popolo. Open Mon.-Sat. 8am-7pm. **Postal Code:** 48100.

Telephones: SIP, via Rasponi, off p. XX Settembre. Very helpful staff. Open daily 8am-8pm. After hours, try **Albergo Diana,** via Rossi, 4. **Telephone Code:** 0544.

Buses: ATR (regional) and **ATM** (municipal) buses depart from outside the train station for the coast and beach towns of Marina di Ravenna, Lido di Classe, etc. Buy tickets at the ATM booth across the *piazza* from the station (L1500 for most towns)—get a return ticket too, as they're difficult to find in the suburbs.

Public Toilets: via Pasolini, off via Cavour. Super-modern and disinfected after every use. L500.

Emergencies: tel. 113. **Police:** (tel. 332 12) in p. del Popolo. **Hospital: Santa Maria delle Croci,** via Missiroli, 10 (tel. 40 91 11). **Medical Assistance:** tel. 330 11.

Accommodations

Most of Ravenna's inexpensive accommodations lie near major transportation lines, and are thus quite noisy. Except during the tanning months of July and August, consider a hotel or campground in one of the quiet beach towns nearby.

Ostello Dante (HI), via Nicolodi, 12 (tel. 42 04 05). 172 beds. Take bus #1 from viale. Pallavicini, left of the station (last bus shortly after 9pm, L1000). A super (but mosquito-infested) no-frills hostel in the eastern suburbs. The women's quarters are among the noisiest in the world. Hot showers 6-9pm only. Six-bed rooms. Reception open 7-9am and 5-11pm. Curfew 11:30pm. L10,000 per person, without HI card L15,000. Showers and breakfast included. Fine dinner L10,000. Bicycle rental L6000 per day (for guests only). Locks for closets, deposit L10,000. Open March-Oct.

Hotel Ravenna, viale Marconcelli, 12 (tel. 21 22 04), on the street running right as you exit the station. Modern (vintage 1960s) and well-kept. Singles L30,000, with bath L35,000. Doubles L45,000, with bath L55,000. Credit cards accepted.

Minerva, viale Marconcelli, 1/A (tel. 21 37 11), across the street from Hotel Ravenna. Clean well-furnished rooms. Singles L35,000. Doubles L45,000, with bath L55,000. Call ahead. Credit cards accepted.

Albergo Al Giaciglio, via Rocca Brancaleone, 42 (tel. 394 03). Walk along viale Farini, then right across p. Mameli. The quietest place in town. All rooms carpeted and clean. Singles L25,000, with bath L29,000. Doubles L37,000, with bath L44,000. Triple L50,000, with bath L64,000. Breakfast in rooms without bath L3500. Full pension L55,000, with bath L65,000. Half-pension L40,000, with bath L45,000. The meals are excellent.

Albergo Mokadoro, via Baiona, 18 (tel. 145 03 67). Take bus #2 northbound and ask the driver to let you off (every 30min. until 11:30pm; about 10min.). 65 modern rooms on an unattractive but quiet road outside town. Singles L22,000, with bath L26,000. Doubles L40,000, with bath L44,000.

Food

Those ravennous for sound local fare will find disappointment in Ravenna—you may find yourself saying, "Nevermore!" If you're staying at the hostel, you may wish to avail yourself of the L10,000 dinner or L4000 plate of spaghetti. Hostelers also benefit from the adjacent bargain **supermarket.** (Open Mon.-Wed. and Fri.-Sat. 9am-noon and 3:30-6pm, Thurs. 9am-noon.) The busy **Mercato Coperto** occupies p. Andrea Costa, up via IV Novembre from p. del Popolo (open Mon.-Sat. 7am-1:30pm and Fri. 4:30-7:30pm).

Mensa Il Duomo Self-Service, via Oberdan, 8 (tel. 239 70), off p. del Duomo. Well-prepared self-service has crowds raving. Come early. Pasta L2600. Full meals L9350. Wine L1000 per glass. Cover L 1000. Open Sept.-July Mon.-Fri. 11:45am-2:30pm.

Ristorante Scai, p. Baracca, 23 (tel. 225 20), a 10-min. walk down boutique-lined via Cavour. At the far end of the *piazza*. A comely restaurant with some interesting dishes. *Strozzapreti,* twisted pasta with tomato and cream, L5500. *San Giovese* wine L5000 per . Cover L2000. Open Oct.-Sept. 10 Tues.-Sun. noon-2:30pm and 7-10:30pm.

Pizza Imperiale, via IV Novembre, 9. Pizza slices to go. Basil L1000, tomato L1100, mozzarella L1300. Open Mon.-Sat. 10am-1pm and 4-8pm; closed Mon. in winter.

Ristorante/Pizzeria Guidarello, via Gessi, 7, off p. Arcivescovado, beside the *duomo.* A huge place with surprisingly good food—the only real *trattoria* in town. Try the *Fantasia della Casa,* 3 differently prepared meats with mixed veggies, a complete meal at L13,500. The *Gran Misto Oliver* combines 3 pastas with different sauces (L7500). Cover L2500. Open daily noon-2:30pm and 7-9pm. Around the corner on v. Mentana at **Galleria da Renato,** (under the same ownership), the same fare is available. Wine L6000 per . Open Mon.-Sat. noon-2:30pm and 7-9:15pm.

Sights and Entertainment

Inside and out, the 6th-century **Basilica di San Vitale,** via San Vitale, 17 (take via Argnetario off via Cavour) is a sight to behold. Restoration of the imposing ancient structure is nearing completion. An open courtyard overgrown with greenery leads to the awe-inspiring interior, where brilliant mosaics depict familiar scenes from the Bible. The courts of the Emperor Justinian and his wife Theodora stand in formal Byzantine splendor; Christ, seated in the dome, rests on a sphere of blue so vivid it belies its 1400 years. (Open daily 9am-7pm. Admission L3000.)

The oldest and most interesting mosaics in the city clothe the interior of the **Mausoleum of Galla Placidia,** behind the basilica. The coin box for illumination is outside. (Open daily 9am-7pm; entrance included with admission to the Basilica.)

Through the gate between San Vitale and the mausoleum, in the cloisters of a one-time convent attached to the church, lies the sprawling **Museo Nazionale,** v. Fiandrini, (tel. 344 24), with collections from a myriad of periods: Roman, early Christian, Byzantine, and medieval. (Open Tues.-Sun. 8:30am-1:30pm. Admission L6000.)

The **duomo** (tel. 391 96), due south in p. Duomo, is the fusion of everyhing Baroque. (Open daily 7am-noon and 3:30-6pm.) In the **Battistero Neoniano** next door on via Battistero (tel. 336 96), some poorly restored mosaics in Hellenistic-Roman style reside on the lower level, with three levels of 5th-century mosaics above. (Church open daily 7am-noon and 3:30-6pm. Baptistry open daily 9am-7pm. Admission L3000.)

A small but precious collection of mosaics from the *duomo* is on display in the **Museo Arcivescovile,** nearby in p. Arcivescovado. While you're there, check out the mosaic chapel and the Throne of Maximilian, perhaps the best piece of ivory carving in the Christian world and the zenith of Ravennine sculpture. (Open daily 9am-7pm. Admission L3000.) Compare the mosaics in the orthodox Battistero Neoniano with those in the **Battistero degli Ariani,** on via degli Ariani off via Diaz, which was used by the Arians, a sect condemned as heretics for doubting the Trinity. (Open 8:30am-noon and 2:30-sunset.) The **Church of Sant'Apollinare Nuovo,** east on via di Roma Sud, showcases some huge mosaics along its nave. (Open daily 9am-7pm.) For more mosaics, continue to the **Church of Sant'Apollinare in Classe** (tel. 47 30 04), a 6th-century basilica 5km south of the city (bus #4 or 44, every 30min. from the train station, L600).

The classical style yields to Byzantine depictions of angels and apostles on the heavily decorated triumphal arch. (Open daily 8am-noon and 2-6pm.)

For those who (unlike Gustav Klimt) grow weary of Ravenna's mosaics, the **remains of Dante Alighieri** (1265-1321) at the end of via Dante Alighieri, will satiate that morbid curiosity. The great poet reposes (and decomposes) next to the ChurchY32 56). There is also a **Dante Museum**, via Dante Alighieri, 1 (tel. 336 67) whose Dante library is 18,000 volumes strong. (Open Tues.-Sun. 9am-noon and 3-6pm. L3000).

Every Sunday in summer, a flea market (books, antiques, etc.) appears in p. Garibaldi, in front of the post office. From the last week in June to the last week in August, the the Church of S. Francesco sponsors **Ravenna in Festival,** featuring operas, concerts, folk music, and drama. The festival culminates in the **concerti d'organo** held in San Vitale, a series of organ recitals. Contact **Teatro Alighieri,** via Mariani, 2 (tel. 325 77) for programs and information. In winter, opera and ballet animate the Teatro Alighieri. An annual **Dante Festival** during the second week in September brings hell to Ravenna with exhibits, readings, and performances. This festival is also given under the auspices of the Church of S. Francesco (tel. 332 56).

Near Ravenna

You'll find endless beach towns and a shoreline akin to New Jersey's along Ravenna's coast. ATM bus A runs in a circuit from p. Farini, in front of the train station, along via Molinetto (by the hostel) to Punta Marina, Marina di Ravenna, Casal Borsetti, and a dozen other beaches and then back inland along via Trieste to the *piazza* (L1200). If you're at the hostel, snag the bus at the via Molinetto stop. There are affordable accommodations along the beach. In Casal Borsetti, try **Cantuccio,** via Casalborsetti, 175 (tel. 44 51 17). (Singles L20,000; doubles L40,000.)

Local fishermen congregate near **Marina di Ravenna**'s two breakwaters, which extend 2.5km into the Adriatic. If you're staying the night, try the hospitable rooms of **Villa Rosa,** viale Spalato, 87 (tel. (0544) 53 04 52), 50m inland from the bus stop in Marina di Ravenna, off via IV Novembre. (Singles L12,000, with bath L15,000. Doubles L25,000, with bath L30,000.) In the neighboring town of **Punta Marina,** try the large two-star **Albergo Elite** at via della Fontana, 11 (tel. (0544) 43 73 09). (Singles with bath L50,000; doubles with bath L90,000.) Farther south at **Lido di Savio, Albergo Rock,** via Cesena, 12 (tel. (0544) 94 92 41) offers soft beds, if not rock-bottom prices. The food is amazing. (Singles L29,000-45,000. Doubles L46,000-62,000. Highest prices July-Sept.) The most pleasant camping option is **Campeggio Pineta,** via Spallazzi (tel. (0544) 44 51 52; L3000-4000 per person, L6000-7000 per tent, L1200 per car, L1500 per light).

Rímini

One face of Rímini, sporting sunglasses and a dark tan, gazes toward the sea: a bohemian Miami Beach with a shortage of bikini tops and an excess of discotheques. Its other face sighs nostalgically toward the inland historic center—an alluring jumble of medieval streets dominated by the Malatesta Temple.

Orientation and Practical Information

Rímini is a major stop on the Bologna-Lecce and Rome-Bologna-Torrino-Lecce train lines, and is served by an airport with service to many European cities (mostly charters). Rímini also forms the gateway to western San Marino, the tiny, tacky mountain republic an hour away by bus. To get to the beach from the station on foot (15min.), walk right from the station along piazzale C. Battisti, turn right again into the tunnel when you see the yellow arrow indicating *al mare,* then follow via Principe Amadeo. By bus, take #10 or 11. Tickets (L700 per hr., L3000 per day) can be bought at the kiosk in front of the station or at *tabacchi.* To reach the historic center of town, take via Dante Alighieri from the station (5min.).

Tourist Offices: APT, p. Battisti, 1 (tel. 279 27), outside the train station to the left. Organized and stuffed with maps and pamphlets. Open daily 8am-8pm. **Branch office,** p. dell'Indipendenza, 3 (tel. 245 11), at the sea next to the Cassa di Risparmio di Rímini. Usually more helpful than the main office. Open daily 8am-8pm, off-season 8am-2pm. **Promozione Alberghiera:** (tel. 522 69), at the same address as the APT branch office. When you arrive at the train station, they will find you a room for a deposit of L10,000—which is later deducted from your bill. Be insistent about what you can or want to pay for a room—if they're unrealistic, start making noises about going to the hostel. They also run an exchange office. (No commission on cash or traveler's checks.) Open Mon.-Wed. and Fri.-Sat. 8:30am-12:30pm and 3-6:30pm, Tues. and Thurs. 8:30am-12:30pm. **Branch office** at the train station, p. Tripoli (tel. 39 16 74). Open July-Aug. daily 8:10am-9:30pm; late April-June and Sept. 1-15 8:10am-7:30pm. **San Marino Information Office:** p. Battisti, 1 (tel. 563 33), 2 doors down from the APT. Bus schedules, shopping and accommodations information. Open May-Sept. Mon.-Fri. 8am-7pm, Sat.-Sun. 8am-noon and 3-6pm.

Budget Travel: CTS, in the **P. A. Viaggi** office at viale Vespucci, 1 (tel 247 81). Open Mon.-Fri. 9am-12:30pm and 3:30-7pm, Sat. 9am-12:30pm. Also **Transalpino** tickets at via Amerigo Vespucci, 11/C (tel. 265 00). Open 9:30am-12:30pm and 3:30-10pm; in off-season Mon.-Fri. 9am-12:30pm and 3-7pm, Sat. 9am-12:30pm.

Currency Exchange: via Pola, 2 (tel. 216 37), near the beach off viale Vespucci at p. Kennedy. Good rates and no commission. Open June-Sept. daily 9am-10pm.

Post Office: corso Augusto, 8 (tel. 78 16 87), near the Arch of Augustus off p. Tre Mártiri. Open Mon.-Sat. 8:20am-1:20pm and 3-7pm. Also at the beach, viale Mantegazza at viale Vespucci. Open Mon.-Fri. 8:15am-1:30pm, Sat. 8:15am-noon. **Postal Code:** 47037.

Telephones: SIP, p. Ferrari, 22, in the mall-like Galleria Fabbri off via Tempio Matestiano, which intersects with via IV Novembre. Open daily 8am-10pm. At other times, try any of the many bars along the beach and near the station. **Telephone Code:** 0541.

Trains: piazzale C. Battisti and via Dante (tel. 535 12). Trains to Bologna (14 per day, L8800) and Milan (12 per day, L23,700). Periodic trains to Rome, Paris, Brussels. Trains hourly to Ravenna (L3900).

Airport: Miramare Civil Airport, via Flaminia (tel. 37 31 32). Mostly charter flights. Rates vary. Check with CTS (under Budget Travel above).

Buses: Intercity bus station at viale Roma at p. Clementini, a few hundred meters from the station. To many inland towns around Rímini. ATM bus tickets at train station and piazza Tre Mártiri (L700).

Car Rental: Hertz, viale Trieste, 16/A (tel. 531 10). Near the beach off viale Vespucci. Special rates for Americans (make reservations in the States). L240,000 per week with unlimited mileage, including 19% tax. Minimum age 21. Open Mon.-Fri. 8:30am-12:30pm and 3-7pm, Sat.-Sun. 8:30am-1pm. Closes later in summer. Also an office at the airport in Miramare (tel. 37 51 08).

Emergencies: tel. 113. **Police:** corso d'Augusto, 192 (tel. 510 00). **Hospital: Ospedale Infermi,** via Settembrini, 2 (tel. 705 11). English-speaking doctors. **Medical Assistance:** on the beach at the end of viale Gounod, beyond viale Pascoli. Free walk-in clinic for tourists. Open in summer daily 9:30am-noon and 3:30-7pm. **Red Cross:** via Savonarola, 6 (tel. 266 12), near the canal.

Accommodations and Camping

During high season (the last week of June through Aug.), your best chance of finding a room is through the tourist or accommodations offices. Reserve in advance by phone to avoid hassles. Those who live on the edge and care little for material possessions make a home on the beach.

Ostello Urland (HI), via Flaminia, 300 (tel. 37 32 16), by the airport, 25min. away on bus #9 (L1200). Get off at via Stokholm (ask bus driver) and follow the signs. Lockout 9am-5pm. Curfew 11pm. L14,000 per person. Non-HI members pay an additional L5000. Breakfast included. Dinners: vegetarian L9000, carnivorous L12,000, pasta only L4000. Call ahead. Open May-Sept.

Pensione Mille Fiori, via Pola, 42 (tel. 256 17), down the street from currency exchange. Large rooms in liveliest section of town. Singles with bath: in June L31,000; July L36,000; Aug.1-20 L50,000; Aug.21-31 L36,000; Sept. L31,000. Make reservations in July and August.

Albergo Filadelphia, via Pola, 25 (tel. 236 79). Clean rooms, soft beds and an owner with a soft spot for Americans. Singles with bath L20,000. Doubles with bath L40,000. Reservations help.

Hotel Pigalle, via Ugo Foscolo, 7 (tel. 264 43). Clean and classy hotel on a quiet street. Jazz posters, a peaceful terrace and young and snazzy staff. All rooms with bath. June and Sept. singles L35,000, doubles L70,000. July and Aug. 23-31 singles L42,000, doubles L84,000. Aug. 1-23 singles L55,000, doubles L110,000.

Hotel Cardellini, via Dante, 50 (tel. 264 12), 100m from the train station, but very respectable. This 2-star offers 63 tidy, tiny rooms with big beds, high ceilings, and remote-control TV at 1-star prices. Very helpful English-speaking manager. High season (begins at end of July): singles L44,500, with bath L59,000; doubles L69,000, with bath L93,500. Low season: singles L29,000, with bath L39,000; doubles L44,500, with bath L58,500.

Camping: Maximum, tel. 37 26 02 or 37 02 71. Take bus #10 or 11 to stop #33 ("Miramare"). July 6-Aug. 24 L5350 per person, L4400 per child, L6600 or L8350 per tent; May 14-July 5 and Aug. 25-Sept. L3900 per person, L3050 per child, L6300 or L8050 per tent. Also try **Italia** (tel. 73 28 82) with campsites and bungalows, via Toscanella, 112 in Viserba di Rímini, 1.5km north of Rímini. From the train station take bus #4 directly to the campsite. L5600 per person, L6000 for a small tent, L9700 for a large tent.

Food

Rímini's seaside swarms with sterile cutpurse eateries. Fortunately, you can survive on the resort's delicious snacks. Look in the center of town for affordable full meals. For brown-baggers, Rímini's **covered market,** between via Castelfidardo and the Tempio, provides an array of comestibles. (Open Mon., Wed. and Fri.-Sat. 7:15am-1pm and 5-7:30pm, Tues. and Thurs. 7:15am-1pm.) The **rosticceria,** in the market, offers cheap seafood and delicious *piadina.* Closer to the beach is the **STANDA Supermarket,** via Vespucci, 133. (Open Mon.-Sat. 8:30am-8pm, Sun. 9am-8pm.)

Mensa Dopolavoro Ferroviario, viale Roma, 70 (tel. 553 88). Near the train station, to the left off via Dante and down a driveway. Food is fresh and service friendly. *Primi* L3500, *secondi* L5800, complete meal L9700. Menu changes daily. Wine L1600 per half-. Open Mon.-Sat. 11am-3pm and 6-9pm.

Ristorante/Pizzeria Pic Nic, via Tempio Malatestiano, 30 (tel. 219 16), off via IV Novembre at the *tempio.* A huge buffet overflowing with gourmet specialties. *Primi* L6000-7000. *Secondi* L9000-17,000. Mozzarella cheese blankets the homemade *lasagne al forno* (L6000). Try the *pizza bianco verde,* a fire-baked cheese and herb delight (L8000). Cover L2000. Open daily noon-3pm and 7pm-1am.

Piade e Cassoni, via Sauro, 10 (tel. 210 66), 2 blocks from the beach. A hangout for Rímini youth. Try *piada,* a local sandwich (L1000-3000) or *Cassoni,* a mini-pizza (L3000). Open daily 4-9:30pm.

Porta Fortuna, via Dante, 39 (tel. 541 19), near the station. Gregarious English-speaking management boasts of having "the only Hong-Kong style place in Rímini." Pork with black mushrooms L6000. Open Mon.-Sat. 11am-3:30pm and 6pm-midnight. In summer open daily all afternoon. **Gelateria Nuovo Fiore,** viale Vespucci, 7 (tel. 236 02), a 2nd location viale Vespucci, 85. Flowered fabric, pseudosteel and neon at this space-age ice-cream bar, the most *di moda* on Rímini's beach walk. The flavor selection is endless. Cones L2000-4000. House *aperitivo* L3000. Open March-Oct. daily 8am-3am; Jan.-Feb. Sat.-Sun. 8am-3am.

Sights

Any tour of Rímini's historic center should begin with the Renaissance **Tempio Malatestiano** on via IV Novembre (tel. 511 30). The church was originally constructed in Franciscan Gothic style; however, in the 1440s the ruling Sigismondo Malatesta ("Sigmund headache") modestly transformed the church into a classical monument to himself and his fourth wife, the lovely Isotta.

Sigismondo Malatesta was canonized to hell by the papacy (a privilege unique in history), burned in effigy, and damned in Rome by Pius II) as a heretic guilty of "murder, violation, adultery, incest, sacrilege, perjury so dissolute that he raped his daughters and sons-in-law and as a boy often acted as the female partner in shameful loves, and later forced men to act as women." But nasty Siggy was also a soldier and patriot who ruled Rímini at its height (1417-1468) and employed such artists as Piero della Francesca and Leon Battista Alberti, who designed the exterior of the new church.

Alberti modeled the front of the temple after the Roman Arch of Augustus, which still stands at the gates of Rímini. The two front arches, originally intended to hold the sarcophagi of Sigismondo and Isotta, are now filled with limestone. The dollar signs perceived by overeager capitalists in the floral frieze are actually the intertwined initials of Sigismondo and Isotta.

The spacious, single-aisled interior and its wooden-trussed roof recall the temple's original Franciscan design. In the chapel to the left of the card shop hangs a looming Giotto crucifix. The sprightly sculptures and reliefs found in almost every chapel are the creations of Agostino di Duccio. (Open daily 7am-noon and 3-7pm.)

A short distance from the temple, **piazza Tre Mártiri,** named after three partisans hanged by the Fascists in 1944, forms the ramshackle, noisy city center on the site of the Roman forum. The most striking vestige of Rímini's former glory is the **Arch of Augustus,** at the end of corso d'Augusto. The oldest Roman triumphal arch (27 BC), it blends together arch, column, and medallion.

Rímini's medieval center and favorite hangout, **piazza Cavour,** off corso d'Augusto, contains one of the oddest ensembles of buildings in Italy. The tall Renaissance arcade of the **Palazzo Garampi** contrasts dramatically with the adjoining fortress-like **Palazzo dell'Arengo** (1207) and the smaller **Palazzo del Podestà** (1334). Between the first two buildings is an Italian version of Brussels's famous *le pisseur,* elaborated in a full Baroque setting. Perpendicular to the Municipal building, the pink brick **Teatro Comunale** (1857), minus its bomb-smashed auditorium, completes a second side of the square. On the third side, a motley collection of shops, bars and offices surround the Renaissance entrance to the **fish market.** Four stone dolphins in the corners of the market once filled the small canals (still visible under the benches) with water used to clean the fish. In addition, two curious sculptures pose in the center of the *piazza:* an eccentric, moss-encrusted fountain (1543), engraved with an inscription recalling the presence of Leonardo da Vinci, and a seated, sumptuously garbed Pope Paul V (1614) brandishing ferocious eagles.

Also worth seeing is the old fortress, **Rocca Malatestiana,** built by Sigismondo between 1437 and 1446 (behind the Communal Theater). Inside the *rocca* is the new **Museo Dinz Rialto** (tel. 239 22), a museum of ethnology with educational exhibits on aboriginal cultures, frequently focusing on Africa and Polynesia. (Open Tues.-Sun. 8am-8pm; Sept.-June Tues.-Sun. 8am-1pm. Admission L2000.) Rímini's last two noteworthy churches are the **Church of Sant'Agostino** with its great cycle of Riminese Gothic frescoes in its choir; and the **Church of the Servi,** with its lush, almost theatrical Baroque interior. The **Museo Civico,** via Gambalunga, 27 (tel. 70 43 25), houses a collection of Roman mosaics and early Italian paintings, highlighted by Giovanni Bellini's *Dead Christ with Four Angels.* (Museum open Tues.-Sun. 8:30am-1pm and 3:30-8:30pm; Sept.-June Mon.-Sat. 8am-1pm. Admission L3000, children L1000.)

Entertainment

Rímini is notorious throughout Europe for its sleazy polysexual pickup scene. *Passeggiata* is a euphemism for the wild cruising you can witness nightly along the *lungomare* spanning **viale Amerigo Vespucci** and **viale Regina Elena.** The discotheques in Rímini are among the largest and most dazzling on the continent—and there are literally hundreds to choose from. For a list of the latest and greatest, pick up a copy of *Kursaal* at the tourist office—it's a free and complete weekly multilingual guide to Rímini's beach and disco culture. Rímini has instituted a **Blue Line**—a bus service (L2000 per night, L10,000 per week) that runs in July and August—for carless discogoers. It originates at p. Kennedy, and runs all night (9pm-5am) to all the clubs. Also in p. Kennedy is the "Night Office," an information service located in a double-decker bus open nightly in the summer from 9pm to 3am.

Beginning in July and continuing through the summer, the **Sagra Musicale Malatestiana** brings international artists and companies to Rímini. Pick up a schedule at the tourist office. Folk groups from all over Italy perform at the *quartiere fieristico* (almost daily at 9:30pm, free).

Near Rímini

San Marino, the "smallest and oldest republic in the world," is a tourist trap to be avoided. From its reconstructed Disneyesque medieval buildings to the cutesy green-and-red uniforms of its toy soldiers, San Marino glares just as much as the thousands of postcards and assorted tourist junk lining its unpardonably cute streets. If, however, you're a true tourist or an avid philatelist, take one of the **Benedettini** or **ATR** buses that leave from outside Rímini's train station (1hr., round-trip L4000; check times at the San Marino tourist office). Pick up the exhaustive *San Marino Practical Guide* at the tourist office if you want to stay for any length of time here.

You're much better off going to **San Leo,** just over the regional border in the Marches. The city meshes an interesting collection of historical buildings with a spectacular setting. The walls and cylindrical towers of the fortress, now the emblem of the city, were designed in the 15th century by Francesco di Giorgio Martini. The oldest building is the beautiful **Pieve,** dating from the 9th century and in miraculously good condition. The 12th-century *duomo* nearby harmoniously blends Romanesque and Gothic styles. At least four buses leave daily from the Rímini train station, making the hour-long trip to San Leo (round-trip L7000).

The seacoast around Rímini is filled with sandy and crowded beach territory. **Riccione,** south of Rímini by bus #10 or 11 (30min., L1500), ranks with Rímini as one of the most active summer resort areas on the Adriatic. North of Rímini, try the resorts of **Viserba** (15min.) and **Torre Pedrera** (20min.), reached by bus #4 from the train station.

Tuscany (Toscana)

The archetypal Italy springs from Tuscany. Its landscapes, familiar from Renaissance paintings, mix sere ochres with ilex groves and lines of cypresses and parasol pines. Grapevines and sunflowers follow the contours of the hills that roll from the rocky, forested Apuan Alps to the marshy Maremma and the metal hills of the south. Its towns, often walled, preen upon the heights, quintessential hill towns. Its Renaissance culture—an unprecedented explosion of art, architecture, and humanist scholarship—became the culture of Italy, while Tuscan, the language of Dante, Petrarch, and Machiavelli, is today's textbook Italian.

Despite its appearance of eternal eminence, everything of importance in this region occurred within an outstanding half-millennium. A backwater in both Etruscan and Roman times, the region was far from the center of the Lombard or succeeding barbarian kingdoms. Toward the end of the 10th century, increasingly powerful local aristocrats wrested control of towns from agents of the papacy or state, creating the free *comuni,* independent city-states. Many of the fortifications that surround Tuscan towns today first sprang up during this period of upheaval. In the 1100s, the free *comuni* of Tuscany began to engage in their two most characteristic activities: inter-city warfare and artistic production. Over the next 500 years, as the aristocracy lost power to the *popolani* (commoners) and the region grew richer through agricultural prosperity and revolutions in banking, these sports continued to preoccupy the Tuscans, with the Renaissance emerging out of the glorious mayhem. The bubble burst in the early 16th century, when the rich, leisured Tuscans, who had long since left their warfare to hired hands (*condottiere*), fell to the invading armies of the French and the Habsburgs. The entire region was then placed under the rule of the Medici, a family of bankers that ruled republican Florence for a century by popular acquiescence and was kicked out before emerging as official nobility to preside over Tuscany's descent from the apex of the High Renaissance into a cultural and political non-entity. Irrelevance is a great preservative fluid, and Tuscany's 20th-century tourism thrives on the region's almost untouched cityscapes.

Though World War II bombing scarred some towns and postwar economic growth has brought others a bit of urban sprawl, collections of medieval streets ornamented by the most brilliant creations of Renaissance architecture remain. The region's only blight: the Germans, Americans, and British who not only overrun the streets, but have bought up villas and set up annexes to their universities here. Though people are generally friendly, your English may induce sighs from natives, especially in Florence. Efforts to speak Italian, however mangled, will be much appreciated.

An extensive and convenient transportation system makes it easy to tour Tuscany's countryside. The state railroad serves all major towns and many smaller ones, though the many hill towns are better reached by bus. Hitching is not uncommon in the area. Given the ease of transportation and the overcrowding of sightseers, plan your itinerary wisely. Florence, Siena, and Pisa are unmissable; consequently, no tourist misses them. Once you've seen them, consider devoting a little time to three of the most hospitable and beautiful of Tuscan cities: Montepulciano in the wine country south of Siena; and Cortona, a great balcony over Tuscany and Umbria in the region's southeast corner; and northern Lucca, which found itself accompanied only by Venice as the last republican hold-outs in Italy after the travails of the 16th century. Many more of Tuscany's best towns, monuments, and monasteries hide among the hills south and west of Siena; in fact, the only area to avoid is the ugly coast. We have room to list only the larger and more art-littered Tuscan spots; if you plan an extended stay in the region, consider exploring on your own—tiny towns crown many hills, and usually if you ask in the town restaurant they'll tell you who lets rooms.

Youth hostels abound in Tuscany, but hotel rooms are on the expensive side. Reservations are advisable all summer, especially in Florence, Siena, and Pisa; otherwise, although you won't be without a place to sleep, it won't be a good deal. Camping is possible at the region's many lakes, mountains, and coastal resorts.

As familiar as Tuscany seems visually, its cuisine may throw you for a loop: neither southern pasta and tomatoes nor northern *risotto* and *polenta* are staples of the Tuscan table. White beans *(fagioli)* are a regional obsession, so join locals and enjoy them in everything; tasteless Tuscan bread, however, is best eaten when hidden, especially in such local concoctions as *crostini* (roasted bread topped with liver pate or cheese) and *panzanella* (bread, tomatoes, and vegetables). Other local specialties include *ribollita* (bean and cabbage stew) and *fiori di zucca fritti* (fried zucchini flowers). Meat dishes include *coniglio* (rabbit), *trippa* (tripe), *lepre* (wild hare), *cinghiale (wild boar)*, *salsicce* (grilled sausages), and the famous and costly beef steak *bistecca alla fiorentina.*

Tuscany's gastronomic triumph, however, is its wine. The region's most popular is *chianti,* from the area around Florence and Siena; *chianti classico* is the highest quality—look for the *gallo nero* (black rooster) label on the neck. Tuscany's premier red wine, however, is the expensive *brunello di Montalcino. Vino Nobile di Montepulciano,* another full-bodied red, hails from the same area. The best white is the light, golden *vernaccia di San Gimignano.* A unique Tuscan wine is *vin santo,* a sweet, sauternes-like wine made from grapes hung in lofts to dry for several months before being crushed; drink it as Tuscans do—with a plateful of *cantuccini di Prato* (crispy almond cookies) for dipping.

Florence (Firenze)

Florence was the epicenter of the Renaissance, home to Michelangelo, Machiavelli and the Medici. Fueled by an innovative banking system, the city evolved from a booming, 13th-century wool and silk trading town into the archetype of political experimentation and artistic rebirth. At its apex in the mid-15th century, Florence was the unchallenged European capital of painting, sculpture, architecture, medicine, astronomy, physics, commerce, and political thought.

Today, too, Florence is unchallenged, not in intellectual or artistic pursuits but in the quest for touristic supremacy. *Everybody* comes here. If you wander around near the station in summer, you may be struck with the bizarre impression you've stumbled onto an open-air session of the U.N. The tourist-to-native ratio gets even worse in August, when every able-bodied Florentine flees to the seaside or to the mountains, leaving Florence's wide streets oddly quiet but for the echoing cadences of tour leaders herding their sweating flocks. Florentines are by and large resigned to the constant inundation, but they certainly make the most of it; most Florentines speak at least some English, enough to swindle the overeager tourist out of those extra few lire. Brave this 20th-century deluge of commercialism to discover the city's incomparable heritage.

Orientation

Florence is easily accessible by train from Milan, Bologna, Venice, and Rome. From the station at p. della Stazione, it is a short walk on via de' Panzani to the center of Florence, the area bordered by the *duomo* in the north, the Arno River in the south, and the Bargello and Palazzo Strozzi in the east and west. This is the old city, replete with cobblestone streets and grand old *palazzi*.

Major arteries radiate from the *duomo* and its two *piazze:* **piazza San Giovanni** encircling the baptistry and **piazza del Duomo** around the cathedral. The city's main street, **via dei Calzaiuoli,** runs from between the baptistry and the *duomo* to **piazza Signoria** in the direction of the river Arno. The **Uffizi** lies off p. Signoria towards the river on the left. Parallel to v. dei Calzaiuoli on the west, **via Roma** leads from p. S. Giovanni through **piazza della Repubblica** (the city's largest open space) to the **Ponte Vecchio,** which spans the Arno to the district called the **Oltrarno.** Parallel to via dei Calzaiuoli on the east, via del Proconsolo runs to the **Badia** and the **Bargello.** Heading north (away from the river) from p. S. Giovanni, borgo San Lorenzo runs to **p. San Lorenzo** and parallel via dei Servi to **p. SS. Annunziata.** Beyond the old city sprawls a vast and ugly suburbia.

For guidance through Florence's tangled center, pick up a free map either inside the station from the booth marked *Informazioni Turistiche Alberghiere,* or just outside at the red and white tourist booth. A more detailed map is the *Litografia Artistica Cartografica* (L3000 at newsstands).

Artistic and historical sights are scattered throughout Florence, but the city's compactness ensures that few sights lie out of the pedestrian's range. Orange ATAF city buses will ferry foot-weary sightseers most everywhere. (See Buses under Practical Information.) Florence's streets are numbered in red and black sequences. Red numbers are for commercial establishments, while black numbers (occasionally blue) denote residential addresses (including most sights and hotels). Black addresses will appear here as a numeral only, while red addresses are indicated by a number followed by an "r." The two sequences almost never coincide (28 black might abut 86r); if you get to an address and it's not what you're looking for, then you've probably got the wrong color.

As in the rest of Italy, most establishments close for two to four hours in the afternoon. On major holidays, including the festival of Florence's patron saint San Giovanni (June 24), everything but the occasional *bar* will close.

For entertainment information, consult the monthly *Firenze Spettacolo* (L2500), sold at newsstands. Hotels, hostels, and most restaurants and tourist information bureaus distribute free copies of *One, Three, Five...Days in Florence,* a slim publication chockfull of museum hours, musical events, and friendly suggestions.

Practical Information

Tourist Offices: Consorzio I.T.A. (tel. 28 28 93) in the train station by track #16, next to the pharmacy. Give them a price range and they will find you a room, though perhaps not the best value and probably near the station. Come in person; no booking by phone. You pay the first night's rent plus a L3000-5000 commission. Open daily 8:30am-9pm. At track #5, the same company has information on all flights departing from Pisa airport, the closest one to Florence. **Azienda Promozionale di Turismo,** via Manzoni, 16 (tel. 233 20), off p. Beccaria; from the *duomo,* take via dei Calzaiuoli, then turn left onto via del Corso. Ignoring name changes, continue straight to p. Beccaria (20min.); turn left to via Manzoni. No accommodations service. Cultural information, maps, and many free pamphlets. Open Mon.-Sat. 8:30am-1:30pm. **Branch offices** at Chiasso Baroncelli, 19r (tel. 230 21 24), and at via Cavour, 1r (tel. 27 60 382). Both open Mon.-Sat. 8am-2pm. Other offices at Piazzetta Guelfa, 3 (tel. 28 40 15) and via Martelli, 6 (tel. 21 38 93.) Open Mon.-Sat. 9am-3pm. **Consortium Italian Tourist Association,** viale Gramsci, 9a (tel. 247 82 31). **Informazione Turistica,** at the red and white booth outside the train station (exit by track #16). Pick

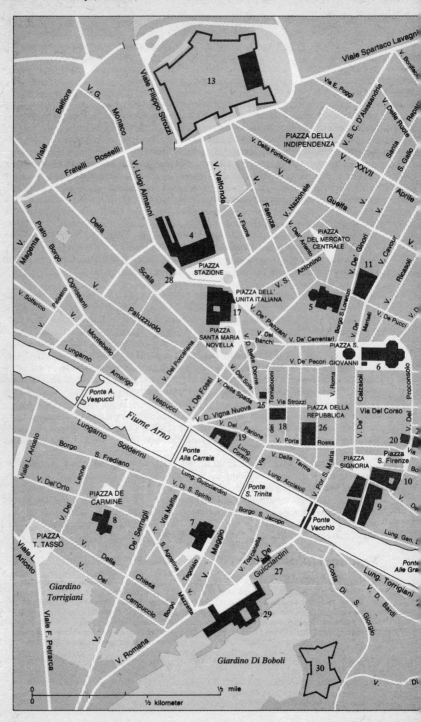

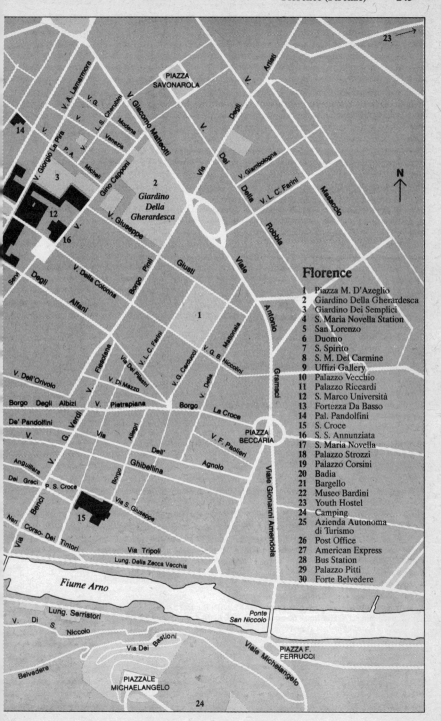

Florence

1 Piazza M. D'Azeglio
2 Giardino Della Gherardesca
3 Giardino Dei Semplici
4 S. Maria Novella Station
5 San Lorenzo
6 Duomo
7 S. Spirito
8 S. M. Del Carmine
9 Uffizi Gallery
10 Palazzo Vecchio
11 Palazzo Riccardi
12 S. Marco Università
13 Fortezza Da Basso
14 Pal. Pandolfini
15 S. Croce
16 S. S. Annunziata
17 S. Maria Novella
18 Palazzo Strozzi
19 Palazzo Corsini
20 Badia
21 Bargello
22 Museo Bardini
23 Youth Hostel
24 Camping
25 Azienda Autonoma di Turismo
26 Post Office
27 American Express
28 Bus Station
29 Palazzo Pitti
30 Forte Belvedere

up a map and a hotel guide here if you bypassed the station accommodation service. Officially open daily 8am-9pm; in practice their hours can be sporadic. **Associazione Cattolica Internazionale al Servizio della Giovane** (tel. 29 46 35), by track #1 in the train station. Free accommodations service. Finally, in p. della Repubblica there is an automated machine by the SIP phone booths that will give listings of hotels, museums and hours, restaurants, discotheques, etc. (L500 per 3min.).

Budget Travel: S.T.S.-Student Travel Service, via Zanetti, 18r (tel. 28 41 83). Sells student discounted train, plane, and bus tickets. Open Mon.-Fri. 9:30am-12:30pm and 3:30-6:30pm, Sat. 9:30am-12:30pm.

Consulates: U.S., lungarno Vespucci, 38 (tel. 239 82 76), at via Palestro near the station. Open Mon.-Fri. 8:30am-noon and 2-4pm. **U.K.,** lungarno Corsini, 2 (tel. 28 41 33). Open Mon.-Fri. 9:30am-12:30pm and 2:30-4:30pm. Call the U.K. Embassy in Rome for after-hours emergencies (tel. (06) 475 55 51). Canadians, Australians, and New Zealanders can choose between their representatives in Rome and Milan.

Currency Exchange: Local banks have the best exchange rates. Open Mon.-Fri. 8:20am-1:20pm and 2:45-3:45pm. A number of banks are open Sat. morning until ll:20am. **Cassa di Risparmio di Firenze** now has automatic tellers that will exchange money at via de' Bardi, 73r; via de' Tornabuoni, 23r; via degli Speziali, 16r; and via dei Servi, 40r. Open 24 hrs.

American Express: v. Dante Alighieri, 20-22r (tel. 509 81). From the *duomo*, walk down v. Calzaiuoli; turn left onto v. dei Tavolini. AmEx is on the little *piazza* at its end. Cashes personal checks for cardholders. They also hold mail (free for card and checkholders, L3000 per inquiry—whether you have mail or not—for everyone else). L3000 to leave messages. L10,000 to forward mail. Does not accept wired money. Handles travel reservations, hotel bookings, and day excursions for card and checkholders. Open Mon.-Fri. 9am-5:30pm, Sat. 9am-12:30pm. Also has a **branch office,** via Guicciardini, 49r (tel. 27 87 51), across the Ponte Vecchio from the old city down via de Guicciardini on the left. If you pass the Palazzo Pitti, you've also passed the office. Financial services and rail reservations only. Open Mon.-Fri. 9am-5:30pm.

Post Office: (tel. 21 61 22), on via Pellicceria off p. della Repubblica. Stamps at windows #21 and 22; Fermo Posta at windows #23 and 24 (L250 per letter). To send packages, go to the back of the building and enter at via dei Sassetti, 4. Open Mon.-Fri. 8:15am-7pm, Sat. 8:15am-noon. **Telegram** office in front open 24 hrs. **Phone books** available Mon.-Sat. 8am-11pm. **Postal Code:** 50100.

Telephones: ASST, via Pellicceria, (tel. 21 41 45) at the post office. Make international collect calls here. Open 24 hrs. Phones also at via Cavour, 21r. Open daily 9am-9pm; winter 9am-8pm. **SIP,** in the train station near track #5. Lines usually shorter than at ASST. 1 booth available for international calls. Open daily 7:30am-9:30pm. Beware: SIP is changing many phone numbers nationally, due to expansion. If you get a busy signal or no one answers repeatedly, the number has probably been changed. Call "12" for information. **Telephone Code:** 055.

Flights: Galileo Galilei Airport, tel. (050) 500 707, in Pisa. Take the airport express (1hr., L5700) from the Florence train station (every hr., 5:55am-8pm). In Florence, call for flight information (tel. 27 88) or ask at the "air terminal" (tel. 21 60 73) at platform #5 in the Florence train station, where you can also check in, register baggage, and get an embarkation card for L2000 (open daily 7am-8pm).

Trains: Santa Maria Novella Station, near the center of town. Information office (tel. 27 87 85) open daily 9am-5pm. You can also use the (English-speaking) computers outside the office to plan your trip. They're bright-yellow, and you probably won't have to wait too long. Every hr. to: Bologna (1hr., L7200, *rapido* supplement L2700); Venice (3hr. 30min., L18,700, *rapido* supplement L6400); Milan (3hr. 30min., L22,000, *rapido* supplement L9300); and Rome (2hr. 30min., L22,000). Almost all trains arrive here except a few trains to and from Rome, which use the **Campo di Marte** station on the east side of town. Bus #19 connects the 2 stations about every 20min. around the clock (25min.).

Metropolitan Transport: City buses (ATAF), p. del Duomo, 57r (tel. 58 05 28). Tickets (L1000 for 70min., L1300 for 2hr., 8 60-min. rides L7500 (8 per day), 24 hr. ticket L5000) must be bought *before boarding* and are available at the train station or at *tabacchi*. L31,000 fine for ticketless passengers. Bus routes are posted at stops; for a comprehensive map go to the ATAF booth in the railway station. Metropolitan bus #7 serves Fiesole.

Buses: SITA, via Santa Caterina da Siena, 15r (tel. 48 36 51 Mon.-Fri., 21 14 87 Sat. and Sun.). Frequent buses to Siena (2hr., L8300), Volterra (6 per day, L9000), San Gimignano (13 per day, L7100), Greve (1 per hr., L3000), and Poggibonsi (many, L5300). **CAT,** p. Stazione, 15 (tel. 28 34 00), to Arezzo (7 per day, 9:30am-6:30pm, 2hr, L6000). **CAP,** v. Nazionale, 4 (tel. 21 46 37), to Prato (L2400). **LAZZI,** piazza stazione 4-6r, (tel. 21 51 54), to Pisa (L8700), Prato (L2400),

Lucca (L7100), and Pistoia (L4000). **LAZZI Eurolines** to Rome, Naples, Scandinavia, Austria, Hungary, and Spain.

Bike and Moped Rental: Promotourist, via B. Bandinelli, 43 (tel. 70 18 63). **Program,** borgo Ognissanti, 135r (tel. 28 29 16). **Ciao and Basta,** via Alamanni, under the Central Station (tel. 21 33 07). **MotoRent,** via S. Zanobi, 9r (tel. 49 01 13). Bikes start at L7000 per 3hr., L15,000 per day. Mountain bikes run about L30,000 per day. Mopeds begin at L5000 per hr., L30,000 per day, L180,000 per wk. No license necessary, but bring ID indicating you are at least 16.

Hitchhiking: Hitchers take the A-1 north to Bologna and Milan or the A-11 northwest to the Riviera and Genoa, or take bus #29, 30, or 35 from the station to the feeder near Peretola. For the A-1 south to Rome and the extension to Siena, they take bus #31 or 32 from the station to exit #23, Firenze Sud. As always, hitchhiking entails risks; *Let's Go* does not recommend hitching. The **International Lift Center,** corso Tintori, 39 (tel. 28 06 21), matches passengers with drivers. Passengers pay a small charge for the arrangement and gas. Open Mon.-Sat. 9am-7:30pm, Sun. noon-3pm.

Lost Property: For objects left on a train, go to the **Ufficio Oggetti Rivenuti** in the train station (tel. 235 21 90). Collect other *oggetti ritrovati* at the **Ufficio Oggetti Smarrito,** via Circondaria, 19 (tel. 36 79 43). If your car gets towed, call **Parco Auto Requisite,** via dell'Artovata, 6 (tel. 35 52 31). They're right next to each other. Take bus #23 (A, B, or C) from the station. Open Mon.-Wed. and Fri.-Sat. 9am-noon.

English Bookstore: After Dark, via del Moro, 86r (tel. 29 42 03), near p. Santa Maria Novella Book-swap (see Shopping). The cheerful Scot who runs this place is a mine of information on almost anything. Sells *Let's Go* for L3000 less than anywhere else (L30,000). Open Mon.-Sat. 10am-1:30pm and 3-7pm, Sun. 3-7pm; in Aug. 10am-1pm. **Paperback Exchange,** via Fiesolana, 31r (tel. 247 81 54). The answer to a traveling bookworm's prayer. Open Mon.-Sat. 9am-1pm and 3:30-7:30pm; mid-Nov. to mid-March closed Monday. **BM Bookstore,** borgo Ognissanti, 4r (tel. 29 45 75). Largest selection of English-language books in Florence. Open Mon.-Sat. 9am-1pm and 3:30-7:30pm, Sun. 9am-1pm; Nov.-Feb. closed Sun. **Libreria Ateneo,** p. S. Marco, 3r (near the Accademia), has an outstanding collection of art books. Open Mon.-Fri. 9am-6pm, Sat. 9am-1pm.

Bulletin Boards: Listings of people seeking Anglophone roommates, English teachers, baby-sitters and notices of Anglophone religious, musical, and theatrical activities. **CarLie's American Bakery,** via Brache, 12r (tel. 12 51 37), near via dei Neri. Open Sept.-July 15 Mon.-Sat. 8am-noon and 4-7pm. **The American Church,** via Rucellai, 16 (tel. 29 44 17), near the train station off via della Scala. Open Mon., Wed., Fri. 9am-12:30pm and Sun. 9-11am. The **British Institute,** via Tornabuoni, 2, between p. Santa Novella and p. della Repubblica. **The Paperback Exchange,** via Fiesolana, 31r (tel. 247 81 54), off p. Salvemini. Open Mon.-Sat. 9am-1pm and 3:30-7:30pm.

Ticket Agency: Box office at via della Pergola, 10r (tel. 24 23 61; fax 234 02 57). Advance booking for shows, concerts, and theater. Open Mon.-Sat. 10am-8pm.

Laundromat: Elensec, via dei Neri, 46r (tel. 28 37 47), near p. San Remigio. L3000 per kg. Open Mon.-Fri. 8:30am-1pm and 3:30-7:30pm. **Lavaria Express,** p. S. Pier Maggiore. L3000 per kg. Open Mon.-Fri. 8:30am-1pm.

Public Toilets: upstairs in the Mercato Centrale, in the Palazzo Vecchio, in the Palazzo Pitti, and in the train stations. All L400.

Public Baths: Bagno S. Agostino, via S. Agostino, 8 (tel. 28 44 82), off p. Santo Spirito. Bath L2500. Soap and towel L1500. Open Tues. and Thurs. 3:30-6:45pm, Sat. 8:30am-noon and 3:30-6:45pm. Another option is to ask at a *pensione* near the station, where an understanding proprietor may let you shower for about L5000.

Swimming Pools: Bellariva, lungarno Columbo, 6 (tel. 67 75 21). Bus #14 from the station or a 15-min. walk upstream along the Arno. Open June-Sept. daily 10am-6pm. Free. **Costoli,** viale Paoli (tel. 67 57 44), in a huge sports complex at campo di Marte. Take bus #17 from p. Unità toward the *duomo.* An Olympic-sized covered pool with separate diving and kiddie pools. Arrive early. Open daily 10am-6pm. Admission June-Sept. L5000, children L1500, over 60 free.

Late-Night Pharmacies: Farmacia Comunale (tel. 28 94 35), at the train station by track #16. **Molteni,** via Calzaiuoli, 7r (tel. 28 94 90). **Taverna,** p. S. Giovanni, 20r (tel. 28 40 13). All open 24 hrs.

Medical Assistance: Misericordia, p. del Duomo, 20 (tel. 21 22 22). They will send an ambulance. **Tourist Medical Service,** via Lorenzo il Magnifico, 59 (tel. 47 54 11). A group of general practitioners and specialists with someone on call 24 hrs. L50,000 for a home visit. Sometimes they give out advice over the phone. **Medical First Aid:** tel. 47 48 91. **Drug Addiction Service:** tel. 48 30 10. A list of French- and English-speaking doctors is available from the U.S. consulate.

Emergency: tel. 113. **Police: Questura** (headquarters), via Zara, 2 (tel. 497 71). On weekends or after hours go around the corner to via Duca D'Aosta. English-speaking personnel usually available. **Ufficio Stranieri** (for visa, work-permit, or passport problems), at the same address and phone number.

Accommodations

Florence abounds with one-star *pensione* and private homes with *affitta camere,* so no matter when you arrive, the search for accommodations shouldn't leave you in a bind. If you arrive late in the afternoon, check with the accommodations service at the train station; they'll know who still has room and at what prices. For L3000 or so, they will also reserve a hotel room for you. The best places go early, so reservations (*prenotazioni*) are wise, especially if you plan to visit at Easter or in summer. The vast majority of *pensioni* prefer to take reservations in the form of a letter with at least one night's deposit in the form of a postal money order, either in dollars or lire. From June to August, and around Easter, there's almost no chance you will find any space in the best lodgings without prior reservations (with a deposit). Calling a day or so in advance may make things easier, but remember that without a deposit most hotels will only hold reservations until noon. Also realize that it is good form to show up if you have called ahead, or to cancel if you can't make it. This simple courtesy avoids untold aggravation not only for proprietors but also for hapless travelers who otherwise may be turned away.

Be aware that prices may increase by as much as 15% from those quoted in *Let's Go.* This edition was published in November 1992; Italian hotels raise their prices in the beginning of January. To make sure you're not paying more than the actual price, check the numbers on the card on the back of the door to your room. The price for a triple, if not posted, should be no more than 135% the price of a double. In theory, many hotels let you choose whether or not to have breakfast; in practice, and especially in summer, they do not: breakfast (usually continental costing upwards of L8000) is "included." Ask, politely, for room prices without breakfast—but don't get your hopes up. Beware also that some proprietors may tack on as much as L3000 for a shower, which sometimes turns out to be just a cool trickle.

Don't be afraid to give proprietors your passport when you check in. They must register you as guests under Italian law. They should not, however, keep your passport to ensure payment. Don't hand over your passport until you've seen the room and are sure you want to stay. If you have any complaints talk first to the proprietor, and then to the **Ufficio Controllo Alberghi,** via Cavour, 37 (tel. 276 01).

Sleeping in Florence's train stations, streets, or parks is a poor idea and police discourage it. In summers past, the city has opened an **Area di Sosta,** or official free sleeping area outside of town (see below under "Camping").

The city's best budget lodgings can be found at **Pensionale Pio X** and **Istituto Gould** in the Oltrarno, but clean and inexpensive lodgings are dispersed throughout the city. **Long-term housing** can be secured rather easily in Florence. If you plan on staying a month or more, check the classified ads in *Le Pulce,* a bi-weekly paper (L3500) that has apartment, sublet, and roommate listings. Prices range from L350,000-L800,000 a month. If you only want to stay a week, try and strike a bargain with someone who's looking for a roommate; they might be willing to take someone short term while seeking a permanent roommie. Also check the **bulletin boards** at CarLie's Bakery, the American Church, the British Institute, and The Paperback Exchange, where people post notices of apartments for rent. (See Orientation and Practical Information.)

Unless otherwise stated, hotels have no curfew.

Hostels

Istituto Gould, via dei Serragli, 49 (tel. 21 25 76), across the river in the Oltrarno. Leave the station by track #16, turn right and walk to p. della Stazione. Go straight ahead down via degli Avelli, with the church Santa Maria Novella on your immediate right. Cross p. Sta. Maria Novella and continue straight down via dei Fossi, over the Ponte alla Carraia, and down via dei Serragli (15min.). Or take bus #36 or 37 from the station to the 1st stop across the river (more trouble than walking). This friendly, beautifully remodeled hostel wins our award for best lodging in Florence. Accommodating staff happy to answer questions, and the sunny rooms are spotless. The only drawback; it's impossible to check in or out on Sundays—the office is closed. Open Mon.-Fri. 9am-1pm and 3-7pm. Sat. 9am-1pm. Singles L30,000, with bath L35,000. Doubles L46,000, with bath L50,000. Triples L57,000, with bath L63,000. Quads L72,000, with bath L80,000. (Lone travelers can take a bed in a quad for L18,000). Sheets and towels included. Rooms are scarce during the academic year, especially in spring. Reserve 3-4 months in advance with deposit in spring.

Pensionato Pio X, via dei Serragli, 106 (tel. 22 50 44). Follow the directions to the Istituto Gould (above) then walk a few more blocks down the street. Quiet, no daytime lock-out, gregarious management, only 4 or 5 beds per room. Clean rooms and bathrooms. 2-day min. stay, 5-day max. stay. Check-out 10am. Curfew midnight. L16,000 per person; showers included, but L3000 more for a room with bath. No reservations. Usually full in summertime, but turnover is such that if you arrive early enough you should find a place. On weekends arrive before 9am.

Ostello della Gioventù Europa Villa Camerata (HI), viale Augusto Righi, 2-4 (tel. 60 14 51), northeast of town. Leave the station by track #5, then take bus #17B (20-30min.). You can also take this bus from p. del Duomo. In a gorgeous villa with *loggia* and gardens. Tidy and popular, though far away. Reception open Mon.-Fri. 9am-1pm and 3-7pm. Check-out 9am. Curfew midnight. L18,000 per person, L5000 per night extra for those without hostel card. Sheets and breakfast included. Dinner L8000. Open 2-11:30pm; off-season 3-10:30pm. Reserve by letter only.

Suore Oblate dello Spirito Santo, via Nazionale, 8 (tel. 239 82 02), near the station. Numbers on via Nazionale are tricky; ask along the street for help. The nuns take in women, married couples, and families. 30 beds in huge rooms with modern bathrooms and a good security. Curfew 11pm. Doubles L52,000, L62,000 with bath. Triples and quads L25,000 per person. Breakfast included. Phone reservations accepted, but it's better still to write in advance. Open July-Oct. 15.

Ostello Santa Monaca, via S. Monaca, 6 (tel. 26 83 38), off via dei Serragli near Istituto Gould. An over-crowded hostel in the Oltrarno. A narrow staircase leads to a maze upstairs where 70 beds crowd into stuffy rooms. Bring your own toilet paper. The hostel is open, with no locks on the doors or any guard. Ask about baggage check, or plan to use the storage at the train station. L15,000, L2500 for sheets. Curfew midnight. No breakfast. Shower included. A sign-up sheet is posted 9:30am-1pm, with as many spaces as there are beds available. No reservations. Open 8-9:30am and 4-11:30pm.

L'Orologio, via Oriulo, 17 (tel. 234 07 06). Simple, adequate rooms. Doubles L65,000, with bath L75,000. Triples with bath L105,000. Breakfast included. Shower L2000.

Piazza Santa Maria Novella and Environs

Standing in front of the station, you will see the back of the Basilica of Santa Maria Novella. Beyond the church and in the immediate vicinity you'll find budget accommodations galore—all excellent alternatives to the tourist-ridden via Nazionale and via Faenza near the station. Ask for rooms overlooking the pigeon-packed *piazza*. In this area you'll be close to the *duomo* and *centro,* and it's a short walk from the station.

Pensione La Mia Casa, p. Santa Maria Novella, 23 (tel. 21 30 61). Dark, cavernous rooms off a green-carpeted hallway. Every night, the proprietor screens—in English, and for free—a documentary on Florence (8pm) and a relatively recent American film (9pm). Curfew midnight. Singles L28,000. Doubles L43,000, with bath L54,000. Triples L58,000, with bath L73,000. Quads L73,000, with bath L92,000. Breakfast L6000.

Locanda La Romagnola and **Soggiorno Gigliola,** via della Scala, 40 (tel. 21 15 97 and 28 79 81). Leave the station by track #5, walk across the street, and turn right onto via della Scala after a block. Friendly, simple, and likely to have rooms. Curfew midnight. Singles L33,000, with bath L42,000. Doubles L49,000, with bath L61,000. Triples L65,000, with bath L81,000. Showers L3000.

Albergo Montreal, via della Scala, 43 (tel. 238 23 31). Clean, friendly, professional. Curfew 1:30am. Singles L35,000. Doubles with bath L57,000 (with shower only L52,000). Triples with bath L75,000. Quads with bath L90,000.

Hotel Visconti, p. Ottaviani, 1 (tel. 21 38 77). Friendly proprietor. Fussily decorated singles L45,000. Doubles L73,000, with bath L85,000. Triples L98,000, with bath L113,000. Quads L126,000, with bath L145,000. Breakfast included.

Hotel Elite, via della Scala, 12 (tel. 21 53 95). Enthusiastic, kindly proprietor is deservedly proud of his well-maintained, 8-room establishment. Single with shower only L40,000; with bath L50,000. Doubles with bath L72,000. Triples L96,000. Breakfast L10,000. Send 1 night's deposit to reserve a room, or call ahead and show up by noon.

Universo Hotel, p. Santa Maria Novella, 20 (tel. 28 19 51). Adequately cleaned rooms, some with views of the church and *piazza*. Singles L55,000, with bath L75,000. Doubles L90,000, with bath L110,000. Breakfast included. Credit cards accepted.

Near the Station

As you leave the station, a left onto via Nazionale will plunge you into a neighborhood of seedy hotels swarming with travelers. If you can't avoid this quarter, at least walk away from the heart of the zone. Here along **via Nazionale, via Faenza, via Fiume, via Guelfa,** and nearby streets, cheap establishments abound—often several to a building.

Ausonia e Rimini, via Nazionale, 24 (tel. 49 65 47). Leaving the station from track #16, take a right, and then a left onto via Nazionale. Welcoming, avuncular owners. The spotless rooms are nicely decorated and well-lit. Curfew 1am. Singles L41,000, with bath L50,000. Doubles L64,000, with bath L76,000. Triples L88,000, with bath L105,000. Quads L112,000, with bath L132,000. Breakfast included. Nov. 10-Jan. prices should be about 10% lower. AmEx, Visa.

Via Faenza, 56 houses no fewer than 6 separate *pensioni*. From the station follow the directions to via Nazionale, on which via Faenza is the 2nd intersection. **Pensione Azzi,** (tel. 21 38 06) styles itself as the "locanda degli artisti"—the artists' inn. Even the art-inept will enjoy the friendly management, large, immaculate rooms, and elegant dining room and terrace. They also boast a small but growing library, ranging from Stephen King to art history (with, as of now, not much in between). Curfew 1am. Singles L35,000. Doubles L58,000. Triples L79,000. Breakfast L3000. Solo travelers can get beds in dorms with 7-8 beds for L25,000 per person. **Albergo Anna,** (tel. 239 83 22). Lovely rooms—some ceilings with frescoes, others with fans. Singles L45,000. Doubles L70,000. Triples L95,000. Breakfast L8000. When it's slow, the proprietress may knock L5000 off the price of a room—but she won't haggle. **Albergo Merlini,** (tel. 21 28 48). Light and airy. Hip and breezy. Breakfast served on the terrace, which looks out over a garden to the *duomo* beyond. Curfew 1am. Singles L38,000. Doubles L50,000, with bath L65,000. Triples L69,000. **Albergo Armonia,** (tel. 21 11 46). Clean and adequate. Doubles L75,000. Triples L105,000. Quads L132,000. Quints L150,000. Breakfast and shower included; prices significantly lower in winter (Nov.-March). **Albergo Marini,** (tel. 28 48 24). Simple white rooms with comfy beds. Curfew 1am. Doubles with bath L60,000. Triples with bath L81,000. Quads with bath L100,000. Breakfast L10,000. **Locanda Paola,** (tel. 21 36 82). Relaxed, but the furniture doesn't all match. Doubles with private shower (but no toilet) L70,000. Triples L75,000, with shower L90,000. Discounts for longer stays.

Hotel Nazionale, via Nazionale, 22 (tel. 238 22 03), near p. Indipendenza. Sunny rooms and friendly management. Breakfast served in your room. Curfew midnight. Singles L45,000, with bath L55,000. Doubles L70,000, with bath L80,000. Triples L94,500, with bath L108,000. Breakfast included. Visa.

Locanda Nella e Pina, via Faenza, 69 (tel. 21 22 31 and 28 42 56). Kindly proprietor will take care of you. One double has view of a spectacular garden. Curfew midnight. Singles L35,400. Doubles L52,000. Triples L70,000. Quads L90,000. **Locanda Giovanna,** (tel. 238 13 53), is located in the same building. Seven small, well-kept rooms, some with garden view. Singles L32,000. Doubles L47,000. Triples L66,000.

Pensione Daniel, via Nazionale, 22 (tel. 21 12 93), near p. Indipendenza. Small and a bit dark but the walls are painted over every Easter in pinks, yellows, and blues reminiscent of a Fra Angelico fresco. Strict midnight curfew. L15,000 per person. Shower L1500. No reservations.

Hotel Marcella, via Faenza, 58 (tel. 21 32 32). Spacious rooms; some overlook a garden. Curfew midnight. Singles L35,000. Doubles L50,000, with bath L60,000. Triples L67,000, with bath L80,000.

Near Piazza San Marco and the University Quarter

Thanks to its location a few blocks off the major tourist axes (Station Duomo-Palazzo Vecchio), this area is considerably calmer and less tourist-ridden than its proximity to the center might suggest.

La Colomba, via Cavour, 21 (tel. 28 91 39). Sunny white modernity. Windows peer out across a charming Florentine roofscape. Italo-Australian proprietor Rosanna is helpful and friendly, and sociable tots Angelo and his little brother Stefano never cry. Curfew 1:30am. Singles L55,000. Doubles L90,000, with bath L100,000. A *real* continental breakfast is included. **Hotel Sofia,** just upstairs, offers pleasant, plain rooms at good prices. Curfew 1am. Singles L33,000. Doubles L50,000. Triples and quads L21,000 per person.

Albergo Sampaoli, via San Gallo, 14 (tel. 28 48 34). A peaceful hotel where you can relax on your own private *terrazzo*. Refrigerators on each floor keep your drinks chilled. Doubles L50,000, with bath L63,000. Triples L75,000, with bath L80,000. Quads L88,000. The proprietor does not accept written reservations; call the night before you're arriving.

Hotel Globus, via Sant'Antonio, 24 (tel. 21 10 62; fax 239 62 25). The sun shoots through these breezy rooms. Outgoing, professional management. Singles L45,000. Doubles L72,000. Triples L88,000, with bath L120,000. Show your *Let's Go* to get these prices. Breakfast included.

Pensione Casci, via Cavour, 13 (tel. 21 16 86; fax 239 64 61). Only 3min. from the *duomo*. A tranquil, recently restored *palazzo* with ceilings and floors as they were in the 14th century. Enthusiastic multilingual proprietors. Singles with bath L60,000. Doubles with bath L90,000. Triples with bath L120,000. Prices fall in low season. All-you-can-eat continental breakfast included.

House for Tourists—Aglietti, via Cavour, 29 (tel. 28 78 24). No authentic Italian name, but authentic flora-phile doing the interior design—the foyer overflows with potted plants. Singles L39,000. Doubles L60,000. Breakfast included.

Hotel San Marco, via Cavour, 50 (tel. 28 42 35) offers 3 floors of airy, modern rooms. Curfew 1:30am. Singles L55,000, with bath L65,000. Doubles L70,000, with bath L85,000. Triples with bath L120,000. AmEx, MC, Visa.

Old City (Near the Duomo)

The daily flood of tourists somehow misses many of the establishments in this ancient quarter. The area boasts a more authentically Florentine atmosphere than neighborhoods closer to the station, which is still only a 10- to 15-minute walk away.

Locanda Orchidea, borgo degli Albizi, 11 (tel. 248 03 46). Dante's wife was born in this 12th-century *palazzo*, which features a still-intact tower. English-speaking proprietor presides over 7 exquisite rooms (some overlook a charming garden). Singles L32,000. Doubles L48,000, with shower L55,000. Triples L66,000, with shower L72,000. Quad L88,000, with shower L92,000. Quint L100,000.

Soggiorno Brunori, via del Proconsolo, 5 (tel. 28 96 48), off p. del Duomo. Sufficiently hygienic rooms in a beautiful and conveniently located building. Friendly manager speaks English and goes out of his way to make your stay pleasant. Curfew midnight. Doubles L48,000, with bath L60,000. Triples L72,000, with bath L85,000. Quads L92,000, with bath L108,000. Breakfast L7000.

Soggiorno Bavaria, borgo degli Albizi, 26 (tel. 234 03 13). From p. della Repubblica walk straight up via del Corso, which becomes borgo Albizi; Bavaria is on the left, inside the courtyard and up the stairs to the right. In oldest quarter of Florence. Kindly management. A little dark and musty, but quiet. Singles L35,000. Doubles L50,000, with bath L60,000. Breakfast L8000. Reserve by July for August stays.

Hotel Aldini, via Calzaiuoli, 13 (tel. 21 47 52 or 21 24 48; fax 21 64 10). If you're contemplating going all-out for a hotel, this is the place to do it. Antique free-standing fireplaces in all the newly renovated and spotless bedrooms. A/C, color TV. Curfew 1:30am. Singles with bath L85,000. Doubles with bath L140,000. Triples with bath L191,000. Breakfast included (we should hope so). MC, Visa.

Albergo Costantini, via Calzaiuoli, 13 (tel. 21 51 28). Big, airy, clean rooms. Curfew 2am. Singles L40,000, with bath L50,000. Doubles L55,000, with bath L75,000. Triples with bath L101,000. Pay in advance. Breakfast L10,000. Call 3 days ahead to get a room.

Albergo Firenze, p. Donati, 4 (tel. 21 42 03 and 26 83 01), off v. del Corso. Tidy, friendly, and centrally located. Singles L41,000, with bath L50,000. Doubles L64,000, with bath L75,000. Triples L93,000, with bath L105,000. Breakfast included.

Hotel Maxim, via dei Medici, 4 (tel. 21 74 74, fax 28 37 29). Another entrance at via dei Calzaiuoli, 11. Cheerful proprietor lets clean and sunny rooms near the *duomo*. Doubles L64,000, with bath L84,000. Triples L97,000, with bath L120,000. Breakfast included. Laundry service L16,000 a load (5kg). AmEx, MC, Visa.

Soggiorno Panerai, via dei Servi, 36 (tel. 26 41 03), near the *duomo*. This tidy, quiet 5-room *pensione* is run by a helpful young American. Doubles L61,000. Triples L83,500. Quad L106,000. All rooms without bath, but 2 rooms share a big shower. Breakfast included. To reserve more than 2 days in advance, send 1 night's deposit.

Pensione Zurigo, via Oriuolo, 17 (tel. 234 06 44). Neat, clean, and simple. Large bathrooms with tubs. Curfew 1:30am. Singles L40,000. Doubles L70,000, with bath L85,000. Triples L75,000, with bath L95,000. Breakfast included. MC, Visa.

Pensi one Esperanza, via dell'Inferno, 3 (tel. 21 37 73). From v. Parione between p. Goldoni and v. Tornabuoni, go through the arch called Volta della Vecchia, turn left on v. Purgatorio, then immediately turn right. 9 rooms with old furniture, some with balconies. Peaceful. Proprietor Ilva is accommodating and attentive. Curfew 1am. Singles L29,000. Doubles L43,000. Showers L3000.

Locanda Davanzati, via Porta Rossa, 15 (tel. 28 34 14), off v. Tornabuoni. On the 2nd floor, not the 11th as the sign on the stairs seems to say. Excellent location and prices. 10 sunny but small rooms—1 great room with a terrace. Some English spoken. Singles L28,000. Doubles L42,000, with bath L53,000. Showers L3000. Breakfast L7000.

In the Oltrarno

Only 10 minutes away from the *duomo,* but literally "outside the Arno," *pensioni* in the Oltrarno offer a welcome respite from the bustle of Florence's hub. Rooms are generally quiet and airy and some overlook the Arno, tranquil *piazze,* or well-kept gardens.

Pensione Sorelle Bandini, p. Santo Spirito, 9 (tel. 21 53 08). Old-world elegance and happy staff on the top floor of a large *palazzo. Beautiful sun-drenched loggia.* Terrace with view of Florence presides over the *piazza.* English spoken. Doubles L83,000, with bath L95,000. Triples L118,000, with bath L133,000. Show your *Let's Go* to get these prices in 1993. Breakfast included. Reservations cheerfully accepted.

Hotel La Scaletta, via Guicciardini, 13 (tel. 28 30 28), across the Ponte Vecchio towards the Pitti Palace. Spectacular views of the Boboli gardens and the city from the rooftop terraces. Rooms furnished with an English touch. Singles L57,000, with bath L69,000. Doubles L83,000, with bath L105,000. Breakfast included. MC, Visa.

Camping

Italiani e Stranieri, viale Michelangelo, 80 (tel. 681 19 77), near p. Michelangelo. Take red or black bus #13 from the station (15min., last bus 11:55pm). Extremely crowded, but offers a spectacular panorama of Florence. Fantastic facilities, including a well-stocked food store and bar. They may post a *completo* sign or tell you the same by phone, but if you show up without a vehicle they will often let you in. L6000 per person, L7000 per tent, L4000 per car, L2500 per motorcycle. Open mid-March to Nov. 6am-midnight.

Villa Camerata, viale A. Righi, 2/4 (tel. 61 14 51), outside the HI youth hostel on the #17B bus route. Catch the bus at the train station or at p. del Duomo. L5500 per person, L6750 per small tent. Open April-Oct. 7:30am-1pm and 3-9pm; if it's closed, stake your site and come back later to register and pay.

Camping Panoramico, via Peramonda, 1 (tel. 59 90 69), outside the city near Fiesole. Take bus #7 from the station to Fiesole (last buses 11:25pm and 12:30am, L1000). L7900 per person, L13,900 per tent, auto included.

Villa Favard, via Rocca Tedalda. Take bus #14. Free youth campsite. Open in summer only.

Food

Florence's hearty Tuscan cuisine is rooted in the peasant fare of the surrounding countryside and reflects the city's unsophisticated side. Yet, Tuscan food, typified by only the freshest ingredients and simple preparations, contends among the world's best cuisines. White beans and olive oil form the two main staples of Florentine food, and most regional dishes will come loaded with one or the other, if not both. Specialties include such *antipasti* as *Bruschette* (grilled Tuscan bread doused with olive oil and garlic, and sometimes topped with tomatoes and basil). For *primi* Florentines have perfected the Tuscan classics *minestra di fagioli* (a delicious white bean and garlic soup) and *ribollista* (a hearty bean, bread, and black cabbage concoction). Florence's classic—and surprisingly familiar—*secondo* is *bistecca alla Fiorentina,* thick sirloin steak (with a characteristic squeeze of lemon), each inch more succulent and expensive than the last. You will gain murmurs of admiration if you order it as Florentines do: *al sangue* (very rare—literally "bloody"). Other typical *secondi* include *trippa alla fiorentina* (tripe cooked in a tomato and cheese sauce), and grilled pork sausages, sometimes made with *cinghiale,* (wild boar). The best local cheese is *pecorino,* made from sheep's milk. Wine is another Florentine staple, and the local *chianti* is superb. Genuine *chianti classico,* the highest quality, commands a premium; it is also called *gallo nero* after the black rooster on its neck label. Many other famous wines such as *Ricasoli* can be just as good. While most restaurants serve good house wines, *vino* bought in a store is a more economical way to sample the local grape. A liter of house wine typically costs L6000-7000 in Florence's *trattorie,* while stores sell bottles of delicious wine, even *chianti classico,* for as little as L4000. Florentine refinement shines through in the local dessert, *cantuccini di prato,* (almond cookies made with tons of egg yolks) dipped in *vin Santo* (a rich dessert wine made from raisins).

For lunch, visit one of the many *rosticcerie gastonomie,* or browse over pushcarts throughout the city. Try the roast meats and pastas, or sample the cold salads and sandwiches (*panini*). Buy your own fresh produce, tripe and meats at the **Mercato Centrale,** between via Nazionale and the back of San Lorenzo, where you can marvel at whole swordfish and skinned rabbits. (Open Mon.-Sat. 8am-1pm; Oct.-May Mon.-Sat. 6:30am-1pm and 4-8:30pm.) For staples, head to **Supermercato STANDA,** via Pietrapiana, 1r (open Tues.-Sat. 8:30am-8pm, Mon. 3-8pm), or to any of the small markets throughout the city.

Santa Maria Novella and Environs

Amon, via Palazzuolo, 26-28r. Some of the best Middle Eastern food to be found on any continent. Try the refreshingly cool and crunchy cucumber salad made with yogurt. Falafel L3000, shish kebab L4000. Beer L1800. Stand-up or take-out only. Open Mon.-Sat. noon-3pm and 7-11pm.

Trattoria da Giorgio, via Palazzuolo, 100r. Not fancy, but serves up filling down-home style meals including *primo, secondo,* salad and wine for L13,000. Menu changes daily. There's usually a wait to get in. Open Mon.-Sat. noon-3pm and 6:30-10pm.

Trattoria Contadino, via Palazzuolo, 69r. Just down the street from da Giorgio, and the same deal. Meals *alla buona* for L13,000.

Il Latini, via Palchetti, 6r. A huge wooden dining room decorated with scores of hams slung from the rafters. They serve up a reassuring bowl of *minestrone Toscano* for L6000. Try the grilled sausage (*salsicce*), perfectly complemented with Tuscan beans, L12,000. Open 12:30-2:30pm and 7:30-10pm.

Il Giardino, via della Scala, 61 (tel. 21 31 41). Enjoy a hearty portion of hand-made *tagliatelle* (L6000) under the vines of the garden inside. The roast veal is enough to encourage anyone on to a 2nd course (L9000). Cover L2000. Service 10%. Open Wed.-Mon. noon-3pm and 7-10pm. Credit cards accepted.

La Grotta di Leo, via della Scala, 41-43r (tel. 21 92 65). This restaurant/pizzeria serves up tasty food at good prices. Their magnum opus, the *pizza della casa,* (L9000), overloads with tomato, cheese, 2 kinds of sausage, ham, mushrooms, artichoke hearts, and a fried egg in the middle. *Primi* L6000-9000. *Secondi* from L10,000. Cover and service included. Open Thurs.-Tues. 11:30am-1am.

Nuova Cina, p. Santa Maria Novella, 9-11 (tel. 21 53 87), offers authentic Chinese food in the middle of p. Santa Maria Novella. No extra charge to sit outside. *Primi* L3000-5000, *secondi* from L7000. Cover L2000. Open Thurs.-Tues. 11am-3pm and 7pm-midnight. Credit cards accepted.

The Station and University Quarter

Trattoria Antichi Cancelli, via Faenza, 73r (tel. 21 89 27). Home-style and hearty. Try a great bowl of vegetable soup (L5000) or a tasty veal scallop with green pepper (L12,000). Open Tues.-Sun. noon-3pm and 7-10:30pm. Credit cards accepted.

Trattoria da Zà-Zà, p. Mercato Centrale, 26r (tel. 21 54 11). Soups are a specialty in this hip-hopping *trattoria;* try the *tris* (mix of 3) bean, tomato, and vegetable for L7000, or the other-worldly *tagliatelle al pesto* made fresh every morning, L7000. *Secondi* around L12,000-14,000. Cover L1800. Open Mon.-Sat. noon-2:30pm and 7-10pm. Reservations are an excellent idea. Credit cards accepted.

Trattoria Mario, via Rosina, 2r. Share huge wooden tables with the crowds of locals that flock here for lunch. Menu changes daily. *Primi* L3000-5000, *secondi* L4500-9000. Open for lunch noon-3:30pm.

Caffé Carocal—Mexican Restaurant, via de Ginori, 10r. Bar atmosphere in which to munch happily on nachos, burritos, (L14,000) or tostadas (L14,000). Open Thurs.-Tues. 6pm-1am.

Mensa Universita, via San Gallo, 25. Worth it just to come away appreciating whatever your school back home slops up. Come here to get a taste of Italian student life: crowded and noisy. Full meal for L8500 includes *primo, secondo,* salad, fruit, yogurt, cheese, bread, and wine. Open Sept.-June Mon.-Sat. noon-2pm and 6:45-8:45pm.

Gran Caffé San Marco, p. San Marco, 9. Pastries, *panini,* hot dishes, and *gelato* that you eat among crowds of students in the *piazza.* Open daily 6am-midnight, Sept.-May closed Sun.

Old City (The Center)

Stazione da Zima, via Ghibbelina 70r. No sign. Healthy food for herbivores. First course choices (L4500) include house specialties like *riso integrale* (brown rice) and *pasta al pesto.* Stuffed tomatoes provide a satisfying *secondo* (L5500). They've also got a great crunchy bulletin board with notices of environmental activities.

Trattoria da Benvenuto, via dei Neri, 47r. Filling portions of *gnocchi* (L4500). Only L7000 for grilled *braciola* (veal chop). Open Mon.-Tues. and Thurs.-Sat. noon-3pm and 7:15-10pm.

Acqua al Due, via Vegna Vecchia, 40r, behind the Bargello. Florentine specialties in a cozy, air-conditioned joint popular with young Italians. The *assaggio,* a dish of 5 types of pasta, demands a taste (L9800); getting a table, however, usually demands a reservation. Open Tues.-Sun. 7pm-2am. MC, Visa.

Aquerello, via Ghibblelina, 156r, (tel. 234 05 54), offers pseudo-Memphis decor and superb, off-beat food. Duck when your *spaghetti flambé all' Aquerello* (L8000) arrives—it's on fire, and it's fantastic. Or, if you like, you can have your duck *à l'orange* (*anitra all'arancia,* L15,000). Cover L3000. Open Fri.-Wed. 11am-3pm and 7pm-1am. Credit cards accepted.

Trattoria le Mossacce, via del Proconsolo, 55r. Between the *duomo* and Bargello. Food to write home about. A succulent *osso buco,* L9500. Open Mon.-Fri. noon-2:30pm and 7-9:30pm.

La Maremmana, via dei Macci, 77r (tel. 24 12 26). A rare combination: simple, generous, and affordable. *Menù* starting at L18,000. Tablecloths, cut flowers, pasta, *secondi,* side dishes, a fruit dessert and wine included. Look for the scrumptious *antipasto* buffet and the *spaghetti scoglio.* Justifiably busy. Open Sept.-July Mon.-Sat. 12:30-3pm and 7:30-10:30pm. MC, Visa.

Osteria e Pizzeria Il Gatto e la Volpe, via Ghibellina, 151r (tel. 28 92 64). A crowded and busy restaurant. The tortellini in walnut sauce (*salsa di noce*) for L7500 are heavenly. Tempting assortment of *antipasti* L7000. *Secondi* start at L10,000. Pizzas L5000-10,000. Cover L2500. Service 15%. Open Wed.-Mon. noon-2:30pm and 7:30-11:30pm. **Trattoria I'che c'è c'è,** via de Mangalotti 11r, (tel. 21 65 89). The owner/chef cares about his food, and you can taste it. *Topini (gnocchi) al gorgonzola,* L7500. Try a classic Tuscan *secondo* like *salsicce e faglioli* (sausage and beans), L10,000. Cover L2000. Open Tues.-Sun. 11:30am-2pm and 7:30-10:30pm. Reserve in advance.

Gran caffé Mozart, via Pietrapiana, 67. Great food in a cheerful self-service restaurant where you can sit outside in the *piazza. Primi* like *gnocchi* or tortellini go for L4000. *Secondi* L6000. Lunch served Mon.-Sat. 12:30-2:30pm.

Jolly caffé, borgo degli Albizi, 80r. A busy bar that also does lunch specials like tortellini (L5000). Get stupid at happy hour every night 9-10pm, when Löwenbräu is only L1200 a pint. Open Mon.-Sat. 8am-1am.

The Oltrarno

The Oltrarno hoards more than its share of fantastic and cheap restaurants. Come here to experience Florentine cooking at its best.

Trattoria Casalinga, via Michelozzi, 9r, near p. Santo Spirito. Delicious Tuscan specialties in relaxed, if crowded, atmosphere. Ravioli made with spinach and ricotta, L5500. *Secondi* about L7500. Menu changes daily. Cover L1500. Open Mon.-Sat. noon-3pm and 7-9:30pm.

Il Borgo Antico, p. Santa Spirito, 61 (tel. 21 04 37). A hip-hopping restaurant with an impressive array of slightly offbeat (but yummy) dishes. Try the *ravioli alla crema di Salvia,* in a sweet-cream rosé sauce (L8000). Pizzas L8000-12,000. Cover L3000. Open Tues.-Sat. 12:30-2:30pm and 7:30-11pm, Mon. 7:30-11pm. (Pizzeria open until 12:30am.)

Il Cantinone del Gallo Nero, via S. Spirito, 6r. (tel. 21 88 98) Don't pass up *fagioli all'uccelletto* (beans with sage and tomato, L6500). A cooler restaurant than most—it's sheltered from the heat in a converted wine cellar. Open Tues.-Sun. 12:30-2pm and 7:30-10:30pm. Always full on Sat. and Sun., so call ahead. AmEx, Diners' Club.

Trattoria Angiolino, via S. Spirito, 22 (tel. 29 89 76). Small menu comprised mostly of daily specials. Lots of happy Italians. Open Tues.-Sun. 11am-3pm and 7pm-midnight.

Rosticceria Alisio, via de Sarragli, 75r. Fill up on their spit-roasted chicken (L3500 for quarter-chicken) and tasty selection of vegetables and *antipasti* (L2500). Don't miss their *fritto misto* of vegetables, including fried zucchini blossoms (L1000 per 100g). Stand-up or take-out only. Open Tues.-Sun. 8am-2pm and 5-9pm.

Baked Goods

CarLie's Bakery, via Brache, 12r (tel. 21 51 37). Behind v. de'Benci, near the river. From P. Signoria, walk between the Palazzo Vecchio and the Uffizi. Head along v. dei Neri and turn left onto v. Brache. If you've lost your passport, head over to the American consulate; otherwise, if you're looking for a genuine American outpost, come to this cheerful bakery where you can load up on the sweets you've been craving. Even non-Americans will wax nostalgic over the deathly fudge brownies and gooey chocolate chip cookies. The 2 outgoing proprietors dole out sympathy and advice to weary American travelers along with their fantastic confections. Open Tues.-Sun. 10am-1:30pm and 3:30-8pm. Open Sept. 1- July 15.

Gelaterie

No dinner in this gelato capital of Italy would be complete without a luscious lick from one of the many *gelaterie*. Set off on your own odyssey, but before plopping down L2000 for a cone assess the quality of any establishment by checking out the banana. If it's bright yellow, it's been made from a mix—keep on walking. You know you've found a true Florentine *gelateria* when the banana is slightly off-grey, indicating only real live bananas are inside.

Gelateria Dei Neri, via dei Neri, 20-22r. A prodigal upstart with sinfully scrumptious gelato. A truly mythical "Mitica" (chocolate ice cream with just about everything mixed in). Open daily 10:30am-midnight.

Il Granduca, via dei Calzaiuoli, 57r. Delicious *gelato* with fresh fruit and other goodies.

Vivoli's, via della Stinche, 7, behind the Bargello. The most renowned of Florentine *gelaterie*, with a huge selection—but no cones, only cups (from L2000). Open Sept.-July Tues.-Sun. 8am-midnight.

Perchè No?, via Tavolini, 19r, off via Calzaiuoli. Though the decor doesn't show it, this is the oldest *gelateria* in Florence—it opened in 1939. Offers a marvelous array of orgasmic flavors. Open Wed.-Mon. 8am-12:30am.

Sights

> *Florence! One of the only places in Europe where I*
> *understood that underneath my revolt, a consent*
> *was lying dormant.*
> —*Albert Camus*

It takes quite a city to reduce an existentialist to acquiescence. The same secret spell that Florence has cast over intellectuals from Goethe to Camus can overwhelm the first-time visitor. Beware the well-documented "Stendhal Syndrome," the dizziness and palpitations of the heart that result from aesthetic overload (named for the famed French author who first described an ailment which overcame him in the church of Santa Croce—no joke, art students on their first trip to Florence should be especially careful). Pick up the museum listings at the tourist office for the most current information on the visual arts scene.

In past years visitors have had to battle the crowds to see the most popular museums—the Uffizi, the Accademia, the Bargello. This is no longer true, but the explanation for this phenomenon is unfortunate for the budget traveler: All Florentine museums (in fact, most Italian museums) recently doubled their admission price, making art-viewing an extremely costly endeavor—L4000-10,000 at most major venues. Florence merits budget-bending for its museums, but choose what you want to see carefully, and plan to spend a healthy chunk of your day at each museum. Before writing off the Uffizi or the Bargello (L10,000), remember that they house the best collections of Renaissance painting and sculpture in the world, and perhaps reconsider. Fill in those gaps left by budget strictures by exploring Florence's churches, most of which double as treasuries of masterpieces.

Piazza del Duomo

Florentines often refer to their cathedral as "Santa Maria del Fiore"; asking a local about *"il duomo"* may leave both of you confused.

In 1296 the city fathers commissioned Arnolfo di Cambio to erect a cathedral and carry out the project "with the most high and sumptuous magnificence so that it is impossible to make it either better or more beautiful with the industry and power of man." Arnolfo died in 1302 and the Florentine elders were left with the task of installing above Arnolfo's monumental structure Europe's largest dome since the Roman Pantheon. Bickering and speculation stalled the construction for decades before Brunelleschi won a competition to direct the construction of the cupola. To accomplish the task, Brunelleschi came up with the revolutionary idea of building a double-shelled dome with interlocking bricks that would support itself as it was built. He also supervised every step of the building process, personally designing the system of pulleys and constructing kitchens between the two walls of the cupola so that the masons would not have to descend for lunch. Alberti described the dome as "large enough to shelter all of Tuscany within its shadow...and of a construction that perhaps not even the ancients knew or understood"—the ultimate compliment in a period awed by the genius of Greece and Rome. Michelangelo paid tribute to its harmonious proportions in a ditty he composed upon receiving the commission for the dome of St. Peter's: *"Io farò la sorella,/Già più gran ma non più bella"* ("I'm going to make its sister/Bigger but not more beautiful.") The cupola was finished in 1436, but the half-completed Gothic-Renaissance façade was taken down by an overly ambitious 16th-century Medici rebuilding campaign and not replaced until 1871, when Emilio de Fabris, a Florentine architect influenced by the Gothic style, received the commission following a victory in another competition. The resulting structure, completed in 1883, fulfilled Vasari's boastful 16th-century prediction that it would be "the most noble, vast, and beautiful building of modern times."

Inside, the nave's sheer immensity overwhelms the art. In the form of a Latin cross, the church claims the world's third longest nave, behind St. Peter's in Rome and St. Paul's in London. The fresco illustrating the *Divine Comedy* in the left aisle, by a student of Fra Angelico, pays tribute to Dante, who was forced to flee to Florence after backing the losing side (white) in the struggle between the black and white Guelphs. Nearby is a fresco of an equestrian statue of the English *condottiere* mercenary general John Hawkwood. Hawkwood was promised a memorial statue in the *duomo* and the ever-frugal republic cunningly delivered only a fresco, albeit one by master-of-perspective Paolo Uccello. The *orologio,* a 24-hour clock designed by Paolo Uccello, is perhaps the interior's most interesting piece. The clock, which hangs on the cathedral's back wall, above the entrance, runs backwards.

Climb up the 463 steps around the inside of the dome (the tallest thing ever built in medieval Italy at 110m) to the lantern (tel. 230 28 85) and on the way survey the city from the external gallery. (*Duomo* open daily 10am-5pm. Masses are held 7-10am and 5-7pm. Lantern open Mon.-Sat. 10am-5pm. Admission L5000.) You can also visit the **crypt** of the church upon which the Santa Maria del Fiore was built to see the tomb of Brunelleschi, some 13th century tombs, and bits of mosaic. (Crypt of S. Reparata open Mon.-Sat. 10am-5pm. Admission L3000.)

Most of the *duomo's* art has been placed in the **Museo dell'Opera di S. Maria del Fiore** (tel. 230 28 85), behind the *duomo* at p. del Duomo, 9. Up the first flight of stairs is a late *Pietà* by Michelangelo. Frustrated by his own work, the sculptor intentionally damaged the figure by taking a hammer to it and severing Christ's left arm. A servant convinced him to stop, and soon thereafter a pupil touched up the work, leaving parts of Mary Magdalene's head with visible "scars" and removing a leg. There are other masterpieces here as well: Donatello and Luca della Robbia's wonderful *cantorie* (choir balconies with bas reliefs of cavorting children and *putti*); Donatello's *St. Mary Magdalene* (1555), a tortured, naked figure draped in her own hair; and a silver altar by Michelozzo, Pollaiuolo, and Verrocchio. The art that once covered the campanile's exterior includes Donatello's prophets and Andrea Pisano's *Progress of Man* cycle of small reliefs. The museum now houses four of the frames from the baptistry's *Gates of Paradise* (see below), and after restoration will house the entire collection. (Open Mon.-Sat. 9am-7:30pm; in winter, Mon.-Sat. 9am-6pm. Admission L5000.)

Though it was built sometime between the 7th and 9th century, by Dante's time Florentines thought their **baptistry** had originally been a Roman temple, a proper medieval complement to this little masterpiece of green and white marble. The interior contains 13th- to 15th-century Byzantine-style mosaics, whose stylized, cartoon-like execution seem to foreshadow modernist art. The lowest circle is thought to be the work of Cimabue. Along the wall rests the elegant, perfect early Renaissance *Tomb of the Anti-Pope John XXIII,* by Donatello and Michelozzo, arranged so that the sculpted figure lies directly in line of Christ's blessing.

The commission to execute the famous bronze doors of the baptistry was among the most coveted in Florence. In 1330, Andrea Pisano (1270-1349) was imported from Pisa, and Venetian foundry-workers were brought in to cast the first set of doors, which now guard the south side (toward the river). In 1401, the cloth guild announced a new competition to determine who would forge the remaining doors. The original field of eight contestants narrowed to two youngsters, Brunelleschi (then 23) and Ghiberti (20). Each was given a year to complete a panel, and Ghiberti, whose entry more elegantly molded its subject to the quatrefoil Gothic frame, was awarded the commission. (The competition pieces, panels depicting the sacrifice of Abraham, now hang in the Bargello.)

Ghiberti's doors, on the north side away from the river, start with Pisano's framework, but add detail, movement, and classical draperies. His work was so admired that the last set of doors was commissioned from him as soon as he finished the first, in 1425. The **"Gates of Paradise,"** as Michelangelo reportedly called them, are nothing like the two earlier portals, abandoning the quatrefoil framing and the 28-panel design for 10 large, entirely gilded squares, each of which incorporates mathematical perspectives to recess the scenes into startlingly deep space. Originally intended to stand as the third set of doors on the north side, they so impressed the Florentines that they were switched with the second doors and placed in their current honored position facing the cathedral. The doors were finished in 1452, after 24 years of labor, and three years before Ghiberti's death. The panels have been under restoration since a 1966 flood and will eventually reside in the Museo del Duomo, while replicas hang in the baptistry. The baptistry's doors open only on June 24, the feast of Florence's patron saint St. John the Baptist. (Open Mon.-Sat. 1:30-6pm, Sun. 9am-1pm.)

Next to the *duomo* rises the 82m **campanile,** the "lily of Florence blossoming in stone." Giotto, then the official city architect, drew up the design and laid the foundation, but died soon after construction began. Andrea Pisano added two stories and Francesco Talenti completed the tower in 1359, but only after doubling the thickness of the walls to support the weight. The original exterior decoration now resides in the **Museo del Duomo.** (The 414 steps are open daily 8:30am-6:50pm; Nov.-March 9am-5:30pm. Admission L5000.)

Palazzo Vecchio and Piazza della Signoria

From p. del Duomo, **via dei Calzaiuoli,** one of the city's oldest streets, leads to p. Signoria. Laid out as part of the original Roman *castrum* (camp), today via dei Calzaiuoli bustles with crowds, chic stores, ice cream shops, and vendors peddling their wares in the sidewalks. At the far end, the area around the **Palazzo Vecchio** (tel. 276 84 65) forms the civic center of Florence.

The fortress-like *palazzo* was built between 1298 and 1314 according to the plans of the ubiquitous Arnolfo di Cambio, who intended it to replace the Bargello as the seat of the commune's government; its interior apartments served as living quarters for the seven members of the *signoria* (council) during their rotating, one-month terms in office. By the time of Cosimo di Medici's autocratic rule, however, the building's role as a symbol of communal government was simply an irony.

The courtyard, rebuilt by Michelozzo in 1444 and ruined by Vasari in 1565 to please a Medici bride, contains a copy of Verrocchio's charming 15th-century *putto* fountain and several stone lions (the heraldic symbol of the city). Michelangelo and Leonardo da Vinci were commissioned to paint opposite walls of the **Salone dei Cinquecento,** the meeting room of the Grand Council of the Republic. Although they did not get around to executing the frescoes, their preliminary cartoons, the *Battle of Cascina* and the *Battle of Anghiari,* were studied by all young Florentine artists and copied for mass production by engravers. The tiny, windowless **Studio of Francesco I,** built by Vasari, is a treasure house of mannerist art, with paintings by Bronzino, Allori and Vasari, and bronze statuettes by Giambologna and Ammannati. The best of the art waits in the **Mezzanino.** Look for Bronzino's portrait of the poet Laura Battiferi and Giambologna's *Hercules and the Hydra.* (Open Mon.-Fri. 9am-7pm, Sun. 8am-1pm. Admission L8000.)

A vast space by medieval standards, **piazza della Signoria** was created in the 13th century by the destruction of the house-towers belonging to the Uberti clan, after they suffered a political decline. For a long time, no one of means wanted to own or build on the site. In 1497, Savonarola convinced Florentines to light off the **Bonfire of the Vanities** in the square, a grand roast that consumed some of Florence's best art. A year later, disillusioned Florence sent Savonarola up in smoke on the exact same spot.

Symbolic sculptures cluster around the front of the *palazzo:* Donatello's *Judith and Holofernes,* Michelangelo's *David* (only a copy is on display; the original stood here over a century ago), Giambologna's *Equestrian Monument to Cosimo I* and Bandinelli's *Hercules.* The awkward Neptune statue to the left of the Palazzo Vecchio occasioned the following quip by Michelangelo: "Oh Ammannato, Ammannato, what lovely marble you have ruined!"

Built as a space for civic speakers, the graceful 14th-century **Loggia dei Lanzi** gradually became a misogynist sculpture gallery under the Medici dukes. Here you can see Benvenuto Cellini's *Perseus Slaying Medusa,* which Cellini signed on Perseus' sash; Giambologna's *Rape of the Sabines* whose spiral quality invites viewing from any angle; and the dynamic and violent *Rape of Polyxena* by Pio Fedi.

The Uffizi

The **Uffizi** (offices, tel. 21 83 41) form a double row behind the *loggia.* Vasari designed the Uffizi in 1554, when Duke Cosimo demanded housing for his consolidated administration of the Duchy of Tuscany. The street makes a strong political statement, framing the tower of Palazzo Vecchio at one end and the Medici Forte Belvedere across the Arno at the other. Giambologna's bust of Cosimo oversees the entire complex at the Arno end. Vasari included a secret corridor in the structure, between Palazzo Vecchio and the Medici's Palazzo Pitti; it runs through the Uffizi and over Ponte Vecchio and houses more art, including a special collection of artists' self-portraits. The city can thank the Medici for the most stunning collection of Renaissance art in the world; the very last Medici, Anna Maria Ludovica (1667-1743) bequeathed the entire clan's hoard of art to the people of Tuscany, provided that it never be moved from Florence.

Before heading up to the main gallery on the second floor, ascend the stairs to the first floor to see the exhibits of the Cabinet of Drawings and Prints. The few drawings displayed here only hint at the wonderful collection they keep squirreled away for scholars. Upstairs, the long main corridor wrapping around the building is stuffed with an impressive collection of Hellenistic and Roman marbles, inspirations for many Renaissance works.

The collection is arranged chronologically, and provides a complete education on Florentine painting of the Renaissance, with detours into a select collection from the German and Venetian Renaissances. Despite the hefty admission, it would be inadvisable to try to see everything in the Uffizi in a day; this is the surest way to come down with Stendhal Syndrome (see above).

Room 2 starts you off in the late 13th and early 14th century with three great *Maestà,* huge panels of the enthroned Madonna by Cimabue, Florence's first remembered genius, Sienese Duccio di Buoninsegna, whose riot of color clearly marks him as a foreigner, and Giotto, whose vastly informed use of perspective and realistic flesh foreshadows the onset of the Renaissance (still 100 years away). **Room 3** drifts off to Siena to fill out the 14th century with the delightful Gothic works of Simone Martini and the Lorenzetti brothers, because, as Room 4 shows, the Florentines weren't up to much then. Rooms 5 and 6 contain some nice Italian bits of International Courtly Gothic, but in no way prepares for the explosion of the early Renaissance in **Room 7.**

Perhaps the most charming room in the museum, Room 7 houses two minor Fra Angelicos, and an over-painted Masolino Madonna and Child (whose central figures are by Masaccio) in addition to its three masterpieces. The softly colored, innovative *Sacra Conversazione* by Domenico Veneziano is one of the master's few known works, and one of the first paintings to incorporate the Madonna and Saints into a unified space. Piero della Francesca's double portrait of Duke Frederico and his wife Battista Sforza, recently restored, glows in translucent color and intricate detail. Rounding off the room, Paolo Uccello's famed *Rout of San Romano* is an absurd and disturbing perspective play where rabbits hop behind huge, toy-like fighting warhorses (this is only the central panel of a triptych—the Louvre and London's National Gallery each have a side). **Room 8** boasts limpid Filippo Lippis, each brown-eyed nun more endearing than the last; the Pollaiuolo brothers share space with a (probably) forged Filippino Lippi in **Room 9.**

Rooms 10-14 are a vast Botticelli shrine: *Primavera, Birth of Venus, Madonna della Melagrana,* and *Pallas and the Centaur,* glow with luminous color after their recent restoration; the recently installed glass and difficult lighting go largely unappreciated. **Room 15** moves into High Renaissance gear with Leonardo's remarkable *Annunciation* and perhaps more remarkable (though unfinished) *Adoration of the Magi,* both of which receive comic counterpoint in Piero di Cosimo's *Perseus Liberating Andromeda.* **Room 18,** an octagonal Tribuna designed by Buontalenti to hold the Medici treasures, is more impressive for its collection of portraits, many by Bronzino. **Room 19** features Piero della Francesca's students Perugino (the *Portrait of a Young Man* is thought to be of his student Raphael) and Signorelli. **Rooms 20** and **22** make an incongruous detour into German territory, and **Room 21** sandwiches the major Venetians between them. Ponder Bellini's famous *Sacred Allegory,* an inexplicably moving work, before examining Mantegna's little *Triptych* in **Room 24.**

As you cross to the gallery's other side, glance out the windows of the south corridor over Florence—the Medici commissioned an impressive view. The second half of the Uffizi rounds out the Florentines in **Rooms 25-27** with Michelangelo's only oil painting, the proto-mannerist *Doni Tondo,* a string of Raphaels unaccountably accompanied by Andrea del Sarto's *Madonna of the Harpies,* and Pontormo's odd *Supper at Emmaus.* Florence cares less for the museum after this, and you'll find rooms sporadically closed. If they're open, the best bits are Titian's influential *Venus of Urbino* and Parmigianino's completely preposterous *Madonna of the Long Neck,* an apparent cross-breed between God and a giraffe, both found in **Room 30;** a clutch of Caravaggios, including his *Sacrifice of Isaac* and *Bacchus* in **Room 43;** and **Room 44's** two Rembrandt self-portraits, one young, one old. (Open Tues.-Sat. 9am-7pm, Sun. 9am-1pm. Admission L10,000.)

The Ponte Vecchio

From the Uffizi, head down to the Arno and turn right. The nearby **Ponte Vecchio** has spanned the Arno at its narrowest point since Roman times. Until 1218 this was Florence's *only* bridge over the Arno. The Medici, in an effort to "improve" the area, kicked out the butchers and tanners, whose shops lined the bridge in the 1500s, and installed the goldsmiths and diamond-carvers whose descendants remain today. The commander leading the German army's retreat across the river in 1944 could not bear to blow up the bridge, and instead destroyed the buildings on either side to make the bridge impassable. Today, the peddlers and artisans who line the bridge by day make way for nocturnal street musicians.

Around the Bargello

The heart of medieval Florence lies between the *duomo* and the Signoria around the 13th-century **Bargello**, in Piazza San Firenze. The Bargello fortress was once the residence of the chief magistrate and later the police headquarters. Now it houses the **Museo Nazionale** (tel. 21 08 01), a treasury of Florentine sculpture. Upstairs on the first floor in the Salone del Consiglio Generale, Donatello's slippery, smooth, and effeminate bronze *David,* the first free-standing nude since antiquity, exemplifies the early period of Renaissance sculpture. Compare it with the marble *David,* also by Donatello, along the wall to the left. Completed about thirty years earlier (1408), this statue appears more a Roman patrician than a shy young boy. Along the wall to the right hang two beautiful bronze panels of the *Sacrifice of Isaac,* submitted by Ghiberti and Brunelleschi for the baptistry door competition (see Piazza del Duomo). Towards the other end of the room resides a series of della Robbia terra-cotta Madonnas. In the *Loggia* (also upstairs on the first floor), one finds a menagerie of bronze animals created by Giambologna for a Medici garden grotto. Backgammon and chess players shouldn't miss the enormous inlaid ivory sets in Sala Della Torce, on the other side of the *loggia.* Downstairs on the ground floor Michelangelo's early works dominate the first room, including a debauched *Bacchus,* a handsome bust of *Brutus,* an early unfinished *Apollo* or *David,* and a tondo of the *Madonna and Child.* Devote your attention to Cellini's work on the other side of the room, especially the models for Perseus and the *Bust of Cosimo I.* Giambologna's *Oceanus* reigns in the Gothic *cortile* outside, while his *Mercury* twirls off his pedestal back in the Michelangelo room. (Open Tues.-Sat. 9am-2pm, Sun. 9am-1pm. Admission L6000.)

The **Badia,** across via del Proconsolo from the Bargello, was the church of medieval Florence's richest monastery. Filippino Lippi's *Apparition of the Virgin to St. Bernard,* one of the most famous paintings of the late 15th century, greets you on the left as you enter. (Open 9am-noon and 4-6pm.) Around the corner in via S. Margherita you can visit the **Casa di Dante** (tel. 28 33 43), the reconstructed house of the great poet. (Open Mon.-Tues. and Thurs.-Sat. 9:30am-12:30pm and 3:30-6:30pm, Sun. 9:30am-12:30pm. Free.) The small museum outlines Dante's life, but you'll get a better idea of a characteristic 14th-century dwelling at **Palazzo Salviati,** a few blocks away on via della Vigna Vecchia at via dell'Isola delle Stinche.

Equidistant from the *duomo* and the Signoria is the intriguing **Orsanmichele,** via dei Calzaiuoli (tel. 28 47 15). Built in 1337, it is the only surviving example of the Florentine Gothic architectural style. Originally built as a granary and *loggia,* and only later partially converted into a church, Orsanmichele today mixes secular and spiritual concerns in the statues along its façade: they represent the patron saints of the major craft guilds. These niched figures make up another gallery of Florentine art: look for Ghiberti's *St. John the Baptist* and *St. Stephen,* Donatello's *St. Peter* and *St. Mark,* and Giambologna's *St. Luke.* Inside, Bernardo Daddi's miraculous *Virgin* is encased in a Gothic tabernacle designed by Andrea Orcagna. Temporary exhibits are shown in the *saloni* on the top floor; it's worth the climb just for the view of the cityscape. (Open daily 8am-noon and 3-6:30pm. Free. Closed in 1992.)

Markets, Palazzi, and Santa Maria Novella

After seeing slews of great Florentine art, visit the area which financed it all. In the early 1420s, 72 banks operated in Florence, most in the area around the **Mercato Nuovo** and **via Tornabuoni.** Trade generated profits that were then reinvested in land and the manufacture of wool and silk. The Mercato Nuovo arcades, constructed in 1547, housed the gold and silk trades. Pietro Tacca's ferocious statue *Il Porcellino* (The Little Pig), actually a wild boar, was added some 50 years later. Its snout remains brightly polished—rubbing it supposedly brings good luck. The starkly neoclassical piazza della Repubblica replaced the Mercato Vecchio, the old market, in 1890. Today, the inscription *"Antico centro della città, da secolare squalore, a vita nuova restituito"* ("The ancient center of the city, squalid for centuries, restored to new life"), seems ironic, emblematic of a more determinedly progressive age. The statue in the center, on the corner near the UPIM store, is a facsimile of Donatello's statue of *Abundance,* which once presided over the square. Here you'll find several of the city's most popular *caffè*.

As Florence's 15th-century economy expanded, its bankers and merchants showed off their new wealth by erecting palaces grander than any seen before. The great Quattrocento boom commenced with the construction of the **Palazzo Davanzati**, via Porta Rossa, 13. Today the *palazzo* has been reincarnated as the **Museo della Casa Fiorentina Antica** (tel. 21 65 18), and illustrates the lives of affluent 15th-century merchants. The building houses furniture, tapestries, utensils, and paintings typical of a wealthy family during the Renaissance. See a video on the history of the building at 10am, 11am, and noon on the fourth floor (about 40min., either in Italian or English, depending on the crowd). (Open Tues.-Sat. 9am-2pm, Sun. 9am-1pm. Admission L4000.)

The relative modesty of the Palazzo Davanzati soon gave way to more lavish *palazzi*. The **Palazzo Strozzi** (tel. 21 59 90), on via Tornabuoni at via Strozzi, begun in 1489, may be the most august of its kind. (Open Mon., Wed., and Fri. 4-7pm. Free.) Alberti's architectural triumph of half a millennium ago, the **Palazzo Rucellai,** via della Vigna Nuova, 16, enjoys world renown for its façade. Its newly renovated interior now houses the **Alinari Museum of Photographic History** (tel. 21 33 70), with temporary exhibits from the vast Alinari photo archives. (Open Thurs.-Tues. 10am-7:30pm. Admission L5000, students, children, and senior citizens, L3000.)

Many owners of the earlier *palazzi* also commissioned family chapels in the **Church of Santa Trinità** (tel. 21 69 12), on via Tornabuoni, so as to spend eternity in the best company. The fourth chapel on the right houses remains of a fresco cycle of the life of the Virgin and, on the altar, a magnificent *Annunciation* by Lorenzo Monaco. Scenes from Ghirlandaio's life of St. Francis illuminate the Sassetti chapel in the right arm of the transept. The famous altarpiece of the *Adoration of the Shepherds,* also by Ghirlandaio, rests in the Uffizi; the one you see here is a copy. (Open Mon.-Sat. 7am-noon and 4-7pm.)

The wealthiest merchants built their chapels in the **Church of Santa Maria Novella** (tel. 21 01 13), near the train station. Built from 1246 to 1360, the church boasts a green and white Romanesque-Gothic lower façade. Giovanni Rucellai commissioned Alberti to design the top half and then had a chapel built inside. Frescoes covered the interior until the Medici commissioned Vasari to paint others in their honor; they ordered most of the other walls whitewashed so their rivals would not be remembered. Fortunately, Vasari respected Masaccio's powerful (but misnamed) *Trinity,* the first painting to use geometric perspective. About halfway down the left side of the nave, Masaccio's fresco creates a tabernacle in the wall; its perspectival sense creates both projection and recession into space to include the worshipper in a brooding and prophetic vision of the mercy seat. Spatial realism is essential to the meaning of the work, which places the body of Christ in the tabernacle of the Holy Ark, and puts the viewer beneath the judgement scene, the path to Christ impeded by the tomb jutting out into the viewer's space. The **Cappella di Filippo Strozzi,** just to the right of the high altar, contains frescoes by Filippo Lippi, including portrayals of a rather green Adam, a wooly Abraham, and an excruciatingly accurate *Torture of St. John the Evangelist.* The tomb of Filippo Stozzi by Benedetto da Mareno lies behind the altar. After making a bet with Donatello over who could create a better crucifix, Brunelleschi made the realistic wooden crucifix that can be found in the **Gondi Chapel,** to the left of the high altar. The **Sanctuary** is covered by a fantastic series of Ghirlandaio frescoes. Unfortunately, the sacristy, off the left aisle, is missing Giotto's masterful wooden crucifix. Under restoration, it should be returned to the church in 1993 or 1994. (Open Mon.-Sat. 7-11:30am and 3:30-6pm, Sun. 3:30-6pm.) Next door, visit the cloister to see Paolo Uccello's frescoes, including *The Flood* and *The Sacrifice of Noah.* Even more fascinating, the adjoining so-called **Spanish Chapel,** the **museo** of the church (tel. 28 21 87), harbors the important 14th-century frescoes of Andrea di Bonaiuto. (Open Mon.-Thurs. and Sat. 9am-2pm, Sun. 8am-1pm. Admission L4000.)

Around San Lorenzo

The Medici staked out an entire portion of the city north of the *duomo* in which to build their own church, the spacious **Basilica of San Lorenzo** (tel. 234 27 31), and the

Palazzo Medici. San Lorenzo was begun in 1419 following Brunelleschi's plans. The Medici loaned the city the necessary funds to build the church and in return were given control over its design. Their coat of arms, with its six red balls, is carved all over the nave; their tombs fill the two sacristies and the Cappella dei Principi behind the altar. (Cosimo's is cunningly placed in front of the high altar, thus making the entire church his personal mausoleum.) Michelangelo designed the church's exterior, but the profligate Medici ran out of money to build it, so it stands bare. (The rough brick is at least consistent with the rusticated Palazzo Medici—officially called P. Medici Riccardi—diagonally across the *piazza*.) Inside the basilica, two massive bronze pulpits by Donatello command the nave. (Open daily 7am-12:15pm and 3:30-5:30pm.) Next door, the **Biblioteca Mediceo-Laurenziana** (tel. 21 07 60) illustrates Michelangelo's architectural virtuosity with its recasting of the vocabulary of classical architecture. Inside is one of the largest and most valuable collections of codices and manuscripts in the world. Changing exhibitions on themes such as Dante or Virgil can be seen in the library from April to June and September to October. At other times of year, atmospheric conditions would damage the collection. (Open Mon.-Sat. 9am-1pm. Free.)

To reach the **Cappelle Medicee** (tel. 21 32 06), go outside and walk around the church through the market to the back entrance on p. Madonna degli Aldobrandini. Intended as a grand mausoleum, Matteo Nigetti's **Cappella dei Principi** (Princes' Chapel) emulates the baptistry. Except for the operatic gilded portraits of the Medici dukes, the decor is oppressive, a rare moment of the Baroque in Florence. Michelangelo's **New Sacristy** (1524) comes as a welcome contrast, its starkly simple architectural design reflecting the master's study of Brunelleschi. Michelangelo sculpted two impressive tombs for Lorenzo and Guiliano de' Medici, representing the four stages of the day. On Guiliano's tomb recline the figures of night (the sleeping woman), and day (the alert man). In contrast, Lorenzo's tomb supports dawn (the woman who refuses to wake up), and dusk (the man tired from a hard day's work). The sculptural treatment of the female figure is especially intriguing; her unnatural look may derive from Michelangelo's refusal to work from female models. (Open Tues.-Sat. 9am-2pm, Sun. 9am-1pm. Admission a steep L9000.)

According to art historians, Brunelleschi proposed a sumptuous design for the **Palazzo Medici** (tel. 276 01), but had it rejected. With its arched window frames and Michelangelo's "kneeling" windows on the southwest corner, Michelozzo's *palazzo* set the trend in palace styles. The private chapel inside features Benozzo Gozzoli's ornate 15th-century tapestry-like murals of the three Magi as well as portraits of the Medici and their family. It's closed indefinitely for restoration. (First floor exhibition hall open Mon.-Tues. and Thurs.-Sat. 9am-1pm and 3-7pm, Sun. 9am-noon. Admission free.)

Around piazza Santissima Annunziata

The complex of religious buildings encircling p. Santissima Annunziata emanates serenity. The *loggia* of the **Spedale degli Innocenti** (tel. 24 36 70; on the right), designed by Brunelleschi and built in the 1420s, was copied on the other side by Antonio da Sangallo a century later. The visual unity so pleased contemporary tastes that the *loggia* was continued across the façade of the church in 1601. The statue of Ferdinando de' Medici stands over the *piazza* in a position intentionally reminiscent of that of Marcus Aurelius in Rome's Campidoglio. The **Galleria dello Spedale degli Innocenti** contains Botticelli's *Madonna e Angelo* and Ghirlandaio's *Epiphany*. (Open Mon.-Tues. and Thurs.-Sat. 9am-1pm and Sun. 8am-noon. Admission L3000.)

The miraculous works of Fra Angelico exalt the **museum** of the **Church of San Marco** (tel. 21 07 41), one of the most peaceful and deeply spiritual spots in Florence. A large room to the right contains some of the painter's major works, including the altarpiece used in the church. Mount the stairs to see Angelico's most famous *Annunciation*, a rainbow celebration that greets you at the top. In the dormitory each cell contains its own Fra Angelico fresco, painted in flatter colors and sparse forms so as to facilitate the monks' meditation on the scene. Michelozzo's library is one of the most successful examples of Brunelleschian serenity, and on the whole, you might feel like following in the footsteps of Cosimo I, the patron of the convent, who retired here. His cell, unsurprisingly, is the largest. Look for Savonarola's cell as well, and imagine that fiery personality contemplating his tender fresco. (Open Tues.-Sat. 9am-2pm, Sun. 9am-1pm. Admission L6000. The exterior is currently under renovation.)

The **Accademia** (tel. 21 43 75) lies between the two churches at via Ricasoli, 60. Most of the museum is off-limits, but the collection itself remains on display. Michelangelo's triumphant *David* stands in self-assured perfection under the rotunda designed just for him. He was brought here from p. della Signoria in 1873 after a stone hurled during a riot broke his left wrist in two places. Note the opaque finish—during a cleaning the original polish was inadvertently removed. Leading up to *David* are Michelangelo's *Prisoners,* a series of five sculptures. The master left these statues intentionally "unfinished;" envisioning a prisoner inside the stone, he sculpted each block only enough to "liberate" it. (Open Tues.-Sat. 9am-2pm, Sun. 9am-1pm. Admission L10,000.)

From p. SS. Annunziata, take bus #6 (get off at via Andrea del Sarto) to Sarto's **Cenacolo di San Salvi,** via di San Salvi, 16 (tel. 67 75 70). This abbey refectory houses the Sarto's stupendous *Last Supper* (1519) alongside other 16th-century Florentine paintings. (Open Tues.-Sat. 9am-2pm, Sun. 9am-1pm. Admission L2000.) The **Cenacolo di Sant'Apollonia,** in the **Museo di Andrea del Castagno,** via 27 Aprile, 1 (tel. 28 70 74), is no less impressive. This mid-15th-century fresco of the Last Supper takes up an entire wall, and is del Castagno's masterpiece. (Open Tues.-Sat. 9am-2pm, Sun. 9am-1pm. Free.)

Around Santa Croce

The Franciscans built the **Church of Santa Croce** (tel. 24 46 19) as far away as possible from San Marco and their Dominican rivals. Despite the ascetic ideals of the Franciscans, it is by far the most splendid church in the city. The church was begun in 1294 on a design by di Cambio, but the façade and Gothic bell tower were not added until the 19th century. Originally the nave was covered by Andrea Orcagna's master fresco cycle. Never heard of Orcagna? Maybe it's through the good offices of Vasari, who not only destroyed the entire cycle, but left Orcagna out of his famous *Lives of the Artists.* On the right of the altar, the tempera murals of the **Peruzzi Chapel** vie with the frescoes of the **Bardi Chapel;** Giotto and his school decorated both. Among the famous Florentines buried here are Michelangelo, who rests at the beginning of the right aisle in a tomb designed by Vasari, and humanist Leonardo Bruni, shown holding his precious *History of Florence* on a tomb designed by Bernardo Rossellino—a wonderful little Brunelleschian piece of architecture. Between the two sits Donatello's gilded limestone *Annunciation,* whose Madonna takes in the news with a somber face. On the same wall Dante's ugly neoclassical sarcophagus stands empty. The Florentines, who banished the living Dante, decided that his corpse would not make much trouble and eventually got a tomb all ready; Dante died in Ravenna, however, and the literary necrophiliacs there have never sent him back. A bit closer to the altar lies Machiavelli, on whose sarcophagus no extravagance was lavished. In the right aisle is the tomb of the Pisan Galileo. The organ here is the largest in Italy. (Open Mon.-Sat. 8am-12:30pm and 3-6pm, Sun. 3-5:30pm.)

The barn-like Gothic of Santa Croce contrasts with the brittle delicacy of Brunelleschi's small **Pazzi Chapel,** at the end of the cloister next to the church. This is an excellent example of the innovations of early Renaissance architecture as well as the perfect place to recover your energy, surrounded by cool *pietra serena* pilasters, Luca della Robbia tondos of the apostles, and rondels of the evangelists by Donatello. The second cloister, also by Brunelleschi, offers even more calm. Doze against a column in perfect tranquility. The **Museo dell'Opera di Santa Croce** (tel. 24 46 19; through the *loggia* in front of the Pazzi Chapel) is still recovering from the disastrous 1966 flood that left many works, including the great Cimabue *Crucifixion,* in a tragic state. The one-time refectory contains Taddeo Gaddi's imaginative fresco of *The Tree of the Cross,* and beneath it, the *Last Supper.* (Open Thurs.-Tues. 10am-12:30pm and 2:30-6:30pm; Oct.-Feb. 10am-12:30pm and 3-5pm. Admission L3000.)

From the museum, follow via dell'Oriuolo two blocks past p. Saluemini and turn right on via Buonarroti to reach the **Casa Buonarroti,** via Ghibellina, 70 (tel. 24 17 52), which houses Michelangelo memorabilia and two of his important early works,

The Madonna of the Steps and *The Battle of the Centaurs*. Both are in the first rooms to the left of the landing on the second floor. He completed these panels when he was about 16 years old; they show his transition from bas-relief to full sculpture. (Open Wed.-Mon. 9:30am-1:30pm, Admission L5000, students L3000.)

A few streets north of via Ghibellina stands the **Synagogue of Florence,** also known as the **Museo del Tempio Israelitico,** via Farini, 4, at via Pilastri (tel. 24 52 52 or 24 52 53). Said to be the most beautiful synagogue in Europe, and built between 1872 and 1874 by the architects Micheli and Treves, the Sephardic temple is decorated in a modified Moorish style, enhanced with elaborate geometrical designs. (Open Mon.-Thurs. 11am-1pm and 2-5pm, Fri. 11am-1pm, Sun. 10am-1pm. Admission L3000, students L2000. Frequent informative tours. Men should cover their heads and women should dress modestly.)

In the Oltrarno

Historically disdained by downtown Florentines, the far side of the Arno remains a lively, unpretentious quarter. Even in high season, when most Florentines avoid public places, p. Santo Spirito bustles.

Start your tour a few blocks west of p. Santa Spirito at the **Church of Santa Maria del Carmine.** Inside, the **Brancacci Chapel** houses a group of revolutionary 15th-century frescoes that were declared masterpieces in their time. In 1424 Felice Brancacci commissioned Masolino and his partner Masaccio to decorate his chapel with scenes from the life of St. Peter. While Masolino probably designed the series, which applies perspective techniques not fully grasped by previous artists, it was Masaccio who executed these revolutionary frescoes before his death in 1428, imbuing his figures with a solidity and sober dignity that built upon the innovations of Giotto. Fifty years later a respectful Filippino Lippi completed the revered cycle. Note especially the *Expulsion from Paradise* and *The Tribute Money,* which are credited to Masaccio alone. (Open Mon. and Wed.-Sat. 10am-5pm, Sun. 1-5pm. Admission L5000.)

As Brunelleschi designed it, the **Church of Santo Spirito** (tel. 21 00 30) would have been one of the most exciting pieces of sacred architecture ever. He envisioned a four-aisled nave encircled by hollow chapels, which the exterior would reveal as a series of convex bumps. Brunelleschi died when the project was only partially completed, and the plans were altered to make the building more conventional. Nonetheless, it remains a masterpiece of Renaissance harmony, similar to but far less busy than San Lorenzo. (Open daily 8am-noon and 3:30-6:30pm, in winter 4-6pm.)

Luca Pitti, a *nouveau-riche* banker of the 15th century, built his *palazzo* east of Santo Spirito, against the Bóboli hill. The Medici acquired the *palazzo* and the hill in 1550 and enlarged everything possible. The courtyard was redesigned by Ammannati; the columns captured in the rough blocks reflect the 16th-century preoccupation with the theme of nature versus art. The **Pitti Palace** (tel. 21 34 40) now houses no less than five museums. The **Museo degli Argenti** (tel. 21 25 57), on the ground floor, exhibits the Medici loot. Browse among cases of precious gems, ivories, and silver, then peruse Lorenzo the Magnificent's famous collection of vases. (Open Tues.-Sat. 9am-2pm, Sun. 9am-1pm. L6000 admission gets you into the costume and porcelain museums as well.) The **Museum of Costumes** (tel. 21 25 57) and the **Porcelain Museum** (tel. 21 25 57) host more Medici debris. (Museum of Costumes open Tues.-Sat. 9am-2pm, Sun. 9am-1pm; admission L6000. Combined ticket with Museo degli Argenti. The Porcelain Museum temporarily closed.) The **Royal Apartments,** (tel. 28 70 96) on the main floor, preserve their furnishings from the residence of the Royal House of Savoy, together with a few treasures from the Medici period. (Open Sat. 10:30-11:30am. Admission by appointment only.) **Museum of Coaches** (tel. 28 46 60) are the carriage collection of the houses of Lorraine and Savoy. The **Galleria Palatina** (tel. 21 03 23) was one of only a handful of public galleries when it opened in 1833. Today its collection includes a number of Raphaels (most, unfortunately, behind glass), and works by Titian, Andrea del Sarto, Rosso, Caravaggio, and Rubens. Note the neoclassical Music Room and the Putti Room, dominated by Flemish works. (Open Tues.-Sat. 9am-2pm, Sun. 9am-1pm. Admission L8000.) The fifth and final museum, the **Galleria d'Arte Moderna** (tel. 28 70 96), houses one of the big surprises of Italian art: the early 19th-century proto-impressionist works of the Macchiaioli school (from Livorno, of all places). The collection includes neoclassical and Romantic works as well. Look for Giovanni Dupré's sculptural group *Cain and Abel.* (Open Tues.-Sat. 9am-2pm and Sun. 9am-1pm. Admission L4000.)

The elaborately landscaped **Bóboli Gardens** (tel. 21 34 40), behind the palace, stretch to the hilltop **Forte Belvedere** (tel. 234 24 25), once the Medici fortress and treasury. Ascend via di Costa San Giorgio (off p. Santa Felicità, to the left after crossing Ponte Vecchio) to reach the villa, an unusual construction with a central *loggia* designed by Ammannati. Buontalenti built this star-shaped bastion for Grand Duke Ferdinand I; now the fortress hosts summer exhibitions and sun-tanning exhibitionism. (Gardens open Tues.-Sun. 9am-7:30pm; April-May and Sept. 9am-6:30pm; March and Oct. 9am-5:30pm; Nov.-Feb. 9am-4:30pm. Admission L5000. Fort open 9am-10pm; in winter 9am-5pm. Free.)

The splendid view of Florence to be had from the fort is matched only by the picture-perfect panorama from **piazzale Michelangelo.** In the middle of the *piazza* stands yet another reproduction of *David,* along with replicas of allegorical statues from Medicean tombs. Go at sunset for the most spectacular vista of the city, from Ponte Vecchio to Santa Croce and beyond.

Above the *piazzale* is **San Miniato al Monte,** one of Florence's oldest churches. (Take bus #13 from the station or climb the stairs from p. Michelangelo.) The inlaid marble façade with its 13th-century mosaics is only a prelude to the incredible pavement inside, which is patterned with lions, doves, and astrological signs. Inside the Cardinal of Portugal's chapel you'll find a collection of superlative della Robbia terracottas (ask the sacristan to let you in). (Church open Mon.-Sat. 8am-noon and 2-7pm., Sun. 2:30-5:30pm; in winter Mon.-Sat. 8am-noon and 2-6pm., Sun. 2:30-5:30pm.)

Entertainment

For reliable information on what's hot and what's not, consult *Firenze Spettacolo* (L2500). The **passeggiata** promenades along via dei Calzaiuoli; afterwards Florentines frequent the ritzy *caffè* in p. della Repubblica. Street performers draw crowds to the steps of the *duomo,* the arcades of the Mercato Nuovo, and p. Michelangelo.

Florence vies with England for the honor of having invented modern soccer, and every June the various *quartieri* of the city turn out in costume to play their own medieval version of the sport, known as **Calcio Storico.** Two teams of 27 players face off over a wooden ball in one of the city's *piazze.* The line between athletic contest and riot is often blurred in these games. Check newspapers or the tourist office for the dates and locations of either historic or modern *calcio.* Tickets (starting at about L15,000) are sold at the Chiosco degli Sportivi on via dei Anselmi (tel. 29 23 63).

To rub shoulders with the most chic of the jet-set Florentines, head over to **La Dolce Vita,** in p. del Carmine, *the* hot-spot of the moment (July 1992) and convenient to the budget lodgings in the Oltrarno. Just two blocks away, p. Santo Spirito hops with a good selection of bars and restaurants. A raucous crowd of Beautiful People frequent **Lo Sfizzio,** on Lungarno Cellini, 1, where they carouse over enormous drinks on the outdoor terrace (open until 1am). For a quieter evening of wine tasting, **Fuori Porta,** Monte alle Croce, 10r, offers an impressive selection of *vino* by the glass, from L4000. (Open Mon.-Sat. 10am-midnight.) **The Red Garter,** via dei Benci, 33r, is definitely the place you want to be if you're a woman scoping out Italian men: pick up a date while listening to classic American rock. (Though there must be nicer ways to meet locals.) For an authentic Irish (you guessed it!) pub serving cider, Guinness, and other draught beers (L6000 a pint), try **The Fiddler's Elbow,** p. Santa Maria Novella, 74. It's crowded and convivial, with a surprisingly high number of Italians among the foreigners. (Open daily noon-12:15am.) **Angie's Pub,** via dei Neri, 35r, (tel. 29 82 45), is an Italian place (despite the name) catering mostly to students, and therefore usually uncrowded in the summer months. A selection of imported beer & cider on tap from L4000 a glass. Angie's also serves hamburgers on its own special rolls (L5000-6000; open Tues.-Sat. 12:30-3pm and 7pm-1am.) For live jazz, **Jazz Club,** via Nuova dei Caccini, 3, at borgo Pinti, lives up to its billing. (Disregard the "members only" sign on the door. Open Sept. 21-July 14.) For entertainment Italian-style, why not—bowl! **Pin's Club Bowling,** via Faenza, 71 (tel. 238 13 80), has 11 regulation lanes. (L5000 per person per game, Sat.-Sun. L6000. Shoes L1000.) There's also pool, ping-pong, and video games. Call ahead to reserve a lane, especially if you want to bowl in the evening. (Open daily 3pm-midnight.)

Dancing

Note that many of the discos listed below cater almost exclusively to tourists, with a sprinkling of Italians who have designs on foreign women.

Space Electronic, via Palazzuolo, 37 (tel. 29 30 82), near Santa Maria Novella. Multitudes of mirrors reflect a young international crowd. Beer L7000, mixed drinks L8000. Free, fun *karaoke*. Open Sun.-Fri. 10pm-2am, Sat. 10pm-3am. Sept.-Feb. closed Mon. Cover with 1 drink L20,000, with a copy of *Let's Go* L15,000.

Yab Yum, via dei Sassetti, 5r (tel. 28 20 18), off p. della Repubblica. Cover with 1st drink L15,000. Open nightly 11pm-4:30am. In summer, Yab Yum's business moves to **Capitale** in the Parco delle Cascinè, in front of the Hotel Michelangelo (tel. 35 67 23). Take bus #17C from the *duomo* or station. Open daily.

Rockafè, borgo degli Albizi, 66 (tel. 24 46 62). The trendy spot for Italian students. American infiltration not yet complete. Cover L15,000. Open Sept.-June Tues.-Sun. 10pm-4am.

Tabasco Gay Club, p. S. Cecilia, 3r (tel. 21 30 00), in a tiny alleyway across p. della Signoria from the Palazzo Vecchio. Florence's most popular gay disco. Minimum age 18. No cover, but minimum 1 drink. Open Tues.-Sun. 10pm-3am.

Festivals

The most important of Florence's traditional festivals, that of St. John the Baptist on June 24, centers around a tremendous fireworks display which rips over the city from p. Michelangelo. Easily visible from the Arno, they start at about 10pm. **Calcio in Costume,** all-out mayhem between two teams of 27 men under the pretext of playing soccer, takes place on three different days around the Festival of St. John the Baptist, more or less in his honor. (For ticket information, see Entertainment.)

The summer swings with music festivals, starting in May with the **Maggio Musicale,** which draws many of the world's eminent classical musicians. The **Estate Fiesolana** (June-Aug.) fills the Roman theater in nearby Fiesole with concerts, opera, theater, ballet, and movies. For information on tickets, contact the Biglietteria Centrale in the Teatro Comunale, corso Italia, 16 (tel. 21 62 53 or 277 92 36), or Universalturismo, via degli Speziali, 7r (tel. 21 72 41), off p. della Repubblica. In September, Florence hosts the **Festivale dell'Unità,** with organized music and concerts at Campi Bisenzia (take bus #30).

The **Florence Film Festival,** generally held in December, is justly famous. For more information contact the film festival office at via Martiri del Popolo (tel. 24 07 20).

Shopping

The Florentine flair for design comes through as clearly in the window displays of its shops as in the wares themselves. **Via Tornabuoni's** swanky boutiques and the goldsmiths on the **Michele Ponte Vecchio** proudly serve a sophisticated, wealthy, Christian-Scientist, big-hair clientele. Some of the best-known *haute couture* shops are **Gucci,** via Tornabuoni, 9 (tel. 21 10 55); **Pucci,** via Pucci, 6 (tel. 29 30 61); **Ungaro,** via della Vigna Nuova, 30r (tel. 21 01 29); **Ferragamo,** via Tornabuoni, 2 (tel. 21 07 56); and its neighbor, **St. Laurent,** via Tornabuoni, 29r (tel. 28 40 40). Unwilling to cede fashion leadership to Milan, Florence makes its contribution to *alta moda* with the bi-annual Pitti Uomo show, Europe's most important exhibition of menswear (held mid-Jan. and July), and its companion Pitti fashion shows. Not all Florentine *couture* is astronomically expensive, however. If you hanker for high-quality used and antique clothing, try **La Belle Epoque,** volta di S. Piero, 8r (tel. 21 61 69), off p. S. Pier Maggiore, or **Lord Brummel Store,** via del Purgatorio, 26r (tel. 28 75 40), off via Tornabuoni. These city boutiques make for great window shopping, but save your shopping money for the better prices you'll find elsewhere.

The city's artisan traditions continue to thrive at the open markets. **San Lorenzo,** the largest, cheapest, and most tourist-oriented, sprawls for several blocks around p. San Lorenzo, trafficking in anything made from leather, wool, cloth, or gold. (Open Mon.-Sat.) High prices are rare, but so are quality and honesty. For clothing and shoes, the market held Tuesday morning in **Parco delle Cascinè** (take bus #9, 17C, 26, or 27 from the station) is a better bet. For a flea market specializing in old furniture, postcards, and bric-a-brac, visit **piazza Ciompi,** off via Pietrapiana (walk out borgo degli Albizi). Virtually undiscovered, it's one of the city's best. (Open Tues.-Sat.) Florentines are not hagglers: bargaining usually won't get you very far, but try it if you feel the asking price is truly outrageous.

Books and art reproductions are some of the best souvenirs you can carry away from Florence. Famed **Alinari,** via della Vigna Nuova, 46-48r (tel. 21 89 75), stocks the world's largest selection of art reproductions and high-quality photographs, L5000-8000 apiece. (Open Mon.-Sat. 9am-1pm and 4-8pm.) Rizzoli's *Maestri del Colore* series of color reproductions is a bargain. **Feltrinelli,** via Cavour, 2 (tel. 29 63 20), opposite the Palazzo Medici, has an unbeatable selection of art books. (Open Mon.-Fri. 9am-7:30pm, Sat. 9am-1pm.) Don't miss the chance to browse at **Franco Maria Ricci,** via delle Belle Donne, 41r (tel. 28 33 12), at via del Moro near Santa Maria Novella. (Open Mon.-Fri. 9:30am-1pm and 4-8pm, Sat. 9:30am-1pm.) **BM Bookshop** offers an extensive architecture and graphic art selection as well as the more standard selections. The English-language selection includes poetry, classics, and new fiction. (Open Mon.-Sat. 9am-1pm and 3:30-7:30pm, Sun. 9am-1pm. Closed on Sun. in winter.) **After Dark,** via del Moro, 86r (tel. 29 42 03), is an English language bookstore with a book swap, magazines and a bulletin board. The atmosphere in the afternoon is that of a literary social club, as a hip English-speaking crowd gathers to browse and converse. (Open Mon.-Sat. 10am-1:30pm and 3-7:15pm, Sun. 3-7pm.)

Cartolerie (stationery stores) and many gift shops carry samples of the famous **carta fiorentina,** paper covered in an intricate floral design. Florentine **leatherwork** is generally of high quality and is frequently affordable. Leather shops fill the city, but p. Santa Croce and via Porta Santa Maria are particularly good places to look. A number of smaller shops, such as **Bagman,** via dell'Alberto, 19, off via della Scala, let you peek in at the artists. Check for such opportunities in other stores too, especially in jewelry stores: many of them sell only goods made on the premises.

One of the best leather deals in the city hides in one of its most beautiful churches. The **Santa Croce Leather School** (tel. 24 45 33/34 and 247 99 13), in the back of the church to the right, offers some of the best quality artisan products in the city, but has prices to match. (Open 9am-12:30pm and 3-6:30pm and 7:30-10:30pm.)

Fiesole

Fiesole, rising on olive-clad slopes 8km to the northeast of Florence, has been a source of inspiration and a resting place for numerous well-known figures—among them Alexander Dumas, Anatole France, Marcel Proust, Gertrude Stein, Frank Lloyd Wright, and Paul Klee. Da Vinci's attraction to the town was somewhat more lofty—he experimented with flying off its hills. Fiesole's location affords incomparable views of both the countryside so beloved by Renaissance masters and of its master, Florence. Bring your hiking shoes and a picnic to set off on a day-long *passeggiata* through Fiesole's olive and fruit groves.

Orientation and Practical Information

Bus and car afford the only access to Fiesole. ATAF city bus #7 from Florence leaves the Florence train station, from p. del Duomo, and from p. San Marco every 15-20min. during the day, less frequently at night (about 20min., L1000, standard ATAF ticket available at the machines). The last bus back to Florence leaves Fiesole at 11pm. The bus from Florence drops you off in **piazza Mino da Fiesole,** at the center of town; the **tourist office** (tel. 59 87 20) is at #37. The well-staffed office offers loads of advice and pamphlets. (Open Mon.-Sat. 8:30am-6:30pm; Nov.-Feb. Mon.-Sat. 8am-2pm.) The principal thoroughfare is **via Gramsci,** also known as *La Principale.* At #5 you'll find the **Post Office.** (Open Mon.-Fri. 8:15am-5:30pm, Sat. 8:15am-noon.) The **Postal Code** is 50014; the **Telephone Code** is 055. In cases of **Emergency,** tel. 113. **Tourist Medical Service** (tel. 47 54 11) is a group of English-speaking general practitioners with someone always on call.

Accommodations, Camping, and Food

Fiesole's natural beauty and tranquility do not come cheap; the town caters primarily to a wealthier crew of tourists. Budget travelers aren't out of luck, though—you can enjoy a full day in Fiesole and still have time to return to Florence for the night. If you're dying to stay, try **Villa Sorriso,** via Gramsci, 21 (tel. 590 27), a plain and simple place with frank, friendly management. (Singles L40,000. Doubles L80,000-some with bath, some with shower only. Breakfast L9000.) **Villa Baccano,** via Bosconi, 4 (tel. 593 41), is 2km out of town on via Gramsci but worth the hike. (Singles with bath L40,000. Doubles L53,000, with bath L64,000. Breakfast L12,000.) **Camping Panoramico,** via Peramonda, 1 (tel. 59 90 69), is 3km out of town with a back-breaking hill at the end of the journey. Take bus #70 from Fiesole, which runs about 12 times per day, the last one at about 7pm (L1000) and encounter beautiful facilities, including a store and a bar. (L7900 per person, L13,900 per tent, auto included.)

Overpriced, tourist-trappist restaurants abound in Fiesole. Opt for one of the several markets and fruit stands on **via Gramsci,** or stop and shop at the **COOP supermarket,** via Gramsci, 20. Indulge in a feast of bread, S. Daniele prosciutto, ripe tomatoes, basil, ricotta, olives, and artichokes. (Open Sun.-Tues. and Thurs.-Fri. 8am-1pm and 5-8pm, Wed. 8am-1pm.) Or head over to **Pizzeria Cappello di Paglio,** p. Mino, 40 with decent *primi* at decent prices. Try the *penne alla puttanesca,* with olives and capers, for L6500. *Secondi* run L10-15,000. (Open Thurs.-Tues. 11am-3pm and 7-11pm.)

Sights and Entertainment

Directly across p. Mino da Fiesole from the tourist office you'll see the 11th-century **Cattedrale di San Romolo.** Note the innovative spacing of the columns of the nave: the distance between the columns diminishes as you move toward the altar, creating an illusion of greater length. Upstairs to the right of the Salutati Chapel lies the tomb of the bishop of the same name and his altar, both works of Mino da Fiesole (1430-1484). The marble of the tomb, with its delicate carvings, resembles a translucent jewel. (Open daily 7:30am-noon and 4-7pm.)

The **Bandini Museum,** behind the *duomo,* houses a select collection of Renaissance works, including an *Annunciation* by Taddeo Gaddi, Cosimo Rosselli's *Crowning of the Virgin,* and paintings by Jacapo di Firenze. (Open Wed.-Mon. 9:30am-1pm and 3-7pm. A ticket to the Bandini Museum, Teatro Romano, and Antiquarium Constanini costs L6000. A separate ticket to the Bandini Museum costs L3000, students L2000.)

Hiding just around the corner from the Museo Bandini, on via Portigiani, 1, are the **Teatro Romano** and **Museo Civico Archeological Zone.** The theater hosts performances year-round, more frequently during the July and August **Estate Fiesolana,** a series of music, dance, and theater performances. Call the theater for details (tel. 594 77). The archeological museum, modeled after an Ionic temple, houses an attractively presented collection of artifacts from excavations in and around Fiesole, including bronze vases, tools, household items, and a fine selection of Roman coins. (Open 9am-7pm; Oct.-March Wed.-Mon. 10am-6pm. Admission L6000, including the Constanini and Bandini museums. L5000 for the theater or archeological museums alone, students L2500.)

If you take via San Francesco up the steep hill from the main *piazza,* you'll be rewarded with an unsurpassed view of Florence and the valley that the Arno has chiseled into the surrounding hills. Trudge further along the street to arrive at the **Church of Sant'Alessandro.** Don't let its white-washed, modern facade dissuade you from entering. Within is the nave of a 4th-century basilica graced by antique Eubean (Greek) col-

Prato   **269**

umns made of rare *marmo cipollina* (onion marble), topped by delicate Ionic capitals.
Off the nave to the left a chapel houses recently restored 15th-century frescoes by Perugino. The basilica itself is built on the site of a temple of Bacchus, fitting considering
the number of vineyards in the surrounding countryside. (The church keeps erratic
hours and is usually closed. Ask at the tourist office or cross your fingers and hike up;
the views outside are spectacular anyway.)

The **Church of San Francesco,** on an ancient acropolis farther up the slope, served
first as a chapel, then as an oratory, next as a convent, and finally as a Franciscan monastery. Through the church and to the left, a tiny cloister opens onto a stretch of sky. In
the church you'll find Raffaelino del Garbo's *Annunciation, Adoration of the Magi* by
Cosimo Rosselli, and Piero di Cosimo's *Immaculate Conception.* Downstairs is the
church museum, with an eclectic collection of Egyptian, Greek, Etruscan, and oriental
art, including a mummy. (Open daily 7:30am-12:30pm and 3-7:30pm. Free.) On your
way back to Florence, don't miss a stop at the tiny hamlet of S. Domenico, in whose
Church and Convent of San Domenico Beato (Fra) Angelico took his vows. The
church houses a spectacular *Madonna and Child with Saints,* and the chapter house
next door a crucifixion and *Madonna and Child,* all by Fra Angelico. (Open daily 8am-
noon and 4-7pm.)

Prato

The machine shops and textile mills outside this hamlet have earned it the nickname
"the Manchester of Tuscany." A self-governing republic in the 12th century, Prato
flourished in textile production and the arts, and maintained schools of mathematics
and theology. The Ghibelline-Guelph feud split the city, and in 1351 paralyzed Prato
became part of the Florentine Republic. The present city is not one of the highlights of
the region, but it does make a pleasant day trip from Florence (30min. by bus or
train)—dig deep for the architectural and artistic treasures masked by its ugly shell.

Orientation and Practical Information

There are two stations in Prato; get off at Stazione di Porta al Serraglio (from Florence 30min., L2100), which is in fact more centrally located than Stazione Centrale.
From the station walk straight down via Magnolfi to the Piazza del Duomo. CAP buses
also run frequently from Florence, ending up in piazza Filippo Lippi, just behind the p.
Duomo (3 per hour, L2400). From the Duomo head down via Mazzoni and take a left
on via Cairoli to find the **tourist office** at #48. The city is surrounded by ancient walls.
Most of its activity centers on the **piazza del Duomo** and **piazza Mercatale** a few
blocks away.

Tourist Office: via Cairoli, 48 (tel. 241 12). Get a map. Extremely talkative and knowledgeable
official will explain anything from soccer to the Crusades. Thorough, detailed brochures. Open
Mon.-Sat. 9am-1pm and 4-7pm.

Post Office: via Archivescovo Martini, 8 (tel. 490 01). Open Mon.-Fri. 8:15am-7pm, Sat.
8:15am-noon. **Postal Code:** 50047.

Telephones: SIP, p. del Duomo, 33. **Telephone Code:** 0574.

All-Night Pharmacy: p. Mercatale, 146/A (tel. 303 27); p. Ospedale, 5.

Emergencies: tel. 113. **Police: Polizia Municipale,** tel. 423 91. **Hospital: Guardia Medica,** via
de' Mazzamati, (tel. 384 38). **Ospedale di Prato,** (tel. 49 42 54), **Misericordia,** via del Seminario,
26 (tel. 216 66). They will send an ambulance.

Accommodations and Food

Hotels are usually available, even in high season.

Albergo Roma, via Carradori, 1 (tel. 317 77; for reservations 370 49). Helpful management.
Beautiful rooms. Doubles with bath L67,000.

Albergo Il Giglio, p. San Marco, 14 (tel. 370 49), 3 blocks from train station. Same management as the Roma, but more upscale. Shower included. Curfew 1am. Singles L46,000, with bath L58,000. Doubles L66,000, with bath L80,000.

Pick up fruit and vegetables at the **market** in p. Filippo Lippi, behind the *duomo* (Mon.-Sat. 8am-1pm.) One of the *bar* should do the trick for lunch: the best is **Pizzeria/Bar Renato,** via Magnolfi, 30, 100m from p. del Duomo. Renato himself, who has been written up in local papers for his friendly countenance and hearty fare, serves delicious slices of his "grand passion" for L1300. (Open Mon.-Sat. 7am-8pm.) A Pratese favorite is **Trattoria Lapo** in boisterous p. Mercatale, 141 which serves simple, filling meals for L15,000, including wine. (Open Mon.-Sat. noon-2:30pm and 7:30-10:30pm.) Don't miss a taste of *cantucci di Prato* at **Pasticceria Mattei,** on via Ricasoli, near via Rinaldesca, the original bakers (since 1885) of this wonderful cookie that proliferates throughout Florence (L16,000 per kilo). Pick up a bottle of *vin santo* there to dip your cookies in (L6000-15,000). (Open Mon.-Sat. 8am-1pm and 4-8pm.)

Sights

In p. del Duomo, the **Cathedral of San Stefano's** Romanesque and Gothic facade, with alternating bands of white stone and green marble, endows the structure with rare elegance. The *duomo's* most unusual feature is the pagoda-like **Pergamo del Sacro Cingolo** (Pulpit of the Sacred Belt), a reproduction of which projects from the cathedral's facade at its right corner. The original resides in the Museo dell'Opera del Duomo next door. The pulpit represents a brilliant collaborative effort: Donatello sculpted the fine bas-relief *putti,* the sprightly and sensuous cherubs that dance around the smooth marble exterior, while Michelozzo contributed the delicately classical canopy and the supporting entablature. The pulpit was commissioned to honor the local legend of the *sacro cingolo.* When the apostle Thomas asked to see Mary's tomb as proof of her Assumption, he found it filled with flowers. Looking to heaven, he saw the Virgin herself, who gave him her belt as confirmation, and doubting Thomas doubted no more. This gift is celebrated five days a year (Easter, May 1, Aug. 15, Sept. 8, and Dec. 25), when church dignitaries ascend to the pulpit and display the *sacro cingolo* to enthusiastic crowds. Other works from the cathedral that are now housed in the museum include the recently revived *Death of St. Jerome* by Prato native Filippo Lippi.

The *duomo* holds a number of artistic treasures. To the left of the entrance is the **Chapel of the Sacro Cingolo,** which Agnolo Gaddi decorated with frescoes depicting the life of the Virgin. Giovanni Pisano sculpted the *Madonna and Child* on the chapel's altar. Halfway up the nave on the left is another pulpit, the work of Antonio Rossellino and Mino da Fiesole, who carved it with scenes from the lives of St. Stephen and St. John the Baptist (the patron saints of Prato and Florence, respectively). In the apse a masterful fresco series by the libertine monk Filippo Lippi depicts the chaste lives of St. Stephen and St. John. The vivid action and attention to courtly detail suggest an artistic temperament ill-suited to monastic life. And in fact, Lippi's model for Salome, a brown-eyed nun, gave birth to their illegitimate son, Filippino, who became a distinguished painter himself. The Pope pardoned the sinning couple and (belatedly) released them from their vows. The **Museo dell'Opera del Duomo** (tel. 293 39), contains Filippo Lippi's *Death of S. Girolamo,* and Filippino's *St. Lucy.* (Open Mon. and Wed.-Sat. 9:30am-12:30pm and 3-6:30pm, Sun. 9:30am-12:30pm. Admission L5000; under 18 and over 60 free.)

The ticket to the museum permits entrance to two other museums in Prato, the **Galleria Comunale** (tel. 45 23 02) and the **Museo di Pittura Murale.** For the Galleria, turn left from the steps of the *duomo* onto via Manzoni and proceed to p. Comune, which is dominated by the **Palazzo Pretorio,** the seat of executive authority under the ancient republican government of Prato. Inside the Galleria offers a small but distinguished collection of painting and sculpture. On the second floor, a gallery of 13th- and 14th-century altarpieces displays works by father and son Lippi, including Filippo's warm and humorous *Nativity with St. Vincent.* **The Museo di Pittura Murale,** p. San Domenico, 18, down via Guasti from p. del Comune, has only recently opened to the public. Bernardo Daddi's important work, *The Story of the Holy Girdle,* can be found in this museum, along with other handily restored frescoes from the Prato area. (Both museums open Mon. and Wed.-Sat. 9:30am-12:30pm and 3-6:30pm, Sun. 9:30am-12:30pm.)

Walk back to p. del Comune, go straight two blocks, and turn right to arrive at the **Church of Santa Maria delle Carceri** (1484-1492), built by Lorenzo de' Medici's favorite architect, Giuliano da Sangallo. Inside, the rounded dome and dignified Corinthian pilasters announce the classical grandeur of the High Renaissance. Andrea della Robbia authored the refined frieze. (Open daily 6:30am-noon and 4:30-7pm.)

Next door looms the **Castello dell'Imperatore,** bulging with massive walls and cyclopean towers. From the battlements (open daily 9:30am-12:30pm), you can see the two faces of Prato: the cranes and smokestacks to the north and east, and the tree-drenched hills to the west. Escape to the real countryside by bus and see Prato's newest contribution to the world of art, the funky **Centro per L'Arte Contemporanea Luigi Pecri** (tel. 57 06 20), which contains a steadily growing collection of modern art in the **Museo d'Arte Contemporanea.** (Center open daily 9am-9pm. Museum open Wed.-Mon. 10am-7pm. Admission L5000. Take bus #10 or 15 from p. San Domenico or p. San Marco, departing every 30min.)

Pistoia

Pistoia came into its own in 1177, when it joined a handful of other Italian city-states in declaring itself a free commune. Despite this bold debut, Pistoia's neighbors soon surpassed it in military, political, and economic sophistication. Coveting Pistoia's metalworkers and dagger-producing smithies, Florence vied with Pisa and Lucca for possession of the city, establishing a difficult hegemony in 1329 after having blamed the city for initiating the struggles between the Guelphs and the Ghibellines. Not until the fall of the Medici did Pistoia regain its independence.

Pistoia's claim to fame (or infamy) is the tool of war it perfected in the 16th century—the pistol. Today, the city is home to one of the world's leading train manufacturers and supplies quite a few subway systems abroad—including that of Washington, DC. Beyond the factories, fields of bright flowers undulate with the rolling hills: this city of steel is also one of Europe's leading greenhouses. Pistoia makes a good day trip from Florence (35min.) with its intact, charming traditional quarter and beautiful *piazze,* but if you're on a tight schedule, head to the less steel-edged towns of Tuscany first.

Orientation and Practical Information

From the train station, the center is easily reached by walking straight up via XX Settembre and straight on to via Vanucci, via Cino, and via Buozzi, at the end of which you turn right for the *duomo* (15min). You can also take bus #10, 12, 26, 27, or 28 to the *duomo* from the station (buy tickets at the COPIT office outside the station, L800). From Florence, you can also take a Lazzi bus (tel. 251 32) which will drop you off in the center of town (L4800), but you'll probably want to avoid this mode of transport, as it is slower and more expensive than the train. The last bus returns to Florence at 9pm.

Tourist Office: in the Palazzo dei Vescovi, p. del Duomo (tel. 216 22). Ask for Paolo Bresci, one of the most helpful tourist officials in Tuscany. Mountains of brochures and a free map. Open Mon.-Sat. 9:30am-12:30pm and 3:30-6:30pm, Sun. 9:30am-12:30pm and 3:30-6pm; off-season Mon.-Sat. 9:30am-12:30pm and 3:30-6pm.

Post Office: via Roma, 5 (tel. 227 56), off p. del Duomo. Open Mon.-Fri. 8:30am-7:30pm, Sat. 8:30am-1pm. **Postal Code:** 51100.

Telephones: p. Garibaldi. Open 24 hrs. **Telephone Code:** 0573.

Late Night Pharmacy: Farmacia, p. del Duomo. If they're not open, they'll have the address of the nearest pharmacy that is.

Emergencies: tel. 113. **Police: Carabinieri,** tel. 212 12. **Medical Assistance: Misericordia,** tel. 20 321. Will send an ambulance.

Accommodations

A reasonable room at a reasonable price is a rare find in Pistoia. The tourist office can call around for you, but with cheaper lodgings in Florence, it makes more sense to see Pistoia on a daytrip.

Albergo Firenze, via Curtatone e Montanara, 42 (tel. 231 41), near via Buozzi at via degli Orafi. Central location. A way-cool Californian couple manages these spotless rooms. High season (April 1-Oct. 15): singles L36,600, with bath L46,200; doubles L56,700, with bath L72,000; triples L86,700, with bath L97,000. Low season: singles L30,000, with bath L40,000; doubles L48,000, with bath L61,000; triples L65,000, with bath L82,000. Breakfast L8000. Visa, MC.

Il Boschetto, viale Adva, 467 (tel. 40 13 36), in Capostrada outside Pistoia. Take bus #10 from the station or from p. Mazzini. Brave the hassle for a lovely setting and a swimming pool. Singles with bath L46,000. Doubles with bath L72,000.

Food

Cruise side streets for grocery and inexpensive specialty shops. Market junkies will want to browse at the slightly touristy **open-air market** held in p. della Sala every Wednesday and Saturday (7:30am-2pm), where you can tickle your tongue with parmesan cheese or stock up on coconuts. A daily fruit and vegetable **market** is also held on weekdays in p. della Sala, near the *duomo* (8am-2pm).

Pizzeria Tonino, corso Gramsci, 159b (tel. 333 30), behind the Palazzo Marchetti. Stellar food at down-to-earth prices. Try the wonderfully tasty and filling *gnocchi* (L7000), or a Tuscan favorite like the grilled *salsicce* (sausage, L7000). Open Tues.-Sun. noon-2:30pm and 7:30pm-midnight. Visa, AmEx.

Tavola Caldo Da Bruno, via Pacinotti, 13, on p. Treviso. The best place for a light lunch. Take-out, or sit at the counter while munching happily on their rice salads (L4000 per portion) or roasted meats (L6000). Open Mon.-Sat. noon-2:30pm and 5-9pm.

Sights and Entertainment

Geographically and culturally, Pistoia converges on the **piazza del Duomo.** On the right squats the **Cattedrale di San Zeno.** Originally erected in the 5th century, the church has since been rebuilt three times. Three tiers of *loggie* mark the black-and-white-striped facade as Pisan Romanesque. Soaring above the cathedral, the eclectic 67m campanile surmounts a Lombard watch tower with its own three tiers of Pisan arcades, a red brick roof, and a bronze spire complete with the ball and cross of the Ghibellines. Inside the *duomo* you'll find an impressive store of early Renaissance art; look for the della Robbia lunette over the central door and several sculptures by Verrocchio. Most remarkable is the *Dossale di San Jacopo,* an enormous silver altarpiece that rests in a plain chapel on the right wall. Ask the sacristan to illuminate the work (L1000), which took Sienese, Florentine, and Pistoian silversmiths nearly 200 years to create. (Cathedral open Mon.-Sat. 7am-noon and 4-7pm, Sun. 7am-1pm and 4-7pm except during services. The chapel is open whenever the sacristan is around to let you in.)

The octagonal 14th-century **baptistry** across from the *duomo* presents a modest exterior enlivened by Nino and Tommaso Pisano's *Virgin and Child* in the tympanum. This work reproduces the canonical form initiated by their grandfather Giovanni in his ivory *Virgin and Child* in Pisa. Inside, the brick ceiling stretches upward in a perfect cone. Fiercely protective of this unusual design, the city has posted a guard to prevent photos and sketches. (Open Tues.-Sun. 9:15am-12:30pm and 4-6:30pm.)

To the left of the *duomo* stands the **Palazzo Comunale.** Built in the 13th and 14th centuries, the *palazzo* sports a curious detail on its facade: to the left of the central balcony an arm reaches out of the wall, brandishing a club above the black marble head below—a tribute to the 1115 Pistoian victory over the Moorish king Musetto. Inside, the ground floor is devoted almost entirely to one of Italy's most important modern artists, Pistoia-born Marino Marini. The **Centro Marino Marini** houses the artist's drawings, etchings, and sculptures. On the first landing is Marini's *Erode* (Herod), a disturbing portrayal of the king holding a dead child at his side. At the top of the stairs, ask the guard to let you into the Assembly Room to the left; in the far corner, you'll

find Agenore Fabbri's horrifying *Ancora una Pietà,* in which the tortured bodies of
Christ and his mother evince a visceral agony. (Open Tues.-Sat. 9am-1pm and 3-7pm,
Sun. 9am-12:30pm. Free.) To improve your mood, head upstairs to the **Museo Civico,**
host to a collection of happier paintings from the 13th through 19th centuries. (Open
Tues.-Sat. 9am-1pm and 3-7pm, Sun. 9am-12:30pm. Admission L3000, under 18 and
over 70 free; Sat. afternoon free.)

Exit p. del Duomo by via del Duca and continue up via dei Rossi; the typical Pisan
Romanesque facade of the **Church of Sant'Andrea** will appear on the left. A generally stark interior sets off the intricately painted wooden ceiling. Here Giovanni Pisano
carved a pulpit that almost shows up his efforts in Pisa. Below the narrative panels,
prophets in the spandrels of the arches display their scrolls, and sibyls seated at the corners appear startled by the messages angels whisper in their ears. The sculptor saved
the most impressive scene, the *Massacre of the Innocents,* for the panel most clearly
visible from the nave. (Open daily 8am-1pm and 4-7pm.)

At the southern end of the city, on via Cavour at via Crispi, don't miss the 12th-cen-
tury **Church of San Giovanni Fuorcivitas.** The left side of the building has taken the
role of facade, since it faces the main street. The single-naved interior is a vast, boxlike space. Against the right wall stands a massive, dramatic pulpit by Fra Guglielmo
da Pisa, supported by two truculent marble lions. Distinctly classical figures re-enact
scenes from the New Testament with a pleasing lack of perspective. This church also
contains Luca della Robbia's vibrant *Visitation,* and a font by Giovanni Pisano. (Open
daily 8am-1pm and 4-7pm.)

If you've had your fill of churches, take a walk on the mild side along Pistoia's picturesque lanes; the areas behind p. del Duomo and around p. Spirito Santo are a marvel
of cobblestone design. Or hop on bus #29 from the station to visit the well-stocked **zoo**
(tel. 93 92 19) 5km out of town. (Open daily 9am-7pm; off-season 9am-5pm. Admission L10,000; 10 and under L7500.)

The thousand or so remaining flower children of western Europe converge annually
on Pistoia for the **Pistoia Blues** concert series held during the last weekend of June.
Now in its 14th year, the concert draws performers like Gatemouth Brown and B.B.
King, as well as groupies living out of camper vans jammed with bongos, bongs, guitars, pipes, and children. For information and tickets (L40,000 for the weekend,
L26,000 for one evening), inquire at the tourist office or the *Comune di Pistoia* (tel. 37
11). The summer festival culminates with the **Giostra dell'Orso** (Joust of the Bear),
held in p. del Duomo on July 25, the feast of St. James (patron saint of the city). The
Giostra began in the 14th century as a bloody contest between 12 mounted knights and
a dressed-up bear. The knights and colorful costumes remain, but a more cooperative
wooden dummy now stands in for the lovable furry.

Lucca

Overshadowed by its neighbors Pisa and Florence, Lucca conserves within its tree-
topped ramparts a hospitable old-world quiescence contentedly undiscovered by the
masses. Once a Roman colony, Lucca was regarded as the capital of Tuscany by the
Goths and Lombards after the fall of the Roman empire. Silk trading from the 12th
through 14th centuries earned Lucca prestige and prosperity that found a lasting expression in fine religious and secular buildings.

Orientation and Practical Information

Trains provide the most convenient form of transportation to Lucca, from either Florence (Florence-Viareggio line, 90min., L5100) or Pisa (30min., L2100). The station
lies just outside the city walls; from the station, walk left on viale Cavour and enter the
first city gate on the right. Inside the walls, head left on via Carrara; via Vittorio on
your right will lead you to **piazza Napoleone** (also known as p. Grande), the hub of the
city. Lazzi buses also run to Pisa and to Florence, stopping in many other towns in the
immediate area (to Pisa L2400, Florence L7100, Prato L5800, Pistoia L4600). Buses

drop you off in p. Verdi; head straight down via S. Paolino until it hits via Vittorio, then take a right to reach p. Napoleone. P. Verdi also has its own tourist office.

Tourist Office: via Veneto, 40 (tel. 49 36 39), off p. Napoleone. Pamphlets and brochures, but no accommodations service. Open Mon.-Sat. 9am-12:30pm and 3-7pm. **Centro Accoglienza Turistica,** p. Verdi. (tel. 535 92). A larger office immures itself within a former gate to the city, from which the enthusiastic, linguistically apt staff doles out brochures and rents bikes (L2000 per hr., L10,000 per day; rental open 10am-7pm). Also **exchanges currency**—though at these rates it's gateway robbery. Office open daily 9am-7:15pm; Nov.-March 9am-1:30pm; exchange open Mon.-Sat. 9am-1pm and 3-7pm.

Post Office: via Vallisneri (tel. 456 90), off p. del Duomo. Open Mon.-Fri. 8:15am-7pm, Sat. 8:15am-noon. **Postal Code:** 55100.

Telephones: via Cenami, 15-19 (tel. 553 66), off p. San Giusto. Open Mon.-Sat. 8:45am-12:30pm and 3:30-7pm. **Bar Casali,** p. San Michele. Open 8am-10pm. **Telephone Code:** 0583.

Pharmacy: Farmacia, p. San Michele, 42. Open Mon.-Sat. 9am-1pm and 4-8:30pm.

Emergencies: tel. 113. **Police: Carabinieri,** tel. 112. **Hospital:** campo di Marte (tel. 97 01). **Medical Assistance: Misericordia,** tel. 49 23 33.

Accommodations

The **CIV-EX travel agency,** at via Veneto, 28 (tel. 567 41), provides an accommodations service.

Ostello Della Gioventú Il Serchio, via Brennero, 673 (tel. 34 18 11). Take bus #1 or 11 from p. Giglio (last bus 8pm), or walk out porta S. Maria; turn right onto via Batoni and then left onto viale M. Civitali and follow the signs for the *ostello* (20min.). Charmless and cheek-by-jowl. Check-out 9am; office open 4:30-11:30pm. Curfew 11:30pm. L15,000 for bunk bed, shower, and breakfast. There is also a bar which serves food (plate of spaghetti L5000). Hostel card required, but they may slip you in if you don't have one.

Albergo Diana, via del Molinetto, 11 (tel. 49 03 68), off p. San Martino. Attractive rooms, grandfatherly manager. Singles L40,000. Doubles L68,000, with bath L80,000.

Albergo Melecchi, via Romana, 37 (tel. 95 02 34). Attractive rooms, but a bit out of the way. Go out the city walls at porta Elisa, and walk straight out viale Cadorna. At its end, 2 or 3 blocks on, turn left onto via Tiglio, and make your first right onto via Romana. Singles L26,600. Doubles L52,000.

Food

Eating out is no problem in Lucca, where an abundance of cheap *trattorie* serve quality Tuscan food and just as many well-stocked *pizzicherie* (delicatessens) offer great sandwiches, fresh fruit, and veggies. The **central market** occupies the large building at the west side of p. del Carmine. (Open Mon.-Sat. 7am-1pm and 4-7:30pm.) An **open-air market** overruns p. Anfiteatro every Wednesday and Saturday (8am-1pm). The **Supermercato STANDA** stands at via Emanuele, 50, off p. Napoleone.

Ristorante Da Guido, via Battisti, 28 (tel. 472 19), at via degli Angeli. Locals thank their lucky stars for the cheap and filling meals. *Penne all'arrabbiata* (made with lots of hot pepper) only L3500. Most *secondi* L6000, including roasted veal or rabbit. Open Mon.-Sat. noon-2pm and 7:30-10:30pm.

Ristorante Margherita, via Sant'Andrea, (tel. 441 46). Get into the groove with home-style cooking, complete with sawdust on the floor and nary a tourist in sight. *Primi* from L4000. Full meal deal L15,000. Open Mon.-Sat. noon-3pm and 7-10:30pm.

Trattoria Da Leo, via Tegrimi, 1 (tel. 422 36), behind p. del Salvatore, off via degli Asili. Tastefully arranged homemade food can be enjoyed outside under the shade of their oversized umbrellas. *Primi* L5000, *secondi* from L8000. Open Mon.-Sat. 11:30am-2:30pm and 7-10pm.

Pizzeria Rusticanella 2, via San Paolino, 30, between p. Verdi and p. San Michele. Float indoors on the aroma of their mouth-watering pizzas. Slices from L1000. If you're not up for pizza, try the *tortelle casalinghe* (L5000) or *salsicce* (sausage, L5000). Open Mon.-Sat. 11am-3pm and 6-10:30pm.

Sights

Piazza Napoleone, in the heart of Lucca, is the town's busy administrative center; the 16th-century **Palazzo Ducale** houses government offices. Head down via del Duomo to the noble **piazza San Martino,** where the ornate, asymmetrical **duomo San Martino** slouches against its bell tower on one side and the post office on the other. Crafty architects designed the facade around the pre-existing bell tower, which had been constructed two centuries earlier. The lopsided whole is testament to the decorative ingenuity of the Pisan Romanesque: it coheres despite the fact that no two columns are alike. Set among the pillars and colonnades, the 12th- and 13th-century reliefs contribute to Lucca's artistic glory; look for Nicola Pisano's *Deposition* and *Nativity* above the right door, and reliefs depicting St. Martin's life and the *Labors of the Months* between the doors. Circle the cathedral to take in the apse and transepts at their best.

Inside, the operatic lightheartedness of the facade gives way to more somber drama. Long *loggie* line the upper part of the nave, their columns concealing vast, dark spaces. Matteo Civitali, Lucca's famous local sculptor, is well-represented in the *duomo;* he designed the floor, contributed the statue of St. Martin to the right of the door, and executed two beautiful sculptures of angels for the altar. His prize piece is the **Tempietto** half-way up the left aisle, which houses the *Volto Santo,* a wooden crucifix said to be the true image of Christ. The beautiful wooden cross bears a wide-eyed and poignantly sad Jesus, now darkened to a deep hue by centuries of exposure to candles. Sculpted by Nicodemus right after Calvary, the statue passed into the hands of Bishop Gualfredo, who was on a pilgrimage nearby. Somewhat ignorant of navigational technique, the bishop set off in a boat without a crew or sails, but, miraculously, the boat landed safely on the beach at Luni. To settle the ownership dispute that arose between Lucca and Luni, the statue was placed on an oxcart and the oxen were left to choose the rightful site; they turned immediately toward Lucca. (The *Volto Santo* is taken for a ride through the town every September 13 in commemoration.) In a peaceful alcove in the left transept is the powerful *Tomb of Ilaria del Caretto,* sculpted with the greatest delicacy by Jacopo della Quercia. The sacristy contains the beautiful and well-preserved *Madonna and Saints* by Ghirlandaio, and Tintoretto's *Last Supper* waits in the third chapel on the right. (Open daily 7am-noon and 3:30-6:30pm; Oct.-Feb. 7am-noon and 3-5:30pm.)

From the cathedral, return to p. Napoleone past the 12th-century Church of San Giovanni, make a right on via Beccheria, and continue to central **piazza San Michele,** the old Roman forum, which is ringed by impressive brick *palazzi* typical of medieval Lucca. The annual **Palio della Balestra,** a crossbow competition dating back to 1443, takes place here. The participants appear in traditional costume on July 12 and September 14 for the competition, which was revived as a tourist draw in the early 1970s. The **Church of San Michele in Foro,** again with multi-patterned columns, epitomizes Pisan-Lucchese architecture. A huge bronze sculpture of the Archangel Michael stands atop the facade, guarding the slim columns and dancing animals set amid geometric designs. The right transept houses a vibrant depiction of four saints by Filippino Lippi. Look for the painted wooden beams that support the organ at the rear of the church. (Open 8:30am-12:30pm and 3:30-7:30pm.) Across from the church, belt it out in the museum at the **birthplace of Giacomo Puccini,** on corte San Lorenzo, 9 (tel. 58 40 28). (Open Tues.-Sun. 10am-6pm ; Oct.-March Tues.-Sun. 10am-4pm.)

From the *piazza,* stroll along nearby **via Fillungo,** Lucca's best-preserved medieval street. Off p. Scalpellini rises the **Church of San Frediano,** an imposing Romanesque structure graced by a huge polychrome mosaic—*The Ascension* by Berlinghieri—on its facade. Within, the second chapel to the right holds the decaying (officially incorruptible) **mummy of Santa Zita,** the beloved Virgin of Lucca. One chapel over to the left are the frescoes of the *Legend of the Volto Santo* by Amico Aspertini; drop a L100 coin into the box to illuminate the intricate designs of the sparkling tiles. (Open 8:30am-12:30pm and 4-7:30pm.)

From the church, cut across p. Anfiteatro (former site of a Roman amphitheater) to via A. Mordini. A right on via Guinigi will bring you to the **Palazzo Guinigi,** a splendidly preserved complex of medieval palaces alternating red brick and white marble columns. Climb the 230 steps to reach the lofty tower of **Torre Guinigi,** crowned by flowers and small oak trees. From here you can survey the entire region and the Apuan Alps. (Open Mon.-Sat. 9am-7pm; off-season 10am-4pm. Admission L3000.)

Conclude your tour of Lucca with a walk or bike ride around the perfectly intact city walls. The shaded, breezy 4km path, which is closed to auto traffic, meets grassy parks and cool fountains along the *baluardi* (battlements) high above the moat. From the wall, you can appreciate both the layout of the city and the beautiful surrounding countryside while mingling with the townspeople who come to jog, socialize, and strut their hounds.

Entertainment

Lucca's calendar groans with dance and classical music events. The musical delights of the **Estate Musicale Lucchese** linger from July to September. The **Teatro Comunale del Giglio's** opera season is September. During the summer, you can take in an Italian-language **film** under the stars in piazza Guidiccioni. (June-Aug. nightly at 9pm, L6000; students, children, and those over 60, L4000.) The **Settembre Lucchese** is a lively jumble of artistic, athletic, and folklore presentations. Pick up a calendar of events from the tourist office.

Pisa

Shameless contemporary exploitation obscures the splendor of Pisa's republican history and cultural clout. Take the time to dig beneath the landscape of leaning plaster towers, ashtrays, and lampshades, and discover Pisa's glorious heritage latent beneath the debris. Medieval Pisa rivaled Genoa, Amalfi, and Venice on the seas, extending its Mediterranean empire as far as Corsica, Sardinia, and the Balearics. From the 11th through 13th centuries, the revenues from these colonies, the profits from ferrying the First Crusade to the Middle East, the spoils from the capture and sack of rival Amalfi (1135), and money from honest trade with the Near East carried the maritime republic to the height of its power. Pisa's renowned ensemble of cathedral, baptistry, and world-famous leaning tower exemplify the Pisan Romanesque, the most innovative architecture of this period, whose instantly recognizable stripes and blind arcades are featured on cathedrals from Sardinia to Apulia.

Pisa's fortunes soured following an unfortunate 12th-century alliance with the papacy that isolated the Ghibelline republic among Guelph neighbors. In 1284 Genoa smashed Pisa's navy at Meloria, ushering in a succession of overlordships that yielded to benevolent Florentine rule in 1405. After five centuries of thumb-twiddling, postwar tourism has once again brought Pisa the riches and world renown that it merits.

Orientation and Practical Information

Pisa lies on the western coast of Italy at the mouth of the Arno, directly west of Florence. **APT** runs both intra- and intercity buses, connecting Pisa with other towns along the coast, including Tirrenia and Livorno. **Lazzi** buses embark on longer routes, serving destinations such as Florence, though hourly trains from that city are more convenient.

The town centers not around its beautiful *duomo,* as do most Italian cities, but rather around the Arno. Most of Pisa's important sights lie to the north of the Arno; the train station unaccountably rests far to the south. To get to the **Field of Miracles** (the *duomo* and leaning tower) from the station take bus #1 (buy tickets to the left outside the station, L800) or walk on via Crispi out of p. Sant'Antonio (next to p. Emanuele), and cross the river; via Roma leads to p. del Duomo (1.5km).

Tourist Office: p. della Stazione, 11 (tel. 42 291). Friendly staff doles out a detailed map. No accommodations service, but will call around to see who has space. Open Mon.-Sat. 9am-1pm and 3-7pm. A **branch** office at p. del Duomo, (tel. 56 04 64), behind the leaning thing, gives detailed info on all types of sights and activities around Pisa. Open Mon. and Fri. 9am-3pm and 3:30-6:30pm, Tues.-Thurs. 9am-3pm, Sat. 9am-noon and 3-6pm.

Budget Travel: CTS, via Santa Maria, 45/B (tel. 454 31). They help with daytrips, international tickets, and boats to nearby islands. English spoken. Open Mon.-Fri. 9:30am-12:30pm and 4-7pm, Sat. 9:30am-12:30pm.

Currency Exchange: Your best bet is a bank near the center of town, but the train station offers reasonable rates and a small commission (L800). *Don't* change money anywhere near p. del Duomo.

Post Office: p. Emanuele, 8 (tel. 242 97), near the station. Open Mon.-Fri. 8:15am-7pm, Sat. 8:15am-noon. **Postal Code:** 56100.

Telephones: at the train station. Open 24 hrs. **Telephone Code:** 050.

Airport: Galileo Galilei (information: tel. 280 88). Charter, domestic, and international flights. Trains make the 4-min. trip (L800) from the train station, coincident with departures.

Trains: p. della Stazione (tel. 422 91 or 413 85), in the southern end of town. Ticket office open 8:30am-8:30pm. Trains run between Pisa and Florence everyhr. (1hr., L6500), stopping in Lucca on the way (20min., L2400). The main coastal line links Pisa to Livorno (L1600), Genoa (L12,100), and Rome (L23,700).

Buses: Lazzi, p. Emanuele, 11 (tel. 462 88). Frequent service to Lucca, Pistoia, Prato, and Florence. **APT,** p. Sant'Antonio (tel. 233 84), near the station. Frequent service to Livorno and Volterra.

Late Night Pharmacy: Farmacia, p. del Duomo. Open all night.

Emergencies: tel. 113. **Police:** tel. 50 15 13. **Hospital:** on via Bonanno, (tel. 59 21 11), near p. del Duomo. **Medical Assistance:** p. San Fredino, 6 (tel. 50 11 00).

Accommodations

Pisa teems with cheap *pensioni* and *locande,* but demand is always high and the new hostel is a bit of a hike. Call ahead and make reservations, or pick up the hotel map at the station, take the bus to the *duomo* and start looking.

Centro Turistico Madonna dell'Acqua, via Pietrasantina, 15 (tel. 89 06 22). Take bus #3 from the station and ask the driver to let you off at the *ostello.* A spanking-new hostel beneath an old sanctuary; opened in April 1992. Check-out 9am. Office open 6-11pm. L16,000 per person includes shower and sheets. L18,000 per person for beds in double or triple rooms. English-speaking management sells cold drinks and bottled water.

Casa della Giovane, via F. Corridoni, 29 (tel. 43 061), a 10-min. walk from the station. Turn right as you leave. An ACISJF hostel for women only. The staff is very accommodating. Reception open 7am-10pm. Curfew 10pm. L20,000 per person in clean and bright doubles, triples, and quads. Breakfast included.

Albergo Gronchi, p. Archivescovado, 1 (tel. 56 18 23), adjacent to p. del Duomo. Pretty gardens in back put you just beyond the range of the Tower, should it topple. Curfew midnight. Roomy, cool singles L25,000 and doubles L40,000.

Hotel Galileo, via Santa Maria, 12 (tel. 406 21). Spacious rooms sporting tiled floors and frescoed ceilings more than compensate for the dark and depressing entranceway. Singles L32,000. Doubles L44,000. Triples L59,000. Quads and quints also available.

Locanda Serena, via D. Cavalca, 45 (tel. 244 91), near p. Dante. Dingy, but spacious and cheap and in the heart of the traditional quarter. Curfew midnight. Singles L24,000. Doubles L37,000. Breakfast L4000.

Albergo Helvetia, via Don G. Boschi, 31 (tel. 55 30 84), off p. Archivescovado, 2min. from the *duomo.* Tidy, spartan rooms. Sweet owners speak English. Curfew midnight. Singles L30,000. Doubles L44,000, with bath L50,000. Breakfast L4000.

Camping: the 3 campgrounds near Pisa can be dreadfully hot and crowded in summer. For information call 56 17 94. **Campeggio Torre Pendente,** viale delle Cascine, 86 (tel. 56 06 65), 1km away, is the closest. Follow the signs from p. Manin. At least L6000 per person and L3000 per tent. Open March 15-Sept. 30. **Camping Internazionale** (tel. 365 53), on via Litoranea in Marina di Pisa, is 14km away. On a private beach with a bar and restaurant. Take an ACIT bus to San Marina di Pisa. Open April-Oct. 15. **Camping Mare e Sole** (tel. 327 57), on viale del Tirreno, in nearby Calambrone. Bungalows on the beach. L6500 per person, L8000 per tent. Open April-Sept.

Food

For a more authentic ambience than that manufactured by the touristy *trattorie* near the *duomo,* wander toward the river. You'll find an **open-air market** in p. Vettovaglie (take via Vigina off lungarno Pacinotti), at the heart of the residential quarter preferred by Pisans; bakeries and *salumerie* also abound. Buy staples at the **COOP supermarket** at p. Don Minzoni and via S. Agostino (open daily 8am-8pm). The local specialty is *torta di ceci* (or *cecina*) a delicious pizza made with chick-peas, available at most *bar-pizzerie* for L2000 per slice.

Mensa Universitària, via Mártiri, off p. dei Cavalieri in the weird modern building with the gaggles of gossiping students outside. Pretty decent cafeteria fare, and perhaps one of the only places in Italy where you can eat a full meal including *primo, secondo, contorno,* and *frutta* for L3000. Crowded with students and both blue- and white-collar workers. Buy tickets at the office noon-2:30pm (no student ID necessary), or ask students outside for extras. Open mid-Sept.- mid-July Mon.-Fri. noon-2:30pm and 7-9pm, Sat.-Sun. noon-2:30pm.

Trattoria da Matteo, via l'Aroncio, 46. Off via S. Maria, near the Hotel Galileo. Jolly proprietor whips up a wide range of culinary treats. The *gnocchi al pomodoro* (L6000) are the way to go. For a *secondo* try the *scaloppina in umido con i funghi* (veal with mushrooms, L7000). *Pizze* L5500-8500. Open Sun.-Fri. noon-3pm and 6:30-10:30pm.

Al Castelletto, p. San Felice, 12, at via del Castelletto. Follow the hordes of locals drifting into this spacious restaurant or simply follow the aroma. Wood-burning brick oven cooks up a wide selection of pizzas (from L5000). *Primi,* including delectably light *gnocchi al pomodoro* L5000-6000. *Secondi* L7000. Open Mon.-Fri. noon-2:30pm and 7-11pm, Sat. 7-11pm.

Pizzeria Nando, corso Italia, 103, between p. Vittorio Emanuele and the river. Piping hot pizzas fly to the customers straight from the mouth of the oven blazing behind the counter (L5500-7000). Fantastic *panini* created before your eyes from bread that's baked to order (L3000-5000). Open Mon.-Sat. 10am-2:30pm and 4-10pm.

Federico Sulza, borgo Stretto, 42. A mammoth selection of *gelati,* bonbons, cookies, coffees, and teas since 1878. Have a seat and ogle Pisa's most chic. Open daily 8:30am-11pm.

Sights

Piazza del Duomo, also known as the **Campo dei Miracoli** (Field of Miracles), contains the shining cathedral, baptistry, *camposanto,* and Leaning Tower, which rise from a plush blanket of green grass enclosed by the ancient city wall. Stretch out on the lawn to study the facade of the **duomo,** the archetype of Pisan Romanesque with its black-and-white geometric decoration and tapered tiers of airy arcades. The winged angels at the upper corners seem to lift the entire structure aloft. Begun in 1063 by Buscheto, the cathedral was the first structure of the Campo, and went quite beyond the architect's comparatively modest original plans. Enter the five-aisled nave through Bonanno Pisano's bronze doors (1180). Though most of the interior decoration went up in smoke in 1595, paintings by Ghirlandaio along the right wall, Cimabue's mosaic *Christ Pantocrator* in the apse, and the remains of the Cosmati pavement on the floor abide in good condition. The artistic highlight of the *duomo* stands at one corner of the crossing: Giovanni Pisano's last and greatest **pulpit,** no doubt designed to outshine his father's in the baptistry. L500 buys you 60 seconds of illumination to study the reliefs, which unabashedly wander from classical to biblical subjects and back. The depictions of the *Nativity,* the *Last Judgement* and *Massacre of the Innocents* are among the most striking panels. Crane your neck to inspect the nave's coffered ceiling, resplendent in its intricate detail. (Open daily 7:45am-12:45pm and 3-6:45pm; in winter 7:45am-12:45pm and 3-4:45pm. Closed for mass 10-10:45am.)

Before moving on, consider your budget and time constraints. The city offers an all-inclusive ticket to the baptistry, Camposanto, the Sinopic, and the Museo del Duomo for L12,000; individual admission for each of these sights is L5000.

The **baptistry,** an enormous barrel of a building decorated with lacelike tracery, mixes the Tuscan Romanesque and Gothic styles—the lower half was completed in typical stripes, but Nicola Pisano and son Giovanni were given *carte blanche* to replan the upper half. They created a glorious Gothic ensemble of gables, pinnacles, and statuary set in lacy tracery. Nicola Pisano's **pulpit** (1260), to the left of the baptismal font, represents the first concerted attempt in Tuscan art to recapture the sobriety and dignity of classical antiquity, and is considered one of the harbingers of Renaissance art in Italy. Ask one of the custodians to walk to the center of the octagonal floor and sing a series of notes, which echo off the dome and leave a major chord suspended in the air (donation expected). Astoundingly, an unamplified choir singing in the baptistry can be heard from 20km away. (Open daily 8am-7:40pm; in winter 9am-4:40pm. Admission L5000, or buy the combination ticket—see above.)

Cultivate a morbid mood to make the most of the **Camposanto,** a long, white-cloistered cemetery filled with earth brought back from Mt. Calvary by the Crusaders. This dirt can supposedly reduce a corpse to a skeleton in a single day. The museum holds Roman sarcophagi whose reliefs inspired Nicola Pisano's pulpit. Fragments of frescoes shattered by Allied bombs during World War II line the galleries. Enter the Cappella Ammannati to view the haunting frescoes of an unidentified 14th-century artist known for these works as the Master of the Triumph of Death. (Open daily 8am-7:40pm; off-season 9am-4:40pm.)

Cross the square from the Camposanto to the **Museo delle Sinopie,** which displays *sinopie* (sketches preliminary to the fresco process) discovered during restoration after World War II. The sketches, originally painted on the walls of the *camposanto* in the 14th and 15th centuries, are by Traini, Veneziano, and Gaddi, among others. (Open daily 9am-12:40pm and 3-6:40pm; off-season 9am-12:40pm and 3-4:40pm. Admission L5000, or buy the inclusive ticket—see above.)

The last and greatest miracle in the Campo dei Miracoli is the **Leaning Tower.** Intended as the *duomo's* campanile, it was begun by Bonanno Pisano in 1173 and had reached the height of 10m when the soil beneath it unexpectedly subsided—the tower took a six-inch lean. Fearing retribution, Bonanno is said to have fled Pisa. A succession of architects were called in to help, and by 1301 the tower had been completed. Tomaso da Pontedera finally inherited the project in the mid-14th century and added the bell tower. (A dark undercurrent of thought has always insisted the tilt was intentional, part of medieval distaste for symmetry. If you've kept your eyes open on the rest of your tour of Italy, you've probably encountered a plentitude of towers at uncomfortable angles: Bologna has a pair, so does Ravenna, and Venice has half-a-dozen that look truly on the brink.) The belfry contains seven bells, each corresponding to a note on the diatonic scale. The tilt intensified as post-World War II tourists ascended in everincreasing numbers, and the tower continues to slip 1-2mm every year, just to tease those anticipating its downfall. The Tower is closed indefinitely, to the dismay of thousands of anxious travelers. More drastic measures have been taken and are being contemplated to halt its slo-mo fall: in the summer of 1992, steel cables were wrapped around the bottom story, whose walls were thought to be in danger of fracturing under the shear. And plans are in the works for the construction of an aqueduct to Pisa which would allow the closure of all wells in the surrounding area. (Groundwater depletion by thirsty Pisans and shower-mad American tourists is thought to cause the Tower's settling.)

The new **Museo dell'Opera del Duomo,** located behind the Leaning Tower, displays artwork from the three buildings of p. del Duomo. Its most significant holding is the ivory *Madonna and Crucifix* by Giovanni Pisano. Another gem is his ivory *Madonna and Child;* the artist's accommodation of the natural curvature of the tusk from which it was carved gives the sculpture its unique sway. (Open daily 8am-7:30pm; off-season 9am-12:30pm and 3-4:30pm.)

Although Pisa makes little effort to woo the tourist beyond the Campo dei Miracoli, museums, Romanesque churches, and picturesque *piazze* pack the city. The **Museo Nazionale di San Matteo,** on the Arno not far from p. Mazzini, houses many important works, including panels by Masaccio, Fra Angelico, and Pietro Lorenzetti, and sculpture by the Pisano clan. (Open Tues.-Sat. 9am-7:30pm, Sun. 9am-1:30pm. Admission L6000.)

Piazza dei Cavalieri, designed by Vasari during Medici rule, intrigues both visually and historically. Once the Roman forum, it remained the civic center through the Middle Ages. Today it is the seat of the **Scuola Normale Superiore,** one of Italy's premier universities, whose prestige weathered Florentine domination thanks to the Medici transferring that city's university here in the 16th century. The administrative offices of the Scuola occupy the beautiful **Palazzo dei Cavalieri.** Its graffiti-kissed facade features busts of the Grand Dukes of Tuscany.

Vasari also designed the 16th-century **Chiesa di San Stefano,** next door to the *palazzo.* Flags taken from the Battle of Lepanto set off the intricately inlaid wooden ceiling. (Open daily 8am-12:30pm and 4-7pm.) The patchy structure of the **Palazzo dell'Orologio,** across the *piazza,* incorporates the remnants of two ancient towers. In one of these, known formerly as the Tower of Hunger, the Pisan government starved Count Ugolino, wrongly accused of treachery at the battle of Meloria. Dante condemns Ugolino to no less than the eighth circle of hell for having devoured his own children, who had been imprisoned with him, in a futile attempt to ward off starvation. Unfortunately, neither tower is visible anymore, but the spot conjures up its own evil visions.

Of Pisa's numerous churches, two merit special attention. Don't miss the **Chiesa di Santa Maria della Spina,** a spectacle of Gothic art, which faces lungarno Gambacorti against the river. To reach the church from the Campo, walk down via Santa Maria and over the bridge spanning the Arno. Originally an oratory, the church was enlarged in 1323 and renamed Chiesa della Spina (Church of the Thorn) because it claims to house one of the thorns from Christ's crown. Inside you'll find works by Tommaso Pisano, but most impressive is the exterior, with its delicate, shining cusps, pinnacles, and spires. (Open daily 8am-noon and 3:30-7pm.) Another worthy sidetrack from the p. del Duomo is the **Church of San Nicola,** between via S. Maria and p. Carrara, dedicated to Pisa's patron saint. See him in the famous altarpiece of the fourth chapel on the right, breaking and deflecting the arrows a wrathful God aims at Pisa. The bell tower of the church inclines slightly, giving it a Son of Leaning Tower effect; until the real thing reopens, this is as tilted as you'll get. (Open daily 8am-noon and 4-6:30pm.)

Pisa's largely untouristed **historic district,** in the area surrounding piazza San Frediano, features serpentine alleyways, cobblestone streets, and relics of a glorious past. Here the stuccoed walls of the old buildings, painted in gold or ochre, give the city a upbeat veneer.

Entertainment

Occasional **concerts** are given in the *duomo,* where the acoustics are astounding. On **via San Zeno,** a former church holds performances of experimental music. On the last Sunday in June, the annual tug-of-war, the **Gioco del Ponto,** revives Pisa's medieval color and pageantry.

Created in 1979, the **Migliarino, S. Rossore, and Massaciuccoli Nature Park and Preserve** extends for 21,000 hectares along the coast between Viareggio and Livorno, and encompasses forest, marsh, lake, and beach. The area invites pleasant strolls, light hiking, picnic lunches, and a refreshing swim. (Take the hourly bus from p. Emanuele to Tombolo, near Calambrone, and then catch the hourly Livorno bus from p. Sant'Antonio.)

Livorno

Overwhelmed by the monstrous liners awaiting departure for Sardinia, Corsica, Greece, and Spain, Livorno seems a rough-and-ready port town. It has long maintained a strong cosmopolitan tradition; already an important trading center by the early 16th century, the city passed legislation providing asylum for any person suffering religious, racial, or political persecution in 1577. The population of Jews, Greeks, and other persecuted peoples subsequently swelled. Liberal thinking has marked Livornese history even into the 20th century; the Partito Comunisto Italiano was established here in 1921. Livorno suffered very heavy Allied bombing during the Second World War which splintered its old city. The largely rebuilt town remains on most tourist itineraries only as a spot to hop a ship to some other destination. Even though Livorno's sights do not merit a special trip, spend your pre-departure hours exploring the few remaining monuments or enjoying the excellent local seafood.

Orientation and Practical Information

A major station on the coastal train line, Livorno is easily accessible by train from Pisa (15min., L1600), Florence (1hr., L8100), Rome (3hr., L22,100), and Piombino (1hr. 30min., L5100). Take bus #1, 2, or 8 from the train station (buy tickets outside at machines or inside at the *tabacchi* for L900) to reach **piazza Grande,** the center of town. Or cross the park in front of the station and walk straight down viale Carducci, which becomes via dei Larderel, to piazza Repubblica. Cross the *piazza* and take via delle Galere to piazza Grande.

Tourist Office: p. Cavour, 6 (tel. 89 81 11), up via Cairoli from p. Grande. Charming and helpful. Open Mon.-Sat. 8:30am-12:30pm. Branch office at Calata Carrara, near the Corsica departure site (tel. 21 03 31). Open June 15-Sept. 30 Mon.-Sat. 9am-noon, and some afternoons.

Post Office: via Cairoli, 12-16 (tel. 89 76 02). Open Mon.-Fri. 8:15am-7pm, Sat. 8:15am-1pm. **Postal Code:** 57100.

Telephones: ASST, p. Grande, 14. Open Mon.-Sat. 7:30am-11:30pm. **Telephone Code:** 0586.

Ferries: It is a good idea to reserve tickets about 2 weeks in advance in July and August, especially if you are traveling with a bicycle, motorcycle, or car. Be sure to check where and when your boat leaves; schedules change unpredictably with little advance notice. To add to the hassle, many of the companies listed apply hellishly complicated fare schedules for their runs to Sardinia, with up to 8 different prices for a one-way ticket. Call ahead to make sure you can afford your planned excursion. **Corsica Marittima,** at the Stazione Marittima (tel. 89 78 51, 89 89 52, or 88 04 56). Sails to **Bastia, Corsica:** mid-April-mid-Sept. Sat. at 3pm or 5:30pm. July-Aug. also Thurs. at 3pm (3hr., L38,000; April-June and 2nd week of Sept., L33,000). From p. Granda, walk down via Logorano, across p. Municipio to via Porticciolo, which becomes via Venezia, which in turn leads to the port and the Stazione Marittima. **Moby Lines:** ferries and hydrofoils to **Corsica** and ferries only to **Sardinia.** Hydrofoils to Bastia, Corsica: mid-June-mid-Sept. Mon.-Fri. at 9:30am (2hrs., L49,000). Ferries to Bastia: Early June-late Sept. 1-3 per day, always a sailing at 8:30am (4hr., L33,000-41,000). Ferries to Olbia, Sardinia: mid-June-early Sept. 1-2 boats per day (at 10:30am or 10:30pm or both). Spottier schedule at other times. (9hr., L72,000—high season and weekends, to L34,000—off-season, morning and midweek departures.) **Corsica and Sardinia Ferries,** Calata Carrara (tel. 88 13 80 or 88 63 28), at the Stazione Marittima. Ferries to, well, **Corsica** and **Sardinia.** To Bastia, Corsica: June-mid-Sept. 1-3 boats per day (always a sailing at 8:30am). Mid-Sept.-June 2-6 boats per week. (4hr., L38,000; L32,000 off-season and midweek. To Olbia, Sardinia: ferries run mid-April-early Oct. Two sailings per day mid-June-early Sept. (at 9:30am and 9:30pm, 9-10hr., L35,000-L72,000).

Emergencies: tel. 113. **Hospital: Pronto Soccorso,** tel. 40 33 51 or 42 13 98.

Accommodations and Food

Finding a room is easy even in summer, since most people stay here only one night before catching a boat. Avoid the train station and port areas and head into the center of town.

Hotel Goldoni, via Mayer, 42 (tel. 89 87 05). Take via Rossi 1 block out of p. Cavour. Clean, modern, and central, though rooms are a bit cramped. Amiable staff. Compact garden. Singles with bath L37,000. Doubles L43,000, with bath L52,000.

Hotel Corsica, corso Mazzini, 148 (tel. 88 22 80). Lovely garden in back features a well-placed copy of Verrocchio's *puttino* fountain. Very quiet. *Caffè* inside. Singles L40,000, with bath L50,000. Doubles L57,000, with bath L70,000.

Livorno owes its culinary specialties, like its livelihood, to the sea. An **open-air market** sprawls along via Buontalenti (Mon.-Sat. mornings). Fill your brown bag at the **STANDA supermarket** off p. Grande at via Grande, 174. (Open daily 8:30am-12:30pm and 4-8pm.)

La Cantonata, corso Mazzini, 222 (tel. 88 14 42). Smiling owner dishes out huge plates of *spaghetti ai frutti di mare* (seafood spaghetti, L7000), the freshest fish, and brimming glasses of *chianti.* Other-worldly *riso nero* (rice turned black from squid ink) only L7000. *Secondi* L8000. Cover L2000. Service 10%. Open Tues.-Sun. noon-2:30pm and 7-11pm.

Trattoria Il Sottomarino, via dei Terrazzini, 48 (tel. 237 71), off p. della Repubblica at the end of via Pina d'Oro. Not cheap, but people come from all over Tuscany just to taste their *cacciucco,* a fiery and delicious seafood stew. Open Aug.-June Fri.-Wed. 12:30-2:30pm and 7:30-10pm.

Sights and Entertainment

Located in the heart of the quarter known as **Piccola Venezia** for the many canals coursing through the neighborhood, the **Fortezza Nuova** is protected by a complete moat. Completed in the early 1600s by the Medici family, this bastion was "new" compared to the Fortezza Vecchia at the port. Open from dawn until dusk, the fortress now houses a well-maintained public garden and park. Compare this fortress to the massive, sprawling **Fortezza Vecchia** (from the new fortress, walk to p. Municipio, and then down via S. Giovanni). Built by the powerful Marquises of Tuscany in the 9th century, the portly tower in the middle was the first fortification on the site. When Pisans conquered Livorno, they built a fort around the tower. In the 16th century the Medici surrounded the ensemble with robust brick walls to consolidate their hold on Livorno, by then the chief Tuscan port.

Livorno has inspired two important contributions to painting. Foremost is the group of 19th-century painters "I Macchiaioli" (literally, "the blotters"), led by Giovanni Fattori (alias Giovanni Flori). In the **Museo Civico Giovanni Fattori** (tel. 80 80 01) in Villa Fabbricotti at via della Libertà, 20, you can see their proto-impressionist work. (Open Tues.-Wed., Fri., and Sun. 10am-1pm, Thurs. and Sat. 10am-1pm and 4:30-7:30pm; admission L4000.) Livorno's second gift to art history was 20th-century painter Amadeo Modigliani.

Livorno's chief festival, the **Palio Marinaro,** takes place just off this stretch of coast. In mid-July, burly rowers from the various neighborhoods of the city race traditional craft toward the old port, to the roars of spectators crammed onto the banks.

Elba

"Lucky Napoleon!" Dylan Thomas exclaimed in a letter written from Elba to his friends; once you've witnessed the island's deep turquoise waters, dramatically poised mountains, and velvety beaches, you'll share the sentiment. A surviving fragment of the giant peninsula that once joined Corsica to the Tuscan shore, Elba first drew Etruscan settlers, who mined its hills for iron. Jason and his Argonauts made a stop, but the jeering Greeks named it Aethalia (Soot Island). Roman patricians saw the island's beauty through the smoke and built their summer villas here. Since then it has changed ownership many times; the present proprietors rent it out to vacationing Germans. Fortunately, the best parts of the island lie off the beaten track, and if you come in the off-season you will have virtually the whole place to yourself.

In July and August, vacationing Italians flock to Elba, so without a reservation made at least several months ahead, it is impossible to find lodging on the island. During June and September the weather is perfect and the beds plentiful. Camping may be the best way to go on Elba, but beware—patches of dirt can come as dear as a hotel on the island and often need reserving. There are three categories of campgrounds: a one-star runs L8600 per person, L12,400 for tent and car/motorcycle; a two-star campground charges L10,300 per person, L14,300 for tent and auto; a three-star is L11,100 a head and L14,950 for tent and auto. Campgrounds with three stars often have incredible facilities, including such amenities as swimming pools, tennis courts and restaurants.

Getting There

The only real way to reach Elba is by ferry from Piombino Marittima (also called Piombino Porto) to **Portoferraio,** Elba's largest city. Trains on the Genoa-Rome line stop at Campiglia Marittima, from which a tiny commuter train leaves for the ferries in Piombino Marittima (wait for the *port* stop). From Florence change at Pisa to arrive at Campiglia Marittima. Both **Toremar** (1hr., L5900; hydrofoil 30min., L12,700) and **Navarma** (1hr., L7000 Mon.-Fri., L10,000 Sat.-Sun.) run frequent boats to Elba, a total of about 18 per day during the summer months. Talk directly to Toremar (tel. (0565) 91 80 80) or Navarma (tel. 22 12 12) at piazzale Premuda, 13, in Piombino.

Transportation

On Elba, **ATL** buses constitute the only form of public transportation between the major cities of Portoferraio, Marina di Campo, Marciana Marina, and Porto Azzurro (all L2300 from Portoferraio). Popular **boat excursions** cover various parts of the coast; contact **Etruria** in Portoferraio (tel. 90 42 73) for details. Renting a **moped** allows you to see the more isolated parts of the island; park it anywhere while you hunt out unexplored beaches.

Orientation

Each of the different zones of the island attracts a distinct variety of loyal visitor, from baby-oriented families in Marina di Campo and Marciana Marina, to party-hard beach fanatics in Capo Civeri, to the private-yacht set in Porto Azzurro. The coast is mostly sandy from Procchio, around Portoferraio, down the east coast and around to Marina di Campo. Elba's western shore, with its stone-slab waterfront, remains relatively unfrequented. Wherever you decide to go, bypass Portoferraio, a chaotic port-city with the most overused and polluted beach on the island. Head over the the **tourist office** as soon as you land to pick up the essential *"notizie Utili per il Turista,"* which gives the lowdown for the entire island on beaches, hotels, restaurants, entertainment of any kind, and a decent map of Elba.

Portoferraio

Practical information

Tourist Office: Azienda Promozionale di Turismo, calata Italia, 26 (tel. 91 46 71), on the 1st floor, across from the Toremar boat landing. Polyglots and information galore: accommodations, a map, bus schedule, and brochure. Open Mon.-Sat. 8am-8pm; off-season 8am-1pm and 2-6pm. There's also a **tourist information booth** at the bus station on viale Elba, 20, which cheerfully provides brochures, reserves rooms, holds luggage (L1500) and sells bus tickets. Open June 15-Sept. 15 Mon.-Sat. 8am-8pm. **Associazione Albergatori,** calata Italia, 21 (tel. 91 47 54). Free room-finding. Open Mon.-Fri. 8:30am-1pm and 3-7pm; off-season 8:30am-1pm and 3-6pm.

Post Office: p. Hutre, off p. della Repubblica. Open Mon.-Fri. 8:15am-7pm, Sat. 8:15am-1pm. **Postal Code:** 57037.

Telephones: SIP, calata Italia, across viale Elba from Hotel Massimo. Open daily 8am-10pm. In Marina di Campo, try **Pietre Bigiotteria,** via Roma, 41. Open Mon.-Sat. 8am-10pm, Sun. 10am-noon. **Telephone Code:** 0565.

Buses: ATL, viale Elba, 20 (tel. 91 43 92). Open June-Sept. Mon.-Sat. 7:15am-1pm, Oct.-May 7:15am-1pm and 5-7pm. A list of places to buy tickets on Sun. is posted on the door. **Luggage storage** is next door, L1500 per piece. Open daily 8am-12:30pm and 1:30-7pm.

Ferries: Toremar, calata Italia, 22 (tel. 91 80 80). Hydrofoil tickets available at the **Toremar Aliscati booth** on the waterfront in front of the main Toremar office. **Navarma,** viale Elba, 4 (tel. 91 81 01).

Bike/Moped Rental: Rent Ghiaie, via Cairoli, 26 (tel. 91 46 66), in front of the Ghiaie beach. Easily the best place to rent mopeds and bikes on the island. Rent a well-maintained bike (L15,000 for 9am-7:30pm, L20,000 for 24hrs.) or moped (daily L30,000, L35,000 for 24hrs., less in Sept.-July). You can also rent from or drop off at any of their other branches around the island (at Marciana Marina, Porto Azzurro, Lacona, or Marina Di Campo; there is a flat L10,000 fee for returning rentals to a different branch, regardless of how many or what kind). They also give lessons to those who have never ridden a moped before. MC and Visa accepted at the Portoferraio office only. Open 9am-1pm and 3:30-7:30pm.

Emergencies: tel. 113. **Police:** (tel. 920 06), on via Garibaldi. **Hospital: Ospedale Civile Elbano** (tel. 91 74 21), off via Carducci. **Ambulance:** p. Repubblica, 37 (tel. 91 40 09).

If you decide that Portoferraio's charm outweighs the drawbacks of its grim port and depressing beach, you might choose to stay a few days. Your best bet for a clean economical bed in this accommodations-starved town is the **Bagni Elba,** via dei Gasperi (tel. 91 51 78), across from the Villa Ombrosa Hotel on the beach, which lets light and breezy doubles with private baths and balconies over the beach for L65,000. Reservations are a must from the middle of June through August; spots fill by Easter. Infested with overpriced tourist restaurants, Portoferraio is not the place to indulge the appetite. Sustain yourself at the *rost icerria* **Pane Calda,** via Carducci, 25, where you can find vibrantly colored rice salads for L7000, and filling *secondi* like *cotoletta alla Milanese* for L8500.

Marina di Campo

Marina di Campo's fine sandy beaches, winding their way for miles along the coast, attract masses of vacationing families with strollers and countless boxes of diapers. The numerous campgrounds around Marina di Campo are popular with young people. You can either bake in the sun or rent sporting equipment like **windsurfers** (starting at L15,000 per hour) at "Tropical Bagni" during the day—no office or phone, just go to the beach and you'll see them. **Hotel Lido** via Mascagni, 29 (tel. 97 60 40), boasts a prime location in the center of town, only a minute from the beach, and clean and comfortable rooms. (Singles L40,000, with bath L50,000. Doubles with bath L63,000.) You must reserve by Easter for July and August. Campgrounds abound in Marina di Campo. Try **La Foce** (tel. 97 64 56), a three-star place, or **Del Mare** (tel. 97 62 37), a two-star campground, both located in La Foce, which borders the left-hand side of Marina di Campo's waterfront. No dope, the **Canabis Resturant,** via Roma, 41-43 (97 75 55), bakes the best food around, including killer crêpes stuffed with cheese and prosciutto for L6000 (open daily 7am-2am). No brownies, though. Via Roma, along the waterfront, is also chock full of *alimentari,* where you can provision yourself for next to nothing. In summer, the party moves to **Marina 2000** at night for dancing and carousing.

Porto Azzurro

If you intend on staying in Porto Azzurro, brace yourself for massive financial outlay. Playspot of the too-thin and too-rich, Porto Azzurro naturally shelters some of the finest beaches on the island, but the beauty comes dear. **La Lanterna,** *affitta camera,* located above La Lanterna restaurant, is the lodging that comes closest to a bargain, charging only L40,000 for a double, with bath L50,000. In summer they might require you to take half-pension for a total of L65,000. **The Grill,** via Marconi, 26, near the Blumarine Hotel, offers copious portions of *penne* with a choice of tomatoes or clams for L7500. (Open daily 8:30am-2:30pm and 6pm-1am.)

Marciana Marina

The strip of pebble beach that borders Marciana Marina's waterfront is just one of the countless beaches that hide in isolated coves along this part of the island. **Casa Lupi,** via Amedeo, (tel. 991 43), is your best bet here. It's a bit of a hike (5-10min. uphill from the beach), but it sports clean rooms and a terrace that looks out over a vineyard to the sea below. (Singles L31,000, with bath L36,000. Doubles L43,000, with bath L52,000. In summer they may require half- or full pension, L60,000 for half, with bath L65,000. Full pension L68,000, with bath L75,000.) Hike along the panoramic road towards Procchio to procure a cove of your own for the day. Marciana Marina is also the perfect base to explore the less developed western half of Elba. From Marciana Marina take the bus (when the bus isn't running many decide to hitch) to Capo Sant'Andrea where you can rent a motorboat along the beach for about L100,000 per day. You can reach the numerous beaches along the western coast that are inaccessible on foot via boat; bring a few friends with you and the mission to secure your own beach doesn't really cost that much. From Marciana Marina, partiers head to the **Claxon** in Procchio to hear live music at night.

From Marciana Marina, an essential side excursion for anyone new to the island is to **Monte Capanne.** From the top of this 1019m mountain one can see the entire island, and even as far as Corsica on a clear day; the view is truly memorable. The uphill trek is a strenuous two hours, but a cable car will take you up for L7500, round-trip L12,000 (open 10am-12:15pm and 2:30-6pm). To get to Monte Capanne take the bus from Marciana Marina to Marciana, and get off at the Monte Capanne stop (15min.).

San Gimignano

The hilltop village of San Gimignano enjoys renown for its stately towers; its medieval center may be the best preserved in all of Tuscany. The 14 towers, survivors of an original 72, recall an odd century in Italian history, when warring families fought pitched battles within the city walls, using their towers for grain storage during sieges, as well as for convenient sites from which to dump boiling oil on passing enemies. Many 13th-century Italian cities emulated San Gimignano's skyline; Florence's towers are said to have numbered in the hundreds. With the rise of the commoners in the 14th century, most towns had them demolished; the towers that remain here are relics of San Gimignano's medieval descent into obscurity.

Tried for centuries by bloody feuds and petty wars, the prosperous pilgrimage-town of San Gimignano finally met its abrupt end with the onset of the Black Death of 1348. The Ardinghelli family made a bid to revive local fortunes by ceding control of the town to a reluctant Florence in 1353, but only succeeded in stripping themselves and the rival Salvucci of power. For the next six centuries San Gimignano stagnated in poverty, until its punctuated horizon proved a sure lure to postwar tourists, whose custom also resuscitated production of the golden *vernaccia* wine. An overnight stay promises blissful tranquility—but joining the hordes of daytrippers will suitably evoke the city's chaotic medieval past.

Orientation and Practical Information

TRA-IN buses run to Florence and Siena every 1-2 hours, and less frequently to Volterra. Change buses at Poggibonsi, also the nearest train station (20min., L2600). Buses arrive at Porta San Giovanni. To get to the center of town, step inside the gates. A tourist office lies to your right. Follow the crowd up the hill to **piazza della Cisterna** and then **piazza del Duomo.**

Tourist Office: Associazione Pro Loco (APL), p. del Duomo, 1 (tel. 94 00 08). Reams of pamphlets. No accommodations service, but a complete list of hotels and rooms in private homes. Also **changes currency** and sells bus tickets. English spoken. Open daily 9:30am-12:30pm and 2:30-6:30pm. **Ufficio Informazioni Turistiche (UIT),** via S. Giovanni, 125 (tel. 94 08 09) will reserve hotel rooms. Polyglot Anna is a dear. Open Mon.-Sat. 9am-8pm.

Post Office: Behind the *duomo.* Open Mon.-Fri. 8:15am-12:30pm and 2:45-6:30pm. **Postal Code:** 53037.

Telephones: at the APL office. Also at **SIP,** via San Matteo, 13. Open daily 8am-midnight. **Telephone Code:** 0577.

Buses: TRA-IN buses leave from p. Martiri outside Porta San Giovanni. Schedules and tickets available in the UIT office, or at the gift shop just outside Porta San Giovanni. Change at Poggibonsi for Florence (75min., L7100), Siena (50min., L5600), Volterra (40min., L3700). Buses run direct to Volterra and Siena mid-June-mid-Sept.

Emergencies: tel. 112. **Police: Carabinieri,** tel. 94 03 13. **Hospital:** via Folgore da San Gimignano (tel. 94 03 12). **Ambulance: Misericordia,** (tel. 94 02 63).

Accommodations

San Gimignano caters almost exclusively to mark-flinging tourists from the north; most accommodations are priced well beyond budget range. Fortunately, though, a fantastic hostel and peaceful convent save San Gimignano from a BMW-clogged fate. Private homes (*affitta camere*) provide another alternative to lire-leeching hotels, with singles running about L40,000 and doubles about L60,000. Get a list from either the tourist office or **La Rocca,** an accommodations service at via dei Fossi, 3/A (tel. 94 03 87), outside the walls near Parco della Rocca. The manager will be more than happy to provide the names and addresses of private rooms to let, or to reserve them for L5000. (Open daily 9am-1pm and 3-9pm.)

Ostello della Gioventù, via delle Fonti, 1 (tel. 94 19 91), at via Folgore di S. Gimignano. A splendiferous place run by congenial young people. The panoramic views, bar, and recently renovated bathrooms make this one of the most welcoming hostels in Italy. English spoken, bus tickets sold, and regional info distributed. No membership required. Reception open 7:30-9:30am and 5-11:30pm. Curfew 11:30pm. L17,000 per person. Showers, breakfast, and sheets included.

Convento di Sant'Agostino (tel. 94 03 83), in p. Sant'Agostino. Marvelous rooms (some with views) set around an otherworldy courtyard. Singles L25,000. Doubles L35,000. Triples L45,000. Write 1 month in advance to secure summer reservations. In a pinch, the manager or the monk in the gift shop will try to squeeze you in.

Ostello del Chianti (HI), via Roma, 137 (tel. (055) 807 70 09), in Tavernelle Val di Pesa. It's not really anywhere near San Gimignano, but it's a nice place anyway. Take the SITA bus to Tavernelle, changing at Poggibonsi (1hr., L3400). Connections are poor, so check the schedule before you go. A splendid 54-bed hostel in a beautiful setting. Membership required. Reception open 6:30-10:30pm, but you may get a key. L12,000 per person. Showers and breakfast included.

Albergo/Ristorante Il Pino, via S. Matteo, 102 (tel. 94 04 15). Rustic simplicity. In the quiet quarter by the convent. Doubles L40,000. Showers included. Breakfast L15,000.

Camping: Il Boschetto, at Santa Lucia (tel. 94 03 52), 2.5km downhill from Porta San Giovanni. Buses run from town to the site (L1000), but it's not a bad hike. Bar, market, and pizzeria. Office open 8am-1pm, 3-8pm, and 9-11pm. L5000 per person, L3500 per small tent, L2100 per car, L1600 per cycle. Hot showers included. Open April 1-Oct.15.

Food

Boar and other wild-game are San Gimignano's specialities, but the town caters to less daring palates with mainstream Tuscan fare at fairly high prices. Whether you're looking to save, or simply to savor, try the **open-air market** in p. del Duomo (Thurs. morning). The famous **Vernaccia di San Gimignano,** one of Italy's finest white wines, can be purchased at the deconsecrated church of **San Francesco** on via San Giovanni.

Rosticceria/Pizzeria Chiribiri (tel. 94 19 48), the 1st left off via San Giovanni as you enter town. Pizza sold by the slice, and plentiful pasta from L4500. The only place in town to get heavenly fare at a down-to-earth price. Open Thurs.-Tues. 11am-10pm.

L'Antica Trattoria, via Cannici, 4 (tel. 94 05 81), just down the hill after you exit through porta S. Matteo. A tame place to catch some of the wild game specialties. Try the *pappardelle alla lepre* (pasta with wild hare, L9500) or the *bocconcini di cinghiale* (boar stew L12,000). Open Tues.-Sun. noon-3pm and 7-10:30pm. MC, Visa.

Osteria Le Catene, via Mainardi. Fast tomorrow, feast tonight. *Primi* from L7000, *secondi* from L10,000. Cover L3000. Service 10%. Call in advance. Open Thurs.-Tues. 12:30-2pm and 7:30-9:30pm. All credit cards accepted.

Sights and Entertainment

Known by the 14th century as *Città delle belle torri* (City of beautiful towers), San Gimignano always had enough tourist appeal that no artist really minded hauling up here for a commission. They came in droves, and the resulting collection of *trecento* and *quattrocento* works luminously (and sometimes ludicrously) complements San Gimignano's asymmetric cityscape. The city rightfully treats itself as a unified work of art—one ticket (L10,000, students L7500; available at any museum or tourist sight) allows entry to almost all of San Gimignano's sights. Opening hours are also coordinated; sights are open April-Sept. daily 9:30am-12:30pm and 3:30-6:30pm; Oct.-March Tues.-Sun. same hours.

Via San Giovanni, the principal street, runs from the city gate to **piazza della Cisterna.** The triangular *piazza,* surrounded by towers and *palazzi,* ajoins **piazza del Duomo** whence rises the impressive tower of the **Palazzo del Podestà.** To its left is the **Palazzo del Popolo** (open 9am-7:30pm) a patchwork structure riddled with tunnels and intricate *loggie.* To the right of the *palazzo* soars its **Torre Grossa,** the highest tower in town and the only one you can ascend; it's well worth the climb. On the left stand the twin towers of the Ardinghelli, truncated thanks to a zoning ordinance that prohibited the building of structures higher than the Torre Grossa.

Within the Palazzo del Popolo, walk through a frescoed medieval courtyard containing a fragment by Il Sodoma to the **Sala di Dante.** Here Dante spoke in 1299 as the ambassador from Florence, hoping to convince the city to join the Guelph league. On the walls, Lippo Memmi's sparkling *Maestà* blesses the accompanying *trecento* scenes of hunting and tournament pageantry. Ascend the stairs to the **Museo Civico,** where Taddeo di Bartolo's altarpiece, *The Story of San Gimignano,* teaches proper respect for the bishop of Mòdena, for whom the city is named. San Gimignano calmed oceans, exorcised demons, saved the city from the Goths, and even fought the devil himself with his trusty cross—which he is pictured bringing with him as he sneaks off in the middle of Mass to relieve himself. The museum maintains an excellent collection of other Sienese and Florentine works, most notably Filippino Lippi's long-fingered *Annunciation,* crafted in two circular panels, and Pinturicchio's serene *Madonna in Glory.* The best part of the museum is the room of wedding frescoes off the stairs, a unique series of *trecento* scenes that take a couple from initial courtship to a shared bath and wedding bed.

Piazza Luigi Pecori, a courtyard behind the *palazzo,* houses the equally dull **Etruscan Museum** and **Museo d'Arte Sacra** in the same building. The latter contains some interesting medieval wood statues among the usual religious robes, but unless you're trying to get the most out of your admission stub, don't bother.

The misnamed **piazza del Duomo** shelters not a cathedral (the town doesn't have one), but the **Collegiata,** whose bare façade hides a Romanesque interior covered with exceptional Renaissance frescoes. Start with the **Chapel of Santa Fina** off the right aisle (open same hours as Museo Civico). A marvel of Renaissance harmony designed by Giuliano and Benedetto Maiano and adorned by Ghirlandaio's splendid frescoes, the chapel is devoted to the most saccharine saint in Italy. At age ten, little Fina accepted an orange from a young boy on the way to the well. Berated by her mother for her wicked ways, Fina fell upon the kitchen table and repented ceaselessly for the next five years, at which point her soul ascended to heaven and the luckless kitchen table bloomed with violets. Ghirlandaio beatifies every goopy moment in loving day-glo colors. In the main church, Bartolo di Fredi contributed Old Testament scenes along the north aisle (look for the excitingly anatomical image of Eve), while Barna De da Siena provided the appropriate, if less enthusiastic, New Testament counterparts along the south aisle. Taddeo di Bartolo's **Last Judgement** frescoes over the entrance are unfortunately a bit faded, but concentrated staring leads one from a judgement of "morbidly imaginative" through "deeply perverse" to "what a sicko" as the nature of the torments endured by the damned becomes clear. Shops around the *piazza* hawk postcards with all the best detail shots in case you miss any through a modest averting of the eyes.

At the other end of town, Benozzo Gozzoli created the poignant and sensitive fresco cycle recounting the life of St. Augustine in the **Church of Sant'Agostino** at the other end of town. (Open 8am-noon and 3-6pm; off-season 2-5pm.) Tuscany's many varieties of wild birds, now largely extinct, can still be seen at the ornithology museum on via Quercecchio, 87.

Dinner finishes early in the hills, and the *passeggiata* along via San Giovanni and via San Matteo (passing by the towers of the Salvucci clan) provides the principal entertainment. During the summer pass the evening under the stars at the **Rocca** fortress where you can take in movies at San Gimignano's outdoor summer music theater (L6000; weekly showings during July and August; check with the tourist office for information).

Volterra

When you finally find Volterra, you'll think that you've reached the edge of the world. Perched atop a huge bluff, the town broods over the surrounding checkerboard of green and yellow fields. Drawn by the cliffs' impregnability, the Etruscans established Velathri, which by the 4th century BC had become one of the most powerful cities of the Dodecapolis, surrounded by three great circuits of still-extant walls. Medieval Volterra shrank to one-third the size of its ancestor, leaving a still-palpable sense of decline and desolation. Today, the medieval mystique gives way to mercantilism: the town depends increasingly on weekend tourists to nourish its alabaster production and trade. Avoid the alabaster onslaught by coming on a weekday, and you'll see the town in all its awesome isolation.

Orientation and Practical Information

Although nearer to San Gimignano and Siena, Volterra is linked administratively to Pisa, from which **TRA-IN** bus service is most frequent (change at Pontederra, L6800). **SITA** buses run from Florence (4 per day, 2hr. 30min., L9000), Siena (5 per day, 2hr., L6300), and San Gimignano (4 per day, 1hr., L5100). There is a small train station 9km west of town at Saline di Volterra, with trains from Pisa (L6500) and the coastal line. **APT** buses synchronized with the trains run between Saline and Volterra (7 per day, L1900). All buses arrive and depart from piazza della Libertà, where you can buy tickets from the vending machine or in the bars down the street. From p. della Libertà, take the only street leading out of the *piazza,* and turn left onto central **piazza dei Priori.** From October to May bus service is less direct and you will have to change buses at intermediate stops. Ask before you go.

Tourist Office: via Turazza, 2 (tel. 861 50), just before p. dei Priori. Provides bus and train information and sells tickets. Distributes a list of those hotels that have registered with the agency, but not those that haven't. Few pamphlets or brochures about the city or environs. Has **telephones.** Open Mon.-Sat. 9am-12:30pm and 3:30-6:30pm; Sun. (in summer only) 9am-noon and 4-6pm. **Telephone Code:** 0588.

Post Office: p. dei Priori, 14 (tel. 869 69). Open Mon.-Fri. 8am-7pm, Sat. 8am-noon. **Postal Code:** 56048.

Public Baths: Albergo Diurno, via delle Prigioni, 3, off p. dei Priori. Toilets L300. Open Fri.-Wed. 8am-7pm.

Emergencies: tel. 113. **Medical Assistance: Misericordia, Pronto Soccorso,** p. San Giovanni (tel. 861 64).

Accommodations and Camping

The spacious youth hostel, convent, campgrounds and inexpensive hotel contribute to the abundance of cheap beds in Volterra. Signs for *affitta camere* frequently appear in shop windows, facilitating a search for rooms in private homes.

Youth Hostel (tel. 855 77), via del Poggetto, across from *fortezza* near Porta A Selci. A squeaky clean hostel with a lush garden out back. Small rooms with terrific views over the city wall to the valley below. Reception open 8am-noon and 6-11pm. Curfew 11:30pm. L15,000; no membership required. Breakfast L3000.

Conventa Sant'Andrea (tel. 860 23), p. S. Andrea, next door to the church, about a 5-minute walk exiting the city from Porta A Marcoli. Quiet, private rooms off frescoed hallways. L20,000 per person, L25,000 per person in rooms with bath.

Camping: "Le Balze," farther down the road at via Mandringa, 15 (tel. 878 80). This attractive campground has bungalows, a restaurant, and a refreshing pool, plus tennis, volleyball, bocce, fishing, horseback riding, and a view over Le Balze. L6500 per person, L6000 per tent, L2000 per car, L1000 per cycle. 4-person bungalow L50,000. 6-person bungalow L60,000. Open early March-late Oct. Reservations accepted.

Food

An excellent selection of Volterra's game dishes and local cheeses is available at **alimentari** on via Guarnacci and via Gramsci. Sample *salsiccia di cinghiale* (wild boar sausage) and *pecorino* cheese. Any of the local *pasticcerie* will sell you *Ossi di Morto,* a local confection made of egg whites, sugar, hazelnuts, and a hint of lemon. Sample them at your own risk; they resemble meringues made of rock. Do your bulk shopping at the **COOP supermarket,** on via delle Casine outside the city walls. (Open Mon.-Tues. and Thurs.-Sat. 7:30am-12:30pm and 4:30-7:30pm, Wed. 7:30am-12:30pm.)

Il Pozzo degli Etruschi, via dei Prigioni, 30. Ample portions of hearty Tuscan fare served in a private garden. Try the *penne ai porcini* (pasta with mushrooms, L5000). For *secondo* hog down a serving of *cinghiale con olive* (wild boar with olives, L9000). Cover L2000. Service 10%. Open Mon.-Sat. 7:30am-12:30pm and 4:30-7:30pm; closed Wed. afternoons. AmEx, MC, Visa.

L'Ombra della Sera, via Gramsci, 70 (tel. 866 63), off p. XX Settembre. Wild boars' heads on the wall create a rustic atmosphere in which you can feast on a copious portion of *tortellini* made with prosciutto and cream, L6500. *Secondi* average L10,000, for which you can procure a superb dish of *coniglio alla contadina* (rabbit with tomatoes and vegetables). Open Tues.-Sun. noon-3pm and 7-10pm. AmEx, Visa.

La Tavernetta, via Guarnacci, 14 (tel. 876 30), near the Porta Fiorentina. Fantastic and plentiful pasta dishes around L7000, *secondi* circa L9000. Mythological personages spy on you from the frescoed ceiling overhead. *Menù* L20,000. Open Fri.-Wed. noon-3:30pm and 6:30-10pm.

Il Porcellino, vicolo delle Prigioni, 16-18 (tel. 863 92). The outside dining and rustic wooden benches make the already *primo* pasta even better. *Primi* L4000-7500, *secondi* from L6500. Cover L2500. Service 10%. Open March-Oct. Wed.-Mon. noon-3pm and 7-11:30pm.

Pizzeria/Birreria Ombra della Sera, via Guarnacci, 16. Great pizza, great prices. Pizzas L5000-7000. Open Tues.-Sun. noon-3pm and 7pm-midnight.

Sights and Entertainment

Volterra's **Fortezza Medicea,** an elegant remnant from the period of Florentine domination used since its 1472 completion as a jail, is the first structure you'll see as you ascend to the town. Volterra revolves around **piazza dei Priori,** a medieval center surrounded by sober, dignified *palazzi*. The heavy and forbidding **Palazzo dei Priori,** the oldest governmental palace in Tuscany (1208-1254), presides over the square. (Open Mon.-Sat. 9am-1pm.) Across the *piazza* sits the **Palazzo Pretorio,** a series of 13th-century buildings and towers.

Located behind the Palazzo dei Priori, the **duomo** documents haphazard construction. Initiated in Pisan-Romanesque in the 1200s, desultory work continued for three centuries without reaching completion. This *duomo* contains a pirate's hoard of frescoes and Romanesque sculpture and is graced by delicate windows of thin-sliced alabaster. Immediately on the left, the oratory houses a series of moving wooden statues depicting the life of Jesus from nativity to crucifixion. The chapel off the transept holds frescoes by Rosselli, including the brilliantly colored *Mission per Damasco*. Over the main altar stands the huge 12th-century polychrome wood sculpture group *Deposition from the Cross*. The pulpit, a lesser-known example of the seemingly ubiquitous pulpits of the overly talented Pisano family, hangs over the left aisle; an intricate alabaster tabernacle by Mino da Fiesole sits above the high altar. (*Duomo* open daily 7:30am-12:30pm and 2-7pm.)

Cross back over the *piazza* and take a right down via dell'Arco to see the massive, 3rd-century BC **Etruscan arch,** one of the city's oldest gates. Note the black globs of stone on the outside, once sculpted human heads that symbolized beheaded enemy prisoners. On the other side of the p. dei Priori on via dei Sarti the **Pinacoteca Comunale** occupies the **Palazzo Minucci-Solaini** (tel. 875 80), an elegant building with a gracefully arcaded courtyard. Inside, Taddeo di Bartolo's graceful *Madonna and Saints* altarpiece will surprise anyone who has seen his gruesome *Last Judgement* in San Gimignano. A Luca Signorelli *Annunciation* and a gleaming Ghirlandaio altarpiece enhance the collection. But the art professors and students making the pilgrimage to Volterra have come for the treasure in the last room on the first floor. In his frenetic *Deposition* (1520), Rosso Fiorentino exploded High Renaissance conventions of order and restraint with a cacophony of colors swirling towards a shockingly green body of Christ. Rosso was never revisited by such dramatic vision, outside the currents of both Renaissance and Mannerist art; after the sack of Rome in 1527, he spent his time covering the walls of Francis I's gallery in Fontainebleau with pre-Baroque fluff. (Open daily 9:30am-1pm and 3-6:30pm; mid-Sept. to mid-June 10am-2pm. Admission L5000, students L2000.)

Volterra's other major attraction is the **Museo Etrusco Guarnacci,** at via Minzoni, 15 (tel. 863 47). It displays over 600 finely carved Etruscan funerary urns from the 7th and 8th centuries, and an enormous collection of dramatic bas-reliefs depicting voyages to the underworld. On the first floor you can find the museum's most famous piece, the oddly elongated bronze figure dubbed *L'Ombra della Sera* (Shadow of the Evening), the present-day symbol of Volterra. The statue, with its spidery limbs, seems to model a man's shadow on the ground at evening. (Same hours as the *pinocoteca*. Admission L8000, students L6000. The ticket is also good for the *pinacoteca*.)

Make a left onto via Lunga le Mura del Mandorlo (before Porta Marcoli) for a spectacular view of the surprisingly intact **Teatro Romano.** Continue past the *teatro* to the **Church of San Francesco** on the edge of town. In the Capella della Pietà off the left aisle a well-preserved 15th-century sculpture group shows the Virgin and St. John mourning over the dead Christ. The more famous **Capella della Croce,** off the right aisle, encloses frescoes by Cenno Cenni relating the story of the True Cross. (Open daily 7:30am-12:30pm and 2-7pm.)

Volterra's most spectacular natural sight lies a 20-minute walk outside of town at **Le Balze.** From on high, view cliffs formed by erosion towering hundreds of feet over the valley floor. These gullies have been growing over the millenia, swallowing churches in the Middle Ages and uncovering an Etruscan necropolis in the 18th century. Precariously perched at the edge of the Balze you can see a 14th-century monastery of the Camoldotesi order, now under restoration and hoping not to be engulfed.

During the second week of July, the city hosts the **Volterra Teatro** drama festival in p. dei Priori. In August, the *piazza* becomes the site of various concerts, mostly of contemporary music. Inquire at the tourist office.

Siena

Today, Siena lies in the shadow of its ancient rival Florence, but during the 13th century its flourishing wool trade, crafty bankers, and sophisticated quasi-republican civil administration marked it as one of the principal cities of Europe—more than Florence's equal. In 1230, the belligerent Florentines catapulted excrement and dead donkeys over Siena's walls in an effort to trigger an irreparable plague. The rude ploy failed, and in 1260 Siena routed the Florentines at the Battle of Montaperti. The century of grandiose construction that followed this brief ascendancy endowed the city with its flamboyant Gothic cathedral, the harmonious piazza del Campo, and a multitude of *palazzi*. In 1348 half of Siena's citizens succumbed to the first of three plagues, and the weakened city bid adieu to its glory days, falling prey to the ambitions of the papacy, the Visconti, and the vengeful Florentines. In 1554, the Medici teamed up with the infinitely ambitious Habsburg despot Charles V to smash Siena into a ghost town. The Florentines then took pains to ensure that Siena would henceforth never amount to anything more than a provincial backwater. It is to this enforced stagnation that Siena owes the unmatched integrity of its medieval Gothic townscape, carefully preserved today thanks to judicious city planning.

Sienese are determined to maintain their identity as more than just a Florentine satellite. They boast their own painting tradition, led by Duccio, Simone Martini, and the Lorenzetti brothers, who built upon the decorative pleasures of Gothic art with exuberant clashes of color and narrative flair, ignoring the sober Renaissance restraint their egg-headed rivals were introducing to the north. They eschew Florentine hard-headedness in other spheres as well, harkening to a mystic tradition that produced the 15th-century Saint Catherine, an ecstatic illiterate who brought the papacy back from Avignon, and Saint Bernadine, who roamed the peninsula reviving the teachings of St. Francis. But there's nothing mystical about the pageantry and bravado of the most characteristic of Sienese rituals, the wild *Palio* and the *contrade* (medieval neighborhood) competition that swirls around it. The *Palio* is the keystone of Siena's principal industry, tourism; the city's avocation is represented by the resurrected 15th-century Monte dei Paschi di Siena, now a major national bank.

Orientation and Practical Information

Siena once lay on the main road between Rome and Paris; modernity finds it on a secondary train line off the Rome-Florence route. Change at Chiusi from Rome and the south, at Empoli from Florence and the north. Frequent buses link Siena to Florence and the rest of Tuscany, making this an ideal base for exploring the smaller Tuscan hill towns (alternately, many of the smaller hill towns make a pleasantly rustic base for visiting Siena). Buses stop outside the city's historic center at p. San Domenico. Across the street from the train station, you can take any bus (buy tickets from the vending machines by the station entrance, L800) to p. Matteotti. Follow the signs to p. del Campo (a.k.a. Il Campo). Walking to the center can be a pleasant way to orient yourself in the city, but be prepared for at least a 45-minute stroll, and procure a decent map before you leave the station.

Tourist Office: Azienda di Promozione Turismo, via di Città, 43 (tel. 422 09). Turn right on the street just before the Campo. Rather harried, but can help students (only students) find rooms to rent for longer stays. Open Mon.-Fri. 9am-1pm and 4-7pm. The **branch office,** p. Il Campo, 56, has a list of private rooms available to non-students for shorter periods (from a few days to a few weeks) for about L25,000 per person. The agency in the Campo also has a travel agency, which **changes money** and sells bus, train, and boat tickets. (Tourist office open in theory Mon.-Sat. 8:30am-7:30pm; travel agency open Mon.-Fri. 9am-1pm and 3:30-7pm, Sat. 9am-1pm.) **Tourist information booths** in the train and bus stations will help with hotels and general orientation.

Budget Travel: CTS, via Cecco Angiolieri, 49 (tel. 28 50 08), off p. Tolomei. Student travel services. Open Mon.-Fri. 9:30am-12:30pm and 4-7pm.

Post Office: p. Matteotti, 36. Fermo Posta at window #12, stamps at #11. Open Mon.-Sat. 8:15am-7pm; last day of each month, 8:15am-noon. **Postal Code:** 53100.

Telephones: SIP, via dei Termini, 40. Open Thurs.-Tues. 7:30am-1:15pm and 2-7:30pm, Wed. 7:30am-1:15pm. Also via Donzelle, 8; open 7am-midnight. Via Cecco Angiolieri; open 7am-10pm. Via Pantaneto, 44; open 7am-11pm. Viale Vittorio Emanuele, 21; open 7am-midnight. All the SIP offices are locally notorious for arbitrary changes in office hours; if the SIP office of your choice is closed, try pay phone booths in piazza Matteotti. Also, SIP offices post a list of other places to go if they're closed. **Telephone Code:** 0577.

Trains: p. Rosselli. Hourly departures to Florence (via Empoli, L7200) and Rome (via Chiusi, L18,700). Open daily 7:30am-6pm.

Buses: TRA-IN/SITA, p. San Domenico, 1 (tel. 22 12 21). Service to all of Tuscany, including Florence (express bus, L8300), San Gimignano (L5600), Volterra (L6300), Montepulciano (L6500), Pienza (L5000), Arezzo (L6600), and Montalcino (L4200). Open daily 5:50am-8:15pm.

Car Rental: Hertz and **Intercar,** via S. Marco, 96 (tel. 411 48). Fiat Panda for L154,700 per day or L666,000 per week. Vespas L77,000 per day. Open daily 8:30am-1pm and 3-7:30pm.

Bike Rental: Poggibonsi Ciclo Sport, via Trento, 82 (tel. 92 85 07), in Poggibonsi.

English Bookstore: Feltrinelli, via Banchi di Sopra, 66. A wide selection. Open Mon.-Sat. 9:30am-8pm. **Libreria Senese,** via di Città, 62-66 (tel. 28 08 45). Penguin classics and bestsellers. Open Mon.-Sat. 9am-8pm.

Laundromat: L'Olandesina Self-Service, via Malta, 38 (tel. 28 81 91), just inside porta Camollia—on your right as you enter the city. Wash those jeans! Leave your load and return 3 hours later to pick it up. Wash and dry L13,000, students, L12,000. Open Mon.-Fri.

Emergencies: tel. 113. **Police: Questura,** via del Castoro, near the *duomo*. **Hospital:** p. del Duomo, 1 (tel. 29 01 11). **Ambulance: Misericordia,** via del Porrione, 49 (tel. 28 08 28).

Accommodations and Camping

Finding a room in Siena is usually simple enough, but call a few days in advance during July and August, and book months ahead for either *Palio*. For stays of a week or more, rooms in private homes provide an attractive alternative, with singles L30,000-60,000. The tourist office has a list and will phone for you (see above).

Ostello della Gioventù "Guidoriccio" (HI), via Fiorentina, 89 (tel. 522 12), in Località Lo Stellino, a 20-min. bus ride from the *centro*. Take bus #4 or 15 across from the station or from p. Matteotti. If coming from Florence by bus, get off at the stop after you see the large black-and-white sign announcing entry into Siena. Considering the availability of inexpensive rooms in the *centro* and the extra expense and inconvenience of bus tickets to the hostel, you might plan on searching assiduously for a spot inside the city's walls before making the journey to the hostel. 120 beds. Curfew 11pm. L17,000 per person. Breakfast included. Dinner L11,000.

La Casa del Pellegrino, via Camporegio, 31 (tel. 441 77), behind San Domenico. A hotel run by nuns—you can enjoy stunning views of the *duomo* from the spotless and secure rooms. Free discourse on the state of sin and salvation. Opens at 7:30am. Curfew 11pm. Singles L30,000, with bath L38,000. Doubles with bath L55,000. Triples with bath L75,000. Quads with bath L90,000. (Prices likely to increase 5% in 1993.) Reservations preferred.

Locanda Garibaldi, via Giovanni Dupré, 18 (tel. 28 42 04), behind the Palazzo Pubblico, close to p. del Campo. A homey establishment with 8 cozy doubles for L48,000. Curfew midnight. Fills early.

Albergo La Perla, via delle Terme, 25 (tel. 471 44), on p. dell'Indipendenza off via Banchi di Sopra. Gregarious management and a central location. Lots of decent rooms. Curfew 1am. Singles with bath L41,800. Doubles L50,000, with bath L71,500.

Piccolo Hotel Etruria, via Donzelle, 1-3 (tel. 28 80 88), off Banchi di Sotto, near Il Campo. Newly renovated rooms and propinquity to the Campo makes this a popular hotel. Curfew 12:30am. Singles L40,000, with bath L50,000. Doubles L50,000, with bath L75,000. Triples L67,500, with bath L100,000. Breakfast L4000. All credit cards accepted.

Albergo Tre Donzelle, via Donzelle, 5 (tel. 28 03 58). Just 1 door up from the Etruria. Airy rooms around a light-flooded stairwell. Curfew 1am. Singles L29,000. Doubles L48,000, with bath L61,000. Triples L65,000, with bath L103,000.

Albergo Cannon d'Oro, via Montanini, 28 (tel, 443 21), near p. Matteotti. Well-decorated, well-maintained rooms with garden and hillside views. 3 singles with bath L55,000. Doubles L60,000, with bath L78,000. Triples L80,000, with bath L105,000. Breakfast L8000. April and Sept. are the busiest months. MC, Visa.

Camping: Colleverde, strada di Scacciapensieri, 47 (tel. 28 00 44). Take bus #8 from p. Gramsci. L9000 including car and tent or camper. Open mid-March to mid-Nov.

Food

Siena specializes in sinfully rich pastries, the most famous being *Panforte,* a dense concoction of honey, almonds, and citron. Sample it at the **Bar/Pasticceria Nannini,** the oldest *pasticceria* in Siena, with branches at via Banchi di Sopra, 22-24, and throughout town. **Enoteca Italiana,** in the Fortezza Medicea, near the entrance off via Cesare Maccari, purveys the finest of the regional wines in Italy, from Brunello to Barolo, Asti Spumante to Vernaccia, at the lowest prices around. Sample before buying, only L2000 per glass. (Open daily 3pm-midnight.) Siena's **open-air market** fills La Lizza each Wednesday (8am-1pm). Shoestringers can pick up supplies at the **Consortio Agrario supermarket,** via Pianigiani, 5, off p. Salimberi (open Mon.-Fri. 7:45am-1pm and 5-8pm, Sat. 7:45am-1pm) or at **COOP,** close to the train station (take bus #1; open Mon.-Tues. and Thurs.-Fri. 8:30am-1pm and 4-8pm, Wed. and Sat. 8:30am-1pm).

Mensa Universitària, via Sant'Agata, 1, tucked away in a courtyard beneath Sant'Agostino. The cheapest meals in town (L10,000). Packed and noisy, but decent stuff in air-conditioned comfort. Open Mon.-Fri. noon-2:30pm and 6:45-9pm, Sat. noon-2:30pm.

Rosticceria, via Calzoleria 12. Where the locals come to buy prepared food. Pick up a crispy and aromatic roast chicken (L3500) or a heaping serving of *gnocchi* cooked to order (L4500). Great Tuscan bean specialties, including bean soup (L3000) and bean salad (L2500). Open Sat.-Thurs. noon-3pm and 6:30-11pm.

Osteria "Titti," via Camollia, 193 (tel. 480 87), near porta Camollia. Prepares wonderful Tuscan specialties and a variety of unique dishes in a relaxed atmosphere. For an unusual treat sample the *gnocchi in crema di carciofo* (gnocchi with an artichoke sauce, L5000). Don't miss *contorni* like the *fagioli all'vecelletto* (beans made with tomatoes and sage; L2500). Open Sun.-Fri. 9am-3:30pm and 7-10:30pm.

Osteria Le Logge, via Porrione, 33 (tel. 480 13), off p. del Campo. A famous and cozy resturant only a short walk from Torre del Mangia. *Primi* offerings include their specialty, *malfatti osteria* (spinach and ricotta in egg pasta, coated with meat sauce and baked, L8000). Amongst their *sec-*

ondi (about L14,000), try the *tagliata alla rucola*, (thinly sliced beef cooked with garlic, olive oil, pepperoncini, and rugola). Cover L2000. Service 10%. Open Mon.-Sat. 12:30-3pm and 7:30-10:30pm. Reservations are a good idea in this popular place. MC, Visa.

Grotta del Gallo Nero, via Porrione, 65-67 (tel. 22 04 46), just down the street from Osteria Le Logge, behind p. del Campo. One of the most popular places in town. Excellent Tuscan specialties at unbeatable prices. Sample a hearty dish of homemade *pici* (fat spaghetti) with porcini and sausage for L8000, or the juicy *vitello arrosto* (roast veal) for L10,000. Open Tues.-Sun. noon-3pm and 7:30pm-1:30am, Mon. noon-3pm.

Trattoria Torre, via di Salicotto, 7-9 (tel. 28 75 48), behind the Palazzo Pubblico. A hole-in-the-wall with truly pleasing fare. *Primi* L5000-7000. *Secondi* L8000-12,000. Avoid the overpriced tourist *menù*. Cover L2500. Open Fri.-Wed. noon-2:45pm and 7-10pm.

Il Grattacielo, via dei Pontani, 8, just off via dei Termini. Don't let the name mislead you; it means "the skyscraper," but nothing's big here but the servings. A tiny locals' place, with just 3 communal tables, this joint serves only cold food—potato salads, *ceci* (chick peas), *fagioli* (white beans), tomato salads, and so on. Watch them slice thin strips of prosciutto from a huge ham behind the counter. A tasty, filling plateful of sumptuous food—with a bottle of water and a hunk of bread—costs around L10,000. Open Mon.-Sat. 7am-11pm.

Bibo, via Banchi di Sotto, 61-63. When the *mensa*'s closed, students come here for cheap, generous sandwiches (L3000) and beer (L3500 for .4-). Also homemade *gelato*. Open Tues.-Sun. 7:30pm-1am.

Forno Indipendenza, piazza Indipendenza, 27. Home to the best breads and fresh pastries in town. Pizza by the slice, L2000. Open Mon.-Fri. 7:30am-1:15pm and 2-7:30pm, Sat. 7:30am-1:15pm.

Caffè Novo, via del Camporegio, 9b. Downhill from P. San Domenico and hard by the Casa del Pellegrino. Even its hip, whitewashed interior can't compete with the panoramic view of the city and the *duomo* from the outdoor tables. Not dirt cheap, but go ahead and splurge; it's much cheaper than the bandits in the *campo*, and peaceful to boot. Open Wed.-Mon. 10am-1am.

Sights

The Campo

Where other Italian towns center on their *duomo,* Siena radiates from the **piazza del Campo,** the shell-shaped, salmon-colored brick square designed expressly for civic events. The paving stones of the *piazza* are allegedly divided into nine sections representing the city's medieval "Government of Nine," though numerate observers count 11. The *campo* has always been the center stage; Dante described the real-life drama of Provenzan Salvani, the heroic Sienese *condottiere* who panhandled around Il Campo in order to ransom a friend. A little later, Sienese mystics like San Bernadino found the *piazza* a natural auditorium. *Il Palio* reduces the Campo to splendid mayhem twice each summer as horses race around the outer edge of the *piazza.*

At the highest point in Il Campo's central axis, you'll find the **Fonte Gaia,** a pool surrounded by reproductions of native son Jacopo della Quercia's famous carvings (1408-1419). Closing the bottom of the shell is the **Palazzo Pubblico,** a graceful Gothic palace. A gluttonous watchman who doubled as a bellringer gave his nickname to the **Torre del Mangia,** the clock tower that rises like a scepter to the left. Siena's Council of Nine commissioned a tower whose republican might would overshadow any skyscraper the nobility or clergy could erect in town; a pair of Perugian architects gave them the second tallest structure raised in medieval Italy (102m; go to Cremona for the tallest). In front of the *palazzo* is the **Cappella di Piazza,** built in 1348 in gratitude for the end of the Black Death which claimed half the population. It took exhausted Siena 100 years to complete the Cappella; you can trace the transition from Gothic to Renaissance architecture as pointed arches give way to gracefully rounded ones halfway up the walls.

The Museo Civico

The Palazzo Pubblico holds the masterpieces of Sienese art in the **Museo Civico.** The two rooms that provide the best introduction to both Sienese art and the spirit of the city are the **Sala del Mappamondo** and the **Sala della Pace.** In the first, named for a lost series of astronomical frescoes, lies Simone Martini's *Maestà* (Enthoned Virgin) and *Guidoriccio da Fogliano.* These two frescoes, facing each other across the vast room, illustrate the contradictions of Sienese medieval government. On the one hand, Siena looked to the Virgin, the town's patron saint, for justification and legitimacy; on the other hand, it hired mercenary soldiers (*condottiere*) like Guidoriccio to defend the city. In the next room, the Sala della Pace (also called Sala dei Nove), Sienese civic pride shines through in Pietro and Ambrogio Lorenzetti's frescoes of the *Allegories of Good and Bad Government and their Effects on Town and Country.* On the right side, in the elaborate, chiliastic *Allegory of Good Government,* people dance in the streets, artisans toil happily, and contented farmers labor on vast stretches of fertile land that unfold to the horizon. The fortunate citizenry's destiny is overseen by Justice, who is counselled by Wisdom and Compassion. On the left side, that of bad government, a gloomy, desolate landscape is populated only by thieves, sinners, devils, and sundry lost souls, their fate sealed by ruling Pride, Wrath and Avarice. The frescoes in the room, once the deliberating chamber of the Council of Nine, might well have shamed the Sienese government into civic decency, but the rule of the Nine came to an end shortly after the frescoes were completed. In a case of life not imitating art—the Allegory of Good Government is remarkably well preserved, while the Allegory of Bad Government is chipping its way into oblivion. Upstairs, on the Loggia dei Nove, you'll find the original della Quercia sculptures from the Fonte Gaia, now sadly debilitated. Step into the next room to witness Matteo di Giovanni's particularly ghastly rendition of the *Slaughter of the Innocents.* Head back downstairs to the entrance, cross the courtyard, and climb the tower's 300-odd narrow steps. At the top, you'll bask in the spectacular view of the *duomo* and the entire city. (*Palazzo* and museum open Mon.-Sat. 9:30am-6:45pm, Sun. 9:30am-1:45pm; Nov.-March daily 9am-1:45pm. Admission L6000, students L3000. Torre del Mangia open daily 10am-7pm, mid-April to mid-June and mid-Sept. to mid-Oct. 10am-6pm, mid-March to mid-April and mid-Oct. to mid-Nov. 10am-5pm, mid-Nov. to mid-March 10am-1:30pm. Admission L4000.)

The Duomo

The zebra-striped **duomo,** perched atop one of Siena's three hills, took so long to build that it spanned two architectural epochs, incorporating Romanesque arches and Gothic pinnacles. Civic pride demanded both enormous scale and prominent position, but the limited size of the hill gave architects some trouble. Because of these limitations, the apse would have hung in mid-air over the edge of the hill, but the Sienese built the **baptistry** below it to support the structure. The obscurely placed baptistry is thus missed by many travelers, but be perverse and go here first for some of Siena's finest art. The miserly lighting makes seeing anything a challenge, but concentrated peering rewards the determined with the epitomal example of the challenge between Gothic and Renaissance styles in the **baptismal font** (1417-30). In the bronze panels that decorate the lower part of the font, compare Ghiberti's *Baptism of Christ* to the adjacent *Herod's Feast* of his close contemporary Donatello. Ghiberti's Gothic panel is a supremely crafted and finished celebration of tactile pleasures, while Donatello's Renaissance work is a more visually reserved, intellectual study of perspective and movement. Other panels are by della Quercia (*Birth of John the Baptist*) and the six bronze angels are by Donatello. (Open mid-March to Sept. 7:30am-7:30pm, Oct. to early Nov. 7:30am-6:30pm, Nov. to mid-March 7:30am-1:30pm and 2:30-5pm.)

Ascending a flight of steps will lead you to the piazza del Duomo and the front façade, but on the way you'll pass a free-standing, zebra-striped wall. This is the sole remnant of Siena's early 14th-century plan to rebuild their cathedral in response to Florence's commencement of their great domed *duomo.* (Siena's was to be the largest in the world but building was halted forever by the bubonic plague.) As you see Siena's present building, you'll hardly regret that they were halted in their ambitions; it would be hard to imagine a more wonderful Christian church than Siena's completely finished, utterly striped, unbelievably decorated edifice. Giovanni Pisano carved the lower part of the façade; the statues of prophets, sybils and philosophers you see are copies of his ground-breaking works, whose interacting postures and oddly proportioned figures were the first to be sculpted with the idea of the awed upward-staring viewer in mind. (The originals are in the Museo dell'Opera Metropolitana, where you can see the rough-cut, deeply grooved chiselling that created the effect.) Above, polychrome inlaid marble and gold leaf illuminate the story of Mary and Jesus. The opulent artistry here, however, pales next to the ornamentation inside. If you're overwhelmed upon entering, perhaps it would be best to look down at the floor, whose inlaid **pavement** is mostly covered (in a rotating cycle) to help preserve the marble masterpieces, the two-century effort of a string of Siena's best artists. The ideal time to visit is August 15 through September 15, when the best works, by the Marchese d'Adamo, are exposed. Look to the excellent stained glass windows next, some based on designs by Duccio. Moving farther up, the striped columns give way to the Gothic vaulted ceiling, its deep blue sky spangled with stars and angels. Halfway up the left aisle you'll find the **Piccolomini altar,** a complete architectural structure designed by Andrea Bregno in 1503. At the bottom on either side are statues of St. Peter and St. Paul, two oft-forgotten works by Michelangelo executed during the same years as his *David.* The **pulpit** nearby is one of Andrea Pisano's best, with allegorical and biblical reliefs wrapping around the barrel (though you may feel an inappropriate urge to laugh at the children-suckling she-wolves that support the mismatched columns of the base).

Farther down this aisle is the lavish **Libreria Piccolomini,** commissioned by Pope Pius III to house the elaborately illustrated books of his uncle Pius II, whose collection still lines the walls. The library also contains the Roman statue **The Three Graces,** and some 15th-century illuminated lyrical scores. The life of Andreas Silvius Piccolomini—diplomat, geographer, poet, historian, religious reformer, creator of Pienza, and generally the quintessential Renaissance man—is celebrated in a series of frescoes by Pinturicchio. These are perhaps more notable for their attention to face and fashion than for any artistic pretention, but are brilliant nonetheless. (*Duomo* open mid-March to Sept. 7:30am-7:30pm, Oct. to early Nov. 7:30am-6:30pm, Nov. to mid-March 7:30am-1:30pm and 2:30-5pm. Strict sartorial standards apply: no tank-tops or shorts above the knee. Library open mid-March to Sept. 9am-7:30pm, Oct. to early Nov. 9am-6:30pm, Nov. to mid-March 10am-1pm and 2:30-5pm. Admission L2000.)

The **Museo dell'Opera Metropolitana** (cathedral museum), under the arches of p. Jacopo della Quercia, which adjoins p. del Duomo, houses all the extra art that formerly graced the cathedral. The first floor contains some of the foremost Gothic statuary in Italy, all by Giovanni Pisano. Upstairs is the *Maestà,* by Duccio di Buoninsegna, originally the screen of the cathedral's altar. (Open mid-March to Sept. 9am-7:30pm, Oct. to early Nov. 9am-6:30pm, Nov. to Dec. 9am-1:30pm, Jan. to mid-March 9am-1pm. Admission L5000.)

Around the City

Siena's **Pinacoteca Nazionale,** down the street from the cathedral museum at via San Pietro, 29, features works by every major artist of the Sienese school: the seven magnificent followers of Onccio, Simone Martini, the flying Lorenzetti brothers, Bartolo di Fredi, Sano di Pietro, Il Sodoma, and many others. (Open Tues.-Sat. 8:30am-7pm, Mon. 8:30am-2pm, Sun. 8:30am-1pm; in winter Mon.-Sat. 8:30am-2pm. Admission L8000.)

The **Sanctuary of St. Catherine,** on via del Tiratoio, pays homage to the most renowned daughter of Siena, a simple girl who influenced popes, founded a religious order, and was proclaimed patron saint of Italy by Pope Pius XII in 1939. The structure offers a pleasant sojourn among roses and geraniums. (Open daily 9am-12:30pm and 3:30-6pm.)

As in other Italian towns, the Franciscans and the Dominicans have set up rival basilicas at opposite ends of Siena. The **Church of San Domenico** contains Andrea Vanni's portrait of St. Catherine and dramatic frescoes by Il Sodoma (1477-1549). The *cappella* also contains the requisite macabre relic, this one depicting Catherine's head. (Church open daily 8:30am-1pm and 4-7pm.) The **Church of San Francesco** houses two mournful frescoes by Pietro and Ambrogio Lorenzetti. The huge, stark space offers a sharp contrast to the *duomo.* (Open daily 9am-1pm and 4-7pm.) The adjacent **Oratory of San Bernardino** (ring the bell at #22 for the doorkeeper) houses several more Il Sodomas.

Via Banchi di Sopra, via Banchi di Sotto, and **via di Città** trisect Siena, intersecting above Il Campo. Via di Città begins with the **Loggia della Mercanzia** and continues past the towers of various medieval families to the **Palazzo Chigi-Saracini,** a magnificent Gothic structure that now houses the Accademia Musicale Chigiana.

Entertainment

The Accademia Chigiana sponsors an excellent music festival, the **Settimana Musicale Senese,** Siena's Musical Week (late July). Siena also hosts a **jazz festival** in July, which features internationally known bopsters. Check the posters or the tourist office for details.

The **Palio di Siena** takes place on July 2 and August 16. As the race approaches, Siena's emotional temperature rises steadily. Ten of the 17 *contrade* (chosen by lot—there's limited space in Il Campo) make elaborate traditional preparations. Young partisans sporting the colors of their *contrada* chant in packs on the street. Five trial races take place over the three days leading up to the race, and a final trial is run the same morning. Just before the race, each horse is brought into the church of its respective *contrada* to be blessed. A procession of heralds and flagbearers prefaces anarchy with regal pomp—the last piece in the procession is the *palio* itself, a banner depicting the Madonna and Child, drawn in a cart by white oxen. Officials pad the buildings of the *piazza* with mattresses, for many a rider has lost control and careened off the track. The horses tear thrice around Il Campo, unsaddled jockeys clinging to their backs. Riders alternate whip strokes between their mounts and their competitors. Packed in the center of Il Campo and hanging from the balconies of the surrounding *palazzi,* the throng roars with excitement. Second place brings dishonor, shame, and occasional suicides.

To stay in Siena during the *Palio,* book rooms at least four months in advance—especially for budget accommodations. Write the APT in March or April for a list of individuals and companies that let rooms, or to reserve a seat in the stands. You can stand in the "infield" of the *piazza* for free. Access to the *piazza* closes early, so stake out a spot early in the day. The two-hour parade takes place immediately before the 7pm race, which lasts about 70 seconds. The night before the race everyone revels until 3am or so, strutting and chanting their way around the city, pausing frequently to eat and quaff. After the race, nine of the 10 competing *contrade* languish in bleary-eyed agony. For the full scoop on *Il Palio* ask at the tourist office and pick up their excellent program. To witness a less touristed phase of *Il Palio,* attend *La Tratta* (the choosing of the horses), which takes place on June 29 and August 13 at 10am.

To do some hoofing of your own, try the **Gallery** (tel. 28 83 78) at via Pantaneto, 13.

Southern Tuscany

Monte Oliveto Maggiore

Perched on a knoll halfway between Montepulciano and Siena, the **Monastery of Monte Oliveto Maggiore** typifies the wealthy Benedictine abbey. Founded by such tired Sienese merchants as Bernardo Tolomei and Ambrogio Piccolomini, both of whom retired here in 1313, the monastery is the mother house of the Olivetan Order, approved by the pope six years after the gold-encrusted monks arrived. Money breeds money, and by the 1400s, Monte Oliveto had so much that a rebuilding program turned the monastery into a Renaissance prodigy. Thanks to its isolation, the place functions today much as it did during the Middle Ages, and remains relatively untouristed. The monks still make their own wine, honey, olive oil, and a strange herb liqueur called *Flora di Monte Oliveto,* all sold at the small shop within the abbey.

The real treasures of Monte Oliveto Maggiore lie in the **Chiostro Grande.** On the wall of this large cloister, to the right as you exit from the church, you'll find a cycle of frescoes depicting the life of St. Benedict. Commissioned to execute the entire cycle, Luca Signorelli died before he completed the job, painting only nine of the 36 panels in 1947-8. Il Sodoma took over the commission, extending the cycle both back into the life of S. Benedict and forward in time from where Signorelli left off. Sodoma's frescoes can thus be found on the first, second and fourth walls of the cycle, and Signorelli's on the third. Don't miss Il Sodoma's *Come Florenzo Manda Male Femmine al Monastero,* in which bewildered monks look to St. Benedict for guidance when confronted with a bevy of voluptuous, scantily clad women. Note the similarity of the positioning and gestures of the women in the foreground here with Botticelli's *Primavera.*

The **Chiesa Abbazia** off the Chiostro Grande, thoroughly renovated in the 18th century, contains treasures from disparate eras. Note the wood-inlaid, 16th-century stalls by master Fra Giovanni da Verona lining the nave and the modern stained-glass work. (Abbey open daily 9:15am-12:30pm and 3-7pm; off-season 9:15am-12:30pm and 3-5:30pm. Ring if the door is closed.)

Rooms are available for visiting students: reserve by mail. (Write to the Abbazia di Monte Oliveto Maggiore, 53020 Siena.) Free **camping** in the area surrounding the abbey is a possibility. At the entrance to the abbey grounds, in the old tower and gate house, **Ristorante La Torre** serves sandwiches (L3000-4000), pizza (L4500-7000), and full meals (around L20,000). The monks also operate a *bar-pasticceria,* which sells basic necessities as well as drinks.

Many people find that the easiest way to reach Monte Oliveto from Siena is to take the train to Asciano (almost hourly, L2800) and then hitch a ride up the 11km of country road to Monte Oliveto. Rides are reportedly easiest to come by on Sundays, when traffic to the monastery is more plentiful. A bus also runs from Siena to **Chiusure,** a walkable 2km from Monte Oliveto (Mon.-Sat. leaves at 2pm, returns at 7am, round-trip L6500).

Massa Marittima

The locals simply call their home "Massa," for indeed even though it's surnamed "Marittima" this burg is anything but close to the waves. An ancient Etruscan mining town, this may not be the place to come for fun in the sun, but it does have one of Tuscany's most spectacular Romanesque *duomos,* and the endearing authenticity of an untouristed Tuscan hill town.

The 13th-century **duomo,** with a marvelous Pisan-Romanesque façade, dominates **piazza Garibaldi,** in the center of town. The stairs leading to the church are a work of art in themselves; at the corner, they converge like a fan into a flat wall. Individually carved heads reign atop the pilasters of the façade's blind arches. To the right of the door lies the enormous baptismal font, sculpted in 1267 from a single block of marble. To the left hangs a charming series of 11th-century bas-reliefs depicting Jesus and his apostles staring out at you. Walk behind the high altar in the choir to see the *Arca di San Cerbone,* the tomb of the city's patron saint (1324). If you look closely at the sharp bas-reliefs, which illustrate the saint's life, you will detect chips of colored paint in the deeper incisions—the entire piece was originally bright polychrome. Peek into the chapel to the left of the high altar to see a *Madonna delle Grazie* by Duccio. (Open daily 9am-noon and 3-8pm.)

Next to the cathedral the medieval **Palazzo del Podestà** now quarters the **tourist office** (tel. (0566) 90 22 89), the **Museo Archeologico,** and the **Pinacoteca Comunale.** The tourist office in the lobby is generous with information and pamphlets. The *museo,* on the first floor, contains prehistoric, Etruscan, and Roman artifacts. Upstairs, the *pinacoteca* displays Sienese paintings, including Ambrogio Lorenzetti's flashy and innovative *Maestà* that infuses a typically iconic subject with narrative focus through the addition of a vast supporting cast of saints worshipping the enthroned Madonna and the trio of allegorical figures on the steps below her. (Open Tues.-Sun. 10am-12:30pm and 3:30-7pm; Nov.-March Tues.-Sun. 9am-1pm and 3-5pm. Admission to both museums L3500; under 18, students and seniors L2500.)

From p. Garibaldi, ascend the steep but charming via Moncini. As you pass through the fortress wall at the top of the street, you will see a soaring arch bridging the wall and the campanile, which dominates p. Matteotti. Hang a right down corso Diaz and a left on via Populonia to come to the **Antico Frantoio,** a house containing an 18th-century olive press, where you can examine the process by which the oil is extracted from the olive. (Open Tues.-Fri. 10am-noon, Sat.-Sun. 10am-noon and 4-7pm. Admission L2000; students, under 18 and seniors L1000.) Back at p. Matteotti, stroll along the path outside the city's walls for a breathtaking aerial view of the surrounding terrain.

Visit Massa on the Sunday following May 20 or the second Sunday of August to catch the **Balestro del Girifalco.** This lively procession in medieval costume culminates in a crossbow match between the *terzieri* (three sections) of the town.

The only hotel in the town's center is the **Hotel Cris,** via Roma, 9-10 (tel. (0566) 90 38 30), on the corner of via Cappellini. (Singles L22,000. Doubles L37,000.) Downstairs a family-run restaurant offers reasonably priced home-style fare. They prepare a delectable dish of *tortelli ai funghi porcini* for only L6000. (The restaurant may be closed in August.)

For a more memorable meal, head to **Trattoria da Alberto,** via Parenti, 35, which serves hearty Tuscan food under grapevines in an outdoor garden. It would be a shame not to try their homemade *tagliatelle* topped with *cinghiale* (wild boar) in a spicy tomato sauce (L6000). Wash it down with a carafe of their respectable house wine. TRA-IN buses link Massa Marittima to Siena, leaving from via Ximenes and arriving at p. San Domenico in Siena (twice daily at 8:30am and 5:30pm, 1hr. 30min., L6600). FMF buses run between Piombino and Massa Marittima, making Massa a convenient stopover ere you see Elba (4 per day, 1hr., L4800). The surest way to reach Massa is by way of Follonica (every 30min., L2100), a local stop on the main Tyrrhenian line from Pisa (L8800). Buy bus tickets at the travel agency at p. Garibaldi, 18 (open 8am-8pm).

San Galgano

Only slightly removed from a winding country pass between Siena and Massa Marittima, the ruined 13th-century Cistercian abbey of San Galgano was once one of the richest and most powerful in Tuscany. Its monks served as treasurers and judges for the communes of Siena and Volterra, helped construct the *duomo* in Siena, and became bishops and even saints. Their vast fortune permitted the monks to construct an abbey of noble proportions, over 70m long, with 16 arches supporting its lofty roof. Then, in the 15th century, the abbey began to decline due to corruption, and by the mid-16th century most of the church had crumbled to dust.

Its very dilapidation makes San Galgano an unforgettable sight. Nature has been kind to the massive old building, the foremost specimen of Cistercian Gothic architecture in Italy; it has removed the roof completely without harming the majestic pillars within. Gothic windows and rosettes frame Tuscan landscapes, and nestfuls of birds chirp from odd corners.

San Galgano, the abbey's patron saint, is renowned for having renounced war for a life of religion and peace with the miraculous gesture of thrusting his sword into a stone. The rock and weapon are enshrined only a short walk away in the **Chapel of Monte Siepi,** a beautiful Romanesque church on a hill overlooking the abbey. The rotund church supports a starkly impressive black-and-white striped cupola and contains, in addition to the miraculous stone, frescoes by Ambrogio Lorenzetti in its chapel. The chapel also contains the hands of a villain who upon trying to burn the hut of San Galgano was torn to shreds by wolves who had befriended the saint. The hands are preserved as a symbol of friendship between the townsfolk and the beasts of the woods. (Open daily 8am-1pm and 4-6pm.)

To reach San Galgano, take the TRA-IN bus that runs between Siena and Massa Marittima, and get off at the San Galgano stop. Four buses run per day between the two cities, so wait for the next one and continue on.

Montalcino

Montalcino has changed little since medieval times, when it was a Sienese stronghold. With few historic monuments to attend to, Montalcino has concentrated on making the heavenly *brunello di Montalcino,* a smooth full-bodied wine that is widely acknowledged as Italy's finest red.

Nearly impregnable behind its walls, in 1555 Montalcino sheltered a band of republicans escaping from the Florentine siege of Siena. There, they and the citizens staged the republic's last stand, holding out against the Medici for another four years. The city walls still stand, along with the remains of the town's original 19 fortified towers. Montalcino's **Rocca,** or fortress, watches over the southeast corner of town. Two courtyards beckon inside the fortress, one sunny and cheered by tiger lilies, the other sylvan and shaded by foliage. You can explore the Rocca's 14th-century walls, chambers, and turrets, which afford a stunning view of the exquisite landscape. (Open Tues.-Sun. 9am-1pm and 2:30-8pm. L2000, with any student ID L1000.) On the way down, stop at the small *enoteca* in the *fortezza's* cavernous main room; try the tasty sandwiches (L3500) as you sample the local wines (L4500 per glass). Montalcino's most inspiring sight lies 9km away down a serpentine country road. Built in the 12th century on the remains of a 9th-century church allegedly founded by Charlemagne, the **Abbazia di Sant'Antimo** (tel. (0577) 83 56 69, ask for Padre Andrea) rates as one of Tuscany's most beautiful Romanesque churches, with its rounded apse and alabaster capitals. (Open daily 10:30am-12:30pm and 3pm to about 5:30pm. Buses run Mon.-Sat. 4 per day, Sun. 2 per day; L1000.)

The most compelling reason to visit Montalcino is its world-class wine. *Brunello*, a dry wine with a pronounced aromatic persistance, is produced from the Sangiovese Grasso variety of grape. The wine pressed from this vine can be given one of three classifications. The first, *vino rosso di Montalcino*, indicates that the wine has been aged only one year in wooden barrels before being bottled, yielding a younger, brighter wine. *Brunello*, the second classification, means that the wine has been aged for four years, and that the wine has aged at least six months in the bottle before sale. Due to its lack of sediment and other special qualities, *Brunello* has an exceptional capacity to age, and should improve for up to thirty years. The final classification, the *Riserva*, denotes a wine that has aged five full years in the bottle, producing a truly exceptional wine. *Rosso* should run around L6000-8000 and the *Brunello* costs roughly L20,000, while the *Riserva* begins at L30,000 a bottle. The best deals on *Brunello* are found at the **COOP Supermarket** off p. del Popolo. To gain a real appreciation for the local vineyards, head 5km down the road to the **Fattoria dei Barbi** in Sant'Antimo (tel. (0577) 84 82 77). You can also visit the **Azienda Agricola Greppo,** which produced the first *Brunello* in 1888, and can be found 3km away from Montalcino on the road to Sant'Antimo. Call before heading out in order to arrange a tour of the cellars (tel. (0572) 84 80 87). Contact the tourist office for information about guided tours of the local vineyards. To sample some of the exotic honey products made in Montalcino hop over to **Apicoltura Ciacci** on v. Ricasoli, 26, up the street from the Chiesa di S. Agostino, where you'll discover every honey product imaginable, including honey soap, honey-biscuits, honey-Grappa, honey-milk and honey candies. (Open 10am-12:30pm and 4-7pm.)

Not only do local products tickle the vinophile's throat, but the superb *trattoria* **Il Moro,** v. Mazzini, 46, is itself reason enough to visit Montalcino. Sample the local catch of *cinghiale* (wild boar) with *pappardelle* (a homemade pasta) for L5000 or the mixed grill for L10,000. (Open Tues.-Sun. noon-2:30pm and 7:30-10:30pm.) Rooms are scarce and expensive in Montalcino, so try to find a bed in a private home. The **Tourist Office,** costa del Municipio, 8 (tel. (0577) 84 93 21), can help you find lodging. You might also try **Affitacamere Casali,** v. Sagna, 3, (tel. (0577) 84 80 83), which lets adequate doubles with bath (L50,000; use of kitchen L15,000).

Ten **TRA-IN** buses make the one-hour trip daily from Siena to Montalcino (L4200). If coming from Pienza or Montepulciano, change buses at Torrenieri. Visit in June, when the old town comes alive for a *Teatro* festival. Contact the tourist office for tickets (about L10,000).

Pienza

Known as "the Pearl of the Renaissance," Pienza was planned and built virtually overnight by Bernado Rossellino to satisfy the utopian vision of Aeneas Silvius Piccolomini. After becoming Pope Pius II in 1458, he fulfilled a humanist dream by transforming his native hamlet into a tiny paradise subsequently dubbed "Pienza" in his honor. The plan called for a group of monumental structures to be erected around a *piazza:* a cathedral, a papal *palazzo,* a town hall, and a public well. Completed between 1459 and 1462, the mini-city exemplifies the Tuscan Renaissance style. In fact, piazza Pio II is in such classical good taste that it verges on boring; you'll yearn for some element of disorder in the textbook façade of the **cathedral.** The luminous interior, however, is purely Gothic, the work of Renaissance masters Vecchietta and Giovanni di Paulo. Ask the custodian in the sacristy on the right aisle to let you visit the underground crypt, which contains a baptismal font by Rossellino and fragments of Romanesque sculpture from the church which formerly stood on this spot. (Open daily 7am-1pm and 3-7:30pm.)

Palazzo Piccolomini, to the right of the *piazza* as you face the church, imitates the Palazzo Rucellai in Florence. Within, various collections of weapons and medals drawn from the pope's personal possessions are on display. (Open Tues.-Sun. 10am-12:30pm and 4-7pm; off-season Tues.-Sun. 10am-12:30pm and 3-6pm. Admission L3500.) Behind the *palazzo,* a three-story *loggia* overlooks an amazing garden hanging along the edge of a cliff. Inside the **Palazzo Civico,** facing the cathedral, you can exhaust the stores of the resourceful **tourist office** (tel. (0578) 74 85 02; open June-July Mon.-Sat. 10:30am-12:30pm and 3:30-5:30pm, Sun. 10am-12:30pm and 3-6:30pm; Aug.-May daily 10:30am-12:30pm and 3:30-6:30pm). To the left as you face the cathedral is the **cathedral museum,** which contains, among a host of fascinating liturgical knick-knacks, a cape worn by Pius II. (Open March-Oct. Wed.-Mon. 10am-1pm and 4-6pm; Nov.-Feb. Wed.-Mon. 10am-1pm and 3-5pm. Admission L2000.)

Aeneas Silvius was baptised at the church **La Pieve di S. Vito,** a 25-minute walk from the center of town along via Fonti (which begins on the back right-hand corner of the park). With a round bell tower and low thick walls, this Romanesque church was begun in the 8th century, but not completed until the 12th century. Go around to the right-hand side of the church to examine the bas-relief sculptures of Jesus' life over the side entrance. Much more peculiar carvings over the entrance include sirens in odd postures, and dragons who whisper in their ears. (The church has been closed for repairs in recent years; it was unclear at press time whether it would be open in 1993.)

August and September bring the "Meeting with a Master of Art" display to the council chamber in the *Palazzo Civico.* This program features the work of a contemporary artist. Come to town on the first Sunday of September for the **Fiera del Cacio,** when Pienza celebrates the local *pecorino* (sheep cheese) by recreating the medieval marketplace. The **Sabato Serenata** is held the day before the sheep cheese fest, and features a philanderer sporting traditional threads, who serenades a matron perched in a window of the Palazzo Piccolomini with old Tuscan folk songs.

Inexpensive lodgings are uncommon in Pienza, but if the tranquility and charm convince you to stay for the night, head over to the **Ristorante il Prato,** p. Dante Alighieri (tel. 74 86 01), which has tiny but clean rooms. (Singles L30,000; doubles with bath L60,000.) More expensive, but with tremendous panoramic views of the countryside from charming balconies, is **Il Corsignano,** via della Madonnina (tel. (0578) 74 81 38). (Singles with bath L60,000; doubles with bath L90,000.) **Trattoria La Buca delle Fate,** corso Il Rossellino, 38/A (tel. (0578) 74 84 48) graces Pienza with exceptional local cuisine, including delicious homemade *pici* (hollow spaghetti, L6000) and a fragrant *coniglio in umido* (rabbit in a light brown sauce, L10,000). (Open Tues.-Sun. noon-3pm and 7-11pm.)

TRA-IN buses run between Pienza and Siena (Mon.-Sat. 7 per day, 1hr. 30min., L5000). Pienza is best seen, however, as a daytrip from Montepulciano (9 per day, L1800).

Montepulciano

This small medieval town, stretched along the crest of a hill, occupies perhaps the finest location in Italy for the melding of beautiful countryside and fine wine. Though the smooth, garnet-colored *vino nobile* has gained the town fame, the landscape and museums alone make the town an excellent choice for a daytrip from Siena.

At the **tourist office,** via Ricci, 9 (tel. (0578) 75 74 42), off p. Grande, pick up the helpful booklet *Montepulciano—Perla del Cinquecento,* in English and French. It contains loads of useful information, including a list of private homes that rent rooms. Check before you trek, however, as such information is subject to change. (Open Tues.-Sat. 10am-1pm and 4-7pm, Sun. 10:30am-1pm and 3:30-7pm.)

TRA-IN buses run to Montepulciano from Siena, Florence, Pienza, and Chiusi. Montepulciano is an easy daytrip from Siena (Mon.-Sat. 6 per day, 2hr., L6600, change at Buonconvento). Hourly trains to Chiusi make Montepulciano a convenient stopover on the Florence-Rome line; take the bus from there (45min., L2700).

Accommodations

The mild trauma of hotel prices in Montepulciano makes the town more attractive as a daytrip from Siena.

> **Affitta Camere Bella Vista** rents small but adequate rooms for short and long term stays. The logical choice at L35,000 for a single, L45,000 for a double with bath (L55,000 for the one double with a bath and balcony). Call for reservations (tel. (0578) 75 73 48).

> **Albergo La Terazza,** (tel. (0578) 75 74 40; fax 75 76 61). Gorgeous, spacious rooms, with access to a charming terrace where *aperitifs* are served among the flowers. Singles with bath L48,000. Doubles with bath L68,000. Triples with bath L75,000. Mini-apartments also available. Breakfast L3500. Reserve ahead; this place is popular.

> **Ristorante Cittino,** vicolo della via Nuova, 2 (tel. 75 73 35), off via di Voltaia nel Corso. A great place to hole up and chao down. Clean and homey. Singles L30,000. Doubles L50,000. The restaurant serves superb homecooked food. Full meals L20,000. Open July to mid-June. Restaurant and hotel closed Wed., but you can check in Wed. night if you call ahead.

Food

Montepulciano offers a smorgasbord of excellent, affordable restaurants. Ristorante Cittino is one of the best deals (see above). There are **minimarkets** all along the *corso* and a larger **supermarket** in p. Savonarola at the bottom of the *corso,* as well as an **open-air market** in p. Sant'Agnese (Thurs. 8am-1pm).

> **Trattoria Diva e Maceo,** via Gracciano nel Corso, 92 (tel. 71 69 51). Where locals go to socialize over a plate of cannelloni stuffed with ricotta and spinach (L7000) or a divine *ossobuco* (L10,000). Open Wed.-Mon. noon-3pm and 7-10pm.

> **Rosticceria di "Voltaia,"** via di Voltaia nel Corso, 86. Tasty homecooked dishes to eat in or take out. Full meals around L20,000, take-out cheaper. Open Mon.-Sat. noon-3pm and 7-11pm.

Sights and Entertainment

Montepulciano boasts an impressive assemblage of 16th- and 17th-century Renaissance and Baroque *palazzi.* The town's main drag, the **Corso,** divides nominally into four parts: via di Gracciano nel Corso, via di Voltaia nel Corso, via dell'Opio nel Corso, and via del Poliziano nel Corso. It winds langorously up the hill, passing near the summit where the Piazza Grande and the *duomo* are located, and is well worth an amble. Impressive *palazzi* line the lowest quarter of the Corso, via di Gracciano. On your right at #91 is the stately **Palazzo Avignonesi** (1507-1575), attributed to Vignola. Notice how the elegant and well-balanced windows of the second floor contrast starkly with the bold protruding windows of the ground floor, marking different stages of construction. The lions' heads on either side of the door belong to the same pride as the lion on top of the **Marzocco Column,** in front of the *palazzo.* The lion, the heraldic symbol of Florence, replaced the she-wolf of Siena in this spot when Florence took the city in 1511. The original lion now rests in the **Museo Civico.** Farther up on the other side of the street at #70 rises the asymmetrical façade of **Palazzo Cocconi,** attributed to Antonio da Sangallo the Elder (1455-1534). Cross the street to #73, the **Palazzo Bucelli,** whose base is inset with Roman and Etruscan reliefs, urn slabs, and inscriptions collected by the 18th-century proprietor, Pietro Bucelli.

The **Church of Sant'Agostino** dominates p. Michelozzo, farther up the street. The lower part of the façade demonstrates Michelozzo's masterful classicism, while the second level "quotes" the Gothic style. Just in front of the church of Madonna di Fatima looms the **Torre di Pucinella,** constructed in 1524 of wood and metal plating. Punctually on the hour, the Pucinella gongs the bell, keeping time for the surrounding neighborhood. Back on the Corso, which becomes via di Voltaia nel Corso at #21, stop at the U-shaped **Palazzo Cervini.** This *palazzo's* external courtyard is typical of country villas but rare in urban residences. Here it serves a double purpose as a symbol of the family's grandeur and as a magnanimous civic gesture in making the clan's private space public.

To reach **piazza Grande** and the **duomo** at the top of the hill you can either meander around and up Il Corso, or scale the steep alleys to the right. The unfinished *duomo,* the Palazzo Tarugi, the Palazzo Cantucci, and the 14th-century Palazzo Comunale ring the *piazza.* The unpretentious *duomo,* with its simple stone and brick exterior and unfinished façade, clothes an even sparser interior. It houses a poignant *Assumption of the Virgin* by Taddeo di Bartolo in a triptych above the altar. (Open 9am-1pm and 3:30-7:30pm.) The austere **Palazzo Comunale** took nearly a century to build, and was finally completed in the mid-1400s by Michelozzo. On a clear day you can take in a view that ranges from Siena's towers in the north to the snow-capped Gran Sasso massif in the south from the palazzo's tower. (Open Mon.-Sat. 8am-1pm. Free.) The remaining two *palazzi* were both designed by Antonio Sangallo the Elder. The elegant white façade of **Palazzo de' Nobili-Tarugi** faces the *duomo;* two arches on the bottom left allow one to enter a deep vaulted *loggia* that cuts through the entire corner of the building. Downstairs in the **Palazzo Contucci** (across from the Palazzo Comunale), an enthusiastic caretaker will discourse on the *vino nobile* he guards in the **Contucci cellars,** a private wine store.

The Palazzo Neri-Orselli, via Ricci, 10, houses the **Museo Civico,** one of Montepulciano's foremost attractions. The museum contains a collection of enameled terra-cotta by della Robbia and Etruscan cinerary urns, but the prime pieces of the collection are the 200-plus paintings. Don't miss the two crucifixions by Filippino Lippi and Luca di Tommè. (Open Wed.-Sun. 9:20am-1pm and 3-6pm. Admission L3000.)

The **Church of San Biagio,** outside the town walls, is Sangallo's masterpiece. Walk the steep half-kilometer down the hill to appreciate the balance of its centralized plan and its graceful details. Stand under the dome and clap your hands for a demonstration of the remarkable acoustics.

Around August 15, the **Bruscello** (a series of amateur theatrical productions) takes place on the steps of the *duomo.* To buy tickets (around L10,000), contact the tourist office. Visit Montepulciano the last Sunday in August to see the raucous **Bravio** (Barrel Race), held to commemorate the eight neighborhood militias who fended off the Florentines and Sienese. Pairs of youths, dressed in costumes bearing their team markings, roll barrels up the steep incline of the Corso, exchanging insults and blows as they battle their way to the piazza Grande. In mid-July and early August of 1992, Montepulciano will hold its 18th **Cantiere Internazionale D'Arte.** Professional and amateur musicians from all around converge for a busy fortnight of opera and classical music—with as many as three different performances per day. Contact the tourist office for details.

Arezzo

Quoth a 19th-century British traveler of Arezzo, "Its subtile air has been asserted to be peculiarly favorable to genius." Indeed, little Arezzo produced a slew of eggheads and visionaries: the poet Petrarch; the humanist Leonardo Bruni; the artist and historian Giorgio Vasari; and Guido d'Arezzo, inventor of the musical scale. Masaccio, Paolo Uccello, Piero della Francesca and Michelangelo were born in the surrounding countryside. Yet most moved on to greener pastures and more cosmopolitan settings. Petrarch left for the papal court in Avignon; Bruni became the intellectual leader and chancellor of Florence; Guido headed for Ferrara; and though Vasari built and frescoed his house in Arezzo, he spent most of his time disfiguring Florence for the Medici. The partial exception to this exodus was local son Piero della Francesca, who stayed here long enough to paint one of the most moving fresco cycles in Italy. But while the cycle undergoes restoration, only an eclectic gathering of good medieval and Renaissance pieces keeps Arezzo on the art pilgrim's tour. The less devoted might better follow the example of the early Aretini—and flee.

Orientation and Practical Information

Arezzo lies on the Florence-Rome train line, an hour from Florence (L6500) and two hours from Rome (L17,100). Buses connect it with nearby hilltowns, including Cortona (LFI, 1hr. 30min., L3400) and Sansepolcro (CAT, 1hr., L4000). Four buses run daily to Siena (1hr. 30min., L6600), returning to Arezzo in the afternoon.

Arezzo's train station and modern quarter lie at the bottom of a hill which ascends through the historic center and peaks at the *duomo*. Follow **via Guida Monaco,** which begins directly across from the station in piazza della Repubblica, up into the medieval and Renaissance old town, and continue with via Cesalpino up to the top. You can leave your bags in **luggage storage,** to your left before you enter the station from the tracks (L1500).

Tourist Office: APT, p. Risorgimento, 116 (tel. 239 52), on the 2nd floor. Take the 1st right off via Monaco after p. della Repubblica. No accommodations service, but will provide a list of hotels with prices. Understaffed but helpful. Open Mon.-Fri. 9am-noon and 4-6pm, Sat. 9am-noon. The **summer branch** of the tourist office is to the right as you leave the station in p. della Repubblica, 22 (tel. 37 76 78). A little overwhelmed by the tourist onslaught, but more than happy to give out free maps and other information. Open June-Aug. Mon.-Sat. 9am-1pm and 4-7pm, Sun. 9am-1pm.

Post Office: via Monaco, 34, to the left of p. Monaco when facing uphill. Open Mon.-Fri. 8:15am-7pm, Sat. 8am-12:30pm. **Postal Code:** 52100.

Telephones: SIP, p. Monaco, 2, in the shopping arcade. Open 24 hrs. Also at via Margaritone, off via Niccolò Aretino near the Archeological Museum. Open Mon.-Sat. 8:30am-12:30pm and 3:30-6:30pm. **Telephone Code:** 0575.

Buses: (tel. 38 26 44), on viale Piero della Francesca in front of the train station. Open Mon.-Sat. 6:15am-8:35pm, Sun. 9:10-11:15am and 3:20-7:15pm.

Emergencies: tel. 113. **Police:** off via Fra' Guittone, near the train station. **Guardia Medica** (tel. 30 04 44). **Hospital:** (tel. 35 67 57; at night and Sun. 35 18 00), on via Fonte Veneziana.

Accommodations

The hotels of Arezzo fill to capacity during the Fiera Antiquaria (Antique Fair) on the first weekend of every month. Reservations are also necessary in the last four days of August during the **Concorso Polifonico Guido d'Arezzo,** a vocal competition. Otherwise, you should have little trouble finding a room.

Ostello Villa Severi, via Redi, 13 (tel. 290 47). Take bus #4 (L800) from the right-hand-side of via Guido Monaco (100yd up v. G. Monaco from the train station), and get off at the stop after the Ospedale Civile (about 7 minutes). A beautifully restored villa in the countryside overlooking hills and vineyards. 68 beds, 6 beds per room. Open 8am-4:30pm and 6:30pm-midnight. L17,000 per person, breakfast included. Dinner L15,000, but if you reserve ahead you can get half-pension (bed, breakfast, and 1 meal) for L27,000, or full pension (room and 3 meals) for L37,000.

Albergo Milano, via Madonna del Prato, 83 (tel. 268 36), near the tourist office. The best in town if you don't feel like schlepping out to the hostel. Curfew midnight. Singles L28,000. Doubles L40,000, with bath L50,000.

Hotel Astoria, via Monaco, 54 (tel. 243 61). A good option in a pinch. Singles L35,000, with bath L48,000. Doubles L56,000, with bath L76,000. Breakfast L7000. Closed Aug. 10-20.

Food

Skip a restaurant lunch and check out alternative food options, such as the **supermarket** at via Monaco, 84 (open Sun.-Fri. 8am-1pm and 4:30-8pm, Sat. 8am-1pm). Try the **open-air market** held Tuesday, Thursday, and Saturday in p. Sant'Agostino. For excellent cheese, especially *pecorino,* a sharp sheep's cheese and local specialty, the best bet is **La Mozzarella,** via Spinello, 25 (open 8am-1pm and 4:30-7:30pm, Wed.

8am-1pm). Eat in the park behind the *duomo,* the one place in Arezzo that affords a peaceful and impressive view onto the Tuscan countryside below.

> **La Scaletta,** p. del Popolo, 11 (tel. 35 37 34), next to the post office. The earthy proprietor/cook takes pride in his tasty and copious cuisine. Try the *scallopa gorgonzola* (L12,000). Pizzas L4000-8000. Open Fri.-Wed. noon-3pm and 7pm-midnight.

> **Otello,** p. Risorgimento, 16 (tel. 22 648), 1 block away from Albergo Milano and in front of the tourist office. Fashionable young customers, tasteful modern decor, and fantastic food. Try the *crostoni,* which look like a sort of post-earthquake pizza (L10,000-12,000). Open Mon.-Sat. 5pm-1am, Sept.-June Tues.-Sun. 5pm-1am.

Sights and Entertainment

The **Church of San Francesco** forms the spiritual and physical center of Arezzo. This 14th-century structure guards Piero della Francesca's famous fresco cycle *Legend of the Cross,* the story of the wood used for Christ's cross from seed to crucifix. The city planned to have finished the restoration for 1992, the 500th anniversary of Piero's birth, but the best laid plans of mice and men often go delayed in Italy. Now that the 500th has passed, the urgency, unsurprisingly, seems to have evaporated. It's now anybody's guess as to when the restoration (now covering the right half) will be completed. (Open daily in summer 8am-noon and 1:30-7pm; off-season 8:30am-7pm.)

Contrast this Franciscan art with the decoration of the rival Dominican order on the other side of town. The **Church of San Domenico** contains a superb Cimabue crucifix (1265), Spinello Aretino's *Annunciation* in the chapel to the right of the altar, and the Marcillat rose window over the door. (Open 7am-noon and 3:30-7pm.) Beyond the church on via XX Settembre is **Vasari's house.** Filled with heroic frescoes, the house merits a trip just for an idea of what Hallmark might have accomplished during the Renaissance. (Open Mon.-Sat. 9am-7pm, Sun. 9am-1pm. Free.)

A right turn up via Domenico, another right on via Sassoverde, and a left on via Ricasoli bring you to the **duomo.** The massive, muted-brown structure encloses Piero della Francesca's *Mary Magdalene* just to the right of Bishop Guido Tarlati's tomb. Light filters into the cathedral through a series of 20-ft. stained glass windows by Marcillat onto the altar, a wildly complex assemblage of 14th-century local carvings. (Open 7am-noon and 3-7pm; off-season 7am-noon and 3-6:30pm.) Between the *duomo* and the fortress, a leafy park gives magnificent views out onto the countryside beyond its edge.

If you backtrack down corso Italia, on the left you'll see the Pisan-Romanesque **Church of Santa Maria della Pieve,** Arezzo's most important architectural monument and something of a city emblem. Its tower is nicknamed "the tower of a hundred holes" for the Romanesque windows that pierce the structure on all sides. The slightly painted arches inside place this 12th-century church in the transitory period between Romanesque and Gothic styles, when architects were beginning to experiment with vaulted ceilings. A brilliantly restored polyptych, *Il Politico* by Pietro Lorenzetti, sits on the elevated presbytery, depicting the Annuciation and the Madonna and Child. (Open daily 8am-1pm and 3-7pm; in off-season 8am-12:30pm and 3-6pm.)

Behind the Pieve is **piazza Grande,** surrounded by a chronological succession of Arezzo's best architecture. Next to the impressive arches of the Pieve's rear elevation, the **Palazzo della Fraternità dei Laici** mixes Renaissance and Gothic styles. A reconstruction of the Petrone, a column where criminals were exhibited and proclamations read, rises at the *piazza's* high point; at the lower point is the requisite fountain, placed there because water refused to climb any farther; still one sees only a reluctant dribble.

The **Giostra del Saracino,** is a medieval joust performed the last Sunday of August and the first Sunday in September. "Knights" representing the four quarters of the town charge with lowered lances at a wooden effigy of a Saracen. Feasting and processions accompany the event, and the winning region carries off a golden lance.

Sansepolcro

Lost in a valley among Tuscany's densely forested hills, medieval Sansepolcro is the birthplace of Piero della Francesca and hosts some of his finest works. The town is most easily accessible by the hourly CAT line bus from Arezzo (1hr., L3300), the last bus returning to Arezzo at 7:30pm. This bus ride is not for the weak of stomach, though the incredible views of the countryside may make you forget your rebelling insides. The bus drops you off on via Vittorio Veneto. To get to the museum, take a left from the bus station, then turn left again at the next street, via Niccolo, and walk three minutes until you come to the street light; the museum will be on your right.

Born here sometime between 1410 and 1420 to a recently widowed Francesca, Piero spent most of his life in this town perfecting the new science of perspective; Sansepolcro's **Museo Civico,** via Aggiunti, 65, houses some of his most famous works. The *Resurrection,* his masterpiece, features a triumphant and determined Jesus sporting a red and white banner as he prepares to stride over the side of his tomb. Also by Piero is the *Madonna della Misericordia,* an impressive polyptych with a huge goddess of a Madonna hiding a confraternity under her cloak. The museum also contains a *Crucifixion* by Luca Signorelli, Piero's best student. Don't miss Antonio and Remigio Cantagallina's *Ultima Cena,* with Judas in the foreground holding his money bag and looking nonplussed as a devil on the floor spits blood on him. (Open daily 9-11:15am and 2:30-7:15pm. Admission L5000.)

The **Palio della Balestra** takes place the second Sunday in September. Stay overnight and join in the revelry generated by this competition between archers of Gubbio and Sansepolcro. To reach Sansepolcro's **tourist office,** on via della Fonte (tel. (0575) 73 02 31 or 74 05 36) from the museum, turn right on via Niccolo and then take the first left on p. Garibaldi; the tourist office is one block ahead on the left. (Open daily 10am-1pm and 4-7pm.) They're more than happy to provide maps and sell guidebooks to the region. Should night fall or hunger strike, try the comfortable **Albergo Fiorentino,** via Luca Pacioli, 60 (tel. (0575) 74 03 50; fax 74 03 70), two blocks from the Museo Civico (singles L24,000, with bath and TV L35,000; doubles L36,000, with bath and TV L60,000; triples with bath and TV L81,000; quads with bath and TV L95,000. Showers L4000. Breakfast L4000-5000) and the **Ristorante Da Ventura,** via Aggiunti, 30 (tel. 765 60), which serves outstanding homemade pasta dishes, including the house specialties: ravioli with spinach and ricotta filling or *tagliatelle* with porcini mushrooms. Whole roasts are carved right at the table. (*Primi* L7000, *secondi* L10,000; open Sun.-Fri. noon-2:30pm and 7-10pm.)

Another important stop on any Piero della Francesca odyssey is the tiny chapel halfway between Arezzo and Sansepolcro, outside the town of **Monterchi.** Twenty-four kilometers outside of Arezzo on highway 73, there is a fork in the road; take the right fork (highway 221) to the chapel. Within, marvel at the unusual *Madonna del Parto,* Piero's rendition of the Madonna immaculately pregnant with Bambino. (Open daily 10am-12:30pm and 3-7pm.) The Arezzo-Sansepolcro bus stops nearby in Le Ville (where you can follow the signs to the chapel, about a 20-min. walk).

Cortona

The ancient town of Cortona preens on a mountaintop with all the hubris of a town that knows it's closer to heaven than earth. Older than Troy, Cortona enjoyed independence on several occasions in its history but earned its reputation under foreign domination. After the usual Guelph-Ghibelline internal strife and some squabbles with neighbors Perugia and Arezzo, the ruling family spent the last years of the 14th century bumping each other off, leaving the city to be plucked by the king of Naples, who promptly sold it to Florence in 1409. Under Florentine rule, Cortona exported Luca Signorelli to its owner and in return received Fra Angelico, who sojourned here for a decade and painted an *Annunciation* that rivals the one in Florence's San Marco. The town's high-altitude perch has allowed little room for expansion; consequently, old

Cortona has changed little in the last 600 years. The inexorable medieval ambience has lured many modern *literati,* Henry James and Germaine Greer among them.

Today the mystique is imperiled by the gaggles of budding *artistes* who come to Cortona under the University of Georgia's art program, but even they can't ruin the spectacular views over Tuscany and Umbria that open from every windowsill.

Orientation and Practical Information

The easiest way to reach Cortona is by train, either from Rome (90min., L13,800), from Florence (1hr., L8800), or from Arezzo (30min., L2400). As Cortona is not directly on the train line, you must get off at either charmless Terontola-Cortona or downright ugly Camucia-Cortona, both of which are connected to Cortona by the LFI buses that run about every 30 minutes to piazza Garibaldi in Cortona (L1700 and L1400 respectively).

Buses leave you at **piazza Garibaldi** just outside the main gate in the city's wall. Enter through this gate and follow **via Nazionale,** passing the **Tourist Office** almost immediately on your left, to the town's center at **piazza della Repubblica.** From there, cross the *piazza* diagonally to the left to reach the other main square, **piazza Signorelli.**

Tourist Office: via Nazionale, 72 (tel. 63 03 52). Friendly and helpful, with lots of maps and brochures. Open Mon.-Sat. 8am-1pm and 3-6pm.

Post Office: off p. della Repubblica. Open Mon.-Fri. 8:30am-7pm, Sat. 8:30am-noon. **Postal Code:** 52044.

Telephones: SIP, via Guelfa, off p. della Repubblica. Open daily 8am-midnight. **Telephone Code:** 0575.

Swimming Pool: tel. 60 13 74, 7km away at Sodo. Take the bus for Arezzo and ask the driver to let you off at the *piscina.* Water slides! Open daily 8am-midnight. Admission L6000.

Emergency: tel. 113. **Police:** via Dardano, 9 (tel. 60 30 06). **Medical Assistance: Servizio Guardia Medica Turistica,** via Roma, 3 (tel. 60 18 17). For emergencies. Open 8am-8pm. **Ambulace: Misericordia,** tel. 60 30 83. **Hospital:** via Maffei (tel. 629 41).

Accommodations

Cheap hotels are scarce in Cortona, but institutional arrangements take up the slack. The hostel is one of Italy's best, a converted 13th-century house with exceptionally friendly management, and the nuns down the hill will do right by you.

Ostello San Marco (HI), via Maffei, 57 (tel. 60 13 92). From the bus stop, walk up steep via S. Margarita, angle to the right before entering the gate, then around left on via Maffei, about 5min. A perfectly clean and cozy place with a cavernous dining room. Up to 10 beds per room. 1 double (open to couples). Laundry facilities available. Open 7-10am and 4pm-midnight. L14,000 per person. Breakfast and sheets included. Showers included, but hot water shuts off late at night. Dinner L12,000. Open mid-March through mid-Oct.; year-round for groups.

Istituto Santa Margherita, viale Cesare Battisti, 15 (tel. 63 03 36). Walk down v. Severini from p. Garibaldi; the *istituto* is at the corner of v. Battisti, on the left. Echoing marble hallways take you to spacious rooms, all with bath. Curfew midnight. Singles L21,000. Doubles (no unmarried couples, please!) L38,000. Triples L48,000. Dormitory-style rooms (single beds in partly enclosed cubicles) for L15,000 per person. Breakfast L3000.

Albergo Italia, via Ghibellina, 5 (tel. 63 05 64), off p. Emanuele. High ceilings, firm beds. In the process of adding another star to their rating, they may or may not jack their prices up in '93 to match. Singles with bath around L50,000. Doubles with bath around L70,000.

Food

With several *trattorie* featuring immense pasta dishes at rock-bottom prices, and an abundance of grocery, fruit, and *rosticcerie* (prepared food) stores, even a pauper won't starve in Cortona. The best local wine is the smooth *bianco vergine di Valdichiana.* True penny-pinchers can pick up a bottle (L3000) at the **Supermercato A&O,** in piazza della Repubblica. (Open daily 8am-1:30pm and 4:30-10pm.) On Saturday, p. della Repubblica metamorphoses into a great **open-air market.**

Trattoria La Grotta (tel. 63 02 71), p. Baldelli, 3, off p. della Repubblica. Delectable fare in a homey atmosphere. Sample the homemade *gnocchi alla ricotta e spinaci* (ricotta and spinach balls in tomato and meat sauce, L7000). Continue sampling with one of their grilled specialties, perhaps the *fegato di Vitello* (calf's liver, L7500). Open daily Aug.-Sept. noon-3pm and 7-11pm; Oct.-July Wed.-Mon. noon-3pm and 7-11pm.

Trattoria Dardano, via Dardano, 24, (tel. 60 19 44) caters mostly to locals in one long, breezy room. *Primi,* including a hearty *lasagne al forno,* L5000-6000. *Secondi* L6000 and up (their specialty is roasted meats, L6000-7000). Open daily noon-3pm and 7pm-midnight.

Trattoria dell'Amico, via Dardano, 12 (tel. 60 41 92). Gregarious owner serves great pasta (L5500-7000), including *spaghetti al pesto* and *penne alla gorgonzola.* For a *secondo,* the wonderful *salsicce al vino* please the carnivorous vinophile in everyone (L6000). Open daily noon-3pm and 7-11pm; in winter Tues.-Sun. noon-3pm and 7-11pm. Closed in Nov.

Trattoria Etrusca, Spaghetteria e Birreria, via Dardano, 55. Specializes in *primi,* serving up marvelously unique pasta creations. Try the house specialty, *tagliatelli colle zucchine* (pasta with zucchini, L7000). Full meals for under L12,000. Kitchen open daily 12:30-2:30pm and 7:30pm-1am; Oct.-May closed Thurs. *Bar* and *birreria* open 9am-2am. MC, Visa.

Sights

The most stunning sights in Cortona are the incredible vistas of the surrounding valleys and hills afforded by Cortona's elevation. From the ancient citadel of the **Fortezza** on the summit of Cortona's rugged hill (Mont. S. Egidio), you can see the entire town spread out below, and gaze out over Tuscany. On the other side of town, at p. Garibaldi, lean out over the iron fence to peer down the jagged cliff to the floor of the valley below, where you can see Hannibal's beloved Lake Trasimeno and Umbria beyond.

In p. della Repubblica stands the 13th-century **Palazzo del Comune,** with a clock tower and monumental staircase. **Palazzo Casali,** to the right and behind the Palazzo del Comune, dominates p. Signorelli. Only the courtyard walls with their coats-of-arms and the outside right wall remain from the original 13th-century structure; the façade and interlocking staircase were added in the 17th century. Inside the courtyard, steps lead to the **Museo dell'Accademia Etrusca,** which cherishes many treasures and artifacts from the Etruscan period, as well as an overflow of carvings, coins, paintings and furniture from the first through the 18th century. In the first gallery is a circular bronze chandelier from the 5th century BC, mounted in a glass case suspended from the ceiling. With 16 voluminous oil reservoirs, it weighs 58kg when empty. A rare example of intricate Etruscan metalwork, the *lampadario* was discovered by a local farmer plowing his field. The same room contains a two-faced *Janus,* depicted as a full figure rather than the usual bust. In the third gallery you'll find 12th- and 13th-century Tuscan art, including works by Taddeo Gaddi, Cenni di Francesco, and Bici di Lorenzo. The museum wraps up with the 20th-century work of local boy Gino Severini, including lithographs, collages, and an intriguing *Maternità.* (Open Tues.-Sun. 10am-1pm and 4-7pm; Oct.-March Tues.-Sun. 9am-1pm and 3-5pm. Admission L5000.)

To the right and downhill from the Palazzo Casali is **piazza del Duomo.** On the façade of the *duomo* note the brick entry of the original Church of S. Maria, poking out like a sore thumb from the stone fronting. During renovations, enter the church from the side door, near the Palazzo Vescovile. Inside, you'll find an impressive Baroque canopied high altar, completed in 1664 by Francesco Mattioli. The two-floored **Museo Diocesano** across from the *duomo* houses a stunning *Annunciation* by Fra Angelico in the upstairs gallery on the right. Across the corridor on the left, Christ's pain-wrenched face confronts you in Pietro Lorenzetti's fresco of *The Way to Calvary.* Vasari's staircase leads to a frescoed oratory on the lower level containing a painted cross by Lorenzetti. (Open April-Sept. Tues.-Sun. 9am-1pm and 3-6:30pm; Oct.-March 9am-1pm and 3-5pm. Admission L5000.) Perhaps the best example of Luca Signorelli's work is *The Deposition,* which resides in the 16th-century **Church of San Niccolò,** up the hill beyond the youth hostel. Ring the bell if the church isn't open, and, after the kind woman shows you the painting, ask her to activate the nifty mechanism that turns the panel around so you can see Signorelli's *Madonna and Saints* on the other side. (Church generally open 9am-12:30pm and sporadically in the afternoon.)

When afternoon sedates Cortona, head up to the **Fortezza Medicea** for a splendid view and a refreshing breeze. Take via San Cristoforo, which winds up the hill between tall cypresses from the small church of the same name. You will pass the remains of Etruscan and medieval city walls, the site of an ancient temple dedicated to Mars, god of war, and a stone explaining how Santa Margherita administered her first miraculous cure. At the top enter the tree-filled fortress, built on the remains of an Etruscan fortification. (Open mid-July to Aug. Tues.-Sun. 10am-1pm and 4-7pm.)

The Renaissance **Church of Santa Maria delle Grazie al Calcinaio,** designed by Francesco di Giorgio Martini, eagerly awaits visitors about 2km down the road near Camucia. The soft gray *pietra serena* stone is beautifully carved in the interior, and the white walls create a cool tonality. Paintings of the Signorelli school hover near the altar and a Marcillat stained-glass window energizes the opposite wall. (Open daily 8:30am-noon and 3:30-7pm.) Ask at the tourist office for information about the **Meloni del Sodo,** recently discovered Etruscan tombs near Sodo.

Entertainment

Cortonese food and wine lives up to its citizens' boasts. Of the numerous gastronomic festivals throughout the year, the most important is August 14-15's **Sagra della Bistecca,** when the whole town pours in to feast upon the superb local steak. Cortonese carry on the gorging and merrymaking well into the night. Various musical and theatrical events take place thoughout the year, clustering in the summer months. The Azienda's informative "Cortona '93" will give you the lowdown. Relax in the **public gardens** or join in the evening *passeggiata* along the park's *parterre*. Italian movies are screened here in summer. Movies are also shown at the grand **Cinema-Teatro Signorelli,** in p. Signorelli (tel. 60 18 82), nightly at 9:45pm.

Umbria

Christened the "Green Heart of Italy," Umbria has enjoyed renown for its wooded hills, valleys, and rivers since ancient times. This region inspired its sons, the Latin poets Plautus and Propertius, as well as Dante and Giosuè Carducci. Often shrouded in an ethereal silvery haze, the landscape also nurtured a mystic tradition that stretches from prehistory through to St. Benedict, who preached the doctrine of the marriage of work and worship, and to Umbria's most famous visionary, the nature-adoring ascetic St. Francis. Generations of visual artists also clambered about these hills, among them Giotto, Signorelli, Perugino and Pinturicchio.

Umbria's earliest inhabitants may have been the eponymous Umbrii, an ancient and reclusive tribe that withdrew to the east as first the Etruscans and then the aggressive Romans sought to expand their frontiers. Barbarian invasions in the 5th and 6th centuries provoked the inhabitants to retreat to the hill towns of the Etruscans, setting the stage for the rise of medieval city-states. More than half a millennium of constant Guelph-Ghibelline warfare followed, finally allowing Pope Paul III to seize the weakened region for his own in the 1530s. Although the yoke of papal governance was lifted during the Risorgimento, its legacy of stagnation lingered well into this century. Umbria has now achieved a measure of prosperity by cultivating interest in its beautifully situated medieval cities and by promoting itself as a center of culture through such summer festivities as the pioneering Two Worlds Festival of Spoleto and the Umbrian Jazz Festival.

While the Italian State Railways (F.S.) link most major towns (Gubbio and Todi are exceptions), buses provide the most convenient access, especially as they drop you off in the center of town rather than at the bottom of a steep hill. Light traffic makes hitching difficult. Lodgings in Umbria are scarce and expensive, although there are youth hostels in Perugia, Assisi, and Foligno. The only real trouble spots are Todi and Spoleto. There are numerous campgrounds near the hill towns (Orvieto, Spoleto, Perugia, Assisi, Foligno) and in the wild (at Passignano and Castiglione on Lake Trasimeno).

Thermal springs, clear streams, Etruscan ruins, and velvety ravines make this an attractive option.

It's possible to feast cheaply in Umbria, particularly in the larger cities. Specialties include *porchetta* (roast suckling pig), black truffles from Valnerina, *funghi porcini* (wild mushrooms), and local sausages. The olive oil is dark green and delicious; the best local wines are white, most notably the dry, straw-colored *orvieto* from the region's southwest corner. Umbria's sweets are justly famous, and though the Perugina chocolates from the region's capital are now shipped all over the world, nowhere else is a kiss of *bacio* so wonderful.

Perugia

The burghers of Perugia will probably be the politest, most pleasant people you'll meet in Italy. Perhaps it's all meant as a grand public apology, for Perugia was long the most violent and disreputable town in quarrelsome Italy. After a childhood spent as an Etruscan polis desperately resisting Roman conquest, and an adolescence spent revolting against the victorious Romans, Middle-Aged Perugia was ready for a career of professional obnoxiousness. Though often busy quashing its Umbrian neighbors or stirring up a little trouble with the Tuscans, Perugia still found time for an annual festival called the *Battaglia de' Sassi* (Battle of Stones), during which two teams threw rocks at each other until a sufficient number of casualties or fatalities left a winner. And besides being celebrated as the town that once imprisoned St. Francis of Assisi (albeit during his dissolute, pre-preaching days), independent Perugia gets religious points as the birthplace of the **Flagellants,** the flesh-mortifying masses who wandered Europe whipping themselves in public, and as the deathbed of three popes (two of whom died by poison). But the good times eventually ended, and Perugia found itself crushed underneath the Papal heel when it fell to Paul III in 1538.

Three centuries of mortification and economic misery as part of the Papal States apparently taught the Perugians some manners (though not subservience—they were rebelling against the Pope as late as 1859), for the present-day capital of Umbria claims a delightfully civilized atmosphere seasoned by the motley international crowd drawn to its universities and art academies. Through the crooked, narrow medieval streets parade a mishmash of well-dressed bourgeoisie, desperately funky students, and pseudo-exotic buskers and vendors. The *palazzi* that crowd corso Vannucci, Perugia's main street, shelter the city's impressive collection of medieval and Renaissance art; interspersed are bars offering the city's contemporary masterpieces, the infamous chocolate *baci* (kisses).

Orientation and Practical Information

A few direct trains run from Florence and Rome to Perugia, but change at Foligno on the Rome-Ancona line, or catch one of the frequent trains from Teróntola on the Florence-Rome route for more service. Leaving from the train station, buses #26, 27, and 36 will leave you in p. Matteotti (L1000). Otherwise it's a difficult 4km trek—uphill. From the bus station in p. dei Partigiani, follow the signs to the escalator (*scala mobile*) which takes you underneath the old city to piazza Italia. Straight ahead, corso Vannucci, the main shopping thoroughfare, leads to piazza IV Novembre and the *duomo;* behind the *duomo* lies the university area. One block to the right of corso Vannucci you'll find p. Matteotti, the municipal center. The new **Digiplan** machines in the train station are extremely helpful, providing instant printout information (in Italian) on sights, museums, stores, restaurants and more. Train information machines speak English.

Tourist Office: p. IV Novembre (tel. 233 27), in the Palazzo dei Priori . Extremely friendly, patient, and knowledgeable staff gives accommodations and travel information. Artistic but misleading city map. Ask for the detailed walking guide, the *Umbria Informazione* brochure and the large map of Umbria. Open Mon.-Sat. 8:30am-1:30pm and 4-7pm, Sun. 9am-1pm; in winter Mon.-Sat. 3:30-6:30pm.

Budget Travel: CTS, via del Roscetto, 21 (tel. 616 95), off via Pinturicchio towards the bottom of the street. Student center with offices for travel and accommodations. Open Mon.-Fri. 9am-12:15pm and 4-7pm, Sat. 9am-noon. **CIT:** corso Vannucci (tel. 260 61), by the fountain. Open Mon.-Fri. 9am-1pm and 3:30-7pm.

Currency Exchange: Best rates at the train station. No commission for exchanges of less than L80,000.

Post Office: p. Matteotti. Open Mon.-Sat. 8:10am-7:30pm. **Postal Code:** 06100.

Telephones: ASST, next to the post office in p. Matteotti. Open daily 7am-9:45pm. **SIP,** corso Vannucci, 76. Open daily 8am-10pm. **Telephone Code:** 075.

Trains: Fontivegge, p. Veneto. **F.S.** south to: Assisi (25min., L2700); Foligno (40min., L3600); Spoleto (1hr. 10min., L5400); Orvieto (1hr. 45min., L8800); Rome via Teróntola (3hr., L18,200). North to: Passignano sul Trasimeno (30min., L3300); Arezzo (1hr. 20min., L6500); Florence (2hr. 30min., L14,200); Siena (L14,200). **Sant'Anna** station in p. Bellucci serves Città di Castello and Sansepolcro to the north and Todi to the south. **Information: F.S.,** p. Veneto (tel. 709 80). Open 8am-noon and 3-7pm. **Ferrovia Centrale Umbra,** largo Cacciatori delle Alpi, 8 (tel. 239 47), near the bottom of the *scala mobile* on the 1st floor. The **ticket window** in the F.S. station is open 6am-9pm. **Luggage Storage:** L1500, open 24 hrs.

Buses: p. dei Partigiani, down the *scala mobile* from p. Italia. City bus #28, 29, 36, or CD (L1000) from the train station. **ASP buses,** p. dei Partigiani (tel. 618 07) to most Umbrian towns, along with Urbino, Rome, and Florence. Information machines are English-competent.

Albergo Diurno: viale Indipendenza, 7 (enter through the *scala mobile* under p. Italia). Open daily 8am-8pm. Toilet L400, shower L5000, bath L5500, towel L1500, soap L1000. Luggage storage L2500 per piece per day.

English Bookstore: Libreria Filosofi, via dei Filosofi, 18/20 (tel. 304 73). Take bus CS from via XIV Settembre. Out of the way, but a good selection ranging from last year's best-sellers to Faulkner and Eliot. Open Mon.-Fri. 9am-1pm and 4-8pm, Sat. 9am-1pm.

Higher Education: Università per gli Stranieri, Palazzo Gallenga, p. Fortebraccio, 4 (tel. 643 44 or 643 45). The university offers courses in Italian language and culture for foreigners. The student *caffè,* replete with pinball machines, is frequented by the young and the restless. A good place to meet other travelers. Check university bulletin board for cultural events and free concerts. Check with the registrar for rooms for rent.

Laundromat: Lavanderia Moderna, via Fabretti, 19, around the corner from the above university. They wash; you pay—L4000 per kg. Open Mon.-Fri. 8:30am-1pm and 4-8pm, Sat. 8:30am-1pm. Or try **Lavanderia GR,** c. Garibaldi, 34. L3000 per kg. Open Mon.-Fri. 8:30am-1pm and 3:30-7:30pm, Sat. 8:30am-1pm.

Swimming Pool: Piscina Comunale, via Pompeo Pellini (tel. 651 60), near Santa Colombata. Open daily 1-7:30pm; off-season Mon.-Fri. 6:30am-8:30pm, Sat. 3-8pm. Admission L5000.

Emergencies: tel. 113. **Police: Questura,** p. dei Partigiani. **Medical Emergency:** tel. 613 41, at night tel. 340 24. **Hospital: Ospedali Riuniti-Policlinico,** via Bonacci Brunamonti (tel. 57 81).

Accommodations and Camping

Reservations are absolutely necessary during the Umbria Jazz Festival in July.

Centro Internazionale di Accoglienza per la Gioventù, via Bontempi, 13 (tel. 228 80). From p. Matteotti walk up via de' Fari, take a right on corso Vannucci and go until you hit p. IV Novembre, then take the road leading off p. Dantu away from the *duomo* past p. Piccinino (a parking lot) and take the right fork (via Bontempi). This clean hostel offers many amenities: the 4-bed rooms have high ceilings, night tables, and firm bunks. The beautiful library is an excellent meeting spot. 3 week max. stay. Lockout 9:30am-4pm. Curfew midnight. L12,000; showers and use of kitchen included. Sheets L1000. Open mid-Jan. to late Dec.

Albergo Etruria, via della Luna, 21 (tel. 237 30), down the passageway by c. Vannucci, 55. This *pensione* sits at the precipitous end of an alleyway; the proprietor will show you through the 12th-century sitting room. Singles L32,000. Doubles L55,000. Showers L3500.

Albergo Anna, via dei Priori, 48 (tel. 663 04), off corso Vannucci. Walk up 4 flights to clean and cool 17th-century rooms, with daunting ceilings and peaceful views. Singles L30,000. Doubles L40,000, with bath L45,000. Showers L6000. Breakfast L5000.

Pensione Paola, via della Canapina, 5 (tel. 238 16). From the train station, take bus #26 or 27 and get off near via della Canapina, across from a large municipal parking lot. Walk up the stairs; the *pensione* is on the right. A charming place with big, beautifully furnished rooms. Singles L30,000. Doubles L45,000. Breakfast included. Reservations recommended.

Camping: Paradis d'Ete, 5km away in Colle della Trinità (tel. 79 51 17). Take bus #36 from the station and ask the driver to leave you in Colle della Trinità. Hot showers and pool at no extra charge. L6500 per person, L5500 per tent, L2500 per car. Open year-round.

Food

Though renowned for chocolate, Perugia also serves up a variety of delectable breads and pastries; be sure to sample the *torta di formaggio* (cheese bread) and the *mele al cartoccio* (the Italian version of apple pie). Both are available at **Ceccarani,** p. Matteotti, 16, or at the **Co.Fa.Pa** bakery two doors down at #12 (both open Fri.-Wed. 7:30am-1pm and 5-7:45pm). For such local confections as *baci* (kisses), a combination of chocolate, nuts, and honey, follow your nose to **Bar Ferrari,** corso Vannucci, 43 (open 7am-midnight). If you prefer your chocolate cold and creamy, head to the student-infested **Gelateria 2000,** via Luigi Bonazzi, 3, off p. della Repubblica (open Mon.-Sat. 8am-midnight), whose product is excellence made edible (cones L1500-3000).

On Tuesday and Saturday mornings you can salivate over the **open-air market** in p. Europa; on other days, try the covered market in p. Matteotti for plenty of fruit, vegetables, and nuts (open Tues.-Sat. 8am-1pm). The entrance is below street level. On summer nights the market becomes an outdoor *caffè.* Buy essentials at the **Supermercato STANDA,** corso Vannucci, 90. (Open Mon.-Sat. 8:30am-12:55pm and 3:30-7:55pm.) Complement your meal with the reasonably priced regional wines *Sagrantino Secco,* a dry, full-bodied red, or *Grechetto,* a light, dry white.

Trattoria Calzoni, via Cesare Caporali, 12 (tel. 290 72), across from Albergo Eden. Home away from home for those who have always wanted (or miss) an Italian grandmother. The distinguished Signora Maria lovingly whips up the pasta of your choice before your very eyes (L8000 including beverage). A full meal will run you L14,000. Open Mon.-Sat. 12:30-2:30pm and 7:30-9:30pm.

Ristorante Dal Mi' Cocco, corso Garibaldi, 12 (tel. 625 11), across from the University for Foreigners. What a deal! A great selection of regional specialties, and *menù* written in Umbrian dialect. Enjoy specially made *vernaccia,* a sweet after-dinner wine that tastes like nectar. A huge meal, including *antipasti,* 2 first courses, meat, vegetable, salad, dessert, mineral water, wine, and *vernaccia,* runs L18,000. Excellent music, too. Open Tues.-Sun. 12:30-3pm and 7:30pm-midnight. It may be necessary to reserve ahead.

Tavola Calda, p. Danti, 16 (tel. 219 76). Wide selection of meat and vegetables available cafeteria-style. Pizza L1200 per slice, sandwiches from L3500, and a decent *rosticceria.* Baked ziti L3300. Rambunctious late-night crowd. Open Sun.-Fri. 9:30am-3:30pm and 7-11pm.

Trattoria La Botte, via Volta della Pace, 33 (tel. 226 79), a few steps from the hostel in a small alleyway off via Bontempi. A family-run place frequented by teenagers. Fixed-price meals L11,000. Specialties include *penne alla norcina* (L6000) and pizza (only at night, L4500). Half-of wine L2500. Open Mon.-Sat. 12:30-2:30pm and 7-9:30pm.

Trattoria Fratelli Brizi, via Fabretti, 75 (tel. 213 86), around the corner and a few blocks down from the University for Foreigners. A pleasant atmosphere cultivated under vaulted ceilings. Well-prepared house specialties include *ravioli tartufati,* made with mushrooms, cream, and truffle oil. Pasta L7500, *secondi* L8000-10,000. *Menù* L20,000. Open Wed.-Mon. noon-2:30pm and 7:30-10:30pm.

Ristorante Del Sole, via della Rupe, 1, (tel. 650 31), off via Oberdan, 18, beyond p. Matteotti. One of the best restaurants in town; local specialties and a terrific wine list in an elegant atmosphere. Try the *umbricelli alla casalinga,* thick pasta with peppers in a garlicky tomato-parsley sauce (L8500). Full meals L24,000-26,000. Open Tues.-Sun. noon-2:30pm and 7-10pm.

L'oca Nera, via dei Priori, 78-82 (tel 218 89). Hidden in the caverns below the north-central quarter, this joint draws a crowd for its delicious food and quick, pleasant service. Best described as a German-American-Italian diner—the massive selection ranges from würtzel to *gnocchi* to hamburgers (avg. L5000 a dish).

Sights

Piazza IV Novembre

The city's most important sights frame p. IV Novembre; all other monuments of distinction are within a 20-minute walk of this spot. In the center of town (the middle of the piazza) lies the **Fontana Maggiore,** designed by native son Fra' Bevignate and decorated by Nicolà and Giovanni Pisano. The bas-reliefs covering the majestic double basin depict scenes from religious and Roman history, the allegories of the months and sciences (lower basin), and the saints and other historical figures (upper basin).

The 13th-century **Palazzo dei Priori** presides over the piazza; its long rows of mullioned windows and toothlike crenellation embody archetypal Perugian bellicosity. This building, itself one of the finest extant examples of Gothic communal architecture, shelters the impressive **Galleria Nazionale dell'Umbria** (tel. 203 16). The immense collection contains fine works by Tuscans Duccio, Fra' Angelico, Taddeo di Bartolo, Guido da Siena, and Piero della Francesca, but look particularly for its Umbrian art. Perugian Pinturicchio's gleeful use of color and disdain for Renaissance seriousness are not as evident in the works here as in Siena's *Piccolomini Library* or San Gimignano's *Chapel of Santa Fina,* but viewing his efforts on the *Miracles of San Bernardino of Siena* is still the visual equivalent of eating a *bacio.* Perhaps too sweet for some tastes (consider the effect of dipping your *bacio* in sugar syrup) are the works of Pietro Vannucci, alias Perugino, the town's most celebrated artist. His newly-restored *Adoration of the Magi* is the gallery's premier piece (unfortunately for the Perugini, many of the Peruginos which formerly graced the city now hang in the Louvre, testament to Napoleon's talents as an art thief). (Open Mon.-Sat. 8:45am-1:45pm and 3-7pm, Sun. 9am-1pm. Admission L8000.)

Next door in the **Collegio del Cambio** (Banker's Guild) (tel. 613 79), Perugino demonstrated what a talented artist could do with even a mundane commission. In his frescoes, he suffuses the entire piece with the characteristic gentle softness that he later passed on to his greatest pupil, Raphael. The latter is said to have collaborated on the *Prophets and Sibyls.* Notice also Perugino's self-portrait (*autoritratto*) on the left wall. In the small chapel adjacent to the chamber hang paintings of scenes from the life of John the Baptist by Giannicola di Paolo (1519), including an especially grisly decapitation scene with a grinning Salomé. Further toward the *piazza,* at #15, visit the **Collegio della Mercanzia.** This richly paneled room, begun in 1390, is the meeting-room for Perugia's merchant guild; to this day the guild's eighty-eight members meet here to debate tax law and local commerce. (Cambio and Mercanzia open Tues.-Sat. 9am-12:30pm and 3-6pm, Sun. 9am-12:30pm. Admission L2000, good for both.) You can visit the **Sala dei Notari,** containing interesting 13th-century frescoes, up the flight of steps across the fountain, for free.

At the end of the *piazza* rises Perugia's austere Gothic **duomo.** Though it was built in the 14th and 15th centuries, the facade was never finished. (Typically, the Perugini were going to use some marble they stole from Arezzo's cathedral-building supply during a battle, but the Aretini made them give it back when they won the next round.) Note the 16th-century door by Galeazzo Alessi facing the *piazza.* Fifteenth- to 18th-century embellishments of varying quality adorn the Gothic interior, but the town is most excited by the **Virgin Mary's wedding ring,** a relic snagged from Chiusi in the Middle Ages. The ring is kept securely under lock and key—15 locks and keys, in fact.

Around Via dei Priori

Stroll along via delle Volte della Pace (off via Bontempi), which follows the city's old Etruscan walls; or follow via dei Priori, which begins behind the palace, and via San Francesco past the church of the same name, to the spartan **Oratory of San Bernadino,** near the end of via dei Priori. Agostino de Duccio built it between 1457 and 1461 in the early Renaissance style, embellishing its facade with finely carved reliefs and sculpture. Look for a panel showing the Bonfire of the Vanities—San Bernadino, the only religious figure the Perugini ever respected, convinced the citizens to burn the superfluous relics of a consumer culture 50 years before Savonarola got Florentines to do the same. Inside San Bernadino, a 3rd-century Roman sarcophagus forms the altar.

Next door, only the pink-and-white facade of the 13th-century **San Francesco al Prato,** where San Bernadino used to stay, remains.

An unbearably medieval walk down via Ulisse Rocchi, the city's oldest street, will take you through the northern city gate to the **Arco di Augusto,** a perfectly preserved Roman arch built on Etruscan pedestals and topped by a 16th-century portico.

Past the newly cleaned **Palazzo Gallenga,** at the end of a little byway off medieval corso Garibaldi, lies the jewel-like **Church of Sant'Angelo.** The 5th-century chruch is the oldest in Perugia; the circular interior incorporates 16 columns appropriated from various ancient buildings. The small park in front of it makes for an alluring picnic spot. Behind the church, the gate **Porta Sant'Angelo** was built by the Perugian *condottiere* Braccio Fortebraccio ("arm strongarm").

The East Side

At the opposite end of town from the Porta Sant'Angelo, near via Cavour, towers the imposing **Church of San Domenico,** the largest in Umbria. A sneeze in here will echo for five seconds. The church's huge Gothic rose window (the largest in Italy) dramatically contrasts with the sobriety of its Renaissance interior. Don't miss the magnificently carved **Tomb of Pope Benedict XI,** finished in 1325, in the chapel to the right of the high altar; his bones lie in a box tied with a red ribbon on the wall. Next to the church, the **Museo Archeologico Nazionale dell'Umbria** occupies the old Dominican convent and showcases Etruscan and Roman artifacts. (Open Tues.-Sat. 9am-1:30pm and 3-7pm, Sun. 9am-1pm. Admission L4000.) Continue on corso Cavour, past the Porta San Pietro, and you'll come to the **Church of San Pietro.** It maintains its original 10th-century basilica form: a double arcade of closely spaced columns leads to the choir. Inside, the walls (and visitors) are overwhelmed by paintings and frescoes depicting scenes of saints and soldiers; among the mass of paint, look for Perugino's *Pietà* along the north aisle. (Churches open 8am-noon and 3:30pm-sunset.)

At the far end of corso Vannucci, the main street leading out from p. IV Novembre, lie the **Giardini Carducci.** These well-maintained public gardens are named after the 19th-century poet Giosuè Carducci, who wrote a stirring ode to Italy inspired by Perugia's historic zeal for independence. From the garden wall you can enjoy a broad vista of the Umbrian countryside: a castle or an ancient church crowns each hill. On the corner of the street below the gardens, a semi-circular lookout point shows you in which direction you're gazing and names the monuments in view. Go around the gardens and down via Marzia to see the **Rocca Paolina,** the 16th-century fortress built by Sangallo, long a symbol of papal oppression; its interior juxtaposes Italian antiquity and dubious modern art. Pope Paul III had Sangallo demolish this section of the city in the 1500s in order to create this prison. In 1860, when Perugia was liberated from the rule of the Papal States and became part of the now-unified Italy, the Perugini spontaneously began hacking it to pieces. Today it serves as a pleasant and fanciful escalator-shelter surrounded by the remains of this medieval quarter. The **Porta Marzia,** the Etruscan gate in the city wall, opens onto via Bagliona Sotterranea. This street within the fortress is lined with 15th-century houses that were buried when the gardens were built above. (Gate open Tues.-Sat. 8am-2pm, Sun. 9am-1pm.) The Rocca is also accessible by the escalator, which runs from 6am until 1am.

Entertainment

Perugia's biggest annual event is the glorious **Umbria Jazz Festival,** which draws performers of international renown for 10 days in July. (Admission L15,000-35,000. Some events free.) For information, contact the tourist office.

July and August bring **Estate in Levare,** a series of musical, cinematic, and dance performances. In September a **Festival of Sacred Music** features concerts in various churches. Check Palazzo Gallenga for listings of English films and other events. The last weekend of every month finds a **Mercato Antiquariato** at p. Piccinino. The two most popular places for drinks are the two *caffè* called **La Terrazza,** one in p. Matteotti and one below p. Grimana by the University for Foreigners. Shake your thing at any of the small discotheques that litter Perugia's streets.

Lake Trasimeno

This placid and somewhat marshy lake, 30km west of Perugia, is the ideal spot to enjoy some arcadian tranquility while watching fishers mend their nets in the hamlets along the shore. Things have not always been so peaceful; in 217 BC, Hannibal's elephant-straddling army, fresh from the Alps, routed the Romans on the plain north of the lake. The names of the villages of Ossaia (place of bones) and Sanguineto (the bloody one) recall the carnage that left 16,000 Roman troops dead.

In the summer, landlocked Umbria becomes so stiflingly hot that splashing in the murky waters of Trasimeno can actually be pleasant. Getting to Castiglione del Lago (on the west shore) and Passignano sul Trasimeno (on the north) is simple. Each day, several buses depart Perugia's p. Partigiani for both lakeside towns (L8400 round-trip). **Passignano sul Trasimeno** is easily reached by bus or train (Perugia-Florence line). You may consider circling through both towns via train (L3300), ferry (L6500), and then bus back to Perugia. The **Pro Loco** (tourist office) is at via Roma, 38 (tel. (075) 82 76 35) overlooking the peaceful city park (make a left if you're coming from the dock; go across the tracks and take a left if coming from the station). Here you'll find maps, hotel listings, and boat schedules. (Open Mon.-Wed. and Fri.-Sat. 9am-noon and 4-7pm, Thurs. and Sun. 9am-noon.) **Hotel Beaurivage,** via Pompili, 3 (tel. (075) 82 73 47) has spic'n'span doubles for L33,000, with bath L52,000. **Hotel Aviazione,** via Roma, 54 (tel. (075) 82 71 62) has the same for L40,000, with bath L56,000. It also offers **bike rental** (1hr. L5000, half-day L10,000, full day L20,000). (Hotel open Dec.-Oct.) Boats leave from the dock for Isola Maggiore (28 per day, 20min., L4500, round-trip L8500). Food in both towns is expensive; plan a picnic on the lakeshore.

Follow in St. Francis's footsteps and spend a delightful day on **Isola Maggiore,** Lake Trasimeno's only inhabited island. A capriciously opened and staffed **tourist information booth** is by the dock. If no one's there, just take a good look at the large map of the island on the other side of the dock. As you leave the dock, take a right and follow the path to the tip of the island (being careful not to squish the green-brown salamanders who will accompany you) to the ruined **Guglielmi castle.** A bit further on is a tiny chapel enclosing the hard rock where St. Francis spent 40 days in 1211. From here, hike five minutes up to the **Chiesa di San Michele Arcangelo,** with a wonderful view of the island. (Open Sun. 10:30am-noon and 3-6pm.) **Castiglione del Lago,** a quiet town appropriately crowned by a castle, is accessible only by road or water. From the bus stop, a flight of steps ascends to the town center. The **tourist office** p. Mazzini, 10 (tel. (075) 96 52 484), will help you find a hotel (singles from L40,000, doubles from L52,000), a room in a private home, or a private flat (from L190,000 per week). You can also **change money** and get boat schedules here. (Open Mon. 8am-1:30pm, Tues.-Fri. 8am-1:30pm and 3-7:30pm, Sat. 8:30am-1pm and 3-7:30pm, Sun. 9am-1pm.) For food, try the shops lining via Vittorio Emanuele, or hop into **Paprika,** via Vittorio Emanuele, 107, whose local specialties include *spaghetti al sugo d'anguilla* (spaghetti with eel sauce from the lake). (Open Fri.-Wed. noon-2:30pm and 7:30-10pm.) To reach the ruined medieval **castle** at the edge of town, walk down v. Vittorio Emanuele and over the grass between the stone wall and the olive trees near the hospital. Ramble along the ramparts for splendid lake views. Take viale Garibaldi down to the dock, where eight boats daily make the 30-min. trip to Isola Maggiore, the largest of the lake's three islands (L3300, round-trip L6400).

Assisi

There is no escaping the legacy of St. Francis in Assisi. The artistic movement he inspired has imparted to this medieval hill town a treasury of 13th- and 14th-century art. The saint's reputation also draws a staggering number of visitors each year, spawning a tacky commercialism which nonetheless gives Assisi a year-long festival atmosphere. Endowed with stunning churches, a medieval fortress, and excellent but expensive restaurants, Assisi merits a tour. Spend a night here to appreciate the charm of its winding streets and pink stone in the absence of herds of daytrippers.

Orientation and Practical Information

Piazza del Comune is the hub of Assisi. Via San Paolo leads off its "top" left-hand corner, via Portica runs from the "bottom" left-hand corner (towards the Chiesa di San Francesco), via San Rufino heads out from the "top" right-hand corner (towards hotels and the *duomo*), while corso Mazzini angles toward the Chiesa of Santa Chiara from the "bottom" right-hand corner. Towering above the city to the north, the **Rocca Maggiore** can help you re-orient yourself with a glance should you become lost among Assisi's winding streets.

Tourist Office: p. del Comune, 12 (tel. 81 25 34), 1 doorway to left of the SIP. Information and accommodations service. Harried, but friendly and extremely helpful. Ask about upcoming musical events. Open Mon.-Fri. 8am-2pm and 3-7pm, Sat. 9am-1pm and 4-7pm, Sun. 9am-1pm. Train and bus schedules posted outside. Beware: the tourist office on corso Mazzini is actually a travel agency.

Post Office: p. del Comune. Open Mon.-Fri. 8am-6:30pm, Sat. 8am-1pm, Sun. 8am-12:30pm. **Postal Code:** 06081.

Telephones: SIP, p. del Comune, 11. The most beautifully frescoed phone building in the world. Open daily 8am-10pm; off-season 8am-7pm. **Telephone Code:** 075.

Trains: Assisi lies on the Foligno-Teróntola **train line,** 30min. and L2400 from Perugia. At Teróntola change for Florence (L13,800); change at Foligno for Rome (L13,000) or Ancona (L10,500). Buses link the station, below the town near the Basilica of Santa Maria degli Angeli, with the town proper, 5km up the hill (every 30min., L1000).

Buses: ASP buses to Perugia (8 per day, L4200), Foligno (8 per day, L2000), and other surrounding hamlets, leaving from p. Matteotti. From p. Matteotti, walk down via San Rufino past the *duomo* to p. del Comune.

Swimming Pool: Centro Turistico Sportivo, via San Benedetto (tel. 81 29 91). Take the bus from p. del Comune. Open late July-Aug. daily 9:30am-7pm. Admission L5000.

Emergencies: tel. 113. **Police: Carabinieri,** p. Matteotti, 3 (tel. 81 22 39). **Hospital:** (tel. 813 91), on the outskirts. Take a city bus from p. del Comune. **First Aid:** tel. 81 28 24.

Accommodations

Reservations are crucial around Easter, and strongly recommended for the Festa Calendimaggio (early May) and in August. If you walk the few kilometers uphill to the hamlet of **Fontemaggio** along the road to Eremo delle Carceri, you will find a **youth hostel** and **campground** (tel. 81 36 36) offering single-sex, 10-bed rooms. The showers are hot, and there's a large market right next door. (Hostel L15,000 per night. Sheets included. Campground L5500 per person, L4500 per tent, L2000 per car. Open year-round.) The recently re-opened **Ostello della Pace (HI),** offers spanking new beds and breakfast for L16,000. (Lock-out 10am-5pm. Curfew 11pm.) If you prefer to be in town, ask the tourist office for a list of **religious institutions.** These are peaceful and cheap, but they shut down around 11pm.

Albergo La Rocca, via di Porta Perlici, 27 (tel. 81 22 84). Follow the signs to the *duomo,* and then take the second cobblestoned street to the left of the *duomo* as you face it. A great choice away from the crowds. Commodious, attractive rooms. Singles L27,000. Doubles L38,000, with bath L51,000. **Alunni Camere Maria Bocchini,** via dell'Acquario, 3 (tel. 81 31 82), off p. Matteotti, very close to Albergo La Rocca. The house is up the stairs by the archway. Signora Alunni Bocchini welcomes with a motherly smile. Clean, cool rooms. Singles L28,000. Doubles L35,000.

Camere Maria Fortini, via Villamena, 19 (tel. 81 27 15). Right on the main drag by p. Matteotti. Not marked as a *camere.* An assortment of colorful flowers on the front steps. Singles L25,000. Doubles L35,000, with bath L45,000.

Albergo Anfiteatro Romano, via del Teatro Romano, 4 (tel. 81 30 25), off p. Matteotti. A large restaurant with modern rooms in a picturesque section of town. Romantic views. Singles L28,000. Doubles L36,000, with bath L60,000. Showers included.

St. Anthony's Guesthouse of the Franciscan Sisters of the Atonement, via Alessi, 10 (tel. 81 25 42). The American sisters treat you like family. No room for asceticism here—the rooms are far too comfy. Gorgeous views of the town, a library full of English-language books, a garden, an orchard, and a relaxing terrace. 2-night minimum stay encouraged. Curfew 11pm. Singles L36,000. Doubles with bath L64,000. Breakfast included. Lunch L16,000. Open mid-March to mid-Nov.

Food

Assisi tempts you with a sinful array of nutbreads and pastries; *bricciata umbria,* a strudel-like pastry with a hint of cherries, is particularly scrumptious. The **bakery** at p. del Comune, 32, offers the widest selection, but the **Pasticceria Santa Monica,** nearby at via Portica, 4, boasts more palatable prices. (open 7am-1:15pm and 4-8pm). On Saturday mornings there's a **market** on via San Gabriele and via Alessi. For well-made *panini* and picnic basics try **Micromarket Baldoni,** via Fortabella, 61, near p. Unità and San Francesco. (Open Mon.-Sat. 8am-1pm and 3:30-8pm; closed Thurs. afternoon.)

Il Menestrello, via San Gregorio, 1A (tel. 81 23 34), off via Portico. A cavernous place encompassing a self-service eatery, a sit-down resturant, and a piano bar. Self-service *primi* L5000-7000, *secondi* L7000-15,000. Open Tues.-Sun. noon-2:45pm and 7pm-midnight.

Pizzeria Manzi Vincenzo, via San Rufino, on the left immediately off p. del Comune. Endearing artist shows you his provocative sociopolitical paintings while feeding you the best pizza in Assisi. He also gives little children free pieces, and speaks halting English with Neapolitan cadences. Slices L1500-3000. Open daily 8am-2pm and 4-7:30pm.

Ristorante La Fortezza, vicolo della Fortezza, 2B (tel. 81 24 18), near p. del Comune. Reputedly the best restaurant in town. The award-winning meals help make up for the pink tablecloths and pseudo-70s decor. Try *faraona alla fortezza* (guinea hen). Full meals run L20,000-35,000, but *primi* start at L9000. Open daily noon-2:30pm and 7-9:30pm.

Pallotta, via San Rufino, 4 (tel. 81 23 07), near p. del Comune. Extremely pleasant; family-run. Try their specialty *strangozzi alla pallotta* (pasta with mushrooms and olives, L8000). *Menù,* including wine and dessert, L17,500. Open Wed.-Mon. noon-2:30pm and 7-10pm.

Il Pozzo Romano, via Sant'Agnese, 10 (tel. 81 30 57), off p. Santa Chiara. The local favorite for pizza (L5000-8000). Scrumptious *crostini.* A huge selection of imported and domestic beers. Open Fri.-Wed. noon-2:30pm and 7-11pm.

Sights

St. Francis, born in 1182, abandoned military ambitions at age 19 and rejected his father's wealth to embrace asceticism. His repudiation of the worldliness of the church, his love of nature, and his devoted humility earned him a huge following throughout Europe, posing an unprecedented challenge to the decadent papacy. He continued to preach chastity and poverty until his death in 1226, whereupon the order he founded was gradually co-opted by the Catholic hierarchy. The result was the paradoxical glorification of the modest saint in churches named for him and for his follower St. Clare, founder of the Poor Clares, the female order of the Franciscan movement.

The **Basilica di San Francesco,** a double-decker celebration of devotion and artistry, bears witness to this conflict of integrity and bureaucracy. When construction began in the mid-13th century, the Franciscan order protested: Francis had adhered to a stark asceticism, and the elaborate church seemed an impious monument to wealth. As a solution, Brother Elia, then vicar of the order, insisted that a double church be erected—the lower level built around the saint's crypt, the upper as a church for services. The subdued art in the lower church commemorates Francis's modest life, while the glittering upper church pays tribute to his sainthood and consecration. This two-fold structure subsequently inspired a new Franciscan architecture.

Enter through the front of the church and you'll be overwhelmed—shafts of light angle sharply across the sky-blue ceiling and the walls are ablaze with Giotto's *Life of St.*

Francis fresco cycle. Giotto's early genius is evident in his illustration of Francis's turbulent path to sainthood, which starts on the right wall near the altar and runs clockwise, beginning with a teen-aged Francis in courtly dress, surprised by a prophecy of his future greatness. The cycle closes with an image of the saint passing through the mystical agony of the "Dark Night," stripping himself of the clothes his father had bought him, signifying a break with his former life. The final stage of his approach to God occurs in the 19th frame, where St. Francis receives the stigmata. Sadly, Cimabue's frescoes in the transepts and apse have so deteriorated that they look like photographic negatives. Most frescoes and sculptures have "History Tell" machines; it costs L1000 to view the history of each work.

Pietro Lorenzetti adorned the left transept with an outstanding *Crucifixion, Last Supper,* and *Madonna and Saints.* Above the altar four sumptuous allegorical frescoes formerly attributed to Giotto are now thought to be the work of the so-called "Maestro delle Vele." Cimabue's magnificent *Madonna and Child, Angels,* and *St. Francis* grace the right transept. Best of all are Simone Martini's frescoes in the first chapel off the left wall, based on the life of St. Martin. Descend through a door in the right side of the apse to a room that houses some of St. Francis's possessions: his tunic, his sandals, and sundry flesh-mortifying instruments. The precious piece which inspired the entire edifice, St. Francis's tomb, lies below the lower church (the steps to it are marked by a sign in the middle of the right aisle.) St. Francis's coffin was hidden in the 15th century for fear the war-mongering Perugians would desecrate it; it was only rediscovered in 1818. The stone coffin sits above the altar in the crypt, surrounded by the sarcophagi of four of his friends. (Mass in English in the upper church Sun. 8:30am. Tours in English of the whole structure Mon.-Sat. at 10am and 3pm; meet in front of the entrance to the lower church. Both churches open daily 6:30am-7pm, closed on Holy Days. No photography, no miniskirts, no short-shorts and no revealing shirts allowed—fashion police abound.)

Don't bypass the modern, well-lit **Museo Tesoro della Basilica,** with its graceful 13th-century French ivory *Madonna and Child,* 17th-century Murano glass work, and a fragment of the Holy Cross. (Open April-Oct. Tues.-Sun. 9:30am-noon and 2-6pm. Closed on holy days. Admission L3000.)

Via San Francesco leads away from the front of the Upper Church between medieval buildings interspersed with 16th-century additions—note especially the **Sala del Pelegrino** (Pilgrim Oratory, under restoration in 1992), frescoed inside and out. Via San Francesco boasts Italy's first public asylum, a 13th-century building at the corner of via Fortebella. At the end of the street p. del Comune marks the old **Roman forum.** Here, bits of Roman Assisi alternate with buildings of the 13th-century commune. (Open daily 9:30am-1pm and 3-7pm. Admission L2500, students with university ID L1500. For non-students, a good deal is the "biglietto cumulativo" which allows entry into the forum, the Rocca Maggiore, and the Pinacoteca, L6500.) As you come upon p. del Comune, you see the **Temple of Minerva,** with its compressed front, next to the Romanesque **torre.** The **Palazzo del Comune,** on the downhill side, contains the **Pinacoteca,** housing Umbrian Renaissance art. (Open daily 9:30am-1pm and 3-7pm, in winter daily 10:30am-1pm and 3-6pm. Admission L2500, university students L1500. Cumulative ticket L6500.) The post office stands on the site of the church in which St. Francis gained his first follower.

Steep via San Rufino climbs up from p. del Comune between closely packed old houses, bursting suddenly onto p. San Rufino to reveal the squat **duomo** with its massive bell tower. The restored interior lacks the facade's verve, but be sure to admire the first-century Roman cistern on your left as you enter. For an ascendant treat, continue uphill on the cobblestoned street to the left of the *duomo* as you face it, and take the steps that branch off to the left. At the top is the towering, dramatic **Rocca Maggiore.** (Open daily 9am-8pm; in winter 10am-4pm. Closed in very windy or rainy weather. Admission L3000, university students L1500. Cumulative ticket L6500.)

The pink-and-white **Basilica of Santa Chiara** stands at the other end of Assisi, on the site of the ancient basilica where St. Francis attended school. (Open Mon.-Sat. 6:30am-noon and 2-7pm; in winter until 6.) Inside you can contemplate the Byzantine crucifix that supposedly revealed to the saint his mission; at his behest, it is kept continually lit. Outside absorb the spectacular view or admire the seemingly weightless flying buttresses which support the church. The **Oratorio di San Francesco Piccolino,** in the upper part of vicolo di Sant'Antonio, is purported to be built around the stable where St. Francis was born, and the **Chiesa Nuova** nearby marks the site of his family's home.

Entertainment

Assisi's religious festivals all involve feasts and processions. An especially long dramatic performance comprises **Easter Week**. On Holy Thursday, a mystery play based on the Deposition from the Cross is acted out, and then on Good Friday and Easter Sunday, traditional processions trail through town. Assisi welcomes May with the **Festa di Calendimaggio** on May Day, a time for dressing up and eating out. A queen is chosen and dubbed Primavera (spring) as banners flutter all over town. The various neighborhoods compete in a noisy musical tournament. Classical concerts and organ recitals occur once or twice per week from April to October in the various churches. October 4 is the **Festival of St. Francis,** when a different region of Italy offers the oil for the Cathedral's votive lamp each year; that region's traditional dances and songs are performed in local costumes. During July and the beginning of August, the **Festa Pro Musica** features internationally known musicians and opera singers. For details, look for posters or ask at the tourist office.

Near Assisi

Several churches associated with St. Francis and St. Clare stand in the immediate vicinity of town. If you travel to Assisi by train, you'll see the huge **Basilica di Santa Maria degli Angeli.** The basilica itself shelters the **Porziuncola,** the first center of the Franciscan order (though actually owned by the Benedictines, to whom the Franciscans still pay the yearly rent—a basket of carp). In order to overcome temptation, St. Francis supposedly flung himself on thorny rosebushes in the garden just outside the basilica, thus staining the leaves forever red. The site grew popular when St. Francis instituted the annual **Festa del Perdono** (Aug. 2), during which an indulgence was (and is) awarded to all who come to the church. When he died in the adjacent infirmary, now **Cappella del Transito,** the chapel began to attract throngs of pilgrims, and a whole ring of supporting chapels sprang up.

A pleasant hour-and-a-half hike through the forest above the town leads to the most memorable and inspiring sight near Assisi, the **Eremo delle Carceri** (Hermitage of Cells). Pass through the Porta San Francesco below the basilica and follow via Marconi. At the crossroads take the left road, which passes by the Seminario Regionale Umbro. The site of St. Francis's retreats, this placid area better conveys the spirit of St. Francis than the opulent basilica. Inside the hermitage stick your head into the small cell where he slept, and outside, examine the stone altar where he preached to the birds. (Hermitage open daily dawn to dusk.)

A 15-minute stroll down the steep road outside Porta Nuova takes you to the **Convent of St. Damian,** where St. Francis received his calling, and later wrote the *Canticle of the Creatures.* The chapel contains fine 14th-century frescoes as well as a riveting woodcarving of Christ. (Open daily 10am-noon and 3-6pm.)

Monasteries, chapels, and churches built where St. Francis spoke or slept are sprinkled throughout southern Umbria, the eastern edge of Tuscany, and the northern Rieti province of Lazio. Those charmed by Francis's taste in central Italian countryside should consult those sections of this book, or ask the tourist office in Assisi about following in his footsteps.

Gubbio

Since 1960 this acutely picturesque town has been home to the National Board of Ancient Towns, an organization dedicated to preserving and restoring Umbria's historic hamlets. Today, cranes swing over the scaffold-dressed ancient stone walls in a desperate attempt to hold on to what once was. A strategic checkpoint on the Roman transapennine road via Flaminia, Gubbio, founded as "Iuvium" by the ancient Umbrian tribe, had long drawn pilgrims to the temple of a mountain god identified with Jupiter. From early on the scrappy city also cultivated an attitude, taking on a succession of intimidating opponents including Romans, Lombards, Perugians, and even Napoleon. In 1387 the Montefeltro forced Gubbio into the Urbino orbit, encouraging artistic endeavors to match martial ones. Gubbio claims Italy's first novelist, Bosone Novello Raffaelli, as well as its own school of painting and ceramic tradition. The dual legacy of art and war survives in the profusion of china and crossbows in the store windows.

Orientation and Practical Information

Despite winding medieval alleyways and bizarre conglomerations of buildings, Gubbio's layout is simple. **Piazza della Signoria,** the civic headquarters, set on a ledge of the hill on which the town is built, forms the center of the web. Buses will leave you off in p. Quaranta Mártiri. A short uphill walk on via della Repubblica, the street bordering the *Loggia dei Tiratori* (Weaver's Gallery), will connect you with corso Garibaldi, where you can find the tourist office.

Tourist Office: piazza Oderisi, 6 (tel. 927 36 93), off corso Garibaldi next door to the local Communist Party headquarters. Extremely helpful staff. English spoken. Open Mon.-Fri. 8:15am-1:45pm and 3:30-6:30pm, Sat. 9am-1pm and 3:30-6:30pm, Sun. 9:30am-12:30pm; off-season, Mon.-Sat. afternoon hours are 3-6pm.

Post Office: via Cairoli, 11 (tel. 927 39 25). Open Mon.-Sat. 8:10am-7:15pm. **Postal Code:** 06024.

Telephones: Easy Gubbio, via della Repubblica, 13. This brand-new office has phones, train information, and other tourist amenities. **Telephone Code:** 075.

Trains: There are no trains to Gubbio itself; the nearest station is at Fossato di Vico, 19km away on the Rome-Ancona line (L5700 from Ancona, L13,700 from Rome). Buses connect Gubbio and the station (Mon.-Sat. 10 per day, 6 on Sun., L2000). For tickets, go to **Clipper Viaggi,** in p. San Giovanni, 15 (tel. 37 17 48), the *piazza* up the hill from p. Quaranta Mártiri. Open daily 9:30am-1pm and 3:30-7pm.

Buses: via della Repubblica, 13-15 (tel. 927 15 44). Ticket office open daily 7:15am-1:45pm. To Perugia (12 per day, 1hr., L6200).

Emergencies: tel. 113. **Police: Carabinieri,** via Matteotti (tel. 927 37 31). **Medical Emergency:** tel. 923 91. **Hospital:** p. Quaranta Mártiri, 14 (tel. 923 91).

Accommodations

Gubbio is an easy day trip from Perugia or on the way to the coast. The town can be seen in a few hours—an overnight stay will drain your wallet unnecessarily. If compelled to stay, cruise for *affitta camere* if you encounter a dearth of hotel rooms.

Albergo Galletti, via Piccardi, 3 (tel. 927 42 47), off p. Quaranta Mártiri. Small and photogenic on the edge of medieval Gubbio. Hospitable proprietor. Singles L30,000. Doubles L45,000, with bath from L58,000. May be closed 2-3 weeks in June/July.

Pensione Grotta dell'Angelo, via Gioia, 47 (tel. 927 34 38), off via Cairoli. The angelic owners offer seraphic rooms. Singles with bath L48,000. Doubles with bath L70,000. Open Feb.-Dec.

Albergo dei Consoli, via dei Consoli, 59 (tel. 927 33 35), 100m from p. della Signoria toward p. Bruno. Ask for rooms with a view. Singles with bath L48,000. Doubles with bath L70,000. Open Feb.-Dec.

Hotel Gattapone, via Ansidei, 6 (tel. 927 24 89), off via della Repubblica. Well-furnished rooms with carpets. Vacancies likely. Singles L48,000. Doubles L70,000. All rooms with baths. Open Feb.-Dec.

Food

Guard against expensive meals in excruciatingly quaint settings. Go for the *salumeria* at p. Quaranta Mártiri, 36, across from the bus station, which makes great sandwiches for around L2500. (Open daily 7:15am-1:15pm and 3:15-8pm). Tuesday morning, there's a **market** under the *loggie* of p. Quaranta Mártiri. Local delicacies await you at **Prodotti Tipici e Tartufati Eugubbini,** via Piccardi, 17. Here you can sample *salumi di cinghiale o cervo* (boar or deer sausage) and *pecorino* cheese or pick up some truffle oil (so your truffles don't get sunburned). (Open daily 8:30am-1pm and 3:30-8pm.)

Trattoria Fiorella, corso Garibaldi, 86 (tel. 927 21 65). Centrally located. Excellent food in a family atmosphere. Complete meals including wine, *primi, secondi,* and fruit L18,000 and a more exotic *menù* for the same. Open Tues.-Sun. 12:15-2:30pm and 7:30-9:30pm.

Ristorante Il Bargello, via dei Consoli, 37 (tel. 927 37 24), in a little *piazza* down the road from p. della Signoria. Vaulted 14th-century ceiling, wine bottles lining the walls, pleasant smiles from the management. Outstanding pizza L4000-8000; Full meals from L25,000. Open Tues.-Sun. noon-3pm and 7-10pm. Major credit cards accepted.

Trattoria San Martino, via dei Consoli, 8 (tel. 92 73 25), near p. Bruno under a flowering trellis. The *paglia e fieno* (pasta with cream, peas, and ham) lingers happily in your tongue's memory. Complete meals around L20,000. Open Wed.-Mon. noon-2:30pm and 7-10pm. May be closed 2 weeks in June-July.

San Francesco e il Lupo, at the corner of via Cairoli and corso Garibaldi (tel. 927 23 44), near the Azienda. A homey place with lupine servings at ascetic prices. *Menù* L20,000. Open mid-July through mid-June daily noon-2:30pm and 7-9:30pm. **Pizzaria,** corso Garibaldi, 48, conveniently located just down from the tourist office. If you're on a strict budget and find yourself in Gubbio, pizza's the only way to go. Excellent inexpensive slices.

Sights

The first sight that greets you as you get off the bus is a pompous Fascist monument, erected in 1927. A grim and muscle-bound soldier stands guard, in a nightmarish martial vision. The ironically juxtaposed **Garden of the Forty Martyrs** (Giardini dei Quaranta Mártiri) honors those shot in reprisal for the assassinations of two occupying officials during World War II.

In **piazza della Signoria** the stark, empty feeling of the square is offset by the panoramic view over its ledge. To the right stands the **Palazzo dei Consoli,** one of Italy's most graceful public buildings. The pre-Renaissance white stone palace (1332) achieves an unpretentious harmony with its rows of asymmetric windows and arcades, its slender campanile, and square Guelph crenellations. Enter to examine the **Museo Civico's** idiosyncratic mix of stone sculpture and old coins, featuring the puzzling *Tavole Eugubine.* Discovered in 1444 near the Roman theater outside the city walls, these seven bronze tablets (300-100 BC) are the main source of our knowledge of the Umbrian language. Their ritual text spells out the social and political organization of early Umbrian society, while providing the novice with good hints on how to take auguries from the livers of animals. Upstairs visit the stately rooms of the **Pinacoteca Comunale,** an eclectic collection of paintings, wooden crucifixes, and 14th-century furniture. From the back room pass onto the *loggia* for the best view of Gubbio. (Open daily 9am-12:30pm and 3:30-6pm; Oct.-April daily 9am-1pm and 3-5pm. Admission L4000. Pinacoteca closed for restoration in 1992. The ticket guarantees admission to both museums.) Across the *piazza* stands **Palazzo Pretorio.** Climb to the top of the town, where the 15th-century **Palazzo Ducale** and the 13th-century **duomo** face off. Federico da Montefeltro commissioned Luciano Laurana, designer of his larger palace in Urbino, to build a miniature version here. The *duomo,* an unassuming pink Gothic building, boasts fine stained-glass windows (late 12th century) and Pinturicchio's *Adoration of the Shepards.*

As you return to p. della Signoria along via Ducale, note the huge barrels tucked in a basement under the *duomo.* Some of these wine casks are over 3.5m high; the largest, from the 1500s, has a capacity of 40,000. Via dei Consoli will take you to the **Bargello** and its fountain. This 13th-century edifice is just one of the many medieval buildings still in use; others nearby include the 13th-century **Palazzo del Capitano del Popolo,** on the street of the same name, and the 15th-century **Palazzo Beni** on via Cavour. Snake your way downhill along the narrow streets that run parallel to the Camignano stream. When you arrive in p. Quaranta Mártiri, the **Church of San Francesco** stands to the right. The church was constructed on the site of the house of the Spadalonga family, friends of St. Francis who gave him a tunic, eventually the prototype for today's Franciscan frock. The central apse holds the splendid *Vita della Madonna* (Life of the Madonna), a partially-destroyed 15th-century fresco series by Ottaviano Nelli, Gubbio's most famous painter. Across the *piazza* is the **weaver's loggia,** under whose shady arcades the 14th-century wool weavers stretched their cloth so that it would shrink evenly.

Besides wool, Gubbio's main industry in the Middle Ages was ceramics. Some particularly fine examples lie in the Palazzo dei Consoli Museum. Wander and enjoy the pottery and antiques at the **Antica Fabbrica Artigiana,** via San Giuliano, 3 (near the Bargello), a cavernous old palace.

During lunch, when all the museums close, take the seven-minute bird-cage chairlift (*funivia*) to the peak of **Monte Ingino** for a splendid view and prime picnicking real estate (round-trip L6000. Open July-Aug. Mon.-Sat. 8:30am-7:30pm, Sun. 8:30am-8pm; Sept. Mon.-Sat. 9:30am-7pm, Sun. 9am-7:30pm; Oct.-Feb. Thurs.-Tues. 10am-1:15pm and 2:30-5pm; June Mon.-Sat. 9:30am-1:15pm and 2:30-7pm, Sun. 9am-7:30pm.) While you're there, visit the **basilica and monastery of Sant'Ubaldo,** Gubbio's patron saint. The basilica houses the three *ceri,* the large wooden candles carried in the **Corsa dei Ceri** (May 15). On your way back to the center of town, stop at the **Church of Santa Maria Nuova** near the funicular station. The church contains the lyrical *Madonna del Belvedere* by Ottaviano Nelli. Ask the custodian at via Dante, 66, to let you in.

Entertainment

Corsa dei Ceri (May 15), a 900-year-old tradition and one of Italy's most noted processions, witnesses the three *ceri,* hourglass-shaped wooden towers brought to p. della Signoria from the basilica of Sant'Ubaldo. They are surmounted by wax statues of Sant'Ubaldo (in whose honor the festival is held), San Giorgio, and Sant'Antonio Abate. After 12 hours of flag-twirling and elaborate traditional preparations, squads of husky runners (*ceraioli*) clad in Renaissance-style tights heft the heavy objects onto their shoulders and race up Monte Ingino at a dead run. Making occasional pit stops for alcoholic encouragement, they eventually reach the basilica of Sant'Ubaldo, and plop down the *ceri* for safe-keeping until the following May.

During the **Palio della Balestra,** held on the last Sunday in May, archers from Gubbio and nearby Sansepolcro gather in p. della Signoria for the latest installment of a fierce crossbow contest dating back to 1461. If Gubbio wins, an animated parade ensues. (Gubbio's major industry these days is the production of toy crossbows for *balestra*—tourists.)

Spoleto

Like its peers in Umbria and southern Tuscany, Spoleto offers a picturesque hilltop setting and almost unbearably charming medieval streets; the town's biggest draw, however, is its summer arts festival, the *Festival dei Due Mondi* (of the Two Worlds). The composer Gian Carlo Menotti selected Spoleto in 1958 to be the test site for his claim that art need not be merely the *dolce* after *pranzo* (sweet after dinner), but could become a community's bread and butter. His optimism has not been betrayed: Spoleto's transformation into an internationally renowned center for the arts has brought prosperity to the town. Prices run as high as the cutting-edge aesthetic sensibility that has spawned expressionist pizza parlors and abstract Mondrianesque one-star hotels. Art of all sorts explodes around the town in late June and usually lingers through the summer. If you wish to rub shoulders with the pretentious and artistically inclined, remember to reserve six months ahead.

Orientation and Practical Information

Spoleto is typically Umbrian in that its narrow, cobblestoned streets make it difficult to navigate. **Piazza del Mercato** is the social center of the city, with many shop-lined streets radiating off it. Via Brignone connects p. Mercato with **p. della Libertà,** home of the tourist office and city bus stop. The adjacent **piazza del Municipio** and **piazza del Duomo** which contain most of the city sights, are close to p. Mercato as well.

Tourist Office: p. della Libertà, 7 (tel. 22 03 11). A warm and savvy office with an excellent if unwieldy map. English spoken. Open daily 9am-1pm and 4:30-7:30pm; off-season 9am-1pm and 3:30-6:30pm.

Post Office: p. della Libertà, 12 (tel. 467 27). Open Mon.-Sat. 8am-12:30pm and 3-7:30pm. **Postal Code:** 06049.

Telephones: During the festival, a **SIP** office appears on via Brignone between p. Mercato and p. Libertà (open daily 10am-midnight). At other times, forage for phones in bars and hotels. **Telephone Code:** 0743.

Trains: (tel. 485 16) in p. Polvani. From: Rome via Orte (2hr., L10,500); Ancona (2hr. 30min., L12,100); Perugia (10 per day, 1hr., L4400). From the station, take any orange bus to **piazza della Libertà** and the tourist office (L1000); otherwise it's a 30-min. uphill trek. Ask for a free city map at the newsstand in the station.

Buses: from p. della Libertà and p. Garibaldi, except service to Urbino and Rimini, which leave Mon.-Sat. mornings in the summer from via Flaminia (near the API gas station). 2 per day to Perugia and Assisi. Check at the tourist office for current schedules.

Emergencies: tel. 113. **Police: Carabinieri,** via dei Filosofi, 57 (tel. 490 44). English speaker available. **Hospital:** via Loreto, 3 (tel. 21 01), outside Porta Loreto.

Accommodations and Camping

Finding accommodations is difficult during the summer music festival. If you're organized enough to make reservations, do so as early as possible. Otherwise, the youth hostel in Foligno is an easy commute, as trains run all night long. Performances take place during the day, so getting back before curfew shouldn't infringe on your festival experience.

HI youth hostel, p. San Giacomo, 11 (tel. (0742) 528 82), in Foligno, 26km away. Curfew 11pm. L13,000 per person. Hot showers and breakfast included. Open March-Aug.

Camere Marcella Venanzi, vicolo II°, 1 (tel. 440 50), off of corso Mazzini, 42. A private home with pleasant rooms, a delightful proprietor, and an optimal location. Singles L25,000. Doubles L40,000.

Albergo Anfiteatro, via Anfiteatro, 14 (tel. 498 53). Whitewashed rooms with modern furnishings. Singles L32,000, with bath L48,000. Doubles L43,000, with bath L70,000.

Hotel Panciolle, via del Duomo, 3-4 (tel. 455 98). Newly graduated from *camere* to hotel. Friendly management and modern facilities. Doubles with bath L70,000.

Fracassa, via Focaroli, 15. Head toward the Roman Theatre, off via del Gesuiti. 7 tidy rooms managed by a charming proprietress. Singles L27,000. Double L35,000.

Camping Monteluco (tel. 22 03 58), behind the church of San Pietro, a 15-min. walk from p. della Libertà. Take viale Matteotti out to the tennis courts, then to the left across the highway. On the far side of the highway, take via San Pietro to the church, to the left, and up the hill. A short distance past the church a dirt path branches to the right and leads directly to the campground. Pleasant and shaded. L6000 per person, L4500 per tent. Open April-Sept.

Camping Il Girasole (tel. 513 35), next to a vast sunflower field (hence the name) near the small town of Petragnano. Hourly buses connect it with the train station. Quiet, with plenty of shade and hot showers. L6000 per person, L6000 per tent. Open Easter-Sept.

Food

An open-air market enlivens **piazza del Mercato** Monday through Saturday from 8:30am to 1pm. At other times, try the **Lo Sfizioso** market at p. Mercato, 26 (open Fri.-Wed. 7:30am-1:30pm and 4:30-7:30pm).

Ristorante Pentagramma, via Tommaso Martini, 4, off p. della Libertà, (tel. 372 33). Spoleto's finest traditional restaurant, cooking up only Umbrian specialties. Try the *zuppa di ceci* (chick pea soup, L8000). (Open Tues.-Sun. noon-2:30pm and 7-10pm.)

Trattoria Del Panciolle, via del Duomo 3-4 (tel. 455 98). Simple country fare; full meals L18,000-25,000. Specialties include *caciotta,* a delectable local cheese (L4000). Some outside tables on a shady porch overlooking the tree-laden *piazza.* Open Thurs.-Tues. noon-2:30pm and 7:30-10pm.

Borgo In, corso Garibaldi, 94 (tel. 22 21 91). Vivacious staff serves excellent calzones for L1500 apiece. *Primi* and pasta from L5000. Pizza from L2000. Open daily 7:30am-10:30pm.

Gelateria, via Mazzini, across from vicolo II° between p. della Libertà and San Filippo Church. The finest *gelato* in Umbria.

Sights

Tucked on a ledge midway between the great papal fortress above and the Roman Anfiteatro below rests Spoleto's monumental Romanesque **duomo.pa r**It was built in the 12th century and then augmented by a portico (1491) and 17th-century interior redecoration. An utter amalgam, its soaring bell tower was cobbled together from fragments of Roman structures and is held up by incongruous flying buttresses. Eight rose windows animate the facade, the largest of which bears the four symbols of the evangelists. Among them glitters a restored Byzantine mosaic (1207). The imposing Renaissance portal below casts an air of solemnity. Inside, look in a chapel off the right nave for some worn yet expressive figures by Pinturicchio, and note Carracci's *Madonna and Saints* in the right transept. Brilliantly colored scenes from the life of the Virgin by Fra' Lippi fill the domed apse. Lippi died here while working on these frescoes. Lorenzo the Magnificent asked the Spoletini to send his body back, but with tourism waning from lack of noble corpses, Spoleto insisted on keeping it. Lorenzo could only commission Lippi's tomb, which lies in the right transept and was decorated by the artist's son, Filippino. (*Duomo* open 8am-1pm and 3-7pm, in winter 7:30am-noon and 3-5pm.)

Santa Eufemia, across the *piazza* to the side of the *duomo,* lacks both the stature and the frescoes of the latter; poor Eufemia never amounted to much in the eyes of the Vatican. The beautiful Romanesque church named for her, however, was built with Umbria's first *matronea* or "womens' balconies." (Open 8am-8pm.)

Spoleto's many classical ruins testify to its prominence in Roman times. The first-century **theater** stands just outside the Roman walls, visible from p. della Libertà. Walk through the theater to the *loggia* next to it and then to the **Museo Archeologico,** with ceramic and statuary finds from the area. (Open Mon.-Sat. 9am-1:30pm and 3-7pm, Sun. 9am-1pm. Free.) The **Arco Romano** at the top of via Bronzino marked the entrance to the town, and farther along, the **Arco di Druso** marked the entrance to the forum (now p. del Mercato). On nearby via de Visiale you can enter a restored **Roman house.** (Open April-Sept. Mon. and Wed.-Sat. 9:30am-1pm and 3-7:30pm, Sun. 10am-1pm and 3-6pm, Tues. 3-7:30pm. Admission L2000; L5000 ticket includes admission to the Pinacoteca and Modern Art Museum as well.) Most of the Roman buildings have been recycled and their stones used to build churches, including **San Salvatore** (1km from the town center), one of the earliest surviving Christian churches in Italy, which retains some of its 4th-century architecture. (Open 7am-7pm; Oct.-May 7am-dusk.)

The **papal fortress,** or **Rocca,** sits on the hillside above Spoleto. The fortress, until recently a prison, was used during the war to confine Slavic and Italian political prisoners; in 1943 the prisoners staged a dramatic escape to join the partisans in the Umbrian hills. Follow the walk that curves around the fortress for panoramic views of Spoleto and the countryside. Farther on, you will reach one of the region's most stunning architectural achievements, the **Ponte delle Torri.** The 80m-high bridge and aqueduct, built in the 14th century on Roman foundations, spans the channel of the river Tessino. On the far bank rise the craggy medieval towers for which the bridge was named.

On the far side of the bridge, take the left fork past elegant villas and ancient churches to **Monteluco,** Spoleto's "mountain of the sacred grove." An invigorating hour-and-a-half climb through an ilex forest leaves you at the tiny Franciscan **Sanctuary of Monteluco,** once the refuge of St. Francis and San Bernadino of Siena. (Open May-Sept. 8am-1pm and 4-8pm. Buses leave p. della Libertà for Monteluco approximately every 1hr. 30min. when it's open. Ask at the newsstand for schedules and tickets; the bus costs L2000.) A five-minute stroll down the right fork brings you to the Romanesque **Church of San Pietro,** on whose façade a menagerie of bas-relief beasties appears, cavorting among cosmological diagrams and scenes from popular fables. Note the wolf wearing a monk's cowl and holding a book to the right of the door. Beyond the bestiary, you'll spot the remains of mosaics laid in the 5th century.

The **Museum of Modern Art** hosts exhibits of art displayed during the summer arts festival. From corso Mazzini, turn left on via Sant'Agata, then right on via delle Terme. The museum lies ahead on your right. (Open Mon. and Wed.-Sat. 9am-1pm and 3-7:30pm, Sun. 10am-1pm and 3-6pm, Tues. 3-7:30pm. Admission with L5000 cumulative ticket.) Spoleto's **Pinacoteca** (art gallery) is located in the Palazzo del Municipio on the *piazza* of the same name. (Admission with L5000 cumulative ticket.)

Entertainment

The **Festival dei Due Mondi** held from mid-June and mid-July has become one of Italy's most important cultural events. The festival features numerous high-quality concerts, operas, and ballets with performances by well-known Italian and international artists. Film screenings, modern art shows, and local craft displays abound. (Tickets L15,000-200,000; a few events are free. Purchase well in advance from travel agents in most large cities or by mail.) Before the Due Mondi, a series of organ concerts runs from April to June in various churches in Spoleto. The opera season, which includes a number of modern and experimental works, runs from late August to September. For one week, beginning the Thursday after Easter, Spoleto also hosts a series of studies about the Middle Ages, with workshops, lectures, and costumed performers.

Near Spoleto: Trevi

Trevi, perched on a hilltop of olive trees, about 30 minutes north of Spoleto by train, is a delightful place to spend an afternoon. The town is splayed in almost complete verticality along a hillside, and sighting it on the approach will simply floor you. Of course, entering also has its rewards. In **piazza del Comune,** the city center, you'll find the **Palazzo del Comune,** home to the **Pinacoteca Comunale.** The museum contains a replica, by Pinturicchio, of his *Madonna e Bambino,* now in London's National Gallery, as well as archeological finds from the area. Halfway along the road to Trevi's center from the train station (2km) is the **Chiesa della Madonna della Lacrime.** The church is on the site of a house on whose wall a Mother and Child with St. Francis had been painted in 1483. Two years later blood-colored tears were seen on the image, inspiring the construction of first a chapel, then a temple, then finally a church on the site. Perugino's frescoed *Adoration of the Magi, Saints Peter and Paul,* and *Annunciation,* from 1521, decorate the interior. The **Illumination Procession,** a candle-lit parade through town in honor of St. Emiliano, is held on January 27 in Trevi, while during the first three weeks in August the town celebrates "Trevi in Piazza," with musical and theatrical performances in p. del Comune.

Trevi is easily reached by train from Foligno (L1100) or Spoleto (L1400). From the station, it's 4km uphill to town. Ten city buses run per day to town (L600), the last at 7:50pm; nine buses per day run to the station, the last at 7:30pm. There is no place at the train station to buy bus tickets, so run into the *tabaccheria* 50m uphill from the stop. The bus leaves you at p. Garibaldi; from there, take via Roma to p. del Comune (also known as p. Mazzini). **Pro Trevi,** the information office, is at the far end of the *piazza* at #16; Trevi's **telephone code** is 0742.

Trevi harbors three sources of overnight accommodation. **Albergo Cochetto,** (tel. 782 29) is off p. Comune/Mazzini down via Dogali, and has well-furnished, if slightly overpriced, rooms. Singles run L31,500, with bath L47,500; doubles are L43,000, with bath L68,500. **La Cerquetta,** is found at via Flaminia, km 144 (tel. 783 66). Singles are L25,000, with bath L36,000. Doubles run L35,000, with bath L52,000. **La Casarecchia,** p. Garibaldi, 19 (tel. 98 03 43), by rights a *pizzeria,* also rents out rooms (about L35,000 per person). (*Pizzeria* open Tues.-Fri. 9am-1:30pm and 3pm-midnight, Sat. 9am-midnight, Sun. 5pm-midnight.)

Todi

According to legend, an eagle led the founders of Todi to this destination when it absconded with a tablecloth to a rocky crag. Reclaiming it, the intrepid ancestors celebrated the recovery of their picnic set by establishing tiny Todi in this aerial setting. History seems to have bypassed the steep, narrow streets of this isolated town; as a result it retains traces of its Etruscan, Roman, and medieval heydays. It also claims an unusually graceful central square and native son Iacopone da Todi, an early Franciscan poet.

Orientation and Practical Information

In the Todi of today, there's barely room for cars, let alone eagles with tablecloths. All areas in the city which don't house an important sight (and some which do) seem to have transmogrified into a parking lot. Piazza del Popolo, the center of town, houses the *duomo* and sundry *palazzi;* p. Jacopone and Umberto lie around the corner. Corso Cavour, mutating into via Roma, via Matteotti, and viale Cortesi, leads steeply downtown and out the ancient city walls to the hotels.

Tourist Office: p. del Popolo, 38 (tel. 88 31 58 or 894 25 26), under the stairs of the Palazzo del Capitano. Buy the map for L3000, since the photocopy they'll hand you is illegible. Open Mon.-Sat. 9am-1pm and 4-7pm, Sun. 9:30am-12:30pm and occasionally 4-6:30pm; in winter closed Sun. afternoon. They also have **telephones. Telephone code:** 075.

Post Office: p. Garibaldi (tel. 894 22 02). Open Mon.-Fri. 8:10am-6:25pm, Sat. 8am-noon. **Postal Code:** 06059.

Trains: The private **Ferrovia Centrale Umbria** (Central Umbrian Railway) provides infrequent service to Todi from Perugia, via Spoleto and Terni. City bus B runs to the station 15min. before every train; it'll carry you the 4km up to the town center (L1000).

Buses: ASP runs 7 buses per day to p. Jacopone from Perugia (80min., L4600). The last bus for Perugia departs at 5pm from the Chruch of Santa Maria della Consolazione, a 1km pleasant downhill walk from the town's center.

Emergencies: tel. 113. **Police: Carabinieri,** via Angelo Cortese (tel. 894 23 23). **Hospital: Ospedale degli Infermi,** via Matteotti (tel. 88 34 47).

Accommodations and Food

Hotels in Todi are expensive, scarce, and inconveniently located. The **Hotel Zodiaco,** via del Crocefisso, 23 (tel. 894 26 25), outside Porta Romana, has singles for L31,500, with bath L47,500, and doubles for L43,000, with bath L68,500. Further down the hill, **Hotel Tuder,** via Maestà dei Lombardi, 13, off v. Cortesi (tel. 894 21 84), proffers luxurious doubles with bath for L92,000. Both of these hotels lie along a busy highway; be careful walking here at night.

Pick up basics at the *alimentari* at via Cavour, 150. (Open Mon.-Sat. 7:45am-1:30pm and 5:30-8:30pm, closed Wed. afternoon.) Fresh fruit and veggies are at the **Frutta and Verdura market** on the corner of p. Jacopone (open Mon.-Wed. and Fri.-Sat. 7am-1:30pm and 4-8pm, Thurs. 7am-1:30pm).

AgriTodi, via San Lorenzo, 1 (tel. 894 23 96). Facing the *duomo* in p. del Popolo, take the small *via* to the right under the portico. Part of a cooperative formed to preserve culinary traditions, it's the place to taste local specialities. Not only do they have the most interesting menu, but they also have the lowest prices in town. *Bruschette* L3000-8000, *primi* L7000-8000, *secondi* L7000-10,000. Lots of local wines for sale. Open Dec.-Oct. Wed.-Mon. 10:30am-2:30pm and 4:30-10pm.

Ristorante Cavour, via Cavour, 21-23 (tel. 894 24 91). Tasty and filling meals L22,000. Excellent pizza about L5000. Specialty is *tortellini al tartufo nero* (with black truffles, L9000). Try to get a seat in the cool medieval dungeon. Open Feb.-Dec. Thurs.-Tues. noon-3pm and 7:30-9:30pm for meals, until 2am for pizza. AmEx.

Ristorante Umbria, via Santa Bonaventura, 13, (tel. 894 27 37) behind p. del Popolo. Serves award-winning Umbrian specialties, but be prepared to part with about L28,000. Magnificent view from the flowered terrace; on a clear night you can watch the sunset over the valley. Delicious pasta *al tartufo* (L15,000). Other *primi* from L9000. Open Wed.-Mon. 12:30-2:30pm and 7:30-11pm.

Bar 'lcopertio, via G. Matteotti, 120 (tel. 894 39 57). For those who wish to avoid the exorbitant expense of full-fledged restaurant dining. It's a trip downhill from p. Jacopone for delicious pizza, lasagna, *bruschettes,* fried vegetables, etc. L10,000 for a healthy portion of 2 items.

Sights

Piazza del Popolo is a stately ensemble of glowering palaces and a somber *duomo;* the square's air of authority is only slightly diminished by the cars which whiz around its edge. This *piazza* has been Todi's focal point since Roman times and remains its high point in altitude and architectural achievement. The **Palazzo del Capitano** (1290) stretches its cavernous portico across the east end of the *piazza* with peaked Gothic windows on the second floor, lending relief to the imposing facade. (Open 10am-12:30pm, 4-8pm.) The **Pinacoteca Civica** occupies the fourth floor; keep climbing for the fascinating frescoes in the **Sala del Capitano del Popolo** at the top of the exterior marble staircase. Huge wooden arches soar across the immense hall. A saw-toothed row of merlons crowns the adjoining **Palazzo del Popolo** (begun in 1213). Across the *piazza* from the *duomo,* the tower and facade of the **Palazzo dei Priori** (1297-1337) retain visages of medieval gloom despite the rows of Renaissance windows carved out in the early 16th century.

Directly across the *piazza* the rosy-faced **duomo** rests solidly atop a flight of broad stone steps. The central rose window and arched doorway command attention with their intricate decoration. Inside, Romanesque columns with Corinthian capitals support a plain wall punctuated by slender windows. The delicate Gothic side arcade, added in the 1300s, shelters an unusual altarpiece: the Madonna's head emerges in high relief from the flat surface of a painting. A strangely halcyon scene of the Last Judgment (16th century) occupies the church's back wall. Above hangs a contorted statue of Todi's mythical eagle. Ask the sacristan to light up the 8th-century crypt for you (L500). The intricate inlay of the chancel's wooden stalls (1530) testify to Todi's woodcarving artistry. (*Duomo* open daily 8:30am-12:30pm and 2:30-6pm.)

Neighboring **piazza Garibaldi** opens to a superb vista. On the right side of the *piazza* stands the Renaissance **Palazzo Atti** with a sadly deteriorated facade but beautiful rusticated stone corners. From the *piazza,* follow the signs leading off corso Cavour to the remaining walls of the **Foro Romano** and the nearby 12th-century **Chiesa di S. Ilario.** From here, it's a brief jaunt to the **Fonti Scarnabecco,** whose 13th-century porticoes still house one solitary working tap. Return to p. del Popolo and take via Mazzini to the majestically angular **Church of San Fortunato.** Built by the Franciscans between the 13th and 15th centuries, the church boasts Romanesque portals and a Gothic interior. The story of the sacrifice of Isaac decorates the space between the first and second columns to the right of the door. Note Masolino's fresco of the Madonna and angels.

To the right of San Fortunato, a path bends uphill toward **La Rocca,** a ruined 14th-century castle. Next to the castle, follow a sinuous path, appropriately named **viale della Serpentina,** to a breathtaking belvedere constructed on the remains of an old Roman wall. Further down stands the isolated **Church of Santa Maria della Consolazione,** an exquisite work of Renaissance architecture that may have been designed by Bramante. The Renaissance appreciation of forms composed of simple shapes finds a particularly serene expression here, with quarter-spheres rising from a central cube. The church's refined white interior shelters a Baroque polychrome altar; statues of the twelve disciples mark its circumference. If you're too beat to hike back up, city buses can transport you, as the church is located on a main road.

The **Mostra Nazionale dell'Artigianato** (National Exhibit of Crafts) takes place in August and September. For some years there has also been a national exhibit of antique and modern woodwork in April, since Todi, after all, is home to some of the finest woodcarvers in Italy. The city's most colorful festival is the **Mongolfieristico,** a three-day hot-air balloon show which occurs in mid-July. For information, contact the tourist office.

Orvieto

Orvieto's forbidding perch atop a volcanic outcropping and the dark closeness of its streets recall its origin as one of the cities of the Etruscan Dodecapolis. However, it is the medieval legacy that colors the city more strongly today. A papal refuge from the Middle Ages through the Renaissance, in the 13th century Orvieto drew Thomas Aquinas to its academies and saw the Crusades planned within its walls. A well-preserved medieval center provides the backdrop for the stunning 13th-century *duomo,* which has rewarded Orvieto's piety with touristic fame and wealth. Sample the product of the other local industry, the excellent white wine *Orvieto classico.*

Orientation and Practical Information

Orvieto lies midway on the Rome-Florence line. The city is also an hour from Perugia. From the train station, you cross the street to take the funicular up the volcano. When you reach the top you can walk up **corso Cavour** toward the center or take a shuttle to p. del Duomo. The journey takes about 15 minutes and costs L1000. Corso Cavour is the town's backbone, site of most of the city's restaurants, hotels, and shops. Via Duomo branches off c. Cavour and ends at p. del Duomo.

Tourist Office: p. del Duomo, 24 (tel. 417 72). Friendly staff is frazzled but patient. Get the incredibly complete pamphlet on hotels and restaurants, sights, and practical information. Complete information on trains and buses; city bus tickets and phone cards for sale. Open Mon.-Fri. 10am-2pm and 4-7pm, Sat. 10am-1pm and 4-7pm, Sun. 10am-noon and 4-6pm. Also has **telephones**. **Telephone Code:** 0763.

Post Office: via Cesare Nebbia, which begins after the Teatro Mancinelli, next to c. Cavour, 114 (tel. 412 43). Stamps are available at tobacco shops and there are mail drops scattered throughout the town. Open Mon.-Sat. 8:15am-6:40pm. **Postal Code:** 05018.

Trains: To Florence (L13,800), Rome (L10,500), and Perugia (L8800). **Luggage Storage:** L1500.

Buses: ACOTRAL, p. Cahen. 7 per day to Viterbo. **ACT,** p. Cahen, 10 (tel. 442 65). To Perugia (L10,500) and Todi (L7700). Buy tickets at the shop next to the station.

Emergencies: tel. 113. **Police:** p. della Repubblica (tel. 400 88). **Hospital:** p. del Duomo (tel. 420 71).

Accommodations

Da Fiora, via Magalotti, 22 (tel. 411 19), just off p. della Repubblica through small p. dell'Erba (take minibus B to Erba). The best deal in town. Not technically a hotel; the proprietress rents private rooms. Modest but spotless. Prices go down in winter. Doubles with bath L30,000. One person L15,000. If it's full, she'll make up beds on the couch or floor for L10,000 per person.

Hotel Posta, via Signorelli, 18 (tel. 419 09), near the Torre del Moro, between corso Cavour and p. Scalza. The location couldn't be better. A leafy garden and pleasant lobby. Curfew 11:30pm. Singles L35,000, with bath L50,000. Doubles L50,000, with bath L70,000. Open March-Dec.

Hotel Duomo, via Maurizio, 7 (tel. 418 87), down the steps to the left of the cathedral. Tidy, with white lace curtains and flowers in front. Large rooms. Curfew midnight. Singles L32,000. Doubles L43,000, with bath L69,000.

Camping Orvieto, (tel. (0744) 95 02 40), on Lake Corbara 14km from the center of town. Call from the station and they'll pick you up. Swimming pool and hot showers included. L7000 per person, L6000 per tent, L2500 per car. Open Easter-Sept.

Food

Most of the fixings will fix you for broke. At least the wine is cheap. An excellent *alimentari* sits below p. della Repubblica at via Filippeschi, 39. (Open Mon.-Tues. and Thurs.-Sat. 7:30am-1:30pm and 5-8pm, Wed. 7:30am-1:30pm.)

Cooperativa al San Francesco (tel. 433 02), on Cerretti off via Lorenzo Maitani off the front side of p. del Duomo. Follow the large signs, your nose, or the crowd. Extremely popular with locals. A huge restaurant, self-service cafeteria, and *pizzeria* all rolled into one. Dine at outdoor tables on a peaceful *piazza* or indulge in the cavernous interior. Pizza (at night only) and wine L11,000. Full meals L15,000. Open daily noon-3pm and 7-11pm.

Da Fiora, via Magalotti (tel. 411 19). Located just below her rent-a-room residence of all trades. Signora Fiora has now established a bustling restaurant enterprise featuring the best deals in town. Pasta, meat, and beer or wine (L12,000) will fill you as you take in a spaghetti Western on TV or enjoy the company of what appears to be the local Boys' Club.

Ristorante Del "Cocco," via Garibaldi, 4/6 (tel. 423 19). From p. della Repubblica walk through the grand archway and enter door on your left. Charming service and an excellent selection of pasta at reasonable prices.

La Volpe e l'Uva, via Ripa Corsica, 1 (tel. 416 12), off via della Pace. Don't be scared away by the murderous eyes of the quick brown fox on their sign—the food and decor here will keep you jumping over lazy dogs for more. Specialties include rabbit (of course) and *tagliatelle all'erba cipollina* (L6000). Live music on Sunday nights. Open Tues.-Sun. noon-3pm and 7:30-11pm.

Sights and Entertainment

The shuttle bus drops you off in p. del Duomo. The first glance at the 1290 **duomo** (Orvieto's fervor and pride) promises to be overwhelming: its fanciful facade, intricately designed by Lorenzo Maitani dazzles and enraptures the admirer with intertwining spires, mosaics, and sculptures. The bottom level features exquisitely carved bas-reliefs of the Creation and Old Testament prophecies, and a final panel of Maitani's highly realistic *Last Judgement;* the bronze and marble sculptures (1325-1964) emphasize the Christian pantheon, set in niches surrounding the rose window by Andrea Orcagna. The fabulous mosaics provide a day-long performance of light and shadow. Thirty-three architects, 90 mosaic artisans, 152 sculptors, and 68 painters worked for over six centuries to bring the *duomo* this far, and the work continues. The bronze doors were only installed in 1970.

The cathedral's 700th anniversary two years ago provoked a flurry of restoration that has left its masterpieces better than ever, among them the **Capella della Madonna di San Brizio** (sometimes called the **Capella Nuova**) off the right transept. Inside are Luca Signorelli's dramatic **Apocalypse frescoes,** considered to be his chef d'oeuvre. Begun by Fra Angelico in 1447, they were supposed to be completed by Perugino, but the city grew tired of waiting and enlisted Signorelli to finish the project. His mastery of human anatomy, dramatic compositions, and vigorous draftsmanship paved the way for the genius of Michelangelo.

On the left wall hangs the *Preaching of the Antichrist.* The prominent Renaissance dandy in a shimmering crimson costume to the left of the Antichrist is the painting's patron; behind the bald man to the patron's left is the red-hatted poet Dante. The woman with the outstretched hand on the other side is Signorelli's mistress; she is seen as a prostitute engaged in the basest act imaginable to a good Catholic of the day, taking money from a Jew. Behind her stand Columbus, Petrarch, Cesare Borgia, and Dante (again). Far off in the corner, Signorelli and Fra Angelico, in black, observe the proceedings. On the opposite wall, muscular humans and skeletons pull themselves out of the earth in the uncanny *Resurrection of the Dead.* Beside it is the *Inferno,* with Signorelli (a blue devil) and his mistress embracing beneath the fiery display.

In the **Cappella del Corporale** off the left transept, Lippo Memmi's *Madonna dei Raccomandati* hangs with abashed pride. In this chapel also sits the gold-encrusted

Reliquary of the Corporale (chalice-cloth), the *raison d'être* of the whole structure. The cloth inside the box caught the blood of Christ which dripped from a consecrated host in Bolsena in 1263, thereby substantiating the doctrine of transubstantiation, which the Papacy was still having some trouble putting over. (The *duomo* is open all year 7am-1pm, but the afternoon hours vary each month—2:30-5:30pm is a safe bet. Free, but bring plenty of L200 coins to illuminate the paintings.)

The austere 13th-century **Palazzo dei Papi** (Palace of the Popes) sits to the right of the *duomo*. Here, in 1527, Pope Clement VII rejected King Henry VIII's petition to annul his marriage with Catherine of Aragon, condemning both Catherine and English Catholicism to a dim future. Now the *palazzo* houses the **Museo Archeologico Nazionale.** Here you can examine Etruscan artifacts from the area, and even walk into a full-size tomb. (Open Mon.-Sat. 9am-1:30pm and 3-7pm, Sun. 9am-1pm. Free.) Across from the *duomo*, the **Museo Claudio Faina,** in the "Museo Civico" building, harbors more Etruscan finds. (Open Tues.-Sun. 9am-1pm and 3-6pm; Oct.-March 9am-1pm and 2:30-4:30pm. Admission L3000.)

A 10-minute walk down via del Duomo and then via Constituente puts you in p. Capitano del Popolo. Here, the 13th-century **Palazzo del Capitano del Popolo** sports the standard motif of Romanesque Orvieto architecture: a checkerboard band surrounding its windows. Return to corso Cavour and continue through p. della Repubblica into Orvieto's **medieval quarter.** The soils of the verdant slope below p. San Giovanni are enriched by the graves of thousands who perished in the Black Death of 1348. Drop by the small church **San Lorenzo de Arari,** with dozens of luminous frescoes and an Etruscan altar beneath its Christian successor.

On the eastern edge of town, down via Sangallo off p. Cahen, you can descend the **Pozzo di San Patrizio** (St. Patrick's Well). Having fled just-sacked Rome, Pope Clement VII wanted to ensure that the town did not run out of water during a siege, and in 1527 commissioned Antonio da Sangallo the Younger to design the well. (Open daily 8am-8pm; in winter daily 8am-6pm. Admission L6500 includes the Museo Greco.) After cooling off in the clammy well shaft, enter the **Fortezza,** where a fragrant sculpture garden and lofty trees crown battlements that overlook the Umbrian landscape. (Open 7am-8pm; Oct.-March 9am-7pm.)

On Pentecost (42 days after Easter), all Orvieto celebrates the **Festa della Palombella.** Small wooden structures filled with fireworks and connected by a metal wire are set up in front of the *duomo* and the Church of San Francesco. At the stroke of noon, the San Francesco fireworks are set off, and a white metal dove shoots across the wire to ignite the explosives. **Concerts** are held in the *duomo* evenings in August. If you're around in early June, don't miss the **Procession of Corpus Domini,** a solemn parade celebrating the Miracle of Bolsena.

Near Orvieto: Civita

Civita, not just another quaint town teeming with tourists, is slightly off the beaten path but well worth the hike. Literally a one-horse town, Civita is crammed onto the pinnacle of a small mountain. It is accessible via foot bridge from Bagnoregio or foot path through the valley between the two mountain towns. Civita's residents (all 20 of them) will invite you into their backyards or basements where you can see their private collections of Etruscan and Roman relics for a small fee. Take a picnic lunch or dine in the sole café. To get there take a bus from Orvieto to Bagnoregio (30min., L3000 round-trip). Civita is a 15-minute hike from the last bus stop. Buses run throughout the day; the last one returns at 5:20pm.

The Marches (Le Marche)

The mountain peaks and undulating hills of the Marches taper into the Adriatic Sea and stunning central Italian hill towns give way to resortdom the farther east you go. Patches of wheat, maize, and olives spangle the region's numerous valleys and coastal plain. Originally inhabited by the Gauls and Picenes, the area later fell under Roman control. It received its present name in the 10th century, when it was a border province of the Byzantine Empire; in the 12th and 13th centuries the powerful Montefeltro family of Urbino and the Malatesta clan of Rímini ruled, sowing the Marches' towns with sumptuous churches and palaces.

Since World War II, summer tourism has emerged as the mainstay of the region's economy. A crowded strip of international beach resorts has sprung up beside the ancient cities that dot the Marches' serene shoreline. Germans predominate in summer, turning the coast into a string of little Munichs-by-the-sea. Senigallia and Fano have retained scraps of charm, but secluded beach is an essentially extinct species along the Adriatic.

Divide your time between the coast and the region's two hilltop gems—Renaissance Urbino and medieval Áscoli Piceno, both less than 90 minutes from the sea. Direct trains roll from Rome to Ancona (4hr. 30min.), and vacation buses cross to Urbino, Áscoli Piceno, and the coast from Tuscany and Umbria. The Milan-Lecce coastal line also serves the region.

Pésaro

Pésaro offers glitzy, crowded beaches to compete with Rímini's, along with a quiet, inviting old city. Not the least of the city's attractions is its proximity to magnificent Urbino, less than an hour away.

Orientation and Practical Information

Pésaro lies on the main Bologna-Lecce route along the Adriatic coast. From Rome, take a train toward Ancona (6 or 7 per day), then change at Falconara to one of the frequent *locali* to Pésaro (4hr. 30min., L19,000). The center of the old city is **piazza del Popolo.** Walk across the small *piazza* in front of the train station onto viale del Risorgimento and then continue on via Branca (5min.). To reach p. della Libertà and the beach, take bus #1, 2, 6, 7, or 11 to viale Trento (in summer only; L600). Buses will drop you either at the train station or p. Matteotti. From the latter, take via San Francesco to p. del Popolo; from there take via Rossini, which becomes viale della Repubblica, directly to the beach.

Tourist Office: EPT, via Mazzolari, 4 (tel. 636 90), off via Rossini near p. del Popolo. A palace of information. Open Mon.-Sat. 8am-1pm. **Azienda di Promozione Turistica (APT),** v. Rossini, 41 (tel. 636 90), Friendly, English-speaking staff can help you find a room. Open June-early Sept. daily 9am-noon and 4-6:30pm. Another branch at the train station (tel. 683 78).

Post Office: p. del Popolo (tel. 691 55), at the beginning of via Rossini. Open Mon.-Sat. 8:30am-5:30pm. **Postal Code:** 61100.

Telephones: SIP, p. Matteotti, behind the AGIP station. Open daily 8am-8:30pm. **Telephone Code:** 0721.

Buses: p. Matteotti, down via S. Francesco from p. del Popolo. Buses #1, 2, 4, 5, 6, 7, 9, and 11 stop at p. Matteotti. To: Fano (frequent buses, 15min.), Ancona and Senigallia (5 per day, 1hr. 30min.), and Urbino (8 per day, 1hr., L2600). Also an express bus to Rome (1 per day, 4hr. 30min.).

Emergencies: tel 113. **Police:** p. Cinelli, 6 (tel. 339 91). **Hospital:** p. Cinelli (tel. 36 11). **Medical Assistance:** tel. 314 44. **Pronto Soccorso,** tel. 329 57.

Accommodations and Camping

Except in July and August, you should have no trouble finding a bed.

Ostello Ardizio (HI) (tel. 557 98), at Fosso Sejore 6km from town. Take the AMANUP bus toward Fano from p. Matteotti (6:30am-10pm every 30min., L600). Quality hostel with 88 beds, in a serene area close to the beach. Fastidiously kept. L14,000 per person. Breakfast included. Meals L12,000. Reservations essential in July and Aug. Open May-Oct.

Hotel Liana, viale Trieste, 102 (tel. 683 30). Big, clean rooms with private bath and euphoric views of the hills and sea. One block from the beach. May-June: singles L35,000, doubles L50,000, full pension L40,000. July: singles L35,000, doubles L55,000, full pension L46,000. August: singles L38,000, doubles L60,000, full pension L54,000.

Pensione Ristorante Arianna, via Mascagni, 84 (tel. 319 27), 100m from the beach. Spotless, basic rooms, excellent food. Singles L35,000. Doubles L55,000. Shower included. Reservations essential. Full pension is a good deal (L57,000, low season L45,000), and the food is tasty.

Hotel Mamiani, largo Mamiani, 24 (tel. 355 41 or 356 19), off p. del Popolo. Away from the beach strip. Unbelievably nice, but you'll pay for it. A little too much pink in the decor. Singles with bath L70,000. Doubles L100,000.

Camping Panorama (tel. 20 81 45), 7km north of Pésaro on the *strada panoramica* to Gabicce Mare. Take bus #1 to the end; from there it's a 20-min. uphill walk. A path leads to a quiet beach. L5500 per person, L9950 per tent. Off-season, L4050 and L7850. Hot showers included. Open May-Sept.

Campo Norina (tel. 557 92), 5km south of the city center on the beach at Fossoseiore. Take the bus for Fano from p. Matteotti (L600). L6200 per person, L7600 per tent. Off-season, L4500 and L6000. 4-person bungalows L52,000, off-season L48,000. Open April-Oct.

Food

Pésaro's **public market** is at via Branca, 5, off p. del Popolo behind the post office (open Mon.-Sat. 7:30am-1:30pm). Booths in the market sell hot *piadini* (round unleavened bread) with prosciutto, cheese, or spinach for about L2000. **Pizzerie** line the beach, while **alimentari** crowd the sidewalk *bars* on corso XI Settembre. Best of all is the **STANDA supermarket** upstairs at via Branca, 52, off p. del Popolo. (Open Tues.-Sat. 8:30am-12:30pm and 4-8pm, Mon. 4-8pm.)

Mensa Arco della Ginevra, via della Ginevra, 3, near Musei Civici. A self-service cafeteria with elephantine portions. Hearty complete meal with wine or water L8900. Open Mon.-Fri. noon-2:30pm.

Harnold's, p. Lazzarini (tel. 687 86), close to Teatro Rossini. The loud rock they play has Rossini dancing on his grave, but it's excused by the wide range of eccentrically named, satisfying *panini* (L3000). Open Thurs.-Tues. 11:30am-2am.

Trattoria da Maria, via Mazzini, 73 (tel. 687 64). The place to go for a home-cooked meal. Gruff owner with no half-baked ideas about the international language of food. *Primi* from L4000. *Secondi* from L7000. Try the fresh *zuppa di pesce* (fish soup). Open Fri.-Wed. noon-3pm and 7-11pm.

Sights and Entertainment

The robust arcade and *putti*-weighted window frames of the 15th-century **Ducal Palace,** home of Pésaro's ruling della Rovere clan, preside over the **piazza del Popolo,** Pésaro's main square. Savor the grace of Pésaro on **corso XI Settembre** and its side streets where narrow passages under blossoming balconies pass open arcades and sculptured doorways. Off the *corso* on via Toschi Mosca, the **Musei Civici** (tel. 312 13) house a superb collection of Italian ceramics and primitives. (Open Tues.-Sat. 9am-8pm, Sun. 9am-1pm; Oct.-March Tues.-Sat. 8:30am-1:30pm, Sun. 9:30am-12:30pm. Admission L4000.) A fine collection of photographs, portraits, theatrical memorabilia, letters, and scores pertinent to the composer's life awaits at the **Rossini Birthplace and Museum,** via Rossini, 34 (Casa Rossini). (Open Tues.-Sat. 10am-10pm, Sun. 10am-7pm. Admission L2000.)

Unfortunately, most of Pésaro's fine Gothic churches languish beneath excessive Baroque ornamentation; wring your hands over the overwrought **Church of San Domenico** on via Branca. An exception is the modest **Church of Sant'Agostino** on corso XI Settembre. Enter to see its beautiful late 15th- and early 16th-century wooden choir stalls inlaid with still-lifes, landscapes, and city scenes. (Open 9am-12:30pm and 3:30-8pm.) For a fine example of art nouveau folly, head toward the beach; just before p. della Libertà on the left, 19th-century **Villino Raggeri** drips with icing-like stucco work.

The evening *passeggiata* (slick threads and *gelato* are *de rigueur*) cruises along viale Trieste and p. della Libertà. Older folk meander through p. del Popolo, window-shopping in riizy stores. Popular watering holes for the youthful are **The Bistro,** viale Trieste, 281, under Hotel Cruiser, and **Big Ben,** via Sabbatini, 14, between the Palazzo Ducale and the Conservatorio Rossini.

Pésaro hosts the **Mostra Internazionale del Nuovo Cinema** (International Festival of New Films) the first two weeks of June. Movies are shown in the buildings along via Rossini, and at the Teatro Comunale Sperimentale off p. del Popolo. The fortune of opera composer Rossini (born here) endowed a music school, the Conservatorio di Musica G. Rossini, which sponsors events throughout the year. Contact the conservatory at p. Olivieri for a schedule. The annual **Rossini Opera Festival** begins in early August. Opera performances and orchestral concerts continue until September. Contact the Azienda for exact dates and prices, or reserve tickets through the information office, via Rossini, 37 (tel. 301 61).

Urbino

If you only visit one town in Italy, make it Urbino. A perfectly harmonious ensemble, under the aegis of philosopher/warrior Federico da Montefeltro (1444-1482) the city exemplified the finest in Renaissance style and tradition. It is no wonder that Baldassare Castiglione described Federico as the "light of Italy" and set the elegant dialogues of his book *The Courtier* in Urbino's Palazzo Ducale. Urbino's fairytale skyline has changed little in the last 500 years. And while tourists shape the character of many cities, Urbino owes its flair to its university students, still imbued with the creative spirit of native sons Raphael and Bramante.

Orientation and Practical Information

The **SAPUM bus** from Pésaro's p. Matteotti or train station is cheap, frequent, and direct (10 per day, 1hr., L3500). After winding up steep hills, the bus will deposit you at borgo Mercatale, above which lies the beautiful city center. A short uphill walk, or a ride in the elevator, takes you to **piazza della Repubblica,** the city's hub.

Tourist Office: p. Duca Federico, 35 (tel. 24 41). Distributes a list of hotels and a small map. Open Mon.-Sat. 9am-1pm and 3-7:30pm; off-season 8:30am-2pm.

Buses: Information tel. 97 05 02. Departures from borgo Mercatale. Timetable posted at the beginning of corso Garibaldi, under the portico at the corner bar on p. della Repubblica.

Post Office: via Bramante, 22 (tel. 25 75), right off via Raffaello. Open Mon.-Fri. 8:30am-5:30pm, Sat. 8:30am-1pm. **Postal Code:** 61029.

Telephones: SIP, p. Rinascimento, 4, off p. Duca Federico. Open daily 8am-10pm. **Telephone Code:** 0722.

Public Toilets: Albergo Diurno, via Battisti, 2, off p. della Repubblica. Toilets L200. Showers L2000. Open daily 7am-noon and 2-7:30pm. Also on via San Domenico, off p. Duca Federico.

Emergencies: 113. **Police:** p. della Repubblica, 3 (tel. 26 45 or 32 04 91). **Hospital:** via B. da Montefeltro (tel. 32 93 51, 32 81 21, or 32 81 22), to the north of the city out of p. Roma.

Accommodations and Camping

Cheap lodging is rare in Urbino. If you can't get into one of the following places, try one of the many *affitta camere,* inexpensive rentals that target Urbino's students. Ask for a list at the tourist office, or check at **Trattoria Leone,** in p. della Repubblica. Signposts around **via Budassi** may also prove helpful. For longer stays, write to the Università degli Studi, calle dei Cappuccini.

Albergo Italia, corso Garibaldi, 52 (tel. 27 01), off p. della Repubblica, near the Palazzo Ducale. A charming hotel with affable management. Patio, great view, and elevator. 48 elegant rooms. Singles L33,000, with bath L39,000. Doubles L41,000, with bath L54,000.

Pensione Fosca, via Raffaello, 67 (tel. 32 96 22). Top floor. Signora Rosina takes good care of her guests. Small, charming rooms. No baths in rooms. Singles L30,000. Doubles L40,000.

Hotel San Giovanni, via Barocci, 13 (tel. 28 27). A relatively modern hotel with a helpful manager. Restaurant downstairs. Singles L35,000, with bath L48,000. Doubles L50,000, with bath L65,000. Triples with bath L75,000.

Camping Pineta, via San Donato (tel. 47 10), in the *località* of Cesana, 2km from the city walls. L6000 per person (L3000 per child), L12,500 per tent. Open June 1- Sept. 15.

Food

Many *paninoteche, gelaterie,* and burger joints lurk around p. della Repubblica. Execute comprehensive shopping at **Supermarket Margherita,** via Raffaello, 37. (Open Mon.-Sat. 7:45am-12:45pm and 5-7:45pm. Closed Thurs. afternoon.)

Ristorante Rustica, via Nuova, 5 (tel. 25 28), across from Club 83. An excellent joint. Delicious pizza from L3000. *Secondi* from L9000. Traditional atmosphere. Open Thurs.-Mon. noon-3pm and 7pm-1:30am.

Ristorante Pasta à Gogo, via Valeria, 16 (tel. 29 42). *Primi* L6000-8000. *Secondi* L12,000-14,000. *Aperitif della casa* is Kyr (L4000). Elegant full meals from L16,000. Service 10%. Open Tues.-Sun. noon-2:30pm and 7-11:30pm.

Ristorante Ragno d'Oro (tel. 22 22), on p. Roma at the top of via Raffaello. Quality home cooking on an outdoor patio. Try their fantastic pasta (L4500). Don't miss their *cresce sfogliate* (an Urbino specialty: flaky, flat bread filled with meats, vegetables, or cheeses, L3000-5000). Open July-Aug. daily noon-3pm and 7pm-midnight.

Pizza Evoé, p. S. Franceso, 3 (tel. 48 94). Very popular with young crowd. Pizzas from L4500. Cover L1500.

Pizzeria Le Tre Piante, via Foro Posterula, 1 (tel. 48 63), off via Budassi. Spectacular view from the outside tables, and delicious food to boot. Pizza dinners L4000-6000, others from L15,000. Open Tues.-Sun. noon-3pm and 7pm-2am.

Sights

Urbino's most remarkable monument is the Renaissance **Palazzo Ducale** (Ducal Palace). The façade, which overlooks the edge of town, boasts a unique design attributed to Ambrogio Barocchi: two tall, slender towers enclose three stacked balconies. Most of the rest of the palace, celebrated in Italy as "the most beautiful in the world," was designed by Luciano Laurana. Enter the palace from p. Duca Federico. The interior **courtyard** is the quintessence of Renaissance harmony and proportion (under disproportionate, discordant restoration in 1992). To the left, a monumental staircase takes you to the private apartments of the Duke, which now house the **National Gallery of the Marches,** a delightful museum whose exhibits, many displaying Duke Federico's penchant for an oddity, are incorporated through the meandering hallways his palace. Eyeball Berruguete's famous portrait of Duke Federico (who sports the world's most famous broken-nosed profile), Raphael's *Portrait of a Lady,* Paolo Uccello's tiny, strange *Profanation of the Host,* and Piero della Francesca's completely unsettling *Flagellation* before considering the *Ideal City,* a perfectly proportionate, perfectly unpeopled Renaissance curio (attribution uncertain). The most intriguing room of the palace is the Duke's study on the second floor, where stunning inlaid wooden panels give the illusion of real books and shelves covered with astronomical and musical instruments. Nearby, descend a circular stairway to the Cappella del Perdono and the Tempietto delle Muse, where the Christian and pagan components of the Renaissance ideal coexist. The chapel once served as a repository for holy relics accumulated by the Duke. Eleven wooden panels representing Apollo, Minerva, and the nine muses at one time covered the walls of the temple, but all have been removed (eight of them are currently in Florence's Galleria Corsini). The **Archeological Museum,** on the far side of the *palazzo's* courtyard, is free with admission to the National Gallery, but you can only enter when the sporadic guide is on duty. (*Palazzo* open Mon.-Sat. 9am-2pm, Sun. 9am-1pm. Admission L8000.)

At the end of via Barocci lies the 14th-century **Oratorio di San Giovanni Battista,** decorated with brightly colored Gothic fresco-work of Lorenzo and Giacomo Salimbeni, representing events from the life of St. John. If you speak Italian, the *custode* can give you a wonderful explanation of how fresco painters used lamb's blood as ink for their sketches. (Open daily 10am-noon and 3-5pm. Admission L2000, but you will be obliged to see S. Giuseppe next door for another L2000.) **Raphael's house,** via Raffaello, 57, is now a vast and delightful museum with period furnishings. His earliest work, a fresco entitled *Madonna e Bambino,* hangs in the *sala.* (Open Mon.-Sat. 9am-1pm and 3-7pm, Sun. 9am-1pm. Admission L4000.) Hike up to the **Fortezza Albornoz** (turn left at the end of via Raffaello) where the awe-inspiring view of the Ducal Palace and the rest of the city demands a picnic. (Open daily 8am-6pm. Free.) For information about English-speaking tours, try contacting Marguerite Laciura at 32 89 40.

Entertainment

Urbino's p. della Repubblica serves as a modeling runway for local youth in their boho threads. Take a walk down this fashion ramp and then stroll (or climb) the serpentine streets at dusk. If you seek more active entertainment, dance the night away at **Club 83** on via Nuova. Throughout July you can attend the **Antique Music Festival** in Church of S. Domenico. A cheaper alternative, and more popular with students, is the **University ACLI,** on via Santa Chiona, a bar with music and small crowds. All this begins in August, when the Italian university summer session convenes. August also brings the ceremony of the **Revocation of the Duke's Court,** replete with Renaissance costumes. Check at the tourist office for the exact date in 1993.

Senigallia

Senigalli's "Spiaggia di Velluto" (Velvet Beach) has lured a swarm of Riviera-style hotels pregnant with sand-crazy tourists. The historic center becomes a nighttime refuge from the dancin' and romancin', but the price for quiet authenticity remains prohibitive.

Orientation and Practical Information

Railroad tracks bisect Senigallia: the old town with its fountains and Renaissance *palazzi* lies on one side, the tidy, modern beachfront on the other. From the station, exit on the beach side (by *binario* #3) and walk straight ahead to the tourist office. From the bus station at Portici Ercolani, follow the river to the train tracks, take the *sottopassaggio* underneath the station and continue on to the tourist office.

Tourist Office: p. Morandi, 2 (tel. 792 27 25), halfway between the station and the beach. Ugly building shelters efficient staff. Pick up the booklet *Estate 93* and their map. English spoken. Open Mon.-Sat. 9am-1pm and 4-7pm, Sun. 9am-noon; Oct.-March Mon.-Fri. 8am-2pm, Tues. and Thurs. also 3:30-6:30pm.

Post Office: via Armellini, 7. Open Mon.-Sat. 8:15am-7:40pm. **Postal Code:** 60019.

Telephones: SIP, on via Marche. Open Mon.-Sat. 8:30am-1pm and 3-9pm, Sun. 3-9pm. Also in front of the train station. **Telephone Code:** 071.

Trains: at viale Bonopera and p. Morandi (tel. 792 41 52), close to the beach. Trains hourly to Pésaro (30min., L2800) and Ancona (30min., L2100). Also to Rome (4hr. 30min., L27,100). **Buses:** Informazioni Biglietteria Autostazione (tel. 792 58 05), on via Montenero next to the stadium. All buses stop at the station and at Portici Ercolani. Daily buses to: Ancona (13 per day, 45min., L1200); Pésaro (5 per day, 45min., L1200); Fano (5 per day, 30min., L1200); Rome (1 per day, 4hr. 30min.); Milan (1 per day, 4hr.). If the ticket office is closed, buy your ticket on the bus.

Emergencies: tel. 113. **Police: Questera,** p. Roma (tel. 662 92 88). **Hospital:** (tel. 662 44), on via Cellini at via Rossini. **Medical Assistance:** Across from Hotel Ritz and next to Hotel Bologna. Officially open July-Aug. daily 9am-1pm and 3-7pm.

Accommodations

Senigallia wields a paralyzing abundance of hotels. The kindly officials at the tourist office will make inquiries for you, so head there first. Some hotels on the beach are true *pensioni* and require a minimum three-day stay, but there are many good hotels in the historic town center, just a 10-minute walk from the beach. In July and August make reservations. At other times of the year you will have the pick of the litter at bargain prices.

Pensione Ambra, via Rieti, 126 (tel. 792 66 34). 1 block from the beach, with 52 clean and comfortable rooms. Hospitable management will nurse you back to health after the hike from the tourist office and station. Good meals at restaurant downstairs. Full pension (L44,000-55,000; off-season L32,000-40,000) isn't a bad deal. Singles with bath L26,500. Doubles with bath L47,000.

Pensione Trieste, via Trieste, 27 (tel. 792 72 79). A couple of blocks from the beach in a breezy neighborhood. High season singles with bath L40,000; doubles with bath L55,000. Low season singles with bath L30,000; doubles with bath L45,000.

Pensione Azzurra, via La Spezia, 1 (tel. 792 64 64), 1 block from the beach. Modern, clean rooms inside a periwinkle-blue building near the free tennis courts. High season singles with bath L50,000; doubles with bath L70,000. Low season singles with bath L35,000; doubles with bath L40,000.

Camping

There are more than 20 campgrounds along the beach. The beaches and waves near the campgrounds are generally better than in Senigallia proper. A complete list is available at the tourist office; always call ahead.

Summerland, via Podesti, 236 (tel. 792 68 16). L3200 per person, L5500 per small tent, L11,000 per large tent. July: L4800, L6500, and L13,000. August: L5200, L6500, and L13,000. Sixteen 4-person bungalows L30,000, June 15-30 and Sept. 1-15 L33,000, July L41,000, August L46,000. Open June 1-Sept. 15.

Helios, lungomare Italia, 3/B (tel. 691 69). L5300 per person, L6300 per small tent, L9800 per large tent. Off-season: L3700, L4250, and L6900. Open May 1-Sept. 10.

Spiaggia di Velluto, lungomare Da Vinci (tel. 648 73). L5200 per person, L8000 per small tent, L9800 per large tent. Off-season: L4500, L5000, and L8000. Open April 15-Sept. 6.

Food

The pizza places along the beach are adequate and inexpensive. Hoard supplies at **Supermarket Sidis Discount,** across from the train station (open Mon.-Sat. 8am-noon and 4:30-7:30pm, Sun. 8am-noon). There is also a **fish and vegetable market** at the Foro Annonario in the old town (open Mon.-Sat. 8am-1pm).

La Taverna, via Bandiera, 55 (tel. 638 09), at via Arsilli, in the city center. Fantastic food and prices. Try any one of their generous pasta dishes (from L7000) and top it off with a plate of fresh figs and prosciutto (L7000). *Secondi* L12,000. Open daily noon-2:30pm and 7:30-10:30pm.

Il Boscaiolo, via Marchetti, 36 (tel. 653 36), off via Massai near p. Saffi in the city center. Eat outdoors at shady wooden tables. Their specialty, *Gnochetti Sardi al Salmone,* is L7500. Pizza L5000-7500. Cover L2000. Open daily in summer noon-2pm and 7:30pm-midnight.

Delize del Centro, via Arsilli, 50 (tel. 646 29). This spiffy *tavola calda* has an endless supply of tasty dishes. *Primi* L4000-5000, *secondi* L5000-L8000. Open daily 9:30am-2pm and 5:30-9:30pm.

Sights and Entertainment

See the tiny old center in half a day, then hit the beach for the circus of vacationing Italian families. Start from the **Portici Ercolani,** long stone arcades that grace the south side of the Misa River and enclose a curving walkway alongside numerous bars and *caffè.* Behind the Portici Ercolani on the via Gherardi hides the superb 16th-century **Chiesa della Croce** (Church of the Cross). Its smoldering, intricately detailed golden interior provides the setting for Federico Barocci's *Transport of Christ to the Sepulcher*

(1592). (Open daily 6:30am-1pm and 5-8pm.) At via Commercianti, 20, off p. Simon-celli, the ancient **synagogue** is the sole remnant of the old Jewish ghetto. The Duke of Urbino lured a sizeable Jewish population here by offering housing and quasi-citizen-ship to anyone willing to live in the malaria-blasted city.

The **piazza del Foro Annonario,** a circular "square" surrounded by 30 Doric col-umns, leads to the **piazza del Duca,** dominated by the "lion's fountain." On one side of the square, the modest exterior of the **Palazzetto Baviera** bears some remarkably ani-mated 15th-century stucco decorations illustrating scenes from the Bible and antiquity, executed by Federico Brandani of Urbino. (Open Mon.-Sat. 10am-noon.) The fortress across the way is the **Rocca Roveresca** (1480), a fine example of Renaissance military architecture. (Open Tues.-Sat. 9am-1pm and 3-7pm, Sun. 9am-1pm. Admission L2000.)

There is life after sunset in Senigallia. Discos abound near the beach area; try **Snoopy, Shalimar Club, Number One,** or **Zero Babele.** Most places charge a L8000-10,000 cover which includes your first drink (drinks average L5000). Women are often admitted free. The **water slide** near the Hotel Ritz on the beach offers slithery refuge from the heat (6 slides L5000, 10 slides L8000).

Ancona

Named by the Greeks for the elbow (*ankon*) shape of the harbor, Ancona is the ar-chetype of a port city. Its value as a center of trade was first recognized by the emperor Trajan, who developed the city in the first century AD; in the Middle Ages, Ancona reached the height of its importance in trade with the East. Today, the cargo is ferry-happy tourists—not spices and silks. But Ancona retains a certain appeal. The old town and Romanesque cathedral are worthy of more than a cursory glance on the way to the dock.

Ferries

Get complete and accurate schedules at the **Stazione Marittima** on the waterfront just off p. Kennedy; bus #1 runs to and from the station (L1000). All the ferry lines op-erate ticket and information booths. The helpful **information office** in the green train car parked outside the station gives free guided tours of Ancona twice a day in summer, as well as free museum tickets and a coupon good for L4000 worth of munchies in a local bar. (English spoken. Open daily 8am-2pm and 3:20-9:30pm.)

Most travel agents have up-to-date schedules, but ferries are fickle, so call and check on dates and prices. An **arrivals/departures board** for the upcoming week hangs in-side the main entrance of the station. Most lines give discounts (up to 50%) for round-trip tickets, and student and senior reductions are usually available, too. Make reserva-tions if you're traveling during July or August. **Be at the *stazione* at least two hours before departure.**

Karageorgis: tel. 27 45 54 or 27 72 04. To Patras (Mon., Wed., and Fri.-Sat., from L82,000; mid-Aug. to late June from L60,000).

Marlines: tel. 20 25 66. To: Igoumenitsa, Patras, and Corfu (Wed. at 1pm and Sat. at 8pm; July-Aug. also Fri. at 10pm, L74,000; mid-Aug. to June L60,000); Iraklion, Rhodes, and Limassol (July-Aug. Fri. at 10pm; L96,000, L80,000, and L210,000 respectively).

Minoan Lines: tel. 567 89. To: Corfu (May-Oct. Fri.-Wed. at 9pm; mid-June to mid-Oct. daily at 9pm; L82,000; mid-Aug. to mid-June L66,000); Igoumenitsa and Patras (May-Oct. Tues.-Wed. and Fri.-Sun. at 9pm, same prices); Cephalonia (May to mid-Oct. Mon. at 9pm, from mid-June also Thurs. at 9am, same prices); Piraeus (same times; L92,000, off-season L76,000); Paros (same times; L128,000, off-season L112,000); Samos (same times, same prices); and Kusadasi, Turkey (same times; L155,000, off-season L135,000).

Strintzis: tel. 286 43 31. To: Corfu, Igoumenitsa, and Patras (Mon.-Tues., Thurs., and Sat., June 20-Aug. 8 L82,000; off-season L66,000; student discount L55,000, off-season L40,000.

Orientation and Practical Information

Ancona is an important junction on the Bologna-Lecce train line and is also served by trains from Rome. The center of town, **piazza Cavour,** is a 10-minute ride on bus #1 from the train station (L800). Buy the ticket at the station or at the *tabacchi* across the *piazza*. **Corso Garibaldi** and **corso Mazzini** connect piazza Cavour to the port.

Tourist Office: in the train station (tel. 417 03). Open daily 8am-6:30pm. Lightly staffed branch office at Stazione Marittima. Open daily 8am-2pm and 3:20-9:30pm.

Post Office: viale della Vittoria (tel. 20 13 20 or 517 28). Open Mon.-Fri. 8:15am-7:40pm, Sat. 8:15am-1pm. **Postal Code:** 60100.

Telephones: SIP, corso Stamira, 50, off p. Roma. Also at p. Cavour. Both open daily 8am-9:30pm. **ASST,** p. Rosselli, in front of the station. Open daily 7am-midnight. **Telephone Code:** 071.

Buses: departures from p. Cavour and the train station (tel. 20 27 66). Timetables posted at p. Cavour. To: Pescara (3hr.), San Benedetto (2hr.), Urbino via Fano (2hr. 30min.), Pésaro (1hr. 30min.), and Senigallia (35min.).

Trains: p. Rosselli (tel. 439 33). To: San Benedetto (1hr., L6500); Áscoli Piceno (1hr. 45min., L9300); Pescara (2hr., L10,500); Pésaro (1hr. 30min., L4300); Rome (4hr., L29,200); and Milan (5hr., L30,000).

Car Rental: Avis, via Marconi, 17 (tel. 20 70 470). From L600,000 per week with unlimited mileage. Free drop-off anywhere in mainland Italy. They speak English.

Public Toilets: at p. Stamira, Stazione Marittima, and Scalone Nappi.

Emergencies: tel. 113. **Police:** tel. 288 88. **Hospital:** at via XXV Aprile, 15 (tel. 59 61).

Accommodations

In summer, people waiting for ferries crash at the Stazione Marittima, but you'll find lots of reasonably priced hotels in the lively town center. Avoid the overpriced lodgings in the area by the train station. Make reservations or arrive early—rooms fill quickly in the summer.

Hotel Cavour, viale della Vittoria, 7 (tel. 20 03 74), 1 block from p. Cavour. Take bus #1 to the beginning of viale della Vittoria. The fragile-looking elevator will take you to large, elegant rooms on the 3rd floor. Doubles with bath L50,000.

Pensione Centrale, via Marsala, 10 (tel. 543 88), on the 4th floor. Fine rooms with high ceilings. Singles L25,000. Doubles L35,000, with bath L50,000. Showers L2000.

Pensione Astor, corso Mazzini, 142 (tel. 20 27 76). Functional rooms and an affable manager. Singles L25,000. Doubles L40,000, with bath L45,000.

Pensione Milano, via Montebello, 1/A (tel. 20 11 47), near the town center. Avoid rooms overlooking the *autostrada* feeder road below. Singles L20,000. Doubles L30,000. Closed during part of the summer.

Food

The port harbors a good number of inexpensive restaurants. Regional specialties include *brodetto* (fish stew), *pizza al formaggio* (cheese bread), and *vinisgrassi* (lasagna with chicken livers and white sauce). Pack a meal for your ferry ride at the old-fashioned **Mercato Pubblico** (across from corso Mazzini, 130), where you'll find the four food groups well-represented. (Open Mon.-Sat. 7:30am-12:45pm and 5:15-7:30pm; off-season Mon.-Sat. 7:30am-12:45pm and 4:30-7pm.) **Supermarket SIDIS,** at via Matteotti, 115, deals groceries at reel-'em-in prices. (Open Mon.-Sat. 8:15am-12:45pm and 5-7:30pm; closed Thurs. evening.)

Trattoria 13 Cannelle, corso Mazzini, 108 (tel. 20 60 12), at p. Roma opposite the eponymous fountain. Packed with locals, this joint really satisfies. *Primi* L8000. *Secondi* L12,000-20,000. Open Mon.-Sat. noon-2:30pm and 8-10pm.

Osteria del Pozzo, via Bonda, a tiny passage off p. Plebiscito. Look for kelly green. Popular, cheery, and cheap. Specialties include fried fish and *spaghetti al frutti di mare* (with seafood). Full meals around L19,000. Open Mon.-Sat. noon-2:30pm and 7:30-10pm.

Trattoria "La Cantinetta," via Gramsci, 1 (tel. 20 11 07), convenient to the old town. Friendly Anconan regulars. *Primi* L5000, *secondi* L7500-10,000. *Menù* L19,500. Also has a bar. Cover L2500. Open Mon.-Sat. 7am-1am; off-season 7am-midnight.

Caffè Diana, viale Vittoria, 1/D (tel. 20 22 16). Behemoth plate of spaghetti an unbelievable L4000! Open Mon.-Sat. 7am-midnight.

Sights

Survey the Anconan sea and sky from **piazzale del Duomo,** atop **Monte Guasco.** Climb up via Papa Giovanni XXIII, or take bus #11 from p. Cavour. If you decide to walk, you'll enjoy the beautiful **Scalone Nappi,** a verdant stairway street. (Follow the left-hand steps at the point where the street forks; there are only 244 steps, and the vista is magnificent.) In p. del Duomo you'll find the **Cathedral of San Ciriaco,** erected in the 11th century on the site of a Roman temple to Venus. Its stolid Romanesque design is the outcome of the confluence of Apulian Romanesque from the south and the remnants of Byzantine from the north. (Cathedral open daily 9-10:30am and noon-6pm.)

Via Pizzecolli, the charming main street of the old quarter, reaches from via Papa Giovanni XXIII to the fine Venetian-Gothic doorway of the **Church of San Francesco delle Scale** (St. Francis of the Steps) before entering the courtyard of the **Government Palace** and **piazza Plebiscito.** Up the street, across from the **Loggia dei Mercanti** (Merchants' Gallery), stands the Romanesque **Church of Santa Maria della Piazza,** its façade overcharged with blind arches and bestial sculptures.

After decades of restoration (World War II bombings and a 1972 earthquake were among its trials), the **Museo Archeologico Nazionale delle Marche** is open for business on via Ferretti above via Pizzecolli. The impressive collection's best pieces include the Ionian *Dinos of Amandola,* some wonderful Greek vases, and two life-size equestrian bronzes of Roman emperors. (Open Mon.-Sat. 9am-1:30pm, Sun. 2:30-7:30pm.) Ancona's painting gallery, the **Galleria Comunale Francesco Podesti,** is housed in the 16th-century **Palazzo Bosdari** at via Pizzecolli, 17. Carlo Crivelli's tiny, flawless *Madonna col Bambino* completely shows up Titian's *Apparition of the Virgin,* recently restored to the full glory of its original colors. Don't miss the eerie and vaguely oriental 13th-century Tuscan sculpture. (Open Tues.-Sat. 10am-7pm, Sun. 9am-1pm. Admission L3000; handicapped, over 60 and students free; Sun. free for all.) Evenings in Ancona demand a stroll on the tree-lined esplanade from corso Garibaldi past p. Cavour (where the statue of tricky political hero Camillo Cavour now entertains dozens of pigeons) to viale della Vittoria. The tourist office's booklet *Estate 93* fills you in on events of interest; also pick up a summer cinema schedule. In mid-July, the **Festa della Birra e del Rock** (Rock'n'Beer Fest) features religious hymns and weak tea with milk.

Áscoli Piceno

According to legend, Áscoli was settled by Greeks who were guided westward by a woodpecker—a *picchio*—which gave the city its surname and provided a symbol for the Marches. Áscoli was the metropolis of the Piceni people, a quiet Latin tribe that controlled much of the coastal Marches and had the woodpecker as their clan totem. Whatever its origins, Áscoli has always been fiercely independent, from its role as a center of anti-Roman power during the Social Wars to its successful resistance to Nazi occupation. In the late 13th century, this independence produced a splendid architecture that remains unspoiled and fantastical. Known as the "town of travertine" for the white limestone of which it is built, Áscoli rests on a plain at the confluence of the Castellano and Tronto Rivers, enclosed by the nearby mountains, which form a natural amphitheater. Stick to the historic center; avoid the ungainly new town.

Orientation and Practical Information

Áscoli is about one hour by bus or train from San Benedetto del Tronto, which is itself one hour from Ancona on the Bologna-Lecce train line. **Cotravat** buses, cheaper, less crowded, and more frequent than the trains, leave San Benedetto del Tronto for Áscoli about every 45 minutes (L2300). If you do take the train, hop the bus (L800) that stops in front of the station and get off at the bus station behind the *duomo*, where the Cotravat buses stop as well. Take via XX Settembre off p. Arringo in front of the *duomo* to via del Trivio, which connects to corso Mazzini and p. del Popolo.

Tourist Office: Ufficio Informazioni, p. del Popolo, 17 (tel. 25 52 50). Very helpful. Open April 15-Sept. 30 9am-12:30pm and 3-7:30pm.

Post Office: via Crispi, off corso Mazzini. Open Mon.-Sat. 8:15am-7:40pm. Fermo Posta open Mon.-Sat. 8:30am-1pm and 4-7:40pm. **Postal Code:** 63100. **Telephone Code:** 0736.

Buses: all leave from viale de' Gasperi (behind the cathedral) except Amadio, which runs from viale Indipendenza. Timetable outside on the wall at **Agenzia Viaggi Brunozzi,** corso Trento e Trieste, 54/56 (tel. 504 60). Buy train and bus tickets here. Open Mon.-Fri. 9am-1pm and 4-7pm. **ARPA** to: Pescara (5 per day, 2hr., L5600) and Rome (daily at 2:20pm, 8hr.). If the Agencia is closed, you can get tickets to S. Benedetto in a *tabacchi*.

Emergencies: tel. 113.

Accommodations

If you're looking for a way to make a lot of money in a beautiful city, open a hotel in Áscoli. The situation here is desperate—the city's youth hostel has been closed indefinitely since 1991.

Albergo Piceno, via Minucia, 10 (tel. 25 25 53), near the cathedral and the bus stop. Close to the center of things, and so clean you could eat off the floor, should the urge strike. If you get a room without bath, you will not have access to a shower. Singles L30,000, with bath L35,000. Doubles L40,000, with bath L45,000. Triples with bath L70,000.

Cantina Dell'Arte, via della Lupa, 8 (tel. 25 57 44 or 25 56 20), behind the post office. In the medieval heart of town, modern rooms with fine furniture, TVs, and private baths. Singles L35,000. Doubles L60,000. Triples L80,000. Quads L100,000.

Hotel Pavoni, via Navilella, 135 (tel. 34 25 75), 3km ahead on the road to San Benedetto. Quiet and affordable, partly because it's in outer exurbia. Take bus #3 from p. Arringo (L800). Singles L30,000, with bath L36,000. Doubles L44,000, with bath L55,000. Extra bed L20,000.

Food

You can fill your tummy without emptying your pockets here—an excellent meal should run L8000. There's also an **open-air market** in p. San Francesco, behind p. del Popolo (Mon.-Sat. mornings). In p. Santa Maria Inter Vineas, the small **Supermarket Gierre** sells local *porchetta*. (Open Mon.-Fri. 9am-1pm and 3:30-8pm, Sat. 9am-1:30pm.)

Trattoria Lino Cavucci, p. della Viola, 13 (tel. 503 58). An excellent choice. *Primi* L3500-L4500. Wine L1000 for half-. Open Sat.-Thurs. noon-3pm and 7-11pm.

Cantina dell'Arte, via della Lupa, 5 (tel. 25 11 35), across from the hotel. A family-run restaurant with long communal tables. Specializes in 2 kinds of dumpling: the square *bauletti* and the donut-shaped *nidi di rondine* (swallows' nests), stuffed with ricotta or meat (both L5000). Complete meal L12,000. Open Mon.-Sat. noon-3:30pm and 6:30-10pm.

Trattoria da Giovanna, rua dei Marcolini, 3, (tel. 252 08), a tiny alley off p. Arringo. Like your mother's kitchen. Giovanna feeds the amiable military crowd regimental portions of food and drink. Mediocre pasta, excellent meat. *Menù* L15,000. Open Mon.-Sat. 11:30am-3:30pm and 6-11pm.

Ristorante da Vittorio, p. Arringa, 3 (tel. 25 93 86). Sample local specialities: stuffed olives L6000, *porchetta* sandwiches L3000. Grilled rabbit, pigeon, and chicken L9500. Open daily 8am-11pm; in winter Wed.-Mon. 8am-11pm.

Restaurant L'Orchida, largo dei Cataldi, 9 (tel. 25 38 70), down a quiet alley. Touristy, a little too fancy, and a lot too pricey. But yummy nonetheless. *Primi* L7000-10,000, *secondi* L12,000-15,000. *Menù* L20,000. Open Fri.-Wed. noon-3pm and 7-11pm.

Sights

Piazza del Popolo, the historic center of town, serves as a calming oasis in this busy city. The 16th-century *portici* which line two sides of the square recall Venice's piazza San Marco. On the third side hunkers the 13th-century **Palazzo dei Capitani del Popolo,** whose massive portal and statue of Pope Paul III date from 1548. The edifice's history is full of Renaissance (and later) intrigue. Originally erected as the palace of the city's hierarch, or captain, the building was burned on Christmas Day 1535 in an inter-familial squabble; the *piazza* smoldered for two full days. A decade later the palace was refurbished and dedicated to the pope, who brought peace to Áscoli. In 1938 the palace was the seat of the principal Fascist party, only to be wrested for partisan use in early 1945. The *piazza* plays forecourt for the elegant eastern end of the **Church of St. Francis** (13th-16th centuries). Its spacious three-aisled interior houses a 14th-century wooden crucifix, the only art object saved from the 1535 fire. At dusk Áscoli's youth gather here for a lively *passeggiata.* (Open 8am-noon and 3-7pm.)

Abutting the church to the south, the gracious **Loggia dei Mercanti** (Merchant's Gallery, 1509-1513), now a favorite meeting place for the town elders, leads to corso Mazzini and the austere 14th-century **Church of St. Augustine** (open 9am-noon and 3-7pm).

Via delle Torri, off p. Sant'Agostino, runs past the stone houses of the old quarter to the 13th-century **Church of St. Peter the Martyr** and tiny via di Solestà. This street, one of the oldest in the city, leads to the single-arched **Ponte di Solestà,** one of Europe's tallest Roman bridges. Around the corner from St. Peter's in p. Venidio Basso stands the diminutive 11th-century Romanesque **Church of SS. Vincenzo e Anastasio** (take via Trebbiani). The low campanile, divided by two arched windows and topped by a conical spire, is characteristic of the city's medieval churches. Legend has it that water from the crypt's miraculous well has healed the lame and brought sight to the blind.

On the other side of town, piazza Arringo derives its name from the harangues delivered there by local leaders. The massive, travertine **duomo** is a pastiche of art and architecture from the 5th through the 20th centuries. A Roman basilica forms the transept, topped by an irregular octagonal dome from the 8th century. The two towers were built in the 11th and 12th centuries, respectively, while the lateral naves and central apse were constructed in the 1400s, giving the cathedral an overall late-medieval tone that is tempered with a modern twinge. Further embellishments included two interior stairways, the 16th-century façade and mosaics depicting Áscoli's role in World War II (1954). The *duomo's* **Cappella del Sacramento** (Chapel of the Sacrament), an intricately framed polyptych of the *Virgin and Saints* (Carlo Crivelli, 1473) surmounts a 14th-century silver altar. (Open daily 9am-noon and 4-7pm.) Next to the cathedral stands the compact 12th-century **baptistry,** decorated with a *loggia* of blind arches. Works by Crivelli, Titian, van Dyck, and Ribera hang amid red velvet curtains and pink walls in **Pinacoteca Civica,** inside the **Palazzo Comunale** (southern flank of the *piazza*). (Open Mon.-Sat. 9am-1pm, Sun. 9am-12:30pm. Admission L2500, seniors free.) Visit the **Museo Archeologico,** also on the *piazza,* for its hall of mosaics. (Open Tues.-Fri. and Sun. 9:30am-1:30pm, Sat. 9:30am-1:30pm and 3:30-5:30pm. Free.)

On the first Sunday in August, Áscoli holds the **Tournament of Quintana,** a medieval pageant in which over 1000 people deck themselves out in traditional costume. The tournament, which features armed jousting and a torchlight procession to p. del Popolo, culminates the four-day festival of Sant'Emidio, the city's patron.

The **carnival** in February is one of the best in Italy. Insanity reigns on the Tuesday, Thursday, and especially the Sunday preceding Ash Wednesday. Residents don costumes, and folk dancers perform in p. del Popolo. Happily, the event is not mobbed by tourists, but you should still make hotel reservations a week ahead.

Rome

Rome's notorious *nomifregismo* (I-don't-care-ness) will inevitably frustrate efficiency freaks and fast eaters. St. Augustine's famed advice, albeit over-quoted, still proves useful. Today, doing as the Romans do means doing lunch for four hours, throwing itineraries to the wind, and leaving your map behind. Getting lost can be one of the most interesting experiences of your Roman holiday. Today's Rome is not so much one city as many cities built on top of and in the midst of one another. Writing in the first century, Livy concluded that "the layout of Rome is more like a squatters' settlement than a properly planned city." Instead of planned preservation, chance, public sentiment, and occasional private patronage have created an eclectic urban landscape. The city's greatest treasures often lie hidden amidst the perplexing tangle of streets, and even the most anticipated encounter becomes a surprise: the Pantheon dawning suddenly over narrow cobbled streets or Bramante's *Tempietto* appearing in the courtyard of a lonely church. Yet Rome is also a city of grandeur—the long approach to St. Peter's is one of the world's most majestic. While Machiavelli praised Rome for its ability to transform the flawed into the flawless, modernity has taken its toll; the Colosseum is crumbling due to urban pollution, maniacal scooters screech through stately *piazze,* and flashy gold-cross pendants have long since replaced sorrowful *pietàs* in Catholic devotions. Romans live and revel in their city, refusing to let it stagnate as a museum, challenging a weighty history with a gleeful defiance. Concerts animate ancient ruins, kids play soccer around the Pantheon, and august *piazze* serve as outdoor movie houses. What may seem sacreligious to the tourist comes natural to the Romans; the capital city is only exercising its rebellious birthright, rejecting the potential paralysis of an overwhelming past.

Getting In and Out of Rome

Plane

International flights touch down at **Leonardo da Vinci Airport** (tel. 659 51), referred to as **Fiumicino** for the coastal village in which it is located. This modern, well-equipped facility has many useful services, including a money exchange and a baggage check. As you exit customs, you'll find a tourist office (tel. 601 12 55) immediately to your left. They'll provide you with maps of the city and try to find you a room. (Open 8:15am-7:15pm.) The train from Fiumicino into Rome leaves from the second floor of the arrivals wing. Look for signs for the *Treno* (not the *Metropolitana*). This new line is the fastest and most convenient way into to Rome, whisking you from the international and national terminals to the spanking new **Air Terminal Ostiense** inside the city. Buy your ticket (L6000) from one of the machines on the second floor; these make change and have English instructions. (Departures 6:30am-12:45am every 15min., 20min.) After 12:45am, blue ACOTRAL buses leave from outside the international terminal for piazza dei Partigiani, where Air Terminal Ostiense is located (L5000; departures at 2:15, 3:30 and 5:00am). Two new "bullet" trains have been installed at the airport, one zipping from Florence's Santa Maria Novella Station and the other from Naples's Mergellina station. Show your Alitalia ticket for a free ride, otherwise, it costs L127,000 (more expensive than the normal train fares, but much quicker and more convenient).

Air Terminal Ostiense provides phones, currency exchange, car rental booths and a branch of CTS (see below). If you arrive there by train from Fiumicino, a series of elevated walkways takes you to either Linea B of the *Metropolitana* (you're at the Piramide stop; Linea B takes you to Termini for transfer to Linea A and the Vatican) or any number of buses outside in piazza dei Partigiani (#57 goes to Termini by way of piazza Venezia; #95 follows via del Corso to via Veneto and Villa Borghese). Both the bus and the subway require you to buy tickets before boarding. Buy subway tickets in the sub-

Rome Overview

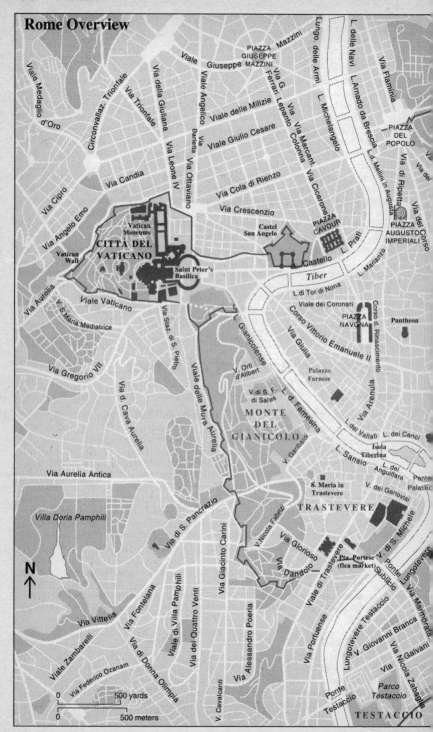

PIAZZA GIUSEPPE MAZZINI
Via G. Mazzini
Viale Giuseppe MAZZINI
Lungo. delle Armi
L. delle Navi
Via Flaminia
Viale Medaglio d'Oro
Circonvallaz. Trionfale
Via della Giuliana
Via Trionfale
Viale
Viale Angelico
Viale delle Milizie
Via G. Ferrari
Via Lepanto
Via Marcant. Colonna
Via Cicerone
L'Arnado da Brescia
L.d. Mellini in Augusta
L. Michelangelo
PIAZZA DEL POPOLO
Via di Ripetta
Via Candia
Via Angelico
Viale Leone IV
Barletta
Via Ottaviano
Viale Giulio Cesare
Via Cola di Rienzo
Via Crescenzio
PIAZZA CAVOUR
Via del Corso
PIAZZA AUGUSTO IMPERIALE
Via Cipro
Via Angelo Emo
Vatican Museums
CITTÀ DEL VATICANO
Castel San Angelo
L. Prati
Vatican Wall
Saint Peter's Basilica
Castello
L. Mariano
Via Aurelia
Viale Vaticano
Tiber
L. di Tor di Nona
V. S.Maria Mediatrice
Viale dei Coronari
Pantheon
Via Gregorio VII
Via Staz. di S. Pietro
Gianicolense
Corso d. Rinascimento
PIAZZA NAVONA
Corso Vittorio Emanuele II
Via Giulia
Via d. Cava Aurelia
V. Orti d'Alibert
V.di S. F. di Sales
Palazzo Farnese
Via Arenula
Viale delle Mura Aurelia
MONTE DEL GIANICOLO
L.d. Farnesina
L. dei Vallati
L. dei Cenci
Via Aurelia Antica
V. Garibaldi
L. Sansio
Isola Tiberina
L. dei Anguillara
Ponte Palatino
Villa Doria Pamphili
Via di S. Pancrazio
S. Maria in Trastevere
V. dei Genovisi
TRASTEVERE
Via Giacinto Carini
V. Nicola Fabrizi
Via Glorioso
Via Dandolo
Viale di Trastevere
V. di S. Michele
Ponte Sublicio
Pta. Portese (flea market)
Lungotevere
Via Marmorata
Via Fontelana
Viale di Villa Pamphili
Viale dei Quattro Venti
Alessandro Poeria
Via Portuense
Lungotevere Testaccio
v. Giovanni Branca
Via Vittela
Viale Zambarelli
Via Federico Ozanam
Via di Donna Olimpia
V. Cavalcanti
Via
Ponte Testaccio
Lungotevere
v. Nicola Galvani
N. Zabaglia
Parco Testaccio
TESTACCIO

0   500 yards
0   500 meters

way station, bus tickets in the bar at the train station. If you need a taxi, a cab from Ostiense is still much cheaper than one from Fiumicino, where the fare can run as high as L70,000. Refuse all offers of special prices or flat rates and insist on the use of the meter.

Most charter and domestic flights arrive at **Ciampino** (tel. 79 49 21 or 79 49 41). From there take the blue ACOTRAL bus to the Anagnina stop on Linea A of the *Metropolitana* (L700; departures 6am-9:30pm every 30min.). Linea A takes you to Termini, the Spanish Steps, or the Vatican. Ciampino is within city limits; do not allow a taxi driver to charge you the long-distance supplement.

Train

Termini (tel. 47 75; all lines open daily 7am-10:40pm; reservations must be made in person), named for the nearby baths (*thermae*) of the Emperor Diocletian, is the transportation hub of Rome, the focal point of most train and both subway lines. Termini is bursting with multilingual information booths, but lines are always long. (Rail information at the front, near piazza dei Cinquecento; tourist information inside between tracks #2 and 3.) Also find currency exchange, baggage services, restaurants, bars, day hotels, barbers, telephone offices, gift shops and even an aquarium.

The various stations on the fringe of town (**Tiburtina, Trastevere, Ostiense, San Lorenzo, Roma Nord, Prenestina, Stazione S. Pietro**) are connected by bus and/or subway to Termini. Be particularly careful of pickpockets in and around the station.

Luggage storage is available along track #1. (Open daily 4am-1am, L1500 per piece per day, no bicycle storage.) For items lost or stolen on the train try the **Oggetti Rinvenuti** office far down track #1 (tel. 473 06 02) or consult the **police** on the same track (tel. 481 95 61 or 488 25 88, open 24 hrs.). For theft within the station, consult the **carabinieri** to the right of the tourist office (between tracks #1 and 2). Thwart theft by using the **waiting room** along track #1 when you can.

If you're interested in traveling from Rome to other cities in Italy by train, see the *By Train* section of *Getting There* for information on how to use Italy's efficient and fairly inexpensive rail system. Sample trip lengths and prices given here are for *diretto* (direct) trains, unless otherwise indicated at the train station. To **Florence:** 2hr., L22,000; *rapido* supplement L9300. To **Venice:** 5hr., L40,000, *rapido* supplement L13,800. To **Naples:** 3hr., L15,400, *rapido* supplement L5300. To get to **Greece** take the train to the port of Bríndisi (7-8hr., L43,500, *rapido* supplement L15,800) and catch the appropriate ferry. Information and tickets are available from **Hellenic Mediterranean Lines**, via Umbria, 21. (Tel. 474 01 41; open Mon.-Fri. 9am-1pm and 2-6pm. English spoken.) Train reservations cost L4000 (the station staff will be honest about whether you need a reservation or not, and not all trains accept reservations). If you don't have a Eurail pass, Bari might make a better point of departure for Greece (see Bari below).

Car

Those entering Rome by car approach the city center by way of the **Grande Raccordo Anulare (GRA),** the beltway that encircles the city. You can take any of several exits into the city. If you are coming from the north, enter on **via Flaminia, via Salaria,** or **via Nomentana.** At all costs avoid **via Cassia,** whose ancient two-chariot lanes can't cope with modern-day traffic. **Via Tiburtina** to the east is even worse. Follow the Grande Raccordo around to **via del Mare** to the south, which connects Rome with **Lido di Ostia.** When leaving the city by car, don't attempt to follow the green **Autostrade per Firenze** signs; get on the Grande Raccordo instead and follow it around; it's longer but faster. From the south, **via del Mare** and **via Pontina** are the most direct connections from the coastal road from Naples. From the Adriatic coast, take **via Appia Nuova** or **via Tuscolana** off the southeastern quadrant of the Raccordo.

Hitchhiking

Those choosing to hitchhike north toward Florence take bus #319 to p. Vescovio and #135 onto via Salaria. They get off at the entrance to the *autostrada*; it's illegal to hitchhike on the highway itself. Those hitching south toward Naples—hardly an advisable way to go if you value your personal safety—often take subway Linea A to Anagnina (the last stop) on via Tuscolana, right at the entrance to the *autostrada*. **Women should not hitchhike anywhere in Italy**.

Orientation

Rome gives priority to coffee and lunch breaks, the *penniccella* (the infamous mid-afternoon siesta), long meals, and extended holidays. Schedules are made in vain here; "we shall simply drift" is a better plan. Most shops and offices are open weekdays and Saturdays 9am-1pm and 4-8pm, in winter 3:30-7:30pm. Nearly everything is closed on Sunday and on Monday mornings, as well as on Saturday afternoons in summer. A few *caffè*, restaurants and tourist services are exceptions. All museums are closed on Monday. Food shops close early on Thursday. But the seven major basilicas of Rome are open all day, every day. Smaller churches usually open with the first mass at 6 or 7am and close around 12:30pm. If no mass is planned, each church follows the caprices of its curate. Many churches reopen at 4pm for a few hours. Most museums and monuments close at 1:30 or 2pm. Plan your day strategically: important business (money changing, travel plans) first thing in the morning, museums and sights until the afternoon, and then, if you haven't drifted into a snoozedom, sights that don't observe siesta (the Forum, Colosseum, *piazze*, fountains, the seven principal basilicas affiliated with the Vatican, S. Pietro, Sta. Maria Maggiore, S. Giovanni in Laterano, S. Paolo fuori le Mure, S. Croce in Gerusalemme, S. Lorenzo fuori le Mure, Sta. Agnese fuori le Mure).

Rome shuts down at the beginning of August, and by *Ferragosto* (August 15), the big summer holiday for Italians, you'll be hard-pressed to find any Romans in the city. Although museums and sights remain open, most offices and restaurants close down completely. Fortunately you won't starve during this time thanks to a humanitarian law preventing bread shops from closing for consecutive days.

The Grand Scheme

No longer defined by the Seven Hills, Rome sprawls over a large area between the hills of the **Castelli Romani** and the beach at **Ostia.** From Termini, the central locus and arrival point for most visitors to Rome, **Città Universitaria** and **San Lorenzo** are to the east, and the major tourist sights lie to the west. You can descend almost on a straight axis through Rome and catch most of its attractions. Starting in the northwest, you can visit Rome's largest park, **Villa Borghese,** the enormous backyard to the **Villa Medici.** Approach Rome's center via the **Spanish Steps** at **piazza di Spagna** for a beautiful view of the city's cupolas and a close-up of Rome's glamorous boutiques and hotels. Directly south by circuitous routes is the **Fontana di Trevi,** (Trevi Fountain), and to the east, the spacious and impressive **piazza del Quirinale.** If you continue your pilgrimage east, you'll hit **piazza Barberini, piazza della Repubblica,** and the **National Museum of Rome.** Migrating south, however, will lead you to the **Forum, Palatine,** majestic **piazza Venezia,** and the **Colosseum.** Travel southwest of Trevi Fountain to find the **Old City, the Pantheon,** and further on, **piazza Navona** and **Campo dei Fiori.** Cross the Tiber to get to **Vatican City** (on a parallel with Termini), the fortified **Castel Sant'Angelo,** and the rowdy nightlife district of **Trastevere.** Accessible by bus, the **Catacombs** are dispersed outside the city walls, concentrated along **via Appia.**

Safety

Rome is congested day and night with lost, bewildered, and distracted tourists, each loaded with cash and valuables in every pocket. The bright side is that Roman thieves, provided with thousands of easy targets, rarely resort to violence. Like any big city, Rome demands caution. As always, carry all your valuables (including your passport, railpass, traveler's checks and airline ticket) either in a **money belt** or a **necklace pouch** stashed securely *inside* your clothing (both available at any well-stocked travel store). If you carry a purse, buy a sturdy leather one with a secure clasp; wear it with the strap across your chest and the purse away from the street, keeping the clasp against you. To avoid having them painfully ripped from your person, don't wear any valuable or valuable-looking jewels.

Never, ever count money in public, and watch to see that you are not followed after changing money. There are as many ways to relieve a tourist of a wallet as there are gypsies in Rome. A favorite trick to watch out for is gypsy children in packs, begging for change and thrusting flat pieces of cardboard or newspaper at your waist, under which they probe pockets and unzip fanny pouches. These buggers are especially thick around the Forum and the Colosseum, and on crowded buses like the #64 and the #492. These kids will do anything for a buck, including pulling down their pants and shrieking. Gypsy women will also approach you, nursing their babies in order to distract you. On the bus and subway, unarmed but devious thieves may brush up against you while the inevitable crush of people is heaviest and grope your bags and pockets. In pairs, one may make an obvious grab or pinch your fanny, diverting you while a subtler hand takes the valuable goods. If you sense that pickpockets have closed in on you or that you are being harassed for any reason, don't be afraid to call attention to yourself or to the offending party; most Romans are embarrassed by these criminals and will move to help you. If you know your wallet has been taken while still on the bus, alert the driver at once; he will lock the doors and drive to the nearest police station.

Rome feels remarkably safe at night. Women and men can walk through the center of town safely during all but the darkest hours. Outside the *centro storico,* however, use caution. The area around Termini and to its south (especially near piazza Vittorio Emanuele and the Colle Oppio, notorious drug areas) and Testaccio demand special vigilance; walk in groups at night. Good old-fashioned bipedal mugging is particularly bad in the suburbs of Cinecittà and Centocelle. If you are robbed, file a report (*denunciare*) with the police—you'll need it for insurance, and it's helpful in case anything is turned in, which sometimes happens. Inquire after lost items at the lost property office, **Oggetti Rinvenuti,** via Nicolò Bettoni, 1 (tel. 581 60 40; open Mon.-Sat. 9am-noon). Also try Termini, at track #1 (tel. 47 30 66 82; open daily 7am-11pm). Check your embassy as well, since cash-drained wallets are often returned there. A last resort is **ACAT,** via Volturno, 65 (tel. 469 51; open Mon.-Fri. 9am-noon and 2-5pm).

Useful Publications

The tourist office has free maps and copies of the invaluable brochure *Here's Rome* and palindromic *Romamor,* which contain important phone numbers, accommodations listings, sample tourist itineraries, and shopping and entertainment options. Also available is *Carnet di Roma e della Sua Provincia,* which lists the month's museum exhibits, concerts, and festivals in the region (in Italian and English). The *Tourist's Yellow Pages* are also free and available at the tourist office and contain, besides advertisements, much useful information. *Tuttocittà,* an indexed pamphlet of maps of the city, showing all the bus routes and listing many useful phone numbers, is printed as an addendum to Rome's yellow pages. It is not for sale, but most offices, *tabacchi,* hotels, and *pensioni* will let you flip through their copy.

Metropolitan is a new bimonthly magazine written by and for the English-speaking population in Rome. Along with lengthier articles on Rome's expatriate scene, there are comprehensive entertainment listings as well as classified ads for jobs, apartments and other services; you can even put your own ad in for free. The magazine is free, and is available at English-speaking bookstores around town. *Wanted in Rome,* a highly informative biweekly English-language newsletter (published Sept.-June), contains job and housing classifieds, a calendar of cultural events, and short articles on topics of interest to English speakers (available at English-language bookstores and English-speaking institutions for L1000). **The Economy Book and Video Center,** via Torino, 136 (tel. 474 68 77) publishes a bimonthly *Happenings* which lists cultural events and discussions available for English speakers; it too is available in English bookstores. *This Week in Rome,* available at newsstands (L4500), is a flashy, tourist-targeted listing in English of events of interest. *La Repubblica*, an invaluable glossy announcing night-clubs, bars, concerts, and special events, comes out with *Trova Roma* on Thursdays.

The circuitous streets make a good map an indispensable. The **tourist office,** via Parigi, 5, and **American Express,** piazza di Spagna, both offer excellent free street maps. The Lozzi *Roma Metro-Bus* office has a helpful map of the city plus a booklet containing all metro, bus and tram routes; it is also available at newsstands and bookstores (L5000). For a thoroughly indexed street atlas, try *Rome A to Z* (sold with *Lazio A to Z*, L14,000) which includes a pocket guide of 20 bike itineraries in Rome.

Transportation

The most disconcerting thing about rush hour in Rome is that it lasts 24 hours a day. Droves of demon mopeds buzz through red lights and over sidewalks. And when thrust into a *piazza*, that cute little Fiat 500 transforms itself into a noisy left-armed bullet. On the upside, with so many Romans darting about, public transportation has developed to meet the demand. Bus and train service is extensive, and the city is doing its best to lengthen metro lines, despite delays caused by workers uncovering ancient ruins with each shovelful. Be attentive when taking public transportation—well-dressed "undercover" pickpockets thrive.

Buses and Trams

Rome's bus system is extensive, although daunting at first glance. Happily, the **ATAC** intracity bus company (tel. 469 51) has ubiquitous booths and a jolly staff which can help you find your way. At the Termini ATAC booth you can buy a detailed map of bus routes (L1000), and you'll need it unless you've already bought Lozzi's city map. Each bus stop (*fermata*) lists all the routes that stop there, key streets on those routes, and routes with nighttime service (*servizio notturno*). Night routes are often different from the daytime routes of the same number. Routes that do not have *servizio notturno* generally stop running at midnight.

Tickets for one ride cost L800. Tickets must be purchased before you board the bus, at *tabacchi* or kiosks throughout the city, and validated in the orange machines at the back of the bus when you board. Tickets are valid on all buses for 90 minutes from time of purchase. The **B.I.G.** daily ticket is valid for 24 hours on the metro and buses (L2800). A weekly bus pass (*biglietto settimanale*) valid eight nights and days (but not for the subway) is L10,000 (sold at piazza dei Cinquecento). Trolleys use the same tickets as buses. The bus network works on the honor system. Bus inspectors roam Rome's buses with greater frequency nowadays. If you are caught without a ticket, there is a strict L50,000 fine; playing dumb tourist doesn't help, and if necessary, they'll drag you to a police station to make you pay the fine. Useful routes for tourists are:

#13 (tram): S. Giovanni-Colosseum-Trastevere.

#19 (tram): San Lorenzo area-Villa Borghese-via Ottaviano-p. Risorgimento. **#27:** Testaccio-Colosseum-via Cavour-Termini. **#30** (tram): Colosseum-S. Lorenzo area-Villa Borghese.

#56 & 60: Trastevere-largo Argentina-p. Barberini-via Veneto. **#62:** XX Settembre-p. Venezia-Vatican.

#64: Termini to Vatican (the wallet-eater).

#118: via Appia Antica-Catacombs of San Sebastian-San Calisto-Baths of Caracalla-Colosseum.

#119 (minibus): p. del Popolo-p. di Spagna-via Repetta.

#170: Termini-Trastevere.

#190: Termini to Villa Borghese.

#492: San Lorenzo-Termini-p. Barberini-p. Venezia-p. Risorgimento.

Night Routes: Be careful at night; sometimes numbers change, and women waiting at bus stops must often endure relentless ride offers and heckling.

#30N: Vatican-Trastevere-south of Termini.

#60N: via Veneto-Trastevere.

#78N: Vatican-Termini.

ATAC also offers a no-frills, three-hour circuit of the city, leaving from p. dei Cinquecento (daily at 3:30pm, Oct.-March Sat.-Sun. and holidays at 2:30pm; L6000). They provide a map and some explanation in Italian and quasi-English, whisking you around the city on an exhaustive excursion. Otherwise, tram #119 winds around many of the more visible monuments in the city.

Subway: (Metropolitana)

The two lines of the **subway** (*Metropolitana)* intersect at Termini and can be reached by descending the stairs at the station. Line A runs from Ottaviano in the northwest (near the Vatican) to Anagnina in the southeast. Line B runs south from Termini to Laurentini in the area of EUR, and to the airport, forking at Magliana. Important stops on line A are p. della Repubblica, p. Barberini, p. di Spagna, and Ottaviano. Important stops on line B are the Colosseum and Piramide (for trains to the beach). For the most part, the subway is safe, but guard your valuables. The majority of Rome's sights are a trek from the nearest subway stop. Line A runs from 5:45am until 11:30pm every day, while line B runs Monday through Friday from 5:45 until 9pm (11:30pm on Saturday and Sunday). Subway tickets (L700; L6000 for a book of 10) can be bought at newsstands, *tabacchi,* or machines in the stations that accept L50, L100, and L500 coins. All stations are equipped with machines that change L1000 bills. Trains to Ostia and the Lido beach are *not* part of the system (L700 extra).

If you will be in Rome for more than a couple of weeks, consider purchasing the *abbonamenti mensili,* which allows unlimited rides on one bus line (L18,000), one bus line and both subway lines (L22,000), or all bus lines and no subway lines (L22,000). It's good for a calendar month, starting on the first day of the month.

Taxis

Taxis are a viable but expensive option. On call 24 hrs., they can be flagged down in the streets. Make sure yours has a meter—at least you'll know that you're being robbed legally. Official rates are L3000 for the first 660m or first minute, then L330 every 330m or each minute. (Night surcharge L3000. L10,000 surcharge from airport and L14,000 to airport. Each suitcase L500.) Radio Taxis: tel. 35 70, 38 75, 49 94, or 881 77.

Car

We hesitate to comment on the sanity of any traveler wishing to get around Rome by car. But if the aggressiveness of other drivers, the weaving antics of moped maniacs, and the suicide squads of pedestrians don't totally unnerve you, keeping a car in the city does guarantee a high-adrenalin (and high-cost) trip. Parking is expensive and elusive, and if you don't keep your eyes peeled for the little signs, you may drive into a car-free zone and incur a fine. Gas (*benzina*) costs four times as much in Italy as in the U.S. (approximately L1500-1550 per liter). **FINA** gas stations will often accept Visa; Exxon, Shell, and Mobil will take AmEx. Rental charges are another expense; L430,000-500,000 per week with unlimited mileage. Non-residents of Italy are eligible for discounts of up to 60%, usually only by reserving from home. Most rates do not include insurance, usually about L15,000 per day. Moreover, all agencies require either a credit card or a deposit of L200,000 in cash. You must be over 21 with a valid international driver's license. An added financial hazard awaits outside the city; if you plan to drive cross-country on major *autostrade,* make sure to budget for extremely expensive tolls. While cruising the *autostrade,* try to buy gas off the highway in smaller towns, although be forewarned that smaller stations may not take credit cards.

If you're still game to rent, Avis, Hertz, Maggiore, and Eurocar all operate booths on the east side of Termini. Otherwise, try their central offices: **Avis,** p. dell'Esquilino, 1/ C (tel. 470 12 16 or 470 11). Open Mon.-Fri. 8am-1pm and 4-7pm, Sat. 8am-noon and 4:20-7pm. Two-day weekend, unlimited mileage, L127,000. **Hertz,** via Veneto, 156 (tel. 321 68 31, reservations 54 79 91), at the corner of via di Porta Pinciana, underground. Open Mon.-Sat. 7am-8pm, Sun. 8am-1:30pm. **Maggiore,** via Po, 8/A (tel. 85 86 98). Open Mon.-Fri. 8:30am-1pm and 2:30-7pm, Sat. 8:30am-1pm. **Budget,** via Sistina, 24/B (tel. 475 57 26). Open Mon.-Fri. 9am-1pm and 3-6pm, Sat. 9am-1pm. **Eurocar,** via Lombardia, 7 (tel. 46 58 02 or 482 43 81). Open daily 7am-8pm. **Prestige,** via Marco Aurelio, 47/B (tel. 48 44 85) and **Eurodollar** via Ludovisi, 60 (tel. 46 09 20 or 474 45 32) both open Mon.-Sat. 8:30am-6pm.

Bicycles and Mopeds

Its hills, cobblestone streets, dense traffic, and lunatic drivers make Rome less than ideal for bikes and mopeds. In some areas, however, bikes are great for exploring the city, and bike rides around Rome's parks can be rejuvenating. In any case, Rome is definitely not the place to take your first moped or scooter ride. Bicycles generally run L4000 per hour and about L10,000-15,000 per day, but the length of that "day" varies depending on how late the shop is open. Try **I Bike Rome,** via Veneto, 156 (tel. 322 52 40), which rents from Villa Borghese's underground parking garage. (Bikes L4000 per hour, L10,000 per day, L30,000 per week; a Hertz card will get you a 50% discount. Open 10am-11pm.) In summer, try the unmarked stands at p. di San Lorenzo at via del Corso or via di Pontifici at via del Corso, both near p. di Spagna (open 10am-1am), or at the Metro Spagna exit at vicolo Bottino (open 9am-11pm). Mopeds and scooters run approximately L55,000 per day. Try **St. Peter Rent,** via Porta Castello, 43 (tel. 687 57 14 and 68 79 09), near the Vatican (open daily 9am-7pm); **Scooters for Rent,** via della Purificazione, 84 (tel. 46 54 85; open daily 9am-7:30pm); or **Scoot-a-long,** via Cavour, 302 (tel. 678 02 06; open daily 9am-7pm).

Practical Information

Tourist Office: EPT, in the Termini Station (tel. 487 12 70 or 482 40 78), between tracks #2 and 3. Horrendous lines. Open daily 8:15am-7:15pm. **Central office,** via Parigi, 5 (tel. 488 37 48). Walk from the station on viale L. Einaudi to p. della Repubblica. Cross the *piazza* and turn right on via G. Gomita, which becomes via Parigi (10min.). Open Mon.-Sat. 8:15am-7:15pm. Pick up a map and copies of *Here's Rome, Romamor,* and *Carnet di Roma e della Sua Provincia.* If you will be traveling in the region around Rome, also ask for *Alberghi di Roma e Provincia,* which lists all hotels and *pensioni* registered with the EPT. Both places will try to help you find a room. **ENIT,** via Marghera, 2 (tel. 497 12 82). No information on Rome. Brochures and hotel listings for all of Italy's regions and important cities. Open Mon.-Fri. 9am-1pm and Wed. 4-6pm.

Budget Travel: Centro Turistico Studentesco (CTS), via Genova, 16 (tel. 44 67 91), off via Nazionale, which veers off p. della Repubblica. Information on student ID cards, non-student plane, train, boat, and bus discounts, plus a free map, and currency exchange. Accommodations service (including out-of-town reservations). Ride board. Open Mon.-Fri. 9am-1pm and 4-7pm, Sat. 9am-1pm. **Branch offices** at via Nuova, 434 (tel. 785 79 06), and corso Vittorio Emanuele, 297 (tel. 654 78 83). Open same hours as main office. Another at via degli Ausoni, 5 (tel. 445 01 41). Open Mon.-Fri. 9:30am-7pm, Sat. 9:30am-1pm. **Enjoy Rome,** via Varese 39 (tel. 445 18 43), 1 block east of Termini, perpendicular to via Milazzo. A new tourist agency with accommodations service, cycling tours, and a discount card valid at various shops and services throughout the city. Open Mon.-Fri. 9am-6pm and Sat. 9am-1pm. **Compagnia Italiana di Turismo (CIT),** in Termini (tel. 448 16 78). Can book and provide information on discount train tickets and tours. Office open Mon.-Fri. 9am-1pm and 2:30-6pm. Also exchanges money. **Italian Youth Hostels Association (Associazione Italiana Alberghi per la Gioventù),** via Cavour, 44 (tel. 487 11 52). Plenty of advice and a list of hostels throughout Italy. HI cards L30,000. Open Mon.-Fri. 8am-3pm. **Transalpino,** p. Esquilino, 9/Z (tel. 487 08 70). 40-50% youth discounts on international train tickets. Ferry information too. Open Mon.-Fri. 9am-6:30pm, Sat. 9am-1pm. Also at a booth in Termini at track #22 (tel. 488 05 36). Open daily 8am-8:30pm.

Embassies: U.S., via V. Veneto, 119A (tel. 467 41). Consular and passport services Mon.-Fri. 8:30am-1pm and 2-4pm. **Canada: Consulate,** via Zara, 30 (tel. 440 29 91). Consular and passport services Mon.-Fri. 9-10am and 1:30-2:30pm. **Embassy,** via G.B. de Rossi, 27 (tel. 841 53 41). **U.K.,** via XX Settembre, 80A (tel. 482 55 51). Consular and passport services Mon.-Fri. 9:30am-12:30pm and 2-4pm; July 13 -Aug. 28 Mon.-Fri. 8am-1pm. **Australia,** via Alessandria, 215 (tel. 85 27 21). Consular and passport services Mon.-Thurs. 9am-noon and 1-4pm, Fri. 9am-noon. **New Zealand,** via Zara, 28 (tel. 440 29 28). Consular and passport services Mon.-Fri. 8:30am-12:45pm and 1:45-5pm. All embassies have 24-hr. referral services in case of emergency.

Currency Exchange: Many inside the train station, but all with low rates and high commissions. The one by the train information booth open daily 8am-8pm. Try **Frama,** via Torino, 21/B (tel. 474 68 70), off via Nazionale near Termini. Open Mon.-Fri. 8:30am-1:30pm and 3-5pm, Sat. 9am-1pm. Or at corso Vittorio Emanuele II, 106 (tel. 68 30 84 06). Same hours. No commission. Also **Numismatica Internazionale,** p. dei Cinquecento, 57/58, on the left side of the *piazza* as you face away from Termini. Open Mon.-Sat. 7am-7pm. 1.5% commission. You can also use the 24-hr. money changing machine at the corner of corso Vittorio Emanuele and corso Rinascimento. No commission. Also via Veneto, 74-76. Beware of street money-changers, who will give you counterfeit money, and be careful when you count your cash; many unsavory characters lurk near small *cambi* and large banks.

American Express: p. di Spagna, 38 (tel. 676 41; lost or stolen checks toll-free 24-hr. 167 87 20 00). Chaotic at times, but fairly efficient. Mail held for free for 30 days for card or checkholders, otherwise L2000. Mail can be forwarded to another address for a L7000 fee upon arrival, or by airmail with prepaid postage. Messages can be left in the office in a stamped envelope for L2000. No need to change checks here, as you will find the same rates and shorter lines at any of the small city's *cambi*; here, however, everyone speaks English and you can count your money in public without fear of being robbed. Excellent free maps of Rome. Open Mon.-Fri. 9am-5:30pm, Sat. 9am-12:30pm.

Post Office: Main Office, p. San Silvestro, 19 (tel. 67 71), near p. di Spagna off via del Tritone. Stamps at booths #22-24. Fermo Posta at booths #58 and 60. Currency exchange (cash only) at booths #25-28. Open Mon.-Fri. 8:20am-6:50pm, Sat. 8:20-11:50am. **Telegrams** can be sent from p. San Silvestro, 18 (tel. 679 55 30). Open 24 hrs. Unsealed packages under 1kg (500g for Australia) can be mailed from San Silvestro; otherwise they must be mailed from **p. dei Caprettari,** near the Pantheon (tel. 654 49 01). Open Mon.-Fri. 8:25am-3:40pm. Packages must be under 20kg and 200cm (sum of the 3 dimensions) and should be tied with a single string. Parcels sealed with tape or glue will be charged more. Another parcel office is on **via della Terme,** entrance on via Viminale. Open Mon.-Fri. 8:25am-7:40pm. Other post offices throughout the city generally open 8:30am-2pm. Stamps (*francobolli*) are available at most *tabacchi* and some newsstands. Letters within Europe L750, postcards L650. Overseas letters L1150, postcards L1050. **DHL Worldwide,** via Labicana, 78B (tel. 794 91), southwest of Termini near the Colosseum. Will deliver packages (up to 500g of documents) anywhere in the U.S., Canada, or Europe within 48hr. Open Mon.-Fri. 8:30am-6:30pm. **Capitalexpress,** via Bresadola, 55 (tel. 855 98 22 or 855 85 31), will deliver your mail anywhere in the world within 2 days for L40,000 up to 500g, L30,000 each additional 500g. Also a fax service. Prices for both places vary depending on customs charges. **Postal Code:** 00100. (See Vatican: Practical Information for a more efficient postal alternative.)

Telephones: ASST, p. San Silvestro, 20 (tel. 679 61 91), next to the main post office. Open Mon.-Sat. 8am-11pm, Sun. 9am-10:30pm. Agonizing lines. Also 2 offices at Termini, one on ground level open 24 hrs., the other downstairs, open 8am-11:30pm. A booth in Termini across from aisle #6 (open Mon.-Sat. 8am-11pm, Sun. 9am-noon and 5-10pm) sells magnetic phone cards available in L5000 and L10,000 units. For **directory information** dial 12. Insert L200 if you are calling from a pay phone; it's returned when you complete your call. Telephone numbers in Rome change as frequently as traffic lights. Phone books often list 2 numbers: the 1st is the number at the time of printing, the 2nd (marked by the word *prenderà*) is what the number will be at some unspecified future time. Numbers don't have a set number of digits (anywhere from 2 to 8), though SIP is now trying to make all numbers uniform. To call overseas, dial 170 for an English-speaking operator. Dial 172-1022 for an American MCI operator for collect or calling card charges to the U.S; the AT&T direct number is 172-1011. **Telephone Code:** 06.

Guided Tours: Generally to be avoided, but for those on a very tight schedule, a hasty but complete air-conditioned bus tour of the city's principal sights is an option. **Carrani Tours,** via V.E. Orlando, 95 (tel. 46 05 10), off p. della Repubblica. The oldest and most reliable firm in the city. 20% student discount. 3-hour tours leave daily at 9am—the Skipper and Gilligan will pick you up at your hotel at 8:15am or 3pm for free. 4 different tours. (Students L25,000-28,000). Open daily 6am-8:30pm. **American Express,** p. di Spagna, 38 (tel. 676 41), offers a series of tours daily at 9:30am and 2:30pm in summer and 3 or 4 times per week in winter (L37,000-45,000). Open Mon.-Fri. 9am-6pm, Sat. 9am-1pm, and for 30min. before each tour Sat. afternoon and Sun.

Lost Property: Oggeti Rinvenuti, via Nicolò Bettoni, 1 (tel. 581 60 40). Open 9am-noon. Also try Termini off track #1 (tel. 473 66 82; open 7am-midnight), and see Police below.

English Bookstore: Economy Book and Video Center, via Torino, 136 (tel. 474 68 77), off via Nazionale, which runs off p. della Repubblica. Italy's largest selection of English-language books, new and used. Also buys books and rents videos. Open Tues.-Fri. 9am-7:30pm, Sat. 9am-1pm, Mon. 3-7:30pm; Sept.-June Tues.-Sat. 9am-1pm and 3:30-7:30pm, Mon. 3-7:30pm. **Anglo-American Book Shop,** via della Vite, 57 (tel. 679 52 52). Lots of new hardbacks and books on Italy. Open Sept.-June Tues.-Fri. 9:30am-1:30pm and 3:30-7:30pm, Sat. 9:30am-1:30pm, Mon. 4:30-8pm; July Tues.-Sat. 9:30am-1:30pm and 3:30-7:30pm. **The Lion Bookshop,** via del Babuino, 181 (tel. 322 58 37). For the literature lover in you. Open Mon.-Fri. 9:30am-1:30pm and 3:30-7:30pm, Sat. 9:30am-1:30pm; Sept.-May Tues.-Sat. 9:30am-1:30pm and 3:30-7:30pm, Mon. 3:30-7:30pm. **Open Door Bookshop,** via della Lungaretta, 25 (tel. 271 69 00). New and used books on literature, music, and art. Open Mon.-Sat. 9:30am-1pm and 4-8pm; Oct.-June Tues.-Sat. 9:30am-1pm and 4-8pm, Mon. 4-8pm. **Esedra International Bookstore,** via Torino, 95 (tel. 488 14 73). English books and novels. Open Mon.-Fri. 9am-7:30pm, Sat. 9am-1pm. **Viale di Termini,** connecting Termini with p. della Repubblica, is lined with outdoor booksellers who often sell dirt-cheap used English paperbacks. The above listed stores carry the *Let's Go* series—proof positive of their high quality.

English Library: USIS (United States Information Service, often referred to as the **American Library**), via Veneto, 119A (tel. 482 66 41), off p. Barberini. Non-fiction and magazines. Only Rome residents can take books out. Open Sept.-July Mon.-Tues. and Thurs.-Fri. 1:30-5:30pm, Wed. 1:30-7pm. **British Council Library,** via Quattro Fontane, 20 (tel. 482 66 41), on the street between p. Barberini and via Nazionale. A fountain of fiction. Also films and lectures in the winter. Borrowing privileges with membership only (1-yr. membership L25,000). Open early Sept.-early July Mon.-Fri. 10am-1pm and 4:30-7:30pm, Sat. 10am-1pm. **Centro Studi Americani,** via Michelangelo Caetani, 32 (tel. 654 16 13), off p. Mattei in a large *palazzo* on the 2nd floor. Borrowing allowed with deposit. Open June 27-late July Wed. and Fri. 8:30am-2:30pm, Tues. and Thurs. 10am-6pm; Sept.-June 26 Mon.-Tues. and Thurs.-Fri. 9:30am-5pm, Wed. 3-7pm.

Laundromat: No self-service laundromats. **Lavaservice,** via Montebello, 11 (tel. 48 95 03), east of Termini. Make sure that they don't put your clothes in more washers than necessary. Open Mon.-Fri. 9am-7pm, Sat. 9am-1pm. **Lavasecco a gettone,** p. Campo dei Fiori, 38 (tel. 678 90 96). Open Sept. to mid-Aug. Mon.-Fri. 9am-7:30pm. Also at via Castelfidardo, 29, near Termini. Open Mon.-Fri. 9:30am-7:30pm, Sat. 9:30am-1pm. Laundromats charge by weight: L12,0000-15,000 for a minimum load of 3-4kg or L4000-L6000 per kilo.

Public Baths: Albergo Diurno Stazione Termini (tel. 48 48 19), underground in the station. Follow the signs in the station towards the metro; showers will be on left. Showers L9000, towel included. Extra towel L1000. Soap L1500. Shampoo L1200. You can leave your bags for L2000 while you bathe. Haircuts, manicures, and pedicures available. Open daily 7:20am-8:30pm.

Swimming Pools: A free list of Rome's 62 watering holes is available from the tourist office. Take your pick or try **Piscina delle Rose,** viale America, 20 (tel. 592 67 17). Take subway line B to the EUR Marconi stop. Outdoor pool. Morning swim L5500 (Sun. L6500), afternoon swim L6500 (Sun. L8000). Open May 28-Sept. 4 daily 9am-12:30pm and 2-7pm.

Beaches: Lido di Ostia, 28km away. The closest to Rome. Take subway line B from Termini to Magliana and switch trains for the beach. Get off at the last stop (every 15min. 6am-10:30pm, 45min., L700 for the subway and train together). Buy tickets at Termini. Not especially clean. See **Near Rome** for other swimming options. Or try the **nude beach** at **Capocotta;** bring a camera. Take train to last stop on Ostia line, then bus #7 to the end. From there, walk 1km on beach before you start getting naked.

Crisis Lines: Samaritans, via San Giovanni in Laterno, 250 (tel. 70 45 44 44), next to the post office. Call or visit the center. Native English speakers. Open daily 1-10pm.

Late-Night Pharmacy: tel. 19 21 for recorded listings in Italian. All pharmacies post the names, addresses, and hours of neighboring pharmacies and all-night pharmacies. **Farmacia Internazionale Antonucci,** p. Barberini, 49 (tel. 482 54 56), between the train station and the Spanish Steps. Take bus #60 or 62. Open 24 hrs.

V.D. Clinic: San Gallicano, via dei Fratte di Trastevere, 52A (tel. 58 48 31). Small inexpensive clinic run by nuns. Crowds and mayhem. Open daily 8-11am.

Hospitals: Salvator Mundi, viale delle Mura Gianicolensi, 67/77 (tel. 58 60 41). Expensive private clinic. English-speaking doctors guaranteed. **Policlinico Umberto I,** viale de Policlinico, 255 (tel. 499 71), near the train station. A free public facility. **Policlinico A. Gemelli,** largo A. Gemelli, 8 (tel. 338 69 22, administration 330 51). A university complex farther from the town center. All open 24 hrs. **Vaccinazoni,** via G. Galilei, 3 (tel. 73 40 43). Shots and vaccines. Open Mon.-Sat. 9am-noon and 3:30-5:30pm.

Medical Assistance: International Medical Center, via Amendola, 7 (tel. 488 23 71, nights and Sun. 488 40 51), 1 block from Termini. On call 24 hrs. English spoken. Will send a doctor to your hotel.

Dental Hospital: G. Eastman, viale Regina Elena, 287 (tel. 445 01 66).

Red Cross: tel. 51 00. An ambulance service.

First Aid (Pronto Soccorso): tel. 115.

Emergency: tel. 113 or for *carabinieri* (military police) 112.

Police: Ufficio Stranieri (Foreigners' Office), via Genova, 2 (tel. 46 86 28 76). English spoken. Report thefts here. Maintains a **lost and found** service. Open 24 hrs. **Police Headquarters,** via San Vitale, 15 (tel. 46 86). **Railway Police,** tel. 481 95 61).

Accommodations

"Everyone soon or late comes round by Rome," wrote Robert Browning, and they usually come round by summer. In July and August, Rome bulges with tourists. A huge quantity of rooms meets this demand, but quality varies significantly and hotel prices in Rome are astronomical. Unfortunately, the one hostel in the city is inconveniently located far from the center of town. Although reservations help, they do not always guarantee a room for the full length of your intended stay—proprietors often prefer the financial appeal of large groups to reserved doubles. Prices vary substantially with the season, and a proprietor's willingness to bargain increases in proportion to the length of your stay, the number of vacancies, and the size of your group. Don't assume that misunderstandings will miraculously disappear on their own; knowing a few key words of Italian can greatly ease communication gaps and make your stay more pleasant (you may want to check the glossary in the back of this book for some basic phrases). Make sure the hotel charges you no more than the price posted on the back of the door to your room; it's the law.

The **tourist offices** will scrounge (reluctantly in peak season) to find you a room. The main office, at via Parigi, 5 (tel. 46 37 48), is the most helpful. The **Centro Turistico Studentesco e Giovanile (CTS),** via Genova, 16 (tel. 47 99 31) and the **Enjoy Rome Agency,** via Varese, 39 (tel. 445 18 43) can also help you find a place. **Protezione delle Giovane,** via Urbana, 158 (tel. 46 00 56) maintains an office in the train station and will assist women in finding convent accommodations and moderately priced rooms.

Steer clear of the many spurious "officials" swarming around Termini and offering to find you a place. They will likely direct you to a run-down location charging 50% more than the going rate. Authentic tourism officials carry photo IDs issued by the tourist office, but the sneaky imposters now issue themselves fake badges; it's best to avoid the officials altogether and head straight to the tourist office.

If the queue at the tourist office extends to Naples, check your bags at the station and investigate nearby *pensioni*. It's usually not hard to find a place—several establishments often operate in a single building. During peak season, some hotels will try to charge more than the official prices and will automatically tell the tourist office they are full. You may do better to call and bargain on your own. There are over 300 *pensioni* in Rome with prices comparable to those listed here. Exercise caution, but don't be afraid to set out on your own. **Always insist on seeing a room first.** Don't be enticed by an included breakfast; a cup of coffee and a stale roll can hike the price up by L8000 or more.

It is illegal and ill-advised to camp out in the public places of Rome, and women should never spend a night outdoors. Although violent crime is infrequent, dozing tourists attract trouble. Those who use this as a last resort check their luggage and valuables at Termini and keep their wallets tucked in their clothes, close to their bodies.

For these listings, reasearched in the summer of 1992, expect price increases of approximately 10% by the summer of '93.

Hotels and Pensioni

North of Termini

The *pensioni* to the north of Termini offer some of the best and safest housing in Rome. Indeed, given the existence of these clean, convenient, often family-run establishments, only desperation warrants a migration south toward dirty, tourist-gouging lodging. If you can't carry your bags another step, take bus #3 or #4 for direct service to this *pensione* area. By foot, find via Marsala running parallel to Termini to the right of the main exit. Head north (left) on via Marsala, and it will become via Volturno. As you walk along via Volturno, you will come to intersections with via Gaeta, via Calatafimi, and via Montebello; turn right onto any of these to find rooms. (Via Calatafimi is a small bent road that connects via Volturno and via Montebello.) Take via Gaeta to get to the streets running parallel to via Volturno (via Palestro and via Castelfidardo).

Pensione Tizi, via Collina, 48 (tel. 474 32 66 or 482 01 28). A 15-min. walk from the station. Take via Goito from p. dell'Indipendenza, cross via XX Settembre onto via Piave, then take the first left onto via Flavia, which leads to via Collina. In a safer location than other accommodations around Termini, this family *pensione* has welcomed students for years to its comfortable rooms. Singles L35,000. Doubles L45,000, with shower L55,000. Triples L64,000.

Pensione Papa Germano, via Calatafimi, 14A (tel. 48 69 19), off via Volturno between via Gaeta and via Montebello. Mama, Papa and the *bambini* Germano run this place with German discipline and Italian warmth. Popular with backpackers and students, reservations are a must during the summer months. Papa speaks English, and will help you find another place if he's full. He may also try to match lone travelers with other groups to fill a room. Singles L35,000. Doubles L48,000, with bath L60,000. Triples L70,000. Reduction of 10% on all rooms Nov.-Dec. MC, Visa.

Pensione Lachea, via San Martino della Battaglia, 11 (tel. 495 72 56), off p. dell'Indipendenza. *Let's Go*'s biggest fan, the warm-hearted owner will ensure every comfort. Doubles L42,000. Triples L60,000. Bargaining isn't out of the question if the place isn't full.

Hotel Gexim, via Palestro, 34 (tel. 444 13 11). A nine-room *pensione* run by a young couple. Guests are expected to stay more than 1 night. Light, airy rooms and no curfew. Singles L38,000. Doubles L55,000, with shower L70,000. Triples L75,000. Laundry L18,000 per load.

Pensione Piave, via Piave, 14 (tel. 474 34 47 or 487 33 60). Definitely worth the extra *lire*. All rooms have private bath, telephone, and carpeted floors. The singles have double beds; one room even has a little fireplace. English spoken. Check-out at 10am, but luggage can be left all day. Singles L50,000. Doubles L70,000.

Pensione Monaco, via Flavia, 84 (tel. 474 43 35 or 481 56 49), around the corner from Tizi and Ercoli. Dim, and no decor to speak of, but bathrooms and beds are spanking clean. Manager won't put up with any funny business; tipsy guests get an extra-cold shoulder. Curfew midnight. 1 shower per day included, another will cost you L2500. Singles L30,000. Doubles L45,000. Triples and quads L20,000 per person.

Pensione Albergo Mary, via Palestro, 55 (tel. 446 21 37 or 446 24 30), and **Pensione Albergo Mary 2**, via Calatafimi, 38 (tel. 47 40 371, fax 482 83 13). Sister establishments. Moderate prices, clean rooms, and some employees speak a little English. Singles L40,000. Doubles L60,000, with shower L80,000. Larger rooms available at Mary 2 for L25,000 per person. Prices soften in the low season.

Locanda Marini, via Palestro, 35 (tel. 444 00 58). Less-than-cheerful interior is warmed by the sprightly proprietrix. Practice your phrasebook Italian with her. L17,000 per person.

Pensione Restivo, via Palestro, 55 (tel. 446 2172). *La donna simpatica* who runs the place takes great pride in the blinding whiteness of her sheets. Large, bright and quiet rooms. Singles L40,000. Doubles L60,000. Triples with bath L80,000.

Hotel Cervia, via Palestro, 55 (tel. 49 10 57, fax. 49 10 56). 21 rooms and 41 beds, so check here if you find the smaller *pensioni* full. A bit musty, but the helpful management speaks English. Curfew 1am. Singles L35,000-40,000. Doubles L60,000-75,000.

Pensione Simonetta, via Palestro, 34 (tel. 444 13 02). A tidy 16-room operation. A little Italian will go a long way with the hospitable management. Singles L45,000, with bath L50,000. Doubles L70,000, with bath L80,000. Triples L108,000.

Pensione Piemonte, via Vicenza, 34 (tel. 44 52 240), off via dei Mille and p. dell'Indipendenza. Practically a hotel. Charming, but prices are on the rise. Singles L50,000. Doubles L70,000, with bath L120,000.

Hotel Home Michele, via Palestro, 35 (tel. 444 12 04). As close to Barbie's dreamhouse as you'll ever find in Rome. Knick-knacks everywhere, especially those of the pink fluffy sort. It's small, so book early. Singles L30,000. Doubles L25,000 per person. Triples L20,000 per person.

Hotel Galli, via Milazzo, 20 (tel. 445 68 59), off via Marsala. Clean and close to Termini. A decent, comfortable choice, especially for garage-sale art aficionados. Singles L35,000. Doubles L55,000. Triples L23,000 per person, but crowded.

Hotel Pensione Cathrine, via Volturno, 27 (tel. 48 36 34). A stone's throw from Termini. Singles L35,000. Doubles L45,000-51,000.

Hotel Castelfidardo, via Castelfidardo, 31 (tel. 474 28 94 or 494 13 78). Completely new rooms, clean showers and helpful management. Singles L40,000, with bath L50,000. Doubles L55,000, with bath L70,000.

Hotel Pensione Domus Mea, via Calatafimi, 31 (tel. 488 11 74). Clean, spacious, and a terrace off almost all rooms. Curfew 1am. Singles with bath L50,000. Doubles with bath L85,000.

Hotel Ventura, via Palestro, 88 (tel. 445 19 51). 1st-floor location is convenient, but noisy at night. Rooms are small but newly renovated. Singles L30,000. Doubles L50,000. Triples L70,000.

South of Termini

In general, the area south of the station is busier, noisier, and seedier than the one to the north, and the proprietors tend to be greedier, grouchier, and less helpful. Many places overcharge the hapless and exhausted tourist who stays one night before moving on to a better scene. However, there are decent places and great bargains to be found with a little perseverance. To avoid confusion among the crisscrossing streets, remember that via Principe Amadeo runs parallel with the west side of the station two blocks over and can be reached by taking any of the side streets that intersect with via Giolitti outside the west exit of the station. The closer you get to p. Vittorio Emanuele, the seedier the area becomes at night. Use extra caution if you're a woman traveling alone.

Pensione di Rienzo, via Principe Amadeo, 79A (tel 446 71 31). A tranquil retreat at a reasonable price. Lovely, large rooms, most with a balcony overlooking a peaceful courtyard. The manager is a kindly gentleman who speaks English. Prices vary by season. Singles L28,000-45,000, with bath L40,000-55,000. Doubles L30,000-55,000, with bath L40,000-72,000.

Albergo Onello, via Principe Amadeo, 47 (tel. 488 52 57). A diamond *pensione* in the rough of south-of-Termini. Pretty, rustic rooms and gracious management. Singles L50,000. Doubles L75,000, with bath L85,000. Triples L90,000, with shower L110,000.

Albergo Terni/Diocleziano/Orbis/Pensione Dina, via Principe Amadeo, 62 (tel. 474 54 28). All 4 establishments reside in a single building. Quality and price vary tremendously, so make sure you see what you're getting. Singles L25,000-35,000. Doubles L50,000-70,000.

Pensione Cortorillo, via Principe Amadeo, 79A (tel. 446 63 94). 7 rooms with wooden beds and flowers on the table. Doubles L55,000, with bath L80,000. Try bargaining.

Pensione Eureka, p. della Repubblica, 47 (tel. 482 58 06 or 488 03 34). Agreeable, and the statues and murals in the entry make you feel right at Rome. English spoken. Curfew 1am. Singles L36,000, with shower L39,000. Doubles L61,000, with shower L70,000. Triples L85,000, with shower L95,000. Showers L2000. Breakfast included. Self-service laundry L15,000 per load.

Pensione Pezzotti and **Hotel Cantilia**, via Principe Amadeo, 79D (tel. 446 69 04 or 446 68 75). The same courteous management runs both places. **Pezzotti:** Singles L40,000. Doubles L55,000. Triples L71,000. **Cantilia:** Singles L60,000. Doubles L89,000. Prices drop dramatically in off-season. Cantilia offers private baths, phones, balconies and TVs.

Pensione Exedra, next door to the Eureka on the 3rd floor (tel. 488 39 12). Comparable in every way, with similarly unglamorous showers. Breakfast included and served in your room. . Doubles L68,000. Quads L120,000. Each extra person L28,000. Showers cost L2000 if staying for only 1 night. Reservations only 1 night in advance.

Hotel San Paolo, via Panisperna, 95 (tel. 474 52 13), at via Caprareccia. The swell proprietor makes up for the questionable decor. Dirt-cheap. Singles L30,000. Doubles L45,000, with bath L50,000. Reservations accepted.

Albergo Teti, via Principe Amadeo, 76 (tel 482 52 40 or 474 35 83). Pricey but exceedingly comfortable. All rooms are tastefully decorated. Those with baths also have a TV. Singles L40,000, with bath L60,000. Doubles L65,000-L70,000, with bath L80,000.

Hotel Orlanda, via Principe Amadeo, 76 (tel. 488 06 37), in the same building as Albergo Teti. Rooms are sparse but clean. One has a charming wooden floor. Official curfew midnight, but is flexible. Singles L35,000. Doubles L50,000, with bath L60,000. Triples L65,000.

Hotel Milo, same building as Orlanda (tel. 474 01 00, fax 474 53 60). 2 floors of immaculate, recently renovated rooms with bath, telephone and TV. Special price for *Let's Go* readers. Singles L65,000. Doubles L100,000.

Albergo California, via Principe Amadeo, 47 (tel. 482 20 02). Not the subtlest neon flowered wallpaper we've ever seen, but the place is clean. Singles L35,000. Doubles L70,000, with bath and TV L85,000. Triples L120,000. You can check out anytime you like, but you can never leave.

Hotel Sweet Home, downstairs from the California (tel. 488 09 54, fax 481 76 13). Home away from home—if you live in the "It's a small, small world" ride at Disneyland. There's also a family room available with a double bed, two twin beds and a crib. Singles L50,000. Doubles L70,000, with shower L90,000. Haggle here.

Hotel Pelliccioni, via Cavour, 47 (tel. 48 44 27). This palatable and pricey *pensione* presents a TV and refrigerator in every room. Singles L51,000, with bath L75,000. Doubles with bath L90,000. Don't bother ordering the expensive breakfast.

Around Piazza Navona

Vecchia Roma (Old Rome) is the ideal, if increasingly expensive, base for living as the Romans do. By day, its winding cobblestone streets, hidden *piazze* and numerous *caffè* charm; by night, the area swarms with boisterous Romans and tourists alike. Most major sights are within walking distance (great for people traveling with children) and the day market at nearby Campo dei Fiori yields bounties of cheap fruit and vegetables. Reservations may be the only way to get a bed, especially in the summer.

Albergo Della Lunetta, p. del Paradiso, 68 (tel. 686 10 80; fax 689 20 28). Take via Chiavari off Corso Vittorio. (If you're coming from Termini, catch bus #64 or at night #70.) An economical Eden in the heart of Old Rome, this is the best value in the p. Navona area. Singles L30,000, with bath L55,000. Doubles L60,000, with bath L90,000. Triples L90,000, with bath L120,000. Reservations recommended.

Pensione Primavera, p. San Pantaleo, 3 (tel. 654 31 09), off corso Vittorio Emanuele south of p. Navona. A good value for its location, but not exactly luxurious. Doubles L65,000, with bath L75,000. Triples L90,000, with bath L105,000. Proprietor may bargain. Prices drop in winter.

Pensione Mimosa, via Santa Chiara, 61 (tel. 654 17 53), off p. di Minerva behind the Pantheon. A matronly woman presides over this kitschy abode. Curfew 1am. Singles L44,000, with breakfast L50,000. Doubles L65,000, with breakfast L76,000.

Albergo Abruzzi, p. della Rotonda, 69 (tel. 679 20 21). Here the humble can contemplate the great; this *albergo* is located smack dab in front of the Pantheon and its noisy admirers. Singles L45,000-55,000. Doubles L70,000-78,000. Reservations recommended in summer.

Hotel Piccolo, via dei Chiavari, 32 (tel.654 25 60), off corso Vittorio Emanuele. Friendly, clean, quiet and comfortable, but perversely small bathrooms—even those with showers. Singles L50,000, with shower L69,000. Doubles L70,000, with shower L80,000, with bath L90,000. Quads with bath L140,000. Reservations recommended in summer.

Albergo Pomezia, via dei Chiavari, 12 (tel. 686 13 71). The recently renovated section is far nicer than the old one; all of the redone rooms have baths. Telephones, heat in the winter, matching furniture, and great bathrooms. Curfew Sun.-Fri. 1:30am. Singles L50,000, with bath L85,000. Doubles L70,000, with bath L110,000. Triples L90,000, with bath L148,000. Prices drop in the winter.

Pensione Navona, via dei Sediari, 8 (tel. 686 42 03). Take via de'Canestrari off p. Navona, cross over corso del Rinascimento, and continue straight. A very helpful Italo-Australian family runs a tight ship in this 16th-century Borromini building. All of the rooms are quiet and clean; most have bathrooms. They tend to fill up with larger groups, so call ahead. Check-out 11am. Singles with bath and breakfast L60,000. Doubles L90,000, with bath and breakfast L95,000. Each extra person L43,000.

Albergo Del Sole, via del Biscione, 76 (tel. 654 08 73). Off p. Campo dei Fiori. Lovely proprietors, clean, and an outdoor garden. Check-out 11:30am. Singles L52,500, with shower L60,000, with bath L70,000. Doubles L75,000, with bath L90,000-96,000.

Hotel Smeraldo, vicolo dei Chiodaroli, 9 (tel. 687 59 29), off via Chiavari. These monkish cells are immaculate and unadorned. Singles L55,000. Doubles 70,000, with bath L90,000. Triples L.90,000, with bath L125,000. Quads L110,000, with bath L145,000. Breakfast L5,000. All major credit cards accepted.

Near the Spanish Steps

The Italian equivalent of Paris's Montmartre, Beautiful People flock here to browse through boutiques and galleries. In an area where designer silk suits, leather loafers, and face lifts abound, inexpensive accommodations are scarce. The neighborhood also suffers from a lack of grocery stores and affordable restaurants.

Pensione Fontanella Borghese, Largo de la Fontanella Borghese, 84 (tel. 687 11 55), off via Condotti after it crosses southwest over via del Corso. The area's only real bargain. Singles L25,000. Doubles L45,000. Triples L52,000. Make reservations 3 weeks in advance.

Pensione Fiorella, via del Babuino, 196 (tel. 361 05 97), off p. di Spagna near p. del Popolo. A nice place with obliging management. Curfew 1am. Singles L40,000. Doubles L70,000. All rooms include breakfast. No reservations—arrive early in the morning to get a room.

Pensione Parlamento, via delle Convertite, 5 (tel. 679 20 82, for reservations 684 16 97), off via del Corso on the street leading up to p. San Silvestro. High ceilings, a gorgeous terrace and wonderful views. Amiable management. Singles L53,000, with bath L90,000. Doubles L70,000, with bath L82,000, with shower and bath L95,000. Each additional person L25,000. Breakfast L12,000 (don't bother). Reservations recommended. Prices are 10% higher for guests who decide to use a credit card.

Pensione Brotsky, via del Corso, 509 (tel. 361 23 39). Tranquil rooms that overlook a courtyard. TV lounge and candy-striped towels. Singles with bath L90,000. Extra person L30,000. Reservations recommended.

Hotel Marcus, via del Clementino, 94 (tel. 68 30 03 20; fax 683 25 67), off of Via della Scrofa (Clementino is an extension of Condotti). Matching wood furniture, telephones, heaters in the winter, secure double windows. All rooms with small bath. Singles L80,000-85,000. Doubles L95,000. Triples L120,000. Quads L140,000. Flash your *Let's Go* and you might get a discount.

Pensione Erdarelli/Pensione Pierina, via due Macelli, 28 (tel. 679 12 65; fax 679 07 05). Clean and centrally located. Breakfast included. Singles L72,500, with bath L92,000. Doubles L110,000, with bath L130,000. Triples L150,000, with bath L177,000. Major credit cards accepted.

Hotel Pensione Suisse S.A.S., via Gregoriana, 56 (tel. 678 36 49), off p. di Trinità dei Monti. In the Swiss tradition of pricey perfection and neutral (yet quaint) location. TV lounge, phone in every room, tidy bathrooms, some with tubs. Singles L65,000. Doubles L98,000, with bath L128,000. Triples L165,000. Breakfast included. Up to half the bill may be paid with a credit card.

Across the River

The *pensioni* on the other side of the Tiber aren't the cheapest in Rome, but they tend to be quiet, clean and friendly. Those in **Ottaviano**, near the Vatican, are attractive for their proximity to popular sights and a safe, residential area. Hedonists and bohemians might prefer to stay in **Trastevere**, scene of much nighttime revelry and home to many young expatriates. Bus #64 from p. del Cinquecento and 81 from via Cavour at Santa Maria Maggiore, as well as subway line A, all run to Ottaviano. Buses #75 from p. Indipendenza, 60 from via XX Settembre, and 170 from p. del Cinquecento all run from near Termini to Trastevere.

Pensione Ottaviano, via Ottaviano, 6 (tel. 38 39 56 or 370 05 33), off p. del Risorgimento north of p. San Pietro. The only hostel-style *pensione* in the area. Temporary home to backpackers from all over. English spoken. Conveniently located, but not a bargain. L20,000 per person for a bunk in a shared room.

Pensione Manara, via Luciano Manara, 25 (tel. 581 47 13). Take a right off viale di Trastevere onto via delle Fratte di Trastevere to via Luciano Manaro. Friendly management runs this homey establishment overlooking colorful p. San Cosimato in the heart of Trastevere. English spoken. Doubles L52,000. Triples L70,000. Quads L90,000. Showers L3000.

Pensione Zurigo/Pensione Nautilus, same building as the Guiggioli, reception on the 5th floor (tel. 372 01 39 or 324 20 50). Not quite as charming as Guiggioli but very serviceable. Spacious spic 'n' span rooms. Fluent English spoken. Doubles L60,000, with bath L80,000.

Hotel Pensione Alimandi, via Tunisi, 8 (tel. 397 239 48 or 397 239 41 or 39 72 63 00; fax 39 72 39 43). Take the steps off viale Vaticano down to via Sebastiano Veniero, and go straight—literally meters away from the Vatican Museum. A gorgeous place with a beautiful garden patio on the first floor and a terrace on the roof. Make reservations in high season, because they sometimes receive large groups. Singles L50,000, with bath L65,000. Doubles L65,000, with bath L85,000. Triples L90,000, with bath L114,000. L10,000 per extra bed. Credit cards of all flavors accepted.

Hotel Amalia, via Germanico, 66 (tel. 397 233 54 or 397 233 56 or 397 23 82; fax 397 233 65). Pastel minimalism, a few plants and a TV lounge. Private baths to be added in the fall of 1992; expect an increase in price. English spoken. Singles L50,000. Doubles L80,000. Triples L106,000. Breakfast is a rip-off at L12,000. MC, Visa.

Hotel Florida, via Cola di Rienzo, 243 (tel. 324 18 72). Clean, sparse modern rooms with telephones. Friendly management. Singles L53,000. Doubles L73,000, with bath L94,000. Triple 130,000.

Pensione Esty, viale Trastevere, 108 (tel. 5881201), about half a kilometer down viale di Trastevere from the Ponte Garibaldi. Simple rooms await in an Orwellian building somewhat removed from the rowdy heart of Trastevere. English spoken. Singles L36,000, Doubles L52,000, Triples L70,000, Quad L85,000.

Institutional and Student Accommodations

If you are looking for a raucous time in Rome, institutions are not the place to go. Curfews at the HI and various religious organizations keep you locked away from late-night Rome, while providing affordable accommodations. Both **CTS**, via Genova, 16 (tel. 467 92 79) and **Enjoy Rome**, via Varese 39 (tel. 445 18 43) will help set you up in various types of accommodations.

Ostello del Foro Italico (HI), viale delle Olimpiadi, 61 (tel. 396 47 09). Take subway line A to Ottaviano and then bus #32. Inconvenient location. 350 beds. 3-day max. stay (extensions granted when vacancies exist). Reception open 2-11pm. Lockout 9am. L18,000 per person. Showers and breakfast included. Lockers provided, though management takes no responsibility for valuables. HI card required—buy one at the desk for L30,000. For information or reservations, contact the regional office of **AIG**, via Carlo Poma, 2, 01195 Roma (tel. 372 92 95; open Mon.-Fri. 8:30am-1:30pm).

YWCA, via Cesare Balbo, 4, off via Torino, west of Termini. Women only. Beds in simple, safe rooms. Curfew midnight. Singles L36,000. Doubles L58,000. Triples L69,000. Quads L92,000. Showers and breakfast (7:30-8:15am) included. No breakfast offered Sunday. Tell reception by 10am same day if you want lunch (1-2:15pm, L15,000).

University Housing: In recent summers, **AIG** (the Italian Youth Hostel organization) has run a program in conjunction with Rome's universities to provide housing for tourists in vacated student quarters (late July to mid-Sept.). The centers are via Cesare de Lollis, 24/B, viale del Ministro degli Affari Esteri, 6, and via D. de Dominicus. 1-week max. stay. L20,000 per person; breakfast included. Contact the tourist office at Termini or at via Parigi, 5 (tel. 46 37 48), or AIG (listed above under Ostello del Foro Italico).

Religious Institutions: Convents, monasteries, and religious houses offer shelter, but rooms often exceed L20,000 per night and strict curfews incarcerate you at 11pm. **Protezione della Giovane** at Termini (tel. 475 15 94; open erratically) or near Termini at via Urbana, 158 (tel. 46 00 56), can make arrangements. A letter of introduction from your own priest, pastor, or rabbi (on letterhead) might help.

Last Ditch: Esercito della Salvezza (Salvation Army), via degli Apuli 39/42 (tel. 49 05 58). Take bus #492 or 415 from Termini. L22,500 per person.

Food

Meals in Rome are lengthy affairs, lasting hours on end. Each course is savored with intent and conversation is loud and liberal. (Breakfast—a gulp of caffeine and a sticky bun—is the only exception.) Accordionists wail out Frank Sinatra (L100 tip expected), corks fly off the local *Castelli Romani* wines, and with the appearance of a crispy *bruschetta* (a piece of toasted bread garnished with oil, garlic, and herbs), the meal begins. Later, the *primo piatto* (first course) arrives, *gnocchi* (potato dumplings) on Thursdays, *risotto* (special rice), or pasta, often prepared *alla carbonara* (with bacon and egg) or *alla matriciana* (with bacon, white wine, tomato, and pepper). Then comes the *secondo* (second course) of meat or fish. Popular main courses include *saltimbocca* (slices of ham and veal cooked together) and *coda alla vaccinara* (stewed oxtail with vegetables). After hours of rumination, and long after the uninitiated are full, fruit and *espresso* are served. The *coup de grace* is a potent shot of *sambuca* (anise liqueur)—try it flaming with the traditional coffee beans floating on top. *Grappa* is another post-prandial option; in its finest form, it is similar to brandy—a doubly distilled, clear liqueur made from old grape pressings.

An alternative to a full Italian meal is a mobile feast. Rome vaunts innumerable **picnic** spots. *Alimentari* are your best bet for standard groceries. They generally have dairy, dry good and deli offerings. For specialty cheeses and fresh bread and meats, try the smaller *panetterie* and *salsamentarie*. These shops will fix you a sandwich or sell you the ingredients. For produce, seek out the Italian greengrocers' *frutta e verdure* shops. Food stores are open roughly Monday through Wednesday and Friday from 8am to 1pm and 5:30 to 8pm, Thursday and Saturday from 8am-1pm only. Get a taste of local produce and local haggling techniques at Rome's many outdoor markets. The largest markets are at p. Campo dei Fiori and p. Vittorio. There is an immense indoor market near the Vatican, in piazza dell'Unità off via Cola di Rienzo. Smaller markets can be found on via Montebello and piazza delle Pace off piazza Navona. **Markets** generally operate Monday through Saturday from 6am to 2pm, and sell goods ranging from food and housewares to clothing and antiques—good to remember if you're planning an extended stay and need kitchen supplies. Catering to real year-round Romans, the fruit and vegetable market on via Montebello in the morning is perfect for breakfast and picnic supplies (Mon.-Sat. 6am-2pm). One of the friendliest food markets in Rome can be found at p. di San Cosimato, in Trastevere. For denizen of the Vatican, there is an indoor food market at the Piazza d'Unità, off via Cola di Rienzo. For easy home fixings with an Italian twist, try *prosciutto e melone* (smoked ham and cantaloupe), *bresaola e rughetta* (smoked beef with bitter greens) or an *insalata caprese* (tomatoes and mozzarella cheese layered with basil leaves). Vendors are usually happy to let you sample the different kinds of cheeses, olives, and meats. A dollop of soft *ricotta*, a slab of *pecorino* (local sheep's cheese) and a baggie of spiced olives are a must. **Pizza** is sold in slices by weight at establishments which brandish the *pizza rustica* sign. An *etto* (100g) repels a snack attack. The rudimentary pizza sold in these shops, however, is a different breed from the real hand-made variety offered with pride at wood-burning *pizzerie*. A well-prepared pizza is light and crispy and blackened a little around the edges, served piping hot by its creator. Other favorite Roman snacks include *baccalà*, deep-fried cod fillets, and *suppli al telefono,* deep-fried rice balls with melted mozzarella in the middle which are named for the long, telephone-cord-like strands that the mozzarella makes as you pull the treat away from your mouth.

For sit-down meals, simple *trattorie* or *osterie* (also *hostarie*) should do the trick. *Rosticcerie* (take-out) are often cheaper, but quality varies. Stay away from the area near the train station—most apparently "bargain" restaurants (offering dirt-cheap fixed-price menus) are actually second-rate tourist snares which serve nothing resembling Italian cuisine. Explore the winding streets around **piazza Navona**, particularly around via del Governo Vecchio, and **Campo dei Fiori**. Some of the rowdiest *pizzerie* call **Trastevere** home. Hop on a bus to reach the university district of **San Lorenzo** or the traditional area known as **Testaccio,** on the eastern banks of the Tiber. These are the last untouristed restaurant districts in Rome. The best places invariably fill up, so set out early to avoid the rush. Romans generally eat dinner late—around 9pm.

San Lorenzo

A five-minute bus ride east of Termini on bus #71 or 492 (get off when the bus turns onto via Tiburtina), San Lorenzo sits in the midst of the Città Universitaria. Many unpretentious *trattorie* and *pizzerie* offer grand cuisine for the university students in an atmosphere that encourages conversation and prevents budget-breaking.

Il Pulcino Ballerino, via degli Equi, 66/68 (tel. 49 03 01), off via Tiburtina. A wonderful, artsy atmosphere with cuisine to match. Try the unusual *tagliolini del Pulcino* (pasta in a lemon cream sauce, L8000) or *polpeltine all'arancio* (meatballs in an orange sauce, L10,000). Cover L1500. Open Tues.-Sun. 8pm-midnight. Closed 1st 2 weeks of Aug.

Pizzeria L'Economica, via Tiburtina, 46 (tel. 445 66 69), on the main bus route. The name says it all. The large family who runs this place cooks up some of the most vicious pizza around (L3000-5000). Or try the antipasto dish for an incredible L4500. Wine L4000. Crowded, with lots of outdoor tables. Go early or late to avoid waiting. Open Sept.-July Mon.-Sat. 6:30-11pm.

Pizzeria Formula 1, via degli Equi, 13 (tel. 49 06 10), off via Tiburtina. Romans know their pizza, so when it's as good and cheap as this, expect to wait. Pizza of all varieties (L5000-7000). Try the zucchini flowers stuffed with mozzarella and anchovies. Theoretically open Mon.-Sat. 6pm-midnight, but it's really anyone's guess—the owner claims the place is "sempre aperto!" (always open).

Il Capellaio Matto, via dei Marsi, 25 (tel. 49 08 41). From via Tiburtina take via degli Equi then the 4th right onto via dei Marsi. Vegetarians rejoice! Numerous pasta and rice dishes for L7000-11,000. Sorceress's salad, with potato, shrimp, corn, carrot and egg L8000. Numerous crêpe dishes around L6500. Tasty chicken dishes available for carnivores. Open Wed.-Mon. 8:30pm-midnight.

Pizzeria il Maratoneta, via dei Sardi, 20 (tel. 49 00 27), off via Tiburtina. Four young marathoners bake pizza on the run (L5500-8500). Tomatoes and marinated seafood cover half of their splendid *Pizza Mare e Monte* (sea and mountain pizza), while tomatoes, mozzarella, mushrooms, eggplant, onion, zucchini, and peppers bury the other half (L8500). *Antipasto di Mare* L6000. Open Mon.-Sat. 6pm-12:15am.

Hostaria da Paolo, via dei Sabelli, 6/8 (tel. 731 42 56). Take via Porta L'Abicana off via Tiburtina and then take the 3rd left. Working stiffs frequent this small *hostaria*, where Swiss Family Robinson decor surrounds incongrously mirthless service. Homemade *pappardelle* pasta (L6000) . Full meals within range: *Insalata* L2500. *Secondi* L6000-9000. Wine L5000 per . Open Mon.-Sat. noon-3pm and 7:30-midnight. Closed most of Aug.

La Tana Sarda, via Tiburtina, 116 (tel. 49 35 50). Personable Sardinians rush from table to table, piling plates with delicacies. Romans rave about the *gnochetti sardi* (twirled pasta with meat sauce, L7000) and the *ravioli sardi* (filled with flavored ricotta, L7000). Cover L2000. Open Sept.-July Mon.-Sat. noon-3pm and 7-10pm.

The Vatican, Trastevere, and Testaccio

The area around the Vatican teems with sinful tourist traps. Save your appetite and take the next bus down the river to Trastevere, site of the city's finest restaurants and its most outrageous *pizzerie*. Farther south, back on the other side of the Tiber, lies Testaccio, the oldest district of Rome (take bus #27 from Termini or bus #92 from p. Venezia). This untouristed area remains a stronghold of Roman tradition, offering intrepid stomachs a true taste of the city—or at least of unusual animal parts. In the Mattatoio neighborhood around the old slaughter houses you may dine as the Romans do, at restaurants that serve authentic local delicacies like the *coda alla vaccinara* (oxtail). Also try the delicious *rigatoni con pajata* (noodles with tomato sauce, liver, and lamb intestines); the latter just resemble noodles.

Hostaria dei Bastioni, via Leone IV, 29 (tel. 31 98 78), off p. del Risorgimento near the Vatican Museums. A miraculous subterranean restaurant which rightly boasts of its seafood specialties. *Risotto alla pescatora* (rice with seafood sauce) L7000. Fresh fish dishes L11,000-14,000. Wine L4000-6000 per carafe. Noisy for outdoor lunch. Cover L2000. Service 10%. Open Mon.-Sat. noon-3pm and 7-11:30pm.

Cucina Abruzzese, via dei Gracchi, 27 (tel. 684 85 89). The somber decor hides some of the area's best home-cooking. A pretty arbor on the street shields you from the sun. Pastas L4500-7000. Cover L2000. Open Tues.-Sun. noon-2:30pm and 7-11:30pm.

Hostaria L'Etrusco, via dei Gracchi, 12 (tel. 31 21 24). Unbelievable pastas (try the tortellini), L5000-8000. Cover L2000. Open Wed.-Mon. noon-2pm and 7:30pm-midnight.

L'Archetto, via Germanico, 105 (tel. 312 55 92). A bit off the beaten track, this hole-in-the-wall joint serves up piping hot pizzas (L6000), *filletti di baccalà* (fried codfish, L4500) and *fiori di zucca* (fried zucchini flowers, L5000). Open Tues.-Sun. 7pm-midnight.

Taverna del Moro, via del Moro, 43 (tel. 580 91 65), off via Lungaretta in Trastevere. Beautiful antipasto spread. *Pizza quattro stagioni* (L12,000). Cheesecake L4000. Bread and cover L2000. Open Tues.-Sun. 7-11pm. Credit cards accepted.

Mario's, via del Moro, 53 (tel. 580 38 09). Take via della Lungaretta off viale Trastevere, and turn right after the church. The L14,000 *menù*, including drink and coffee, makes this place a steal. Pasta is consistently phenomenal (and very cheap—L4500-6000). Cover L800. Open Sept. to mid-Aug. Mon.-Sat. noon-4pm and 7pm-midnight. Credit cards accepted.

Birreria della Scala, p. della Scala, 58/60 (tel. 580 37 63). Take via della Lungaretta off p. Sonnino; follow it past p. Santa Maria onto via della Paglia and turn right at p. di Sant'Egidio. This hub of the Trasteverian social scene packs rowdy Romans into enormous booths. Pulsates with live music daily 8-10pm. Endless menu offers 26 types of pasta (L6000-8000). Sip notoriously anaesthetic mixed drinks at the bar (L8000-10,000). Open Thurs.-Tues. 7:30pm-2am.

Pizzeria Ivo, via di San Francesca a Ripa, 157/158 (tel. 581 70 82). Take via delle Fratte di Trastevere off viale Trastevere. Alas, the tourists have finally discovered this Trastevere legend (no thanks to us), but the mouth-watering pizza's still worth the long wait and chaos. Pizza L8000-11,000. Cover L1000. Open Sept.-July Wed.-Mon. 6pm-1am.

Il Duca, vicolo del Cinque, 56 (tel. 581 77 06), off via del Moro on the left as you head toward the river. A classic Roman *trattoria* on a lively nighttime street. Divine *bruschetta* (try *al carciofo*—with artichoke paste, L2500), *lasagne* and other pastas (L7000-10,000). Wine L8000 per liter. Cover L2000. Open Tues.-Sun. 12:30-2pm and 7:30pm-midnight.

L'Ape sul Melo, via del Moro, 17 (tel. 689 28 81). Great for wimpier foreign appetites. Bistro atmosphere with a good beer and wine selection. Salads and snacks L6000-L8000. 18 types of hot sandwiches (around L6000). Great desserts, including chocolate mousse (L4000). Open Thurs.-Tues. 7pm-2am.

Il Tulipano Nero, via Roma Libera, 15 (tel. 581 83 09), in p. San Cosimato. A friendly, hopping *pizzeria*; dine outdoors in the summer months. Iron palates can attempt the *rigatoni all'elettroshock* (very hot indeed, L8000), or try the interesting pizza combos. Wine L9000 per . Cover L1500. Open Thurs.-Tues. 7:15pm-1am.

Trattoria Turiddo, via Galvani, 64 (tel. 575 04 47), in the Mattatoio district of Testaccio (take bus #27 from Termini or the Colosseum). Locals come here for food they grew up on, like *rigatoni con pagliata* (with tomato and lamb intestine—not as gross as it sounds, L8000), *Coda alla vaccinara* (stewed oxtail, L14,000) and *Animelle alla griglia* (grilled calf's veins, L11,000). More standard Roman specialties are available for the weak of stomach. Vegetarians might want to stay away. Cover L2000. Open Sept. 21-Aug. Mon.-Tues. and Thurs.-Sat. 1-2:30pm and 7-10:30pm, Sun. 1-2:30pm.

Trattoria Al Vecchio Mattatoio, p. Giustanini, 2 (tel. 574 13 82), next door to the above. A gutsy Roman eatery. Their *tonarello sugo coda* (thick spaghetti with tangy tomato oxtail sauce, L8000) followed by *arrosto misto di frattaglie* (a mixed grill of liver, intestines, veins and back muscles, L14,000), washed down with some extra-strong wine (L7000 per), will put hair on anyone's back. Cover L2000. Service 12%. Open Sept.-July Wed.-Sun. 12:30-4pm and 7:30-11pm, Mon. 1-3pm.

Piazza Navona and Campo dei Fiori

Unspoiled and traditional *trattorie* are rivaled here by creative and unusual dining spots. Steer clear of the main *piazze* and venture into the alleys for repasts true to native tastes. Via del Governo Vecchio and via del Monserrato brim with some particularly homey and romantic *trattorie* and *pizzerie*. The former Jewish Ghetto, behind via Arenula, boasts some of Rome's best home-cooking—and it's even Kosher.

Uno, via del Portico d'Ottavio, 1/E (tel. 654 79 37), around the corner from the Teatro Marcello. Wonderful fresh anchovies with green beans. Delicious kosher pastries. Fully kosher kitchen. Open Tues.-Sat. 12:30-3pm and 7:30pm-midnight. Closed Fri. for dinner and Sat. for lunch.

Palladini, via del Governo Vecchio, 29. No sign or place to sit, but bustling with a Roman lunch crowd eating seconds-old *panini.* Point to the fillings of your choice. Favorites include *prosciutto e fichi* (smoked ham and figs—not kosher) or *bresaola e rughetta* (smoked meat with the herb rughetta) sprinkled with parmesan cheese and lemon juice. Hearty sandwiches about L3500. Open Sept.-July Mon.-Sat. 8am-2pm and 5-8pm.

Pizzeria Baffetto, via del Governo Vecchio, 114 (tel. 686 16 17), on the corner of via Sora. This humble *pizzeria* has made Baffetto a household name among Romans. The *pizza gigante* could feed the entire Christian Democratic party. The service is harried; sit, eat and you're outta there. Pizzas L5000-10,000. Wine L6000. Cover L1000. Open Mon.-Sat. 6:30pm-1am.

Il Giardinetto, via del Governo Vecchio, 125 (tel. 686 86 93). An oasis among the district's hard, dusty cobblestones. Linger over the well-seasoned pastas (L7000-10,000; try the *gnochetti* or the *pasta gorgonzola*) and the house wine (L8000 per). Portions generous enough to skip the *secondi* (L12,000-16,000). Open Tues.-Sun. 1-3:30pm and 8pm-midnight. Reservations and credit cards accepted.

Filetti di Baccalà, largo dei Librari, 88 (tel. 686 40 18). Take via dei Giubbonari off p. Campo dei Fiori; largo dei Librari will be on your left. Don't miss this busy, unpretentious establishment located in a miniature *piazza* beneath a quaint church. The ideal spot for informal *antipasti* and wine, this self-service joint makes an unforgettable *filetto di baccalà* (deep fried cod fillet, L3200-3500). Wine L5000 per . Cover L1000. Open Sept.-July Mon.-Sat. 5:30-11:30pm.

Ristorante del Pallaro, largo del Pallaro, 15 (tel. 654 14 88). Italian food prepared with gusto. Dole out a worthwhile L24,000 for a humongous full-course meal, including wine and dessert. No choices—you get whatever they're inspired to make. Pleasant outdoor tables. Open Sept.-July Tues.-Sun. 12:30-3pm and 8pm-midnight.

Da Sergio, vicolo delle Grotte, 27 (tel. 654 66 69). Go left out of p. Farnese to p. della Quercia; vicolo delle Grotte leads left back up to via dei Giubbonari. Da Sergio is legendary for its delicious pasta plates (don't pass up the *carbonara*). One of Rome's quieter and more romantic outdoor spots to dine. Cover L2500. Open Mon.-Sat. 7pm-midnight.

L'Insalata Ricca, largo di Chiavari, 85 (tel. 654 36 56), off corso Vittorio Emanuele near p. Sant'Andrea della Valle. Funky modern art, innovative dishes, and an offbeat ambience are successfully combined with neighborly service and savory, traditional *trattoria* fare. Try the *gnocchi al sardi* (L6500) or request their title dish *insalata ricca,* a robust salad with everything on it (L6500, smaller portion L5000). Cover L2000. Open Thurs.-Tues. 12:30-3pm and 7-11pm. Open during *Ferragosto* except Aug. 14-16. **Insalata Ricca 2,** p. Pasquino, 73 (tel. 68 30 78 81), at the beginning of Governo Vecchio.

La Creperie di St. Eustachio, p. St. Eustachio, 50 (tel. 68 30 74 46). Crêpes as delicious and more creative than those of Italy's snooty Lombard League neighbors to the North. Salted crêpes with cheese and prosciutto (L7000-9000) and dessert crêpes are served by the friendly chef. Try the obscenely rich *nutella e ricotta* crêpe (L8000). Open Tues.-Sun. 5pm-2am. Closed Aug. 5-18.

Near the Spanish Steps

The high prices in this flashy district are no guarantee of quality: *caveat edax* (let the diner beware!). But before shrugging into the **McDonald's** at p. di Spagna, stop, look at the Big Mac wrappers on the Spanish Steps, remember that you're in a culinary capital, and reconsider. Opt for a hot *panino* with mozzarella and prosciutto, a fresh salad, or a piece of *pizza rustica* at one of the many bars in this area. There's an *alimentari* at via Laurina, 36 (open Mon.-Sat. 8am-2pm and 5-8pm).

Centro Macrobiotico Italiano, via della Vite, 14 (tel. 679 25 09), on the 3rd floor, just off via del Corso. Membership costs L30,000 per year (in the summer months, membership is only about L13,000). They allow tourists 1 meal for L2000 and a passport-check. The dishes are all fresh and contain no butter. No Parkay either. A full meal comes to about L15,000. *CousCous vegetale* L6800. Natural *gelato,* made with soy milk and honey, L5000. Open Mon.-Fri. 10am-7:30pm.

Ristorante da Ugo al Gran Sasso, via di Ripetta, 32 (tel. 321 48 83). Ugo's da great guy with da sassy-o name, and his *spaghetti al vongole* (spaghetti with fresh clam sauce, L8000) is just gran. Other pastas L6000-8000. *Secondi* L7000-10,000. Cover and service L2000. Open Sun-Fri. noon-4pm and 7-11pm. Closed Aug. 1-20. Credit cards accepted.

Pizzeria Al Leoncino, via del Leoncino, 28 (tel. 687 63 06), at via dell'Arancio. Take via Condotti from p. di Spagna, cross via del Corso, then take via del Leoncino off via Tomacelli. Fast, inexpensive and informal. The traditional, hand-prepared pizzas are baked in front of you and the hordes of Romans who adore this place. Pizza L6000-8500. Wine L4000 per . Open Sept.-July Thurs.-Tues. 1-2:30pm and 7pm-midnight.

Al Piccolo Arancio, vicolo Scanderberg, 112 (tel. 678 61 39), near the Trevi Fountain in an alley off of via del Lavatore, which runs off p. di Trevi. The sign says "Osteria." Unconventional and delicious pastas and appetizers. Try the *Fiori di Zucca* (fried zucchini flowers stuffed with mozzarella, L7000) or the *Carciofi al Judaica* (a whole fried artichoke). Arrive early. Cover L2500. Open Sept.-July Tues.-Sun. 12:30-5pm and 7-11:30pm. Credit cards accepted.

Trattoria Da Settimio all'Arancio, via dell'Arancio, 50 (tel. 687 61 19). A favorite for Romans in the know. Run by the same family that runs Al Piccolo Arancio. Excellent 3-course meals L23,000-26,000. Try the *ossobuco* (braised veal shank in sauce, L12,000) or *abbacchio* (roast lamb, L15,000). Huge portions of fresh vegetables (L4500) and delicious *antipasti*. Cover L3000. Open Mon.-Sat. 1-3:30pm and 7pm-midnight. Closed Aug. 7-Sept. 6. Credit cards and reservations accepted.

Near the Station

There is no reason to subject yourself to the gastronomic nightmare of the tourist-targeted resturants flanking Termini. Walk 10 minutes away for a real meal. There are some fine resturants near Termini, sufficiently removed from the station flux, that cater to a voracious clientele of workmen.

Le Caveau, via Conte Verde, 6 (tel. 731 02 66). Follow via Giolitti along the train station until you hit via Cairoli. It intersects via Conte Verde about 600m down. Follow the slightly seedy path to this rambunctious hideout overflowing with happy Roman youth. Lots of loud music and 24 types of pizza (L4000-8000). Try the *gnocchi verdi al gorgonzola* (L7000). Excellent beers (L2000-4000). Open Tues.-Sun. noon-3pm and 6:30pm-midnight.

Osteria con Cucina de Andreis Luciano, via Giovanni Amendola, 73/75 (tel. 46 16 40). Take via Cavour west from p. dei Cinquecento; via Giovanni Amendola is the 1st intersecting street. A green bead curtain screens the entrance to this haven for ravenous budget travelers. Inside, enjoy a good belch with the burly workers who yell "Big Bear—99¢" and fill the place in the afternoon. Or work the backpacker crowd that wanders in around dusk. Generous portions of standard pasta dishes (L3300-3600). Huge marinated half-chicken L5000. *Pollo e pepperoni* (chicken and peppers) is L5000. Those who lack a workin' appetite can order half-portions for half-price, plus L300. Wine L3000 per . Bread and cover L1000. Open Mon.-Fri. 9am-3pm and 7-9pm, Sat 11:30am-5pm.

Pizzeria Giacomelli, via Faà di Bruno (tel. 38 35 11), near viale Mazzini. A notorious *pizzeria* bursting with Roman *ragazzi*. One of the few *pizzerie* open for lunch. Have it your way—3 different sizes, hundreds of garnishes and they'll even make the crust thicker if you ask. Their monster pizza is not for beginners; it comes with everything from mini artichokes to beans and snausages. Pizza L7000-15,000. Try one of their homemade dessert pies, if you dare. Open Tues.-Sun. 12:30-3pm and 6:30pm-midnight.

Restaurant Monte Arci, via Castelfidardo, 33 (tel. 474 48 90). Take via Solferino past p. dell'Indipendenza off the east side of the station and then take the 1st left past the *piazza*. Boisterous waiters serve delectable *paglia e fieno al Monte Arci* (a pasta and spinach dish, L10,000) and *gnocchi* with mushrooms and asparagus (L7000). Cover L2500. Open Thurs.-Tues. noon-3pm and 7-11:30pm. Credit cards accepted.

Desserts

If you have a sweet tooth, the road from Rome will lead straight to the dentist. Simply glancing at the glazed pastries in endless bakery windows may get you cavities, and the spectrum of the *gelato* rainbow will make each cone the most difficult choice of your life. Chocolate is the purist's choice but don't miss out on exotica like tiramisù, kiwi and bacio (a "kiss" of hazelnut and chocolate). You'll usually have the option of a free dollop of heavenly whipped cream (*panna*) to top it off. At larger establishments, pay first and take the receipt to the counter to order. Here are some shrines along the *gelato* and pastry road to Nirvana. Come as you are.

Giolitti, via degli Uffici del Vicario, 40 (tel. 679 42 06), near the Pantheon off via della Maddelena. A Roman institution as venerable as the Vatican. Indulge yourself with their gargantuan 10-scoop "Olympico" sundae for L8000. The homemade *panna* is unbeatable. Cones start at L2000. Open Tues.-Sun. 7am-2am.

Fassi Palazzo del Freddo, via Principe Eugenio, 65/67 (tel. 73 78 04), off p. Emanuele west of Termini. This century-old *gelato* factory is a confectionery altar duly worshiped by many. Some heretics argue that the *gelato* here beats Giolitti's hands down. Try both and blaspheme your calories away. Cones L1500-3000. Open Tues.-Fri. 3pm-midnight, Sat.-Sun. 10am-2am.

Gelateria Trevi di A. Cercere, via del Lavatore 84/85 (tel. 679 20 60), near the Trevi Fountain. A small, family-run *gelateria* of yesteryear, whose fare puts the glitzy *gelaterie* down the street to shame. The infamous *zabaione* is the house specialty. Small cones L2000. Open June-Sept. daily 10am-1am; Oct.-May Fri.-Wed. 10am-1am.

Pascucci, via Torre Argentina, 20 (tel. 656 48 16), off corso Emanuele, east of p. Navona. The 6 turbo-charged blenders on the bar have earned this place a reputation throughout the republic; they grind fresh fruit into colorful, frothy frippified *frulatti* frappes (L2700-4000). Open Tues.-Sat. 6:30am-midnight.

Ai Tre Tartufi, p. Navona, 27. Neighboring Tre Scalini perfected the killer tartufo, a menacing hunk of chocolate ice cream rolled in chocolate shavings, but the tourists there have sent the price through the roof. Next door, Tre Tartufi serves up practically the same confection for a mere L4000 (L8000 if you want to sit outside), as well as *gelato* and coffee. May be the only place you can afford to sit in p. Navona. Open Tues.-Sat. 8pm-1am.

Caffè

Coffee is Rome's foremost fuel, and languorous pit stops are *de rigueur.* By night, the *caffè* come alive with thunderous, cross-table conversation, bustling waiters and shrill cashiers. In most *caffè* you pay one price to stand and drink at the bar and a higher price to sit down at a table. There is usually a menu on the wall of the bar listing the prices *al bar* (standing up) and *a tavola* (at a table); check the prices before you get comfy in your seat. Especially around the historical center and the major *piazze*, the price of a *cappuccino* tends to jump from L1500 to L5000 as soon as your derriere hits the chair. Still, if you want to lounge for an hour over your coffee, no one will bother you. Popular hunting grounds are Trastevere and the winding streets around Campo dei Fiori.

Caffè Sant'Eustachio, p. Sant'Eustachio, 82 (tel. 686 13 09), in the *piazza* southwest of the Pantheon. Take via Monterone off corso Emanuele. Rome's coffee empire. Once a favorite haunt of Stendhal and other literary expatriates, now bursting with Romans. Neither the recipe nor the decor has changed since its opening in 1938. Sit out on the *piazza* and nurse a steaming cappuccino (L4000; L2000 at the bar). Open Sept.-July Tues.-Sun. 8:30am-1am.

L'Antico Caffè Greco, via Condotti, 86 (tel. 678 25 54), off piazza di Spagna. Waiters in tuxes serve the renowned cappuccino (L1600) in this *caffè* dating back to 1760. Pot of tea L1900. Pimm's L6700. Open Mon.-Sat. 8:30am-8:30pm.

Caffè della Pace, via della Pace, 3/7 (tel. 686 12 16), beneath vines and church façades. Chic and expensive. Comes alive at night with hip Romans "in the know." Cappuccinos, daytime L2000 at bar, L4000 at table; nighttime L5000 at bar, L10,000 at table. Open daily 10am-2am.

Tazza D'Oro, via degli Orfani, 84/86 (tel. 679 27 68). No place to sit down, but the best brew around and at fantastic prices (*caffè* L800). Superlative *Granita di Caffè* (L1500) after a hot day of sight-seeing. Open Mon.-Sat. 6:45am-8:15pm.

Strasté, via della Lungaretta, 76 (tel. 589 44 30). Haiku composers, herbal tea drinkers and mellow souls rejoice. A mega-artsy *caffè* with floor cushions and soft jazz in the midst of beer-swilling, foot-stomping Trastevere. 22 varieties of tea (L4000). *Torta mimosa* L4500. Wine and beer L4500. Open Tues.-Sun. 7-10pm.

Bar S. Calisto, p. S. Calisto, 4 (tel. 589 56 78), in Trastevere. *Il favorito* across the river, where Trasteverean youth, expatriates and Roman elders socialize outdoors over inexpensive cappuccino (L1200—sitting or standing) and *granita di limone* (L2000). Open Mon.-Sat. 6:30am-3am.

Sights

> *Roma, non basta una vita (For Rome, one life is not enough).*
>
> —*A Roman saying*

The saying applies both to the diligent tourist and to the city itself, which has risen from the ashes of nine sackings, occasional civil wars, endless feuds among its aristocrats, and intermittent desertion by the political and religious leaders who made it the center of the world for millennia. Before any exploration of this tangled 2700-year legacy, a brief review of Rome's history might be of some good to the bewildered traveler. **Romulus** and **Remus,** the twin children of a Vestal Virgin and the war-god Mars, founded the city in 753 BC but didn't leave the city any vintage monuments— just a precedent for fratricide and a tolerance for the children of the supposedly celibate. The Etruscans, who became dominant over the region in the 7th century BC, actually built the first temples and racetracks. A few of their monuments linger in the city, most notably the statue of the **Capitoline wolf,** the permanent symbol of the city. In 507 BC, the Romans expelled the Etruscans and established the Republic after the son of the Etruscan king raped the Roman maiden **Lucretia,** setting off a popular revolt. The liberated citizens promptly set about living up to their wolf protectress by pouncing on all their neighbors. The next four centuries (after a slight setback when the Celts sacked the city in 390 BC) were occupied by the gradual conquest of everything worth bothering about in the vicinity of Europe, North Africa, and Asia. Having beaten up on the rest of the world and taken their wealth, deities, and peoples back to Rome to decorate the capital, Romans began beating each other up over control of the treasure-filled city. The first half of the first century BC was consumed by crises of leadership and the Social Wars, which in turn were resolved by the death of the Republic at the hands of **Pompey the Great** and then **Julius Caesar.** Caesar and Pompey set the standard for self-promotional construction which was to be carried to extremes by Caesar's great-nephew **Augustus,** the first emperor, who claimed that he had found Rome a city of brick and left it a city of marble. After Augustus, every Roman emperor down to Constantine left something with his name on it; from the **Arch of Tiberius** to the **Baths of Caracalla,** a Roman expedition may eventually lead to an acquired ability to list all their names. Exactly when Rome began to decline is debatable, but by 275 AD things were hairy enough that the emperor **Aurelian** had a wall built around the city. By the 4th century AD the emperors had moved out, and Roman citizenry enjoyed a kinder, gentler 5th century: the Goths (410) and the Vandals (455) sacked the city, with the Goths returning in 476 just to make sure they hadn't missed anything. Over the next 500 years, Romans transformed the classical remains into Christian churches and fortresses as the popes attempted to lend relevance to what had become a backwater town. In the 10th century, the *populus* started to give them trouble, attempting several times over the next few centuries to turn the city into a free commune in emulation of both its glorious past and the republican administrations of Northern Italian towns. The popes sheltered in nearby Viterbo for a while, then fled to Avignon in 1305, stranding Rome in a chaotic and destructive period called "The Babylonian Captivity."

The Church soon returned to the sagging city, and the popes, in the properly rapacious traditions of the metropolis, drained enough money out of pious Europeans and their personal fiefdom (the Papal States of central Italy) to hire squadrons of out-of-town talent to decorate the city during the Renaissance. Under **Pope Julius II** (1503-1513), the papacy began rebuilding **St. Peter's,** and Julius's chief architect, **Bramante,** was given free reign to demolish parts of medieval Rome and build according to his fancy; he earned well his nickname "ruinante" by destroying a major chunk of medieval architecture. Rome survived yet another sacking in 1527 at the hands of the army of Holy Roman Emperor **Charles V,** which included Spanish and German soldiers; numerous artistic treasures were destroyed or lost in the chaos. Over the next two centuries, Rome built or rebuilt the majority of its churches. Even more of the medieval city was destroyed to create *piazze* in front of churches or space for grand *palazzi,* while many ancient Roman buildings were pillaged for their marble in what was a sort of municipal self-sack. Much of the ancient city disappeared under the Baroque excesses of the Counter-Reformation; arch-rivals **Bernini** and **Borromini** fought their artistic battles in the streets and piazzas of Rome and their legacy remains inescapable. Like the rest of Italy, Rome drifted into irrelevance during the 18th century, and despite attempts to restore a Roman republic in 1798 and 1849, little happened in Rome until the army of Italy finally kicked the Pope out of power by entering the city in 1870. The Popes locked themselves inside the Vatican for the next 59 years, perhaps to avoid seeing the new nation scrap yet another part of the eternal metropolis. New streets were carved into town and gigantic, garish public squares and buildings (including the awesomely bombastic **Vittoriano** in piazza Venezia) were erected to celebrate the new capital of united Italy. More recent building has been less monumental, mostly comprising an accretion of apartment and business blocks to house and service the spiraling population.

Present-day Rome offers a stunning (and often stunningly incongruous) array of monuments, museums and churches; the sheer number, erratic opening times, ubiquitous scaffolding, jammed buses, and thousands of competing tourists render sightseeing a formidable challenge. Plan your day carefully if you want your wanderings to coincide with Roman schedules; many sights are open only in the mornings and all but the Vatican close on Mondays. Keep in mind that the Roman lunch lasts from about 1-4pm, and the entire city shuts down. Use this time to explore non-lunching monuments (like the Forum, *piazze*, or the major basilicas) or do as the Romans do and lunch. Remember to carry a pocketful of L100 and L200 coins to illuminate the treasures of discreetly extortionate churches; try to avoid murderous thoughts for the other tourists who will gather around the monuments your change has illuminated and drift away when your 60 seconds are up instead of contributing. Summer visitors should beware the debilitating effects of windless, fume-filled, 110° air and the unbearable mid-day sun. Protect yourself with a hat and frequent beverage breaks. (Safe, cool, very potable water gushes from public spigots though bottled-water vendors will insist otherwise.)

Piazza del Popolo

Piazza del Popolo (1816-1824), the northern entrance to the city, was the first sight that greeted 19th-century travelers who arrived in Rome through the Porta del Popolo. The "people's square," is a favorite arena for communal antics; after a victory by one of the city's soccer teams or the downfall of a political leader, the *piazza* resounds with music and merriment. As you walk around the serenely symmetrical square, you'll see buildings in one quadrant echoing those in another, all the handiwork of Guiseppe Valadier. Tucked away on the north side of the *piazza* near the Porta del Popolo, the small **Church of Santa Maria del Popolo** contains two iridescent canvases by Caravaggio in the chapel to the left of the altar: the *Conversion of St. Paul* and the *Crucifixion of St. Peter.* The **Chigi Chapel** was begun by Raphael for the wealthy Sienese banker Agostino Chigi, reputedly the world's richest man. Work on the obscenely expensive chapel ceased in 1520 when both men died, only to be taken up anew and completed by Bernini for Cardinal Fabio Chigi, who became Pope Alexander VII in 1655. Notice the Pinturicchio frescoes in the apse of the church as well. (Open daily 7am-12:30pm and 4-7:30pm.)

Via di Ripetta, twin street of via del Babuino, leads out of p. del Popolo toward the Tiber. The huge brick mound of the **Mausoleum of Augustus** and the glass-encased **Ara Pacis,** a monumental first-century BC altar erected in honor of Augustus's peaceful empire, stand near the confluence of via di Ripetta and the Tiber. Both ancient monuments warrant contemplation—the former from a distance for its overall effect and the latter close up for its detail. (Ara Pacis open Tues.-Sun. 9am-1pm, Tues. and Sat. also 4-7pm. Admission L2500. To visit the mausoleum, contact *Ripartizione Antichità e Belle Arti del Comune di Roma* at tel. 67 10 36 13.)

Farther south, via del Corso spills onto **piazza Colonna,** named after the **Column of Marcus Aurelius** which towers over the square. The prime minister lives in **Palazzo Chigi,** directly on the *piazza,* while the convex, almost polygonal building to its right, the **Palazzo di Montecitorio** of Bernini, houses the powerhouse of the Italian legislature, the **Chamber of Deputies.** (Both closed to the public.) The office of the newspaper *Il Tempo* faces via del Corso. At the side of the building, pedestrians gather to read the latest edition, displayed in the windows.

East along via Sabina rises the newly restored **Fontana di Trevi.** Occupying most of the tiny *piazza,* Nicola Salvi's (1697-1751) figures mount the back of the *palazzo.* The water for the fountain flows from the **Acqua Vergine aqueduct,** which also supplies water to the spouts in p. Navona, p. di Spagna, and p. Farnese. The aqueduct's name derives from the maiden who allegedly pointed out the spring to thirsty Roman soldiers. Completed in 1762, the present fountain is a grandiose elaboration of an earlier basin. Tradition claims that travelers who throw a coin into the fountain will return to

Rome. However, the fountain is eroding (despite its restoration) from the rust of coins (especially British and American ones). Do the fountain and future generations a favor, and refrain from tossing coins.

The Spanish Steps and piazza di Spagna

Designed by an Italian, funded by the French, named for the Spaniards, occupied most ferociously by the British, and now conquered by the American ambassador-at-large Ronald McDonald, the Spanish Steps exude a truly international air, serving as the center toward which most foreigners gravitate. Women beware—every eligible man in Rome (usually a self-granted title) prowls here at night. Recent police crackdowns, including a clearing of the steps at around 1am, have put a damper on the *vivace* nature of the place, but this may be only temporary. The Spanish Steps and p. di Spagna take their names from the Spanish Embassy, located since 1647 in the other triangle of the hourglass-shaped *piazza*. Piazza di Spagna possesses all the requisite elements of a *piazza,* but you have to search for them. The fountain at the foot of the steps, by Bernini's father, mimics the shape of a boat, supposedly inspired when the sculptor witnessed a barge washed up in the *piazza* after a flooding of the Tiber. Despite its simple design (by Carlo Maderno), the rosy façade of the **Church of Santa Trinità dei Monti** provides a worthy climax to the stairs' grand curves, not to mention a sweeping view over the city. The Zuccari brothers who frescoed Santa Trinità in the 16th century built their *palazzetto* at the corner of the *piazza* on via Sistina, bestowing upon it one of the most imaginative façades in the city.

Today you're more likely to see con artists than true artists, but in its day the *piazza* attracted many a creative spirit. Stendhal, Balzac, Wagner, and Liszt all stayed near here; Henry James and the Brownings lived on via Bocca di Leone, a small side street in the area. Above via Frattina, 50, amid the glitter and glamor of chic boutiques, you'll see a plaque announcing James Joyce's former residence. Another small plaque on the side of the house to the right of the Spanish Steps marks the place where Keats died in 1821. The second floor of the house at p. di Spagna, 26, now houses the charming **Keats-Shelley Memorial Museum** (tel. 901 42 46). You can scrutinize a lock of Keats's hair, his deathbed correspondence, an urn containing Shelley's bones, and even some of Keats's curious drawings. Byron is also honored on the grounds at p. di Spagna, 66, where he once lived, even though he didn't have the good sense to die in Italy. The library contains an extensive collection of books dealing with the work and lives of the three poets, as well as manuscripts of some of their works. (Open Mon.-Fri. 9am-1pm and 2:30-5:30pm; Oct.-June Mon.-Fri. 9am-1pm and 2-6pm. Admission L4000.)

The streets between p. di Spagna and via del Corso, not long ago home to bohemians and brothels, are now some of the most elegant in Rome, gleaming with plate-glass windows and people preening. Boutiques litter **via Condotti** and **via Frattina; via Borgogna** sparkles with jewelry stores; **via della Croce** tempts with sumptuous foodstuffs; and **via del Babuino** and **via Margutta** supply conservative, expensive art fodder.

Along viale Trinità dei Monti on the other side of Santa Trinità, the **Villa Medici** houses the **Accademia di Francia** (tel. 676 11). Founded in 1666 to give young French artists a chance to come to Rome (Berlioz and Debussy were among the beneficiaries), the organization now keeps the building in mint condition and arranges excellent exhibits, primarily of French art. Behind the villa's severe Tuscan front lie a wonderful garden and an elaborate rear façade. (Academy open Nov. to mid-July Wed. and Sat.-Sun. 10am-1pm. Admission L2000 by guided tour only. Villa closed to the public except during exhibits. Admission varies.) The **Pincio,** a rather formal public park, extends up the hill beyond the villa.

Piazza Barberini

Indifferent to the modern hum around the square, Bernini's Baroque **Triton Fountain,** with its musclebound figurehead, spouts a perfect stream of water high into the stirring air of p. Barberini. This cascade marks the fulcrum of Baroque Rome. Twisting north is the opulent stretch of **via Veneto,** which has seen its 1950's *dolce vita* replaced by airline offices, embassies, and a flood of tourists 40 years too late. It showcases the Bernini **Fontane delle Api** (Bee Fountain). Intended for the "use of the public and their animals," the fountain buzzes with the same motif that graces the aristocratic Barberini family's coat of arms. The 1624 Counter-Reformation **Church of Santa Maria della Concezione,** further up via Veneto, is a mausoleum housing the tomb of Cardinal Antonio Barberomo, who also founded the church; in the crypt, the bones of 4000 Cappuchin friars keep him company. The bone stacks are artfully arranged and can be visited daily 9am-noon and 3-6pm. (Donation requested.)

In the other direction, up via delle Quattro Fontane, the sumptuous **Palazzo Barberini,** at via delle Quattro Fontane, 13, houses the **Galleria Nazionale d'Arte Antica** (tel. 481 45 91), a collection of paintings dating from the 13th to 18th centuries. Maderno, Borromini and Bernini all had a hand in the architecture. Of the earlier works, note Fra Angelico's triptych, Filippo Lippi's *Annunciation and Donors,* Piero di Cosimo's *La Maddalena,* Holbein's *Portrait of Henry VIII,* and the superb canvases by Titian, Tintoretto, Caravaggio, El Greco, and Poussin. Most startling, however, is the entrance hall, whose ceiling glows with Pietro da Cortona's *Triumph of Divine Providence,* a glorification of the papacy of Urban VIII and his family, the Barberini. The family apartments on the second story merit a peek. In addition to preserving the rooms of the *palazzo* as they were during the height of the Barberini family's influence (mid-1600s), these galleries display period ceramics, silver, and a collection of ornate gowns. (Open Mon.-Sat. 9am-2pm, Sun. 9am-1pm. During renovation, visits to the apartments are allowed every half-hour. Admission to both galleries and apartments L6000.)

Along with the four fountains that give it its name, the juncture of via delle Quattro Fontane with via XX Settembre hosts the unique **Church of San Carlino alle Quattro Fontane.** This Borromini masterpiece, small enough to fit inside one of the pillars of St. Peter's, attests to his mastery of curves. (Open Mon.-Fri. 9am-12:30pm and 4-6pm, Sat. 9am-12:30pm. If the interior is closed, ring at the convent next door.) And wherever Borromini is, Bernini is not far away. The simple façade of **Sant'Andrea al Quirinale** masks a domed, elliptical interior. The elliptical plan of both churches forged a momentary compromise among the Latin cross, Greek cross, and circular church plans. (Open Wed.-Mon. 10am-noon and 4-7pm.)

Piazza del Quirinale, at the end of via del Quirinale, running from via XX Settembre, occupies the summit of the tallest of Rome's seven hills. The **Palazzo del Quirinale** is the official residence of the president of the Italian Republic. In the middle of the *piazza* are the famous renditions of Castor and Pollux, the *Dioscuri.* The twins were parted in the 18th century to accommodate the obelisk now separating them.

Returning on via del Quirinale past San Carlino, visit the **Church of Santa Maria della Vittoria,** which houses Bernini's orgasmic *St. Teresa in Ecstasy.* Her description of her hallowed moment: "The pain was so sharp that I cried aloud but at the same time I experienced such delight that I wished it would last forever." (Open daily 7am-noon and 4:30-6pm.)

Following via della Consulta south from the *piazza* to via Nazionale, trek east or hop on any of the buses headed to p. della Repubblica, site of the **Church of Santa Maria degli Angeli.** Built above the Baths of Diocletian, the vast interior gives a sense of the magnitude and elegance of that ancient sauna. (Open precisely 6:55am-noon and 3:55-7pm.) Around the corner on viale E. di Nicola, the **Museo Nazionale Romano delle Terme** (tel. 488 05 30) combines several important patrician collections with sculptures and antiquities found in Rome since 1870. Don't miss the *Sala dei Capolavori* (Room of Masterpieces) and the so-called Ludovisi throne, a Greek statue dating from the 5th century BC. Upstairs, the frescoes from the Villa di Livia at Prima Porta, a town north of Rome, remain remarkably vivid. (Open Tues.-Sat. 9am-2pm, Sun. 9am-1pm. Admission L3000.)

Off via Cavour, four blocks down from Termini, the **Basilica of Santa Maria Maggiore** occupies the summit of the Esquiline Hill. As one of the seven major basilicas of the city, it is officially a part of the Vatican City. Both its front and rear façades are rococo works, but its interior, built in 352 AD, is the best-preserved example of a paleochristian basilica in the city. The coffered ceiling is believed to have been gilded with the first gold sent back by Columbus from America. The apse mosaic, from the 13th century, glitters with a magnificent scene of the *Coronation of the Virgin*; the artisan had to depict biblical scenes to be read by the (mainly illiterate) church-goers, and at a great distance. The subterranean confessional before the altar contains a relic of the baby Jesus' crib (now sheathed in globs of silver). To the right of the altar, a simple marble slab marks the tomb of Gian Lorenzo Bernini. In contrast to the medieval simplicity of the central church, the Pauline and Sistine Chapels on either side of the nave are monuments typical of High Renaissance excess, each lined with extravagant slabs of colored marble pillaged from nearby Roman ruins. (Church open daily 8am-7pm; dress code often enforced.)

Piazza Rotonda

The **Pantheon** (tel. 36 98 31) is one of the few classical buildings left largely undamaged by the Catholic Church's millennia-long crusade to eradicate pagan monuments and quarry their marble. The inscription across the portico explains that Marcus Agrippa, three times consul, erected the building in 27 BC. Hadrian replaced the conventional temple with the innovative structure you see today, but preserved its portico down to Agrippa's name on the frieze. The proportion and harmony of the interior are breathtaking and surprising. The classical façade and useless brick structure hiding the dome from the back were designed to deceive the visitor into expecting a square, classical interior; since the level of the pavement was some 20 feet lower than today, you can imagine how completely concealed the enormous dome was. The only source of light is the central oculus of the dome—an unprecedented structural feat not repeated until the 20th century.

The Pantheon originally served as a temple to all the Roman gods. The first Christian emperors tried to close it, but popular opposition proved too strong; the popes compromised and converted it into a church in 609. In the Middle Ages it functioned as a fortress and even a fish market. By the Renaissance it had gained such renewed esteem that when Pope Urban VIII Barberini melted down the bronze beams from the portico in 1590 to make the *baldacchino* (canopy over the altar) for St. Peter's, wags blasted him with *"Quod non fecerunt barbari fecit Barberini"* ("What the barbarians didn't do, Barberini did"). He also enlisted Bernini to add two clumsy turrets, which became popularly known as the "ass-ears of Bernini." The tombs of Raphael and the first two kings of Italy lie along the sides of the interior. (Open Mon.-Sat. 9am-4pm, Sun. and holidays 9am-1pm; Oct.-June Mon.-Sat. 9am-2pm, Sun. and holidays 9am-1pm. Free.)

As you exit, examine the recently restored Baroque fountain by Giacomo della Porta (1537-1604). The Egyptian obelisk on top was added in the 18th century, when obelisks, popular among ancient Romans, were once again in vogue. With the Pantheon behind you, go right and back around it to reach **piazza Minerva.** Here, Bernini's winsome elephant statue supports another obelisk, upstaging the unassuming **Church of Santa Maria sopra Minerva.** To the right of the entrance to the church, six plaques mark the high water level of floodings of the Tiber over the centuries. Inside the church, stained glass windows cast a soft radiance across the only Gothic interior in Rome and its celestial ceiling. Head right to visit the **Caraffa Chapel,** full of frescoes by Filippino Lippi (1457-1504) depicting the life of St. Thomas. Watch out for Michelangelo's famous sculpture of *Christ Bearing the Cross* to the left of the altar as you enter and the statue of St. Sebastian in the sixth chapel now attributed to him as well. (L200 coins needed to illuminate the chapels.) The 15th-century artist Fra Angelico is buried in the church's north transept behind a bronze fence. (Church open daily 7am-noon and 4-7pm.)

The Jesuit **Church of Sant'Ignazio di Loyola,** opposite the church in its own delicate rococo *piazza,* by contrast, demonstrates the artistic exuberance of the Baroque. (The façade was under restoration in 1992.) Its sumptuous interior celebrates the sainthood of the founder of the Jesuit movement. The masterwork of the church is Padre Andrea Pozzo's *trompe l'oeil* painting *Triumph of St. Ignatius,* which creates the illusion of a soaring dome on the flat ceiling. (Church open daily 7:30am-noon and 4-7:15pm.)

Via del Corso

Originally the Broad Street for the Roman Republic, via del Corso became a prestigious address when the popes widened the street in the 15th century to accommodate the wild (often cruel) antics of Carnival. The storm of riderless horses and the hunchback races of the 18th century have been replaced by streams of crazed shoppers and the apocalyptic onslaught of buses and scooters. Nearby is the **Galleria Doria Pamphili** (in the *palazzo* of the same name at p. del Collegio Romano, 1A; tel. 679 43 65), which houses the most important surviving Roman patrician art collection. The gallery harbors treasures from the 15th through 18th centuries, including Caravaggio's *Flight into Egypt* and *Mary Magdalene,* Bellini's *Madonna,* Rubens's *Portrait of a Franciscan,* and Velázquez's *Portrait of Innocent X.* The private apartments contain some of the best paintings: Fra Filippo Lippi's *Annunciation* and Memling's *Deposition.* (Open Tues. and Fri.-Sun. 10am-1pm. Admission L4000. Guided tour of private apartments a worthwhile extra L3000.)

Around the corner from Palazzo Doria lurks **piazza Venezia,** not so much a *piazza* as a deadly expanse of asphalt where all the frustrated would-be Mario Andrettis of Rome try to hit fourth gear before reentering Rome's narrow and crowded streets. **Palazzo Venezia,** the first great Roman Renaissance *palazzo* and onetime papal residence, overlooks the *piazza.* Mussolini occupied the building and delivered some of his most famous speeches from its balcony. The arches of the portico in the courtyard and the arched façade of the **Church of San Marco** (facing the Campidoglio)—founded in 336, restored in 833, and restored again in the 15th century—exemplify the Renaissance appropriation of antiquarian motifs. The mosaic in the apse (829 AD) depicts Christ and Pope Gregory IV (elected 827 AD) holding a model of the recently restored church. (Rome has been *in restauro* since time immemorial.) The **Museo Palazzo Venezia,** via del Plebiscito, 118 (tel. 679 88 65), maintains a humdrum permanent collection of papal art objects supplemented by more exciting exhibits announced on banners flying outside. (Open Mon.-Sat. 9am-noon and 4-7pm, Sun. and holidays 9am-1pm. Admission L8000.)

Piazza Navona

Modern times sustain the true-to-Rome uproar of this ancient chariot track and 15th-century festival and marketplace. Races, wrestling matches, and javelin tosses were held in the *piazza's* circus, and according to 17th-century paintings, the *piazza* was sometimes flooded for staged naval battles among fleets of convicts. At night, it throbs with unbridled energy. Lighten your wallet at the pricey outdoor *caffès* and have your fate augured by the turn of the *tarocchi.* Very early in the mornings or too late at night, the crowds abate and you can appreciate the tranquil harmony of the *piazza's* arrangement.

Three Bernini fountains grace p. Navona. In the center, the magnificent **Fountain of the Four Rivers** (1653) represents the Nile, Ganges, Danube, and Rio de la Plata, all identified by characteristic fauna and flora. The obelisk was originally ordered from Egypt by Domitian and moved to piazza Navona from the Circus of Maxentius by Pope Innocent X. One story holds that Bernini designed the Nile and Plata statues with their arms shielding their eyes so as to express derision for the **Church of Sant'Agnese** opposite, which was designed by Bernini's great rival Borromini. The legend continues that Borromini then added the statue of St. Agnes to the façade looking haughtily out beyond the *piazza,* not deigning to drop her gaze to Bernini's work.

Off the northeastern corner of the *piazza* sits the 15th-century **Church of Sant'Agostino,** which shelters a Raphael fresco and Caravaggio's *Madonna of the Pilgrims,* on the left as you enter. (Open 8am-noon and 5-7pm.)

The scarred torso of a classical statue stands against the back corner of Palazzo Braschi. It's all that remains of poor **Pasquino,** a communal bitchboard ever since Cardinal Caraffa put him here in 1501. Early activists affixed satirical comments against city authorities, the pope, and other targets to Pasquino's base for all to read. You may still find some graffiti on Pasquino, although authorities try their darndest to keep him clean.

Browse along **via del Governo Vecchio** leading out of p. Pasquino and eventually to **piazza dell'Orologio.** Borromini's slender clock tower rises on the corner of the Philippine **Chiesa Nuova Convent,** which holds three paintings by Rubens. The **Oratorio** next door is another example of Borromini's work. (Open 7:30am-noon and 4-7pm.)

East of p. Navona, across corso del Rinascimento, stands **Palazzo Madama,** seat of the Italian Senate since 1871. When the Senate is in session (and only then), you may enter the gallery and witness Italian politicos' inaction. The **Church of San Luigi dei Francesi,** around the corner on the left, is the French community's church. The three Caravaggio paintings in the Chapel of St. Matthew (in the back, left-hand side) depict the saint's spiritual life. *The Vocation of St. Matthew* is especially compelling, with down-to-earth, realistic details. (Church open Fri.-Wed. 7:30am-12:30pm and 3:30-7pm, Thurs. 7:30am-12:30pm.) When you come out on corso del Rinascimento behind San Luigi, turn left to reach the **Palazzo della Sapienza,** formerly the seat of the University of Rome, now the home of the State Archives. It features an exhibition room in the Borromini-designed library, whose spiral cupola can be seen kilometers away. (Enter at corso del Rinascimento, 40.) Within the deceptively plain front door of **Sant'Ivo's Church** (1660) flowers Borromini's glorious creation with its curved, extending lines. (Open Sept.-May Sun. 9am-noon, or ring for the porter.)

Campo dei Fiori

Across corso Emanuele from p. Navona, wonderful little Campo dei Fiori is a haphazard clearing in the middle of a dense medieval quarter. "Campo dei Fiori" means "Field of the Flowers," a name whose promise is fulfilled by a bright and colorful market each morning (7am-2pm). During papal rule, the area was the site of countless executions. A statue of one victim, Giordano Bruno (1548-1600), rises above the bustle, arms folded over his book. Scientifically and philosophically ahead of his age, Bruno sizzled at the stake in 1600 for taking Copernicus one step farther: he argued that the universe had no center at all.

The streets around the *campo* are the most picturesque in Rome and merit a few hours of wandering. The deceptive alleyways may lure you to a cloistered fountain, a secluded *piazza,* or a hidden church, or spill you back into the bustling marketplace. Watch for fugitive figs underfoot.

An imposing stone coat of arms identifies the **Cancelleria,** an early Renaissance *palazzo* northwest of the *campo.* Designed in 1485, it impressed various popes and cardinals who appended their insignia to it. Today, the Cancelleria is the seat of the three Tribunals of the Vatican and is legally considered part of Vatican City. The building's designer remains anonymous, but its unprecedented size and style have led the scholars to suspect Bramante. The courtyard, a three-story arched *loggia* of Doric columns, resembles his masterful restoration of the adjoining **Church of San Lorenzo in Damaso.** (No admittance beyond the Cancelleria's courtyard. Church open Mon.-Sat. 7:30am-noon and 4:30-8pm. In summer, 7am-12:45pm and 4:30-7:30pm, Sun. and holidays 7:30am-12:45pm and 4:30-7:45pm.) Continuing up to corso V. Emanuele and following it right for one block will lead you to the **Church of Sant'Andrea della Valle,** which, begun in 1591 by Grimaldi and completed by Carlo Moderno, claims the second-tallest cupola in Rome. The setting of Puccini's opera *Tosca* opens in this church, continues in p. Farnese, and concludes at the prison Castel Sant'Angelo, across the river at the end of corso Emanuele.

Piazza Farnese

Several streets lead from Campo dei Fiori toward the Tiber into p. Farnese. The square is dominated by the huge **Palazzo Farnese,** begun in 1514, a building which marks the apogee of the Renaissance fascination with *palazzi.* The Farnese, a noble family from Lazio, eventually rose from obscurity to claim dukedoms in Parma and Piacenza. As the first Counter-Reformation pope, Pope Paul III (Alessandro Farnese, 1534-1549) reinstated the Inquisition and—on a more humane note—commissioned the best architects of his day to design his dream abode. Unfortunately Antonio da Sangallo, Michelangelo, and Giacomo della Port were so advanced in their careers that they died before the project's completion. Sangallo's façade and entrance passage are indeed remarkable, but the most impressive parts of the building are Michelangelo's elaborate cornice and courtyard. Today, the French Embassy rents the *palazzo* for one lira per 99 years. (Palace not open to the public.) In the 16th and early 17th centuries, the Farnese family hosted great spectacles in the square. The two huge tubs that today comprise the fountains were brought from the Baths of Caracalla to serve as "royal boxes" from which members of the self-made patrician family could spectate. While in the *piazza,* peer at the **Church of San Brigida,** whose ornate portal curiously upstages its *palazzo* façade. Go around the back of the Palazzo Farnese for a glance at the gardens, and to see Michelangelo's beautiful vine-covered bridge over via Giulla. Note the *vanitas* skull motif in the little **Church of Santa Maria della Morte,** on via Giulla.

The elaborate façade of **Palazzo Spada,** a short distance down vicolo dei Venti off the south corner of Campo dei Fiori in p. Capo di Ferro, contrasts vividly with the Palazzo Farnese's. The thinning columns behind the library create an optical illusion (designed by Borromini) in which the gallery seems longer than it is. One can best appreciate this from the *palazzo's* intricately ornamented courtyard, which is lined with dozens of statues. Cardinal Spada's art collection is preserved the way he saw it at the **Spada Gallery** (tel. 686 11 58). The collection is comprised mostly of various portraits of the Cardinal by Guido Reni (1575-1642), but also includes Titian's early *Portrait of a Musician* and Pietro Testa's *Allegory of the Massacre of the Innocents.* (Open daily 9am-2pm. Admission L4000.)

Piazza Mattei

In p. Mattei, the graceful 16th-century **Fontana delle Tartarughe** (Turtle Fountain) by Taddeo Landini marks the center of the ghetto, the quarter to which Jews were confined from the 16th to the 19th centuries. There are no less than five Mattei *palazzi* in the surrounding area. Historically, these have been controlled by that noble family. Heading out of the *piazza* toward the river along via Sant'Ambrogio, you'll come to via Portico d'Ottavia. Several houses on this street, notably #13, 17, and 19, date from medieval times. Note in particular the inscription on the building at via Portico d'Ottavia, 1, which, after the patriotic invocation *Ave Roma,* praises the owner for beautifying Rome.

The Roman ruins at the end of the street are the **Portico d'Ottavia** and **Teatro di Marcello.** The church installed inside the portico, **Sant'Angelo in Pescheria,** gets its name from Rome's fish market, which operated there from the 12th to the 19th century. Until the 1700s, Jews were forced to attend mass here; they resisted this aggressive evangelism by plugging their ears with wax to block out the priest's voice. The theater, begun by Julius Caesar and completed by Augustus, was transformed into a fortified *palazzo* by various Roman families starting in the 12th century. (No admittance to either the theater or the portico. Church open sporadically.)

In a city overrun with Catholic iconography and classical designs, the **Sinagoga Ashkenazita** (Synagogue of Rome, tel. 687 50 51) proudly proclaims its divergent heritage. Built between 1874 and 1904, the synagogue incorporates Persian and Babylonian architectural devices. The synagogue also houses a museum that displays some ceremonial objects of the 17th-century Jewish community. (Synagogue open Mon.-Thurs. 9:30am-2pm, Fri. 9:30am-1:30pm, Sun. 10am-noon. Museum open Mon.-Fri. 10am-1pm and Sat. 10am-noon. Admission L4000.) Confronting the synagogue on the south side, the façade of the **Church of San Gregorio** carries a Hebrew and Latin inscription admonishing Jews to convert to Catholicism.

At the end of via del Teatro di Marcello, two blocks to the left of the theater when facing the Tiber, stands the **Church of Santa Maria in Cosmedin,** erected in the 6th century on the site of an ancient temple. The 12th-century portico holds the famous *Bocca della Verità,* originally a drain cover in the shape of a huge face with an open mouth—the mask of a river god. The Mouth of Truth, it was said, would close on the hand of a liar, cutting off the fingers; the priest would sometimes place a scorpion in the mouth to bite suspected liars. The building is an excellent example of an early medieval Roman church, incorporating both Imperial Roman and early Christian styles. Unfortunately, 19th-century restoration has diminished its original charm. (Portico open daily 9am-5pm. Church open daily 9am-1pm and 3-5pm.)

Returning to via Portico d'Ottavia, retrace your steps up via Catalana past the synagogue, and note the **Palazzo Cenci** at the end of the street. The *palazzo* was the scene of the September 9, 1598 scandal when Beatrice Cenci, aided by her brother and her stepmother, succeeded in having her sexually abusive father Francesco Cenci murdered. The whole clan was beheaded two days later at the command of Pope Clement VIII, but the public sympathized with the group's plea of self-defense against the incestuous drug addict Francesco. Every year on September 11, a mass is held at piazzata di Monte Cenci in memory of the wronged Beatrice.

In the other direction from p. Mattei, off via Caetani, lies **via delle Botteghe Oscure.** At the intersection with via Aracoeli, the imposing headquarters of the former Partito Communista Italiano challenge the nearby headquarters of another organization salient in European history, the Society of Jesus. The construction of **Il Gesù,** the Jesuits' principal church in Rome, began in 1568 under Vignola (1507-1573) with the patronage of Alessandro Farnese. The façade and plan by della Porta became the prototype for countless churches built or rebuilt during the Counter-Reformation. Grandiose decorations, especially Baccicia's fresco *The Triumph of Jesus* in the vault of the nave, testify to the order's ambition. Also look for the Chapel of Sant'Ignazio di Loyola, dedicated to the founder of the order, who lies buried under the altar. (Open daily 6am-12:30pm and 4-7:15pm.)

Campidoglio (Capitoline Hill)

As you approach **Capitoline Hill,** the smallest of Rome's seven hills, a flight of stairs will lure you upward from p. d'Aracoeli (to the right and rear of p. di Venezia as you face the monument to Vittorio Emanuele). The political and religious center of the ancient empire, it has been the seat of the city's civic government since the 11th century. The hill has always been associated with Republican virtues and civic liberty; in 1143 rebelling Romans met here to reestablish the Senate. The **Palazzo Senatorio** now serves as the office of the mayor of Rome. From in front of the two Egyptian lions (ancient Roman imports converted into Baroque fountains) at the base of the hill you have a choice of three paths up the hill. To the left, the steep, brick medieval staircase leads to the Church of Santa Maria d'Aracoeli; to the right lies a curved road, via delle Tre Pile (built in 1692); in the center rises Michelangelo's magnificent staircase, the *cordonata.*

Tackling the *cordonata,* you'll pass the statue of Cola di Rienzo, leader of a 1347 popular revolt that sought to revive the Roman republic. The top of the cordonata opens out onto a *piazza* fronted by the matching **Palazzo dei Conservatori** and **Palazzo Nuovo** to the right and left, and the **Palazzo dei Senatori** to the rear. A statue of Marcus Aurelius on horseback used to grace the center, but both man and steed succumbed to Roman pollution and were removed for restoration. (A replica will eventually replace them.) The equestrian bronze was revered throughout the Middle Ages as it was believed to represent the first Christian emperor, Constantine. The statue has also been immortalized by a legend: the end of the world will supposedly arrive when the last piece of gilding flakes off the horse. When Pope Paul III commissioned Michelangelo to improve the neglected Campidoglio in 1536, and transferred the statue here from the Vatican, the artist made it the focal point of his symmetrical plan. He put a new façade on the Palazzo dei Conservatori and placed the Palazzo Nuovo opposite for balance. Notice the oval geometrical pattern and the gentle slope of the ground to the base of the non-statue—some have called this spot the navel of the world.

Today, the two palaces of the **piazza del Campidoglio** house the treasures of the **Musei Capitolini** (tel. 698 28 62), the world's oldest museum. The collection of classical sculpture was conceived under Pope Sextus IV in 1471. Exhibits are poorly labeled; an abridged guide runs you L5000. In the **Palazzo Nuovo** note the dramatic *Dying Gaul,* a copy of the 3rd-century BC Roman statue commemorating victory over the Gauls at Pergamum, and the bronzes of the *Old and Young Centaurs,* one weeping

because he is old, the other because he is young. In the courtyard of the Palazzo dei
Conservatori, fragments of a colossus of Constantine speak, like Ozymandias, of shattered glory. Among the statues in the rooms above stand the delicate *Boy with a Thorn*
and the famous Etruscan *Capitoline Wolf,* the symbol of Rome itself. Romulus and Remus were added to the piece during the Renaissance, to depict more vividly the ances-
tral myth of Rome. The new wing of the museum, on the Palazzo dei Conservatori side,
divided into the **Museo Nuovo** and the **Braccio Nuovo,** shelters some statues from the
Temple of Jove that stood on this site (fragments of the temple remain in the courtyard). The Greek statues *Apollo Shooting* and *Athena* are the best of the group. On the
top floor, the **pinacoteca** contains a representative collection of 16th-century paintings
(somewhat diminished after a quick raid by the Vatican Museum). The remainders include Bellini's *Portrait of a Young Man,* Titian's *Baptism of Christ,* and Caravaggio's
Fortune Teller. (Open Tues.-Sun. 9am-1:30pm, Tues. and Sat. also 5-8pm, Sat. also 8-
11pm; Oct. 1-March 31 closed Sat. 5-8pm. Last admission 30min. before closing. Admission to both the Palazzo Nuovo and the Palazzo dei Conservatori L10,000, students
L5000; last Sun. of the month free.)

Up the Capitoline Hill's medieval staircase, in the **Church of Santa Maria d'Aracoeli,** a glorious Pinturicchio fresco cycle of the life of St. Bernardino (1454-1513) circles the first chapel on the right as you enter. (Open daily 7am-noon and 3:30pm-
sunset.) Piazza del Campidoglio hosts a series of concerts in July by the Accademia di
Santa Cecilia. Inquire at via Vittoria, 6 (tel. 678 07 42), or at the tourist office.

From the terrace on the right side behind Palazzo Senatorio and down some stairs,
the view over the Forum is regal, especially at night. Original Roman flagstones pave
the downhill road on this side. From below, the Roman base of the Palazzo Senatorio
inserts itself neatly between the ruins of the Temples of Vespasian and Concord, which
flank via del Foro Romano along the hill. From the other side of the *palazzo,* a double
flight of stairs leads to the **Mamertine Prison,** now consecrated as **San Pietro in
Carcere** in commemoration of St. Peter's imprisonment here. (Open Thurs.-Tues.
9am-12:30pm and 2:30-6:30pm, Wed. 9am-12:30pm. Donation requested.)

The Forum and Palatine

Once a marshy valley prone to flooding, the area which is now the Forum evolved
first into an Etruscan market and later into Rome's chief public and civic square. The
Forum was at its busiest in the 2nd century, after the conquest of ancient Greece: Senators debated the fates of other nations over the din of haggling traders, the Vestal Virgins built their house over a street full of prostitutes, priests carried out sacrifices in the
temples, and victorious generals led triumphal processions. All the while, pickpockets
cased the tourists, as they do today. Dwindling at one point to a cow pasture, the Forum
underwent its first excavations in 1803, and they continue today. Unfortunately, archeologists have rendered the site extremely confusing—to understand the chaotic collage
of stone and brick, invest in a copy of Pietro Romanelli's *The Roman Forum* (on sale at
the ticket office, L8000). To best avoid the headaches of the Forum, brace for them:
slow tour groups, confusing sites, heat and dust. Go early, take a bottle of water and
take it easy. The entrance to the Forum on via dei Fori Imperiali lies halfway down via
Sacra, the processional street that runs through the Forum from the **Arch of Tiberius,**
in the west, to the **Arch of Titus,** in the east. (Tel. 679 03 33 or 678 07 82. Forum
grounds open Mon. and Wed.-Sat. 9am-6pm, Sun. and Tues. 9am-2pm; admission
L10,000.)

On your right as you enter, the Augustan edifice **Basilica Aemilia** housed the *argen-
tarii* (money-changers) who operated the first *cambi* in the city; in the pavement you'll
see bronze coins melted during several fires. The open space in front of the basilica is
the original Forum, and was the site of all civic ceremonies and religious festivals until
the Imperial period. **Via Sacra,** the oldest street in Rome, runs through the Forum right
to the slopes of the Capitol Hill.

The brick building at the end of the Basilica Aemilia is the **Curia,** meeting place of
the ancient Roman Senate. The present structure, built by Emperor Diocletian in 283
AD, owes its survival to its sanctification as St. Hadrian's Church in the 7th century.

Male citizens came to vote at the **Comitum Well**, or assembly place in front of the Curia, until Julius Caesar moved the gathering point to the *campus martius,* today's Campo dei Fiori. The so-called **Tomb of Romulus**, an ancient temple, lies below the Curia. The nearby **Arch of Septimus Severus** is an anomaly in its republican surroundings. Celebrating Severus's victories in the Middle East, the arch's reliefs depict the imperial family; Caracalla scraped off a portrait of Severus' brother after having him killed and seizing the throne. Traces of the original inscription are still visible. To the left of the arch, marking one end of the Forum proper, are the **rostra,** or speakers' platforms, named for the beak-shaped prows of ships that were mounted here after a naval victory in 338 BC. Halfway up the Capitol Hill, the **Tabularium,** former repository of the Senate archives, now serves as the basement to the Renaissance Palazzo dei Senatorio and is currently under excavation. The eight columns halfway up the hill herald the porch of the **Temple of Saturn** (inaugurated in 500 BC), one of the most revered sanctuaries in Republican Rome, now emerging gingerly from scaffolding.

Bordering the south side of the Forum is Julius Caesar's **Basilica Giulia** (54 BC), from whose halls justice was administered. Look for inscribed grids and circles in the steps where Romans, anxiously awaiting verdicts, distracted themselves with an ancient form of tic-tac-toe. The **Column of Phocas** in front of the basilica honors the man who seized the throne of Byzantium and awarded the Pantheon to Pope Boniface IV. At the east end of the Basilica Giulia, the **Temple of Castor and Pollux** celebrates the Roman rebellion against their Etruscan king in 510 BC. The twin gods descended and routed the Etruscan army at the Battle of Lake Regilles in 499 BC. Across the street is the Temple of the Deified Julius, which Augustus built in 29 BC to honor his murdered adoptive father and proclaim himself divine progeny.

Via Sacra continues through what was the **Arch of Augustus,** and then passes between the Regia and the restored, circular **Temple of Vesta,** honoring the goddess of home and hearth. This is where the Vestal Virgins tended the sacred fire of the city, keeping it alight for over 1000 years. As long as they kept their vow of virginity, the Vestals were among the most powerful and respected women in ancient Rome; those who strayed, however, were buried alive. Statues of the more famous virgins surround the courtyard of their house; one base, with the name scraped off and the statue gone, commemorates an upstart who eloped with her lover. North of the Regia, the **Temple of Antonius and Faustina** displays an elegant frieze. East of the temple, the excavation of the **ancient necropolis,** the cemetery of the original inhabitants of the area, gave credence to the once legendary founding date of Rome (753 BC). The bronze doors of the nearby **Temple of Romulus** (son of Maxentius) survive from the 4th century AD.

The **Basilica of Maxentius and Constantine,** to the left along via Sacra, is the largest monument in the Forum and one of the most important existing examples of Roman architecture, inspiring numerous Renaissance constructions. The immense main barrel vault extended the full length of the three vaults you see today. Finally, dominating the east end of the Forum, the **Arch of Titus** commemorates Titus's destruction of Jerusalem in 70 AD. The famed reliefs inside the arch, covered for restoration in 1992, depict the sack of the great Jewish temple, including the pillage of a giant menorah.

Here at the end of via Sacra, turn right and ascend the **Palatine Hill,** where Romulus supposedly founded Rome. The hill served as a prime residential area during the days of the Republic; today its flowering gardens and grassy environs are an ideal place to picnic and escape the starkness of the Forum. Though there are ruins aplenty, cool breezes and sweeping views are the real reason to make the steep climb. **Clivus Palatinus,** the main road of the Palatine, leads up to the **Farnese Gardens,** built over the site of the Palace of Tiberius. Inspect the rare Roman wall-paintings of the **Casa di Livia,** which belonged to Augustus's wife Livia, the first Roman empress and (according to Robert Graves' *I Claudius*) "an abominable woman." Augustus's own early imperial residence seems to have been a modest building, at least when compared to the immense **Domus Augustana**, a palace built for Emperor Domitian (81-96 AD), which burdens the rest of the hill. Look for the curious central courtyard of the **Domus Flavius** with its octagonal basin. The unpopular Domitian allegedly lined the walls of this courtyard with polished stone so he could observe the reflections of any potential assailant. The throne room of the palace is north of the peristyle, flanked by a basilica and a room for public ceremonies. To the south reclines the **Triclinium,** or banquet hall. East of the official palace stood the private residence of the emperor, organized around a central courtyard (with fishpond). The fragmented pavement in some of the rooms exposes the ingenious system of central heating ducts, a common Roman installation. Nearby, the **Palatine Antiquarium** remains closed for restoration. Along the south side of the Palatine lie the unimpressive remains of the **Circus Maximus,** where crowds of a quarter million spectators once gathered to watch great chariot races.

Across the street from the Forum sprawl the **Fori Imperiali,** a conglomeration of temples, basilicas, and squares built by emperors of the first and 2nd centuries, partly in response to increasing congestion in the old forum. In the 1930s, with imperial aspirations of his own, Mussolini cleared the area of medieval constructions and created the via dell'Impero (now the via dei Fori Imperiali) as a thoroughfare for his military parades. This barren concourse cuts across the old fountains at an awkward angle. Of the remainders, the **Forum of Trajan** (107-113 AD) is the largest and most impressive. Eight years of restoration helped reveal the perfectly preserved upper half of the famous **Trajan Column,** which commemorates the emperor's conquest of the Dacians, denizens of present-day Romania. **Trajan's Market,** a semi-circular ancient **shopping mall** that housed 150 *tabernae,* or single-room stores, holds frequent art exhibits. (Forum and market open Tues.-Sat. 9am-1:30pm, Sun. 9am-1pm, and in summer 4-7pm. Admission L3750. Entrance at via IV Novembre, 94.) The **Forums of Caesar and Nerva** are open for the same hours as Trajan's, but are best appreciated from street level. **Augustus's Forum**, accessible at via Campo Carleo off p. del Grillo, is better viewed from above at via Alessandria, where you can see the remains of the temple to Mars Ultor (Mars the Avenger). (Open April-Sept. Tues.-Sat. 9am-1pm and 3-6pm, Sun. 9am-1pm; Oct.-March Tues.-Sat. 10am-5pm, Sun. 9am-1pm.)

While standing amid the ruins of the Forum, glance northward to ogle a neoclassical wedding cake surmounted by a winged chariot. This is the rear view of the **Vittoriano** (1885-1911), p. Venezia's bombastic monument to King Vittorio Emanuele II and Italian unification. For a closer look, walk to the hilltop along via dei Fori Imperiali, or enjoy the frontal view from p. Venezia.

Colosseum and Testaccio

The **Colosseum,** the internationally recognizable symbol of Rome, was begun under the emperor Vespasian and finished under Emperor Titus in 80 AD. Built mostly by Jewish slaves, the amphitheater seated 50,000 spectators and was equipped with a retractable linen awning to protect the crowds from sun or rain. The arena could be flooded for mock naval battles, and a series of trenches led to a labyrinth of tunnels and cages from which wild animals, imported from the far corners of the Empire, were brought to the surface by elevator. The interior is a bit of a disappointment, since Renaissance Popes used most of the marble blocks for their own grandiose constructions. Not until Benedict XIV (1740-1758) consecrated the Colosseum in the memory of martyred Christians did the destruction stop. The Venerable Bede (672-735) remarked that "as long as the Colosseum stands, Rome stands; when the Colosseum falls, Rome will fall; but when Rome falls, it will be the end of the world." So keep an eye on it: Mussolini paved a road around the Colosseum to emphasize its greatness, and now it faces serious deterioration due to the traffic and pollution. (Tel. 700 42 61. Open Mon. and Wed.-Sat. 9am-sunset, Tues. and Sun. 9am-1pm. Upper decks open Sun. and Wed. 9am-1pm, all other days 9am-3pm in winter, 9am-6pm in summer; admission L6000.)

On one side of the Colosseum you'll find the remarkably intact and majestic **Arch of Constantine** (315 AD). Constantine built the arch to commemorate his victory over rival emperor Maxentius at the Battle of the Milvian Bridge in 312. The well-proportioned triple arch is mostly constructed from fragments pillaged from other monuments; the circular medallions were originally part of a monument to Hadrian.

On the Esquiline Hill off via Cavour rises the **Church of San Pietro in Vincoli** (St. Peter in Chains). The church houses Michelangelo's unfinished tomb of Julius II, with its famous statue of Moses. The anomalous goat horns protruding from Moses' head result from a mistranslation of the Hebrew Bible. When Moses emerged from Sinai with the Ten Commandments, according to scripture, "rays" (similar to "horns" in Hebrew) shone from his brow. Flanking the Moses statue are Leah and Rachel, who represent the active and the contemplative life. Under the altar of the church dangle the chains of St. Peter. (Open daily 7am-12:30pm and 3:30-6pm.)

The **Church of San Clemente,** an early Christian structure of several layers, stands one and a half blocks east of the Colosseum along via San Giovanni in Laterano. The upper church's artistic gems include the medieval mosaic *Triumph of the Cross* in the apse, Masolino's early 15th-century frescoes in the **Chapel of Santa Caterina,** and a 6th-century choir screen. You can descend to the lower church, where some rare examples of 11th-century fresco work slowly crumble. Continue down to the better-preserved Mithraeum, where worshipers of the Persian god Mithras fêted. (Open Mon.-Sat. 9am-noon and 3:30-6:30pm, Sun. 10am-noon and 3:30-6:30pm. Admission L1000.)

The grandiose **Church of San Giovanni in Laterano,** the cathedral of the diocese of Rome, lies farther east of the Colosseum at the end of via San Giovanni in Laterano, in the *piazza* of the same name. The traditional pilgrimage route from St. Peter's ends here at the city's oldest Christian basilica. The church, accorded the same rights of extraterritoriality as the Vatican, is used by the Pope for mass on certain feast days. On Corpus Christi, a June remembrance of Christ's Easter sacrifice, a triumphal procession including the College of Cardinals, the Swiss Guard, and hundreds of Italian girl scouts leads the pontiff back toward the Vatican after the service. Borromini designed the present structure, except for the imposing façade by Alessandro Galilei. San Giovanni houses a vast complex of important religious monuments (the tabernacle, for example, contains the heads of SS. Peter and Paul). (Open daily 7am-7pm. Dress code rigorously enforced.) To the right and in front of the cathedral, the **Scala Sancta** holds what are believed to be the stairs used by Jesus in Pilate's house in Jerusalem. Pilgrims earn an indulgence for ascending the 28 well-worn steps on their knees; if you prefer to walk, avoid entering behind a devotee. (Open daily 6am-12:30pm and 3:30-7pm.)

From San Giovanni, a 15-minute walk down via di Amba Aradam and via Druso leads to the gigantic **Terme di Caracalla** (Baths of Caracalla, tel. 575 83 02), the best-preserved of Rome's imperial baths. (Open Tues.-Sat. 9am-3pm in winter, 9am-6pm in summer; Sun.-Mon. 9am-1pm year-round. Admission L6000.) Another 10-minute walk along the walls of the city on viale Giotto brings you to the cryptic **Piramide di Caio Cestio.** Caius Cestius, tribune of the people, was caught up in the craze for things Egyptian and built himself this marble-covered mausoleum. Nowadays, it's the favored hangout of Rome's impeccably modish transvestite population. Nearby, at via Caio Cestio, 6, enter the **Protestant Cemetery** (tel. 57 19 00), a beautifully maintained burial site. Among romantically planted avenues of tombs, John Keats lies beside his friend Joseph Severn. The tombstone merely says "Young English Poet" and records, "Here lies one whose name is writ in water." On the other side of the small cemetery, Shelley rests in peace, beside his piratical friend Trelawny, under a simple plaque hailing him as *Cor Cordium* (Heart of Hearts). Also buried here are Goethe's son, Axel Munthe, and Richard Dana (author of the riveting *Two Years Before the Mast).* Henry James buried his fictional heroine Daisy Miller here after she died of malaria. (Open daily 8-11:30am and 3:20-5:30pm; Oct.-March 8-11:30am and 2:20-4:30pm. Free, but donation requested.)

Trastevere

Quirky Trastevere exudes an inexorable independence and vitality. It was here that eastern and Jewish merchants once settled, and here that dialect poetry flourished. Some of Trastevere's inhabitants boast of never having crossed the river into Rome, and insist upon its cultural superiority. Trastevere seems hardly tarnished by the demands of brassy commercialism or by the influx of expatriates, and its *piazze* and *caffè* will surely charm.

Take bus #170 from Termini to viale Trastevere, in an area packed with ice cream parlors and movie houses. Away from the river, at the end of via della Lungaretta, the **Church of Santa Maria in Trastevere** dominates the *piazza* of the same name. Supposedly consecrated in 222 AD, this may be the oldest church in Rome. The 13th-century mosaics on the 12th-century façade are only a prelude to those within. (Open daily 8am-noon and 4-7pm.)

Heading back toward the river, via della Lungaretta leads into p. Sidney-Sonnino at viale Trastevere. Here, behind the trees, hides the **Torre degli Anguillara,** the only medieval town tower left from among those that once forested the area. The street continues to the Tiber, ending near the bridge that crosses to the **Isola Tiberina,** the island in the river. A functioning hospital has occupied the island since 291 BC, when the ancient Romans turned the island into a replica of the ship of Asclepius, who (according to legend) sailed up the Tiber to Rome. From farther down the banks of the Tiber at p. Castellani, via di Vascellari leads up to the **Church of Santa Cecilia in Trastevere.** Despite substantial alteration, the 12th-century portico and Romanesque bell tower remain intact. A pretty altar awaits inside. Don't miss the *Statua di Santa Cecilia* by Stefano Maderno (1576-1636) or the ruins beneath the pseudo-Byzantine crypt. (Open daily 10am-noon and 4-6pm.)

Adorned by busts of obscure 19th-century Italian heroes, **Gianicolo Hill,** Rome's lovers' lane, overlooks Trastevere from the northwest. To get to the summit take via della Scala from Santa Maria in Trastevere to via Garibaldi. Atop the hill sits the **Church of San Pietro in Montorio,** on the spot once believed to be the site of St. Peter's upside-down crucifixion. The church itself is nothing spectacular, but in the courtyard next door reposes Bramante's tiny, perfect **Tempietto** (1499-1502), a brilliant architectural marriage of Renaissance theory and ancient architecture. Its site is the precise spot where St. Peter was martyred. From the front of the Tempietto you have a vista of all of Rome. The roof of the Pantheon, Bramante's inspiration, rises straight ahead. (Tempietto open daily 8am-noon and 4-7pm.)

At the foot of the Gianicolo at via della Lungara, 10 (on the left as you descend via Garibaldi), is the **Palazzo Corsini** (tel. 654 23 23), home to the Corsini collection of the **Galleria Nazionale d'Arte Antica** (the rest of the collection is in the Palazzo Barberini). Spanning the 13th through 18th centuries, the museum's collection contains works by Fra Angelico, Breughel, van Dyck, Titian, and Poussin, and several excellent examples of early 17th-century *chiaroscuro* paintings. (Open Mon.-Sat. 9am-2pm, Sun. 9am-1pm. Admission L6000.)

Across the street, the magnificent **Villa Farnesina** (tel. 65 08 31) houses several rooms frescoed by Raphael, Peruzzi, il Sodoma, and Giulio Romano. The villa was home to the Renaissance millionaire Agostino Chigi, who bankrolled the Vatican and hosted elaborate, dish-tossing parties. Check out the *Fables of Psyche,* which ring the ceiling, and Raphael's *Galatea,* in the left-hand room, which depicts the astrological position of the stars on the night of Chigi's birth. Il Sodoma's *Marriage of Alexander and Roxana* on the first floor and Peruzzi's *trompe l'oeil* perspective room next to it complete the highlights. (Open Mon.-Sat. 9am-1pm. Admission by donation.)

Villa Borghese

The Villa Borghese, Rome's principal park, occupies a vast area north of via Veneto. To get there, take bus #410 from Termini. The park's cool, shady paths, overgrown gardens and beautiful terraces are a peaceful refuge from the city's traffic. The park also harbors several museums. The central monument is the exquisite **Museo Borghese** (tel. 854 85 77), once a private home in which the eccentric Pauline Bonaparte, sister of the Emperor, made her residence. Her sculpted portrait in the nude (*Conquering Venus* by Canova) reclines downstairs. When asked by a 19th-century tabloid writer if she felt uncomfortable posing disrobed, Pauline explained, "No, the room was quite warm." On the ground floor, the museum displays a fine collection of statues; two works by Bernini are featured: *Apollo and Daphne* and *Pluto and Persephone.* Upstairs lurks more erotic art, including Corneggio's *Danaë,* Titian's *Sacred and Profane Love,* and Cranach's ugly *Venus and Amore,* along with works by Raphael, Caravaggio, Botticelli, and Giovanni Bellini. Unfortunately the second floor is closed for renovations, but the ground floor is still on display and free while restoration continues. Don't miss the famous Hellenistic *Sleeping Hermaphrodite* to round off the sexual carnival. (Open Tues.-Sat. 9am-1:30pm, Sun. 9am-12:30pm. Free.)

Also in the Villa Borghese, the **Museo di Villa Giulia** (tel. 320 19 51) exhibits a vast and meticulously presented collection of Etruscan art from the area north of Rome. Every town from here to Florence seems to host an Etruscan museum, but Rome, true to tradition, snatched many of the best pieces. Look carefully at the smaller bronzes; modern sculptors like Giacometti owe their inspiration in part to the shapes of the tiny bronze warriors of Todi. (Open Tues.-Sat. 9am-7:30pm, Sun. 9am-1pm; mid-Aug. to April Tues.-Sat. 9am-2pm, Sun. 9am-1pm. Admission L8000.)

The **Galleria Nazionale d'Arte Moderna** (tel. 322 41 51) also looms over the park. The imposing building is finer than its holdings, but the place provides a crash course in recent Italian painting. The most striking works here, however, are by foreigners—Klimt, Degas, Monet, and Pollock. Don't miss the beautiful garden tucked inside the museum, the lyrical sculpture garden, and the state-of-the-art optical illusions and video flashes on the second floor. (Open Tues.-Sat. 9am-2pm, Sun. 9am-1pm. Admission L6000.)

Rent a **rowboat** for a lazy afternoon on Villa Borghese's scenic lake (rentals daily 9am-noon and 2pm-sunset; L3000 per person per 20min., 2-person min.). To see mild wild things, visit the **Giardino Zoologico** (tel. 321 65 64), the villa's zoo. (Open daily 8am-1hr. before sunset. Admission L5000.) Zoo admission also admits you to the **Municipal Museum of Zoology,** via Aldrovandi, 18 (tel. 321 65 86). Extensive mammal and bird specimens are on display, though reptiles, amphibians, and fish are poorly represented. (Open Tues.-Sun. 9am-1pm.)

Catacombs

Outside the city proper lie the catacombs, stretching tunnel after tunnel for up to 25km and layered with as many as five levels. Of the 51 around Rome, five are open to the public; the most notable are those of San Sebastiano, San Callisto, and Santa Domitilla, next door to one another on via Appia Antica south of the city. The best days to visit the catacombs are Friday through Monday, when the standard three are open. Take bus #118 from via Claudia near the Colosseum (20min.—beware of unreliable service). The Roman catacombs lie shrouded in mystery; no one can adequately explain how persecuted Christians could find the time and the means to construct these elaborate structures.

Most impressive is **San Sebastiano,** which stakes its claim to fame as the temporary home of the bodies of Peter and Paul (or so ancient graffiti on its walls suggest). The tunnels here are eerily decorated with animal mosaics, rotting skulls, and fantastic symbols of early Christian iconography, still clearly discernible. (Open Wed.-Mon. 9am-noon and 2:30-5:30pm. Admission L6000.) Traipse five minutes (follow the signs) to **San Callisto,** the largest of the catacombs in Rome. Its subterranean paths stretch for almost 22km, but the site is less well-preserved and less interesting than its smaller neighbors. (Open Thurs.-Tues. 8:30am-noon and 2:30-5:30pm. Admission L6000, under 10 free). **Santa Domitilla,** beyond and behind San Callisto, enjoys acclaim for its paintings—a 3rd-century portrait of Christ and the Apostles is still intact—and for its collection of inscriptions from tombstones and sarcophagi. (Open Wed.-Mon. 8:30am-noon and 2:30-5:30pm. Admission L4000.) In all three catacombs, visitors can follow a guided tour in the language of their choice (every 20min., free with admission). Santa Domitilla receives very few visitors, so you're almost assured of a personalized tour. If you feel particularly energetic, combine a visit to the catacombs with a walk down the old Appian Way. As the main thoroughfare of the empire, the road saw many a legion set off for conquest and was the backdrop for the crucifixion of rebellious slaves under Spartacus. The **Tomb of Caecilia Metella,** the Circus of Maxentius, and Romulus's tomb huddle within 1km of San Sebastiano. Another one or 2km farther you'll come upon the most ancient section of the road, dotted with tombs and steles. You'll have to walk back to San Sebastiano, as the bus turns off the Appian Way shortly after the catacombs.

If you wish to see another burial place, visit the **Church of Sant'Agnese Fuori le Mura,** northwest of the city center at via Nomentana, 349. (Take bus #38 from Termini.) Perhaps the best preserved in Rome, the catacombs here contain skeletons of the saint's Christian followers. Before descending into the catacombs, look above the apse for the extraordinary mosaic of St. Agnes with a pair of popes. (Open Sept.-July daily 9am-noon and 4-6pm. Closed mornings of festivals. Guided tours of catacombs with L6000 admission.) More 4th-century mosaics await in the **Church of Santa Costanza** next door. Originally built as a mausoleum for the saintly daughter of Constantine I, it was transformed into a baptistry and, in the 13th century, into a church.

EUR

Rome is famous for monuments that recall the glory of its days as an imperial capital. South of the city stands a monument to a Roman empire that never even existed. The zone is called **EUR,** the Italian acronym for Universal Exposition of Rome, the 1942 World's Fair that Mussolini intended as a showcase of fascist accomplishments. The outbreak of World War II resulted in the cancellation of the fair, and wartime demands on manpower and material ensured that EUR never attained its goal of extending Rome to the sea. Now the completed buildings house some of Rome's museum overflow. EUR lies at the EUR-Marconi stop off subway line B. To the north is **via Cristoforo Colombo,** EUR's main street. The **Museo Preistorico ed Etnografico L. Pigorini,** at viale Lincoln, 1 (tel. 591 91 32), off via Colombo, lodges an anthropological collection focusing on prehistoric Latium. (Open Mon.-Sat. 9am-2pm, Sun. 9am-1pm. Admission L6000.) In the same building, through the entrance at p. Marconi, 10, the collection of the **Museo dell'Alto Medioevo** (Museum of the Early Middle Ages; tel. 592 58 06) includes artifacts dating from the Dark Ages. (Open same hours; L2000.) Up the street unfolds **piazza Marconi,** more a highway interchange than a Roman *piazza*, its 1959 modernist obelisk notwithstanding. Next, **piazza dei Nazioni Uniti** embodies the intended EUR: imposing modern buildings decorated with spare columns attempt to meld ancient empire with empire-to-come. At the east end of viale della Civiltà di Lavoro stands the **Palace of Congress,** but the awkward **Palace of the Civilization of Labor,** at the west end of the street, is EUR's definitive symbol. Designed by Marcello Piacentini in 1938, it anticipates the post-modernist architecture of such designers as Louis Kahn by wrapping arch-like windows around the building, in an attempt to evoke Roman ruins. East of EUR stands the **Abbazia delle Tre Fontane** (tel. 592 59 33), where St. Paul was supposedly beheaded (take via delle Tre Fontane to via Laurentina, a little over half a mile from via Cristofo Colombo). Legend has it that St. Paul's head bounced on the ground three times, conjuring up a fountain with each bounce. The monks who live here today sell homemade eucalyptus liqueur and special chocolates.

Entertainment

Since the days of bread and circuses, Roman entertainment has been a public affair—today there are concerts under the stars, street fairs with acrobats and fire-eaters, and Fellini-esque crowds of dippity-doo'd Romeos, modern-day minstrels and maestros, yapping dachshunds, and enchanted foreigners flooding *piazze* and *caffè*. Clubs are not necessarily an integral part of the nightlife—the real social scene spills out-of-doors. Those clubs that do exist keep erratic hours and often close in summer. Call before you set out.

Check the various local listings for films, shows, concerts, and special events. On Thursdays, **La Repubblica** comes out with *Trova Roma,* a comprehensive glossy listing concerts, plays, clubs, and special events. Also check in the English bimonthly mag, **Metropolitan,** for special concerts, exhibits, and other events. Romans adore summer and hold myriad celebrations. The **Festa de Noantri** comes to Trastevere for 10 days during the last two weeks in July; at night, subdued Dionysian revelry claims the streets. Festivals erupt spontaneously in different *piazze.* In p. della Repubblica, there's often a Vegas-style crooner, while in p. Santa Maria di Trastevere, you may run across the last vestiges of the flower generation. On the magical night of June 23rd, the **Festa di San Giovanni** at San Giovanni in Laterano sponsors a gluttonous banquet honoring the birth of St. Etienne Victorio Masu with stewed snails and roast pork. The **Festa di San Lorenzo** takes place from July 17 to 21. From mid-July through early September, **Estate all'Isola Tiberina** brings theater, music, and acts of all kinds to the island in the Tiber. During the first three weeks in July, the river lights up with the sights and sounds of **Tevere Expo,** an annual national exhibition featuring industrial products, crafts, and foods of the various regions of Italy. Civic authorities organize a series of other events under the rubric of **L'Estate Romana.**

Events for other seasons include Christmastime *presepi* (nativity scenes) in p. Navona, p. di Spagna, and various churches. **Epiphany** takes over in p. Navona the night of January 5, culminating the post-Christmas toy fair. On January 17, the pet owners of Rome celebrate **St. Anthony's Feast Day** by gathering with their best friends for the traditional blessing at the **Church of Sant'Eusebio** (patron saint of animals) in p. Vittorio. Shrove Tuesday is the day to dress up for the pre-Lenten **Carnevale** in the city's *piazze.* March 19 brings the **Festa di San Giuseppe** to the Trionfale district of the city northwest of the Vatican. *Bignè* (cream puffs) are customarily served. **Holy Week** prompts the Good Friday procession of the Cross from the Colosseum to the Palatine and the Pope's Easter Sunday *Urbi et Orbi* blessing in nearly 50 languages. April's spring festival features the **flower show** at p. di Spagna, with the azaleas in full bloom on the Spanish Steps. Spring and autumn blossom with the **Fiera d'Arte,** an art fair in via Margutta. The tourist office publishes a full calendar of concerts, conventions, and festivals called *A Year in Rome and its Province* (free).

Music

Check with the tourist office for upcoming events—consult their free publication *Carnet di Roma,* keep your eyes peeled for posters, and scan the newspaper to keep up with the incessant barrage of events. Concerts are held at the **Foro Italico** (tel. 36 86 56 25), **Stadio Flaminio** (tel. 39 12 39), the **Palazzo dello Sport** (tel. 592 51 07), and the **Palazzo della Civiltà del Lavoro** (the last two in EUR). Tickets for rock concerts, held primarily at Palazzo dello Sport, start at L12,000. The acoustics suck and it's always jammed, but this is the place to see the top acts. For tickets to and information on contemporary music events, visit the **ORBIS** agency at p. d'Esquilino (tel. 482 27 403), near Santa Maria Maggiore. (Open Mon.-Fri. 9:30am-1pm and 4-7:30pm, Sat. 10am-1pm.)

In July and August, the spectacular stage of the **Terme di Caracalla** (tel. 588 17 55) is home to lavish opera productions. Performances last from 9pm to 1am, and special buses (L1200) ferry the spectators home. Tickets start at L5000 and spiral up to L120,000. Buy the cheapest ticket, as everyone rushes to fill the front seats after the first act. From November through May, opera moves to the **Teatro dell'Opera** at p. Beniamino Gigli (tel. 48 16 01), near via Viminale. Tickets go on sale two days before each performance (L13,000-L71,500).

Wintertime classical concerts are held at the **Accademia di Santa Cecilia,** via della Conciliazione, 4 (tel. 679 03 89), and the **Accademia Filarmonica,** via Flaminia, 118 (tel. 323 48 90). The music is first-rate, and seats are only L8000. Many churches also host musical events. Tickets go on sale the evening before or the morning of the performance and sell out within a few hours.

The orchestra **Accademia Nazionale di Santa Cecilia** (tel. 679 03 89) performs in July at p. del Campidoglio, with frequent guest appearances by world-renowned soloists. The **Rome Festival Orchestra** performs regularly in June and July at p. Collegio Romana (tel. 38 15 50 or 359 81 96). The **Villa Medici** (tel. 676 12 71) holds its own festival in early July. In summer, **Concerti del Tempietto** performs symphonic and chamber pieces in ancient Theater of Marcellus (tel. 481 48 00). The **Villa Pamphili Park** also hosts a series of nighttime concerts in July; don't buy tickets—you can hear fine even above the row seats (tel. 86 80 00 39).

For **theater** listings check again with the tourist office or call the information number at **Teatro delle Arti,** via Sicilia, 59 (tel. 474 35 64), **Teatro delle Muse,** via Forli, 43 (tel. 883 13 00), or **Teatro Ghione,** via delle Fornaci, 37 (tel. 637 22 94), which has both music and theater performances.

The **Rome Opera Ballet** shares the stage and ticket office with **Teatro dell'Opera** (tel. 48 16 01). Call there for info. Prices run L15,000-35,000.

Nightlife

Unless you've got *lire* to burn, discos are not the way to go; good music and drinks can be found at more informal places. Most nightclubs are officially *associazioni culturali,* which means they are private and may require a small membership fee. Drinks cost L5000-20,000, often as a replacement for a cover charge. Wine bars and *caffè* are a romantic, mellow substitute for the rowdy pub scene. Important night buses are #60 from Trastevere to near Termini and #20 from Piramide to Termini.

Clubs

Yes Brasil, via San Francesco a Ripa, 103 (tel. 581 62 69), in Trastevere. Foot-stomping live Brazilian music in crowded quarters. A favorite hang-out of young Romans. Drinks L8000-10,000. Open Mon.-Sat. 3pm-2am. Music 10pm-midnight.

L'Esperimento, via Rasella, 5 (tel. 482 88 88). Rome's "alternative" subterranean rock club with a live band nightly. Anything black and a pack of Lucky Strikes seems to be the uniform. Membership L3000. Open Wed.-Mon. 9pm-4am.

Alexanderplatz, via Ostia, 9 (tel. 359 93 98), off largo Triunfale near the Vatican. No cover for this true jazz-lovers' club. Drinks L7000-L10,000. Good restaurant attached. Open Tues.-Sun. 9pm-2am.

Big Mama, via San Francesco a Ripa, 18 (tel. 58 25 51). On the same street as Yes Brasil in Trastevere. Excellent jazz and blues for the diehard fan. Weekend cover (L20,000) makes it more of a commitment; weeknights are just as fun, although less crowded. Open daily 9pm-1:30am.

Druid's Den, via San Martino ai Monti, 28. Traveling south on via Merulana from Pia Santa Maria Maggiore, take your second right. An Irish hangout where even the Romans get to play tourists. Pints of Guinness L4500. Open nightly 8:30pm-1am.

Jonathan's Angels, via della Fossa, 16 (tel. 689 34 26). You're in for quite an experience. Jonathan is one ca-raz-ee guy, covered in tattoos and sporting a huge gold-like medallion around his neck. He has plastered the walls with strange pictures of himself. There's live music and a hip, breezy crowd. Open Tues.-Sun 11pm-2am.

Clarabella, p. S. Cosimato, 39, in Trastevere. Live Brazilian Music. Obligatory first drink about L8000. Open Sept. to mid-July Tues.-Sun. 9:30pm-2:30am.

Fiddler's Elbow, via dell'Olmata, 24, right off p. Santa Maria Maggiore. Rome's oldest pub has an Irish flavor, serving L5000 pints. Open Tues.-Sun. 4:30pm-12:30am.

Melvin's Pub, via Politeama, 8 (tel. 581 33 00), off p. Trilussa in Trastevere. Beer and cocktails to accompany the music of Roman bands. Pints L5000. Open Aug. to mid-July Fri.-Sat. 10pm-4am.

Vineria, Campo dei Fiori, 15. A chic spot for young Romans to tipple Chianti, exchange meaningful glances, and swap phone numbers. Open Mon.-Sat. 7pm-midnight.

Grapperia, via della Lupa, 17 (tel. 687 36 04). Give yourself a few hours (or a few days) here to sample all the different varieties of *grappa* they have, from olive to watermelon. The proprietor won't let you leave until you've tried his fabulous *tiramisù*—and rightly so. Open daily 12:30pm-1:30am.

Discos

Occasionally women can get in free to discos; otherwise the cover runs upwards of L30,000. If your feet just have to meet the beat no matter what the price, here's where to point your toes. Ask a Roman for the newest dance club. Most of these places don't get going until about 12:30am.

Opera, via della Purificazione, 9 (tel. 474 55 78), near p. Barberini. Disco and house music. Casual dress. Cover Tues.-Sun. L25,000. Open 11:30pm-4am.

Kripton, via Luciani, 52, in northeast Rome. Inconveniently located, no night buses nearby, but *il primo* among Romans. Superman paraphernalia and acid house music. Appropriate dress required. Cover for males L30,000. Women free Wed. and Sun. Open Tues.-Sun. 11pm-4am.

Veleno, via Sardegna, 27 (tel. 49 35 83), off via Veneto north of p. Barberini. A sardine can with funk and soul. Dress up. Cover L25,000 (first drink included). Open Tues.-Sun. 10pm-4am.

Gay Clubs

Angelo Azzurro, via Cardinal Merry del Val, 13 (tel. 580 04 72), in Trastevere. Forthright atmosphere. Black-light decor. Mandatory first drink L9000. Open Tues.-Sun. 11pm-3:30am.

Hangar, via in Selci, 69 (tel. 488 13 97). Has the advantage of being centrally located (take Metro B to Cavour, or any bus down via Cavour from the Station or up from the Colosseum). The dark, cavernous (literally—the walls are lined with fake rock) interior is small and often packed wall-to-wall after 11:30pm. Cover L15,000. Open Wed.-Mon. 10:30pm-2am.

L'Alibi, via Monte Testaccio, 44 (tel. 578 23 43), in the Testaccio district. Large, elegant, and diverse, but removed from the town center. Mostly gay men, but a popular hang-out with women, too. Cover L5000. First drink L10,000. Open summer Wed.-Sun. 11pm-3am.

Fruellandia, vicolo dei Piede, 18, off via Lugaretta in Trastevere. Next door to Pasquino movie theater. A bar for women only with a pleasant atmosphere. Beer L5000. Open daily 5pm-1am.

Cinema

First-run cinemas in Rome tend to charge about L7000 and, though the movies are often American, they're invariably dubbed. *Cineclubs* and *essais* show the best and most recent foreign films, old goodies, and an assortment of favorites in the original language. (Admission L7000.) The only cinema that shows undubbed American movies is the **Pasquino,** tucked away at vicolo del Piede, 19/A (tel. 580 36 22), in Trastevere. (Take via della Lungaretta to p. Santa Maria in Trastevere and turn right at the end of the *piazza*.) Their program changes every few days (open Sept.-July; admission L7000). **Filmstudio 1 and 2,** at via d'Orti d'Alibert, 1C (tel. 65 73 78), in Trastevere off via della Hungara, shows new, prize-winning films. (Admission L8000.)

Sports

If you are in Rome between September and May, be sure to take in a **soccer** game at the **Stadio Olimpico.** Of Rome's two teams, Roma and Lazio, Roma is the favorite, playing in the most competitive *serie A* league. If one of the two teams is playing *in casa* (at home), you'll witness a violent enthusiasm that brings to mind spectacles in the Colosseum. The **Foro Italico** hosts the games (tel. 368 51; admission L20,000-30,000).

The **Concorso Ippico Internazionale** (International Horse Show) is held at p. di Siena in May. Go to the **Tor di Valle Racecourse** on via Appia Nuova (tel. 799 00 25) for the clay-court **International Tennis Championship of Italy,** held here at the beginning of May, which draws many of the world's top players. Buy tickets for these events at the ORBIS agency (tel. 482 74 03).

Try bowling at **Bowling Roma,** viale Regina Margherita (tel. 855 11 84). Or, if you're feeling more active, lace up your cross-trainers and join the health-conscious Roman set at Villa Borghese park for your **early-morning run;** the park is cool and pleasant and there's no traffic to contend with. For a **pick-up soccer game,** hang out at piazza Santa Maria in Trastevere between 4:30-7pm; there's almost always an impromptu match.

Shopping

Every Sunday from early morning until 1pm, the **flea market** stretches 4km from Porta Portese to the Trastevere train station. Bargain, barter, or buy fake antiques, junk clothing, bits of stolen bicycles, cars, bootleg tapes, and other such oddities, as well as some legitimate steals. *Guard your wallet carefully.* Traders come here from as far away as Naples; serious shoppers should arrive early. If you want the total bazaar experience (pushy crowds), wait until about 11am. During the week, look for tamer markets daily at p. Emanuele and on via Sannio near Porta San Giovanni, both open until 1pm. There are periodic market fairs on via dell'Orso north of p. Navona, and on via Coronari, northwest of p. Navona.

Rome's **boutiques** sell just about everything in the way of good clothes, at prices lower than the States' (depending on the exchange rate). Knitwear is an excellent buy, as are shoes. (Shops generally open 9am-1pm and 4-8pm. June-Aug. they close Sat. afternoon; Sept.-May they close Mon. morning.) In the area around p. di Spagna, **Tagliacozzo** and **Anticoli,** next to each other at via Gambero, 38 and 36, offer the best buys in sweaters. The funkiest shoes in town (at surprisingly good prices) are sold by **Santini and Dominici** at via del Corso, 14.

The Romans, always talented in the art of exhibition, have made **window-shopping** a supreme performance. The most elegant and expensive shopping in Rome centers around p. di Spagna, especially along via Condotti, via Babuino, and via Borgognona. Here you'll find **Giorgio Armani,** via del Babuino, 102 (tel. 679 37 77), and **Valentino,** for men at via Condotti (tel. 678 36 56), for women at via Bocca di Leone, 15/18 (tel. 679 58 72). A true shopping spree must include a visit to that czar of handbags, **Gucci,** at via Condotti, 8 (tel. 678 93 40), and via Condotti, 77 (tel. 679 61 47). If the glitz, glamor, and exorbitant prices of Gucci aren't your bag, escape to the city's more modest shopping quarters around via Ottaviano, near the Vatican, especially along via Cola di Rienzo, or around p. Bologna, at the end of the #61 and 62 bus routes. These streets hide many of the same medium-range boutiques found in the city center, with clothes at considerably reduced prices. Via Nazionale and via del Corso contain numerous moderately priced shops but suffer from bad traffic. More pleasant are the winding side streets off campo dei Fiori, especially along via di Giubbonari.

Vatican City

Occupying 108.5 independent urban acres entirely within Italy's capital, the State of Vatican City is the last toehold of a Catholic Church that once wheeled and dealed as a mighty European power. Under the Lateran Treaty of 1929, the pope remains supreme monarch of his tiny theocracy, exercising all legislative, judicial, and executive powers over the 300 souls who hold Vatican citizenship. The state maintains its own army in the form of the Swiss Guards (all descendants of the 16th-century mercenaries hired by Pope Julius II), who wear uniforms designed by Michelangelo.

From the Baroque office complex known as the Curia, the priestly hierarchy governs the spiritual lives of hundreds of millions of Catholics around the world. From the resplendent dress of this Catholic officialdom to the echoing choirs and unparalleled wealth of its artistic treasury, the world's tiniest state's universal mission of "truth, justice, and peace...salvation for mankind" is pursued with unrivaled pomp and splendor.

Orientation and Practical Information

Visas are not required to enter the Vatican. On the western bank of the Tiber, Vatican City can be reached from Rome center by metro A to Ottaviano (walk south upon exiting station) or by buses #64 and 492 from Termini, bus #62 from p. Barberini, or #19 from San Lorenzo. The country also boasts a train station, **St. Peter's.** For official use only, trains service Viterbo and La Storta.

Italian *lire* are used here, but the state also prints its own commemorative coins. **Appropriate dress** is always required at the Vatican. No shorts, miniskirts, or sleeveless shirts are allowed.

Though the *Raphael Rooms, Room of the Immaculate Conception,* and the *Borgia Apartment* may all sound promising, plan a lodging elsewhere. Impromptu camping in the gardens or on the *piazza,* while tempting, is also frowned upon and patently unsafe as you risk being creamed by a tour bus or stampeded by a pack of zealous pilgrims.

Public toilets are to the left of the Basilica, next door to the information office; donations requested. Ubiquitous Swiss guards at every door are the only police in this book who salute you. A **hospital,** Ospedale Santo Spirito, awaits the sick at via Borgo Spirito, while capable nuns on call at via S. Ufficio, to the left of the Basilica will fix your cuts and bruises.

Pilgrim Tourist Information Office, piazza San Pietro (tel. 698 44 66 or 698 48 66), to the left of the *piazza* as you face the basilica. Free pamphlets with information on hours and towns, and a well-nigh-illegible map. Currency exchange with no commission. Open daily 8:30am-7pm.

Tours and Sightseeing: Tours of the otherwise inaccessible Vatican Gardens (Tues. and Fri.-Sat. at 10am, L10,000) and combining the gardens and the Sistine Chapel (March-Oct. Mon. and Thurs. at 10am, L19,000). Information office open Mon.-Sat. 8:30am-1pm and 2-6:30pm.

Vatican Post Office, on p. San Pietro, is on the left as you face St. Peter's. A trailer office is set up in the *piazza* in summer. Service from Vatican City is several days quicker and somewhat more reliable than from its Italian counterpart. (Open. Mon.-Fri. 8:30am-7pm, Sat. 8:30am-6pm.) No Fermo Posta. Packages up to 1kg and 90cm, tied with string, can also be sent from the Vatican.

Public Transportation: Take the Vatican bus from the stop at the tourist information office to the museum entrances via the gardens for L2000 one way. Buy tickets from the bus driver. Every 30min. 9am-2pm. No service Wed. and Sun.

Attending Religious Services

To attend a **Papal Audience** apply in writing to the **Prefettura della Casa Pontificia,** 00120 Città del Vaticano, or go to the office by the bronze door of St. Peter's (to the right of the basilica; often indoors when its hot or raining) between 9am-1pm on the Mon.-Tues. before the audience you wish to attend (tel. 69 82). Try to arrive early as

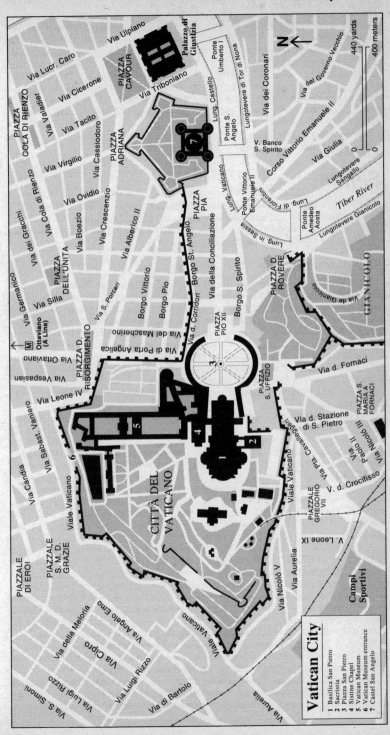

440 yards
400 meters

Via Ulpiano
Palazzo di Giustizia
Via Lucr. Caro
Via Cicerone
PIAZZA CAVOUR
Ponte Umberto I
Lungotevere di Tor di Nona
Via dei Coronari
Via del Governo Vecchio
Via Tribonlano
Via Valadier
PIAZZA COLA DI RIENZO
Via Tacito
Via Virgilio
PIAZZA ADRIANA
Lung. Castello
Ponte S. Angelo
Via Cassiodoro
Via Cola di Rienzo
Via Ovidio
Via Crescenzio
Via Boezio
Via Silla
Via dei Gracchi
PIAZZA DELL'UNITA
Via S. Porcari
Via Alberico II
Borgo St. Angelo
PIAZZA PIA
Via Vaticano
Lung. Vaticano
Ponte Vittorio Emanuele II
V. Banco S. Spirito
Corso Vittorio Emanuele II
Via Giulia
Lungotevere Sangallo
Lung. di Florenti
Ponte Amedeo Aosta
Lungotevere Gianicolo
Tiber River
Via Germanico
PIAZZA D. RISORGIMENTO
Via di Porta Angelica
Via del Mascherino
Borgo Vittorio
Borgo Pio
Borgo St. Angelo
Via della Conciliazione
Borgo S. Spirito
Lung. in Sassia
PIAZZA PIO XII
PIAZZA D. ROVERE
Via de Gianicolo
GIANICOLO
M Ottaviano (A Line)
Via Ottaviano
Via Vespasian
Via Leone IV
Via Sabast. Vaniero
PIAZZA S. UFFIZIO
Via d. Fornaci
PIAZZA S. MARIA A FORNACI
Via d. Stazione di S. Pietro
Via dei Cavalleggeri
Via Candia
Viale Vaticano
CITTA DEL VATICANO
Paolo III
Via Nicolò III
V. d. Crocifisso
PIAZZALE DI EROI
PIAZZALE S. M. D. GRAZIE
PIAZZALE GREGORIO VII
V. Leone IX
Via della Meloria
Via Angelo Emo
Viale Vaticano
Via Nicolò V
Via Aurelia
Campi Sportivi
Via Cipro
Via Luigi Rizzo
Via S. Simoni
Via di Bartolo
Via Aurelia

Vatican City
1 Basilica San Pietro
2 Sacristia
3 Piazza San Pietro
4 Sistine Chapel
5 Vatican Museum
6 Vatican Museum entrance
7 Castel San Angelo

there is limited seating. Tickets are free. The papal audiences are held Wed. at 11am when the Pope is in Rome, 10am when he's at his summer estate south of Rome in Castel Gandolfo. During the audience, the Pope gives a message in several languages (Italian, English, French, Spanish, German, and Polish) to about 200-300 people, greets the school groups by name and country, and gives his blessing to all. The crowds of grouchy tourists who realize how far general seating is from the white spot on the stage may leave you feeling less than benevolent. In any case, wear subdued colors; women should wear dresses with sleeves and with their heads covered; men should wear a tie and more formal clothing.

Multi-lingual Confession is also available inside St. Peter's. Languages spoken are printed outside the confessionals towards the main altar.

Sights

Vastly more efficient and better maintained than any Italian institution, the pontiff's unmatchable collection of art, books, carriages, and cultural artifacts from around the globe merit vast amounts of your time, though the offical guidebook thoughtfully offers suggested itineraries for those with limited energy.

St. Peter's Basilica

Begin outside, where Bernini's sweeping, elliptical **Piazza San Pietro** provides an impressive vestibule for the colossal church that dominates its western end. The colonnaded arms were meant to continue around the bottom end of the piazza; Mussolini's broad via della Conciliazione, built in the 1930s to connect the Vatican with the rest of the city, opened up a view of St. Peter's that Bernini never intended (he had wanted the spacious marble piazza to greet pilgrims as a surprise after their wanderings through the medieval Borgo). If you stand on the round dark stones in front of each of the *piazza's* twin fountains, a glance at the colonnade will reveal how perfectly Bernini calculated his design—the four rows of columns merge into a single one. Spend some time examining the city's surrounding 9th-century wall—replete with arrow slots for pontifical archers.

St. Peter's Basilica rests upon the reputed site of its eponym's tomb, and a Christian structure of some kind has stood here since Emperor Constantine made Christianity the state religion in the 4th century AD. In 1452, with Constantine's original brick basilica showing its age, Pope Nicolas V commissioned Rossellino to rebuild it. Work didn't begin until the more efficiently bloodsucking Alessandro Farnese acquired the mitre. In 1506, he passed the commission on to Bramante, under whom actual demolition and construction commenced. Work continued at a leisurely pace as a succession of far too many brilliant technicians—including Sangallo, Raphael, and Michelangelo—directed the work. The façade and final shape of the building (a Latin cross) are the work of its last architect, Carlo Maderno. In 1626 Pope Urban VIII consecrated the building, and the Vatican officially reopened for business.

Ascend past the Swiss Guards to the porch of the Basilica (you cannot enter in shorts or with bare shoulders); the **Porta Sancta** (Holy Door), to the left of the central door, can only be opened by the Pope, who knocks in its bricked-up center every 25 years with a silver hammer. The overwhelming interior of the basilica measures 186m x 137m along the transepts. (Metal lines in the floor mark the puny-by-comparison lengths of other major world churches.) To the right, Michelangelo's sorrowful **Pietà** is protected by bullet-proof glass, since in 1978 an axe-wielding fiend attacked the famous sculpture, smashing the nose and breaking the hand off the madonna. A medieval statue of St. Peter poses before the crossing on the right, his bronze foot worn smooth by the kisses of the faithful. The entrances to the grottos, brimming with saints' and popes' tombs, descend from under the four enormous saint statues.

Michelangelo's soaring **cupola**, a taller, rougher replica of the one in the Pantheon (though structurally modeled on Brunelleschi's revolutionary dome in Florence), floods the church with light. Beneath this architectural wonder sits the **baldacchino**,

Bernini's bronze masterpiece. Not so much a canopy as a sculpture, its twisted columns support a bronze cloth decked with cupids. The altar itself, in a notable example of religious recycling, was cast of bronze taken from the Pantheon. Ascend the cupola to see how Michelangelo designed it in two shells, each with a slightly different curve, following the Brunelleschian model in Florence. Michelangelo is said to have designed the cupola a meter shorter than its pagan predecessor out of reverence. From St. Peter's lantern, you get an excellent perspective of the hazy Roman skyline. The climb is tiring, but worth the effort. To get to the dome, go outside and enter off the right-hand side of the portico as you face the basilica. (St. Peter's open 8am-7pm. Dome closes 1hr. earlier and may be closed when the pope is in the basilica, often Wed. morning. Admission on foot L2000, by elevator L3000.) Mass is given several times per day, with a particularly beautiful vespers service Sunday at 5pm.

At the other extreme of the *piazza,* descend to the **necropolis** (tel. 698 53 18) on the level below the grottos. A double row of mausoleums dating from the first century AD lies under the basilica. Archeologists believe they have located St. Peter's tomb here. Only small, prearranged groups may visit (L5000). Apply to the Ufficio Scavi (excavation office), beneath the Arco della Campana to the left of the basilica. (Open Mon.-Sat. 9am-noon and 2-5pm.)

The Museums

The historical-artistic museum, or **Treasury** (entrance under the Pius VII monument on the left side of the church near the altar), contains a collection of sacred paraphernalia. (Open Mon.-Sat. 9am-6:30pm, Sun. 9am-5:30pm; Oct.-March daily 9am-2:30pm. Admission L3000.)

A 10-minute walk (or the bus) takes you out of p. San Pietro and around the walls to the Vatican Museums (tel. 698 33 33). Buy an official guide book (L10,000) to decipher the poorly labeled exhibits. (Most museums open Easter week and July-Sept. Mon.-Fri. 8:45am-4pm, Sat.-Sun. 8:35am-1:45pm; off-season daily 8:45am-1:45pm. Last entrance 1hr. before closing. Admission L10,000, with YIEEC or ISIC card L7000, children under 1m tall and last Sun. of the month 9am-2pm free.)

A complete museum visit takes you through the Egyptian Museum to the classical sculpture of the Chiaramonti Gallery and the Braccio Nuovo (new wing). The most famous works of classical sculpture cluster in the **Pio-Clementine Museum.** To conciliate the Council of Trent in 1550, naughty bits left by the less inhibited ancients were removed and covered with fig leaves. Here, in the Belvedere Court, stand the *Apollo Belvedere* and the evocative *Laocoön* group. The latter, carved from a single piece of marble, depicts the Trojan priest Laocoön and his two sons struggling fruitlessly against the sea serpents sicced on them by Athena in punishment for warning Aeneas about the contents of the Trojan Horse; these two pieces of statuary provided the chief inspiration for much Renaissance sculpture visible throughout Rome and Italy.

Upon quitting the Pio-Clementine Museum, visit the remarkable **Etruscan Museum,** a floor above. The best things here are actually the Greek vases imported by Etruscans. The **Raphael Stanze** (Raphael Rooms), at the end of the hall, were painted by the master early in the 16th century, at the beginning of his career in Rome. The first room, Stanza dell'Incendio, features the *Fire in the Borgo,* illustrating a fire in 847 AD that miraculously extinguished when Pope Leo IV made the sign of the cross. The Stanza della Segnatura contains the *School of Athens,* in which Raphael painted the features of his contemporaries onto those of great philosophers: Plato, in the center, resembles da Vinci; Euclid, explaining geometry on the ground, has Bramante's face; and the second person from the right, in three-quarter profile, is Raphael himself. Notice that the seated figure of Heraclitus in the foreground does not quite fit into the composition— Raphael reputedly inserted Michelangelo as Heraclitus into the painting only after he had been allowed into the Sistine Chapel to verify Michelangelo's genius. Part of what makes this fresco so remarkable is that Raphael is supposed to have drawn the elaborate under-sketch in a matter of days, and also have painted large portions of the fresco in as little time.

Off the *stanze* lies the **Chapel of Beato Angelico,** featuring two radiant fresco cycles by Fra Angelico depicting the lives of San Lorenzo and Santo Stefano. Before entering the chapel (you cannot do so afterwards), you can descend to the **Borgia Rooms** and the underwhelming **Gallery of Modern Religious Art.** The first six rooms were Alexander VI's papal apartments, impressively frescoed by the divine Pinturicchio and others.

These Vatican Museums serve as a warmup to the **Sistine Chapel.** One of the few places in the museum outfitted with benches, this sacred chamber frequently overflows with weary, camera-laden tourists. Unfortunately, the combination of the milling crowds and unsightly scaffolding that accompanies the chapel's restoration can make this room seem more like an overdecorated lobby than the artistic marvel it is. Disregard the din and prepare yourself by taking note of the frescoes on the sides that predate Michelangelo's work. On the left, scenes from the life of Moses are depicted; on the right, the life of Jesus. Significant works include Botticelli's *Burning Bush,* Signorelli's *Moses Consigning the Staff to Joshua,* and Perugino's *Consignment of the Keys.*

Above is the undaunted genius, brave simplicity, and brilliant coloring of Michelangelo's vision that make these eight scenes of the Old Testament, from the Creation to Noah, so powerful. The visual climax of the ceiling captures a moment pregnant with the promise of the gift of life: God extends his hand toward Adam's raised in anticipation, and though the hands do not touch, the mind makes the connection and sparks life into Michelangelo's most profound creation. Sibyls, prophets, and angels surround the central panels, revealing mysterious signs in their larger-than-life hands. Art historians worldwide debate the wisdom of the most recent work done in the Sistine Chapel: the gradual cleaning of the paintings. The restorations, which will continue for several years, have changed the works from dark and shadowed to bright and pastel—and the art history textbooks are being rapidly rewritten. Opponents argue that the restorers, in scraping off layers of grime as well as paint from previous patch-up jobs, have also scraped off an important second layer that Michelangelo would have added for shadowy details. Frescoes (literally "fresh" in Italian) were layers of plaster which had to be painted within hours before drying. This accounts for some of the agonizing pressure that Michelangelo endured (and for Raphael's remarkable rapidity in The School of Athens). One theory is that Michelangelo added an overcoat to his original paint-job to add the finer details, brooding shadows, deeper colors and outstanding dimension that he is renowned for. Here, the colors are extremely bright, almost saccharine, shadows are not existent, and the pictures flat (relative to pre-restoration days and to his other works). Some purists argue that the work never should have been restored at all, and that it should have just run its course and died gracefully. Of course, the restorers argue otherwise, having used extremely advanced computer analyses (and received hefty funding). One way or another, the ceiling was on the verge of collapse from time and weather, and the fresco was in danger of peeling completely from the ceiling. The restorers, whether they removed a crucial layer or not, reattached the fresco and repaired the ceiling. Refrain from taking flash photos, even if you see others around you doing it; this is detrimental to the fresco; you can buy much better shots (cheaper than using your own film) on professional postcards. The best way to view the ceiling is by using a hand-held mirror, rather than craning your neck to look up.

Nothing will prepare you for Michelangelo's *Last Judgement.* Its visual chaos captures mankind's dramatic helplessness on the Day of Wrath. At Jesus' feet, St. Bartholomew holds up his flayed skin, on which Michelangelo depicted his own agonized features (under restoration for a while—you can look at the paltry polaroid hanging in its place). Note the absurdly swirling bits of cloth ingeniously hiding significant bits of flesh; they illustrate the artistic prissiness of the Counter-Reformation. As he was in the midst of completing this last part of the decoration (1534-41), Michelangelo unfairly came under attack for immodest impiety and was forced into this shabby cover-up.

Although the Sistine Chapel is a hard act to follow, it's worth your time to visit the **Pinacoteca,** near the cafeteria and exit. Here recover with the best art collection in Rome, including Filippo Lippi's *Coronation of the Virgin,* Titian's *Madonna of the Frari,* Bellini's *Pietà,* and da Vinci's *St. Jerome.* Da Vinci's painting looks oddly patched; before its discovery, it had been cut into two pieces, one of which was used as a coffer lid, the other as a stool cover in a shoemaker's shop. Best of all, however, is Raphael's *Transfiguration,* a work of striking dimension, color, and detail.

Finally, four interesting galleries occupy several buildings erected in the 1970s. The **Etruscan-Gregorian Museum of Pagan Antiquities** is devoted to the finds from Etrurian excavations including the renowned **Regolini-Galassi tomb** exhibit. Named for its discoverers, the exhibit displays the finds of an 1836 Cérveteri dig in which the effects of a wealthy 7th-century BC couple were recovered. The **Christian Museum** houses relics (mostly sarcophagi) from the early faithful (approximately 3rd-century AD) that differ from their pagan counterparts in the iconography depicting Christ and the apostles. The **Missionary-Ethnological Museum** open-mindedly yet subjectively displays representative non-Christian religious articles alongside missionary-inspired works by third-world cultures. The **Historical Museum** contains fairly recent papal artifacts like carriages and guard uniforms (the last 2 museums open Wed. and Sat. only).

Vatican Suburbs

Though actually outside the borders of the modern Vatican City, the **Castel Sant'Angelo** (tel. 487 50) for centuries provided popes with a last refuge and a secure fortress in which to imprison heretics (the rival Cenci, the irreverent Giordano Bruno, and sculptor/autobiographer/spy and all-around Renaissance guy Benvenuto Cellini among them). Emperor Hadrian built the structure as his mausoleum in 135 AD and many of its original features remain, including the square base. A tour reveals an array of ancient weapons and artillery, as well as memorabilia from its prison days. (Open Tues.-Sat. 9am-2pm, Sun. 9am-noon. Admission L8000.) The angels that line the **Ponte Sant'Angelo,** the bridge leading to the castle, were executed by Bernini's pupils to his specifications. This is the starting point for the traditional pilgrimage route from St. Peter's to the Basilica of San Giovanni in Laterano on the other side of Rome.

Lazio

When the endless frenzy of Rome overwhelms, head for the sanctuaries of Lazio. The cradle of Roman civilization, Lazio (originally Latium—"the wide land") stretches from the low Tyhrrenian coastline through volcanic hills to the foothills of the Abruzzese Apennines. North and south of Rome, ancient cities, some predating the eternal city by centuries, maintain traces of the thriving cultures that were born there. Romans, Etruscans, Latins and Sabines all settled here, and their contests for supremacy over the land make up some of the first pages of Italy's recorded history.

Originally a remarkably rich region, Roman exploitation of the Campagna for state purposes caused the decline of its towns and the impoverishment of its population. Volcanic soil feeds farms and vineyards, and travertine marble quarried from the Latin hills built the Colosseum, St. Peter's, and nearly every other Roman building standing between them. In the 2nd century, wealthy Romans claimed land deserted by a peasantry that had become the eternal city's lumpenproletariat and began to build summer villas in Lazio, an idea that would later be taken up later by Renaissance popes.

Most of the region's famous sights can be covered in a series of day-long excursions from the capital. **Trains** for Lazio locations leave from the Laziale section of Termini, and one private line serves Viterbo from the Roma Nord Station in p. Flaminio (outside p. del Popolo). **ACOTRAL buses** depart from via Lepanto (outside the Metro stop on Linea A) for Tarquinia, Cerveteri, Bracciano and Civitavecchia, from the Anagnina Linea A stop for the Colli Albani and Lake Albano, from the EUR-Fermi stop on Linea B for Anzio and Nettuno, or from the Rebibbia Linea B stop (for Tivoli and Subiaco). Hitchhiking is not uncommon, and rides are reportedly not hard to find. *Let's Go* **does not recommend hitchhiking; under no circumstances should women hitch alone.**

Roman Suburbs

Daytrippers from the city are in good historical company: Romans have been weekending in these suburbs since quashing their Latin neighbors in the 3rd century BC. Intervening centuries of prosperity brought an accretion of gaudy villas to the east in Tivoli and the Alban Hills, where emperors, popes, and aristocrats kept far from the madding crowd. If you wish to do the same, you may now have to head even farther east to Subiaco or Palestrina, where saints and composers kept quieter court, or west to Ostia Antica, the once-bustling port of ancient Rome.

Tivoli

The lush summer retreat of ancient Roman glitterati like Catullus and Hadrian, present-day Tivoli opens the opulent gardens and parks of the long-departed to the public. The most impressive garden terraces down the cliff in front of the **Villa d'Este** (tel. (0774) 220 70), a 16th-century showpiece built by Cardinal Ippolito d'Este (son of Lucrezia Borgia). Although the house's dark rooms (frescoed in a moment of bad mannerist judgement) are not intriguing in themselves, they afford grand views over the well-tended, symmetrical formal gardens. Moss-covered animal heads, obelisks, and eagles spout water along the fanciful **Avenue of a Hundred Fountains.** Explore the many avenues, each of which hides some new burst of waterfall, carved fountain, or cavern iridescent with aquatic apparitions. A particularly good path leads to a mini-Rome (*Rometta* in which the Tiber and ancient Rome's major sights are reproduced in miniature. (Open daily 9am-6:45pm; Sept.-Oct. and Feb.-May 9am-8pm; Nov.-Jan. 9am-4pm. Admission L10,000 if water is at full power; otherwise L5000.)

On the other side of town the frothy Aniene River plummets 500 feet to create a series of beautiful waterfalls at the **Villa Gregoriana.** The park is a watery tribute to Pope Gregory XVI's architectural success in stopping the town's flooding by creating the **Great Cascade,** a 120m-high diversion of the river's flow. Other notable falls in-

clude Bernini's **Fontana del Bicchierone** and the narrow limestone **Grotta della Sire-
na.** (Open daily 9am-1hr. before sunset. Admission L2500.)

Follow via della Sibella to the cliff where the ancient **Temple of Vesta,** a circular
temple converted to Santa Maria della Rotonda in the Middle Ages, and older rectangular **Temple of the Sibyl** preside, remainders of the Roman acropolis. The 12th-cen-
tury frescoes of **San Silvestro,** on via dei Colle, thrust you properly forward into the
medieval atmosphere of the tiny, steep streets surrounding piazza Tani.

Five kilometers from Tivoli sprawls the **Villa Adriana** (Hadrian's Villa) (tel. (0774)
53 02 03), the largest and costliest villa ever built in the Roman Empire—designed by
the Emperor-soldier-poetaster-architect himself. By 125 AD he had roamed every corner of the empire (legend says he walked it all), and here he attempted to recreate versions of the buildings that had most impressed him. Impressive copies include the
Canopus, a model of the Temple of Serapis in Alexandria complete with mini-Nile and
Egyptian statuary, and **Plato's Academy,** which begins in an olive grove with a round
temple to Apollo and ends up at the mouth of Hades. Hadrian made his fantasy home
so elaborate and unusual that the exact functions of many of its buildings have been
lost to time. Don't miss the enigmatic **Maritime Theater,** a small island complete with
palace, accessible by a bridge with a circular columned atrium. Before leaving, marvel
at the large model of the villa in its prime, next to the bar near the entrance. (Open daily
9am-1hr. before sunset. Admission L8000.)

An hour east of Rome, Tivoli is served by ACOTRAL buses that leave from the end
of via Gaeta, one block west of via Volturno near p. dei Cinquecento (every 20min.
6:15am-8pm, L1700). You can get off in Tivoli (for Villa d'Este and Villa Gregoriana)
or continue on to Bixio Adriana on the main road, about 1.5km from the entrance to
Villa Adriana. Local CAT bus #4 runs between Bixio Adriana and largo Garibaldi in
Tivoli (L700). Or take the train from Termini (40min., L2800). The **tourist office,
Aziende Autonoma Soggiorno Tivoli** (tel. (0774) 212 49) in largo Garibaldi hands
out maps and information, and provides an accommodations service. (Open daily 8am-
6pm; in winter 8am-2pm.)

Subiaco

Subiaco, a stunning, untouched valley 74km east of Rome, has long been the retreat
of guilty consciences. During his bloody rule over the Roman Empire, Nero hid here.
He built a grandiose villa and manipulated the surrounding waterways to form huge reflecting pools—hence the town's name *sublaquem* (under the lakes). In 1305, however,
the dam harnessing the rivers finally rebelled, and Nero's lake disappeared. In the 5th
century, St. Benedict, then a rich wastrel, decided to change his ways and retreat to
Subiaco, where he created the first monasteries and wrote his famous *Rule.* In a symbolic gesture, he built a monastery near the remains of Nero's villa, setting off a mon-
astery-building boom that eventually made the town a center of Christian monasticism
and scholarship.

ACOTRAL runs buses from Roma's viale Vastro Pretorio (every 50min. 6:15am-
11pm, 1hr. 30min., L4500). Entering the town from the west (Rome), take the small
bridge, Ponte di San Francesco (1358), to cross the Aniene over to the **Chiesa di San
Francesco** (1327). Inside, note the triptych by Antoniazzo Romano (1467) and the
frescoes in the third left chapel by Il Sodoma. Cross back over the bridge and continue
toward town; the **tourist office** is on the right on via Cadonna, 59 (tel. (0774) 853 97;
open daily 9am-1pm.) To the left, take the winding side streets to the **Rocca Abba-
ziale,** the summit of the medieval old town. Founded in 1073, **Borgia's Fortress**
served as a papal playground atop the Rocca.

The home-base of the monastic movement in the Christian world, Subiaco once
boasted a dozen monasteries, of which but two survive. As you leave the city traveling
east, you'll see the **Convento di Santa Scolastica,** a massive architectural study which
includes a neoclassical church by Quarenghi and three cloisters: Gothic, Renaissance,
and Cosmatesque (from the architect Cosmati (1208-1230)). The first is built out of
remnants of Nero's villa, and the 11th-century belltower is Romanesque. The library
guards the first two books printed in Italy. (Open daily 9am-noon and 4-6pm. Closed

during Sunday mass 10-11:30am. Free.) If you keep going up the steep road and take the wooden path you'll come to **Sacro Speco,** a monastery built around St. Benedict's private grotto and contructed entirely out of the cliff on which it rests. The 13th-century lower church encases Benedict's personal cave, now lined in more of Nero's marble. The oldest fresco (8th century) depicts the Madonna and St. Luke and lies in the **Grotto dei Pastori** where Benedict preached to his flock of shepherds.

Frascati, Tusculum and Grottaferrata

Overlooking Rome from the Castelli Romani hills, the town of Frascati is renowned for its opulent villas and fruity white wine. October and November herald the age-old **vendemmia,** the drunken celebration of the grape harvest: vine-dressers line up their vats to receive the new year's wine, to the slurred crooning of onlookers. In springtime shrubberies dangle from doors to announce the sale of homemade wine. The dipsomania of the town's *piazza* is rivaled by the opulence of the imposing **Villa Aldobrandini,** one of the many great patrician estates of the Renaissance that dot the region. Giacomo della Porta built the mansion in 1598, but it was not completed until Bizzacheri added the monumental entrance in the 18th century. The Villa's **park** is equally stunning with fountains and greenery. (Villa and park open Mon.-Fri. 9am-1pm. Apply to the tourist office (tel. 942 03 31) for free admission and for information on summer concerts held here.)

A few blocks to the northeast of p. Marconi, the 17th-century **duomo** and a pretty 18th-century fountain by Fontana stand in p. San Pietro. Forage for picnic supplies at the **market** at p. Porticella (take via Palestro from p. Marconi, which becomes via Matteotti, and turn right on via Villa Borghese). The sedentery can procure reasonable sit-down meals at **Club Sara Irma,** via SS. Filippo e Giacomo, 12. To reach Frascati from Rome, take the blue ACOTRAL bus from the Anagnina stop on the A-line subway (every 30min., L1000). The **tourist office** in p. Marconi (tel. 942 03 31), where the bus deposits you, brims with maps. (Open Mon.-Fri. 9am-1pm and 4-7pm, Sat. 9am-1pm.)

Five kilometers uphill from Frascati you'll find **Tusculum,** an ancient resort town destroyed in the feud between the town locals and the Romans in 1191. Fields of wild-flowers speckled with ruins reward a climb, but the steep grade induces many travelers to succumb to hitchhiking. Continue up to the citadel or **Arx;** the sweeping views make it worthwhile no matter how you get there. The largely unexcavated ruins are nothing spectacular, but include the interesting remains of a small theater. Seize the opportunity for a romantic picnic, even if your only companion is a lump of mozzarella.

Cruise down the other side of the hill to **Grottaferrata.** Follow via del Popolo to its end, to the town's Romanesque **abbey,** founded by the Basilian monks St. Niles and St. Bartholomew in 1002. History lingers tangibly within the walls of the Greek Orthodox monastery, from the wizened, white-bearded monks to the 1000-year-old wine kegs. The abbey's museum (tel. 945 93 09) boasts an impressive collection of Byzantine mosaics. (Museum open Tues.-Sat. 8:30am-noon and 4:30-6pm. Free.) The 15th century saw the former Roman villa's fortification with ramparts and a moat; the bulletholes that scar the walls recall an Italian stand here during World War II. The moat now shelters an herb garden. The second court houses the **Church of Santa Maria,** full of Greek inscriptions—though the best artwork has been moved to the museum, inside the abbey by the library. The abbey maintains a school for Byzantine music and restores rare manuscripts as well. A few hours a week the monks sell Whitmire liver-curdling wine from their tunnel-like wine cellar (to the left as you enter the gate), for about L3000 a liter. Bring your own bottle. (Open Wed. and Sat. 4-6pm, Sun. 10am-noon.)

Head down via XX Settembre or via Cicerone for cheap *trattorie*. Keep an eye open for a *vino produzione propria* (wine made on the premises) sign. Catch the bus back to Rome on via Santovetti at the other end of via del Popolo until 9pm (L1000).

Ostia Antica

The classical Roman remains of Ostia Antica (tel. 565 00 22) rival those of the more famous (and more crowded) Pompeii. Proper exploration merits the better part of a day, so bring your own lunch and a bottle of water. To reach Ostia, take the Metro Line B to the Magliana stop (L700; ask for the through ticket to Ostia), change to the Lido train and get off at the Ostia Antica stop (20min.). The bar outside the train station has the only food or drink before the site. Cross the overpass and continue straight to the "T" intersection. Make a left and follow the signs to the entrance. (Site open daily 9am-6pm in summer, in winter 9am-4pm; admission L8000.)

The city, named for the *ostium* (mouth of the Tiber), was apparently founded around 335 BC, when Rome was just beginning its rise to power. The growth of Ostia parallels that of its mother city's expansion into the world of Mediterranean trade and politics. First a mere fortified camp established to guard the salt fields of the Tiber delta, the settlement was developed as a commercial port and and naval base during the 3rd and 2nd centuries BC. After Rome won control of the seas in the Punic Wars, almost every bit of food and material imported to the city passed across the docks of Ostia.

The ruins that remain in Ostia all speak of the thriving commercial activity the port once saw. An eclectic mix of warehouses, shipping offices, hotels, bars, and shrines to the polyglot religious cults of slaves and sailors combine to fill the site. Ostia's fortunes declined as Rome's did: The port fell into disuse during the onslaught of the Goths, and the silty Tiber eventually moved the coastline a mile or so to the west. After the city was sacked by the Goths in the 800s, Pope Gregory IV built a new fortified town (up the road from the entrance gate) and the ancient city receded into malarial swampdom. (Happily, though, the mud served as a remarkable preservative.) Once a town of 80,000, the site was nearly desolate until papal excavations began in the 19th century; archaeologists have uncovered about half of the city—they continue to dig. Practical Ostia's buildings were built of brick. The site was thus quarried and pillaged far less than the monumental marble precincts of Rome; what remains today is in many ways more impressive. Walking its main streets and narrow alleyways, you can imagine the din and flow of ancient city life.

Ostia's main road, **Decumanus Maximus**, runs through the middle of the city from the Porta Romana, curving around to the Porta Marina, which once opened onto the sea. Traveling from Porta Romana down the Decumano Massimo, you'll see tombs from different periods in a cluster to the left. The **Baths of the Cisiarii**, on the far side of the warehouses (to the right of the road), hold fascinating mosaics. Often, you can brush away the gravel to reveal an extension of the visible mosaic. The marine mosaics in the **Baths of Neptune** are even more spectacular; find the one illustrating the courtship of Neptune and Amphitrite. For an excellent view of the gymnasium, climb the stairs on the side. At the top, looking away from the baths, you can see the **theater.** Restored in 1827, the theater now hosts classical plays; it is also home to a souvenir shop and bar. (Contact the tourist office in Rome for information.) Behind the theater, **piazzale delle Corporazioni** (forum of the Corporations) housed the offices of Ostia's commercial associations. Their trademarks emblazon the mosaic floors outside each store, identifying merchants from all corners of the ancient world.

Ostia's **museum,** near the parking lot on the north side of the site, displays a diverse and delightful collection of artifacts recovered from the excavation. The collection ranges from a triumphant statue of Emperor Trajan to cooking utensils. Be sure to investigate the well-preserved sarcophagi in Room IX.

As in Rome, Ostia Antica's **Capitolium** and **forum** command the center of town. A civic center and elegant showcase for Ostia, as well as its principal temple, the 2nd-century Capitolium was intended to recall the Capitol in Rome. Across from the Capitolium explore the forum and the best **baths** in the city. Nearby, a small first-century temple dedicated to Rome and Augustus houses a statue of the goddess Roma, the only extant personification of the city besides the statue on Rome's Capitoline Hill. The 3rd-century **Tempio Rotondo,** on vicolo del Pino, is a miniature anthropocentric Pantheon dedicated to the cult of all emperors. Across from it stands the **Curia,** or Senate House, where the city council played politics. The residential areas of Ostia comprise an architectural digest of all classes of Roman housing, from the *insula* (apartment block) to the *domus-villa* (detached house).

Swimming and Otherwise: Around the Lakes-Lago Vico

If you're addicted to the ocean, your only chances for swimming in Lazio are the unspectacular beaches at **Lido di Ostia** or the spectacular-for-other-reasons nude beach at **Capocetta.**

For those not pledged to acquiring a sand-flecked tan, some delightful water awaits in Lazio's great lakes. Placed in the craters of extinct volcanoes, these three round puddles see a lot of Roman traffic, but they're large enough to comfortably absorb everyone. The best place to go swimming near Rome is **Lake Bracciano,** Rome's reservoir. You can take a train from Termini to Bracciano (on the Rome-Viterbo line, L5200) and the early Renaissance **Orsini-Odescalchi Castle** (tel. 902 40 03), which has frescoed ceilings, an impressive collection of arms and armor, and quite a few stuffed, wild boars (open Thurs., Sat., and holidays 9am-noon and 3-6pm). Walk down the hill to the lake about 1km (there are signs to the *lago*), and continue right until you find an appealing patch of shore. There are numerous stands renting windsurfers, paddle boats and other diversions as well as ferries to the neighboring towns of Anguillara and Trevignano.

Farther away, little **Lake Vico** is both prettier and better supplied with amusements. Take a car down the serpentine road, or get off at the bus stop on top of the hill and walk down 2km from Caprarola. A train runs to Caprarola from Stazione Ostiense (leaves 11:03am, change at Orte, arrives 1:40pm, L8800 one way, L15,800 round trip) or you can take a bus from Lepanto (about every hr.; L4500). Lago Vico is a nature reserve, campground, and recreational facility. You must make a reservation to stay at the campsite (tel. (0761) 61 23 47; L6000 per person, L5000 per tent, L3500 per car). The campground management also offers guided tours of the reserve (mostly in Italian) for a group of at least four: on horseback (6hr. tour, L75,000 per person); in a jeep (4-8hr., L20,000 per person); on mountain bikes (you must have your own bike, 4-8hr., L35,000); in a canoe (L10,000 per hr.); by foot (8hr., L18,000 per person); or by flying carpet (you must have your own rug, 25min., a devilish L6666 per load). You can also take instructions in canoeing (L15,000 per hr.) and archery (L7000 per hr.). The management is young and eager to show the reserve to visitors.

Nearby **Caprarola's** one street, via Filippo Nicolai, leads up to the top of a hill on which perches the citadel-shaped **Palazzo Farnese,** built by that notoriously rich organizer of the Council of Trent, Alessandro Farnese (Pope Paul III). Old men sun on the walls of the slightly overgrown entrance, but the Zuccari frescoes depicting *The Splendors of the Farnese Family* and *The Council of Trent,* the views, and the gardens are nevertheless impressive. (Open June-Aug. 9am-7pm; Mar.-May and Sept. 9am-6:30pm; Oct. 9am-5:30pm; Nov.-Feb. 9am-4pm. Admission L5000.) There's not much reason to go farther north in search of fresh water or scenery (Vico has the best of both), but **Lake Bolsena** can boast status as Italy's fifth largest lake, and a miracle of its very own. In 1263 in the town of Bolsena, a Bohemian priest, on his way to Rome, stopped to say mass. Doubting Peter, who had previously had some trouble swallowing the notion that the host really became Christ's body, was properly startled when the host began dripping blood onto the altar linen. Happy Pope Urban IV received the miraculous linen in Orvieto and gratefully ordered that a wonderful church be built there (see Orvieto in Umbria). Bolsena didn't get anything, and doesn't really have anything, but those who like to swim alone can take a bus from Viterbo (ACOTRAL bus, every hr., L2300). Bolsena is also the best location for camping near Viterbo (see Viterbo for listings).

Etruria

The Etruscans dominated central Italy from the 7th to the 3rd centuries BC and left vestiges of a flourishing culture. Ambitious Rome, annoyed by former Etruscan dominance and the Etruscan trade alliance with the Carthaginians, demolished and absorbed the Etruscan confederation of 12 city-states, the Dodecapolis, and Etruscan culture gradually disintegrated. What is known of the Etruscans has been dug up with difficulty from a few ruins; most of these are tombs, replete with art objects and frescoes but barren of information about the political or economic organization of Etruria. The best-excavated necropolises are those at Cervéteri and Tarquínia, both easy daytrips from Viterbo or Rome. The Apollo Sanctuary at Veio is all that's left of this largest Etruscan city. All the movable objects found at these sites have been taken to various museums—the Villa Giulia museum, the Museo Nazionale Etrusco in Tarquínia, and the Vatican Museum.

Cervéteri

You can marvel for yourself over the mystery of the Etruscans at Cervéteri's extensive tombs, the best and best-known Etruscan archeological site near Rome. The **necropolises** that extended around Etruscan towns were designed to imitate Etruscan settlements of the day, and interiors were furnished with objects from daily life. Only some 50 of an estimated 5000 tombs have been excavated; but the visible ghost town encompasses large residences, including the Tomb of the Shields and Chairs; smaller houses such as the Tomb of the Alcove (note the carved-out matrimonial bed); and even row houses. The triangular shape on the right as you enter a room marks the woman's grave, and the horizontal semicircle on the left indicates the man's grave. Look for the remarkable colored reliefs in the Tomba dei Rilievi.

ACOTRAL buses run to Cervéteri from Rome at via Lepanto (every 30min., 80min., L3500, take subway line A to Lepanto). From the village, it's another 2km to the necropolis on the road leading west; follow the signs. A train from Rome's Trastevere station also serves the city (L3800, round-trip L6400). (Open Tues.-Sun. 9am-7pm; Oct.-April Tues.-Sat. 9am-4pm, Sun. 11am-4pm. Admission L4000, under 18 free. Maps L700.) Bring a flashlight. Also worthwhile is the **Museo Nazionale di Cervéteri,** p. Santa Maria Maggiore (tel. 995 00 03), located in Ruspoli Castle, a fairy-tale edifice of ancient walls and ornate crenelations. The museum displays those relics excavated from the Cere necropolis within the last ten years. (Open Tues.-Sun. 9am-2pm and 4-7pm; in winter Tues.-Sun. 9am-4pm. Admission L4000.) Inquire at the **tourist office,** on via delle Mura Castellane, about organized archeological walks to the necropolis.

Tarquínia

Great Tarqínia socked it to the early Romans, imposing on the city a short-lived dynasty of Tarquin kings. The city of 100,000 died out in proper style, leaving a vast (understaffed) necropolis whose best moveable objects have landed in the national museum here, but whose unmoveable frescoes are also worth exploring.

Trip over Tarquínia by day. The site is a popular local stop on the Rome-Grosseto line, and buses run from the station and beaches into town every 30min. until 9:10pm. Buses also link the town with Viterbo (1hr., L3500), Civitavécchia (45min., L3200), and Rome (8 per day, 2hr., L6300). The bus from Rome leaves from via Lepanto, not p. Flaminio (as erroneously stated in the tourist office's brochure). For information on Southern Etruria (the province of Viterbo), inquire at the **Azienda Autonoma di Turismo** at p. Cavour, 1 (tel. (0766) 85 63 84), or at the **EPT** in Viterbo, p. dei Caduti, 16 (tel. 22 61 61). The cheapest hotel in hilltop Tarquínia, **Hotel San Marco,** p. Cavour, 18 (tel. 84 08 13), offers commodious, comfy rooms. (Singles L42,000. Doubles L60,000.) In Tarquínia Lido, a beach 2km from where the train stops, **Albergo Miramare,** viale dei Tirreni, 36 (tel. 880 20), right on the beach, lets beautiful doubles for only L35,000 (with bath L49,500). Camp at **Tuscia** (tel. 882 94), and revel in a *pizzeria,* market, clean bathrooms, and a separate grove for tents (L7000 per person, L8000 per tent, 4-person bungalow L50,000). Take the bus from Tarquínia or from the train station (3km), and get off at the last stop along the beach. Eating in Tarquínia is cheap and enjoyable. An absolute must for lunch or dinner is **Trattoria Corneto** (tel. 95 78 26), under the *cucina e pizzeria* sign at via Garibaldi, 12, at via Cavallotti. This nondescript establishment cooks up monumental plates of spaghetti (L6000-7500) and loaded pizzas (L4500-6000).

Buses arrive in the **Barriera San Giusto** outside the medieval ramparts. The **tourist office** here (tel. 85 63 84; open Mon.-Sat. 8am-2pm and 5-7pm) provides a wealth of information and bus schedules. In adjoining p. Cavour stands the **Museo Nazionale** (tel. (0766) 85 60 36), one of the best collections of Etruscan art outside of Rome, occupying the huge Gothic-Renaissance **Palazzo Vitelleschi.** Inside the entrance loom the sepulchral monuments of many of the important Tarquinian families. On the second floor, pet the museum's mascot, the Etruscan sculpture of the noble *Winged Horses* (4th century BC). The impressive array of Greek ceramics includes a vase shaped like a woman's head and a huge cup depicting the assembly of the gods. Also on the second floor are several reconstructed tombs with fine frescoes. (Open Tues.-Sat. 9am-2pm, July 15-Sept. 15 also 4-7pm. Guided evening tours Tues.-Fri. Admission L8000.)

The same ticket admits you to the **necropolis,** Tarquínia's main attraction. Take the bus from the Barriera San Giusto (any that go to the "cimitero" stop), or better yet, walk (15min. from the museum). Head up c. Vittorio Emanuele from p. Cavour and turn right on via Porta. Then take via Ripagretta and then via delle Croci, which leads to the tombs. You must wait for a group to form and a guide to let you into any of the excavated tombs. Because of their sensitivity to air and moisture, only four to six may be seen on a given day (and those only peered at from behind a metal railing in the doorway). All of the tombs are splendid works of art, decorated with astonishingly fresh paintings. (Tombs open Tues.-Sun. 9am-2pm and 4-7pm.)

Veio

The Sanctuary at Veio is particularly fiendish in that it contains the only set of Etruscan ruins that is easy to visit—and the one least worth the bother. If you won't have another Etruscan opportunity, take bus #201 to **Isola Farnese** from Rome's p. Ponte Milvio (8 per day, L1200). Isola Farnese, a tiny feudal hamlet, surrounds Castello Ferraioli. Before the bus goes up to the *castello,* it passes a small dirt road marked "Veio." The path descends to a waterfall where a tiny bridge crosses a babbling stream. On the other side, the path on the right leads up to a large stone gate, the entrance to the excavations. From here, the original Roman road, paved with broad stones, winds to the summit where temples once stood.

Viterbo

Heavy Allied bombing shattered Viterbo's old city walls, and reconstruction has been slow. You'll see the results as you step from the station into traffic and rubble. Across the busy highway, amid hovering carbon fumes, is the forbidding entrance to a city tinctured black. But don't be deterred: the vestiges of Viterbo's eminence warrant a stop.

Viterbo began as an Etruscan center but earned prominence as a papal refuge from Frederick Barbarossa's siege on Rome in the 12th century. The real architectural splurge commenced during the next century, as Viterbo became a Guelph stronghold in the aristocrats' civil war. It was here that the torturous process of papal elections first took shape. The *capitano* (city dictator) locked the cardinals in their palace until they chose a new pope. Threats to cut off food deliveries and to remove the roof from the conference room (so that the cold could creep in more easily) were added incentives for a quick decision. Today Viterbo also serves as an induction point for draftees of the Italian military; its streets brim with an eclectic mix of boys in uniform, punks, window shopppers, and senior citizens. And it still draws many to its sulphurous hot **Bulicane spring,** (3km from center) famous for its curative powers.

Orientation and Practical Information

Enter the city through the arched thresholds of the great stone wall, and venture out at your own risk. Don't chance getting lost in the suburbs—there's plenty to check out within. At first glance, the inner city might intimidate you with its incongruous passages and what seem to be haphazardly scattered yellow signs misleading you down dead-end alleys. But don't worry—do follow the signs. There are few dead ends and several ways of getting to each of the many significant buildings and *piazze*. The town is easily navigated, its walls forming a trapezoid with the wide parallel side lining the eastern sector. **San Francesco** and **Santa Rosa** are in the northeast region, **San Sisto** and **San Pellegrino** (the historical center) in the southeast, and **San Lorenzo** west of center. **Piazza dei Caduti** is just north of **del Plebiscito** (which is practically dead center). The bus station is located just outside the northeast corner. Via Marconi and via Cavour/via Ascenzi lead to a point at the tourist office. When you arrive at the bus or train terminal, walk right along the city wall to the first opening, Porta Fiorentina, and descend along via Matteotti to p. Verdi at the bottom of the hill. Via Marconi on the right takes you to p. dei Caduti and the EPT; the Azienda di Turismo is on the left, and corso Italia, sloping up to the right, leads to the medieval San Pellegrino district.

Tourist Office: EPT, p. dei Caduti, 16 (tel. 22 61 61). All sorts of printed materials, including a map and self-guided tour of Viterbo. English spoken. Limited hours, but large map displayed outside. Open Mon.-Sat. 8am-2pm. **Azienda di Turismo,** p. Verdi, 4 (tel. 22 66 66). No English, but a helpful wall map. Open daily 8am-1:20pm.

Post Office: via Ascenzi (tel. 23 48 06), between del Plebiscito and the tourist office. Open Mon.-Fri. 8:10am-7:35pm, Sat. 8am-noon. Also p. della Rocca. Open Mon.-Fri. 2-7pm. **Postal Code:** 01100.

Telephones: SIP, via Calabresi, 7. Open Mon.-Fri. 8:10am-7:50pm, Sat. 9am-12:30pm. **Telephone Code:** 0761.

Buses: Tickets can be purchased at the theater/snack bar at viale Trento or at the ACOTRAL on via Sauro (1 block away). All buses board passengers across from the theater. Buses to: Orvieto (1hr. 30min. L4300); Civitavécchia (1hr. 45min., L4800); Tarquínia (1hr., L4300); Caprarola (L1500); and Bolsena (L3000) as well as other cities in Etruria. To get to Viterbo from Rome take city transit bus #490 or any bus going to p. Flaminio. At the Flaminio station buy a combination train/bus ticket (L5300) to Viterbo. A train will take you 10min. to Saxo-Rubio (the sticks) and buses bound for Viterbo will be waiting.

Emergencies: tel. 113. **Police: Questura,** località Pietrare (tel. 34 19 55). **Hospital:** via dell'Ospedale, 101 (tel. 23 28 61), at via San Lorenzo. **Red Cross:** tel. 23 40 33.

Accommodations and Camping

Albergo Milano, via della Cava, 54 (tel. 34 07 05). Family-managed hotel located in northeast by San Francesco and not far from the bus station. Stoic (but kind) grandmother will direct you to a clean room equipped with short-wave radio. Jam to worldwide tunes. Singles L27,000, with bath L35,000; doubles L40,000, with bath L60,000.

Pensionè Trieste, via N. Sauro, 32 (tel. 34 18 82), right down the street from the bus station headquarters (just outside of the wall). Offers rooms with bath. Singles L35,000. Doubles L50,000.

Albergo Roma, via della Cava, 26 (tel. 22 72 74 or 22 64 74). If Minerva is filled, look for Roma just a few doors down. Comfy quarters at 2-star prices. Singles L33,390, with bath L49,350. Doubles L49,350, with bath L71,000.

Pensione Minerva, via della Caserma, 7 (tel. 34 09 90). Clean, cheap, and affable. Singles L23,000. Doubles L34,000, with bath L47,000. Triples L60,000.

Camping: the nearest campgrounds are on the immaculate beach of **Lago di Bolsena,** 30km north. Most accessible by public transport are those in Bolsena itself (ACOTRAL bus, L3000): **Il Lago,** viale Cadorna (tel. 79 91 91), L6000 per person, L4500 per tent, L3500 per car (open March-Sept.), and **Pineta,** via A. Diaz (tel 79 98 01), L4400 per person, L3700 per tent. (Open April-Oct.) You can find prettier campgrounds near Bolsena off the Cassia in the towns of Capodimonte and Montefiascone. Check with the tourist office for a full list of campgrounds in the province of Viterbo.

Food

Local specialties include the exotic-looking *lombriche* (earthworm) pasta and a chestnut soup known as the *zuppa di mosciarelle*. Try Viterbo's native *sambuca,* a sweet anise-flavored liqueur. One of the most celebrated local wines exults in the effer-vescent name *Est! Est!! Est!!!*, which are the first words of the epitaph on the grave of a German traveler who died of the drink in 1113 while on a journey to Rome. Accord-ing to legend, he sent a servant ahead of him to search out good local wineries to be marked with the word "Est" ("here it is" in Latin). He arrived in Montefiascone to find "Est! Est!! Est!!!" on a winery. He agreed with the servant's taste wholeheartedly, to the point of his own demise. Pope Martin IV experienced a doom of a different sort—the sufferings of purgatory, according to Dante—for his weakness for another local dish, roasted eel from Bolsena. Less exotic, if no less sinful, freshwater fish can be had in the towns surrounding Lake Bolsena. *Alimentari* can be found along via dell'Orolo-gio, or check out the huge **outdoor market** (Saturdays 7am-2pm) in p. della Rocca.

> **Trattoria del'archetto**, via Cristoforo, 1 (at the open end of a dead end). Dine under the eyes of our patron saint of travel. Outdoor tables rain or shine (*primi* L6000-10,000, *menù*—full meal L18,000).

> **Porta Romana**, via della Bontà, 12 (tel. 237 18). You tell her how much you're willing to pay, she tells you how much you're entitled to eat. Provincial specialties lauded by locals. Full meals about L18,000. Cover L2000. Open Mon.-Sat. 7-11:30pm.

> **Taverna del Padrino,** via della Cava, 22. Tasty pizzas and a lively atmosphere. Popular with con-scripts. Pizzas average L7000. Cover L2000. Open daily noon-2:30pm and 7pm-3am.

Sights

At the southern end of town is the medieval quarter's administrative center, **piazza del Plebescito.** The medallion-decked building with the tall clock tower is the Palazzo del Popolo, across from the Palazzo della Prefettura. Large stone lions, the symbol of Viterbo, guard both. Between them lies the **Palazzo Comunale** in full Renaissance sprawl. The odd frescoes in the **Sala Regia,** painted in 1592, depict the history of Vit-erbo, mixing in Etruscan, classical, Christian, and medieval legends. (Open 8am-7pm. Free. Go upstairs to the office on your right and ask to have the Royal Room opened.) Outside, the façade of the church of Sant'Angelo incorporates a late Roman sarcopha-gus that contains the body of the ineffably beautiful and virtuous Galiana. When she re-fused to marry an amorous Roman baron, he besieged the city, promising to spare it if she came to the wall. As soon as Galiana appeared, the baron shot her with an arrow, thereby ensuring her fidelity.

Curious *palazzi* line **via San Lorenzo,** which wends its way from p. del Plebescito into Viterbo's medieval heart, p. San Lorenzo. There, in the Siena-influenced bell tow-er of the **cathedral,** pairs of slender, arched windows climb to a sharp peak. The **Palaz-zo Papale,** topped by a row of toothlike merlons, fills the far end of the *piazza.* From the *loggia,* enjoy a bird's-eye view of a complex of early Christian churches. This has been the site of three papal conclaves, including the one in which the roof was removed to freeze the clergy into a decision. (Open Mon.-Sat. 10am-12:30pm. Free.)

Via San Pellegrino stumbles its way through the medieval quarter of **San Pellegrino.** Churches and towers block the path completely, belittling the sky to a scant strip of blue between the dark *peperino* walls of volcanic rock. At the northwestern boundary of San Pellegrino at the end of v. San Lorenzo is the charming yet unfortunately named **piazza delle Morte** (Square of Death), at the center of which is a vibrant fountain as well as the 13th-century **palazzetto of San Tomaso.** Note the medieval balcony next to the Church of Santa Giacinta, also on the square. At the northern end of town, the **Ba-silica of San Francesco** contains the tombs of two popes who died in Viterbo: Adrian V (1276, whom Dante put in hell with the misers) and Clement IV (1265-68). Both mausoleums sport exemplary 13th-century sculpture. At the **Church of Santa Rosa** (near the Basilica), the 700-year old corpse of Viterbo's celebrated saint is preserved in a glass case.

Entertainment

At 9pm on September 3, the people of Viterbo honor Santa Rosa. One hundred burly bearers carry the *Macchina di Santa Rosa,* a towering construction of iron, wood, and papier-mâché about 30m high, through the illuminated streets. The bearers of the tributary lug it around town and then sprint uphill to the **Church of Santa Rosa** (where the well-preserved remains of the saint lie). In 1814 the *macchina* fell on the *facchini* (bearers), and in 1967 it had to be abandoned in the street because it was too heavy. Several days of frenzied celebration surround this event. The **Festival Barocco** brings excellent classical music to Viterbo's churches in June. Ask at the tourist office about tickets (L12,000) and schedules.

Near Viterbo

Villa Lante, in the picturesque town of **Bagnaia** outside Viterbo, is a particularly enjoyable example of the grandiose villas that were in vogue among 16th-century church bigwigs. The local (orange) bus #6 leaves Viterbo from p. Mártiri d'Ungheria every half-hour for Bagnaia (15min., L1300, last bus back leaves Bagnaia at 8:30pm).

From the *piazza* where the bus drops you, walk uphill and enter the right-hand gate. Most of the estate now serves as a public park, and you can wander among the fountains and avenues as you please. To enter the gardens immediately adjacent to the villa, however, you must ring at the gatehouse on the left as you enter and wait for a keeper to give you a tour of the verdant glories designed by Vignola in the 1570s. In a manner characteristic of Renaissance gardens, water rushes down the hill behind the villas through a sequence of elaborate fountains before disappearing underground. (Villa Lante open Tues.-Sun. 9am-7:30pm; March-April and Sept.-Oct. 9am-5:30pm; Nov.-Feb. 9am-4pm. Tours of the inner gardens every 30min., L2000.)

A little farther along the same road lurks a pleasure garden of a different sort: the **Parco dei Mostri** (Park of the Monsters). Blue ACOTRAL buses depart from viale Trento in Viterbo (6 per day, L1300) and drop you off in **Bomarzo,** 1km from the park, 3km from the farmhouse *pensione* outside of town. From where the bus leaves you, walk downhill and follow the signs for Palazzo Orsini (not Parco dei Mostri). Turn left down the stairs marked via del Lavatio, and continue downhill to the park. If the picturesque towns and landscape of this region have left you longing for a tourist trap, this offbeat 16th-century Disney World supplies the diversion. A surreal wilderness of grotesque forms here mocks overdone aristocratic sculpture gardens of the time (e.g., Villa Lante's). A walk through the mossy paths here is anything but pastoral, as you amble into the mouths of snarling beasts and past a giant ripping another apart limb by limb. (Open 8:30am-7pm; admission L8000.)

The Orsini who commissioned the gardens may also have owned what is now Bomarzo's only lodging. The **Club Agrituristico** is a converted 16th-century hunting lodge. Its new owners moved from Rome to this idyll, in which they've established two quaint rooms which they rent for L60,000 per night per room (each room accommodates up to four people). They also have horseback riding (L15,000 per hr.), their own organic produce, camping (L8000 per person, L3000 per tent), and kitchen facilities. Call ahead and they'll gladly pick you up at the bus stop (tel. (0761) 92 44 66).

Civitavécchia

Numerous powers have sought control of Civitavécchia's deep port. Emperor Trajan was first (108 BC), followed by the Byzantines in the 6th century, and the popes two centuries later. The Saracens in 826 caused the entire population to flee to La Tolfa where Pope Leone II had a town built for them; the inhabitants missed their old city so much, however, that they decided to move back en masse. Today, Civitavécchia serves as an important port linking the Italian mainland with the vast mountainous island of Sardinia. Fill a few hours' layover with a pleasant waterside walk, at the city's museum, or in the open-air market.

Civitavécchia is a major stop on the Genoa-Rome line, accessible from Rome (1hr. 30min., L6500) and Pisa (2hr. 30min., L18,700). To get from the train station to the port, turn right on viale Garibaldi, which follows the shore. You'll pass the **tourist office** at #42 (tel. (0766) 253 48; open Mon.-Sat. 8:30am-12:30pm and 3:30-7pm). To get from the port to the station, walk along the shore to the right as you face inland.

Tirrenia is the biggest ferry line conecting Civitavécchia with Sardinia. Ferries connect with **Olbia** daily both ways at 11pm, and in July and August additionally at 11am. Prices vary depending on the class and season. Consider booking two weeks in advance for late July and the month of August. Otherwise just show up at the port. If you're willing to sit or sleep on the floor or deck, passage (*posto ponte*), the trip to Olbia is L16,900. Tickets for Poltrone start at L27,000. For Cagliari, it's the same for *posto ponte*. Seats start at L47,700. There is also a **Ferrovie dello Stato** connection to **Golfo Aranci,** 19km from Olbia (4 per day, 8hr. 30min., L15,400), a better option if you have a car; if you're on foot, you can catch the train to Olbia from there (L2400). **Store luggage** at the station or the port (L2000 per piece per day).

The **post office** welcomes at via Giordano Bruno, 11 (tel. 233 07; open Mon.-Fri. 8:25am-7:40pm, Sat. 8:25-11:50am). **Telephones** ring next door at #13. The **telephone code** is 0766. Avoid spending the night if you can; you can nap on an overnight ferry to Sardinia. If you must sleep, try the unspectacular **Albergo Miramare,** viale della Repubblica, 6 (tel. 261 67), on the waterfront between the port and the train station. (Singles L30,000, doubles L50,000.) **Roma Nord,** via Monte Grappa, 27 (tel. 38 01 05 or 38 02 81), northeast of the port has shabby but ridiculously cheap rooms. It's often full, so call first. (Singles L18,000, doubles L23,000.) Nix the numerous *pizzerie* near the port and head for **Pizzeria Santa Lucia,** viale Garibaldi, 34 (tel. 252 35), where they cook their pies in wood-burning ovens (L5500-10,000). **Trattoria Alla Lupa,** via S. Fermina, 5 (tel. 257 03), serves ample portions of spicy Lazio favorites for about L17,000. For shipboard meals, hunt and gather at the *alimentari* across from the train station (open Mon.-Wed. and Sat. 9am-1pm and 4:30-8:30pm, Thurs. 9am-1pm). Better yet, venture into the abundant **open-air market** on via Doria, parallel to corso'Centrocelle (open daily 7:30am-2pm).

The Sabine Hills: Rieti and its Province

Covering the Sabine mountains and the Salto lake basin east of Rome, Rieti province is one of the most naturally verdant in all of Italy, and was coveted long before St. Francis claimed it as a spiritual home. The natives' constant wars against the Romans and Latins often turned ugly—the rape of the Sabine women a brutal example—and presaged later invasions by Saracens, French, and the Napoleonic Empire. A brief calm spell under the protection of the Papal State (12th and 15th centuries) and the preoccupation with building upon spots where St. Francis slept endowed the tiny mountain villages and countryside with a plethora of medieval and Baroque churches, sanctuaries, and castles. Carved into the promontories on which they perch, these towns peer out over beautiful vistas.

Rieti

Some Romans are better than others. When Curius Dentatus captured this Sabine capital in 290 BC, he did the region a favor and made the land fertile by draining the nearby swamps and diverting the water into what is now Terni's Marmore Falls. The resultant greening later made the town a favorite of St. Francis. Easily accessible from Rome, the wee provincial capital makes an excellent base and introduction to the hill country. ACOTRAL buses run almost every hour from Rome's Castro Pretorio (1hr., L5300). Trains run frequently from Termini to Rieti station (L12,100, round-trip L20,600).

The most convenient place for comprehensive **tourist information** is the Alitalia office, via Vittorio Emanuele II, where via Garibaldi ends. Cross p. Mazzini from the train station and walk through the park. Turn right onto via D. Pesheria and make your first left. The office will be on your right as you enter the *piazza*. (Tel. 27 07 02; open Mon.-Fri. 9am-1pm and 3:30-7pm, Sat. 9am-1pm.) The post office is on via Garibaldi, 283 (to your left). (Open Mon.-Fri. 8:30am-6pm, Sat. 8:30am-noon.) Telephones are also available there. The **postal code** for Rieti is 02100; its **telephone code** is 0746. If you plan to sleep in Rieti while traveling throughout the Sabines, consider doing so at the three-star **Europa,** centally located in the old town on via San Rufo, 49 (tel. 49 51 49), one block south of via Garibaldi behind the Centro d'Italia. (Singles L40,000, with bath L60,000. Doubles L60,000, with bath L80,000. Breakfast L3000.) Or try **Hotel Serena,** on v. della Gioventù, 17/A (tel. 27 09 30), outside the fortified walls off v. Ludovico Canali. The helpful management offers clean rooms with TVs. (Singles L28,000, with bath L55,000. Doubles L47,000, with bath L75,000.)

Fallone, a calzone stuffed with herbs and olive oil, and *fregracce alla Sabinese,* a pasta dish with black olives, mushrooms, artichokes, tomatoes, and olive oil, are particularly savory Sabine specialties. Try **Al Calice d'Oro,** on v. Marchetti, 10 (tel. 442 71; open Tues.-Sun. 7-11:30pm), or **La Fontanella,** on v. San Francesco, 36 (tel. 456 85), for these and other dishes.

Piazzo Vittorio Emanuele, encloses the **Palazzo Comunale** which in turn encloses the **Museo Civico.** The museum's collection includes some Iron Age pieces, statues of Diana and Kouros, and the only work signed by Venetian Zannino di Pietro, *Stories of St. Francis.* (Open Tues.-Thurs. and Sat.-Sun. 9am-1pm. Free.) Smack in the center of town at p. Cesare Battisti is the 12th-century **Cathedral of Santa Maria Assunta,** with superb vaulted ceilings and a square bell tower. Inside, the ornate, domed **Chapel of St. Barbara** contains a Bernini statue of the saint. At the end of via Roma, make a left and continue to the 13th-century **Chiesa di San Francesco,** and gaze at the 14th-century copies of Giotto's Assisi frescoes.

Rieti Province

The pocket of charming villages in the province are best seen by car, since bus service is infrequent and few excursions are worth an entire day's effort. Among the best spots to stop are **Roccasinibalda,** 23km south of Rieti, a little village with one of the prettiest castles in Italy—a scorpion-shaped edifice fortified and embellished by the Medici Pope Clement VII and Alexander Cesarini. Its hanging gardens and some of the interior are open to the public. Further south **Fara in Sabina** is a village of severe medieval buildings, whose **Church of Sant'Antonio** boasts Vignola's **tabernacle,** a stellar exemplar of the Renaissance search for the perfect temple form. Check out the incredible view from the terrace on the square—on clear days you can make out the dome of St. Peter's. Nearby, the itsy-bitsy hamlet of **Roccantica** lies at the base of Monte Pizzuto, its romantic placement a proper tribute to its patron saint, St. Valentine. You can arrange a free tour of the town by calling the **tourist office** (tel. (0765) 630 15).

Eighteen kilometers west of Rieti is St. Francis's stomping ground, **Greccio.** The convent **Santuario di Greccio,** built right into a cliff, was the saint's private sanctuary for one year in 1217. Francis liked Greccio so much that in 1223 he returned to celebrate Christmas and demonstrated his acumen as a handyman by building a *presipio* (crèche). This crèche, the first ever, earned the convent a reputation as the Franciscan Bethlehem. The convent lies 2km from the town center, a beautiful wooded walk along the main road. Tired pilgrims can rest at the **Hotel della Fonte** (tel. 75 31 10). (Singles L22,000. Doubles L40,000, with shower L60,000.) Buses run frequently to Greccio (L4600 round-trip).

The Pontine Islands

A weekend playground for city-weary Romans, the Pontine Islands are the most splendid asset in all of Lazio. After housing a series of exiles from ancient Rome, this stunning volcanic archipelago with its mountain spines and turquoise water was given to Bourbon King Charles III of Naples by his mother Elisabetta Farnese in 1730. The Islands' subsequent inhabitation by wood-hungry Neapolitans led to the contemporary landscape of tiny vineyards, fragrant wild herbs, and flowers. Though crowded in July and August, the islands are geared mainly to Italians—a welcome change from the rampaging Germans on Elba and the international mayhem of Cápri.

The Pontine Islands can be reached by ferry from Anzio, Terracina, Fiumicino and Formia by several ferry lines including **Med Mar** (via Ofanto, 18, tel. 841 90 57; or piazza Barberini, 5, tel. 482 85 79) and **CAREMAR** (in Naples, tel. (081) 551 38 82; in Ponza, tel. (0771) 46 16 00 or 227 10). From Rome the most inexpensive option is CAREMAR from Anzio (L16,700; train to Anzio L4300). The most convenient route is via Fiumicino (to Ponza L40,000, Ventotene, L47,000). The Terracina-Ponza commute is L10,000 (once daily). If you're on an island spree, consider the journey from or to Cápri and Íschia. (Cápri-Ventotene on Med Mar is L25,000 but only runs June-Sept.)

Fiumicino-Ponza-Ventotene: Med Mar departures daily 9am and 4:15pm, 2hr. 30min.; L47,000 to Ponza, L44,000 to Ventetone. Free shuttle bus runs from the airport to the port. Make reservations with a travel agent in Rome especially for weekend travel.

Formia-Ponza: CAREMAR departures 9am and 4:30pm, L16,700. Returns 5:30am and 1:30pm.

Formia-Ventotene: CAREMAR departures 9:10am and 1pm, 3hr., L41,000. Return 5:30pm. If no one is at the information booth at the Ventotene port, inquire at the bar next door.

Ponza-Ventotene: Med Mar departures 11am and 6pm, 30min., L15,000. Return 11am. CAREMAR departure 6:10pm, 35min., L14,500.

Ponza

Orientation and Practical Information

Tourist Office: Pro Loco (tel. 800 31). The office is on your left as you mount the main staircase leaving the dock. Useful brochure available. Open Mon.-Sat. 9:30am-1:30pm.

Post Office: corso Pisacane, 32. Make your 1st right after the tourist office; the sign is on the left. Open Mon.-Fri. 8:30am-1:30pm, Sat. 8:30am-noon. **Postal Code:** 04027. **Telephone Code:** 0771.

Buses: main station Autolinee Ponzesi, via Dante (tel. 804 47). Buses depart from here every 15min. to Le Forna (L1500). On the way back, flag down buses anywhere along via Panoramica.

Emergencies: tel. 113. **Police:** molo Musco (tel. 801 30). **First Aid and Medical Care: Poliambulatorio,** via Panoramica (tel. 806 87).

Accommodations and Camping

Prices have skyrocketed over the past few years due to increasing tourism. Unfortunately, Ponza isn't the fishing village it once was. Random camping was outlawed three years ago due to fire hazards. There are two helpful agencies to save you the trouble of searching for a site: **Agenzia Immobiliare "Arcipelago Pontino,"** corso Pisacane, 49 (tel. 806 78), and **Agenzia Afari "Magi,"** via Branchina Nuova, 21 (tel. 80 98 41). They will help you find a room in *affitta camere* (private homes) for L40,000 in July and August, less during the off-season.

Pensione-Ristorante "Arcobalene," via Scotti D. Basso, 6 (tel. 803 15). As you ascend the stairs you may be cursing the writer who sent you here. When you reach the summit, however, you will understand why you were sent. Straight up the ramp, follow the street until it ends, then veer right until you pass the Bellavist Hotel. Turn left and follow the signs up, up, up. Wonderful people, the best views in Ponza and excellent food. Singles L30,000, doubles L60,000; off-season L25,000 and L50,000. English spoken. Call ahead in summertime.

Casa Vitiello, via Madonna, 28 (tel. 801 17). In the historic part of town, this family-run *affitta camere* has simple rooms in a quiet location. Follow the signs to La Torre dei Borbini and it'll be across the street. Singles, L40,000, doubles, L70,000; off-season L35,000 and L60,000.

Food and Entertainment

The Pontine Islands are known for their lentil soup, fish, and lobster. Several comparable restaurants and bars surround the port and spark the island's nightlife. (Be careful if you're staying in Le Forna; Sept.-June the last bus is at 10pm; July-Aug. last bus at 3am.) Most resturants also rent boats and organize island excursions by day.

Ristorante Lello, strada Panoramica, 10 (tel. 803 95), next door to the bus station. Specializes in regional dishes. Their *zuppa di lenticchie* (lentil soup, L5000) is especially tasty. *Primi* L7000, *secondi* L10,000.

Le Note Blu, via Banchina T. di Fazio (tel. 805 07). Located directly on the waterfront, this "piano bar" with live music nightly is a good bet for jazz and drinks. (First drink L5000. Open 10:30pm-5am depending on the crowd.)

Sights

Ponza is full of grottos and hidden beaches. Explore either on foot (the best way to savor the breathtaking panoramic views) or by renting a boat (try the jutting pier to the right of the main launch; L80,000 and up for the entire day depending on boat size). For a guided boat tour, inquire at any of the portside resturants that advertise (around L16,000 per person). Most trips visit the **Pilatus Caves,** an ancient Roman breeding ground for Muraena fish. Underwater types should consider going to **Noi e il Mare,** Banchina Mamozio (tel. 80 99 99 or 86 81 40), located right under the ascending ramp from the main disembarkation pier; both scuba diving expeditions and lessons are offered. (Equipment rental L40,000. Seven-day certification course L450,000—equipment not included.)

Ventotene

If the crowds of Campania are driving you mad, there's at least one refuge for regrouping—tranquil Ventotene. Despite a barren landscape, this tiny island's unexploited charm will rejuvenate your weary traveling bones. Over the centuries, Ventotene has served in various capacities as a prison: ancient Roman women were succeeded in the 18th century by a co-ed clan of convicts (from Naples) sent to the island to reform themselves in arcadian bliss. After four scandalous years of license (1768-1772), they were tossed off the island and replaced by farmers. The tiny **tourist office** is located right on the port and is managed by an affable English-speaking staff. **C.S.V.,** at p. Castello (via Pozzo di S. Candida, 13), will help you find a room in a hotel, *affitta camere*, or private home for L30,000 (single) and L60,000 (double) during July and August. Prices drop from September through June. There are two **supermarkets,** one at p. Castello and the other at via Roma. The **Archeological Museum** is also at p. Castello (open 10am-1pm and 7pm-midnight). Two splendid **beaches** flank either side of the port.

Abruzzo and Molise

For the Abruzzo, the postwar economic boom proved as much of a boon as a ruthless barbarian invasion. Like a medieval onslaught of Visigoths, "progress" reduced the coastal regions to a shapeless cultural shambles. The hills and mountains were able to turn the assault to their advantage, but Pescara and the surrounding coast are a vapid tumble of *pizzerie*, discos, and skin-cancer fiends, completely alien to the rugged, pristine highland. L'Áquila, the capital, is an ethereal fantasy out of Calvino's *Invisible Cities;* nearby, Sulmona offers world-famous poets and candy stores. The Gran Sasso, highest of the Apennines, and the Abruzzo national park offer a glimpse of an Italy before all the civilization: wild animals, mountainous vistas, and pure air.

The nation's second smallest region, **Molise** is deservedly the least known Italian corner, lacking any cities of distinction. Nevertheless, its mountain areas abutting the Abruzzo national park offer more unspoiled wildnerness, where bears, wolves, and boars roam, trying to avoid assimilation into the local cuisine, which includes *sopprfessate* (smoked boar sausage). Also scattered through the region are several ancient towns, and some ruins dating back to the Golden Age of Greece.

In both regions, train lines are painfully circuitous, so make use of the **ARPA** bus service. Avoid traveling on Sundays, when bus traffic is sharply reduced. If you want to explore Molise, plan on using a car, since the best wilderness and villages lie beyond the scope of public transportation.

Pescara

Juxtaposed with archetypal Italian hill towns like L'Áquila and Áscoli Piceno, Pescara is a custard pie thrown in the face of dignified Italy. Obsessed with regaining its prominence on the Adriatic Riviera, it can offer few claims to cultural grandeur; its most revered citizen is the poet Gabriele D'Annunzio, widely scorned in the rest of the country for his glorification of fascism. The clean beach is a 20km string of resort hotels. Inland, the city suffers from an adolescent awkwardness which it tries to mask with high-tech architecture and prices that are just plain high.

Main train lines run from Pescara to Bologna (4hr., L21,100), Ancona (2hr., L9300) and Rome (4hr., L15,200), making Pescara a transport hub. Buses leave from p. della Repubblica (connected to the train station by a vendor-lined tunnel through the old station) and run to Sulmona (Mon.-Sat. 5 per day, 1hr. 30min., L5900), L'Áquila (9 per day, 4 on Sun. 1hr. 30min., L6900) and Áscoli Piceno (Mon.-Sat. 6 per day, 2hr. 30min., change at Alba Adriatica, L5700). Most hotels and restaurants lie between the bus station and the beach, or on the northern wharf. From the station, turn right off corso Umberto at p. Salotto to reach the harried but informative **EPT tourist office** at via Fabrizi, 173 (tel. 421 17 07; open Mon.-Sat. 8am-noon and 5-8pm). The **post office** on corso Vittorio Emanuele, 106 (tel. 424 21) is open Mon.-Fri. 8:30am-7:30pm, and Sat. 8:30am-noon. The **postal code** is 65100. The ASST **telephones** on corso Umberto, 21, are near the train station (open 24hrs.). The **telephone code** is 085. For **beach first aid,** call 223 33; for other **emergencies,** dial 113.

Accommodations and Food

Hotel Alba, via Forti, 14 (tel. 38 91 45), off corso Vittorio Emanuele. Clean rooms and gregarious management. Singles L30,000, with bath L40,000. Doubles with bath L70,000. L1000 less in off-season.

Hotel Roma, via Piave, 142 (tel. 421 16 57). From the station make a left on corso Vittorio Emanuele and then take a right. Affable manager. Singles L19,000. Doubles L34,000, with bath L42,000.

Camping: Internazionale (tel. 656 53), on lungomare Colombo by the water. Take bus #10 from the train station. July 11-Aug. L6500 per person, L6500 per small tent, L8000 per large tent; off-season L4500 per person, L4500 per small tent, L5500 per large tent. Open May 30-Sept. 20.

Local specialties include two liqueurs: *aurum,* made from grapes, and *centerba,* distilled from 100 herbs. A handful of excellent restaurants hide near **corso Umberto.** A cooperative **food market** holes up in a warehouse on p. Muzii (open Mon.-Sat. 9am-1pm and 4-7pm).

Black Bull Pub, via Regina Elena, 32 (tel. 351 98). Not a pub but an excellent pizza joint. *Primi* L4000-8000, *secondi* L7000-15,000. Pizza L4000-8000. Cover L1500. Service 10%. Open Thurs.-Tues. noon-3pm and 7pm-midnight.

Ristorante Cinese Hai Bin (tel. 318 28), viale Riviera Nord, 44 (tel. 422 28 28). Italy's biggest Chinese restaurant is the epitome of Pescara; chintziness is glorified in this huge pagoda surrounded by the restaurant's own beach umbrellas. The food has managed to stay authentic, though. *Menù* L12,000. Open daily 12:30-3pm and 7:30pm-midnight.

Sights and Entertainment

Pescara's only attraction is its beach, but to make up for that, in mid-July the town hosts the **Pescara Jazz Festival** at the open-air Teatro d'Annunzio on the waterfront. Some big names perform here annually; check with the tourist office for the 1993 line-up or call (085) 37 41 98. (Tickets run L17,000-L22,000, on sale at the EPT.) Live jazz bebops at the **Happy Time** club, signposted off corso Umberto. Sets begin at 11pm and women often get in free. The **Museo Ittico,** via Raffaele Paolucci, 3 (tel. 37 82 33), showcases seashells, stuffed aquatic birds, and even the skeleton of a sperm whale. (Open Mon.-Sat. 9am-1pm and 3:30-7pm; in winter Mon.-Sat. 8am-2pm. Free.)

Térmoli

Overrun with tourists in the summer, the stimulating resort town of **Térmoli** retains enough authenticity to be interesting, and it's also the cheapest and most convenient Apulian point of departure to the Trémiti Islands. A 90-minute train ride on the Bologna-Lecce line from Pescara to the north and from Fóggia to the south (both L5700), the city flaunts the standard Italian beach scene and a fairly enticing old quarter. Walk down corso Umberto I from the train station and take the first left onto corso Nazionale to reach the **Borgo Vecchio,** the historic center. Early risers will thrill to the aquamarine collision of sea and sky, framed by medieval streets. The most titillating feature of the Borgo Vecchio is the lacy, racy **Castello Svevo,** built in 1247 by Swabian Frederick II of Hollywood. The castle was subsequently abandoned for 500 years, inhabited only by cavorting elves, until 1799, when the Bourbons used it as a prison to hold 300 revolting *termolesi* (closed to the public). The **cathedral,** cuddling up behind the castle, manifests a uniquely suggestive 13th-century interpenetration of Byzantine, Moorish, Abruzzese, and Umbrian forms. (Open daily 7:30am-6:30pm.)

Térmoli thrives on summer festivals. For three days around the last weekend in July, the **International Festival of Folklore** lures innocent young dancers, singers, and storytellers from around the world. Every August 4 Térmoli celebrates the **Festa di San Basso** with a bawdy parade of fishing boats and fireworks in honor of the city's patron saint. The **Sagra del Pesce** occurs the last Sunday in August, when scantily clad fish smolder in large outdoor cauldrons. Every August 15, an impertinent Saracen pass at the city is reenacted by "burning down" the Borgo Vecchio with fireworks. Off via Duomo (in the Borgo Vecchio) at **Osteria Dentro le Mura,** via Salvatore, 36, yield to the temptation of *crostini* (pieces of grilled bread with sundry toppings, L2500-L3000; open daily 8pm-2am). **Rosticceria Pizzeria Bar Morelli,** on v. Roma, 27 (tel. 70 32 86), hustles full meals for around L12,000 and pizza for L1500 a slice. (Open daily 8am-11pm.) **Pensione Villa Ida,** via Milano, 27 (tel. 26 66), to the left of the train station toward the beach, is hardly a rough trade. (Singles with bath L33,000. Doubles with bath L43,000. Obligatory half-pension in July, L45,000 per person; obligatory full pension in August, L66,000.) The **post office** (tel. 24 05) offers itself on corso Milano, 18. (Open 8:15am-5:30pm. Fermo Posta 8:15am-1pm. Reduced potency July-Aug. Mon.-Fri. 8:15am-1pm, Sat. 8:15am-noon.) The **postal code** is 86039, and the **telephone code** 0875. Térmoli's responsive **tourist office** at p. Bega (tel. 27 54), through the arcades off corso Umbergui, has the best information on the Trémiti Islands, and posts bus and train schedules; buses leave from the same *piazza.* (Open Mon.-Sat. 8am-7pm.)

L'Áquila

L'Áquila (The Eagle) seems a fitting name for this busy commercial city, perched on a lofty plateau in the heart of the Gran Sasso massif, the highest segment of the Apennines. A 1703 earthquake partially demolished the medieval city; the rebuilding left it with a half-modern character. The city is most famous for the curious preponderance of the number 99: exactly 99 churches, 99 *piazze,* 99 luftballoons, and 99 fountains gracing its streets. Every night, in fact, at 9:09pm the bell in the civic tower rings 99 times and another of the 99 bottles of beer on the wall is consumed. According to legend, the builders of the city were the inhabitants of the 99 castles situated in the Aquilan basin; their effigies can still be seen at the Fontana delle 99 Cannelle near the train station. And Áqulians always party like it's 1999.

Orientation and Practical Information

The city's historic district centers on **piazza del Duomo,** joined to the commercial district near the bus station by **corso Vittorio Emanuele II.** On the other side of the *piazza,* corso Federico II runs to **via XX Settembre,** which circumscribes the southern half of the city, and completes the numeric theme.

Tourist Office: EPT, p. Santa Maria Paganica, 5 (tel. 41 08 08). Take corso Vittorio Emanuele to via Leosino; hang a right and the office will be on your right. Ask for their map of the Gran Sasso Mountains if you're planning on hiking. Open Mon.-Fri. 8am-2pm and 4-6pm, Sat. 8am-1pm. **Azienda di Turismo:** via XX Settembre, 8 (tel. 223 06), on the other side of town from the bus station. Some English spoken. Useful maps and information about L'Áquila and the surrounding countryside. Open Mon.-Sat. 9am-1pm and 3:30-6:45pm, Sun. 10am-1pm.

Post Office: on p. del Duomo (tel. 616 41). Open Mon.-Sat. 8:15am-7:40pm. **Postal Code:** 67100.

Telephones: SIP, via XX Settembre, 75. Open Mon.-Sat. 8:30am-1pm and 3:30-7pm, Sun. 9am-12:30pm and 3:30-6:30pm. **Telephone Code:** 0862.

Trains: at p. della Stazione (tel. 204 97), in the outskirts. Take bus #1, 3, or 3/5 (L600) from outside the station to the center of town, or follow the signs to the Fontana Delle 99 Cannelle and then hike up the hill to corso XX Settembre (about 1km total).

Buses: ARPA (tel. 694 64). To: Rome (16 per day, 9 on Sun., 1hr. 30min., L11,300); Pescara (9 per day, 5 on Sun.; in winter 2 per day, none on Sun., 2hr., L8700); Sulmona (Mon.-Sat. 9 per day, 1hr., L6100); Avezzano (30 per day, 2 on Sun., 1hr. 30min., L5300). Bus tickets in the information booth at Porta Paganica, near the *castello* whence the buses leave. **Ognivia,** v. Tre Spigne, 3 (tel. 42 05 20), near the bus station. To Rome (1 per day, 1hr. 30min., L11,300) and Bucharest, Romania (every Fri., 2 days, L220,000, round-trip L330,000).

Hiking Information: Club Alpino Italiano, via XX Settembre, 15 (tel. 243 42), on the 3rd floor. The best maps, books, and information on local trails and refuges, though you'll be lucky if you find an English speaker. Open Mon.-Sat. 9am-1pm and 4-8pm.

Emergencies: tel. 113. **Police: Questura,** via Strinella, 2 (tel. 113). **Red Cross:** tel. 223 33.

Accommodations

Albergo Aurora, on via Cimino, off p. del Duomo (tel. 220 53). Walk through the courtyard and take stairs up to 2nd floor. Large, quiet, dilapidated rooms. Singles L25,000. Doubles L36,000.

Il Portichetto, on highway S.S. 80 (tel. 31 12 18). A serious hike, but you haven't many choices left in L'Áquila. Singles with bath L35,000. Doubles with bath L60,000.

Food

L'Áquila overflows with *torrone,* a nougat made of honey and almonds, occasionally covered with chocolate. **Fratelli Nurzia,** corso Frederico II, 50, sells the confection directly from its factory near p. del Duomo (L22,000 per 880g; open Mon.-Sat. 9am-8pm). There is an **outdoor market** held every morning except Sunday in the same *piazza.* Concoct your own meal at **Supermercato STANDA,** via Indipendenza, 6, off p. del Duomo under the STANDA department store. (Open Mon.-Sat. 9am-1pm and 4-8pm; in winter closed Mon. afternoon.)

Trattoria Stella Alpina, via Crispomonti, 15 (tel. 41 31 90), off p. del Duomo. Serves hearty regional dishes like *agnello ai ferri* (grilled lamb, L9000) and *spaghetti alla chitarra* (thick spaghetti, L6000). Ask for the *crostini,* a delicious concoction of toasted bread, melted mozzarella, and prosciutto drenched in green-as-grass olive oil (L8000)—it ain't on the menu. Request the *schiaffoni* and, instead of getting whacked repeatedly across the face, you'll get delicious rigatoni-like pasta in a sauce of cream, peas, and mushrooms (L5500). Cover L2000. Open Sat.-Thurs. 11:30am-3:30pm and 6:30-10pm.

Trattoria San Biagio, p. San Biagio, 1 (tel. 221 39), down via Sasso from p. del Duomo. The local favorite. You will be satisfied with any selection, but the *minestre mediterraneo,* a soup of minced rice and vegetables (L7000) is particularly satisfying. Cover L2000. Open Mon.-Sat. 11:30am-3:30pm and from 6:30pm until the crowd leaves.

Ristorante Renato, via dell'Indipendenza, 9 (tel. 255 96), near p. del Duomo. The quality merits the higher price. *Orecchiette con cime di rapa* (pasta with turnip shoots; L7000) and *agnello ai ferri* (grilled lamb;L15,000) are house specialties. Local wines L6000 per bottle. Cover L2500. Open Mon.-Sat. 7pm-midnight.

Sights and Entertainment

L'Áquila's **castello** dominates the pleasant park at the end of corso Vittorio Emanuele, across and up the hill from the bus station. The Spanish built this hilltop fortress in the 16th century as a defense against rebellious townspeople. Its thick walls now house the outstanding **National Museum of Abruzzo**, which showcases the region's early art. The museum's extensive collection of sacred medieval art includes delicate wooden doors carved with New Testament scenes from a 12th-century church. The paleontological section contains a fossilized mammoth found near the town in 1954. (Open Tues.-Sat. 9am-2pm, Sun. 9am-1pm. Admission L3000.) In the evenings, the path around the fortress's moat is the site of the *passeggiata,* which continues up and down corso Vittorio Emanuele.

From via XX Settembre, take viale Crispi to viale di Collemaggio to reach the **Basilica of Santa Maria di Collemaggio.** Begun in 1287 at the urging of local hermit Pietro da Morrone (who later became Pope Celestine V), the church boasts a façade of checkered pink and white marble, punctuated by rose windows and rounded doorways. The stripping away of baroque embellishments in 1972 and the earlier loss of medieval frescoes account for the church's dearth of ornamentation, with only the striking white limestone Renaissance **Tomb of San Celestino** left. Sin much? Well, August 29 is your lucky day. Simply walk through the church's main door and, according to tradition, all will be forgiven. Each year on this day, important political figures from all parts of Italy march in procession through the door in hopes of attaining absolution. (Open 8:30am-12:30pm and 4-7pm.)

Closer to the heart of town, walk down via Sassa (off p. Duomo) for a short tour of L'Áquila's minor architectural prizes. Stop at Palazzetto Franchi, #56, which encloses a graceful Renaissance courtyard made unique by its double *loggia* (now partially sealed). For a real surprise, walk to the courtyard of #29A and ring the doorbell on the side. Mysteriously, the door opens and a clear voice rings out, "Avanti!" This is the **Church and Convent of Beata Antonia,** run by cloistered nuns. Ask to see the *affresco* (fresco) and you will be escorted to a magnificent 15th-century crucifixion scene covering an entire wall. (Ring between the hours of 9am-noon or 4-6:30pm.)

Down via San Bernadino lies the **Church of San Bernardino,** built in honor of Bernadino of Siena, who spent the last years of his life here hoping to revive the pure Franciscan faith. Inside the Renaissance-façaded structure you'll find two mausoleums (for San Bernadino and Maria Pereira) by Silvestro dell'Aquila, a student of Donatello. The exquisite Baroque wooden ceiling is like butter and was built after the 1703 earthquake ravaged the original interior.

Before leaving L'Áquila, admire to the city's emblem, the 13th-century **Fontana delle 99 Cannelle** (Fountain of the 99 Spouts), near the train station in Porta Rivera. Each of the fountain's distinct (and distinctly deteriorating) stone faces, which portray the original 99 barons of L'Áquila, spews a steady stream of water from an unknown source, uninterrupted since the fountain's construction in 1292.

From November to May, the **Società Aquilana dei Concerti** holds classical concerts in the *castello* (admission L8000-L18,000). Also of interest are the recitals at the **Festival of Classical Guitar** in August. For ticket and schedule information, check the Azienda di Turismo. L'Áquila claims one of central Italy's best snow sport resorts, **Campo Felice.** (Weekly lift tickets L100,000, children L80,000.) *Settimana bianca* (white week) packages, covering room, board, and lift tickets, begin at L350,000. Write to the Azienda di Turismo for information.

Near L'Áquila

The craggy terrain around L'Áquila conceals isolated medieval towns, ancient churches and monasteries, and vacant fortresses. East of the city lie the extraordinary ruins of the 15th-century **Rocca Calascio,** one of the world's most sophisticated works of military architecture. It's surrounded by the medieval towns of **Santo Stefano di Sessanio** and **Castel del Monte,** as well as the 9th-century **Oratorio di San Pellegrino** in the town of Bominaco. To the west of L'Áquila lie extensive Roman ruins at **Amiternum,** and the enormous **Lago di Campotosto,** the largest man-made lake in Italy, which supplies electricity to the Abruzzo and surrounding regions. ARPA buses service these sights from both L'Áquila and Sulmona (2-3 departures per day, 1hr. 30min.-2hr. 30min., L3000-4000). North of L'Áquila, the town of **Assergi** contains a beautiful 12th-century abbey, **Santa Maria Assunta,** with well-preserved frescoes reminiscent of Byzantine art. To get there, take one of the hourly #6 municipal buses (1hr., L1200) from Porta Paganico.

Twelve kilometers above L'Áquila rises the snowcapped **Gran Sasso d'Italia** (Big Rock of Italy), the highest peak entirely within Italy and a mountaineer's delight. First procure a map marked *wanderkarte* or *carta topografica per escursionisti.* Make sure it includes *sentieri* (trails marked by difficulty) and *rifugi* (hikers' huts charging L8000-14,000 per night). Always call these refuges before setting out, and bring food, as prices rise with the altitude. **Club Alpino Italiano** in L'Áquila (tel. 243 42) has the most up-to-date Apennine advice. The accommodations booklet available at L'Áquila's **EPT** contains a list of Abruzzo refuges. From L'Áquila, take bus #6 from Porta Paganico; make sure it is going all the way to the *Funivia.* (about 5 per day, 1hr., L1200; buy an *extraurbano* ticket in a *tabacchi*). Get off at the base of the cableway. If you don't feel like hiking to the top, you can take the *funivia* halfway up (L10,000, Sat.-Sun. L12,000; descent L8000, Sat.-Sun. L10,000; round-trip L15,000, Sat.-Sun. L18,000). The *funivia* runs every half-hour from 8:30am-5pm, except at 1:30pm. Camp and munch at **Camping Funivia del Gran Sasso** (tel. 60 61 63), an immaculate, grassy area down the hill from the eponymous cableway. (L6000 per person, L6000 per small tent, L8000 per large tent; off-season L5000 per person, L5000 per small tent, L7000 per large tent. Electricity L2000. Showers L1000. Eggplant parmesan L3000.) The campground also provides massive *panini* for L3000. (Restaurant open daily 9am-1pm and 3-9pm. Campground open Nov.-April and June-Sept. 15.)

The area around the *funivia* offers several pristine trails. Walk down the road about 500m to reach trail #10, which will take you up to **Monte Della Scindarella,** with a stupendous view of the Gran Sasso and L'Áquila. The upper *funivia* station provides access to several trails; to tackle the Great Pebble itself, take trail #3 to trail #4. In the winter, the Gran Sasso teems with skiers. Skiing at **Camp Imperatore,** the upper end of the *funivia,* starts at L100,000 for a weekly lift pass (valid throughout the season except Dec. 26-Jan. 6 and the Tuesday after Easter). If you're a novice, take a lesson from the Gran Sasso ski school (L30,000 for individuals, less for groups of 2 or more).

Sulmona

Sulmona's most famous son, the poet Ovid (43 BC-17 AD) stands immortalized in **piazza XX Settembre,** his gaze cast toward the curtain of mountains that drapes the city. Despite its preoccupation with the poet, Sulmona owes its beauty to the late middle ages, when prosperity spurred the construction of innumerable churches and palaces. Sulmona maintains a distinct sweetness, thanks not only to the residents' friendliness but also to the proliferation of candy stores. Sulmona has been the home of *confetti* candy since the 15th century. These flower-shaped, sugar-coated almonds, now most often supplanted by horrible paper imitations, are thrown at weddings worldwide. Sulmona is easily reached by ARPA bus from L'Áquila (8 per day, 1hr. 30min., L4800), and Pescara (5 per day, 1hr. 30min., L5900). For more bus information, call 522 58. Buy tickets on the bus. The city is on the Rome-Pescara train line, with 15 daily trains in each direction (Rome, 3hr., L10,800; Pescara, 1hr. 15min., L4400). To get to the town center from the station, take bus A (every 30min., buy tickets in *tabacchi,* L700) or walk the 2km uphill. The **telephone code** is 0864; use the **SIP** phones behind the **Church of the SS. Annunziata** on largo San Tommasi. (Open daily 8am-10pm.) The **tourist office,** is at via Roma, 21 (tel. 532 76), off corso Ovidio. (Open Mon.-Sat. 9am-2pm.)

Albergo Italia, p. Tommasi, 3 (tel. 523 08), off p. XX Settembre, may be packed, but it offers classy rooms overlooking the dome of the church of the SS. Annunziata and the mountains. (Singles L22,000, with bath L30,000; doubles L33,000, with bath L43,000.) At the **Nuova Madrigal,** via Paoline (tel. 517 85), you'll find quiet in the heart of the old quarter. (Singles L20,000; doubles L37,000.) **Ristorante Stella,** beneath the hotel, serves a decent four-course meal for L18,000 (open daily noon-2pm and 7-10pm). Buy pizza by the slice for as little as L1000 at **Pizzeria Candida,** corso Ovidio, 75. (Open Mon.-Sat. 8am-1pm and 3:30-10pm.) **Ristorante Cesidio,** p. Solimo (tel. 527 24), a family-run escape from busy corso Ovidio and the main *piazze,* is clearly *the* place to eat here. Munch a full meal for as little as L18,000. (Open Sat.-Thurs. noon-3pm and 7:30-midnight.) Those with a sweet tooth will collect many a cavity in this town. **G. Di Carlo e Figlio,** corso Ovidio, 185, does bonbon business in *confetti.* (Open daily 8:30am-1pm and 2:30-7pm.) Pick up picnic staples at **Supermercato STANDA,** corso Ovidio, 15. (Open Mon.-Sat. 9am-1pm and 4-8pm.)

At one end of corso Ovidio, the gardens of Sulmona offer shade to the weary. Next comes the **Church and Palace of SS. Annunziata,** Sulmona's architectural showpiece and one of the Abruzzo's most magnificent structures. An extravagant Baroque church façade abuts a delicate Gothic-Renaissance *palazzo,* where the lazy intricacy of Gothic windows and portals complements the symmetric Renaissance purity of the central and right portals. The *palazzo* now houses a small museum focusing on Renaissance Sulmonese goldwork. (May be closed for restoration.) Throughout the summer months, free classical music concerts fill the *palazzo's* courtyard (check the billboards or with the tourist office).

Beyond the church, head down to colossal **piazza Garibaldi** to eyeball the Renaissance-era **Fontana del Vecchio,** which gushes clear mountain water from a rare Gothic aqueduct (1256). A daily **market** takes place here. Farther down corso Ovidio, on p. del Carmine, stood the **Church of San Francesco della Scarpa** (St. Francis of the Shoe), but all that remains is a 12th-century portal. Off corso Ovidio near the gardens, peek into the **Palazzo Tabassi.** Note the intricate façade, built in 1449 by Matro Petro Da Como, and the frescoed lunettes of the gothic arches. (Erratic hours. Free.)

Prohibitively expensive accommodations mean that the mountain resort town **Scanno** is better visited as a daytrip from Sulmona. Its lake is one of the few remaining in Italy that has not been reduced to an enormous pee-puddle. Incredible vistas accompany the twisting, stomach-punishing bus ride (14 per day, 1hr., L2500).

National Park of Abruzzo (Parco Nazionale d'Abruzzo)

The National Park of Abruzzo, a huge wildlife preserve, occupies a vast, mountainous tract in the southwest corner of the region. It contains perhaps the only genuine wilderness in Italy, with vast glaciers and forests, and extensive fauna. Furthermore, the park's villages, with their *pensioni* and restaurants, offer more than just the usual trappings of civilization.

Pescassèroli, the park's administrative center, provides the ideal base for exploration. According to yet another ridiculous legend, the town was founded by a nasty old count who had taken advantage of Pesca, the beautiful wife of the knight Serolo. After the young lovers died (Pesca of shame, Serolo of grief) the penitent count joined their names and built the town around their (the dead people's) tomb.

Orientation and Practical Information

Pescassèroli, like most towns in the preserve, is served by ARPA's **Avezzano-Castel di Sangro** bus line (6 per day). Unfortunately, five out of six ARPA drivers are "60 Minutes" fans; there is only one bus on Sunday. **Avezzano** (on the Rome-Pescara train line) lies one and a half hours by bus from Pescassèroli (L3400), one and a half hours from Rome (L5400), two and a half hours from Pescara (L6900), and two hours from L'Áquila (L6000). An ARPA bus links L'Áquila with Avezzano hourly (50min., L3400). **Castel di Sangro** (on the Sulmona-Carpinone train line) is one hour from Pescassèroli (L2500). In July and August an ARPA bus leaves p. Esedra in Rome for Pescassèroli daily (7am) and returns to Rome in the evening (7:30pm, L8000). For more information, call ARPA at (0863) 265 61 or 229 21.

In Pescassèroli, the helpful **tourist office** (tel. 91 04 61) waits on via Piave across from the police station. Get accommodations and transportation information here. (Open daily 9am-1pm and 4:30-6:30pm.) For an essential park map (extortionately priced at L8000—you might try to pilfer one) and similarly expensive books on its plants and critters, try the **Ufficio di Zona** (tel. 919 55), off p. Sant'Antonio. (Open daily 9am-noon and 3-7pm.) At least it's for a good cause; profits go toward maintaining the park.

The dreary town of **Avezzano** is notable only for its location on both the Rome-Pescara train line and the main bus route though the National Park. The **tourist office,** via Garibaldi, 35/39 (tel. 352 67), lies directly across the *piazza* from the train station and ARPA bus stop. (Open Mon.-Sat. 9am-1pm and 4-6pm.)

The town of **Alfedena**, 1km from its train station and 33km from Pescassèroli, showcases picturesque archeological sites. Its **tourist office** (tel. 873 94), in the main square, stocks information on the ever-open Roman **acropolis** and **necropolis.**

The **telephone code** for Pescassèroli, Opi, and Avezzano is 0863; for Civitella Alfedena, Alfedena, Castel di Sangro, and Pescocostanzo, 0864.

Accommodations, Camping, and Food

Avezzano: If you must stay overnight here, opt for **Creati,** via XX Settembre, 208 (tel. 41 33 47), with singles for L25,000 and doubles for L40,000 (private bath included). Most restaurants in Avezzano charge exorbitant prices.

Pescassèroli: Most reasonably priced accommodations in Pescassèroli do not offer single rooms, but solo travelers can often finagle a double or quad room to themselves for the price of a single. **Locanda Al Castello** (tel. 91 07 57), across from the park office, is comfortable, charming, and convenient to the bus stop and trails. Full pension is a good deal, as the meals are plentiful and delicious. (L25,000 per person, L30,000 Aug. and last week of Dec.; half-pension L45,000 per person, L55,000 Aug. and year's end; full pension L65,000, L70,000 Aug. and the 6 days of Christmas.) Two kilometers uphill from town, but with mountain views, the **Albergo Valle del Lupo,** via Collachi (tel. 91 05 34), rents fresh new rooms. Walk down viale S. Lucia off p. S. Antonio and turn right along viale Colle dell'Oro. Follow the signs from there. (Doubles L50,000, with bath L57,000. Single and off-season prices are negotiable.) There are four campgrounds within 21km of town; the best is **Campeggio dell'Orso** (tel. 919 55), by the river on the Opi road (L5000 per person, L5000 per tent).

The best restaurant in town is **Pizzeria Ristorante Picchio** on via Lungo Sangro (tel. 91 23 33). Enjoy delicious *funghi sott'olio* (L3000) and broccoli-stuffed *tortelloni* (L7000) in the shadow of two huge wooden mills that once ground flour for pasta. Cover is L2000. A full meal, including drinks, will cost around L20,000. (Open daily noon-3pm and 7-11:30pm; Sept.-June Thurs.-Tues. noon-3pm and 7-11:30pm.) Get a pre-hike carbo-boost from **Pizzamama,** via Colli dell'Oro, 18 (tel. 91 27 69); don't confuse this street, off p. S. Antonio, with the road out of town. Pizza is L1000 per slice, including *pizza al jurapi,* made with a spinach-like plant that only grows at altitudes above 1600 meters. (Open daily 11am-3pm and 5-10pm.) The **A&O supermarket** is on via S. Lucia, the main highway (open daily 8:30am-1pm and 4-8pm).

Opi: ARPA buses follow the winding road through the park to the village of **Opi** (5km). Two kilometers past the village on the bus route lies the campground **Vecchio Mulino** (tel. 91 22 32; L6000 per person, L5000 per small tent, L10,000 per large tent). At the turn-off to Camosciara there's an **information center** (tel. 891 70) for foreign visitors. (Open July 10-Aug. Mon.-Sat. 9am-1pm and 2-5pm.)

Civitella Alfedena: 10km past Opi, the bus reaches the village of **Villetta Barrea;** 200m down, the turn-off to Civitella Alfedena leads to the **Pinas Nigra Campground** (L5000 per person, L5000 per tent. Aug. L1000 extra). The site is large and pleasant, bordered by the River Sangro. In Civitella Alfedena, make yourself at home at the **Alberghetto La Torre,** via La Torre (tel. 89 01 21; doubles L40,000; extra bed L15,000). The ice-cold **Barrea Lake** cuts majestically into the mountains, stretching 7km between Villetta Barrea and the next village of **Barrea.** The **Colle Ciglio** campground, on the banks of the lake, is 500m above town on the way to Alfedena, 10km southeast of Barrea.

Alfedena: Stay at **Leon D'Oro** (tel. 871 21; singles L20,000, with bath L22,000; doubles L34,000, with bath L40,000). **Alimentari Crispi,** off the main square, makes *panini* (sandwiches) from L2000. A track leads from Alfedena to **Lago Montagna Spaccata** (3km away), where the intrepid and insulated can brave the freezing mountain waters.

Food Festivals

During August, eat your way through the park by stopping at a food festival free-for-all. On the 24th day of the eighth month, Opi hosts the **Sagra degli Gnocchi** (gnocchifest), a nationally renowned eat-along that causes an accommodations squeeze as thousands converge to consume *gnocchi,* sausages, and cheese while watching exploding *gnocchi* fireworks. (*Gnocchi,* in case you've been wondering, are potato-flour dumplings whose consistancy ranges from delicate puffs that melt in the mouth to chewy lumps that land with a thud at the bottom of the stomach before creeping their way through your GI tract.)

Excursions

You don't really enter the park until you begin the scenic ascent on the bus ride from Avezzano to Pescassèroli. Fields of poppies, rock outcrops, dazzling valleys, and dizzying vistas will delight you. To avoid gastronomic *déjà vu,* don't eat too much before this twisting climb. If you don't see any wildlife in the park, compensate in Pescassèroli by checking out the **zoo** on via S. Lucia, which includes animals indigenous to the park and information on natural history. (Open daily 10am-noon and 3-6pm. Admission L3000.)

Once you get off the bus, you'll find the region undeveloped and its trails poorly marked. Begin by purchasing a trail map (L8000) from the Ufficio di Zona in Pescassèroli. The clear, detailed map points out where the different animals protected in the preserve—brown bears, chamois, deer, wolves, and eagles—are most likely to be found. Some of the best trails are within walking distance of Pescassèroli. From the town center, turn right at the intersection of viale S. Lucia with the state road to reach trail B2, a two-and-a-half-hour climb skirting Monte Di Valle Carrara; you might see a bear (hope it's at zoom-lens distance). Make the beautiful two-and-a-half-hour hike to **Valico (Pass) di Monte Tranquillo** (1673m). Take trail C3, which starts at the southern end of town, up through the green Valle Mancina past the Rifugio Della Difesa. Keep climbing and you'll eventually reach the pass, with its impressive view of the mountain peaks to the north. For a more extended excursion, take trail D6, across the stream from town, up to trail E3, which leads to the town of Opi (total time 3hr. 30min.). Or take trail D1, at the same starting point, to trails A9 and A1 (3hr. 30min.). To increase your chances of seeing wildlife, continue on trail A2 (1hr.) to A3 (1hr. 30min.), or bring Frán.

If you can tune your hiking timetable to that of the ARPA bus line, venture further afield. A scenic hike snakes its way to the **Valle Fondillo,** 9km from Pescassèroli. To reach it, take a bus to the south-bound road just after Opi (it's at km #51; ask the driver). At the end of this road, trail F2 guides you on a pleasant stroll up to the *Valico Passaggio dell'Orso* (1672m, 2hr. 30min. to the top). If you prefer lumpier terrain, **La Camosciara** is the place for you. To get there, hop the bus to Casone Antonucci, just west of Villetta Barrea (at km #55-56). A paved road leads south for about 3km to p. Camosciara. From here, embark on the strenuous one-hour hike to the **Rifugio Della Liscia** (1650m), at the foot of the rocky peaks.

In winter, this area has excellent skiing, due to the unique combination of mountainous hills and copious snowfall. Package deals on **settimane bianche** (white weeks) can run as low as L380,000 for room, lift tickets, and half-pension (full pension L425,000).

For more information, contact the tourist office in Pescassèroli. For a regional snow bulletin, call (0862) 665 10.

Inland Molise

If your yen for wilderness is unfulfilled after the National Park, consider trekking into the remote interior of Molise. Avoid staying in **Campobasso,** the Akron of Italy and Molise's capital, accessible by a one-hour bus ride from Térmoli (L3600; 2hr. by train, L5700) and a four-hour train ride from Sulmona or Naples. Stop just long enough to make the connection to **Isernia,** a small town one hour by train from Campobasso (L4300; by bus L3600), and an ideal base for day-long explorations of the nearby hill-towns. Despite a modern appearance, Isernia is believed to be one of the oldest settlements in Europe: in 1979 primitive stone tools used by the town's namesake *Homo aeserniensis* (a human genus believed to have migrated from Africa one million years ago) were discovered here. You can examine some of these tools at the small **archeological museum** (tel. (0865) 41 35 26) 1.5km from the train station down corso Garibaldi. (Open Tues.-Sat. 8:30am-1:30pm and 4-7pm. Free guided tours.) Unwind at **Il Vecchio Mulino** (tel. 595 17). On the bank of a racing mountain stream, it provides an excellent meal of local specialties for under L20,000. (Open Mon.-Sat. 1:30-10:30pm.) An eager **EPT** awaits on via Mario Farinacci, 11 (tel. 39 92), off corso Garibaldi to the left of the station on the eighth floor. Inquire about information on the region. (Open Mon.-Fri. 9am-1pm.) You'll hate bidding farewell to the comfortable and modern **Hotel Sayonara** at via Berta, 131 (tel. 509 92). From the train station, take the third right four blocks down. (Singles with bath L45,000. Doubles with bath L65,000.) For information on **tours** of the Isernia area in English, contact Anna Giancola (tel. (0865) 41 42 86).

From Isernia, you can tour the tiny towns of Molise, where a slew of festivals take place. On July 26, **Jelsi** hosts the **Sagra del Grano,** where different characters and even a cart are sculpted from grain and paraded about in honor of Santa Anna. July whips through **Scápoli** with an international festival dedicated to the *zampogna,* a particularly reprehensible breed of bagpipe (check with the Isernia EPT for dates). A rip-roaring good time can be had in **Montenero Valcocchiara** on the last Sunday in August, when the **Rodeo Pentro** comes to town. Hikers and nature-lovers can reach the **Mainarde Mountain Range,** one of Italy's largest, by taking the bus to Scápoli (under L5000).

SOUTHERN ITALY

Campania

In the shadow of Mount Vesuvius, the fertile crescent of Campania cradles the Bay of Naples and the larger Gulf of Salerno. Campania, Italy's most spectacular natural setting, greets its scores of tourists with famous hospitality and a wealth of historic sights. The island of Cápri, a delicious pleasure palace in the Tyrrhenian Sea, is in danger of sinking under the combined tonnage of the summer's invading tourists. To escape the masses, explore the oft-ignored.inland towns, the ruins of Paestum, or the fiery fields west of Naples. Or revel in the festival of humanity cruising the stunning Amalfi coast, the ruins of Pompeii and Herculaneum, and the bubbling baths on the isle of Íschia.

The area's commercial and cultural history has long been bound up with that of Naples, its capital and major port. Strategically located Naples has been coveted ever since it was established as a Greek colony, Neapolis (New City), around 600 BC. Conquered by the Romans in 327 BC, it became a favorite residence of emperors (Nero made his theatrical debut here) and literary personages, including Virgil, largely because of its insistence on retaining the Greek language and customs. A Byzantine dukedom in the 7th century and later subject to Norman Sicily, Naples reached the zenith of its medieval prosperity when Charles I of Anjou made it his capital in 1266. Along with his Angevin and Aragonese successors, Charles enlarged the city and embellished it with palaces and churches. The Spanish Habsburgs (1502-1704) were followed by Bourbons, Bonapartes, and finally the Savoys. Campania became part of the unified Italian nation in 1860.

Naples (Nápoli)

At its core, Naples is true to the melodrama of the mandolins. It is home to unwavering fatalists, united by family and tradition, not to mention an ever-sacred soccer team despised by the rest of the boot. Rich museums, grand palaces, and a proudly extroverted populace define this city far better than the powerful criminals of the invisible Neapolitan Camorra. Petty thievery does abound, however, so empty your car and leave cameras, jewelery, and other *scugnizzi*-bait in a safe place at the hotel as you venture out to explore this musical city.

Getting In and Out of Naples

Naples is southern Italy's transportation hub; frequent **trains** from Stazione Centrale connect the city to Italy's other major cities, including the port city of Bríndisi on the Rome-Lecce line (where the ferries to Greece accept Eurail passes). (See Trains for more information.)

Ferries run from Naples's Molo Beverello to the islands of Cápri, Íschia, and Prócida. The tourist office brochure *Qui Napoli* and the newspaper *Il Mattino* both carry up-to-date ferry schedules. Ferry schedules and prices change constantly, so it's best to check ahead. **Caremar** hydrofoils and ferries serve all three islands. (To Cápri, 5 per day, 70min., L8000; to Íschia, 9 per day—5 of these by way of Prócida—70min., L8000; to Prócida, 6 per day, 60min., L7000. Less frequent in off-season. Ticket office on Molo Beverello open daily 6am-11pm.) Other key ferries:

Naples-Lípari Islands: Siremar Lines, Agenzia Carlo Genovese, via Depretis, 78 (tel. 551 21 12; open daily 9am-1pm and 3-7:30pm). Ferries leave at 9pm from the Molo Angioino at the Stazione Marittima Thurs.-Tues.; June 1-15 Mon., Thurs., and Sat.; Sept.27-May 31 Tues. and Fri.

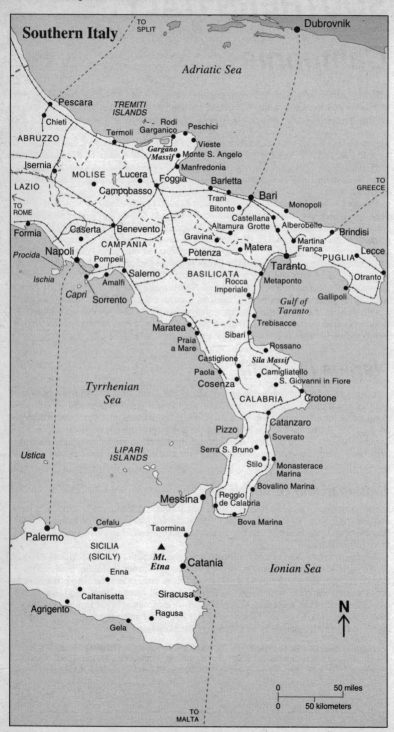

Southern Italy

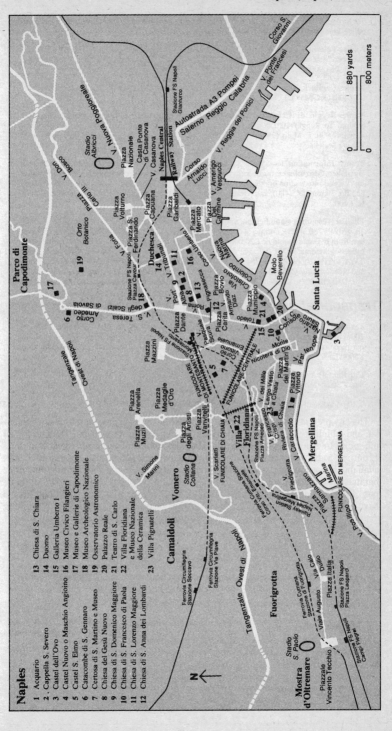

Naples

1 Acquario
2 Cappella S. Severo
3 Castel dell'Ovo
4 Castel Nuovo o Maschio Angioino
5 Castel S. Elmo
6 Catacombe di S. Gennaro
7 Certosa di S. Martino e Museo
8 Chiesa del Gesù Nuovo
9 Chiesa di S. Domenico Maggiore
10 Chiesa di S. Francesco di Paola
11 Chiesa di S. Lorenzo Maggiore
12 Chiesa di S. Anna dei Lombardi
13 Chiesa di S. Chiara
14 Duomo
15 Galleria Umberto I
16 Museo Civico Filangieri
17 Museo e Gallerie di Capodimonte
18 Museo Archeologico Nazionale
19 Osservatorio Astronomico
20 Palazzo Reale
21 Teatro di S. Carlo
22 Villa Floridiana e Museo Nazionale della Ceramica
23 Villa Pignatelli

To: Strómboli (8hr., L57,480), Lípari (12hr., L64,560), and Vulcano (13hr., L65,160). Fares quoted are June-Sept.; at other times they will be somewhat lower.

Naples-Palermo: Tirrenia Lines, Molo Angioino, Stazione Marittima (tel. 551 21 81); ticket office open Mon.-Sat. 8:30am-1:30pm and 2:30-7pm, Sun. 3:30-7:30pm). To: Palermo daily at 8pm (11hr., L61,900; Oct.-May L47,900). There is a L2000 port tax upon leaving Palermo.

Naples-Cagliari: Tirrenia. Thurs. and Sat. at 5:30pm; Oct.-May Thurs. at 7:15pm (16hr., L48,400; Oct.-May L37,800).

Naples-Règgio di Calabria-Catania-Syracuse-Malta: Tirrenia. Departs Naples Thurs. at 8:30pm. To: Règgio (10hr. 30min.), Catania (15hr.), and Syracuse (19hr.). All fares L61,900; Oct.-May L47,900. To Malta (25hr., L137,600; Oct.-May L114,000). There is a L15,000 port-tax upon leaving Malta.

Trains: Information, tel. 553 41 88; lines usually busy. Ticket prices and schedules in English and Italian. Also **information booths** and **Digiplan machines** at the Stazione Centrale. Telephone service and information booths open daily 7am-9pm. To: Milan (7hr., L56,700), Rome (1-2 per hr., 2hr. 30min., L15,400), and Syracuse (10hr., L41,900). To Bríndisi (for Greece), 6hr. 30min., L27,100.

Flights: Aeroporto Capodichino, viale Umberto Maddalena (tel. 780 57 63; departures 780 32 35; arrivals 780 30 49), northwest of the city. Take bus #14 from p. Garibaldi in the city center. A taxi from p. Dante should be L20,000. Connections to all major Italian and European cities. **Alitalia,** via Medina, 41/42 (tel. 542 53 33), off p. Municipio. Open Mon.-Fri. 8:45am-5:30pm. **TWA,** via Partenope, 23 (tel. 764 58 28). They don't handle flights from Naples, but cover Rome and other airports. Open Mon.-Fri. 9am-5:30pm. **British Airways,** via Partenope, 31 (tel. 764 55 50). Daily flights to London. Open Mon.-Fri. 9am-1pm and 2-5:30pm.

Transportation within Naples

Taxis: tel. 556 44 44. A rollercoaster ride. Take only taxis with meters. Fare L2800 plus L100 per 100m or 25 seconds. Sun. and holidays L1200 supplement; 10pm-7am L2000 supplement. L400 per piece of luggage. L400 per dog. Taxis to the airport should be about L20,000. Minimum L5000 fare.

Car Rental: Avis, at Stazione Centrale (tel. 28 40 41). Open Mon.-Fri. 8am-1pm and 3-7:30pm, Sat. 8:30am-1pm and 4-6pm. **Hertz,** p. Garibaldi, 69 (tel. 20 62 28). Open Mon.-Fri. 8am-7pm, Sat. 8am-1pm, Sun. 8am-12:30pm. **Europcar,** p. Garibaldi, 69 (tel. 20 65 96), open daily 8am-7:30pm. A small car should be L450,000-550,000 per week at any of these locations.

The city presents numerous public transportation options: bus, tram, subway, funicular, and a high-speed suburban train line (Ferrovia Circumvesuviana). The fare for all inner-city transport is L1000 per ride. Half-day non-subway passes (6am-2pm or 2-11pm) are valid on all buses, trams, and funiculars (L1500, whole-day passes L2500; available in convenience stores throughout the city). Subway passes are the same price but must be purchased separately, and they cannot be used on the other modes of transport. Bus service, especially in the morning and late afternoon, can be a drag. People have been known to fall out of or be crushed inside overcrowded buses. To cover long distances (especially from Mergellina to the station), use the efficient and cool subway or tram #4.

Buses #150 and 106: From p. Garibaldi to the center of the city, p. Municipio, and onward to the bay (Riviera di Chiaia) and Mergellina (for the youth hostel and Pozzuoli).

Buses CS and CD: From p. Garibaldi to p. Cavour (CD) or via Pessina (CS, for the Museo Archeologico Nazionale), and to p. Dante, a good area for restaurants and hotels.

Bus #185: The most direct route to p. Dante from p. Garibaldi.

Bus #152: From p. Garibaldi through p. Municipio, p. Vittoria, and Mergellina.

Trams #1 and 4: A picturesque and practical way to get from the station to Mergellina. Stops at the Molo Beverello port. Hop on in front of the Garibaldi statue near Stazione Centrale.

Metropolitana: The subway system is convenient from the train station to points west: p. Cavour (Museo Nazionale), p. Amedeo (funicular to Vómero), Mergellina, and Pozzuoli. Go to platform #4, 1 floor underground, at Stazione Centrale.

Ferrovia Circumvesuviana: The fastest way to get to Herculaneum (15min.), Pompeii (45min.), and Sorrento (80min.). One floor underground at the train station.

Funicolare Centrale: The most frequently used of the 3 cable railways to Vómero, connecting the lower city to the hills and S. Martino. Leaves from p. Duca d'Aosta, next to the Galleria Umberto on via Roma/Toledo.

Hitching to other cities from Naples is extremely risky.

Crime

Accompanied by tinkling mandolins, Neapolitans love to glorify their city with a "canzone napolitana," a felicitous and flighty ballad of sun, sea, and *amore*—the three pillars of this legendary city. The Naples of song, however, is only an operatic respite from the modern, urban Naples, a promiscuous and anarchical landscape of haggling market crowds, hell-bent motor vehicles, and packs of volatile youngsters known as *scugnizzi*. Like its *scugnizzi,* Naples possesses an unkempt and dangerous charm that is often difficult to appreciate, especially for the many visitors who fall prey to *lo scippo,* the local term for petty kleptomania.

Naples is poorer and more industrial than many of the cities which tourists frequent. Its crime problems are concomitantly more serious (and worth taking seriously). Women travelers and solo travelers should be especially on guard in Naples. Follow those common sense safety rules warranted by large cities, and review the Safety and Women Travelers sections in the General Introduction of this book; you should also note the following advice for circumstances when common sense isn't enough. Wear your backpack on both shoulders at all times and be sure that your money belt or necklace pouch is securely hidden inside your clothes, away from prying eyes (and grabbing hands). (One *Let's Go* researcher/writer was attacked on a main street in Spaccanapoli at 8pm by two men attempting to rip off her money belt.) Never wear expensive or bulky jewelry, and don't wear an expensive watch. If *anything* happens to you, scream as loudly as possible. Always walk on major streets, moving quickly and confidently. Solo travelers may want to join up with another person or a group at their hotel to explore the city. Women should be especially careful—never sit alone in a train compartment. One thing to do is ask couples or men you trust if you can wait with them in train stations. If you think suspicious-looking characters are following you, duck into the nearest *caffè* and call a taxi. One more piece of advice: If you're getting around by car, stow valuables in the trunk and keep your doors locked—thieves are known to ransack cars stopped at red lights and run off with purses and cameras.

Orientation and Practical Information

Naples consists of several *piazze* and quarters. Immense **piazza Garibaldi,** on the eastern side of Naples, contains the central train station and the major city bus terminal. Broad, tree-lined corso Umberto I leads southwest from p. Garibaldi, ending at p. Bovio; from here via Depretis branches to the south, leading to p. Municipio and nearby p. del Plebiscito, an area of stately buildings and statues. On the water at the foot of p. Municipio lie **Molo Beverello** and the Stazione Marittima, the point of departure for ferries. Turn north from p. del Plebiscito and go up via Toledo (also called via Roma) to reach **piazza Dante,** the **university district,** and **Spaccanapoli** (literally "splitting Naples"), a straight, narrow street that changes names every few blocks (becoming via Capitelli, via Benedetto Croce, via San Biagio dei Librai, via Vicaria Vecchia, and via San Gregorio Armeno). Lined with palaces and churches, Spaccanapoli runs through the middle of historic Naples with Roman rectitude. But be careful you don't get yourself *spaccato* by the hordes of youngsters on mopeds who use this alley, only three or four meters wide, as a racecourse. To the west, at the foot of the hills, you'll find the **Santa Lucia** and **Mergellina** districts, with their celebrated bayside walks of via Partenope and via Caracciolo. Farther west are the most scenic areas of Naples: hillside **via Posillipo, via Petrarca** winding up above Mergellina, and **via Manzoni** running along the crest of the ridge, with stunning vistas from its western end. A park crowns the cliffs of panoramic **Capo di Posillipo.** The hilltop **Vómero** district above Santa Lucia commands a view of Mount Vesuvius to the east, historic Naples below, and th Campi Flegrei (Phlegraean Fields) to the west. The Vómero can be reached by funicular from via Roma/Toledo or the Montesanto station (northwest of p. Dante).

Tourist Offices: EPT, at the central train station (tel. 26 87 79). Helpful, almost to a fault—you'll have to wait as they exhaustively help the people in front of you. They will also call hotels and ferries for you. Pick up a map and the indispensable guide *Qui Napoli* (Here's Naples), featuring everything from train schedules to entertainment listings. For specific information on arts and entertainment, check out the *Posto Unico,* a poster/calendar covering theaters, restaurants, and clubs. English spoken. Open Mon.-Sat. 9am-8pm, Sun. 9am-1pm. **Information office,** p. Gesù Nuovo (tel. 552 33 28). Take bus #185 up via Roma toward p. Dante, get off at via Capitelli, and follow it to the *piazza*—right in front of the Chiesa del Gesù Nuovo. The most helpful (particularly for sights in the Old City) and professional office in the city. Open Mon.-Sat. 9am-7pm, Sun. 9am-2pm. **Main office,** p. Martiri, 59, scala B, second floor (inside Ferragamo's *palazzo)* (tel. 40 53 11). Take bus #150. Open Mon.-Fri. 8:30am-2:30pm. Also at Stazione Mergellina (tel. 761 21 02) and the airport (tel. 780 57 61). In theory open Mon.-Fri. 8:30am-2pm and 5-7:30pm. **Information booth,** p. Garibaldi, outside the train station. Has little to offer. Other offices at Castel dell'-Ovo (tel. 764 56 88) and at the hydrofoil port in Mergellina (tel. 761 45 85). **Qui Napoli Computer Information,** terminals located throughout the city in public buildings and sights, offers tourist information and more. Yes, the computers speak English.

Budget Travel: Centro Turistico Studentesco e Giovanile (CTS), via Mezzocannone, 25 (tel. 552 79 60), off corso Umberto, northeast of p. Bovio. Student travel information, ISIC and FIYTO cards, and booking service. Open Mon.-Fri. 9:30am-1pm and 3-6pm, Sat. 9:30am-12:30pm. **CIT,** p. Municipio, 70-72 (tel. 554 54 26). The city's most complete travel agency. Train, plane, and ferry reservations. Open Mon.-Fri. 9am-1pm and 2:30-6pm. For ferry reservations to Greece, go to **Travels and Holidays,** via Santa Lucia, 141 (tel. 41 41 29). Take bus #150 from p. Garibaldi. Open Mon.-Fri. 9am-1:30pm and 3-6:30pm, Sat. 9am-1:30pm. **Italian Youth Hostel Organization (Associazione Alberghi Italiani per la Gioventù),** p. Carità, 40 (tel. 552 00 84), north of the central post office. An excellent resource for information on youth hostels and special HI and Transalpino plane, train, and ferry discounts. HI cards L30,000. Open Mon.-Fri. 9am-1pm and 4:30-7pm, Sat. 9am-1pm; Oct.-June 9am-1pm and 4-7pm, Sat. 9am-1pm.

Consulates: U.S. (tel. 761 43 03; phone lines open 24hr.), on p. della Repubblica (sometimes called "p. Principedi Napoli" on maps) at the western end of the Villa Comunale. Passport and consular service'Passport and consular services Mon.-Fri. 8am-1:30pm; mid-Sept. to June Mon.-Fri. 9am-12:30pm and 3-5:30pm. **Malta:** via Ponte di Tappia, 82 (tel. 552 15 73) off via Roma/Toledo near p. Municipio. Open Mon.-Fri. 9am-1pm and 4-8pm. All others should contact their embassies in Rome.

Currency Exchange: The few banks willing to change money charge commissions of L3000. Try one of the banks' main offices for the most efficient transactions. Closest to the train station is **Banca Nazionale del Lavoro,** p. Garibaldi (tel. 799 71 13), at the corner of corso Umberto. Open for exchange Mon.-Fri. 8:30am-1:30pm and 2:45-4pm. You can also exchange in the Stazione Centrale, which has the longest hours but bad rates. Open daily 8am-1:30pm and 2:30-8pm.

American Express: Ashiba Travel, p. Municipio, 1 (tel. 551 53 03). Holds mail 1 month "for free" and replaces lost cards and checks (lost checks must be replaced during the banking hours of Banco di Roma). Open Mon.-Fri. 9am-1pm and 3:30-7:30pm, Sat. 9am-1pm. AmEx works with the **Banco di Roma,** via Verdi, 31 (tel. 785 41 11), right around the corner. Open Mon.-Fri. 9am-1:20pm and 2:45-3:45pm.

Post Office: p. Matteotti (tel. 551 14 56), off via Diaz, which runs off corso Umberto at its western end. Fermo Posta L250 per letter retrieved. Offers special *CAI post* service (Posta Celere), which delivers packages anywhere in the world in 3 days (in Europe, starting from L28,900, to USA, starting from L49,500 for packages up to 1kg). Open Mon.-Fri. 8:15am-1:30pm, Sat. 8:15am-12:10pm. Also at Galleria Umberto and Stazione Centrale (both open same hours). **Postal Code:** 80100 (for Fermo Posta at p. Matteotti).

Telephones: ASST, at Stazione Centrale. Also at via Depretis, 40, on the street off p. Bovio at the end of corso Umberto, heading south towards p. Municipio. Both open 24 hrs. **SIP,** at Galleria Umberto. Open daily 9am-5pm. Also at via Petronio, 8-18, off via N. Sauro along the water in Santa Lucia. *Gettoni* and *scheida* cards only. Open daily 8:30am-10pm. The via Depretis office has the shortest lines. **Telephone Code:** 081.

English Bookstore: Feltrinelli, via S. T. d'Aquino, 70/76 (tel. 552 14 36). Turn off via Roma/Toledo onto via Ponte di Tappia at the Motta restaurant; the store is 20m ahead on the left. An extensive selection, including yours truly. Open Mon.-Fri. 9am-8pm, Sat. 9am-1:30pm. **Universal Books,** Rione Sirignano, 1 (tel. 66 32 17), upstairs on the 1st floor, near Villa Comunale, 1 block east of via Santa Maria in Portico. Books in a multitude of tongues. Open Mon.-Fri. 9am-1pm and 4-7pm, Sat. 9am-1pm.

Luggage Storage: around the corner from the pharmacy in the train station. L1500 per piece per day. Open 24 hrs.

Late-Night Pharmacy: tel. 26 88 81, at Stazione Centrale (leaving the tracks, head to the left by the fountain). Open Mon.-Sat. 8am-8pm. Pharmacies rotate late-night responsibilities. Call 192 for the 24-hr. recording of nighttime pharmacies (in Italian).

Emergencies: tel. 113. **Police:** tel. 794 11 11. English speakers always available. For problems, go to the *ufficio stranieri* (Office for Foreigners) at the Questura, via Medina, 75, at via Diaz. **Medical Assistance: Ambulance,** tel. 752 06 96. **Guardia Medica Permanente** (tel. 751 31 77), in the Municipio building, for medical assistance at night or during holidays. **Psychiatric First Aid:** tel. 743 43 43.

Accommodations

When you arrive at the central train station, hotel-hawkers will invariably approach you. If you do need to stay near the train station, and all you want is a cheap bed for the night, this may be the easiest route. Check *Let's Go* first, though, and seek out a good-quality, safe place (some offer a special *Let's Go* price). However, unless you're only staying over in Naples to catch an early train or ferry the next day, you really should avoid the area around Piazza Garibaldi. Filth, noise, and vice are pervasive—it's particularly unsafe at night, and will leave you with a drastically skewed impression of Naples. There are better alternatives in the area around the **university,** between p. Dante and the *duomo*. Hotels here cater primarily to students and offer well-furnished, immaculate rooms at low prices, though vacancies decrease when school is in session. The **Mergellina** area at the far end of the waterfront (served by subway and trolley) commands outstanding views of Vesuvius and Cápri, but ranges in price from expensive to exorbitant. The costly hostel also resides here.

Seriously consider paying more for added comfort, security, and respectability in Naples. Always agree on the price *before* you unpack your bags, never give up your passport before seeing your room, and be alert to hidden shower charges, obligatory breakfasts, and the like. When selecting a place to stay, check for double-locked doors and door buzzers. The **International Catholic Association for the Service of Women (ACISJF),** at the Stazione Centrale (tel. 28 19 93) near the EPT, helps women find safe and inexpensive rooms. (Open Mon. and Wed.-Thurs. 3-7pm, Tues. and Fri. 9:30am-1pm and 3-7pm, Sat. 9:30am-1pm.) Phone numbers are posted at the booth in case nobody's home (or try tel. 40 41 28). If you have a legitimate complaint, call the EPT's special number: 40 62 89. An English-speaker is on hand to help you. For information on **camping,** see Near Naples below.

Ostello Mergellina (HI), salita della Grotta, 23 (tel. and fax. 761 23 46). Take the Metropolitana to Mergellina and make 2 sharp rights onto via Piedigrotta. Follow the street underneath the overpass and follow the signs up to your right (*before* you get to the tunnel). A 15-min. walk from the subway and not far from the waterfront. Overpriced, but one of the safest places to stay on a budget in Naples. Well-maintained 2-, 4-, and 6-person rooms, all with bath. Although there are 200 beds, it's best to reserve in July-Aug. Someone is always there, so you can leave luggage. Lockout 9:30am-4:30pm. Check-out 9am. Curfew 11:30pm. L16,000 per person (likely to increase to L17,000 soon). If you are not a member, you must pay L5000 extra per night. Each such payment earns you a stamp, and with 6 stamps you receive a hostel membership that's good for one year. Breakfast, sheets, and shower included. The self-service cafeteria downstairs offers à la carte items and full meals for L11,000.

Near piazza Dante and Vómero

Take bus #185, CS, or CD from the train station to the bargain rooms around p. Dante. Although we wouldn't advise walking around here late at night, it makes an acceptable central base for cautious tourists. To reach the more serene Vómero, get off any of the buses running up via Roma/Toledo toward p. Dante near Galleria Umberto, and take the funicular up.

Soggiorno Imperia, p. Miraglia, 386 (tel. 45 93 47). From p. Dante, walk east through the arch to the left of the clock tower. Continue on via San Pietro a Maiella, to the right of Pizzeria Bellini.

Continue walking through a small *piazza*. At the end, look for two large grey doors on the right side of the narrow street. A 4-floor climb to bright, clean, and recently renovated rooms. Young, extremely helpful management accustomed to working with students. Convivial TV room makes a great meeting place. English spoken. Pay telephone. Singles L21,000. Doubles L34,000. Showers included. Call 1 or 2 days in advance July-Aug. and at Easter.

Albergo Duomo, via Duomo, 228 (tel. 26 59 88). No need to go out to dinner—just eat off the immaculate floor here. Capacious white-and-baby-blue-trimmed rooms, all with bath. Doubles L70,000. Triples L90,000. Quads L110,000. *Matrimoniale* L50,000. Curfew 1-2am.

Allogio Fiamma, via Francesco del Giudice, 13 (tel. 45 91 87). Walking from the Imperia, turn right as you go out the door, and take the second left. The Fiamma's kindly owners offer vast and not-so-vast old rooms at good prices. All rooms with bath. Doubles L50,000; triples L69,000; quads L88,000. Children under 14 stay free. Small discounts for large groups or long stays. Current renovations (appearing to be in early stages) scheduled to be completed in 1993.

Pensione Margherita, via Cimarosa, 29 (tel. 556 70 44 and 578 28 52), on the 5th floor, in the Vómero outside the central funicular station. A fancy hotel that charges the lowest prices in this posh district. Pleasant breakfast room with paintings, color TV, and oriental rugs. Often full. English spoken. Curfew midnight. Singles L40,000. Doubles L72,000. Triples L99,000. Breakfast and showers included (L1000 for a towel).

Near Piazza Bovio

Albergo Orchidea, c. Umberto, 7 (tel. 552 40 07), scala B, on the 5th floor. On this noisy but relatively safe *piazza* you'll find dazzling, high-ceilinged rooms with small balconies and great views (some with views of the sea). All rooms with private shower. Doubles L80,000. Triples L100,000. Quads L120,000.

Near Mergellina and Santa Lucia

More scenic and serene than p. Garibaldi or p. Dante, Mergellina and Santa Lucia harbor a few choice accommodations. Keep on the main streets along the waterfront at night, though, as the small sinewy alleys can be dangerous.

Pensione Teresita, via Santa Lucia, 90 (tel. 764 01 05). Cozy and feels secure inside. Singles L25,000. Doubles L35,000. Some rooms have refrigerators.

Near piazza Garibaldi

Casanova Hotel, via Venezia, 2 (tel. 26 82 87). Take via Milano off p. Garibaldi and go left at its end. A good (though noisy) option in this ramshackle region. Airy, clean rooms, knowledgeable management, and a rooftop terrace with bar service. Doubles L40,000, with bath or shower L52,000. Quad with bath L90,000. Breakfast L4500.

Hotel Ginevra, via Genova, 116 (tel. 28 32 10). Turn right immediately as you exit the station; walk 2 blocks up Corso Novara, and take the second right onto via Genova. Pleasant, bright rooms, some with TV. Singles L25,000. Doubles L45,000, with bath L50,000. Breakfast L3500. Laundry service (L4000 per load). Show them your *Let's Go* guide to obtain these rates.

Hotel Prati, via Rosaroll, 4 (tel. 554 18 02, fax. 26 88 98). Take corso Garibaldi to the right from the far end of p. Garibaldi to p. Principe Umberto. Well-decorated rooms complete with mini-balconies, phones, wooden dressers, and tiled bathrooms. Very professional, but at the expense of charm. Color TV and fridge in room. English spoken. Special prices for *Let's Go* users: doubles with bath L80,000. L27,500 per additional person. Breakfast L6000; lunch and dinner L20,000 each. Credit cards and traveler's checks accepted.

Albergo Zara, via Firenze, 81 (tel. 28 71 25). From the train station, turn right onto corso Novara, then take the 1st left. Clean rooms with peeling neoclassical ceilings. Cozy TV room. Singles, doubles, and triples, with and without bath. L25,000 per person.

Hotel de la Ville, vico S. Alessio al Lavinaio, 16 (tel. 554 03 97). Take a left onto corso Garibaldi from p. Garibaldi and hang a right on "Il Traverso Garibaldi," which becomes via Alessio. Less grandiose than its name would imply, the Hotel de la Ville nonetheless offers fine rooms at good rates. Singles L25,000. Doubles L38,000, with bath L46,000. Flash your *Let's Go* to get the best prices. Traveler's checks accepted.

Food

Pizza, that world-famous concoction of crust, tomatoes, and cheese, was an invention of Neapolitans, though it had to travel to the United States and back before the rest of Italy caught on. To this day, this is the only place you will get the true, unadulterated product. Pizza-making is an art here; the *pizzaioli* (pizza chefs) begin their apprenticeships as tots and perfect their craft over a lifetime. The unique combination of the skill of the *pizzaiolo,* the sweet local tomatoes, fresh mozzarella cheese, extra-light dough, and a wood-burning oven makes for an exquisite pie. Stands throughout the city sell slices of pizzas fresh out of the oven for L1000 each; they're popular late-morning snacks. (Try the stands around p. Capuana and p. Mercato, to the north and south of the train station.) Naples's most venerable—though not oldest—*pizzeria* is **Antica Pizzeria Da Michele,** via Cesare Sersale, 1/3 (tel. 553 92 04), to the right off corso Umberto not far from the train station. They make only the two original types of pizza here, *Marinara* (with tomato, garlic, oregano, and oil, L3000) and *Margherita* (with tomato, mozzarella cheese, and basil, L3000). (Open Sept.-mid-Aug. Mon.-Sat. 8am-10pm.)

Seafood in all of its glorious incarnations is the pearl of Neapolitan cuisine. Enjoy the mussels of the gulf in *zuppa di cozze* or *cozze al limone,* or savor *vongole* of all varieties, including razor clams and their more expensive cousin, the oyster. *Aragosta* (crayfish) are sweeter than lobster, and *polipi* (octopus) is one of the cheapest sources of protein around. The city's most notable wines are *lacrima christi* (Chirst's tears) which accompanies the seafood, and the red *gragnano.*

Spaghetti, now an Italian staple, was first boiled in the pots of Neapolitan kitchens—and don't mumble any nonsense about Marco Polo and China to the Neapolitans if you want to stay on their good side. Today, Naples's most famous pasta dishes are the savory *spaghetti alle vongole* (with clams) and *alle cozze* (with mussels); both are served in their shells atop the pasta. Hungry paupers favor *spaghetti alla marinara* (with a simple tomato and garlic sauce).

Naples's most beloved pastry is *sfogliatella,* filled with sweetened ricotta cheese, orange rind, and candied fruit. It comes in two forms, *riccia,* the original flaky-crusted variety, and *frolla,* a softer, crumbly counterpart. The city's foremost *sfogliatella* producer is **Pintauro,** via Roma/Toledo, 275 (tel. 41 73 39), a tiny, worn-marble bakery that has been around since 1785. It sells both varieties, piping hot, for L1300 each. (Open May-July Mon.-Sat. 8:30am-7:30pm; Sept.-April Wed.-Mon. 8:30am-7:30pm.)

Have fun at Neapolitan **markets. On via Soprammuro,** off p. Garibaldi, you can create your own repast from the street market's edible grab bag. (Open Mon.-Sat. 8am-1:30pm. Find food downstairs (and clothes upstairs) at the **STANDA supermarket** at via Roma/Toledo, 128. (Open Mon.-Fri. 9am-1pm and 4-7:45pm, Sat. 9:10am-1pm.)

Near piazza Dante

The historic center around p. Dante, served by buses #185 and CD, shelters some of the city's most delightful *trattorie* and *pizzerie.* Amidst its narrow, winding streets, you'll find some of the cheapest eats on via dei Tribunali.

Pizzeria Sorbillo, via Tribunali, 35. A testimony to Neapolitan pizza-making culture. The cheapest pizza in the area (from L2500). In summer, try your pizza with *filetto* (fresh tomato chunks) for L1000 extra. Beer L2000. Service 10%. Open Mon-Sat. 11:30am-3pm and 7-11pm.

Pizzeria Port'Alba, via Port'Alba, 18 (tel. 45 97 13), inside the Port'Alba arch on the left side of the p. Dante clock tower. Established in 1830, this is the oldest *pizzeria* in Italy. The *vecchia pizza Port'Alba* is the chef's chef d'oeuvre, split into quarters, one with shrimp and calamari, one with tomato and mozzarella, one with capers and olives, one with mushrooms, and in the center a little surprise (L8000). The *pescatore* is loaded with seafood (L8000). The restaurant's non-pizza offerings are also good. Cover for *pizzeria* L1000, for restaurant L2000. Service 15%. Open Thurs.-Tues. 9am-2am.

Le Bistrot dell'Università, via Sedile di Porto, 51 (off via Mezzocannone near corso Umberto). Picnic tables draw an informal college crowd. You'll be hard pressed to beat their L11,000 lunch including cover and service (but not drinks). *Primi* from L3500. Open for lunch Sept. to mid-Aug. Mon.-Fri. noon-4pm. In Sept.-June the menu goes South American at night (open Wed.-Mon.).

Trattoria Fratelli Prigiobbo, via Portacarrese, 96 (tel. 40 76 92). Turn off via Roma at the Motta restaurant and walk 2 blocks. Dirt cheap seafood *secondi* like roasted *calamari* (L6000). *Primi,* including *gnocchi alla mozzarella,* around L3000. They also have pizza (L3000-5000). Wine L2000 for a half-bottle. Cover L500. Open Sept. to early Aug. Mon.-Sat. 9am-11pm.

Ristorante Dante e Beatrice, p. Dante, 44-45 (tel. 549 94 38), An elegant restaurant serving up seafood specialties. *Primi* L3000-6000 (try the heaping *gnocchi sorrentina* L5000), *secondi* L7000-10,000. *Menù* L20,000. Open Thurs.-Tues. 12:30-4pm and 8pm-midnight.

Ristorante-Pizzeria Bellini, (tel. 45 97 74) at the corner of strada Sta. Maria Costantinopolo and via San Pietro, by Port'Alba. Service is slow, but the scrumptious entrees make up for it. Fresh fish. Try the *bucatini alla Bellini,* thick spaghetti-like pasta with eggplant, peppers, peas, tomatoes, mushrooms, basil, and mozzarella (L7000). Cover L1500. Service 13%. Open Mon.-Sat. noon-2:30pm and 7:30-10:30pm.

Gelateria Della Scimmia, p. della Carità, 4 (tel. 552 02 72). The bronze monkey that hangs in the storefront has come to symbolize superior ice cream and desserts. Try the *formetta,* an ice cream sandwich made with thin crispy wafers—you pick the flavors (L2000). Cones L1500-3000. Open Thurs.-Tues. 10am-midnight.

Piazza Amedeo and Santa Lucia

Piazza Amedeo, with its own *metropolitana* stop, is a favorite hangout of Naples's chic youth. Along its scenic avenues, just north of the Villa Comunale park, you'll find several trendy *caffè* and pubs. Restaurant prices are high, but explore the streets for great snack-bars.

Osteria Canterbury, via Ascensione, 6 (tel. 41 35 84). Take via Vittoria Colonna off p. Amedeo, make the 1st right down a flight of stairs, then turn right and immediately left. The best affordable meals in the area. The elegant interior, with lots of wood and fresh flowers, prepares your senses for a delicious meal. Devour the classic *penne di casa Canterbury* (pasta with eggplant, cheese, and tomato sauce, L9000). Cover L2000. Open Sept.-July Mon.-Sat. 1-3pm and 8:30pm-midnight.

Pizzeria Trianon da Ciro, via Parco Margherita, 27 (tel. 41 46 78), off p. Amedeo. Same old name, but it's on the cutting edge of Neapolitan *pizzerie.* This stylish and modern place caters to a snobby crowd, but has gained a popular following for its gigantic pizzas (L6000-10,000). *Pizza Trianon* is their hallmark, with 4 different sections (L10,500). Cover L2000. Open daily noon-4pm and 6pm-1am. All credit cards accepted. Reservations may be necessary Saturday nights.

Mei Lin, via Riviera di Chiaia, 165 (tel. 66 49 94). Sick of spaghetti? Peevish over pizza? Come here to fulfill all your Chinese food desires. This super-friendly, air-conditioned Chinese restaurant has spring rolls for L1800, chicken dishes for L8000-10,000. Special tourist menu available at lunch (L15,000-18,000). Open daily noon-2:30pm and 7pm-midnight. Credit cards accepted.

Mergellina

Take tram #1 or the subway to **Mergellina,** southwest of p. Amedeo on the waterfront. It's an excellent area for informal but hearty Neapolitan dining. **Piazza Sannazzaro,** in the center of Mergellina, is famous for its many *trattorie,* which serve the beloved local *zuppa di cozze.* Via Piedigrotta and the surrounding streets also present affordable alternatives.

Antica Trattoria al Vicoletto, via Camillo Cucca, 52 (tel. 66 92 90). From the subway exit, walk across the street onto via Piedigrotta. Follow it about 150m until you see the sign, then turn left into the narrow alley. The food here is *puro, genuino,* and *economico.* An incredible full meal 12,000 (served during the day only; cover and service—but not drinks—included). Try the *tagliatelle al vicoletto,* with eggplant, peppers, tomato, and pesto (L7000). Cover L2000. Service 15%. Open Sept.-July Mon.-Sat. noon-3pm and 7pm-1am.

Pizzeria Da Pasqualino, p. Sannazzaro, 79 (tel. 68 15 24). Outdoor tables and amazing pizza (L4000-8000). Also terrific seafood and fried snacks. The *cozze impepata* (mussels in pepper broth, L7000) really spices things up. Wine from L4800 per . Cover and service included. Open Nov.-Sept. Wed.-Mon. noon-midnight.

Vómero

A cable car up to Vómero brings you to the city's favorite culinary enclave. Restaurants are generally pricier, but **via Bernini** and **via Kerbaker,** both off via Scarlatti near the funicular stations, offer some traditional *trattorie.*

Trattoria La Pentolaccia, via Kerbaker, 124 (tel. 556 71 34). Enter around the corner at p. Durante, 1. A sweet place with lots of locals. Excellent house wines L3000 per . Go for the house fish specialty, *farfelle salmone* (L6000). *Pasta e fagioli* L4000. For a savory *secondo* try stuffed squid (L6000). Cover L1000. Open Sept.-July Mon.-Sat. 12:30-3pm and 8-11:30pm.

Trattoria da Sica, via Bernini, 17 (tel. 556 75 20). Unblemished and family-run. Traditional Neapolitan fare like *vermicelli alla puttanesca* (pasta with tomatoes, olives, and capers, L6000) and *pasta e fagioli* (pasta and bean soup, L5000). Terrific wines from L4000 per . Frequented almost solely by natives. Cover L1000. Service 12%. Open Oct.-Aug. Fri.-Wed. noon-3:30pm and 8pm-midnight.

Osteria Donna Teresa, via Kerbaker, 58 (tel. 556 70 70). Wonderful, homey place. Most dishes less than L5500. Try the excellent *pasta al forno* (baked pasta, L5000). Their specialty is *spaghetti alle vongole* (L7000). They offer a complete meal (*primi* and *secondi*, plus a glass of wine) for L15,000. Wines L2000 per . Bread L500. Open Sept.-July Mon.-Sat. noon-3pm and 8pm-midnight.

Near piazza Garibaldi

Tourist-ridden, expensive, and mediocre restaurants dominate p. Garibaldi. Fortunately, high-quality low-cost meals lurk on the side streets off the *piazza*. These areas become seedy at night, so eat early.

Trattoria Da Maria, via Genova, 115, the 2nd right off corso Novara. No sign. In a city where tradition, simplicity, and hospitality come first, Papà Riccio and his family have kept their small, unrefined *trattoria* true to the Neapolitan style. All pasta L4000. The local favorite is *bucatini alla puttanesca* (pasta with tomatoes, olives, and capers). *Secondi* from L5000. Local wines L3500-5000. No cover, no service. Open Mon.-Sat. noon-3:30pm and 6:30-10pm. Closed Aug. 15-30.

Pizzeria Trianon da Ciro, via Pietro Colletta, 44/46 (tel. 553 94 26), near Antica Pizzeria da Michele. From p. Garibaldi, take corso Umberto, make a right 200m down on via Egizaca a Forcella, then a left at the 1st *piazza*. With marble tables and wood-burning ovens, this ancient *pizzeria* is just as famous as Da Michele down the street, and many prefer its larger and more innovative selections (such as *8-gusti*, a pizza divided into 8 differently flavored sections, L10,500). Beer or cola L1700. Service 15%. Open Mon.-Sat. 10am-4pm and 6-11:30pm, Sun. 6-11:30pm.

Pizzeria alla Brace, via Spaventa, 14-18 (tel. 26 12 60), across from Avellinese. Dine outdoors in relative elegance. Mixed *antipasti* L5000. *Primi* L3000-9000. Pizzas L3500-6000. Cover L1000. Service 12%. Open Mon.-Sat. noon-12:30am.

Avellinese da Peppino, via Silvio Spaventa, 31/35 (tel. 28 38 97). From the train station, take the 3rd left on p. Garibaldi. In a well-lit area. Locals and tourists dine in harmony at the outdoor tables, lured by the tasty seafood dishes. Unparalleled *spaghetti alle vongole* (L8000). *Gragnano* wine L4000 per bottle. Cover L1000. Service 8%. Open daily 11am-midnight.

Trattoria Spina, piazza Portanova, 1 (tel. 553 99 53). From p. Garibaldi, walk down Corso Umberto, through p. Nicola Amore, and take your 1st right onto via Starace. On the left in the little *piazza* just ahead. *Primi* from L3500; try their specialty, *pasta e ceci* (pasta with chick peas, L3500). Or cool off with their splendid *insalata caprese* (buffalo mozzarella, tomato, and basil, L6000). Cover and service included. Open Tues.-Sun., noon-4pm.

Sights

Don't be deceived or disheartened by the unpleasant scene that greets you as you exit the train station—not all of Naples is like this. **Piazza Garibaldi,** locally known as the "Zona Vasta," is a confusing conglomeration of hotels, small bars, parked cars, buses, vendors, and black-market dealers. Naples's main artery, **Corso Umberto,** leading away from the *piazza*, is an impressive boulevard lined with beautiful cast-iron street lamps and 19th-century buildings that inexplicably metamorphoses into a sleazy transvestite strip at night. A couple of detours lead off the *corso* into the interesting alleys of old Naples. Off to the north, **via Sant'Agostino alla Zecca** leads to the dilapidated 18th-century church of the same name. The dramatic interior features a mighty Christ sharing a cloud with St. Augustine. (Church open daily 8am-12:30pm and 4:30-7pm.)

Corso Umberto ends in **piazza Bovio** at the 17th-century **Fountain of Neptune,** with a view over p. Municipio to the massive **Castel Nuovo.** Charles of Anjou built it in the 13th century to replace the waterfront Castel dell'Ovo, which was too susceptible to attack. The finely modeled central panel of the remarkable double-tiered **Laurana Arch** (1467) adorning the entrance portrays King Alfonso I in his chariot, surrounded by his court. It is one of the earliest examples of Renaissance sculpture in the city, built to commemorate Alfonso's 1443 arrival in Naples. In the courtyard, the elegant Renaissance portal at the entrance to the 14th-century Chapel of Santa Barbara is surmounted by a Madonna and a flamboyant Gothic rose window. The castle proper houses the offices of the city government and is closed to the public, but you can enter the **museo civico,** containing sculptures and frescoes from the 14th and 15th centuries, along with 15th- to 20th-century bronze and silver works. (Open Mon.-Sat. 9am-1pm. Chapel open same hours as museum. Both free.) Continue away from the station past p. Municipio to **piazza del Plebiscito,** the most decorative square in the city, dominated by the neoclassical **Church of San Francesco di Paola** (1816-1831). The dome, based on Rome's Pantheon and raised high on a drum, overpowers everything in the square. The impressive interior, meanwhile, feels more like a Supreme Court chamber than a church. (Open daily 7am-noon and 4-7:30pm.)

In front of the church stand two equestrian statues, one of Charles III (Don Carlos) and the other of Ferdinando I. The 18th-century Palazzo Salerno and the 1815 Palazzo della Prefettura flank them. The plain, three-story facade of the **Palazzo Reale** (1600-1602) balances the curving mass of the San Francesco church. In the series of niches below the facade, fierce late 19th-century statues represent the eight dynasties that ruled Naples. From the courtyard, enter the huge Staircase of Honor. Its 15th-century bas-reliefs depict the battle between Ferdinand of Aragón and René of Anjou. Above, on the second floor, the former royal apartments now house the **Palazzo Reale Museum** and the plush 18th-century **Court Theater.** Many of the rooms are decorated with Gobelins tapestries, and the palace houses an impressive collection of Romantic paintings. (Palace and museum open Tues.-Sun. 9am-2pm. Admission L6000.) Next to the palace presides the **Teatro San Carlo,** the most distinguished opera theater in Italy after Milan's La Scala. Its gray and white neoclassical facade dates from an 1816 rebuilding. The ticket office is open Tues.-Sun. 10am-1pm and 4:30-6pm when there is a performance. Season runs Oct.-June. (Ticket office tel. 797 23 31 or 32, theater tel. 797 21 11.) Stroll into the neighboring **Galleria Umberto,** a four-story arcade of shops and offices constructed between 1887 and 1890 in imitation of Milan's Galleria Emanuele. Its skillful blending of glass and iron exemplifies a late-Victorian wedding of technology and art.

Spaccanapoli (Historic Naples)

Via Roma, a.k.a. **via Toledo,** begins to the side of p. del Plebiscito at small and busy p. Trieste e Trento and runs through the heart of the city's historic district. The Spanish built the street and gave it its original name, via Toledo; they also bear the responsibility for the small checkerboard of streets that climb the hill to the west, where their garrison resided. At the corner of the *piazza,* the typically Jesuit **Church of San Ferdinando** (1622) boasts a single wide aisle. The lectern, fonts, and chairs bear the emblem of the king of Spain. Look for the Ribera painting of Sant'Antonio tucked away in the sacristy. (Church open daily 8am-12:30pm and 4:30-7pm.)

From here, walk up the street, angling to your right through p. Carità to reach p. Monteoliveto, where you'll encounter the unassuming **Church of Sant'Anna dei Lombardi,** a venerable museum of Renaissance sculpture. Its most noted work, Guido Mazzoni's *Pietà* (1492), sits in the chapel at the end of the right transept. In the Piccolomini Chapel, to the left of the entrance, note the beautiful monument to Maria d'Aragona by Antonio Rossellino and Benedetto da Maiano. Walking up calata Trinità Maggiore from the church, you'll reach **piazza Gesù Nuovo,** which testifies to Naples's architectural diversity. On one side of the *piazza* broods the **Church of Il Gesù Nuovo.** Erected between 1584 and 1601, its dark pyramid-grid facade is left over from a 15th-century Renaissance palace. Colored marble and typically florid Neapolitan frescoes adorn the light interior. (Gesù open daily 7:15am-1pm and 4-7:15pm. Sant'Anna open daily 7:15am-1pm, but closed as of June of 1992. It may re-open in 1993 for organized tours.)

On the other side of the square rises the **Church of Santa Chiara,** one of the principal monuments of medieval Naples. Constructed in 1310, it was rebuilt in a spare Gothic style after being destroyed during World War II. The large, single-aisled apse-less interior is littered with medieval sarcophagi and tombs, many decorated with beautiful Gothic canopies. Exit the left side of the church and walk to the right down the side alley to the entrance of the **Cloister of the Clarisse.** Straying from the customary intimacy and delicacy of a medieval cloister, two alleys of trellises—decorated with majolica tiles depicting rural and town scenes, carnivals, and myths—crisscross the overgrown courtyard. This lovely, peaceful spot is a welcome rest. (Church open daily 8am-12:30 and 4:30-7:30pm. Cloister open Mon.-Sat. 8:30am-12:30pm and 4-6:30pm, Sun. 8:30am-12:30pm.)

Return to via Roma/Toledo and walk right past p. Dante onto via Pessina to the **Museo Archeologico Nazionale** (tel. 44 01 66), Europe's most important archeological museum. The collection includes the astonishing treasures of Pompeii and Herculaneum. Pick up an English guidebook at the museum's souvenir shop (L8000), since few pieces are adequately labeled. To get to the museum, take the subway to p. Cavour, or take bus CS, CD, or any other going up via Roma/Toledo, and get off at p. Museo.

Dominating the Great Masters Gallery on the ground floor are the *Farnese Hercules* and the *Farnese Bull,* the largest surviving sculpture from antiquity, carved from a single block of marble. The back hall exhibits some powerfully realistic portrait busts. Among them find Socrates, with his pug nose, swollen face, and balding head, and Seneca, with his protruding tongue and loose folds of skin.

The real treasures, however, await upstairs. Subtle, intricate mosaics from Pompeii rest on the mezzanine; don't miss the large *Mosaic of Alexander,* which portrays a young and fearless Alexander routing a terrified army of Persians. The *Medea* captures the anguish of the mythical sorceress as she contemplates killing her children. (Museum open Tues.-Sat. 9am-2pm, Sun. and holidays 9am-1pm. Admission L8000.)

The **Church of San Domenico Maggiore** forms one side of a small *piazza* of the same name off via Roma/Toledo between p. Carità and p. Dante. A 14th-century church with a 19th-century Gothic interior, San Domenico combines two styles: the pointed arches, windows and the vaulted side aisles are Gothic, but the color and texture of the decor are strictly Neapolitan Baroque. The 13th-century painting that spoke to St. Thomas Aquinas, a resident of the church's adjoining monastery, hangs in the Chapel of the Crucifix (on the right side of the altar in the nave). To the painting's question, "Well hast thou written me, Thomas. What wouldst thou have as a reward?" St. Thomas replied, "None other than thee." The small **Church of Sant'Angelo a Nilo,** across from San Domenico, takes its name from the ancient statue erected here by the Alexandrian colony. The church sports beautiful 15th-century carved wooden doors and the sepulchre of Cardinal Rinaldo Brancaccio, the product of a collaborative effort by the Florentine artists Donatello, Michelozzo, and Portigiana. (San Domenico open daily 8am-12:30pm and 4:30-7pm, Sant'Angelo a Nilo open daily 8am-12:30pm.)

Naples's best-kept secret is the **Cappella di San Severo,** which hides on via De Sanctis, a small side street north of p. San Domenico Maggiore. The chapel, now a private museum, features the *Cristo Velato* (*Veiled Christ*) by Giuseppe Sammartino, consummated in 1753. Sammartino's remarkable marble veil over the statue of the wounded, prostrate body of Christ continues to confound experts. Many believe he poured a molten substance over the body to create the incredibly lifelike veil. To the right of the altar in a group titled *Disillusion,* a man extricates himself from marble netting with encouragement from a seated angel. The altar depicts cherubs opening up the empty tomb below a representation of the Deposition, all sculpted from a single block of marble. Downstairs through a door to the right, two truly grisly 18th-century corpses, one of them an obviously pregnant woman, stare from glass showcases. One legend claims that the alchemist Prince Raimondo of the San Severos, who built the chapel, killed his wife and her lover by injecting them with a poisonous elixir that happened to preserve their veins, arteries, and vital organs. The guard claims that the veins are reconstructions, but we're not so sure... (Open Mon. and Wed.-Sat. 10am-1pm and 5-7pm, Tues. 10am-1pm. Sun. 9am-1:30pm. Admission L3000.)

Via Benedetto Croce, via San Biagio dei Librai, and via Vicaria Vecchia are just three of the names Spaccanapoli takes as it follows the course of the old Roman Decumanus Maximus. This is the heart of the old city, a narrow way enclosed by tall tenements and decaying *palazzi.* On via San Biagio dei Librai alone lie the Renaissance

Palazzo Sant'Angelo (#121), **Monte di Pietà** (Banco di Napoli, #114), and **Palazzo Marigliano** (#37). The street continues, widening at intervals to accommodate churches and monuments. Via San Biagio ends at via del Duomo, where you'll find the 18th-century **Church of San Giorgio Maggiore.** In the vestibule of its warm yellow interior stand the antique columns and walls of a primitive paleochristian structure. Diagonally across from the church rises the beautiful Renaissance **Palazzo Cuomo** (1464-90). You can enter the foyers of most of these private palaces Monday through Friday roughly 9am-2pm.

The venerable shops of Naples's traditional artisans line Spaccanapoli and the surrounding alleys. Off the *piazza* of the church of San Domenico Maggiore at **Calace Strumenti Musicali,** vico San Domenico Maggiore, 9 (up the stairs on the left of the courtyard to the first floor), mandolins, guitars, and other intstruments are still crafted by hand with techniques passed from master to apprentice over generations. (Open Mon.-Sat. 8:30am-6:30pm.) **Scultura Sacra Lebro,** via San Gregorio Armeno, 41, a family operation, is one of the last to produce hand-carved and painted religious statues. Come in to admire their skillful work. (Open Mon.-Fri. 9am-1:30pm and 4-7:30pm, Sat. 9am-1:30pm.) The most endearing shop in Old Naples may be the tiny **Ospedale delle Bambole** (doll hospital), via San Biagio dei Librai, 81, near via Duomo, founded in 1899. The mirthful shopkeeper is perfectly suited to his merciful calling. (Open Mon.-Fri. 10:30am-1:30pm and 4:30-8pm, Sat. 10:30-1pm. Closed three weeks in August.)

Unlike the cathedrals of other Italian cities, Naples's **duomo** loiters on an obscure side street. The church began as a 5th-century paleochristian basilica. The facade, late 19th-century neo-Gothic, retains its original doors. A Baroque veneer covers the Gothic outlines of all the pointed arches in the interior, except in the two chapels on either side of the high altar. The latter are decorated with 14th-century frescoes, which retain their original form. Halfway down the left side enter the **Church of Santa Restituta,** the first Christian basilica of Naples. Built in the 4th century, it preserves its ancient forms in the nave's columns and in a 5th-century baptistry, whose primitive font was hacked out of the floor (the entrance to the baptistry lies at the end of the right aisle). Also note the early 14th-century mosaic of the Madonna with two saints (6th chapel off the left aisle). A beautiful 17th-century bronze grille protects the Baroque **Chapel of San Gennaro.** Relics of St. Januarius are said to have stopped lava from Mount Vesuvius at the gates of the city. A silver reliquary is secreted behind the high altar, bearing the head of the saint and two vials of his coagulated blood. According to legend, disaster will strike the city if the blood fails to liquify at appointed times (the first Saturday of May, Sept. 19, and Dec. 16), when boisterous and confident crowds jam the *duomo.* Under the *duomo's* altar in the crypt you can enjoy some peace beside the bones of S. Gennaro. (Cathedral open daily 8:30am-1pm and 5-7:30pm.) Beneath the *duomo,* excavations have exposed remarkable vestiges of Naples's past. Here you can wander the impressively intact Greek and Roman roads which run under the modern city. (Excavations open for special tours Sat.-Sun. at 10:30am and 11:30am. Tickets must be reserved in advance from the Azienda di Turismo at p. del Gesù.)

Piazza Capuana, between the *duomo* and p. Garibaldi, forms the center of a vibrant quarter of old Naples. Two ponderous towers frame one of the most beautiful Renaissance archways in Italy, the **Porta Capuana.** On one side of the *piazza,* the elegant Renaissance **Church of Santa Caterina a Formiello** (built in 1519) matches the gray stone and white stucco of the gate. (Open daily 9am-12:30pm and 5-7:30pm.) Via Carbonara serves as the quarter's main street. Its neighborhood church, officially **San Giovanni a Carbonara** (closed in 1993), is known by locals as **Santa Sofia;** its *piazza* doubles as a soccer field for hyperactive neighborhood kids.

Santa Lucia and Mergellina

Walk along the bay in the late afternoon or early evening to see the Villa Comunale fill with *passeggiata*-prone locals. Via Sauro in the Santa Lucia section is the traditional place to watch the sunset. The 12th-century **Castel dell'Ovo** (Egg Castle; open for exhibits only), a massive Norman structure of yellow brick and incongruously converging angles, stands on the promontory of the port of Santa Lucia, dividing the bay into two parts. To the west lies the **Villa Comunale,** a waterfront park dotted with sycamores and palms and graced by sculptures, fountains, and an **aquarium.** The oldest in Europe, it features a collection of 200 species of fish and marine fauna native to the Bay of Naples. (Tel. 583 31 11. Open Tues.-Sat. 9am-5pm, Sun. 9am-6pm. Admission L2000, students L1400, under 6 L1000.) Off the rocks near the Castel dell'Ovo Neapolitans come to sunbathe and swim. A streetcar runs along the Riviera di Chiaia, where at #200 you'll find the **Villa Pignatelli,** one of the few verdant villa grounds left in the city.

At the foot of the hills of Posillipo, **Mergellina** affords the most celebrated view in Naples: climb via Petrarca to see the panorama to which no postcard can do justice.

Vómero and the Hills

The breezy calm of the hillside residential district of Vómero is an antidote to the frantic pace of the rest of Naples. A full morning, or perhaps two, should be reserved for visiting Vómero's important historical sights, the Villa Floridiana and the Monastery of St. Martin. Funiculars to this area leave from via Roma/Toledo across from the Galleria, from p. Amedeo, and from p. Montesanto.

The **Villa Floridiana** (entrance at via Cimarosa, 77) crowns a knoll notable for its camellias, pine trees, and terrace overlooking the bay. The villa itself, a graceful white neoclassical mansion (1817-19), houses the **Duca di Martina Museum,** which contains porcelain, ivory, china, pottery, and a small group of 17th-century Neapolitan paintings (tel. 578 84 18). The park surrounding the villa is tranquil. (Museum open Tues.-Sat. 9am-2pm, Sun. 9am-1pm. Admission L4000; free for children under 18 and adults over 65. Park open 9am-one hour before sunset—generally 7pm in summer and 4pm in winter.)

The huge Carthusian **Certosa di San Martino** (Monastery of St. Martin) rises from a spur of the Vómero hill near Castel Sant'Elmo. Erected in the 14th century, it was remodeled during the Renaissance and Baroque periods. It now houses the **Museo Nazionale di San Martino** (tel. 578 17 69), whose stern rooms document the art, history, and life of Naples from the 16th century to the present. (Open Tues.-Sat. 9am-2pm, Sun. 9am-1pm. Admission L6000; free for those over 65 or under 18). The **Castel Sant'Elmo,** begun in 1349 under the Anjou reign, affords a remarkable view from its ramparts. (Open Tues.-Sat. 9am-2pm, Sun. 9am-1pm. Free.)

The **Museo e Gallerie di Capodimonte** occupy a restored 18th-century royal palace set in the sylvan hills north of the National Museum. Collections of both masterpieces and kitsch compete for attention along the walls; the former are usually on the second floor, the latter on the first. Among the many masterpieces look for Massacio's *Crucifixion* with a golden-haired Mary Magdalene, Filippino Lippi's *Annunciation and Saints,* with Florence in the background, Raphael's portrait of Pope Leo X and two cardinals, Michelangelo's stunning drawing of *Three Soldiers,* and two superb Breughels—*The Allegory of the Blind* and *The Misanthrope.* In addition, keep an eye peeled for Luca Signorelli's decrepit *Adoration,* Pinturrichio's stunning *Assumption,* and works by Botticelli, Perugino, and Martini. A haunting *Flagellation* by Caravaggio and a copy of Michelangelo's *Last Judgment* (with the figures unclothed as they were originally painted) by Marcello Venusti also hang here. (Open Tues.-Sat. 9am-2pm, Sun. 9am-1pm. Admission L8000.) Take bus #110 or 127 from Stazione Centrale, #22 or 23 from p. del Plebiscito, or #160 or 161 from p. Dante. (The gardens surrounding the museum are open daily 7:30am-8pm; off-season 7:30am-5pm or 6:30pm.)

Down via Capodimonte from the museum, head into the **Chiesa della Madonna del Buon Consiglio,** which Neapolitans refer to as "Little St. Peter's." Inside, in the third chapel on the left (the Chapel to the Duchesses of Aosta), resides a smaller (but still sizeable) copy of Michelangelo's *Pietà.* Outside under the portico sits a copy of his *Moses.* Outside the church, enter the 2nd-century **Catacombe di San Gennaro,** noted for their frescoed early Christian chapels. (Tours given Fri.-Sun. at 9:30, 10:15, 11, and 11:45am. Admission L3000.)

428   **Campania**

Entertainment

The monthly *Qui Napoli (Here's Naples)* and the weekly poster *Posto Unico,* both available at the tourist office, provide excellent information on happenings in Naples. Most of the information in *Qui Napoli* is translated into English, including brief descriptions of the city's major sites and tour listings. *Posto Unico* publishes lists of films, discos, and clubs (in Italian).

Luglio Musicale a Capodimonte, a series of free classical music concerts, brings top-notch performers to the Museo di Capodimonte grounds on July nights. The tourist office sponsors free folk concerts with typical Neapolitan and Italian songs throughout the year. The concerts are given Tuesday through Sunday from 9:30 to 11:15pm in the Partenope Hall of the Royal Hotel, via Partenope, 38. Get a free pass from your hotel or the tourist office.

Naples is liveliest during its many religious festivals. The **Festa di Piedigrotta** on September 7 and of **San Gennaro,** the patron saint of Naples, on September 19, explode with a communal ardor that is unique to Naples. The festival of **Madonna del Carmine,** held on July 16 at p. del Carmine at the southern end of corso Garibaldi, culminates in fireworks at the Fra' Nuvolo tower. During Christmas, hundreds of crèches (*presepi*) decorate the city. The sepulchre decorations during Easter and the grand Easter parade in the center of town are also noteworthy.

If you want to enjoy the sun but not stray too far from the city, head to the huge rocks off Castel dell'Ovo. Neapolitans gather here in the heat, and many intimate *caffè* lurk on the promontory below the castle proper.

Naples slumbers at night, except for the Sunday evening *passeggiata,* when the Villa Comunale along the bay fills with folks taking in the cool air. The young elite strut their new threads around **piazza Amedeo.** Via Posillipo beckons those who savor the smell of the sea (take bus #140 from p. del Gesù) and via Petrarca is ideal for a romantic stroll (take bus #C21 at p. Plebiscito). Or join legions of amorous couples at the scenic park at Capo di Posillipo (take bus #140 to the end). While strolling via Posillipo, titillate your tastebuds with an ice cream from **Bilancione,** via Posillipo, 398/B, near p. San Luigi. It's a Naples tradition. (Open Sept.-July Thurs.-Tues. 10am-11pm.)

Naples's nighttime hotspots include **Casablanca,** via Petrarca, 101 (tel. 769 48 82); **Chez Moi,** Parco Margherita, 13 (tel. 40 75 26; take the Metropolitana to p. Amedeo); and the large **KissKiss,** via Sgambati, 47 (tel. 46 65 66) in Vómero. A respectable crowd frequents all three. They feature dancing Friday through Sunday from 10pm and charge a L15,000-20,000 cover. (KissKiss puckers up during the week as well. All open Sept.-July.) Ask around to get the latest on the club scene. **The Shaker Club,** via N. Sauro, 24 (tel. 41 67 75; take bus #150 to via Partenope—it's in the Albergo Miramare), caters to an older crowd with its more refined nightclub atmosphere. Gay men and women hang out at **Bagatto,** via Partenope (close to the Hotel Royal) and **Jimmy Club,** via Manzoni, 28 (take bus C21 from p. del Plebiscito). The Villa Comunale is another gathering spot for gay people at night, as is **Bar Marotta** in p. Vittoria. None of these bars is exclusively gay, however. Also, if the discos are too pricey for you, on summer evenings **p. Bellini** closes to traffic; *caffés* and bars set their tables out, and young people fill the *piazza.* You don't even need to order a costly drink (beer L5000 and up) to sit down.

Shopping

Throughout the city, and particularly in the **Duchesca** region off via Mancini near p. Garibaldi and the **Pignasecca** region off p. Carità, street markets peddle belts, radios, shoes, and other inexpensive items. Never buy electronic products here, and hold tight to your valuables on the crowded streets. (Markets are generally open Mon.-Sat. 9am-sunset; many close Tues. at 2pm.)

If you feel more comfortable window-shopping at fancy stores, the main shopping districts center around **corso Umberto, via Roma/Toledo, via Chiaia** near p. Trieste e Trento, and **via dei Mille** in the Santa Lucia region. The most modern and expensive shopping district is in the hills of Vómero along perpendicular **via Scarlatti** and **via**

Luca Giordano. Two affordable clothes chains that sell contemporary Italian casual wear are **Wiscky & Coca** and **Omonimo.**

The Bay of Naples

West of Naples: Campi Flegrei (Phlegraean Fields)

The Bay of Naples originally served as a strategic trading port for the Greeks, who associated its westerly peninsula with the underworld. The volcanic lakes and bubbling mud baths of the Phlegraean (Burning) Fields did not, however, intimidate either the Greeks or Romans: Both built major cities here, and scattered the area with imposing monuments.

Although somewhat shabby and neglected, **Pozzuoli** has several worthwhile ruins of its own, and makes the best base for exploring the Campi Flegrei and also the most convenient jumping-off point for the islands of Pócida and Íschia. The town is serviced by subway from Naples's Stazione Centrale and by the Ferrovia Cumana train from Montesanto in Naples (southwest of p. Dante, L1000). Allow a full day to see the sights of the fields, since they are far apart. Numerous signs point the way, but if you feel more secure with a map in hand visit Pozzuoli's **tourist office,** via Campi Flegrei, 3 (tel. (081) 526 14 81 or 526 24 19), off p. Capo Mazza. (English spoken. Open Mon.-Fri. 9am-2pm.) **Caremar** ferries (tel. (081) 526 13 35) run three times a day to Íschia (1hr. 30min., round-trip L9000) and Prócida (30min., round-trip L5800). Buy tickets at the **biglieterria marittima** on via Roma.

From the Ferrovia Cumana, take the pedestrian bridge over the tracks, turn left and then right at the big intersection; from there follow the curving road to p. Capo Mazza. Pozzuoli's **Anfiteatro Flavio,** built under Vespasian between 69-79 AD, boasts unusually well-preserved underground galleries and arenas which show the complicated mechanics necessary for raising and lowering the animal cages. (Open daily 9am-2hr. before sunset. Admission L4000.) From the Metropolítana station, turn right onto via Solfatara, turn right again on via Anfiteatro, and follow it to the entrance. The **Tempio di Serapide** was not a temple at all, but an ancient city market that just happened to enclose a statue of the god Serapis. A weird form of volcanic activity, bradyseism, which causes slow earthquakes that can raise or lower the entire region by several feet over the course of a few months, has intermittently submerged, shaken, and lifted this site. With its puddles of water and eerie, half-submerged pillars, the marketplace looks like a miniature Atlantis just risen from the sea. On via Solfatara, to the right of the Metropolitana station, snag any of the city buses going uphill to get to the still-active **Solfatara Crater.** Alternately, you can easily walk (20min.) from the train station to see the steaming fissures and bubbling mud; just don't fall in. (Open 9am-1hr. before sunset. Admission L4000.)

Many fascinating sights are within easy bus or car ride from Pozzuoli. You might want to pack a lunch before setting out, though, as the areas offer only small overpriced snackbars to appease grumbling bellies. From any of the SEPSA bus stops located throughout Pozzuoli or by way of the Ferrovia Cumana, take the 20-minute ride to **Baia** (L1000), notable for the Roman baths that have recently been excavated there and for its history as an hotbed of ancient hedonism. (Baths open daily 9am-2hr. before sunset. Admission L4000.) A bit to the north is **Lake Averno,** a spooky haunt that Homer and Virgil described as the entrance to Hades.

From the Baia area, you can take a bus (L1000 on the Napoli-Torregaveta line) or the Ferrovia Cumana train line to **Cumae,** the most impressive site in the Campi Flegrei. Cumae was the earliest Greek colony on the Italian mainland (founded in the 8th century BC), and the mother of Pozzuoli, Naples, and many cities of the Magna Graecia. Its highlight is the **Antro della Sibilla,** a long gallery built for the Cumaean Sibyl, the most famous oracle west of Greece. In this great hallway, used as a pizza oven prior to its rediscovery in 1932, devotees awaited the Sibyl's prophecies. Ascend the acropolis to the ruined Temple of Jove (take the steep stairs that tunnel up through the rock) which rewards the climb with a vantage to the curving coast. You may be able to sneak into the huge gallery underneath the promontory; it leads past subterranean cisterns to other ruins farther inland. The whole sprawling site requires at least an hour's visit. Bring a flashlight. (Open daily 9am-2 hrs. before sunset. Admission L4000.)

If you are intrigued by the Campi Flegrei's combination of volcanic coastline, ancient ruins, and provincial modernity, continue out to **Bácoli** and **Miseno,** at the tip of the peninsula. Hike **Bácoli's** steep streets, then visit its cisterns: the **Cento Camerelle,** on the *via* of the same name, whose two subterranean levels supplied a Roman villa; and the **Piscina Mirabile,** a huge, pillared underground reservoir that supplied the Roman fleet at Miseno. Under Augustus, the port of **Miseno** was joined to the nearby lake to provide a secure anchorage; various remnants of the Roman camp survive above and below water. Explore the village or climb the towering cape; some also hitch through the tunnel to reach the lighthouse.

There are only two semi-budget hotels in Pozzuoli. The accommodating management of the **Hotel Flegreo,** via Domiziana, 30 (tel. 526 15 23), about 1km down the road from the tourist office, lets small rooms. (Doubles with bath L60,000; triples with bath L75,000.) **Albergo Paradiso,** via Campi Flegrei, 52 (tel. 866 54 69), falls short of its name, but still offers fairly roomy, clean doubles; with or without bath for L55,000. (Sept.-July try to knock off at least L5000). You can reach it either by walking 3km past the tourist office and following the left-curving road when you reach the Arco Felice locality, or by taking the #1 CTP or the SEPSA bus. The **AVERNO** Campsite, SS. Domiziana, 21 (tel. 804 26 66), offers three-star camping for L8000 per person, L8000 per tent. For cheap picnicking, grab your supplies at the **supermarket** across the street from the tourist office. **La Lampara,** via dell'Emperio, 9 (tel. 526 37 62), serves its well-prepared fish dishes and pizza at outdoor tables overlooking the bay. *Farfelle al salmone* is L8000 and pizza ranges L4500-L8000. (Open Thurs.-Tues. 12:30-2pm and 7-11:30pm. Credit cards accepted.) **Trattoria Da Don Antonio,** via Magazzino, 20 (tel. 526 79 41), off the port in shabby but ebullient surroundings, caters to the voracious, serving a full meal of fresh seafood with drink for under L21,000. (Open Sept.-July Mon.-Sat. 12:30-3:30pm and 7-9pm.)

Further out on the cape, delve into fabulous beaches and countryside. Many visitors camp unofficially near the sea or by one of the many volcanic lakes. There are several sites with facilities in the area—opt for these safer spots if there are less than three in your group. **Vulcano Solfatara,** via Solfatara, 47 (tel. 526 74 93), offers sites next to the crater for L8600 per person, L6600 per tent (open Apr.-Oct. 15); Pozzuoli's tourist office provides further information on camping.

Inland from Naples: Capua, Caserta, Benevento

Caserta

Caserta, 45 minutes from Naples by train (the first leaves from Stazione Centrale at 7:15am; L2800), claims as its main attraction the Versailles-like **Palazzo Reale** (Royal Palace), locally referred to as the "Reggia." Luigi Vanvitelli (actually Van Wittel, a Dutchman) built the palace and its magnificent gardens between 1752 and 1774 for Bourbon Charles III. The absurd, overwrought building contains 1200 rooms, 1790 windows, and 34 staircases. In the three libraries you can admire the original books, a telescope, and a pyramidal bookcase, but the most intriguing sight in the Palace is the "Presepe," an immense nativity scene in the room after the libraries. Enclosed in a walk-around glass case, this scene makes the Holy Family appear to be plopped down in the middle of a movie set, or at least a southern Italian town in the 1790s. Giants, Arabs, camels, and monkeys, all out of proportion, cavort pell-mell with Mary and Joseph; one side of the scene is a view of an Italian market day. The contents of every room in the palace are labeled extensively on a placard prominently displayed (in Italian). (Tel. (0823) 32 14 00. Open Mon.-Sat. 9am-1:30pm, Sun. 9am-12:30pm. Admission L6000.) Bring a picnic lunch and enjoy the birds and the bees in the extensive gardens behind the palace. The waterfall runs daily from 11am-3pm. (Gardens open daily 9am-6pm. L4000.)

After chuckling through the palace, walk around the haunting medieval town of **Caserta Vecchia.** The Apulian-Romanesque cathedral dates from 1153 and reveals distinct Middle Eastern influence. (Six buses per day (Bus #11) run to and from Caserta Vecchia from Caserta's train station and from piazza Vanvitelli, 30min., L1600.)

Caserta doesn't abound with cheap places to stay, but if you decide to sleep over, the **Albergo Eden,** via Verdi, 26 (tel. 35 56 17), to the right of the train station as you exit it, should have room. (Singles with bath L30,000. Doubles L40,000, with bath L49,000.) For excellent, economical eats, try **Farina R&V,** via S. Giovanni, 7-9 (tel. 32 61 38), off corso Trieste. They offer *primi* for L3000-4000 and *secondi* for L8000-10,000. (Open Mon.-Sat. noon-3:30pm.) **Ristorante Soletti,** largo San Sebastian, 1 (tel. 32 80 22), off p. Dante, serves up pizza and other goodies under the stars (and streetlamps). (Open Sat.-Thurs. noon-2:30pm and 7:30-10:30pm.)

Caserta's **EPT** is located at corso Trieste, 37 (tel. 32 11 37), at the corner of p. Dante. Pick up their brochure on the Palazzo Reale and free detailed map of town. (Open Mon.-Fri. 8:30am-1:30pm, Sat. 8:30am-noon.) Caserta's **postal code** is 81100; its **telephone code** is 0823.

If you happen to be in town in July, you may catch the **Festa Sant'Anna,** when music and fireworks light up the town. The beginning of September brings concerts to Caserta Vecchia, in a festival known as **Settembre al Borgo.**

Capua

Just 15 min. by train from Caserta (L1400), Capua appears to be a typical small town with one great attraction—its museum. The **Museo Provinciale Campano,** through the arch at the end of via Duomo (tel. 96 14 02), has an extensive, important collection of Etruscan, Egyptian, and Roman artifacts to amaze and delight. (Open Tues.-Sat. 9am-2pm, Sun. 9am-1pm. Free.) Capua, founded 47 years before Rome on the banks of the Volturno river as Casilinum, gradually transformed into the Roman outpost Santa Maria Capua Vetere, 5km from today's present city. The pillaging and burning of Santa Maria by Saracens forced the inhabitants to escape to Capua Nova, present-day Capua; the tumble-down *duomo* dates from 856, its unclimbable campanile from 861. The castle, which you'll spy on your way into the center of town from the station, and which now houses the local police force, was begun for protection against invading Normans in 1065.

Capua's Cápriciously opened **Pro Loco** slumbers at p. Giudici, 12, the town center. Here you can pick up a map and a guide to the sights. (Theoretically open Mon.-Sat. 8:30am-noon and 4-8:30pm.) For excellent edibles, try **Da Nino/La Taverna Fieramosca,** with two entrances, one on via Amalfitano and one on p. Ethiopia. (Pizza in the evenings from L3000, delicious pasta with the sauce of the day L5000. Open Tues.-Sun. noon-3:30pm and 7pm-midnight.) Even cheaper food can be found at the **mercato** in p. Ethiopia (Mon.-Sat. 8am-1pm).

To get into the center of the old city from the station, head straight down viale Ferrovia and across what used to be the town moat; go through the 16th-century Porta Napoli arch, make a right as you face the Teatro Ricciardi, and then your first left, which heads straight into p. Giudici.

Benevento

The countryside around Benevento is enchanting. The town was first called *Maleventum* (Ill Wind); after the Romans finally defeated Pyrrhus here in 275 BC, however, they decided it might be a "good wind" (*Benevento*) after all. Although a car is the most convenient way to get here, you can catch a direct bus or train from Naples (7 trains per day, 2hr., L6100), or come from Caserta (70min., L4400). Visit the village of **Montesarchio,** with its 15th-century castle, or **Sant'Agata dei Goti,** with its Romanesque cathedral. Benevento's solemn, unhurried atmosphere is itself a delightful contrast to Naples. Sights include **Trajan's Arch,** constructed in 114 AD and decorated with fine bas-reliefs, and the huge Roman theater from the 2nd century BC—one of the largest in Italy. Before returning to Naples, sample Benevento's *Strega* (witch) liqueur—it will leave you spellbound.

East of Naples: Pompeii, Herculaneum (Ercolano), and Vesuvius

Mount Vesuvius's fit of towering flames, suffocating black clouds, and seething lava meant sudden death for the prosperous Roman city of **Pompeii** in 79 AD. The eruption buried the city—tall temples, patrician villas, massive theaters, and all—under 10 meters of volcanic ash. Archeological findings indicate that Pompeii was inhabited as early as the 8th century BC and that during the 7th century BC, it fell under the influence of Greeks and Etruscans, who developed it as a commercial center. By the 2nd century BC, Pompeii was a mature city with a Hellenic culture typical throughout southern Italy. Falling under Roman influence around 180 BC, the city developed further both as a trading port and as an aristocratic enclave. Successive layers of ash, dust, pebbles, lava, and rock from the sudden eruption preserved not only the buildings but also the remains of a few of its inhabitants, asphyxiated by the heavy cloud of poisonous gas which preceded the lava. On the other side of the mountain, Herculaneum was discovered when 18th-century farmers sank shafts for wells. The analysis of ancient texts soon revealed another, larger city nearby—Pompeii. Covered with soft material (in contrast to the hard tufa stone over Herculaneum), parts of Pompeii were quickly unearthed beginning in 1748, and the remains have provided us with a basic understanding of daily life in the Roman era.

The quickest route to Pompeii (25km south of Naples) is the **circumvesuviana** train line from Naples's Stazione Centrale (L2500; Eurail passes valid). A less frequent state train leaves from the main track at the station, stopping at Pompeii en route to Salerno (7 per day 7:10am-1:15pm, L2500). Most travelers take the *circumvesuviana's* Naples-Sorrento line, which lets you off at the Pompeii-Villa dei Misteri stop just outside the west entry. An alternative is to take the *circumvesuviana* from Naples toward Poggiom-arino and hop off at the Pompeii Santuario (*not* the Pompeii Valle) stop. Then walk straight from the station, take a right across your first *piazza,* and head about 300m down via Roma to the east entrance. (Entrances open 9am-1hr. before sunset. Admission L10,000.)

The **tourist office,** via Sacra, 1 (tel. 850 72 55), across from p. Barto Longo on the way to the east entrance, provides free maps and the informative pamphlet *Notizario Turistico Regionale.* (Open Mon.-Sat. 8:30am-1:30pm.) Another tourist office sits near the west entrance on via Villa dei Misteri (tel. 861 09 13), to the right of the *circumvesuviana* stop.

The east side entrance to the site admits you by the amphitheater, the west side entrance by the Antiquarium. A comprehensive walk-through will probably take four or five hours; pack a lunch and a water bottle as the two snackbars are rather expensive, although good in a pinch.

As you enter from the east, the **Grande Palestra** sprawls to your left. The large structure, enclosed on three sides by a colonnade and pine trees, was used by Pompeian youths for gymnastic exercises and competitions.

The **amphitheater** across from the gymnasium, built in 80 BC, is the oldest extant, and best-preserved in Italy. With seating for 15,000, it looms over a vista of Pompeii and the mountain beyond. Next to the gymnasium, the **House of Loreius Tiburtinus** preserves the essentials of a Roman garden—long rectangular pools surrounded by trellises and formal paintings. Walking toward the Forum, which is near the west or "sea" entrance, you'll pass the **teatro grande,** constructed in the Hellenistic Age (200-150 BC) in the hollow of a hill. In July, August, and September, classical concerts featuring big-name performers are held here, usually Friday, Saturday, and Sunday at 9pm (L10,000-30,000). Parallel to the stage to the left is the much smaller **teatro piccolo,** built later for concerts and ballet. North of the theater stands the **Temple of Isis,** testimony to the strength of the cult of the Egyptian fertility goddess in Pompeii. Going north from the temple, you will reach **via dell'Abbondanza,** Pompeii's main street (1km long), lined with small shops, taverns, and electoral campaign propaganda.

From via dell'Abbondanza, backtrack toward the east entrance and turn off to the **Casa di Menandro.** Named after Menander, the Greek poet whose fresco was found in the courtyard, the house is one of the largest and most intact in the city. The entrance leads to an atrium, in which the pool was once used to catch rain water from the ceiling opening. Bedrooms open off the atrium; a small shrine for a household god meditates in the corner. On the left is a fresco depicting the Trojan War. The unassuming room at the far wall of the court houses the yellow fresco of Menander.

Head west on via dell'Abbondanza toward the Forum to reach the **Terme Stabiane** (Stabian Baths), and enter through another *palestra.* The separate men's and women's sides each included a dressing room, cold baths (*frigidaria*), warm baths (*tepidaria*), and hot or steam baths (*caldaria*). The world's oldest profession claimed its own territory one street over in the red-light district of **Vico del Lupanare.** At the top of this street is a small brothel consisting of several bed-stalls. Above each of the stalls a pornographic painting depicts with unabashed precision the specialty of the women who inhabited it.

Via dell'Abbondanza ends at the **Forum,** the commercial, civic, and religious center of the city, framing a wonderful view of Vesuvius. The **basilica** (law courts building), which encloses the south side of the Forum, was the largest building in Pompeii and retains parts of its impressive dais in the southeast corner. Three temples also graced the Forum. On the northern side rises the **Temple of Jupiter.** The **Temple of Apollo** sits across the side street from the basilica, almost hidden from the rest of the city (unlike a Greek temple, which usually reigns from atop a hill). The stone in the middle was used as a sacrificial altar. In the **Temple of Vespasian,** on the western side across the forum from the Temple of Apollo, a delicate frieze on the center altar illustrates the preparation for a sacrifice.

Showcases along the western side of the Forum display gruesome plaster casts of some of the volcano's victims, including a crouching pregnant woman and a running boy. The contorted positions of the humans and even a dog are sufficient to convince that the inhabitants were suffocated by the gases of the eruption rather than crushed by its ashen discharge.

North of the Forum, rest in the cafeteria (go up to its roof for the only aerial view of Pompeii) before starting on a walk to the northwest corner of the site and out to the Villa dei Misteri. Walk up to the massive **Casa del Fauno,** in front of the **Casa dei Vetii.** The Casa dei Vetii contains Pompeii's most remarkable frescoes, all crafted in the latest of Pompeii's styles, involving fantastic architectural designs in grandiose perspective. For a chuckle, follow the halls to a tiny room on the right. This Jesse Helms special contains a two-and-a-half-foot marble statue of Priapus proudly displaying his colossal member. This legendary child of Venus and Adonis is pictured elsewhere in town and phallic images are ubiquitous, but your smirks prove you more dirty-minded than the Romans; phalli were believed by the ancients to ward off the evil eye. Next to the room a smaller *triclinium* contains some of the most intact examples of the late style of Roman painting.

You can rent a tour guide for L300,000 or save your cash—a short search is bound to land you in an English tour to savor the gory details of life and death in the ancient Pompeiian culture.

A short walk from the Casa dei Vetii brings you to **Villa dei Misteri.** A renowned cycle of paintings (in the room directly to the right of the entrance) depicts a ritual of initiation into the forbidden cult of Dionysius.

One kilometer outside the archeological zone, the second floor of the **Museo Vesuviano** displays Pompeiian threads, while the first floor houses a boring collection of items from the Barto Longo estate. The museum calls Big Bart's old villa home; you can find it on via Colle S. Bartolomeo, 10 (tel. 863 10 41), off the p. Barto Longo, the corner diagonally opposite the road to the train station. (Second floor open daily 9am-1pm.) The **basilica** presides over p. Barto Longo; its crypts hold the remains of rich ol' Barto—Christian Laettner-esque $90 perm and all. (Crypts open daily 9am-1pm and 3-6pm.)

Unless you wish to tour Pompeii extensively, there is no reason to stay overnight in the dull modern city. The cheapest alternative is to stay at one of the local campgrounds, all near the ruins. Unfortunately, all are somewhat ruined themselves. **Camping Zeus** (tel. 861 53 20), outside the Villa dei Misteri *circumvesuviana* stop, boasts a swimming pool and restaurant (L8000 per person, L5000 per large tent, L4000 per small tent). Not far away, on via Plinio, the main road that runs from the ruins, **Camping Pompeii** (tel. 862 78 82), with the same ownership and prices as Zeus, has attractive bungalows for L60,000 for two people and L75,000 for three. You can sack out on the floor of its indoor lobby for L8000 per night. These places are eager for customers, so you can usually bargain them down at least 25%.

La Vinicola, via Roma, 29, tempts with a pleasant outdoor courtyard and abundant *gnocchi con mozzarella* (potato dumplings with tomato and cheese, L5500). Also try the *zuppa di cozze* for L5000. (Wine L2500 per half-liter. Cover L1500. Service 15%. Open daily 9am-midnight; Nov. to mid-July Sat.-Thurs. 9am-11pm.) Gulp down more expensive meals at the **Trattoria Pizzeria dei Platani,** via Colle San Bartolomeo, 8 (tel. 863 39 73), up the street from the Museo Vesuviano, where L7000 buys you a plate of cannelloni. (Cover L2000. Service 15%. Open daily 9:30am-7:30pm.)

Closer to Naples (12km), **Ercolano (Herculaneum)** would have a sublime seaside view if it weren't 10m underground. Take any *circumvesuviana* train toward Pompeii from Naples's central train station to the Ercolano stop (15min., L1200). Walk 500m down the hill from the station to the **ticket office.** (Open daily 9am-1hr. before sunset. Visitors may remain until 30min. before sunset. Admission L8000.) Before entering, consider purchasing the *Amadeo-Maiuri* guide to Herculaneum, the most comprehensive guidebook, available in the bar across the street (L9000). Neatly excavated and impressively intact Herculaneum contradicts the term "ruins." Once a wealthy residential enclave on the Roman coast road, Herculaneum does not evoke the same sense of tragedy that Pompeii does—all but a handful of its inhabitants escaped the ravages of Vesuvius. In a much less disorienting (and less crowded) tour than those offered in Pompeii, you can wind your way through the 15 or so houses and baths that are now open to the public. There are no colossal buildings, temples, or off-color frescoes to grab your imagination here, but the houses, with their fresh interior decoration, attest to the cultural development of this affluent community. Two-thousand-year-old frescoes, furniture, mosaics, small sculptures, and even wood paneling seem as vital as the day they were made, preserved by a mud avalanche that tumbled off the volcano on a cushion of gas. The **House of Deer,** so named for a statue of a deer being savagely attacked by greyhounds, is one of the more alluring villas. Probably big partiers, the owners had a statue of a *Satyr with a Wineskin* and an all-too-recognizable statue of the town's patron "saint" Hercules in a drunken stupor trying to take a leak. The **baths** are quite interesting and largely intact. **The House of the Mosaic of Neptune and Amphitrite** belonging to a rich shop owner is famous for its mosaic depicting—well, take a guess.

From the Ercolano stop, it's also possible to take a blue bus to **Mount Vesuvius** (round-trip L4500), still the only active volcano on the European continent. Rest assured—it's safe for now; the last eruption occurred on March 31, 1944. You can ramble to the top (1hr.) for a look inside the astounding crater, but you must be accompanied by a guide (L4000). (From the Ercolano stop to Mt. Vesuvius 6 buses daily; Oct.-March 5 buses daily; last return bus 5:50pm.)

Islands

Lingering languidly off either shore of the Bay of Naples, the pleasure islands of **Cápri, Íschia,** and **Prócida** beckon the culture-weary traveler.

Large ferries (*traghetti*) and hydrofoils (*aliscafi*) leave daily from Naples's **Molo Beverello** at the end of p. Municipio in Naples. (Take bus #150 or tram #1 or 4 from Naples's *stazione centrale.*) **Caremar,** Molo Beverello (tel. 551 38 82, in Cápri 837 07 00) runs the main line to the islands; **Navigazione Libera del Golfo (NLG),** Molo Beverello (tel. 552 55 89, in Cápri 837 08 19), has slightly lower prices and less comfortable boats. Avoid purchasing a round-trip ticket which will subject you to the whims of a single company for the duration. The islands are also accessible via Sorrento. Ferries run throughout the day from both ports. Check schedules and prices at *biglietteri* located at all ports. Transport is very affordable; Naples to Íschia, for example, is only L7300. Eight ferries leave for Cápri between 6:40am and 7:40pm (L6300; first departure Sun. 7am). The last boat returning to Naples leaves at 7:20pm. Ferries to Íschia charge the same prices and follow similar schedules, leaving Naples from 6:30am (Sun. 7:05am) to 7:30pm, with a late ferry (via Prócida) at 11pm. Direct ferries to Prócida run between the same hours (5 per day, L5500). There is also service between Íschia and Prócida (L2700), Cápri and Sorrento (L4250), Íschia and Sorrento (L10,000), Amalfi and Cápri (L9000), Íschia and Pozzuoli (L9800), and Prócida and Pozzuoli (L6400). Hydrofoils for all islands leave from the Mergellina marina more frequently, but cost about twice as much. Between late September and June, ferries run at about half their high-season frequency.

Cápri

The Roman emperor Augustus became enamored of the fantasy island beauty of Cápri in 29 BC and swapped more fertile Íschia for it. His successor Tiberius passed his last decade here in wild imperial debauchery. Today's tacky tourists may harbor a yen for debauchery, too, but in Cápri they are generally content to pay through the nose for en masse ferry excursions to the renowned Blue Grotto, or to gawk at the rich and famous in Cápri town's *piazzeta.* **Ánacapri,** clinging to the side of nearby **Monte Solaro** (589m), is less frequented by daytrippers, and qualifies as a budget version of paradise, with two *affita camere,* privately rented rooms at affordable rates. Carry your *Let's Go* with you (it may land you discounts). You might consider renting a moped in Sorrento (see below) and bringing it over on the ferry, as the distances between sights, ports, and hotels are long. Otherwise the bus system will efficiently get you to the most important sights.

Orientation and Practical Information

Most ferries dock at **Marina Grande** on the north side of the island, from which you can take the **funicular** to the town of Cápri (every 15min. 6:35am-9:15pm, L1500). Buses leave from town to **Marina Píccola** (on the south shore) and **Ánacapri** (every 15min. 6:30am-1:40am, L1500). Less frequent buses run directly from Marina Grande to Ánacapri (L1500). The funicular ejects you into **p. Umberto; via Roma,** Cápri's ritzy strip, leads off to the left. The bus to Ánacapri takes you to **p. Vittoria. Via Giuseppe Orlandi,** running in both directions from the *piazza,* leads the cheapest and best establishments.

Tourist Office: in Cápri, at the end of the dock at Marina Grande (tel. 837 06 34). Open Mon.-Sat. 8am-8pm; Sept.-June 9am-1pm and 3:30-6:45pm. Also in p. Umberto, (tel. 837 06 86). Open Mon.-Sat. 8am-8pm, Sun. 8:30am-2:30pm; Oct.-May Mon.-Sat. 9am-1pm and 3:30-6:45pm. In Ánacapri, an information office hunkers at via Orlandi, 19/A (tel. 837 15 24), off the main *piazza,* to the right as you get off the bus. Open Mon.-Sat. 9am-1pm and 3:30-6:40pm; Sept.-May 9am-1pm. These offices provide a vague map, an updated list of hotels, and ferry and bus schedules. English spoken.

Currency Exchange: Cambio, via Roma, 33 (tel. 837 07 85), across from the main bus stop in Cápri. Open March 15-Nov. 15 daily 9am-9pm. Also at p. Vittoria, 2 (tel. 837 31 46), in the center of Ánacapri. Open March 15-Nov. 20 daily 8:30am-7:30pm. No commission at either location.

Post Office: central office in Cápri on via Roma (tel. 837 72 40), a couple of blocks downhill from p. Umberto. Open Mon.-Fri. 8:15am-6:30pm, Sat. 8:15am-12:10pm. In Ánacapri at viale de Tommaso, 4 (tel. 837 10 15). Open Mon.-Fri. 8:15am-1:30pm, Sat. 8:15am-12:10pm. **Postal Code:** 80073.

Telephones: SIP (tel. 837 83 60), behind the funicular stop in Cápri. Open daily 9am-1pm and 3-10:45pm; Oct.-May 9am-1pm and 3-8pm. Public phones in Ánacapri at p. Vittoria, 4 (tel. 837 12 07). Open daily 8am-1:30pm and 5-9pm; Oct.-May 8am-1:30pm and 2:30-7:30pm. **Telephone Code:** 081.

Buses: tel. 837 04 20. In Cápri, buses depart from via Roma for Ánacapri, Marina Píccola, and points in between. In Ánacapri, buses depart from p. Barile off via Orlandi for the Grotta Azzurra (Blue Grotto), the *faro* (lighthouse), and other points nearby. There's also a direct bus line between Marina Grande and p. Vittoria in Ánacapri. Buses cost L1500 per ride.

Luggage Storage: Caremar ticket office (tel. 837 07 00), across from the Marina Grande dock. L2000 per bag. Open daily 8am-7pm.

Public Showers and Swimming Pool: Bagni Nettuno, via Grotta Azzurra, 46 (tel. 837 13 62), above the Blue Grotto in Ánacapri. Take the bus from Ánacapri center. Full use of outdoor pool, private beach, reclining chair, shower, and changing room in scenic cliffside surroundings for a special *Let's Go* price of L8000 per day. Open mid-March to mid-Nov. daily 9am-7pm.

Emergencies: tel. 113. **Police,** via Roma (tel. 837 72 45). They'll connect you with an English speaker. **Hospital: Ospedale Capilupi,** via Provinciale Ánacapri (tel. 837 00 14 or 837 87 62), between Cápri and Ánacapri. For minor medical assistance in summer, call the **Guardia Medica Turistica** in Cápri (tel. 837 20 91).

Accommodations

Call in advance and confirm reservations; Ánacapri is your best bet. It's possible to find vacancies impromptu in July, but not in August. Makeshift camping is frowned upon and heavy fines are strictly imposed. But don't be put off by the inconvenience of finding a place to stay; the natural splendor of this legendary island should not be missed.

Ánacapri

Villa Eva, via La Fabbrica, 8 (tel. 837 20 40). Set high among the gardens and trees in the deep interior of Ánacapri, this is the perfect vacation setting. From the port at Marina Grande, take the direct bus to Ánacapri and get off at p. Vittoria. From here, telephone Villa Eva and they will pick you up. Once you enter this secluded sanctuary, it will be hard to bid *ciao* to warm-hearted Mamma Eva and her hubby Vincenzo. The tidy, tasteful rooms (with bath) were built by Vincenzo himself. Kitchenette available. L20,000 or L25,000 per person depending on the room you ask for. Private doubles L50,000. Telephone a few days in advance to confirm your reservations. Reservations valid until 3pm.

Hotel Il Girasole, via Linciano, 43 (tel. 837 23 51). Take the Ánacapri bus to the p. Caprile stop and walk down the hill to your left. Take the tiny alleyway with the "Girasole" sign for about a 7-min. walk straight ahead. A real treat for *Let's Go* users—the management loves the Book and anglophones in general. Very accommodating, offering use of cooking facilities, and occasional free access to their surplus of garden vegetables. All rooms have private baths. Plans are in the works to convert this paradise to a hostel. Bed in a double L25,000, in a triple L23,000, in a quad L20,000. Light breakfast included.

Hotel Caesar Augustus, via Orlandi, 4 (tel. 837 14 21), on the main bus route (from the port, L2500) before the town center. It's difficult to dispute their claim to the "most beautiful view in the world." Once the most expensive luxury hotel on the island, today a comfortable, weathered monument with a gorgeous garden entrance. English spoken. L30,000 per person upon mention of *Let's Go*. Open Easter-Oct.

Cápri Town

Albergo La Tosca, via Birago, 5 (tel. 837 09 89). Walk up the stairs at p. Umberto at the exit of the funicular and through the 2nd alley on the left, via Padre S. Cimino. Follow the twisting path, bearing right on via Valentino, and take a left where the street ends. Spacious rooms, some with ecstatically scenic views and terraces. Singles L30,000. Doubles L55,000, with bath L70,000. Oct.-May singles L25,000, doubles L50,000, with bath L60,000. Breakast L10,000. Discounts in off-season for stays of 3 or more days.

Pensione Quattro Stagioni, via Marina Piccola, 1 (tel. 837 00 41). From p. Umberto at the top of the funicular walk downhill on via Roma. Turn left at the 3-pronged fork in the road and look for the 1st house on the left. Flower-filled coziness with hot but clean rooms, sensational views, and an outgoing, English-speaking owner. One single L35,000. Doubles L70,000, with bath L80,000. Breakfast L15,000. Less of a deal in July and Aug. when half-pension of 1 meal or the costly breakfast is required (L25,000 added to room price). Open March 15-Nov.

Food

Caprese food is as glorious as the panoramas from the island's cliffs. Savor their local *mozzarella* alone, or with tomatoes, oil, and basil in a dish known as *insalata caprese,* respectfully considered the best summer meal in the world by many. The *ravioli alla caprese* is hand-stuffed with the tastiest of local cheeses. Don't miss the *torta di mandorla* (chocolate almond cake). Accompany meals with the local red and white wines, which bear the *Tiberio* label.

Restaurant and bar prices in the town of Cápri will make you gasp—buy food from one of the groceries instead. Take the right prong of the fork at the end of via Roma to reach **Supermercato STANDA** (open daily 8am-1:30pm and 4:30-9pm; in winter Mon.-Sat. 8am-1pm and 3:30-8pm). Ask at Girasole and Villa Eva for local low-cost restaurants.

Ánacapri

Ristorante Il Cucciolo, via della Fabbrica, 52 (tel. 837 19 17), near the bus stop for the Damecuta ruins on the road to the Blue Grotto; a 5-min. walk from Villa Eva. Follow the path from the sign. An outdoor restaurant with expansive views of the bay. Homemade *agnolotti* (stuffed pasta) and their fresh fish are the friendly owner's pride and joy. Wine L7000 per . Open June 21-Sept. 21 daily 12:10-2:30pm and 7:30-10:45pm; March 15-June 20 and Sept. 22-Oct. 30 Wed.-Mon. 12:10-2:30pm and 7:30-10:45pm.

Trattoria Il Solitario, via Orlandi, 96 (though the tile says #54; tel. 837 13 82), off p. Vittoria. An amazing, ivy-covered hideaway. *Cannelloni alla caprese* L8000, homemade pasta L7000-8000, salads L3500. Wine L5000 per bottle. Cover L1500. Open daily 12:15-3pm and 7pm-midnight; Sept. 21-June 19 Tues.-Sun. 12:15-3pm and 7pm-midnight.

La Quercia, via della Migliari, 46 (tel. 837 88 20). Only a 5-min. walk from Girasole. Supreme view and divine seafood at discount prices.

Cápri Town

La Cantina del Marchese, via Tiberio, 7/E (tel. 837 08 57). From p. Umberto, follow via delle Botteghe into via Fuorlovado, which leads up, up, up to via Tiberio (15min.). A truly distinctive restaurant, sheltered from tourists by the horrendous climb. They offer such creative pasta dishes as *bucatini del prete* with fresh tomato, basil, wine, and parmesan (L8000) and *pasticcio alla cantina,* baked with mixed pasta, squash, zucchini, ham, and parmesan (L9500). Homemade cheeses and cold cuts (large plate L6000-8000), as well as wine (L6000 per carafe). Service 10%. Open daily noon-3pm and 7pm-midnight; Oct.-June Fri.-Wed. noon-3pm and 7pm-midnight.

Moscardino, via Roma, 28 (tel. 837 06 87). Under new management. Limited but excellent selection. Open daily noon-3pm and 7pm-midnight.

Sights

To appreciate Cápri's Mediterranean beauty from on high, take via Longano from p. Umberto in Cápri center and then make the trek up to the left on via Tiberio to **Villa Jovis** (1hr.). This is Emperor Tiberius's ruined but still magnificent pleasure dome. Legend has it that Tiberius chucked those who displeased him over the precipice. *Let's Go* advises walking down. (Open daily 9am-1hr. before sunset. Admission L4000.) On the descent along the path, a short detour takes you to the **Arco Naturale,** a majestic stone arch, off via Matermania on the eastern cliffs. On a clear day you can see as far as Paestum through the weathered arch.

Toward the southern edge of the town of Cápri lies the **Certosa,** a 14th-century Carthusian monastery. The Gothic chapel remains unruffled and angular as ever, despite 18th-century Baroque frescoes. (Open Tues.-Sun. 8am-2pm. Free.) The nearby **Giardini di Augusto** (Gardens of Augustus) aren't noted for their horticultural beauty, but a superb series of belvederes makes the visit worthwhile. In one corner of the gardens a small statue is dedicated to Lenin, who fled to Cápri after the failed revolution of 1905. (Garden open daily 8am-1hr. before sunset.) Descend the coiled trail below the gardens if it's open, or take any of the frequent buses to **Marina Píccola** on the southern coast (every 15min., L1500), one of Cápri's most beautiful seaside stretches. Though the beach is a glorified pile of rocks, you can cavort in the clear water among immense lava stones or rent a boat and paddle to even better spots to the west. You can also swim at Marina Grande, near the port.

Take any of the boats near the port or descend north between vineyards from p. Umberto to **Bagni di Tiberio,** a bathing area amidst the ruins of an imperial villa (also accessible by boat from Marina Grande, L7000).

Until the completion of the cliffhanging roadway a few decades ago, only a narrow Phoenician staircase joined **Ánacapri** (literally "over Cápri") to the lower town. From p. Vittoria in Ánacapri, take a 10-minute chairlift (round-trip L5500) to the top of **Monte Solaro.** (Open 9:30am-2hr. before sunset.) The view from the top is terrific: on a clear day, you can see the Apennines to the east and the mountains of Calabria to the south. Another Ánacapri attraction is the **Villa San Michele.** Built earlier this century on the site of another of Emperor Tiberius's villas, it was the lifelong work of the Swedish author and physician Axel Munthe. Classical sculptures throng the villa, many retrieved from Cápri's sea bottom where they were hurled after Tiberius's death, allegedly by the ghosts of his victims. (Open daily 9am-1hr. before sunset. Admission L4000.) From Ánacapri center, take a bus to the **faro,** Italy's second-tallest lighthouse, where you can snorkle, tan, or leap from volcanic rocks among countless Italians.

Cápri's most famous attraction, the **Grotta Azzurra** (Blue Grotto), has become the area's most fearsome tourist trap. A motorboat from Marina Grande, barely 2km away, costs L8000 round-trip and leaves regularly from 9am until two hours before sunset. From the motorboat you are transferred unceremoniously to rowboats for a tour of the grotto (L10,500, tip expected). The "captains" take you through at such a speed that your eyes scarcely have time to adjust to the remarkable blue glow, best seen in the early evening. You can skip the motorboat ride by taking a bus from Ánacapri to the cliff above the grotto (every 20min., L1500). Many visitors dive into the clear water of the grotto, but swimming is permitted only before 9am and after 6pm when the rowboats are not running. Don't go alone or if the surf is heavy. There is a tiny public "beach" (really a rock and concrete ledge) at Gràdola, just west of the Grotta, poised for diving board action.

Íschia

Across the bay from overrun Cápri, larger, less glamorous Íschia has managed to cram many of the characteristics of Campania onto its small surface. Íschia has beautiful beaches, natural hot springs, ruins, forests, vineyards, lemon groves, and a once-active volcano. Unfortunately, the island hasn't escaped the hideous overpricing of a resort island. Íschia's main towns are: **Íschia Porto,** which surrounds a perfectly circular port formed by the crater of an extinct volcano; **Cassamícciola Terme,** an expensive spa sporting an overcrowded beach; **Lacco Ameno,** another spa town but one with a lofty pedigree (it's the oldest Greek settlement in the western Mediterranean); and **Fório** on the western coast, sheltering many *pensioni* and the popular **San Francesco beach.** Between tanning and swimming sessions, the occasional visitor can take in Íschia's scattered sights. Near Íschia Porto, the **Castello d'Íschia** (1441), built by the King of Spain on the site of a 5th-century BC Greek fortress, is located on a little island of its own connected to Íschia by a 15th-century footbridge. When Íschia's volcano **Mt. Epomeo** erupted for the last time in 1301, the island's inhabitants fled to the tiny island for safety; after the castle was completed, it sheltered Íschia's entire population, forced to flee the mainland this time due to eruptions of pirates along the shore. When you visit, be sure to check out the **nun's cemetery** where the Poor Clares resided in the 18th century. When nuns died, the order built stone thrones with drains resembling royal potty trainers to prop the decomposing bodies as a constant (and redolent) reminder to the other nuns of death's presence. The castle also features an exposition room with changing modern art exhibits. (Open daily 9am-8pm. Admission L5000, elevator to top L1000.)

The ruins in Lacco Aveno testify to its antiquity, but the town's most distinctive characteristics are the **Il Fungo** (Mushroom) finger-shaped promontory off the coast, and an expensive thermal spa featuring radioactive waters. If you're staying in Fório, stop by its 14th-century sanctuary, **Santa Maria di Loreto,** and the 15th-century tower **Torrione.** Just south is **Citara,** a large beach with giant diving rocks. **Barano d'Íschia,** the southern region of Íschia, contains the **Spaggia dei Maronti,** the most tranquil and scenic swimming area (serviced by boat-taxi from Sant'Angelo) and a convenient base for hikes up the volcano, Mt. Epomeo.

Practical Information

Tourist Office: scalo Porto Salvo (tel. 99 11 46 or 98 30 05), in Íschia Porto. Open Mon.-Sat. 9am-8pm, Sun. 9am-1pm. A 2nd Azienda Turismo operates on corso Vittorio Colonna, 104 (tel. 98 30 66). Open daily 8:30am-12:30pm.

Budget Travel: CIT Viaggi, via Roma, 41 (tel. 99 10 12).

Buses: Land and Water, to destinations all over the island. Main office and depature point on Íschia Porto. Bus #1 covers Cassamícciola Terme, Lacco Ameno, Fório, and Sant'Angelo. (Every 30min., L1200.) **Tours** of the island by boat (L13,000) and by minibus (L16,000) are available and can be booked through agents along the waterfront.

Ferries: Two major lines, **Casemar** and **Linee Laura,** have the same prices and schedules—they only vary by 30min. To Íschia from: Naples (every 2hr. 6:10am-11pm, Sun. 7:05am-11pm, L7300); Pozzuoli (5 per day, L4900); Amalfi (L13,000); Sorrento (L10,000); Positano (L12,000); and Prócida (L2700).

Accommodations

Hotels in Íschia run the gamut from reasonable to exorbitant. By late July and August rooms are hard to come by without reservations made at least three months in advance. Few hotels offer singles, and since rooms are in such high demand, hotel owners may not rent rooms for less than a week. Prices plummet from October to May. Get the hotel list from the tourist office for the most detailed maps of the island, or try the most economical way to overnight in Íschia: camping. Íschia is an easy daytrip from both Sorrento and Naples, so you might consider avoiding the search for affordable accommodations altogether.

Íschia Porto

Albergo A. Macri, via Jasolino, 96 (tel. 99 26 03), near the port off the street that runs along the water. Respectable rooms far from the beaches. Singles L27,000, with bath L35,000. Doubles L55,000, with bath L65,000. Oct.-June singles L23,000, with bath L32,000. Doubles L50,000, with bath L58,000. Flash your *Let's Go* book to get these prices.

Il Crostolo, via Cossa, 32 (tel. 99 10 94). From the tourist office take via Jasolino right, but don't follow it to the port. Take the ascending road to the hotel at the top of the curve to the right. Terrace and several of the rooms have super views of the port. Singles with bath L38,000. Doubles with bath L62,500. Sept.-June singles L26,000; doubles with bath L60,000. Breakfast included. Half-pension (L60,000) required in July and Aug.

Cassamícciola Terme

Pensione Quisisana, p. Bagni, 34 (tel. 99 45 20). Take bus #3 from the port to the *piazza.* Tiny, family-run establishment with plenty of comfort. A 10-min. walk from the beach. Curfew midnight. July-Aug. obligatory full pension L54,000 per person. Open May-Oct.

Fório

Pensione Di Lustra, via Filippo Di Lustro, 9 (tel. 99 71 63). A 2-second walk from the beach. At first you might think you've mistakenly stumbled into botanical gardens. Gorgeous views inside and out. Doubles with bath L55,000-65,000 including breakfast. Half-pension often required in July and Aug. (L50,000). **Pensione Villa Franca,** strada statale Lacco, 155 (tel. 98 74 20). Take bus #1 from Íschia Porto and get off at the stop for the San Francesco beach. On the street traversed by the bus. Well-kept rooms, a pretty patio, and a swimming pool. A 15-min. walk from the beach. English spoken. Singles L28,000, with bath L32,000. Doubles with bath L56,000.

Camping: The most economical source of accommodations. 2 delightful campgrounds lie near Íschia Porto. The better is **Eurocamping dei Pini,** via delle Ginestre, 28 (tel. 98 20 69), a 10-min. walk from the port. Take via del Porto onto via Alfredo de Luca, walk uphill and take a right on via delle Terme, where you will see the arrow indicating *Camping.* L9500 per person, L9000 per large tent, L5000 per small tent; Sept.-June L8000, L7000, and L5000. Bungalows with bath and kitchen facilities for 2, 3, 4, or more run L64,000 (reserve ahead). The tent site is more scenic than the bungalow site. Open June-Oct. **Camping Internazionale,** via M. Mazella (tel. 99 14 49), a 15-min. walk from the port. Take via Alfredo de Luca from via del Porto and bear right onto via M. Mazzella at p. degli Eroe. (Note that there are 2 via Mazzellas—Michele and Leonardo—running parallel.) Luxuriant foliage and tranquil surroundings. L12,000 per person (L8000-10,000 off-season), L6000 per tent. Showers included. Immaculate 2-person bungalows with bath L65,000, L15,000 per additional person; off-season L40,000 and L14,000. Bathless bungalows are slightly cheaper. Open May-Oct. 20.

Food

Íschia has ubiquitous outdoor eateries, numerous *alimentari,* and a plethora of fruit vendors.

Íschia Porto

Da Mastu Peppe o Fraulese (tel. 98 19 12), located behind the tourist office on the waterfront. Lovely outdoor restaurant with a view of the port. Standard spaghetti L5000. *Risotto alla pescatore* (with fresh seafood, L11,000). Open Tues.-Sun. 12:30-2pm and 8pm-midnight.

Emiddio, via Porto, 30, right by the docks. Here the *ravioli alla panna* (L5000) are supreme. Other *primi* L4000-7000. Cover L1500.

Prócida

A small island of fisherfolk and farmers, Prócida prefers to remain a spectator to its neighbors' summertime transformation into country clubs. Though crowds also swarm to Prócida, they don't stay on long enough to taint its beaches. Take a ferry from Naples (5 per day, L6400), Pozzuoli (L5200), or Íschia (L2700). The 14km volcanic coast offers three principal beaches: *Spiaggia Chiaia, Spiaggia Ciraccio,* and *Chiaiolella.* From the main port, the interior sights of the island can be covered in one beautiful trek. From the town center, take via Principe Umberto out and up the long steep haul (no buses) to the **Abbazia Arcangelo San Michele** (St. Michael's Abbey) on the easternmost and highest hilltop in Prócida. On the way up you'll see the medieval walls of the **Terra Murata** (citadel) on via San Michele just below the monastery. The abbey's pastel yellow facade, redone in 1890, belies the interior, where you'll find ornate 15th-century gold-lead frescoes and bleeding Christ figures. (Open daily 9am-6:30pm.) On the way down, revel in the view of the island's second port on the southern side and stop to admire the ochre Pantheon-domed **Santuario Mariano** with an 1810 facade at p. Vittorio Scialoia. Buses don't serve much of the island, but it's only 4km wide and taxi service is available from Marina Grande (tel. 896 87 85). From the center, via Vittorio Emanuele, buses do wheel you to **Chiaiolella,** a little port where you can cross the footbridge to the islet of **Vivara,** preserved as a wildlife sanctuary and breeding ground for the rabbits Procidano cook up in their famous stew. **Angolo di Paradiso,** via Salette, 14 (tel. 896 76 57), on the Ciraccio beach, serves excellent, inexpensive dishes. *Spaghetti alla scarpara* is a fried spaghetti dish with myriad spices (L6000). Their *coniglio alla procidana* (local rabbit) will make you hop for joy and wiggle your nose (L11,000). (Cover L1500. Service 10%. Open May-Sept. daily 1-4pm and 7-10:30pm.)

Of the island's four hotels, only two are affordable. The **Riviera,** at via G. Da Procida, 36 (tel. 896 71 97), is in the Chiaiolella beach area. (Singles with bath L35,000; doubles with bath L60,000; full pension L80,000. Open April-Sept.) The **Savoia,** on via Lavadera, 32 (tel. 896 76 16), also has decent rooms. (Doubles L50,000; full pension L60,000.) You can reach the campground **Graziella,** at via Salette (tel. 896 77 47) on the beach, by taking the island bus from the port to p. Urno and walking one-half km to Spiaggia Ciraccio. Facilities are few but tranquility abounds. (L8000 per person, L7000 per tent. Open May-Sept.) The **tourist office,** via Principe Umberto (tel. 894 90 67), also lets apartments from one night to a month depending on availability. (Open Mon.-Sat. 9am-1pm and 4-8pm, Sun. 10:30am-1pm.)

Sorrento

Odysseus's crew shielded their ears from the spellbinding song of the Sirens, who inhabited Sorrento's peninsula. If the Sirens still exist, chances are they chant in English and German to camera-laden foreigners. Nevertheless, there are fates far worse than being shipwrecked on Sorrento's rocky beaches where rooms with views are still affordable and access to Cápri and the Amalfi coast is convenient.

Orientation and Practical Information

On the tip of the peninsula that leaps for Cápri's throat, 48km south of Naples, Sorrento is served by frequent *circumvesuviana* trains. Buses run regularly from Sorrento to the towns of the Amalfi coast.

There's a short throughway which leads you from the stairs outside the station (by the phone booths) to **corso Italia,** Sorrento's main street. To the left lies **piazza Tasso,** the center of town. Several smaller *piazze* surround it, as do most of the town's restaurants, bars, and shops.

Tourist Office: via L. De Maio, 35 (tel. 878 11 15). Cross p. Sant'Antonino (behind p. Tasso toward the water) to via L. De Maio; the office is to the right within the Circolo del Forestiere complex, in the room on the left as you enter the building. A large, well-run, English-speaking office with maps, accommodations service, and information on cultural events. Grab a free copy of *Surrentum,* the monthly tourist magazine. Open Mon.-Sat. 8:30am-12:30pm and 4:30-8pm; Oct.-June 8:30am-2:30pm and 4-7pm.

American Express: Acampara Travel, p. Angelina Lauro, 13 (tel. (081) 878 48 00).

Post Office: corso Italia, 210T-U (tel. 807 28 28), near p. Lauro. Open Mon.-Sat. 8:15am-7:30pm. **Postal Code:** 80067.

Telephones: SIP, p. Tasso (tel. 878 24 00), at via Correale under the church on the far side. Open daily 9am-1pm and 4-9:30pm. **Telephone Code:** 081.

Buses: SITA (tel. 878 27 08). All buses to towns on the Amalfi coast leave only from the *circumvesuviana* station. Frequent buses to Positano (L1500), Praiano (L2100), and Amalfi (L2800). From Amalfi, change buses and pay an additional L2100 to go to Salerno or an additional L1100 to go to: Atransi, Ravella, Scala, Minori, or Maiori.

Ferries: the cheapest route to Cápri. Descend the stairs at p. Tasso. **Caremar** (tel. 878 12 82) is the most reliable. Boats leave daily at 8am, 10am, 2:45pm, 5:45pm, and 7:40pm (less frequently in winter). Tickets L5000. Ferries also to: Íschia (L10,000), Amalfi (L10,000), and in summer, Ponza (L40,000), and Ventotene (L30,000).

Car and Moped Rental: Sorrento Rent A Car, corso Italia, 210/A (tel. 878 58 61), and **Thomas,** p. S. Antonino, 4 (tel. 878 58 61) both offer fair rates and the most comprehensive services. Credit cards accepted. Rent **bicycles** and **tandems** from **Guarracino,** via S. Antonino, 19 (tel. 878 17 28). Open 9am-9pm; 7am-midnight in summer.

Emergencies: tel. 113. **Police:** vico 3° Rota, (tel. 878 11 10), a left off corso Italia 1 block after viale Nizza, past the hostel. Ask for the English-speaking foreigners' office (*Ufficio Stranieri*). **Hospital: Ospedale Santa Maria Misericordia,** corso Italia (tel. 878 34 96). English speakers on hand.

Accommodations and Camping

Some Sorrento hotels allegedly charge more than their official prices but escape municipal reprimand. Still, many bargains lurk about. The prices below are the officially quoted ones. It's sensible to call ahead for reservations in July and August.

Ostello Surriento (HI), via Capasso, 5 (tel. 878 17 83). From the train station, go down the stairs by the phone booths and follow the through street to corso Italia. Make a right then look for the old church on your left; via Capasso runs along its side. Savvy young management, wild decorations, and a waterfront location redeem the primitive and many-bedded rooms. Free shower. Lockout 9:30am-5pm. Curfew 11:30pm. L11,000 per person. Breakfast L2000, dinner L11,000. Open March-Oct.

Hotel Linda, via degli Aranci, 125 (tel. 878 29 16), behind the train station. Despite the barren area, the rooms are cozy and comfortable. Doubles with bath L56,000. Sept.-July singles with bath L35,000.

Pensione Mara, via Rota, 5 (tel. 878 36 65). Turn right on corso Italia from the train station, take via Capasso past the youth hostel, and then make your 1st right. Immaculate rooms (some with terraces) in a beautiful quiet area. English spoken. One single L30,000. Doubles L60,000. (Make reservations for a summer stay.)

Hotel Elios, via Capo, 33 (tel. 878 18 12). Clean rooms with lovely bay views. Doubles with bath L64,000. Bringing your *Let's Go* could get you a discount if you ask politely and smile.

Hotel Nice, corso Italia, 257 (tel. 878 16 50). Not the most picturesque hotel in this beautiful city but reasonably clean rooms. Nice proprietors. Nice singles L37,000. Nice doubles L56,000.

Hotel City, corso Italia, 221 (tel. 877 22 10), on the main street that heads toward p. Tasso from the train station. A colorful, art-filled place. A bit noisy at night. English spoken. Comfortable doubles with bath (some with garden patios) L50,000. Singles available Sept.-June L45,000. Breakfast L7000. Reserve at least 2 months in advance for Aug.

Hotel Savoia, via Fuorimura, 48 (tel. 878 25 11), on the street off the right hand of the statue in p. Tasso. The best bet if you're arriving in the summer without reservations. Friendly English-speaking management. A few small singles with bath L35,000-40,000. Doubles L60,000-65,000. Breakfast L7000.

Hotel Loreley et Londres, via Califano, 2 (tel. 878 15 08). Take via Capasso past the youth hostel all the way to the waterfront. The Sorrento hotel you've dreamed of, with view of cliffs and sea. Worth the slightly higher price. Doubles with bath and breakfast L75,000. July-Sept. obligatory half-pension L65,000.

Camping: Nube d'Argento, via del Capo, 21 (tel. 878 13 44). From the train station, follow corso Italia past p. Tasso until it becomes via del Capo. L10,000 per person and per tent, L5000 per small tent; Sept.-June L8000 and L4000. **Villaggio Verde,** via Cesarano, 12 (tel. 878 32 58), a 10-min. walk from the town center off via degli Aranci. L7500 per big tent and L6000 per little tent; Sept.-June L6000 and L4500. Two-person bungalows with kitchen and bath L60,000.

Food

Sorrento is famous for its *gnocchi,* plump potato dumplings smothered in a zesty to-mato sauce and mozzarella cheese. Also popular are the *cannelloni. Nocillo* is a dark liqueur made from the hefty local walnuts. Unfortunately, few of the affordable restau-rants in Sorrento offer local fare, opting instead to cater to the Germans with *Würstel* and to the English with fish and chips. However, if you've been dying for a real eggs-and-bacon breakfast, you'll find it here. Otherwise, flee the city center and explore the local hangouts in the surrounding area. **Supermercato STANDA,** at corso Italia, 221, sells the cheap stuff (open Mon.-Wed. and Fri.-Sat. 8:30am-12:55pm and 5-9:25pm, Thurs. 8:30am-12:55pm). Follow San Cesareo out until it turns into San Puoro for fresh fruit, fish, or bargain shoes sold at a variety of market stands. (Go in the morning for the best deals.)

Outside the City

Taverna del Curato, via Casarlano, 10b (tel. 877 16 28). 30min. uphill walk from town center in the locality of Casarlano, or take the infrequent bus #1 from p. Tasso. From p. Tasso, take via Fuo-rimura to via Atigliana and follow it uphill. Food just like mamma's (if mamma were an expert cook living in the Sorrento hillside). They make their own *fettucine del Curato* (hand-cut pasta with cream, ham, mushrooms, and bacon, L7000) and bottle their own wine (L5000 per). Cover L1500. Open daily noon-1am; Oct.-May Thurs.-Tues. noon-1am.

Gigino Pizza a Metro, via Nicotera, 11, at Vico Equense (tel. 879 84 24), a 10-min. train ride from Sorrento. Take the *circumvesuviana* to the Vico Equense stop, go left as you exit the station, and follow the winding road uphill to its end at p. Umberto. Finally, take a left on via Roma and another left on via Nicotera. This is unofficially the world's largest *pizzeria,* a massive 2-story fa-cility with monstrous wood-burning ovens that cook *pizza a metro* (1m-long pizza), supposedly famous throughout Italy. A meter will feed at least 5 starving tourists. Overeat *pizza margherita* with fresh tomato and mozzarella (L22,000) or *quattro stagioni* with cheese, prosciutto, mush-room, and tomato (L24,000). Chug a half-liter of beer for L2500. Cover L1000. Service 13%. Open daily noon-1am.

In the City

Ristorante e Pizzeria Giardiniello, via Accademia, 7 (tel. 878 46 16). Take the 2nd left off via Giuliani (way to the right of via Dinkins), which runs off corso Italia at the cathedral. Mamma Luisa does all the cooking in this large family-run establishment. Her *gnocchi* transcend poetry (L5000). Don't miss the *bocconcini al Giardiniello,* tiny oven-baked pizzas with prosciutto and mushrooms (L6000 for about 10). *Vino di Sorrento* L4000 per bottle. Cover L500. Open daily 11:30am-midnight; Oct.-May Fri.-Wed. 11:30am-midnight.

Ristorante Sant'Antonino, via Santa Maria delle Grazie, 6 (tel. 877 12 00), off p. Sant'Antonino. Popular with locals as well as tourists for its flora-filled patio and low prices. *Farfalle con zucchine* (butterfly-shaped pasta mixed with zucchini, L6000) and yummy-and-a-half *gnocchi alla sorrentina* (L5500). Long wine list. Open July-Sept. daily noon-midnight; Feb. 16-June and Oct.-Dec. closed Monday.

Ristorante 2000, largo Sedil Dominova, off via San Cesareo. The "2000" dominates a tiny *piazza* with outdoor tables, a liquor store, and a small *alimentari.* The *menù* is surprisingly good with lasagne and veal cutlet at L13,000.

The westerly orientation of the beaches makes sunset swims truly memorable. To get to the lovely **Punta di Sorrento,** walk down the Ruderia Romana off via Capo; after 400m, it turns into a footpath that leads to the water, passing the ruins of a medieval fortress. A bit farther, southwest of the city, the **Villa di Pollio,** a public park, harbors ruins and a fantastic swimming hole. To get there, take a bus to Capo di Sorrento and then walk 12 minutes past the stop.

Nearby **Sant'Agata** (12km by SITA bus from p. Tasso), a tiny city perched high in the hills, is known as the "city on the two gulfs" because from its majestic height you can see both the Bay of Naples and the Gulf of Salerno. The city's church, the **Chiesa di Sant'Agata,** boasts a 13th-century mother-of-pearl altar by the Florentine school. From the church, take an uphill path to the locality of **Deserto,** a tranquil and eponymously deserted plain from which you can survey the Campanian coastline far below.

Sorrento hosts several interesting spectacles throughout the year, including an elaborate procession on Good Friday and an international film festival in October. One of the most notable events of the year is the February 15 **Festa di Sant'Antonino,** when the town's fishermen let loose with a market to beat all markets, processions from the church, and a parade of Sant'Antonino's statue through town. Several miracles are attributed to the saint, among them his success in convincing a nasty whale to return a swallowed child to its mother at the *marina grande.* Classical music is performed roughly every other night throughout July and August at the outdoor atrium of the **Chiostro di San Francesco,** near the Villa Comunale on the water. (Showtime 9pm. Admission L16,000, students under 26 L10,000, some shows half-price.) Free events from July through September take place in the Villa Comunale, the Chiostro di San Francesco, and the town's two ports. From November to March, the Sorrento Tourist Board organizes **Sorrento Inverno,** a free entertainment program that includes movies, concerts, local folklore exhibits, and guided tours of town. The area around p. Tasso heats up and gets down after dark. People swarm the streets, look out over the bay, and career around on mopeds. **La Boutique della Birre,** in Ville Pompeiana, via Marina Grande, 6 (tel. 877 24 28), has gorgeous frescoed rooms, pool tables, over a hundred kinds of beers, and music saturating the air. Food is also available (sandwiches and pasta). (Open nightly 7:30pm-1am.)

Amalfi Coast

The Amalfi Coast is worth every superlative a tourist brochure could heap upon it. Stretches of bold, arresting bluffs typify the region's alluring scenery. A limestone range marked by deep gorges and fantastically sculpted rocks, the harsh southern shore of the mountainous peninsula separating the Bay of Naples from the Gulf of Salerno is tempered by prolific lemon groves, grape vines, olive trees, almonds, camelias, and oleander.

The coast is accessible by frequent SITA buses leaving Sorrento and Salerno every two hours, and *circumvesuviana* service from Naples on a less regular basis (the Meta stop). Some find the route via Salerno more convenient as Eurail passes are not honored by the *circumvesuviana* to Sorrento and Meta. You will revere the bus drivers after this voyage; they manage the dizzying, semi-aerial roads with aplomb. Rent a motorbike for an exhilarating—and treacherous—coastal experience. Due to the character of the road, hitchhiking is inadvisable for hitchers and drivers alike.

Positano

Ten miles from Sorrento, Positano looks as if it might slip off its tenuous rock perch right into the sea. As Steinbeck wrote of his old vertical haunt, "You do not walk to visit a friend, you either climb or slide." Steinbeck wasn't the only *artiste* so taken with this town; a flux of postwar creative types, Tennessee Wiliams among them, hit this quiet fishing village. In recent years, Positano has perhaps traded some authenticity for tourist appeal, but it remains one of a kind, especially when seen from the direction of

Sorrento, or at night when the Positano cliff glows in an effervescence of sparkling lights.

Positano is located one hour from Sorrento by SITA bus. From the bus stop at Chiesa Nuova, either walk down the winding stairway to the village (affectionately referred to as the "Thousand Steps,") or take the bus, which runs every half-hour up and down the main street (L1200). When leaving, buy tickets in advance from the **Bar Internazionale.** The terse but well-informed **tourist office** is at via del Saracino, 4 (tel. 87 50 67). Stop by to pick up a map and a neat, glossy booklet on the town. (Open Mon.-Sat. 8:30am-2pm.) A row of 10 **SIP telephones** is located directly behind the tourist office in the alley. The **telephone code** for Positano is 089. A **pharmacy** is located at via dei Mulini (tel. 87 58 63). The **emergency number** is, as always, 113; the **police** are at Chiesa Nuova (tel. 87 50 50).

Ferries provide extensive service; buy tickets at the *biglietteria marittima* on the port. Boats run to Cápri (departures 9am and 3:20pm, L12,500), Amalfi (11am, 5:20pm, and 6pm, L7000), Íschia (9am, L14,000), Salerno (5:20pm and 6pm, L12,500), Naples (3:20pm, L13,000), and Sorrento (3:20pm and 4:10pm via Cápri, L13,000).

Homer's Sirens allegedly inhabited the three rocks off Positano's beach. If you too feel the pull of the Sirens' call, try one of the many *pensioni* in the area. (Reserve early in the busy summer season.) **Villa Maria Luisa,** via Fornillo, 40 (tel. 87 50 23), 10 minutes from the top of Positano near Fornillo beach, leases splendid views, relaxing terraces and doubles with baths (L45,000-55,000). Literally next door is the quaint **Casa Guadagno** with spotless well-lit rooms. Call ahead as the 10 rooms with bath are a quick sell. (Singles L38,000, doubles L55,000. Oct.-May singles L35,000, doubles L50,000.)

As you descend on the right of via dei Mulini, the aroma emanating from **Trattoria Giardino degli Aranci** will entice you to their outdoor and indoor tables. Their specialties are spaghetti with mussels (*cozze*) for L9000 and grilled fish for L14,000. (Tel. 875 157. Open daily 8am-1am; in winter Tues.-Sun. 1-3pm and 8-11pm.) **O'Capurale,** Marina di Positano (tel. 87 53 74), dishes up heaping plates of *bucatini alla caporalessa* (baked pasta with eggplant and cheese) for L7000 (other pasta specialties L7000-11,000), and serves them at outdoor tables facing the beach. Main dishes run L9000-11,000. Wine is L6000 per . (Cover L2000. Service 10%. Open March-Oct. daily 12:30-4pm and 7:30-11pm.)

Spiraling upwards from **Marina Grande,** Positano's grey but attractive beach, **via dei Mulini,** with its many boutiques and well-clad foreigners, is a study in the well-heeled tourist. For more traditional sight-seeing, however, the 17th-century church of **Santa Maria Assunta,** located in the piazza Flavio Gioia, crowns the memorable Positano landscape with a beautiful tiled dome. Boats from **Marina Grande** will take you on minicruises to the islets of **Li Galli,** and **La Porta** beach with its 15,000-year-old grotto, the legendary Sirens-ville. Hop the bus from the top of Positano or hike the 45-minute trail to **Monte Pertuso.** On the way, stop at the locals' favorite freshwater spring at the foot of a small Madonna. Monte Pertuso, a high cliff pierced by a large *pertuso* (hole), towers over the beautiful and hamlet of **Praiano,** which basks in new-found popularity.

Praiano

Three and a half miles down the coast, Praiano is a rocky city built in the image of Positano, but less touristed than its neighbor and rival in the fish trade. This tiny town has a lovely beach but no tourist office and no real center. A spread of a few shops meets the needs of its 1500 inhabitants. Enjoy the rapturous panorama from the excellent campground-hotel **La Tranquillità,** Praiano 84010 (tel. (089) 87 40 84), on the road to Amalfi (ask the busdriver to stop at the Ristorante Continental/La Tranquillità). The rooms here hold a monopoly on the coast's most awe-inspiring views of the surrounding caves, castles, gorges, and sea, while the spotless campsite (the only one on the coast) clings miraculously to precipitous cliffs that hang over the coast. (L12,000 per person; off-season L10,000. Tent included. Bungalows with bath and often a terrace L25,000-30,000 per person including breakfast.) Don't leave the coast without savoring a meal at the open-air **Ristorante Continental,** above La Tranquillità. The mountain air, the endless views, and the exquisite food will leave you in a state of bliss. *Primi* cost L6000, *secondi* are L9000-15,000, and the local wine runs L6000 per . *Let's Go* bearers receive a 15% discount. (Cover L2000. Open daily noon-3pm and 8pm-midnight. Hotel and restaurant both open March-Nov.) The hotel has a direct staircase to the beach. There's another marvelous beach up the road toward Positano but you must be willing to descend 400 steps (keep the return trip in mind). Alternate accommodations may be found at **Open Gate** (tel. 87 41 48), just up the street from the campground, which offers views and steps to the beach (doubles are about L50,000.)

Turn the bend as you leave Praiano and you immediately encounter both the sign for the **Grotto Smeraldo** and the steps leading to the miniscule fishing village of **Conca dei Marini,** which boasts a Norman tower. The SITA bus from Sorrento to Salerno will drop you off at the elevator entrance to the grotto, to the left of a bar/restaurant/ceramics shop. The grotto is sensitive about its rivalry with Cápri's azure equivalent. The water—of a pleasant green hue due to the light entering through an underground tunnel—isn't as stunning, but the cave is large, and the tour long as multilingual guides show you stalagmites and stalactites in different forms above and below the water level. As you enter the grotto look to the left to see a well-hidden profile (ask the guide if you can't find it). An Italian television station ruined the natural beauty of the site by sinking a nativity scene in the middle of the cave. The guides tend to dwell on this rather distressing feature. The elevator down from the road is free; entrance to the cave and boat tour is L4000. (Open daily 9am-5pm.)

Amalfi

> God created Amalfi one day when he was in a great mood.
>
> —A. Cutole

The first Sea Republic of Italy, Amalfi has been a bustling seaside town since its foundation by the Romans. After a downfall caused by Norman conquest and the 1343 earthquake, Amalfi became the first city to reestablish commercial ties with both the East and West, and created its own coin. Home of Flavio Gioia (inventor of the compass), Amalfi was also the point of origin of the famous *"Tabula de Amalpha,"* an important development in the governing of sea navigation. Today, however, tourism has replaced exotic sea trading. Fortunately, the crunch isn't as intense as in Sorrento, and the milieu is far more enchanting. Amalfi attracts passive lingerers who stroll the beautiful bayside promenades, sip coffee in the intimate *piazza* in front of the cathedral, or step off on forays into the high hills and winding roads of the surrounding coast.

Orientation and Practical Information

Buses stop in piazza Flavio Gioia, named after the developer of the European magnetic compass. Head away from the water and pass through the white, arched portal or the street to the right of piazza del Duomo.

Tourist Office: corso delle Repubbliche Marinare, 19/21 (tel. 87 11 07). On the water in the direction of Salerno from the bus stop. Gentle staff has limited information; ask for the city pamphlet, hotel list, and street map if they're in stock. Open Mon.-Sat. 8am-2pm and 4:30-7pm; Oct.-May 8am-2pm.

Post Office: corso delle Repubbliche Marinare, 29 (tel. 87 13 30), on the road running along the waterfront. Open Mon.-Fri. 8:15am-6:30pm, Sat. 8:15am-12:15pm. **Postal Code:** 84011.

Telephones: Bar Della Valle, via Marino del Giudice, 8 (tel. 87 12 65). Take the road that leads uphill from p. del Duomo. Open daily 8am-2pm and 3:30-10pm; Oct.-May closed Sun. **Telephone Code:** 089.

Buses: terminal at p. Flavio Gioia, 1 (tel. 87 10 09), at the waterfront. Buses leave regularly for: Sorrento (L3200), Positano (L1600), Salerno (L2400), Ravello (L1500), and other coastal destinations.

Boats: several companies sail from the port near p. Flavio Gioia. Among them, **Gabbiano** propels thrice daily to Cápri June-Sept. (L9000), and to Íschia (L12,500); April 9-May to all locations once daily. To Salerno June-Sept. 4 times daily (L5000). Private boats sail regularly for the Grotta Smeraldo from the docks next to the bus terminal (about L10,000 per person).

Scooter Rental: from the Travel Tourist Office, p. Flavio Gioia, 3 (tel. 87 24 67). L54,000 per day.

Emergencies: tel. 112. **Police:** via Casamare, 19 (tel. 87 10 22).

Accommodations

Staying in Amalfi is a pricey treat. Accommodations fill in August, so reserve at least one month in advance. The best bargain is a stone's throw away in the less crowded village of Atrani.

A'Scalinatella, in Atrani, p. Umberto, 12 (tel. 87 19 30). From Amalfi walk 5min. along the waterfront. Just before you arrive at the tunnel descend the stairs that pass through the Ristorante Zaccaria to the water and take a left. Cross the parking lot and go under the arch into the town's only *piazza.* Follow signs from there. The congenial family that manages this quasi-hostel caters to students and budget travelers. Special *Let's Go* price of L10,000 (L12,500 in Aug.) for bed and bath. Sheets, use of kitchen facilities and washing machines, and towel are extra.

Pensione Proto, salita dei Curiali, 4 (tel. 87 10 03). Take via Lorenzo d'Amalfi from p. Duomo and go right into the tiny alley where you see a sign for the Church of Maria Addolorata. Comfy but run-down rooms. Proto-English spoken. Half-pension required July-Aug. L30,000-35,000 depending on room. June and Sept. singles with bath L14,000, doubles with bath L25,000. Cheaper in off-season.

Hotel Amalfi, via dei Pastai, 3 (tel. 87 24 40), to the left off via Genova as you go uphill. A 3-star establishment with immaculate rooms, attentive management, terraces, and citrus gardens—simply Amalfi's best. All rooms with bath. English spoken. June-Sept. doubles L70,000, with breakfast L80,000. Oct-May doubles L65,000. These are the special *Let's Go* prices, so be sure to mention the book.

Hotel Lidomare, via Piccolomini, 9 (tel. 87 13 32), through the passageway off via Genova across from the *duomo.* Take a left up the flight of stairs, and then go up the steps through the arch on the far right side of the *piazza.* Posh, pristine, and small. Antique lounge sports color TV and piano. Run by a delightful duo. 1 single with bath and breakfast L55,000; Oct.-May L45,000. Doubles with bath and breakfast L80,000-85,000; Oct.-May L75,000. A/C L7000.

Food

Countering the low-quality, high-priced outlets that feed the charter busloads, grocer **N. Anastasio** (tel. 87 10 07) at via Lorenzo d'Amalfi, 32, the street that runs by the *duomo,* provides cold cuts (about L1500-3800 per *etto*) and *passolini,* a regional specialty of plump raisins wrapped in inedible lemon leaves (L2000). Also consider a bottle of *Ravello* wine for L4000-7000. (Open Mon.-Sat. 8am-1:30pm and 4:30-9:30pm, Sun. 8am-1pm; off-season closed Sun.)

Bar Il Tarì, via P. Capuano, near #9 (tel. 87 18 32), on the street that via Genova runs into. Don't let the name or location throw you; the restaurant Il Tarì is a few doors down, but the snack bar is unmarked. Delectable hot and cold food at delectable prices. *Gnocchi* L5000, sandwiches L3500-4000. Wine L5000 per . Open daily 10am-3pm and 7-11:30pm; Nov.-May closed Tues.

Ristorante La Piazzetta, in Atrani on p. Umberto I (tel. 871 930), also unmarked but easy to find on the town's only *piazza.* Special student and *Let's Go* prices of L10,000 for full *menù* including beverage and service. Codfish is their sensational specialty. Run by the same family as A'Scalinatella.

Trattoria La Perla, salita Truglio, 3 (tel. 87 14 40), around the corner from the Hotel Amalfi. Elegant but moderately priced. Terrific seafood. Bounteous *spaghetti al profumo di mare* (with seafood, L9000) and terrific homemade *cannelloni amalfitana* (pasta stuffed with veal and spices, L5000). *Sammarco vino* from Ravello L6000 per bottle. Try mentioning *Let's Go.* Open daily noon-3:30pm and 7pm-midnight; Oct.-May closed Tues.

Bar-Gelateria Royal, via Corenzo d'Amalfi, 10 (tel. 87 19 82), near the *duomo.* The excellent hand-churned ice cream here is Amalfi's best. Their specialty is the *pastiera napoletana,* with bits of Neapolitan Easter fruitcake. Cones L2000-3000. Open daily 11am-2am; Oct.-May closed Mon.

Sights

The town's principal monument is the **duomo,** off via Mansone I, at the top of a long flight of stairs overlooking p. del Duomo. Rebuilt in the 19th century according to the original medieval plan, the incredible cathedral (originally 9th-12th century) boasts a startlingly brilliant façade of varied geometric designs typical of Arab-Norman style, but very unusual in Italy. The bronze doors are exceptional, crafted in Constantinople in 1066. The interior's unusually narrow bays augment its taut elegance. Downstairs, the crypt houses the remains of St. Andrew (all except his head, which the Pope kindly donated to St. Andrew's church in Patras, Greece) and a bronze statue of the apostle sculpted by a pupil of Michelangelo. The two smaller statues on either side are attributed to Bernini's father. (Cathedral open daily 7am-1:30pm and 3-8pm. Appropriate dress required.) To the left of the church the **Chiostro Paradiso** (Cloister of Paradise), a 13th-century cemetery, has become a graveyard for miscellaneous column fragments, broken statues, and sarcophagi. Its Arabic arches create a romantic setting for piano and vocal concerts on Friday and Saturday nights July through September. Tickets cost L8000. (Cloister open daily 9am-1:30pm and 3-8pm. Admission L2000.)

The old 9th-century **arsenal** located on the waterfront by the entrance to the city contains relics of and information on Amalfi's erstwhile maritime glory. Continue up the street to the ceramic laboratory **Ceramiche Giovanna Fusco,** via delle Cartiere, 22, where some of the pottery that saturates p. del Duomo's shops is made before your very eyes. (Open Jan. 7-Aug. 17 and Aug. 26-Dec. 22 Mon.-Sat. 9am-1pm and 3-6pm.) Just before the ceramic lab, several yellow signs point to a path that leads up into one of the treasures of Amalfi, the **Valle dei Mulini** (Valley of the Mills). A short hike up and away from the sea along a stream bed by the old paper mills affords a pastoral view of hillside lemon groves and narrow, rocky mountains.

Near Amalfi: Atrani

Your first excursion from Amalfi should be to **Atrani,** (if you haven't escaped there already), a shimmering beachside town of 1200 inhabitants, a mere 10-minute walk from Amalfi (or 1 bus stop, L800). Nestled in the entrance to a ravine, the **Valley of the Dragons,** Atrani has beachfront with no stairs screened by stunning mountains in the background. The investiture of Amalfi's vacationing doges took place in the town's **Church of San Salvatore dei Birento,** facing you as you enter the town's main archway to the central *piazza.* The church has been remodeled but the 11th-century Byzantine bronze doors are still intact. Thirteenth-century **Santa Maria Maddalena** is also beautiful, with its tiled cupola and gorgeous view of the coast.

As you climb up the main street (via dei Dogi) from the port, **public toilets** are on the left, **phones** are on the right, and the town's best restaurant, **A'Paranza,** crowns the top of the hill on the right.

Ravello

Ravello's origins are shrouded in mystery; it probably began as a Roman refugee camp in the 6th century AD. By the end of the 11th century the town had blossomed to 36,000 inhabitants, whose numbers dwindled progressively as a result of Pisan raids. Today, with a population of 2500, the town has retained the medieval beauty and landscaping prized by Boccaccio, who dedicated part of the *Decameron* to it, and by Wagner, who made it the setting for the second act of *Parsifal.* Whether or not you sense yourself on the brink of a *magnum opus,* it's worth the journey up the mountain. Hike the 7km up from Amalfi for the most spectacular views.

Orientation and Practical Information

Ravello is a short bus ride from Amalfi (every hr., 7am-10pm, L1200). **Piazza Vescovado** hosts most municipal services, while the hotels and restaurants are generally to the left of the *piazza* when you face the *duomo.* The **tourist office,** at p. Vescovado, 13 (tel. 85 70 96), to the left of the cathedral, is very helpful, offering pretty brochures, maps, and up-to-date accommodations information. (Open Mon.-Sat. 8am-8pm, Sun. 8am-2pm; Oct.-April Tues.-Sat. 8am-7pm, Sun.-Mon. 8am-2pm.) To the left of the tourist office is the **post office** (open Mon.-Sat. 8:15am-1:30pm). The **postal code** is 84010. Next along the street is the **pharmacy,** while **public toilets** are to the right of the *duomo* by the corner bar. **Exchange currency** at the **Banca Populare,** via Roma, on the left walking away from the *duomo*. (Open Mon.-Fri. 8:20am-1:15pm.)

Accommodations and Food

> **Hotel Villa Amore** (tel. 85 71 35), en route to Villa Cimbrone. Column-filled niches in the hall-ways and a garden overlooking cliffs and sea make for a special treat. July-Aug. half-pension re-quired at L77,000. June and Sept. singles with bath L48,000, doubles L87,000; Oct.-May singles with bath L41,000, doubles L77,000.

> **Albergo Toro,** via Emanuele Filiberto (tel. 85 72 11), up the street to the left of the tourist office. Clean, comfortable rooms on an oleander-filled side street. Pretty covered terrace, restaurant downstairs. Half-pension July-Aug. L65,500; Oct.-June singles L36,000, with bath L40,000. Doubles L72,000. AmEx.

Several *alimentari* and assorted specialty food shops line via Roma off p. Vescovado. If you're in a mood to be served, however, try **La Colonna,** at via Roma, 20 (tel. 85 78 76). The affable young owner Alfonso speaks English and is well-known throughout the town for his delectable fish and homemade pasta. Try his cheese crêpes (L9000) or ask for his specialty (not listed on the menu), *tagliatelle con melanzane* (pasta with eggplant, L9000). He's also proud of his tasty *tarta capese,* an almond chocolate cake (L5000). (Open Tues.-Sun. noon-2pm and 7-11pm.) If you're taken by the pottery on the tables and walls, visit brother Pasquale's gallery next door.

Ravello decants some of southern Italy's best wines. Three famous types, *Sammarco, Gran Caruso,* and *Episcopio,* are savored around the globe. Pick up a few bottles of *Sammarco* (L4000-5000) at the vineyard's warehouse, **Casa Vinicola Ettore Sammarco,** via Civita, 9 (tel 87 23 89), at the SITA bus stop 3.5km from Amalfi on the road to Ravello. (Open Mon.-Sat. 8am-1pm and 3-7pm, Sun. 8am-1pm.)

Sights

Trees and flowers, small churches, and winding byways enhance the already spectac-ular setting of Ravello's **Villa Rufolo,** perched 360m above the sea. This 11th-century country estate, built by a wealthy Ravellian family, later housed several popes, Charles of Anjou, and the embittered expatriate Wagner, who exclaimed upon seeing it, "The garden of Klingsor is found." Enter through a medieval tower whose beautiful Nor-man-Saracen vault and statues represent the four seasons. Continue on to the famous Moorish cloister, overgrown with flowers and foliage, where the rich polychrome dec-oration retains its original magnificence. (Enter from the bus stop at p. Vescovado. Open daily 9:30am-1pm and 3-7pm, Oct.-May 9:30am-1pm and 2-5pm. Admission L2000.)

Outside Ravello's **duomo** you can see the Amalfi coast's third set of spectacular bronze doors (these 12th-century ones were modeled on Amalfi's). Inside, a simple nave arcade of antique columns sets off two fantastic Cosmatesque pulpits, one large enough to be a separate building. Marble, mosaics, and depictions of curious beasts cover each. A small niche to the right of the high altar contains a reliquary holding the skull of Santa Barbara. To the left of the altar stands the chapel of San Pantaleone, pa-tron of the town, whose "unleakable" blood is preserved in a cracked vessel. (Open dai-ly 9am-1pm and 3-7pm; Oct.-May 9am-1pm.)

Follow the signposts for **Villa Cimbrone** on the small road passing to the right of Villa Rufolo. Floral walkways and gardens are the prelude to some of the most magnif-icent views in all the Amalfi coast. The villa, designed in the 1900s, merits a stroll through its dreamy cloisters. (Admission L3000.)

San Pantaleone was beheaded at Nicomedia on July 27, 290. On this day every year the city holds a **festival** and the saint's blood reputedly liquifies.

Ravello's **classical music festival,** held June 20-30, hosts internationally renowned musicians. Concerts draw crowds to the cathedral and the gardens of Villa Rufolo. Tickets run L12,000-15,000.

Scala

Established in 400 BC by a group of Roman shipwreck victims, Scala lies 1.5km up the hill from Ravello. The tiny little burg spawned both Ravello and Amalfi; unfortunately, those greedy Pisans got to it between 1135 and 1137 and the town has never fully recovered.

Scala faces Ravello from the northwest, dominating the coast from its 400m elevation. Take any of the buses from Amalfi (7am-9pm, L1500) or Ravello (10:30am-9:30pm, L1500). The still air, ebbing mist, and glimmer of the sea behind the cliffs of Ravello below make Scala's inspiring landscape the consummate Amalfi coast image.

Don't be daunted by the unappealing façade of the **cathedral.** Stunning and fully worth a look, this immense structure has three exceptional frescoed plates on its vaulted ceilings. The nave has a tile depiction of Scala's coat of arms, a lion ascending a ladder (logical when you see how high the town is perched). The **Pro Loco** (tel. (089) 85 73 25), in p. Municipio around the corner from the pharmacy, hands out pamphlets (open daily 9am-noon and 5:30-9:30pm). They can also direct you to the **Torre dello Ziro,** the remaining tower in the castle ruins with a lofty panorama of the coast.

After your hike to the tower, savor the views from a table at **Ristorante-Pizzeria Belvedere,** via d'Amata (tel. 85 73 76), in the Campidoglio area of Scala, 1km uphill from the bus stop. The huge plates of *pasta al sugo di pesce* (with fresh seafood, L11,000) confirm your arrival in heaven. (Cover L1500. Service 10%. Open daily noon-3pm and 7pm-midnight; Oct.-March Sat.-Sun. noon-3pm and 7pm-midnight; April-June Thurs.-Tues. noon-3pm and 7pm-midnight.)

Minori

Minori was once Amalfi's arsenal and as such suffered attacks from all of the bigger port's enemies. In these more settled times, however, the city has developed a reputation for its lemons, exported all over the world, and for its beaches and family atmosphere. Accommodations are reasonable, so Minori is a sensible stopover point on your way along the coast.

The coastal SITA bus (L1500) stops right at the center of town, which opens right onto a gravel beach. The **Pro Loco** at p. Umberto I, 18 (tel. (089) 87 70 87 or 87 76 07), is often out of pamphlets. (Open Mon.-Sat. 9am-noon and 4-8pm.)

For lodging, **Albergo Cápri,** via Dietro la Chiesa, 19 (tel. 87 74 17), on the second floor, is a good bet, though far from luxurious. Take the road through Church San Trofimena's bell tower. (Doubles L41,000, with bath L46,000.) The **Caporal Hotel,** via Nazionale (tel. 87 74 08), is a prettier hotel with more professional services. (Doubles with bath and breakfast L57,000.) For a satisfying meal, try **La Botte,** via S. Maria Vetrano, 15 (tel. 87 78 93). The management is accommodating, there are wooden outdoor tables, and the *spaghetti con ronsole* (clam sauce) is splendid (L9000).

Salerno

Home to Europe's first medical school, Salerno was where medieval patients received the latest drugs and submitted to the newest surgical techniques; even today it maintains the intellectual snobbery of a university town. After the picturesque and mountainous coastal villages, the big-city atmosphere and dearth of sights are a shock to the system. Nevertheless, inexpensive accommodations and extensive bus and train connections (Eurail passes are good here) facilitate transit to the Amalfi coast and the archeological sites of Pompeii and Paestum.

Orientation and Practical Information

Salerno is a major stop for trains headed toward Calabria from Rome and Naples. You'll exit the train station onto piazza Veneto, from which the expansive and remarkably clean corso Vittorio Emanuele strikes off to the northwest, leading to via dei Mercanti. Parallel to corso Vittorio Emanuele but closer to the sea, corso Garibaldi runs northwest into via Roma, and southeast into corso Torrione. Closer to the water piazza della Concordia separates lungomare Trieste from lungomare Marconi to the southeast.

Tourist Office: EPT (tel. 23 14 32), on p. Ferrovia to the right as you leave the train station. Maps and pamphlets on the Amalfi coast. *Memo* is an excellent guide to Salerno's *alberghi*, with map, bus schedule, and entertainment listings. The helpful employees speak English. Open Mon.-Fri. 8:30am-2pm and 3-8pm, Sat. 8:30am-1pm and 3-7pm. **AAST**, p. Amendola, 8 (tel. 32 07 93), across from via Roma, 232. Information on Salerno itself. Open Mon.-Fri. 9am-1pm and 4:30-7pm, Sat. 9am-noon.

Budget Travel: CTS, corso Vittorio Emanuele, 22. Student IDs and special fares.

Post Office: corso Garibaldi, 203 (tel. 22 41 54), at via dei Principati. Open Mon.-Sat. 8:30am-7:30pm. **Postal Code:** 84100.

Telephones: SIP, corso Garibaldi, 31/2, set in from the street to the left as you leave the train station. Open daily 8:15am-8pm. **Telephone Code:** 089.

Trains: in p. Ferrovia (tel. 23 14 15), behind p. Veneto. Trains depart regularly 5am-11pm to Pompeii (40min., L2400) and Naples (1hr., L4300). Also several trains to Paestum on the Salerno-Règgio di Calabria line (45min., L3200).

Buses: SITA, corso Garibaldi, 117 (tel. 22 66 04). Information office open Mon.-Sat. 8am-1pm and 4:30-8pm. Buses to Naples (every 10-15min. 6am-9pm, L4300) leave from corso Garibaldi outside SITA information office. Buses for the Amalfi coast depart from p. della Concordia: Amalfi (frequent buses 6am-10:30pm, L2400); Sorrento (9 per day 6am-7pm, L5000) with stops at the coastal towns of Praiano (L3200) and Positano (L3900). Buses run less frequently Sun. **ATAC** (tel. 22 58 99) city bus #41 leaves regularly from outside the train station to Pompeii (every 20min. 5:55am-9:55pm, 30min., L2800). Several bus lines run from p. Concordia to Paestum (direction "Sapri," L4000).

Swimming Pool: Piscina Comunale Torrione, lungomare Marconi (tel. 23 90 41), across the street from the fort-like structure. Admission L5400, under 14 L3800, Sunday L6500 and L5000. Open June-Sept. daily 10am-4pm.

Emergencies: tel. 113. **Police:** tel. 23 18 19. **Hospital: Ospedale Ruggi d'Aragona,** via San Leonardo (tel. 75 00 22). **Medical Assistance:** tel. 30 19 99.

Accommodations

The hotel supply is just adequate: nothing more, nothing less. Establishments fill rapidly in late July and August, so arrive early in the morning to secure a place.

Ostello della Gioventù "Irno" (HI), via Luigi Guercia, 112 (tel. 79 02 51). Exit the train station and make a left. Via Torrione runs along the tracks. After about 300m you'll come to via Mobilio which will take you left under the tracks. Approximately 300m more and you'll see a staircase on your right leading up to via Luigi Guercia. Clean rooms, kitchen facilities, TV room and gentle management—who could ask for anything more? Curfew midnight. Lock-out 10:30am-5:00pm. L15,000 per person, L2000 for sheets. Ask at desk for directions to eateries which offer special prices to hostel clientele.

Pensione Fabio Rossetti, lungomare Marconi, 18 (tel. 22 64 46). Take the *lungomare* east and keep your eyes peeled for a white building down by the beach. There's a small road leading down to it (on your right). Industrious family is getting this place together. Spiffy rooms, all with telephone. Top floor with balcony and larger rooms L25,000 per person. Bottom floor L20,000 per person. Morning coffee and kitchen use included.

Albergo Cinzia, corso Vittorio Emanuele, 74 (tel. 23 27 73), down the street from Santa Rosa. Chintz galore. One single L20,000. Doubles L40,000. Make reservations for July and Aug.

Albergo Santa Rosa, corso Vittorio Emanuele, 14 (tel. 22 53 46), off the *piazza* in front of the train station. Clean, bright, and a bargain. English spoken. Curfew 12:30am. Singles L30,000. Doubles L45,000.

Hotel Salerno, via Vicinanza, 42 (tel. 22 42 11). The sign's across the street from Albergo Santa Rose. Furniture was new in the 50s and hasn't died yet. Singles L28,000, with bath L31,000. Doubles L43,000, with bath L50,000.

Food

Salerno lays claim to no dish in particular but partakes of the general Campanian culinary genius, serving delightful specialties like *pasta e fagioli* (pasta and bean soup) and all sorts of seafood-based treats. Nearby Battipaglia produces the famous *mozzarella alla buffala,* fresh mozzarella cheese made from water buffalo's milk. Shop cheap at **Supermercato STANDA,** corso Vittorio Emanuele, 228 (open Mon.-Tues. and Thurs.-Sat. 9am-1pm and 4-8pm, Wed. 9am-1pm).

Pizzeria Ristorante Fonzie, via S. Mobilio 22 (tel. 239 208). Richie, Potsie and the gang cook up excellent, very inexpensive food on the way to the hostel. Delicious mini-pizzas L1000. Open 12:30-2:30pm and 4:30pm-midnight.

Pizzeria Del Vicolo della Neve, vicolo della Neve, 24 (tel. 22 57 05). Take the side street that intersects with via Roma before #160; go right and then right again. In the old city, this piece of Salernitan history hasn't changed since its opening 500 years ago. Try traditional dishes like *baccalà in cassuola* (salt cod with tomatoes, oregano, and oil, L7000) or *giambotta* (a mix of potatoes, eggplant, and peppers, L5000). Cover L2000. Service 12%. Open Thurs.-Tues. 8pm-3am.

Trattoria-Pizzeria Da "Sasà" La Casereccia, via Diaz, 42, off corso Vittorio Emanuele. Black chairs and pink tablecloths demonstrate that this popular restaurant can accessorize. Full meals of delicous fish L15,000-25,000. Cover L2000. Open Mon.-Thurs. and Sat. noon-3pm and 8-10:30pm, Sun. noon-3pm.

Ristorante Il Caminetto, via Roma, 232 (tel. 22 96 14). Across the street from the tourist office. A family-run restaurant that keeps its prices low. Savor *risotto alla pescatore,* a delicious mix of rice and seafood, for only L7000. Pizzas bake in the wood-burning oven at night (L4500-7000). *Gragnano wine* L5000 per . Cover L2000. Service 12%. Open Thurs.-Tues. noon-3:30pm and 7pm-midnight.

Sights and Entertainment

Taking via Molo Manfredi off of the Villa Comunale at the western end of via Roma, you can stroll onto the seawall that juts into the bay. Once there, revel in the divine Amalfi coastline and in the sights and sounds of the nearby fishing harbor. Unfortunately, Salerno's sea is filthy. To swim in the area either wear a wetsuit, or hop over to another town on the Amalfi coast—the hamlet of **Vietri sul Mare** is closest (take the SITA bus toward Sorrento, 15min., L1500).

For a spectacular view of Salerno's majestic environs, take bus #19 from Teatro Verdi (L1000), west of the Villa Comunale, to the medieval **Castello di Arechi,** which dates from the 8th century. (Open daily 9am-1pm and 3-6pm. Free.) Back at city level, visit Salerno's medieval quarter. Walk along corso Vittorio Emanuele until it fades into narrow via dei Mercanti. The medieval city won acclaim in its day as capital of the Norman empire (1077-1127) and home of Europe's oldest medical school. (Ninth-century codices were already calling it ancient.) Watched over by a 12th-century Norman tower, the **cathedral,** built between 1076 and 1085 by decree of the Norman leader Robert Guiscard, honors Salerno's patron saint, San Matteo. An ancient pool lies in the center of its colorful atrium. The revered tooth, the holy tooth, and nothing but the tooth of San Matteo awaits worship in the crypt. (Cathedral open daily 9:30am-12:30pm and 4-7pm.)

Don't miss the Sunday evening *passeggiata* when the *lungomare* overflows with people strolling and enjoying ice cream. In June, July, and August, an **arts festival** features free concerts and drama in the atrium of the cathedral and at the city's stadium. Salerno also hosts an **international film festival** in October at Cinema Capitol in the center of the city (admission L6000).

The area around Salerno rocks with throttling and throbbing discos. June through September, the nighttime hotspot is the renowned **Fuenti** (tel. 21 09 33), in the locality of Cetara, 4km west of Salerno. Uniquely situated on the coastal cliffs, it features three full floors of open-air dancing. Hot hot hot. (Cover L15,000, first drink included. Open Sat.-Sun. 10pm-4am.) In the winter, Salerno lives it up at **Living,** via Gelsi Rossi (tel. 39 92 01), northeast of the train station in the city center. (Open Oct.-May Thurs.-Fri. 8:30pm-2am, Sat. 9:30pm-3am, and Sun. 6:30pm-3am. Free, except Sat.-Sun. cover L15,000, first drink included.)

Paestum

Paestum's ruins rise up in an open field amid flowers and wild grasses. Founded in the 7th century BC as Poseidonia by a group of Greek colonists from Síbari (near Crotone in the Ionian Sea), Paestum quickly grew into a flourishing commercial center, enjoying an expansive trade with the Etruscans and the lands to the north. Conquered in the 4th century BC by native Italians, it revived under Roman rule with the addition of baths, forums, and amphitheaters. Decline set in when the extension of the Appian Way to the Adriatic allowed Rome to bypass Tyrrhenian trade routes. Recurrent malaria epidemics and Saracen raids during the 9th century hastened the city's demise. A final takeover by malarial mosquitoes saved the city from further raiding but also cancelled possibilities for future rehabitation.

Hotels and restaurants lie north and south of the site. It's most convenient to stay in Salerno, only an hour away and connected by frequent buses and trains. Buses on the Salerno-Sapri line leave from p. Concordia, near the Salerno train station, about every half-hour (first bus at 5:45am); trains run about every two hours. The last bus back to Salerno leaves at 8:10pm, the last train at 9:30pm. Both cost about L2800. Nunzio Daniele's *Paestum: Hypothesis and Reality* earns the *Let's Go* seal of approval.

The three major temples lie along the **via Sacra.** The **basilica** (6th century BC) dedicated to Hera is thought to be the oldest, based on its archaic form. The temple is extremely wide (9 columns across—even the Parthenon is only 6), and the tapering of its columns so extreme that it makes the temple's outer colonnade seem to lean outward on both sides. The neighboring **Temple of Neptune** (450 BC) is the largest, most intact Doric structure in the city. The six-by-fourteen column plan is responsible for the long, graceful form. In contrast to the basilica, a slight upward curving of the temple floor corrects the optical illusion that the columns sag outward. Sit facing Neptune on the far wall of the basilica for a remarkable view of this petrified forest of columns. In front of the temples lie the remains of large altars, an imposing block of limestone in front of the basilica, and two basins (the small one Roman and the other Greek). At the opposite end of the grounds, past the forum and amphitheater, stands the small **Temple of Ceres** (circa 500 BC), whose Ionic capitals now grace the museum. Sacrificial altars wallow in front of the temple, and to the right towers a lone votive column.

The **museum** (tel. (0828) 81 10 23), outside the temple grounds on the other side of via Aquila, displays a fascinating collection of sculpture, architectural fragments, terracottas, and unusual tomb paintings hailing from Paestum and excavations in the nearby plain of Sele.

Visit the site early in the morning, when silence and stillness reign. (Temple grounds open daily until 2hr. before sunset. Admission to both museum and site L10,000.)

In July and August, Paestum hosts its own international festival of music, drama, and dance. For a program and information, contact the **tourist office** on via Aquila (tel. (0828) 81 10 16; open Mon.-Sat. 8am-2pm).

A popular beach lies about 2km east of the temples, sprinkled with several campgrounds. **FLIC** (tel. (0828) 81 12 91) rents spots with electricity and running water for L9000 (July-Aug. L15,000) plus L4000 per person (July-Aug. L5400). Nearby **Villaggio Desiderio** (tel. 85 11 35 or 72 50 24) has a pool and markets. (July-Aug. L8000 per person; Sept.-June L4000 per person. Use of pool L7500.)

Apulia (Puglia)

The heel of Italy's boot, Apulia has paid the price for its strategic location relative to the East. The region fell prey to a variety of predators as a key point of European offensives and the first point of attack from the Muslim world. Apulia's fertile, flat territory is especially valuable for its position on the thirsty, rocky Mediterranean coast. The ancient Greeks left few traces of their stay here, but made Apulia one of the flourishing regions of Magna Graecia. For the Romans, the area was an outlet to half the Empire; the Appian Way led to now-dismal Bríndisi. The Middle Ages brought an onslaught of invaders (Normans, Lombards, Saracens, and Goths), whose combined and conflicting influences created a fantastic conglomerate culture. In fact, the single most important Apulian and the best representative of interfusion was originally a foreign invader: Frederick II of Swabia (1220-1280), eccentric and enlightened, left dozens of castles and established the region as a center of medieval culture. His half-Muslim, half-Italian court, parading through Apulia with elephants, eunuchs, Arab scholars, and dancing girls, was the scandal of Europe, the *stupor mundi* (wonder of the world). After Frederick's death and his son Manfred's defeat, the conquering French sent forth a slew of barons to squeeze the wealth out of Apulia. Their successors, the Spanish Habsburgs, wrung the last bits of lucre from the increasingly improverished region, leaving behind an extensive and unique Baroque architectural presence.

Modern Apulia, having served its time on skid row, is regaining its prominence as the richest and most educated region in the *mezzogiorno*. In Apulia's interior, whitewashed, cone-roofed *trulli* houses and remote medieval villages dot a cave-ridden plain; along the shore, ports conjure up an Eastern air. The region's diverse landscape also endears, from the forested Gargàno Massif and the fertile chessboard plain to the Grecian Salentine Peninsula. Unfortunately, the Spanish and the barbarians left a legacy of *machismo* which women may find threatening, especially in the large cities. In public, pointed obliviousness or a withering insult is usually sufficient to dissuade continued obnoxious behavior.

Apulia is as accessible to contemporary tourists as it was to ancient invaders. Direct train lines run from Naples to Bari and from Bologna to Lecce. **Rail service** is supplemented within the region by the private Ferrovie Bari-Nord, Ferrovie Del Sud-Est, Ferrovie del Gargàno, and Ferrovie Calabro-Lucane lines. If you hold a Eurailpass or *cartaverde*, remember that the plastic has no power on these lines. The transportation hubs of Fóggia, Bríndisi, and Táranto are perhaps best viewed from the station as you make your connections; base yourself in Bari and Lecce instead. Bari, the end-point for two of the private rails, and home of the miraculous "Stop-Over in Bari" program, is unbeatable as a budget base from which to explore the small sea towns, *trulli* houses, obscure castles, assorted ruins, and limestone caves of central Apulia. Stay in dizzyingly Baroque Lecce while exploring the Salentine Peninsula in the far south, and plan on reserving some time for the virgin forests and white cliffs of less accessible Gargàno Massif, the spur of Italy's boot. Public transport in Apulia is not always a paragon of convenience and dependability; unless you've got wheels, flexibility is imperative. But if you come with a plan, tolerance, and curiosity, Apulia will reward you richly.

Fóggia

Fóggia is one of the few Italian cities where architectural modernity is not synonymous with monstrosity. Its broad streets and ample gardens are spacious, well-proportioned, and pleasant.

Fóggia's no doubt a nice place to live, but you wouldn't want to visit there. Nevertheless, its position at the cross-tracks of the Naples-Bari and Bologna-Lecce train lines makes it the logical point of departure for the beautiful terrain of the Gargàno peninsula, and for easy daytrips to the medieval cities of Lucera and Troia.

Orientation and Practical Information

Viale XXIV Maggio leads from the train and bus station to **piazza Cavour;** to the right, **via Lanza** runs to **piazza Giordano,** continuing as **corso Vittorio Emanuele,** which leads to the **old quarter.**

Tourist Office: EPT, via Perrone, 17 (tel. 236 50), a 10min. walk from p. Giordano. From the station, follow viale XXIV Maggio straight past p. Cavour to corso Giannone, take the 3rd left onto via Cirillo, which becomes via Bari, then take a right just before the gas station. Or take bus MD. Or don't bother at all—they have little information about Fóggia. Open Mon.-Fri. 8am-2pm, Tues. also 3:30-7:30pm.

Currency Exchange: Banca Nazionale del Lavoro, via della Repubblica, 18 (tel. 79 94). Standard rates, no commission, long waits. Security system à la Star Trek. Open Mon.-Fri. 8:20am-1:20pm for exchanges; 3-4:30pm for other transactions.

Post Office: viale XXIV Maggio, 30 (tel. 211 33), about 3 blocks from the station. Open Mon.-Sat. 8:15am-7:10pm. **Postal Code:** 71100.

Telephones: SIP, via Contę Appiano, 14-18, near p. Cavour. Open daily 8am-9pm. **Telephone Code:** 0881.

Buses: SITA, p. Veneto (tel. 236 18), across the *piazza,* to the left of the station. To: Vieste (6 per day, 3hr., L6900), Monte Sant'Angelo (7 per day, 1hr. 30min., L4300), and Campobasso (3 per day, 2hr., L6300). **ATAF,** information at via Isonzo, 35 (tel. 724 91), the 4th right off viale XXIV Maggio coming from the station. Board buses at p. Veneto, to the right of the station. To Troia (every hr., 45min., round-trip L3600). **Ferrovie dello Stato,** to Lucera (every hr., 30min., round-trip L2800). Buy your ticket in the train station.

Accommodations and Food

Many of Fóggia's cheaper *pensioni* huddle together near the station, particularly on **via Monfalcone,** two blocks from p. Veneto. For cheap hunger busters, a **STANDA supermarket** (groceries downstairs) beckons from corso Vittorio Emanuele, 55. (Open Mon.-Fri. 8:30am-1pm and 4:45-8:30pm, Sat. 8:30am-1pm.)

Albergo Centrale, corso Cairoli, 5 (tel. 67 18 62). From the station, follow viale XXIV Maggio to p. Cavour, then turn right on via Lanza and bear left after p. Giordano onto corso Cairoli. Luxurious rooms are the result of a 350-million-lire renovation project. Help the charming proprietor make back the investment. Singles L21,000-25,000, with bath L30,000. Doubles L42,000-46,000, with bath L54,000. Triples L63,000, with bath L75,000. Reduce the price by selling foreign coins to the owner.

Hotel Asi, via Monfalcone, 1 (tel. 62 33 27 or 62 33 28). A grand entrance lobby, but the elegance of the 1930s has faded into dinginess. Kind manager is extremely proud of his elevator. Singles L33,000, with bath L43,000. Doubles L62,000, with bath 72,000. Triples L85,000, with bath L95,000. Discounts for "workers and students" (25% off rooms without bath, 10% off rooms with bath).

Ristorante del Cacciatore, via Pietro Mascagni, 12 (tel. 200 31), off the end of corso Vittorio Emanuele. More than just a restaurant, this establishment also lets yummy, fresh rooms. Singles with bath L30,000. Doubles with bath L55,000. Full pension L75,000. Streamline your plans by **dining** in air-conditioned luxury downstairs. Delicious homemade *tagliatelle verdi* (spinach noodles) L6000. *Secondi* L9500-10,500. *Menù* L18,000, including L1500 cover and 10% service. Open Mon.-Sat. noon-3pm and 7:30-10pm.

Trattoria Santa Lucia, via Trieste, 57. Loving service and delicious meals. *Pasto completo* includes *primo, secondo,* beverage, fruit, vegetable, cover, and service (about L20,000). *Menù* L17,000. Open Mon.-Sat. noon-3:30pm and 6:30-10:30pm.

Risorante Cinese Ton Fen, via Piave, 60 (tel. 67 02 12). Luckily, the province's only Chinese family is composed of genial and talented ambassadors of good cuisine. Four steamed dumplings L3000. Entrees L5000-9000. *Menùs* L12,000, 15,000, and 20,000. Cover L2000. Open Wed.-Mon. noon-3pm and 7:30pm-midnight.

Sorrento Cucina Casalinga, via Trieste, 37. A great little find. *Menù* L15,000. Try the *pasta e ceci* (pasta with chick peas) and *frittura di pesce* (fried fish). Open daily noon-4pm and 7-11pm.

Sights

Fóggia's historic interest doesn't extend much beyond the **duomo,** now embellished by an overscaled Baroque tower added after a 1731 earthquake. World War II bombardment revealed an interesting Pisan-style arcade along the church's lower flanks, probably dating from a 14th-century restoration. The church, constructed in 1155, retains its original Romanesque crypt. (From p. Cavour, take a right onto via Lanza, then another right at p. Giordano onto corso Vittorio Emanuele.) The open *loggia* at p. de Sanctis, 88, across from the cathedral, and a few remaining pilasters on nearby via Arpi are all that's left of Renaissance Fóggia.

The city's ancient past can be relived at the **Museo Civico** off the end of via Zara on via della Repubblica. Well-organized displays exhibit vases, ceramics, figurines, and coins from the two nearby archeological sites of Arpi and Sipontum.

Lucera

Thirty minutes from Fóggia, **Lucera** surmounts a high plateau, its enormous castle dominating the region for miles. In the 13th century the ubiquitous Frederick II populated a defunct Roman township with 20,000 Sicilian Saracen mercenaries, who clad the city in Islamic architecture. Fifty years later, Lucera fell to Charles of Anjou. He added 140 families from Provence who tore down mosques and built a series of Gothic churches. The two groups continued to coexist for another few decades, until King Charles II decided to massacre the Arabs and give the town the short-lived, ironic name "City of St. Mary."

To enter the old city, pass through the archway in front of the bus stop. Follow the routes marked by the yellow signs to the castle and Lucera's other sights. The **cathedral,** one of the great architectural creations of medieval Apulia, was begun by Charles II of Anjou in 1300 to commemorate the slaughter of the Saracens. Inspect the nearby 14th-century **Church of San Francesco,** a Lombard-French barn which houses Gothic and Baroque frescoes. (Both open daily 8am-noon and 5-8pm.)

Behind the cathedral is the **Museo Civico.** A guide will whisk you past Roman coins, Arab pottery, antique marble, and other artifacts excavated in Lucera. The **tourist office** dozes in the same courtyard. (Both open Tues. and Fri. 9am-1pm and 4-7pm, Wed.-Thurs. 8am-1pm, Sat.-Sun. 9am-1pm. Museum admission L1000.) The pentagonal medieval **castle,** built by Frederick II in 1230, more than 1km in circumference, is topped by 24 towers, almost all intact. The castle commands a fine view of the fertile plain below, known as the Tavoliere (chessboard). (Castle open Tues.-Sun. same hours as museum. Free.) Buy groceries on the way and throw a picnic in Fred's honor.

The **Anfiteatro Romano,** built for Augustus in the first century BC, rests at the foot of the hills in the eastern end of the city. Underbrush now covers its terraced stands. In April, the amphitheater hosts stagings of the Passion. (Open Tues.-Sun. 7am-1pm and 2-8pm. Free.)

Lucera sports only two hotels. **Albergo Al Passetto,** p. del Popolo, 28 (tel. 94 11 24), is a pleasant joint built into the old city wall. (Singles with bath L31,000. Doubles with bath L45,000. Adequate meals start at L20,000. Under renovation in summer of 1992.) **Hotel Gioia** (tel. 94 52 07 or 94 52 24), is nearby at viale Ferrovia, 15. Here you can find singles for L31,000 (with bath L35,000), and doubles for L49,000 (with bath L55,000). Full pension L50,000, half-pension L40,000. Groups may get a discount.

Southwest of Lucera is the old town of **Troia.** Formerly the Daunian village of Aecae, it later fell into the hands of several of the rich, famous, and debauched, including Hannibal and Emperor Fabius Maximus. Some of the remains of the ancient settlement reside in the **Museo Civico,** but most are still hobnobbing with the earthworms. The most significant to-do in Troia is the **cathedral,** one of the prime Romanesque edifices in southern Italy, complete with Byzantine bronze doors and the most fantastic rose window in the south. Yearning for festivities? Troia honors five of its favorite saints with several days of fireworks and games in mid-July.

The Gargàno Massif

The Gargàno Massif once ranked among the most popular pilgrimage destinations in Europe: the Archangel Michael was said to have appeared here in a cave here in the 5th century, and in ancient times the same cavern was occupied by a respected dream oracle. In these more secular times, the peninsula is renowned for the 65km of beaches on the northern and eastern coasts, some of the best in continental Italy. The inland is covered by the **Foresta Umbra,** which shelters some of Italy's rare old-growth stands. The forest abruptly gives way to classic Mediterranean terrain on the southern half. The

Gargàno is succumbing to the twin blights of southern coastal areas—smokestacks and beach umbrellas—so visit the region soon, before it becomes an industrial tract interrupted by the occasional *villagio turistico.*

Manfredónia

Manfredónia's waterfront reeks of rotting fish, but this factory town could serve as a possible base for exploring the southern coast and Monte Sant'Angelo. From Fóggia, you can reach Manfredónia by taking either a **SITA** bus (every 2hr. until 5:25pm, 45min.), or one of the many **Ferrovie dello Stato** trains (9 per day, 30min., L2800). The **tourist office,** corso Manfredi, 26 (tel. 219 98), off p. Marconi, has up-to-date bus and boat information. English spoken. Walk to the right from the train station 10 minutes on viale Aldo Moro. (Open Mon.-Sat. 8:30am-1:30pm.) The town's only cheap hotel, **Albergo Santa Maria,** p. D'Acquisto, 14 (tel. 224 65), off p. Marconi, offers antiseptic green singles for L30,000, doubles for L40,000. Eat cheap on the beach at **Pizzeria Capriccio,** viale Miramare, 6 (tel. 271 57), past the castle. (Pizza L3000-7000; cover L2000. Open daily noon-3pm and 7pm-midnight.) The **telephone code** for Manfredónia and environs is 0884.

Siponto

Three km southwest of Manfredónia, the ancient city of Siponto was abandoned after a 12th-century earthquake and plague. The sole survivor is the remarkable **Church of Santa Maria di Siponto,** which stands in a grove of pines amidst modest pre-Roman ruins. Built during the 11th century in Puglian-Romanesque style, the church's blind arcade shows strong Pisan influence, while the square plan and cupola also point to Byzantine roots. Siponto is the next-to-last stop on the Fóggia-Manfredónia train line.

Monte Sant'Angelo

The most impressive town in the Gargàno interior is Monte Sant'Angelo, a pilgrim's haven hugging a narrow 240m precipice. Ropes of garlic hang against doors where eyelet curtains flutter in the sunlight; in the evening, old women sell fresh oregano and chick-peas on streets that a few hours earlier held only the echo of church bells. The town is most famous for its **Santuario di San Michele** (St. Michael's Sanctuary). In the 5th century, the area's lord, who bore the now-unfortunate name Elvis Emanuel, lost his prize bull. He eventually found the bull kneeling before a dark, inaccessible cavern, previously shunned by superstition. The Archangel Michael subsequently appeared and commanded Elvis to consecrate the cave to Christianity. Note the inscription above the entrance: "Horribilis est locus iste" ("this place is horrible"), which reveals both the pagan superstition and the medieval view of the avenging angel. Enter the **grotto** through handsome 11th-century bronze doors wrought with biblical scenes. Inside, a Gothic vestibule (1273) spills into a dripping cavern. Behind the altar, a wooden canopy supported by four antique columns covers a small fountain (actually just an opening in the rocks) said to possess miraculous powers at certain times of the day. (Open daily 8:30am-noon and 2:30-7pm. The hours of the fountain's "mysterious powers" are unknown to mere mortals.)

Across from the upper entrance of San Michele stands the **Tomba di Rotari** (Tomb of Rotharis), actually a 12th- or 13th-century baptistry, whose odd elliptical dome complements the weird carvings on the walls. Exiting San Michele, above and to the right you'll see a **Norman castle** dating from the late 1400s; modeled on Frederick II's Castel del Monte (see below), it supports the octagonal "Giant's Tower." (Castle closed to the public.) Follow the signs to the left of San Michele and visit the **Museo Tancredi** (tel. 620 98), which displays a carefully arranged collection of folk art and tools from Gargàno. (Open Tues.-Sat. 8am-2pm and 2:30-8pm, Sun. 10am-12:30pm and 2-7pm, Mon. 8am-2pm. Admission L1000.)

The only place to stay in Monte Sant'Angelo is **Albergo Moderno** (tel. 613 31), where comfortable, quiet singles go for L25,000, and doubles for L50,000. You can take the **SITA** bus to Monte Sant'Angelo (30min., L1500). Three buses per day (Mon.-Sat.) run directly from Fóggia to Monte Sant'Angelo (1hr. 30min., L4300).

Farther north spreads the beautiful **Foresta Umbra** (Shady Forest). The isolated forest is extraordinarily peaceful except on Sunday, when it becomes a picnic area for Fóggian families. Unfortunately, Umbra is difficult to reach by public transport. **SITA** buses leave Manfredónia daily at 11:15am and 1:10pm and take one hour to reach the intersection in the middle of the forest on their way to Vico del Gargàno. (July 15-Aug. 31, 4 buses per day go to the forest from Peschici; see below.) Routes are highly seasonal and subject to cancellation; check at the bar in p. Marconi, Manfredónia, or at the Edicola Millecose in Peschici on via XXIV Maggio for precise information. Hitchhikers find the going to be slow; the Vico-Monte Sant'Angelo road is busy enough, but the road to Vieste (30km away) is trafficked only on Sundays, when tourists flood the place.

Vieste

The touristed seaside town of Vieste lies opposite a rocky promontory, the "pizzomunno" or "tip of the world," which forms a natural harbor. According to legend, the site originally was home to an anonymous fishing village inhabited by the handsome fisherman Pizzomunno and the beautiful maiden Vieste. The nearby Sirens (of *Odyssey* fame), jealous of Pizzomunno's love for Vieste, drowned her in the abyss. Pizzomunno turned into white stone, petrified by sorrow; every hundred years, the lovers come to life for one night (tickets L50,000). While Vieste's graceful authenticity abides in spite of the suntanned masses, a certain frivolity undermines the legend.

Orientation and Practical Information

There are two ways of getting to Vieste, and both are picturesque. If you're coming from the north on the Bologna-Lecce line, get off at San Severo and catch the Ferrovie del Gargàno train to Peschici; a bus continues to Vieste (San Servo-Vieste, 3hr.). A direct Ferrovie del Gargàno **bus** from San Severo to Vieste leaves daily at noon (3hr. 30min.). **SITA** buses run from the south to Vieste from Fóggia via Manfredónia (6 per day, 3hr., L6900). The **centro** lies a 10-minute walk down viale XXIV Maggio from the bus stop at p. Manzoni.

Tourist Office: p. Kennedy, 1 (tel. 70 88 06). From the bus stop, walk up viale XXIV Maggio, which becomes corso Mazzini. Bear left at the end onto viale Italia. Tables piled with tourist guides, maps, and practical information on Vieste. English affably spoken. Open Mon.-Sat. 8am-2pm and 4-10pm, Sun. 8:30am-1pm; Sept. 21-June 21 Mon.-Fri. 8am-1:30pm and 3:30-9:30pm, Sun. 8:30am-1pm.

Post Office: via Veneto (tel. 70 80 00), next to the public gardens. Open Mon.-Fri. 8:15am-6:30pm, Sat. 8:15am-noon. **Postal Code:** 71019.

Telephone Code: 0884.

Buses: schedules are posted in the kiosk at the bus stop. **Ferrovia del Gargàno,** tel. (0882) 32 14 14. Buy tickets at one of the *agenzie* in p. Vittorio Emanuele. **SITA,** tel. (0881) 731 17. Buy tickets on the bus.

Ferries: to the Trémiti Islands daily (see Trémiti Islands below).

Emergencies: tel. 113. **Police:** tel. 70 62 22.

Accommodations and Food

Vieste is a summer resort without budget provisions. If you plan to visit between mid-July and August, make reservations or be prepared to dance 'til dawn. Prices change monthly in summer, peaking in August. For information on the **Agriturismo** program, which places tourists at local farms, call 762 04. Rates vary according to season and participants.

Pensione Al Centro Storico, via Mafrolla, 32 (tel. 70 70 30), at the end of via Pola. From the bus stop take viale XXIV Maggio to p. Vittorio Emanuele, which leads to via Pola. A splendid old *palazzo* kept spotless by the peachiest proprietor in Vieste. She'll give you keys to come and go as you please. Singles L30,000, doubles L45,000. Prices go up by L6000 in July and even more in August. Delicious breakfast included.

Albergo Riviera, via IV Novembre, 2 (tel. 70 50 00), off via Veneto. Fastidiously kept. Airy, spartan lodgings. Singles L30,000, doubles with bath L35,000; off-season, singles L20,000-25,000, doubles L25,000-30,000.

Pensione Giada, lungomare Europa, 18 (tel. 70 74 79), on the north beach. From the bus station take viale XXIV Maggio, make a quick left onto via Tommaseo, and walk to the end of the street. Turn left and down to the sea, then turn on to lungomare Europa. Large rooms with double beds, modern baths, and balconies. Charming owner. Doubles with bath L65,000.

Camping: More than 80 campsites line the beaches north and south of the city. Call ahead to check for vacancies. **Apeneste** (tel. 70 51 91), off lungomare Mattei. L6500 per person, L7000 per small tent, Ll6,500 per large tent; July-Aug. 20 L7000 per person, L7500 per small tent, L18,500 per large tent. Open June-Sept. **Baia degli Aranci** (tel. 70 65 91), on lungomare Europa, 1km from town. A large site among evergreens and olive groves. L3000-7900 per person, L5000-14,000 per tent. Open May 11-Oct. 5.

Around the old town, restaurants occupy basements and stuccoed corners, while a daily produce **market** on viale XXIV Maggio near the bus station supplies the less table-inclined. At night, wooden carts selling nuts and candies line the streets of **La Villa,** specializing in *torrone* (nougat with hazelnuts). Stock up at the **supermarket** on v. XXIV Maggio near the bus station. (Open Mon.-Wed. and Fri. 8am-1pm and 5-8pm, Thurs. 8am-1pm, Sat. 8am-1pm and 5-9pm.)

La Ripa, near the *duomo.* Pricey tourist-trap appearance is just a guise; 3 generations of women serve *troccoli al sugo di seppia* (long, canoe-shaped noodles in cuttlefish ink, L5000) and *cozze piriene* (stuffed mussels, L7000). Other *secondi* L4500-L8000. Cover L1500. Open May-Oct. 1-2:30pm and 7:30pm-midnight.

Locanda La Macina, via Alessandro III, 49, at the foot of the *duomo.* One of Vieste's best dining experiences can be had at outdoor wooden tables between 2 400-year-old walls. Entrees start at L6000. Open daily 12:30-2pm and 6-11pm.

Ristorante Box 19, via Santa Maria di Merino, 19 (tel. 70 52 29), off corso Mazzini, near lungomare Europa. The town favorite. Pasta dishes L4500-6000. Try the *melanzane ripiene* (stuffed eggplant) L6000. Wine L4500 per . Cover L1500. Service 10%. Open daily noon-3pm and 7pm-midnight.

Il Fornaio, corso Mazzini, 12, at the end of the street. For Vieste's cheapest and most satisfying meal, partake of the *panzerotti* (deep-fried dough filled with cheese and tomatoes, made fresh every 10min., L1000). Open daily 8am-midnight.

Sights and Entertainment

In southern Vieste, at the end of via Battisti, the buildings of the well-preserved old town crowd up against the *duomo* in seeming adoration. Architecturally, the weathered **duomo** is the embodiment of understatement. Near the entrance note the wooden statue of Santa Maria; legend has it that the statue sweats, but one can't be sure. From the *duomo,* head southeast on via Cimaglia to the **Chianca Amara,** a rock where in 1554 the lives and bodies of thousands of *Viestini* were cut short by Turks. A **castle** rising from the town's summit offers a tremendous view of the Gargàno coast. Join the massive swarm of people in Vieste's popular *passeggiata,* which passes around the **Giardini Pubblici Vittorio Veneto** and **corso Lorenzo Fazzini.** Of Vieste's three **beaches,** the southern beach, **Pizzomunno,** parallel to lungomare Mattei, is the freshest (a.k.a. spiaggia della Scialara or del Castello). To get to the beaches of postcard fame, however, you must travel farther up or down the coast. Throughout this area, the water is so clear that you can see to the sandy bottom for hundreds of feet out from the shore.

The best way to see the famed Gargàno coastline is to take a two hour 30 minute motorboat excursion from Vieste to the local **grottos.** Boats depart from the port daily in summer at 8:30am and at 2:30pm if enough people show (L15,000, under 12 L7000). Buy tickets at hotels or at any of the ubiquitous kiosks.

Worthwhile Vieste festivals include that in honor of **San Giorgio** in late April, featuring a procession, fireworks, and a horse race on the beach; the **Festival of Santa Maria** in early May; and the mid-June **Festival of Sant'Antonio.**

Peschici and Rodi Garganico

An attractive alternative to Vieste is **Peschici,** 45min. away on the Ferrovie del Gargàno bus line (L1900, buy tickets in one of the kiosks on p. Vittorio Emanuele). Stroll through the bright white labyrinth of the *centro* and savor the authentic, relatively untouristed ambience. From the bus stop, backtrack along the highway in the direction from which the bus came, and then follow the signs to the *centro.* To enter the historic center, pass through the portal in the old city wall, leading to the oft-renovated **castle** on the left. After sweating your way through the old town, descend one of the flights of steps off via Roma toward the beach. The seaside sunset is a spectacular event, as the town on the hill lights up in a postcard-perfect pose.

Peschici's modest size precludes bountiful budget sleeps. Contact the **Pro Loco** (tel. (0884) 96 44 25; open in summer daily 9am-noon and 5-9pm) for assistance. An extremely pleasant proprietor at the **Locanda Al Castello,** via Castello, 29 (tel. 96 40 38), lets homey rooms, some overlooking the water. (Singles with bath L35,000. Doubles with bath L70,000.) Otherwise try any of the many campgrounds nearby. **Campeggio Baia San Nicola** (tel. (0884) 96 42 31), near the beach, charges L8300 per person and L9000 per tent; L4500 for either in the off-season (light L1200). Food in Peschici is priced for richer tourists than thou. Buy roasted chickens (sold in ubiquitous *rosticcerie*) or grab **groceries** from **Scudo/VeGe** (tel. 96 40 55) on via XXIV Maggio off p. IV Novembre. (Open Mon.-Sat. 7am-1pm and 5-11pm.)

A sorry alternative to Vieste is **Rodi Garganico,** an unspectacular, justifiably inexpensive beach town. A bus from Peschici (4 per day, 35min., L1200) or a train from San Severo (7 per day, 1hr. 30min., L2700) deposits you in town—both are on the Ferrovie del Gargàno. Rodi sports a beach wider and longer than Peschici's, but remember size isn't everything—better to hit the beach just west of the town.

On the western beach consider renting one of the well-maintained rooms of **Pensione Sabbia D'Oro** (tel. (0884) 952 89). From the Esso gas station on the main road in town, turn on to the street that heads toward the water and follow it to the beach. Doubles with bath cost L46,000; ask for a room on the water. Off the east beach, behind a parking lot, is the mediocre **Albergo la Scogliera,** via Scalo Marittimo, 13/15. The rooms are fine, but some overlook the parking lot. (Singles with bath L30,000. Doubles with bath L60,000.)

In Rodi, as in Peschici, *pizzerie, rosticcerie,* and markets offer the most economical fare. The **Super Conad supermarket** on the main road lacks only fruit, which is available at stands in town. The **port** for ferries extends past the east beach.

Trémiti Islands (Isole Trémiti)

The Homeric king Diomedes, it is said, came here with his army on the way home from the Trojan War. The defeated Trojans, seeking revenge, transformed the army into albatrosses, which are only seen at sunset and sunrise and are said to emit the cry of a newborn baby. The birds' mythical origin is still the only plausible explanation to the evolutionary puzzle of why the species exist in three isolated pockets: here, in Japan, and in Calais, France. Now called *Trémiti* after the small tremors which continually rattle them, the islands provide a woody, sandy escape from the competitive summer tanning of the Adriatic resorts. In July and August, the bronzed ones invade these isles as well, but happily cluster on just one beach. If you're planning a daytrip, bring your own provisions, since all food bears the price tags of imports. The islands make easy daytrips from Vieste, Térmoli, and several other points. The **tourist office** in Térmoli has the most comprehensive information on the Trémiti (see Térmoli listings under Molise).

Getting There

Ferries and hydrofoils ply the islands from a number of Adriatic ports, though Térmoli is now the most convenient departure point. **Adriatica Navigazione** runs **ferries** and **hydrofoils** from the largest number of ports, and can be contacted in Manfredónia at Ditta Antonio Galli e Figlio, corso Manfredi, 4-6 (tel. (0884) 228 88); in Vieste at Gargàno Viaggi, p. Roma, 7 (tel. (0884) 70 85 01); in Térmoli at Intercontinental, corso Umberto I, 93 (tel. (0875) 70 53 41); in Rodi Garganico at Soc. Fratelli delle Fave de' Manonghia, via Trieste, 6 (tel. (0884) 96 63 57); in Vasto at Massacesi, p. Diomede, 3 (tel. (0873) 36 26 80); and in Ortona at Agenzia Marittima Giuseppe Fratino e Figli, via Porto, 34 (tel. (085) 906 38 55). **Motonave Vieste,** via S. Maria di Merino, 8 (tel. (0884) 70 74 89), runs service from Vieste, and **San Lucia Lines,** Bar Del Porto, 2707 (tel. 48 59), runs the cheapest boats from Térmoli. Depending on from whence you come and which ship you take, you will arrive at either **San Nicola** or **San Domino.**

> **Térmoli-Trémiti: Adriatica Navigazione,** May 26-Sept. 30 daily at 9:20am, additional departure Fri. at 7:30pm, 1hr. 45min., round-trip L20,800; call for departure times in other seasons. (Also offers expensive—L40,000—hydrofoil service.) **Santa Lucia Lines,** daily at 9:15am, 2hr., round-trip L20,000.

> **Vieste-Trémiti: Motonave Vieste,** daily at 8:40am, 2hr., round-trip L28,000.

> **Ortona-Trémiti: Adriatica Navigazione,** June 8-Sept. 22 at 8am, 3hr. 30min., round-trip L54,000.

> **Térmoli-San Domino: Motonave Zaffiro,** tel. (0875) 70 59 90. The cheapest and best way to go. July-Aug. daily at 8:20am and 4pm, return at 10:15am and 5:30pm, 1hr. 15min., round-trip L24,000. Sept.-June daily at 8:45am, return 5pm. **Adriatica Navigazione** also has service May 26-Sept. 30 daily at 9:20am, additional departure Fri. at 7:30pm, 1hr. 45min., round-trip L28,000.

Adriatica hydrofoils also link these and other cities with the islands, but are more expensive (from Vieste round-trip L37,000 plus port tax, from Térmoli L40,000). Hydrofoils run daily between the islands and Peschici, Rodi Gargánico, Manfredónia, and Vasto in Abruzzo. Call them for further information.

Note: for all departures, be at the port about 45min. before departure.

Whether you've landed on San Nicola or San Domino, you will immediately be assailed by announcements for boat tours of San Domino and its grottoes (about L10,000), but be forewarned—the excursion is nothing spectacular. **Luggage storage** at each port is L1500.

Ferries between the two islands run frequently (L1500; don't buy a round-trip ticket or you may be stuck without a return boat). Make sure your boat is just going across, and not on a tour; you may be asked to shell out L10,000 once on the high seas.

Once There

Your choice of island will be guided by the parable of Mary and Martha. If you prefer the contemplative life, head to **San Nicola,** dominated by a massive Benedictine abbey predating the millenium. Access to the sea, the town of San Nicola itself, and the **Church of Santa Maria** all lie within the abbey's boundaries. The church houses a Byzantine crucifix brought to the islands in 747 (the year, not the plane), an 11th-century black Madonna, and the fully visible mummified remains of the blessed Tobias, in surprisingly good shape for his 434 years. Also note the Venetian altar and the remnants of Byzantine mosaics on the floor. To the left of the church lies a **courtyard,** lined by Roman and Gothic cloisters, which opens to a remarkable view of the entire archipelago. The abbey is impossible to miss coming from the ferry dock, as it is the only opening in a vast sheet of rock.

If you prefer the pleasures of the active life, hit the beaches of **San Domino,** the largest of the Trémiti. All affordable accommodations are here. To reach the bathing paradise along the island's eastern coast, follow the signs off the main road to town to "Villaggio Internazionale," veering right just before the "Villaggio" itself. This will lead you to the northern tip of the island, where you can search out a *cala* (cove) you like.

Pitching tents is strictly forbidden on all the islands, but **Punta del Diamante** (tel. 66 30 34), on San Domino, rents prefab aluminum tents (half-pension L69,000, full pension L75,000; off-season half-pension L66,000, full pension L72,000). Most places require full pension in summer, but it's not a bad deal especially since the food beats restaurant offerings. The best deal in town is at the **Hotel Paradiso,** (tel. 66 30 14).

(L45,000 per person with breakfast; off-season L35,000. Half-pension doubles L80,000-103,000, depending on season.) A pair of semi-affordable *pensioni* sit atop the hill across from **Bar Diomede,** overlooking the sea. **Pensione Giovanna** (tel. 66 32 13 or, from October through March, (0875) 70 10 69) has doubles with bath and balcony (full pension L80,000; less in off-season). Next door and almost identical is **Pensione La Bussola** (tel. 66 30 68), which lets rooms without pension (doubles with bath L70,000, full pension L75,000). To get here from the port, follow the road to the left and hook left at the Hotel Paradiso. **Pensione Rossana** (tel. 66 32 49), up the steep hill to the left of the port, requires full pension in July and August. (All double rooms. Half-pension L70,000, L75,000 in July, L80,000-90,000 in Aug.) **Albergo Villa Olimpia** (tel. 66 30 46), to the left off the main road on the way to the island's center, is home to over 40 felines. For humans, the hospitable owner offers rooms without pension. (L40,000 per person; off-season L30,000 per person. Full pension is L85,000 per person; off-season L60,000.) All supplies must be brought in by ship, so restaurants are expensive. Bring your own provisions and save, or shop at the *alimentari* in the center. **Da Michele,** on the way to Pensione Giovanna, will make you a Dagwood-size sandwich for L2000-3000. (Open daily 8am-10pm.) The **telephone code** on the islands is 0882.

Bari

> Se a Parigi ci fosse il mare sarebbe una piccola
> Bari. (If Paris had the sea it would be a little Bari.)
> —Local Saying

Baresi have good reason to boast. A center of Byzantine power in southern Italy, their city went on to become a major embarkation point for the Crusades, and later the keystone of Frederick II's Mediterranean empire. The new city, a model of 19th-century urban planning, serves as the region's cultural and economic hub. Not the least of Bari's accomplishments is a concerted effort to make the city enjoyable for backpackers, an enterprise conducted in the spirit of the city's most famous resident: Santa Claus.

Du calme, Parisiens! No need to go about flooding Normandy *just* yet. Bari's old city, reminiscent of an Arab *medina,* is a nucleus of old-style poverty coupled with modern twists: pitiless maniacs on wheels, racism against Albanians and other minorities, street crime, and a widespread drug problem. Nevertheless, Bari can be safe as long as you exercise the precautions you would in any large city, and the "Stop-Over in Bari" program makes it an excellent base for daytrips to the surrounding countryside.

The "Stop-Over in Bari" Program

Six years ago, local government and grass roots organizations came up with a unique idea (and it had better stay unique, or budget travel guides will become obsolete)—to make Bari a mecca for backpackers from all over. The agent would be the "Stop-Over in Bari" program, and the original philosophy would be emblazoned on a flyer distributed across Europe: "Free vacations!" Well, almost free. Between **mid-June** and **mid-September,** Stop-Over can be of immeasurable assistance to travelers **under 30** who are not residents of the region.

Your first stop in Bari should be the Stop-Over **booth** in the train station or the *stazione marittima.* The affable, English-speaking student staffers will provide you with maps and limitless information on Bari and its province. Pick up a daily Stop-Over **newsletter** for information on discounted restaurants, shops, museums, and cultural events. For additional daily information, tune in to Stop-Over **radio** in English at 102 FM. If you have a sleeping bag or tent, take Bus #5 or 3 to Pineta San Francesco, a free **campground** with bar, free showers, and free luggage storage; free kitchens, and pizza, along with daily recipes, are also available. All city buses are free to Stop-Over qualifiers with proof of residence and age. Be aware, though, that Bari's bus system is lousy—strikes are frequent and service is slow.

If you are bereft of sleeping bag or simply want a more luxurious sojourn, take advantage of Stop-Over's **Package,** which puts you up in a private home for two nights for a mere L30,000. You'll be put up with college students and their ilk, most likely in neighborhoods safer than those in which Bari's squalid *pensioni* cluster. (Call (080) 521 45 38 or fax 521 18 22 to reserve; reservations appreciated but not essential.)

Stop-Over also offers two free weekly **concerts** and occasional events throughout the summer, free use of **bicycles** and **skateboards,** and, projected for the very near future, free copies of an English edition of Luca Conti's *Inter-Rail Man,* a funny and detailed guide to railpass travel from a personal perspective.

Stop-Over's **main office** at via Dante Alighieri, 111, has more detailed information on sights and events (tel. 521 45 38; open daily 8:30am-8:30pm). The 24-hr. **summer hotline** is 44 11 86.

Ferries

Getting to Greece from Bari is cheaper and more appealing than going by way of Bríndisi. Ferries ply to **Corfu** (11hr.), **Igoumenitsa** (12hr. 30min.), and **Patras** (15-20hr.). There are no discounts for Eurail passes or *cartaverde,* but most lines offer special student rates. The following are ferry companies with their destinations; the lowest prices (deck class) for each are shown. The **high season** varies slightly from company to company, year to year, and place to place, but is generally from the first week of July to the last week of August. The **port tax** for Greece is L11,000. Tickets and information can be obtained directly at the **stazione marittima** or at the offices listed below. **You must check in at the stazione marittima two hours before departure.** After buying your ticket and paying the tax, you will be given a boarding card to be stamped at the **police station,** conveniently located in the *stazione marittima.*

Morfimare, corso de Tullio, 36/40 (tel. 521 00 22). Boxes #11 and 12 at the port. To: **Patras** (L50,000, high season L60,000; students pay L10,000 less; departs at 9pm, odd-number days June-July, evens in Aug.); **Igoumenitsa-Corfu** (same prices as Patras; departs at 8pm, even days June-July, odds in Aug.).

Ventouris Ferries, c/o Pan Travel, v. S. Francesco d'Assisi, 95 (tel. 524 43 64). To: **Patras** (L50,000, high season L65,000, students pay L5000 less; departs daily at 8:30pm); **Corfu** and **Igoumenitsa** (all prices L5000 cheaper than Patras; daily departures July-Aug.).

Orientation and Practical Information

Via Sparano leads north from the train station two blocks to **piazza Umberto,** the main square in town. Two blocks east of the *piazza* and parallel to via Sparano runs **corso Cavour,** Bari's main street. About nine blocks north is **corso Vittorio Emanuele,** separating the old city to the north and the new city to the south. The main square in the old city is **piazza Mercantile.**

Tourist Office: Stop-Over should satisfy your every need, but...**EPT,** p. Aldo Moro, 33A (tel. 524 22 44), to the right as you leave the station. Regional and local maps of Apulia. English spoken, sort of. Open daily 8am-2pm and 3-8pm.

Budget Travel: OTE, via Dante, 111 (tel. 521 45 38). From the station, walk 1 block past p. Umberto and to the left. Information on student discount travel from the people who run Stop-Over. Open Mon.-Fri. 9:30am-1pm and 4:30-7:30pm, Sat. 9:30am-5pm.

Currency Exchange: at the information desk in the F.S. train station when banks are closed (open until 8pm). Also at the **Automobile Club Italiano** at the ferry terminal, but only when boats are arriving or departing.

American Express: Morfimare, corso de Tullio, 36/40 (tel. 521 00 22), near the port. Open Mon.-Fri. 9am-12:30pm and 3:30-6:30pm.

Post Office: p. Battisti (tel. 39 61 11), behind the university. From p. Umberto, take a left on via Crisanzio, then the 1st right on via Cairoli. Open Mon.-Fri. 8:20am-7pm, Sat. 8:20am-1pm. **Postal Code:** 70100.

Telephones: SIP, via Oriani, near the castle. Open daily 8am-9pm. **ASST,** outside the station to the right. Better for international calls. Open daily 7am-10pm. **Telephone Code:** 080.

Trains: Bari lies on train lines from Rome (6 per day, last at 9pm, 7-8hr., L33,000) and Milan (15 per day, last at 11:25pm, 8-10hr., L53,700). Frequent **trains** connect Bari with Apulia's larger towns: Fóggia (1hr. 30min., L7800), Táranto (2hr., L7800), Bríndisi (2hr., L7800), and Lecce (2hr. 30min., L9300). The station is also home to several private lines, including the **Ferrovie del Sud-Est** (to Castellana Grotte, Alberobello, and Martina Franca), on the last track of the central station, and the **Bari-Nord** (to Bitonto and Barletta) and the **Ferrovie Calabro-Lucane** (tel. 572 52 22; to Matera in Basilicata), both on the western side of the square.

English Bookstore: Feltrinelli Bookstore, via Dante, 91/95, one-half-block from Stop-Over's main office. A decent collection of classics and moderns. Open Mon.-Sat. 9am-1pm and 4-8pm.

Emergencies: tel. 113. **Police:** tel. 113; **Carabinieri:** tel. 112. **Ambulance:** tel. 522 15 14. **Fire Department:** 115.

Accommodations

Unless you're over 30 or it's not summer, you won't stay in a Bari hotel unless you are a well-heeled masochist. The two-day Stop-Over "Package" is a better deal than most of the following, even if you don't use the second day. Exercise caution in the following locations.

Ostello del Levante (HI), Palese Marina, lungomare Colombo (tel. 32 02 82). Take the train to the Bari-Palese stop (L600) or bus #1 from corso Cavour to Palese and walk to the beach. The hostel resides in safer territory outside the city. It doubles as a home for the mentally handicapped, so watch which column you check when you register. Six beds per room. Lockout 9am-5pm. Curfew 11pm. L12,000 per day (includes breakfast).

Pensione Darinka, via Calefati, 15/A (tel. 523 50 49), off corso Cavour. From p. Umberto, walk down via Argiro and turn right. English-speaking Brando-voiced proprietor keeps the place pleasant. Renovated in the summer of 1992. Call for new prices (doubles were L40,000 before renovations).

Pensione Giulia, via Crisanzio, 12 (tel. 523 50 30). From the station, turn left just before p. Umberto. Clean and spacious, the rooms have semi-vaulted ceilings painted with idyllic scenes. Singles L42,000, with bath L55,000. Doubles L57,000, with bath L73,000.

Pensione Romeo, via Crisanzio, 12 (tel. 521 63 80), in the same *palazzo* as the Pensione Giulia. Recently remodeled. The ground floor is clean and modern, but avoid the upstairs rooms. Sepulchral singles with bath L35,000. Lovelorn doubles with bath L50,000.

Food

Sandwiched between bountiful sea and rich pastures, Bari specializes in seafood, horse, and lamb dishes. Zesty seafood sauces like *ciambotto* (made of fish, olive oil, onions, and tomatoes) accompany pasta. Ricotta cheese made with sheep's milk is Bari's splendid modification on cottage cheese. Many *macellerie* sell whole roasted chickens to go for about L8000. The daily morning **market** at p. del Ferrarese is a vegetable frenzy. **Supermercato Vito Caldarulo,** via de Giosa, 97 (tel. 54 43 26), one street east of corso Cavour, vends at reasonable prices (open daily 8:30am-1pm and 5-8pm).

Osteria delle Travi, largo Chiurlia, 12, at the end of via Sparano. Turn left through the arches at the entrance to the old city. Support the *Mezzogiorno* in this charming stone cellar by ordering local specialties: pasta with arugula and ricotta, and *braciola* (horsemeat wrapped around stuffing). Full meals L14,000 without drinks. Other prices vary. Open Tues.-Sun. 12:30-2:30pm and 7:30-10:30pm.

Taverna Verde, largo Adua, 18/19 (tel. 54 03 09), on the *lungomare* between Molo San Nicola and La Rotunda, at the end of corso Cavour. Black-tie service at ripped-jeans prices. *Orecchiette alla barese* (the regional pasta speciality) L5000. Local wine L3000 per . Cover L2000. Service 15%. Open Mon.-Sat. noon-3pm and 8pm-midnight.

Vini e Cucina, strada Vallisa, 23, in the old city. Follow corso Cavour to p. Mercantile; it's to the left. Looks like a dungeon, but a charming one. Full meals with house wine L12,000. Open Mon.-Sat. noon-3pm and 6-10pm.

El Pedro Self-Service, via Piccinni, 152 (tel. 521 12 94). Not a Mexican restaurant but a great cafeteria serving authentic Pugliese specialties, different every day. Complete meal with drink L14,000. Open for lunch only.

Sights

Enjoy Bari, but don't make yourself a target for crime. **Women should not venture alone into the old city, especially at night.** As in other southern cities, avoid flashy watches and jewelry, keep valuables in front inside pockets, and hold purses and bags where drive-by thieves can't grab them.

Enter the **old city** at p. Mercantile, the site of a colorful morning **market.** The *piazza* lies under the open porch and clock tower of the **Sedile,** the medieval meeting place of the Council of Nobles. Debtors were once tied to the Column of Justice (far right of square).

Yes, Virginia, there is a Santa Claus, and he's dead. His remains were brought to Bari from Asia Minor by 60 sailors in 1087, after the clever Baresi outran some Venetians who had planned to nab the remains of this patron saint of sailors and pawnbrokers. The victorious sailors refused to hand over the saint to the local clergy, saying they had vowed to construct a special temple for the remains, thought to possess miraculous properties. From p. Mercantile, follow via Palazzo di Città to the **Church of San Nicola,** built in the 12th century to shelter the remains of St. Nicholas (Santa Claus), who is renowned not only for Christmas loot but also for resurrecting three children who were sliced to bits and plunged into a barrel of brine by a nasty butcher. The church's spartan appearance is better suited for a fortress; in fact, the tower on the right survives from a Byzantine castle that originally occupied the site. The central door exemplifies the motley sources of the Puglian-Romanesque style: Saracen in the arabesques and symbolic figures around the door, classical in the rosettes of the cornice, Byzantine in the solemn angels surrounding the arches, and Lombard in the crude animal carvings of the bases. An 11th-century episcopal throne hides behind the high altar. The crypt, with its windows of translucent marble, houses the remains of St. Nick beside a beautiful silver reliquary. (Open daily 8am-noon and 4-7pm.)

Bari's Puglian-Romanesque **cathedral** is a short walk from the church. Passing down **strada del Carmine,** you'll be greeted by the vibrant old streets: narrow alleys lined with small whitewashed houses and thronged with children, vendors, and black-swathed women. Begun at the end of the 12th century during the peaceful years of Norman rule, the **cathedral** displays a typically austere Gothic façade, somewhat modified by Baroque decorations around the doors. Its interior is a fine example of Romanesque architecture, with a choir and chapel protruding gently from the nave. (Open daily 8am-noon and 4-7pm.)

On the outskirts of the old city, not far from the cathedral, the **Castello Svevo** (Swabian Castle) evokes the grandeur and power of three different periods. The castle proper and its four keeps are of Byzantine-Norman origin, rearranged by Frederick II (1230-1240) into a trapezoid with two of the towers still standing in the interior. In the north, toward the sea, a pointed door and beautiful mullioned windows also hearken to the 13th century. The bulwarks and angular keeps that jut outward were 16th-century additions. Much of the castle is closed for the excavation of a recently discovered Roman city on the site. (Open daily 9am-1pm and 3:30-7pm. Admission L4000; under 18 free.)

Beyond the castle lies a seawalk that trails past the ferry port to a small fishing harbor then on to **Molo San Nicola** (San Nicola's Wharf). The gray-and-white towered building in the distance, the **Palazzo della Provincia** on lungomare N. Sauro (tel. 39 24 23), houses the **Pinacoteca Provinciale** on its top floor. The museum displays paintings by Veronese, Tintoretto, and Bellini, including the latter's *Martyrdom of St. Peter.* Despite perforation by a staggering collection of cutlery, the painting's hero is coolness incarnate. Ask to see the works of Francesco Netti, Bari's greatest artist and Italy's only impressive Impressionist painter. (Open Thurs.-Tues. 9am-1pm and 4-7pm, Sun. 9am-1pm. Free.)

Entertainment

Bari rivals Naples as the south's cultural nucleus. Stop-Over has the latest news on events and hotspots, and sponsors everything from recycling workshops and kite festivals to comic-strip shows. The two-month opera season at the **Teatro Petruzzelli** (tel. 524 17 61) begins in January, along with a concert season at the **Teatro Piccinni** (tel. 521 37 17). In summer, occasional concerts are held in the *castello*. Entertainment listings crowd *Ecco Bari*, the tourist office's entertainment guide, and the *Bari Sera* section of *La Gazzetta del Mezzogiorno* (the local newspaper). Stop over at "Stop-Over" for the scoop on the latest in the nightlife scene.

The great commercial event of the year, the **Levante Fair,** runs for 10 days in mid-September. The largest fair in southern Italy, it displays goods from all over the world in the huge fairgrounds by the municipal stadium, off lungomare Starita.

Excursions from Bari

Bari's environs are ideal for whistle-stop daytrips. Bitonto, Ruvo di Puglia, Barletta, and Castel del Monte lie on or near the **Bari-Nord** line to the north of the city, while Ostuni, Egnazia, and Trani are served by the **FS** main line. The **Trulli district** falls in the domain of the **ferrovie del sud-est,** while the High Murge are accessible by the **ferrovie Calabro-Lucane.** Remember that Eurailpasses and *Cartaverde* hold no clout on private railways. (Only FS is non-private.)

Bitonto

For a potent dose of Puglian-Romanesque architecture, take the half-hour train ride from the Bari-Nord station to Bitonto (every hr., L1400). When you arrive, a 1km walk down via Matteotti and a right turn deposits you in the medieval quarter. Once there, many signs with detailed maps will help direct you. Bitonto's glorious **cathedral** stands in the medieval quarter; it was constructed between the 12th and 13th centuries from mellow golden stone in loose emulation of San Nicola in Bari. Majestic side arches enhance the church's compact form, while sculptured lions, griffins, and bas-relief New Testament scenes enliven the main portal. Inside, windows illuminate a finely carved wooden ceiling (a late 19th-century reproduction of the original design), while a splendid pulpit crowns the nave (1229). The **crypt** rests on 30 columns salvaged from a Roman temple. Their capitals were the gifts of 30 members of the city's medieval nobility. (If closed, contact the sacristan in early morning or late afternoon; small tip expected.)

The rest of medieval Bitonto boasts several interesting buildings, including the Gothic **Church of San Francesco d'Assisi** (1286) and the 16th-century **Palazzo Sylos Calo,** whose Catalan-Gothic doorway opens to an elaborate Renaissance courtyard. In addition to these, almost all of the buildings in Bitonto's *centro storico* can claim provenance in the Middle Ages. Walk around the narrow street for a dose of the Apulian dialect and of village life as it must have been three-quarters of a century ago.

Ruvo di Puglia

Midway between Bari and Barletta on the Bari-Nord line (from Bari 30min., L2800), Ruvo di Puglia began as a Greek colony in about the 8th century BC and reached the pinnacle of its influence four to five centuries later. Ruvo later passed into Roman hands; in 463 AD those fun-loving Goths destroyed the town in a fit of good-humored mayhem. Patient Ruvo whiled away the dog days of the Middle Ages in gradual rebuilding; one of the best products of this epoch is the three-nave Apulian Romanesque **cathedral** begun in the 13th century and restored several times from the 16th to the 19th centuries. Note the exterior ornamentation and the church's large, ornate rose window; other highlights include a 14th-century wooden crucifix and M. Pino da Siena's 1576 *L'Adorazione dei Pastori*. On the façade, note the statue of a man on a throne, reading the Book of the Seven Seals; this is believed to be a portait of our dear friend,

Frederick II. To the right of the cathedral stands the resolute **campanile,** antedating the millennium. To get to the museum from the station, turn right and then onto corso Duca della Vittoria; follow the signs from there. The cathedral is to the left of the museum, on the other side of the wooded *piazza.*

Castel del Monte

Situated halfway between the Murge and the sea, Castel del Monte is the subject of much speculation. It was originally built for the pleasure of Frederick II around 1240; lacking defensive structures, it probably served no strategic purpose. The edifice is straight out of a *Dungeons and Dragons* module: a perfect octagon, with eight octagonal towers, containing sixteen trapezoidal rooms, connected by three differently structured stairways embellished with twenty-sided dice. It is surmised that charismatic Frederick designed it himself as a pleasure dome, meeting place, and astronomical observatory. In fact, rays of sunlight converge on certain points at each semi-annual equinox, à la Indiana Jones.

The grounds are always open, but unless you're a 12th-level paladin, you can only visit the inside on Sunday mornings. To get there, take the Bari-Nord train to Andria (35min., L3800) and then board one of six daily buses on the Andria-Spinazzola route (45min.; call 209 48 for information on departure times).

Barletta

Barletta is a compact city with a few bursts of fun to offer. Its star attraction is an amusing pageant on the first or second Sunday in September. The city reenacts the 1503 **Disfida** (Challenge), a battle in which 13 Italian knights handily defeated 13 Frenchmen. The victory was somewhat hollow, as the Spanish would later use the pretext that the knights had received Spanish aid to occupy the entire southern half of Italy. Other attractions include some interesting Romanesque churches, a massive bronze statue from antiquity, and an outstanding collection of paintings by Giuseppe de Nittis, one of Italy's great 19th-century artists. To reach all of Barletta's sights, walk from the station and turn right on via Garibaldi. Barletta is 15 minutes north of Trani on either the Bologna-Lecce or Bari-Nord train lines (from Bari 40min., L4400).

The 12th-century **Church of San Sepolcro** graces the center of town on corso Vittorio Emanuele at corso Garibaldi. Corso Vittorio Emanuele itself runs beneath a fanciful jumble of wrought-iron arches, which are illuminated in a multicolor display at night. The façade preserves remnants of an original porch, a pointed doorway, and two blind arches. The only decoration remaining in the recently restored church interior is the large 13th-century baptismal font to the left of the entrance, and the tender 16th-century Byzantine-style Madonna at the end of the right aisle. (Open Mon.-Sat. 10am-noon and 3-7pm.) On a low podium next to the church towers the 5m **Colosso.** This 4th-century bronze statue from Constantinople represents a Byzantine emperor, possibly Valentinian I, holding the cross and globe, symbols of the two realms of his power. As the Venetians were hauling home the loot from the sack of Constantinople (the Fourth Crusade), shipwreck sent the Colosso to Barletta's shore. It was then dismembered by a group of friars who melted its bronze limbs for use as church bells. The limbs you see were fashioned by a 15th-century sculptor commissioned to restore it.

Continue on corso Garibaldi and venture into the old town to reach the **Cantina Della Disfios,** where the fabled confrontation of the knights took place. The "cantina" itself is simply the basement of a Gothic palace; note the huge stone cistern in the back.

The **Museo e Pinacoteca Comunali** (City Museum and Art Gallery), on via Cavour at corso Garibaldi, houses archeological material and satirical paintings by Giuseppe de Nittis. His works chronicle the gluttonous world of the 19th-century *haute bourgeoisie.* (Open Tues.-Sun. 9am-2pm. Free.) Continue along v. Cavour to reach the massive **Anson Castle,** a military behemoth from which the Third Crusade was launched. Unfortunately, you'll have to admire it from the outside.

The only game in town for budget accommodations is the **Pensione Prezioso,** via Teatini, 11 (tel. 52 00 46), on p. del Plebiscito at the end of corso Vittorio Emanuele.

(Singles with bath, L30,000; doubles with bath L45,000). For nourishment, try the **Bella Napoli** (tel. 322 31), across from the museum at corso Garibaldi, 129. The food and service are superb, full meals are L15,000, cover L2000, service 15%. (Open daily noon-3pm and 7pm-midnight.) Less classy (but with outdoor tables), **Pizzeria Dai Saraceni**, p. del Plebiscito, 65 (tel. 51 71 00), offers complete meals for L18,000. Try their tasty *pizza al Saraceni* (with ham, artichokes, olives, capers, etc.) for L5000. (Cover L2000, service 15%; open daily noon-4pm and 7pm-1am.) Off corso Garibaldi, **Supermarket DOK** is on via G. de Nittis. (Open Mon.-Sat. 8:30am-1:30pm and 4:30-7:30pm.)

Trani

A captivating fishing village, Trani prospered as a free port in the 14th and 15th centuries. Its *ordinamenta maris,* a 1063 maritime commercial code, was the first written set of sea laws since antiquity. The city's well-preserved medieval quarter evokes the period of Trani's ascendancy, and its streets, heirs to structural fragments from the Middle Ages onwards, are a veritable architectural history book. At the harbor, leather-faced fishermen perform the daily ritual of untangling and mending their nets. While yachts now outnumber fishing sloops in the harbor, modern Trani's function as a bedroom community for well-to-do *Baresi* has not affected the classic character of the old quarter. From the train station, walk down via Cavour to the lovely p. della Repubblica, site of a **tourist office** (tel. (0883) 432 95), whose knowledgeable staff dispenses pamphlets and maps. (Open Mon.-Fri. 8:30am-12:30pm and 3:30-5:30pm., Sat. 9am-noon.) Continuing down via Cavour to p. Plebiscito, you'll reach the flourishing **public gardens.** A small fishing harbor separates the gardens from the 11th-century **duomo,** which rises on a promontory surveying the sea. The patron of this cathedral is Nicholas the Pilgrim, a religious fanatic who chanted the *Kyrie Eleison* incessantly. The miniature panels of saints and biblical scenes on the bronze front doors are the work of Barisano da Trani. Measuring 24m by 11.5m by 5.5m, the primary crypt of San Nicola Pellegrino is one of the world's largest.

Down the waterfront from the cathedral stands the **Castello Svevo** (1249), presently "closed for renovation and re-use," whatever that means. An old-world flavor prevails along the harbor and parallel **via Ognissanti.** Here workshops (mostly of antique-furniture restorers) crowd against medieval palaces and churches. The **Ognissanti,** a 12th-century church with three naves and no transept, will thrill fans of Umberto Eco's *Foucault's Pendulum.* Built by the Knights Templar on their way back from the Crusades, it may still hold cryptic evidence of their plans for world domination. (Closed in 1992.) Further down the street, the 15th-century **Palazzo Caccetta,** now a middle school, evokes the more sumptuous palaces of Florence.

The heritage of Trani's medieval Jewish community endures in street names (via la Giudea, via Sinagoga, via Mosè di Trani) and within two small **churches** (Santa Maria Scuolanove and Sant'Anna), which were synagogues until the Spanish imported the Inquisition and exported the Jews in the 16th century. The latter, on via la Giudea off via Prologo across from the Palazzo Caccetta, was built in 1247 and preserves a Hebrew inscription on a marble plaque inside. (Closed in 1992.)

A morning fish and produce **market** takes place daily from 8:30am to noon at the end of via Ognissanti.

In summer, the tourist office organizes a number of musical and cultural activities nightly at p. Quercia. If you're in Trani during the last weekend in July, be sure to see the festivities of the **Festa di San Nicola Pellegrino.**

Albergo Lucy, p. Plebiscito, 11 (tel. 410 22), near the public gardens, is a low-priced, elegant hotel run by a caring proprietor. Its huge doubles with bath cost L60,000. Parrots (lamentably in chains) greet visitors at the entrance of **Trattoria Emanuele** (tel. 58 36 02), by the port at supportico della Conca, 2, which serves full meals for L20,000. Pasta dishes cost L6000-7000. *Secondi* L8000-10,000. (Cover L3000; open Thurs.-Tues. noon-3pm and 4pm-midnight.) **La Fattoria,** via Cavour, 98 (tel. 58 91 89) sells wonderful *focaccia* (L500 per slice), and has provisions for a lunch in the park. (Open Mon., Wed., and Fri.-Sat. 7am-1pm and 5:30-9pm, Thurs. 7am-

1pm.) Try **Cittadella,** v. Amedeo, 274 (tel. 58 21 69), for great pizza (L4000) and other goodies.

Egnazia

Just south of the Bari-Bríndisi border slumber the ruins of Egnazia. In olden times, this Messapian city was famed for its pottery, characteristically superimposing yellow, purple, and white designs on a glossy black background. You can view examples of these wares at the **archeological museum.** (Tel. (080) 72 90 56. Museum open daily 8:30am-1:00pm and 2:30-7pm; archeological zone open 8:30am-7pm. Free.) Egnazia eventually became a Greek port, taking the name Gnathia, and then a Roman stronghold. The ruins of the port are the most extensive Roman remains in Apulia; unfortunately, they're mostly underwater, and are currently being studied by scuba archeologists. Above ground, see the three-aisled **basilica,** the **forum,** a road leading to Bríndisi, and the **acropolis** atop the hill. Several tombs and sections of the ancient fortifications survive from the Messapian period.

Travel to Egnazia via Monópoli, which is 45 minutes from Bari by train (almost every hr., L3500) and one hour from Bríndisi (about every 2hr., L4400). From the Villa Comunale in Monópoli (nowhere near Park Place), take the bus towards Torre Canne and get off at Egnazia (you will not pass Go; you will not collect $200). There is an Egnazia train station but it's a bit removed from town and the ruins.

Ostuni

Ostuni seems to come straight out of Calvino's *Invisible Cities*. Rising out of a landscape of sea, red earth, and olive trees, the *città bianca* (white city) appears completely ethereal. The walls and even the pavement of the *centro storico* are kept pure as the driven snow by local ordinance; walking through the old town, you'll feel surrounded by icebergs. Nevertheless, the most important monuments in Ostuni are polychromatic. The **Convento Delle Monacelle** (Convent of the Little Nuns) on via Cattedrale sports a Baroque façade and is topped by a blue-, yellow-, and white-tiled dome of evident Moorish inspiration. Further along via Cattedrale, surprisingly, is the **cathedral.** Built in 1437, it was the last Byzantine building erected in southern Italy. On via Cavallo, the more modest **Chiesa di San Giacomo di Compostella** (1423) served as a chapel to a noble family.

By far the most breathtaking sight on Ostuni, however, is the panoramic view of the fields rolling out to the sea, from a foreground of white houses. From via Cattedrale, turn left and head downwards until you reach the edge of the old town. Keep going left, and you'll hit the **Porta Nuova,** a gate commissioned by Robert D'Anson to boost commerce in Ostuni.

From the **train station,** take the shuttle bus (every 30min., every hr. on Sun.; L700) to p. Libertà, which abuts on via Cattedrale at the edge of the old town. (Return buses same times.) The **AAST Tourist Office** (tel. 97 12 68; open Mon.-Fri. 9:30am-12:30pm and 6:30-9pm; July-Aug. Mon.-Sat.) is at p. Libertà, 63.

For replenishing and a change of color, go to the kitschy **Osteria del Temp Perso,** v. G. Tanzarella, 47 (tel. 30 33 20). Good food for easy-to-stomach prices. (Open evenings 8:30pm-midnight.) Frequent **trains** run to Ostuni from Bríndisi (40min., L2800) and Bari (1hr., L5100).

Trulli District

Hundreds of unusual, cone-shaped dwellings, known as *trulli,* cluster in the **Valley of Itria,** between Bari and Táranto. Originally built in the 16th and 17th centuries by pioneers in the great Italian pastime of tax evasion, the mortarless buildings follow a design of concentric stone circles of decreasing radii, stacked and topped by a limestone cap. The Spanish levied a harsh tax for each dwelling; however, unfinished houses were exempted. The *trulli* were designed so that the roof could be knocked down in minutes, as soon as the tax man was spotted. The tax codes were changed when the

Spanish caught on, but the style persisted. The *trulli* have been incorporated into modern life as residences, restaurants, and even boutiques.

Alberobello

The greatest concentration of *trulli* is in Alberobello, 90 minutes south of Bari on the Ferrovie del Sud-Est line to Táranto (15 trains per day, fewer on Sundays, more on school days, L2800).

From the train station, bear left and take v. Garibaldi until you reach p. del Popolo. Any left turn will bring you into the thick of the *trulli* zone. Unhappily, the *trulli* are crawling with tourists, and most have become curio shops. Beware the limpid-eyed souls who beg you to "visit" the interior of their *trullo:* you will be expected to buy at least a postcard.

Turn right from p. del Popolo to find the **Pro Loco Tourist Office,** at corso Vittorio Emanuele, 15 (open Mon.-Sat. 8:30am-12:30pm and 5-7pm). Continue on corso Vittorio Emanuele and bear left past the nondescipt church at the end. Straight ahead is the **Trullo Sovrano,** or Sovereign Trullo. This mammoth two-story structure, the *only* two-story trullo, was built in the 19th century as headquarters for a religious confraternity and *carbonari* sect. Alberobello's eateries and sleeperies are overtouristed and expensive; make it a Bari-based daytrip.

Locorotondo

The next stop after Alberobello coming from Bari is Locorotondo, which merits a quick tour despite its paucity of monuments and *trulli.* From the train station, turn left, then turn right at the junction with the main road, and follow the *centro storico* signs. The whitewashed medieval streets sport a Baroque fresco here, a wrought-iron, balloon-shaped balcony there. Enjoy a terrific view of *trullo* territory from **via Cavour,** at the northern edge of the *centro storico.*

You can stay in the heart of *trulli* land under the auspices of the **Agriturismo** program. Call Franco Conte (tel. 931 78 97) to arrange a stay at Contrada Cerrosa, outside Locorotondo (L25,000-35,000 per person per day; stays of several days preferred).

Martina Franca

You can see other *trulli* sprinkled among fields of flowers in the surrounding Itria Valley by taking the train to Martina Franca, 6km away and the next stop on the train line. Founded in the 14th century as a free (*franca*) city by Philip D'Anson, Martina Franca doesn't have that many *trulli,* but it charms with movie-set preciousness. From the train station, follow via della Stazione to via del Lecci, then turn left on corso Taranto, which becomes corso Italia. Turn left and go through the arch at p. XX Settembre to reach p. Roma, where you can (possibly) pick up a map at the **tourist office,** #35 (tel. 70 57 02; open Mon.-Sat. 9am-12:30pm and 4:30-7:30pm, Nov.-March Mon.-Sat. 8:30-2pm). Next door towers the grandiose **Ducal Palace** (1669) with more than 300 rooms, most of which are now offices. To tour the few accessible rooms, climb the left-hand stairs to the third floor. The walls are draped with multicolored Baroque frescoes depicting contemporary and ancient scenes of leisure and pleasure. Ironically, the rooms host the meetings of the Martina Franca city council. (Open Mon.-Sat. 8am-8pm. Free.) The fanciful Baroque façade of the 18th-century **Church of San Martino** presides over p. Plebiscito (open daily 8am-noon and 4-7:30pm). From viale de Gasperi, enjoy the vista of the Itria Valley and its *trulli.*

There are no cheap hotels here. Your optimal wager may be **Albergo La Cremaillere,** 7km away in Locando San Paolo at via Orimini, 1 (tel. (080) 70 02 65). Singles go for L35,000 and doubles (all with bath) for L60,000. To get there, take a Ferrovie del Sud-Est bus, which leaves from p. Crispi off via Taranto for Locando San Paolo. Another option is the aforementioned *Agriturismo* deal in Locorotondo. For a good meal, stop by **La Tavernetta,** corso Vittorio Emanuele, 31 (tel. 70 63 23), off p. Roma. Homemade *orechiette al sugo* go for L6000, main dishes for L8000-12,000; local wine is L5000 per . (Cover L2500. Open daily noon-3pm and 7:30pm-midnight.) Shop at **Supermercato Fontana,** on via Taranto to the left after turning off via dei Lecci. (Open Mon.-Sat. 8am-1pm and 5-8pm.)

Martina Franca's **Festival della Valle d'Itria** brings concerts and opera to the city from late July through early August. Tickets for the events range from L5000 to L30,000. During the first weekend in July, the **Festa di San Martino** rouses the town with the outdoor concerts and parades.

Martina Franca is about 45 minutes by train from Táranto (9 per day, round-trip L4000) and 90 minutes hours from Bari. (Trains leave at 7:15am, hourly from 8:30am-12:30pm and 2:30-6:30pm, and less frequently until 9pm; L4700.) Bus service from Ferrovie del Sud-Est connects Martina Franca with Táranto's p. del Castello (11 per day, L2400; for information call 40 44 63 in Táranto).

Castellana Grotte

Take a Sud-Est train from Bari toward Alberobello to reach Castellana Grotte, home to Italy's finest caverns (30min.). They are a 2km hike away from the station, though many hitch successfully. Those folk follow the Grotte signs from the train station. You enter from an enormous pit called *La Grave,* which, despite its beauty, was used as a garbage dump until the rest of the caverns were discovered in 1938. The real highlight waits at the end of the tunnel—the *Caverna Bianca* (White Cavern), a landscape of sta-lactites. Tours (1hr. 45min., L20,000) run from 9am-noon and 3-7pm. Partial tours (40min., L10,000) do not include the *Caverna Bianca,* and leave hourly from 8:30am-12:30pm and 2:30-6:30pm. For information, call (080) 896 55 11.

The High Murge

Trains on the **Ferrovia Calabro-Lucane** line from Bari to Matera (frequent depar-tures, 1hr., L5800) cross gently rolling paths to the quiet town of **Altamura.** Although the town is one of the largest in the Murge region, the old town has managed to hold on to a timeless tranquillity. From the FCL train station, go right, through the underpass, and straight on via Regina Margherita to the gate; feel free to peek through the gates of the villas that line the approach. A portal through the old city wall leads to via Frederi-co II di Svevia. On the left down via Federico you can see the petite **Church of San Nicolò of the Greeks,** a simple church serving the Greek Orthodox community. A bit further down towers the campanile of the **cathedral,** built in Frederick's time. The façade's two towers reveal northern European influences. Inside, look for the treasury and women's gallery. The **Pro Loco** (Tourist Office) is in p. della Repubblica.

The only reasonable sack shack in town is the **Albergo Mercadante,** via Frederico, 74 (tel. (080) 84 24 92), conducting rooms almost as musical as the hotel's namesake—composer Francesco Saverio Mercadante (1795-1870), born across the street. (Singles L18,000. Doubles L26,000. No private baths.) Bow to **Il Rè della Griglia** and he'll grant you scepter-blessed calzone (L4500), pizzas, and other regal fare at via La Mag-giore, 2, off via Federico. (Tel. 84 10 53. Open Tues.-Sun. 9am-1pm and 6pm-mid-night.) A **supermarket** is at via Fillippo 58. (Open Tues.-Sun. 9am-2pm and 5-8pm.)

Gravina in Puglia seems even more rustically tranquil than Altamura until you dis-cover the oddities on the far side of town most natives avoid. To get there, take a Grav-ina train on one of the FS or FCL lines from Altamura (10 per day, 6am-10pm, 10min., L1400). To the right of the station as you exit stands the church of the **Madonna delle Grazie,** with an apparently annoyed eagle sprawled across its façade. The big bird symbolizes the Orsini clan, a powerful Roman family that sat around making popes. Though the bird has pals all over town, flee this particularly horrid avian to the far side of the tracks and follow the sign to the *centro* until you hit the big intersection. Go straight onto corso Aldo Moro, continuing on via Vittorio Veneto past the **Palazzo di Città.** About 300m up via Veneto, at the intersection with via del Museo, laments a fad-ed blue sign pointing towards the **Museo Ettore Pomarci Santomasi,** via del Museo, 20 (tel. 85 10 21), which exhibits archeological finds from the area. (Open Tues.-Sat. 9am-noon.)

Eerie material lurks at the end of via Matteotti (coming from p. della Repubblica). In p. Domenico, pray that your sins aren't too mediocre because **Purgatory Church** on the right would be a very creepy place to spend eternity. The two skeletons on the por-tal are supported by bears, which were also Orsini mascots. To the left of the church and right of the **Biblioteca** (built in 1743) lies a street leading to the **Basílica,** an immense four-aisled edifice. Back and towards the left of the Biblioteca, a narrow path runs through a particularly decrepit section of town. At the bottom lies the entrance to the district avoided by all locals. Ravines and the teeming vestiges of antedeluvian cave dwellings bring home the meaning of the name *gravina.* Some of the vestiges take the form of bones, which now rattle around in the **Grotto-Church of San Michele,** their deceased possessors minced by Saracen scimitars. The gate to the grotto area and church stays locked, but pay a few hundred lire to one of the kids nearby to summon the caretaker. Do this as well for the **Church of San Vito Vecchio** on the right towards the top of the hill. You'll soon see why the whole area is riddled with superstition. Yikes.

Bríndisi

> *Aye! This is the most repugnant city I've ever been to!*
>
> —*Paolo Damsci*

Want to *really* look forward to going home? A visit to Bríndisi will undoubtedly do the trick. Most people linger here just long enough to catch a ferry to Greece, but even rational folk sometimes get stuck overnight.

A look at the architecture indicates that Bríndisi must once have been quite pleasant. The narrow medieval alleys and flowered 19th-century streets remain, sadly obscured and overshadowed by the by-products of a busy port: cheap postwar buildings, piles of garbage, and prostrate transients. The latter are usually young backpackers, but recently they have come to include thousands of Albanian refugees.

Bríndisini react to their city's dreariness in two ways. Some people accept their fate with a wry sense of humor; others bitterly resent anyone who comes from more tolerable climes.

Ferries

Bríndisi is Italy's major departure point for ferries to Greece. There is regular service to **Corfu** (8hr. 30min.-9hr. 30min.), **Igoumenitsa** (10hr. 30min.-11hr. 30min.), **Patras** (15-20hr.), and **Cefalonia** (Adriatica lines, 16hr. 30min.). From Patras, there is bus service (4hr., L14,000; buy tickets at the *stazione marittima*) and train service (railpasses valid) to Athens. All ferries leave in the evening.

Bríndisi is served by **Adriatica,** via Regina Margherita, 13 (tel. 52 38 25) near the *stazione marittima;* **Marlines** c/o **Pattimare,** corso Garibaldi, 97 (tel. 52 65 48 or 52 65 49); **Hellenic Mediterranean Lines,** corso Garibaldi, 8 (tel. 52 85 31); and **Fragline,** corso Garibaldi, 88 (tel. 56 82 32).

In 1992, the lowest regular rates were on average as follows: to Corfu or Igoumenitsa, deck-class L55,000, students L50,000; from the third week of July through the second week of August L95,000, students L80,000. To Cefalonia or Patras L65,000, students L55,000; in high season L100,000, students L95,000. Deck class is fine in summer—sleeping horizontally outside is more comfortable than spending the night in an airline-type seat in a smoke-filled room. Be sure to bring warm clothes and a sleeping bag if you're on the deck. Bicycles travel free; motorcycles are L15,000-20,000, high season L35,000-45,000.

Most lines offer discounts to those under 27 and to ISIC-holders. **Eurailpass** holders get free deck passage on Adriatica Lines and Hellenic Mediterranean Lines (space-available basis—you could get bumped by a paying passenger), but must pay a L18,000 supplement from June 10 through September (this includes the port tax); at other times the only charge is the L11,000 **port tax. Cartaverde** holders get a 50% reduction on the same two lines. Buying a round-trip ticket in the off-season saves 10%.

Finally, there are group reductions of approximately 10% on one-way and 20% on round-trip tickets (usually 10 people minimum).

Eurail holders should go directly to the main offices listed above to get their tickets, because many travel agencies will advertise either Adriatica or Hellenic Mediterranean tickets and then try to double-talk their way to your money with commission-based services. Those without railpasses should seriously consider leaving from the much more palatable port of **Bari,** where departures can be up to L30,000 cheaper (see Bari listing above).

When you buy your ticket, you must pay the obligatory port tax (11,000), and the office will give you a boarding card, which you must have stamped at the police station on the first floor of the maritime station.

You lose your reservation on most lines if you don't check in at least two hours before departure. Allow plenty of time for late trains and the 1km walk from the train station to the ferry station. From mid-July to mid-August, it may be worth the effort to purchase ferry reservations at line offices or travel agents in other cities before you get to Bríndisi.

Practical Information

All that ferrygoers need to know about Bríndisi is that **corso Umberto** runs straight out from the train station, punctuated by fountainous **p. Cairoli. Corso Garibaldi** meets corso Umberto at **p. del Popolo,** then veers left, leading to the *stazione maritti-ma.* Bríndisi is generally unsafe and crime-ridden; women should beware in the evenings. Lone backpackers are considered particularly easy targets. If your ferry connection is late at night, be aware that theives often stalk tourists along corso Umberto. Try to walk with a group of people (the more the better; wait until you can collect at least a quartet, preferably of mixed gender).

Tourist Office: Don't follow the bright signs to "tourist information"; they'll lead you to a bare room in the *stazione marittina.* **EPT,** lungomare Regina Margherita, 5 (tel. 52 19 44), is at the dock to the left of the *stazione marittima,* 1 block to the side of p. Vittorio Emanuele. Charming official speaks English flawlessly. Open daily 9am-1pm and 4:30-7:30pm.

Budget Travel: CTS, via Bastioni Carlo V, 9 (tel. 56 01 87), the 1st right out of p. Crispi at the train station. Student ID cards and all that jazz.

Currency Exchange: Go to **Banca Nazionale del Lavoro** at via Santi, 11, off p. Vittoria. Avoid the ripoff rates at the *stazione marittima;* change money at one of the many outfits lining corso Umberto and c. Garibaldi, all of which offer direct U.S.-Greek conversions.

Trains: p. Crispi. Both **FS** and **Ferrovie del Sud-Est.** From: Naples (8:52pm, 8hr., L27,100); Rome (via Fóggia, 3 per day, 8hr., L38,900); Milan (via Ancona and Bologna, 6 per day, 10hr., L59,600). To: Bari (frequent departures, 1hr. 30min., L7800); Táranto (every hr., 75min., L4400); Lecce (frequent departures, 30min., L2800). **Luggage storage**: L1500 per bag.

Buses: Ferrovie del Sud-Est, at the train station (52 59 91). Handles buses throughout Apulia. **Marozzi** c/o Pattimare, corso Garibaldi, 97 (tel. 52 65 48), on the *lungomare,* wheels twice daily to Rome (7hr. 30min., L53,000).

Post Office: via San Francesco, off the *lungomare* (tel. 239 56). Open Mon.-Sat. 8:15am-8pm. **Postal Code:** 72100.

Telephones: SIP, via XX Settembre, 6, to the left on your way from the station to the port, near Albergo Venezia. Full service on international calls. Open daily 9am-1pm and 3:30-6:30pm. **Telephone Code:** 0831.

Public Showers: via del Mare, behind the Stazione Marittima. Not the cleanest facilities. Showers L3000. Toilets L300 when they're not on strike. Open daily 9am-1pm and 4-8pm.

Emergencies: tel. 113. **Police:** tel. 113. **Hospital: Ospedale di Summa,** p. Antonio (tel. 20 42). **Ambulance:** tel. 52 14 10.

Accommodations

Not many people choose to stay the night in Bríndisi. If they do, it's usually on top of a backpack in one of the *piazze* along corso Garibaldi—a miserable and dangerous experience.

Ostello della Gioventù "Bríndisi," is 3km away in Casale (tel. 41 31 23). L11,000 per person. Meals L10,000. Breakfast L3,000. Take the ferry across the port (every 10min., L200) then follow the signs for 1500m, or take bus #3 or 4 from the center (L700). Open 7am-midnight.

Hotel/Pensione Altair, via Tunisi, 4 (tel. 52 49 11), off via Garibaldi, near the *Stazione Maritima*. Clean, quiet and comparatively safe. Singles L25,000. Doubles L40,000, with bath L60,000.

Hotel Europa, p. Cairoli, 5 (tel. 528 46). A modern sleeping experience. Tiny, sterile rooms with TVs. In a relatively safe area. Singles L30,000. Doubles L40,000, with bath L70,000.

Food

This is one place where *Let's Go's* suggestions result in overcrowding of restaurants. Beat the crush by boldly going where no researcher has gone before: stroll around to *pizzerie* and *trattorie* and check posted menus. A wonderful **open-air market,** off corso Umberto on via Battisti, sells fresh fruit by the metric ton. (Open Mon.-Sat. 7am-1pm.) Pizza and *focaccia* are made in huge sheets and sold by weight. **Supermarket Eurospar,** at the end of corso Garibaldi, near the port, is modern and well stocked but crowded with Greece-bound backpackers. (Open Fri.-Wed. 8:30am-1pm and 4:30-8pm, Thurs. 8:30am-1pm.)

Trattoria da Emilia Spaghetti House, vico dei Raimondo, 11, off via San Lorenzo. A selection of fresh pastas runs L7000, including salad, beverages, and cover if you bring your *Let's Go*. Open daily 9am-10pm; ring bell if the owner isn't there.

Spaghetti House Osteria Cucina Casalinga, via Mazzini, 57, parallel to corso Umberto, not far from the station. Delicious fare and a proprietor who loves *Let's Go* readers. *Lasagne* L4000. Full meal of pasta, beverage, and bread, about L6000. Cover L500. Open Mon.-Sat. 11am-2:30pm and 4-8:30pm.

Trattoria L'Angoletto, via Pergola, 3 (tel. 52 50 29), near the port, off corso Garibaldi. Pleasant, elegant outdoor eating. Pizza L5500-8000. Open daily 9am-11pm.

Sights and Entertainment

Stand with your back to the port and turn right; on the stairs facing the water you will find the only remaining terminal **column** of the Appian way. If you look closely, you'll see a marble capital graced by the sculpted figures of Jove, Neptune, Mars, and eight tritons. On the other side of the port rises another pillar. This modern counterpart to the Roman relic is a monument to Italian sailors. Surrounded by a vast seaside park, the **Marinaio d'Italia** takes the shape of an oversized rudder 55m high. You can easily hop over on one of the **Casale** ferries that leave every 10 minutes from Banchina Montenegro, opposite via Montenegro (round-trip L2000).

Back in Bríndisi, wander through the nooks and crannies of the old town. Just above the Appian Way column, you'll stumble across the ruins of the Roman house in which Virgil died on his way home from Greece. P. Duomo introduces the *duomo* itself (12th-century, rebuilt in the 18th century), where Frederick II wed Jerusalem's Yolande.

If you follow the water for 2km or take the Casale ferry, you'll end up at the **Santa Maria del Casale.** The pride of Bríndisi, this multicolored, elaborately adorned building is reminiscent of Byzantine design but also incorporates Gothic ornamentation. It was built by Prince Phillip of neighboring Táranto, who enlisted his countryman Rinaldo da Taranto to paint an impressive Last Judgement fresco. If you're stuck overnight between June 27 and July 14, and suicide is not a viable option, kill time at the **Festa de L'Unità.** The erstwhile Italian Communist Party subverts the minds of capitalism-weary Brindisini with nightly dancing, movies, music, and even a fashion show. (Most events are free and take place in via Grandi.

Lecce

Variously dubbed the "Florence of the Baroque" and the "Athens of Apulia," Lecce is both a happily untouristed cornucopia of 17th-century architecture and one of southern Italy's most important intellectual centers.

A cosmopolitan succession of conquerors—Cretans, Romans, Saracens, Swabians, and more—passed through here, but the city's modern form was defined under the dominance of Habsburg Spain in the 16th and 17th centuries. Competitive merchants, aristocrats, and the religous orders of the Counter-Reformation spawned a plethora of palaces, churches, and arches in the distinctive *barocco Leccese*. Carved from soft, golden sandstone, the exuberant architecture resembles a sumptuous theatrical set. Cornices curl around columns, draperies drip with fatuous *putti*, balconies resemble fruitbowls, and windowsills become flower stalls.

Lecce remains an important center of agricultural trade, which around here means an abundance of olives. The University of Lecce is responsible for restoration projects and archeological studies around the area, as well as a vivacious student scene. The city provides a good starting point for a trip down the Salento Peninsula, Italy's high heel. Small Turkish- and Greek-looking towns dot the peninsula, and in some places you'll hear a dialect similar to Greek.

Orientation and Practical Information

The southeastern terminus of the state railway system, Lecce lies some 35km south and inland of Bríndisi. Twenty-five daily trains connect the Athens of Apulia with the Newark of Apulia (30min., L2800). To get to the center from the train station, walk down viale Quarta and turn right onto the broad via Gallipoli. Turn left at viale Otranto and continue to the end. Past the castle on your left is **p. Sant'Oronzo,** the center of town. The immense Portale Napoli can be reached by following via Umberto from p. Sant'Oronzo to via Principi di Savoia, then turning left. Many intersections are bereft of street signs, so trace your path along a map or pleasantly lose yourself.

Tourist Office: EPT and AAST, (tel. 464 58, 244 43 or 30 44 43), in the "Il Sedile" monument in p. Sant'Oronzo. Maps, pamphlets, hotel listings. Helpful, informed, and occasionally English-speaking. Open Mon.-Fri. 9am-1pm and 5:30-7:30pm, Sat. 9am-1pm.

Budget Travel: CTS, via Palmieri, 89 (tel. 218 62). A student travel service. Air and train information, tickets, and discounts. Open Mon.-Fri. 8:30am-1pm and 4:30-8pm, Sat. 8:30am-1pm.

Post Office: in piazzetta Libertini (tel. 230 00), at the end of viale Otranto next to a large indoor market. Open Mon.-Sat. 8:15am-8pm. **Postal Code:** 73100.

Telephones: SIP, via Oberdan, 13 (tel. 68 64 22), near p. Mazzini. Open daily 9:15am-12:45pm and 3:30-6:30pm. **Telephone Code:** 0832.

Trains: in p. Stazione (tel. 210 16), about 1km from the town center. F.S. travels north to Táranto (change at Bríndisi, 8 per day, 2hr., L7800). The provincial **Ferrovie del Sud-Est** (tel. 419 31) runs down the Salento Peninsula to Gallipoli (8 per day, 1hr., L7600 round-trip) and Otranto (change at Maglie, 4 or 5 per day, 1hr. 30min., L6800 round-trip).

Buses: STP, via Adua (tel. 228 73), parallel to via Taranto. Connections to the Salento Peninsula. **Sud-Est,** via Boito, easily accessible by urban bus #7 (L600) from the train station (tel. 64 76 34). To: Otranto (2 per day, 1hr. 30min.); Gallipoli (5 per day, 50min.); Táranto (2 per day, 80min.); and other Apulian destinations.

Emergencies: tel. 113. **Police:** viale Otranto (tel. 47 16). **Hospital: Ospedale Vito Fazzi,** p. Bottazzi (tel. 68 51). **Ambulance:** tel. 68 54 03 or 63 54 11.

Accommodations and Camping

An affordable, decent bed is a rare find indeed.

Ostello della Gioventù Adriatico (tel. 65 00 26), 12km from Lecce on the beach of San Cataldo. Take the bus toward San Cataldo from the Villa Comunale (near p. Sant'Oronzo), Porta Rudiae, or viale Bríndisi (every hr. on the hr.; Sept. 4 per day; last at 7pm; L1200). L7000 per person. Open July-Sept.

Hotel Cappello, via Montenegrappa, 4 (tel. 288 81). From the station, take the 1st left off viale Quarta onto via Don Bosco and follow the signs. Nice and modern but be prepared for a rude awakening by the morning trains next door. Bathless singles have toilet, bidet, and sink, but no access to a shower; however, the affable owner will probably let you shower in an empty room. Singles L30,000, with bath L40,000. Doubles with bath L65,000. Triples L70,000. Quads L92,000.

Camping: Camping Torre Rinalda (tel. 65 21 61), 3km from the beach in the zone of Litoranea. Take bus #18 to Litoranea. July 7-Aug. 26 L7400 per person, L10,600 per tent. Off-season L5400 per person, L6700 per tent. **Camping Pinimar** (tel. 428 43), 12km northeast of Lecce at Marina di Frigole. 7 buses depart daily from Lecce's Villa Comunale. L3600 per person, L4100 per small tent. Use of kitchenette L2200.

Food

Regional specialties include *ciceri e tria* (pasta cooked in chick pea broth), *cappello da gendarme* (a pastry shell stuffed with eggplant, zucchini, and veal), and *mercia,* a sheep's-milk mozzarella. Buy picnic supplies at **Salumeria Loiacono,** via Fazzi, 11, in p. Sant'Oronzo, a 150-year-old cheese store. The **indoor market** next to the post office provides a chance to haggle. (Open Mon.-Fri. 5am-1pm, Sat. 5am-1pm and 4-8pm.)

La Capannina, via Cairoli, 13 (tel. 241 59), 700m from the station. Delicious food outdoors, in the middle of an imposing neoclassical *piazza.* A fun atmosphere—don't miss the *antipasti self-serve* (L6000). Meat dishes L8000-10,000. Wine L2000 per half-liter. Cover L1500. Service 15%. Open Tues.-Sun. noon-3pm and 7-11:30pm.

Ristorante Cinese Chinatown, via della Saponea, 15 (tel. 30 85 58), past the Church of Santa Croce on the right. Complete *menùs* L15,000, L20,000, and L25,000. Open Mon.-Sat. noon-3pm and 7-11pm.

Ristorante-Pizzeria Da Claudio, via Cavour, 11 (tel. 49 529), 1 block down from Alloggio Faggiano. Complete dinner L15,000 (includng cover). Pasta from L5000. Meat dishes L5000-7000. Pizza L3500-5000. The excellent house red wine is L3000 per . Cover L1200. Open Thurs.-Tues. 7-11pm.

Sights and Entertainment

The best way to see Lecce is to wander around the old quarter, bumping into Baroque monuments at every turn. Start with the **Church of St. Irene** (1591-1639) off p. Sant'Oronzo, a fine example of both Roman Baroque and the more florid Lecce style. Unfortunately, like many of the city's arhitectural treasures, the church is closed for restoration. You can fulfill the architectural longings awakened in you by the church in the marvelous complex of **piazza del Duomo,** a short distance away on via Vittorio Emanuele. In front looms the **cathedral,** rebuilt between 1659 and 1670 by Giuseppe Zimbalo, the architect of many of Lecce's most celebrated buildings. The interior dates mostly from the 18th century, with the exception of two Leccese altars. (Open daily 8-11am and 4:30-7:30pm.)

To the right of the cathedral (the first building as you enter the square), you'll encounter the **seminary** (1709) by Cino, a pupil of Zimbalo. Cino was also well-versed in flamboyant architectural idiom here, stopping just short of debauchery with the help of a little bilateral symmetry. The solid center portal keeps the windows in line; their frames swirl like icing on a cake.

The **Palazzo Vescovile** (Bishop's Palace), distinguished by its open portico, has been remodeled several times since its original construction in 1632. The porticoes held shops in the days when an annual fair took place in the *piazza.* The final component of the *piazza,* the **campanile** (1682), exhibits a more restrained elegance. A stroll down via Libertini takes you to the **Porta Rudiae** (1703), past the unfinished Baroque façade of the **Church of Santa Teresa** to the simple Renaissance façade of the **Church of Sant'Anna.** At the end of the street awaits the phantasmagorically complicated **Church of the Rosary,** Zimbalo's last work.

Return to p. Sant'Oronzo and walk north across p. Castro Mediano to Lecce's most uninhibited monument. No amount of extravagant architecture quite prepares you for the **Church of Santa Croce** (1548-1646), the supreme expression of Leccese Baroque and the city's most vaunted possession. Fantastic monsters and caryatids adorn the façade; the great rose window resembles an upside-down wedding cake. Instead of the surfaces lavished with sculpture and painting favored by many Baroque buildings, two simple rows of Corinthian columns support plain white walls within the church. A wonderfully animated altar (1614) by F. A. Zimbalo, Giuseppe's papa, adorns the chapel to the left of the apse. (Open daily 9am-1pm and 5:30-7:30pm.)

To the left of Santa Croce rises the **Palazzo del Governo.** Zimbalo designed the lower half of the façade while Cino worked on the upper portion. Diagonally across the street sprawls the Florentine-style **Palazzo Adorni,** with a secret enclosed garden in back. (Both open daily 8am-1pm.) From here via Umberto and via Principe di Savoia take you to the **Arco di Trionfo,** erected in 1548 in honor of Charles V, whose coat of arms adorns the front. Located in an ancient cemetery beyond the arch, the **Church of SS. Nicolò e Cataldo** was founded in 1180 by the Normans and modified in 1716 by Cino (closed for restoration). Note the Arabic influences, especially in the portal. Small mausoleums of every conceivable style cluster around the narrow paths of the cemetery next door.

Little remains of Lecce's Roman city except the 2nd-century AD **amphitheater,** which is camouflaged by the scenery at **piazza Sant'Oronzo.** The **Column of Sant'Oronzo** next to the amphitheater is one of the two that once marked the termination of the Appian Way in Bríndisi.

Still more Baroque churches await the as-yet-unsatisfied visitor. The **Church of Santa Chiara** (1694; closed for restoration), at the end of p. Vittorio Emanuele, houses fine Leccese Baroque altars. **Via Arte della Cartapesta,** so named for its manufacture of papier-mâché figures of saints, runs to the left of the church. The **Church of Carmine,** whose whimsical façade (1717) was Cino's last work, contrasts perfectly with the plain façade of the **Church of the Gesù** (1579), providing a definitive expression of Leccese Baroque.

On viale Gallipoli toward the station, you'll find the urbane **Museo Provinciale.** It houses a collection of bronze statuettes, inscriptions, vases, and rare 4th-century commemorative fish plates. Traipse up to the *pinacoteca* on the third floor to see a stunning 13th-century gospel cover inlaid with gold, blue, and white enamel. (Open Mon.-Fri. 9:30am-1pm and 2:30-7:30pm, Sun. and holidays 9am-1:30pm. Admission L2000, Sun. free.)

This quiet city comes alive in July and August. **Estate Musicale Leccese** (July 1-Aug. 15) is a festival of music and dance. Ask at the EPT for *Calendario Manifestazioni 1993,* which details seasonal goings on in the whole province.

Salento Peninsula

While in Lecce, take the time to visit the many medieval fortresses and castles scattered along the **Salento Peninsula.** The castle closest to Lecce (11km away on the road to Struda) is **Acaia,** now a forgotten ruin overgrown with weeds. Huge vaults, remnants of mosaics, narrow staircases, and a desolate courtyard stir medieval fantasies. (Three buses per day leave for Acaia from the via Adua station in Lecce.)

Other spots in the Salento Peninsula are hard to reach by public transport. The **Ferrovie del Sud-Est,** a private railway, serves most of the larger communities (Gallipoli, Otranto, Gagliano), but is slow and infrequent. People are known to take the train to one of the larger towns by the sea and then use the EPT map to guide them in hitchhiking.

Otranto

Otranto is the best starting point for a tour of the Adriatic Coast (9 per day, 1hr. 30min., round-trip L7000; change at Maglie). An ancient city of Greek origin and the easternmost point of habitation in Italy, Otranto was once the capital of Byzantine territory in Apulia and remained a key strategic site throughout the Middle Ages as a Norman outpost and embarkation point for the Crusades. In 1480, the Ottoman Turks attempted to conquer the Italian Peninsula and started the project in Otranto. The invasion was turned back early on, but Otranto's 800 citizens were slaughtered and the town ravaged. The remains of the "martyrs of Otranto" are still found in the phenomenal **cathedral,** which also preserves an 11th-century mosaic pavement of the Tree of Life that extends the entire length of the nave. The crypt houses 42 columns pilfered from Greek, Roman, and Arab structures, all of varying marbles. Alterations over the centuries have left the once-austere exterior with an elaborate Baroque portal from the 18th century and a fine Gothic rose window. The Byzantine **Church of San Pietro** poses covertly in an enclosed square. Built between the 10th and 11th centuries in the shape of a Greek cross, its richly articulated interior contrasts with its staid exterior.

Otranto's **tourist office,** at via Basilica, 8 (tel. (0836) 80 14 36), rests at the foot of the *duomo.* The independent **Cooperativa Turismo Iniziativa Otranto,** on largo Cavour near the *duomo,* is staffed by a jolly bunch who'll help you find a room. They also participate in the national *Agriturismo* program, by whose good graces tourists can stay at local farms. The cost is usually around L31,000 per person including meals. You can also rent bikes at this agency (L10,000 a day) or join their bike tours to local sites (L8000-10,000, bike included). (Open Mon.-Sat. 9am-12:30pm and 5-9pm.) If you plan to stay, try **Albergo Ester,** via Papa Giovanni XXIII, 19 (tel. (0836) 80 12 06), near the Aragonese castle, rents doubles with bath for L65,000. (Reserve in Aug.) **Il Gabbiano** (tel. (0836) 80 12 51), dispenses singles for L37,500 (with bath L45,000) and doubles for L59,600 (with bath L70,000). Full pension is L72,000 and breakfast L6000. From Sept. 15 to July 30, bring your favorite green-garbed budget travel guide and receive a 15% discount. **Pensione La Plancia,** near Il Gabbiano, (tel. (0836) 80 12 17), has well-scrubbed singles with bath for L40,000, doubles with bath for L60,000. All of Otranto's hotels have obligatory full pension on the order of L70,000 per person in August. The **Ristorante/Pizzeria Pub 90,** lungomare Kennedy, 2 (tel. (0836) 813 25), offers pizza for L3000-8000. *Primi* L5000-6000, *secondi* L8000-10,000<italicxd1 fish is a specialty. (Cover L2500. Service 10%.) You'll find fast food and pizza by the slice at **Profumo di Mare,** lungomare Terra d'Otranto, 3. Or sate your hunger with a roast chicken, (*pollo arrosto,* L7000) from one of the many *rosticcerie.* A dilapidated **ferry** runs from Otranto to Corfu and Igoumenitsa (Greece), operated by **Roana Lines.** You'll have to check the byzantine schedule yourself. Fares average L40,000 (students L35,000), but they jump to L70,000 (students L50,000) from July 29 to August 10. Make inquiries and reservations at the **Stazione Marittima** (tel. (0836) 80 10 05).

Venture a few miles north of Otranto to **Torre dell'Orso,** a *lido* cradled in pine woods at the end of a beautiful inlet. A bemused Madonna sits at the **Grotta della Poesia,** a small pool of clear water enclosed by low cliffs and a natural bridge.

The coast south of Otranto is more rugged, bordered by limestone cliffs and dotted with flat-roofed homes. **Santa Cesárea Terme** is an important resort in the area, famous for its thermal springs and spectacular location. The **tourist office** gathers dust at via Roma, 209 (tel. (0836) 944 40 43). A mere 6km south of here is the marine cave **Zinzulusa Grotto,** filled with stalactites and stalagmites (*zinzuli* in the local dialect). Two Ferrovie del Sud-Est buses per day run to Santa Cesárea Terme from via Adua in Lecce.

Gallipoli

To explore the peninsula's Ionian Coast, start at **Gallipoli** (*not* the Gallipoli of World War I fame, which is located in Turkey). (From Lecce by train every 30min., 1hr., L3200, or by bus 1hr., L3200). Named "beautiful city" by the Greeks, the port has traditionally traded in olive oil and wine. Its insular old city possesses a distinctly Greek air. Pastel houses enclose narrow winding streets that lead to the seaside promenade that has replaced the city's ancient walls. Stretching along Gallipoli's northern coast are two picturesque beaches, **Santa Maria al Bagno** and **Santa Caterina.** Several secluded beaches lie close to town and south of Gallipoli (admission around L500). **Lido San Giovanni,** on the beach road, harbors pebbly sand and clear water. Gallipoli's extremely modest **Pro Loco tourist office,** corso Roma, 225 (tel. (0833) 47 62 02), huddles next to p. Fontana Greca. (Open Mon.-Fri. 10am-noon and 5-7pm.) Continue up corso Roma over the bridge and into the old town. On the left at corso Roma, 3, ripens an indoor fruit market. (Open 7am-1:30pm and 5-8pm.) Across the street on p. Imbriani is the **post office.** (Open Mon.-Fri. 8:30am-1pm.)

Unfortunately, Gallipoli has no bargain lodgings. Either stay in Lecce or camp. **Camping Vecchia Torre** (tel. (0833) 20 90 83), about 3km from town, lets bungalows for two people at L20,000 (off-season L11,000). Or pay L6500 per person, off-season L4500. (Open May 15-Sept.) **Baia di Gallipoli** (tel. (0833) 47 69 06), about the same distance from town, rents two-bed bungalows for L60,000, and charges L6300 per tent, L8700 per person, off-season L4500 per tent, L6200 per person. (Open June- Sept.) Both have tennis courts and are close to the beach.

Táranto

Legends say Taras, son of Neptune, founded Táranto 1200 years before Rome's creation. As a metropolis of Magna Graecia, Táranto was an important trading port and center of philosophical thought. Spartans, Normans, and their kin periodically reduced Táranto to smithereens; only a few premodern traces remain.

Contemporary Táranto is a fascinating microcosm of the ups and downs of the 20th-century *mezzogiornio*. The old city, with its noisy markets and tiny fishing boats, retains the trappings of the preindustrial South. Flanking this area is a naval base, the result of Táranto's military build-up during Fascist times; to the north, postwar smokestacks churn out steel.

Orientation and Practical Information

Táranto is divided into three parts: the **port area** to the north, with the train station; the **old city,** a small island across Ponte di Porta Napoli from the station; and the **new city,** to the southeast across the *canale navigabile,* which houses the majority of hotels, restaurants, and offices. Pick up a city map at the information window at the station and then take any bus (L800) to the new city. Don't walk through the old city with a pack on unless you're eager to part with it. At night, stick to the brightly lit, well-populated seaside boulevards.

Tourist Office: corso Umberto, 113 (tel. 212 33), in the new city. Take bus #8 from the station; get off 3 stops after the bridge into the new city. Make a left on via Acclavio and follow it to corso Umberto; the office is across corso Umberto on the corner. Well-equipped, genial. Provides a good map and help with accommodations. Open Mon.-Fri. 9am-1pm and 5-7pm, Sat. 9:30am-12:30pm.

Budget Travel: CTS, via Matteotti, 1 (tel. 43 33 50, fax 452 62 38), just across the bridge in the new city. ID cards and student discounts. Open Mon.-Sat. 10am-1pm, Sept.-June 9am-1pm and 3-8pm.

Post Office: lungomare Vittorio Emanuele II (tel. 259 51), a few blocks up from the *canale navigabile.* Open Mon.-Sat. 9am-1pm and 5:30-7:15pm. **Postal Code:** 74100.

Telephones: SIP, lungomare Vittorio Emanuele, 20 (tel. 290 91), near the post office. Open 8am-9:30pm. **Telephone Code:** 099.

Trains: in p. Duca d'Aosta for both **F.S.** and **Ferrovie del Sud-Est.** Pick up the transportation timetables at the tourist office. Trains to: Bríndisi (frequent departures, 1hr. 30min., L4400), Bari (also frequent, 1hr. 30min., L7800), Naples (departs 6am, 6hr., L19,600), Rome (2 per day, 8hr. 30min., L35,900), Martina Franca (9 per day, 45min., L2800), and Alberobello via Martina Franca (14 per day, 1hr., L3500). For Alberobello there is 1 direct train daily at 4:30pm.

Buses: AMAT city bus tickets cost L800; buy them at *tabacchi* or at the small office outside the station. **Ferrovie Autobus del Sud-Est** (tel. 35 35 85) buses to Martina Franca (11 per day, 7am-9pm, 1hr., L2800) and Bari (4 per day, 2hr., L7800) leave from p. Castello (in the old city, just across from the *canale navigabile*). Buses to Lecce (4 per day, 2 hr., L5700) leave from via Magnaghi in the northeastern outskirts of the new city. **SITA** buses depart from p. del Castello for Matera (5 per day, 1hr. 45min., L3400; some require a change at Laterza).

Emergencies: tel. 113. **Police:** tel. 112 or 113. **Hospital: SS. Annunziata,** via Bruno (tel. 98 51).

Accommodations and Camping

Unlike other Apulian cities, Táranto is not lacking in cheap, comfortable lodgings. Fortunately, most hotels congregate in the brightly lit *viali* of the new city, and at the end of the well-traveled *lungomare* in the old city. Nevertheless, exercise caution all throughout Táranto at night. The campgrounds here boast four stars and correspondingly astronomical prices.

Albergo La Cremaillere, in Locando San Paolo at via Orimini, 1 (tel. (080) 70 02 65). Quite far out; take the Ferrovie del Sud-Est bus from p. Castello for Martina Franca, and get off at Locando San Paolo (6 per day, 50min.). Right on the *autostrada.* Singles L35,000. Doubles L60,000, all with bath.

Pensione Rivera, via Campania, 203 (tel. 33 88 90), on the outskirts of town. Take the "Circolare Rossa" bus (L800) from via Regina Margherita and get off at via Campania (15min.). Contemporary, comfortable rooms in a residential area. Singles L25,000. Doubles L42,000.

Hotel Ariston, p. Fontanta, 15 (tel. 40 75 63), across the bridge into the old city from the station. Right on the fishing port; clean, spacious rooms, some with balconies overlooking the sea. Genial desk manager. Singles L21,600. Doubles L34,800, with bath L44,000.

Albergo Pisani, via Cavour, 43 (tel. 240 87), across bridge in the new city off p. Garibaldi. The brightest, newest place in town. Singles L33,000, with bath L40,000. Doubles L63,000, with bath L77,000. Triples with bath L90,000.

Albergo Sorrentino, p. Fontana, 7 (tel. 47 18 390), next to Hotel Ariston. Family-run. Large but run-down rooms. Singles L22,000. Doubles L35,000, with bath L40,000. Showers included.

Food

Táranto swims with seafood. Try *cozze* (mussels) in basil and olive oil. Inexpensive restaurants flood the new city, and the *menù turistico* is a good catch here, often as varied as the regular menu. Grab your daily bread at **Supermercato STANDA** in p. Immacolata (open Mon.-Fri. 9am-1pm and 4:45-8:30pm, Sat. 9am-12:45pm). The daily **market,** in the *piazza* just across the bridge into the old city, supplies pop music, live snails, stingrays, and yes, fruits and vegetables. (Open daily 7am-1:30pm.)

Trattoria Gatto Rosso da Rino, via Cavour, 2 (tel. 298 75). Specializes in seafood. The *spaghetti mare misto* (literally "mixed sea") is a *primo primo* (L4500), as are the *tubetti alle cozze* (tubular pasta with mussels, L5000). Open Tues.-Sun. 11am-3pm and 7-11pm.

Ristorante Basile al Ristoro, via Pitagora, 76 (tel. 452 62 40), across from the Giardini Pubblici, 1 street up from corso Umberto. An excellent value—pleasant atmosphere, prompt service, and delicious food. Offerings vary according to availability of fresh ingredients. *Primi* around L6000, *secondi* L7000. Pizza and beer, L7000. *Menù* L15,000. Open Sun.-Fri. 9:30am-3pm and 6pm-midnight.

Birreria Amstel, via d'Aquino, 27 (tel. 937 58), in the new city, parallel to corso Umberto off p. Immacolata. Tasty *risotto alla marinara* (rice with seafood, L5500). If you eat in the *tavola calda,* you'll save L1000 per dish and be spared the cover to boot. Splendid pizzas in the evening L3000-6000. Full-choice *menù* L15,000. Wine L3000 per . Cover L1500. Open Aug.-June Thurs.-Tues. 12:30-2:30pm and 7-11:30pm.

Sights

Other than the cathedral and the superb National Museum, little remains of the city's past glory. Nonetheless, the waterside and main square abide with a certain graciousness. Visit the tree-lined **lungomare Vittorio Emanuele** in the new city for a far-reaching view over the Mar Grande. On the horizon, between Rondinella Point to the right and lighthoused Capo San Vito to the left, you can spy the islands of San Pietro and San Paolo, which enclose the outer harbor. Both are military outposts, however, and can be visited only with permission. The fecund gardens of **Villa Peripato** (or *giardini pubblici*), on the other side of the city, bloom toward a terrace overlooking the Mar Piccolo and the Italian naval base.

Situated across the bridge into the old city, the **Aragonese Castle** was built with a view of both waters and with a hold over the *canale navigabile.* Unfortunately, it still seems to have strategic value; the navy occupies nearly all of it, and only the small **art gallery** (first door on your left crossing into the old town) may be visited. (Gallery open daily 9:30am-1pm and 6-9pm. Free.)

The **old city** invites visitors to wander its dark byways, but exercise appropriate caution. It is home to a remarkable **cathedral,** built in the 10th century and rebuilt in 1713. The church was originally a Greek cross; the Latin arm was added in 1170. The Byzantine exterior walls and cupola are still visible at the sides of the church. Under the chancel, the crypt is doused with 12th-century Byzantine frescoes. Welcome relief from the solemnity of the old town is supplied by the flamboyant decoration of the **San Cataldo Chapel** (end of the right aisle), whose multicolored, intricate marble designs exemplify the Leccese Baroque influence. Compare this structure with Táranto's other prominent cathedral in the eastern part of the new city. Designed by Gio Ponti, this modern Gothic creation takes the shape of a sail. (Both open daily 1-5pm.)

The most telling testimony to Táranto's former importance is found within the excellent **National Museum,** corso Umberto, 41, at corso Cavour. This museum's collection of Magna Graecian art now rivals Reggio's and Naples's as the best in Italy; its terracotta figure collection is the world's largest. Mostly excavated from the city's necropolis, the collection also includes sculpture and mosaics, imported and local pottery, jewelry, coins, and prehistoric materials. (Open Tues.-Sat. 9am-2pm and 3-7:30pm, Sun. 9am-1pm, Mon. 9am-2pm. Free daily tours in Italian 9:30 and 11am. Admission L6000.)

In summer, an ACTT city bus stops along the *lungomare* (10 per day, 8:15am-7:30pm, L800), carrying you to the most beautiful, least crowded **beach** in the area, **Lido Silvana.**

Entertainment

Every night from about 6 to 8pm, the entire stretch of **via d'Aquino** throngs with scoping crowds. The action centers on **piazza della Vittoria.** Giovanni Filippo Sousa fans sound out a nightly cheer at sundown as the navy band toots to the lowering of the flag where lungomare Vittorio Emanuele meets the *canale navigabile.*

Táranto's **Holy Week festival** draws crowds and acclaim from around the country. In a ceremony rooted in medieval Spanish ritual, men don masks and long white robes with pointed hoods and parade a cart through the streets, on a pilgrimage to the Holy Sepulchres housed in Táranto's churches. The festivities begin the Sunday before Easter. Two processions occur Thursday, at 3pm and midnight, and one on Good Friday at 5pm. The Procession of Our Lady of Sorrows leaves at midnight from the Church of San Domenico. A river of people floods the city, walking until noon on Good Friday.

On May 10, the city celebrates the **Festa di San Cataldo** with a procession of boats that escorts the statue of San Cataldo around the harbor. As it passes the Aragonese Castle, the castle lights up beneath a stirring display of fireworks.

Basilicata

When Carlo Levi first came to Basilicata, he found a desperately backward and seemingly God-forsaken land. His novel *Cristo si è fermato a Eboli (Christ Stopped at Eboli)* portrayed the plight of the inhabitants with such urgency that it helped launch the *Cassa per il Mezzogiorno,* a national effort to integrate southern Italy into the 20th-century economy. Remote Basilicata exemplifies the outcome of government efforts: peasants still live in marked isolation, while cement cities have sprung up throughout the region, thanks to billions of lire sent from Rome.

Part of Basilicata's problems is its affinity for earthquakes; the epicenter of the 1980 quake that leveled distant Naples was here. This was once part of Magna Graecia, but the shaken Greeks abandoned the region long ago. Metaponto, the chief Greek city in the Basilicata, was alternately rocked by earthquakes and sacked by passers-through (including Spartacus) before the entire region fell to the Lombards in the 6th century

AD. Metapontoremains home to the best ruins on the Ionian coast, though even these are meager; the sandy beaches lining the southern coast remain the most potent offering of southern Basilicata. Inland, Matera harbors the unusual *sassi,* rock dwellings which date from the Paleolithic Age and sheltered persecuted monks in the 9th century; Maratea in the west presides over Basilicata's 20km of rocky Tyrrhenian coast.

Matera

A few decades ago, Matera represented the quintessence of Italian poverty, its destitute inhabitants forced to live in caves (*sassi*) together with pigs and chickens. A river of lire, the source of which is Rome, produced the prosperous, self-satisfied town you see today. Rome's munificence helped build adequate housing, which drew most of the citizens out of their rock caverns. In the 1970s, radicals and visionaries moved to reinhabit the ancient dwellings. Ongoing renovations reflect the effort to provide many Materans with a life in the "interesting" part of town, and the *sassi* are now undergoing rapid gentrification.

Orientation and Practical Information

Ten **SITA** buses depart each day from Metaponto's train station at p. Matteotti (8:25am-9:55pm; 6 per day in winter, 8am-4:50pm; 1hr., L2900) and one from Potenza (at 3:45pm, 1hr. 45min., L5100). Seven **Ferrovie Calabro-Lucane** buses leave from Ferrandina's train station on the Potenza-Táranto line (6:30am-9:35pm, 45min., L2400). Calabro-Lucane **trains** also leave every one to two hours from Bari's central train station (6:50am-10:57pm, 1hr. 30 min., L3800). Six SITA buses leave daily from Táranto's bus terminal at p. Castello for Matera (5:50am-7:20pm, 1hr. 45min., L3400). Most service is drastically reduced Sunday and holidays. The heart of the new city is piazza V. Veneto. Via Roma links it to the train and bus stations at p. Matteotti; via delle Beccherie leads to p. Duomo in the *sassi.*

Tourist Office: EPT, via de Viti de Marco, 9 (tel. 33 34 52 or 33 19 83). From the station walk down via Roma and take your 2nd left. Pamphlets in English and a map. Acquire the comprehensive guide to Basilicata. English spoken. Open daily 8am-2pm and (tentatively) 4-7pm—afternoon hours may not be continued in 1993. **Cooperative Amici del Turista** (tel. 31 01 13), in p. San Pietro Caveoso in the *sassi,* gives out maps and advice on exploring the cave dwellings. Open daily 9:30am-12:30pm and 4-7pm; March-May 9:30am-1pm; Oct.-Feb. erratic morning hours. In summer, begin your information odyssey at one of the **information gazebos** near the entrance to the *sassi.* There is one at via Ribola and another between p. Veneto and via del Corso. Open daily 9am-1pm and 3-7:30pm.

Post Office: on via del Corso (tel. 33 18 22), off p. Veneto. Open Mon.-Fri. 8:15am-5:30pm. **Postal Code:** 75100.

Telephones: SIP, via del Corso, 5 (tel. 24 21). Open Mon.-Sat. 9am-1pm and 2-7pm; Sun. 9am-1pm and 3:30-6:30pm. At night, try **Autonoleggio Tommaso,** vico XX Settembre, 2 blocks from p. Vittorio Veneto. Open 9pm-8am. **Telephone Code:** 0835.

Emergencies: tel. 113. **Police:** tel. 33 42 22. **Ambulance:** tel. 33 35 21. **Hospital:** on via Lanera (tel. 21 14 10).

Accommodations

Insidious rate creep has set in among Matera's former budget hotels as they seek more stars and higher profits. It's possible to find a room if you arrive early in the day, but you'd be best off making reservations a few days in advance.

Albergo Roma, via Roma, 62 (tel. 21 27 01), downhill from the bus station at p. Matteotti. Friendly, clean, and conveniently located. Fills up fast during festival period (late June-early July). Curfew midnight. Singles L22,000. Doubles L36,000, with bath L40,000.

Hotel President, via Roma, 13 (tel. 33 57 91, fax. 33 58 21). The President promises a few affordable rooms without baths and no new taxes. Singles L33,000. Doubles L60,000. Credit cards accepted.

De Nicola, via Nazionale, 158 (tel. 38 51 11). Follow viale A. Moro from p. Matteotti to via Anunzia Tella. To the left, via Anunzia Tella turns into via Nazionale. A bit of a hike from the station, but might still have a free room late in the day. Singles with bath L42,000. Doubles with bath L68,000.

Food

Matera offers several culinary specialties, including *favetta con cicore* (a soup of beans, celery, chicory, and croutons, all mixed in olive oil) and *frittata di spaghetti* (pasta mixed with anchovies, eggs, bread crumbs, garlic, and oil). Experience true Materan grit by gnawing on *pane di grano duro;* made of extra-hard wheat, this bread stays fresh almost as long as Twinkies. **Panificio Perrone,** via dei Sariis, 6 (tel. 38 56 56), off via Lucana, sells large, fluffy loaves (L1600 per kg). They also sell tasty *biscotti al vino,* cookies baked with wine (L7000 per kg). (Open Mon.-Wed. and Fri.-Sat. 8am-2pm and 4-8pm, Thurs. 8am-2pm.) The **market** nestles between via Lucana and via A. Persio, near p. Veneto. (Open Mon.-Sat. 7am-1pm.) Down the block from the tourist office sits **Supermercato Divella,** via Spine Bianche, 6 (open Mon.-Wed. and Fri.-Sat. 8:30am-1:30pm and 5-8:30pm, Thurs. 8:30am-1:30pm).

Ristorante Pizzeria Il Terrazzino, Bocconcino due, 7 (tel 33 25 03), off p. Veneto to the left of the Banco di Napoli; follow the path to the sign. Savor local delicacies in a cave dug into the cliffs, or on the outdoor terrace that offers a breathtaking view of the *sassi.* Try hand-made pastas like *cavatelli alla boscaiola,* with a sauce of tomato, mushrooms, and prosciutto (L8000). Pizzas L6000-12,000. Finish with the dazzling *spumoni* (chocolate, coffee, and vanilla ice cream, made *in casa*) L4000. Wine L4000 per . Cover L2000, L1000 for pizza. Service 10%. Open Wed.-Mon. noon-4pm and 7pm-midnight, Tues. noon-4pm (summer only).

Trattoria Lucana, via Lucana, 48 (tel. 33 61 17), off via Roma. Matera's best *trattoria.* For *primi,* try the hearty *sfoglia alla lucana,* a lasagna made with local cheeses (L6000). For *secondi,* the *boccancini alla lucana,* their specialty (diced veal with mushrooms), is a steal at L12,000. Cover L2000. Service 10%. Open daily 12:30-3pm and 8-10pm; Oct.-June Mon.-Sat. 12:30-3pm and 8-10pm. Closed most of Sept.

Sights

Before venturing to the *sassi,* take a quick peek in one of the churches on the city's fringes. Walking up via San Biagio away from p. Veneto, you'll arrive at the 13th-century **Church of San Giovanni Battista,** notable for its decorative portal. The interior is a harmonious Gothic blend of arches, vaults, and columns. Enter the heart of the *sassi* zone by following the *iternario touristico* leading from via delle Beccherie away from via Fiorentilli. You'll ultimately find yourself at via Duomo, which surprisingly leads to the *duomo* in p. del Duomo. Erected between 1268 and 1270, the church is a fine Puglian-Romanesque construction with reaching nave, projecting moldings, rose windows, and richly carved portals. Inside, the 15th-century carved choir stalls compete with the stunning 16th-century **Cappella dell'Annunziata** for your attention. (Churches officially open daily 9am-noon but most remain unlocked until 7 or 8pm.)

From here, you can begin your tour of the *sassi* in the valleys **Sasso Caveoso** and **Sasso Barisano** by following via Madonna delle Virtù (called the Strada Panoramica dei Sassi) just down the hill from the *duomo.* Of obscure origin, the *sassi* come in four types. The oldest—and crudest—are simply niches in the rock lining Sasso Barisano (across the canyon formed by the Gravina River), in which townsfolk lived over 7000 years ago. The second type includes the carved nooks around Sasso Caveoso dating from around 2000 BC. Third are the homes more elaborately carved from the rock around via B. Buozzi (stemming from via Madonna delle Virtù); these are around 1000 years old. Finally come the intentionally constructed dwellings around via Forentini, no more than 750 years old. Although the *sassi* were almost completely evacuated after the new city was erected, young couples have been renovating and jazzing up nearly all the ancient homes, with the exception of the 6th-century *chiese rupestri* (rock churches). Many still display remnants of Byzantine frescoes dating from the 12th to the 16th centuries. Follow via Madonna delle Virtù south (to the right) to the **Churches of San Pietro Caveoso** and **Santa Maria d'Idris,** and farther down to the **Church of Santa Lucia alla Malve.** Although the Church of San Pietro Caveoso is currently closed to the public, the two other churches preserve beautiful 11th-century Byzantine frescoes painted on the tufa of the caves. Neither keeps regular hours, but you can try asking for the claviger who will let you in and provide a brief tour of the place (tip him about L2000).

As you roam the Sasso Caveoso, you'll be approached by children who get their spending money by giving "tours." You are better off going with the Amici dei Sassi (tel. 33 10 00) or the Amici del Turista, listed above. Call them first before paying for some kid's *gelato*.

Down via Buozzi in the direction of p. Veneto, the **Museo Nazionale Domenico Ridola,** via Ridola, 24 (tel. 31 12 39), off via Lucana outside the *sassi,* houses an excellent, boldly displayed prehistoric and early classical collection, all in a former 17th-century monastery. (Open Tues.-Sat. 9am-2pm; Sun. 9am-1pm. Free.)

Entertainment

Matera lets it all loose during the **Festival of Santa Maria della Bruna,** held during the last week of June and first week of July. The festival reaches its climax on July 2. At dawn, a procession of shepherds leaves the *duomo,* and at dusk a cart holding a Madonna follows. The ornate cart rumbles along via XX Settembre, illuminated by thousands of small lights, while warriors in medieval costume and clergy on horseback march solemnly alongside. At the end of the procession, everyone participates in the *Assalto al Carro,* in which relic-hungry spectators tear apart the cart holding the Madonna after the Madonna itself and other valuables have been removed to safety.

Matera showcases itself in July with **Luglio Materano,** a feast of classical music, dance, and theater. Call ahead to the tourist office to be sure that they're continuing this (new) tradition in 1993. The best evening amusements lie with Matera's 55,000 townspeople: any Friday night you can join them as they strut along p. Veneto and via del Corso talking up a storm during breaks in *gelato* snarfing.

Metaponto

Like many other towns on Italy's southern coastline, Metaponto is feeling the effects of increased development. A well-known beach resort, its lonely train station and scattered Greek ruins have been joined by a meager (albeit expanding) community development project. A profusion of clothing stores and food markets testify to Metaponto's metamorphosis. The **tourist office** on viale delle Sirene (tel. 74 19 33) is open July-Sept. daily 8am-8pm. There is a **post office** across from Metaponto's Archeological Museum in the new settlement (open Mon.-Sat. 8:30am-5:30pm) and a **bank,** Casa di Risparmio di Calabria e di Lucania, located by the beach (tel. 74 19 13; open Mon.-Fri. 8am-1pm). Metaponto's **telephone code** is 0835.

To reach the clear water and fine sand of Metaponto's **beach,** catch one of the few buses from the train station (L600, plus L400 for every big bag), or—better yet—walk straight from the station (50m) and take a right onto via Ionio, being careful not to electrocute yourself on the recently completed pass over the train tracks. From the base of the overpass, it's a 2km walk. Concessions cover only part of the beach; much of it remains untouched and bordered by grassy dunes. Only two reasonable lodging options serve the traveler. To get to the **Hotel Oasi,** via Olimpia, 12 (tel. 74 19 30), turn right at the fork in via Ionio about 100m from the beach. It's at the far end, past the bend in the road and the minimarket in the large, unmarked white building with a red fence. The Oasi rents spacious doubles with bath for L30,000. In July and August the owner usually demands full pension (L55,000 per person). A luxurious alternative is the **Hotel Kennedy,** via Ionio (tel. 74 19 60), on the right side of the fork. Gorgeous doubles with balconies and bath go for L50,000. Full pension is generally required in August (L80,000 per person). **Camping** is probably the best idea if you plan to hang out on the beach for a few days. Attractively situated, **Camping Magna Grecia,** via Lido, 1 (tel. 74 18 55), lies one-half km off Via Ionio from the strand. (Aug. 1-20 L8000 per person., L7000 per tent; less at other times.) Magna Grecia is really an amusement park in the guise of a campground, complete with shuttle to the beach, tennis courts, swimming pool, game rooms, snack bars, and a disco. The cheapest option is **Camping Comunale,** viale Europa, 16 (tel. 74 19 12). Follow the signs from via Lido. On public land, it only charges L1500 per person, L4000 per tent, and L1200 for electricity.

To reach Metaponto's **archeological sites,** follow the road that leads away from the station. Immediately past the turnoff onto via Ionio and to the left lies Metaponto's brand new shopping/apartment complex and recently completed **Archeological Museum.** In addition to maps and photos which detail the development of Metapontum (founded in 773 BC by the Greek inhabitants of Sybaris, a city notorious for its hedonism), the museum houses dozens of Greek artifacts from the area. (Open Tues.-Sat. 9am-1pm; Oct.-March Tues-Sat. 9am-noon. Admission L4000.) Further down the road from the station (one-half km) lies the turnoff to Metaponto's **Parco Archeologico.** Following the signs, you'll be led to the scanty ruins of the Doric **Temple of Apollo Licius** and the remains of a **Greek Theater** (1.5 km). The theater was the first to be constructed from a mound of dirt rather than dug out of a hillside. Continuing on the road from the station for about 3km and turning right on the coastal highway bound for Táranto, it's another 2km to the **Tavole Palatine—**ruins of the Greek temple of Hera. The famous Greek mathematician Pythagoras supposedly taught here until his death in 479 BC. The ruins, 15 standing columns and part of the flooring and entablature, have been called Tavole Palatine since the Crusades when *paladini* (knights) gathered here before leaving for the Holy Land.

Metaponto is an important **train junction** on the Táranto-Règgio line (16 per day to Táranto, 1hr., L3900; 5 per day to Règgio, 6hr., L30,300) with a connection to Naples by way of Potenza (5hr., L18,700). **Bus** service connects the Metaponto station with Matera (8 per day 7am-9pm; in winter 5 per day 7am-5:30pm, L2400).

Calabria

Calabria is Italy's last continental foothold before its lunge for Sicily. Though it is surrounded by water—the Ionian and Tyrrhenian Seas and the Strait of Messina—little moisture reaches the sere Calabrian interior. Farms in this region are kept verdant only by dint of endless irrigation. In contrast to fecund Sicily, water was so scarce only 30 years ago that pharmacies sold it to desperate farmers. "Cultural" ties, however, knit the two regions together—Calabria is rife with organized crime, where the fearsome mob is called the *'ndrangheta.* As in Sicily, its kingpins stage covert resistance to the liberalizing influences of the national government, seeking to secure and maintain power, prestige, and profit for themselves. Their efforts have helped perpetuate the region's vestigial feudalism and its poverty, sending waves of Calabrian hopefuls to northern Italy and North America in search of a better life.

Calabria shares the hot-potato history of most of southern Italy. Beginning with the ancient Greeks, legions of Byzantines, Saracens, Normans, Aragonese, and others couldn't quite keep hold of it, but left behind their marks on the region's population and cities.

Of the region's four major towns, only two warrant time and energy. Set in the heart of the Sila Massif, a huge granite plateau (1100-1700m), Cosenza appeals to visitors not only for its environs but also for its picturesque old town and Romanesque cathedral. Magnificent pine and oak forests (some of the last virgin forest in Italy), emerald lakes, and carpets of flowers adorn the Sila in summer; steep mountains and steady snowfall make for perfect skiing in the winter. Near the southern tip of Calabria is Règgio di Calabria, a dull place whose superb archeological museum houses the famous Bronze Warriors from Riace. On a venture north along the sandy but often bleak beaches of the Ionian Coast, visit Rossano and Gerace, two little-touristed towns that preserve numerous Byzantine monuments.

Taking public transportation seems as fast as a stroll in the *'ndrangheta's* cement boots—don't expect to cover large distances quickly.

Cosenza

Cosenza is two-faced: while a flat urban metropolis bursts out of its shell on one side of the Busento River, an old city clings to a hill topped by a citadel— Cosenza's greatest treasures lie between the two. Deep in the Busento River still wallows loot from the first sack of imperial Rome. Besides being *the* site for a spot of speculative fishing, Cosenza's greatest attribute is its location, which makes it the perfect base for hiking in the Sila Massif.

Orientation and Practical Information

Getting around Cosenza isn't difficult, once one realizes there are two train stations *and* two bus terminals. Outside the city, on the Crati River, lies the new train station from which trains service **Paola**, on the Rome-Règgio di Calabria coastal line (12 per day, 20min., L2000), and **Metaponto** (11 per day, change at Sìbari, 3hr., L9500). Then there's the old train station, from which trains depart for **Camigliatello, San Giovanni,** and other cities in the Sila. Bus #5 connects the stations (every 15min. 6am-12:30am, L1000). The small bus terminal is right outside the old train station at piazza Matteotti. One block away stretches **corso Mazzini,** a main thoroughfare which runs parallel to the tracks extending from the old station and connecting the small bus station with the large one at piazza Fera. Once on corso Mazzini with your back to the old train station and small bus depot, turn left for the old town and right for the central bus station and SIP.

Tourist Office: EPT information office (tel. 48 26 40), at the new train station. Maps, hotel listings, and information on the Sila. Open Mon.-Fri. 7:45am-2:15pm. There is another one in town (tel. 39 05 95), on via Rossi. From p. Fera near the central bus station, follow via Simonetta until you come to viale della Repubblica. From here, bear up the hill to the right on via Rossi and cross the rotary at the beginning of the *autostrada*. The office is on the opposite side of the rotary to the left. The same material, but the staff speaks better English. Open Mon.-Fri. 8:15am-8:15pm. The central **EPT office** advises at viale Trieste, 50 (tel. 278 21). With your back to the old train station, Simon says go right and quickly left if you have any questions the others can't handle. Open Mon.-Fri. 8am-2pm.

Post Office: tel. 264 35, on via Vittorio Veneto at the end of via Piave off corso Mazzini. Open Mon.-Sat. 8:15am-7:30pm. **Postal Code:** 87100.

Telephones: SIP, via dell'Autostazione, above the bus station. Open daily 8:10am-8pm. At other times, try **Croce Bianca,** via Beato Angelo d'Acri, 29. **Telephone Code:** 0984.

Trains: tel. 48 23 23. The new station (Cosenza) is on via Popilia at the *superstrada*. The old station (Cosenza Centrale) is off p. Matteotti near the old city. Cosenza Monaco, Cosenza Campanella, and Cosenzo Casali are three other stations in and near the city.

Buses: off p. Fera, at the opposite end of corso Mazzini from the train station. Get schedules at the information booths in the new train station. (FCL bus, tel. 368 51.) Gate #5 for Catanzaro, #14 for the Tyrrhenian coast. Snackbar open 24hrs. Buses run erratically on Sun. and holidays.

Emergencies: tel. 113. **Police: Questura** tel. 360 01. **Hospital: Ospedale Civile dell'Annunziata** (tel. 68 11), on via Felice Migliori. On weekends, call 318 31.

Accommodations and Food

The most affordable lodging clusters around the old station, just a few blocks from the old city, a quarter blessed with good *pensione* and cursed with evil tourist traps. **Albergo Bruno,** corso Mazzini, 27 (tel. 738 89), just one block from the train station, offers singles for L30,000, with bath L40,000. Doubles L38,000, with bath L54,000. Triples L50,000, with bath L66,000. Quad with bath L74,000. Already enhanced by newly renovated bathroom facilities, your stay is topped off with free use of the kitchen and pool-tabled TV room. Those aspiring to the high life can check into the **Nuovo Hotel Excelsior,** p. Matteotti, 14 (tel. 743 83), facing the old train station. The management equips the large, bright rooms of this once-grand hotel with color TVs and phones. (Singles L46,000. Doubles L70,000. Triples L90,000. Quads L105,000. Accepts AmEx, Diners' Club.) The best **camping** in the area is at the Sila Massif (see

Near Cosenza) and in the seaside towns of **Scalea** and **Marina di Belvedere** (at least 4 buses per day to each location 6:35am-6pm, 1hr. 15min., L3000-5000 depending on season). Two sites on Scalea's Tyrrhenian waterfront are **Camping il Gabbiano** (tel. (0985) 205 63), at L2000 per person and L5000 per tent, and **Campeggio Moby Dick** (tel. (0985) 202 78), at L1500 per person and L6000 per tent (open mid-May to mid-Sept.). In **Marina di Belvedere,** dozens of campsites abound, offering complete package deals (tent, electricity, and space) for as little as L10,000.

Consenza's best dishes are prepared *ai funghi,* with fresh mushrooms from the forests of the Sila. Fungus lovers should proceed to **Trattoria Peppino,** p. Crispi, 3 (tel. 732 17), reached by taking a right when you come to the Mario Martire bridge (two blocks from the old train station) leading into the old city. Full meals with drink go for L13,000. (Open Mon.-Sat. noon-10pm.) Crossing over the bridge and going left leads to **Pizzeria Tavola Calda,** corso Telesio, 214, with its tiny brick oven that churns out the giant *pizza grande* for only L3000. Serves only stand-up or take-out orders. (Open Mon-Fri. 9am-12:30pm and 5-8:30pm, Sat. 9am-12:30pm.) The **Supermercato Standa** vends to do-it-yourselfers at corso Mazzini, 98 (open Mon.-Fri. 8:45am-12:45pm and 4-8pm, Sat. 8:45am-12:45pm).

Sights and Entertainment

All sights of interest in Cosenza lies in the old city across the small **Busento River** from the old train station. Cross the river, turn left onto corso Telesio, and climb uphill to the **cathedral.** Keep your head up and your mouth closed, for there's no telling what will be tossed from the medieval windows. Despite an excess of garbage, these dark, winding streets are as intriguing as the cathedral itself. Note the mural of the Madonna and Child on the right side of the cathedral, painted in 1863. After the completion of the cathedral in 1222, Frederick II donated what is today the city's most prized possession—the tiny, ornate **Byzantine Cross.** The colorful jewel (204x264mm) bears a Christ and mourning Madonna on the left arm, a supplicating St. John the Evangelist on the right, and the archangel Michael above. These days the cross beautifies the Arcivescovato, near the cathedral. Though most bells in the town are rung with the push of a button, you can sound this cathedral's bells the old-fashioned way (Mon.-Fri. 10am-noon). Perched atop the hill, p. XV Marzo guards the **Museo Civico** (tel. 733 87), which houses an impressive collection of prehistoric bronzes. (Open Mon.-Sat. 9am-1pm. Free.)

Next to the museum sits the 9th-century **Teatro Rendano,** completely rebuilt after its destruction in World War II. The theater resonates with opera from January to April. From p. XV Marzo, you can make the climb to the 12th-century **Norman Castle.** (The castle's doorman may grant you admission—chances are better in the morning. If not, make an appointment with the *Assessorato al Turismo* (tel. 225 42) off p. del Burzi.)

The Sila Massif

Located smack dab in the middle of Calabria is the **Sila Massif,** 2000 square kilometers of pristine wilderness spread among three main zones: La Greca, the area to the north; La Grande, the central area that features Camigliatello, San Giovanni in Fiore, and Lakes Arvo and Cecita; and La Piccola, a coastal area that contains Lago Ampolino. Those three areas together constitute one of Italy's last mountain chains still covered with virgin forest.

La Sila's two main villages, **Camigliatello Silano** and **San Giovanni in Fiore,** lie within easy reach of Cosenza. To reach Camigliatello you can take either a bus (7 per day, 45min., L3200) or a train (9 per day, 1hr. 30min., L1800); San Giovanni is also accessible by both bus (7 per day. 1hr., L4500) and train (8 per day, 2hr. 15min., L2500). Though slower, train travel should not be missed; from the old station in Cosenza (Cosenza Centrale), trains no more than 20m in length inch their way up and through the mountains, accessing incredible views. You'll be awed by the feats of engineering it took to build the route.

Camigliatello

The first major stop you'll come to on the train line from Cosenza is Camigliatello, a lilliputian alpine town with fairytale streets and chateux, and the area's best base for exploration. Upon arrival you should immediately confer with the hiking experts at **Pro Loco** (tel. 57 80 91) on via Faigitelle 150m to your left as you exit the train station. They give out useful maps of the Sila and offer advice as to where you should and shouldn't go and what's worth seeing. (Generally open 9am-12:30pm and 3-7pm.) They'll also tell you more about what you'll see on two particularly interesting hikes from Camigliatello's *castro*. The first involves walking (1hr. 30min.) to **Lago Cecita,** one of five major lakes in the region, sharing a border with the **Parco Nazionale.** Following the signs in front of the station, keep walking until you reach the small pine forest; several dirt roads then branch from the highway, leading ultimately to Cecita's shores. A second, more demanding, and potentially confusing hike from Camigliatello is the three-hour climb to the top of the highest peak in the Sila, **Monte Botte Donato** (1930m). To get there, follow the highway toward Cosenza for about 4km and take the left turn at the *Fago del Soldato* intersection. As you begin climbing, bear left—you'll come to a ski-lift—climb below it until you reach an unmarked road. Turn left onto the road and you'll eventually reach the summit. From the peak of Monte Botte Donato on a clear day, you can see both the Tyrrhenian and Ionian Seas.

Less adventurous souls can visit the nearby pine forest or just savor the fresh mountain air. Pro Loco will help with lodging inquiries. In August and December, **Hotel Mancuso,** via del Turismo, 55 (tel. 57 80 02), on a street running parallel to via Roma to your right as you exit the station, requires full pension at L80,000 for pleasant rooms with baths. (Curfew midnight. Off-season singles with bath L35,000, doubles with bath L78,000, triples with bath L96,000, quads with bath L130,000.) The **Baita,** via Roma, 97 (tel. 57 81 97), to the right as you exit the station, lets singles with bath for L40,000; doubles with bath L78,000; and triples with bath L93,000. In the off-season, Sept.-July 20, doubles with bath are L60,000; triples with bath L75,000. For campers, **La Fattoria** (tel. (0984) 57 83 64) lies about 3km from Camigliatello on the road to Lago Cecita. The nicer **Villaggio Lago Arvo** (tel. (0984) 99 70 60) awaits on the banks of Lago Arvo in Lórica, 37km from Camigliatello, but is inaccessible by public transportation. Your best bet is to take the bus or train toward San Giovanni in Fiore and get off at Silvana Mansio, which is 15km from Lórica. (Campsite open May-Sept.) For assistance in Lórica, try the **Pro Loco** (tel. (0984) 53 70 69) on via Nazionale.

While in Camigliatello, picnic on the local specialties—cheeses, cured meats, and marinated mushrooms. The main drag overflows with *salumerie* that will provide you with sandwich fixins. On v. Roma, 44, grab an amazing, freshly-baked *cornetto al cioccolata* (chocolate croissant) at **Bar Leonetti** for just L1000. (open Tues.-Sun. 7am-8:30pm.) To reach some comfortable refuges in the woods, take the path starting at the Cultara Residence Sign .5 km along the highway toward Cosenza. Within 10 minutes you'll be surrounded by trees. **Da Sasa Video,** via Roma, 12, rents bicycles for L3000 per half-hour and tandems for L5000 per half-hour. (Open May-Sept. daily 9am-10pm; rentals only conducted on Sunday in May, June, and September.)

Amazing **skiing** conditions draw downhill diehards from Christmas until the Ides of March. Camigliatello's **Tasso Ski Trail** (tel. 57 80 37), on Monte Curcio, is about 3km from town, up via Roma and left at Hotel Tasso. A lift ticket is L20,000 per day. Hop a ride in summer for memorable views. (Lift runs daily 8:30am-6:30pm; Oct.-June 8:30am-5:30pm. Round-trip L4200.) You can rent skis and boots at **Da Sasa** for L18,000 per day whenever there's snow on the ground.

San Giovanni in Fiore

The last stop on the train from Cosenza is at the center of the Sila (8 trains per day from Camigliatello, 45min., L2000; 7 buses per day, 20min., L2500). Alpine plateaus laden with pine and oak forests nestle among hundreds of green fields laced with rushing mountain streams and the winding streets of the town. While there aren't any hikes from San Giovanni itself, visit for the scenery and the spectacular approach by train. From the train station follow viale della Repubblica to your right until it splits. Follow via Roma to your right and after some torturous twists and turns you'll pass a hospital to your right; take the stairs to your right past the hospital dorm to via Mateotti. The **tourist office** is down on your left off p. Municipio *(tel.* (0984) 99 21 47) and can help you make the most of your stay.

Just a few blocks from the tourist office lies San Giovanni's **Arco Normanno,** an arch of stones leading to the **Abbazia Florense,** an abbey first constructed in 1195 and since renovated and expanded. While the inner sanctum is unimpressive save for its intricately vaulted wooden roof, the masonry on the weathered facade is noteworthy. Adjacent to the church and accessible from the inner sanctum is the **Museo Demologico,** with dozens of photographs detailing the life and times of San Giovanni in the early decades of this century. To get to all the sights, turn left on via Matteotti from the front of the tourist office and then left again down the incredibly steep and winding via Sele. At the base of the hill, another left at the fork onto via Vallone will lead you to via Archi. A right (finally) on via Archi brings you under Arco Normanno; 50m farther down are via Cognale and the Abbazia.

There are a few pitiful campgrounds around San Giovanni (they are comparatively new and the trees have yet to grow to a reasonable height), but a reasonable housing option is **Kursaal** at via Panoramica, 263 (tel. (0984) 99 25 59). Rooms run L30,000 per person; in August full pension is usually required at L50,000 per person. If the **Standa supermarket** to your left as you exit the station doesn't suit your fancy (open Mon.-Sat. 9am-1pm and 3-8pm), try the **Osteria Bologna,** via Gramsci, 327 (tel. (0984) 99 15 33) to the right off via Matteotti about 100m to your left as you exit the tourist office.

Tyrrhenian Coast

The western coast of Calabria and Basilicata tempts with mountainous terrain and relatively little resort development. Going as far south as **Pizzo** will bring you back to rocky terrain and tourist crowds. The best stretch of territory hugs the northern coast between Praia a Mare and Sangineto; white beaches and the towering rocks of inland mountains meet here to compose a majestic landscape.

From Pizzo, any local train headed away from Règgio will take you to the western coast's other seaside villages, **Sangineto, Diamante, Cirella,** and **Scalea;** and in every case you'll travel through Paola (a necessary stopover if you're on your way to Cosenza). If the train workers should suddenly go on strike during your visit, you can also reach Paola's beach by taking a right turn immediately outside the train station and another right under the trestle at the base of the exit camp.

Further up the coast lies **Praia a Mare** (train station Praja; from Naples 2hr. 30min., L14,000; from Règgio 3hr., L17,000). If crowded beaches don't turn you off, just head to the **Isola di Dino,** less than 800m down the strand from Praia. Here you can enjoy the same blue Tyrrhenian waters as, according to legend, did the wayward Ulysses when he dropped by. From the train station, via Stazione leads straight to the beach; a left onto the first big street, via Longo, heads toward **piazza Halia,** the center of town. The main strip of hotels and restaurants on via Guigni begins past the *piazza;* about 200m down the strip is a small yellow sign to the left pointing towards the *santuario.* Follow the sign down via Nicola Maiorano to piazza F.G. Lomongco and go under the train tracks—the eerie town grotto and church await up on the hill. Once there, explore the caves carefully; the stalagmites ooze a sticky pus-like substance. At the foot of the hill off p. F.G. Lomongco resides the aptly named **Pensione la Piedigrotta** (at the foot of the grotto), on via Nicola Maiorano (tel. (0985) 721 92), whose compassionate hostess will help you recover from run-ins with the pus. Singles are L25,000, with bath L27,500. Doubles run L40,000, with bath L55,000. (Aug. 1-20, the proprietress requires full pension—L75,000-85,000 per person. In July, depending on the crowds, you may be required to take half-pension—L55,000 per person.) On the beach is the fancier **Hotel Chiaia,** via da Vinci, 18 (tel. (0985) 724 45), off viale della Libertà. (Singles L25,000. Doubles with bath L50,000. Triples with bath L60,000. In July and August the proprietor requires full pension—L65,000 per person in July, L85,000 per person Aug. 1-24.) Among the *pizzerie* that crowd the main drags, **Pizzeria Nautilus** bakes the meanest pie on via Lungomare (tel. (0985) 74 105), at the beach off p. Italia. For hungry throngs, they offer the humongous *pizza lo gusti* (twenty-flavor pizza), serving four, for L30,000. (Humbler pizza L4000-10,000. Service 15%. Open in summer daily noon-3pm and 8pm-1am.) To the north and just off the beach, **Game Park Ondasud** will suit you to a miniature tee, then amuse you with bumper boats and the like. Finally, rock formations, caves, and a cozy, pebbled beach await you a few minutes north of Praia in **Maratea Marina.** Officially part of Basilicata, Maratea makes a great daytrip (6 trains per day from Praia, 20min., L600), but don't go on Sundays unless you crave crowds. The closest chow to the beach is **Il Patriarca Pizzeria** (tel. (0973) 87 90 16), 30m up the road to the right as you face away from the train station. (Pizzas from L3000; open daily noon-3pm and 8-11pm.)

Two worthwhile spots to visit around Maratea Marina are the **Grotte di Marina,** a group of stalactite- and stalagmite-coated caverns discovered in 1929 during construction of the *superstrada,* and the town of **Maratea** proper. To reach the caves, simply turn left at Il Patriarca Pizzeria (directions above) and head up to the *superstrada;* the caves are 2km down the road. (Open daily 9am-12:30pm and 4-7pm; in winter call the Maratea tourist office for an appointment.) To get to the town of Maratea, simply catch a train from the Marina or travel 3km on the *superstrada* away from the caves. Once in Maratea, orient yourself with your back to Maratea station, then follow the parking lot left, descend along the road to the right, turn right through the tunnel, and continue until the main road with directional signs points right. Follow, follow, follow, and once you've walked about 1.5 km from the station, some more signs point left for **Maratea Porto** and right for **Maratea Santa Vénere** and the historic center. In Santa Vénere, just past the signs, you can pick up a few mildly helpful English booklets from the **AAST tourist office** (tel. (0973) 87 69 08) in the *piazza* (open Mon.-Sat. 9am-8:30pm, Sun. 9am-12:30pm and 5-8pm; reduced hours in winter); you should head downhill, however, for more interesting sights. The port, an attractive inlet from the Gulf of Policastro, harbors fishing and pleasure boats as well as ritzy restaurants. The best eating option, **Paninoteca Perro Caliente,** opposite the road leading to the port, serves up spicy sandwiches for L5000-7000. (Service 10%; open April-Sept. daily 10:30am-midnight.)

Uphill from Santa Vénere, the **historic center** blankets the side of Monte San Biagio with an extraordinary array of winding, directionless streets. On the top of the mountain lies Maratea's **basilica,** built over the site of a temple where dread pagans once made grisly sacrifices to Minerva. Hovering nearby, looking a tad like an overgrown Christmas ornament, a 22m **Statue of the Redeemer** spreads cheer and redemption throughout the land. Buses run, albeit infrequently, between Maratea Marina, the port, Maratea's central station, Santa Vénere, the historic center, and even up to the basilica (L700; current schedules posted at train stations, tourist offices, and at all ticket sellers). One bus in the morning and two in the late afternoon roll to Maratea Castrocucco, site of **Camping Maratea,** the only accommodation even approaching affordability. (Tel. (0973) 87 90 97. In Aug. L22,500 per person with parking, light, and hot shower.)

Règgio di Calabria

Completely rebuilt after a 1908 earthquake and currently brimming with designer clothing stores, Règgio just plain lacks mystique. Fortunately, it houses the National Museum, where bronze figures harken to Calabria's ancient heyday as part of Magna Graecia, and provides access to the countryside, where olive groves and flower fields cultivated by the perfume industry reflect the sensuous side of Italian life. Less than 35km north lies the tiny village of Scilla, from which one can see Sicily and the Aeolian Islands without difficulty.

Trains and Ferries

Règgio has two train stations. All trains stop at **Stazione Centrale,** p. Garibaldi (tel. 981 23), at the southern end of town. The much less frequented (albeit more convenient) **Stazione Lido** sits at the northern end of town off via Zerbi and near the museum, port, and beaches. As the terminus of the western north-south train line, Règgio is linked to most major cities, including: Milan (3 per day 7:40-10:50pm, 14hr., L74,700); Rome (3 per day 7:20am-2:20pm, 7hr., L46,800 plus L16,800 *rapido* supplement, also 1 "express" train per day; 8:27pm, 10hr., L46,800); Florence (3 per day 7:40-10:50pm, 11hr., L68,600); Venice (1 per day 6:38pm, 14hr., pre-reserved couchettes only, L72,700 plus L18,500 couchette supplement); Naples (7 per day 1:30am-11:30pm, 5hr., L33,600, also 3 *rapido* trains per day, 7:20am-7:20pm, 4hr. 30min., L12,800 *rapido* supplement.). Though several ferries cross the strait to Messina in Sicily, a greater number of ferries and all trains make the crossing from the nearby city of **Villa San Giovanni** (30min. north by train, L1200). Nevertheless, three companies do provide service from here to Sicily, Malta, and points throughout Italy. **Ferrovie dello Stato** (tel. (0965) 981 23), at the port five blocks to the left of Stazione Lido facing away from the sea, accepts all InterRail, Eurail, and kilometric tickets for the Sicily crossing. **Tirrenia,** via B. Bozzi, 31 (tel. 940 03), sits off via III Settembre three blocks from the Lido station. (Ticket office open Mon.-Fri. 8:30am-1pm and 4-7pm.) **SNAV** (tel. 295 68), next to Ferrovie dello Stato, specializes in hydrofoil service from Règgio to points beyond.

Villa San Giovanni-Messina: Ferrovie ferries 3:20am-4:45pm (14 per day, 20min., L800).

Règgio-Messina: Ferrovie ferries 6:55am-9:55pm (10 per day, 50min., L1600 one-way, L3000 round-trip). **SNAV** hydrofoils Mon.-Fri. 7:15am-8:40pm (24 per day) and Sat. (18 per day, 20min., L5000).

Règgio-each of the Lípari Islands: SNAV hydrofoil (June 1-Sept. 30; 4 per day per isle, 2hr., L29,300 (Vulcano)- L48,100 (Alicudi).

Règgio-Catania-Syracuse-Malta: Tirrenia ferries Tues., Fri., and Sun., stopping in Catania (3hr.) and Syracuse (7hr.); both for L20,000 (Oct.-May L16,000); continuing to Malta (11hr.) for L86,000 (Oct.-May L74,000).

Orientation and Practical Information

Most travel in Règgio is along **corso Garibaldi,** connecting Stazione Centrale in the south with Stazione Lido in the north. City buses continuously traverse the route (L800), though it is only 1.5 km from S. Centrale to S. Lido.

Tourist Office: AAST booth (tel. 271 20), at the central train station. Useful maps and directions, but irregular hours. "Here is spoken English." Occasionally open Mon.-Sat. 8am-2pm and 2:30-8pm. Two other booths with similarly mythic hours at the airport (tel. 32 02 91) and at via Roma, 3 (tel. 211 71).

Luggage Storage: at both Centrale and Lido stations (L1500).

Budget Travel: Azienda Viaggi Rossana (CTS), corso Garibaldi, 238 (tel. 930 01). Student travel information and service, if you're stuck and need to get out of Règgio fast. Open Mon.-Fri. 9am-1pm and 4:30-7:30pm, Sat. 9am-1pm.

Post Office: via Miraglia, 14 (tel. 245 08), near p. Italia. Open Mon.-Fri. 8am-7pm, Sat. 8am-2pm. **Postal Code:** 89100.

Currency exchange: At corso Garibaldi, 211.If you're desperate. Open 9am-noon and 4-7pm.

Telephones: SIP, corso Garibaldi 187 (tel. 36 01), 200m past the Azienda toward the port. Open Mon.-Sat. 9am-1:50pm and 4-7:30pm, Sun. and holidays 8am-3pm. **Telephone Code:** 0965.

Airport: Svincolo Aeroporto, south of town. Catch Yellow Bus #113, 114, or 115 from p. Garibaldi outside S. Centrale (L1000). Planes service all major cities in Italy.

Emergencies: tel. 113. **Police:** tel. 471 09, on via Santa Caterina, in the northern end of town near the port. **Medical Assistance:** tel. 34 71 06. **Hospital: Ospedale Riuniti,** via Melacrino (tel. 34 71 13).

Accommodations

Staying in Règgio often means depleting your wallet. Hotel quality is notably low and the campgrounds which exist are distant from the city center.

Ostello Principessa Paola del Belgio (HI), via Nazionale, 2 (tel. 75 40 33), in Scilla (7 trains per day, 45min., L1800; 10 buses per day, last bus 8pm, L2000). In an old castle overlooking the sea. A 10-min. walk from the beach. HI card required. Lockout 9am-5pm. Curfew 11pm. L8000 per night in advance. Open April-Sept. Closed in 1992.

Pensione S. Bernadetta, corso Garibaldi, 585 (tel. 945 00), right across p. Garibaldi from the central train station all the way up on the 5th floor. Cozy, but acrophobics beware. Singles L26,000. Doubles L35,000.

Albergo Noel, viale Zerbi, 13 (tel. 33 00 44 or 89 09 65), a few blocks north of Stazione Lido. With the sea behind you, turn left as you exit the station. Great location. TV room and decent restaurant. All rooms with bath. Singles L34,000. Doubles L45,000. Triples L60,000. Breakfast L5000. All credit cards accepted. Reserve in advance in June-Sept.

Pensione Callea, via Verona, 2 (tel. 941 54). Go up via S. Vollaro 2 blocks from the museum and climb the stairs—it's to your right. A bit run-down and almost always filled. Singles L20,000. Doubles L30,000.

Food

Règgio's chefs feel most at home making *spaghetti alla Calabrese* (noodles dressed in a potent pimento sauce), *capicollo* ham (salami spiced with local hot peppers), and *pesce spada,* swordfish caught off neighboring Bágnara Calabra. A large **market** lies at p. del Popolo, off via Amendola near the port. (Open Mon.-Sat. 6am-1:30pm.) At corso Garibaldi, 103, towards the Stazione Lido end also in front of S. Centrale, a **STANDA supermarket** supplies the basics. (Open Mon. and Wed.-Sat. 8:30am-1pm and 5-8:15pm, Tues. 8am-1pm.)

Trattoria Del Villeggiante, via di Tripepi, 31 (tel. 89 90 01), in the northern end of town up the hill from the market. A happy little establishment serving fresh, tasty food. Hook the *pesce spada,* L10,000. *Primi* L5000; try the *linguine checca,* made with a sauce of tomatoes and *pepperoncini.* Wine L4000 per . Cover L1500. Open Mon.-Sat. noon-3pm and 7-11pm.

Cordon Bleu, via corso Garibaldi, 203 (tel. 33 24 47), not far from the Museum and STANDA Supermarket. It's more Italian than it looks. Calamari (L6000) and assorted pastries (from L1000) especially tasty. Wine L2500 per . Cover L1000. Open Thurs.-Tues. 7am-1am.

La Pignata, via Demetria Tripepi, 122 (tel. 278 41), up via Giutecca from corso Garibaldi near the SIP. An elegant pizzeria-restaurant with carved wooden ceilings and leather seats. One-eyed giant *pizza polifemo* (with mussels) L6000. *Maccheroni calabresi* L7000. All meals, including pizzas, come with a tasty appetizer of *bruschette,* pieces of toasted bread rubbed with garlic and topped with a spicy red sauce. Cover L2000. Open Aug.-June Thurs.-Tues. noon-2:45pm and 7:30-11pm.

Paninoteca Da Enzo, via II Settembre, 17. A hole in the wall with great sandwiches (L2000-3000) and lively clientele. Open Mon.-Sat. 10am-2:30pm and 6-11pm.

Sights and Entertainment

If passing through Règgio, you might as well pass the day by the sea. The **lungomare,** a pleasant park overlooking the water and the rugged Sicilian coast, stretches from one end of Règgio to the other. The main reason visitors stop in Règgio is, however, the world-renowned **Museo Nazionale,** at p. de Nava, on corso Garibaldi near the Stazione Lido. Documenting Magna Graecia civilization with material from excavations in Calabria and underwater treasure-hunts off the coast, many of the museum's splendid pieces have spent years shuttling about the museums of the world, so expect a few vacant spots along the walls. Especially notable in the non-traveling collection are the works in the upstairs gallery by southern Italian artists such as Antonello da Messina and a set of dramatic Greek tablets from the 5th and 6th centuries BC telling the stories of Persephone, Castor and Pollux, and Achilles and Agamemnon. The two masterpieces of the museum are the extraordinary **Bronzi di Riace** (Bronze Warriors of Riace), two Herculean Greek statues found off the coast of Riace, Calabria, in 1972. These overwhelming figures were miraculously preserved for over 2000 years in the gentle waters of the Ionian. After painstaking restoration, the two-meter statues have been identified as Greek originals and dated to the middle of the 5th century BC, the Golden Age of Greek sculpture. (Open Tues.-Sat. 9am-1:30pm and 3:30-7:30pm, Sun. 9am-1pm, and Mon. 9am-1:30pm. Admission L4000, over 60 and under 18 free.)

Règgio becomes more inviting as the sun sets and corso Garibaldi, p. de Nava, and the waterfront fill for the evening *passeggiata*. **Feste di Settembre** in an annual pandemonium of folklore exhibitions, concerts, and religious ceremonies.

Near Règgio

Scilla and Bágnara Calabra, two fishing villages, each lie about 30km from Règgio along the Tyrrhenian coast. The picturesque hamlet and beach resort of **Scilla** sits above the famous rock behind which, according to Homer, a female monster with six heads, 12 feet, and a voice like a yelping puppy hid before devouring entire ships that were skirting the harrowing whirlpool of Charybdis. Scilla is accessible from Règgio by train (12 per day, 45min., L2400) or by bus (12 per day, last bus 8:30pm, L2200). Avoid Scilla on Sunday, when half of Calabria flocks to its small rocky beach. If you're lucky, you can get a tidy room in the **Pensione Le Sirene,** via Nazionale, 57 (tel. (0965) 75 40 19 or 75 41 21). Just one block from the beach (v. Nazionale runs parallel to the sea, one block back from the *lungomare*), Le Sirene offers shady communal terraces that overlook the sea and cool rooms with ceiling fans. (Singles with bath L40,000. Doubles with bath L55,000. Triples with bath L70,000. Reservations a good idea June-Aug.) You'll find the cheapest meals around at **Pizzeria San Francesco** on the beach (tel. 75 46 91). Pizza starts at L4500. (Open June 1-Sept. 15 daily noon-2pm and 7pm-1am.) Walk 10 minutes from the beach to **Paper Ros** (tel. 75 42 62), an enjoyable locals' *caffè* with a superb view (open daily 10am-midnight). The town peaks at night after the daytrippers have left and yellow submarine lights illuminate the square-jawed castle. Appreciate its nocturnal majesty with a relaxing drink at **Virtigine,** p. San Rocco, 14. The outdoor seats overlook the castle. Drinks from L1500. (Open daily 7:30pm-midnight.)

Bágnara Calabra, 8km north of Scilla, nestles among cliffs and grottoes. Painted swordfishing boats with tall lookout towers bob just offshore. The road north of town commands a view of Sicily and the Lípari Islands.

Aspromonte, a protuberance Calabria developed after kicking Sicily one night, presides over the southernmost tip of the Italian peninsula in pine-and-birch covered glory, awaiting those who can't get all the way to the Sila for their nature break. To reach the center of the area, take one of the nine daily blue buses (#127 or 128) from in front of Règgio's central train station to **Gamberie** (L2000). Here visitors enjoy a fabulous view of Sicily and the straits of Messina from the heights of Puntone di Scirocco (1660m), accessible by chairlift.

The Ionian Coast

The barren beaches which stretch between Règgio di Calabria and Metaponto are sparsely populated with Italian and German tourists and rarely frequented by anyone else. If a strip of sand is all you desire, consider hopping onto the Règgio-Catanzaro line and checking out whatever comes your way. **Soverato** (130km from Règgio, L10,500) offers one of the most expansive, scenic, and popular strips; however, the beaches at **Bovalino, Marina, Palizzi,** and **Brancaleone** are closer and almost as agreeable. All travelers should be forewarned before planning their itineraries that trains traversing the Ionian coast often have erratic schedules and multiple connections: give yourself ample time to get where you want to go.

Locri and Gerace

Locri (80km from Règgio, L6200) is a sleepy modern town with a seemingly endless, smooth beach, a surfeit of tennis courts, and some standard Roman ruins. If you're there for the night, drop by the **Ristorante and Albergo Orientale,** via Tripoli, 33 (tel. (0964) 202 61). We can't vouch for the restaurant side of things, but the *albergo* offers airy, pleasant rooms with balconies. To get there from the train station, walk away from the sea two blocks on viale Garibaldi. Then turn right on viale G. Matteotti, a major thoroughfare; via Trípoli is to the left three blocks away (right after you pass Euromoda di Riganello). (Singles L30,000. Doubles L60,000. In August, the owner requires guests to take half-pension L18,000 per person.) An inferno of flavor and spice, the **Trattoria Manglaviti,** via Roma, 116, cooks up a L12,000 *menù* for elderly card-shuffling locals who have been drinking and dealing here for years. (Open daily noon-11pm, but food is not served noon-3pm.)

To get to the taciturn town of **Gerace,** 10km inland from Locri and high above the Calabrian countryside, grab a bus from in front of Locri's train station (Mon.-Sat. 6 per day 7am-4:30pm, 20min., L1400, round-trip L2300, return 30min. after each of the Locri departure times). Gerace lives and breathes medieval architecture, and its heart is the **cathedral,** Calabria's largest. As you enter, you'll immediately notice the structure's imperial crypt, supported by 26 ancient Greek columns pilfered from Locri. From the crypt, climb the stairs into a Romanesque interior of the grandest proportions. Outside, to the left of the entrance, note the exquisitely detailed Gothic portal. Another extraordinary portal graces the **Church of San Francesco** (1252), down the street to the right of the cathedral entrance. Its geometric design reveals Byzantine influence. For information about Gerace and Locri, consult the **tourist office** in Locri, via Fiume, 1 (tel. (0964) 296 00). To get there, follow via G. Matteoti towards the library (#160) and park/maze off via Umberto; via Fiume is a small street to your left. (Open Mon.-Sat. 8am-1pm and 3-6pm; Sept.-June Mon.-Fri. 8am-1pm.)

Stilo and Serra San Bruno

About 40km north of Locri reposes the small coastal town **Monasterace Marina** (from Locri L2900), from which buses leave for **Stilo** (Mon.-Sat. 11am-4pm, 6 per day, 40min., L1600). The dreamy hilltop village of **Stilo** houses the famous church **La Cattolica**; head up the hill in front of the bus station. (Open daily 9am-noon.) From Stilo one can also get to **Serra San Bruno,** a pretty village surrounded by forests, even further inland and higher up in the Sila mountain range. Erratic bus schedules change with the season (at least 4 per day 9am-5pm, 1hr. 15min.). If you survive the circuitous roads, you'll be able to check out the church of **San Biagio,** with reliefs depicting events in the life of Bruno of Cologne (after whom the city is named) and a particularily notable altarpiece depicting an elated Madonna. If you have time (and you're a male) visit the monastery 2km west of the village. (Ask a local to direct you.)

Crotone and Cirò Marina: More Beaches

Approximately 90km north of Locri sits **Crotone,** the once-dignified hometown of Pythagoras, now recognizable by its smokestacks and sulphur-filled air (2hr. from Locri, L6200). Its only asset is its bus connections to **Capo Rizzuto.** Take a city bus to Crotone's *centro* and then another bus to Capo Rizzuto, a defiant extension of land into the sea (Mon.-Sat. 3 per day 7am-3pm, 45min., L2000). Squish sand and clay between your toes as you savor the cliff and beach terrain. Hotels and *pensiones* charge a lotta lire here, but there's no shortage of campgrounds. **Camping La Rondine** (tel. (0962) 79 91 60), overlooking the sea on the main road in town, is run by a chipper family. (L8000 per person, L1500 per small tent, L2500 per large tent, L4800 for light. Open June-Sept.) The population explodes exponentially in August, but at other times you shouldn't have a problem finding a place. If La Rondine is full, try any of the dozens of other campsites advertised throughout town. Catch some munch at the **Supermercato Capo Rizzuto** off the main road (open daily 8am-1pm and 5-9pm). **Warning:** do not try to arrive by train at the Isola Capo Rizzuto station, or you'll be stuck in the middle of the boondocks, a long way away from Isola C.R. and an even longer one from Capo Rizzuto itself.

Le Castella, also accessible by bus from Crotone (Mon.-Sat. 1 per day, 1hr. 30min., L2300) is more serious about its beaches, and has a genuine Aragonese castle. (Open daily 8am-8pm. Free.) Campgrounds blanket the waterfront here as well.

Thirty-five kilometers north of Crotone lies **Cirò Marina** (on the Síbari line, 25min. from Crotone, 15 per day, L2900), site of yet another beach. This incarnation flaunts brightly colored fishing boats, dozens of *pizzerie,* and a ton of gargantuan concrete blocks piled along the coast to preserve the town from inundation. From the train station, walk to the first main road, then turn left and left again at the gas station; a 1.5km stroll carries you to the beach. **Albergo Sellaro Mario,** via Roma 147/149 (tel. (0962) 310 23), en route to the beach, offers rooms which have seen better days, but management which looks enthusiastically toward their future guests. (Singles L30,000, with bath L40,000. Doubles L40,000, with bath L60,000.) You can sleep under the stars at **Camping Punta Alice** (tel. (0962) 311 60). (In August L7300 per person, L4400 per small tent, and L7100 per large tent; at other times rates approximately L1000-2000 cheaper.) Just head to the left as you arrive at the beach, past the benches and street lamps straight out of a Picasso painting.

Rossano and Trebisacce

Rossano, about 45km northwest of Cirò Marina, merits a visit for its church. The Rossano train station is a precipitous 5km down the hill from the main village; simply hop on one of the orange city buses that stop in front of the yellow and black curved median (L1000). To best appreciate Rossano's magnificent Byzantine **Church of San Marco,** pick up a local "tour guide"; any of the children or elderly men hanging around the main square will help you for a few thousand lire. Built circa 1000 AD, San Marco, on a square plan with five drum-shaped domes and three apses, is considered Calabria's most important Byzantine monument, along with the similar La Cattolica at Stilo. The recently restored interior mixes symmetrical arches and vaults; worn remains of frescoes and fragments of the original altar add color to the stark white walls. (Open daily 9am-noon.)

After San Marco, visit the cathedral and the little **Museo Diocesano,** which packs in more per square meter than most museums in Italy. Its most exalted treasure is the 5th-century *Codex Purpureus,* a 188-page manuscript of the Gospels of St. Mark and St. Matthew. Also fine oil paintings and a few 15th-century Gregorian chant-books. (Open Mon.-Sat. 9am-noon and 5-7pm, Sun. and holidays 9am-noon. Free.)

Rossano has its share of inexpensive hotels, but better bets can be found in **Trebisacce,** 35km north of Rossano and 40 minutes by train along the coast, another town boasting another beach strip. The family-run **Albergo Noia,** via Vuo Foscolo, 185 (tel. (0981) 513 21), offers tidy, pretty rooms with good plumbing and kind management. (Singles L35,000. Doubles L55,000. Triples L73,000. All rooms with bath. July-Aug. obligatory half-pension L47,000, but present your *Let's Go* book for a possible discount.) If it's full (likely in Aug.), consider the **Albergo Parnasso,** off via Alturi at Traversa sa S. di Via Alturi, 5 (tel. (0981) 511 97), with singles for L20,000 and doubles for L40,000, all with baths (and televisions on request). In August, the owner requires half- or full-pension (L40,000 and L60,000 per person respectively). To find either hotel, turn right onto via Alturi from outside the station and walk about 10 short blocks, past the Esso station; both are near the **STANDA supermarket,** via Avocato d'Alba, 389 (via Alturi changes name 3 times; via Avocato d'Alba is just one incarnation).

The best *trattoria* in Trebisacce is the **Trattoria del Sole,** via Piave, 14bis (tel. (0981) 51 7 97), near the church at p. Matteotti. *Primi* L4500-8000. *Secondi* L7000-15,000. Try their homemade specialty, *penne alla trattorie del Sole,* made with bacon, eggplant, and mozzarella and *pecorino* cheese (L7000). Cover and service L2500. (Open daily noon-3pm and 8-11pm; closed Sundays in winter.) The STANDA is open Mon.-Sat. 7:45am-1:30pm and 5:15-9:30pm, Sun. 8am-12:30pm.

SICILY (SICILIA)

Throughout the ages, many civilizations—among them the Greeks, Romans, Arabs, Normans, and Spaniards—have directed their attention at Sicily. Enamored of the island, they each decided to stay, usually with the support of an invading army. This uninterrupted series of hostile takeovers may have been bad fortune for the island's residents at the time, but it's a boon for the modern traveler: Each of the insurgent peoples has left its own imprint upon the island, presenting the twentieth-century visitor with a fascinating cultural array. Today, Sicily is invaded only by tourists eager to take in the legacy of three millenia and more. Despite its tattered history, oft-conquered Sicily remains indomitable. The great civilizations of the Mediterranean have come and gone, leaving the island littered with their ruined monuments. Nonetheless, Sicily emerges intact, the synthesis of centuries of occupation, creation, and destruction.

In the 5th and 6th centuries BC, the city-states of Sicily were the most powerful and populous in the Magna Graecia, the flourishing extension of Greek civilization in the western Mediterranean. In the 9th century, the island became a Muslim outpost second in importance only to Spain. The island later served as the seat of the Norman court, one of the most enlightened in medieval Europe, and subsequently become the pawn of Renaissance dynasties. The island ultimately fell under harsh Spanish rule. The Bourbons' shortsighted agricultural policies bled the rich volcanic soil and reduced much of the Sicilian interior to a parched wasteland. The island was "liberated" by Garibaldi in the 1860s, but economic conditions failed to improve.

The bloodshed of Sicilian politics has been matched by the cruelty of Mother Nature. To Giuseppe Lampedusa, Sicily was a "landscape which knows no mean between sensuous sag and hellish drought." The island's position at the edge of the European geologic plate has resulted in a succession of seismic and volcanic catastrophes that have periodically wiped away the accumulated gains of human endeavor (not to mention a fair number of the humans themselves). Those not destroyed seem to have drawn strength from survival; the fruits of Sicily's artistic and intellectual climate range from Selinunte's stark grandeur to Noto's baroque frivolity, from the irrefutable logic of Pythagoras to the wry irrationalities of Pirandello. Not all of Sicily's children have thrived in its harsh territory, however; in the late 19th and early 20th centuries, hundreds of thousands left Sicily behind in favor of the promised lands of the United States and Argentina.

Modern Siciliy bears the scars of its history with a quiet dignity. Unlike other regions of Italy, Sicilians do not revel in their island's traditions; they speed, instead, toward the future, installing condom vending machines in front of medieval cathedrals and raising petrochemical refineries beside Greek acropolises. For years a point of exodus, Sicily now attracts thousands of immigrants from North Africa. And the mafia—which dominates most outsiders' image of Sicily—has somewhat faded from sight. Visitors who expect to see black limousines slinking through Palermo and corpses bobbing in the Gulf of Catania will be disappointed.

Because of Sicilian immigration to the United States, and to some extent because of the welcomed American invasion in 1942, *Statiunitensi,* (particularly *Sicilo-Americani)* are greeted with exceptional warmth. Women, however, should be aware that male attention in Sicily is often aggressive, and foreigners, unequipped with the extensive lexicon of Sicilian cut-downs, are particularly susceptible. Though this behavior often extends to verbal harassment, cases of physical harassment and assault are few. But whereas violent crime is rare (by American standards), petty crime is rampant. The larger cities (Palermo, Catania, Messina, and Trápani) enjoy notoriety for their pickpockets and purse-snatchers, and their downtown districts can be unsafe at night. Travel in groups if you can, or stay close to frequented areas.

In summer Sicily swelters for weeks at a time (35-45°C). The burning African *scirocco* winds can scorch your vacation in July and August. In addition, haze and random

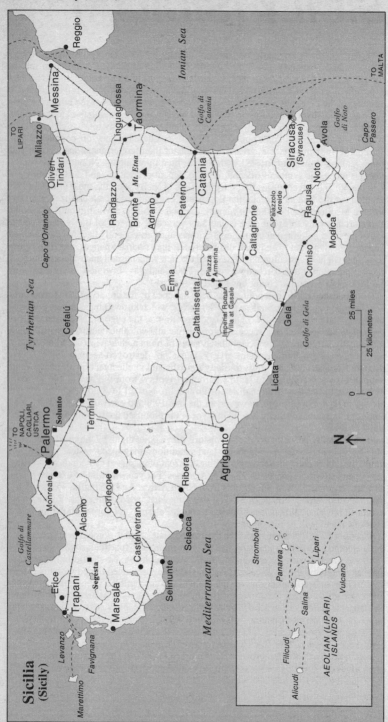

Sicilia
(Sicily)

Reggio

Ionian Sea

TO MALTA

Messina

Linguaglossa
Taormina

Golfo di Catania

TO LIPARI

Milazzo

Oliveri
Tindari

Mt. Etna

Catania

Siracusa
(Syracuse)

Golfo di Noto

Capo Passero

Avola

Capo d'Orlando

Randazzo

Bronte
Adrano

Paterno

Noto

Palazzolo
Acreide

Ragusa

Tyrrhenian Sea

Modica

Enna

Caltagirone

Comiso

Cefalù

Caltanissetta

Piazza
Armerina

Imperial Roman
Villa at Casale

Gela

Golfo di Gela

25 miles

25 kilometers

Licata

0
0

TO
NAPOLI,
CAGLIARI,
USTICA

Soluto

Termini

Palermo

N

Monreale

Agrigento

Golfo di
Castellammare

Corleone

Alcamo

Ribera

Castelvetrano

Sciacca

Erice

Segesta

Selinunte

Stromboli

Lipari

Trapani

Marsala

Panarea

Mediterranean Sea

Vulcano

Levanzo

Salina

Favignana

Filicudi

AEOLIAN (LIPARI)
ISLANDS

Marettimo

Alicudi

fires often obscure vistas in the summer months. Spring and autumn are ideal times to visit to the island. Holy Week in Sicily is noted for its colorful processions: the most celebrated are Good Friday in Enna, where marchers don white, hooded costumes in the Spanish tradition, and Easter Sunday in Prizzi, featuring the dance of the devil and of death. For complete details, pick up the booklet "Easter in Sicily," available at most tourist offices. For the traditional tour of Sicily, follow the coast; for a tour of traditional Sicily, venture into the heartland. If you do visit in summer, follow local custom: eat a big lunch, take a two-hour nap, and enjoy the island in the cool early evenings.

Transportation

Flights from all major Italian cities service Palermo and Catania. The cheapest way to reach Sicily is a train-ferry combination to Messina (from Rome via Règgio di Calabria, L46,000). **Tirrenia** (tel. (0923) 218 96), the largest private ferry service in Italy, is the most extensive and reliable, although you should still expect considerable delays; **Grandi-Traghetti** (tel. 091 58 79 39) offers better off-season rates to Palermo from Genoa and Livorno. Prices vary according to specific dates, although approximate prices are given below. Listings are for Tirrenia lines unless otherwise stated.

Règgio di Calabria-Messina: 12 per day on the state railroad ferry 5am-10pm; 1hr.; L1400. To cut this scenic 50-min. crossing to 20min., take the *aliscafo* from the same terminal at the Règgio port (L5000).

Villa San Giovanni-Messina: 22 per day on the state railroad ferry 3:20am-10:05pm (L1000).

Genoa-Palermo (22hr.): **Grandi-Traghetti Lines** Sat.-Mon. at 1pm, Wed. at 4pm. *Poltrona* L98,000; July 25-Aug. 10 L118,000; Oct.-June 14 L78,000. **Tirrenia Lines** year-round Tues., Thurs., and Sat. at 4pm; July 16-Sept. 10 also Sun. noon; July 9-Sept. 30 also Sun. at 4pm. *Poltrona* L102,200; Oct.-May L80,300.

Naples-Palermo (10hr. 30min.): 1 per day at 8:00pm. *Poltrona* L61,900; Oct.-May L47,900.

Cagliari-Palermo (14hr.): Fri. at 7pm. *Poltrona* L44,300; Oct.-May L34,500.

Livorno-Palermo (18hr.): **Grandi-Traghetti** Tues. and Thurs. at 6pm and Sat. at 5pm. *Poltrona* L91,000; July 23-Aug. 10 L117,000; Oct.-June 17 L78,000. Deck seats L80,000, available only if all other classes are filled.

Naples-Catania-Syracuse (15hr. 30min., 18hr. 45min.): Thurs. at 8:30pm. Deck seats L44,000. *Poltrona* L61,900 for either destination. Off-season L47,900.

Règgio di Calabria-Catania-Syracuse (3hr. 15min.): To Syracuse Tues., Fri., and Sun. at 8:30am. A bargain. Deck fare to either port L14,700. *Poltrona* L22,000; off-season L20,400.

Cagliari-Trápani (11hr.): From Cagliari Sun. at 7pm, from Trápani Tues. at 9pm; *Poltrona* L44,300; Oct.-May L34,500.

La Goulette (Tunisia)-Trápani (8hr.): Mon. at 8pm. *Poltrona* L84,700; Oct.-May L71,000.

Kelibia (Tunisia)-Trápani: SNAV hydrofoils Tues., Thurs., and Sat. at 8:45am (3hr.); Tues.-Wed., Fri., and Sat.-Sun. at 8:45am (3hr. 45min., via Pantelleria). Fare L75,000.

Trains in Sicily only partially deserve their reputation for tardiness; the diminutive *Elettromotrici* are reasonably reliable and convenient. Two major bus companies, the private, air-conditioned, and punctual *SAIS,* and the public, often steamy *AST,* serve many of the destinations inaccessible by train. There's no central transportation authority in Sicily, so check in every city and with every driver for the bus schedules to your next destination. Give yourself a few extra hours to get where you're going, especially if you're heading for isolated ruins.

Hitchhiking is difficult on long hauls; hitchers are reputed to have better luck near the turn-off to roads for short, specific trips. **Solo women in particular should not hitchhike in Sicily. Driving** in Sicily is only for the very brave. You'll need an International Driver's Permit (available at AAA; see Documents and Formalities in General Introduction), a rental car, and nerves of steel. Travelers (drivers and pedestrians alike) should be aware that most Italians drive as if they're behind the wheel of a Ferrari F40, even if it's actually a Fiat 500. And Sicilians seem to be particularly fond of using their car horns. When cruising down a highway, a cryptic Italian highway pictogram may or may not indicate "imminent death." **Pedestrians** should note that simple tasks like crossing the street can become a real challenge here. One strategy is to follow other people across, using them as a buffer between you and the speeding cars. Another alternative is to treat oncoming traffic like a charging rhinoceros: make eye contact and pray to the local saint. Incidentally, Italy is a small country, and the Italians do not waste space—their streets are just wide enough for a car to pass through. Make your mother happy, and look both ways before crossing the street. Being run over—even just once—could ruin your entire day.

Messina

History has handed Messina misfortune after misfortune. Initially colonized in the 8th century BC, the city was first captured (and renamed Messene) by Anaxilas in 493 BC. One hundred years later the Carthaginians came and razed the site. Thereafter, the city began its life as a trading card, falling into the hands of everyone from the Marmertines to the Normans to Richard the Lionheart. The city grew to prosperity under Norman rule and burgeoned as a Crusader port, for 600 years remaining a proud bastion at the periphery of European civilization.

Since the 17th century, though, Messina has been on a downhill slide. After rebelling against Spanish rule in the late 1600s, the city lost its special privileges and declined to one-eighth of its former size. Its slow convalescence was only temporary, for Messina was devastated by plague in 1743, demolished by an earthquake in 1783, bombarded from the sea in 1848, struck by cholera in 1854, slammed by more earthquakes in 1894 and 1908 and flattened by both Allied and Axis bombs during World War II. What is left is a city that has struggled time and again to rebuild itself, and now seems to have taken a few too many body blows to get up off the canvas anymore. Buildings in Messina generally date back no more than several decades, and nearly all appear to have been hastily constructed; even the cathedral seems of recent origin. A sense of impermanence hangs about, as if Messina's inhabitants know that yet another disaster will soon prove the futility of their efforts.

Unfortunately, Messina is the main point of entry into Sicily from the mainland, so you will probably have to pass through here. Although no city is without its virtues (the bar at the train station has satisfying snacks and good *gelato* for L1700), you'll probably want to move on as soon as possible, if only because your money is much better spent elsewhere in Sicily. Messina has all of the costs of a place like Taormina, and none of the charm.

Orientation and Practical Information

Major transportation routes and tourist offices cluster around the train station at p. della Repubblica. **Via 1° Settembre** connects it with **piazza del Duomo,** intersecting with **via Garibaldi** en route. Via Garibaldi runs along the harbor to both the hydrofoil dock and corso Cavour. Two blocks from p. della Repubblica (to the left as you exit the station), is via Tommaso Cannizzaro, which leads to the center of town, meeting viale San Martino at **piazza Cairoli.** Women should not walk alone in Messina at night. Be wary of pickpockets and purse-snatchers; keep your money in a secure place.

Tourist Office: Ufficio Informazioni Communali, outside the Central Station to the right in p. della Repubblica (tel. 67 29 44). Affable, English-speaking, and replete with materials and maps. Also has information on Lípari Islands, Taormina, and other areas within the province of Messina. **APT,** via Calabria, 301 (tel. 67 42 36 or 67 53 56), to the right of the station past the information office. A deluge of maps and information. The English-speaking agents can provide information and help you find a room. **AAST,** p. Cairoli, 45 (tel. 293 35 41). All offices open Mon.-Sat. 9am-7:30pm.

Post Office: at p. Antonello, off corso Cavour near the cathedral (tel. 67 53 56). Italy's only outdoor post office. Fermo Posta at window #12. Open Mon.-Sat. 8:30am-6:40pm. **Postal Code:** 98100.

Telephones: (ASST), on your right from the train station. Open daily 8am-9pm. **SIP,** via Natoli, 59, left off via Cannizzaro and across from the Banca di Credito Populace. Open 24 hrs. **Telephone Code:** 090.

Trains: at p. della Repubblica (tel. 69 49 45). To: Palermo (19 per day, 5hr., L17,100); Syracuse (12 per day, 3hr., L13,800); Rome (7 per day, 11hr., L46,000); Milazzo, the main port for the Lípari Islands (at least 12 per day, 40min., L3200). **Luggage Storage:** L1500 per bag.

Buses: SAIS, at p. della Repubblica, 46 (tel. 77 19 14), and at the train station. To: Taormina (11-14 per day, 1hr. 30min., L5100) and Catania (9 per day, 3hr., L9000). **Giuntabus** (tel. 77 37 82), viale San Martino at via Terranova. To Milazzo (11 per day, 30min., L5000).

Public Transportation: Buses, from p. della Repubblica into town, L500. Purchase tickets at any *tabacchi* or newsstand.

Ferries: Central Station, p. della Repubblica. **Hydrofoils: SNAV** (tel. 36 40 44), on corso Vittorio Emanuele II, 1km north of Central Station off via Garibaldi. To the Lípari Islands (5 per day June 1-Sept. 30, 2hr., L28,200). Save L15,000 by going to Milazzo and catching the ferry there.

Lost Property: tel. 77 37 52. In the state building on via Vettovaglie, to the right of the station.

Late-Night Pharmacy: check listings outside any pharmacy for the rotating 24 hr. service. **Centrale,** corso Garibaldi, 69 (tel. 67 90 34). Open Mon.-Fri. 8:30am-1pm and 4:30-8pm.

Emergencies: Police, tel. 113. **Hospital: Policlinico Universitario,** p. Maurolico (tel. 293 49 81).

Accommodations and Camping

Some smaller establishments are wary of foreign backpackers; check your bags at the station while searching.

Hotel Monza, viale San Martino, 63 (tel. 77 37 55), at via Cannizzaro. Sylvan lobby welcomes you to comfortable, tranquil, modern rooms. Singles L32,000, with bath L55,000. Doubles L55,000, with bath L90,000.

Hotel Touring, via Scotto, 17 (tel. 293 88 51), directly to the left of the train station. Opulent hallways conceal tiny rooms reminiscent of monastic cells. A convenient choice for travelers stranded between trains. Singles L30,000. Doubles L50,000.

Albergo Roma, p. Duomo, 3 (tel. 67 55 66). Ideally situated, to the left of the cathedral. Dreadfully sagging beds. Come for the high charm, not high-temperature water. Front door kept locked at all times. The management is stickly about rules. Singles L13,000. Doubles L26,000. Showers L1000.

Camping: Il Peloritano, (tel. 34 84 96). Take bus #28. L3300 per person, L3300 per small tent. Open May-Oct.

Food

Relatively inexpensive restaurants and *trattorie* crowd the area around via Risorgimento, reached by following via Cannizzaro (see Orientation above) one block after it becomes via Tommaso. In summer, try the legendary *pescespada* (swordfish) direct from the Straits of Messina, delectable enough to earn Homer's mention in the *Odyssey*. On via S. Cecilia, eight blocks from p. Maurolico down via Cesare, there is an evening outdoor **market** (daily 6-11pm).

La Grande Muraglia, via Nicola Fabrizi, 73 (tel. 71 80 15), right off via Risorgimento 3 blocks from p. Maurolico toward the station. Not the best bargain, but a multicultural experience. Whoever said wonton soup doesn't go with *spaghetti bolognese*? *Menù* L19,000. *Coperto* L2500. Open daily noon-3pm and 6-11pm.

Trattoria "Lasqualo," via N. Bixio, 151. Brave the other customers breathing over your shoulder and try some of the *antipasto di cozze* for L5000. *Primi* L8000, *secondi* L9000-12,000. Wine L4000 per . Cover L1500. Service 10%. Open 9am-3:30pm and 6-11pm.

Sights

The disasters that have befallen Messina have left few of its monuments intact. The government has recently been pouring in buckets of lire to revive the faded testaments to past glory, and many sights are currently shrouded in scaffolding and large white tents.

Graceful p. Duomo contains the 12th-century **duomo** (open 8am-12:30pm and 4-7pm, currently under restoration) and the squat **Church of SS. Annunziata dei Catalaní** from the same period. The cathedral's stark exterior features an ornate portal portraying the Archangel Gabriel and the Madonna with saints. The Arab-influenced sidings of SS. Annunziata are more reserved. In front of the church is the **Fontana di Orione** (circa 1547, also under restoration), the work of Michelangelo's pupil Angelo Montorsoli, where lazy nudes recline on a richly embellished base. The clock tower houses what is supposedly the world's largest astronomical clock. The grim reaper keeps time until the grand spectacle at noon, when a mechanical procession of animals, angels, and legendary figures re-enacts the local legend of the Madonna della Lettera, patron saint of the city. A **festival** in her honor takes over the town every June 3; another festival, the **Ferragosto Messinese,** takes place Aug. 14-15, featuring a procession 150,000 strong.

Just down the road from the port is the **Civic National Museum.** Founded in 1806 with five private collections, it was adopted by the state in 1904 as a repository for the furnishings, valuables, and works of art recovered from churches and civic buildings after the 1894 earthquake. Today it includes a collection of Renaissance and Baroque masterpieces, among them *The Polyptych of the Rosary* (1473) by local hero Antonello da Messina, an Andrea della Robbia terra-cotta of the Virgin and Child, and Caravaggio's *The Adoration of the Shepherds* (1608) and *Resurrection of Lazarus* (1609). Take bus #8 from the station or p. Duomo (20min.); walk part of the way back to view the harbor's scythe-shaped form, which gave Messina its original name Zanclon, from the Greek *zancle* (scythe). (Museum open daily 9am-1pm; Tues., Thurs., and Sat. also 3-7pm.)

A few nearby beaches provide relief from Messina's heat. **Spiaggia Mortelle** (bus #8 or 28) is on the Tyrrhenian Sea to the north, while **Santa Margherita** (bus #9 or 34) is on the Ionian Sea to the south. A string of pleasant beaches decorates the route to Palermo past Mortelle (bus #28, every 30min., 50min. from town), but only disembark at **Spaggia S. Saba** if you're into tar balls and broken glass.

Lípari Islands (Isole Eolie)

Seven jewels set in the sparkling Mediterranean, the Lípari or **Aeolian Islands** are all places of diverse and remarkable beauty. They are first mentioned in Homer's *Odyssey* as the domain of Aeolus, King of the Winds. According to this tale, Aeolus gave Odysseus the gift of a bag of winds (the original windbag) to help quicken his return trip. His sailors—not the brightest of seafarers—ignored the warning labels and opened the bag, blowing themselves right back to the islands. Upon beholding the splendor of these islands, you too may want to consider a return visit.

Things have changed somewhat since Homer's day, although the islands can still get pretty blustery. Today's Lípari Islands are renowned for their fiery volcanoes and long (if rough) beaches. Long overlooked, the islands have been discovered recently as one of the last chains of unspoiled seashore in Italy. Food and accommodations are more expensive than in the rest of Sicily; prices peak, unsurprisingly, in the August high season, for which you'd better make reservations on the main islands no later than May. Fortunately, there is a youth hostel. Of the seven isles, visit Lípari for a well-equipped tourist center, a castle, and easily navigable vistas; Vulcano for bubbling mud baths and a billowing sulfurous crater; Strómboli for luxuriant vegetation and a restless volcano; Panarea for inlets and a more elite clientele; Salina for grottoes and pilgrims; Filícudí for winding trails and coastal rock formations; and Alicudi for a rare dose of solitude.

Getting There

The seven-island archipelago lies off the Sicilian coast north of Milazzo, the principal and least expensive embarkation point (on the Messina-Palermo train line; 1hr.

from Messina, L3200; 4hr. from Palermo, L13,800). **Giuntabus** also services the town. (Tel. 090 67 37 82; 19 per day from Messina 5:45am-7pm, 4 on Sun., 45min., L5500; also daily from Catania airport June-Sept., L20,000.) Ferries leave much less frequently from **Naples's** Molo Beverello port. Hydrofoils (about twice the price of ferries) run regularly in late July and August from **Messina, Naples, Cefalù, Palermo,** and **Règgio di Calabria.** Both **SNAV** and **Siremar** have complete hydrofoil schedules available at every port (ask for *un orario generale).* The staff is generally helpful and will usually let you leave your luggage at the ticket offices. To get to the port in Milazzo, it's easiest to take the blue bus in front of the station. Get your ticket at the bar (L600) and ask to get off at the ferries *(traghetti).* If you're walking, cross piazza Marconi from in front of the train station and bear left on via XX Luglio. Three blocks later you'll hit the port as via XX Luglio becomes via dei Mille and then, as it curves to the right hugging the port, via Luigi Rizzo. Ferry offices can be found on via dei Mille, while *aliscafi* (hydrofoils) and their owners repose on via Rizzo.

Siremar (tel. (090) 928 32 42 in Milazzo) and **Navigazione Generale Insulare** (tel. 928 34 15) run reliable ferries out of Milazzo. Siremar also services several smaller islands and Naples (tel. (081) 551 21 81 or 551 12 13 in Naples). Frequencies listed are for June through September. Prices are the same for both lines. Connections can be made between any stops in a line.

Milazzo-Vulcano-Lípari-Salina: To: Vulcano 1hr. 30min., L8200; Lípari 2hr., L8700; Salina 3hr., L11,200. **Siremar:** 4-5 per day 7am-6:30pm. **NGI:** 2-3 per day 6:30am-10pm.

Milazzo-Panarea-Strómboli via Vulcano and Lípari: To: Panarea 3hr. 15min., L9700; Strómboli 5hr., L14,100. **Siremar:** 1 per day 8-9am. **NGI:** Friday only, 6:30am and 10pm.

Milazzo-Salina-Filicudi-Alicudi via Vulcano and Lípari: To: Salina 3hr. 15min., L11,200; Filicudi 4hr. 30min., L15,200; Alicudi 5hr. 30min., L18,700. **Siremar:** 1 per day 6:45-7am.

Naples-Strómboli-Panarea-Salina-Lípari-Vulcano: To: Strómboli 8hr., L47,900; Panarea 10hr. 30min., L51,100; Salina 11hr. 30min., L51,100; Lípari 12hr. 30min., L53,800; Vulcano 13hr. 45min., L54,300. **Siremar:** Daily (except Wed.) 9pm from the Molo Beverello port.

Running twice as often as ferries for twice the price and in half the time are the increasingly popular **hydrofoils (aliscafi). Siremar** and **SNAV** (tel. 928 45 09 in Milazzo, 36 40 44 in Messina) run the show here. From May 15 to October 15, SNAV runs to Lípari from Messina (5 per day 7am-6:20pm, L28,200), Règgio di Calabria (5 per day, L29,600), Cefalù (3 per week, L36,000), Palermo (2 per day, L55,100), and Naples (2 per day, L103,200). Siremar's cabins are air-conditioned; SNAV's are not. Again, frequencies listed are for June through September; connections can be made between any two points in a route.

Milazzo-Vulcano-Lípari-Salina: To: Vulcano 35min., L15,200; Lípari 50min., L16,300; Salina 1hr. 15min., L20,500 Siremar/L33,300 SNAV. **Siremar:** at least 6 per day 6:30am-7:15pm.

Milazzo-Panarea-Strómboli via Vulcano and Lípari: To: Panarea 1hr. 40min., L19,500; Strómboli 2hr. 30min., L25,900. **Siremar:** at least 3 per day 7:05am-3:05pm.

Milazzo-Filicudi-Alicudi via Vulcano and Lípari: To: Filicudi 2hr., L28,000; Alicudi 2hr. 30min., L34,500. **Siremar:** at least one per day 2:15-3:15pm The above information should be accurate for high season (June-Aug.), but always be sure to verify details at the ticket office.

The **telephone code** for the islands is 090. (You must pay extra for inter-island calls.)

Lípari

> ... a floating island, a wall of bronze and splendid
> smooth sheer cliffs.
>
> —Homer

Lípari, the largest and most beautiful of the islands, conceals a town by the same name. Pastel-colored houses hug a small promontory crowned by the walls of a medieval *castello,* the site of an ancient Greek acropolis. Its placid appearance belies an effusion of summer activity, from folk festivals to discos. Lípari makes an ideal base for daytrips to the other six islands and their splendid beaches. The town's best beaches, **Spiaggia Bianca** and **Spiaggia Porticello,** are easily reached by bus.

Orientation and Practical Information

The looming *castello* sits at the heart of the town, with the ferry dock to the right and the hydrofoil landing just to the left as you approach by sea. From piazza Ugo di Sant'Onofrio in front of the hydrofoil dock, **via Garibaldi** runs around the base of the *castello* to piazza Mazzini, shadowing the ferry dock. Farther inland the main street **corso Vittorio Emanuele** darts off parallel to the harbor.

> **Tourist Office:** corso Vittorio Emanuele, 202 (tel. 988 00 95), up the street from the ferry dock. English spoken. Useful free handouts. Open Mon.-Sat. 8am-2pm and 4:30-7:30pm, in Aug. 4:30-10pm.
>
> **Currency Exchange: Banca del Sud** and **B.A.E.,** both on corso Vittorio Emanuele. Open Mon.-Fri. 8:30am-1pm. Unofficial exchanges will change money at rip-off rates, but are always available in an emergency. Compare with exchange available at the post office (cash only).
>
> **Post Office:** corso Vittorio Emanuele, 207 (tel. 981 13 79) 1 block up from the tourist office, in the building that looks like 2 stacked steam-pipes. Fermo Posta. Open Mon.-Fri. 8:30am-6pm, Sat. 8:30am-1pm. The **postal code** for Lípari is 98055, for Canneto-Lípari 98052, and for the rest of the islands 98050.
>
> **Telephones: SIP,** (tel. 981 12 63) in the no-name boutique with the yellow awning on via Maurolico, off corso Vittorio Emanuele. Open Mon.-Sat. 8am-12:45pm and 4-9pm, Sun. 9am-12:45pm. At other times use the Hotel Augustus, via Ausonia, the first right off corso Vittorio Emanuele from the port. Open daily 9am-1pm and 4-11pm. **Telephone Code:** 090.
>
> **Public Transportation: Autobus Urso Gugliemo,** via Cappuccini (tel. 98 12 62). **Taxis:** corso Vittorio Emanuele (tel. 981 11 10) or Marina Corta (tel. 981 11 95). **Bike/Moped Rental: Foti Roberto,** via F. Crispi, 31 (tel. 981 23 52), on the beach to the right of the ferry port. Bicycles L5000 per hr., L20,000 per day. Mopeds and scooters L9000 per hr., L27,000 per day. Open Easter-Oct. 15 daily 9am-6pm.
>
> **Public Showers: Salone Docce,** at the barbershop of the Fratelli Acquaro, corso Vittorio Emanuele, 261, across from Officina Fonti motor service near the ferry dock. Hot showers for men L5000. One of the pleasant Acquaro brothers will give you a pampering chair shave for L4000. Open Mon.-Fri. 9am-noon and 4-8:30pm, Sat. 9am-noon.
>
> **Pharmacy: Farmacia Internazionale,** corso Vittorio Emanuele, 128 (tel. 981 15 83). English-speaking doctor often on duty.
>
> **Emergencies:** tel. 113. **Police:** tel. 981 13 33. **Medical Emergency:** tel. 988 52 26. **Night Emergency:** tel. 988 52 67. **Hospital:** tel. 988 51.

Accommodations and Camping

As you ply the port or walk the streets, locals will ask if you are looking for *affitta camere* (private rooms and apartments). These are often the best bargains but prices vary according to demand; proprietors ask for higher prices earlier in the day, then lower the costs later if their rooms haven't filled up. Try bargaining, but expect to pay at least L12,000-15,000 per person from September to June; start at L20,000 in August. Inquiring at local shops (try the bait-and-tackle store on via Garibaldi near the hydrofoil dock) is often a useful route for finding *affitta camere.*

Lípari is invaded by more and more tourists as the summer progresses, reaching capacity in August. Hotels fill almost instantaneously and owners raise their prices by as much as 25%. Make reservations as far in advance as possible.

> **Ostello Lípari (HI),** via Castello, 17 (tel. 981 15 40), 120 beds, on the hill within the walls of the fortress, next to the cathedral. Strict management sternly enforces 11pm curfew. Nevertheless, it's probably the best deal on the islands. Reception open daily 7:30-9am and 6pm-midnight, downstairs only noon-2pm (to check in luggage). L10,000 per person. Cold showers only. Sheets and blankets available on request. Kitchen facilities. Breakfast L2500. Lunch and dinner each L13,000 if demand calls for them (book them in the morning). HI card only required when near capacity. Reservations recommended in July and Aug. Open March-Oct.

Locanda Salina, via Garibaldi, 18 (tel. 981 23 32), near the hydrofoil port. Beautiful rooms overlooking the water. Singles L25,000. Doubles L50,000. Breakfast L5000 (no breakfast in Aug.). Reserve several days in advance for June, months ahead for August.

Hotel Europeo, corso Vittorio Emanuele, 98 (tel. 981 15 89). Singles L35,000, with bath L40,000. Doubles L50,000, with bath L70,000. Showers L1500. Breakfast L3000. Reserve early for June-Aug.

Camping: Baia Unci (tel. 981 19 09), 2km from Lípari at the entrance to the hamlet of Canneto. This diminutive, shady expanse has an amiable management and a cheap self-service restaurant (roasted swordfish a bargain at L11,000). L8500 per person, tent included. Open April-Oct. 15. Restaurant open Mon.-Sat. noon-2pm and 7-10pm.

Food

Try any dish with the island's famous *cápperi* (capers), and accompany it with the indigenous *Malvasia* wine. But unfortunately, eating cheaply on Lípari is something of a challenge. The **Upim Supermercato d'Anieri Bartolo,** corso Vittorio Emanuele, 212, stocks the basics. (Open Mon.-Tues. and Thurs.-Sat. 8:30am-1pm and 4-9:30pm, Wed. 8:30am-1pm. Visa, MC.) The *alimentari* lining corso Vittorio Emanuele are generally open Sunday.

Trattoria d'Oro, via Umberto I, 32. Look for the pink sign pointing off corso Vittorio Emanuele. The *menù* is an especially good buy (L15,000). Try the *polpo all'insalata* (marinated octopus salad, L10,000). Open daily 11:30am-3:30pm and 6:30pm-midnight.

Trattoria A Sfiziusa, via Roma, 39 (tel. 981 12 16), right off Anime d. Pugatorio where the hydrofoils dock and their crews dine. They make a mean pasta. *Primi* L5000-7000, *secondi* L10,000-13,000. Best bet is the *menù* at L16,000. Open daily noon-2:30pm, 6pm-midnight; closed Fridays in winter. Visa accepted.

Il Galeone, corso Vittorio Emanuele, 214 (tel. 981 14 63). Good pizzas and a handy location, close to the ferry docking site. Tempts with 34 types of pizza, L6000-12,000 apiece. Open 8am-11pm (pizza in the evenings only, other courses in the daytime). Closed Dec.-Feb.

Self-Service "Dal Napoletano," via Garibaldi, 12 (tel. 988 03 57), down the block from Locanda Salina, above. As suggested by the name, this is a self-service joint, which means you can avoid the *coperto* and service charge common elsewhere. In fact, they'll bring your order to you at the outdoor tables. *Maccheroni alla Norma,* L8000. *Menu* L15,000. Beer on tap. June-Sept., open 24hrs. Oct.-May, daily, 9am-3pm and 6pm-midnight. Closed Mon.

Sights and Entertainment in Lípari Town

A medieval **castello** crowns the town; within its walls stand four churches and a **duomo.** The latter contains an 18th-century silver statue of San Bartolomeo (above the high altar) and a 16th-century Madonna (in the right transept). The ruins opposite the cathedral in the *parco archeologico* reveal layers of civilization that date back to at least 1700 BC. Many of the artifacts found here decorate the exterior of the superb **Museo Archeologico Eoliano,** which occupies the two buildings flanking the cathedral. Inside the museum is the *serione geologico-vulcanologica,* an exposition of the volcanic history of the islands. (Open Mon.-Fri. 9am-2pm, Sun. 9am-1pm.) A neoclassical amphitheater inside the fortress hosts events during July's riotous **Festival delle Isole Eolie** (9am-2pm and 3pm-6pm in summer; 9am-4:30pm in winter). But even just a walk around the island or town is itself a treat. The twilight view of the Marina Lunga from near the *municipo* is unbelievably picturesque (right at the base of the *castello* entrance—look for the illuminated cross on the far peak). Even better—for both your eyes and your camera—is a sunset ferry ride to the islands.

As the sun sets and the zephyrs meander in from the sea, squeeze into your spandex and bop over to the **Discoteca Turmalin,** outside the castle walls and to the right as you exit. (Tel. 981 15 88. Cover L12,000. Open July-Aug. daily 10am-2am; Sept.-June Sat. only 10am-2am.) For a dose of American pop culture, visit the **Megaton Bar** at via XXIV Maggio, 51 (tel. 981 26 19). Enjoy big-screen TV and loud music while sampling a variety of teas, beers, sandwiches, and cocktails. (Open daily 8am-4am, Sept.-May 8am-1pm and 2pm-2am.) In a blowout party to mark the end of the summer tourist season, Lípari goes crazy with a colorful procession, fireworks, and other festivities on **August 24**—the day of the cathedral's patron saint, St. Bartholomew.

Around the Island

Lípari is known for its beaches and hillside panoramas. Go all out—rent a moped, and party on. Work your way counterclockwise from Lípari's marina, where you'll first stop at **Canneto,** home to a rocky beach and plenty of softer mammals bronzing on them. To get to the **Spiaggia Bianca** (White Beach) north of Canneto, take the water-front road to the "No Camping" sign, then walk up the stairs of via Marina Garibaldi and bear to your right down the narrow cobblestoned path along the water's edge for one-third of a kilometer. The beach is the spot for topless (and sometimes bottomless) sunbathing (and burning). Protect your delicate flesh, though—those pebbles are sharp. And watch out—or maybe don't—for public autoeroticism by the shameless locals. From Canneto center, explore the secluded sandy coves flanking Spiaggia Bianca by renting one of the rafts, kayaks, or canoes that line the beach at via M. Garibaldi. (L6000-8000 per hour, L25,000-35,000 per day.) Buses leave the Esso station at Lípari's ferry port for Canneto nine times per day (16 in July and Sept.; 21 in Aug.; L1200), and for Porticello (Cave di Pumice) 7 times per day (9 in Aug., L1200).

Just a few kilometers north of Canneto lies **Pomiciazzo,** where dozens of pumice mines line the road. On clear days, spectacular views of Salina, Panarea, and Strómboli hang on the horizon. Travel a few kilometers north and you're at **Porticello,** where you can bathe at the foot of the pumice mines while small flecks of the stone float on the sea's surface. As you dive beneath the waves for polished black obsidian, note the red and black veins (pumice and obsidian) which stretch from the beach into the seabed.

After passing through Acquacalda, the island's northernmost city, you'll see signs for the **Duomo de Chisea Barca,** right on the border of **Quattropani.** Head up the slope toward the church and check out some of the homes chopped into the obsidian hills. After a series of twists, turns, and some *very* steep inclines you'll finally reach the church and be granted a vista only those of saintly stature deserve.

Traveling south, across the island from Lípari Town, you'll pass through **Varesana** where the road splits: one route leads to **M.S. Angelo** (dominating the center of the island; follow signs for **Pirrera**) and the other runs to **Pianoconte,** where lava-coated battle gear has been unearthed. Here the road splits again, with one path leading to the **Thermal Baths** at **San Calogero** (on the west side of the island opposite Lípari), noto-rious during Roman times. The salty sulphate-bicarbonate waters bubble at a steamy 54°C (130° F), but don't be tempted to jump in; a doctor must first certify that you need the jolt. In the opposite direction perches **Quattrocchi** (Four-Eyes), so-called for its view of the four headlands that lie off the island's coast. If you make it to the Quattroc-chi Belvedere (4km from Lípari, but a heady climb), you receive in return a noble vista of Lípari's *castello,* Vulcano, and the *Faraglione,* a series of monoliths rising from the sea between Vulcano and Lípari.

South of Quattrocchi sits **Monte Guardia,** home to UNESCO's **Geophysical Observatory** and, for the rest of us, a close-up view of Vulcano (see below).

Infrequent buses wend their way all the way around the island (3 per day, 1 hr., round-trip L1400; check with tourist office for current times). More often visitors grab boats from the hydrofoil port in Lípari and tour around Lípari and its neighboring is-lands. Excursions are run by **SEN** (Società Eolie di Navigazione, tel. 981 23 41), which conducts tours of Lípari (Mon., Wed., Thurs., and Sat. at 10:15am, return 6pm, L40,000); Salina and Vulcano (L30,000); Alicudi and Filicudi (Tues. and Fri. at 9am, return 8pm, L45,000); Panarea (L27,000); Strómboli (daily at 3pm, return 11pm, L38,000); and Vulcano (daily at 9am, return 1pm, L15,000 for tour around island, L6000 for direct trip). If these prices are too high, try privately contracting a fishing boat for a personalized excursion. Bargain for a decent price—about L12,000 per person per hour is reasonable. Consult the NGI office (via F. Crispi, 96, near the ferry port) for other ways to experience the islands.

Vulcano

> *Stretch out and immerse yourself; the hand of the*
> *god Vulcan will hold you gently, transforming*
> *thoughts into bubbles of music and culture.*
> *—a signpost in Vulcano.*

The psychedelic sensations promised by these words may elude you, but this island is still a delight. Escape the crowds of Lípari and climb up to the sulfurous crater; take a dip in the bubbling sea or sink deeply into the therapeutic mud. But beware: some geologists think the gurgling volcano may explode within the next twenty years. For now, though, the great crater lies dormant at the island's center. Easy access from Lípari (by hydrofoil, L3300; by ferry, L1800) makes Vulcano an excellent daytrip. For those who can stomach the smelly fumes, longer stays are affordable and relaxing. The island has had an interesting history, inevitably tied to its volcano. The Greeks (among them Aristotle and Thucydides) repeatedly mention eruptions on Vulcano, including the one which created Vulcanello in 183 BC. Ancients believed this was the primary residence of Hephaestus (Vulcan), god of fire and blacksmiths, while medieval lore took the crater to be the entrance to hell. The 19th century introduced industry to the island, which a series of enterprising entrepreneurs purchased with the aim of extracting alum and sulfur. These industrial high hopes, however, were blown to bits by the earthquake of 1890. Today, Vulcano simmers away, huffing and puffing but not blowing any houses down—yet.

Orientation and Practical Information

Ferries and hydrofoils dock at **Porto di Levante,** on the eastern side of the isthmus between **Il Cardo** (the mountain to the left as you approach the port) and the Vulcanello peninsula (to the right). **Porto di Ponente,** along with **Spaggia Sabbie Nere** (Black Sands Beach—the only smooth one on the Aeolian Islands), lie across the isthmus on the west side of the isle. From the dock at p. di Levante, via Piano curves to the left (toward the volcano) and via Provinciale to the right. About 60m from the port, via Provinciale intersects via Porto Levante, and they merge to become via Porto Ponente. For information about Vulcano, try calling 985 20 28 (summer only) or following the signs to the information center. On via Piano sits a **post office** (tel. 985 20 49; open Mon.-Fri. 8am-1:30pm, Sat. 8am-11:20pm). Another post office is found at via Vulcano (985 24 65). A pharmacy, **Farmacia Bonarrigo,** is at via Faualauoro, 1 (tel. 985 22 44). For **medical emergencies,** dial 985 22 20; for **police,** call 985 21 10. There are lots of places to rent boats, autos, scooters, or bicycles, including **Porticciolo di Ponerte** (tel. 985 24 77) and **Pino Marturano** (tel. 985 24 19). For information on **public transportation,** contact **Scaffidi Rindaro** on via Piano (tel. 985 20 94).

Accommodations and Food

Keep in mind that all of Vulcano reeks with pervasive sulfur vapors—the island's accommodations are no exception. The comfortable **Togo Bungalows,** at the far end of via Levante (tel. 985 21 28), furnishes small, four-person bungalows with stoves for L20,000 per person; there are lockers for valuables. **Agostino,** via Favoloro, 1 (tel. 985 23 42), has comparatively simple doubles at decent prices (Sept.-June L45,000; July-Aug. L60,000). The amiable couple that runs the **Residence Lanterna Blù,** via Lentia, 58 (tel. 985 21 78), rents cozy apartments for longer stays. Each has a kitchen, a bath, and a private terrace shaded by flowering vines. (Two-person apartments May-June L40,000-50,000; July and Sept. L70,000; August L90,000. Extra bed L15,000; L18,000 one-time fee will be charged for cleaning the apartment at the end of your stay. Open Jan. 16-Dec. 14.) Somewhat cheaper is the **Pensione La Giara,** via Provinciale, 18 (tel. 985 22 29) with twenty rooms at L35,000 per person (breakfast included). The largest and most conveniently located campground is **Campeggio Togo** (tel. 985 23

03), 800m from the port in the Vulcanello area behind the Sabbie Nere beach. Its rather rudimentary facilities cost L7500, Sept.-June L5500-7000. L3500 per tent.

The **general store Agostino** is located on via Favoloro, 30, off via P. Ponente next to via Provinciale. (Open Mon.-Sat. 8am-1pm and 4-8:30pm, Sun. 8am-1pm.) **Panificio Alongi,** via Mercalli, 28, is the island's best bakery. To get there, hook a left on via P. Levante from via Provinciale as you're heading away from the port; via Mercalli is near the **Ristorante Lanterna Blù,** which offers a respectable L20,000 *menù*.

The only truly stellar eating experience on the island is the **Ristorante al Cratere** (tel. 985 20 45), just past the entrance to the path to the crater. Its *fettucine fresche al cratere* and aromatic grilled swordfish (L16,000) can be savored with excellent imported beer (from L3000). The L19,000 *menù* is a bit closer to the moderate price range. (Open daily 12:30-3pm and 6-10pm.) If you're seeking a more spartan gastronomical experience, the **Taverna del Marinaio,** just across from Agostino on via Favoloro, vends pizzas from L7000. (Open noon-3pm, 5:30pm-midnight.) Quality *gelato* can be had at the **Ristorante-Bar Vincenzino,** via Porto Levante (tel. 985 20 16). Finally, for some fun, check out **Il Diavolo Dei Polli,** in Vulcano Piano (tel. 985 21 97). It's a bit out of the way, but worth it for the view and conversation (Italian only) with the owner, Franco. (Grilled specialties; *primi* L5000-6000, *secondi* L10,000-12,000. Open noon-3pm, 6pm-midnight. Franco also drives the island's taxis, so if you try calling and he isn't busy, he may give you a ride up.)

Sights and Entertainment

Once on Vulcano, you should immediately tackle the one-hour hike to the **Gran Cratere** (Great Crater) along the snaking footpath beside the crater's fumaroles. Be warned: between 11am and 3pm the sun transforms the side of the volcano into a furnace, so head out in the early morning or late afternoon. The climb is not too difficult, but there are some steep inclines to look out for. On a clear day, having reached the top, you'll be able to see all the other islands. Don't linger long, however: the sulfur smoke spouting from the volcano is saturated with toxins. To get to the path from the port, follow via Piano for 100m to the bird statues; the path to the crater (**Sentiero per il cratere**) begins on your left on via Provinciale, just past the **Pizzeria Steak House** and the small yellow sign reading "Marcelleria," and follow the cobblestones from there.

Just up via Provinciale from the port sits the **Laghetto di Fanghi** (mud pool) to your right, a bubbling pit where hundreds of zealots come to spread the allegedly therapeutic glop all over their bodies. If you have no dermatological crises or just think the whole thing is a tad too silly, wade in the nearby waters of the **acquacalda** just behind the *laghetto*. Here, underwater volcanic outlets make the sea percolate like a jacuzzi; don't scald your feet! For cooler pleasures, visit the crowded beach and crystal-clear waters of Sabbie Nere, just down the road from the *acquacalda* (follow the signs off via P. Ponente through the black sand).

A **bus** runs from the pier to **Volcano Piano** on the other side of the island (6-7 per day 9am-6pm, L2000). There's little to do except visit the skeleton of the **Church of Saint Angelo,** admire the vistas, and savor the aroma of sun-ripened ginger. In the opposite direction from the pier lies **Vulcanello** with a peninsula all to itself. Like its bigger (and more interesting) sibling across the way, it comes complete with noxious fumes; on the other hand, the colors of the rocks along the way help to compensate for the odor.

Strómboli

Simply stated, the island of Strómboli is a volcano. This becomes evident on the approach as you catch sight of the fuming, conical mountain jutting straight out of the sea. But despite the volcano's year-round activity, Strómboli town (pop. 370) lies dormant until the frantic summer months bring with them the annual eruption of tourists. When the gushing streams of tourists are about (mid-June through early September), cheap accommodations are almost impossible to find—don't plan on staying unless you camp overnight. On the other hand, in the slow off-season, owners are often reluctant to rent rooms for fewer than three nights at a time. If you can manage it, see Strómboli on a day trip out of Lípari or Salina. (Ferry times and fares may make it difficult; shoot for the less expensive *nave* if possible.) Otherwise, camp out on the volcano's peak and watch the rocks roll.

Two towns cling to the volcano's slopes. Miniscule **Ginostra** huddles in the southern corner, essentially cut off from the rest of the island. On the opposite side, the adjoining villages of Piscità, Ficogrande, San Vincenzo, and Scari have fused to comprise Strómboli town on the island's northeast corner. The **Church of San Vincento** rises above the town and commands a tremendous view from its *piazza*, replete with Rodinesque sculptures of the Holy Trinity. From the ferry and hydrofoil dock, via Roma leads up the hill to the church at piazza Vincenzo. Via Filzi leads from p. Vincenzo across to via V. Nunziante, which descends past a few fast-food joints back to the sea where it hits via Marina at the black sand beach of **Ficogrande** (big fig). From here 2km in the distance rises **Strómbolicchio,** a gigantic rock with a small lighthouse perched on its rim. The ravages of the sea have eroded the rock (56m high only 100 years ago) to a mere 42m and dropping. **Boats** for hire make their way out to the base of Strómbolicchio (L10,000-15,000), from which one can climb the stairs (reinforced with concrete in the 1920s).

Hiking the volcano unguided has been officially illegal since mid-1990, although virtually everyone appears to do it anyway. If a solo trip (or the letter of the law) worries you, go with one of the island's authorized guides. (April-Oct., L20,000 per person; you may be able to negotiate for less.) Trips leave daily from Ficogrande at the stairs of v. Nunziante between 5 and 6pm, returning between 11pm and midnight. (Visit CAJ down the stairs, directly across the *piazza* from the church, for more information about the hike.) Despite large warning signs, it is entirely possible to hike the volcano unguided. (If doing so, don't go by the CAJ people waving your copy of *Let's Go*—the folks in the office are concerned about the fact that backpackers are ignoring local ordinances and because they're missing out on L20,000 at the same time.) It's likely you'll have trouble stashing your bags anywhere in town (especially in the CAJ office); you might try asking politely further down the road. In an emergency, hike up to where things start getting difficult, and hide your heavy, non-valuables somewhere until you can pick them up on your way back down. Be sure to take sturdy shoes, a flashlight, snacks, warm clothes for the exposed summit (sleeping bag is a real bonus), and *at least* 2 liters of water. The hike takes about three hours up and two down. Ideally, try to reach the summit around dusk—you can't see anything but smoke during the day—in order to camp out and see the brilliant lava flows by night. Remember to bring high-speed film to get good nighttime photos.

The trail to the volcano's mouth has three parts. First, take via Marina as it passes Ficogrande, bearing right at the large warning sign a half-kilometer down the road. If you stifle the urge to follow the small blue signs leading to "Centro Mare Strómboli," then duck under the cacti, and walk 20m on the narrow cobblestone path, you'll soon end up at a rather secluded stretch of beach, home to nude sunbathing and, at dusk, other corporeal pleasures. Resist temptation—keep walking on the cobblestone path another 300m past the homages to the Madonna and the garbage dump until you see a faded blue sign for a restaurant. Unless you're already dying of thirst, ignore this trap too and head to your left, where the trail cuts a clean swath through 3m reeds. After 70m of reeds, follow any path up the switchbacks, taking all shortcuts except those marked "No." Halfway up the slope is the island's best view of the tremendous **Sciara del Fuoco** ("Trail of Fire") streaming down the mountain into the sea, and a glimpse of the crater. Finally, the trail degenerates into a scramble up volcanic rock and ash, where it pays to follow the red-and-white striped rock markings. Heed the warning signs at the top ridge: several years ago a photographer fell to her death in search of a closer shot. If you see a red triangle with a black vertical bar, it means "danger," not "no parking." Be intelligent about climbing with heavy loads or in the dark, since the last part does get steep. Europe's most active volcano belches forth a thundering shower of molten boulders every 15 minutes or so to the cheers of onlookers. For an overnight trip, bring a sturdy food bag, plastic to place between you and the wet sand, warm clothing, and foul weather gear for the frigid fogs that envelop the peak. SEN runs an evening **boat**

trip from Strómboli to see the molten crimson trail of the *Sciara del Fuoco*. Boats leave Strómboli port at 5pm and return at 8pm (L20,000).

Hotels on Strómboli are booked solid in August by the previous winter. In other months, check via Roma for the occasional bargain. **Pensione la Nassa** (tel. 98 60 33) is a good bet, to the left off via Marina just 20m before the beach at Ficogrande as you depart from the port. A charming woman rents little houses on a daily basis (L40,000 per person, with bath). **Pensione Roma** (tel. 98 60 88), next to the Bar Roma, is five minutes from the ferry dock up on via Roma, almost at the top of the hill to the right. The rooms are cool and comfortable. (July-Aug. doubles L60,000; March-June 14 and Sept.-Oct. singles L20,000, doubles L40,000. In winter, singles L15,000.) Farther past the church is **Locanda Stella,** via F. Filzi, 14 (tel. 98 60 20), where two grandmothers rent warm doubles and triples. (Obligatory half-pension L35,000 per person including breakfast. Open June-Aug.) **Villa Petrusa,** via Soldata Panetrieri, 3 (tel. 98 60 45) has singles and doubles ranging from L24,000-45,000 per night. **Affitta camere** are available for extended periods of time. Inquire at bars and stores, or check with the tourist office.

For food, the best deals can be had at the **Duval Market** (tel. 98 60 52), to the left off via Roma right before the church. (Open daily 8:30am-12:30pm and 4:30-8:30pm.) Just a few meters down on via Roma is the *rosticceria* **La Trattola.** Half a roast chicken is L5500 and pizza runs L9000-12,000 per pie. (Open daily 8:30am-11pm.) On a breezy terrace overlooking the sea you'll find **La Lampara,** on via F. Filzi between the church and via Nunziante. Grilled swordfish (L12,000) and myriad pizzas (L6000-9000) are unequivocally filling. Try the *tiramisù,* a heavenly conglomeration of coffee-and-rum-soaked cake and sweet mascarpone cream (L4000). (Cover L1000. Open May-Oct. daily noon-2:30pm and 6pm-midnight.) After the tiring trek to the crater, you can replenish your stocks at the aptly named **General Store,** v. Vittorio Emanuele, 786 (tel. 98 61 63; open 8:30am-1pm, 4:30-8pm, closed Wed.) or at any of the comparable stores further along the way back. **Il Gabbiano,** on via Nunziante above the beach at Ficogrande, moonlights as a free disco, vying for dancing dynamos with the outdoor **La Nassa** (cover L5000 with 1 drink), located on via Marina toward the ferry dock. (Both open July-Sept. 10pm-2am.)

Strómboli's **post office** lies on via Roma (open Mon.-Fri. 8:05am-1:30pm, Sat. 8:05-11:20am), and the island's only bank, **Banco Agricola Atriea,** is next to the Gabbiano (open June-Sept. Mon.-Fri. 8:30am-1:30pm). The town **pharmacy** is also on via Roma. (Open 8:30am-1:30pm and 4-10pm, Sept.-June 14 9am-noon and 4-7:30pm.) For **medical emergencies** call 98 60 97 or go to the Guardia Medica on the Ficogrande side of the church; for **police** call 98 60 21. If you find yourself stuck in Ginostra in an emergency, you have no choice but to wait for a ferry or a hydrofoil to come along and try to hail it in a rowboat.

Other Islands

The remaining four *Eolie* provide a refreshing and uncrowded detour from the ordinary, whether you're in the mood for a rural fishing village or an overindulgent resort.

A verdant paradise and the second-largest isle, **Salina** brims with some of the best *Malvasia* wine (available at Malfa, on the north coast). It also bristles with the renowned rock formations at Semaforo di Pollara and Punta Lingua. Salina is still relatively uncorrupted by tourism; its beaches are uncrowded, its sleepy character intact. From the port, via Lunga Mare heads to the right toward Malfa and Pollara, site of the last eruption on the island some 12,000 years ago. From Malfa a road cuts through the center of the island through Valdichiesa and down the slopes of Pinella, where some of the hydrofoils dock. The town of Lingua, famed for its lucid water, lies just south of Salina's main port, 3km to the left on via L. Marel. From Lingua and Valdichiesa, paths extend to the peak of **M. Fossa delle Felci,** which presides over the isle at an impressive 962m. If you show up on August 15 for the Feast of the Assumption of the Virgin you'll be surrounded by pilgrims en route to the **Sanctuary of the Madonna del Terzito,** nestled in Valdichiesa and dating back to the early 1600s.

Near the port, **Pensione Mamma Santina,** via Sanità, 26 (tel. 984 30 54), has singles and doubles with bath for L35,000 and L55,000 respectively from October to June (July-Sept. obligatory half-pension L70,000). To get there, traipse along via Lunga Mare about 25m to the right of the port; via Sanità is a narrow staircase woven into the hill. **Villa Orchidea,** on via Roma in Malfa (tel. 984 40 79), is run by a friendly Australian woman. (Doubles with bath L72,000-95,000 in low season. July-Aug. obligatory half-pension L100,000.) At Rinella, **Camping Tre Pini** (tel. 980 91 55) charges L8000 per person, L8000 per tent. (Open June-Sept.) For a cozy dinner, **Trattoria Isola Verde,** via Risorgimento, 142/ 150, has some creative entrees. *Riso ai funghi* (rice and mushrooms) goes for L7000, while *scaloppine alla Malvasia* (veal cooked in Malvasia wine) can be savored for L9000 (open daily 11am-4pm and 7-11pm); heading right from the port on via L. Mare, walk up any street to your left one block toward via Risorgimento. Isola Verde is right next to the church off via Roma. **Mamma Santina** also runs a small eatery, especially convenient if you're staying there for the night. The *menù* goes for L28,000, wine included. (Open 1-2pm and 8:30-9:30pm.) **Posta Telegrafo** is at v. Risorgimento, 130 and is open Mon.-Sat. 8am-1:20pm. **Carabinieri** for Salina are at 984 30 19.

If *La Dolce Vita* were being filmed today, it would be set in **Panarea.** In the last three or four years, this tiny island (3.5 sq. km) midway between Salina and Strómboli has become the favorite spot for wealthy northerners, who come to private villas or to hotels that run a steep L150,000 or more per person. The island is renowned for its immaculate waters and striking natural rock sculptures. **Punto Milazzese,** on the southern tip of the island was the site of a Bronze Age prehistoric village, while the opposite end is marked by a sulfurous fumarole. Noleggio Bancha (tel. 98 30 74) rents **boats** of all sorts for exploration of the isle's coastal coves and hidden shores (one rental office located in Drauto, about 1.5km down the road to the left of the port). Come here for a daytrip from Lípari (plan your boat trips carefully); there are few cheap accommodations and no inexpensive dining options. If you're hungry, you're best off dropping by the *alimentari* on via S. Pietro.

West of Lípari, **Filicudi** presents an array of volcanic rock formations and the enchanting **Grotta del Bue Marino** (Grotto of the Monk Seal) on the side opposite the port (accessible only by boat). Heading to the right up the hill of **Montepalmieri** as you arrive at the port brings you rapidly to the rocky terraces of **Fossa Felci** (774m) and the island's **post office,** adjacent to (and located in the same building as) the **Pensione La Canna.** (Tel. 988 99 56; doubles with bath L65,000; full pension L80,000.) As you head further up to the town of **Valdichiesa** with its rapidly deteriorating church (note its precariously balanced bell tower), paths run around to the western edge of the Fossa and down to **Pecorini,** home to a set of ancient Greek inscriptions. The island's one paved road carries you back to the port from here, as the peninsula **Capo Graziano** reaches effortlessly into the sea from the right. **La Canna,** an impressive rock phallus (71m high, 9m wide), skyrockets from the sea a kilometer from Filicudi's west coast. It's easily visible if you make it on the footpath around the Fossa; otherwise rent a boat (L15,000-20,000) or grab a ferry to **Alicudi** which will pass right by the suggestive rock.

On the westernmost fringes of the Aeolian islands sits **Alicudi,** at five square km, little more than a speck in the sea. With one telephone, a hotel, 120 inhabitants, no paved roads, and recently installed electricity (Feb. '91), Alicudi is just the place to go if you're headed nowhere in particular. Heading up via Regina Elena leads you rapidly to the island's **church,** as well as, farther on, the **castle.** It's rumored that women used to hide from pirates in the nooks and crannies of the **Serra della Farcona;** if you reach **M. Filo d'Arpa's crater** (675m) you'll see why—just getting up there is a task. Left of the port, make your way over the stones to untouristed **Tonna.** The **Albergo Ericusa** (tel. 988 99 02, it's *the* phone) caters to the few visitors who aren't visiting family; half-pension runs at L60,000 and full pension at L85,000. (Open June-Sept., but call before you come—it's a long way back to civilization.) Full pension is advisable; with their isolation, vendors sell food at inordinately high prices, so be prepared.

Cefalù

Ostensibly named for the head-shaped promontory (now called the Rocca) that stares down upon what once was a sleepy fishing village, Cefalù remains a cache of Arab, Norman, and medieval architecture. Unfortunately, the flood of visitors drawn to its pleasant streets and sandy beaches has banished tranquility. Hotels fill up during the summer, and the prospects of finding an inexpensive *pensione* are fairly dismal even in the off-season. Visit Cefalù as a stopover or daytrip from Palermo, only an hour away by train (14 each weekday, L5000; 6 trains per day to Milazzo, 5 hr., L10,500—if you're en route to the Lípari islands). You can easily tour the town in half a day and still have time for a swim.

Practical Information

Tourist Office: corso Ruggero, 77 (tel. 210 50), in the old city. From the train station turn right onto via A. Moro, which first becomes via Matteotti then corso Ruggero (10min.). English-speaking staff helps with accommodations and stocks a map of the city. If you don't see anyone, check in back. Open Mon.-Fri. 8am-2pm and 4:30-7:30pm, Sat. 8am-2pm. Also at the train station. English spoken. Open Mon.-Sat. 8am-8pm.

Post Office: via Vazzana (tel. 215 28), off via Roma. Open Mon.-Fri. 8am-7pm, Sat. 8-11:20am. **Postal Code:** 90015.

Telephones: Agenzia San Mauro, via Vazzana, 7 (tel. 243 40). In front of the *lungomare.* Open Mon.-Sat. 9am-1pm and 4-7:30pm. **Telephone Code:** 0921.

Buses: SAIS, to Castelbuono and Geraci. **SPISA,** via Umberto I, 28 (tel. 243 01), in front of Bar Musotto. Take via A. Moro (right of the the train station) to the first intersection, and go right 1 block on via Mazzini. Serves all local towns for under L1500.

Emergencies: tel. 113. **Police:** tel. 113. **Hospital:** via A. Moro (tel. 211 18). **Nighttime Medical Emergency:** tel. 236 23.

Accommodations, Camping, and Food

Cefalù's hotels cater primarily to deep-pocketed northern Europeans; cheap lodgings are an endangered species. If you've ever considered camping, now's the time.

Locanda Caneglosi, via Umberto I, 28 (tel. 215 91), off P. Garibaldi. *The* budget shack. Only half-a-dozen rooms, so call in advance. Jun.-Aug. singles L12,000. Doubles L17,000. Showers included.

Pensione delle Rose, via Gibilmanna (tel. 218 85). Turn right on via A. Moro from the station. At the first stoplight, turn right onto via Mazzini and right again on via Umberto which soon turns into via Gibilmanna. Make a final right at the *pensione* sign, and left up the tree-lined stairs. Rooms with spectacular views of the town. Singles L30,000. Doubles L40,000, with bath L50,000. Oct.-May singles L22,000, doubles L35,000, with bath L45,000.

Pensione La Giara, via Veterani, 40 (tel. 215 62), off corso Ruggero, a block from the beach. Comfortable rooms with balconies opening onto a picturesque street with a sea view. Singles L34,000. Doubles L63,000. Oct.-May singles L33,000, doubles L55,000.

Camping: Costa Ponente (tel. 200 85), 3km west at Contrada Ogliastrillo (a 45-min. walk or a short ride on the Cefalù-Lascari bus, L1000). Swimming pool and tennis court. L6000 per person, L5500 per small tent, L7800 per large tent; Sept.-June L5400 per person, L4800 per small tent, L6900 per large tent. Nearby **Camping Sanfilippo** (tel. 201 84) charges L4500 per person, L4000 per small tent, L6000 per large tent.

Affordable restaurants cluster around corso Ruggero and via Vittorio Emanuele, and many fine *pizzerie* converge on via C.O. di Bordonaro and the *lungomare,* some with balcony dining. Shop for basics at **STANDA,** via Vazzana (tel. 245 00) near the post office. (Open Mon.-Sat. 8:30am-1pm and 5-8:30pm.)

Al Bastione, cortele Pepe (tel. 232 28), off via Umberto to the left past the *duomo* as you head toward the sea. Eat outdoors in a tiny courtyard under a grapevine, or indoors in the air-conditioned basement. Fabulous seafood dishes during the day and pizza at night (from L5000). Open daily 11:30am-3:30pm and 6:30pm until they decide to close.

Arkade Grill, via Vanni, around the corner from the tourist office. Break the pasta habit with the Tunisian *menù* (L13,000), or try other Tunisian specialties like *couscous* (L10,000) or *ejgia merguez* (spicy sausages, L6100). Wine L3500. Cover L1000. Open daily noon-4pm and 7-11:30pm; Sept.-June Fri.-Wed. noon-4pm and 7-11:30pm.

Sights and Entertainment

In p. Duomo off corso Ruggero you'll find Cefalù's austere 11th-century Norman **cathedral,** supposedly erected by Roger II in gratitude for divine protection from a shipwreck. There are also some indications that this structure was constructed as a fortress. The golden stone and square-towered solidity echo the monumentality of the Rocca behind it. Inside, 16 Byzantine and Roman columns support superb capitals as well as elegant horseshoe arches that manifest the Saracen influence on Norman architecture in Sicily. The bright Byzantine mosaics depict angels, a compassionate Christ, the Madonna, and the Apostles. (Open daily 9am-noon and 3:30-7pm. Proper dress required—shoulders and knees should be covered.)

Opposite the cathedral, down via Mandralisca, the private **Museo Mandralisca** houses a fine collection of paintings, Greek ceramics, Arab pottery, antique money, and Antonello da Messina's *Ritratto di Ignoto* ("Portrait of an Unknown Man," 1470-1472), the face featured on most Sicilian tourist brochures. (Open Mon.-Sat. 9am-12:30pm and 3:30-6pm, Sun. 9am-12:30pm. Admission L3000.)

At the end of via XXV Novembre on via Vittorio Emanuele (hugging the beach) is the curious semi-subterranean 16th-century **lavatoio medievale** (medieval laundromat). Don't drink the water coming from its fountains and try your best not to inhale the noxious fumes spewed from the ancient tubs.

For a bird's-eye view of the city, make the half-hour haul up the **Rocca** by way of the Salita Saraceni, which begins near p. Garibaldi off corso Umberto I. On the mountain, walkways lined with ancient stone walls lead to the **Tempio di Diana** (Temple of Diana). Dating back to the 4th century BC, it was first used for sea-cult worship and later as a defensive outpost.

Frolic under the stars at one of the town's discos, such as **Astro,** via Martoglio (tel. 231 03) or **Le Sabbie d'Oro,** loc. S. Lucia (tel. 213 40). From July to September, Cefalù hosts the **Incontri d'Estate,** which features classical, contemporary, and Sicilian folk music, as well as opera, in outdoor concerts. The Sicilian Symphony Orchestra is a featured performer at these concerts. Shows are moved to the *duomo* August 4-6 to accommodate the **Fiesta di San Salvatore** in honor of Cefalù's patron saint, celebrated with a rousing display of fireworks and marching bands.

Cefalù's best beaches, **Spiaggia Mazzaforno** and **Spiaggia Settefrati,** are located west of town on SPISA's Cefalù-Lascari bus line (L1000).

Near Cefalù: The Ruins of Tyndaris

Seventy-five kilometers east of Cefalù and just 15km west of Milazzo (whence ferries depart to the Aeolian Isles) lies **Tíndari,** site of the ruins of **Tyndaris.** Dating from the 4th century BC, the Greek settlement was founded high on a hill as a fortification against enemy attacks. Tindaris chose wisely, siding with Rome in the Punic Wars and supplying ships for the expedition that destoyed Carthage in 146 BC. However, an earthquake in 365 AD destroyed the city, and the Arabs mopped up the remains in 836. Unearthed only in the mid-1900s, the ruins are now home to a museum, several archeological curiosities, olive groves, and spectacular views of the Aeolian Isles.

Ironically, the first sight you'll see upon climbing the hill to the ancient site is the **Santuario di Tíndari,** erected less than 30 years ago for the **Madonna Nera** (Black Madonna). Across from the entrance to the sanctuary, a path leads to the heart of the ruins where a **basilica** and **agora** abide to the right. The **theater** perches 125m further down, characteristically cut into the hill with an impressive panorama of the surrounding seascape. The **museum,** adjacent to the theater, has a series of knick-knacks uncovered from the site as well as some drawings illustrating what life was like in the ancient town. (Museum open daily 9am-2pm. Site open daily 9am-1 hr. before sunset. Both free.) Just in front of the museum proceeds the main street of the town, the **decu-**

manus. Follow it to the right as you exit the museum; it will curve past the base of the basilica and lead you to the **Casa Romana,** an old Roman house replete with intricate mosaics. All around the site stand bits and pieces of the city's walls, as well as the original city gate on the main road en route to the *santuario.* If you have the chance, drop by Tíndari to see **Greek drama** in the theater; the tourist office in Cefalù has listings of current plays and performance times.

To get to the ruins at Tíndari either take a train to **Patti,** departure site for direct buses to the site (approximately every 45min., L1000), or take the train to **Oliveri-Tindari** and hike 3km uphill to the site. Be sure to double-check when buses are returning; Tíndari ain't no mecca and you can readily find yourself stranded there late in the day.

Palermo

The people and palaces of Palermo, capital of Sicily, proclaim it as a crossroads of Mediterranean cultures. First in the Phoenician orbit, then under Roman and Byzantine sway, Palermo blossomed under Saracen (831-1071) and enlightened Norman rule (1072-1194), emerging as one of Europe's most prominent cities. Hohenstaufen, Angevin, Aragonese, and Bourbon overlords followed. Enjoying unusual goodwill and tolerance, the city became the intellectual bastion of southern Italy and a junction for trade between East and West (thus its original name, "Panoiamus," meaning "all harbor"). Today Palermitans are reputed to retain an Arabic outlook commensurate with their physical heritage, although their Norman ancestry has left a balance of blondes unique in southern Italy. In modern times, Palermo has earned notoriety as the cradle of Italian organized crime. Having risen to prominence in the late 19th century, the loose affiliation of *uomini d'onore* (men of honor) known as the Mafia saw its power diminished by Fascist-era purges, then augmented by cooperation with invading Allied forces during World War II. Since the mid-80s the government has once again tried to curtail Mafia influence, with inconclusive results. Although the ongoing battle of intimidation and assassination continues to make headlines and coffee-shop conversation, petty thievery and drive-by snatchings are far more likely to trouble the traveler. Women should be especially alert in Palermo. Be cautious, especially as you stray further from the center of this fascinating, patchwork city.

Orientation and Practical Information

Palermo and its crescent-shaped harbor lie at the end of a fertile basin called the **Conca d'Oro** (Golden Conch). To the north, 610m of Monte Pellegrino's limestone mass separate the city from **Mondello,** its beautiful beach. As you exit the front of the station onto p. Giulio Césare, **via Roma** runs straight into the bowels of Palermo, spanning the old city. Ten blocks from the station it is intersected by **corso Vittorio Emanuele,** racing from the sea toward the mountains and, 10 blocks after that, by **via Cavour,** running parallel to corso Vittorio Emanuele. Just a few blocks to the left of via Roma as you exit the station lies **via Maqueda,** paralleling via Roma through its intersection with c. Vittorio Emanuel at **piazza Vigliena** all the way to the Teatro Mássimo at via Cavour. At this point it transforms into **via Ruggero Séttimo,** and at via E. Amari (in p. Castelnuovo) into **via Libertà.**

Behind the once-grand *palazzi* lining the main avenues you'll find a maze of alleys and courtyards. These innards of historic Palermo are a sharp contrast to the sterile grid of the modern quarter west of p. Castelnuovo. Shop for food at markets off via Roma on via Divisi, and between the Palazzo dei Normani and the station at p. Ballaro; for clothing, try via Bandiera near the Church of San Domenico. Ritzier shops plume themselves along via Roma, via Maqueda, and viale della Libertà. With the exception of restaurants, everything in Palermo closes from noon to 3pm and then again around 8pm.

Crime

Don't let crime ruin your stay in Palermo. Pickpockets and moped-mounted bag-snatchers will get you if you fail to take precautions. Keep wallets in moneybelts or neck pouches, *not* in front pockets or handbags. Leave all bags, valuables, expensive watches and other jewelry at your hotel; if your room is not secure, however, you may have to choose between two evils. Avoid the dark, deserted back streets of old Palermo at night—and hit the sack by 9pm; any wandering after that hour invites trouble.

Tourist Office: p. Castelnuovo, 34 (tel. 58 38 47), 2km north of the train station. Take bus #7 or 46 going toward Teatro Politeama. In the building with the huge Sicilcasa sign, but the trip here is hardly worth it. The Branch at the **train station** is a superb alternative, with detailed information on Palermo and other places of interest such as Cefalù, Monreale, and Ústica; it's also a lot more convenient (open Mon.-Sat. 8am-8pm). There is another branch office at p. San Sepolcro (tel. 616 13 61), off via Maqueda to the right just a few blocks before you hit corso Vittorio Emanuele going from the station (open Mon.-Sat. 8am-2pm). The booth at the airport (tel. 59 16 98) is open daily 8am-8pm.

Budget Travel: CTS, via Garzilli, 28/G (tel. 32 57 52). Take via Maqueda to piazza Castelnuovo; go 1 block past p. Castelnuovo on via Libertà and turn left on via Carducci. Two blocks farther you'll hit via Garzelli. The office is then to your right. Harried but efficient. Open Mon.-Fri. 9am-1pm and 4-7:30pm, Sat. 9am-1pm.

Consulate: U.S., via G.B. Vaccarini, 1 (tel. 30 25 90), off viale della Libertà. Take bus #14 or 15. Open Mon.-Fri. 8am-12:30pm and 3-5pm. Emergencies only. **U.K.** (tel. (081) 66 35 11) citizens should contact their consulate in Naples; **Australian** citizens should contact their embassy in Rome (tel. (06) 83 27 21); **New Zealanders** should also call Rome (tel. (06) 440 29 28).

American Express: G. Ruggieri, via E. Amari, 40 (tel. 58 71 44). Follow via E. Amari from p. Politeama toward the water. Very busy. Open Mon.-Fri. 9am-1pm and 4-7pm, Sat. 9am-1pm.

Post Office: via Roma, 322 (tel. 160), by the Museo Archeologico, 2 blocks from via Cavour. Open Mon.-Sat. 8:15am-7:30pm for letters, 8:15am-1:20pm for packages. Fermo Posta at windows #15-16. Open Mon.-Sat. 8:15am-7:30pm. **Postal Code:** 90100.

Telephones: ASST, via Lincoln, across from the train station. Open 24 hrs. **SIP,** via Principe di Belmonte. Follow via Maqueda until it metamorphoses into via Ruggero Séttimo and you reach piazza Castelnuovo. Across from Castelnuovo is piazza Ruggero Séttimo; take the first right off that *piazza* before the Politeama Garibaldi. Open daily 8am-8pm. **Telephone Code:** 091.

Flights: Cinisi-Punta Raisi (tel. 59 16 90), 31km west of Palermo. Public buses connect the airport to p. Politeama (15 per day 5:30am-10:20pm, L3500), as do private buses that operate until the last flight leaves or arrives (L4000). Taxis charge at least L50,000 for the same route.

Trains: p. G. Césare (tel. 616 18 06), on the eastern side of town. To: Milan (22hr., L78,700); Rome (15hr., L63,200); Naples (13hr., L51,000).

Public Transportation: City buses (AMAT), tel. 22 23 98. Fare L1000 for a 1hr. ticket, L3000 for a 1-day pass. Buy tickets from coin-operated machines inside buses (exact change only), from *tabacchi,* or at the bus depot. The main terminal is in front of the train station.

Buses: Filli Camilleri-Argento, (tel. (0922) 390 84). To Agrigento (2-3 per day, 2hr., L9200) from via Balsamo around to the right of the train station as you face piazza G. Césare and via Roma. **Autoservizi Segesta,** via Balsamo, 26 (tel. 616 79 19) has over 20 departures per day direct to Trápani (1hr. 45min., L10,500). **SAIS,** via Balsamo, 16 (tel. 616 60 28). To Catania (16 per day, 2hr. 30min., L16,000) and Syracuse (Mon.-Sat. 5 per day, 4hr., L21,200).

Ferries: Tirrenia (tel. 602 11 11) in Palazzina Stella Maris within the port. Entry to port off via Francesco Crispi. Open 8:30am-1pm and 3-5pm. **Grandi Traghetti,** via M. Stabile, 53 (tel. 58 78 32). Open Sun.-Fri. 8:30am-5pm. **Siremar,** via Francesco Crispi, 120 (tel. 58 24 03). Open 8am-1pm and 3-5pm. **SNAV,** via P. d. Belmonte, 51 (tel. 58 65 53). Open 9am-1:30pm and 3:30-7pm. Siremar has daily ferries to Ústica (Mon.-Sat. at 9am, Sun. at 7:30am, 2hr. 20min., L14,100) as well as hydrofoils 3 times daily in July and Aug. (at 7am, 2:45pm, and 6pm, 1hr. 15min., L28,300).

Gay Men's Resource Center: Arci-Gay, via Trápani, 3 (tel. 32 49 17 or 32 49 18). Information on events. Open Mon.-Fri. 9:30-11:30pm.

Lost and Found, in the Palazzo del Municipio, p. Pretoria (tel. 33 93 30), off via Maqueda near via Vittorio Emanuele. Open daily 8:30am-1:30pm.

Public Toilets and Showers: Albergo Diurno, at the train station. Clean and convenient. Showers L7500. Shampoo L3500. Open daily 8am-8pm.

Late-Night Pharmacy: Lo Cascio, via Roma, 1 (tel. 616 21 17), near the train station. Open Sun.-Fri. 5:30pm-1pm, Sat. 8pm-9am. Consult tourist office for seasonal openings.

Emergencies: tel. 113. **Police:** tel. 112. **Hospital: Civico Regional e Generale,** via Lazzaro (tel. 48 45 44). **Medical Emergency:** tel. 48 45 44.

Accommodations and Camping

Finding a decent and inexpensive place to stay here is a breeze. A surfeit of *alberghi* blesses **via Roma** and **via Maqueda,** but women should avoid the eastern part of town by the train station after dark.

Pensione Sud, via Maqueda, 8 (tel. 617 57 00), in the busy part of town just 2 blocks from the station. Handsomely furnished rooms and caring, helpful owner make it one of the best deals in town. Keep an eye out for Rocco, the *pensione's* guard-cat. Singles L20,000. Doubles L28,000-30,000. Triples L40,000. Scalding showers L2000. In the same building is **Albergo Vittoria** (tel. 616 24 37), a 2-star with simple modern rooms. Singles L26,000. Doubles L36,000. Triples L50,000.

Hotel Cortese, via Scarparelli, 16, (tel. 33 17 22). From the train station, walk 10min. down via Maqueda to via dell'Universita; look for the sign to the left. Turn left and go another 200m. Probably the nicest hotel in its price range. Impeccable, modern rooms with new furniture. Singles L20,000, with shower L26,000. Doubles L34,000, with shower L42,000. Hall showers free. Half or full penion available. Visa, MC.

Albergo Rosalia Conca d'Oro, via Santa Rosalia, 7 (tel. 616 45 43). Turn left off via Roma as you leave the station. Spacious rooms with balcony views of neighborhood. Run by an older couple always willing to provide helpful advice. A perk: June 15-Sept.15 you get free tickets to beaches at Mondello and Sferracavallo—sun umbrellas and cabanas included. Singles L22,000. Doubles L35,000. Triples L48,000.

Albergo Letizia, via Bottai, 30 (tel. 58 91 10). From via Roma head on corso Vittorio Emanuele toward the water. Via Bottai is the 8th street on your right, just before the entrance to p. Marina. A little out-of-the-way, but the modern rooms are as fresh as the bottles of rainwater the owner collects in his spare time. Singles L25,000, with bath L30,000. Doubles L36,000, with bath L45,000. Extra bed L13,000.

Hotel Ariston, via M. Stabile, 139 (tel. 33 24 34), in the busy part of town far from the station. Head up via Roma 3 blocks past via Cavour or take bus #7 or 46 and jump off before via E. Amari. Modern rooms overlooking a quaint courtyard. Singles L25,000, with bath L28,000. Doubles L35,000, with bath L45,000.

Petit Hotel, via Principe di Belmonte, 84 (tel. 32 36 16), to the left off via Roma 2 blocks before via E. Amari as you head from the station. Quiet, clean, and in a safe neighborhood crowded with posh *caffè.* Drop by Frankie's place downstairs (Bar Fiore) for a late-night snack. Doubles with bath L48,000.

Albergo Cavour, via Manzoni, 11 (tel. 616 27 59), on the 5th floor. From p. G. Césare in front of the station hang a right on via Lincoln; via Manzoni is the 1st street on your left. Well-sized rooms, sweet Transylvanian elevators. Singles L22,000. Doubles L32,000. Showers L3000.

Albergo Orientale, via Maqueda, 26 (tel. 616 57 27), just a few blocks from the station. Don't come for the stark rooms; come for the surreal experience of meandering through the halls of this gloriously run-down 17th-century *palazzo.* Singles L25,000. Doubles L40,000, with bath L45,000. The only triple (with bath) has a balcony Mussolini would have died for (L55,000).

Albergo Alessandra, via Divisi, 99 (tel. 616 70 09), off via Maqueda. Recently renovated, with beautifully decorated ceilings. Singles with bath L30,000. Doubles L40,000, with bath L50,000.

Hotel Odeon, via E. Amari, 140 (tel. 33 27 78). Directly to the right of the Teatro Politeama as one faces it from p. Castelnuovo. Clean but depressing rooms in a super-convenient location. Singles L18,000, with bath L22,000. Doubles L32,000, with bath L40,000.

Hotel Capri, via Maqueda, 129 (tel. 616 82 49). Clean though charmless rooms, all with brand-new bathrooms. Singles L20,000-25,000. Doubles L35,000-40,000.

Camping: Trinacria, via Barcarello (tel. 53 05 90), at Sferracavallo by the sea. Take bus #28 from Teatro Mássimo. L4600 per person, tent included. Also at Sferracavallo is **Campeggio dell'Ulivo,** via Pegaso (tel. 53 30 21). It's cheaper, but lower quality. L2700 per person, tent included.

Food

Palermo is famous for its *pasta con le sarde* (with sardines and fennel) and *rigatoni alla palermitana* (with a sauce of meat and peas). The best seafood platter is swordfish, either plain (*pesce spada*) or rolled and stuffed (*involtini di pesce spada*). Eggplant comes in every shade of purple, in forms ranging from slender to stout. Have it cold in a tasty sauce, deep-fried in sandwiches, or in a dish called *caponata di melanzana,* stewed with onions, celery, green olives, and capers. At certain stands in the markets you can get octopus simmered to order (snack portion about L1500). Also try *panelle,* tasty fried balls of chick-pea flour sliced and sandwiched. For the apotheosis of local cuisine, have *spaghetti al broccoli affogati alla palermitana,* spaghetti combined with spicy fried broccoli. And, of course, partake of the heady local wines.

The **STANDA supermarket** has outlets at via Libertà, 30 (tel. 33 16 21), in the northern end of town past piazza Castelnuovo, and at via R. Séttimo, 16/22 (tel. 58 60 19), on the stretch of pavement linking via Maqueda and via Libertà. (Both open daily 9am-1pm and 4-8pm.)

Trattoria Shanghai, vicolo de Mezzani, 34 (tel. 58 97 02), overlooking piazza Caracciolo. Hook a right on corso Vittorio Emanuele off via Roma as you journey from the station and then a left on via Vuccíria just 1 block farther. As you enter p. Caracciolo, bear right onto vicolo de Mezzani. Despite this *trattoria's* name, the food here is pure Palermo. Arrive for lunch and watch the marketeers do their stuff. Great *gamberi* (shrimp) L8000. Cover L1000. No set hours; drop in for lunch or dinner. Service 10%.

Hostaria al Buar 2, via E. Amari, 92 (tel. 32 16 78), off via Roma as you angle towards the port. Award-winning Italian and North African cuisine. Experience Tunisia's finest with the *Completo Tunisio* (L14,000, food, drink, and cover included). Cover L1000. Open Thurs.-Tues. noon-3pm and 6-11:30pm.

Trattoria-Pizzeria Enzo, via Maurslico 17, to the right as you exit the station onto p. G. Césare. Filling and fabulous for the fantastically frugal. Full meals (*primi, secondi,* and beverage) L13,000. Open Sun.-Fri. for lunch and dinner.

Il Cotto e il Crudo, p. Marina, 45. From via Roma, head toward the water on corso Vittorio Emanuele, then right on via Bottai into piazza Marina. So diminutive and peaceful you'd never know it was there. Look for the *trattoria* sign in front. Don't miss the *penette con tofu e salvia* (pasta in a sauce of tofu and fresh sage, L5000). Well-presented self-serve antipasto table L5500. Cover L1000. Service 10%. Open Mon.-Sat. noon-3pm and 7-11pm.

Hotel Patria, via Alloro, 104 (tel. 616 11 36). Take via Paternostro off corso Vittorio Emanuele until you see the fading red Hotel Patria coat of arms to your left past piazza Fiances. Palermitans line up to eat delicious food al fresco in one of the city's most romantic courtyards. Try the *spaghetti al pescespada* (L7000). *Secondi* L6000-12,000. Cover L500. Service 10%. Open Mon.-Sat. 1-3pm and 8-11pm.

Trattoria dei Vespri, p. Sta. Croce dei Vespri, 6/A (tel. 617 20 19), 2 blocks south of corso Vittorio Emanuele. Turn left off via Roma onto via Discesa dei Giudici at the large Tarantino sign heading away from the station, then bear left and walk 1 *piazza* past the church of Santa Anna. A gourmet oasis in the midst of the dark old city. Enjoy the food at an outdoor table in an otherwise deserted *piazza.* The *pescespada arrosto* (roasted swordfish) is unbeatable (L10,000). Service 10%. Open Mon.-Sat. 1-3pm and 6:30pm-midnight.

Osteria Lo Bianco, via E. Amari, 104 (tel. 58 58 16), off via Roma as you're headed towards the port. Local crowds wipe the sweat from their brows between each delectable bite. They have a printed *menù,* but, in truth, it changes daily. If you're lucky they'll have some *pesce spada* (swordfish, L8000), but everything's a treat. Sample local wines from the stainless steel barrels perched safely overhead (L2500 per). Open Mon.-Sat. noon-3pm and 7-11pm.

Bar Fiore, via Principe di Belmonte, 84 (tel. 33 25 39), off via Roma near the Teatro Politeama. A cheap and decent eatery in this otherwise expensive pedestrian mall. If you have a whole meal, jovial owner Frank, Palermo's greatest extrovert, will treat you to a glass of *zibbibbo,* an Olympian ambrosia that Bacchus brought to Palermo. Pasta of the day L3000; large and light *insalata mista* L5000. Try his superb *frullata,* the Italian milkshake (L3500). Top it off with some amazing pizza, your choice of artichoke, spinach, or mushroom (L2500). Draft beer on tap. Possible discounts for groups carrying *Let's Go*. (Frank's a big fan.) Open daily 6am-midnight.

Antica Foccacceria S. Francesco, via Paternostro, 58, off corso Vittorio Emanuele across from the Church of S. Francesco on the *piazza.* A 150-year-old *pizzeria:* dark wood, cast iron, and aged cacaphony. Supposedly Garibaldi took his first meal here after liberating Palermo. Pizza about L2000 per slice. A tribe of locals lines up for *pane ca' meusa,* small sandwich of ricotta and marinated tripe, for L2000. *Arancina,* a fried-rice-and-meat ball, costs L1500. Beer L2500-3000. Eat outside (you bring it out yourself) on the steps of S. Francesco. Open Tues.-Sun. 11am-3pm and 7pm-midnight.

Trattoria Trápani, p. Giulio Césare, 16 (tel. 61 61 642). On the right side of the square as you exit the train station. A real handy cheap-eat. *Primi* L2800-3000, *secondi* L4500-6000. *Coperto* L300. Service 10%. Open Mon.-Sat. noon-3pm and 6pm-10:30pm.

Sights

After ancient glory and then seven centuries of neglect, Palermo is an incongruous mix of the splendid and the shabby. The bizarre sight of Palermo's half-crumbled, soot-blackened 16th-century *palazzi* startles visitors accustomed to the cleaner historic districts of northern Italy. In the past several years, however, efforts have begun to clean, rebuild, and reopen structures like the magnificent Teatro Mássimo, closed due to water damage for the past—get this—20 years. Peek into random courtyards on your path to find the *cortili* for which the city is famous. The courtyards themselves often seem to be held together only by the ivy laced across their facades. Visit the one at corso Vittorio Emanuele, 452 (across from the *duomo*); the sylvan interior of via Maqueda, 83 (halfway between the *duomo* and the train station); and the arches of via Paternostro, 48 (off corso Vittorio Emanuele to the right as you're headed toward the water). For a glimpse of Palermo's ravaged splendor, climb the red marble staircase at via Maqueda, 26, across from the Orfeo cinema, to the tremendous balustrade on the top floor.

From Quattro Canti to San Giovanni degli Eremiti

The intersection of corso Vittorio Emanuele and via Maqueda forms the **Quattro Canti,** where each corner celebrates a season, a king of Spain, and one of the city's patron saints. The Canti date from the early 17th century when Sicily was under Spanish rule. Just a few steps away to your left as you proceed down via Maqueda toward the station sits **piazza Pretoria** with a fountain (1555-1575) originally intended for a Florentine villa, but currently more likely to be found in the pages of *Penthouse.* Palermitans were so shocked when it was unveiled that they nicknamed the sculpture "the fountain of shame." Flanking the *piazza* are the 16th-century **Palazzo del Municipio** and the splendid baroque **Church of Santa Caterina** (1566-1596).

Next to the statue of Philip III in the Quattro Canti, the dismal gray facade of the **Church of San Guiseppe dei Teatini** (1612) belies its "as much as you can put on the walls without tearing them down" Baroque interior. Don't miss such details as the upside-down angels supporting the fonts at the entrance, or the frieze of children playing musical instruments on the wall of the south transept. (Open daily 7:30am-noon and 6:30-8:15pm.)

Farther down via Maqueda and to the left as you approach the station, **piazza Bellini** embraces the **Church of San Cataldo** (1154), a Norman building whose red domes and arches give it the air of a mosque. **La Martorana,** or, more properly, **Santa Maria dell'Ammiraglio** (built for an admiral of the Norman king Roger II), shares San Cataldo's leafy platform. Mediocre Baroque additions partially conceal its 12th-century structure. The Byzantine mosaics inside are the 12th-century equivalent of celebrity photos: here's Roger I and Jesus, there's George the Admiral with the Mother of God. (Both open Mon.-Sat. 8:30am-1pm and 3:30-7pm, Sun. 8:30am-1pm.)

Across via Maqueda from p. Bellini and to the right as you close in on the station, **via Ponticello** winds through a crowded neighborhood to the **Chiesa del Gesù** (or Casa Professa, built 1363-1564). Look for its green mosaic dome. The ochre stucco facade conceals a dazzling, multicolored marble interior and an almost Warhol-like depiction of the Last Judgment. Standing in Il Gesù's courtyard, you can see traces of American bombing during World War II; the **Quartiere dell'Alberghería,** the inner core of the city, never quite recovered from the war's destruction—as evinced by the numerous shattered buildings, including the one next to the Chiesa. (Church open daily 7am-noon and 5-6:30pm.)

Farther along via Ponticello, **piazza Ballarò** combines a lively market and a view of the 17th-century **Church of the Carmine,** whose mosaic dome is simply dumbfounding. This area, replete with narrow streets and hidden gardens, warrants further exploration. Venturing from the Quattro Canti onto **corso Vittorio Emanuele,** heading away from the harbor, you will pass the dilapidated *palazzi* of the **piazza Bologni** to the left and a spindly statue of Charles V (1630) before confronting the striking exuberance of Palermo's **cattedrale** up on the right. Begun by the Normans in 1185, it absorbed elements of every architectural style from the 13th through 18th centuries, though the best exterior elements are the original Norman towers and the three-apsed grandeur of the eastern side. Inside, the chapels on the left contain six royal tombs (four canopied and two set in the wall) of Norman kings and Hohenstaufen emperors dating from the 12th to 14th centuries. The *tesoro* (treasury, L1000), to the right of the apse, contains a dazzling array of sacerdotal vestments from the 16th and 17th centuries as well as episcopal rings, chalices, and croziers. (Open daily 7am-noon and 5-7pm.) The cattedrale is connected by the flying buttresses to the former Archbishop's palace (1460).

Set behind a tropical garden across from the church, the **Palazzo dei Normanni** contains the **Cappella Palatina** (1132-40, currently under partial restoration). Built by Roger II, it too exhibits a fantastic fusion of styles—a carved wooden stalactite ceiling, a cycle of golden Byzantine mosaics rivaled only by those of Ravenna and stanbul, and marble walls with geometric designs. In the apse, an enormous Christ looms above a 19th-century mosaic of the Virgin. Before leaving, visit the **Sala di Ruggero** (King Roger's Hall, one floor above the Palatina), a room adorned with mosaics in flora and fauna motifs. Because the *palazzo* is now the seat of the Sicilian Parliament, you must wait at the desk for an escort. (Palace open Mon. and Fri.-Sat. 9am-noon unless Parliament is in session. Chapel open Mon.-Fri. 9am-noon and 3-5pm, Sat.-Sun. 9-10am and noon-1pm. Chapel closed Sunday and holiday afternoons.)

Walk back to corso Vittorio Emanuele to see the **Porta Nuova,** a huge gate topped by a pyramidal roof. The gate was erected to commemorate Charles V's triumphal entrance in 1535, but modified in 1668 with the rugged figures which now embellish the entrance arch.

Perhaps the most romantic spot in Palermo is the garden and cloister of the **Church of San Giovanni degli Eremiti** (St. John of the Hermits), via dei Benedettini, 3, a hike from via Maqueda. Built in 1132 by fanciful Arab architects, it is topped by winsome pink domes. Beside the church a tropical garden shades 13th-century cloisters. (Open Mon., Thurs., and Sat. 9am-2pm; Tues., Wed., and Fri. 9am-1pm and 3-5pm; Sun. 9am-1pm. From April to September 30, closes at 6pm.) To get there take bus #9 or 34.

From the Church of San Francesco to the Villa Giulia

The churches and palaces east of via Roma toward the old port (La Cala) lie in a maze of tiny, serpentine streets. The 13th-century **Church of San Francesco d'Assisi,** via Paternostro, off corso Vittorio Emanuele about five blocks from via Roma and to the right as you head toward the harbor, features an intricate rose window and a zigzag design on the outside common to many other churches in the area. The church's restored Gothic interior was augmented by side chapels in the 14th and 15th centuries and adorned with Renaissance and Baroque accessories. (Open daily 7-11am and 4-6pm.)

The **Oratory of San Lorenzo,** just a few doors down via Imarolatella (to the left as you face the church of San Francesco), was decorated by the master of stucco, Giacomo Serpotta (1656-1732). This monochrome stucco has a hard finish that seems to be carved stone when looked at from afar. Caravaggio's last known work, *The Nativity* (1609), was stolen from the altar in 1969—hence the seven locks on the oratory door. The inlaid mother-of-pearl benches are too impressive to sit on. (Open erratically; the oratory is curated by an elderly neighbor in her spare time. There is no entrance fee, but a small *offerta* is expected.)

The **Giardino Garibaldi,** a park several blocks further toward the sea on corso Vittorio Emanuele, is replete with royal palms, fig trees, and giant banyans. Intriguing but dilapidated buildings surround the square; check out the **Museo delle Marionette** in the Palazzo Fatta, which exhibits marionettes exemplifying Sicily's proud tradition of puppetry. (Open Mon.-Sat. 9am-1pm and 4-7pm, ring the bell to enter. Puppet shows on request.) From the nearby **Church of Santa Maria della Catena** you can see the small inlet of **La Cala,** once the harbor and now a fishing port. Corso Vittorio Emanuele ends at the war-scarred remains of the **Porta Felice** (begun in 1582). Once a fashionable seaside drive, the **Foro Italico** is now a tacky boardwalk strip. The part-Gothic, part-Renaissance **Palazzo Abatellis** (1495) houses one of Sicily's superb regional galleries. Upstairs, an entire room is devoted to painter Antonello da Messina (1430-1479), Sicily's number-one son. Works by Leandro Bassano (1557-1622), Vincenzo da Pavia, and Leonard Macaluss round out the Sicilian gang. Take bus #3, 5, 8, 23, or 24. (Open Mon., Wed., and Sat. 9am-1:30pm, Tues., Thurs., and Fri. 9am-1:30pm and 3-7:30pm, Sun. and holidays 9am-12:30pm. Admission L2000.)

To the east, down Foro Umberto I along the harbor, **Villa Giulia** has a weary garden, which harbors a little something for everyone: band shells, playgrounds, menageries, sculpture and floral gardens, cenotaphs, and a small amusement park.

From the Church of San Matteo to the Museo Archeologico

Most of Palermo's other noteworthy sights lie along **via Roma** west of corso Vittorio Emanuele as you amble away from the station. The Baroque **Church of San Matteo** (on corso Vittorio Emanuele) conceals an ornate marble interior and four statues by Serpotta in the pilasters of the dome. (Open daily 8am-noon and 4-7pm.) On via Roma to the right just a block from its intersection with corso Vittorio Emanuele, again as you move away from the station, is the 12th-century **Church of Sant'Antonio,** revamped in the 14th and 19th centuries. You can still see the original structure in the square frame and the columns of the chancel. (Open Mon.-Sat. 7:30am-noon and 6:30-8:15pm, Sun. 7:30am-1pm. Closed for restoration in 1992.) Just past the intersection, on via Vucciría off corso Vittorio Emanuele, is Palermo's main food **market.** Dozens of varieties of fish, seafood, fruits and vegetables, including six-foot eggplants, tantalize the palate and the eye.

The **Church of San Domenico** fronts the *piazza* of the same name on via Roma, to the right with the station behind you. Rebuilt in 1640, the church is Sicily's Pantheon, containing tombs and cenotaphs of distinguished citizens. The **Oratorio del Rosario,** behind San Domenico on via dei Bambinai (ring at #16), houses a famous altarpiece by Van Dyck, *Madonna of the Rosary with St. Dominique and the Patroness of Palermo* (1628). (Both open 7:30am-noon.)

Via Meli extends from piazza San Domenico and leads, appropriately enough, to piazza Meli. By bearing left on via dei Bambinai, through piazza Valverde, and onto via Squarcialupo, you'll find the **Church of Santa Cita** on your left. The exterior was damaged during the war, but a rose window remains, showering the interior with baroque color and texture. The marble arches on the east wall of the choir and the sarcophagus in the second chapel on the left remain from the original Renaissance structure. The **Oratorio di Santa Cita,** behind the church (ring at via Valverde, 3), is decorated with Serpotta's *Virtues,* reliefs of New Testament scenes, and, on the short wall near the entrance, a depiction of the Battle of Lepanto, where Cervantes lost a hand. (Both open 9am-noon and 4-6pm.)

The **Museo Archeologico Regionale** is found at p. Olivella, 4 (tel. 58 78 25) and is accessible by hanging a left on via Bara two blocks before via Roma hits via Cavour as you head away from the station. This museum occupies a 17th-century convent and displays a relatively unremarkable collection in two beautiful courtyards. Unfortunately, it is undergoing renovation, and its priceless collection of metopes from Selinunte are all packed away. The renovations on the first floor are mostly completed, but the second floor will be closed for some time yet. See the building for its *cortile.* In the bronze collection is the *Ram of Syracuse* (Greek, 3rd century BC), renowned for its realism. (Open Mon., Wed.-Thurs., and Sat. 9am-2pm., Tues. and Fri. 9am-1:30pm and 3-6pm, Sun. and holidays 9am-1pm. Admission L2000.)

Other Sights

Across via Maqueda from the Archeological Museum, the **Teatro Mássimo,** constructed between 1875 and 1897 in a robust neoclassical style, is the largest indoor stage in Europe after the Paris Opera House. The Mássimo unfortunately has been undergoing reconstruction since 1985; the projected completion date is in 2010 (or maybe 3010, given the pace of progress in Sicily). The exiled opera and symphony perform in the **Politeama Garibaldi** (farther up via Maqueda, which becomes via Ruggero Settima), a huge circular theater built in 1874. The entrance is a triumphal arch crowned by a bronze chariot and four horses. The theater also houses the **Galleria d'Arte Moderna.** (Theater performances Jan. to late May and mid-July to Aug. Admission from L15,000. Gallery open Tues. and Fri.-Sun. 9am-1pm and 4-8pm, Wed.-Thurs. 9am-1pm. Admission L2000.)

The **Convento dei Cappuccini** welcomes amateur pathologists into its catacombs; 8000 bodies, some mummified and intact, inhabit lengthy subterranean corridors. (Open daily 9am-noon and 3-5pm; tours offered by friars intermittently. Admission free, but *offerta* expected.) Take bus #27 from p. Castelnuovo or bus #5 from Stazione Centrale.

Monte Pellegrino, an isolated mass of limestone rising from the sea, is Palermo's principal natural landmark, separating the city from the beach at Mondello. Near its summit, the **Santuario di Santa Rosalia** marks the site where Rosalia, a young Norman princess, sought ascetic seclusion. Her bones were discovered in 1624 and brought to Palermo, where they vanquished a raging plague. The present sanctuary is built over the cave where she performed her ablutions; its trickling waters are said to have thaumaturgic powers. The summit of Monte Pellegrino (a half-hour climb from the sanctuary) offers a gorgeous view of Palermo, Conca d'Oro, and on a clear day, the Lípari Islands and Mount Etna. Take bus #12 from p. XIII Víttime to the sanctuary.

Entertainment and Seasonal Events

Palermo shuts down entirely at night. After about 9 or 10pm, there is virtually nothing to do—which is just as well, since walking any later is not a particularly wise idea. Summer nights belong to the *lido* of **Mondello,** on the cape beyond Monte Pellegrino. To join the crowds of young Palermitans in their *passeggiata,* take bus #14, 15, or 77 from p. Sturzo behind the Teatro Politeama and get off at the last stop (L600). In summer, express bus #6 ("Beallo") also runs to Mondello, beginning at the train station and stopping along via della Libertà. Here people mill about sampling seafood from the waterfront stalls (a complete dinner can come to a mere L5000), sipping coffee, and exchanging glances. The bar and disco at **Villa Boscogrande,** the gorgeous *palazzo* where director Lucino Visconti filmed *The Leopard,* attract a posh crowd. Take bus #28 from via della Libertà.

The major summer event in Palermo takes place at the **Teatro del Parco di Villa Castelnuovo.** From the first week of July through the first of August, an international festival of ballet, jazz, and classical music jams in this open-air seaside theater. For tickets and information, contact the **Politeama Garibaldi,** p. Ruggero Séttimo (tel. 58 43 34; open Tues.-Sat. 10am-1pm and 4-7pm), across from the tourist office. The **Festa di Santa Rosalia,** held July 10-15, gives the city an excuse to shed its usual sobriety and go on a binge of music and merriment.

Palermo resorts to two other beaches aside from the Lido at Mondello. **Sferracavallo** is a roomier but rockier beach (take bus #28 from via della Libertà), while **Addaura** entertains the young Palermitan jet-set crowd in summer (bus #3 from the train station or via della Libertà).

For more in-depth information on cultural events and nightlife, pick up a copy of *Un Mese a Palermo,* a monthly brochure in Italian, available at any APT office.

Ardent mafia buffs may want to see the **Carcere Giustiziario,** an imposing structure looming where via Francesco Crispi becomes via Monte Pellegrino. The prison, reputedly Italy's most secure, houses *Cosa Nostra* kingpins and terrorists.

Near Palermo

About 30km east of Palermo at the base of Monte Calógero sits **Términi Imerese,** a rapidly developing resort first frequented by Greeks and Romans, who began taking advantage of the town's supposedly therapeutic springs in 600 BC. Home to an impressive Baroque *duomo,* a wonderful view of the northern coast, and some decent accommodations, Términi makes a reasonable choice as a stopover on the way to Cefalù. All trains from Palermo (30min. away) stop at the base of the hill on which the city stands. As you exit the station onto via Aurora, orange AST buses head to the top of the town (L600); hopping off at via Garibaldi will land you just a block away from piazza Duomo, with its 16th century statues. Inside the **Duomo** check out Marabitti's *Madonna del Ponte* and a crucifix painted by Ruzzolene in the late 1400s. Near p. Duomo you'll find the **Museo Civico** (thoughtfully located on via Museo Civico) which contains some archeological goods from the ruins of ancient Greek Himera and a few simple paintings. Since the museum (tel. 812 82 79) is only open from 9am-2pm and 4-8pm, hang out with the young people in the afternoon shade just in front of the *duomo;* a small *caffè* serves *gelato,* pastries, and drinks at halfway decent prices.

To stave off an ornery appetite, visit **Magras Supermarket** at piazza Francesco Crispi, 14, off via Aurora two blocks to the left as you exit the station en route to the *duomo.* For convenient accomodations you might try **Le Gabbiano (Dipendenza)** at via Libertà, 221 (tel. 811 32 62). It's over 1000m to the left as you exit the station, but brings you all the comforts of home without overdoing it. (Singles L28,000, doubles L36,000; prices do not include bath or breakfast. Reservations recommended.)

Between six and 12 buses leave from Términi Imerese's train station to **Cáccamo,** home to 8600 vivacious Sicilians and a gargantuan 12th-century **castle.** A Duke of Cáccamo lived here until the early 1900s, at which time it was handed over for public use. If the front door is closed, turn around and head toward the war memorial; buzz Signor La Rosa at corso Umberto, 6. He'll take you to all the spots worth seeing— down deserted alleys and secret passageways (generous tip expected). After seeing the castle, float around the town and check out the **duomo** dedicated to St. George; note the fiery reliefs about the door by Gaspare Guercio. Unfortunately, Cáccamo doesn't offer travelers any places to stay; head down the hill to Términi Imerese instead.

About 10km southwest of Palermo lies the golden city of **Monreale** and its magnificent Norman-Saracen **duomo** (circa 1174). The church's incredible medieval mosaics supposedly inspired Jacques Cartier to name his Canadian city Montreal. Against a brilliant gold background, the Old and New Testaments are depicted in 130 panels, over which a massive Christ Pantocrator (Ruler of All) presides. To read this brilliant Bible, start at the upper right-hand corner of the inner nave with the creation and work your way back to the present under Christ Pantocrator where Virgin and Child sit with attendant angels, among whom you can find Thomas à Becket, cannonized just as work on the mosaics began (L500 to light up mosaics). The net overhead testifies to Monreale's nemesis—termites have been making a meal of the carved and gilded timber ceiling since the early 19th century. The *tesoro,* off the transept, is housed in one of the most raucously rococo chapels in Italy. Outside, circle around to see the Arab-style inlay behind the apse, and a spectacular view of the *conca d'Oro* below. Then step in to see the intricate arches and multicolored inlays of the cloister (partially under restoration in 1992), renowned for the capitals of its colonnade, each one unique. Considered to be the richest collection of Sicilian sculpture anywhere, the capitals run the gamut of styles: Greco-Roman, Saracen, Norman, Romanesque, Gothic, and various combinations. In the corner by the lesser colonnade and its fountain, look for the capital depicting William II offering the Cathedral of Monreale to the Virgin. Be sure to climb up to the roof and look down on the central apse. (Cathedral open daily 8am-12:30pm and 3:30-6:30pm. Cloister open April-Sept. daily 9am-7pm; Oct.-March Mon.-Sat. 9am-1:30pm, Sun. 9am-12:30pm. Admission to cloister L2000; to roof L2000.) From Palermo take bus #9 from the far side of via Lincoln and to the left as you leave the train station (L1000). The *duomo* is up via Roma to the right when you hop off the bus in Monreale. (As you turn the corner, on the right you can see the marble sign commemorating the local captain of Carabinieri who was killed there by the Mafia in 1983.) **Tourist information** (tel. 65 64 270) resides in the building to the left of the church.

Sate your hunger at **Trattoria-Pizzeria da Peppino,** via B. Civiletti, 12 (tel. 640 77 70), off via Roma to the right as you're headed toward the *duomo*. *Primi* start at L3000, *secondi* at L5500. The *pizza bastardo* sports the local cheese *caciocavallo* (L4500). (Open Sat.-Thurs. 12:30-2:30pm and 6pm-1am.) For picnics, plunder the produce stores that line via Roma. The **Salumeria Fratelli Madonia,** via Roma, 22 (tel. 640 44 97), will provide not only a quick nutrition fix, but a lesson in pasta nomenclature. (Open Mon.-Sat. 7am-1:30pm and 4-8pm.) For cookies, cakes, pizza, and other delights, the bloodhound consumer heads for **Panifico Conca D'Oro,** via P. Novelli, 25 (tel. 640 45 13, open until 8pm), whose enticing aromas you can smell over a block away.

If windswept ruins make you swoon, you might consider paying a visit to the Phoenician and Roman site at **Soluntum** (Solunto), perched on a precipitous promontory about 15km east of Palermo on Cape Zafferano. Come to poke around the remains of dwellings, sewers, cisterns, a forum, and a theater, or just to take in the panorama of Palermo and environs. Take strada statale 113 to Porticello, then turn left and continue past Aspra to the site.

The volcanic island of **Ústica** also lies within reach of Palermo, 36 miles off the coast. Settled first by our phriends the Phoenicians, then by pirates and exiled convicts, this marine reserve features prime snorkeling and waterborne grotto-hopping opportunities. Inquire at the Palermo tourist office for further details. **Siremar** runs ferries and hydrofoils out to the island (see Orientation and Practical Information: Ferries).

Trápani

Unlike much of urban Sicily, Trápani is a remarkably livable and energetic city. You'll find the center surprisingly clean and traffic-free; the major arteries are closed to automobiles for much of the day. Its residents display a combination of Sicilian candor and North African effusiveness that has earned Trápani its designation as "Sicily's friendliest city." While its sights are not at the top of most tourists' itineraries, it makes a perfect base for expeditions to the beaches of the western coast, the luckless ruins of Greek temples, and the breathtaking mountain-town of Érice. If you're in Trápani for more than a few hours, the Baroque churches peppered throughout the town, fashioned at the crossroads of European and African influences, merit more than just the harried glance of a traveler in transit.

Ferries

Ferries and hydrofoils leave Trápani for the Égadi Islands (Lévanzo, Favignana, and Maréttimo). Tickets for both are available from **Siremar,** via Ammiraglio Staiti, 61 (tel. 54 05 15), right on the port just a few blocks south of corso Italia (open Mon.-Fri. 6:30am-1:30pm and 3:30-6:30pm, Sat. 6:30am-1:30pm and 3:30-4:30pm, Sun. 6:30am-3pm). You can also get ferry tickets from **Traghetti delle Isole,** via Ammiraglio Staiti, 13 (tel. 217 54; open Mon.-Fri. 9am-1pm and 4-7pm, Sat. 9am-noon); and hydrofoil tickets from **Alivit** (tel. 240 73) or **Aliscafi SNAV** (tel. 271 01), both with clearly marked ticket booths on via A. Staiti off p. Garibaldi. The following departure times are for mid-June through mid-September only. The prices are the same on all lines.

Trápani-Favignana: 6 per day (7am-2pm, 1hr.-1hr. 30min., L4100). 11 hydrofoils per day (7am-7:15pm, 20min., L7600).

Trápani-Lévanzo: 6 per day (7am-2pm, 1hr.-1hr. 30min., L4100). 11 hydrofoils per day (7am-7:15pm, 20min., L7600).

Trápani-Maréttimo: 1 per day at 9am (2hr. 30min., L9300). 5 hydrofoils per day (8:15am-6:15pm, 1hr., L17,400).

Trápani-Pantelleria: Ferries depart daily at 9am (4hr. 30min., L29,800). SNAV hydrofoils depart Mon., Thurs, and Sun. at 8:45am (2hr. 15min., L39,000).

Trápani-Kelibia (Tunisia): SNAV hydrofoils depart Mon., Thurs., and Sun. at 8:45am via Pantelleria (3hr. 45min., L85,000). **Tirrenia** runs to Tunis every Monday at 9am (9hr., L84,700).

Orientation and Practical Information

Trápani sits on a peninsula, three hours west of Palermo by train (L13,800). An express bus makes the trip in two hours, rolling from via Paolo Balsamo, 26, near the train station in Palermo, to p. Garibaldi in Trápani (L10,500). Trains run from Marsala (13 per day, 45min., L3700). From Agrigento, take a bus from p. Garibaldi (behind the movie theatre, near the post office) at 6:20am, or 1:10pm (**S. Lumia,** tel. (0922) 204 14, L14,500 one way, L23,200 round-trip.) **Corso Vittorio Emanuele II** runs through the old town, intersecting **via Roma,** which spans the peninsula. The old town lies directly in front of the train station; the new town is behind it. The **bus depot** is just around the corner to the left as you exit the station.

Tourist Office: p. Saturno (tel. 290 00). Take via Osorio from the Mobil sign, turn left at the end, and then go right onto corso Italia all the way to the *piazzetta.* Armfuls of handouts. English spoken. Open Mon.-Sat. 8am-8pm, Sun. 9am-1pm. **Information booth** at airport. Open for incoming flights. **APT main office,** via Vito Sorba, 15 (tel. 270 77),4 blocks behind the station to the right. Open Mon.-Sat. 8am-2pm, Tues. and Thurs. 4-7pm.

Post Office: p. Veneto (tel. 291 28), up via Osorio and then right on via XXX Gennaio. Open Mon.-Sat. 8am-2pm. **Postal Code:** 91100.

Telephones: SIP, via Scontrino, near the station. Open daily 8am-9pm. **Telephone Code:** 0923.

Flights: V. Florio Airport (tel. 84 11 30), 16km outside the city in Birgi en route to Marsala. Buses leave 1hr. before flight time from outside **Salvo Viaggi,** corso Italia, 52/56 (tel. 274 80, fax. 284 36). To Rome (L174,000), Pantelleria (L37,000), and special chartered flights on Saturday from Milan (price varies). **Trains:** at piazza Stazione (tel. 280 71 or 280 81). **Buses: AST** (tel. 216 41) buses to Érice leave from p. Malta, around to the left of the train station (Mon.-Sat. 11 per day 6:30am-7pm, Sun. 5 per day 9am-6:15pm; L2000, round-trip L3400). Catch the return bus in Érice on via Pepoli (7:30am-7:55pm). For information, call 200 66. To Segesta: **Tarantola,** tel. 310 20 or 325 98. To Palermo: **Segesta** leaves from p. Malta.

Luggage Storage: at the train station, L1500 per piece. Open 24 hrs.

Emergencies: tel. 113. **Police:** via Orlandini, 19 (tel. 271 22). **Hospital: Ospedale Sant'Antonio Abate,** via Cosenza very far from town (tel. 80 91 11).

Accommodations and Camping

Hotels are much better and only slightly more expensive in the beach resort **Capo San Vito;** take a bus from p. Malta (9 per day, 1hr., round-trip L7300).

Pensione Messina, corso Vittorio Emanuele, 71 (tel. 211 98), on a Renaissance courtyard just a few blocks from piazza S. Agostino. Spacious rooms, firm beds, and a rather loud pink bathroom. Run by a slightly rambunctious family. Singles L15,000. Doubles L30,000.

Albergo Moderno, via Genovese, 20 (tel. 212 47). Turn right off corso Vittorio Emanuele (heading away from piazza S. Agostino) onto via Roma, then take a left on via Genovese. Trápani's oldest hotel, this once-proud *palazzo* hosted the Princess of Spain. Quiet, clean rooms. Singles L25,000, with bath L35,000. Doubles L40,000, with bath L48,000.

Sabbia d'Oro, via Santuario, 49 (tel. 97 25 08), on the beachfront in San Vito Lo Capo. Impeccable, great location, and a bargain for the area. Singles L27,000. Doubles L39,600. Sept.-June singles with breakfast L26,000. The same management runs **Pensione Ocean View** (tel. 97 26 13) in the same building. Less opulent rooms. L17,500 per person, L20,000 with bath.

Albergo Maccotta, via degli Argentieri, 4 (tel. 284 18), behind the tourist office on p. Saturno. Quiet location, airy rooms. Singles L30,000-40,000. Doubles L70,000.

Camping: Capo San Vito and Castellamare del Golfo, on the opposite side of the cape, harbor most of the nearby campgrounds (buses daily to Castellamare at 12:30pm and 2:30pm, 1hr. 30min., round-trip L6400). **Near Capo San Vito: Camping La Fata,** via Mattarella (tel. 97 21 33), and **Camping Soleado,** via della Secca (tel. 97 21 66). Both charge L7000 per person, L6500 per small tent, L9000 per large tent. **Camping El Bahira** (tel. 97 25 77), 2km before Capo S. Vito in Salinella, on the water. Better location and facilities. L9000 per person, L12,500 per small tent, L17,000 per large tent. All open June-Sept. **Near Castellamare del Golfo: Baia di Guidaloca** (tel. 59 60 22); **Lu Baruni** (tel. 391 33); **Nausicaa** (tel. 315 18), and the cheapest, **Ciauli** (tel. 318 33), which charges L5500 per person, L5500 per small tent, L7500 per large tent. The other places charge about L1000 more. All open June-Sept., except Lu Baruni, which is open year-round.

Food

Take your money to the **open-air market** in p. Mercato di Pesce (at the end of via Torrearsa), and let it loose. (Open Mon.-Sat. 8am-2pm.) On the way from the train station to the port, pick up essentials at **Discount Alimentari,** via San Pietro, 30. (Open Mon.-Sat. 8:30am-1:30pm and 4:30-8pm.) Trápani is known for its sardines and its *couscous con pesce,* in which said sardines often lurk.

Mensa Ferrovieri, at the train station. This employees' cafeteria is also open to tourists. All dishes made to order. Full meals (bread, pasta, meat, salad and beer or wine) L8000. Open daily 11am-3:30pm and 6-10:30pm.

Pizzeria Calvino, via Nasi, 77 (tel. 214 64), 1 block off corso Vittorio Emanuele as you're headed toward the port. All of Trápani comes here for take-out pizza (small L4500) before soccer games. Sit-down or take-out. Savor *lasagne al forno* (L4500). Open daily noon-2pm and 7pm-1am.

Pizzeria Mediterranea, corso Vittorio Emanuele, 195 (tel. 54 71 76). Only 2 choices: *pizza origanata,* with whole tomatoes, garlic, oregano, anchovies, and *pecorino* cheese; or *pizza quattro gusti* with ham, basil, anchovies, and mozzarella. Small L5000, large L15,000. Both pies are drool-worthy. Beer L4000 per mug. Open Fri.-Wed. 9am-1pm and 4pm-midnight.

Trattoria la Botte, corso Vittorio Emanuele, 191 (tel. 8711 50). Full of merry locals. The hearty food is good but the atmosphere is the prime (and primal) draw. *Primi* L6000, *secondi* L6000-8000. Try the local wine from one of the wooden casks above the bar (L3000 per). Cover L1500. Open Sat.-Thurs. 8:30am-2pm and 4:30-9pm.

Casablanca, via San Francesco d'Assisi, 69 (tel. 200 50), near the port at via Serisso. More soothing than Bogart's voice. Bubbling fountain, a large ceiling fan, and soft classical music. Pricey, but worth it. Try the great *crêpe caprese* (stuffed with tomatoes, basil, and mozzarella, L4000). Wine L4000 per . Cover L1000. Service 10%. Open Tues.-Sun. noon-3pm and 7:30pm-midnight.

Sights and Entertainment

You can knock off Trápani's major sights in a pleasant afternoon. Begin one block off corso Italia on via Selisabetta, where the Gothic-Renaissance **Church of Santa Maria** displays a beautiful marble baldachin (1521) sheltering a Della Robbia terracotta. Farther up corso Italia you'll hit piazza S. Agostino which runs right into piazzetta Saturno by way of via S. Agostino; this area is one of the city's most charming. Here you'll find the facade of the former **Church of Sant'Agostino** (14th century), which preserves a Gothic portal and rose window. The **Fountain of Saturn,** a triple-tiered basin supported by sirens, dates from the late 16th century.

The main street of the old city, **corso Vittorio Emanuele II,** around the corner, is lined with elaborate façades. At one end, the 17th-century **Palazzo Seratorio** houses temporary art exhibits on its main floor; the **Collegio dei Gesuiti** (1636) contains an 18th-century carved walnut cupboard; and the **cattedrale** displays a striking green-tiled dome and pink stucco walls. Down a small street to the left on via Giglio, the tiny Baroque **Chiesa del Purgatorio** sports a free-standing sculpture and a small emerald dome outside, and a group of 20 incomprehensible wooden statues inside. This collection, called *I Misteri* (The Mysteries), is carried in a procession around the town on Good Friday. The bearers call out, asking if anyone knows whose they are or what they're for. No one ever does, so they are returned to the church for another year. Their identification has been a mystery for over 600 years.

Viale Regina Elena runs along the port to **viale Duca l'Acosta,** where fishermen dry and mend their nets. For a treat, get up at the crack of dawn, head down to see the fishermen do their stuff, and continue up to the tip of the city to see the sunrise at the **Torre di Ligny.** From the Torre you can take via Libertà past the fish market at piazza Mercato de Pesce to **via Garibaldi,** the handsomest street in the city. A broad flight of steps to the right brings you to the **Church of San Domenico.** Via Garibaldi continues past the pink, twisted columns of the **Chiesa di Carminello.**

Farther out in the new section of town visit the **Museo Nazionale Pepoli.** (It's a grueling walk; take bus #1, 10, or 11, L700.) The museum's magnificent Baroque interior staircase leads to a collection of local sculpture, painting, coral carvings, and folk-art figurines. (Open Fri.-Tues. 9am-1:30pm, Wed.-Thurs. 9am-1:30pm and 4-6:30pm. Admission L2000, Sun. free.)

Trápani sponsors a festival of opera, ballet, and drama, **Luglio Musicale Trapanese** (tel. (0923) 229 34), which attracts troupes from abroad. It takes place in an open-air theater in the city park, the Villa Margherita, during the last three weeks of July. (Shows begin at 9pm. Admission from L12,000.) **Settimana dell'Egadi,** in late May, greets the new crop of tourists with music, food, and archeological tours, and of course there's the **Processione dei Misteri,** where you can moan and groan to the beat of the bemasked and becolored townsfolk as they march through the city on Good Friday, quizzing their clueless comrades about the statues they carry.

At night the young and the restless populate the beer gardens in p. XVIII Novembre or the *gelaterie* along via Turetta, but only until 8:30pm, when the entire town passes out.

Around Trápani

San Vito Lo Capo

The gentle shores of San Vito Lo Capo present an immense, sandy beach and a vast selection of *gelaterie.* Although it's a major resort for northerners, the town remains inexpensive, genuine, clean, and an ideal place to relax for a day. For more seclusion, drive 12km, or make the bus connection through Castellamare to Guida Loca, to the **Riserva dello Zingaro,** a nature preserve whose pastoral, cow-studded trails lead to crystalline coves and a grotto that could serve as the entrance to Dante's *Inferno.* Buses to San Vito leave from the Trápani *autostazione* at p. Malta (Mon.-Sat. 9 per day 7am-8pm; Sun. 8:30am-7pm, 1hr. 15min., L4400 one way, L7300 round-trip). The last bus back to Trápani on weekdays leaves at 8:15pm (Sun. return trips from 10am-8:15pm). For more on the Zingaro nature reserve, ask for information (in English) at the Trápani tourist office.

In recent years more and more visitors have been flocking to the cement-city **Gibellina Nuova** whose ruins were paved with a labyrinth of concretepassageways. (From Trápani 6 buses per day 6:50am-2:30pm, returning 6:25am-2:45pm, 1hr., L2500.)

Érice

Only a short distance from the coast, Érice soars 750m above sea level. In ancient times, Érice was one of Sicily's most revered sites. As such, the city has been the mythical home to successive goddesses of fertility: first the Elymnian Astarte, then the Greek Aphrodite and the Roman Venus. Both the city itself and the vistas it affords are a visual delicacy. The outer walls date back to the 16th century BC, and the town is virtually unchanged from medieval times. The city has a number of worthwhile sights to visit, particularly the **Norman castle,** with its medieval towers (in typical Sicilian fashion, adorned with TV broadcast aerials), and the lush adjoining gardens. There is also a 14th-century **duomo** with a 13th-century bell tower. But the greatest pleasure is in strolling Érice's cobblestone streets, savoring the well-preserved buildings and the overwhelming views. The panoramas out over Trápani (occasionally reaching all the way to Tunisia) are tremendous.

The **Tourist Office (AAST)** is at via C.A. Pepoli, 56, on the hill near the bus stop (tel. 869 388 or 869 173). The **bus** from Trápani leaves from p. Malta (Mon.-Sat. 12 per day, 6:30am-9pm., Sun. 5 per day 9am-6:15pm. Last bus back weekdays at 10:15pm, Sun. at 7:15pm, 45min., L4300 round-trip). As hotel prices tend to be as lofty as the altitude, Érice is best as a daytrip from Trápani. If you're stuck, the cheapest place is the **Edelweiss,** cortile p. Vincenzo (tel. 86 91 58); singles with bath L60,000, doubles L95,000. Good cheap food is also hard to come by, and **La Pentolaccia,** via Guarnotti, 17, is as close as you'll come (tel. 86 90 99). *Primi* run L7000 and *secondi*

L8000; try the *Scaloppine alla marsala* for a real treat. (Cover L2500. Open Sun.-Fri. noon-3pm, 7:30-10:30pm. Closed Dec.-Feb.) Just down the block, the **Antica Pasticceria del Convento,** via Guarnotti, 1, makes sinfully good sweets for the nuns and the public alike. L16,000 buys a kilo, enough to earn four people an afternoon in purgatory. (Open daily 8:30am-1pm and 3pm-midnight; tel. 869 005.)

Égadi Islands (Isole Égadi)

The mid-afternoon summer sun is far kinder to the Égadi Islands than to their scorched neighbor, Sicily. Cats and local elders lounge on the terraces of the white-washed tufa houses nestled above the harbors, soothed by the warm massage of the sirocco. Pass by Favignana, tourist trap and home to the remnants of the archipelago's tuna trade, and head straight for the outlying islands of Maréttimo and Lévanzo. Connected by frequent ferry and hydrofoil service (both between islands and between the islands and Trápani; see Trápani, Ferries), these rough and barren islands—strewn with bushes, wildflowers, and lost sheep—offer archeological wonders, cool sea grottos, and hiking trails with incredible views.

Favignana

Site of a large military camp, industrial, gritty Favignana sports a traditional beach, the Lido Burrone, 3km across the island from the main harbor. Rent a bike and pedal to one of Italy's hidden treasures, an old quarry by the sea called the **Bue Marino** (Elephant Seal). A small number of overpriced *pensione* and vaguely satisfying campgrounds await on Favignana; hop the hydrofoil to Maréttimo or Lévanzo. For food, raid the *alimentari* on via Mazzini.

Lévanzo

The prehistoric cave art in the **Cava del Genovese,** about an hour on foot from the port, is only viewable on a guided tour (in decipherable Italian only). Signor Castigliano, who will lead you to the caves on his burro, generally meets all hydrofoil arrivals and can be found at the Siremar office above the dock. The Paleolithic incisions are the most fascinating for their veracity and curvilinear form; one shows a horse with its head turned in a style of representational depth that predates the Renaissance by centuries. The Neolithic paintings of animals (such as pigs and cows) no longer inhabiting the islands illuminate the geological history of the archipelago. The island also offers a number of secluded beaches and grottos for swimming.

Lévanzo offers budget accommodations and some barely affordable food, making it the best base for a visit to the Égadi Islands. **Pensione Paradiso,** on the main road overlooking the port, is the only budget option. Ask for the newly renovated rooms overlooking the sea. No breakfast is available, and the dinner of spaghetti or fish is eminently skippable. Prices vary by room but run L34,000 to L48,000 (price for off-season and longer stays is bargainable). Pick up groceries or bring food, or for a splurge, try the fresh fish at the restaurant up the hill.

Sundown draws locals, travelers, and resident expats to the seaside café, where an evening of cards and a warm North African sirocco can easily stretch one cappuccino (L1500) into four. (Open until 11pm.)

Maréttimo

Maréttimo, the farthest and most remote of the Égadi Islands, offers the most remote atmosphere as well. Newly established hiking trails take you up and down the rocky cliffs of the island, and on clear days, the view stretches as far as Tunisia. There are no official accommodations on the island; people ask around when they arrive for someone to put them up for about L20,000 per night. A handful of cafés, *gelaterie,* and the **Torrente Trattoria,** on piazza Umberto across from the Siremar office, vend sandwiches and *gelato.*

Western Coast

Pantelleria

The appeal of this sun-baked volcanic island is rooted in its North African feel, tranquil, eminently strollable countryside, and characteristic dome-roofed *dammuso* dwellings. Try climbing the extinct volcano or meandering through the terraced vineyards which yield raisins and Tanit, a famous raisin wine. The *sesi,* resembling the *nuraghi* of Sardinia and the *trulli* of Apulia, are the neolithic remnants of the island's earliest inhabitants. Ferries and hydrofoils connect the island daily with Trápani, but cheaper **Alitalia** flights leave from Trápani daily (call for current flight information) and from Pantelleria for the return trip (30min., L75,000). The cheapest place to stay is at the **Miryam,** corso Umberto #1 (tel. 0923 91 13 74). Singles with bath L45,000, doubles with bath L70,000. The **Agadir,** via Catania #1 (tel. 91 11 00), offers half-pension for L60,000. In low season, singles with bath run L29,000 and doubles L48,000. People investigate lodging in private homes, which can save a lotta lire.

The **Pro Loco,** via San Nicola (tel. 94 18 38), can help you find a place if you're desperate. (Open Mon.-Sat. 9am-12:30pm and 5-8pm.) A **post office** and **bank** sit in the center of piazza Cavour. Somewhere nearby is the home of Gianni Gabriele, who rents mopeds for only L15,000 a day (tel. 91 17 41); call to find out if anybody's home and to get directions to his unmarked house.

Segesta

One of the best-kept secrets of the archeological world is the unfinished 5th-century Greek temple at Segesta. As you approach from the train station, you'll catch glimpses of the temple ahead; note the ancient theater crowning the hill on the left. The ruins constitute the sole remains of the once-flourishing city of the native Sicilian people (Sikels). From mid-July until the first week of August during odd-numbered years, classical plays are performed in the ancient theater. Special buses leave p. Politeama in Palermo (1hr. 45min. before showtime) and p. Marina in Trápani (1hr. before showtime). Buy the L12,000 tickets from a travel agent in Palermo or Trápani. To reach the theater, walk up the road from the *bar* (20min.). Only two trains from Palermo and three from Trápani make daily stops at Segesta's station (Palermo-Segesta L10,200; Trápani-Segesta L3200). **Buses** to Segesta are run by Autoservizi Tarantola (tel. 310 20), leaving Trápani at 8am, 10am, and 2pm Mon.-Sat., returning at 11am, 1pm, and 6pm. (L4000 one-way, L6700 round-trip.)

Marsala and Mozia

The city of **Mozia** began as an outpost of nearby Carthage, and passed an uneventful four centuries producing textiles until its destruction at the hands of the Syracusans in 397 BC. The survivors hightailed it to Cape Lilybeo and founded what is now Marsala. The Arabs renamed it "Mars-Alí," port of Alí. In 1575, Emperor Charles V successfully averted pirate attacks by hastily blocking off the port itself, but the unfortunate side effect of this action was a decline of the city which lasted several centuries. Garibaldi landed here in 1860 with his famed thousand, to begin his campaign of unification. In today's calmer times, the city is best known for its delectable wine. Although Marsala is best visited as a springboard to the unique and mysterious Mozia, the city's two museums are intriguing in their own right.

The 18th-century **Palazzo Comunale,** and the bland-at-best Baroque **duomo** stand in **piazza della Repubblica.** A variety of sculpture from the 16th-century school of Gagini decorates the church's vast interior. Behind the *duomo* at via Garraffa, 57, the **Museo degli Arazzi** contains Philip II's eight elaborate 16th-century tapestries illustrating Titus's war against the Jews. A polite request will get you a guided tour from the enthusiastic custodian. (Open Mon.-Sat. 9am-1pm and 4-6pm. Admission L4000.) The **Museo Lilybeo,** at the end of viale N. Sauro off p. della Vittoria, houses a 35m Carthaginian warship believed to have sunk during the Battle of the Égadi Islands, which ended the First Punic War in 241 BC. (Open 9am-1pm, Wed. and Sat.-Sun., also 3-6pm. Free.) The nearby **Insula Romana** (Roman Tenement), one of the few buildings excavated in the vast archeological zone, further documents Marsala's ancient past. (Open upon request at the Museo Lilybeo.) The small **Church of San Giovanni,** at the opposite end of the archeological zone of viale Sauro, covers Grotta della Sibilla, a cave where a mythical Sibyl proclaimed her oracles.

To witness the production of Marsala wine, embark on a free tour of the **Cantina Florio** facilities, located on lungomare Mediterraneo just past via S. Lipari. (Open to the public Mon.-Sat. 9am-noon and 3-6pm.) Marsala's **Pro Loco,** at via Garibaldi, 45 (tel. 95 80 97), off via XI Maggio, will direct you to other Marsala distillers and help find accommodations. (Open Mon.-Sat. 8am-8pm, Sunday 9am-noon and 3-6pm.) **Trattoria da Pino,** via San Lorenzo, 25, (tel. 71 56 52) offers a decent L18,000 *menù*. To get there from p. Repubblica, head away from the station on via XI Maggio and bear left on via Curatolo, which eventually becomes via Lorenzo. The cheapest hotel in town is the **Garden,** via Gambini, 36 (tel. 98 23 20), near the train station. (Singles L27,000, with bath L40,000. Doubles L50,000, with bath L65,000.)

San Pantaleo (ancient Mozia or Motya) was the scene of a monumental naval battle in which Dionysius of Syracuse annihilated the Carthaginian Himilco in 397 BC with the aid of that new super-weapon, the catapult. The near-deserted islet lies 8km north of Marsala, across a thin strait traversed hourly by a scrawny boat (Mon.-Sat. 9am-7pm, L3000). Remains of the original, child-sacrificing Phoenician inhabitants are plentiful, from the ritual altar to the dry dock on the other side of the tiny island. Many of the island's archeological finds are displayed in the tiny museum at the port.

To get to Marsala from Trápani, take a bus from via Malta (4 per day, departs 6:50am-2pm, returns 7:10am-2:15pm, L3600 each way). The bus company in Marsala (**Municipilizatta,** tel. 95 11 05) runs six buses a day to and from Mozia, leaving from p. del Popolo. (Bus #4, L800, Departs 6:45am-4:45pm, returns 7am-5pm.)

Selinunte

A magnificent jumble of ruins atop a plateau overlooking the Mediterranean, Selinunte (from the Greek *Selinus,* the wild celery that once grew in the valley) awes with its immensity and desolation. Composed primarily of a trio of temples to the east (the only one standing was reconstructed in 1958) and an acropolis across the valley to the west (restructured 1925-1927), these piles of rubble recall Selinunte's glory as an ally of Syracuse in the 6th century BC. The city fortunes took a decided downturn after 409 BC, when the place was sacked by Segesta and Carthage; it was finally destroyed by its own people in 241 BC in anticipation of a Roman attack. Selinunte remains shrouded by an air of mystical isolation that justifies the sobriquet given it by the Arabs: "the place of the idols." (Open 8am-sunset. Admission L1000.) About a kilometer inland, the enormous half-quarried drums for unbuilt columns lie abandoned in a stone outcropping. In the field below is the one that got away.

Getting to Selinunte is a hassle. From Palermo, Trápani, or Marsala, take the bus or train to Castelvetrano. Buses leave for Selinunte from Castelvetrano's train station (4 times per day, 30min., L1100). From Trápani allow three and a half hours travel time, from Palermo four and a half hours, from Marsala two hours. Selinunte is best seen on a daytrip from Castelvetrano, where you can stay at the **Hotel Ideal,** via Partanna, 26 (tel. 442 99), to the left as you exit the station. Singles L18,800, with bath L26,500. Doubles L26,500 with bath L39,000. If you're desperate, see if the staff at **Pro Loco** in piazza Garibaldi can help. (Open Mon.-Sat. 8am-8pm.) **Tourist Information,** v. Marco Polo, 98 (tel. 46 057) may also be able to help.

Agrigento

The Greek poet Pindar once lauded Agrigento as "Man's Finest City." Some may argue that the centuries since Pindar have introduced tough competition for the title, but that Agrigento nevertheless retains its title. It boasts, above all, some of the world's

best-preserved classical Greek architecture. The city is also known as the birthplace of
Luigi Pirandello, winner of the 1934 Nobel Prize in Literature. Visitors to modern
Agrigento will find an atmosphere of congeniality hovering above its web of winding
streets.

Orientation and Practical Information

Agrigento marks the midpoint of Sicily's southern coast. The transportation terminals, along with a park in piazza Moro, divide the medieval from modern cities. The
train station spits passengers out at **piazza Marconi,** whence viale della Vittoria cruises down the hill. **Via Atenea,** just north of the station toward the bus terminal, is the
main street, lined with shops and restaurants; it snakes through the old city from p.
Moro to piazza Pirandello. Trains run from the station to Palermo (11 per day, 2hr.
30min., L10,500), Catania (10 per day, 4hr., L13,800), and Enna (7 per day, 21/4hr.,
L8800). Buses gather at the station in p. Roselli, off via Cicerone up the hill from the
train station. From Marsala, take the train to Castelvetrano (15 per day, 1hr., L2900)
and then one of four daily buses to Agrigento (L6300) via Selinunte and Ribera. From
Ragusa, AST buses run at 6:50am and 4:10pm daily with a direct connection at Gela
(4hr., L6600). For information, call **Fratelli Camilleri ed Argento** (tel. (0922) 390
84). **Cuffaro** (tel. (0922) 91 63 49) runs buses from Palermo's via Lincoln station (21/
4hr., L7500) and from Catania's p. Bellini station (23/4hr., L12,700).

Tourist Office: viale delle Vittoria, 255 (tel. 269 22), a stone's throw from the train station. Helpful. Open Mon.-Fri. 9:30am-12:30pm. **AAST:** via Atenea, 123 (tel. 20 454). Also helpful and
friendly.

Post Office: p. Vittorio Emanuele (tel. 200 21). Open Mon.-Fri. 8:10am-7:30pm, Sat. 8-11am.
Postal Code: 92100.

Telephones: SIP, via Atenea, 96. Open daily 8am-7:30pm. **Telephone Code:** 0922.

Buses: Most city buses depart from the train station. #8, 9, and 11 run to the Valley of Temples,
#9 and 10 to San Leone. Fare L600. Buy tickets at any newsstand or *tabacchi.*

Ferries: Siremar, Porto Empedocle. L1600 by bus from p. Roselli (every 30min.). To the Pelágie
Islands Linosa (L35,700) and Lampedusa (L45,000). (Daily at midnight; Oct. 16-May Mon.-Sat.
at midnight; arrive 5:30am at Linosa, 8:15am at Lampedusa.) Return boats leave Lampedusa at
10:15am and Linosa at about 1pm. Tickets available through Siremar at the port or by calling 63
66 83. You must be at the port 1 hour before departure.

Emergencies: tel. 113. **Police:** p. Moro (tel. 50 63 22). **Hospital: Ospedale Civile San Giovanni
di Dio** (tel. 20 755), off p. S. Giuseppe on via Atenea.

Accommodations and Camping

Bella Napoli, p. Lena, 6 (tel. 204 35), off via Bac Bac, which leads uphill from the western end
of via Atenea. Clean rooms, savvy staff, and a rooftop terrace overlooking the valley. Singles
L28,000, with bath L30,000. Doubles L38,000, with bath L45,000.

Concordia, via San Francesco, 11 (tel. 59 62 66). Take via Pirandello from the corner of p. Alto
Moro. Close to the train station. A modern hotel whose small but clean rooms and bathrooms
counter the spirit of the dirty market street on which it lies. Singles L23,000, with bath L25,000.
Doubles L33,000, with bath L39,000.

Hotel Villa Belvedere, via San Vito, 20 (tel. 200 51), up the stairs where viale della Vittoria intersects with p. Marconi at p. S. Giuseppe. Cool and quiet, modern rooms and personable staff.
Singles L30,000, with bath L50,000. Doubles L50,000, with bath L60,000.

Camping: Internazionale San Leone at San Leone (tel. 416 12). Take bus #9 or the "San Leone"
bus to the beach and walk to the left. L5200 per person, L5200 per 2-person tent. Sleeping bag
only L5500 per person. Open April-Oct. **Camping Nettuno** (tel. 41 62 68), 6km from Agrigento,
past San Leone on bus #9. Less green and less comfortable than San Leone. L3000 per person,
L3000 per small tent, L6000 per large tent. Open year-round, but check with the tourist office before heading out.

Food

Walk down the steps from p. Marconi to the soccer field to find an all-purpose **market.** (Open Mon.-Sat. 9am-early afternoon.) Lower prices and less atmosphere come your way at **STANDA,** in Agrigento's tallest building at via Gioeni, 41, behind p. Moro. (Open Tues.-Sat. 9am-1pm and 4:30-8:30pm, Mon. 4:30-8:30pm.)

Trattoria Atenea, via Ficani, 12 (tel. 202 47), the 4th right off via Atenea from p. Moro. Think nothing of the ominous "We speak English" and "Nous parlons Français" signs. 2-course lunch L15,000; dinner *menù* L12,000. *Calamari* (squid) or *gamberi* (shrimp) L9000. Wine L4000 per . Open Mon.-Sat. noon-3:30pm and 7-11pm.

Ristorante Pizzeria, la Corte degli Sfilzi, 4 (tel. 59 55 20), in the cortile (garden) Contarini off via Atenea. The fancy floral-print tablecloths bear witness to fine victuals. Go for the *pizza menù*, your choice of pizza, *insalata mista,* and wine or beer, including cover and service (L10,000). Regular *menù* L14,000. Open Thurs-Tues. 1-3pm and 7:30pm-midnight.

Trattoria Black Horse, via Celauro, 8 (tel. 232 23), off via Atenea. An interesting family-run establishment. Ask the cook to sing as you wait and you'll be treated to some Verdi. *Tronchetto dello chef* (L6500) is the specialty: a thick lasagna packed with peas, ham, and meat sauce. Veal Scallopine "Black Horse" is a worthy *secondo.* Wine L5000. Cover L2000. Open Mon.-Sat. noon-3pm and 7-11pm. AmEx, MC, Visa.

Paninoteca Manhattan, salita M. Angeli, 9, up the steps to the right off via Atenea near p. Moro. Creative Italian sandwiches with creative American names. The "Rokhfeller" combines tuna, pepper, lettuce, *insalata russa,* tabasco, and a healthy dose of whiskey (L3500), while the "Brooklin" sports 'shrooms, cheese, lettuce, and *pancetta* (L3500). Innumerable brands of beer L2500. Open Mon.-Sat. 8:30am-3pm and 5:30pm-midnight.

Trattoria La Forchetta, p. San Francesco, off via Atenea. Authentic Agrigentean cuisine in a restful setting. *Primi* from L6000. *Secondi* from L8000. Excellent *calamari fritto* (fried squid) L9500. Cover L1000. Service 10%. Open Mon.-Sat. 12:30-3pm and 6:30-11pm.

Sights and Entertainment

The most interesting building of the medieval city is the small, 11th-century Norman **Church of Santa Maria dei Greci**, which occupies the site of a 5th-century BC Doric temple. (Follow the signs up the hill from the end of via Atenea.) Part of the wooden Norman ceiling remains, as well as a portion of the 14th-century Byzantine frescoes. Look for the astonishing secret tunnel, which you can enter from the courtyard. It preserves the stylobate (the platform beneath the columns) and the six stumps of the ancient temple. (If closed, call 255 62 for the custodian; L500 tip expected.) At the top of the same hill is Agrigento's Baroque **Cattedrale.**

Ambling down via Girolamo, which flanks via Atenea, will take you past the former Consulate of the British Empire (#63), replete with lions and royal insignia, to **Santo Spirito,** a complex containing a chapel, charterhouse, and refectory (now used as a library), founded by Cistercian nuns at the end of the 13th century. The church displays beautiful stuccos (1693-1695) by Serpotta. These illustrate scenes from Christ's life; ring the bell on the church door to enter. For more Serpotta stucco, take a walk down via San Spirito and via Foder to the **Chiesa del Purgatorio** (Church of the Purgatory), which houses eight statues representing the Virtues. To the left of the church, underneath a sleeping lion, is the entrance to a network of underground channels and reservoirs built by the Greeks in the 5th century BC.

To get to the **Valle dei Templi** (Valley of the Temples), take bus #8, 9, 10, or 11 from the train station (last bus back at 8:30pm; L600) and ask to be dropped off at the *Quartiere Ellenistico-Romano* (Hellenistic-Roman Quarter). With its four roads and Ellenistico-Romano terraced building complex, it provides an excellent idea of the old city's organization. Descend the hill to the **Museo Nazionale Archeologico di San Nicola** to orient yourself. The museum contains a notable collection of artifacts, especially vases from Agrigento and the rest of central Sicily. (Open Tues.-Sun. 9am-2pm and 3-7pm. Free.) Visit the adjacent **Church of San Nicolà,** a small 13th-century Romanesque-Gothic church on the site of a Greek sanctuary, which preserves Roman sarcophagi with reliefs depicting the death of Phaedra (second chapel on the right; open sunrise-sunset).

With the exception of the temples of Concord and Juno, the structures here were destroyed by a combination of earthquakes and early Christian anti-paganism. Walking down from the museum, the first site you encounter is the **Tempio dell'Olimpico Giove** (Jupiter). Had its construction not been halted by the Carthaginian sack of the city in 406-405 BC, it would have been one of the largest Greek temples ever built. Now little is left; most of the temple's stone was carted away in the 18th century to build a jetty at nearby Porto Empedocle. The temple's 38 18m columns were supported by 8m *telemones*—figures standing in as supporting columns. A reconstructed *telemon* lies alongside the ruins. The four columns supporting an entablature represent the piecemeal effort to rebuild the 5th-century BC **Tempio di Castore e Polluce** (Castor and Pollux). Bear right as you leave this complex. The next temple, the **Tempio di Giunone** (Juno), also dates from the 5th century BC.

Uphill from the Temple of Juno looms the **Tempio della Concordia,** the most intact (34 columns!) Greek temple in the world after the Temple of Theseus in Athens. The temple was erected in the mid-5th century out of volcanic rock, now faded golden. It owes its remarkable preservation to early sanctification as a Christian church by the then-Bishop of Agrigento San Gregorio delle Rape (St. Gregory of the **Turnips**). The niches in the interior walls originally created for Christian worship are still visible. Poke around the nearby Christian necropolis, just left of the **Tempio di Ercole** (Hercules), the oldest temple (6th century BC) here.

Heading back up the hill to town, tourists in search of Mr. Write should visit the birthplace of playwright **Luigi Pirandello** in piazza Kaos (named for Pirandello's most famous work). Take bus #8 to this small museum of books and notes, honored by his gravestone in the backyard. (Open Mon.-Sat. 9am-noon. Free.) The **Settimana Pirandelliana** (tel. (0922) 235 61), a week-long festival of plays, operas, and ballets performed out-of-doors in p. Kaos takes place in late July and early August (admission L12,000).

The first Sunday of February brings the **Almond Blossom Festival,** an international folk event in the Valley of the Temples. In early July, townsfolk throw bread to the effigy of St. Calogero in gratitude for curing the city of a deadly yeast epidemic. **San Leone,** 4km from Agrigento (very easily accesible by bus #9 or 10), is laden with splendid stretches of beach. At night it hops to the tunes of **Discoteca Aster** (tel. 423 66; free). Buses stop running at 9pm, but visitors have been known to finagle rides.

Somewhat Near Agrigento: Pelágie Islands

The islands of **Lampedusa** and **Linosa,** though geologically part of the African continent, belong politically to the province of Agrigento. They're an easy, budget-busting ferry ride from Porto Empedocle (one-way to Lampedusa L45,000, to Linosa L35,700). Lampedusa exploded to now-faded fame when a Libyan missile barely missed it in 1986. Besides good luck, the island is noted for its peculiar Arab-style architecture, peregrine falcons, seals, and virile sea turtles; revel in fauna at the Isola dei Conigli nature reserve. Linosa's greatest riches lie underwater: the island is famous for unbeatable snorkeling and diving. Unfortunately, the port areas have become infested with bacteria and tar balls from the isle's sewage facilities.

Accommodations aren't cheap on the islands. **Albergo Oasi** (tel. 970 630) lets singles for L40,000 and doubles with bath for L80,000; **Albergo Belvedere** (tel. 970 188), offers half-penisone at L75,000 per person. On Linosa try **Hotel Algusa.** (Tel. 972 052. Singles with bath L40,000, doubles with bath L75,000.)

Ragusa

The provincial capital of Ragusa has quietly avoided the frenetic pace of other Sicilian cities, simultaneously managing to escape inclusion on most tourist itineraries. Its placid atmosphere has been carefully cultivated for millennia. The city has grown uphill from its beginnings at **Ibla Ragusa,** so that walking the streets is tantamount to following an architectural timeline. The old city begins with a well-preserved Baroque center, then winds its serpentine way up and down the hills toward a frenzy of construction in the new city, near the station. Along the way, the city displays all of the intervening stylistic periods along the way. The streets here evolve from an orderly grid into a chaotic weave of terraced alleys. The citizens seem to acknowledge the taxonomy of new and old town: the young hang out in the former, while their elders congregate in the latter. Though the Ragusan pace of life is somewhere between comatose and dead, the city will reward the dedicated street-wanderer with architectural treasures and near-perfect solitude.

Orientation and Practical Information

The train and bus stations are in p. del Popolo and nearby p. Gramsci, respectively. To reach the city center from these adjacent *piazze,* hang a left as you exit either station onto **viale Tenente Lena,** go through p. Libertà, and walk up to the Ponte Senatore F. Pennavaria, the northernmost of three bridges crossing the Vallata Santa. The *ponte* runs directly into **via Roma,** which continues across town to its abrupt end at the edge of a moonscape. **Corso Italia,** off via Roma, leads downhill to the stairs to Ragusa Ibla at **Santa Maria delle Scale.** AST **buses** run regularly from Syracuse's piazzale Marconi (Mon.-Sat. 8 per day, Sun. at 8am only; 3hr., L13,000 round-trip). Two AST buses run daily to Gela (6:50am and 4:10pm, 1hr. 30min., L4500), where a connection can be made to Agrigento (1hr. 30min., L5900). From Enna, take the bus to Gela (2hr., L8500) and then the train (2hr., L5600).

Tourist Office: via Natalelli, 131 (tel. 62 14 21), up 1 flight. Turn left off via Roma 1 block past p. Libertà before the Ponte Senatore. Open Mon.-Sat. 8:30am-1:30pm.

Post Office: p. Matteotti, (tel. 62 23 21), 2 blocks down corso Italia from via Roma. Open Mon.-Sat. 8am-2pm. **Postal Code:** 97100.

Telephones: SIP, via Maiorana, on the city side of Ponte Vecchio (the middle bridge). Open Mon.-Sat. 9am-12:30pm and 4:30-8pm. **Telephone Code:** 0932.

Buses: AST (tel. 62 12 49), in p. Gramsci. Schedules posted on side of building bordering the depot. Buy tickets on bus. **ETNA** to Catania (5 per day, 3hr., L7800). A ticket office is located inside p. Gramsci's only *caffè.*

Emergencies: tel. 113. **Police:** tel. 113. **Hospital: Ospedale Civile,** right across from the train station (tel. 62 27 33 during the day; tel. 62 39 46 for nighttime and holiday emergencies).

Accommodations

Hotel San Giovanni, via Transpontino, 3 (tel. 62 10 13), off the center bridge on the station side. A quiet, clean hotel with great beds and marble bathrooms; you can hear the trains behind the hotel go thump in the night. Singles L35,000, with bath L50,000. Doubles L45,000, with bath L80,000.

Ionio: via Risorgimento, 4a (tel. 62 43 22). Closest to the train station. Singles L24,000-28,000, with bath L50,000. Doubles with bath L80,000.

Camping: Ragusa's campgrounds are at Marina, 30km to the south. Tumino buses (tel. 62 31 84) run regularly from p. Gramsci in Ragusa to p. Duca degli Abruzzi in Marina (30min.; L2900, round-trip L4900). **Baja del Sole,** (tel. 398 44). L5000 per person, L6000 per small tent, L8000 per large tent, L6000 per person with sleeping bag. **Villa Nifosì** (tel. 391 18) runs L6000 per person, L6000 per tent, L6200 per person with sleeping bag.

Food

While in Ragusa, make a point to try some *mpanatigghie,* thin pastries filled with cocoa, cinnamon, and ground meat. Unfortunately, they aren't cheap, and neither are the *trattorie* where they're sold. If you're tapped for cash, try the **Supermercato STANDA** instead, at via Roma, 187 (tel. 62 20 27), at the end of the bridge into town. (Open Tues.-Sat. 9am-1pm and 4-8pm, Mon. 4-8pm.)

Latalena Self-Service, via Risorgimento, 30 (tel. 65 25 88), just a few blocks from the station, to the left off viale Sicilia. Savor the L12,000 *menù* or pizza as you explore the delicacies under the glass next to the register. Open Tues.-Sun. noon-2:30pm.

Pizzeria La Grotta, via G. Cartia, the 2nd right off via Roma at the sign. Amazing pizzas and *calzoni* with draft beer for only L1500. Open Wed.-Mon. 12:30-3pm and 6-10pm.

La Valle, via Risorgimento, 66 (tel. 293 41). From the station take a right onto viale Sicilia, then walk downhill past the gas station. *The* place young Ragusans recommend, though on the pricey side. Pasta L5500-8000. A wide variety of pizzas L6000-8000. Open Sat.-Thurs. noon-3pm and 8pm-midnight. AmEx, Visa.

Caffè Trieste, corso Italia, 76 (tel. 62 21 10), across from the post office. Superior Sicilian pastries (L1500-2000) and perfect iced espresso (L1400). No seats, just pit-stop consumption. Open Mon.-Sat. 6:30am-9pm.

Sights and Entertainment

Judge Ragusa and Ibla by their exteriors—church interiors rarely match their elaborate Baroque facades. The many side streets delight with their quaint doorways. The upper town boasts an **Archeology Museum** (tel. 62 29 63) that lies one floor down and in back of the STANDA, with artifacts from the nearby Syracusan colony of Camarina. (Open Mon.-Sat. 9am-2pm, daily 3-6:30pm, Sun. 9am-1pm. Free.) On the way down to **Santa Maria delle Scale,** note one of the few 14th-century structures that survived the massive 1693 earthquake. Via delle Frecce and via dei Vespri, two small streets off via Santa Anna, are lined with some of Ragusa's most charming homes.

The stairs at Santa Maria offer a stellar spread of Ragusa Ibla, crowned by a monastery and the 18th-century dome of **San Giorgio.** Descend under the roadway to p. Repubblica. A dirt road down here circumscribes the town, passing abandoned *palazzi* and monasteries. At the far end of the hill, ascend the steps to **corso XXX Aprile.** From here go left for the beautifully arranged **piazza del Duomo** and **S. Giorgio,** or downhill and to the right for the shady **Giardini Iblei.** In front of the garden, you can catch buses #1 and 3 back to via Roma in Ragusa (every 30min., L600). On August 29 the town celebrates the **Festival of San Giovanni.** An **Antique Market** takes place the last Sunday of each month at Giardini Iblei.

In summer, any citizen who can fit into a swimsuit spends the weekend at **Marina di Ragusa,** a drab resort strip. Autolinee Tumino (tel. 390 51) runs 10 buses per day to Marina (last bus leaves Mon.-Sat. 8:15pm, Sun. 6:15pm; last bus returns Mon.-Sat. 9:30pm, Sun. 10:40pm; L2900, round-trip L4900). A complete schedule is posted in the Polleria Giarrosto in Marina's p. Duca degli Abruzzi. In the same *piazza* savor Marina's best ice cream at **Delle Rose,** where the scoops are so enormous they give you *two* cones.

The resort's most animated eatery, **Pub Shaker,** is located at the beginning of lungomare Mediterraneo, and serves a variety of *panini,* including the oddly stuffed *tropicale,* with prosciutto, pineapple, lettuce, and mustard. Bottled beers are L2200 and up. (Open daily 7pm-4am.)

Betwen Marina and Ragusa you can find the intriguing **Castle of Donnafugata,** an eclectic villa constructed and enlarged between the 17th and 19th centuries. Pick up a glossy pamphlet at the tourist office.

Syracuse (Siracusa)

Sicily's dignified Grecian city, Syracuse radiates the classical romance of Rome and harbors the climate of a vacation island. *Siracusani* lament their city's millennia-long decline. Some say the city began to slide in 668 AD, when the bathing Byzantine emperor Constans was bludgeoned to death with a soap dish. Others set the fatal date at 211 BC: Syracuse just hasn't been the same since being sacked by the Romans. Certainly the glory-days were long ago; from the 6th to 3rd centuries BC, Syracuse was arguably the greatest city in the world, cultivating such luminaries as Pindar, Theocritus, and Archimedes, and claiming among its diverse feats the creation of both the world's largest theater and the first known cookbook. The young metropolis wielded a military might unrivaled in the Mediterranean. Syracuse can no longer claim to be the center of the civilized world, but the decline of this ancient New York has been slow, enough to make a visit still worthwhile, as the busy *caffè* and businesses of ancient Ortigia and the latter-day *palazzi* of Neapolis attest.

Orientation and Practical Information

Syracuse rests on and off the southeastern coast of Sicily. Most businesses are on the island of Ortigia, which is connected by two bridges to the mainland. The principal bridge leads to **corso Umberto** on the mainland, which becomes **via Francesco Crispi** at p. Marconi, passing by the train station.

Tourist Office: EPT, at lungo Paradiso in the archeological park off corso Gelone where it intersects with viale Teocrito. Open daily 8am-2pm and Tues.-Fri. 3-6pm. **APT:** via San Sebastiano, 45 (tel. 67 710). Ask for the brochure *campeggi e villaggi turistici* for information on camping in the area. Open 8am-2pm and 4-7pm.

Post Office: p. delle Poste, 15 (tel. 684 16), in the old city near the bridge. Fermo Posta (tel. 669 95). Open Mon.-Fri. 8am-7:45pm, Sat. 8am-1pm. **Postal Code:** 96100.

Telephones: SIP, via Brenta, 33, behind the train station. Open daily 8am-8pm. At other times, try **Bar Tamanaco,** p. Marconi, 19. **Telephone Code:** 0931.

Trains: via Francesco Crispi, midway between the old city and the archeological park. To: Catania (15 per day, 1hr. 30min., L6500); Taormina (14 per day, 2hr., L10,500); Messina (13 per day, 3hr., L13,800); Ragusa (4 per day, 3hr., L8800).

Buses: From the depot at piazzale Marconi at the end of corso Umberto in Ortigia. **SAIS** (tel. 667 10), off c. Umberto, near the train station.. To Catania (9 per day, 1hr. 30min., L6500) and Palermo (4 per day, 4hr., L22,100); **AST,** tel. 656 89. To: Catania (14 per day, L5400); Noto (13 per day, 45min., L3500); Piazza Armerina (at 5:15am, 3hr., L8000).

Ferries: Tirrenia, via Mazzini, 5 (tel. 669 56). Open Mon.-Sat. 9am-1pm and 3-5:30pm. To: Naples (Wed. at 3:30pm from Molo San Antonio, arriving Thurs. at 9:30am, about L50,000); Règgio di Calabria (Mon., Wed., and Sat. at 3:30pm, arriving at 10pm, L16,300); Malta (Sun., Tues., and Fri. at 4:30pm, arriving at Vittoriosa at 9:30pm, about L75,000; Oct.-May L55,000). Open 9am-noon and 3-6pm.

Emergencies: tel. 113. **Police:** via S. Sebastiano (tel. 211 22). **Hospital:** via Testaferrata (tel. 92 41 11). **Late-night Emergencies: Guardia Medica,** on via Reno just a block from the station (tel. 225 55).

Accommodations and Camping

Syracuse offers copious cheap accommodations in the new city and by the train station, but, if you'd prefer seashells and cobblestones, a room in charismatic Ortigia is well worth the expense. Women should be wary of the hotels around the station.

Pensione Bel Sit, via Oglio, 5 (tel. 602 45), on the 5th floor. Close to the station overlooking the Foro Siracusano. White rooms, caring proprietors, convenient locations, and *way* up high. Singles with bath L25,000. Doubles L30,000, with bath L36,000.

Hotel Milano, corso Umberto, 10 (tel. 669 81). At the entrance to the bridge to Ortigia. Modern, spacious rooms on a busy street. Fall asleep to the sound of motorcycles gunning their engines. Singles L23,000, with bath L30,000. Doubles L35,000, with bath L45,000.

Pensione Pantheon, via Foro Siracusano, 22 (tel. 229 85), off corso Umberto. Clean and cheery. Soft beds. Singles L20,000, with bath L25,000. Doubles L35,000, with bath L36,000.

Gran Bretagna, via Savoia, 21 (tel. 687 65), across the bridge in Ortigia. A weathered but charming hotel—the only one left in Ortigia. Some rooms have huge 19th-century frescoes. Curfew midnight. Singles L35,000, with bath L45,000. Doubles L60,000, with bath L70,000. Breakfast included.

Camping: Minareto, across the harbor from Ortigia (tel. 72 13 98). Take bus #34. L5000 per person, L5000 per small tent, L8000 per large tent. Open March-Sept. **Fontane Bianche** (tel. 79 03 33), near the beach. Take bus #34. 20km from Syracuse. L6000 per person, L7000 per tent, L10,000 per large tent, L5000 per sleeping bag. Open April-Oct.

Food

Pizza is about the only budget option in Syracuse other than the **market** on via Trento, near the Temple of Apollo. (Open Mon.-Sat. 7am-early afternoon.) For staples, try the **Supermercato Linguanti,** corso Umberto, 186, across from the Hotel Centrale just a block from the station. (Open Mon.-Tues. and Thurs.-Sat. 7am-1pm and 3-8pm, Wed. 7am-1pm.) *Panini*-mobiles motor about the Foro Siracusa some nights. A grilled steak sandwich, fries, and a beer come to about L8000.

Self-Service Santuario, p. della Vittoria, 14 (tel. 643 49), near the Santuario della Madonna at the end of via M. Carabelli. Offers divine protection from high prices with restaurant-quality meals. Get there before 2pm; they run out of food quickly. Menu varies daily. *Primi* around L4000, *secondi* L5500. Open daily 8am-3pm.

Stella del Porto, via Pripolo, 40 (tel. 605 82), just a few doors down from p. Marconi. Mostly locals; the cooks will drag you into the kitchen to choose your fare. Menu changes daily. Full meals L20,000. Open Mon.-Sat. noon-3pm and 6-10pm.

Trattoria la Foglia, via Capodieci, 39 (tel. 46 15 69), in the south side of town. Very chic and worth the price. A sculpting couple has switched from stone to a more malleable (and palatable) medium. Savor exquisite vegetables under the ancient wooden beams. Pasta from L7000, vegetable plates L8000-10,000. Cover L3000. Open Wed.-Mon. noon-4:30pm and 7:30pm-midnight.

Spaghetteria do Scugghiu, via D. Sciná, 11, off p. Archimede. An ancient Syracusan institution. Twenty-two delicious types of pasta, all L6000. *Secondi* L8000-10,000. Cover L1500. Open Tues.-Sun. noon-3pm and 7-10:30pm.

Del Forestiero, corso Timoleonte, 2 (tel. 644 76). Enjoy a meal by the sea. God's own tortellini (L6000). *Secondi* from L7000. Wine L4000 per . Open Tues.-Sun. 1-3pm and 7-10pm.

Tuttopizza, lungomare Alfeo, 12, below the Fontana Aretusa. Investigate the wonderful results of trysts between dough and tomato sauce, all served outside at candlelit tables (L3000-8000). Try the *Alfeo,* their finest match, topped with eggplant, prosciutto, olives, mushrooms, tomato, and mozzarella. Beer L3500. Cover L1000. Open Wed.-Mon. 9pm-1am.

Sights

The historic sights are concentrated in two areas a few kilometers apart: the enclosed archeological park in the north part of town, and the island of Ortigia.

Ortigia

It was here in 413 BC that Archimedes' mirrors saved Syracuse from invasion, decimating the massed fleet of jealous Athens in one of the great naval battles of antiquity. The ruins of two Greek temples and several charming Gothic and Renaissance churches and palaces are sprinkled along the winding streets of the island. Upon crossing the bridge to Ortigia you'll stumble over the ruins of the **Temple of Apollo.** This is the oldest Doric temple in Sicily, erected around 565 BC. All that remain are two columns supporting a piece of entablature and parts of the *cella* wall, which manifests traces of the subsequent Byzantine church.

Up corso Matteotti to the right, remnants are scattered through **piazza Archimede,** the principal square of the old city. Special treats await at the Palazzo Lanzo (#6), a 15th-century building graced by original Gothic fenestration and a beautiful Catalan 14th-century staircase in the courtyard. Down via dei Montalto, a small passageway leads to a fantastic external view of the **Palazzo Montalto** (1397), the fanciest of the Gothic palaces in town, with triple windows set in Arab-decorated pointed arches. From here, backtrack to p. Archimede and walk up vie Roma and Minerva to p. del Duomo. The **duomo** is one of the most extraordinary buildings in all of Italy. More than 2300 years separate the 18th-century baroque facade from the attached 5th-century BC **Temple of Athena,** and the intervening centuries each made their own additions. The cumulative effect is the representation of every period of Italian architecture. Once admired by Cicero, the temple was converted to a three-aisled Christian basilica in the 7th century. The columns were embedded in a solid wall, and arches were carved out of the interior (as at Agrigento's Temple of Concord). Twenty-six of its original 34 columns remain, not only on the sides but also in the entrance and in the Byzantine chapel at the end of the north aisle. The 16th-century wooden ceiling sports an inscription, actually an exerpt from a papal bull issued by Leo X in 1517 asserting the importance of the church. Also of interest are a marble font from the Catacombs of San Giovanni, supported by 13th-century bronze lions (first chapel on the right), and an altar that was made from the temple's entablature.

Piazza del Duomo, in front of the cathedral, is lined with fragrant oleander trees and surrounded by a collection of extraordinary buildings. At #24, the graceful facade of the **Palazzo Benevantano,** reconstructed in 1788, conceals an elegant serpentine balcony. A restrained facade with a wrought-iron balcony introduces the church at the far end of the square, **Santa Lucia alla Badia** (1695-1703; open only during church services and closed for restoration in 1992).

From the *piazza,* a trip down via Picherale will bring you to the ancient **Fonte Aretusa,** a "miraculous" freshwater spring by the sea. Legend has it that the nymph Arethusa escaped through a tunnel from her admirer Alpheus and was transformed into this fountain by the goddess Diana. Alpheus in turn was transformed into the eponymous river in Greece, which supposedly feeds the spring to this day through a getaway tunnel. Steps lead to the **Foro Italico,** a tree-lined walk along the harbor.

Archeological Park.

The larger monuments, among them the Greek theater and the famous Paradise Quarry, cluster in the park. (Open Mon.-Sat. 9am-2hr. before sunset, Sun. 9am-1pm. Admission L2000.) The **Greek theater,** scooped out of solid rock at the beginning of the 5th century BC, is the largest of its kind in existence. The c*avea,* or auditorium, originally had 59 rows of seats (now 42) in nine wedges, seating up to 15,000 people. You can still distinguish the three divisions of the theater—the c*avea,* the semi-circular orchestra pit, and the rectangular stage, which had a two-story permanent set with niches and colonnades.

The **Paradise Quarry,** outside the entrance to the Greek theater, is a merry flowered area in front of the chalk cliffs. It consists of two large grottoes: the **Orecchio di Dionigi** (Ear of Dionysius) and the **Grotta dei Cordari** (Cordmakers' Cave). The former is an artificial grotto of cathedral proportions (65m long, 5-11m wide, 23m high). Its name is derived from its resemblance to a giant earlobe and its exceptional acoustics. Supposedly its echo allowed the tyrant rex Dionysius, poet manqué, to overhear the conversations of prisoners confined in a lower room. Nearby, also carved out of the rock, is the **tomb of Archimedes** with a stone triangle atop the entrance.

In proximity to the park is the immense **Roman amphitheater,** constructed in the 2nd century AD, and next to it is the **Altar of Hieron II** (241-215 BC), which was used for public sacrifices. At 198m by 23m, it is the largest altar known. Only the lower part, cut out of the living rock, remains; the upper part, constructed of blocks, was filched by the Spanish in the 16th century for building material. The long flat surface is used today as a stage for dance and theater performances. Contact the tourist office for ticket and program information.

The **Catacombe di San Giovanni,** a few blocks away down viale Teocrito, are extensive, sporadically frescoed catacombs dug between 315 to 360 AD. Outside the catacombs lie the ruins of a building said to be the first Christian church in Sicily. Below the ruins hides the 4th-century crypt of San Marciano. L2000 gets you a whirlwind tour of a few of the hundreds of rooms underneath the church. (Tours given Thurs.-Tues. hourly 10am-noon and 4-6pm, Dec.-Feb. 10am-noon.) The entire city is rumored to rest on a labyrinth of similar underground galleries, some running all the way to Catania, dug to provide refuge from invaders. Located down viale Teocrito from the park, the three-year-old **Museo Archeologico Regionale Paolo Orsi,** on the grounds of the Villa Landolina, is credited with one of the world's best collections of Greek artifacts. (Open Tues.-Sun. 9am-1pm and 3-6:30pm. Admission L2000, under 18 or over 60 free.)

Entertainment

Every even-numbered year, **Greek classical drama** is performed in the spectacular setting of the Greek Theater during May and June. The cheapest seats cost L15,000-20,000; ask for details at the EPT office. July and August bring all kinds of music and theater to **Ara di Ierone II.** (Admission L7000-25,000.)

Beachcombers can bus the 18km from Syracuse to **Fontane Bianche** (bus #21 or 22, L600), an endless, silken beach frequented by a jet-set crowd. A smaller, less spectacular beach, more popular with the locals, is **Arenella,** 8km from the city (bus #23, L600). To play in waters of a different sort, take a daytrip to the **Fiume** and **Fonte Ciane,** home of the world's only major papyrus groves outside of Egypt. Take AST bus #21 or 22 from the post office to the Fiume Ciane bridge (15min., L1200; let the driver know where you want to go); then walk along the path up to the source.

Natives rate Ortigia nightlife a *"niente"* (nothin'), but don't give up so easily. Much tax money has been spent on lighting the monuments, and the tiny island becomes a stage for the *passeggiata*. **Flirt,** via Cavour, 4, off p. Duomo, is home to the artsy and demure. (Open daily 8pm-1am.) **La Dolce Vita,** via Roma, 118, not far from the *duomo,* is a snazzy piano bar with a slick interior. (Open daily 9pm-3am. Expensive.) For either a more rowdy or more mellow scene, choose from the bars along foro Vittorio Emanuele II. During the winter, boogie 'til your boots burst at **Il Trabochetto,** via delle Vecchio Carceri, 30, near the *duomo* (L12,000).

Near Syracuse: Noto

After suffering complete destruction in a 1693 earthquake, Noto, 32km southwest of Syracuse, was rebuilt in Baroque opulence by the Syracusan Landolino family. A cascade of palaces and churches, some set atop monumental staircases and others behind tropical gardens, glitters along **corso Vittorio Emanuele.** The local stone has aged to give all the buildings a wonderful soft golden-brown coloring, especially beautiful in the light of early afternoon. The **tourist office,** p. XVI Maggio (tel. 83 67 44), on corso Vittorio Emanuele, provides a free map of the most beautiful buildings. (English spoken. Open daily 8am-2pm and 3-6pm.) You'll note that while proud Noto lavishes care on its 18th-century edifices, its Romanesque, Gothic, and modern structures languish in acute disrepair. Evidently the architectural rule of thumb is, "If it ain't Baroque, don't fix it." (**Cattedrale** (1693-1770) under restoration in 1992.) **Trattoria del Carmine,** via Ducezio, 9 (tel. 83 87 05), on the first street off via S. La Rosa from p. XVI Maggio, serves home-cooked *ravioli di ricotta* (L5000). Full meals are L12,000-15,000. (Open Tues.-Sun. noon-3pm and 7-midnight.) Try Spanish *paella* (L8000) at the more spacious **Trattoria il Giglio,** p. Municipio, 8/10 (tel. 83 86 40), near the *duomo,* or sample *spaghetti in nero di seppia,* (cooked in cuttlefish ink, L6500). Quaff wine for L3000 per ; cover is L1000. (Open daily noon-4pm and 7pm-midnight; in winter noon-4pm and 6-10pm.)

On the third Sunday of May, Noto hosts the **Infiorata: Saluto alla Primavera,** the city's greatest festival. On this day, the length of via Niccolaci is blanketed with mosaics painstakingly assembled from thousands of flower petals. The second week in August, a folk festival invigorates the normally sedate town. The tourist office distributes a schedule of events, most of which are free.

SAIS and AST **buses** leave from Syracuse in a steady stream from 4:15am to 7:50pm (23 per day, L8100 round-trip), and the last bus back heads out at 9:10pm. Noto can also be reached by the local train for Modica, which departs every hour from the central train station (L4300 round-trip), but it's a 20-minute walk uphill to town from the station. Fine beaches are only 7km away at **Marina di Noto;** buses leave from the Giardini Pubblici (4 per day, L1800). Noto's one hotel is the clean and pleasant **Albergo Stella,** via F. Maiore, 40 (tel. 83 56 95). (Singles L22,000. Doubles L40,000, with bath L45,000. Showers L2000.)

If you are independently mobile, the remote, eerie neolithic necropolis at **Pantalica** merits a visit. In a river gorge about 30km northwest of Syracuse near Sortino, the gouged-out sockets of hundreds of tombs stare out from looming cliffs. Bring a flashlight.

Catania

Catanians claim their city prepares them for every surprise the rest of the world has to offer. Certainly the metropolis is intimidating, with its chaotic traffic, immense, collapsing housing projects, and unfortunate status as Italy's most crime-ridden city. Behind the squalid veneer, however, lies an intriguing urban mosaic. Perpetual prey to the nearby volcano, this ancient city has been leveled and rebuilt many times; the present appearance dates from reconstruction following the monstrous 1692 earthquake, after which G. B. Vaccarini embellished the city with sumptuous Baroque buildings. The walls of dark volcanic stone lend a characteristic pall to the historic quarters, matched by gray concrete elsewhere.

Orientation and Practical Information

Catania lies between Messina and Syracuse on Sicily's eastern coast. The main street, **via Etnea,** runs north from p. del Duomo to p. Gioeni, but there is little of interest beyond p. Cavour. From the train station walk inland along corso Mártiri della Libertà to bank-laden **corso Sicilia,** which intersects with via Etnea. From here thrifty accommodations and boutiques await to your right all the way to piazza Cavour; to the left is the **duomo** and **via Vittorio Emanuele II** running to the water and p. dei Mártiri.

Don't just avoid specific neighborhoods in Catania—treat the *entire city* as a bad neighborhood. And be particularly wary of anything which might be intended as a distraction—a (staged) fight, someone pointing out a stain on your clothes, even an intentional fender-bender to get you out of your car. Be cautious walking around the city, especially at night; single women should be particularly watchful. Leave expensive watches or clunky jewelry somewhere safe (in your hotel, *if secure*), and don't be afraid to make a scene if you feel threatened. Check the General Introduction sections on Safety and Security and Women Travelers, and refer to the Crime section for Naples or Palermo, for further important information on safety and security.

Tourist Offices: AAPIT, largo Paisiello, 5 (tel. 31 21 24 or 31 77 20), up via Pacini, off via Etnea near the post office. Open Mon.-Fri. 9am-1pm and 4:30-6:30pm, Sat. 9am-1pm. **Train station branch office,** (tel. 53 18 02). Open Mon.-Sat. 9am-1pm and 4-7pm. **Airport branch office,** (tel. 34 19 00). Open Mon.-Fri. 8am-8pm.

Budget Travel: CTS, via Garofalo, 3 (tel. 715 04 34). Student travel information. Open Mon.-Fri. 9am-1pm and 4-7:30pm, Sat. 9:30am-12:30pm.

American Express: La Duca and Co. Viaggi, via Etnea, 65 (tel. 31 61 55). Book catamaran tickets to Malta here. Open Mon.-Fri. 9am-1pm and 4-7:30pm, Sat. 9am-noon.

Post Office: via Etnea, 215 (tel. 31 15 06), in the big building next to the Villa Bellini Gardens. Open Mon.-Sat. 8:15am-7:40pm. **Postal Code:** 95100.

Telephones: SIP, corso Sicilia, 67. Open daily 9am-12:30pm and 4:30-7:30pm. **ASST,** p. Papa Giovanni XXIII, 12 (tel. 53 35 01) across from the train station. Open 8am-8pm. **Telephone Code:** 095.

Flights: Fontanarossa, (tel. 34 63 38). Take bus #24. Two flights weekly to Malta (Mon. at 2:30pm and Fri. at 7:30pm, L221,000) with **Air Malta,** via Ventimiglia, 117 (tel. 32 51 83).

Trains: (tel. 53 16 25), in p. Papa Giovanni XXIII. To: Syracuse (every hr., 1hr. 45min., L7200); Messina (every hr., 2hr. L6200); Enna (9 per day, 1hr. 30min., L6500); Palermo (5 per day, 4hr. L17,100).

Buses: Interurban buses arrive in front of the train station. **SAIS,** v. D'Amico, 181 (tel. 53 61 68). Open 6am-9pm. To: Messina (14 per day, 1hr. 30min., L8700); Taormina (13 per day, 1hr. 30min., L5100); Syracuse (9 per day, 1hr. 30min., L5700); Enna (7 per day, 1hr. 15min., L7700); Palermo (4 per day, 3hr., L16,600). **ETNA** will take you from the train station to piazza Armerina (2hr., L7800). All bus services are reduced Sun. **City Buses:** From via Etnea, headed south, buses #29, 33, and 36 to the central train station; bus #24 to the airport; and bus #27 or D (June-Sept. only) to the beach. Tickets L800, L1100 per 2hr., L1400 per 9hr.

Ferries: Gozo Channel, office at Fratelli Bananno, via Anzalone, 7 (tel. 32 66 08); open Mon.-Fri. 9:30am-12:30pm and 4-6pm, Sat. 10am-1pm. **Tirrenia,** p. Grenoble, 26 (tel. 31 63 94). **Port Information,** tel. 53 16 67 or 53 11 34.

Late-Night Pharmacy: Crocerossa, via Etnea, 274 (tel. 43 10 71 or 43 41 29).

Emergencies: tel. 113. **Hospital:** via Vittorio Emanuele, off via Plebiscito (tel. 32 65 33).

Accommodations

Pensione Gresi, via Pacini, 28 (tel. 32 27 09), off via Etnea near Villa Bellini and the post office. Don't let the charred doors on the 1st floor discourage you; the *pensione* on the 3rd floor is spotless. Pleasant rooms. Singles L35,000. Doubles L55,000, with bath L70,500.

Pensione Südland, via Etnea, 270 (tel. 31 24 94), across from the post office. Immense and elegant, though somewhat noisy and often full. Singles L35,000, with bath L46,000. Doubles L48,000, with bath L61,000. Breakfast L5000.

Pensione Ferrara, via Umberto, 66 (tel. 31 60 00) off via Etnea just a few blocks from via Pacini. Well-kept accommodations on Catania's most fashionable shopping street. Bright, cheerful rooms. Singles L28,000, with bath L35,000. Doubles L50,000, with bath L70,000.

Pensione Rubens, via Etnea, 196 (tel. 31 70 73). Rooms of Rubenesque proportions. The proprietor will give you keys for entering whenever you please. Singles L28,000. Doubles L46,000. Showers L3000.

Camping: Villagio Turistico Internazionale (Catania Plaja), lungomare Kennedy, 47 (tel. 34 08 80). Luxurious, with stove, refrigerator, and other niceties. L3800-5000 per person, L4000-6000 per small tent, L6600-9000 per large tent. Two-bed bungalows L46,000-65,000.

Food

Don't leave Catania without trying their famous spaghetti, named after Catanese composer Vincenzo Bellini's well-known opera, *Norma.* Topped with tomato sauce, eggplant, and salted ricotta cheese, it is a toccata for the tastebuds. A lively **fish market** is located south and west of p. del Duomo.

Trattoria la Paglia, via Pardo, 23 (tel. 34 68 38), across from the duomo behind the erotic fountain near the middle of the fish market. Catch of the day, *spaghetti marinara,* vegetable, fruit, and wine L18,000. Try *insalata di polpo* (octopus salad) L6000. Area not recommended for single women at night. Open Mon.-Sat. noon-11pm.

Trattoria Casalinga, via Biondi, just 2 blocks off via Antonio di Sanguiliana. Menu changes daily, but you can be sure it'll be something delightful. Full meals L14,000. Open for lunch only and for as long as the clientele stays.

Pizzeria Mungibeddu, via Corodoni, 37, off via Umberto I east of via Etnea. Delicious pizza L4000-7000. *Coperto* L1000. Three-course *menù* L10,000. Open Mon.-Sat. 10am-3pm and 5pm-10pm.

Gastronomy C. Conte, via Etnea, 158 (tel. 31 10 89). An excellent eatery. *Pizzette* and other *tavola calda* snacks L1800-2000. Counters only, so come early. Also take-out service. Open Mon.-Sat. 7am-11pm.

Spinella, via Etnea, 300 (tel. 32 72 47). Super pastries and coffee right across from the Bellini gardens. Open Wed.-Mon. 7am-10:30pm. For comparison, try **Pasticceria Savia** (tel. 32 23 35) next door.

Sights

At the center of Catania's **piazza del Duomo,** Vaccarini's lava-built **Fontana dell'Elefante** (Elephant Fountain, 1736) boasts a unique anatomical feature. Vaccarini, true to reality, carved his elephant without visible testicles. When the statue was unveiled, horrified Catanian men concluded that this was a slur on their virility and demanded corrective measures; Vaccarini's acquiescence was monumental. Residents pledge that visitors may attain citizenship by smooching the elephant's massive tush, but the altitude of the pachyderm's posterior precludes any such aspirations. Stand behind the lewd fountain on the far end of the square for a good view of the **cathedral,** introduced by an open space at its side, allowing the full play of Baroque regalia. The other buildings on the square (the 18th-century Palazzo del Municipio on the left, the former Seminario dei Chierici on the right) employ an elegant white-stripe motif that contrasts with the cathedral's facade.

The church interior, now with a Baroque barrel-vaulted nave and domed side aisles, once looked quite different, as 1950s restoration work revealed. Stumps of the old columns were found, as well as the tall pointed arches of the original three apses. The two transept chapels have exquisitely paneled Renaissance frames (1545). One of them, the Norman **Cappella della Madonna** (right), also preserves a beautiful Roman sarcophagus and a 15th-century statue of the Virgin. Back in the main altar, Catania's patron saint Sant'Agata is depicted amongst the wooden choir stalls, performing the daily miracle (1588).

Via Crocíferi, which runs parallel (three streets away) to via Etnea from p. del Duomo to Villa Bellini, is packed with Baroque churches. Via Gesuiti, which branches off from via Crocíferi at the church with an octagonal tower, climbs a hill to the **Church of San Nicolò,** the largest and most frightening in Sicily. A giant unfinished facade with amputated columns and black protuberances encloses a cavernous interior. In the chancel is the empty shell of a once-sumptuous organ and the tomb of the man who built it. From the dome, there's a magnificent view of the city and the slopes of Etna. (Church open 8am-2pm.) Next to the church is a former convent (partially under restoration), with ornate windows and balconies. One of the two courts encloses a beautiful **garden**— it's easy to miss, so ask where it is. Along sloping via Vittorio Emanuele on the way to via Etnea are the **Teatro Romano** and **Odeon,** two theaters whose marble Mt. Etna's 1669 eruption coated in lava. (Open Tues.-Sun. 9am-1 hr. before sunset.)

Two 17th-century buildings enclose **piazza dell'Università,** north of p. Duomo. Both by Vaccarini, the **Palazzo San Giuliano** is on the right and the **Palazzo dell'Università** stands opposite. Next comes the vibrant **Collegiata** (1768), once a college for priests, which contrasts with the more restrained **Church of San Michele** nearby. The church organ once knew the hands of composer and Catania native son Bellini. Farther up via Etnea his namesake, **Bellini Gardens,** offer a lush refuge against Mt. Etna's backdrop.

Entertainment

The **Teatro Bellini** (tel. 31 20 20) opened in 1890 with a performance of the composer's opera *Norma;* it is now the city's principal theater for opera and concerts. The four-month opera season begins in the middle of January, following the three-month symphonic season. Tickets for regular performances run L3000-8000. From July to September, the city and province host performances as part of the **Catania Musica Estate,** held at Ente Fiera (from June-Sept. only take bus #27 or D from p. del Duomo, 20min., L700). All events are free and schedules are plastered about town.

If you'd rather listen to the waves, but have left your New Age tapes behind, try **La Plaja,** a pleasant but crowded beach (take bus #27 or D, June-Sept. only). Farther away from Catania's port, **La Scogliera** is a clear bathing area spread out beside igneous cliffs (bus #34 from p. Duomo, 30min.).

Near Catania: Mount Etna

If in Sicily, you must visit **Mt. Etna,** one of the world's largest active volcanoes and (at 3350m) the largest and highest in Europe. The Greek poet Hesiod envisioned Etna as the home of Typhon, the last monster conceived by the Earth to fight the gods before the dawn of the human race. If so, Typhon remains restless; a 1985 eruption destroyed much of the tourist station near the summit. Etna blew its top again in 1992, unsettling residents of some of the towns along its slopes.

The trains of **Ferrovia Circumetnea** circumnavigate the volcano's base, stopping at local villages. From Catania use **Stazione Borgo,** via Caronda, 352/A (tel. 54 12 43), off viale Leonardo da Vinci. On Sundays in July and on Sundays and Thursdays in August and September, the *giro turistico,* a round-trip tour from Stazione Borgo, begins at

8:55am; reserve at corso delle Province, 13 (tel. 37 48 42; L16,000, under 10 L7200). An **AST** bus leaves from the central train station (station #5) at 8:05am for Reffugé Sapienza, making a rest stop at Nicolosi (where you can fill your empty picnic basket), and returns at 4pm (round-trip L6500). From Sapienza you can hike to the top in four or five hours or take the recently completed cable-car service (up the mountain from 9am-4:45pm, last down at 5:15pm; closed if winds are high). Stock up on food before you leave; as a last resort the self-service cafeteria at the tourist station will serve you decent L1500 pizzas and pasta dishes for L4500-5000. Based in Taormina, **SAT,** corso Umberto, 73 (tel. (0942) 246 53) runs pricey package tours which ascend all the way to the summit by bus. **CIT,** corso Umberto, 101 (tel. 233 01) offers similar deals. Trips to 1,900m are L28,000 and trips to the top are L60,000.

Taormina

Taormina hovers precariously on a high terrace overlooking the sea and a stretch of precipitous coastline, with Mt. Etna looming behind. Its spectacular natural beauty, however, is becoming increasingly obscured by a profusion of hotels, bars, and lava ashtrays. Despite all the tacky trinkets, Taormina's charm still shines through. Stop in, admire the vistas, and do your best to ignore the curio shops, camera-laden tourists, and souvenir sun-hats.

Orientation and Practical Information

The easiest way to get to Taormina is by bus from Messina (18 per day, L5100) or Catania (14 per day, L5200). Although trains are more frequent—from Messina (26 per day, 50min., L3800) and Catania (30 per day, 45min., L3100)—the train station is located far below Taormina, and access to the city depends on buses which make the run uphill every 15 to 75 minutes until 9:15pm (L1200).

From the bus depot, hang a left up via Pirandello until you hit **corso Umberto I,** the main drag, which runs the length of the town. Innumerable stepped side streets branch from the *corso.* **Via Bagnoli Croci** heads downhill to the public gardens, while **via Circonvallazione,** above corso Umberto, has a stepped path up to the **Castel Taormina.** Via Teatro Greci leads, appropriately enough, to the widely acclaimed Greek Theater.

Tourist Office: p. Santa Caterina (tel. 232 43), off corso Umberto at p. Vittorio Emanuele in Palazzo Corvaia. Helpful and well organized, if they slow down enough to notice you. Will help with your accommodations search (difficult in Aug.). English spoken. The **ticket office** (tel. 62 58 56) sells tickets to summer's many artistic events; pick up a program. Open daily 10am-1pm and 5-8pm.

Currency Exchange: Costana Viaggi, p. San Pancrazio, 32/A (tel. 234 94). Open Mon.-Fri. 9am-12:30pm and 4-7pm, Sat. 9am-noon. Also, hordes of other places on corso Umberto I.

American Express: La Duca Viaggi, p. Aprile IX, 1 (tel. 62 52 55), off corso Umberto. Will hold mail for 1 month. Open Mon.-Fri. 9am-1pm and 4-7:30pm, Sat. 9am-noon.

Post Office: p. S. Antonio (tel. 230 10), at the end of corso Umberto near the hospital. Open Mon.-Sat. 8:10am-7:30pm; last day of the month closes at noon. Another branch at via Nazionale, 200 (tel. 239 82). **Postal Code:** 98039.

Telephones: SIP, via San Pancrazio, 6 (tel. 246 69), at the top of via Pirandello in the Avis office. Open Mon.-Sat. 8am-12:30pm and 4:30-8pm, Sun. 9am-12:30pm. **Telephone Code:** 0942.

Buses: SAIS, tel. ((0942) 234 94). To Catania, Messina and local destinations. **Etna Tramonto** gives a full trip around the mountain, including ascent to the central crater (Mon. at 3pm, L57,000). **SAT** (tel. 501 98; 246 53 for fare information) offers similar excursions. Etna trips June-Oct. Mon. and Wed., April-May Mon., Wed., and Fri.; L28,000 for a ride up to 1900m; L60,000 for a trip to the crater.

Car Rental: Avis, via San Pancrazio, 6 (tel. 230 41). Open Mon.-Sat. 8:30am-12:30pm and 4-8pm, Sun. drop-off only 9am-noon.

Moped Rental: California, via Bagnoli Croce, 86 (tel. 237 69). Scooters L22,600 per day, L148,000 per week. Vespa 2-seaters L41,750 per day, L281,000 per week. Must be over 15. Open daily 9am-1pm and 4-8pm. **Sicily on Wheels,** down the street at #90. Offers similar rates and services.

English Bookstore: Libreria Interpress, corso Umberto, 37 (tel. 249 89).

Emergencies: tel. 113. **Police:** tel. 112. **Medical Emergency:** tel. 231 49. **Hospital: Ospedale Civico San Vincenzo** (tel. 533 10), in p. San Vincenzo.

Accommodations and Camping

Reservations are a must in August. The following *pensioni* usually have vacancies in the off-season, but most will not accept phone reservations from late June through September. If you are determined to stay overnight in summer, have the tourist office book a room for you. Cheaper accommodations are available in the nearby towns of Mazzarò, Spisone, and Giardini-Naxos, but bus service to these areas stops about 9pm; the only alternative for the first two is a long hike down steep trails.

Pensione Svizzera, via Pirandello, 26 (tel. 237 90; fax. 62 59 06). Turn right at the eastern end of corso Umberto. Between the bus station and the town center. A little expensive for the budget traveler, but well worth every *lire*. The rose- and ivy-colored building looks out over the magnificent coastline. Kept so neat, even the Swiss would be impressed. All rooms with bath. Singles L35,000. Doubles L60,000. Triples L66,000. Breakfast included. Open March-Nov.

Villa Pompei, via Bagnoli Croci, 88 (tel. 238 12), across from the public gardens. You can smell the flowers from the rooms. Run by sweet, caring sisters. Singles L18,000. Doubles L34,000, with bath L46,000. Extra bed L10,000. Showers L2000. Reservations for June-Sept. required a month in advance with deposit.

Pensione Columbia, via Iallia Bassia, 11 (tel. 234 23). Go down the steps by the entrance to the Greek theater. Clean rooms and a pleasant lounge. Singles L23,000. Doubles L36,000, with bath L42,000, with bath and breakfast, L52,000. Breakfast (obligatory July-Aug.) L5000. Reserve for summer 1 month in advance. Open irregularly in winter.

Camping: Campeggio San Leo (tel. 246 58), on the cape. L4500 per person, L6000 per small tent, L5000 per large tent. **Eurocamping Marmaruca** (tel. 366 76), 5km from Taormina in the Letojanni area. L5400 per person, L4300 per small tent, L6500 per large tent. Both sites reached by taking a SAIS bus toward Messina (L1200).

Food

Cheap eateries are few and far between; avoid everything off corso Umberto I. Even buying bread, cheese, and fruit can be expensive unless you try the **Supercato STANDA** on via Apollo Arcageta, at the end of corso Umberto, one block up from the post office. (Open Mon.-Sat. 8am-1pm and 4-8pm.)

Pace, p. San Pancrazio, 3 (tel. 231 84), at the end of via Pirandello. Outdoor tables, plenty of company, and a great location. Bright lights, big pizza (L5000). *Cannelloni alla Siciliana* L6000. Pizza slices to go L1800. Open Wed.-Mon. noon-3pm and 7-11pm.

Piccolo Mondo, p. San Pancrazio, 18 (tel. 243 22), across from Pace. *Pennette arrabbiate* (a spicy pasta with peppers) L6000. *Pizza del piccolo mondo* (salmon, capers, olives, and onions) is yummy at L9000. Other pizzas L5500-7500. Wine L8000 per . *Coperto* L1500. Open Tues.-Sun. noon-3pm and 6pm-midnight.

Pizzeria L'Arco, via C. Patricio, 28 (tel. 211 21), on the continuation of via Pirandello. The young clientele doesn't wait for the savory pastries to cool; a burned tongue is a small price to pay for such *buon gusto*. The *cipolline* is stuffed with mozzarella, prosciutto, tomatos, and onions (L2500). Take-out available. Open Tues.-Sun. 9am-2pm and 4:30pm-11pm.

U Lantirnaru, via Apollo Arcageta, 14 (tel. 245 65), at the end of corso Umberto. Watch the chickens spinning in their huge wood-burning oven. Half a big bird, a large plate of french fries, bread, and a beer or soda for L15,000. Plate of mixed roasted garden vegetables L3000. Open Mon. and Wed.-Sat. 9am-2pm, 5-11pm. Sun. 10:30am-2pm.

Odeon Bread Roll (tel. 245 01), on via Ingegnere, off corso Umberto, near the Odeon Romano. A quiet *paninoteca* with inexpensive, filling sandwiches. The speciality is the *parmigiana*, a sandwich of baked eggplant, prosciutto, egg, tomatoes, and cheese (L5000). Other *panini* start at L3500. Open Thurs.-Tues. 6pm-3am.

Sights

Goethe thought the 3rd-century **Greek Theater** in Taormina commanded one of the most beautiful views in the world; see if you would sell your soul for the vista. (Open daily 9am-1 hr. before sunset. Admission L2000, under 18 or over 60 free.)

A few blocks away at the end of corso Umberto is the **Roman Odeon,** a small theater now partly covered by the Church of Santa Caterina next door. At the other end of corso Umberto lies the 13th-century **duomo,** rebuilt during the Renaissance. ("It's open when the Monsignor wants it to be open.") The Gothic interior shelters paintings by Messinese artists and a fine alabaster statue of the Virgin. Crowning the rock pinnacle that towers above Taormina, the **castello** commands a perfect view.

The **public gardens** on via Croce provide a secluded spot for appreciating Taormina's marvelous scenery and the view of Etna. Each olive tree along the promenade bears the name of a Taorminian soldier killed in World War I.

Entertainment

In the summer, the city hosts **Taormina Arte,** an international festival of theater, music, and film (July-Sept.). Most performances are in the Greek Theater or in the public gardens. (Admission L7000-50,000. For information call 62 58 56 or visit the outdoor offices in p. Vittorio Emanuele.) Taormina is home to a number of overpriced, uneventful discotheques. The nightlife mostly concentrates in nearby Giardini-Naxos (see below). One worthwhile nightspot is **Tout Va,** via Pirandello, 70 (tel. 238 24), an open-air club with great views, although it's a tiring half-hour trek from town. (Cover with first drink L14,000. Open in summer daily 10pm-3:30am.) **Le Perroquet** (tel. 248 08), on via Roma and p. S. Domenico de Guzman, is a popular gay club. (Cover L15,000. Open daily July 15-Sept. 15.) At the end of May, Taormina welcomes the **Raduno del Costume e del Carretto Siciliano,** a traditional parade of vibrant costumes and horse-drawn carriages.

Near Taormina

Beachniks should descend to the **Isola Bella** in preparation for the evening *passeggiata*. This tiny island, a national nature preserve, is accessible by the funicular from via Pirandello in Taormina (every 15 min.; L1000, after 9pm L1500; last car up at 2am). Huge lines form for the return trip at "rush hour" from 5 to 7pm. (Some have been known to hitch the short distance.) Some of the nearby towns—**Castelmola** in particular—are also very pretty, and a short bus ride out of town.

Nearby **Giardini-Naxos** was the site of the first Greek colony in Sicily (725 BC). Recent excavations in the **archeological park** have revealed the outlines of the city walls, built with monstrous irregular blocks of solidified lava. (Open Mon.-Sat. 9am-1hr. before sunset, Sun. 9am-1pm. Free.) A long sandy beach, not entirely overrun by hotels, is the town's other attraction. Along via Roma you'll find affordable accommodations; many of the places are cheaper than the options available in Taormina. **Ristorante Fratelli Marano,** via Naxos, 181 (tel. 523 16), serves tasty *spaghetti alle melanzane* (with eggplant) for L4500, but the main attraction is their pizza (L3000-6500). (Open daily noon-3pm and 6pm-midnight.) SAIS buses leave from Taormina's bus terminal every 15 to 45 minutes (L1300, round-trip L2100).

Enna

Soaring above the poorest and only landlocked province in Sicily, inviolate Enna invites you to view the life of the island's interior. Ennans are prone to modesty and self-deprecation, and coastal Sicilians view them with a condescending eye, a combination which has made Enna Sicily's best-kept secret: a cool, animated city with numerous *pi-*

azze offering panoramas of the surrounding countryside. Ennans are quick to point out that theirs is a city of true tranquility, and the only capital without a mafia presence. They take their time and rarely fret: perched atop a mountain 948 meters above sea level, watching over the entire land, there is no need to worry.

Throughout its history, the town has been a popular military base, passing from the hands of its original Sikan inhabitants to Greek, Roman, Arab, Norman, Lombard, and Bourbon rule. The only vestiges of this past are a huge medieval castle, a Lombard tower, and a curiously remodeled 13th-century cathedral.

Orientation and Practical Information

Enna is known as the "navel of Sicily" as it is located in the center of the island. It is easily accessible by bus from Palermo or Catania; voyaging from the south requires transfers at either Caltanissetta (L3600) or Gela (Mon.-Sat. 5 per day, 1hr., L8700). Buses leave Catania from the train station (Mon.-Sat. 5 per day, 1hr. 15min., L8000) and Palermo from via P. Balsamo, 16 (2hr., L11,000). Train service from both cities is cheaper, but the train station is 5km from town; a bus runs to the terminal on viale Diaz (every 2hr., L1300). To get to the center of Enna from the bus depot, turn right onto viale Diaz in front of the station and then take another right onto corso Sicilia; walk until via Sant'Agata branches off to the right. This runs directly into **via Roma,** Enna's main strip, at p. Matteoti. This *via* then leads past p. Vittorio Emanuele and up to the **Castello di Lombardia** on the left, and down through the residential section of town to the right.

Tourist Office: AAPIT, via Roma, 413 (tel. 50 05 44 or 50 05 48). One of Sicily's best. Extremely informative and well-organized, with loads of brochures. Pick up the fine map of Enna with a very detailed map of the whole island on the obverse. Open Mon.-Fri. 8:30am-1:30pm and 3:30-6:30pm, Sat. 8:30am-1:30pm. **ASST,** p. Colajanni, 6 (tel. 261 19), to the left of the Albergo Sicilia. Open daily 8:30am-2pm and 4:30-7pm.

Post Office: via Volta, 1 (tel. 217 29). Open Mon.-Sat. 8am-2pm. **Postal Code:** 94100.

Telephones: SIP, p. Scelfo (tel. 240 34), in front of San Francesco. Open daily 8am-8pm. At other times, try **Albergo Sicilia,** p. Colajanni. **Telephone Code:** 0935.

Buses: SAIS, viale Diaz (tel. 50 09 02), outside the city center. Open daily 6am-9:30pm.

Emergencies: tel. 113. **Police:** tel. 112. **Hospital: Ospedale Umberto I,** tel. 452 45. **Guardia Medica:** tel. 454 89.

Accommodations and Food

The town's only hotel is the **Grande Albergo Sicilia** p. Colajanni, 5 (tel. 50 08 50), on via Roma behind the AAPIT sign. This modern building is posh and clean. (Singles with bath and breakfast L60,000. Doubles with bath L100,000. Triples L130,000.) If there are no vacancies at the hotel, take city bus #4 to the town of Pérgusa (every hr., L600), a lakeside retreat 7km from Enna. In Pérgusa, go to lakeside p. Scelfo and you will find both **La Pergola** (tel. 423 33), which charges L17,000 for singles with bath and L26,500 for doubles with bath, and **Miralago** (tel. 362 72), which offers bathless singles (L14,000) and doubles (L22,800). The city government manages seasonal campsites around Pérgusa (June-Sept. L8000 per person); inquire at the *Municipio* on Umberto.

Enna's most famous comestible is its *piacentino* cheese, sharp, spicy, and best sampled at the **market** on via Mercato Sant'Antonio, off via Roma at p. Umberto I. (Open Mon.-Sat. 6am-2pm.) **Centro Formaggi** at via Mercato Sant'Antonio, 33, is the other *formaggio* connection. Pick up the cheapest bread and circuses at **Max Market Romano,** behind the bus station. (Open Mon.-Fri. 8am-1:30pm and 4-8pm, Sat. 8am-8:30pm.) For a quick fix, try **Knulp,** via Restivo, 14, off via Roma, to the right a few blocks before you hit the *duomo.* What is Sicily's coolest bar-eatery doing in provincial Enna? Don't ask, just groove to James Brown and try the *Panino Funny Bread,* with strong gorgonzola cheese, prosciutto, and radicchio (L3000). Large beer runs L3500. (Open Tues.-Sun. 11am-2pm and 6pm-2am.)

Sights and Entertainment

Via Roma ascends through the old city, leading to the **cathedral.** Founded in 1307 and renovated in the 16th century, it has a slender Baroque facade. The polygonal transepts, the apses, and the south door remain from the original medieval structure. Bring a L100 coin for the excellent recording (in English, Italian, Lithuanian, or French) about the *duomo's* history and numerous artworks. (Erratic hours.) Behind the church, the small **Museo Alessi** displays the *duomo's* treasury and some Greek and Roman artifacts and medieval paintings. (Open Tues.-Sun. 9am-1pm and 4-7pm. Free.) The nearby **Museo Varisano,** on p. Mazzini across from the *duomo,* is magnificent. It houses temporary exhibits as well as an archeological collection with artifacts dating back 5000 years. (Open Mon.-Sat. 9am-1:30pm and 3:30-6:30pm, Sun. 9:30am-1pm and 3:30-6:30pm. Free.)

The **Castello di Lombardia,** constructed on a 5000-year-old foundation at the eastern end of town, was built by Frederick II to maintain control of the center of the island. Six of the original 20 towers remain. One of its three courtyards is now used as an open-air theater. The castle offers a thrilling view of the meteor-impressed Lago Pérgusa; myth has it that Hades abducted Demeter's daughter Persephone from its shores. Behind the castle, at the summit of the mountain, is Demeter's sacred ground, the **Rocca di Cerere,** imparting a view of the fertile fields below. (Castle open Tues.-Sun. 10am-12:30pm and 3:30-6:30pm. Free.)

The **Torre di Federico II,** an octagonal lookout with excellently preserved Gothic vaulting, rises 24m at the opposite edge of the city, surrounded by the city's public garden. (Garden open daily 9am-1pm and 4-8pm. Free.) A secret tunnel, still visible from the tower's third level, once connected the tower with the Castello di Lombardia. (Access to the tower only by permission from the gatekeeper, whose house is on the grounds of the public gardens. Tower under restoration in 1992.)

In July and August, Enna holds its **Estate Ennese,** a series of concerts and performances, including popular contemporary artists, in the theater at Castello di Lombardia. (Tickets run about L15,000; performances are suspended during *castello* restorations.) The **Autodromo di Pergusa** (tel. 256 60) hosts international Gran Premio car races from April through September. One of the largest festivals is the **Festa della Madonna,** held on July 2, marked by the incessant popping of firecrackers and the interminable eating of renowned *mastazzoli* (apple cookies). Parties also accompany the feasts of **Saint Anna** on the last Sunday in July and **Saint Valverde** on the last Sunday in August. Enna's most renowned festival, however, is its **Holy Week.** On Good Friday Ennans participate in a huge and very solemn procession. Different groups and religious orders don unique costumes, revealing the Spanish influence once quite strong in Sicily.

Near Enna

The golden Baroque buildings of **Piazza Armerina** rise gracefully on three knolls overlooking the Ennese countryside. Nearby is the **Villa Imperiale,** a Roman country house that preserves some of the ancient world's finest mosaics.

The villa lies 5.5km southwest of town. Officially known as the Villa Romana del Casale, it was probably a hunting lodge of Maximanius Heraclius, co-emperor with Diocletian under the Principate. The villa was built around 300 AD and was occupied until the Arab period. Sacked in 1160 and buried by a landslide soon after, it remained undiscovered until 1916. The **mosaics** are the largest and most intact of their kind in the world. In the Corridor of the Big Game Hunt, a varied landscape of hills, trees, rocks, and villas surrounds hunters pursuing their game while the hunted animals themselves chase smaller prey. In the Triclinium (the large banquet hall), a muscular Hercules stands amidst nudes of remarkable detail, and bikini-clad women play with beach balls. Unfortunately, there is no bus service to the villa, but vans periodically shuttle tourists to the site; some have been known to hitchhike. Otherwise, gear up for a long walk under the possibly scorching Sicilian sun. The best guide to the villa, *Piazza Armerina: Town of the Mosaics* by Ignazio Nigrelli, is available at the Enna tourist office.

(Villa open daily 9am-1 hr. before sunset. Admission L2000.) Also ask for information about some of the other nearby villas, such **Morgantina, Ardone,** and **Nicosia.**

Piazze filled with pine, eucalyptus, poplar, and cedar trees punctuate Piazza Armerina's narrow medieval streets. In the center is **piazza Garibaldi,** with several 18th-century buildings. The **duomo** (1627) at the summit of the town peers down with its imposing Baroque facade (17th-18th centuries) and a 15th-century Gothic-Sicilian belfry. Inside, the painted crucifix and the Madonna in the chapel to the left both date from the 15th century. Above the high altar, a baroque tabernacle contains a Byzantine icon of the *Madonna della Vittoria,* a gift of Pope Nicholas II. It is carried in procession during the **Feast of the Assumption** (August 15). The Feast of the Assumption is preceded on August 14 by the **Palio dei Normanni,** a costumed horse race commemorating the presentation of the key to the city to the Norman Count Roger III.

Piazza Armerina is a 45-minute bus ride from Enna (7 per day, 3 on Sundays and holidays; L3700). Buses also run directly to Palermo, Catania, and Syracuse. To reach Ragusa on the way east or south, take a bus to the petrochemical wasteland of Gela (several per day, 1hr., L2650; ask at least 3 bus drivers hanging out in p. Gen. Cascino to triangulate the correct times). From Gela, the best option is the train (3 per day, 2hr., L3750). Be sure to allow time to catch the last bus out, or you'll find yourself stranded.

City **tourist information** is at p. Garibaldi, 1 (tel. 68 02 01; open Mon. and Sat. 8:30am-1:30pm, Tues.-Fri. 8:30am-1:30pm and 5-7pm). The town has no inexpensive accommodations, but if you're stuck, try the **Park Hotel Paradiso** (tel. 857 00) or the **Selene** (tel. 802 54); each offers singles for L32,000 and doubles for L49,000, bath included. There is also a campground, **Campeggio La Ruola** (tel. 68 05 42), which features helpful owners, a restaurant with yummy food, and a souvenir shop. La Ruola sits at the turn-off to the villa 4km outside of the town (L4500 per person).

SARDINIA (SARDEGNA)

"Not a bit like the rest of Italy..." declared D.H. Lawrence, inspired by Sardinia's harsh, mountainous terrain and diffident rusticity. These persist in the untamed interior, but 20th-century concrete beehive condominiums and tourist amenities have long since cluttered the coast. In the major cities, people dress as elegantly, drive as recklessly, and profess the same passion for *gelato* as the "continentals." The Sardinians, however, retain their keen sense of honor and hospitality. Most proudly speak the native Sardo dialect, an orphan Romance language bearing little resemblance to Italian.

Nonetheless, an old Sardinian legend reveals a sense of inferiority: when God finished making the world, he had a handful of dirt left over, which he chucked into the Mediterranean and stepped on, thus creating Sardinia. Other curious landscaping phenomena took place over 3500 years ago; the island is dotted with nuraghi, intriguing monuments constructed around the 2nd millenium BC. Cone-shaped fortified tower-houses, they were built of huge blocks of stone without the aid of mortar. Over 7000 survive. The same civilization erected the 500 **Giants' Tombs** to house *en masse* the remains of its rich and famous.

The first historically recorded invaders of Sardinia were the seafaring Phoenicians and the Carthaginians. It was the methodical and business-minded Romans, however, who turned the island into an agricultural colony. Sardinia's history has been one of violent and almost constant struggle against foreign invaders, including the Pisans, the Aragonese (who took over Alghero and kicked out the inhabitants), and the cruel and oppressive Spanish who were finally overpowered in the 18th century. Even Napoleon tried (and failed) to take Sardinia in 1793 in an offensive launched from Corsica. Vittorio Emanuele, who became king of Italy in 1861, began his campaign from Sardinia (birthplace of the wildly popular Garibaldi, who played no small part in achieving unification) and made it part of the unified whole. Mussolini did much for the island and its transport networks, and is still fondly remembered. These days, twenty-four NATO bases "occupy" the island. Throughout the centuries of foreign influence, however, Sardinians have clung firmly to their traditions.

Well into this century, the economy of Sardinia still depended exclusively on agriculture. Only decades ago, *padroni* (landlords) still held the land and poor farmers toiled under a system akin to serfdom. Owing to the growing influence of the Italian Communist Party (both its founder, Antonio Gramsci, and its late Secretary General, Enrico Berlinguer, were Sards), much of the land is now owned by those who work it, although large sections of Sardinia's scenic coastline have fallen into the hands of foreign speculators. Industrialization and modernization have polarized Sardinian society, sidelining many who cling to traditional ways of life. Recently, tourism and industry have emerged as significant forces in Sardinia's existence. Still, despite a massive campaign launched on the continent to promote Sardinia as a vacation destination, many of the island's attractions remain virtually inaccessible without a car, and despite (or perhaps because of) the American military base on La Maddelena, few Sards care for Anglophones.

Getting There

The cheapest way to go is *posta ponte* (deck class) from Civitavécchia to Olbia (L16,900). Beware the summer tourist rush (late July and August) and the omnipresent possibility of strikes when planning your trip to Sardinia. If you plan on traveling at the height of the season, reserve two weeks prior to departure. Prices listed below are for *poltrone* (reserved reclining chairs). *Posto ponte* fares are often available only when all the *poltrone* are taken. **Tirrenia** operates the most ferries and offers the cheapest fares,

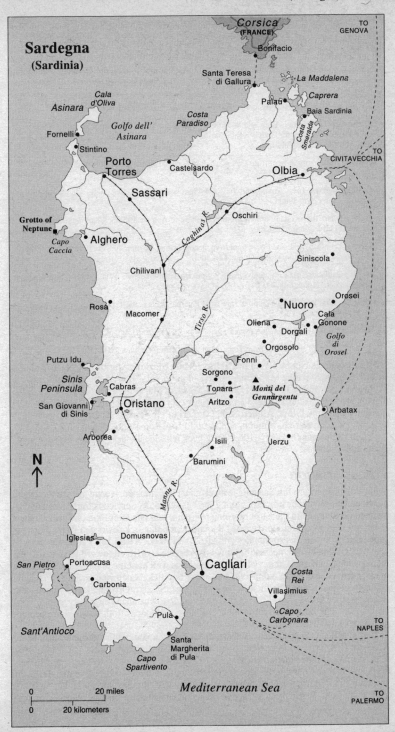

Sardegna
(Sardinia)

Corsica
(FRANCE)

TO
GENOVA

Bonifacio

Santa Teresa
di Gallura

La Maddalena

Asinara

Cala
d'Oliva

Golfo dell'
Asinara

Costa
Paradiso

Palau

Caprera

Baia Sardinia

Fornelli

Stintino

Costa
Smeralda

TO
CIVITAVECCHIA

Porto
Torres

Castelsardo

Olbia

Sassari

Grotto of
Neptune

Oschiri

Siniscola

Coghinas R.

Capo
Caccia

Alghero

Chilivani

Orosei

Rosà

Macomer

Tirso R.

Nuoro

Oliena

Cala
Gonone

Dorgali

Orgosolo

Golfo
di
Orosel

Putzu Idu

Fonni

Sinis
Peninsula

Cabras

Sorgono

San Giovanni
di Sinis

Oristano

Tonara

Aritzo

Monti del
Gennargentu

Arbatax

Arborea

Isili

Jerzu

N

Barumini

Mannu R.

Iglesias

Domusnovas

San Pietro

Portoscusa

Cagliari

Costa
Rei

Carbonia

Villasimius

Sant'Antioco

Pula

Capo
Carbonara

TO
NAPLES

Santa
Margherita
di Pula

Capo
Spartivento

Mediterranean Sea

TO
PALERMO

0   20 miles

0   20 kilometers

but long delays occasionally mar the service. Tirrenia is represented in the U.S. by **Extra Value Travel,** 683 S. Collier Blvd., Marco Island, FL 33937 (tel. (800) 255-2847, in FL (813) 394-3384).

Civitavécchia-Olbia: daily both ways at 11pm, July-Aug. also at 11am (7hr., L27,000). There is also a **Ferrovie dello Stato** connection to Golfo Aranci, near Olbia (4 per day, 8hr. 30min., L15,400), a better choice if you've got a car.

Civitavécchia-Cagliari: daily at 8:30pm from Civitavécchia and Cagliari (13hr., L47,700).

Civitavécchia-Arbatax: Tues. and Fri. from Civitavécchia at 8:30 and 10pm; in winter 8:30pm only. Departs Arbatax for Civitavécchia Sun. and Thurs. 10pm and midnight; in winter midnight only. (8hr. 30min., L36,400.)

Genoa-Olbia: daily at 6pm from Genoa, Aug. at 5 and 11:45pm. Daily at 8:30pm from Olbia, Aug. 8:15am and 8:30pm. (13hr., L57,400.)

Genoa-Cagliari: Tues., Thurs., and Sun. at 4:45pm from Genoa. Mon., Wed., and Sat. at 3pm from Cagliari (20hr. 30min., L77,200).

Genoa-Porto Torres: daily at 8pm from both cities, in Aug. at 8:15am, 10am, 5pm, 7pm, and midnight (12hr. 30min., L50,500).

Genoa-Arbatax: Mon. and Fri. at 6pm from Genoa, in Aug. at 7pm. Tues. and Sat. at 2pm from Arbatax, in Aug. at 4pm. (19hr. 30min., L53,500.)

Naples-Cagliari: Tues., Fri., and Sun. at 5:30pm from Naples. Mon., Wed., and Sat. at 6:30pm from Cagliari. (16hr., L48,400.)

Palermo-Cagliari: Fri. and Sun. at 7pm from Palermo. Thurs. and Fri. at 7pm from Cagliari. (13hr., L44,300.)

Trápani-Cagliari: Tues. at 9pm from Trápani. Mon. at 7pm from Cagliari. (11hr., L34,500.)

Tunis-Cagliari: Tues. at 8pm from Tunis. Mon. at 7pm from Cagliari. (21hr., L100,400.)

Tirrenia offices can be found in **Civitavécchia,** Stazione Marittima (tel. (0766) 288 01 23); **Genoa,** Stazione Marittima, Ponte Colombo (tel. (010) 25 80 41); **Palermo,** via Roma, 385 (tel. (091) 33 33 00); **Livorno,** Agenzia Marittima Carlo Laviosa, via Scali d'Azeglio, 6 (tel. (0586) 89 06 32); and **Rome,** via Bissolati, 41 (tel. (06) 474 20 43).

Flights also link Olbia, Alghero, and Cagliari to most major Italian cities, as well as to Paris, Geneva, Zurich, Munich, and Frankfurt. A Rome-Olbia flight runs L131,500, but night flights are cheaper (L106,000). Check with local tourist offices for schedules, fares, and discounts.

Transportation

Public transportation in Sardinia is an efficient and inexpensive way to see the island provided you plan your itinerary around the bus schedule. Service is fairly frequent but tends to concentrate in the early morning (6-10am) and late afternoon (4-7pm). Try not to get stuck in the middle or (worse) the end of the day in a town you're ready to escape. The two main bus companies are ARST and PANI. **ARST** links almost every village on the island to the nearest big town. Its service is oriented toward local residents; the bus stops on request at any cluster of houses as well as at the planned stops. Service is inexpensive and fairly extensive. You must buy tickets before boarding. **PANI,** by contrast, connects only the major cities—Cagliari, Sássari, Oristano, and Núoro—and although some buses stop at one or two intervening towns, many stop only at their final destination. The buses are comfortable and air-conditioned. Both services are prompt and stick close to schedule.

Tourist office officials shake their heads sadly when you inquire about **Italian State Railway (FS)** train service. Ask about the other Sardinian railways (FCS and SFS, which connect some smaller towns) and they laugh. Suffice it to say that trains in Sardinia are slow and unreliable at best, though significantly less expensive than buses. If you aren't in a hurry, they can provide pleasant vistas of the countryside that highway travel sacrifices. Particularly attractive is the Sássari-Alghero line, which runs through greenery and mountainous areas (while the bus takes you through dry scrub). Bus and train passage are rigorously controlled in Sardinia; hang on to your ticket.

The easiest way to cover the smaller, less touristed areas of Sardinia is by renting a **car.** The best deals will be found in larger cities. **Mopeds** are another option, running about L50,000 per day; finding rental outlets, however, is a challenge. **Bikes** seem an enticing option, but unless you have the leg muscles of an Olympian, Sardinia's mountainous terrain will reduce you to a hiker with a two-wheeled backpack. Anyone traveling alone should think twice about bicycling in some of the less populated inland areas south of Nuòro, and women are especially cautioned. Though *Let's Go* does not recommend hitchhiking, many find it a reasonable option. **Thumbing in Sardinia can be highly dangerous, especially for women—even when traveling in pairs.**

Accommodations and Food

Virtually all growth in Sardinia's rapidly expanding vacation industry has been in the luxury sector. Most cities lack an adequate selection of moderately priced accommodations. Consult the local tourist office, and ask for the semi-reliable and comprehensive *Annuario Alberghi,* which lists prices for all hotels, *pensioni,* and official campsites on the island. You can usually find a decent single in town for about L30,000, but during peak season single travelers will probably have to scrounge for roommates. Beware of hotel managers who quote low prices and, when it comes time to pay, point innocently to a higher figure posted on the room door. Try to get something in writing, or ask outright why the posted price is higher. Rooms are scarce in August. The two **youth hostels** (in Alghero and Porto Torres) provide an inexpensive but unreliable alternative, as they often fill up or shut down unexpectedly. Both lie near the beach and have crowded but airy rooms. If you have a car or motorcycle, consider camping. Campsites tend to boast magnificent locations right on the water, often with Roman ruins scattered about. **Camping** outside official campsites is illegal, but discreetly practiced nonetheless. **Agriturismo** is an excellent alternative to *pensioni;* tourists live on farms in the countryside and eat dinners with their host families (bed and breakfast approximately L25,000, half-pension L37,000, full pension L50,000). Ask the tourist office for a list of participating farms in the area or write ahead to: **Agriturismo di Sardegna,** Cooperativa Allevatrici Sarde 09170, Oristano, Caselle Postale 107.

Sardinia's cuisine, like its terrain, is rustic and rugged. Sards serve up hearty dishes like *sa fregula* (pasta in broth with saffron—a spice rarely used on the mainland), *malloreddus* (dumplings with saffron), or *culurgiones* (ravioli stuffed with cheese and beetroots, covered with tomato sauce, lamb, and sausage). The most celebrated dishes are a vegetarian's nightmare: grilled pigs or goats, *cordula* (lamb entrails), and pork cooked in lamb's stomach. Fish and shellfish (even on pizza) abound on the island and are bound to titillate your tongue in a novel way. Unfortunately, it's hard to find these typically Sardinian dishes except in expensive restaurants. Still, don't leave the island without sampling such distinctive local specialties as *pane frattau,* a thin bread covered with eggs, cheese, and tomato sauce, and *sebada,* a delicious dough stuffed with cheese, sugar, and honey. For the cheapest meals, eat at *pizzerie, rosticcerie,* or *tavole calde,* or prepare your own meals (most hostels have facilities). Look for daily outdoor markets in older neighborhoods, where you can get fresh bread and fruit, goat and sheep cheese, and then go tend your own flock for the completely authentic experience. Sardinia's wines, often sweet and strong, reward a swig or two. Try *vernaccia d'Oristano* (with a heady almond aftertaste) with fish, or the robust *cannonau di Sardegna* with meat.

Cagliari

Cagliari earns the superlatives among Sardinian cities; it is the island's capital, its largest metropolis, the chief and most agreeable port, and one of the best destinations on the island. The city yields such improbable and delightful surprises as Roman ruins, Spanish churches, medieval citadels, exquisite beaches, and a large pink flamingo population. Founded and raised to prosperity under the Carthaginians, Cagliari passed through the hands of numerous conquerors, Romans, Spaniards, and Pisans among them. The city's present disposition, however, seems more influenced by the sun and pleasant climate than by its sanguinary history. From Cagliari, you can make daytrips to the nuraghic ruins near Barumini, the Phoenician-Roman city of Nora, and the Costa del Sud beaches.

Orientation and Practical Information

Via **Roma** (where the PANI bus drops you) hugs the harbor, framed on one side by p. Matteotti, which houses the tourist office and town hall (the train and ARST stations are nearby). On the other flank are p. Deffenu, the PANI station, and the Tirrenia docks. The city sweeps upwards onto a steep and unforgiving hill crowned by the **castello**, which commands a fantastic view of the city and sea. The summit is also the historic center of town, where churches, ruins, narrow streets, and towers contrast sharply with the mobile meat market of Cagliari youth cruising via Garibaldi to shop, scope, and flirt.

Azienda di Turismo, p. Matteotti (tel. 66 92 55 or 66 49 23), in the park/garden in the weirdly-shaped cubicle. Wonderfully helpful and pleasant. Free maps, detailed picture pamphlets, etc. Open Mon.-Sat. 8am-2pm.

Budget Travel: CTS, via Cesare Balbo, 4 (tel. 48 82 60). Information on discounts and travel packages for students. Sells HI cards. Open Mon.-Fri. 9am-1:30pm and 4-7:30pm, Sat. 9am-1:30pm. **Associazione Italiana Studenti Sardi: Memo Travel,** via Pitzolo, 1/A (tel. 40 09 07). General travel information, English-speaking staff. Open Mon.-Fri. 9am-1pm and 4:30-8pm, Sat. 9am-1pm. To get to either agency, take the M-bus going east on via Roma, and get off at via Bacaredda, near p. Garibaldi. Via Balbo is immediately off via Bacaredda; follow it until it becomes via Tola, and via Pitzolo will be on your right. If you hit via Dante Alighieri, you've gone too far.

Currency Exchange: (tel. 65 62 93), in the train station at the information desk. Open Mon.-Sat. 7am-10pm.

Post Office: p. del Carmine near p. Matteotti (tel. 66 83 56). Fermo Posta L250 per letter. Open Mon.-Sat. 8am-4:40pm, but some services close at 1pm. **Postal Code: 09100.**

Telephones: ASST, via Angioy, off p. Matteotti. An efficient but expensive office. Open 24 hrs. for international calls. **SIP,** via Cima, 9, off via Manno. Open daily 8am-9:30pm. **Telephone Code:** 070.

Airport: in the village of **Elmas** (tel. 24 01 11, 24 00 46, or 24 01 69). Free ARST buses for ticketholders run between the airport and the city terminal at p. Matteotti (20min.) before each flight.

Trains: Ferrovie dello Stato (tel. 65 62 93), p. Matteotti. In summer, 9 trains per day to: Olbia (L18,200), Porto Torres (L19,500), Sássari (L18,700), and Oristano (L6300). **Ferrovie Complimentaríe della Sardegna** (tel. 49 13 04), p. della Repubblica. A private railroad.

Buses: PANI, p. Darsena, 4 (tel. 65 23 26). Nonstop service to Sássari at 7am and 2:15pm (L26,000). Open Mon.-Sat. 9am-2pm and 5-7pm, Sun. 1-2pm and 5:15-6:15pm. **ARST,** p. Matteotti, 6 (tel. 65 72 36), serves local towns (see above for more info). Office open 5am-10pm.

Ferries: Tirrenia, via Campidano, 1 (tel. 66 60 65), at the end of the via Roma arcade. Service to Genoa (L77,200), Civitavécchia (L47,700), Palermo (L44,300), and Tunis (via Trápani, L100,400). Open Mon.-Fri. 9am-1pm and 4-7pm. The new office in Stazione Marittima in the port opens 1hr. before ships depart.

Car Rental: Ruvioli, via dei Mille, 11 (tel. 65 89 55). Minimum age 18. Credit card recommended. Open Mon.-Sat. 8:30am-1pm and 3:30-8pm.

Laundry: Lavanderia a Gettone, via Concezione, 3/A. Open Mon.-Fri. L3000 per kg. Open 8:30am-1pm and 3:30-7:30pm.

English Bookstore: La Bancarella, via Roma, 169. Classics and a complete selection of romance novels (sigh). Open Mon.-Fri. 9am-1pm and 4:30-8pm, Sat. 9am-1pm.

Pharmacy: Farmacia Dr. Spano, via Roma, 99 (tel. 65 56 83). Gives out a free booklet with helpful phrases concerning illness (in 4 languages). Open Mon.-Sat. 9am-1pm, and 4:30-10:10pm.

Emergencies: tel. 113. **Police: Questura,** via Amat, 9 (tel. 602 71). **Hospital:** military hospital on via Ospedale, 46 (tel. 66 57 55), by the Chiesa di San Michele. Near the beach Il Poetto, try **Ospedale Marino,** viale Poetto, 12 (tel. 37 36 73). **First Aid:** tel. 267.

Accommodations

Cagliari has an ample stock of inexpensive pads, but there is fierce competition year-round: university students from September until mid-July, tourists from July to mid-September. Ask the tourist office in p. Matteotti for help. Check the curfew if you are staying at a small *allogio,* or put on a trustworthy face and ask for a key to the front door.

Albergo Firenze, corso Vittorio Emanuele, 50 (tel. 65 36 18), on the 5th floor. Motor City Fred is gone, but current proprietress is sweet as can be. Singles L20,000. Doubles L26,000.

Albergo Centrale, via Sardegna, 4 (tel. 65 47 83), by La Perla. Certainly central, a decent place with an aquarium (budget seafood?). Singles L25,000, with bath L28,000. Doubles L39,000, with bath L45,000.

Allogio Londra, viale Regina Margherita, 16 (tel. 66 90 83), right next to the PANI station. The huge, chipping wooden doors, high ceilings, and lace curtains house comfortable rooms. Singles L25,000, with bath L30,000. Doubles L38,000, with bath L45,000.

Flora, via Sassari, 45 (tel. 65 82 19), around the corner from the post office. Ignore the tacky panelling and lack of natural light—this place is a bargain. Singles L27,000, doubles L42,000.

Locanda La Perla, via Sardegna, 18B (tel. 66 94 46), on the 1st road parallel to via Roma, near p. Matteotti. A big black-and-white pictographic sign welcomes you to this clean and friendly pearl in the oyster of Cagliari. Midnight curfew. Singles L34,000. Doubles L44,000. Showers L2000.

Locanda Las Palmas, via Sardegna, 14 (tel. 65 16 79), next to La Perla. Good location and adequate rooms. Microscopic singles L33,000. Doubles L39,000. Showers L2500.

Pensione Vittoria, via Roma, 75 (tel. 65 79 70) on the 3rd floor, next to the movie theater. A small, elegant *pensione* with cavernous, majestic rooms, inlaid mosaic floors, beautiful furnishings, and views of the sea. Singles L35,000, with bath L41,000. Doubles L54,000, with bath L70,000.

Food

For inexpensive food, go to via dei Mille (off via Roma), where several *pizzerie* and *trattorie* serve delicious meals amidst the squalor. Via Sardegna and via Cavour, the first two streets parallel to via Roma, offer a more refined fare and setting for an additional few thousand lire. For basic picnic fare, try **La Marina,** via Sicilia, 13, a small but well-stocked market with a deli section. (Open Mon.-Fri. 8am-1pm and 4:30-8:30pm, Sat. 8am-1pm.)

Da Bruno, via Cavour, 17 (tel. 653 54). True Sardinian cuisine in a warm, hospitable atmosphere. Try the *malloreddus alla Campidanese* (traditional cornflour dumplings with saffron and *peccorino* cheese, L7000) and the *porchetto sardo* (roast pork with Sardinian seasoning, L12,000). Open Tues.-Sun. L12:30-2:30pm and 7:30-11pm. Credit cards accepted.

Trattoria Ci Pensa Cannas, via Sardegna, 37 (tel. 66 78 15). A mainstay on the "Sardegna strip." Mounds to munch at moderate prices. Try the *gnochetti Sardi Campidonese* (potato dumplings with *peccorino* cheese, L5000) or the full *menù* for L15,000. Cover L1500. Open daily 11:30am-3pm and 7-11pm.

Basilio, via Satta, 112 (tel. 48 03 30), tucked away on a side street. From p. Deffenu, go uphill on via XX Settembre, continue on via Sonnino, and turn right 3 blocks later on via Grazia Deledda—via Satta is on the left. Largely Italian crowd. Complete dinners L18,000. Cover L2000. Open Mon.-Sat. noon-2:45pm and 8-11pm. Credit cards accepted.

Trattoria Gennargentu, via Sardegna, 60 (tel. 65 82 47). Heaping plates of lasagne and *gnocchetti sardi,* tasty shish kebab, and sublime squid—this place has it all, plus a cozy atmosphere, warming house wines, and reasonable prices. Open Mon.-Sat. noon-3pm and 7-11pm. Credit cards accepted.

La Cantina, via dei Mille, 3 (tel. 66 64 30). A cavernous interior with fast-food offerings and prices. Stuff yourself for less than L4000. Open Mon.-Sat. 9am-3pm and 5-10:30pm.

Trattoria da Serafino, via Sardegna, 109. Not the most cordial environment, but large and luscious portions in a modest yet elegant setting. Low cost (courses L4000-7000).

Beverly Fast Food, via Garibaldi, 1. Hamburgers, hot dogs, pizza, ice cream at Micky D prices. Open Mon.-Sat. 8am-8pm.

Sights

The conspicuous pink towers of the **Bastione di San Remy** mark the division between the modern port and the cramped medieval quarter on the hill above. Climb the stairway to the terrace for a spectacular view of the Golfo degli Angeli, the marshes to the west, and the "Devil's Saddle," a rock formation set amidst the mountains surrounding Cagliari. Up the slender steps behind the *bastione* lies medieval Cagliari, where wrought-iron balconies overflow with flowers. Narrow streets lead uphill to the **duomo,** a charming exemplar of Pisan geometry refinished in 1933 by Giarrizzo in the Romanesque style of the Pisa cathedral. The pulpits at the entrance, depicting scenes from the New Testament, are the work of Guglielmo Pisano, as are the four wrestling lions at the base of the 12th-century altar. Before leaving, glance below at the sanctuary carved into the island rock in 1618. The colorful marble inlays with animated miniatures of Sardinian saints cover the 292 niches containing the relics of early Christian martyrs.

The age-blackened **Torre di San Pancrazio** (1305) is up the hill on p. Indipendenza, and its mate, **Torre dell'Elefante** (1307), lies below on via Università. Keep in mind that these former bulwarks and prison towers were erected without the help of the cranes currently being used to restore them. The towers shade the **Museo Nazionale Archeologico,** a repository of grave artifacts from the earliest period of Sardinian history. Prehistoric figurines stand beside elegant Greek statues, and the curves of Roman vases reflect sparkling Phoenician jewelery. Most impressive are the broad-shouldered warriors and pot-bellied gods crafted in bronzed stone by the people of the mysterious nuraghic civilization. (Open Tues.-Sat. 9am-2pm and 3:30-6:30pm, Sun. 9am-1pm and 2-5pm. Admission L4000.)

Pass under the Torre di San Pancrazio to the **Arsenale,** from whose lofty towers you can admire the model-like cityscape. There you will find the **Cittadella dei Musei,** a modern complex of research museums that houses Oriental art. Stroll down a curving lane to the public gardens at the end of viale R. Elena. To the left of the **museo civico** is a contemporary Sardinian gallery of painting and sculpture. (Open Tues.-Sat. 9am-1pm and 4-7pm. Free.) To the left of viale Buon Cammino is the **Roman amphitheater,** the most significant Roman ruin in Sardinia. It was constructed in the 2nd century from a natural depression in the rock. Continue down via San Ignazio da Laconi to the university **botanical gardens** with over 500 species of plants. (Open Tues.-Sun. 8:30am-1:30pm; admission L1000, children L500.)

A small pagan temple from the Roman era was incorporated into the **Church of San Saturno** in 470 AD. The oldest church on the island, it was built in the shape of a Greek cross with a dome to designate the site where Saturnus was martyred during the reign of Diocletian. The church now stands closed and forlorn in an empty lot in p. San Cosimo off via Dante near the cemetery.

Entertainment

A **flea market** fires up on Sunday mornings at the **Bastione di San Remy** (Terrazza Umberto). Comb through used clothes, toys, and assorted junk to the thumping beat of reggae and rap. Also on Sundays, explore the **food market** on the far side of the stadium in borgo Sant'Elia. Stroll and bargain for fresh sea creatures or fresh fruit in the huge local gathering.

During the first four days of May, Sardinians flock to Cagliari for the stupendous **Festival of Sant'Efisio,** faithfully honoring a vow made 300 years ago to the deserter from Diocletian's army who saved the island from the plague. A costumed procession escorts his effigy from the capital down the coast to the small church that bears his name.

From July to September, the city hosts an **arts festival.** The amphitheater rejuvenates with classic plays, and outdoor movies are shown at the Marina Piccola, off Spiaggia del Poetto (take Bus P). Get a schedule from the Azienda. Bus P runs every 20 minutes from p. Matteotti to the **beach,** packed sardine-tight with locals. Stay on the bus for five to 10 minutes to reach less crowded areas (L1200).

Near Cagliari

Partially submerged, **Nora,** said to be the oldest city in Sardinia, was settled by the Phoenicians (circa 850 BC), who coveted its strategic position at the end of a high, narrow peninsula. The town prospered, becoming in time a Roman stronghold. Its luck faltered, however, with the onslaught of pirate raids, and by the 8th century, Nora was abandoned completely. The site intrigues with motley ruins—from Phoenician temples to a 16th-century Spanish watchtower—and with its rugged location, strong winds whipping across the ancient walls. (Open daily 9am-8pm; off-season 9am-12:30pm and 2-5pm. Admission L3000, children over 10 L1500, 10 and under free.) Nearby is a pleasant beach. ARST buses make a run to Pula every hour (30min., L3300). From Pula, it's a 4km walk to Nora; follow corso Emanuele, turn left when it ends, and follow the signs.

Continue beyond Pula to the unspoiled **Costa del Sud,** which originates about 50km southwest of Cagliari. A small road follows the shore, with paths branching down to the coves. No industry exists here to taint the lucid azure water, no campground to clutter the windswept shore. Eight ARST buses per day run to Chia (1hr., L5500), on the Costa del Sud's eastern edge, and a few continue on to **Teulada** (1hr. 30min., L7000), an inland town only 8km from the more deserted western end.

Originally set on the coast, over a period of centuries Teulada gradually moved inland as its inhabitants sought refuge from seaborne invasions. This isolation has facilitated the preservation of mores that are only memories elsewhere in Sardinia. Although it seems an excellent base for excursions to the Costa del Sud, Teulada has very few hotels. Desperation may lead you to **Hotel Sebera** (tel. 927 08 76), off p. Garibaldi where the bus stops, which boasts clean, private baths and TVs in the rooms (singles from L55,000, doubles with pension L80,000).

The tiny village of **Uta** (20km west of Cagliari) shelters the **Church of Santa Maria,** one of the island's most notable Romanesque buildings. Built around 1140, the church is a deft fusion of French and Pisan architectural styles. Eleven ARST buses per day depart for Uta (40min., L2500).

Barúmini, an agricultural bastion in the rolling countryside 60km north of Cagliari, lies 1km west of the **Nuraghi of Su Nuraxi.** (Open daily 8am-dusk.) These ruins are the best-preserved complex of nuraghi in Sardinia. Set atop a hill, the village is constructed of huge, rough-hewn blocks in an intricate layout, vividly illustrating the defensive nature of this civilization. The only direct service from Cagliari to Barúmini is the daily ARST run at 2:10pm (1hr. 30min., L7000). To return, take the FCS bus at 6:30pm (L3200) to San Luri. Once in San Luri, go to the FS train station to catch the commuter train to Cagliari at 7:10pm (L4200).

C.S. Elia and **Il Poetto** (4km and 6km southeast of the city, respectively) are grand sandy beaches. The latter stretches 10km from the mountainous Sella del Diavolo (Devil's Saddle) to the Margine Rosso (Red Bluff); behind it are the salt-water **Stagno di Molentargius** (Ponds of Molentargius), a popular flamingo hangout. This place was once extraordinary, but now as half of Cagliari flocks in every Sunday it's getting increasingly grubby. City bus P leaves from via Roma (20min., 1200, ticket must be bought beforehand at a newsstand).

Núoro and Its Province

Invasions and foreign domination have defined the political history of coastal Sardinia; older Sardinian culture was forced to retreat inland. If true *Sardi* exist today, they must live in Núoro, where the jagged terrain of Sardinia's interior has sculpted a diffident *campagnola* (rural) mentality in its inhabitants. Proud peasant women, dressed in magpie black, drape Spanish *fazzolletti* (shawls) over their shoulders and murmur in a dialect studied by academics worldwide for its similarity to Latin, while their children sport Levi's and cruise the streets on mopeds. A car is ideal for visits to the Núoro province's smaller villages, as much of the region is inaccessible by public transport and is less well-adapted to tourism than Sardinia's larger cities.

Núoro

Practical Information

From the station, follow via Lamarmora to **piazza della Grazie.** From there corso Garibaldi then leads to piazza Vittorio Emanuele II, the ARST station, the *duomo,* and the main shopping area on via Manzoni. Behind you and up the hill along via IV Novembre you'll find the piazza d'Italia, the tourist office, and the PANI station. To the right of the **Chiesa della Grazie** lie the privately run train station and a residential area.

Tourist Office: p. Italia, 9 (tel. 300 83). Armed with an array of booklets and brochures, the staff is eager to evoke Núoro's past. English spoken. Usually open Mon.-Fri. 9am-1pm and 4-7pm.

Post Office: p. Crispi, 8 (tel. 302 78), off via Dante. Open Mon.-Sat. 8am-7:40pm. **Postal Code:** 08100.

Telephones: SIP, via Brigata Sassari, 6, at p. Italia 1 block from the tourist office. Open Mon.-Sat. 8:30am-12:30pm and 3-7pm, Sun. 8am-1pm. **Telephone Code:** 0784.

Trains and Buses (PANI): Station located at the corner of via Lamarmora and (appropriately) via Stazione. At piazza Emanuele (2 blocks from the *duomo*), is a center of youth activity and also the local **ARST** station where you can catch a bus to the train/PANI station. Daily service to: Cala Gonzone (L4500); Dorgali (L3500); Oliena (L1500); Orgósolo (L2500); Cagliari (L18,500); and Monte Ortobene (L1200). Trains unreliable. Tickets for PANI available at Tobacco/Bar attached to the Lamarmora station.

Car Rental: Autonoleggio Maggiore, via Convento, 32 (tel. 304 61). Open Mon.-Sat. 8am-1pm and 4-7pm.

Emergencies: tel. 113. **Ambulance/Medical Emergency:** tel. 363 02. Volunteer ambulance service only.

Accommodations and Food

Inexpensive establishments are few and far between in Núoro, and the campgrounds are miles away.

Il Portico, via Mons. Bua (tel. 375 35), near the end of p. Vittorio Emanuele. Lovely, clean rooms with private showers and baths. Pleasant management runs great restaurant below. Singles L35,000. Doubles L50,000. Reserve ahead.

Mini Hotel, via Brofferio, 13 (tel. 331 59), off via Roma. Overlooks an enormous construction site. Homey, clean, and noisy, with an effusive staff. All rooms with baths. Singles L45,000. Doubles L65,000.

Hotel Grillo, via Mons. Melas, 14 (tel. 386 78), off via Manzoni. Reisdential neighborhood away from center, across from the judo school. Baths in every room, and full of fine touches. Singles L60,000. Doubles L80,000.

Cheap restaurants are scarce. Try the well-hidden but very friendly **supermarket** on via Manzoni, next to the Alitalia office. (Open Mon.-Fri. 8am-1pm and 4-7:30pm, Sat. 8am-1pm.) For fresh fruit, cheese, and meat, explore the enclosed **market** at p. Mameli, 20, also off via Manzoni. (Open Mon.-Tues. and Thurs.-Sat. 8am-1pm and 4:30-7pm, Wed. 8am-1pm.)

Pizzeria Del Diavolo, via Dante, 10, near the post office. A variety of sinfully good pizzas (cheese L1800, mushroom L2300). Come see black-garbed locals munch take-out. Open Mon.-Sat. 8:30am-1pm and 5-10pm.

Bar Loriga, p. Vittorio Emanuele, 41. *Panini imbottiti* (stuffed rolls) from L1800. Open Mon.-Sat. 7:30am-2pm and 4-11pm.

Il Portico, via M. Bua (tel. 331 59), off the north end of p. Vittorio Emanuele. Connected to the hotel, this restaurant serves delicious, elegant meals to locals. Try their *risotto alla pescatora* (rice in a creamy fish sauce, L8000) and the *fritto di calamari* (fried squid, L15,000). Start with *salsiccia sarda e olive,* a well-known hard Sardinian salami (L6000). Pizzas L5500-7000. Cover L2000. Open Tues.-Sun. noon-2:30pm and 7-11pm.

Sights and Seasonal Events

Despite Núoro's provincial appearance, there are a few small treasures to be found. As you walk in the streets above p. Mazzini, keep your eyes open for stark leftist **murals,** similar to those at Orgósolo. The surreal **piazza Sebastiano Satta,** named for the local poet, lies off via Roma. Alcoves cut into twisted pillars of rock cradle statuettes that tell his story. The recently renovated *duomo* in p. Santa Maria della Neve merits a look. The major attraction in town is the **Museo della Vita e delle Tradizioni Popolari Sarde** (Museum of Sardinian Life and Popular Traditions), via Mereu, 56. Follow the signs up from the cathedral. The museum has masks, traditional costumes, and various artifacts recalling the pastoral past of Núoro's inhabitants. One of the better known masks is the farmer's mask and costume replete with sheep fur, cowbells, and a grimace worn during primitive Sardinian festivals. (Open Tues.-Sat. 9am-1pm and 3-7pm, Sun. 9am-1pm. Free.) Núoro celebrates one such festival—the **Sagra del Rendetore,** on the last two Sundays of August. Núoro's natives claim that while in other parts of Sardinia such rites exist to placate tourists, here they are "proprio sentiti" (truly felt).

Núoro also provides housing to the **Museo Regionale del Costume,** viale San Francesco, with exhibits of more traditional clothing, and the **Museo Civico Speleo,** an archeological museum of items found in the Nuraghic province. The latter is a great way to learn about the region's geography. (Both open Tues. and Thurs. 9am-1pm and 3-7pm, Wed., Fri., and Sun. 9am-1pm. Free.) The **Casa di Grazia Deledda** has been preserved as a museum exhibiting the personal effects of the 1926 Nobel Prize winner in literature. (Open daily 9am-1pm. Free.) Sardinians are very proud of their writer; myriad *vie* and *piazze* are named in her honor.

The Province

For a picnic, take the orange APT bus from p. Vittorio Emanuele up to **Monte Ortobene** (3 per day, 10min., L1200). At the peak lies a shady park from which a large bronze statue of Christ the Redeemer overlooks the neighboring hamlets. From the bus stop on top of Monte Ortobene, walk 20m down the road to get a good view of colossal **Monte Corrasi,** dwarfing the town of **Oliena** below.

If the view intrigues you, hop on a bus and check out Oliena up close (30min., L1500). In this undeveloped heartland village the black-clad women attend mass daily while old men cluster in the *piazze* and discuss the weather and their wives' cooking. There are several churches in Oliena; modestly beautiful **Santa Croce** on via Grazia Deledda, begun in 1580, is still largely intact and well worth a visit. The stone exterior is surrounded by flowers, and the interior contains an ancient wooden tabernacle with an eerily life-like wooden sculpture of Christ's body in a coffin (used during the rites of Saints' Week). Ask the **Pro Loco** (tourist office; tel. (0784) 28 87 77) for the keys to visit; to reach the office continue straight on via Vittorio Emanuele II (after the bus drops you off at the little white chapel) and take the large stairway to your left. The office is in the middle of a flight of stairs on your right. No maps of the city exist, but they can give you directions. (Open daily 9am-1pm and 3:30-7:30pm.)

Ci Kappa, on via Martin Luther King (tel. (0784) 28 87 33) is a famous bar, restaurant, and hotel, with a lovely view onto corso Vittorio Emanuele II and the mountain. The rooms are modern and comfortable, and all have private baths. (Singles L48,000;

doubles L65,000.) Another acclaimed hotel/restaurant in the area is **Su Gologone** (tel. (0784) 28 75 12), advertised throughout Sardinia for its "traditional" cuisine and snazzy accommodations with horseback riding, pool, bars, and disco. The only hitches are the price (of course) and the fact that it rests 8km outside of Oliena toward Dorgali. Singles are L76,500 and doubles are L95,000; while a complete meal will run you upwards of L45,000. **Carrus,** via N. Bixio, 11 (tel. (0784) 28 90 66) is an Agriturismo farm. Bed and breakfast are L25,000 if you stay one night, and drop to L20,000 per night for extended stays.

Venturing past Oliena is problematic since the scarcity of public transportation limits exploration of the hill towns south of Núoro. **ARST** buses run round-trip at ungodly hours. One remote town easily accessible from Núoro is **Orgósolo,** a pleasant 40-minute ride (L2400) through rolling, ochre-colored countryside punctuated by vineyards. The area's bloody history of *banditismo* (banditry) was made famous throughout Italy by the 1963 film *The Bandits of Orgósolo.* Check out Orgósolo's colorful 1960s **murals,** a series of leftist and nationalist paintings covering walls on **corso Repubblica,** the town's main street. A local teacher initiated the paintings after studying art in Latin America. Check out the ironic location of a mural decrying American imperialism—on via John Kennedy. In **piazza Caduti in Guerra,** a spring trickles from a water-gouged rock, a memorial to the town's war dead. Across the street, a mural depicts an old man resting, decorated with a war medal. A Brechtian inscription reads, "Happy are the people who have no need of heroes."

If you desire repose and an evening in town, stay at **Hotel Sa'e Jana,** via Lusu (tel. (0784) 40 24 37), near the elementary school, a family-run hotel with large rooms, balconies, private baths, and a rustic atmosphere. Ask the proprietor about his tri-weekly "peasant" feasts accompanied by traditional Sardinian folksongs. (Singles L55,000; doubles L70,000.) Closer to the center of town lies the **Petit Hotel,** via Mannu, 9 (tel (0784) 40 20 09), off corso Repubblica, offering comfortable rooms and prices (singles L20,000, with bath L25,000; doubles L32,000, with bath L36,000). If you miss the last bus back to Núoro and are tempted to hitch after dark, reconsider—hitching is not safe here even at the best of times, and *bandito* activity occasionally resurfaces in the countryside.

Just over one hour east of Núoro by ARST bus (5 per day via Dorgali, L4000) lies **Cala Gonone,** the gateway to a number of spectacular beaches and caves. Take the steps through the wooded area when you get off the bus.

The beaches at Cala Gonone are pebbly and crowded. A walk or hitch down the dirt road along the coast rewards the effort with sandier, less-populated beaches. Boats leave four times per day, more often in July and August (L13,000), for the stunning **Grotta del Bue Marino** (Cave of the Monk Seal), one of the last haunts of this elusive creature. The seals rarely appear during the day, however, and the cave itself is the main attraction. Nearly 1km of its more than 5km expanse of caverns, stalactites, and lakes is illuminated. However, stampeding crowds and the locked gate isolating the glowing grotto mar the experience. Just down the coast is the vast beach of **Cala Luna.** Encircled by marshes and caverns, the beach is accessible only by boat (L12,000, combined grotto/Cala Luna ticket L19,000). Boats also run to the more remote and equally breathtaking beaches of **Cala Sistre** (L20,500), **Biriola d'Aguglia** (L27,500, reservation required), and **Cala Mariolu** (L27,500), all accessible only by boat. **Consortto Marittimo Transport** has monopolized the boat transport market to beaches. Call for reservations (tel. (0786) 933 05). **Cala Osal** is accessible only by car.

Cala Gonone has wholeheartedly embraced the creed of tourism, making budget accommodations a sacrilege. Try the convenient (if noisy) **Albergo Gabbiano** in the port (tel. 931 30). (Singles L35,000, doubles L45,000.) One step up is the newly renovated **Piccolo Hotel,** via Colomba, 32 (tel. 932 32). The gracious proprietor lets elegant, immaculate rooms with balconies overlooking a quiet garden. (Singles with bath L50,000; doubles with bath L80,000, with mandatory summer pension for two L90,000.) A large, well-equipped, and expensive **campground** on via Collodi (tel. 931 65), across from the city park, charges L11,900 per person (L17,600 in July and August), and L2000 for a lamp. (Open April-Sept.)

Oristano and Its Province

Obsidian-rich soil and coastal geography made Oristano province prime property on the ancient real estate market. The first settlers to the area came during the Neolithic Age. Settlers attracted by the region's mineral wealth continued to flock to Oristano during the Nuraghic period. From these different groups of immigrants, the "protosards" (the original Sardinians) came to be. Native Nuraghic peoples fought Phoenician-Punic colonizers for control; both left significant ruins. The town of Oristano, capital of the province, saw the height of its independent splendor in the 14th century when the princess Eleanora d'Arborea led the last stages of native resistance to mainland invaders and wrote a massive legal code in ancient Sardinian that was adopted throughout the island. Today Oristano sustains a quiet life, keeping the beauty of the Sinis peninsula beaches and ruins to itself.

Oristano

Orientation and Practical Information

Piazza Roma is the center of town. The **ARST** station and **tourist office** are located on the south end of via Cagliari. There is a large map outside of the ARST station. To get to p. Roma form there, follow via Emanuele from nearby p. Mannu. From the PANI station (located on via Lombarda on the other side of town—north of p. Roma) head toward via Tirso. Make a right and then a quick left onto via Cagliari. When you come to via Tharros, turn left and this will take you directly into the square.

Tourist Office: via Cagliari, 278 (tel. 731 91 or 741 91), 6th floor, near p. Mannu across from the ARST station. Extremely helpful, well-informed staff with information on the town and region. Open Mon. and Thurs.-Fri. 8am-2pm, Tues.-Wed. 8am-2pm and 4-8pm. **Pro Loco,** vico Umberto, 1 (tel. 706 21), off via de Castro, between p. Roma and p. Eleonora d'Arborea. Independent tourist office with information on Oristano only. Open Mon.-Fri. 9am-noon and 5-8pm, Sat. 9am-noon. A Pro Loco **trailer** summers on piazza Roma. Open daily 9:30am-9pm. A new Pro Loco office is in the works on via Vittorio Emanuele.

Post Office: via Mariano IV, 10 (tel. 30 27 34). Open Mon.-Sat. 8:15am-7:40pm; stamps only sold until 12:50pm. **Postal Code:** 09170.

Telephones: SIP, p. Eleonora d'Arborea, 40, opposite the Church of San Francesco. Open Mon.-Fri. 8:30am-12:30pm and 3-7pm, Sat. 8:30am-12:30pm. **Telephone Code:** 0783.

Trains: p. Ungheria (tel. 722 70), about 1km from the town center. Trains to: Sássari (4 per day, 3hr., L12,200), Olbia (4 per day, 4hr., L13,800), and Cagliari (15 per day, 1hr., L7200).

Buses: PANI, via Lombardia, 30 (tel. 212 68), at a bar. Three buses leave daily to: Cagliari (8:55am, 4:19pm, and 9:35pm, 1hr. 30min., L11,000); Núoro (7am, 3:30pm, and 7:50pm, 2hr., L11,000); Sássari (7am, 3:30pm, and 7:50 pm, 2hr. 15min., L13,000). **ARST,** via Cagliari (tel. 780 01), connects local routes and runs 2 slower buses to Cagliari (7:10am and 2:10pm, 2hr. 15min., L11,000).

Laundry: Lavanderia Espresso, via Sardegna, 137, across from the Bonsai restaurant. L3000 per kg. Open Mon.-Fri. 8:30am-1pm.

Emergencies: tel. 113. **Ambulance/Medical Emergency:** Tel. 782 22. **Main hospital,** via Fondazione Rockefeller (tel. 742 61). **First Aid:** tel. 743 33.

Accommodations and Camping

Prices and quality here are consistent with those of northern cities, and Oristano caters more to traveling Sardinian businessmen than to tourists; moreover, competition is low, keeping prices bloated.

Piccolo Hotel, via Martignano, 19 (tel. 715 00), off via Crispi. From p. Eleonora d'Arborea, walk in the direction of the statue's stare; take a right, an immediate left, the 3rd right, and then a left. Tidy, tiny rooms, all with baths, several with massive balconies overlooking the medieval city. Helpful, philosophically inclined management. Singles L40,000. Doubles L60,000.

Hotel Amiscora, viale San Martino, 13 (tel. 30 21 52), 1 block beyond p. Mannu. Newly renovated with large baths, carpeted floors, and neat beds. All rooms with baths. Singles L50,000. Doubles L60,000.

Camping: Torre Grande, via Stella Maris (tel. 222 28), 100m out of Torre Grande on the road to Oristano (7km). Facilities galore, but packed in summer. L5000 per person, L8300 per tent. Open July-Sept. There are also bungalows available for rent. They house up to 4 and are a bargain at L50,000 (low season) or L80,000 (high).

Agriturismo: ask at the tourist office for information. Spots generally run L35,000 per person including half-pension.

Food

You can buy the basics for rock-bottom prices at the **Euro-Drink market,** p. Roma, 22. (Open Mon.-Sat. 8am-1pm and 5-8pm.) The **STANDA supermarket** is at the corner of via Diaz and via Cavour. (Open Mon.-Fri. 8:30am-1pm and 4:30-8pm, Sat. 8:30am-1pm.)

Bonsai, via Sardegna, 140 (tel. 735 46). Sit down in the back or take out from the bar to take advantage of this eatery's fantastic sandwich menu (L3500-4500); or try a full sit-down meal with wine (L15,000-16,000). Very friendly service; worth the walk. Open Wed.-Mon. 7:30am-11pm.

Arborea, p. Roma, 15 (tel. 703 63). Boisterous locals dine under huge murals that portray the astounding and rapid succession of Sardinian civilizations, invasions, and governments. Try the outstanding *spaghetti alle arselle* (scallops, L9000). *Menù* L25,000. Open daily noon-3pm and 7-11pm.

Sights and Entertainment

The center of town is **piazza Roma,** dominated by the chunky 13th-century **Tower of St. Christopher.** On summer evenings, young *oristanesi* rock and ramble through the *piazza* and the adjoining **corso Umberto.** The pastel **Church of San Francesco** (1838) stands at the end of via de Castro, at p. Eleonora d'Arborea. In the sacristy of this Pantheon-inspired building, the 16th-century polyptych of *St. Francis Receiving the Stigmata* and the 14th-century statue of San Basilio by Nino Pisano evince deep reverence. The main sanctuary displays a wooden crucifix, a simple, straight cross on which the emaciated and tortured body of Christ is draped (typical of 14th-century German art; left altar), and a balustrade formed from fragments of an 11th-century pulpit (right transept).

A statue in p. Eleonora d'Arborea by the *municipio* commemorates **Eleonora d'Arborea,** Sardinia's Joan of Arc. This local heroine was a 14th-century princess who successfully defended independent Sardinia against the encroaching Aragonese. She is remembered for drafting the *Carta de Logu* (Code of Laws) in 1395, setting down the Sardinian legal system for almost 500 years and preserving the ancient Sardinian language in which it was written. The matriarchal tradition continues in Oristano to this day—many provincial officials, including the most recent governor and mayor, have been women.

Down via E. d'Arborea from p. E. d'Arborea is the **duomo,** a delightful amalgam of a 13th-century skeleton and 18th-century embellishment. Outside, a rainbow-colored cupola sits on top of the octagonal bell tower. Inside are chandeliers, tapestries, paintings, and even some stained glass. Patterns of yellow, blue, and lavender create halos around the icons and altars. Three kilometers out of town on the road to Cagliari is the equally remarkable 12th-century **Basilica of Santa Giusta,** typically Sardinian in its synthesis of Lombard and Pisan influences. The sculpted facade depicts two lions dismembering and devouring a deer. Set against this macabre backdrop is a tremendous square cross of dark blocks. The interior is simple and severe, so as not to distract the pious during uninspiring sermons.

On the last Sunday of **Carnevale** (March) and the following Tuesday (inquire at the tourist office), Oristano celebrates the **Sartiglia,** a traditional race first run in the 16th century in which masked horsemen try to pierce six-inch metal stars with their swords as they gallop down the street. Those who pierce many stars bring *Fortuna* upon the next harvest. In nearby Cabras (on the road to Tharros), **La Corsa degli Scalzi** is performed the first Sunday in September. This procession of white-clad, barefoot runners, bearing a statue of San Salvatore, reenacts the brave feat of Oristanese women at the time of the Moorish invasion. While the men remained to defend the town of San Salvatore, the women carried the statue of the town's saint away to safety in neighboring Cabras. On July 6 and 7, **Ardia** sponsors a frenzied and occasionally fatal horse race in which zealous riders circle a church seven times to commemorate Emperor Constantine's victory at the Milvian Bridge in 312 AD. Go early to get a good standing place; the horse cavalcade begins between 6 and 7pm. There is no public transportation to the event.

Sinis Peninsula and the Costa Verde

The coastal areas surrounding Oristano offer everything that the better-known resorts do—except the concrete and crowds.

Twenty kilometers west of Oristano, in the southernmost tip of the peninsula, lie the ruins of the ancient Phoenician port of **Tharros.** Much of the city remains submerged, but recent excavations have revealed Punic fortifications, a Roman temple dedicated to Demeter, a paleochristian baptistry, and a Punic shrine. The impeccable beaches here are as beautiful as they are serene. To reach Tharros, take an ARST bus (40min., one way L2500, round-trip L5000) directly to the site. Student guides paid by the Council of Cabras lead informative free tours of the ruins in Italian. On the way to Tharros you'll pass two interesting churches: **San Salvatore,** built above a pagan temple whose Roman deities (Venus, Cupid, and Hercules) are still visible on an underground wall, and **San Giovanni in Sinis,** a part-pagan, part-Christian structure dating from the 5th century that seems, in structure and spirit, to be a distant ancestor of Oristano's Santa Giusta. During the 1960s San Salvadore was converted into a Mexican-American "Old West" village for several spaghetti westerns.

On the other side of the isthmus from Tharros are the beaches and village of **San Giovanni di Sinis.** To go directly there, take the ARST bus (4 per day at 8am, noon, 2pm, and 6:50pm; L2500, round-trip L5000). The two sites, Tharros and San Giovanni, are close enough that you might buy a ticket for the ruins and then cross over to San Giovanni on foot. Don't be fooled by the elderly sisters who manage the only hotel in this tiny beach village—they have a habit of advertising bargain prices to lure you out and then zap you for full pension at L70,000!

Fifteen kilometers north of San Giovanni on the peninsula are the beaches of **Putzu Idu** and **Cala Saline.** Beautiful, virgin-white, and largely empty, they're worth a swim or even a few quiet days of lolling. Three villages lie in close proximity on this remote corner of the peninsula. The only affordable accommodation is at **Hotel "Su Pallosu"** in Marina di S. Vero Milis (tel. (0783) 580 05). The local fishing community frequents the bar. They'll warm you with local spirit. Look for Marco, a small man wearing a baseball cap. He'll point you in the direction of cheap food and Club Tomoka, where you can find live music and a friendly gathering on a nightly basis. To get to Putzu Idu from Oristano, take the ARST bus (direction Barátili or San Pietro) and get off at Riola (25min.). Walk down via Roma, which dead-ends onto via Umberto, and turn right. Wait for the connecting bus a few meters down the street, across from the motocycle repair shop. The connecting bus (use the same ticket) will be marked "Cala Saline"; take it for another 8km (10-15min.) right to the beach. (Bus leaves Oristano 9:50am; returns at 1pm and 7pm; L3000.) Walk a few kilometers south along the coast to see the stunning cliffs at **Capo sa Starraggia.** Approximately 7km south, the lovely cliffs and white beach of **Is Arustas** await the hardy hiker; the less ambitious can take an ARST bus directly to Is Arutas (same line as San Giovanni, L3500).

About 35km south of Oristano, the **Costa Verde,** stretches nearly 40km, a happy mingling of sandy coves and scintillating ocean. Yet apart from the two coastal towns of Porto Palma and Marina di Arbus (where there is a rudimentary campsite), there are few denizens to speak of, and even fewer travelers. ARST buses take you part of the way to Arbus (*not* Marina di Arbus or Diane) at 8:10am, 2pm, and 5:45pm (1hr. 30min., L5500) but you'll have to fend for yourself from there.

Alghero

For a place originally labeled "L'Aleguerium" because of the abundance of seaweed cluttering its shores, Alghero has come a long way. Its serpentine cobblestone streets, stately eucalyptus trees, and parasol pines overlook a magnificent expanse of ocean. In the 11th century, the Genovese transformed Alghero from an insignificant fishing village into a major trading post; in 1350 a wave of Catalonian immigrants repopulated the city. Natives still speak the melodious Catalan language, a number of restaurants serve *paella,* and many of the *piazze* are called *plaças.* In fact, the town's Spanish air has earned it the nickname of the "Barcelonetta of Sardinia."

Orientation and Practical Information

Getting to and from Alghero via public transport usually requires going through Sássari. Alghero is one hour from Sássari by ARST bus (5 per day, L4200), SFS bus (10 per day, L4200), and by train (10 per day, L3200). ARST buses also run directly to Porto Torres (4 per day, 50min., L4500).

Tourist Office: p. Porta Terra, 9 (tel. 97 90 54), near the bus stop. Walk toward the old city from the park. Provides a street-indexed map, list of accommodations, and bus and train schedules. English spoken. Open daily Mon.-Sat. 8am-8pm; Oct.-June Mon.-Sat. 8am-2pm and 5pm-8pm.

Currency Exchange: largo San Francesco, 21. 24 hr. automatic machine. Also **Banca Commerciale Italiano**, viale Giovanni XXIII. Open Mon.-Fri. 8:20am-1:35pm and 3:15-4:45pm.

Post Office: via XX Settembre, 108 (tel. 97 93 09). Open Mon.-Sat. 10am-7:30pm, Fermo Posta 10am-1:20pm. **Branch Office,** via Colombano, 44, near the tourist office (tel. 97 92 45). Open Mon.-Fri. 8:10am-1:15pm, Sat. 8am-12:45pm. **Postal Code:** 07041.

Telephones: booths at p. Sulis. Phone cards available in bars on the *piazza.* **Telephone Code:** 079.

Trains: at via Don Minzoni and via Castelsardo (tel. 95 07 85), in the northern part of the city. Take the city bus from the *fermata* 1 block north of the tourist office (every 20min.) or stroll 1km along the port. Open daily 5:30am-9:30pm. There is also a tiny and more convenient terminal beyond the main station on via Garibaldi, adjacent to the port, with Sássari service only (40min., L3200, more scenic and cheaper than the bus).

Buses: ARST and SFS buses depart from via Catalogna, by the park. Purchase ARST tickets on board, SFS tickets at *caffè* or kiosks in the park. To Sássari (L4200) and Porto Torres (L4500). ARST information tel. 26 00 48.

Taxis: p. Porta Terra (tel. 97 53 96), across from the tourist office.

Bike/Moped Rental: Noleggio di Tilocca Tomaso, at the harbor (tel. 97 65 92). Bikes L12,000 per day, mountain bikes L18,000 per day, tandem bikes L20,000 per day. Mopeds L25,000 per day. Scooters L50,000 per day. Open Mon.-Sat. 8:30am-1pm and 4-8:30pm, Sun. 8:30am-noon. **Velosport,** via Veneto, 90 (tel. 97 71 82). Similar prices and a much larger stock. Discount of 10% if you rent for 3 or more days. Open Mon.-Sat. 9am-1pm and 4:30-8:30pm.

Car Rental: Budget, via Sassari, 7 (tel. 93 51 67). L87,000 per day.

Horse Rental: Club Ippico Capuano (tel. 97 81 98), 3km from Alghero.

Emergencies: tel 113. **Police:** p. della Mercede, 4, tel. 113. **Hospital: Ospedale Civile** (tel. 95 10 96), Regione la Pietraia, a few blocks north of the main train station on via Don Minzoni.

Accommodations and Camping

Prices escalate and rooms vanish in July and August. Finding singles is particularly difficult. Don't expect much help from the *azienda.* If all else fails, friendly **Masia Margherita** at via Angelo Roth, 12 (tel. 97 53 93), may have a room in a private house for about L22,500 per single and L45,000 per double with shower.

Ostello dei Giuliani (HI), via Zara, 3 (tel. 93 03 53), 7km from Alghero in Fertilia. Take the yellow AF city bus (from via La Marmora next to the train station, every hr., 15min., L1100). ARST buses around the corner also go there. Curfew 10pm. L14,000 per person. Showers L2500. Breakfast L3000. Scrumptious lunches and dinners L12,000. (Meals served July and Aug. only.) *Always* reserved to capacity in July and August, but call and ask about cancellations.

Pensione Normandie, via Mattei, 6 (tel. 97 53 02), a 10-min. walk from the port. From via Cagliari (which turns into via Papa Giovanni XXIII), turn right on via Mattei. Adequate rooms in friendly, family-run place. Singles L20,000. Doubles L35,000.

Hotel San Francesco, via Machin, 2 (tel. 97 92 58). From the tourist office, follow via Simon along the old city boundary and take the 2nd right. Tranquil, comfortable rooms in the church cloister, each with private bath. Occasional concerts. Reserve ahead in summer. Singles L37,000.

Hotel Coral, via Fratelli Kennedy, 64 (tel. 97 93 45), off p. Sulis. Pretty tree-lined patio on a quiet block. Simple, neat rooms. Singles L32,000, with bath L40,000. Doubles L47,000, with bath L55,000.

Camping: Calik (tel. 93 01 11), 6km away, before the bridge into Fertilia. Large and crowded, 50m from the beach. L12,000 per person. Open June-Nov. **La Mariposa** (tel. 95 03 60), via Lido, 3km away on the Alghero-Fertilia road and near the beach. Packed in summer. L13,000 per person. Open June-Oct.

Agriturismo: available at **Dulcamara** (tel. 99 91 97) and **Carboni Margherita** (tel. 99 90 93) in S. Maria la Palma. Minumum stay 3 days. Bed and breakfast L25,000 per person; L10,000 booking tax per person. Inquire at tourist office.

Food

Investigate the **market** by the park at the bus stop; enter from via Cagliari (open Tues.-Sun. 7am-1pm). Every Wednesday, crowds engulf the **open-air market** on via de' Gasperi (open 8am-1pm). Down the street, the **Supermercato STANDA** via XX Settembre, 3, permits less claustrophobic indoor shopping. (Open Mon.-Sat. 9am-1pm and 4:30-8:30pm.)

Marechiaro, via La Marmora, 44 (tel. 97 99 83). Small and cozy, sequestered from the trodden tourist path. Good all around. Full meals roughly L15,000. Open daily 7-11:30pm.

Maristella, via Kennedy, 9 (tel. 97 81 72). Right next door to the bowling alley, this sidewalk *trattoria* with bright yellow awnings wins for atmosphere. All the traditional *primi* L7000-10,000, *secondi* L10,000-18,000. Open noon-2:30pm and 6pm-midnight. Credit cards accepted.

Ristorante El Pultal, via Colombano, 40 (tel. 97 80 51), in the old city near the post office branch. Expensive main dishes, but reasonable prices on large pizzas (L4500-8500). Relaxing interior with white Catalonian arches. Open daily 9:30am-3:30pm and 7pm-midnight.

Filli Leoni, (in Fertilia) via Fiume trav. Porti ci (tel. 93 04 75). One of the few eating establishments in the area. The tasty, inexpensive pizza is worth the trip from Alghero.

Pesce D'Oro, via Catalogna, 12 (tel. 95 26 02). Pleasant atmosphere with outdoor tables by the park. *Primi* L7000-10,000. *Secondi* L9000-15,000. Pizza L4000-9000. Dine to piano accompaniment by whomever decides to mount the bench.

Sights and Entertainment

Wander at leisure through the **Città Vecchia** (Old City). Creep down the alleyways, peek into the churches, and surface occasionally to circle the ancient walls and behold the shimmering sea beyond. From p. Sulis, via Carlo Alberto takes you to the 14th-century **Church of San Francesco,** whose heavy neoclassical facade conceals a gracious Gothic presbytery. In July and August, the classical music of the **Estate Musicale Internazionale** (Summer Music Festival), sponsored by the tourist office, fills the cloisters. Schedules and tickets are available from the tourist office. Brown and green shutters complement the beige facades along nearby via Principe Umberto, a perfectly medieval street. At #7 you'll find the **Casa Doria,** with its beautiful 16th-century front, built by the powerful Doria clan of Genoa who fortified the fishing village of Alghero in the 11th century. Down the street you can get the most interesting view of the cathedral—the backside. Begun in 1552, the cathedral took 178 years to build, resulting in a motley Gothic-Catalan-Renaissance facade. Redone in the 19th century, the church retains its striking Gothic choirs and campanile.

There are three strategically located medieval **towers** in Alghero. **Torre del Portal,** on piazza Porta Terra, was one of two access routes to the fortified Catalan city, complete with a drawbridge and (at the time) an artificial moat. **Torre de l'Espero Reial,** in piazza Sulis, is a circular fortification with a grand view of the ocean. The **Torre de Sant Jaume** is commonly known as the **Torre dels Cutxos** (Dog's Tower) since it served as a 15th-century dog pound.

For a look at what's doing 'neath the waves, visit the **Mare Nostrum Aquarium,** via XX Settembre, 1 (tel. 97 83 33), across from the old city. The aquarium displays representatives of the local fish and reptile populations, along with those beloved carnivores, piranhas and sharks. (Open daily 10am-1pm and 5-11pm; Oct.-June Mon.-Fri. 10am-noon and 4-8:30pm, Sat.-Sun. 4-9pm. Admission L8000.)

After a day in the sun, head for **Birdlands,** via Roma, 50 (tel. 97 79 03) in the historic center. Live music blares nightly in the lounge upstairs (open 9:30pm-1am); a bar and *gelateria* occupy the downstairs (open 11am-1am). Ask at the *azienda* about seasonal events, which include Catalan music and folk performances.

Near Alghero

The **Grotte di Nettuno** (tel. 94 65 40) is a vast natural wonder, an eerie cavern complex of dagger-like stalactites and mushrooming stalagmites. The caves delve into Capo Caccia, a steep promontory which projects from Porto Conte (25km by land from Alghero, 15km by sea. Groups are admitted hourly 8am-8pm; Oct.-April 9am-2pm. Admission L9000.) Boats leave Alghero's Bastione della Maddalena at 9am, 10am, 3pm, and 4pm (round-trip 3hr., L13,000). The SFS bus combs the beautiful coast (leaving at 9:15am, 2:50pm, and 5:15pm, returning at 1pm, 4:35pm, and 6:55pm, 50min., round-trip L6000). Mopeds can reach the *grotte* in 30 minutes. Once there, descend the memorable 654 steps that plunge between massive white cliffs all the way to the sea. If you're on moped, stop at the beaches of Porto Conte and exquisite Capo Caccia, as well as the **Nuraghe of Palmavera** (10km out of Alghero), where an intriguing central tower dates from 1500 BC. (Mandatory tour L3500. Open daily May-Sept. 9am-1pm and 3-8pm.) If you've rented a moped for the whole day, ride 10km toward Porto Torres to the **Necropolis of Anghelu Ruju,** the largest in Sardinia, a group of 38 tombs built by the local fishing tribes around 3000 BC. You can also take the ARST bus from Alghero (departures at 7:05am, 1:45pm, and 4:35pm, L1500).

At **Bosa,** 45km south of Alghero, make a short climb down the hillside away from town to several outstanding beaches. A bus departs from Alghero at 9:55am and 6:50pm, and returns via an interior route at 5:30pm. Follow the sea away from Alghero to the magnificent beaches of **Spiaggia di San Giovanni** and **Spiaggia di Marta Pia,** north of town, where you'll find lots of clear water and few tourists. The **Spiaggia Le Bombarde,** close to Fertilia and the hostel, is even less crowded but is receding rapidly into the sea. A determined walk to **Torre del Lazzaretto** farther along the shore will be more rewarding. The ASP city buses serve Porte Corte and the beaches.

Sássari

Sardinia's second-largest city sits atop a limestone plateau, where its medieval founders sought refuge from the invasions and malaria epidemics more common to coastal territory. Today Sássari is an important petrochemical center, with modern suburbs nestling around its compact medieval core. In the capital of Italy's largest province, Sassarians enjoy the highest standard of living in Sardinia, as well as the continental pretensions of its grandiose 18th-century piazza d'Italia and sole boulevard, via Roma.

Orientation and Practical Information

All roads radiate from the newly restored **piazza d'Italia.** As you stand facing the Banco di Napoli in the *piazza,* **via Roma** and the **PANI station** are on your left; **emiciclo Garibaldi** and the **ARST station** are straight ahead, with the leafy **piazza Castello** behind it; the main shopping street, **corso Vittorio Emanuele,** and the **train station** are on your right. The towns of Alghero and Porto Torres are conveniently located 37km southwest and 18.5km northwest, respectively.

Tourist Office: (tel. 23 35 34) via Brigata Sassari, 19, and at the northwest corner of piazza d'Italia. Basic brochures and a polite staff. Open Mon.-Fri. 8am-2pm and 4-6pm, Sat. 8am-noon.

Currency Exchange: Banca Commerciale Italia, piazza d'Italia, 23. Open Mon.-Fri. 8:20am-1:35pm and 3:15-4:45pm.

Budget Travel: CTS, via Costa, 48 (tel. 23 45 85), off viale Italia. Open Mon.-Fri. 10:30am-1pm and 5-7:30pm.

Post Office: via Brigata Sassari, 13 (tel. 23 21 78), off p. Castello. Open Mon.-Fri. 8:15am-7:40pm. Many services not available after 1pm. **Postal Code:** 07100.

Telephones: SIP, viale Italia, 7/A. Open Mon.-Fri. 9am-12:30pm and 4:30-7:30pm. **Telephone Code:** 079.

Flights: 28km south, near Alghera Fertilia. Free ARST buses leave for airport from station 75min. before departures. **Airport Information:** tel. 93 50 33.

Trains: p. Stazione (tel. 26 03 62), 1 block from p. Sant'Antonio. To: Olbia (9 per day, 2hr., L8800); Oristano (7 per day, 2hr. 45min., L10,800); Cagliari (6 per day, 3hr. 30min., L18,700); Porto Torres (9 per day, 20min., L1600); Palau (2 per day, 4hr., L10,500); Alghero (10 per day, 40min., L3200).

Buses: PANI, via Bellini, 25 (tel. 23 69 83 or 23 47 82), off via Roma, 1 block from p. d'Italia. To: Cagliari (at 6:35am, 2pm, and 7:15pm, 4hr., L26,000; direct at 6am and 2:15pm, 3hr. 15min.); Núoro (3 per day, 2hr. 30min., L13,000); Oristano (3 per day, 2hr. 15min., L13,000). Open Mon.-Sat. 5:30am-6:30am, 9:15am-2:15pm, and 5:30-7:15pm. **ARST,** emiciclo Garibaldi, 23 (tel. 26 00 06). Serves most local routes. **SFS,** next door at #26 (tel. 24 13 01). Runs buses to Alghero (10 per day, 90min., L4500), Porto Torres (L2000), Castelsardo (L3500), and Torrelba (L4000). Open Mon.-Sat. 7am-1:30pm and 2-8pm. Buy tickets at the newsstand in the *emiciclo.* **Luggage Storage-ARST:** L2000. Open Mon.-Sat. 10am-4:30pm.

Car Rental: Avis, via Mazzi, 2/A (tel. 20 30 55 46). One day L90,000. One week L450,000.

All-Night Pharmacy: Simon, via Brigata Sassari, 2 (tel. 23 32 38). Posts a weekly list of other all-night pharmacies.

Emergencies: tel. 113. **Police:** via Copino (tel. 23 23 43). **Medical Emergency: Ospedale Civile,** via de Nicola, off via Costa (tel. 22 05 00). **First Aid:** tel. 22 06 21.

Accommodations

Cheap rooms in Sássari are tough to find in July and August.

Pensione Famiglia, viale Umberto, 65 (tel. 23 95 43). Friendly owners let large rooms with cathedral-high ceilings; however, the beds are cots, and hot water is scarce. Don't let the flies in the lobby deter you. Curfew midnight. Doubles L25,000.

Hotel Giusu, p. Sant'Antonio, 21 (tel. 23 33 27). Very clean, modern, and professional. All rooms with private bath. Singles L40,000. Doubles L56,000.

Food

A wide selection of *pizzerie* lines **corso Emanuele.** Any student ID allows you to eat at the **University Mensa,** via Padre Manzella, 2 (tel. 21 91 11), off p. Gramsci. A basic, filling meal is yours for L6500; better yet, see if you can get a student outside to sell you a ticket for about L1000. (Open Mon.-Sat. 12:30-2:20pm and 7:30-9pm.) The large, enclosed **market** occupies p. Mercato, down via Rosello from via Vittorio Emanuele. (Open Mon.-Fri. 8am-1pm and 5-8pm, Sat. 8am-1pm.) The **STANDA supermarket** is on viale Italia at via Sardegna. (Open Mon.-Fri. 8:45am-1pm and 4:30-8:15pm, Sat. 9am-1pm.) Or try the well-stocked minimarket (tel. 26 02 13), to the left as you exit the station (open Mon.-Fri. 8am-1pm and 5-8pm, Sat. 8am-1pm). Even better is the daily outdoor **market** at piazza Tolo which sells fruit, vegetables, clothes, and housewares (7am-2pm).

Florian Ristorante, via Belleini, 27 (tel. 23 62 51 27). A lovely restaurant on p. d'Italia with hearty authentic cuisine. Traditional calamari L6000, and *tagliatelle alla lepre* (pasta in rabbit sauce) L15,000. Open Mon.-Sat. noon-3:30pm, and 6-10:30pm. Credit cards accepted.

Pizzeria Al Corso, corso Emanuele, 148 (tel. 23 42 10). Perhaps the island's best pizza, loaded with cheese and toasted to perfection in a wood-burning oven (L6000-9000). Even the plain mozzarella *margherita* will catapult you into an orbit of exultation. Delightfully strong, sweet house wine. Open Tues.-Sun. 7pm-1am.

Trattoria Da Peppina, vicolo Pigozzi, 1 (tel. 23 61 46), off via Emanuele. A small, simple place filled with locals. *Primi* L4000-7000, *secondi* L6500-10,000.

Al Fornaio, via al Rosello, 23, in the corso Trinità area. The best bread bakery in town. Packed constantly. Open Mon.-Sat. 8am-2pm.

Sights and Seasonal Events

The **Museo Giovanni Antonio Sanna,** via Roma, 64 (tel. 27 22 03), houses reconstructed nuraghi, gripping Sardinian paintings, traditional costumes, and a robust garden. The graceful Roman statues and mosaics are also a treat, but best of all is the droning rhythm of Sardinian pipe music played in the ethnographic section. (Open Mon.-Sat. 9am-2pm, Sun. 9am-1pm, 2nd Wed. of each month 4:30-7:30pm. Admission L4000.) The **Cathedral of San Niccolò,** originally a 13th-century Romanesque structure, gained a Spanish Colonial Baroque facade in the 17th century, dubbed "an immense flower of stone," by Elio Vittorini. Entry is not allowed, however. The **Church of Santa Maria di Betlem,** near the train station, is another hybrid: its 14th-century Gothic vaults shelter elegant Baroque altars, and the adjacent cloister preserves a bronze-spigoted medieval fountain. (Open 10am-6pm.)

The lavish **Sardinian Cavalcade,** held on the second-to-last Sunday in May, is Sardinia's most notable folk festival. The festivities include a morning procession of costumed emissaries from dozens of villages all over Sardinia, an afternoon *Palio* (horserace), and an evening song-and-dance show.

I Candelieri, the festival of the candlesticks (great wooden columns in the shape of enormous tapers), takes place on Assumption Day (August 14), when the *Gremi,* or farmers' guilds, parade giant replicas of candles and matches through the streets. The festival dates back to the 16th century, when people reasoned that it was a lack of candle offerings to the Virgin causing the latest plague.

Near Sássari

Castelsardo's striking location on a lofty promontory and its proximity to sandy beaches make it a popular junction along Sardinia's Costa Paradiso. Only 34km northwest of Sássari, it is also a convenient daytrip (10 ARST buses per day, L3500). The hilltop town offers few cultural sights other than a late-Gothic **cathedral,** tastelessly replastered in drab stucco, which shelters an impressive 15th-century painting of the *Madonna with Angels.* The **castle** at the top of the hill affords a tremendous view of the northern coast (open daily 8am-8pm).

There are no rooms in the old town. Try **Pensione Pinna,** lungomare Anglona, 7 (tel. (079) 47 01 68), across the street from the harbor. (Singles L22,000-35,000. Doubles L40,000-60,000.) For a tasty, satisfying lunch, try one of the *foccacine* (L4200) at **Pizzeria Number One,** p. La Pianetta, 33.

Some easily accessible nuraghi await you 30km south of Sássari—most notably **Nuraghi Santu Antine** at **Torralba.** Some of the most interesting prehistoric architecture in the western Mediterranean idles just off the road. The central tower dates from the 9th century BC and the fortifications surrounding it from the 7th. (Site open daily 8:30am-8:15pm.) The must-see **Museum of the Valley of the Nuraghi** at via Carlo Felice, 97 (tel. 84 72 98), in Torralba, provides information on the nuraghi, next to excavated relics. (Open Tues.-Sun. 9am-1pm and 3-8pm. Admission L3000, under 18 free.) The Torralba train station (on the Cagliari-Sássari line) lies 1km from the monument, and PANI and ARST buses also run to the town (4km from the site, L3600).

Northern Coast

The crowded northern shore of Sardinia includes the Emerald Coast, arguably the area of Italy most victimized by the Eurotourist deluge; Santa Teresa di Gallura, a coastal retreat rapidly succumbing to the same tourist-glutted fate; and the Costa Paradiso, which developers are trying to push as the "next Costa Smeralda." To round things off, there's the justly untouristed petrochemical center of Porto Torres, and the once-charming town of Stintino. Unless you're longing to find a hotel that literally charges a million lire a night, or you miss the crush of Rimini and piazza San Marco, travel elsewhere.

Porto Torres

There is little to rave about in a town whose most scenic spot is a three-bench park next to the main bus stop. Founded by Caesar, it once enjoyed considerable importance as an ancient Roman harbor. Today it is a major petrochemical center and ferry terminal for boats to and from Civitavécchia, Genoa, and Toulon (France). Do as Caesar would have done: come, see, and leave quickly.

Orientation and Practical Information

Trains, buses, and ferries come and go from the port. As you stand with your back to the water, straight ahead is **corso Vittorio Emanuele II**, the main street, which leads from the port to the church of San Gavino.

Tourist Office: Pro Loco, via Roma, 30 (tel. 51 50 00). The office is hidden down a back street. Head from the port into town with the water at your back. This is via Emanuele II. Via Roma will be the 1st cross street. Turn left. English-speaking attendants will present you with maps, brochures, and information. Open July-Sept. 8am-7pm with 1hr. off for lunch.

Post Office: via Pacinotti, 4 (tel. 50 21 90). Open Mon.-Fri. 8:10am-1pm, Sat. 8am-12:45pm. **Postal Code:** 07046. **Telephone Code:** 079.

Trains: via Ponte Romano, 89 (tel. 51 46 36), next to the port. To: Sássari (L1600). Trains stop in the middle of the street. Open daily 5:30am-8:30pm.

Buses: ARST buses run to and from **Sássari** incessantly (L2000) and **Alghero** (5 per day, L4500). For service to **Stintino**, walk 2 blocks from the port to p. Umberto, where you can also catch the bus to Sássari. It's best to purchase tickets in advance at the **Bar Acciazo** on corso Vittorio Emanuele, halfway between the port and p. Umberto (look for the big pink sign).

Ferries: Tirrenia, Stazione Marittima in the port (tel. 51 41 07). Service to Genoa, Livorno, and Toulon. Ticket office open Mon.-Sat. 8:30am-noon and 3-8pm, Sun. 3-6pm.

Car Rental: Mureddo, via Mare, 8 (tel. 51 01 81, after hours 27 46 29), across from the port. Must be 18. Also **bike rental.** *Let's Go* gets you 20% off. Open daily 8:30am-1pm and 3:30-7:30pm.

Emergencies: tel. 113. **Medical Emergency: Pronto Soccorso**, via delle Terme, 5 (tel. 51 03 92), off via Ponte Romano. Some English spoken.

Accommodations and Food

There's no need to stay or eat in Porto Torres, since Sássari is only 30 minutes away by bus. Prices for rooms (when available) are high, the **HI youth hostel** is tiny, and the windows of restaurants on the main street are plastered with outrageous "tourist menus." **Ostello per la Gioventù Balai (HI)** is an option at via Balai (tel. 50 27 61). Walk 2km from the port along the coastal road to Castelsardo until you reach the intersection of via Balai and strada Litoranea, or take the local bus which leaves every half-hour from the *fermata* in front of the port. It's often full, so call ahead. (Reception open 6-11pm. L14,000 per person. Dinner L12,000. Open July-Oct.) Stock up on munchies at the immense **Turrismarket**, via Pacinotti, 1, at via Sacchi beyond San Gavino. (Open Tues.-Sat. 8:15am-12:45pm and 5:30-8pm, Mon. 8:15am-12:45pm.) Choose from a variety of *panini* (L4500-7000) at **Pizzeria Il Drago**, via Ponte Romano, 54 (open Tues.-Sun. 6-11:30pm), or settle down for a superb seaside meal at **Ristorante**

Scaglio Lungo, via Lungo Mare, 12 (tel. 50 13 00). Meals start at L16,000. (Open daily 7pm-4am.) You can also try **Cristallo,** p. XX Settembre (tel. 51 49 09) for some great *spaghetti agli scampi* (spaghetti with shrimp, L12,000). (Open Tues.-Sun. 12:30-3pm and 7:30pm-midnight.)

Sights

To the untrained eye, the ruins of a Roman bath (*Terme Centrale*) next to the train station look like marble rubble. Medieval townspeople, themselves uncertain, named them "Il Palazzo del Re Barbaro" (Palace of the Barbarian King). In the museum, you can see headless statues, cornucopias, and ancient gamblers' dice, all excavated from the bath. A guide is usually free to take you through the ruins and recount tales of their once-licentious use. (Open daily 9am-1pm and 3-7pm.) You'll need no assistance to identify the seven marble arches that span the narrow Turitano River nearby as part of a **Roman bridge.**

Porto Torres's finest sight is the **Church of San Gavino,** a masterpiece of Sardinian architecture. An 11th-century variation on a Pisan Romanesque theme, it has a second apse in front replacing the formal facade. The somber interior, lit only by tall slit windows, shelters a double row of 28 ancient columns and a wooden truss ceiling. Outside, tiny, dilapidated houses with external staircases enclose antique courtyards.

Near Porto Torres: Stintino

Stintino, 24km northwest of Porto Torres on the Capo del Falcone, was until recently a legitimate fishing village; it is now a prototypical victim of development. The winter population of 746 increases to almost 20,000 in summer. Much of Stintino's transformation can be attributed to the stunning beauty of **Spiaggia di Pelosa,** a beach 4km outside town, whose sparkling turquoise waters glisten against the bone-dry **Isola Asinara,** a penal colony. An easy 500m wade through thigh-deep water takes you to a tiny islet and its marooned 18th-century Aragonese tower. One bus per day in summer (at 2:20pm, 30min., L3500) serves Stintino from Porto Torres, and doesn't return until the next morning. Return through Sássari (4 per day, 1hr., L4500), or better yet, leave from Sássari in the morning. Don't miss the last bus, as impromptu camping is well-nigh impossible. If you're desperate, try **Albergho Silvestrino** at via Sassari, 12 (tel. 52 30 07), where singles run L27,000, with bath L32,000, and doubles are L52,000, with bath L57,000.

Santa Teresa di Gallura

Perched on Sardinia's northwest tip, Santa Teresa di Gallura is a pastel beach town; it's very *pleasant,* in a banal, soporific kind of way. From the tiny, immaculate beach **Rena Bianca,** though, Bonapartophiles can leer at Corsica across the turquoise waters.

A dirt path leads away from the beach up the hill. At the fork, the lower path leads to **Isola Municca,** a stadium-like islet with high rocks that ring a field of grass. The higher trail twists between magnificent granite formations and offers an excellent view of Corsica and Capo Testa, especially in the morning. Follow the hill to reach the isthmus connecting **Capo Testa** with the mainland. Otherwise, go back into town and take via Capo Testa (3km) or the ARST bus from the post office mornings and afternoons. There are beaches on both sides of the isthmus—check the direction of the wind and choose the leeward side. From Capo Testa's lighthouse, you can walk down to a secluded series of scenic coves. Paths lead south through the spectacular granite quarries of the *Valle della Luna.*

Santa Teresa's **Azienda,** p. Vittorio Emanuele, 24 (tel. (0789) 75 41 27), can assist you accommodations. (Open daily 8:30am-1pm and 4:30-7pm; Oct.-May Mon.-Sat. 8:30am-1pm and 4:30-7pm.) From Santa Teresa, daily **ferries** sail to Bonifacio in Corsica (1hr., L11,500; French visa required). Both **Tirrenia** (tel. 75 41 56) and **Navarma** (tel. 75 52 70) staff offices at the tiny port. If you wish to cross into French waters yourself, rent a sailboat or motorboat from **Circolo Nautico Capo Testa** (tel. 75 54 56) on the isthmus, which also runs a scuba-diving school (Open May 15-Oct.15 daily 8am-8pm). Alternatively, explore *terra firma* by renting a horse at **Centro Ippico Ruoni** (tel. 75 15 90), 5km out of town in Ruoni. Bike and moped rentals are available from **GULP,** via Nazionale, 58 (tel. (0789) 75 56 89). Mountain bikes go for L25,000 per day, Piaggios for L35,000; Vespa 125's are L60,000 per day, and scooters are L45,000 per day. (Open Mon.-Fri. 9am-12:30pm and 5-7:30pm, Sat. 9am-12:30pm.) All-day (9:30am-5pm) boat excursions to the archipelago islands are available for L15,000 (L40,000 with lunch) from **ONDA,** via Carlo Alberto, 9 (tel. 75 41 49). **ARST buses** travel to Olbia (5 per day, 1hr. 30min., L6500), Sássari (2 per day, 3hr., L11,500), and Palau (40min., L3000) from via Eleonora d'Arborea, adjacent to the post office off via Nazionale. Tickets can be purchased at the Black and White Bar across from the station on via Nazionale.

Accommodations, Camping, and Food

Cheap hotels are often full in July, *always* in August. Most demand at least half-pension. Prices are listed for low and high seasons respectively where possible.

Hotel Bellavista, via Sonnino, 8 (tel. 75 41 62), at the edge of town overlooking Rena Bianca. Huge rooms, private baths, and balconies. Singles L35,000-50,000. Doubles L50,000-60,000.

Riva Hotel, via Galliano, 26 (tel. 75 42 83). Pleasant rooms, nice management, no pension. Singles L40,000. Doubles L55,000.

Hotel Al Porto, via del Porto, 2 (tel. 75 41 54). From via Nazionale turn onto via del Porto and follow it to the port. Worth the walk: large, almost elegant rooms with peaceful views of the water, and the Sardinian countryside. Singles L25,000-30,000. Doubles L50,000-60,000. Credit cards accepted.

Camping: Arco Balleno, 10km from Porto Pozzo (tel. 75 20 40). L12,500 per person, including tent and car.

Most local restaurants are astronomically expensive. For hearty low-cost basics, an *alimentare*, fruit and vegetable market, and delis are easy to find on via Aniscara off p. Vittorio Emanuele (open during regular business hours).

Papa Satan, via La Marmora, 20/22. No phone. Look for the sign off via Nazionale. Futuristic flaming patio in back. Wood-burning ovens. Try the devilishly good *spaghetti alla Papa Satan* (L11,000-13,000). Open daily noon-2:30pm and 7pm-midnight.

Panino's Shop, via XX Settembre, off p. Emanuele. Ultracool owner plays rap while making chewy pizza (L3000). Open daily 7am-3am.

Costa Smeralda

Once upon a time, the windy, craggy coastline above Olbia was nothing but a series of poor fishing villages. Then, in 1962, a consortium of foreign investors led by the Aga Khan developed the area into a posh resort and renamed it the Emerald Coast. Today, the fine sand beaches and clean waters are blocked off by a swarm of luxury hotels, restaurants, and shops. Accommodations and food run to outrageous sums, and the alert police force actively discourages unofficial camping. Crowds are sizeable year-round, and downright unbearable in July and August. It is impossible to find a room anywhere on the coast in August. Travel instead to the less touristy, less expensive, more appealing southern coasts, many of which are lovelier than this over-priced petri dish of tourist culture.

A bland town of pastel stucco and reinforced concrete, **Arzachena** is notable mainly for its nearby gulf. The town is a central depot on the northern coast, halfway between Olbia and Santa Teresa di Gallura on the ARST bus route, one hour from each (10 per day from Olbia, L3000). If you must pause here, the **Azienda di Turismo** has an office on via Risorgimento (tel. 826 24; open Mon.-Fri. 8am-1:30pm and 3-7:15pm, Sat. 8am-1:30pm). Catch all buses two blocks down the hill behind the *azienda*.

Summer tourists clog **Palau,** essentially one large condominium complex which functions as the main departure point for the outlying islands. For L42,000, boats will take you on a daytrip to three of the more remote islands—**S. Maria, Budelli,** where you'll find the famous *spaggia rosa* or pink beach (go to see tourists loading Zip-Loc bags with the rosy sand), and **Spargi.** (Operates June-Sept., inquire next to the Tirrenia ticket office at the port.) More conventional itineraries follow the hourly ferries to the once-beautiful islands of La Maddalena and Caprera (L1700-2000). These excursions sell out quickly. Although a major port of call for the U.S. Navy, **La Maddalena** is in reality little more than one enormous, tourist-saturated campground. The road encircling the island passes small fishing harbors, tourist villages, and beaches. **Locanda da Raffaele** at La Ricciolina (tel. 73 87 59) has doubles for L50,000. Or try camping at **Il Sole,** via Indipendenza (tel. (0789) 72 77 27) for L6000 per person, L8000 per tent. To the **tourist office,** via Nizza, 2 (tel. (0789) 73 66 55), follow the main quay to the right with your back to the water; Nizza is a small alleyway on the left-hand side. (Open daily 8:30am-1pm.) A bus runs from La Maddalena's docks to **Caprera** (L2400), the birthplace and final home of **Giuseppe Garibaldi,** the flamboyant and popular hero of Italy's unification. His house is now a museum housing an impressive array of artifacts relating to the *Risorgimento.* (Open Tues.-Sat. 8:30am-1:30pm. Admission L3000.) On Sundays, you can visit the gardens, but not the museum. Boat tours from La Maddalena to the archipelago islands are offerred by several private boat companies along the quay. These tours are all-day affairs (roughly 10am-5pm), and the L35,000 fare includes a spaghetti lunch.

Olbia

While not particularly seedy, Olbia is hardly the stuff of which poetry is made—it's just another dot on Italy's map of lackluster, well-trafficked ports. Celebrate your arrival in Sardinia by stocking up on essentials and escaping to further destinations as quickly as possible.

Practical Information

Ferries arriving at the port are greeted by blue ARST buses and a train timed to meet incoming passengers. The decrepit cluster of buildings to your left as you disembark is the train station *Olbia Marittima,* where bus and train tickets can be purchased. To reach Olbia's *centro,* take the waiting train to the first stop. (The train continues on to Sássari, a much better choice if you can handle a bit more travel.) To get to the tourist ofice, walk directly from the station up via Pala until it intersects with **corso Umberto,** with the ARST station to your right. Turn left and continue past **piazza Margherita** on your right (Olbia's youth hangout) until you reach via Catello Piro (also on your right), where you will find the tourist office. It's likely, however, that your boat will arrive long before business hours. If this is the case, consider walking the short distance from ferry into town. When you reach Principe Umberto, make a left, and you will end up at the other end of corso Umberto. Make a right and discover several *caffè* where you can chug espresso and devour cream-filled pastries with other weary travelers while waiting for the tourist office to open.

Tourist Office: via Catello Piro, 1 (tel. 214 53), off corso Umberto. The best thing in Olbia: excellent map of the town supplied by very friendly English-speaking staff. Ask for the *Annuario Alberghi,* an invaluable list of prices for almost every hotel in Sardinia. Open Mon.-Sat. 8:30am-1pm and 4-7pm, Sun. 8:30am-noon; Oct.-May Mon.-Sat. 8am-1pm and 4-7pm, Sun. 8am-noon.

American Express: Avitur, corso Umberto, 139 (tel. 243 27). Check-cashing for cardholders on weekday mornings. Open Mon.-Fri. 9am-1pm and 4-7pm, Sat. 9am-1pm.

Post Office: on via Acquedotto (tel. 222 51), 2 blocks off p. Matteotti. Open Mon.-Sat. 8:30am-7pm. **Postal Code:** 07026.

Telephones: SIP, via de Filippi, 14, off p. Matteotti. Open 24 hrs. **Telephone Code:** 0789.

Trains: via Pala, off corso Umberto by the bus station (tel. 224 77). Before the ferry departure, trains run directly from the station to the port. Trains depart regularly for Sássari (L8800) and Golfo Aranci (L2400).

Buses: ARST, at the far end of corso Umberto, 168 (tel. 211 97). To: Núoro (4 per day, about L9000); Arzachena (10 per day, L3000); Santa Teresa di Gallura (5 per day, L6500); Palau (L4000). Schedule posted in station. Open 4am-1am. Local buses (orange) traverse the town and trek from Olbia's center to the airport (#2). Local rides cost L1200-1300; buy tickets on board from coin-only machines.

Ferries: Tirrenia, corso Umberto, 17 (tel. 226 88). Service to Civitavécchia and Genoa. Open Mon.-Sat. 8:30am-1:30pm and 4:30-6pm. **Port office** (tel. 224 82) open when ferries are running—check 1hr. 30min. in advance for schedule changes. **Linea dei Golfi** (tel. 221 26), in the port office, runs lines to Piombino (the port for Elba) and Livorno in Tuscany.

Bike and Moped Rental: Smerelda Express (tel. 691 92), at the Olbia airport. A Vespone PX moped runs L50,000 per day, a Piaggio Bravo bike L25,000 per day. Unlimited mileage. Open 6am-midnight.

Pharmacy: Farmacia Lupacciolu, via Porto Romano, 2 (tel. 213 10). Open Mon.-Sat. 9am-1pm and 4:40-10pm, Sun. 8-10am.

Emergencies: tel. 113. **Hospital: Ospedale Civile** via Aldo Moro (tel. 522 00 or 522 01). Some English spoken. **Guardia Medica,** via Fern, 4 (tel. 224 91), near the Church of San Simplicio. For medical assistance evenings and weekends. Open Sat. 2pm-Mon. 8am, Tues.-Fri. 8pm-8am.

Accommodations and Food

Albergo Terranova, via Garibaldi, 3 (tel. 223 95). One of the cheapest. Singles L25,000-32,000. Doubles L45,000-50,000. Sinks in rooms.

Albergo Minerva, via Mazzini, 6 (tel. 211 90). Clean, well-lit rooms and friendly young management. Singles L30,000, with bath L38,000. Doubles L50,000, with bath L70,000.

Dining in Olbia can either be inexpensive and unremarkable or very expensive and delicious. Either way, it's usually a bummer. For self-service bargains, shop at the **Mercato Civico** on via Acquedotto (open Mon.-Sat. 7:30am-1pm and 4:30-8pm), or at the **STANDA Supermarket** at corso Umberto, 156 (open Mon.-Sat. 9am-1pm and 4-8pm).

Il Golosone, via Corso Umberto, 41. Savory crêpes, moderate prices, super-friendly crew. Try the *prosciutto e formaggio* (Italian ham and cheese, L4000) or *al Grand Marnier* (L3300). Open Mon.-Sat. 10am-1pm and 4:30pm-midnight, Sun. 4:30pm-midnight.

Pizzeria Al Ciclope, via Acquedetto, 24. No telephone number, no drinks, no one-eyed clientele, nothing but fine pizza. Cheese slice L1500. Open daily 10:30am-1pm and 5:30-10pm.

A Tavole di Leone o Anna, via Barcelona, 90 (tel. 263 33). A hike northwest of the train station, or take bus #1. Via Sassani turns into via Barcelona. Cute floral booths, lovely wooden bar, and superb Sardinian cuisine. *Spaghetti alla pescatora* (spaghetti with a fresh fish sauce) L18,000. Homemade ravioli L14,000. *Aragosta alla Catalana,* their lobster specialty, L20,000. Open Wed.-Mon. noon-3pm and 8-11:30pm.

Sights and Near Olbia

Nearly all traces of Olbia's Greek, Roman, and medieval past have disappeared. The one exception is the 12th-century **Church of San Simplicio** behind the train station. Built in the Pisan Romanesque style, the structure features an attractive asymmetrical facade of off-white granite. Inside, half-formed faces leer out from stone pillars. (No set hours.)

Excursions from Olbia include trips to **S'Abe** (6km away) on the road to **Castello Pedrese,** and the "Giants' Tombs" of **Su Monte.** If you're taking the bus to Núoro, not far out of Olbia you'll pass the surrealistic **Isola Tavolara,** an immense prism of rock protruding 450m out of the sea. Five buses per day run to **San Teodoro,** 30km from Olbia (L3000), where a long, luxurious beach eases into the ultramarine water. Especially in July and August, you'll be marching straight into the ranks of the tourist phalanxes, but go ahead—it's worth it. Stay at the **Albergho L'Esagono** (tel. 86 57 83), a complex of red clay buildings right on the beach, off via Cala d'Ambra (doubles with obligatory half-pension L80,000; full pension required in August for L95,000). Up the road is the **Cala d'Ambra campground** (tel. 86 56 50) with satisfactory facilities (L7900 per person, tent included).

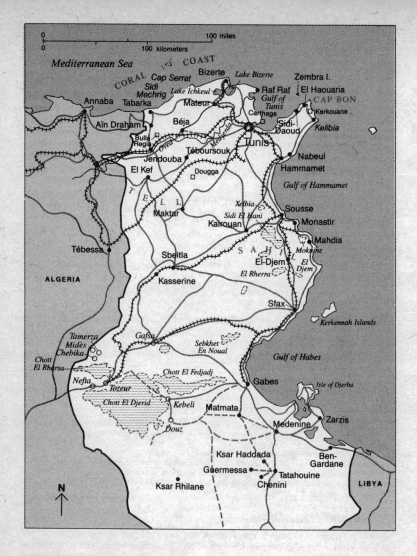

TUNISIA

US $1 = 1.16 dinar (D)	1D = US $0.87
CDN $1 = 1.00D	1D = CDN $1.00
UK £1 = 2.29D	1D = UK £0.47
AUS $1 = 0.83D	1D = AUS $1.21
NZ $1 = 0.63D	1D = NZ $1.60

Imagine a long ago and far away place, a place with seemingly endless dunes, Sand-people, Jawas, and droids. The shooting location for Luke Skywalker's desert planet in *Star Wars* is probably the first—and maybe only—image that most people have of Tunisia. But if you take Tatooine, zoom in to the present day, and add to this backdrop surprisingly modern cities, mysterious *medinas*, impressive ancient ruins, spectacular beaches, and intricately decorated mosques, you have today's Tunisia.

Queen Dido of Phoenicia sailed to Carthage in the 9th century BC to found a nation "rich in wealth and harsh in the pursuit of war." Thousands of years later, Tunisia's people are far from wealthy, and little is harsh in this gentle land of vast open spaces, remote green oases, and secluded Saharan villages. Sadly, mass tourism of the package-holiday variety dominates the Tunisian travel scene. The least effort to escape the European crowds and coastal resorts, however, reveals a hospitable people proud of their Islamic and North African culture.

Planning Your Trip

No visa is required of U.S. citizens to enter Tunisia for up to four months, or of Canadians and U.K. citizens for up to three months. Australians and New Zealanders must obtain a visa before departure from the nearest Tunisian consulate.

The **Tunisian National Tourist Office (ONTT)** is a good source of information and brochures about the country and its regions. They distribute the handy *Tunisia Practical Guide* and a detailed map (both free). The country's central tourist office is at 1, av. Mohammed V, 1002 Tunis (tel. 34 10 77, fax 35 09 97). In the U.S., write or call the **Embassy of Tunisia,** Cultural Section in Charge of Tourism, 1515 Mass. Ave. NW, Washington, DC 20005 (tel. (202) 862-1850). The ONTT in the U.K. is at 77a, Wigmore St., London W1H 9LJ (tel. 071 224 5561; fax 071 224 4053). In Italy, contact the Centro Turistico della Tunisia, 10, via Baracchini, 20123 Milan (tel. 87 11 26). For the U.S. State Department's *Background Notes* on Tunisia, write to the Superintendent of Documents, U.S. Government Printing Office, Washington, DC 20402. Major Tunisian cities also operate a local tourist office called the **Syndicat d'Initiative.**

Money

The dinar (D) consists of 1000 millimes (ml). Sums are written with periods: 14.300 means 14 dinars, 300 millimes. Amounts under 5D are frequently expressed in thousands of millimes. Change is often scarce, so hang on to it, especially the precious 100ml pieces used in pay phones. Save your exchange receipts: with them, only 30% of what you originally change can be reconverted, up to a maximum of 100D; without them, you can't reconvert any currency at all. It is illegal to import or export Tunisian currency.

Banks are generally open for exchange in summer Monday through Friday 8 to 11am and in winter Monday through Thursday 8 to 11am and 2 to 4pm, Friday 8 to 11am and 1:30 to 3pm. During Ramadan (see Festivals and Holidays), banks are open Monday through Friday 8 to 11:30am and 1 to 2:30pm. A few large hotels and all airports provide exchange services outside regular hours.

Safety and Security

When wandering in the crowded, labyrinthine *souks* (market streets) of the *medina* (old city), cling to your bags, mind your pockets, and seek safety in numbers. The *medinas* are extremely dangerous after dark. Even the police stay out of them, and won't be sympathetic if you wander in and survive to come out and complain.

Carry sums of over 10.000D or 15.000D in a moneybelt or necklace pouch. When purchasing a souvenir or hiring a guide, keep your money securely in hand or belt until you have agreed on a price. Always pay with small bills—request them when you exchange. Be suspicious of locals who may show you around their city or give you directions, and then demand a fee as a "guide." If there's something you don't want and won't pay for (a guide, a rug, whatever) make this absolutely clear right up front. As a rule, always negotiate a price for a service (a tour, a taxi ride) *beforehand*. In contrast to much of North Africa, Tunisia has very harsh laws regarding the possession or use of drugs. *Do not attempt to bring drugs in, take them out, buy them or use them.* Don't even talk to dealers, who are likely to approach you with hashish in the more heavily touristed areas. Being caught in any drug-related incident will likely lead to your being whisked off to defend yourself in Arabic in front of an extremely unsympathetic Tunisian authority.

Women traveling alone in the touristed cities of the north will encounter only minor hassles if they remain near hotels and tourist areas. If you want to venture into the interior or the south, however, you should travel only in groups which include men whom you trust. Note that Americans are not universally popular in the Arab world, particularly given recent U.S. intervention in the Persian Gulf and U.S. support for Israel. To avoid a potentially hairy situation when traveling in the south, carry something with you which shows that you're not affiliated with the Tunisian army—the military likes to check cars and buses for deserters. Women and those eager to be inducted into a foreign military need not worry. And as a general rule of thumb, be wary of anything marked *"Danger de Mort"*—"Beware of Death." Most of Tunisia's **electric current** runs at 220v AC.

Tunisia's nationwide **emergency phone number** is 197.

Health

The two major health problems you're likely to encounter in Tunisia are diarrhea and overexposure to the sun. Dysentery is also common. Select produce that can be peeled, or wash it thoroughly with *bottled* water. Don't eat creamy pastries or any food that has been standing out. Sandwiches and salads, even those served in restaurants, may also prove regrettable. If you want to play it safe, always stick with things that have been bottled, boiled, baked or broiled. Always wear a sun hat in the interior to prevent heatstroke and carry plenty of bottled water. Don't drink the local water in any form. Don't be lured by the treacherous, ice-cold glasses of *citronade*. Beware as well of ice cubes, and be careful even when brushing your teeth. Finally, be sure that, along with sunscreen, your medical kit includes chewable Pepto Bismol or Kaopectate tablets. The only vaccination recommended for travelers to Tunisia is a gamma globulin; consult your doctor for specifics.

Keeping in Touch

Tunisian **telephones** take 100ml coins—about six are needed to call anywhere in the country briefly. The unused balance will be returned. Dial direct using the regional area codes: Tunis and suburbs 01, Bizerte-Cap Bon region 02, Sousse-Mahdia-Monastir region 03, Sfax region 04, Gabes-Jerba region 05, Gafsa region 06, Kairouan region 07, and El Kef and the North 08. Certain rural areas can be reached only with the operator's assistance (tel. 15). International calls may be placed from telephone offices and from major hotels. The quickest, cheapest way to call abroad is to find a phone that accepts 1D and 500ml coins, and dial direct (00—country code—area code—phone number). Direct calls to the U.S. cost 2.400D per minute. Expect a 20-minute wait if you call collect ("en P.C.V.").

Letters to the U.S. and Canada weighing up to 20g cost 500ml; postcards are 400ml. Letters to Europe are 450ml; postcards are 350ml. Post offices (called the "P.T.T." for Poste, Téléphone, & Télégraphe) are generally open from 8am to noon and from 3 to 6pm Monday through Friday and Saturday mornings; in winter from 7:30am to 1:30pm Monday through Saturday. Ramadan hours are usually 8am-3pm. Allow at least three weeks for mail sent from Tunis to the U.S., two weeks for European addresses. Send **telegrams** and telexes from telephone offices or post offices. (Stamps are also sold at newsstands and tobacconists.)

Language

The official language is Arabic, but all Tunisian secondary school students study French, and most people who commonly deal with tourists speak a smattering of English and German as well. French is common among educated Tunisians even in the interior. You would do well to brush up on your sign language.

Getting There

By Plane

There are no direct flights between North America and Tunisia. North Americans should fly to London or Rome, and then make their way to Tunis by plane, train, or boat. **Tunis Air** flies from most major European and North African cities and offers a confusing array of round-trip deals. Flights to London cost 142D, but a charter company will reduce that by about 50%. Tunis Air flights to and from France are about the same price. Flights between Tunis and Marseille cost around 155D.

By Boat

As far back as 204 BC, boatloads of visitors were coming from Italy to present-day Tunisia. Back then, the plan was to land, travel around some, destroy Carthage, and head back to Italy. Now you too can make this same exciting trip (minus the razing of the capital city). Try calling **Tirrenia** (tel. (0923) 238 19 in Trápani) for ferry information:

Trápani-Tunis (7hr. 30min.): Chair L81,400; Jan.-May L71,000. Departures from Trápani Mon. at 9am; From Tunis Mon. at 8pm; arrives Tues. at 6:30am.

Calgiari-Tunis (20hr.): Chair L100,400; Jan.-May L84,700. Departures from Cagliari Sun. at 7pm; from Tunis Mon. at 10pm. Weather permitting, **SNAV** (tel. (0923) 240 14) hydrofoils depart Wed. at 11am and Fri. at 10pm from Trápani for Kelibia, east of Tunis on the Cap Bon Peninsula (7-10hr., L78,000.) High season rates for ferries apply from June through September. As always, consult updated schedules.

Report for all ferries leaving the port of La Goulette (a 15-min. ride on the TGM commuter train from downtown Tunis, get off at Vieille Goulette) *two hours in advance,* or you'll miss the boat. During the last two weeks of August, all boats from Tunisia are packed with Europe-bound migrant workers. Book tickets well in advance. To buy a ferry ticket, you must show your bank receipt for the purchase of dinar and obtain a Bons de Passage from the bank itself—a minor but requisite bureaucratic hassle. You can buy tickets from all major travel agents. In the late summer crunch, fight it out at the crowded **Tirrenia Ticket Office,** 122, rue de Yougoslavie. All boat lines are supervised by the **Compagnie Tunisienne de Navigation (CTN),** which provides passenger information and runs ticket offices at 5, rue Dag Hammarskjold in Tunis (tel. 24 28 01); at La Goulette; at Ponte Colombo (Gare Maritime) in Genoa (tel. (01) 25 80 41); at Rione Sirignano, 2, in Naples (tel. (081) 66 03 33); and at 61, bd. des Dames in Marseille (tel. 91 91 92 20). On arrival, you will have to fill out a detailed customs declaration, although it is unlikely that you will be carrying any of the items asked about (refrigerators, firearms).

Once There

Transportation

A major **train** line runs south from Tunis to Sousse, and then splits into an eastern line through Sfax, which ends in Gabes, and a western line to Tozeur and Gafsa. Another line runs west through Jendouba to the Algerian border and splits into northwest branches ending in Bizerte and Tabarka. Although service is infrequent, the trains are pleasant and air-conditioned. Second-class prices compete with the cost of other modes of transportation. For information, contact **Société Nationale de Chemins de Fer Tunisienne (SNCFT)** at the train station (Gare Tunis-Ville) in pl. de Barcelone, between rue de Hollande and av. de Carthage at av. Farhat Hached (tel. 24 44 40). Pick up a train schedule for the entire country (all on one page!) at the information booth in the Tunis train station. Student discounts are available.

Buses are the most common form of intercity transit. They are inexpensive and convenient, but crowded. Try to board at the terminal (*gare routière*)—this increases your chance of finding a seat and may get you onto an express coach. Schedules change frequently and service can be painfully slow, especially in rural areas. The **Société National des Transports (SNT),** 74, av. de Carthage, Tunis, operates buses between Tunis and its suburbs. The **Société du Métro-Léger du Tunis (SMLT),** av. Muhammad V, Tunis, operates the light rail system, and the **Société de Transports Rural et Interurbain (SNTRI),** passage Mazaguan, Tunis, operates rural, intercity, and international routes.

Louages, usually Peugeot station wagons, serve as intercity taxis. They depart as soon as they get five people with a common destination and will travel as far as the distance from Tunis to Jerba (over 500km). Since no stops need be made along the way, *louages* are the quickest form of ground transport. Prices are fixed and each *louage* lists the rates. If the car doesn't fill, the policy is to charge more per person. On standard routes, per person rates compete with bus and train fares. Such *louages* often indicate the name of their destination on a plaque. Special requests, such as remote archeological sites, can be negotiated but usually cost more than trunk routes of equivalent distance; if the driver can't fill the car for the return voyage, the fare will be doubled. While *louages* have the advantages of speed and convenience, they can be dangerous: the drivers are not known for cautious driving. In addition, the points of departure in each city for a particular destination may be hard to determine, and could even change periodically. Nevertheless, to reach some of the more out-of-the-way locations, a *louage* may be your only option.

A **private car** is indispensable for touring the Sahara, where public transportation is scarce. You must be at least 21 and have a valid international driver's license. Get four people together and rent a cozy two-door four-seater with unlimited mileage, and you can cover transportation costs with 20D per day per person. The Renault 4 is the cheapest option and a reliable vehicle, though it's likely to be in poor condition. Ask to inspect the car *before* you sign. If you're planning to travel through the desert, be sure to bring ample water, since breakdowns do occur.

Hitchhiking is illegal in Tunisia, but many foreigners find it fairly easy. Keep in mind that many Tunisians consider hitching tantamount to freeloading, and may request a contribution. Hitching doesn't save money, since public transportation is so cheap, but it does save time. **Women should never hitch alone in Tunisia.** *Let's Go* does not recommend hitchhiking (see General Introduction above).

Accommodations

In Tunisia, toilet seats and hot showers are a rare luxury. Bring your own toilet paper.

Tunisia supports nearly 30 Youth Centers and HI **youth hostels,** all designed to house soccer teams. They tend to be large, functional, and clean. Some are as charming as locker rooms, and while convenient to the local stadium, they are often far from the center of town. Not all are safe for women. The HI affiliate in Tunisia is the Association Tunisienne des Auberges de Jeunesse, 10, rue Ali Bach Hamba, BP 320-1015 Tunis, RP (tel. 24 60 00).

The ONTT classifies **hotels** on a zero- to four-star scale, and provides listings of all official hotels. Budget travelers should stick with the unrated (1-4D per person), one-star (5-8D per person), and two-star (9-12D per person) establishments.

Organized **camping** hasn't yet come of age in Tunisia, except in the south, where it may be your only alternative. Nevertheless, a handful of campgrounds do exist. As for unofficial camping, the ONTT guide states, "You can pitch your tent where you wish on beaches and in parks after having first obtained permission from the property owner or from the nearest Police or National Guard station." In practice, it can be hard to get such permission, or even to find the right people to ask. In a pinch, most youth hostels will allow camping on their grounds for 300ml-1D per person, including use of the facilities. Public beaches are the most popular places for setting up camp. Freelance camping could be dangerous, though—think twice before pitching your tent (especially given the low cost of regular accomodations). Don't ever camp alone.

Food

Tunisian cooking reflects the competing foreign influences in the country. A single bakery may sell French pastry, Berber date cake, and Near Eastern *halvah*. The staple starch is potatoes, usually cooked in a spicy tomato sauce. All restaurants serve *couscous*, a steamed semolina wheat preparation, topped with almost any kind of sauce. Beef and chicken are Tunisia's principal meats, typically served roasted, either plain or skewered (*en brochette*). *Merguez,* one of the country's most common meat dishes, is spicy sausage, often served with tomatoes and other vegetables. *Odja* consists of eggs and tomato sauce with a bit of sausage, and *koucha* is a meat and potatoes mixture in a spicy red sauce. *Tajine* resembles quiche. Vegetables, mostly tomatoes, cucumbers, and onions, are finely chopped in *mechouia,* Tunisia's national salad. Fast-food stands serve *brik à l'oeuf* (eggs, potatoes, and a green vegetable in a puff-pastry shell). When in the south, fresh almonds (*looz*) are a readily available, satisfying snack.

In cafés, try the abraisive yet soothing *thé vert,* tea richly steeped with mint and heavily sugared. Although Islam frowns on drinking, beer and wine are widely served. *Celtia,* the most common brand of beer, costs 1.200D per bottle. Tunisian red wines are heavy, but *gris de Tunisia* and *Koudiat,* both rosés, are quite good. The local liqueurs *bookha* (distilled from figs) and *thibarine* (distilled from dates) merit sampling.

Bargaining

The name of the game is hard bargaining. Asking prices are about ten times the actual value. If you really intend to buy, avoid mingling with tour groups, and shop late in the day when salespeople are anxious to unload their wares. Refusing, turning your back, and walking away will decrease the price substantially. It is often possible to barter in Tunisia; pens, T-shirts, and sport caps are especially coveted items.

Gabes, off the usual tourist itinerary, is a good place to shop. Here you won't find the kitschy knick-knacks that litter the *medinas* of Tunis, Hammamet, and Monastir.

Life and Times

History and Politics

Tunisia has long treasured its physical and ideological openness. Centuries of immigration and empire-building as well as various foreign influences have left their mark on this tiny nation, which today belongs as much to the Mediterranean as to the Maghreb.

The earliest evidence of settlement in Tunisia dates from about 750 BC, but legend attributes the founding of **Carthage** to the Phoenecian Queen Dido in 814 BC. By the 6th century BC, already prosperous from coastal and North African trade, the city had become a major power in the Mediterranean. When both Carthage and Rome intervened in Sicily, the two empires went to war one another in a series of conflicts known as the Punic Wars, comparable in size and scope to the World Wars of our century. Of the three wars, the second was the most spectacular and devastating. **Hannibal,** the Carthaginian general, led an army that included 370 elephants over the Alps to surprise the Romans from the north, and kicked some Roman butt at Lake Trasimeno and Cannae. Nevertheless, the clever Roman leader Fabius Cunctator ("the delayer") prevailed over Hannibal in the end, with his strategy of "delaying," or avoiding combat. Subsequent Italian governments appear to have hung onto this delaying concept, though without the same fortuitous outcomes. The Second Punic War ended with a Roman victory in 201 BC, but the influential Roman Senator Cato the Elder made *Cartago deleda est* ("Carthage must be destroyed") his cry, and eventually people listened. Perhaps quiet Cato, the Romans declared the Third Punic War, which permanently settled the conflict in their favor (146 BC).

Despite the Romans' attempt to prevent Carthaginian resurgence by sowing the city site with salt, Carthage soon flourished as a provincial capital. Tunisia was Rome's primary African granary; the richness of its archeological remains attests to the colony's wealth. Like much of the Empire, it was sacked by the Vandals and reconquered by the **Byzantine Empire.** As the Arabs began to dismember Byzantium, the region was overrun in 698 and incorporated into the Abassid Empire centered in Baghdad. The four dynasties that ruled Tunisia established the Islamic faith locally and built the *medinas* (old cities) at the center of present-day Tunisian cities.

In the late 16th century, the **Ottoman Turks** seized the area, but within a century had relinquished control to the **Beys,** a dynasty of Turkish origin. Under these rulers, Tunisia acquired its present-day name and borders. When they weren't cavorting within their Bardo Palace, the Beys supervised the adoption of the 1861 constitution—the first in any Arab country—and pushed Tunisia toward Westernization. The latter efforts led to economic dislocation and allowed European nations to "manage" Tunisia's economy.

After invading Tunisia in 1881, the **French** did a great deal to organize and develop the country; they also seized all the best land for their own settlers. Their lasting legacy is the Tunisian civil service, one of the best in the Third World. Although French rule remained relatively liberal in Tunisia, a nationalist consciousness developed among the intelligentsia, who formed the reformist **Destour Party** shortly after WWI. They were soon superseded by a new generation of young agitators led by a lawyer named Habib Bourguiba, who split and formed the more radical Neo-Destour party. Bourguiba, whom the French jailed before he escaped into exile, returned triumphantly on June 1, 1955, to negotiate Tunisia's relatively painless transition to independence, which came on **March 20, 1956.** A year later he deposed the last Bey, then the titular head of state, and became President-for-Life.

A pragmatist, Bourguiba encouraged the French to stay, to the benefit of Tunisia's economy. Social reforms were introduced, including equal rights for women, liability reform, and greater and more equitable educational opportunities; the country stands a model of civic freedom in the Arab world. By the last decade of Bourguiba's reign, however, Tunisia was in financial turmoil and a state of civil unrest. After 31 years in office, the elderly Bourgiba was deposed in a bloodless coup on November 7, 1987. His influence, though, is still strongly felt and his face continues to adorn the currency. He was replaced by President Aine el Abidine ben Madj Hamita Ben Ali, or President Ben Ali for those who don't have all day. General Ben Ali has attempted to reverse the economic decline with new economic programs and active pursuit of Middle Eastern unity. While Tunisia today faces high unemployment and a tradition of autocracy, it also remains one of the more open and stable of the Arab states.

Festivals and Holidays

Islam is the primary cultural force molding Tunisian life; the major celebration each year is **Ramadan,** the Muslim month of fasting that comes at different times of the Gregorian year, depending on the lunar calendar. Ramadan affects all aspects of daily life. Shops and services close down for the afternoon. Muslims are forbidden to eat, drink, or smoke between sunrise and sunset. After sunset, streets swell with people, shops and businesses reopen, and the festivities last until well past midnight. The end of Ramadan is marked by Id al-Fitr, a three-day celebration during which all commercial activity comes to a standstill. In rural areas and smaller towns, restaurants and cafés close throughout the day. Concerned about how little work gets done during the month-long holiday, President Bourguiba once moved to cancel Ramadan—an action akin to outlawing Lent in the Vatican. A nationwide revolt quickly compelled Bourguiba to abandon his ill-advised position.

Southern Tunisia tends to host national festivals, which invariably include camel fights as well as such less-raucous forms of traditional culture as folkloric presentations and parades. The most extensive festival takes place in Douz and Tozeur in late December and in Nefta in April. A similar spectacle is held in the north at El-Haouaria on Cap Bon in June.

Tunis

Tunis is a Maghreb city that tries very hard to be Paris. Modern and prosperous by North African standards, its million-and-a-half inhabitants cloak themselves in a swirling mixture of Western fashion and traditional garb. The ancient heart of the city, the *medina,* where tumultuous *souks* (bazaars) unfurl around immense mosques, possesses a specious Arab authenticity belied by the tawdry clutter of a tourist trap. The stately structures and tree-lined boulevards of colonial Tunis vacillate between a bizarre imitation of European culture and a pleasant Islamic variation on the City of Light. On the outskirts sprawls a typical third-world urban margin: innumerable, identical blocks of ugly high-rises and miles of muddy shantytowns.

Originally an appendage of Carthaginian Thynes, Tunis survived the destruction of its mother city to become a prominent outpost in Roman and Byzantine times. By the 13th century it had matured into a bastion of Islam. Under the Hafsid Dynasty, the city acquired a reputation for liberal ideas and progressive ways that it continues to cultivate.

Orientation and Practical Information

The new downtown was laid out by the French in their beloved colonial checkerboard fashion. Major boulevards often change names after large intersections. The primary east-west axis is **avenue Habib Bourguiba,** which becomes **avenue de France** several blocks before the *medina.* The avenue is intersected by the major north-south artery, **avenue de Carthage,** which becomes **avenue de Paris** and then **avenue de la Liberté** as it proceeds north. The former stretches from the water's edge to the *medina;* the latter extends from the southbound bus station to the verdant **Belvedère Park.** Av. Habib Bourguiba is *the* thoroughfare, home to most of the city's major banks and travel agencies. The body of water at the end of the avenue is not the Mediterranean, but **Lac de Tunis,** an enclosed expanse of salt water. A causeway carries the electric TGM commuter train across the lake to the harbor at **La Goulette,** where the ferries dock. To get to the TGM station from the port road on the left, take a right at the castle, a left at the statue, and walk straight (10min.). The train will take you to Tunis for 180ml. The *Métro,* a newly opened above-ground trolley, connects the TGM station with the train station. The TGM line continues north to the archeological sites of Carthage, the village of Sidi Bou Said, and the beaches at La Marsa.

Tourist Office: ONTT Reception Office (tel. 34 10 77), pl. d'Afrique at av. Bourguiba and av. Mohammed V. Not too informed and not too helpful. Many brochures, little information, no English. Ask for a map of the city and hope it isn't in Arabic. Open Sat.-Wed. 8:30am-1:30pm and Thurs.-Fri. 7:30am-1:30pm. For advice and intelligible maps, try the ONTT branch offices at the **train station** (same hours), on the 2nd floor of the Tunis-Carthage **airport,** or at the **port.**

Budget Travel: Sotutour-Stav, 2, rue de Sparte (tel. 24 70 48), off av. de Paris. They sell ISICs and operate "vacation villages" at Hammamet, Tozeur, and near Tunis. Open Mon.-Sat. 8:30am-12:30pm and 2:30-8:30pm.

Embassies: U.S., 144, av. de la Liberté (tel. 28 25 66). **Canada,** rue du Senegal (tel. 28 65 77). **U.K.,** 5, pl. de la Victoire (tel. 24 51 00), at the entrance to the *medina.* Also the only service for citizens of Australia and New Zealand. **Algeria,** 18, rue du Niger (tel. 28 31 66). For a visa—required of U.S. and Canadian citizens staying longer than 3 mo., and of Australian citizens visiting for any length of time—bring 7.500D to the consulate at 136, av. de la Liberté (tel. 28 00 55). Minimum sum for **money exchange** about 1000 Algerian Dinars.

American Express: Carthage Tours, 59, av. Habib Bourguiba (tel. 25 43 04). No banking services. Emergency check cashing for cardholders only; others can only report lost or stolen traveler's checks here. Don't expect a warm reception. Open Mon.-Fri. 8am-noon and 2:30-7pm, Sat. 8am-6pm.

Post Office: 30, av. Charles de Gaulle, (tel. 65 01 21), off av. de France. Limited services only in the afternoon. **Poste Restante** (150ml per letter received). Open Mon.-Fri. 7:30am-1pm and 5-7pm, Sat. 7:30am-1pm, Sun. 9-11am.

Telephones and Telex: 29, rue Gamal Abdel Nasser, entrance around the corner from the post office. Inefficient. Some phones here take 1D and 500ml pieces, so you can make direct international calls. Send **telegrams** from here or the post office. Open 24 hrs. 24-hr. payphones also in the underpass at av. de Paris-av. du Ghana intersection. **Telephone Code:** 01.

Flights: Tunis-Carthage International Airport (tel. 23 60 00). 24-hr. **currency exchange.** Take bus #35 from av. Bourguiba to the airport (*aérodrome*) and back (about 320ml). Note: the TGM Aéroport stop is actually a beach named Aéroport—not the airport. **Tunis Air,** 48, av. Habib Bourgiba, (tel. 25 91 89).

Trains: SNCFT Tunis Ville Station, pl. de Barcelone (tel. 24 44 40), between rue de Hollande and av. de Carthage. The new *Métro* connects this station to the TGM station. To: Hammamet and Nabeul (1.800D); Sousse (2.600D); Sfax (5.900D); Gabes (8.800D); Bizerte (1.700D). **Commuter Trains: TGM,** at the foot of av. Bourguiba. Carthage-La Marsa via La Goulette and Sidi Bou Said. Speedy, frequent tram service 5am-midnight. 350ml to Carthage and La Marsa, 200ml between middle stops.

Buses: City buses at av. Dr. Habib Thameur at **Jardin Thameur** before av. de Paris; also next to the **TGM Tunis-Marine Station.** Buses also stop at pl. de Barcelone, in front of the Tunis-Ville train station and along av. Bourguiba. Fare 140ml and up, depending on distance traveled. **Southbound** and **Hammamet-Nabeul Buses: SNT** (tel. 49 52 55 or 49 03 58). The SNT station is at the end of av. de Carthage across from the cemetery to the right. Walk or take municipal bus #8 from av. Bourguiba or #50 from Gamal Abdel Nasser (140ml).

Ferries: La Goulette (tel. 27 50 00). Take the TGM train to Vieille Goulette, 1km from the port. Ferry tickets at any of the travel agencies along av. Bourguiba. Arrive at least 2hr. before departure.

Taxis: tel. 25 22 11. Always metered. Three passengers is the usual maximum. 50% surcharge after 9pm. To airport about 2D.

Car Rental: Europcar, 17, av. Habib Bourguiba (tel. 34 03 03). The cheapest. Renault Super 5s cost 240D for 3 days, 535D for a week. Open daily 8am-12:30pm and 2-7pm. **Hertz,** 29, av. Bourguiba (tel. 24 85 59), or at the airport (tel. 23 60 00). **Avis,** 90, av. de la Liberté (tel. 28 25 08). It is illegal for a rental car to carry more than 5 people including the driver. Always have passports ready for security checks. You must be 21 to rent and drive, or have had a license for more than 1 yr.

Swimming Pool: in the **Parc du Belvédère,** at the end of av. de la Liberté. Open July-Sept. 10am-5pm. Admission 500ml. Take bus #5, 28, or 38 from av. Bourguiba.

Laundromat: There are no coin-operated laundromats in Tunisia, but some dry cleaners take laundry by the kilo. Try **Laverie,** 15, rue d'Allemagne, across from the produce market. Open Mon.-Sat. 7am-6:30pm.

Late-Night Pharmacy: 43, av. Bourguiba (tel. 25 25 07), or 20, av. de la Liberté (tel. 24 35 20).

Hospital: Hôpital Charles Nicolle (tel. 66 30 10), bd. du IX Avril 1938 at rue Paul Bourde.

Emergencies: Police, tel. 197 or 24 21 11. Less than helpful. **Ambulance:** tel. 190 or 24 53 99. **Medical Emergency:** tel. 24 73 30.

Accommodations

Finding a budget hotel in Tunis is no problem except in the height of summer; the problem is finding one that isn't sleazy. Think twice before staying in the cheapest hotels or in the *medina*.

Hotel Cirta, 42, rue Charles de Gaulle (tel. 24 15 82), near the post office. One of the best deals in town. Tiny but unsullied rooms, many with balconies overlooking the bustling street. Singles 5D. Doubles 9D. Triples 12D. Quads 14D. Showers 1D.

Hotel Bristol, 30, rue Mohamed el Aziz Taj, (tel. 24 48 36), off av. de Carthage behind the Café de Paris. Clean, cheap cubbyholes. Singles 4D. Doubles 6D. Triples 9D. Quads 11D.

Hotel Agriculture, 25, rue Charles de Gaulle (tel. 24 63 94), across from the Cirta, which it resembles. Decent and well-kept. Absolutely no livestock or vegetables allowed. Singles 4.500D. Doubles 8D, with bath 10D. Triples 12D, with bath 14D. Showers (cold in summer) 1D.

Victoria Hotel, 79, av. Farhat Hached (tel. 34 28 63), across from the bus stops in front of the train station. Singles 7D. Doubles 10D. Triples 10D, with shower 11D, with bath 14.500D.

Hotel Commodore, 17, rue d'Allemagne (tel. 24 49 41), 2nd right off av. Charles de Gaulle from av. de France. A cut above, and not much more expensive. Polished wood lobby and spotless rooms. Singles 7.5D, with bath 10D. Doubles 14.500D, with bath 16.500D. Triples 20.500D, with bath 22.500D.

Hotel Rex, 65, rue de Yougoslavie (tel. 25 73 97), at rue Ibn Khaldoun. Good-natured management. Breezy rooms with imitation parquet floors. The bathrooms (in every room) are an architectural landmark. Singles 11.500D. Doubles 15.500D. Triples 20.500D.

Hotel de Suisse, 5, rue de Suisse (tel. 24 38 21), in a narrow alley between rue de Hollande and rue Gamal Abdel Nasser, by the train station. Tidy and affordable. Singles 7D. Doubles 10D, with bath 11D. Showers 1D. Across the street, **Hotel Central** (tel. 24 04 33) provides mediocre rooms at unspectacular prices. English-speaking, friendly, but more suitable for men than women. Doubles 7D. Triples 10D. Quads 13D. Mat on roof 2D. Shower 1.2D.

Hotel de France, 8, rue Mustapha M'Barek (tel. 24 58 76), off pl. de la Victoire. Dingy hallways, but the most amiable management in town. Singles 9.800D, with shower 11D. Doubles 12.200D, with shower 14.800D. Breakfast 1.600D.

Food

Tunis is most cosmopolitan when it comes to cuisine. You can feast on *spaghetti alla bolognese* cooked to an *al dente* perfection that would be the envy of any Italian chef, continue with a savory platter of spiced roast lamb, and finish with a delicate *éclair au chocolat* worthy of the finest french *pâtisseries*—all for under 4D. Unfortunately, this gastronomic ideal is surrounded by pitfalls: many places are dirty, many clean places are overpriced. The stand-up *rôtisseries* and sandwich shops of av. Bourguiba and av. de la Liberté are usually rip-offs. The farther away from av. Bourguiba you go, the fewer dinar will leave your pocket. Budgetarians can survive on the hot snacks sold at most *pâtisseries:* mini pizzas, hot anchovy rolls, tuna rolls, and meat pies (about 350ml). Peruse the stalls of the comprehensive **central market,** on rue Charles de Gaulle between rue d'Allemagne and av. d'Espagne (open daily 6am-2pm). **Monoprix,** a large supermarket with stores off av. Bourguiba on rue Charles de Gaulle and on rue de la Liberté at rue du Koweit, also stocks a selection of inexpensive edibles. (Open Mon.-Sat. 8am-12:30pm and 4:30-8pm, Sun. 9am-1pm.)

M'Rabet (tel. 26 17 29), at the center of the *medina* in Souk Et-Trouk. The 300-year old building contains the *sarcophagi* of an Ottoman sheik, his servant, and his daughter, for whom the restaurant is named. Smoke a *sheeshah* (water pipe, 1.500D) or sip Turkish coffee (300ml). Upstairs is a tea salon, decorated with old curved mirrors and paintings, and a copper furnace reminiscent of Aladdin. Main courses are served (dinner 11-12D) as a belly dancer gyrates to the plinking of a *sitar* (6D for the show). Open Mon.-Sat. noon-3 pm and 8pm-midnight. Shows in the evening only.

Restaurant Carcassonne, 8, av. de Carthage (tel. 25 67 68). Clean, serene, friendly, and efficient. Try the *tajine* (a bit like quiche, 1.500D). Four-course Ménu du Jour a super-bargain at 2.800D. Open daily 8am-10pm.

Mic Mac (tel. 34 28 67), at rue de Yougoslavie and Ibn Khaldoun. One of the few stand-up sandwich shops that's not a rip-off. Reasonably clean. Massive, greasy *schwarma* sandwich and fries 1.100D. Open Mon.-Sat. 7am-10:30pm.

Restaurant Des Palmiers, 11, rue d'Egypte (tel. 28 54 07), off av. de la Liberté. Worth every second of the 10-min. walk from av. Bourguiba. Dishes are fresh, Tunisian, and served quickly. Try the *meloukya,* a delicous meat dish which looks extremely unappetizing (1.350D). Open Mon.-Sat. noon-10:30pm. Closed mornings during Ramadan.

Restaurant Neptune, 3, rue du Caire (tel. 24 48 20), across from Hotel Africa. The complete, 4-course *ménu* is a fantastic deal (1.900D). Prompt service, large portions, decent fare, but no tridents. Nothing on the menu over 3.5D. Open daily 11am-3pm and 6-10pm.

Restaurant Ennil, 9, rue du Caire (tel. 34 93 80). Mediocre food at reasonable prices. Open daily 10am-10pm. Across the street at #6, **Restaurante du Caire** (tel. 25 77 01) serves similarly uninspired but affordable fare. Open 11am-10pm.

Sights

Tunis is as rich in colors, images, and textures as the mosaics for which it is renowned. The labyrinthine *souks,* the thousand and one secrets of the *medina,* the sun-baked cupolas, and the exultant minarets stimulate endless wonder.

The New City

The best introduction to French-built modern Tunis makes itself available as you stroll up **av. Habib Bourguiba,** known as the city's Champs Elysées. Including its tree-filled park median, the boulevard spreads nearly 70m. The strip testifies to the Tunisian passion for flowers—florist stalls and young boys vending jasmine blossoms line its entire length. Along the way, you can also stock up on such Tunisian souvenirs as Levis 501 T-shirts and Bee Gees bootlegs. The **place d'Afrique,** at the intersection of av. Muhammed V, was once occupied by an equestrian statue of Bourguiba. That statue now resides in front of La Goulette, and in its place rises a four-legged clock tower. The site has been officially renamed **place du 7 Novembre 1987,** commemorating the recent *coup d'état.*

Nowhere is the stamp of the French colonial period clearer than at the juncture of av. Bourguiba and pl. d'Afrique, in the heart of the city. After you cross av. de Carthage on the boulevard, you will reach the **Artisanat** (a bastion of overpriced local crafts) on the left, and after it, the wedding-cake white **National Theater.** At **place de l'Indépendence,** where av. Bourguiba comes to an abrupt halt, you may suddenly feel you are in Paris: on the left is the oversized French Embassy, a miniature Elysées palace hiding behind its elegant black iron fence. Then the street narrows suddenly and av. Bourguiba becomes av. de France. The next block on the same side forms a continuous arcade in the manner of a 19th-century Parisian boulevard. Across the street looms the massive Roman Catholic **cathedral,** which incorporates keyhole-shaped Islamic arches into its Gothic form (1882). The blend is only slightly more successful than the French efforts the French made within the edifice to convert Tunisians to Christianity. The interior houses one of the eight Mollins-Cervailles-Coll Romantic organs in the world. (Cathedral open for Mass: weekdays 8:15am and 6:30pm., Sun. 8:30am and 11:00am.) If you are in search of a little leafy peace, head to the **Jardin Thameur,** av. Habib Thameur.

Medina

In most Arab cities, the fortified medieval city, or *medina,* seems worlds apart from its 19th- and 20th-century surroundings. This is true only of the fringes of Tunis's *medina,* however, since the central areas have become so infested with vulgar souvenir shops that they seem a continuation of av. Bourguiba, which leads directly toward them. The medieval *souks*—itinerant weekly markets specializing in handmade wares—have become so commercialized that there is now a Souk Burger, next to the Mustang Jeans by the mosque. Stuffed toy camels decorate every curb, and for your convenience, the street vendors do take VISA and American Express.

Nevertheless, the *medina* is certainly worth a few hours; if you avoid the main drags, you may even be enchanted. Exploring the *medina* by day is less risky than at night, when it's unsafe for anyone. (The police will be unsympathetic if you're mugged.) On av. Bourguiba and by the mosque, young men claiming to be students will offer either to guide you around the sights (they will expect payment) or to accompany you to the grossly over-priced artisan shops (they will receive a commission). Also beware of merchants who drag you upstairs to see their "terraces," and then request an outrageous fee for the exalted privilege of having entered their shop.

To escape the tourist traps, take route de la Kasbah (on the right) rather than rue Djamaa ez Zitouna (on the left) from pl. de la Victoire. Both are lined with shops, but the shoppers on the former are Tunisian. Near the mosque, turn right and wind slowly up the Bab Souika. **Place Bab Souika,** just outside the *medina* walls to the north but at the core of the old city, numbers among the most atmospheric spots in Tunis. Head across the street, up rue Halfouine, the pungent butchers' street, to the benches and stalls in front of the **mosque Saheb Ettabaa,** stronghold of Arab culture.

To "do" the medina, start back at the **Great Mosque,** in the center of the *medina,* rue Djamaa ez Zitouna. Known formally as Djamaa ez Zitouna (Mosque of the Olives), the Great Mosque—also home to the first university in the Arab world—maintains vague visiting conditions for non-Muslims—especially during the summer. Generally, you are permitted to visit the courtyard between 8:30am and noon (except on Fri.) if your arms and legs are fully covered. Alternatively, visit the terrace of one of the surrounding shops and look down into the courtyard—prayer times are quite a sight. As you enter the courtyard of the mosque, a long row of carved wooden doors studded with iron stands on your left. These conceal the prayer area and the *mihrab,* which faces east toward Mecca. Opposite, you'll find the gigantic minaret, soaring over the entire *medina.* Modified in the 19th century, it is far more decorative than the courtyard or prayer room. The prayer room's 184 columns were salvaged from temples and other abandoned buildings of Roman Carthage.

Be prepared for aggressive salesmen who will sprinkle your hand with fragrance if you stop for a moment in **Souk el-Attarine** (the perfumers' market). At the end of Souk el-Attarine, take a right and a few steps on Sidi Ben Arous to come to the stylish 17th-century **Hamouda Pacha Mosque** with its elegant minaret and adjoining mausoleum. Souk el-Attarine leads into **Souk et-Trouk,** a market of tailors whose stacks of red fezzes would turn any Shriner green with envy. Follow Souk et-Trouk to rue Sidi Ben Zaid. On your left, you'll see the handsome 17th-century **Sidi Youssef Mosque,** dominated by its octagonal minaret, while on your right stands the 18th-century **Dar el Bey** palace, now housing the Ministry of Foreign Affairs. Walk back toward the minaret of the Grand Mosque and along its back wall through the **Souk el-Koumach** (also called Souk des Etoffes). Multicolored scarves, light dresses, and other women's garments hang in high rows in this 15th-century alleyway. Don't miss the narrow turn-off onto **Souk el-Leffa,** the luxurious *souk* of spangled carpets.

Many of the larger emporiums boast intricately tiled **terraces** from which you can peer at and admire the rooftops of the *souks* and the surrounding *medina.* The most famous is that of the **Palais d'Orient,** the large bazaar at #58 Souk el-Leffa. Their enameled tile terrace dates from the 15th century and its view is featured on hundreds of postcards of Tunis.

Souk el-Leffa turns into **Souk es-Sekkajine,** the saddlemakers' *souk,* still proffering reins and halters. Retrace your steps, turn right onto Souk el-Kouafi, and on your right will be the miniature maze of Souk des Orfèvres—the jewelers' neighborhood. In this beehive of shops, hunched artisans cut stones, engrave silver, and fashion pendants out of ancient coins.

Walk back in front of the main porch of the Grand Mosque and cut uphill along Souk el-Attarine for a quick turn-off right onto Souk el-Blag-Djia, which becomes tiny rue el-Jelloud. Where you see the sign "el-Jelloud," take a left into a cul-de-sac (Impasse Echemmahra). At the far end, you can ring the doorbell at #9 and ask to visit the small, elegant 17th-century **Tomb of Princess Aziza,** now a private residence. Other sights of interest in the *medina* lie farther from the central market area. The stately **Mosque of Sidi Mahrez** at the far northern tip of the *medina,* can be reached by passing through completely untouristed *souks* where local residents do their shopping. From the area of the Grand Mosque, walk back toward the new city along rue de la Kasbah, and take the left fork onto the narrow **Souk du Cuivre** (copper souk), which rings with a chorus of metalworkers' hammers. You can buy teapots, lamps, pipes, and hammered metal plates here directly from the artisans (5.000-25.000D). At the end, turn left onto Souk el-Grana, which eventually turns into Souk el-Out. If you follow the covered market route, the *souks* will eventually give way to **Sidi Mahrez,** a large white mosque on the street of the same name. The 17th-century edifice is noted for its strong Turkish influence, with four small domes grouped around a single large central dome. (The domes are not visible from the street and entrance is off limits; catch a glimpse from the rooftop bar of the Hotel International.) Across the street, through two bronze doors, lies the fascinating **Zaouïa Sidi Mahrez.** Walk straight in and turn left to find a well where women come to bathe in holy fertility water. Bring condoms.

Make the stroll over to the southern corner of the *medina.* From the Grand Mosque, follow rue Djamaa ez-Zitouna, and take the first right onto Souk el-Balat, which leads to rue des Teinturiers. Here, at #31, you'll find the **Mosquée des Teinturiers**—dyers' mosque, built in 1716. Although closed to non-believers, the mosque is worth seeing for its fancifully colored eaves in red, green, and yellow. A few steps farther, signs point the way to **Dar Ben Abdallah,** an ornate 18th-century palace that houses the **Museum of Traditional Arts.** (Open Tues.-Sun. 9:30am-4:30pm. Admission 500ml.) If you follow rue Ben Abdallah from the courtyard of the palace, you'll eventually reach the **Souk des Teinturiers,** the dyers' colorful *souk,* where looms rattle and dye trickles into a gutter in the middle of the street.

The Bardo Museum

While a trip to North Africa generally means escape from the endless "must-see" museums of Europe, Tunis offers no better diversion than the **Bardo Museum,** home to one of the world's finest collections of ancient art. The Bardo is most renowned for its Roman mosaics; the finest works have been transported here from various archeological sites throughout the country and compensate for the uninspiring ruins at Carthage and other sites.

Initiate yourself on the ground floor at the cross-shaped baptistery in the **Paleochristian Room,** which also features brightly colored mosaic tombstones with dyspeptic icons and Latin admonitions. Around the corner in the jovial **Tophet Room,** ritual slabs informatively illustrate the Carthaginian procedure for sacrificing children to their dark goddess. If you don't intend to try this out, move on to Room VI, which features the findings from **Bulla Regia,** highlighted by twice-life-size statues of Roman gods, as well as a fine mosaic of Perseus and Andromeda. The ornate geometric mosaics uncovered at **Thuburbo Majus** are in Room VIII. Take refuge from the dead by ascending the staircase into the land of the immortal: Room IX, the central exhibition hall, is a courtyard with a Turkish twist, used by the bey's harem. Now it houses sculpture and mosaics excavated at Carthage. The **Hadrumetum Room** is decorated below by an immense mosaic from Sousse, the *Triumph of Neptune,* while the walls above are a backdrop for three semi-circular works depicting rural houses and a 4th-century piece entitled *Mosaïque du Seigneur Julius.* The adjacent Room XI mounts a superbly preserved *Neptune in his Chariot.* Room XXVII houses the finds from **Dougga,** including a celebrated mosaic that depicts *Ulysses and the Sirens,* the latter quite homely and the former frightened nonetheless. Complete your odyssey at the **Uthina Room,** where a wall-mounted mosaic depicts the love-lorn Orpheus enchanting the beasts with his inspired strumming.

The Bardo is open Tuesday through Sunday from 9:30am to 4:30pm; during Ramadan until 4pm. (Admission 2.000D; Fri. and Sun. afternoons 800ml. Photo permits 1.000D.) Take bus #3 from av. Bourguiba (240ml), or take bus #3 or 4 from Bab Souika east of the *medina.* Or think about catching a cab (1.500-2.000D) to avoid a crowded bus.

Near Tunis

Tunis's environs were made for daytrips. The efficient TGM commuter trains make **Carthage** (30min.) and **Sidi Bou Said** (35min.), easy, quick rides. Trains come every 15 minutes or so, and the fare is 600ml round-trip to either of these destinations. The spectacular 30km beach of **Raouad** begins just past **Gammarth;** but both these towns (and La Marsa as well) are now overrun tourist nightmares.

Carthage

> *There was an ancient city (Tyrian settlers inhabited it), Carthage, opposite Italy and the far-off mouths of the Tiber, a city rich in wealth and terribly harsh in the pursuit of war. Juno is said to have loved this one city more than all lands...*
> *—Virgil, The Aeneid I 12-16*

> *Carthage must be destroyed.*
> *—Cato*

If you come to see the ruins of this great city you will understand Juno's sentiment; if you visit the modern town which has taken its place, you will probably side with the Senator. Contemporary Carthage is a bland, pretentious collection of mansions and tourist traps. A bottle of soda costs 600ml here—be sure to drink up in Tunis. The ruins are scattered over a wide area that coincides with the stops of the TGM train line. Successive stops are close together and can be traversed easily on foot. If you're short on stamina or time, get off at the **Carthage-Hannibal** station, visit the Roman baths, then get back on the TGM to **Carthage-Byrsa** and visit the Tophet and the Punic Ports. The nearby beaches of the Bay of Tunis offer a refreshing alternative to yet another ruin. Buy a ticket for all Carthage sites at either the Carthage Museum or the Roman baths (2D, free with student ID. Be ready to fend off guides or use up some loose change.)

Carthage-Byrsa: Though most of the uncovered ruins of Carthage date to the Roman era, evidence of the original Punic settlement has been discovered here in the form of a cemetery. At the site of the **Tophet** (also called the **Sanctuary of Tanit**) quiet bushes conceal stones shaped like the planks of picket fences, engraved with a simple design: a circle atop a rectangle that balances on a triangle. The pictogram represents the figure of the bloodthirsty goddess Tanit, who demanded the sacrifice of first-born 12- and 14-year-olds in time of hardship. Each stone mourns one of the 1200 children who were sacrificed here. (Open daily 7am-7pm.) To reach the Tophet, cross the tracks and head towards the sea, then take a right onto rue Hannibal.

Almost nothing remains of what was the world's greatest harbor in its time, but determined archeologists have reconstructed the contours of the original **Punic Ports.** Inside the "Antiquarium" (the custodian will unlock it for you) are detailed models of the military port from the Punic and Roman periods. (Site open daily 7am-7pm.) To reach the ports, walk toward the water from the Carthage-Byrsa station and take your third left to circle the swamp.

Carthage-Dermech: the **National Museum of Carthage** occupies the site where an immense Roman temple once stood. The remains are scattered throughout the surrounding gardens. Inside you'll find only a few Punic funerary steles and two expressive 4th-century sarcophagi made from Italian Carrara marble—an indication of the city's former wealth. (Open daily 8:30am-7pm.) To reach the museum from the station, cross the tracks and walk down rue J.F. Kennedy until you see a steep flight of stairs (rue 18 Janvier) leading up the hill to the left.

Carthage-Hannibal: The most substantial rubble of Carthage lies in the village named after the general who struck fear into the hearts of thousands of Romans. From the station, walk toward the water and turn left on rue Septime Severe to find the 2nd-century Roman **Baths of Antonius**—the single most impressive ruin in Carthage.

Once rivaling Rome's Baths of Caracalla in size, the baths were gradually destroyed by villagers who used the site as a quarry. You can't enter this forest of humpbacked pediments and fallen pillars; the sea breeze is your only solace as you wander around them. Further away from the water, beyond the overgrown ruins, you'll discover a tiny underground Christian chapel, whose floor is patterned with an ornithological mosaic. (Open daily 8:30am-7pm; off-season 8:30am-5pm.)

Head farther up the road, cross beneath the railway tracks, and follow the signs to the **Roman Villas** and **Archeological Gardens,** where you'll find two Byzantine churches and a Punic necropolis. The guides will tell you that the elegant villa was Hannibal's Palace; they refuse to admit that Hannibal wasn't Roman and died 400 years before the villa was built. Over the hill lies the well-preserved 3rd-century **Odeon.** (Open daily 8am-7pm.) From the station, cross the tracks and go uphill to reach the remnants of the Roman **amphitheater.** Another 2km ahead, the scrupulously restored **Theater of Carthage,** provides the backdrop for the **Festival of Carthage** (July to mid-Aug). For information, contact the tourist office in Tunis or see the schedule in *La Presse.*

Sidi Bou Said

Perched on the rocky promontory of Cape Carthage at the northern tip of the Bay of Tunis, the beautiful Tunisian village of Sidi Bou Said is a 35-minute train ride from downtown Tunis. This hill-top city of whitewashed, cube-shaped houses and brilliant blue doorways has inspired artists and attracted scores of Europeans for many years. During summer evenings and late into Ramadan nights, Europeans and Tunisians alike make merry in the cliff-top cafés. Decorative detail is the secret to Sidi Bou Said's charm: doors studded with patterns of giant black nails, metal knockers in the shape of the Hand of Fatima, brightly painted metal window grills, and wooden window boxes thick with flowers.

From the TGM station, proceed to the right and turn left at the police station. Walk up the hill along av. Docteur Habib Thameur to the tiny **town square.** The **TGM** whisks you back to Tunis until midnight. Follow rue Sidi Bou-Fares from the main square, turn left, and hike up the hill. A small tip will persuade the guardian to let you climb the **lighthouse.** Or continue from the town square until you see the steep flight of 254 stairs to the right; these descend to the small beach. Before 10am or after 9pm, ask around the port about lending a hand on one of the fishing boats that ply the sea all night and return at dawn. You'll have a great time, and if you can spare several days, you may even get paid. The **Hotel Sidi Bou-Fares,** up the hill from the main square at #15 (tel. 74 00 91), maintains eight simple, spotless rooms with stone floors around a garden courtyard in the shade of an immense fig tree. The ambience here suggests something between a luxurious Mediterranean villa and a 1960s commune. The genial owner occasionally cooks lunch, and trades insults with the guests. Call ahead; a room here is the most pleasant base for exploration in Tunis. (Singles 8.500D. Doubles 13D. Triples with bath 18D. Breakfast 2D.)

Restaurant Chergui, off the main square (tel. 74 09 87), is the cheapest and one of the most appealing restaurants in town. Try the excellent *couscous poulet* for 1.800D, the *brik à l'oeuf* for 600ml, or the *tajine de fromage* (a meatless quiche) for 1.800D, all served in a large courtyard at low, Arab-style tables. (Open daily noon-10pm.) For dessert, pick up some *bambolini,* a fried dough concoction swamped in sugar, for 200ml from the stands that line the beach.

Sidi Bou Said exists only for the evening. As the sun sets, the city's unrivaled cafés jolt awake from mid-day slumber. Avoid the expensive and trendy restaurants at the bottom of the cliff. Instead, contemplate the ocean from atop the cliff at **Café Sidi Chabaane,** an exotic place with irregular tiers and delicate teas.

Cap Bon Peninsula

Stretching northeast toward Sicily, Cap Bon defines the Bay of Tunis on one side and the Gulf of Hammamet on the other. The cape's hillsides, rich with olive and orange groves, and its shimmering sea provide welcome relief from both the scorching heat of the south and the wearying bustle of Tunis. Droves of vacationing Europeans seek the blessings of the peninsula's fine beaches and baptism in its azure waters in the crowded beach towns of Kelibia, Hammamet and Nabeul. Frequent and packed buses link the villages of the peninsula with Tunis and each other. Unfortunately, inexpensive hotels are rare; save your budget by hitting hostels.

Nabeul

Nabeul is both a pleasant, inexpensive place to spend a few days and an excellent anchor for excursions throughout the rest of the Cap Bon Peninsula. Its beaches may be less spectacular than the more famous ones at nearby Hammamet (12km south), but Nabeul's lower prices and less artificial atmosphere more than compensate. Locals and foreigners alike come here to relax and swim in what is perhaps Tunis's only authentic beach town. Nabeul's other claim to fame as tile and ceramics capital of Tunisia makes it a nexus for tourists who equate travel with shopping. The place becomes a madhouse on Friday mornings, when myriads of tourists are bused in for a contrived, so-called **camel market**. Flee for the beach when you hear the din approaching.

If you arrive by train (from Tunis, 12 per day, 20min, 680ml round-trip), and exit the **train station,** in front of you will be (yet another) **place du 7 Novembre,** with a tree growing out of a massive ceramic vase. Across the street and slightly to the right is a small **museum** of Carthaginian and Roman findings (open Tues.-Sun. 9am-4:30pm). To get to the **tourist office,** av. Taïeb Mehiri (tel. 868 00), head straight one block, and make a right onto av. Taïeb Mehiri. Proceed almost to the beach; it's on your right. By Tunisian standards, they're outstandingly helpful: they speak English *and* they have a map. (Open 7:30am-1:30pm and 4-7pm, Sept.-June 8:30am-1pm and 3-5:45pm.) If you come by bus (tel. 852 61), you will arrive somewhere on the main street in town, which changes name (from west to east) from av. Thameur to **av. Farhat Hached** (the major shopping street) to rue Zarrouk. **Av. Bourguiba** is a perpendicular cross street; the train station and pl. 7 Novembre are two blocks south of the intersection. The **post office** (tel. 850 00) and **police station** (tel. 854 74) both reside on av. Bourguiba. (Post office open Mon.-Fri. 7am-1pm and 5pm-7pm., Sat. 7am-1:30pm.)

Louages for the south and for Tunis (2.500D) leave from the intersection of av. Thameur and av. Bourguiba. (Negotiate a price *before* you get in.) Every half-hour, buses leave for Tunis (1hr. 30min., 1.680D) and Hammamet (12km away, 360ml). Buses and *louages* to Kelibia and other cities in northern Cap Bon depart from the El-Mahfar station (tel. 854 07) at the far end of av. Farhat Hached, a half-block beyond the town square. If that sounds too farhfetched or you don't feel like waiting for one of the 12 daily buses to Kelibia (1.700D), take a local bus from El-Mahfar to **Korba** (8 per day, 600ml) and transfer to a bus en-route from Tunis (780ml).

Nabeul is blessed with a magnificently located and painstakingly managed **HI Youth Hostel** (tel. 855 47), lodged between two luxury beachside hotels. Walk several blocks away from the train station and turn right on rue Mongi Slim, where you can wait for the local bus or walk the mile to the beach. Groups fill the crowded bunks in summer, but getting a mattress and camping out in the courtyard is never a problem. Half-(4.000D) or full (6.000D) pension is now required, but the simple, delicious food is well worth it, and you don't have to stray from the beach. Membership is not required for short stays. Lockout's at midnight, but if there aren't many lodgers the manager will give you keys. Back in town, you'll find the **Pension Les Roses** on rue Sidi Abdel Kader (tel. 855 70), off av. Farhat Hached. Rooms are pleasant and clean, and one is graced by a pair of marble arches (5.000D per person; July-Aug. 6.000D; Shower 500ml). The **Hotel Les Jasmins** (tel. 853 43), 2km from the bus station down the Hammamet road, allows **camping** on its grounds for 1.100D per person, 700ml per tent (showers included).

Restaurant de la Jeunesse, 76, av. Farhat Hached, attracts a healthy mix of tourists and locals. Dishes run 1-2.500D; the *merguez grillé* is excellent at 2.000D. (Open daily 9am-9pm.) Try **Ideal Restaurant,** up rue Mongi Slim from the youth hostel, a friendly, family-run place where most dishes run 1.000D and a tasty steak 2.000D. The Friday specialty is *couscous,* and you can gobble up a meal with a main course, salad, and beverage for 5.000D. (Open daily 8am-11pm.)

Near Nabeul: Hammamet

Whatever beauty Hammamet once had is now lost in a slick, commercial, money-sucking vortex, its 20th-century incarnation. (Not even the Garden of Eden could maintain its charm if invaded by sixty-odd hotels.) Admittedly, the beaches are impressive, but there is little to do in Hammamet except stare disapprovingly at the relentless tides of tourists. The most entertaining sights in Hammamet are the signs advertising various establishments, which range from "Ismail's Deutsches Restaurant" to the cross-cultural "Pizzeria-Restaurant L'Orient" to "Sinbad's Bazar-Snackbar-Cafe-Boutique-Frisör." Moving from the ridiculous to the sublime, Hammamet's one impressive sight is its handsome 15th-century **fort,** which presides over the rows of hotels and restaurants (open 8:30am-9pm, Oct.-April 8:30am-6pm, 1.000D). However, the adjacent **medina** is, predictably, an artificial, latter-day cave of thieves. As always, hang onto your dinars, or they're apt to leave your pocket by means both fair and foul.

To get to the beach from the **train station** (tel. 801 74), head left as you exit the station and go downhill along av. Bourguiba. **Tourist Information** (tel. 804 23) is at the foot of the avenue, within sight of the beach and the fort. **Trains** leave Tunis for Hammamet (8 per day, 1hr. 30min., 1.840D, change at Bir Bou Rekba). **Buses** leave from Tunis' Gare Routière Sud (10 per day, 1.560D) and arrive at av. Bourguiba, near the fort in Hammamet.

Kelibia

Kelibia is the gem of the Cap Bon region, a quiet town of beaches and fishing boats. Presiding over Kelibia is its magnificent fortress, which has changed hands more than half a dozen times since its construction in the 6th century BC. Nearby are the gorgeous white sands of **El-Mansourah** (2km north), probably the peninsula's finest beach. Further north at **Kerkouane** are the best-preserved Punic ruins in all of Tunisia. Kelibia's one drawback is the scarcity of affordable lodgings and food; it's probably best seen as an easy daytrip from Nabeul.

Arriving by either bus or *louage,* you will be deposited in Kelibia town, a dusty, modern place noteworthy only for its 10 mosques, all with varied minarets. To get to the more attractive seaside section (2.5km away), head right with the arches of the bus station behind you. Walk a short distance until you come to a large street with a flower-laden divide. Turn right onto this street; you'll pass the **supermarket** on your left. After one block you should see a sign for the **Hotel Florida** and **Nabeul Plage.** Catch a cab (250-350ml), walk a couple of blocks further to the **bus stop** (every 30min, only in July and August), or hoof it from there.

The amazingly intact **Borj,** or fortress, sits between Kelibia and Mansourah. Along with the fort at Hammamet, it controlled the eastern portion of the Cap Bon peninsula. Little remains of the original 4th-century BC walls; most of the present battlements were added by the Romans and Byzantines in the subsequent centuries. In the 16th and 17th centuries, the Spanish wrested control of the fort from its Fatimid occupants and built the crenellations atop the walls. It was later occupied by the Turks and then the French. The anti-aircraft gun emplacements are adornments from our own century; the fort's Axis occupants came under attack by Allied aircraft. The fort is generally open all day during the summer, but accessibility depends on whether the local occupant and guardian is there to greet you.

The best value for accommodations is the signposted **Hotel Florida** (tel. 962 48), which has singles for 13.500D and doubles for 22.000D. Although a bit pricey, it's right on the sand and gazes toward the fortress. The Florida also has a pretty good restaurant, with a 5.000D *menu.* **Club Nautique,** a windsurfing school next door, rents sailboards in high season for about 5.000D an hour. Across the street, the **Restaurant de la Jeunesse** (tel. 961 71) serves reasonable grilled fare at 6.000-7.000D for a full *menu.* A little further down the road, around to the right as the road to El-Mansourah splits off to the left, is the **Cafe Sidi El-Bahri.** Stop in, sit on a terrace overlooking the sea, and sample some of the most marvelous *café au chocolat* you'll ever taste (250ml). One kilometer farther, off to the left along the road to El-Mansourah, the **HI youth hostel** (tel. 961 05) fills rooms for 2.000D per person. Your only other option for budget accommodations is the **Pensione Anis** (tel. 857 77). Free-lance **camping** is often tolerated along Mansourah beach and the long stretches of deserted beach further north. Again, try to check with any possible owner of the site or the police, and be sure to consider safety.

Fourteen buses per day leave Tunis for Kelibia from the SNT station at the end of av. de Carthage (2hr., 2.640D). Twelve buses per day run to and from Nabeul (1hr. 30min., 1.700D); a *louage* is about the same. Kelibia is also linked to Trápani (Sicily) by a hydrofoil (Tues.-Sun., 3-4hr., L78,000 or 110.000D).

El Haouaria

Situated at the far northern tip of Cap Bon, El Haouaria is the home of one of the most unusual and unexpected sites in all of Tunisia: the **Grottes Romaines.** These, the Roman Caves, are a labyrinth of underground pyramids carved out of the limestone rock along the shore.

You can either explore the grottos yourself (be sure to bring a flashlight), or ask one of the local people nearby to show you around. The first you'll come to is the Ghar el Kebir, or "Big Cave," which is a big cave. In the center sits a crude but massive sculpture of a camel. Linked to this, and with numerous other ground-level entrances and exits nearby, is a whole series of other man-made grottos. Most are pyramidal; the holes at the top served to admit light and allowed the quarried stone to be lifted out. In some places, you can see small pits in the rock, where food could be cooked. Shafts of light streak down at angles, and vines hang down from the holes at ground level; the combined effect is stark and eerie.

El Haouaria can be reached by bus from either Tunis or Kelibia. Buses depart daily from Tunis's Gare Routière du Nord (near the Bab Saadoun), itself a bus trip on the #3 from the center of town (5 per day, 2hr. 15min., 2.930D; check return times with the driver). Service is much more frequent to and from nearby Kelibia, running every hour or so. To reach the caves themselves, walk straight through town along the unavoidable av. Bourguiba and then head 1.5-2km past the end of town and towards the shore. You'll come to an umbrella-bedecked café patio; the rocks slope down to the sea from here. The entrance to the cave with the camel is a short distance off to the right.

Between Kelibia and El Haouaria lies **Kerkouane,** an abandoned site which was buried under the sand; you can clearly see the layout of the town in the Punic ruins (12km north of Kelibia, open 9am-noon and 2-5pm).

Sousse

In spite of Sousse's popularity as one of Tunisia's major tourist locations, it remains clean, inexpensive, and basically agreeable. The city was first founded by the Phoenicians, possibly as early as the 3rd century BC. Between the 3rd century BC and the 8th century AD, two tourist activities were consistently in vogue here: capturing the city and changing its name. The place became, in sequence, Hadrumetum under the Romans, Hunsericopolis under the Vandals, Justinopolis under the Byzantines, and finally Sousse under the Aghlabid Arabs. Its glory days came in the 9th century AD, when the Aghlabids built the existing city walls and most of the major monuments. In recent years the city has enjoyed rapid growth and prosperity. (Tunisia's President Ben Ali hails from Sousse—a little pork barrel politics never hurt any city.) Take in Sousse itself, and then branch out to see the other cities of the Sahil.

If you come in by train, you will arrive at the **train station** (9 trains per day from Tunis, 2hr. 30min., 3.660D; 8 per day from Nabeul, 2-3hr., 2.740D; change at Bir Bou Rekba). Turn right as you exit and walk about 100m until you see **place Farhat Hached,** where pedestrians, buses, cars and even the occasional train all compete for the same space. Just as you arrive, the **tourist office** (tel. 251 57) will be on your left at 1, av. Bourguiba. (Open Mon.-Sat. 7:30am-7:50pm, Sun. 9am-noon in summer; 8:30am-1pm and 3-5:45pm, half-day Fri.-Sat., closed Sun. rest of year.) The entrance to the *medina* will be visible partway across the plaza off to your right. Most buses and *louages* end their routes at the **bus station,** alongside the walls of the *medina*. Walk a short distance toward the water; the entrance will be to your right and the tourist office off to your left. Buses to and from nearby locales congregate in pl. Farhat Hached itself, along the water. (Before attempting bus transport, get out your flash cards and brush up on your Arabic Tunisian place names.) The **post office** is on av. de la République, which also branches off pl. Farhat Hached; most everything else is on av. Bourguiba. These include the Monoprix **supermarket** (open daily 8am-1pm and 3:30-7:30pm), numerous **banks,** and the **police station** (tel. 255 66). Round the corner from the Monoprix, on rue du Caire, is another bank of available **telephones** (open 8am-midnight).

The **medina** itself is the heart and soul of Sousse, even more so than in most Tunisian cities. It is also distinctive, if only by its size—almost everything of interest lies within the old city. The streets are noticeably wider, the merchants somewhat more civilized. But most striking are the remarkably preserved outer walls. One look at the extensive fortifications serves as an unforgettable reminder of what the *medinas* really were before the introduction of fast-multiplying T-shirt vendors; entire fortified cities once could and did resist sieges. Enclosed within the walls is the **Ribat,** a fortress-within-in-a-fortress constructed in the 8th century. The coastal *ribats* served as "fighting sanctuaries," wherein a special class of warrior-monks (sort of the Islamic counterpart to the Christian Knights Templars) divided their time between prayer and practice smiting their fellow man. Climb the tower for an excellent view of the *medina*. (Open Tues.-Sun. 8am-7pm, May 1-Sept. 30, admission 1.000D, photo permit 1.000D.) Close nearby is the **Grand Mosque,** constructed under the Aghlabites in 850 AD. While (as elsewhere) the prayer hall is closed to non-Muslims, the simple but elegant courtyard is open to all visitors. (Open 8am-1pm; admission 300ml.) Outside the *medina* walls is a small but pleasant **Museum of Antiquities,** with one of the best collections of mosaics outside of the Bardo Museum in Tunis. To get there, head uphill from the main entrance to the *medina* (created by an Allied bomb during Word War II) and walk about half a kilometer along blvd. Maréchal Tito. The museum is just beyond the point where the Army and Police barracks guard each other across the street. (Open May 1-Sept. 30 Tues.-Sun. 8am-7pm; admission 1.000D, photo permit 1.000D.)

A good choice for accommodations is the (perhaps wistfully named) **Hotel de Paris,** 15, rue du Rampart Nord (tel. 205 64). Angle to the right as you enter the *medina*; it's just inside. Rooms can be miniscule (i.e. exactly as long as a bed) but they're neat, the showers are hot, and there's a rooftop terrace to boot. (Singles 6.000D. Doubles 10.000D.) Around the corner at 19, rue de l'Eglise is the **Hotel Tunis,** which is slightly cheaper but not as nice. More upscale is the **Hotel Medina,** (tel. 217 22) right off one corner of the Ribat. It's got ample rooms, so it's a good fallback. The entry room is something right out of Ali Baba. (Singles 13.000D. Doubles 19.000D.)

Eating out in Sousse is generally expensive. As a rule, avoid anyplace along av. Bourguiba or pl. Farhat Hached; both the food and the prices are clearly targeted at tourists. For good, family-style food, **Restaurant du Peuple** next door to the Hotel du Paris is a wise pick. A tasty, filling meal here won't set you back more than 2.500-3.500D. Otherwise, for fair, fairly cheap fare try the three alleys opposite the two big movie theatres on av. Bourguiba. (If you're lucky, you can stop in and see a Hindu-original action-romance subtitled in French and Arabic; you'll never again think an American movie atrocious.) The inauspiciously titled **Big Mac** serves food more or less worthy of the name; **Restaurant de la Jeunesse,** (tel. 277 49), one block over on rue Ali Bach Hamra is in essentially the same league. A plate at either place runs about 1.500-2.500D.

The North (Coral) Coast

In comparison to the rest of the country, Tunisia's northern, or coral, coast has little to offer and is less touristed than Cap Bon and the east. Of its cities, only Bizerte and Tabarka merit your attention.

Bizerte

Situated at Africa's northernmost point, Bizerte has long been seen as an important strategic port. The Carthaginians were the first to settle here, and dug the canal linking the Mediterranean Sea to the inland Lake Bizerte. In 310 BC, Agathocles of Syracuse adopted the "best defense is a strong offense" tactic while besieged by Carthage, landing in North Africa and (literally) burning his boats behind him. The Greeks named their colony here "Hippo Diarrhytus," and while this might sound like an African animal with a digestive problem the name stuck for several centuries. The Romans built atop the Greek and Carthaginian contributions, and were followed in their turn by the Byzantines and Arabs. The city changed hands repeatedly during the 16th-century Hapsburg-Ottoman wars. In the 17th century, the city gained notoriety as a pirates' nest, serving as a base for raids on European ships. World War II again demonstrated the city's importance, as it was a key objective during the see-saw North African battles of the Axis and the Allies. The French were so attached to the site that they ceded control of the city when Tunisia was granted independence in 1956, but refused to abandon the port and naval base. Five years of mounting tensions led to a major confrontation and over 1000 Tunisian military casualties. The Bizerte Crisis if 1961 led to the opening of diplomatic discussions, and two years later the French withdrew entirely. Only bitter memories and the solemn cemetary remain from that time; the white beaches and old quarters of the town remain timeless.

Orientation and Practical Information

The compact town center may perplex because many roads run diagonally. A good benchmark is avenue de l'Algérie, diagonally connecting the new town square (place 7 Novembre 1987) to the base of place Slah-Edine Bouchoucha, by the Old Port. The main **bus station** is on the other side of the new square, at the waterfront near the drawbridge. Blue buses depart either from the main station or from another stop nearby on av. d'Algérie for Ras Jebel (12 per day, 740ml), Ghar-el-Melh (3 per day, 1hr., 740ml), Jendouba Le-Kef (1 per day, 5.650D), and to Tunis's Bab Saadoun station (every 30min., 1hr. 30min., 2.130D). *Louages* for Tunis (1.600D) and occasionally for Ras Jebel leave from rue du 1er Mai, off the canal and in the shadow of the drawbridge. The **train station** rails to the south of the main bus station (walk left parallel to the water). Four slow trains crawl daily to Tunis (1hr. 30min., 1.720D).

Ask for a map of Bizerte at the friendly but poorly informed regional **tourist office** at 1, rue de Constantinople (tel. 327 03 or 328 97). From the main bus station, walk toward the bridge, turn left at the park, then turn right one block after the park. (Open Mon.-Sat. 7:30am-1:30pm and 4:30-6:30pm; off-season Mon.-Sat. 8:30am-1pm and 5-7:45pm.) The **post office** and **currency exchange** (tel. 315 85) wait a half-block from the new square on av. de l'Algérie. (Open Mon.-Thurs. 7:30am-1pm and 5-6pm, Fri.-Sat. 7:30am-1:30pm.) Around the corner on rue du 1er Mai, the **telephone office** is open daily from 7:30am to 8pm. On av. Bourguiba, several small shops rent **bicycles** for around 2.000D per hour and **mopeds** for about 4.000D per hour.

Accommodations and Food

The expensive resort hotels along the beach ooze with tour bus discharge. Most cheap hotels in town fill in July and August, so arrive early.

Remel Youth Hostel (HI; tel. 408 04), 4km south of town on the road to Tunis. Take "Menzel Jemil" bus #8 (140ml) and ask to get off at Remel Plage. A funk-o-matic ramshackle place. Isolated and idyllic Remel Beach lies 100m away through the trees. Non-members often manage to talk their way in. 1.500D per person. Shower included. Breakfast 500ml. Lunch or dinner 1.500-2.000D. Cooking facilities available. Sheets 350ml.

Maison des Jeunes, tel. 316 08. From the bus station, walk at a right angle 4 blocks across av. Bourguiba, and walk 10min. on bd. Hassan en-Nouri; the hostel lies up a driveway to the left. Looks like Mao Tse-tung's mausoleum, minus the charm. Still, it's clean. Frequented by soccer teams in summer. Some beds held for foreigners. 2.000D per person. Showers 300ml.

Hotel Zitouna, 11, place Slah-Edine Bouchoucha (tel. 387 60), 1 block from the Old Port. From the bus station, walk diagonally through the new square. Spartan and pleasant. Rooms are tiny, sheets a bit dingy. Singles 3.000D. Doubles 5.000D. Showers 500ml.

Hotel Continental, 24, rue du 2 Mai 1934 (tel. 314 36). Walk diagonally through the new square on av. d'Algérie; it's slightly off to your right, 1 block past. Fair-sized rooms, somewhat dark corridors. Singles 4.500D. Doubles 7.000D. Showers included.

Fruit vendors sprout in great numbers in **place Slah-Edine,** and a lively **market** flourishes near the base of the old port.

Rôtisserie du 1er Mai (tel. 380 87), on the corner next to the telephone office. Steaming, scrumptious spaghetti or *couscous* 1.000D. Open daily 6:30am-11pm.

Pizzeria du Vieux Port, Chez Belahouel, on the old port. A restaurant name that runs through 3 languages and the place to stop if you've had *couscous* once too often. Pizza 550ml per 100 grams.

Sights

In the celebrated **Old Port,** the smells of coffee and rotten fish wed and waft through the air. Facing the Old Port, **place Slah-Edine Bouchoucha** is ringed with fruit and vegetable stalls, above which rise the twin minarets of the Debaa and Grand Mosques. Through the ramparts away from the Old Port, the gallant 18th-century **kasbah** houses cozier cafés; its crenellated battlements command a broad view of the port and coast. Rock it. The **Andalusian Quarter,** with its ancient archways, winding alleys, and nail-studded doors, lies just to the north. Sheep wander the streets and chew hay, and in every other shop, a caged parakeet or two twitters merrily. On the neighboring hilltop, the 16th-century **Spanish Fort** is now an open-air theater. Confusingly, the fort was actually built by the Turks, and received its name when the Arabs captured it from Don Juan of Austria.

Cap Blanc, which forms Africa's northernmost point, is perhaps the most spectacular sight near Bizerte. To get there, follow av. de la Corniche along the beach and up the coast to the *Radiophare du Cap Blanc* sign, where you turn right. The rough road struggles to the top of **Jebel Nador** (288m), the perfect perch for a glorious sunset vista. Below, chalky Cap Blanc protrudes into the sea. To reach its tip, descend the mountain and follow the trail leading off the road. The bike ride is scenic and challenging; count on three hours round-trip.

The three "luxury" beach hotels, **Corniche Palace, Jalta,** and **Nadhour** monopolize sports and entertainment. Equipment rentals run high for waterskiing, windsurfing, and boating. The three hotels rent **horses** for around 9.000D per hour (with guides). Jalta also rents bikes for 2.000D per hour.

Near Bizerte: Utica (Utique) and Raf Raf

Utica is North Africa's oldest port and was once its greatest, but the passage of three millenia has seen the city fall into decline and abandonment. What remains today dates from a late period in the city's history and consists mostly of first to 4th century aristocratic Roman residences. To get to Utica, take any non-direct bus along the Bizerte-Tunis line in either direction (every 30min., 40min., 890ml) and get off at Utique. From the rather lonely bus stop in town, cross over the highway and follow the signposted road 2km to "Utique ruines"; you'll come to a small **museum** with two rooms of Punic and Roman exhibits, and some of the mosaics not taken to the Bardo Museum. Get your ticket to enter 800m farther along at the site marked by a yellow sign so rusted it looks like an antique itself. The only remnant of Utica's Carthaginian period is the ancient (8th century BC) **Punic necropolis.** Most of the rest of the site consists of Roman Houses, the most noteworthy of which is the **Maison de la Cascade** (House of the Fountain). Herein, you'll find splendid mosaics, intricate marble work, and of course, a fountain. (Site open 9am-7pm; museum closed Mon. Admission 1.000D; photo permit 1.000D.)

Along the coast east of Bizerte, the mountains at **Raf Raf** plunge into the sea, forming a crescent-shaped beach by the water. The beach itself isn't bad, though it may be quite crowded in the summer. The view is complemented by the island of Pilau, a huge rock which juts out of the sea in front of the shore. Frequent buses make the trip to and from Bizerte (take #36 or 512, 12 per day, 1hr., 2.280D, last bus returns from Raf Raf at 6:30pm). If you get caught overnight, there's one hotel in town, the **Hotel Dalia** (tel. 41 630), which charges 13.000D for singles, 18.000D for doubles. From the bus stop, follow the signs to "Raf Raf Plage", about 150m, to reach the beach.

Tabarka

The pleasant, likable city of Tabarka is the great prize of the North Coast. Despite this, it remains almost entirely untouched by tourism, something which (at least for the moment) only increases its charm. Welcome breezes blow through the cheerful streets of Tabarka town, which is flanked on one side by a beach and on the other by rocky cliffs. Tabarka's splendid fortress rises dramatically above it all, keeping a watchful eye on everything below.

There are only a few hotels in Tabarka; the cheaper ones are the **Hotel Mammia,** two blocks uphill from av. Bourguiba, and the **Hotel de la Plage** (tel. 44 039) at 7, rue du Pêcheur. The latter is right near the beach and charges 8.500D for singles and 13.000D for doubles. Cheap eating is possible at the far end of av. Bourguiba and along its side streets. Rue Farhat Hached, off av. Bourguiba and one block from the Hotel Mammia, is home to both **Restaurant Triki** and **Restaurant El Hana.** Lunch or dinner at either runs about 2.500-3.000D.

Tabarka's most captivating sight is its **Genoese Fort,** an integral part of the city's history. It was built by the Lomellini famili, who received the Isle of Tabarka as ransom for the release of the Turkish pirate Dragut, who spent four years rowing a Genoese galley after being captured. Dragut proceeded to prove himself worthy of such a price; after his release, he captured Tripoli, destroyed a Spanish fleet, and conquered Jerba. Meanwhile, Tabarka remained in the hands of the Lomellinis for over 200 years. Tabarka's other sight of note is the cluster of rocks at the very end of town known as **Les Aiguilles** ("The Needles"). These huge (20m) natural spires shoot out of the water and are framed against the sky. There is also a museum at **La Basilique,** the site of a French basilica, featuring mostly mosaics. (Admission 600ml.)

Eight buses per day head to and from Tunis (5.400D), 180km away. One bus daily runs directly to Le Kef; otherwise you'll have to make your own connections by bus or *louage* south via Ain Draham and Jendouba.

Near Tabarka: Ain Draham

Halfway between Tabarka and Teboursouk lies **Ain Draham,** a town whose fame rests upon its mountaintop location and the surrounding cork forests. The 8-10km along the way to Ain Draham do provide some winsome vistas, although the effect of seeing a cool mountaintop forest may not be quite the same for people who haven't spent their life living in a desert. The other thing Ain Draham is known for is boar hunting. If this pastime floats your boat, inquire locally for details; there's some red tape you'll have to cut through if you want to get a gun or hunting license, or take a boar out of the country with you (bring a big duffle). To get to Ain Draham, take a bus or *louage* from either Tabarka or Jendouba (from Tabarka 40min., 700ml; from Jendouba 1hr., 1.280D). Four buses per day also run directly to Tunis (5.920D).

Tell

The mild climate and fertile fields of this northern interior region have made it a preferred spot throughout history. Bulla Regia and Dougga, the finest Roman colonial sites in Tunisia, testify to Tell's five centuries as Rome's primary granary. The walled city of El Kef has attracted worshipful Romans, Christians, Muslims, and legions of plundering mercenaries.

Bulla Regia

With your first glance around the site, the trip to remote Bulla Regia will hardly seem worth the trouble. But look a bit deeper (literally) and you'll see that your efforts have paid rich dividends. Bulla Regia's treasures remain buried beneath the ground, in a series of underground mansions and sites. The city was the capital of the Numidian kingdom (hence the suffix "Regia," or "of the King") until the last of the Numidian heirs, Jugurtha, was defeated by the Romans 25km away. Affluent Romans of the 2nd and 3rd centuries AD gentrified the location, rebuilding the city and then duplicating their villas below ground to escape the summer heat. A 7th-century earthquake destroyed most of the above-ground sections, but left numerous subterranean rooms and mosaics intact.

Purchase your entrance ticket at the **museum** across the road from the site. (Open daily 7am-7pm. Admission 1.000D. Photo permit 1.000D.) Here, you can wise up on your Bulla Regia history (assuming you read French or Arabic); relics include a relief of a Numidian horseman and a mosaic of Medusa. The main entrance to the site stands by the extensive 2nd-century **Baths of Julia Memma,** dominated by a massive arch. Wander north to the **Maison du Tresor** (House of the Treasure) for its sunken mosaics. The above-ground **Christian Basilica,** a few steps west, holds badly blotched but surprisingly vivid mosaics. Back by the House of the Treasure, take the road farther north to discover steps leading down to the most intact and evocative site, the **Maison de la Chasse** (Hunting Villa). Five entire rooms survive, surrounding the most beautiful courtyard in Bulla Regia. Graceful Corinthian columns support the underground ceiling, while the blue sky looks down upon the central patio. In the adjacent house to the north, mosaics vividly display gazelles, birds, and other animals, as well as a scene of porters bearing the prey. The **Maison de la Pêche** (Fishing Villa), to the east, shelters two shell-shaped fountains, one above ground with a colorful mosaic of fishermen in the act, and a larger one underground. The house served as a tribunal and prison: the judge sat by the underground fountain and sent miscreants into cells behind him. About 100m farther north, the **Maison d'Amphitrite** displays a vast and truly remarkable mosaic of Venus. To the southeast, you can see the **Temple of Apollo** and the substantial remains of the **theater;** off to the west is a small **Byzantine fort.**

To reach Bulla Regia, catch one of the four morning buses from La Kef to Jendouba (2hr., 1.560D). A cab may set you back 1.500-2.000D for the 6km ride to the museum, though the fare should be as little as 400ml. If you're lucky you can catch one of the hourly blue-and-white buses from Jendouba to Bulla Regia from pl. 7 Novembre 1987 (280ml), though the presence of three bus companies may confound. Buses also run north to Ain Draham (1hr., 1.280D) and on to Tabarka. The last bus back to Le Kef is at 1pm; *louages* (1.850D) make the run until mid-afternoon. *Don't* get caught in Jendouba after about 4pm, or you'll find yourself stranded in a no-horse town with absolutely no way to get out.

Le Kef

Le Kef (also "El Kef") means "The Rock," an appropriate name for a fortress town built atop a craggy mount. Le Kef's commanding position was important as late as 1956, when it proved an invaluable post for the French, who wished to observe Algerian rebel stations during the Franco-Algerian war. Even after Tunisian independence was granted, the French troops abandoned the vital position only after a judicious combination of diplomatic requests and incessant sniping.

The city's reputation dates far back, to when the rulers of Carthage shipped their rowdy Sicilian mercenaries here. Arab refugees from the Christian *Reconquista* of Spain later settled the town, reminded of the rocky plains and sweeping plains of Andalusia. However, the city's association with gentler things also dates back to ancient times. The Romans built a libidinous temple to Venus at Le Kef, and perpetuated the belief that every year Venus flew between Rome and Le Kef, accompanied by a flock of doves. Islamic pilgrimages to Kairouan and to Mecca traditionally pass through Le Kef to solicit the doves' blessing.

Orientation and Practical Information

Le Kef's *medina* lurks under the towering *kasbah*. Below, the new city tumbles down the hillside into the valley. The bus and *louage* station lies in the new city, five minutes from the *medina*—walk down the main road, turn right, and take your second left on rue Ali Belhaouane. Frequent *louages* supplement bus service to Jendouba (4 per day, 1hr., 1.560D), Tunis (17 per day, 4hr., 5.300D), Bizerte (1 per day, 4hr. 30min., 5.650D), Sfax (2 per day, 5hr., 5.850D), and Gafsa (1 per day, 5hr., 5.650D).

Next to Café Dinar at pl. de l'Indépendance stands a highly competent **tourist office** (tel. 211 48). Mohamed Tlili, the friendly volunteer director of the bureau, also heads the *kasbah* restoration effort; he can give you an authoritative history of any Kefian monument. (Open daily 7am-noon and 3-7pm.) The town **post office, telephone office,** and **currency exchange** huddle together on rue Hedi Chaker and rue d'Algérie (tel. 200 00). From the tourist office, bear left at the fork and walk two blocks. (Open Mon.-Sat. 7:30am-6:30pm, Sun. 9-11am.)

Accommodations and Food

The drab **HI youth hostel** (tel. 216 79), 2km down the road to Tunis, allows **camping** for 700ml. Otherwise, a sojourn is 2.000D per person, only 1.000D cheaper than **Hôtel L'Auberge,** on pl. de l'Indépendance (tel. 200 36). L'Auberge is the least expensive hotel in town, charging 3.000D per person for cheery, albeit dilapidated, rooms. The newer **Hôtel Medina** is at 18, rue Farhat Hached (tel. 202 14). From pl. de l'Indépendance, walk 20m on av. Bourguiba and bear left (uphill). The hotel charges 6.000D for singles, and 4.000D per person in doubles or triples. Request a blanket. (Strong showers 500ml.)

Le Kef has few sit-down restaurants. For 1.500D each, sample delicious *couscous, mermez,* and *mloukia* at **Restaurant de l'Afrique,** (tel. 220 79) on rue Hedi Chaker, one block from the main square. (Open daily 5am-11pm.) A few doors down and slightly cheaper is the **Restaurant El Andelous.** Still farther down the street, behind the Esso station, a congenial Paris-trained chef runs **Restaurant Dyr** (tel. 207 85). He cooks local delicacies such as *agneau au Rômarin* (lamb with rosemary, 4.000D; open Sat.-Thurs. noon-3pm and 6pm-midnight).

Sights

Climb up through the *medina* from the steps starting at Hôtel de la Source. These will lead you to the foot of the *kasbah* (1601), crowning the peak of Le Kef's once impregnable rock and affording a fine vista of irrigated plains and the bustling new town. The *kasbah* is currently under restoration, but if you wander inside, a delighted guide will give you a tour *gratis.* Beneath the *kasbah,* the well-preserved 4th-century **Christian Basilica** surrounds an open-air court with massive, oblong columns. During the 8th century, the basilica was converted into a mosque, making it one of the oldest in the country; villagers call it Djamaa el-Kebir, or Grand Mosque. (Open daily 8am-noon and 3-6pm. Free.) Across from the basilica stands the picturesque **Mosque of Sidi Bou Makhlouf,** with its array of creamy fluted domes and a slender, tiled octagonal minaret. Beyond the **Bab Ghedive,** nicknamed the Gate of Treachery after Governor Ghedive opened the gates for the French in 1881 (up rue de Jendouba and past the square), in the countryside on the left, you'll discover the **Roman cisterns** as you abruptly step from the city out into a deserted outdoor area facing a stone cliff face.

On the street behind Hotel Medina, the **Église de Saint Pierre** predates both the French and the Arabs, who call it Dar el-Kous. This 4th-century Roman basilica stands empty now, save for a few pillars. For an unusual outdoor excursion you can take a hike up the inspiringly named **Jugurtha's Table,** a huge slab of stone with an exhaustive vista. To get there, take a *louage* from Le Kef to the village of **Kalaat Senan** (1.950D). A 4km path leads to a 1,500-year-old staircase cut into the living rock. From the top, you can look out over Algeria and the fields of the Tell.

Sbeïtla

Most visitors to Tunisia would at least recognize Sbeïtla—it's one of the sites most often photographed by the Tunisian Tourist Office. The Capitoline temple with its slim columns, which graces so many "Tunisie" posters, is the best-preserved building in a complex of ruins which were once the Roman town of Sufetula. Step through history as you walk through Roman, early Christian, and Byzantine ruins dating from the first through 6th centuries AD.

The origins of Sufetula remain uncertain, but the Romans appear to have built the town from scratch early in the first century AD. The place never attained real prominence, except possibly for a short time in the 7th century. In the year 646, the Patriarch Gregory elected to challenge the Byzantine authorities in Constantinople, proclaiming himself Emperor and making Sbeïtla his capital. He chose poorly—the following year a horde of 20,000 Arabs under Abdullah ibn Saad came by and beat the daylights out of Sbeïtla. At this point, the Patriarch Gregory caught a severe case of death. Neither he nor Sbeïtla ever really recovered.

On arrival at the one-room bus station, turn right with the train tracks behind you. Walk two blocks to av. Belhaouane, and turn left. Walk straight along av. Belhaouane 1km until you come to the ruins, nicely heralded by the **Triumphal Arch,** which formerly marked the entrance to the city. A little further along is the small but well-kept **museum** and the entrance to the site. (Open sunrise-sunset. Admission 1.000D, photo permit 1.000D.) Entering opposite the museum and disregarding anyone attempting to sell you real, authentic Roman coins and statues, turn left and pass the 7th-century **Byzantine Forts.** You can head through the still-discernible town grid to the three-bayed **Arch of Antonius Pius.** Step right through it into the ever-dignified **Forum** and view the high point of your tour—the **Temples to the Capitoline Trinity.** Although they are characteristically combined into one temple, Sbeïtla for some reason constructed separate, adjacent temples to the trio of Jupiter, Juno, and Minerva. Exiting between the temples, you can head off to the right to find some early (3rd- to 6th-century) **Christian basilicas** and a superbly preserved stone baptistry.

To reach Sbeïtla, you'll probably have to deal with the confusion of the Kairoun bus station (5 buses daily, 2hr., 3.430D). Sbeïtla is also connected to the Roman ruins at Makthar (6 buses daily, 1hr. 30min., 2.760D) from which connections can be made to Tunis and Le Kef. There are also direct connections to Le Kef. Be sure to check the time of the last bus out, or you may end up as ruined as Sufetula.

Dougga

The Roman metropolis of Dougga, the largest and best-preserved ancient site in Tunisia, is everything you expected from Carthage but failed to find. From its temple to its toilets, the ancient city remains almost completely intact; indeed, it was inhabited up to a century ago, when a new town was built down the hill for its denizens who, it was felt, were distracting the tourists. Framed by pastures, olive trees, and grain fields, perched on a high bluff, Dougga is also the most scenically situated of Tunisia's ruined Roman cities. A thorough tour of Dougga, which extends over several square miles, demands the better part of a day. Fortunately, the major ruins are concentrated in a small area around the ancient forum.

The main entrance to the site leads directly to the wonderful 2nd-century **theater.** The Tunisian National Tourist Office now schedules performances of classical drama here during the annual **Dougga Festival,** in July and early August. Tickets for shows (in French and Arabic) cost 3.000-4.000D. Ask at the tourist office in Tunis. A short walk uphill from the theater brings you to the remains of the **Temple of Saturn.** The god of time (and Ford automobiles?) has left only six pillars standing, silhouetted against the skyline and staring out over miles of grain fields.

Continuing down the road from the theater, you will come to the former center of town and the **Capitol of Dougga.** Despite its small size, this 2nd-century building deserves its reputation as one of the finest examples of Roman construction in Tunisia. Six slender, fluted columns, 10m high and crowned with a full triangular portico, recall the grandeur that was Rome. Inside there's just a large marble head of Jupiter, gazing upward, seemingly distraught over the loss of the rest of his body. Adjacent to the capitol are the **Forum** and the **Plaza of the Twelve Winds,** where the careful eye will discern a circular compass rose carved into the marble pavement. A series of steps descend toward the main street and the large structure below, the **Lycinian Baths.** The baths are well-preserved, with many of the massive walls and interior colonnades still standing; below, you can step down to the service tunnels. Exiting from the service tunnels drops you in the residential part of town, more or less in front of the **House of Ulysses.** As far as we know, Ulysses was not actually the owner of the house; rather, the place takes its name from a particularly well-preserved mosaic, since moved to the Bardo Museum and copied onto many a tourist brochure. Across the street, stairs lead down to the **House of Trifolium.** No, Dougga's largest building was not a temple or government structure—it was a brothel. Numerous small rooms, about whose functions archeologists can only speculate, branch off the central courtyard. In its day, Old Trifolium would have been heralded by a stone stele depicting a huge erect penis. At some point over the centuries, this was removed, leaving behind two elegant but much more subdued Corinthian columns atop the staircase.

Farther off to the east are the feet of the now-broken **Arch of Septimus Severus.** The pagoda-like structure is the **Lybico-Punic Mausoleum,** built in the 2nd century BC by architect Abarish for a Numidian prince. It is probably the most significant example of Punic architecture in Tunisia, because it is just about the *only* example of Punic architecture in Tunisia. The Romans held the Carthaginians in high esteem, but that didn't mean they had any intention of leaving their monuments standing.

Turning back to the Capitol and heading west, one comes to the blocky 3rd-century **Arch of Severus Alexander.** Heading slightly further west, one stumbles upon the particularly attractive **Temple of Juno Calaestis.** A dozen freestanding columns and a semicircular wall form a courtyard surrounding a central pillared platform. (Site open 8am-7pm. Admission 1.000D. Photo permit 1.000D.)

Dougga must be reached by way of **Teboursouk,** a drowsy agricultural village. Daily buses run from Le Kef to Teboursouk (17 per day, 1hr., 2.250D) and from Tunis (1hr. 45min., 3.450D). The last bus back to Tunis leaves at 5:45pm. No public transportation accesses the 6km between Teboursouk and Dougga except during the July festival, when special buses and cabs frequent the route in the afternoon and early evening. Otherwise, you'll have to rely on a thumb, walking shoes, or a taxi (which will try to stick you for 5.000D, if you can find one); the walk is agreeable, if tiring. Grab some water before you go. At the entrance, an urgent guide will tell you that your visit will be immeasurably poorer without his services. Unless you can agree in advance on a reasonable price (1.000-2.000D), shrug him off.

Sahil

Bulging from Tunisia's central eastern shore is a wide stretch of land called the Sahil, or "coastal plain." The hot, arid landscape sustains endless groves of olive trees. Myriad sheep forage aimlessly in unlikely places—courtyards, public squares, and even supermarkets. Diversity reigns in this region: while the northern city of Sousse swells its massive *medina* with package-tour visitors, the southern city of Sfax has industrialized with nary a tourist in mind. Monastir, the coastal birthplace of former president Bourguiba, offers only the inflated trappings of a personality cult. Down the coast, the ancient port of Mahdía enchants with its forthrightness. Inland, Tunisia's most sacred mosque reposes in Kairouan, while at sleepy El Jem, a Roman coliseum bears witness to a great and cruel civilization.

Kairouan

For centuries the faithful have made their way across the desert to pay their respects at the most sacred mosque in the Maghreb region—the **Mosque of Sidi Oqba** at Kairouan, dedicated to the saint who spread Islam across North Africa. Kairouan is the fourth holiest city in Islam, eclipsed only by the sacred triad of Mecca, Medina, and Jerusalem. Religious fervor and a strategic location have accounted for the fortified city's growth in the inhospitable steppe of central Tunisia. Popular convention holds that seven pilgrimages to Kairouan equal one to Mecca—sufficient to absolve your sins entirely. As Kairouan is also home to some of the most interesting architecture and decorative work in all of Tunisia, it is a worthy destination for pilgrim and tourist alike. Kairouan is one of only two Islamic holy cities that admit non-Muslims (Jerusalem is the other). According to legend, Sidi Oqba ibn Nafi, a companion of Muhammed, founded the city in 670 when a spring suddenly sprouted at his feet, revealing a precious gold chalice that had mysteriously disappeared from Mecca. For good measure, Oqba banished all the scorpions, snakes, and reptiles from the region. After all this, the sanctity of the spot was immediately acknowledged, and the city became known as "Kairawan"—camping place for camels.

Kairouan's first century or so was a bit rocky—the city was captured and pillaged, then captured and pillaged again. But beginning in the year 800 AD, Kairouan flourished under the Aghlabid dynasty, which made the city its capital until it was conquered in 1057. During this golden age, most of Kairouan's major buildings were constructed, and the city attained a religious and cultural preeminence which (despite occasional reversals) it retains to this day.

Orientation and Practical Information

Kairouan can be reached most easily by bus from Tunis (11 per day, 3hr., 4.890D). *Louages* to and from Sousse (1hr., 2.300D) run until about 8pm. The biggest problem with Kairouan's bus connections are not the bus schedules themselves, but rather *determining* the schedules. Kairouan's Kafkaesque bus terminal is, alas, not Tunisia's finest. Departure times to some locations (such as archeological sites like Sbeïtla and Makthar) seem to be a state secret. Be certain to ask at least three independent sources (tourist information, bus station information, and a couple of bus drivers) when buses leave for your destination, and don't believe everything you hear.

All of Kairouan's historical sights cluster around the sprawling *medina,* while most of the town's services line **av. 7 Novembre,** which runs south from **Bab Ech Chouhada,** the main southern entrance to the walled city. **Place de la Victoire,** marked by a giant pedestal that once supported a statue of Habib Bourguiba, lies several blocks off av. 7 Novembre by way of av. de la Republique. **Note:** old maps and pamphlets show av. 7 Novembre as av. Bourguiba, and av. de la Republique as av. Farhat Hached.

Tourist Office: Syndicat d'Initiative, (tel. 204 52), and **tourist information** (tel. 217 97) in adjacent offices, on pl. des Martyrs facing Bab Ech Chouhada. From pl. de la Victoire, walk down av. de la Republique (to the left of the post office), then turn left. A special combined admission ticket to all the sights is available here (2.000D). Ticket required for entrance to the Great Mosque, the Mausoleum of Abou Zama, the Mausoleum of Sidi Abid Al Ghariani, and the museum. Pick up a map here and ask them to mark the sights on it. Open daily 7:30am-5:30pm; Sept.-May 8:30am-1pm and 3-5:45pm.

Post Office: pl. de la Victoire (tel. 225 55). Open daily 7:30am-12:30pm and 5-7pm, Sun. 9-11am.

Telephone Office: a few blocks from the post office. Take the 2nd right off pl. de la Victoire onto the road for Tunis. The office is on your right past Budget Rent-A-Car. Open daily 8am-8pm.

Swimming Pool: the **Hotel Continental,** near the Aghlabite Pools, and the **Hôtel des Aghlabites,** near the youth hostel. Admission 2.000D.

Accommodations and Food

Kairouan perpetuates the Tunisian tradition of cheap, commodious accommodations for bone-weary pilgrims.

Youth Hostel (HI), av. de Fès (tel. 203 09), near Hôtel des Aghlabites. Pass in front of the municipality building, to the left of av. 7 Novembre, and take the circuitous route hugging the buildings on the right side. Dormitory beds. Members-only when full. Curfew midnight, in winter 10pm. 2.000D per person. **Camping** 700ml.

Hôtel Sabra (tel. 202 60), on rue Ali Belhaouane next to the tourist office outside the *medina.* Comfortable and affordable with a panoramic terrace. One triple has a curved balcony with a view of the *medina* (10.500D). Singles 4.500D. Doubles 8.000D. Showers and breakfast included.

Hôtel Sidi Belhassen (tel. 203 51), bd. Sadikia. Follow signs from Bab Et Tounes. Clean beds squeezed into shoebox rooms, some with no windows. Singles 3.000D. Doubles 6.000D. Triples 7.500D. Showers included.

There are few bargains for hungry visitors. Most of the cheaper restaurants in Kairouan inflict fixed-price menus upon unsuspecting stomachs. Due to the high mercury levels and the greedy vendors, beverages go for a whopping 500ml. (Café Sabra next to the tourist office sells soda for 200ml.) Always inquire about prices before you chow or chug. Your cheapest eating options are the roast chicken places along av. de la Republique. Make a pilgrimage to Kairouan's sweet shops for the divine *makroudh,* pastries stuffed with dates and smothered in honey.

Restaurant Barrouta, behind the Barrouta. Here, small dinar will buy an ample dinner. Walk through the kitchen to get to the tables or eat outside. Most entrees 1.200-1.500D. The *macaroni-agneau* satiates nicely, and a wonderful spicy sauce blankets omelettes. Open daily 11am-10pm, except when they're closed.

Restaurant Fairouz (tel. 218 62), marked by large signs off av. 7 Novembre in the *medina.* Tasty Tunisian fare served with French folksongs blaring from the radio. *Couscous d'agneau* 2.200D. Open daily 9:30am-10:30pm.

Restaurant Sabra, av. de la Republique, 2 blocks from pl. de l'Indépendance. Neat and prompt. 3-course *menu* 3.500D. Open daily 10am-10pm.

Sights

Plan your walking tour of Kairouan around the comprehensive ticket available at the tourist office. The sights included are the most interesting and the only ones open to non-Muslims. As usual, you can enter the courtyard of the **Great Mosque** but not the main prayer room. (Trappings provided for those not in proper attire, i.e. knees and shoulders covered.) Peer through the tall carved door of banana wood on the right to catch a glimpse of the *mihrab* (prayer niche) and *minbar* (pulpit) brought from Baghdad in 862, two of the oldest examples of luster tile decoration in the world. Also check out the 296 columns throughout the prayer hall, with Roman, Greek, and Punic capitols collected from all over Tunisia. The oldest Islamic monument in the Western world, the mosque was erected in 688 and rebuilt in 695. Most of what you see today is 9th-century Aghlabite work that has been renovated and altered over the centuries. Opposite the sanctuary stands the oldest minaret in the world, built in 836. Its ponderous appearance hints at a secondary, defensive purpose—note those decorative arrow-slits in the crenellations near the top. Ten minutes west of the Great Mosque, just beyond the northern entrance to the *medina,* lie the **Aghlabite Pools,** commissioned by the son of Muhammed the Aghlabite in the 9th century.

The **Mausoleum of Abou Zama** is also known as the **Zaouia de Sidi Sahab,** in reference to Abou Zama's role as a companion to the Prophet. The Zaouia is home to a religious brotherhood and its founder's tomb. From the baseboards to eye-level, flowery blue tiles cover the walls, and then from eye-level up, minutely filigreed gypsum. A colonnaded corridor and a second, domed foyer are paneled similarly. The final courtyard, surrounded by cells and vessels containing saints' remains, is clad in tiles patterned with buildings and trees. The gypsum and the tile work mingle artfully here; the resulting masterpiece wins recognition as the high point of Islamic decorative art in Tunisia. (The Great Mosque is open Sat.-Thurs. 8am-1pm, in winter 8am-2pm, on Fridays during Ramadan 8am-noon. The other monuments, except when noted, are open Sat.-Thurs. 8am-6pm, Fri. 8am-1pm.)

Head back toward the tourist office to visit Kairouan's carpet-walled *souks* along av. 7 Novembre. In the **Souk des Tapis** from noon to 3pm on Fridays, women auction the rugs they've knotted and woven to eager merchants. Across from the Souk des Tapis, up the stairs in a brown building is the **Bir Barrouta.** Within its narrow confines a blindfolded camel circles endlessly, powering a 14th-century contraption that lifts water from a sacred spring far below the chamber. For a small donation you can sample this refreshing water that, according to legend, flows directly from Mecca. Up the side street, the 9th-century **Mosquée de Trois Portes** glorifies its namesake three portals with a delicate façade.

Close by the Bab Ech Chouhada is the **Zaouia Sidi Abid El Ghariani.** It is hard to imagine a more serene final resting place than the tiny courtyard of striped black-and-white Moorish arches. In a side room, the saint rests in peace under an ornate wooden ceiling. (Open Mon.-Thurs. 8am-2pm, in winter 8am-6pm.) A new **museum** housing treasures from Kairouan lies 7km outside the city on the road to Sfax. Inquire at the tourist office for directions and information.

Kairouan draws a crowd from across Tunisia for its festive celebration of **Mouled,** the prophet Muhammed's birthday.

Near Kairouan: Makthar

Although one of the least-visited archeological sites in the country, Makthar features a surprisingly extensive spread of ruins. Located 110km west of Kairouan, the site is that of the former Carthaginian and later Roman city of **Mactaris.** The Roman-built **Bab el Ain arch** serves as the divider between modern Makthar, a small and unremarkable little town, and ancient Mactaris. Just beyond, a three-room **museum** serves as the entrance to the site; inside are a few well-crafted funerary steles and a rare example of Latin carved in its elegant, cursive script. (Open April-Sept. 9am-noon and 2-6pm; Oct.-March 9am-noon and 2-5:30pm. Admission 1.000D, photo permit 1.000D.)

Most impressive are the ruins of the **Roman baths.** Even now, the walls tower 18m above the ground, an indication of the Roman reverence for that which comes next to godliness: cleanliness. Traces of the mosaics remain upon the floor. Most picturesque is the 2nd-century **Arch of Trajan,** which now presides over the site from atop the crest of a hill; the scene has an aura which is at once both dignified and slightly Ozymandian. The remnants (mostly foundations) of a number of other buildings and temples are scattered about the site, which you can inspect virtually undisturbed.

A few buses run daily from Kairouan; inquire about details and be certain about the last return time. Two buses per day leave from Le Kef, at 8am and 3pm. Note that there are two bus stations in town (SNTRI and S.T. Kef). Buses to Le Kef (2hr., 2.030D) depart opposite the Hotel Restaurant Mactaris.

Monastir

Monastir's rich historical legacy is now barely tangible. Its origins go back to the Phoenicians and the Romans; the city enjoyed a stint in the limelight when nearby Kairouan slipped into decline in the 11th century. More recently, Monastir was the birthplace of ex-President Bourguiba, and his association with the city is still quite salient. In fact, unless you happen to be an ardent personal fan of the man, don't bother spending more than a half-day here. (If, however, you do have a fixation with a certain former Tunisian head of state, then you'll love the huge **Bourguiba Mosque,** the twin-towered **Bourguiba Family Tombs,** and the ultimate in self-indulgence, the gold-leafed **Statue of Bourguiba,** all on or near **Avenue Bourguiba.** Get the picture?)

Although the government (believe it or not, under Bourguiba) poured money into "improving" the old quarters of Monastir, the end result is a sterile, artificial tourist locale. The one item of interest which remains both genuine and unharmed is the **Ribat** (a monastery-fortress like that of Sousse), founded in 796 AD and expanded in the 9th and 11th centuries. (Open 8am-7pm; admission 1.000D.) Climb the tower for a splendid view of the sea in one direction, and Bourguiba-land in the other. Then catch the next train at the Gare du Metro, rue Salem B'chir, for the equally historic and much more charismatic city of Mahdía one hour south (8 per day, 1.080D). Buses (#52) to or from Sousse run hourly (690ml).

Mahdía

A bit removed from the well-worn tourist track, Mahdía remains a peaceful location almost entirely free of the milling crowds so common elsewhere. The city's fortunes have waxed and waned since the Fatimid leader, Obeid Allah, first realized the tremendous strategic importance of the long, thin peninsula upon which the city resides. Obeid Allah, reverently known as *el-Mahdi* ("the Deliverer") proceeded to occupy the peninsula of Cape Africa between 916-921, establishing a fortress and a city. The wisdom of these defenses, which included a 30-foot wall across the peninsula, was proven in 945, when Mahdía resisted an 8-month siege led by Muslim puritan Abu Yazid. After his failed siege attempt, the good Mr. Yazid was stuffed and used as a toy for the Caliph's monkeys; this pretty much ended his career in the puritan business. (Tough neighborhood.)

Shortly thereafter, Mahdía began to flourish as the capital of the (Shiite) Fatimid Dynasty, and for a time it even eclipsed Kairouan in importance. Obeid Allah had constructed the main fortress facing east toward Cairo in the hope that his rule would soon extend that far. In 968, the Fatimids did gain control of Cairo, fulfilling Obeid Allah's dream. However, their capital's glory proved short-lived—within a century, Mahdía was sacked by the first of a succession of Christian and Muslim occupiers. The city was left with a handful of impressive monuments and the memory of a heroic past. Present-day Mahdía is a pleasant little fishing village with a lively port and a *medina* unencumbered by aggressive merchants hawking souvenirs. Someday, this may change: sooner or later, resort hostels will exploit the 17km of beautiful beaches nearby. At least for now, though, Mahdía remains untouristed, quiet, and endearing.

Orientation and Practical Information

Upon arrival by bus or train, walk with the water to your right until you see the Obeidite Mosque on your left; the Skifa is nearby if you walk that way. If you overshoot, you'll come upon the easily recognizable **Borj. Rue Oubad Allah el-Mahdi,** the *medina's* charming, narrow main street, originates at the massive stone gateway of the Skifa Bab Zouila and passes through place du Caire and then place Kadi Noamene, thus hitting all three of the old city's focal points. Just inside the Skifa, the **Syndicat d'Initiative** occupies the first building on the street (tel. 810 98). The office doubles as a paint shop and distributes hand-sketched maps, but the knowledgeable official speaks several languages and may invite you for coffee. **Buses** depart from the port area for Monastir (10 per day, 1hr., 950 ml), and Sousse (14 per day, 1hr. 45min., 1.460D). The last buses leave around 8:30pm. **Louages** are a more convenient option to and from Mahdía, as service is frequent and competitively priced to Sousse (1.900D), Ksar Hellal (650ml), and El Jem (1.200D). *Louages* leave from the Esso station next to the port, two blocks from the Skifa across from the **train station.** Eight metro trains per day leave for Monastir (1hr., 1.080D), and continue on to Sousse's Bab Jedid station (1hr. 30min., 1.480D), along the port a few blocks from pl. Hached. **Avenue Habib Bourguiba** is the new city's main artery; along it you'll find most banks and travel agents. A **police station** sits at #71 (tel. 816 73). Nearby are a **post office** and **telephones** (open Mon.-Sat. 8am-6pm) and a **supermarket** (open Tues.-Sat. 8am-12:15pm and 3:15-7:30pm, Sun. 8am-12:30pm. MC, Visa).

Accommodations and Food

The paucity of visitors to Mahdía means few budget accommodations, but what does exist is great. Avoid arriving late in the day in summer without reservations. Mahdía's handful of restaurants clusters in the port area. Evenings in the *medina* revolve around cozy **place du Caire,** where outdoor café tables brim with locals.

Hotel Al Jazira, 36, rue Ibn Fourat (tel. 816 29). Walk from the Skifa to pl. du Caire, turn left onto rue du Corrique, and walk to the water. Jazira is on your left. An incredible bargain. Clean, cozy rooms, some overlooking the sea. Genial family management, attractive rooftop terrace. Vacancies hard to come by in summer. Women should exercise caution crossing the *medina* at night. Singles 10.000D. Doubles 13.000D. Shower included.

Hotel Rand, 20, av. Taïeb Mehiri (tel. 804 48), several blocks from an excellent beach. From the Skifa, walk up av. Bourguiba, bear left at the fork, and turn left at the *gouvernerat* (10min.). Spacious, spic-and-span rooms and gracious management. Singles 4.500D, with bath 5.500D. Doubles 7.000D, with bath 8.000D. July-Aug. supplement 1.000D per person. Breakfast 1.000D.

Grand Hotel, on av. Bourguiba at av. Bechir Sfar (tel. 800 39). Walk up av. Bourguiba from the Skifa until the road splits (10min.); it's right in the middle. The sign says "Hotel Panorama"— don't fall for this clever ruse, or you'll walk to the ends of the earth. Impeccably clean. The shady courtyard in front serves as the local watering hole. Singles 8.000D. Doubles 18.000D. Sept.-June singles 7.000D, doubles 14.000D. Breakfast included.

Camping: El Asfour, on the public beach along the Sousse road, between the El-Mehdi and Sables d'Or hotels. Nothing actually there; it's just a place. 2.000D per person.

Restaurant El Madina (tel. 806 07), in the market building behind the large Banque de Tunisie. Don't look for the sign (it's in Arabic), look for the Maitre d' in the bright orange suit with the Salvador Dali moustache. Somewhat spicy fare at mild prices. Amazing *brik à l'oeuf* (500ml) and *couscous au poisson* (1.700D). Open daily 7am-11pm.

Restaurant El Moez, 2nd alleyway after turning to the right inside the Skifa. Quiet place with fresh seafood. Octopus and fish dishes 800ml-2.000D. Open daily 8am-9pm.

Sights

The **Skifa Bab Zouila** (Dark Entrance) is pretty much what the name suggests. This imposing gateway to the *medina* is a logical place to start a tour of Mahdía. Originally, it served as the only land gate to the heavily fortified Fatimid capital. Keep in mind that the Skifa was just the gateway of the fortifications—it's clear that the architects of Mahdía's defenses really meant business. The Skifa's walls are over 10m thick, while its dark namesake passageway stretches over 44m. From the Skifa, walk down rue Oubad Allah el-Mehdi to **place du Caire** and the glazed tile façade of the **Moustapha Hamza Mosque.** Mahdía's most venerable monument lies a little farther toward the water at place Kadi Noamene. The **Obeidite Mosque** is Islam's oldest Fatimid mosque, and after the Great Mosque in Kairouan, Tunisia's holiest. Obeid Allah first erected the structure in 921, but a cycle of gradual deterioration and restoration has continued, with the most recent restoration occuring in 1961-65. Despite major reconstructions, the simple linearity of the original Fatimid design has been preserved. The arcaded courtyard conducts you to a colonnaded sanctuary. Unadorned pillars separate modest rush mats that cover the floor of the prayer room. At all times, visitors are restricted to the main courtyard, and extremely modest attire is required. (Inquire at the *syndicat* for the entrance hours. If they're closed, check the mosque Sat.-Thurs. in late afternoon.) Continue from the Great Mosque along the *medina's* waterfront, where you're likely to see young locals diving for octopus. The **fishing port,** Tunisia's busiest, is the scene for intriguing arrivals (human and ichthyoid) in the early morning and at dusk. Ahead looms the immense **Borj el-Kebir** (literally "big fart") which is also fittingly named. Built by the Turks in 1595, the Borj, with its strategic location, commands a view of all approaches to the city. (Open Tues.-Sun. 9am-1pm and 2-6pm. Admission 1.000D, students 600ml with ID, photo permit 1.000D.) From mid-July to August, the Borj hosts **The Nights of Mahdía,** the equivalent of the International Festival of Sousse, featuring the same shows. Tickets are sold at the gate (1.000-5.000D, students half-price).

Farther along the peninsula, hewn out of the rocky shoreline, the 1000-year-old **Fatimid Port** continues to harbor fishing boats. At the tip of windblown Cape Africa, a solitary lighthouse presides over Mahdía's sprawling cemetery. The famous treasures from a sunken Roman ship discovered off the cape in 1907 are currently on display at the Bardo Lynne Museum. After the circuit of the peninsula, continue down the coast toward Monastir and you'll come upon the **municipal beach.** Farther along the route to

Sousse, the beaches remain unmarred (so far) by the debris of resort hotels that have littered the coastline to the north.

Near Mahdía

South of Mahdía, off the road to Ksour Essaf, lies **Salakta.** Turn off at the sign and follow the road to the coast; then veer left and you'll reach **Sullecthum,** an ancient Roman seaport that once engaged in lucrative trade. Though small, the **archeological museum** houses interesting relics, including a remarkable mosaic of a lion. (A tip to the caretaker will open the museum anytime.) South along the white, sandy beach and all around the museum are found the ruins of the port.

El Jem

The Roman coliseum at El Jem is one of the most remarkable sights in all of Tunisia. It seems to rise up suddenly out of nowhere, surrounded by nothing but olive trees for miles in all directions. The huge structure towers formidably over the collection of ramshackle buildings at its feet. The modern-day town of El Jem clusters around the coliseum, which looks for all the world as if the Roman Empire fell just yesterday.

During his brief 3rd-century reign, the rebel emperor Gordian constructed the amphitheater by an old Roman road, exactly halfway between Sousse and Sfax. However, he neglected to buy the support of the Third Augustan Legion, which promptly beat up on both Gordian and the rest of the province. In its day, the amphitheater held 30,000 spectators and hosted games of all sorts—a testament to what life was like before TV. The sixth largest coliseum in the world, the amazingly intact arena reflects the skill of the Roman engineers responsible for its construction. The damage you see is no fault of theirs, but rather of an overzealous government official, who in 1695 ordered artillery fired at the coliseum in an attempt to flush out a band of tax evaders who had fortified themselves within. (Arena open sunrise-sunset. Admission 2.000D; photo permit 1.000D.) From mid-June to July, the colosseum is the spectacular setting of the **Festival International de Musique Symphonique** (with the catchy slogan, "El Jem que j'aime"). For information call (01) 78 58 64 in Tunis or 902 24 in El Jem. On the road south to Sfax (a 10-min. walk from the amphitheater) lies the **Archeological Museum** and another, smaller amphitheater. Mosaics in the museum once adorned Roman villas at Thydrus, the predecessor of the modern village. (Open daily 7am-7pm and 3-6pm. Admission 2.000D. Ticket is the same as for the amphitheater.)

The drab main avenue of El Jem still bears the once-obligatory name of Bourguiba and is home to some auto mechanics and a couple of goats. At the end opposite the arena and next to the **train station,** you will find El Jem's only hotel: **Hotel Julius** (tel. 900 44 or 904 19), with plush singles for 7.500D, doubles for 13.000D. (Breakfast and private bathrooms included.) There are a few hole-in-the-wall eateries in El Jem, but the only good bargain is **Restaurant de Bonheur** (tel. 904 21), one block from the hotel down the road to Sfax. Go with the *poulet rôti* (2.000D) and salads (1.200D) or request an excellent omelette (800ml, not on the menu; open daily 8am-midnight). The **post and telephone office** (tel. 901 39; open Mon.-Thurs. and Sat. 8:30am-2pm, Fri. 8:30am-1pm) and a couple of **banks** also reside on av. Bourguiba.

Three buses (1.800D) and seven trains (2.020D) per day stop here en route to Sousse and Sfax. (*Louages* to Mahdía 1.000D.) Buses and *louages* depart from the square in front of Hotel Julius, across from the train station. The train station **stores luggage** for 500ml per piece.

Sfax

Sfax may be Tunisia's second city in terms of size (a quarter of a million residents), but it has not yet assumed corresponding importance as a cultural or tourist center. Sfax has the look and feel of someplace modern and commercial, rather than historical. The

most notable feature of the city is the massive and unmistakeable wall surrounding the
medina. The interior is relatively devoid of tourists, and (whether by cause or effect)
also somewhat lacking in items of interest. The **Great Mosque,** almost exactly in the
center of town, is unfortunately closed to non-Muslims; the exterior decorations and a
look through the corner windows provide a tantalizing preview of the inaccessible,
marvelous colonnaded interior. In the new town, the **Archeological Museum** (tel. 217
44) is on the ground floor of the town hall on av. Bourguiba; inside are mostly Roman-
era mosaics and sculptures. (Open Tues.-Sun. 8:30am-1pm and 3-6pm; admission
600ml.)

   Tourist Information (tel. 246 06) is located in a glass pavilion on av. Bourguiba, on
the right a few blocks straight ahead from the **train station.** Seven trains run daily from
Sousse via El Jem (2hr., 2.790D one-way, 5.580D round-trip), three per day to and
from Gabès (3hr.). The **bus station** is right by the train station, slightly to the left as
you exit. Occasional buses run to the mostly nearby cities, including eight daily to
Gabès (4.180D). If you own a jet, the **airport** (tel. 408 79) is located 10km out of town.
The **ferry dock** is the point of departure for SONOTRAK ferries to the Kerkennah
Isles. To get to the ferry terminal, walk 12 long blocks (about 900m) straight from the
train station, and turn left (about 400m more).

Near Sfax: Kerkennah Islands

   Only 21km off the coast and due east of Sfax, the Kerkennah Isles are the consummate antithesis of that busy, metropolitan city. In fact, these isles are almost completely
undeveloped. While lacking amenities, they also lack the typical mobs of tourists
found at Hammamet and Jerba. It's one of the rare places in Tunisia where you stand a
reasonable chance of finding a beach all to yourself. Kerkennah is an excellent place
for unwinding on the sand (the water is too shallow for real swimming) or watching the
sunsets—and not much else. Given its isolation and solitude, Kerkennah's great advantage (or problem) is that there is absolutely nothing to do.

   To get to the Isles, catch a ferry from the terminal at Sfax (tel. 22 216) for the unbelievably small fee of 500ml. (Ferries leave 8 times daily in each direction, 1hr. 30min.
Departures from Sfax every 2hr. 6am-10pm, from the islands, every 2hrs. 5:30am-
7:30pm.) On arrival, you will be at the westernmost point in the archipelago, which is
interconnected by causeways. Of the two major islands, Gharbi is the westernmost and
Chergui is the easternmost. Five hotels cluster together in Sidi Frej, on Chergui. Take
the municipal bus (or possibly sneak onto the Hotel Farhat bus) and ask to be let off at
the hotels (*Zone touristique*). It's about a 15-minute ride; be sure to get off at your stop,
or you'll end up someplace disturbingly nowhere with about a two-hour wait to catch
the bus heading the other way. Along the way, you'll marvel at the flat appearance of
the islands. The Kerkennah are very low (no point on the islands is more than 35 feet
above sea level—no doubt leading to great local consternation over global warming),
and punctuated only by countless palm trees. When you get off the bus, follow the
signs and walk about 200m to the hotels. Of the bunch, the **Hotel el Kastil** (tel. 812 12)
and the **Hotel el Jazira** (tel. 81 058) are the cheapest. The Jazira charges 8.000D for
singles, 12.000D for doubles (with breakfast); the Kastil is usually 1.000D more per
person, but they'll pick you up at the port if you call ahead. Next door, the **Hotel Cerci-
na** is a step up the price ladder, with 14.500D singles and 22.000D doubles, breakfast
included. The Farhat and Grand Hotels are both 20.000D a head. Eating options are
limited by location; the hotel restaurants are pretty much the only candidates. The restaurant at the Kastil is moderately priced (dinner about 4.000D) and you can watch a
glorious sunset over the waves.

Southern Tunisia

   The vast emptiness of the Sahara stands as a reminder of humanity's insignificance.
Villages cling to hilltops or huddle in oases; the immense desert scarcely deigns to acknowledge them except with continual gusts of sand. Berbers still dwell in caves, Be-

douins still herd camels and harvest dates, and human presence is still a rare mirage in the vast ocean of sand. The diversity of the desertscape is surprising. The **Great Eastern Erg** undulates with endless sand dunes. But the Sahara of southern Tunisia has many other faces: the marshy salt flats of **Chott el Jerid,** the jagged **Ksour Mountains,** the lunar landscape of Matmata, and the bursts of green foliage in the oases.

Desert Survival

Summer temperatures soar in the Sahara. The body loses a gallon or more of liquid per day—*Drink a liter of water every hour and a half or so.* Light-colored, breathable long sleeves and trousers actually keep you cooler and protect you from the sun. *Always keep your head covered*—you can buy a wide-brimmed straw hat on the street for about 4.000D. Also wear a good pair of sunglasses. Temperatures fluctuate unpredictably; bring a sweater or jacket. In winter temperatures in the Sahara approach the freezing point, and it occasionally snows.

Gabès

Gabès is a Saharan frontier town *par excellence.* According to tradition, modern Gabès was founded on an old Roman site by Muhammed's barber, Sidi Boulbaba. Mr. Boulbaba resides in Gabès to this day, tucked away cozy in his grave. The poetic reason for Gabès's existence since the 7th century is its beautiful oasis; the more pragmatic reasons are its strategic location and the presence of its barracks. Gabès has always been the gateway to the Sahara and has an atmosphere to match: you know you're venturing off the beaten path when you witness both little lost lambs and wind-blown sands scattered about the streets. Like myriad others through the ages, stop off in Gabès, wander amidst the low, white houses along the dusty streets, and prepare yourself before trekking inland.

Gabès consists of two major streets, which intersect to form a V. The first bears the remarkably original name of **Avenue Bourguiba;** the other bears the equally unique appellation of **Avenue Farhat Hached.** Note that these streets are long; it's over 2km from the bus station to the sea. Most items of interest are found on av. Hached. The **tourist office** (tel. 702 54; open loosely Mon.-Sat. 9am-noon and 3-6pm) is about 300m towards the sea from the intersection of the two. There's also a **Syndicat d'Initiative** (tel. 703 44) right at the intersection; check out the handy list of 1974 phone numbers posted by the door. To get to either office, turn right onto av. Farhat Hached if arriving by train or bus. Between the train and bus stations on av. Farhat Hached (left from the train station, right from the bus station) you'll find a **late night pharmacy** and, several blocks away, a **post office** and **money exchange.** (Open Mon.-Thurs. 8am-noon and 2-5pm, Fri.-Sat. 8am-noon.) Across the street, *louages* wait in a dirt lot. Farther down av. Farhat Hached, the **telephone office** rings daily 8am-midnight. Also on av. Farhat Hached is the **bus station,** where rival companies run to Jerba (6 per day, 3hr. 30min., 5.100D), Matmata (9 per day, 1hr., 1.840D), Kebili (5 per day, 2hr., 2.600D), Douz (2 per day, 3hr., 4.100D), and Gafsa (2 per day, 3.300D). *Louage* fares run slightly higher. For travel north along the coast, the train is the best option. Two air-conditioned trains per day zoom to Tunis (8.850D, *direct-climatisé*). **Hertz,** 30, rue Ibnou El Jazzar (tel. 705 25), is near the intersection of av. Farhat Hached and av. Bourguiba. A **police station** (tel. 703 90) guards av. Bourguiba near the Hotel Regina.

The **Centre de Jeunesse (HI)** (tel. 702 71), on the northern edge of town, is a **youth hostel** with large, clean dorms and a **campground.** From av. Farhat Hached, between the train and bus stations, turn at the Hotel Salama onto rue Sadok Lassoued. Continue to the end of the street, then turn right and take an immediate left. The youth center is 200m ahead on the left. They admit members-only when the hostel is almost full, usually late July through August. (Curfew midnight; 2.000D per person. Well-shaded camping sites, kitchen facilities included.) The **Hotel Medina** (tel. 742 71), on rue Ali Jemel off av. Farhat Hached, to the right from the train station lets spacious, well-furnished rooms with balconies. (Singles 6.000D. Doubles 8.000D.) The gregarious manager of the **Hotel Ben Nejima,** 66, rue Ali Jemel (tel. 210 62), at av. Farhat Hached near Hotel Medina, maintains immaculate rooms near the bus stations. (Singles 5.800D. Doubles 8.000D.)

La Bonne Boufe, 62, av. Bourguiba, near the intersection with av. Hached, serves an immense, immensely tasty *couscous d'agneau* for 1.600D (open daily noon-10pm). The **Restaurant Marhaba,** 338, av. Farhat Hached, below Hotel Marhaba, has no dishes over 2.000D. Their *couscous à la viande* is somewhat dry but tasty nonetheless. (Open daily 8:30am-midnight.) **Restaurant Bouka Chouka,** rue Ali Jemel (tel. 203 87), next to Hotel Ben Nejima, prepares delicious food served lightning fast for about 3.000D a meal. *Pommes de terre à la viande* is 1.600D. (Open Sat.-Thurs. 6am-11pm.)

Near Gabès: Isle of Jerba

The island of Jerba was supposedly the residence of the mythical "Lotus Eaters" from Homer's *Odyssey.* According to the narration, Odysseus's crew, while on shore leave, got themselves really smashed on local lotus Mai Tais, and decided that going home wasn't such a pressing concern after all. Roughly three millenia later, Jerba still bills itself as a haven of R&R, although massive inebriation and subsequent mutiny are frowned upon. Despite the best efforts of the tourist industry, Jerba does still manage to retain some of its natural beauty.

While the fictional description of Jerba is of a merry island where inebriated inhabitants stumble around smashed out of their minds, the reality of the island's history has been much less serendipitous. The Phoenicians first arrived in the 6th century BC; the Carthaginians later built the 7km El Kantara causeway connecting the island to the mainland (still in use today). Thereafter, the island passed into the hands of the Romans, the Ibadite Muslims, the Hilalian Arabs, the Kings of Sicily, and the Hafsids. The island's heyday came in the 16th century, at a time when Jerba was notorious as a pirate's haven. In 1560, French, Spanish and Neapolitan troops attacked the island in an effort to wrest it from the control of the infamous pirate Dragut. An excessively bloodthirsty fellow, Dragut massacred the invading forces with the help of the Turkish fleet and constructed a tower out of their 5000-odd skulls. The tower was given an annual whitewash and remained until 1848, when some concerted pleading led to the bones' removal and burial.

Despite this nasty lesson, Europeans still invade Jerba. Modern Jerba is an agreeable place to rest for a couple of days, but it falls well short of a mythical paradise: the towns are basically dull, and the beaches often overrun with tourists. It's wisest to avoid the string of expensive shoreline hotels and instead stay in **Houmt Souk,** the island's largest city and transportation hub. From Houmt Souk, at the center of the northern shore, a short bus trip or about a 2.500D taxi ride takes you to the start of the beaches, about 12km east. A bus trip (#10 or 11) around the island costs about 1.500D. About the only item of interest is the El Ghriba Synagogue in Er Ridah. The synagogue is modern but the site is supposedly one of the oldest in the world. Jerba's small but enduring Jewish community claims to be descended from a group that fled Jerusalem in 584 BC.

Arriving at the bus station and following the downhill road to the right, you will be on the omnipresent **Avenue Bourguiba.** After 200m, on your left will be the **Syndicat d'Initiative,** (tel. 509 15) in a nice pavilion; on your right will be the confusing tangle of streets where most of the hotels are found. The Syndicat can give you a handout with a map but not much else. **Tourist Information** (tel. 505 44) can do the same but is much farther away, in the direction of the shore and the **Borj el Kebir,** Houmt Souk's fortress and another Dragut memento. (Tourist office open 7am-1pm. Borj open 8am-noon and 3-6pm. Admission 600ml, 1.000D photo permit.) Accommodations are predictably expensive. **Hotel el Arischa** (tel. 50 384) is on rue de Bizerte, to the left from the front of the Catholic church. A former villa, it vaunts a beautiful courtyard which makes up for the apparently medieval door locks. (Singles 7.000D. Doubles 12.000D. Breakfast included.) **Hotel Sables d'Or,** one block over, is quite nice and only slightly costlier. (Singles 7.500D. Doubles 13.500D. Triples 19.000D. Breakfast included.) **Hotel Essalem** (tel. 510 29) is cheaper and near the bus station. Head one block down av. Bourguiba and turn right at the police station. (Singles 5.100D. Doubles 10.200D.) Avoid renting the antiquated bicycles at the Hotel Sindbad; the owner does not refund money for such minor problems as punctured tires or handlebars that snap off. The going rate for bicycles elsewhere is about 1.000D per hour, 6.000D per day. Thankfully, one can eat relatively cheaply at either the **Restaurant du Palmiers,** 45, rue de Bizerte, or the **Restaurant du Sportif** on av. Bourguiba. A meal at either runs about 3.000D. **Buses** run from Gabès (4 per day, 3hr. 30min., 5.100D) and depart via Gabès once daily each for Sfax (7.060D), Sousse (10.300D) and Tunis (13.400D). **Louages** generally run slightly more often and aggregate in front of the bus station. **Tunis Air** also flies once daily to Jerba.

Matmata

When the makers of *Star Wars* were searching for a setting for a desert planet, they came upon the otherworldly scenery surrounding Matmata. If box-office receipts are any indication, the choice was certainly a good one. And, indeed, the sun-scorched landscape along the way to Matmata does look decidedly extraterrestrial: twisted mountain and sprawling craters stretch to the horizon. (Don't miss the incongruous sight of "Welcome to Matmata" appearing suddenly in large letters in three languages on the side of a mountain in the middle of the desert.) Although the film crews and jawas packed up long ago, nature adds its own special effects at sunset, when the ominous landscape assumes an eerie red glow. With moonrise, all becomes peaceful. Walk just a kilometer or so along either the Tamezret or Gabès roads and savor some memorable images. Brief but repetitive rains have carved gutters and valleys into the rock; the Berbers now build dams to reroute the water to their olive trees.

At first glance, the desert surrounding Matmata appears entirely uninhabited. The Berber population has developed a remarkable mode of habitation in which a large central pit is carved in the ground (usually about 10m deep and 10m wide), while tunnel passageways connect a constellation of adjoining chambers. The present-day Berbers of Matmata have made some 20th-century concessions—many of their "primitive" dwellings sprout television antennas at ground level. Local children will be more than delighted to show you their homes for a few hundred millimes.

Matmata is easily seen as a daytrip from Gabès, but you might consider an overnight stay: the daylight hours are an endless parade of tour buses deploying batallions of tourists and the town becomes vastly more pleasant in the evenings, when the buses depart and sunset introduces a cool, serene nightfall. And finally, there's the added novelty of staying in Matmata's unique hostels ("Luke Skywalker slept here"): if you've always wanted to go underground, here's your chance.

Three of Matmata's hotels are, of course, pits. The famous cantina scene in Star Wars was filmed at **Sidi Driss** (tel. 300 05). Unfortunately, nearly all of the decor from that period has since been removed, so you'll have to use the Force of your imagination. The one-bulbed, polybed rooms are cool and reasonably clean (4.500D per person, including breakfast). **Les Berberes** (tel. 300 24) is almost a rerun of Sidi Driss: same prices, same facilities, but nicer management; you're also less likely to get stomped on by tourists. It's never been toasted by aliens, but it cooks tasty, down-to-earth three-course meals for 2.200D. The **Marhala Touring Club Hotel** (tel. 300 15) puts fewer beds into cleaner rooms. It's also more expensive and more touristed. If you arrive in high season early in the day, they may insist on full pension (10.500D), but the meals of soup, egg pastry, and couscous are well worth it. (Singles 5.500D. Doubles 9.000D. Showers 1.000D. Breakfast included.)

Nine buses per day run between Matmata and Gabès (1.390D), supplemented by *louage* service. Confirm that your ride is going all the way to "Matmata *ancien*," and not "Matmata *nouvelle*," 15km short of the village.

Near Matmata

The sleepy subterranean village of **Haddej** remains untainted by mass tourism and George Lucas. Take one of the Gabès-Matmata buses and get off at Tijma, 5km outside of Matmata; a sign points out the paved road leading east to Haddej, 3km away. If you prefer or want to be environmentally conscious, you can hire a donkey from locals in Matmata (20.000D per day). **Tamezret,** 10km to the west of Matmata, is a well-preserved Berber village carved into the cliffs along the side of a mountain, commanding a dramatic view of the bleak landscape. Its stone houses huddle tightly together in defensive Berber style, and are best seen from above. At the top of the town by the steepled building, enjoy a cup of mint tea with almonds in the café (400ml) or clamber onto the roof for a look at the village below. One bus per day runs at noon from Matmata to Tamezret (500ml), supplemented very sporadically by covered pickup trucks (1.000D). Even if you don't make it to the village, a hike on the road is worthwhile for the dramatic landscape above. More spectacular scenery awes along the bumpy road to **Toujane,** 23km east. Scenically perched on the edge of a cliff, the village is split in two by a deep gorge. There are no restaurants or cafés here, but children tote small buckets with bottles of lukewarm soft drinks for 300ml.

Tataouine and Chenini

Venturing out south from Gabès, one comes to the Berber towns, on the fringes of inhabited Tunisia. The Berber villages, or *ksars*, have noticeably different names and styles from the Arab cities to the north. As often as not, these settlements are located in astoundingly inhospitable settings, unforgettable evidence of the Berbers' ability to adapt themselves to their harsh desert surroundings.

The most convenient base from which to explore the Berber homelands is **Tataouine** (which does indeed sound suspiciously like Luke Skywalker's desert homeworld), sometimes also called Foum Tataouine. The 125-km journey from Gabès south to Tataouine proceeds by way of **Medenine,** itself a Berber city of some interest until the 1960's, when the government in its proven wisdom decided to bulldoze the entire place as part of a plan to improve it. Don't stay in the new, improved Medenine longer than it takes to change buses (Gabès to Medenine, 4 buses per day from 7am, 1hr. 30min., 2.070D). From Medenine take a connecting bus to Tataouine (1hr., 1.500D). On arrival, the **bus station** is on rue 1 Juin 1955, about a block from the two main streets, our old friends av. Bourguiba and av. Farhat Hached. **Louages** depart from a plaza with a clock tower on av. Farhat Hached (about 2hr. and 4.000D back to Gabès). Accommodations and eating in Tataouine are generally affordable, and both are options in the inelegant but inexpensive **Hotel Ennour** (tel. 601 31) at one end of av. Bourguiba. Rooms are 3.000D per person, and plates in the restaurant below run 1.300-2.200D.

Chenini is the most impressive (and most touristed) of the Berber villages in the vicinity of Tataouine; less-frequented ones include Guermessa, Ghomrassen, and Ksar Hadada. Far to the south (78km) is Remada (which does not have an eponymous inn). To make the 18km trip to Chenini, you'll have to take a **louage,** since there's no other transport. At least you'll get to see some good deserted landscape along the way. Bargain for a taxi trip there and back; it shouldn't come to more than about 10.000D total. You'll be dropped off at the **Relais Chenini,** which serves a standard, fixed-price meal for 3.000D. Below you will be the **post office (PTT)** and the town's lone **telephone.** Above, the stone path snakes upwards towards the village itself, cut and built into the side of the mountain. Follow the path around the mountain to the other side for some fantastic views of vast expanses of nothing.

Douz

After visiting Douz, you'll have a lasting impression of what the word "oasis" means. It may not be what you expect, though; it isn't the archetypal pool of water accompanied by Bugs Bunny or Lawrence of Arabia. Rather, it is a sizeable expanse (acres and acres) of cultivated palm trees, surrounded by a substantially larger expanse of desert in all directions. Situated between the Great Eastern Erg and the vast *Chott,* Douz makes an ideal base for desert adventures and is perhaps the best of the Tunisian oases to visit. The town began as a rallying point for the M'Razig, a nomad tribe. Legend has it that Douz got its name when the French army's 12th batallion bivouacked here in the 19th century—*douze* means "twelve" in French. Modern Douz still has an army barracks (don't try to take photos—it's *not* appreciated), but the town is also becoming increasingly touristy. Between 10am and 7pm, the streets here are a sizzling frying-pan of heat and humidity. Twilight among the cultivated plots brings the only respite. Wandering boys may pour you a cup of palm sap for 50ml; try it in the morning when it's sweetest.

The **Hotel Bel Habib** (tel. 953 09), on av. 7 Novembre, one block from the bus and *louage* station, rents out immaculate rooms with elegantly decorated showers for 3.000D per person. Some rooms have balconies overlooking the market square. Take your mattress out on the terrace for a snooze *en plein air.* The hotel **20 (Vingt) Mars** (tel. 954 95), on the main square, lets slightly dustier rooms at the same price. The battered rooms and wafer-thin mattresses of the **Hotel Essaada** (tel. 950 19) go for 2.500D, including showers; beware the persistent resident guides. (Breakfast 50ml.) Down the main road (av. des Martyrs) into and past the oasis, convoys of tour buses disgorge hapless tourists at expensive hotels with swimming pools. **Hotel Rose des Sables** (tel. 954 84) parts with singles for 11.000D, doubles for 16.000D. (Breakfast included.) **Hotel Saharien** (tel. 953 37) provides fans and polished wood desks in comfortable rooms. (Singles 18.000D. Doubles 24.000D. Breakfast included.)

You won't leave your heart at the **Desert Club Camping** on rue des Affections, off av des. Martyrs. It's absolutely shadeless, and at 5.000D per person, more expensive than the hotels.

The **Restaurant Bel Habib** (tel. 953 09), below the hotel, serves meat-filled *tajine* for 1.000D. The friendly people at the **Restaurant El-Kods** (tel. 954 95), besides conversing in about five languages, prepare tasty, sizeable meals for 2.000D. The **Restaurant Ali Baba,** one block up the Kebili road, is only slightly bigger than its two tables, but cannot be accused of being pretentious. (*Couscous* 1.500D.)

From a café on av. des Martyrs, the well-informed **tourist office** (tel. 953 51) arranges three-hour **camel rides** (2.500D) and buggy rides (1.800D). (Open Mon.-Sat. 8am-noon and 3-6pm.) The **post office, telephone office,** and **currency exchange** (tel. 953 00) give to their causes on av. des. Martyrs. (Open Mon.-Thurs. 8am-noon and 3-6pm, Fri.-Sat. 8am-12:30pm.) For longer journeys into the Sahara by car and camel, drop by **Abdelmoula Voyages.** (Tel. 952 82. 25.000D per day, meals and camping included. Open Mon.-Thurs. 8am-1pm and 3-6pm, Fri.-Sat. 8am-1pm.) You can also explore the rippling, powdery dunes by the fort-like Hotel Mehari, on the edge of the desert, 2km past the tourist office. Vacant 51 weeks of the year, the stadium on the town's outskirts comes to life in late December for Douz's **Festival International du Sahara,** when you can watch Berber tribes playing sand hockey with a bran-filled ball or cheer on fighting, racing camels. Hundreds of tourists saturate the town during that week, and most hotels tack extra dinars onto their prices.

Public transportation puts Douz within easy reach. Buses run to Tozeur (6 and 8am, 3.300D) and Gabès (7am, 2:30 and 8:30pm, 4.100D). Additional buses cruise to nearby Kebili, 20 minutes away by *louage* (750ml).

You can take buses to smaller, less-touristed towns deeper in the desert. At 7am and 3pm, buses run to **Zaafrane** (500ml) along a predominantly paved road. You can usually return at 5:30pm (but check). Two more buses run in winter. The **Zaafrane Hotel** offers rooms for 9.000D per person., 11.000D in July and August. The buses continue through fantastic scenery to **Nouil, Es-Sabria,** and finally **El-Faouar** (1.500D), where beautiful palms shade squat modern buldings. The only hotel in El-Faouar, the creatively named **Faouar Hotel,** offers half-pension for 13.000D. For 3.000D, you can camp in Nouil. Buses return from El-Faouar at noon and 5pm.

Tozeur

Situated over 120km across the Chott el Jerid (salt flats) from Douz, Tozeur is the largest (and almost the only) city in southwest Tunisia. Like Douz, it's an oasis and makes an excellent base for desert excursions. Tozeur's distinctive characteristic is its 8th-century Mesopotamian-style brickwork, which incorporates geometric designs into the walls themselves. The designs are particularly visible in the walls of mosques and the *medina.*

Two major avenues (remarkably enough, named **av. Farhat Hached** and **av. Habib Bourguiba**) cross to form a T. Arriving by bus or *louage*, you will find yourself on av. Farhat Hached to the east of av. Bourguiba, which runs north-south. The **Syndicat**

d'Initiative (tel. 500 34), located at the intersection, isn't much help unless you want to book a tour somewhere. The regional **tourist office** (tel. 505 03) is much more helpful, but they're 3km away—all the way to the end of av. Bourguiba and then down av. Abou el-Kacem ech Chabbi, which heads off to the west. **Telephones** are near the Syndicat, **currency exchanges** are found on the two main avenues, and the **post office** (tel. 500 00) is just off av. Bourguiba. The **police** (tel. 500 16) are 1km away on the Gafsa road; the **hospital** (tel. 504 00) is located in town. **Buses** run to Nefta (5 per day, 45min., 700ml) as do *louages*. Both provide service to Douz via Kebili (2 per day, 3.300D) and Tunis via Kairouan (5 per day, 4hr., 8.470D to Kairouan; 7hr., 12.480D to Tunis) as well.

Tozeur's *medina* extends off to the left as you walk down av. Bourguiba past the Syndicat. Don't bother with the **Museum of Popular Arts** (tel. 500 34) within; three small rooms present more dust than exhibits. (Open 8am-1pm and 4pm-7pm; admission 1.000D.) Instead, admire the geometric design laid out in the sand-baked bricks of the walls and arches. When bricks grow tiresome, head over to Tozeur's park, **Le Paradis,** for lovely flowers and a profusion of palm trees. From the end of av. Bourguiba, veer right and walk about half a kilometer; still farther along, past the tourist office, is the **Belvedere** and **cultural center.** The Belvedere features a view of 2500 acres of palm trees, and part of the Chott. The cultural center boasts an impressive new building, lots of places to spend money, and another touristy, skippable museum, the private **Musée Dar Cherait** (tel. 51 100; admission a lofty 2.500D).

Tozeur has a number of reasonably priced accommodations options. Its conveniently located youth hostel, the **Auberge de Jeunes** (tel. 505 14—walk east on av. Farhat Hached and follow the sign at the clock tower 100m) is less depressing than most Tunisian hotels (3.000D per person). Only slightly more expensive, **Hotel Essalem** (tel. 50 981) is more upbeat and is located in the same area. It's the closest to the bus station; walk 150m due east along av. Farhat Hached. Engage Sukander, the Essalem's owner, in conversations in French, Italian, Spanish, or Arabic; if you're lucky he may invite you to join him for dinner or to smoke a *sheeshah* (water pipe). (5.000D per person, with breakfast at any time you like—almost as good as Denny's.) At the **Hotel Essaada** (tel. 50 097), you'll rest better with your mattress on the floor rather than on the sagging beds—but at 2.500D per person, you can't really gripe. A step up are the **Hotel Splendid** (tel. 50 053), off av. Bourguiba (singles 10.200D, doubles 15.000D, breakfast included, showers 1.000D) and the **Residence Warda** (tel. 50 597), on av. Abou el-Kacem Chebbi. The Splendid features a swimming pool, and both the Splendid and Warda offer a desert miracle—air conditioning—for an extra 3.000-3.500D. Tasty cheap eats aren't tough to find either. Among the options are **Restaurant le Paradis** (tel. 51 432) off av. Bourguiba, **Restaurant le Soleil** (tel. 50 220) on av. Abou el-Kacem Chebbi, and the **Restaurant du Sud** on av. Farhat Hached.

Near Tozeur: Nefta & Vicinity

Nefta is another of the Tunisian oases, lying 23km due west of Tozeur. It is famous for its numerous non-volcanic hot springs, which are scattered about the area. (Unless you've got a thing for pools of hot water, they aren't hugely exciting.) As is evidenced by the many mosques in town, it is also known as a lesser religious center. But Nefta is most noteworthy for the **Corbeille de Nefta,** a natural dome-shaped depression filled with palms. The site is eye-catching, but the view is marred by an architectural eyesore—the Sahara Palace Hotel. More worthy occupants of the dome's edge are the several mosques that comprise the **Ridge of Domes.** While the Corbeille is attractive, it's not quite as fabulous as the tourist offices might claim—especially if you've already seen the oases at Douz and Tozeur. After you've seen your first 50,000 palm trees, they all start to look the same.

To get to Nefta and the Corbeille, take the bus from Tozeur (700ml); you'll pass the **Syndicat d'Initiative** (tel. 571 84) on your way in. Then walk down av. Bourguiba until it splits just past the post office, take the right fork then the first street to the right, and keep heading in that direction for about 250m. On reaching the rim, take the dirt track down and past a heap of rubbish to enter the Corbeille itself.

To clamber around some authentic Saharan sand dunes, ride the bus 10km past Nefta or hire a *louage* to take you there and back at a designated time (1.100D each way). Ask to be taken to a place called the **Marché de Roses du Sahara.** The Marché itself is an outdoor market for the omnipresent "Roses of the Sahara," curious rock formations (crystallized gypsum) found locally. Bypass the market and head off to the right about 800m, where you will begin to encounter the shifting sand dunes of the Sahara. Here, you can explore the trackless desert in complete solitude, except, of course, for other groups of tourists or bands of locals who will run out at you and try to sell you unidentified souvenirs for 1.000D. (As always, be sure to bring at least a liter of water per person per hour.)

Upon returning to the road, on the left side you'll see the vast, flat expanse of the *Chott*. Moving past the market, you can walk out onto these salt flats (in general, more flat than salted). The location is also a particularly good one for seeing mirages (or, at least, things which *look* like mirages).

Another 24km along the same road is the **Algerian frontier,** along which one of the few points of entry is found at Hazoua. You can reach Hazoua by bus directly from Tozeur once daily at 10am (1hr. 30min., 1.580D). Once there, be prepared for a long wait at the Tunisian border and a 3km walk to the Algerian frontier post unless you can snag a *louage*. At present—especially in the aftermath of the assassination of the Algerian President in July 1992—the Algerians are likely to give you a cool reception. You'll need an entry visa and will probably be required to change 1000 non-convertible Algerian Dinars (US $250-300) which you cannot take back out with you. Good luck.

Also Near Tozeur: Chebika, Tamerza, & Mides

The mountains, deserts, and oases surrounding Tozeur constitute some extremely difficult terrain, but they also offer what is without question some of the most spectacular scenery in all of Tunisia. The three towns of Chebika, Tamerza, and Mides reward the intrepid traveler with something unique and marvelous to behold. Ideally, see them all as a full-day trip from Tozeur; otherwise at least try to reach Tamerza, the most accessible of the three.

By and large, the roads in the region are impassable in anything less than a Range Rover; along some stretches you may wish you had a Patton tank or Bradley Fighting Vehicle. Given this, your best option is to hire a 4x4 automobile and a guide for the day. Get together a group and pile as many people as you can into the car—they can seat up to nine passengers. Bargain for the total price of the trip: typical rates will be 90.000-120.000D for the day. A good deal on a full car can run as low as 12-13D per head. You can try asking at the Syndicat for information, but a good source of vehicles and guides is **Mehari Voyages** (tel. 503 87) in Tozeur, on av. Farhat Hached. Your other option is to take a bus from Tozeur to Metlaoui, then a bus or train to Redeyef, and to improvise from there. With luck you can get a *louage* to go the 20km or so to Tamerza and then back.

After traversing roads which challenge even the best shock-absorbers, you first encounter **Chebika,** an classic oasis. Although the inhabitants have recently relocated to newer buildings alongside the old village, Chebika itself is an ancient village community perched on a mountainside, with an unbelievable cluster of palms nestled between mountains to one side and desert to the other. For a handful of change, a local will take you along the path that climbs through the hills to the source of the spring, which flows downhill as a small stream. Striking though it is, the stream is dwarfed by the one at **Tamerza**, which is famous throughout Tunisia for its two waterfalls—cool, lush and beautiful sanctuaries in the midst of the parched desert. The last location, only 3km from the Algerian border, is **Mides,** where you can gawk at a gorgeous gorge which cuts into the rock.

Throughout your trip you can take in breathtaking desert vistas and remarkable mountain panoramas. (Don't be put off if you round a deserted mountain bend and suddenly encounter a traffic jam of ten or twenty Range Rovers lined up at a photo spot.) And on the way home, don't miss out on that desert sunset. Try to leave in the early morning or after midday to avoid the most oppressive heat, and tote loads of water (buying it later will cost you plenty).

Appendices

Language

Modern Italian, a descendant of medieval Latin, was standardized in the late Middle Ages, thanks to the literary triumvirate of Dante, Petrarch, and Boccaccio, who all wrote in the Tuscan dialect. Today, although most Italians still converse at home in local dialects, they can also communicate in "standard" Italian, which is taught and spoken at school, and which reigns though the universal medium of television. If you don't speak Italian, you'll probably be able to manage with English. More Italians are likely to know a smattering of French than English, and cognates often help Spanish speakers.

Knowing a few basic terms, however, will make your trip much easier, and you'll find that even mangled Italian can evoke enthusiastic appreciation. Take a phrase book (the *Barron's* book is fairly useful; and *Berlitz* has some useful phrases, though the vocabulary is geared toward business travelers) and practice with it before you leave. Better yet, teach yourself with a tape and book set: Barron's provides thorough drilling in basic vocabulary and grammar at a budget price ($75). If you can learn only one complete sentence, learn *Parla inglese?* (PAHR-lah een-GLAY-say: Do you speak English?). Remember that when writing numbers, Italians often cross their sevens and use a comma instead of a decimal point (and vice versa). Even more often, what they write is completely illegible to the American-trained eye—once you've learned the numbers, ask the train information people to speak rather than write the time and track you want.

Pronunciation is easy: it's almost entirely phonetic, but remember that no letter (except H) is ever silent.

Vowels

There are only 7 vowel sounds in Italian. **A, I,** and **U** are always pronounced the same way, whereas **E** and **O** each have two possible pronunciations, depending on whether the sound is stressed or unstressed.

a	(**fa**ther)	*casa*	*papa*
e	(b**e**d)	*è*	*bello*(stressed)
e	(**a**te)	*sete*	*e*(unstressed)
i	(mar**i**ne)	*bigoli*	*misti*
o	(r**o**sy)	*dove*	*nome*(stressed)
o	(l**o**st)	*cosa*	*posta*(unstressed)
u	(r**u**se)	*lusso*	*virtù*

Consonants

Italian consonants will give you few problems, except the few quirks noted here.

C and G: before **a, o,** or **u c** and **g** are hard, as in *cat* and *goose* or as in the Italian *colore* (koLORay) or *gatto* (GAT-to). They soften into "ch" and "j" sounds when suceeded **i** or **e,** as in the English *cheese* and *jeep* or the Italian *ciao* (chow) and *geLAto* (jehlahtoh).

CH and GH: The consonant combinations **ch** and **gh** are always followed by an **i** or **e** and return c and g to their hard counterparts, thus *chiave,* (KYAvay) and *laghi* (LAgee).

GN and GL: pronounce **GN** like the **NI** in *onion,* thus *bagno* is "BAHNyo." **GL** is said like the **LI** in *million,* so *sbagliato* is said "sbalYAHto."

S and Z: An intervocalic **s** is pronounced as the English z, thus *casa* sounds like "kahza." A double **s** or an initial **s** has the same sound as English s, so *sacco* is "SAHC-co." **Z** always has a ts sound; *stazione* is thus "statSYOHnay."

SC and SCH: when followed by **a, o,** or **u, sc** is pronounced as "sk," so *scusi* yields "SKOOzee." When followed by an **e** or **i,** however, the combination is pronounced *sh* as in *sciopero* (SHOpe-hroh). The combination **sch** only precedes an **i** or **e** and is always hard (sk) as in *pesche* (PEHs-kay).

Doubled consonants: most likely to cause the English speaker difficulties and blank stares is the difference between double and single consonants in Italian. When a doubled consonant appears, a good approximation of proper pronunciation is to tack the consonant to both the end of one syllable and the beginning of the next, thus *sette* should be "SEHT-te" while *sete* is said "SEH-te." This may seem minor, but if you mean "I'm thirsty" ("Ho sete"), you don't want to end up saying "I'm seven years old" ("Ho sette").

Stress

For most Italian words, stress falls on the next-to-last syllable. When a word's stress falls on the last syllable, it is written with a grave accent: *città, unità*. In general, the endings **-ia, -ie,** and **-io** act as a single syllable for stress purposes, with the stress falling on the preceding syllable, which you'd otherwise consider the third-to-last. The main exception to this last rule is the group of words ending in the **-ria** suffix that indicates a shop; their stress falls on the last **i**: *trattoRIa, rosticceRIa, paneficeRIa, salumeRIa, lavandeRIa,* etc. Because place names so often deviate from these rules, *Let's Go* indicates stress in the names of cities throughout the book by the use of acute accents, which Italians are phasing out of their language: Pésaro, Táranto, and so on (some of the accents are standard to written Italian, thus Règgio di Calabria is written, as in Italian, with a grave accent—and when referring to the island Cápri (CAHpri), remember only the car is named cuhPREE.

Italians do not pluralize by adding an **s**, but change the last vowel of a word. A word that ends in an **a** in the singular (mela—MEH-lah) ends with an **e** in the plural (mele—MEH-lay). A word that ends with an **o** in the singular takes an **i** (*conto* to *conti* the plural, as does a word that ends in an **e** in the singular (*cane/canie* A word whose last letter is accented, such as **caffè**, stays the same in the plural. A word that doesn't end with a vowel is also stable (one *autobus,* two *autobuse*

Reservations by phone

Mastery of the following phrases should allow you to get through the process of reserving a room on the telephone. Remember, many proprietors are using to dealing with the minimal Italian of callers; even without any real knowledge of Italian, it is quite possible to get a room.

Pronto! (prohn-toh): phone greeting.

Parla inglese? (PAHR-lah een-GLEH-say): Hopefully, the answer is "Sì," or better yet, "Yes." If not, struggle gamely on ...

Potrei prenotare una camera singola (doppia) senza/con bagno per il due agosto? (POH-tray preh-noh-TAH-ray OO-nah cah-MEH-rah seen-GO-lah (DOHP-pyah) SEHNT-sa/kon BAHN-yoh pehr eel doo-ay ah-GOS-to): Could I reserve a single (double) room without/with bath for the second of August?

Mi chiamo (mee KYAH-moh): My name is ...

Arriverò alle quattordici e mezzo (ahr-ree-veh-ROH ahl-lay kwaht-TOR-dee-chee ay MET-tsoh): I will arrive at 14:30 (remember, Italian use the 24-hour clock, so add twelve to afternoon/evening arrival times).Return phrases to watch out for: *Mi dispiace* (mee dis-PYAH-chay, I'm sorry); *No, siamo completo* (noh, syah-moh com-PLEH-toh, Nope, we're full); *Non si fa prenotazioni per telefono* (nohn see fah preh-no-tat-SYO-nee pehr te-LEH-fo-no, We don't take telephone reservations); *Deve arrivare primo delle quattordici (DEH-vay ahr-ree-VAH-ray PREE-moh dehl-lay kwaht-TOR-dee-cee, You must arrive before 2pm).*

Numbers

1	uno	19	dicianove
2	due	20	venti
3	tre	21	ventuno
4	quattro	22	ventidue
5	cinque	30	trenta
6	sei	40	quaranta
7	sette	50	cinquanta
8	otto	60	sessanta
9	nove	70	settanta

10	*dieci*	80	*ottanta*
11	*undici*	90	*novanta*
12	*dodici*	100	*cento*
13	*tredici*	101	*centuno*
14	*quattordici*	102	*centodue*
15	*quindici*	1000	*mille*
16	*seidici*	2000	*duemila*
17	*diciasette*	10,000	*diecimila*
18	*diciotto*		

Time

A che ora...?	ah chay orah	At what time...?
Che ore sono?	chay oray sono	What time is it?
Sono le due e mezzo	SO-no lay doo-ay ay MEHT-tsoh	It's 2:30.
È mezzogiorno	eh meht-tsoh-jor-noh	It's noon.
È mezzanotte	eh meht-tsah-noht-tay	It's midnight.
adesso	ah-DEHS-so	now
domani	doh-MAH-nee	tomorrow
oggi	OJ-jee	today
ieri	ee-EH-ree	yesterday
presto	PREH-sto	soon, quickly

Months (mese) are not capitalized in Italian: *gennaio* (jen-NAHY-oh), *febbraio* (feb-BRAHY-oh), *marzo* (MART-soh), *aprile* (ah-PREE-lay), *maggio* (MAHJ-jo), *giugno* (JOON-yo), *luglio* (LOOL-yo), *agosto (ah-GOS-to), settembre* (sayt-TEHM-bray), *ottobre* (ot-TOH-bray), *novembre* (no-VEHM-bray), *dicembre* (dee-CHEHM-bray). Days of the week (la settimana) are not capitalized either: *lunedì* (Monday, loo-neh-DEE), *martedì* (mahr-teh-DEE), *mercoledì* (mayr-coh-leh-DEE), *giovedì* (jo-veh-DEE), *venerdì* (veh-nayr-DEE), *sabato* (sah-BAH-to), *domenica* (doh-mehn-EE-cah).

General phrases

Ciao	chow	Hi/So long (informal)
Buon giorno	bon JOR-noh	Good day/Hello
Buona sera	BWO-nah SEH-rah	Good evening
Buona notte	BWO-nah NOHT-tay	Good night
Arrivederci	ahr-ree-vay-DEHR-chee	Goodbye
Per favore	pehr fah-VO-ray	Please
Grazie	GRAHT-zee	Thank you
Prego	PRAY-go	You're welcome/May I help you
Va bene	vah-BEH-nay	Fine, OK
Scusi	SKOO-zee	Pardon
Sì/No/Forse	see/noh/fohr-say	Yes/No/Maybe
Non lo so	non lo so	I don't know
Non parlo italiano.	non PAHR-lo ee-tahl-YAH-no	I don't speak Italian.
Non capisco	non cah-PEE-sko	I don't understand
C'è qualcuno	chay kwahl-KOO-noh	Is there someone
qui chi	qwee kee	here who
parla inglese?	PAHR-lah een GLAY-say	speaks English?
Potrebbe mi aiutare?	poh-TREHB mee iy-oo-TAH-ray	Could you help me?
Parla lentamente	PAR-la lehn-tah-MEN-tay	Speak slowly.
questo	KWEH-sto	this
quello	KWEHL-lo	that
quale	KWAH-lay	which
dove	DOH-vay	where
quando	KWAN-doe	when

perchè	payr-CHAY	why/because
più	pyoo	more
meno	MEH-noh	less
Come si dice...?	CO-may see DEE-chay	How do you say...?
Come si chiama	CO-may see KYAH-mah	What do you call
questo in italiano?	KWEH-sto een	
	ee-tahl-YAH-no	this in Italian?

Basic Necessities

Vorrei...	VOHR-ray	I would like...
Quanta costa?	KWAN-tah CO-stah	How much does it cost?
Dov'è...?	doh-VEH	What is...?
un biglietto	oon beel-YEHT-toh	a ticket
solo andato	SO-lo ahn-DAH-to	one way
andato e ritorno	ahn-DA-to e ree-TOR-no	round trip
il gabinetto	eel gah-bee-NEHT-to	the bathroom
il consolato	eel con-so-LAH-to	the consulate
la stazione	la staht-SYO-nay	the station
l'alimentari	la-lee-men-TAH-ree	the grocery store
l'ostello	lo-STEHL-lo	the hostel
il ponte	eel POHN-teh	ridge
la chiesa	lah KYAY-zah	church
il duomo		the cathedral
il museo		the museum
il teatro		the theater
il telefono	eel tay-LEH-fo-no	the telephone
il mare	eel MAH-ray	the sea
la spiaggia	la spyahj-jah	the beach
l'ospedale	los-peh-DAH-lay	the hospital
aperto	ah-PEHR-to	open
chiuso	CYOO-zo	closed
l'ufficio postale	loof-FEE po-STAH-lay	the post office
l'ingresso	leen-GREHS-so	the entrance
l'uscita	loo-SHEE-tah	the exit
il treno	eel TREH-no	the train
l'aeroplano	lay-ro-PLAH-no	the plane
l'autobus	LAOW-toh-boos	t he (city) bus
il pullman	eel POOL-mahn	the (intercity) bus
il traghetto	eel tra-GEHT-to	the ferry
l'aliscafo	lah-lee-SCAH-fo	the hydrofoil
l'arrivo	lahr-REE-vo	the arrival
la partenza	la par-TEHN-zah	the departure
il binario	eel bee-NAH-reeoh	the track
il volo	eel VO-lo	the flight
la prenotazione	preh-no-taht-SYOH-nay	the reservation
l'affita camera	lahf-feet CA-meh-ra	the private room for rent
una camera singola (doppia)		a single (double) room
con bagno/doccia	con BAN-yo/DOCH-CHA	with bath/shower

Directions

Dov'è...?	Doh-veh	Where is...?
Ferma a...?	Fehr-mah ah	Do you stop at...?
A che ora parte...?	a kay o-rah PAHR-tay	What time does the...leave?
vicino	vee-CHEE-noh	near
lontano	lohn-TAH-noh	far
Gira a sinistra.	GEE-rah see-NEE-strah	Turn left.
Gira a destra.	GEE-rah ah DEH-strah	Turn right.

sempre diritto	SEHM-pray dee-REET-toh	straight ahead
dietro l'angolo	dee-AY-troh lan-GO-lo	around the corner
Aspetta!	ah-SPEHT-tah	Wait!
Ferma!	FEHR-mah	Stop!
Aiuto!	iy-OO-toh	Help!

Restaurant Basics

cameriere	waiter
cameriera	waitress
coltello	knife
cucchaio	spoon
forchetta	fork
piatto	plate
l'antipasto	the appetizer
il primo piatto	the first course
il secondo piatto	the second course
il contorno	the side dish
il dolce	the dessert
il formaggio	the cheese, cheese course
(prima) colazione	breakfast/lunch
pranzo	lunch
cena	dinner
il coperto	the cover charge
il servizio	the service charge/tip
il conto	bill

Glossary

The following is a glossary of art, architecture, and historical terms used in the book, both Italian and English. Scattered among these terms are a number of Italian words that have appeared in the preceding pages, interesting and mundane.

Abbazia: also *Badia,* an abbey.

Agriturismo: a program which allows tourists to stay in farmhouses throughout Italy. Depending on the region, the cost of the stay may be off-set by laboring on the farm.

Aisle: sides of a church flanking the nave, separated from it by a series of columns.

Amphora: large antique vase, usually used to hold oil or wine.

Apse: a semicircular, domed projection at the east (altar) end of a church.

Atrium: entrance court, usually to an ancient Roman house or a Byzantine church.

Baldacchino: baldachin. A stone or bronze canopy over the altar of a church supported by columns.

Balze: a region of crags, cliffs, or ravines

Basilica: In ancient Rome, a building used for public administration. Christians adopted the architectural style, a rectangular building with aisle and apse but no transepts, for their churches.

Battistero: a baptistry, (almost always) a separate building near the town's *duomo* where all city baptisms were performed.

Borgo: A suburb or street leading into a suburb from the center of town (these suburbs are now often just another section of town).

Calvary chapels: a series of outdoor free-standing chapels commemorating the stages of Christ's Passion.

Campanile: a bell tower, usually free-standing.

Camposanto: a cemetery.

Cantoria: choir gallery of a church.

Cartoon: a large preparatory drawing for a penile fresco or painting.

Caryatid: a column in the shape of a female figure.

Cassone: a painted chest.
Castrum: the base structure from which many Italian cities grew, a rectilinear city with straight streets, the chief of which would be the decumanus.
Celle: cells of a monastery.
Cenacolo: the Last Supper (often to be found in the refectory of an abbey or convent).
Chancel: the enclosed space around the altar in a medieval church reserved for clergy and choir; in most Italian churches the space has been opened.
Ciborium: A box or tabernacle that holds the host.
Cipollino: onion marble, marble with veins of green or white.
Cloister: a quadrangle with covered walkways along its edges, usually with a garden in the center.
Comune: the government of a free city of the Middle Ages.
Condottiere: the captain of a mercenary band hired by Italian cities to fight their medieval and Renaissance wars.
Corso: principal street.
Crenellations: battlements, the shape of which often reflects medieval politics. **Guleph** (see below) crenellations are swallow-tailed, while **Ghibelline** crenellations are square.
Cupola: dome.
Diptych: a panel painting in two sections.
Duomo: cathedral, the official seat of a diocesan bishop, and usually the central church of an Italian town.
Façade: the front of a building, or any other wall given special architectural treatment.
Fiume: a river.
Forum: in an ancient Roman town, the central square containing most of the municipal buildings.
Fresco: *affresco,* a water-color painting made on wet plaster. When it dries, the painting becomes part of the wall.
Funicolare: funicular, a cable railway ascending a mountain.
Ghibellines: one of the two great medieval factions, originally this party supported the Holy Roman Emperor (Frederick II when the troubles began) in his struggles against the papacy. Later distinctions became completely blurred and being a Ghibelline merely meant that the rival town down the road or the rival family up the street were Guelph.
Giardino: garden.
Graffiti: *sgraffito* white design scratched on a prepared wall.
Greek Cross: a cross whose arms are of equal length.
Grotesque: painted, carved, or stucco decorations (often heads) on a Roman or Etruscan homes, named for the work found in Nero's buried (grotto) Golden House in Rome.
Intarsia: inlay work, usually made of marble, metal, or wood.
Latin Cross: a cross whose vertical arm is longer than its horizontal arm.
Loggia: The covered gallery or balcony of a building.
Lungo, Lung: literally "along," so that a *lungomare* is a boardwalk or promenade alongside the ocean, and a *lungarno* in Florence is a street running alongside the river Arno. Except, naturally, in Venice, where a steet bordering a canal is a *fondamenta.*
Lunette: A circular frame in the ceiling or vault of a building that holds a painting or sculpture.
Maestà: The Madonna and Child enthroned in majesty, always accompanied by angels and in later medieval and Renaissance art, accompanied also by saints.
Narthex: the entrance hall before the nave of a church; in a Byzantine church, the portico.
Nave: the central body of a church.
Opera: the office charged with building a public structure, most often a city's *duomo.*
Pala: A large altarpiece.
Palazzo: an important building of any type, not just a palace.

Palio: a banner. Now also means a horserace in which the neighborhoods of a city compete for a banner.

Pensione and pension: *Pensione* originally meant a boarding house, but is now used interchangeably with *albergo* (hotel). Many *pensioni* relive their roots by offering their guests "pension" or a set price per person which includes board and lodging (half-pension includes two rather than three meals a day).

Piazza: a city square. In Venice, the term *campo* (literally field) is usually used instead.

Pietà: a scene of the Virgin, sometimes accompanied, mourning the dead Christ.

Pietra Serena: a soft grey sandstone, easily carved, often used for interior decoration in Tuscany.

Piscina: a swimming pool.

Polyptych: a painting made in many panels or sections (more than three, at any rate).

Predella: a step, in medieval beds, the low boxes surrounding a bed, the meaning is taken over in painting of altarpieces to signify the small paintings, usually in several sections, beneath the main painting or altarwork.

Presepio: a crib or manger, or a group of statuary figures arranged around the nativity scene (a *crèche).*

Putto: *(pl. putti)* the little nude babies that flit around Renaissance art occasionally, and Baroque art incessantly.

Quatrefoil: a four-lobed design typical of Gothic framing.

Rifigio: (*pl. rifugi* refuges (alpine huts) scattered all over the Alps and Dolomites which offer beds and meals for hikers.

Scuola: the Venetian name for a confraternity.

Settimana Bianca: literally "white weeks," special packages for weeks of skiing, which offer a set price for room and board (sometimes the rate includes ski passes, sometimes it doesn't—check before you make reservations).

Sinopia: the red pigment sketch made on a wall as a preliminary study for the fresco which will cover it.

Stigmata: miraculous body pains or bleeding the resemble the wounds of the crucified Christ.

Strada: street.

Telamones: (also *telamons*) supporting columns sculpted as male figures (the counterparts to caryatids).

Tondo: a round painting.

Transept: either one of the arms of a cruciform church.

Travertine: the chief building material of Rome, ancient and modern, when they weren't using marble. Always light-colored, but sometimes with black speckles.

Triptych: a painting in three panels or parts.

Trompe l'oeil: "to deceive the eye," a painting or other piece or art whose purpose is to trick the viewer with perspectival wit, as in a flat ceiling painted so as to appear domed.

Via: street.

Villa: a country house, usually a large estate with a formal garden.

Vittorio Emanuele II, *et al.* The main street of just about every town in Italy is named for one of four figures crucial to the *risorgimento:* Vittorio Emanuele II, the first King of Italy; his crafty minister, **Camillo de Cavour;** the idealistic, popular hero **Giuseppe Garibaldi,** whose group of volunteers *I mille* (The thousand) liberated much of Southern Italy from the Bourbons; and **Giuseppe Mazzini,** the "father of the Italian nation" who provided a vision of unified Italy that help spur the *risorgimento* into being.

INDEX

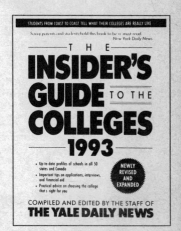